Ethical Leadership
A Primer on Ethical Responsibility in Management

John W. Dienhart
Seattle University

Terry Thomas
Attorney

MEMORANDUM TO THE READER

These are challenging times in business ethics. I could not allow current events and controversies to pass without calling special attention to issues of personal ethics and ethical leadership that are so important today.

A unique author team developed this ethics primer as a prologue to the special "Ethical Leadership" update edition of *Management 7/E*. John W. Dienhart is the Boeing Frank Shrontz Chair for Business Ethics at Seattle University; Director of the Northwest Ethics Network, and past President of Society of Business Ethics. Terry Thomas is an attorney and lecturer, and was formerly Director of Ethics Operations at The Boeing Company.

I urge you to read and participate in the activities of this ethical primer as a prelude to the rest of the book. Read it as an essay, one that should provoke your critical thinking. As you read, ask and answer for yourself important questions such as these:

- What is ethics and what is ethical behavior?

- How can one understand and develop personal ethics?

- What can we learn from recent cases of failures in business ethics?

- How can you best prepare to master personal ethical challenges in your career?

The world at large needs ethical leaders to guide our governments and social institutions. The businesses and organizations of your community and mine need them also. Please join with me in grounding your study of management with commitment to the ethical leadership of organizations and to socially responsible business and organizational practices.

John R. Schermerhorn, Jr.
Charles G. O'Bleness Professor of Management
Ohio University
Author: *Management 7/E*

The recent news has been full of sensational cases of corruption and ethical failures in the world of business. If you haven't been following the reports, and if you don't pay attention to the others that are sure to come, you will miss valuable information. These cases introduce us squarely to an issue that is center stage to your future career and professional well-being—"ethics" and its role in guiding the leadership of society's organizations.

This primer, "Ethical Leadership," will help frame your introductory study of management in an ethical context. It should be helpful, even indispensable, in building your confidence in dealing with ethical dilemmas and challenges in the workplace. It should also help you to further develop your personal moral framework as a guide for ethical decision making and ethical leadership in even the most complicated management situations.

Let's begin with a look at four scenarios, all drawn from real life. Consider each and answer for yourself the accompanying thought questions. We'll refer to these cases throughout the coming discussion.

Case 1　A midlevel manager at Fran-Tech, a Seattle software company, receives a CD-ROM containing the source code for a competitor's software product. The competitor is the market leader in the software niche in which both companies compete and is crushing Fran-Tech in the marketplace. An anonymous note accompanying the package states that the package was sent by a disgruntled employee of the competitor, and urges the recipient to use the data "as you see fit." The manager is considered to be a "star" performer by her boss and her peers. Once the manager realizes the contents of the CD-ROM, she picks up the telephone and calls her counterpart at the competitor. "I think I have something that belongs to you," she says. She returns the CD-ROM to the competitor.

> *Thought Questions*: (1) Why did she do this? (2) Why didn't she, at the very least, first make a copy before returning the CD-ROM? (3) Shouldn't she have called her supervisor or the legal department first before acting?

Case 2　Johnson & Johnson, a major global drug manufacturer, learns that seven users of Tylenol capsules, a popular over-the-counter pain reliever, have died in the Chicago area. Further investigation reveals that the poisonings were not accidental; the capsules had been tampered with, laced with deadly cyanide. The company is certain that the tampering occurred after the product was shipped from its plants, i.e., it was not the work of a disgruntled Johnson & Johnson employee. Top managers at the company, led by the CEO, take the following actions: Johnson & Johnson immediately withdraws all Tylenol from the market nation-wide, stops all Tylenol advertising, issues warnings to the public not to use any of its Tylenol products—not simply the capsules—and recalls all Tylenol products from the shelves, a total of 31 million bottles valued at over $100 million.

> *Thought Questions:* (1) was the company's reaction too drastic and too swift? Should the decision makers have waited until more facts were available? (2) Should the recall have been limited to the Chicago area? (3) Since the poisonings occurred after the product had left Johnson & Johnson's control and were clearly the work of some criminal, should J&J have denied responsibility for the acts?

Case 3 Merck, a large multinational pharmaceutical firm, discovers that a drug the company has marketed to treat horses against parasitic worms can also be developed into a drug for humans that prevents river blindness, a horribly disfiguring disease that causes total blindness in its victims. The disease afflicts millions of poor people in sub–Saharan Africa. The cost to develop the drug for use in humans, including the necessary clinical trials, will run into the hundreds of millions of dollars. Additional millions will be necessary to deliver the drug to the victims in Africa, as well as to educate them as to its effectiveness and proper use. Because the victims live in abject poverty, they cannot pay for the drug. Moreover, although Merck will receive some help from international relief agencies and governments, it will bear the majority of the costs of this project itself. Aside from acting as a cure for river Blindness, there is no other use for the drug. More than 20 years after beginning the project, Merck continues to distribute the drug free of charge, and thus to lose money.

> *Thought Questions:* (1) Why did Merck develop a drug whose only customers could not afford to buy it? (2) Is this type of public service better left to governments than to private companies? (3) Does Merck have the right to "waste" shareholders' money on products and activities that have no hope of ever turning a profit?

Case 4 Costco Wholesale Corporation, is an international members-only discount retail store. While investigating a move into the United Kingdom, its bankers are recommending a way of structuring a borrowing transaction so that both principal and interest on the loan are tax deductible, as opposed to interest only, as is generally the case. The transaction would provide both significant tax savings to and a lower effective rate of interest to Costco. The company's top management decides that although the transaction would follow the letter of the law, it would not fall within the "spirit" of the law. As Richard Galanti, CFO, said, "It did not pass the smell test." The company foregoes the tax benefits.

> *Thought Questions:* (1) Why should a company decline to do something that is legal, and that will deliver more profits to its shareholders? (2) What is the "spirit" of the law, and why should a company consider it?

ETHICS

In Chapter 6, "Ethical Behavior and Social Responsibility," **ethics** is formally defined as a code of moral principles that sets standards of what is "good" and "right" as opposed to "bad" or "wrong" in the conduct of a person or group. When we read the articles and hear the news reports about the corporations and people behind today's scandals—those of Andersen, Enron, WorldCom, and others—there is much to be concerned about. They inform us about trusted senior executives engaged in unethical behavior; they describe organizations that tolerated decisions and actions that enrich the few while damaging so very many. Those harmed by the unethical practices range from company employees who lost retirement savings, to stockholders whose investments lost value, to customers and society at large who paid the price of business performance gone sadly off course. Society deserves much better than this.

○ **Ethics** is the code of moral principles that sets standards of what is "good" and "right" as opposed to "bad" or "wrong" (see Chapter 6).

ETHICAL LEADERSHIP AND INTEGRITY

○ **Ethical leadership** is moral leadership that meets the test of being "good" rather than "bad," and "right" rather than "wrong" (see Chapter 13).

○ **Leadership integrity** is the leader's honesty, credibility, and consistency in putting ethical values into action.

We expect and demand today that organizations be run with **ethical leadership**, which is moral leadership that meets the ethical test of being "good" and not "bad," and of being "right" not "wrong." As discussed in Chapter 13, "Leading," ethical leadership is distinguished by the presence of true **leadership integrity**—the leader's honesty, credibility, and consistency in putting ethical values into action. The recent highly publicized scandals inform us of failures in ethical leadership and integrity. But let there be no mistake about it, there is a plethora of positive examples and ethical role models to be studied as well.

You will find in *Management 7/E,* many examples of people and organizations that are exemplars of ethical leadership and integrity unquestioned. You can find them also in this primer's opening scenarios. At Fran-Tech, the manager voluntarily gave back competitor information that could have greatly helped her own struggling company. Johnson & Johnson probably destroyed millions of dollars worth of perfectly good Tylenol products as a result of a few isolated incidents. At Merck, the decision led to a financial loss and the firm has no hope of ever recouping its investment. Costco executives elected to forego a perfectly legal tax strategy that would have increased profits. The managers in all four cases took ethical actions. The underlying question is: "Why?"

THE ETHICS REFLEX

○ **Ethics reflex** is a nearly automatic tendency to do what is right, even when it might be contrary to the employer's interest.

These decision makers did what they thought was right, even though it was not—at least in the short run—in their best financial interests. We call this response the **ethics reflex**—ethical action taken without extensive delay or analysis. At times nearly automatic (see manager's notepad 1), it is a characteristic of ethical leadership. Individuals and organizations that exhibit the ethical reflex very often do not engage in cost–benefit calculations and/or engage in lengthy consultations with lawyers about ways to avoid liability or "manage" the situation. They tend to do what feels right; they do it reflexively; and, they let the consequences fall where they may.

At Costco the ethics reflex is evidenced by Richard Galanti's comment that the rejected alternative, with all of its potential advantages, just "did not pass the smell test." In the Tylenol case, we see it as Johnson & Johnson destroyed millions of dollars worth of perfectly good product. Although there could also have been hundreds or even thousands of cyanide-laced pills among the destroyed packages, it is also possible that they were only in the seven bottles already discovered. While these scenarios were surely considered, the decision makers acted decisively and ethically to address the immediate problem without wasting time. Their ethics reflex was to take what they considered to be the right steps—withdraw all Tylenol from the market.

CORPORATE CULTURE AND THE ETHICS REFLEX

Why do some people, when faced with choices between alternatives—some of which are legal, profitable, but ethically suspect—consistently choose the ethical course of action? The answer, we believe, lies with individual ethical integrity and corporate culture. The ethics reflex is common

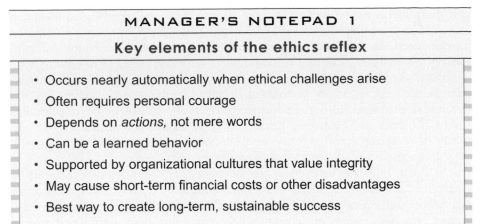

MANAGER'S NOTEPAD 1

Key elements of the ethics reflex

- Occurs nearly automatically when ethical challenges arise
- Often requires personal courage
- Depends on *actions,* not mere words
- Can be a learned behavior
- Supported by organizational cultures that value integrity
- May cause short-term financial costs or other disadvantages
- Best way to create long-term, sustainable success

to individuals acting within a consistent **corporate culture** that values integrity. In Chapter 2, "Environment and Diversity," this culture is defined as the system of shared values that guides the behavior of organizational members.

Organizational cultures that support and create the ethics reflex are incubated by the statements and, more importantly, by the actions of their leaders. When corporate leaders make it clear that the needs of customers come before profits and then act consistently with that promise, for example, they will attract employees with the same values. In this way a firm's ethical culture builds and continually reinforces itself over time. When surrounded by peers who expect and follow high ethical standards, even persons of somewhat lower personal integrity will often act in accordance with the higher standard. When executive leadership consistently demands ethical behavior and develops an organizational culture that supports the ethics reflex, it becomes a learned behavior on the part of employees. Over time this culture becomes so ingrained that when a situation arises, such as the Fran-Tech dilemma or the Merck river blindness project decision, the ethics reflex guides people toward the type of behavior the company values.

> ○ **Corporate culture** is the system of shared values that guides the behavior of organizational members (see Chapter 2).

ON THE WRONG SIDE OF THE ETHICS REFLEX

The ethics reflex results when people have individual integrity and work in organizational cultures that support integrity. Unfortunately, the recent reports about business corruption, accounting scandals, and the like make it abundantly clear that some companies are not like this. They possess what might be termed a "negative" ethics. They develop cultures where the decision-making reflex is solely to promote short-term corporate profit, as well as personal gain and power for top executives. Such organizations have little or no regard for the moral correctness of behavior. Actions and decisions are viewed solely in terms of cost and benefit analysis of what is best at the time for the company and/or its privileged managers.

We would see quite different behaviors in the opening examples if the governing cultures in each case tolerated unethical behavior. In a negative ethical culture the manager at Fran-Tech would almost certainly choose to copy the source code that was offered to her. Why not use it and try to overcome her firm's competitive disadvantage? In the Tylenol case, Johnson & Johnson executives may have turned first to lawyers and financial analysts to quantify the risks of allowing their product to remain in the marketplace. At the extreme, they might have made their decision by comparing the costs of potential future deaths with the benefits of saving from destruction millions of dollars of product. In the Merck example, a culture that placed less value on customers would likely have led decision makers to cancel the river blindness project. After all, it would be a pointless waste of corporate resources. Finally, Costco executives would almost certainly have seized upon the tax loophole when entering the U.K. markets. Why forgo the obvious, and legal, advantages it offered?

In these negative examples, the decisions and behaviors exhibited by employees are the product of a prevailing organizational culture that does not place high value on ethical behavior. Importantly, such negative outcomes may occur even in settings where corporate documents and executive speeches carry ethical themes. Unless the leadership behavior matches the leadership and corporate messages, they will have little positive impact.

People in organizations are influenced by what company leaders both *say* and *do* in ethical situations. While nearly all companies have platitudes and slogans extolling the virtues of acting to high standards of integrity, too many executives fail to follow through by setting positive examples and consistently taking ethical actions. People in all organizations are keen observers of leadership behavior; they will quickly note any disparities between what leaders say and do. Once employees discover that the ethical culture is different from that stated in official documents or that executive leaders operate by a different set of rules, they will likely respond accordingly. Some will adjust their behavior, lowering personal standards to fit the actual culture. Others will seek alternative employment with an organization whose ethics and values are more compatible with their own.

DISCOVERING (AND DEVELOPING) PERSONAL ETHICS

The roots of the ethics reflex are found within the character of the individual. A person of integrity has a coherent set of ethical standards and acts on them even when it is difficult to do so. While we may be urged to develop integrity by our parents, teachers, church leaders, and government authorities, it is still a matter of personal choice and development. Simply put, you and we will only have integrity if we choose to have it and work hard to maintain it.

What choices, exactly, does a person of integrity make? To help answer this question, let's look at a series of actions that the majority would think lacks integrity.

Scene 1. A person is competing with a good friend for an assignment overseas. The person lies about the friend to secure an advantage.

Scene 2. A person pads their expense reports over a period of many years, costing the company tens of thousands of dollars.

Scene 3. A person refuses to grant a promotion to the most qualified candidate because he is Hispanic.

Scene 4. A person who does well in college and in preparatory courses is invited to a party the night before his CPA exam. He wants to leave, but ends up staying late and drinking too much. He goes to the exam blurry-eyed and confused.

In contrast to the behavior exhibited in scenes 1 and 2, people of integrity care about their personal relationships and the well-being of the groups of which they are members. In contrast to what happens in scene 3, a person of integrity respects human dignity (fairness, justice, and rights). And in contrast to scene 4, people of integrity can control themselves and follow through on their plans. Those who successfully master the challenges of personal integrity—to have it and consistently maintain it—possess at least two important understandings.

1. *Persons of high integrity have clear beliefs about what is ethical and what is not.* Having clear beliefs does not mean holding fixed and unchangeable beliefs or ignoring the views of others. We are always learning new, unintended consequences of our beliefs, and a mature decision maker takes this information into account. Thus, our ethics reflexes change over time as we see the results of our actions.

2. *Persons of high integrity have the commitment and creativity to act on these beliefs in efficient ways.* It is difficult to follow through on our ethics reflexes if others push back. Being a person of integrity does not always mean directly confronting others with whom we disagree. While some confrontations are unavoidable, many situations can be handled with integrity and finesse.

ETHICAL DEVELOPMENT IN FOUR DIMENSIONS

Ethics is essentially the study of how to live a good life. If the ethics reflex relies on a person having clear ethical beliefs about what is right and wrong in life, how can ethics be better understood at the personal or individual level? How can one best approach the challenges of personal ethical development? It helps to view ethical development in four dimensions: (1) self-development, (2) personal relationship development, (3) group development, and (4) human dignity development.

Ethics and Self-Development   The self-development dimension of personal ethics focuses on the goals we have and how we pursue and attain these goals. Individually, for example, we can define our self-development in terms of financial, career, spiritual, family, and many other goals. If we look back on the Fran-Tech case, the manager involved saw her self-development in terms of honesty, integrity, and respect for the law. The software she received was stolen property. Because an honest citizen returns stolen property, the case for her was closed and the decision she made was not debatable. Importantly, by returning the code, she not only acted from her good character she also strengthened it. Our individual characters are built and reinforced one act at a time. The more we act in a particular way, ideally an ethical way, the easier it becomes to do so the next time.

Your ethical development

What kind of person do you want to be?

How do you want others to think of you?

How do you *not* want others to think of you?

Ethics and Personal Relationships Development   The second ethics dimension, personal relationships development, focuses on the relationships we have with other persons. In the management context this is especially important in respect to the relationships we have with the people we work with, and in the groups in which we participate as members and leaders. It is important for people in organizations to work together. Cooperation builds as people help each other with projects and tasks. A business and its members benefit when employees act on the

Your ethical development

How do you define good relationships at work?

If someone asks you to return a favor, are you obligated to help if you feel uncomfortable doing what the person asks?

"you help me and I help you" principle, while mutually supporting high ethical standards.

In the Fran-Tech case, for example, the manager who returned the software strengthened the already trusting relationships she had with her boss, peers, and employees. She further increased her integrity in the eyes of others, with fellow employees likely to feel even more comfortable going to her for advice about difficult problems. She also began a trusting relationship with the competitor that could bear fruit for her and her company, should future opportunities for joint ventures or other forms of legal cooperation arise. At Costco, the decision not to take a legal but ethically suspect tax reduction publicly confirmed a key ethical value. The common vision of Costco held by each of the senior managers was supported. This reinforcement of shared understandings and ethical commitments likely further enhanced the trust in their working relationships.

Ethics and Group Development   The third ethics dimension focuses on the development of the groups in which we participate. Like individuals, groups and organizations can define their well-being in terms of financial, market, religious, civic, or other standards. These standards of the group will influence how we make individual decisions.

Your ethical development

What kind of groups do you want to identify with?

When are you uncomfortable with the decisions of a group?

How do you define the good of a business organization?

In the Fran-Tech case, the manager sent a positive message to the competitor about Fran-Tech's culture and goals, as well as her own character. By showing that Fran-Tech is an honest company that plays by the rules, she defies the notion that "dirty business" is the group norm. She also sent a powerful message within Fran-Tech that honest behavior on the part of the executive team is part of the culture, even if it seems to have short-run costs. Culture and group norms were also at play in the decisions of Merck, Johnson & Johnson, and Costco. Each of these companies has a strong statement of values that is not just window-dressing. The values are integrated into decision making throughout the firms, from the top down. With clear messages about how to act, decisions that would otherwise be agonizing, costly, and delayed can be made easily, efficiently, and quickly.

Ethics and Fairness, Rights and Human Dignity   The fourth ethics dimension focuses on the extent to which the practices in which we engage and the organizations in which we participate are fair and just and respect human rights. We can evaluate fairness in terms of outcomes, processes/procedures, or both. Outcome fairness works in situations where the outcomes are easy to evaluate. If you and your friend split the cost of a pizza, the fair outcome is easy to determine—you each get half to eat. In many business situations, however, the fair outcome is not easy to determine. Thus, we try to develop fair *processes* so that results are considered fair. This idea should have a familiar ring; it underlies the notion of *due process* that is embedded in the United States's constitutional form of government.

Your ethical development

How do you define fairness, rights, and human dignity in the context of business operations?

How important is it for you to work in a business that is fair and respects the rights of all?

In the financial world of business, people invest their money in public companies by buying stock. They expect a fair return on their money, just as the pizza buyers expect a fair return on their purchase price. There are two ways a company rewards investors. One way is through an increase in stock price. A well-run company should draw more investors. As people compete for the stock, the stock price goes up, and previous owners are rewarded. The second way is through dividends. Companies take some of the profits and distribute them to shareholders. Besides giving owners a cash return, the announcement by a company that it will pay dividends can also increase the stock price, thus giving owners a double reward. The question is: What constitutes a fair reward for investors?

The answer to this question of fairness is not as easy to determine as is the case of two friends splitting a pizza, and there is more room for unfair rewards to be made. A company's financial statements and forecasts, for example, heavily influence stock price. If those reports are good, the stock price can increase quickly. Inaccurate financial reports that overstate the performance of the company completely disrupt the process. Those unaware of the inaccuracies will frequently drive up the price of the stock by buying in reliance on the false information, only to lose money when the lies are revealed. Those who know that the reports are false, however, will sell their stock while it is still high, reaping an unfair reward before the stock loses its value.

○ **Corporate governance** is the oversight of management decisions and company actions by Boards of Directors that are supposed to represent the interests of stockholders.

There are two processes designed to protect against such corrupt practices, and to ensure that the financial reports and forecasts made by businesses are accurate and that no one unfairly gains rewards. The first is **corporate governance**—oversight of management decisions and company actions by Boards of Directors that are supposed to represent the interests of stockholders. The second is **auditing**, an external assessment by independent and certified accounting firms that guarantees the accuracy of financial reports. In our imperfect world of business, as illustrated by the recent cases of Andersen, Enron and WorldCom, both of these processes can break down.

○ **Auditing** is an external assessment by independent and certified accounting firms that guarantees the accuracy of financial reports.

WHEN BUSINESS ETHICS FAILS

Businesses and other organizations operate in complex civic, political, and economic environments. They both influence these environments and are influenced by them in return. In this setting, ethical business decision making creates value for a business entity by promoting sustainable networks of individuals, personal relationships, and groups in a context of human dignity. This perspective on business ethics starts with the responsibility of business decision makers to look after the well-being of their organization. That is what they have promised to do, and the many business stakeholders depend on their performing that role well.

Corporate social responsibility, as discussed in Chapter 6, "Ethical Behavior and Social Responsibility," refers to the obligations a business has to many stakeholders. The narrowest view considers corporate social responsibility an obligation to obey the law. However, the developing consensus supports a more expansive definition that includes commitments to work with employees, their families, the local community, and society at large to improve the quality of life. Businesses, like societies, are increasingly evaluated by the extent to which they are fair, just, and respect the rights of all.

○ **Corporate social responsibility** is the obligation of a business to external stakeholders (see Chapter 6).

The actions and decisions in the four cases that began this primer reflected the ethics of corporate social responsibility. And, although the managers did not focus on the short-term financial well-being of their company as their first or only priority, their companies benefitted or at least were not harmed by their ethical actions. Fran-Tech avoided the risk of having to battle civil or even criminal charges for using stolen information. Johnson & Johnson remained one of the most trusted names in the pharmaceuticals industry. Merck was able to initiate important relationships with developing nations. Costco avoided damage to its reputation as it entered the United Kingdom.

When business ethics do not support corporate social responsibility, by contrast, the costs of failure can be very high for all concerned.

THE CASE OF ARTHUR ANDERSEN

Arthur Andersen, LLP was until recently one of the largest certified public accounting firms in the world. Its client base included a diverse mix of companies and organizations ranging from huge global corporations to the City of New York. Andersen, like many other accounting firms, provided two types of services to its clients: auditing and consulting.

Andersen's auditing business involved the traditional auditing of financial statements. When it provides this service, an accounting firm examines the financial books and records of the client and compares its business dealings to generally accepted accounting practices. If it finds the financial activities of the client in order, the accounting firm issues a letter included in the client's annual report, certifying that the client meets the accounting standards of the industry. This certification is important; it is legally required for all companies that are publicly traded in the United States. Investors, from individuals to large institutions, rely on the accounting firm's certification as part of their decision to buy the client's stock.

Over the last several years major accounting firms, like Andersen, added business management consulting to their business portfolios. Management consultants provide advice to clients on a wide variety of business matters, ranging from how best to structure business transactions to how to manage suppliers or employees. Because public accounting firms become so familiar with their clients' businesses during the auditing process, it seems logical to use that knowledge for the additional purpose of management consulting for the same clients. Management consulting is very lucrative; often, the fees generated from this activity dwarf those generated from the auditing activity.

○ **Conflict of interest** is where one goal or business task is compromised in service to another.

This dual role of auditor and management consultant has led to **conflicts of interest,** where one goal or business task is compromised in service to another. For example, an auditor is supposed to maintain a skeptical independence, acting as a sort of watchdog, and questioning the client closely about its financial practices to ensure that they are proper. When, however, the auditing firm is also trying to sell its business consulting services to that same client, its incentive to maintain its independence may be compromised, out of fear of angering the client, who may send its consulting business to a competitor. Further, when an accounting firm provides both management consulting advice and auditing services to the same client, it may find itself in the awkward position of passing judgment as an *auditor* of the very management practices it recommended as a *management consultant*. This places the accounting firm into a direct conflict of interest situation, because its duty to perform a thorough audit may conflict with its desire to provide innovative business consulting strategies, the propriety of which might be questioned by an aggressive auditor.

One of Andersen's most important clients was Enron, a huge Houston-based energy company. Andersen provided both auditing and manage-

Enron The Consequences of Ethical Failure

When the news hit, it was almost unbelievable. How could a major multinational company fail so miserably and so dramatically? How could the employees of a major American business lose their hard-earned retirement savings almost overnight? How could highly paid senior business executives go so sadly off course, apparently placing individual gain and self-interests above all else? Visit Internet sites, read as much as you can, and follow the daily news reports as the Enron debacle further unfolds and the firm and some senior executives face the justice system. Included with this update edition of *Management 7/E* is the Enron Case on CD-Rom. Take advantage of it as an opportunity to further your understanding of the ethical context of business and advance your quest for the strongest possible foundations of personal ethical development.

ment consulting services to Enron, thus performing the dual role described above. In November 2001, after years of extremely high profits, Enron disclosed that certain accounting problems, which occurred while Andersen was its auditor, would force it to restate, or change, prior financial reports. These changes caused Enron to report a huge $618 million net loss for the third quarter of 2001. The effect on Enron's stock was devastating—by late fall it had plunged to a mere fraction of what it had been less than a year before. Investors—many of them Enron employees—lost billions of dollars as a result.

Blame for Enron's bad news has been laid in part at the feet of Andersen. As the entity responsible for auditing Enron's financial statements, many commentators assert that it should have been aware of the large transactions that were now being called into question. Many further asserted that Andersen had been caught up in the conflict of interest problem that arises from the dual role of providing both auditing and business management consulting services. Making matters worse was the revelation that, at the same time the problems at Enron came to the public's attention, a senior Andersen employee ordered the destruction of documents relating to the audit work. This action, which was a deliberate effort to withhold evidence that government regulators would be seeking in its investigation of Enron's problems, constituted the serious crime of obstruction of justice. The employee who directed the document destruction soon after plead guilty to the crime, and Andersen itself was indicted, tried, and convicted of the same crime in spring 2002.

Andersen's ethical and legal failures in the Enron case can be summarized as follows:

- Andersen failed in its audit duty to question certain Enron transactions.
- Andersen had an inherent conflict of interest because it performed the dual roles of auditor and management consultant to Enron.
- Andersen, acting through its employees, committed the crime of obstruction of justice in an attempt to cover up its unethical acts.

BUSINESS COSTS OF ETHICAL FAILURE

Andersen's ethics failures in the Enron matter were extensive. Figure 1 divides the business costs of such ethical failures (see also manager's notepad 2) into three categories. The first cost, represented by the inner-

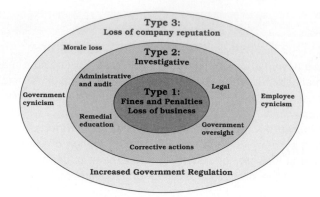

Figure 1   Business costs of ethics failure.

most circle on the chart and labeled *Type 1 costs,* is the easiest to show. At sentencing for its conviction of the crime of obstruction of justice, Andersen will in all likelihood receive a huge fine. In addition, as soon as the company was indicted, even before it was tried and convicted, it began losing business. Dozens of the Andersen's longstanding clients deserted it, choosing to fire Andersen and send their work to its competitors. This loss of present and future business was devastating to Andersen.

Andersen also suffered a further category of costs, shown as *Type 2 costs* in the figure. Type 2 costs include such things as attorney's fees, investigative costs, and the other costs shown. To defend itself against lawsuits filed by clients, investors, and the government, Andersen had to retain the services of expensive lawyers, auditors, and other professionals who are called in when a firm gets into serious trouble. These costs can run into the multiple millions of dollars. Further, on August 16, 2002 Andersen lost its Texas state accounting license, and was thus forbidden from doing further accounting work in that state.

The outer ring of the diagram shows *Type 3 costs,* which include such things as reputation loss, morale loss, employee and government cynicism, and increased government regulation. These costs are abstract and difficult to quantify, but they can be devastating to a firm. In the Andersen case, the Enron matter left the firm's reputation in shreds; the firm's problems became the subject of front-page news, late-night television jokes, and editorial cartoons. Morale among employees, the vast majority of whom had done nothing wrong and had had no involvement in or responsibility for the Enron debacle, plunged. Many, fearing for their jobs, left the firm, causing a severe talent drain. Finally, in direct response to the Arthur Anderson/Enron disaster, the U.S. government got involved. Congress began considering legislation that would add significant new accounting oversight responsibilities and stiff new penalties for financial reporting crimes such as may have occurred in this case.

Each Type 3 cost in the Andersen case proved to be enormously expensive. But the damage from this ethics failure is more widespread than just the devastating costs to Andersen. Sadly, the costs of ethics failures are almost never limited to the wrongdoers themselves. Other firms in the same line of business also feel the sting of additional regulation and the loss of public trust. As it becomes more costly to do business, this is passed on to the consumer, who ends up paying more for products and services.

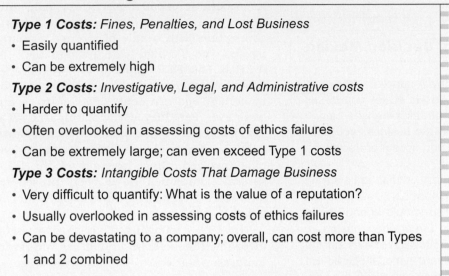

GOVERNMENT RESPONSES TO ETHICAL FAILURES

When a series of spectacular failures such as Enron, Andersen, and WorldCom occurs, regulatory authorities, spurred by public outcry, often move to act. Their goal is to pass laws that will force companies to act ethically. Typically, this is done in two ways: (1) new, stricter regulation and (2) more severe penalties for failures.

BUSINESS ETHICS AND THE LEGAL ENVIRONMENT

The U.S. Government has a long history of passing laws in response to ethical lapses by companies. In 1863, following fraudulent "war profiteering" by companies engaged in rebuilding the nation after the Civil War, Congress passed the Federal False Claims Act. This law, still in effect today, provides stiff penalties for any person or company that makes a false claim, generally for payment of money, against the government. Companies convicted under the law face not only criminal sanctions, but also civil monetary penalties of three times the dollar loss suffered by the government, plus fines of $10,000 for each false claim submitted. For a large company, such a penalty may be a mere monetary nuisance, though the negative publicity and other costs of such an ethics failure, as described in the previous section, are likely to be far greater. For a small company, however, a large judgment against it under the False Claims Act can be a death knell, particularly if its proprietors also face personal criminal charges.

The False Claims Act has another powerful provision regarding **whistleblowers**—employees who discover and report ethical misconduct. In respect to this act, whistleblowers are able to bring private civil actions, called *qui tam,* or whistleblower suits, against their employers. If the suit is successful, the whistleblower can recover a portion of the amount recov-

○ **Whistleblowers** are employees who discover and report ethical misconduct (see Chapter 6).

ered as a reward. Whistleblowers have thus obtained rewards in the millions of dollars for turning on their employers.

In 1977, following a scandal where American aerospace executives paid huge bribes to Japanese government officials in connection with a sale of aircraft, Congress passed the Foreign Corrupt Practices Act (FCPA). The FCPA makes it a criminal offense for American businesses to pay bribes to foreign government officials to secure business. Penalties for violating the FCPA are severe; they can amount to millions of dollars in fines, plus jail time for the individuals involved. Since passage of the FCPA, several companies have been prosecuted, and several executives have been sentenced to jail.

In 1991, following a series of scandals involving the defense and other industries, Congress passed a comprehensive set of guidelines to be used when sentencing corporations convicted of committing crimes. These guidelines greatly increased the penalties for corporate wrongdoing. In addition to the "stick" approach of enhanced penalties, however, the guidelines introduced something new, a "carrot." Companies who can demonstrate that they have in place an effective program to detect and prevent violations of law can receive a significant reduction in their fines. The thinking behind this provision is to encourage companies to create programs of codes of ethics, ethics training, employee reporting systems such as hotlines, and other methods aimed at preventing wrongdoing. If a company can show that it has taken such good-faith steps, but that employees nevertheless committed a crime, it may have its fine reduced to as little as 5% of the base amount.

In 2002, in response to the accounting scandals at Enron, Andersen, WorldCom, and others, Congress passed the Sarbanes-Oxley Bill (H.R. 3763, § 201). This law creates a new national accounting oversight body, called the Public Company Accounting Oversight Board, which will operate under the auspices of the federal Securities and Exchange Commission. The Board has vast powers to oversee the accounting industry. The Act also forbids companies that do auditing work from also providing management consulting services, although the Act does provide for limited pre-approval of such dual activities in some cases. Thus, the dual role of auditor and management consultant played by accounting firms, such as Andersen, for many years has been made unlawful by government regulation. This change in the law will have a profound effect on accounting firms that have developed their management consulting businesses in tandem with their auditing practices. In addition, the Act imposes strict new reporting requirements on companies and their upper management. For example, the CEO and CFO now must personally certify the accuracy of financial data disclosed in financial reports. The Act also provides for far stricter penalties for financial frauds.

BEYOND LAWS AND GOVERNMENT REGULATIONS

With all the laws on the books aimed at preventing corporate wrongdoing, one might be tempted to think of it as a thing of the past. Yet even as more and more regulation is put on the books, corporate wrongdoing continues. If nothing else, the fact that lawbreaking continues in the face of all these strict regulations proves that it is simply impossible to control through written law all aspects of human behavior. Many people will willingly violate any law on the hope or belief that they will not be caught. Others will violate laws that they consider unnecessary or insignificant, such as speed-limit laws. Still others will devise schemes that, while technically legal, are nevertheless morally or ethically wrong.

For these reasons, we contend that corporations must create their own ethical environments—cultures of integrity based upon shared values that are clearly set forth, embraced by all employees, and evenly applied. This will support and establish a climate for the positive ethics reflex described earlier in this primer.

Cultures of integrity in businesses can manifest themselves in both internal and external ways. Internally, companies may devise codes of conduct or codes of ethics that govern how the business will be run and how, for example, employees will be treated. Externally, businesses can choose to interact in certain ways with the world beyond the narrow interests of the company itself, in an effort to improve the lot of all of society.

Virtually all businesses have some sort of culture of integrity. Some value it highly, considering it a key competitive advantage; others largely ignore it. Most companies begin their efforts to develop an internal culture of integrity by adopting a written **code of ethics**—a formal written statement of ethical commitments and expectations. This can be either detailed and elaborate, or fairly simple. Costco, for example, has a simple yet highly effective mission statement that sets forth its code of ethics:

> ○ A **code of ethics** is a formal and written statement of ethical commitments and expectations (see Chapter 6).

> Costco's mission is to continually provide our members with quality goods and services at the lowest possible prices. In order to achieve our mission, we will conduct our business with the following Code of Ethics: A. Obey the Law B. Take Care of Our Customers C. Take Care of Our Employees D. Respect Our Suppliers E. Reward Our Shareholders

From this statement of values, Costco has developed a culture of integrity that forms the basis for far more complex decisions such as those faced in the examples that began this primer. Some businesses, unfortunately, *talk* about their integrity while their actions display that no such culture exists. A good example is Enron. This company had an elaborate code of ethics, but ignored it in several significant dealings that eventually caused the company to disintegrate.

ETHICAL LEADERSHIP: A PERSONAL CHALLENGE

In the final analysis, we must each ask ourselves an important question: Why be ethical? In the best of circumstances the ethical course of action often goes unrewarded. In the worst circumstances it can cost us opportunities for success, or threaten our livelihoods or even our very lives. There

Remember the Key Terms

- Auditing
- Business ethics
- Code of ethics
- Conflicts of interest
- Corporate culture
- Corporate governance
- Corporate social responsibility
- Ethics
- Ethical behavior
- Ethical leadership
- Leadership integrity
- Whistleblower

are examples all around us of unethical behavior going unpunished or, in some cases, even being rewarded. With wildly successful yet unethical public figures ranging from CEOs of Fortune 500 companies to government leaders, it may seem that ethics remains the quaint province of the hopelessly old-fashioned, the out-of-touch. But this is simply wrong.

We have communicated throughout this primer what we believe to be the core truth about ethics in business and in life: *Long-term, sustainable success can only be built upon a foundation of solid ethical behavior.* We should not endeavor to be ethical out of fear of being caught, but rather because of the freedom and success that it brings. Our experience is that the most ethical people are those who have the least fear. They are blessed with the confidence that comes with knowing that their actions are beyond reproach. And in contrast to the few notorious cases of ethics failures that are the stuff of the evening news, history has proven time and time again that those who do good eventually win.

We encourage you to examine all of the topics in *Management 7/E* from the standpoint of ethics. When viewed through the lens of what is truly the right thing to do, many business and management decisions become easier, not harder. It is perhaps that ease, that peace of mind, that is the most reliable indicator of a strong and consistent ethics reflex—the one that we sincerely hope you develop, maintain, and protect throughout your life and professional career.

Management

7th EDITION

7th EDITION

Management

JOHN R. SCHERMERHORN, JR.

John Wiley & Sons, Inc.

New York • Chichester • Weinheim • Brisbane • Singapore • Toronto

ACQUISITIONS EDITOR	*Jeff Marshall*
MARKETING MANAGER	*Charity Robey*
SENIOR PRODUCTION EDITOR	*Patricia McFadden*
SENIOR DESIGNER	*Harold Nolan*
FREELANCE PRODUCTION MANAGER	*Jeanine Furino*
SENIOR PHOTO EDITOR	*Hilary Newman*
PHOTO RESEARCHER	*Teri Stratford*
PHOTO EDITOR	*Sara Wight*
ILLUSTRATION COORDINATOR	*Anna Melhorn*
OUTSIDE PRODUCTION SERVICE	*Ingrao Associates*

COVER PHOTOGRAPH—Photo Credits listed Clockwise from top: ©Photo Disc; Paul Edmondson/Stone; ©Photo Disc; ©Photo Disc; ©Photo Disc; ©Photo Disc; ©Photo Disc; ©Digital Stock; and (center photo) ©Digital Stock.

This book was set in 10/12 Garamond Book by Progressive Information Technologies and printed and bound by R.R. Donnelley and Sons. The cover was printed by Lehigh Press.

This book is printed on acid-free paper.

The paper in this book was manufactured by a mill whose forest management programs include sustained yield harvesting of its timberlands. Sustained yield harvesting principles ensure that the number of trees cut each year does not exceed the amount of new growth.

ISBN: 0-471-43570-8

Printed in the United States of America
10 9 8 7 6 5 4 3

To my sons John Christian and Charles Porter

While you played *It's later now.* *Think* *Home,* *Time* *Hurry home*
I wrote. *Don't worry.* *of all the fun* *now and forever,* *has its ways,* *when you can.*
But always, *Time* *we have.* *will always be* *doesn't it?* *Come laughing, sons.*
I was listening *means love shared,* *Here, there, everywhere,* *wherever* *Not enough,* *Tell us*
and loving *by you* *doing things* *I can be* *not enough,* *your*
you. *and me.* *together.* *with you.* *I often say.* *wonderful stories.*
1984 *1986* *1989* *1992* *1996* *1999*

Songs riding winds.
Mimi,
Uncle George,
Uncle Nelson.
Whispers and choirs.
Silence speaks.
2002

Memorandum

To: **Management 7/E Readers**
From: **Professor Schermerhorn**
Subject: **Getting Connected!**

Welcome to *Management 7/e* and its theme—"Get Connected!"

This is the age of information. The wonders of the Internet and all of its possible connections are transforming the ways we live, work, study, and enjoy leisure. *Management 7/e* was written in the spirit and with the great opportunity of these new times. It was written while I continuously moved back and forth between my writing and resources on the Internet. Doing so opened a vast array of examples, reports, cases, and information that I hope have enriched this book as much as they enhanced my own understanding about the new emerging workplace.

I'd like you to read *Management 7/e* in the same fashion—while connected to the Internet. So, why not open your web browser and use the *Management 7/e* student web site to explore the many informative web links built into the text? Let the Web help you take full advantage of the many interactive learning enhancements that support and extend Reality Checks, Take-It-To-The-Cases, Career Connections, and other features that are found throughout the text.

"Get connected" is the theme, but the goal of *Management 7/e* is to advance your Career Readiness! I have spent many years studying and writing about management, management education, and workplace trends. I also teach management every year to students like yourself. My classes are both large and small, undergraduate and graduate. Increasingly, they utilize the Internet and computer technology to enrich the learning experience. This book is very much a product of what I learn from my teaching and my day-to-day work with students. It was written to bring to you the best of my knowledge and experience, combined with the power of information technology.

Although we can't be in class together, we can meet through the pages of this book and in the on-line experiences of the companion web site. I'm very excited about *Management 7/e*. My students will be on-line as they work with it and participate in my classes. Please join with us in the study of management. Get connected! It's the future.

The *Management 7/E* Philosophy

Management today is like the colorful collage featured in the cover art and throughout the design of *Management 7/e.* Now is a time of cultural pluralism, globalization, and significant change. Just as a beautiful collage offers the beholder a dynamic mix of colors, forms, and impressions, so too does the new workplace. There is no better time than the present to embrace its rich opportunities and prepare for an exciting future.

Today's students are tomorrow's leaders and managers. They are the hope of the 21st century. Just as the workplace in this new century will be vastly different from today's, so too must our teaching and learning environments be different from days gone by. Even while continuing to emphasize cultural diversity, information technology, ethics and social responsibility, the global economy, and the imperatives of quality and high performance, management educators must confidently move students forward on paths toward an uncertain future. New values and management approaches are appearing; the nature of work and organizations is changing; the age of information is not only with us, it is transforming our lives.

Management 7/e is part of the same transformation. This edition has been extensively revised with a sincere commitment to continuous improvement and customer service for both students and instructors alike. Students tell us they liked the self-tests at the end of each chapter in the prior edition. The tests have been continued. Students tell us they want real-world examples. This text is rich in examples embedded in the normal flow of chapter discussions. Students tell us they want more career support and focus on career development. This edition offers an extensive *Career Readiness Workbook* with many professional development opportunities—including a unique Career Advancement Portfolio and systematic skill and outcome assessment format.

Instructors tell us they appreciated the reasonable length of the prior edition and its commitment to straight talk about management theory and practice. The new edition is like one of today's high-performance organizations—neat, trim, fast, web-linked, and highly capable for the task at hand. Instructors tell us they want solid content that covers the major theories and concepts while staying closely tuned to the issues and developments of the day. The new edition still offers solid management foundations while centering them in the real themes, demands, and opportunities of a new and still-developing workplace.

Importantly, instructors tell us they want evermore support for innovative, flexible, and integrative course designs. *Management 7/e* is rich in opportunity as a true resource for learning; in this edition it has become a learning instrument, not just a textbook. It is also a very flexible instrument that easily accommodates a variety of instructional needs and approaches. The chapters are presented in logical order, but can be used in different sequences according to preference. The end-of-book Career Readiness Workbook offers under one cover an extensive array of options that allows for innovative course enrichment tailored to fit the needs of your students.

As management educators, we all face common problems and opportunities when developing courses, working with students, and trying to uphold accreditation standards. *Management 7/e* is based on four constructive balances that I believe remain essential to the agenda of higher education for business and management.

- *The balance of research insights with introductory education.* As educators, we must be willing to make choices when bringing the theories and concepts of our discipline to the attention of the introductory student. The goal should always be to set the best possible foundations for lifelong learning. It should not and cannot be to provide, in one course or program of study, everything a student will ever need to know about management or anything else.
- *The balance of management theory with management practice.* As educators, we must understand the compelling needs of students to sense the potential applications of the material they are reading and thinking about. We must continually bring to their attention good, interesting, and recognizable examples. This holds true both for students with very limited work experience and for those already progressing along established career paths.
- *The balance of present understandings with future possibilities.* As educators, we must actively search for the directions in which the real world of management is heading, and we must actively help students explore and address these directions. We must select and present materials that can both lead students in the right directions and help them develop the confidence and self-respect needed to best deal with them.
- *The balance of what "can" be done with what is, purely and simply, the "right" thing to do.* As educators, we are role models and we set the examples. We must be willing to take stands on issues like equal employment opportunity, quality of work life, managerial ethics, and corporate social responsibility. We must be careful not to let the concept of "contingency" betray the need for positive "action" in managerial practice. And, we must not allow it to draw students away from understanding the many dimensions of performance "accountability" in a fair and just society.

Today, more than ever before, our students have pressing needs for direction as well as suggestion. They have needs for application as well as information. They have needs for integration as well as presentation. Our instructional approaches and materials must deliver on all of these dimensions and more. My goal is to put into your hands and into those of your students a learning resource that can help meet these needs.

Whether your classroom is small or large, the opportunities for progress through educational excellence are equally great. *Management 7/e* and its supporting web sites are my contributions to the future careers of your students and mine.

John R. Schermerhorn, Jr.
Charles G. O'Bleness Professor of Management
Ohio University

Management 7/E Learning Connections

Just like the rich and diverse cultures of our world, today's workplace offers a bold and stimulating mix of people, forms, and impressions. All, of course, are increasingly linked together by the wonders of new technology. Consistent with our dynamic and ever-changing times, *Management 7/e* creates connections between management theory and practice in a new workplace. It offers a mosaic of learning resources and opportunities integrated with the core text. You will find a comprehensive web site connected to every page in the text, as well as interactive case studies, a skills and outcome assessment framework, self-assessment inventories, exercises in teamwork, and a student portfolio builder, all designed to help focus and refine your career readiness.

As you read through this new edition of a popular classroom text, you will discover a focus on the dynamics of management in the context of a challenging and new work environment. You will learn about the responsibilities of a manager and what this means for your future career through many practical examples that are interwoven with core concepts and theories. You will appreciate the clear, concise, and engaging writing style that has made this text very successful year after year. And, you will benefit from the solid foundation of research covered, as well as the high quality of examples presented.

Now is the time to "Get Connected" with management and your career readiness! Let *Management 7/e* and its supporting web sites help you obtain the tools and understanding needed to pursue a successful career in our new and challenging workplace.

CHAPTER FEATURES

Management 7/e was written and designed to serve as an integrated and interactive learning resource. Chapter pedagogical features were chosen to fit a learning model based on clear learning objectives, integrated textual examples, useful end-of-chapter study guides, and extensive on-line interactivity and support.

PLANNING AHEAD AND STUDY QUESTIONS

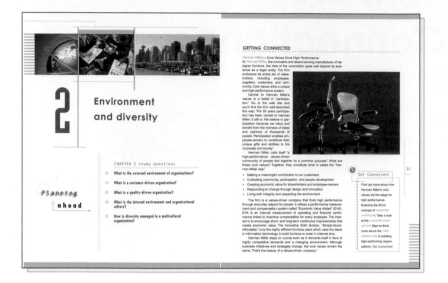

Each chapter opens with two very helpful sections. Planning Ahead presents a set of basic study questions that provide students with the desired learning objectives of the chapter, as well as a framework for a later end-of-chapter review. This is followed by a brief Opening Vignette offering a timely real-world example that highlights the chapter themes.

STUDY GUIDE

Each chapter concludes with an integrated Study Guide. Designed for self-study in preparation for examinations and to consolidate learning, it begins with a Chapter Summary. The summary offers bullet-list responses to the study questions first posed in the chapter-opening Planning Ahead section. Key issues for each major subject heading in the chapter are highlighted. The summary is followed by a list of Key Terms that is keyed to page numbers in the chapter where definitions can be located. Next comes a complete chapter Self-Test—consisting of multiple-choice, true-false, short response, and application essay questions. This is an excellent way to prepare for examinations, and the author's responses to each question are provided on-line. A guide to suggested Career Readiness Activities found in the end-of-text Career Readiness Workbook and in on-line electronic resources concludes the section.

THEMATIC BOXES AND MARGIN PHOTOS

To exemplify the importance of timely issues in the new workplace, Thematic Boxes with special photo-illustrated examples are embedded as part of the general text discussion for each chapter. The boxes provide concise and relevant examples without interrupting the flow of the material. The examples range from small and entrepreneurial firms to large multinational organizations to organizations in the nonprofit sector. Themes for the boxes include Diversity, Ethics & Social Responsibility, Globalization, High-Performance Organizations, and more. Additional, brief, real-world examples are featured as Margin Photo Essays in each chapter.

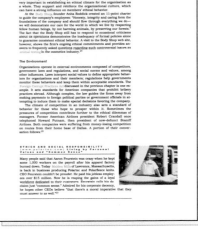

CAREER CONNECTION SIDEBARS

Each chapter includes a Career Connection Sidebar that links text material to realitics and developments in the new workplace. Written and designed in the style of a professional business magazine, these sidebars pose questions to the reader that are relevant to one's career development and professionalism. With Internet links and an on-line version, readers can follow the career connection in more depth and detail.

TAKE-IT-TO-THE-CASE!

Each chapter is identified with a Critical Thinking Case from the end-of-text Career Development Workbook. This case is introduced as part of chapter content with the feature Take-It-To-The-Case. The feature introduces the case with application to the material being addressed, and directs the reader to explore further information and engage in critical thinking about the organization and the situation described.

REALITY CHECKS

There are a lot of facts and figures available regarding developments in the new workplace and the way people and organizations are responding to them. The innovative Reality Checks in each chapter introduce a key fact or survey result relevant to text discussion. Each is linked to an interactive on-line activity that asks the reader to respond to further questions regarding the issue at hand. Actual results on-line from surveys and data sources are then provided to complete the "reality check" experience.

MANAGER'S NOTEPADS

To assist in developing practical applications, Manager's Notepads are provided in each chapter. These notepads consist of concise lists of helpful hints that describe the "do's" and "don'ts" of managerial behavior. They appear as boxed inserts conveniently placed throughout the text.

MARGIN LIST NOTES AND MARGIN RUNNING GLOSSARY

The margins of the book offer a built-in study guide and chapter outline. Special Margin List Notes call attention to key bulleted or numbered lists of information as they are presented throughout the text. Boldfaced key terms are also called out and defined in the margins. They form a Margin Running Glossary of key concepts from the chapter discussion.

Career Readiness Workbook

The innovative Career Readiness Workbook provides many ways to take full advantage of the management course and advance your career readiness. Included as a major component in the workbook is an updated version of the unique Career Advancement Portfolio®—a student portfolio builder, for both print and on-line formats, inclusive of a skill and outcome assessment framework. Also included is an extensive set of learning resources and activities: Cases for Critical Thinking, Integrative Learning Activities, Exercises in Teamwork, Self-Assessment Inventories, and guides to The *Fast Company* Collection on-line.

CAREER ADVANCEMENT PORTFOLIO

The Career Advancement Portfolio® provides print and on-line templates for personal student portfolios that document one's academic and personal accomplishments. This resource allows the students to frame and summarize their credentials for external review in the quest for internships and full-time employment. It also offers a way for course assignments to be inventoried for purposes of both academic assessment and competency demonstration. The special option for building and putting on-line an Electronic Career Portfolio is especially consistent with the expectations and opportunities of the information age. Both the print and electronic student portfolios can be easily maintained and updated for purposes of outcome assessment within a course or program of study, as well as for the student's personal development and career development.

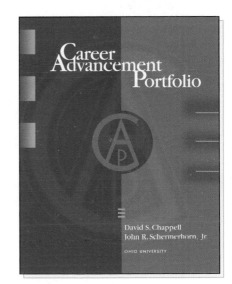

To facilitate portfolio development *Management 7/e* is linked with a Skill and Outcome Assessment Framework that focuses students on six critical skill and outcome assessment areas: Communication, Leadership, Teamwork, Self-management, Critical Thinking, and Professionalism. Each of the workbook features and resources is indexed within this framework to identify learning activities with potential contributions to each skill and outcome area. Master writing and presentation projects for individuals and teams are also suggested to apply the various features to the development of essential written and oral communication skills.

CASES FOR CRITICAL THINKING

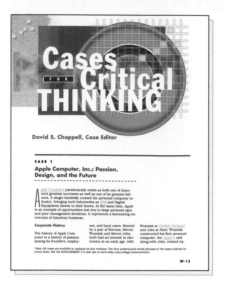

The Cases for Critical Thinking section contains a case specifically developed for each text chapter. Individual cases bring to life the decisions managers must make every day on both a national and global level. The case studies describe situations faced by organizations and their managers in a range of contexts. Each case concludes with a list of questions for the student to answer concerning the in-depth scenarios they are given. Interactive versions of cases are available on-line through the *Management 7/e* student web site. These on-line cases are updated regularly and new cases will be posted to enrich the alternatives for classroom use.

INTEGRATIVE LEARNING ACTIVITIES

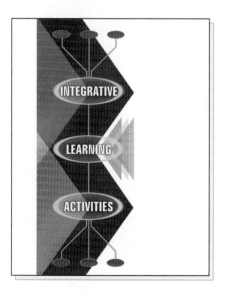

Integration is one of the important thrusts in management and management education today. Included in the workbook are easy-to-use and highly involving integrative learning activities that can supplement various aspects of a course. A set of Internet Research and Presentation Projects helps students gain familiarity with important real-world issues while further building their skills in using the Internet, gathering and interpreting information, and making written and oral presentations. Integrated Cross-Functional Cases on Outback Steak House and Richard Branson's Virgin Enterprises further allow for the management process and the new workplace to be examined in the context of entrepreneurship and old economy–new economy transitions. The cases can be used in whole or in parts to best fit the instructor's course design. They are very useful to reinforce the importance of functional integration, technology utilization, and strategic thinking in management today.

EXERCISES IN TEAMWORK

A rich portfolio of Exercises in Teamwork offers opportunities to explore, in the team setting, a variety of issues and topics from chapter and class discussions. Many options are available in the complete set of 30 exercises, with all presenting situations that provide the basis for group discussion or individual analytical exercises. Through participation in the exercises students can gain a better understanding of how text concepts and ideas get put into practical use. They gain self-insight also through the experience of participating in real team situations. Instructions are clear and self-explanatory, and formats for group discussion and class interaction are also provided.

SELF-ASSESSMENTS

Self awareness and insight are critical to one's continued personal and professional development. The workbook appropriately provides a diverse set of Self-assessment inventories of managerial tendencies and perspectives. This set and additional assessments are also available in interactive self-scoring formats on-line at the student web site. By completing the self-assessments, students analyze their knowledge of management issues and their possession of the skills necessary to tackle these issues. Each assessment is broken down into instructions on how to complete the assignment, directions for scoring, and an interpretation of the score along with guidelines for understanding its meaning in a larger context.

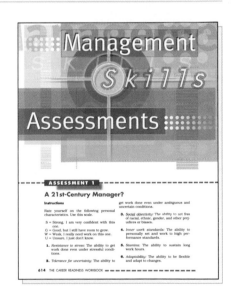

THE *FAST COMPANY* COLLECTION ON-LINE

A unique collection of readings was selected by Prof. Schermerhorn from the popular new economy magazine, *Fast Company*. Each reading was chosen for its insights into developments in the current world of work and organizations, and for its strong career readiness themes and implications. Look for the following articles, which are available on-line on the student E-Resource center.

- Scott Kirsner, "Collision Course"
- Robert Reich, "The Company of the Future"
- Alan Weber, "Danger: Toxic Company"
- Tony Schwartz, "How Do You Feel?"
- Tom Peters, "The Brand Called 'You'"

INTEGRATED MANAGEMENT 7/E WEB SITES

There is no better way to "Get Connected!" than to experience and utilize the rich opportunities of the *Management 7/E* web site, both as a student and an instructor.

STUDENT WEB SITE

An extensive Student Web Site has been developed in support of *Management 7/e* both for classroom applications and for distance learning environments. This site is available at www.wiley.com/college/schermerhorn. It includes the following special resources for enrichment of the student learning experience.

- PowerPoint downloads for text and supplementary figures
- PowerPoint downloads for special class activities
- Interactive on-line versions of in-chapter Reality Checks
- Interactive on-line versions of all cases
- Interactive on-line versions of self-assessments
- Internet links to organizations and information sites relevant to chapter materials
- A full electronic version of the Career Advancement Portfolio®
- An on-line study guide for students, including chapter self-tests
- The *Fast Company* Collection on-line.

INSTRUCTOR'S WEB SITE

An extensive Instructor's Web Site supports *Management 7/E* for classroom applications and distance learning settings. This site is available at www.wiley.com/college/schermerhorn. It includes the following special resources to support instructors in their commitments to rich and stimulating student learning environments.

- PowerPoint downloads for text figures
- PowerPoint downloads from Prof. Schemerhorn's actual classes
- Supplementary in-class exercises and activities, with supporting PowerPoint downloads and presentations
- Special "quick-hitters" for in-class use and with special value for large-section courses
- Instructor's versions of on-line cases
- Complete on-line Instructor's Resource Guide containing teaching support for the textbook, for all features in the Career Readiness Workbook, and with additional recommendations for course enrichment
- And . . . The Author's Classroom!

The Author's Classroom

Prof. Schermerhorn teaches management on a regular basis to undergraduate students in both large and small class sections. At Ohio University he has won the University Professor Award, the school's campus-wide honor for outstanding undergraduate teaching. The Author's Classroom is a special on-line resource that he has designed to bring to all instructors the activities, approaches, and materials from his actual classroom. Updated on a regular basis, this unique feature enables instructors to enrich their courses by building upon Prof. Schermerhorn's approaches with his students. By going on-line with The Author's Classroom, instructors find additional teaching ideas and resources for each chapter, including Prof. Schermerhorn's personal PowerPoint presentations, special in-class activities, preferred web sites for browsing during class, and more. By using *Management 7/e* you get more than a textbook, and you get more than your students' access to a complete learning resource with integrated text, Career Development Workbook, and student web site. You also get to join The Author's Classroom.

Management 7/E
Highlights of the New Edition

Like its predecessors, *Management 7/e* introduces the essentials of management as they apply within the contemporary work environment. Its first goal is to cover the appropriate topics in a manner relevant to the dynamic environment of management today and changes taking place in the new workplace. Its second goal is to always do so with sufficient depth so that the introductory student gains a solid foundation in management. The third goal is to do all of this in an interesting, engaging, and applied way—one that holds students' attention and stimulates them to actively relate to both the material at hand and the everyday examples that abound in their experiences.

The subject matter of *Management 7/e* remains carefully chosen to meet AACSB accreditation guidelines while allowing extensive flexibility to fit various course designs and class sizes. The book is thorough from a curriculum standpoint but written to meet the needs of the introductory student. Importantly, this is done with special attention to an integrated treatment of the environment, quality operations, cultural diversity, the global economy, and ethics and social responsibility, and the growing influence of new information technologies as paramount concerns and themes of our day.

There are many new things to look for in this edition. Along with updates of core material, *Management 7/e* offers a number of changes in the organization, content, and design that respond to current themes and developments in the theory and practice of management.

ORGANIZATION

- The fundamentals of the management process—planning, organizing, leading, and controlling—are thoroughly addressed in the timely context of change leadership and the challenges of work and careers in an emerging new economy.
- The book is organized into five parts with themes relevant to today's organizations: (1) Management Today, (2) Context, (3) Mission, (4) Organization, (5) Leadership.
- *Part 1: Management Today*—opens the book with a clear focus on the exciting and dynamic new workplace, environment, and diversity, and the importance of information technology and decision making.
- *Part 2: Context*—sets the context for management by reviewing historical foundations, examining the forces of globalization, and highlighting the importance of ethics and social responsibility.
- *Part 3: Mission*—integrates planning and controlling as management functions, includes a full chapter on strategic management and an all-new chapter on entrepreneurship and new ventures.

- *Part 4: Organization*—covers the essentials of organizing as a management function, with special attention to new developments in organization structures, designs, and work processes and systems.
- *Part 5: Leadership*—offers extensive coverage of leadership, including in-depth coverage of motivation and rewards, individual performance, job design, stress, teams, and teamwork, communication and interpersonal skills, and change leadership.

CONTENT

Throughout *Management 7/e*, every effort is made to bring in the latest thinking and concepts facing managers and organizations today. In addition to core themes of diversity, competitive advantage, quality, globalization, and empowerment, specific coverage has been enhanced in this edition on the following topics and more:

multicultural organizations • ethnocentrism • cultural relativism • strategic leadership • competitive advantage • self-management • change leadership • customer relationship management • supply chain management • e-business • entrepreneurship • organizational learning • lifelong learning • emotional intelligence • horizontal organizations • cross-functional teams • virtual teams • career readiness • virtual organizations • process value analysis • reengineering • work-life balance • strategic human resource planning • boundaryless organizations • performance-based rewards • job stress • alternative work arrangements • cross-cultural communication • conflict management • negotiation • teamwork •innovation processes • career portfolios

DESIGN

The design of *Management 7/e* has been created in specific response to the author's experience as a classroom instructor and with the assistance of helpful feedback from management educators using the prior edition. With a clean and open look in a four-color format, the design is our attempt to provide introductory management students with a book that is consistent in style with the professional literature they can and should be reading. Look for the following features in *Management 7/e*.

- Chapter Opening Vignettes with Chapter Study Questions
- Thematic boxes on timely workplace themes
- Career Connection Sidebars
- Manager's Notepads
- Reality Checks
- Take-It-To-The-Case!
- Margin List Identifiers and Margin Running Glossary
- Margin Photo Essays
- Chapter Study Guide ending chapters with a Summary, Key Terms, Self-Test, and suggested Career Readiness Activities
- Career Readiness Workbook with Career Advancement Portfolio®, Cases for Critical Thinking, Integrative Learning Activities, Exercises in Teamwork, Self-Assessments, and The *Fast Company* Collection on-line

INSTRUCTOR'S SUPPORT

Management 7/e is supported by a comprehensive resource package that assists the instructor in creating a motivating and enthusiastic learning environment. As previously mentioned, the on-line support and the Instructor's Web Site are exceptional—including PowerPoint slides, The Author's Classroom, and more. In addition, instructors have available to them further support:

- Complete Instructor's Resource Guide—a unique, comprehensive inventory of resources for building a system of customized instruction. The guide offers helpful teaching ideas, advice on course development, sample assignments, and chapter-by-chapter text highlights, learning objectives, lecture outlines, class exercises, lecture notes, answers to all end-of-chapter material, and tips on using cases. The entire guide is also available on disk.

- An updated comprehensive Test Bank is available, consisting of 2,700 multiple-choice, true-false, and essay questions categorized by pedagogical element (margin notes, margin terms, or general text knowledge), page number, and type of question (factual or applied). The entire test bank is also available in a computerized version, MICROTEST Diplone for Windows, created by Brownstone Research Group, for use on an IBM PC computer (or a compatible) running on MS-WINDOWS.

- The comprehensive Nightly Business Report Video Package offers video selections from the highly respected business news program. These video clips tie directly to the theme of the management mosaic and bring to life many of the case examples used in the text as well as others from outside sources. Video supplements are also available for the Integrative Cross-Functional Cases.

- The Business Extra Program, a partnership between Wiley and the Dow Jones Company, offers an exciting new way to extend your textbook beyond the walls of the classroom. The program is comprised of the On-Line Business Survival Guide—which includes a special password for Wiley's Business Extra web site, through which your students get instant access to a wealth of current articles, as well as a special offer for *The Wall Street Journal Interactive Edition.*

- Web CT and Blackboard support for *Management 7/E* is available for on-line teaching and learning designs supported by these systems. Wiley will provide basic content based upon material accompanying the text. Instructors have the option of uploading additional material and customizing existing content to fit their needs.

- Mastery Testing a web-based testing system that provides the student with an interactive on-line bank of quantitative problem sets which includes coaching and feedback comments on incorrect responses. The student can test him/herself repeatedly by answering the randomly generated questions which allow for self-paced drilling in preparation for a quiz or exam. This particular program contains an Adaptive Mastery Testing Feature which customizes each student's session based upon his or her demonstrated learning needs. A student can only proceed to a more difficult set of questions once he or she has answered correctly a certain number of less challenging questions.

Acknowedgments

Management 7/e was made possible through the extraordinary efforts of many people. The project was initiated and completed with the support of my editor, Jeff Marshall, with the assistance of Marian Provenzano, Developmental Editor. As always, a unique team at John Wiley & Sons worked together to build and complete the many facets of this book. Special thanks go to the following superb group of Wiley personnel who worked tirelessly on the project: Susan Elbe (publisher), Harold Nolan (designer), Hilary Newman (photo research), Suzanne Ingrao (Ingrao Associates), Patricia McFadden and Jeanine Furino (production), Cindy Rhoads (supplements), and Charity Robey (marketing). I also wish to thank Anna Melhorn for overseeing the illustrations and Fred Courtright for his work compiling the permissions.

In this edition, we wanted to offer the best possible selection of cases and to bring them alive on the Internet. To do that, we turned to a great teacher—David Chappell of Ohio University. As Case and Web Site Editor for the project, he responded with just what we'd hoped for—exceptional quality and great sensitivity to the needs of instructors and students. The Integrated Cross-Functional Video Case on Outback Steakhouse is a result of the fine work of George Puia of Indiana State University and Marilyn Taylor, University of Missouri, Kansas City. To Michael K. McCuddy of Valparaiso University, for PowerPoint presentations, and Bonnie Fremgen, University of Notre Dame, for the In-Basket Exercise, goes a special thank you for their original and exceptional contributions.

We also wanted a truly useful instructor's resource guide. For that, we turned to Michael K. McCuddy of Valparaiso University, who also provided a top-quality product. We wanted a substantial test bank. To do that we relied on the skills of Michael K. McCuddy as well. Finally, we wanted a stimulating and relevant web site. For that, we turned to David Kear of the New Technology Group of John Wiley & Sons. For the highly substantial and informative NBR Videos, we thank Jack Kahn and Emily Richardson of Nightly Business Report.

Writing and revising *Management 7/e* came at a new time in my family life—sons Christian and Porter emerging as young men intent on living their ways, not ours, wife Ann growing still in beauty and insight as we together step into the future. It's nice now to be able to think more about all that, to prepare for the next border crossings. And as always, I sincerely hope that the results of my work meet their expectations.

I offer this final word of thanks to the following colleagues whose willingness to review and critique parts of this book at various stages of its life added immensely to my understanding. Always, I tried to listen to and deal constructively with your suggestions. Every point was considered and appreciated. I hope that you, too, feel the final product justifies your fine efforts. Special thanks to Felix Kamuche, *Morehouse College;* Dr. Roosevelt Butler, *The College of New Jersey;* Donald R. Schreiber, *Baylor University;* Gerald F. Smith, *University of Northern Iowa;* Charles Goodman, *Texas A&M University;* Karen Eboch, *Bowling Green State University;* Nancy M. Carr, *Community College of Philadelphia;* Abigail Hubbard, *University of*

Houston; David M. Hall, *Saginaw Valley State University;* Joseph Kavanaugh, *Sam Houston State University;* Pamela Lieb, *The College of New Jersey;* Nathan Himelstein, *Essex County College;* Margaret Hill, *Texas A&M University;* Dr. Bruce Charnov, *Hofstra University;* Linda W. Ross, *Rowan University;* Taggart F. Frost, *University of Northern Iowa;* Sheila J. Pechinski, *University of Maine;* Frederick D. Greene, PhD, *Manhattan College;* Mark J. Weber, PhD, *University of Minnesota;* and James Phillips, *Northeastern State University.*

For past reviews, I would like to thank: Bonnie Baker, *Siena College;* Santanu Borah, *University of North Alabama;* Mark Butler, *San Diego State University;* Clarence Butz, *Azusa Pacific University;* Kent Carter, *Westminster College;* Bert Connell, *Loma Linda University;* Elizabeth Cooper, *University of Rhode Island;* Kenneth Everard, *The College of New Jersey;* Bonnie Fremgen, *University of Notre Dame;* Terri Friel, *Eastern Kentucky University;* William Gardner, *University of Mississippi;* Gerson M. Goldberg, *Oklahoma Panhandle State University;* Carnella Hardin, *Glendale Community College;* David Hoag, *St. Louis Community College Merimec*; William LaPorte, *Capital Community Technical College;* Lloyd Letcher, *Kansas State University;* Douglas McCabe, *Georgetown University;* Kevin McCarthy, *Baker University;* William Moor, *Arizona State University;* Benjamin Morris, *Saint Leo College;* Ilona Motsiff, *Trinity College;* Chuck Nuckles, *Concordia University;* Vernon A. Quarstein, *St. Leo College;* Michael Raphael, *Central Connecticut University;* James G. Salvucci, *Curry College;* Roy Simerly, *East Carolina University;* Cynthia Singer, *Union County College;* Margaret Sprenz, *David N. Meyers College;* Shanthi Srinivas, *California State University;* Ram Subramanian, *Grand Valley State University;* Burley Walker, *University of Texas;* Bobbie Williams, *Georgia Southern University;* Cheryl Wyrick, *California State Polytechnic University;* and Jiaquin Yang, *University of North Dakota.*

Brief Contents

Contents

*The *Fast Company* Collection does not appear in this textbook but is available on-line on the student E-Resource center.

PART TWO | CONTEXT

• Chapter 5
Global Dimensions of Management   114

• Chapter 6
Ethical Behavior and Social Responsibility   144

CAREER READINESS WORKBOOK   W-1

About the Author

Dr. John R. Schermerhorn, Jr. is the Charles G. O'Bleness Professor of Management in the College of Business at Ohio University, where he teaches graduate and undergraduate courses in management. Dr. Schermerhorn earned a Ph.D. in organizational behavior from Northwestern University, an MBA (with distinction) in management and international business from New York University, and a BS in business administration from the State University of New York at Buffalo. He has taught at Tulane University, the University of Vermont, and Southern Illinois University at Carbondale, where he also served as Head of the Department of Management and Associate Dean of the College of Business Administration.

Highly dedicated to serving the needs of practicing managers in all types of organizations, Dr. Schermerhorn has written *Management 7/e* to help others bridge the gaps between the theory and practice of management. At Ohio University Dr. Schermerhorn has been named a University Professor, the university's highest campus-wide honor for excellence in undergraduate teaching. He is committed to instructional excellence and curriculum innovation, and is working extensively with technology utilization and Internet applications in the classroom. He serves as a guest speaker at colleges and universities, lecturing on developments in higher education for business and management, as well as on instructional approaches and innovations.

Dr. Schermerhorn's extensive international experience adds a unique global dimension to his textbooks. He has worked in China, Egypt, Indonesia, Thailand, Malaysia, Vietnam, the Philippines, Poland, Hungary, Venezuela, and Tanzania. He has also served as a Visiting Professor of Management at the Chinese University of Hong Kong, as on-site Coordinator of the Ohio University MBA and Executive MBA programs in Malaysia, and as Director of the Interdisciplinary Center for Southeast Asia Studies at Ohio University. He is also a member of the graduate faculty at Bangkok University, Thailand, and serves as advisor to the Lao-American College in Vientiane, Laos.

A dedicated scholar, Dr. Schermerhorn is a member of the Academy of Management, where he served as chairperson of the Management Education and Development Division. He is known to educators and students alike as senior co-author of *Managing Organizational Behavior 7/e* (Wiley, 2000), *Introducing Management* (Wiley, 2000), and *Basic Organizational Behavior 2/e* (Wiley, 1997). He has also published numerous articles in the *Academy of Management Journal*, *Academy of Management Review*, *Academy of Management Executive*, *Organizational Dynamics*, *Asia-Pacific Journal of Management*, and the *Journal of Management Development*, among other scholarly journals.

Management

7th EDITION

1

The dynamic new workplace

Planning
ahead

GETTING CONNECTED

Monster.Com—Smart People Create Their Own Futures

As the leading global on-line career site, Monster.com represents the growing field of on-line job placement services available on the Web. Along with JobDirect, Careerbulder, and others, they open new career development options.

Job candidates and employers can connect easier and faster by utilizing these on-line services, including resumé postings, interview tips, company research, and job searches. College students can use Monstertrak.com to serve their career development needs. For those relocating, Monstermoving.com offers help in planning a move, finding a moving company, mortgage financing, and even finding temporary housing.

Monster.com supports over 8 million registered job seekers and a resumé database containing over 4 million unique resumés and 380,000 unique job opportunities. According to Media Metrix, it is the number-one destination for job seekers and the 79th most visited domain on the Internet.

The Monster.com web site boasts an impressive 38.6 pages viewed per user and experiences over 15.2 million visits per month. Monster.com represents itself as a "lifelong career network" that includes services to help everyone from recent college grads all the way up to seasoned executives.

The "Monster" isn't just a domestic resource for job seekers and employers. It has gone global, and you can too. Sporting a list of Who's Who among Corporate America, Monster.com provides research on companies throughout the United States and overseas in several foreign countries, including France, Germany, Singapore, Australia, and others.

There's no complacency here, no becoming too comfortable with success. The "Monster" keeps changing as its markets develop. It launched a service recently that supports "free agents"—the service claims to be the world's first on-line, auction-style marketplace for talent. Contract workers can link up with employers interested in hiring their services. Services are offered and "bids" are exchanged between workers and potential employers.

Monster.com is headquartered in Maynard, Massachusetts. It is the flagship brand of the Interactive division of TMP Worldwide Inc., one of the world's largest search and selection agencies. TMP's clients include more than 480 of the *Fortune* 500 companies.[1]

@ **Get Connected!**

You too can create a monster. Explore Monster.com or any other on-line career site of your choosing. Use resources from the end-of-text Career Advancement Portfolio® to write and post your on-line resumé. Get connected!

The 21st century has brought with it a new workplace, one in which everyone must adapt to a rapidly changing society with constantly shifting demands and opportunities. Learning and speed are *in*; habit and complacency are *out.* Organizations are fast changing, as is the nature of work itself. The economy is global, driven by innovation and technology. Even the concept of success, personal and organizational, is evolving as careers take new forms and organizations transform to serve new customer expectations. All such developments, say the editors of *Fast Company* magazine, affect us all, offering both "unparalleled opportunity and unprecedented uncertainty." In this age of continuous challenge, a compelling message must be heard by all of us—smart people and smart organizations create their own futures![2]

Speaking about the future, what do companies like the The Container Store (consumer retailing), SAS Institute (software development), Cisco Systems (network technology), Southwest Airlines (airline transportation), and Charles Schwab (financial services), all have in common? They represent very different industries, but together they are ranked at the top of *Fortune* magazine's list of the 100 Best Companies to Work For in America.[3] Unlike the once-mighty Xerox, on the verge of bankruptcy as this is being written, they are all companies with futures.

In the quest for the future the best employers share an important commitment to people. Amidst high performance expectations, they offer supportive work environments that allow people's talents to be fully utilized while providing them with both valued rewards and respect for work-life balance. At the best of the best, for example, employees benefit from flexible work schedules, on-site child care, on-site health and fitness centers, domestic partner benefits, as well as opportunities for profit sharing, cash bonuses, and competitive salaries. In short, the best employers are not just extremely good at attracting and retaining talented employees. They also excel at supporting them in a high-performance context so that their talents are fully utilized and their contributions highly valued.

After studying high-performing companies like those just mentioned, management scholars Charles O'Reilly and Jeffrey Pfeffer conclude that success is achieved because they are better than their competitors at getting extraordinary results from the people working for them. "These companies have won the war for talent," they say, "not just by being great places to work—although they are that—but by figuring out how to get the best out of all of their people, every day."[4] This, in large part, is what *Management 7/e* and your management course are all about. Both are designed to introduce you to the concepts, themes, and directions that are consistent with career success and organizational leadership in today's high-performance work settings. As you begin, consider further the challenge posed by the title of O'Reilly and Pfeffer's book: *Hidden Value: How Great Companies Achieve Extraordinary Results with Ordinary People.* Let your study of management be devoted to learning as much as you can to prepare for a career-long commitment to getting great things accomplished through working with people.

@
Get Connected!

Follow the Web links for all items printed in blue to enrich your learning experience. They can be easily accessed by turning on your Internet browser and visiting the *Management 7/e* student web site.

WORKING IN THE NEW ECONOMY

Yes, we now live and work in a new economy ripe with challenging opportunities and dramatic uncertainty.[5] The new economy is a networked economy in which people, institutions, and nations are increasingly influenced by the Internet and continuing developments in information technology.[6] The chapter opener on Monster.com is but one example of how the Web and its vast networking capabilities are changing our lives. The new economy is a global economy, whose scope increases daily. The nations of the world and their economies are increasingly interdependent, and with this globalization comes great challenges as well as opportunities. The new economy is knowledge driven. We must all accept that success must be forged in workplaces reinvented to unlock the great potential of human intelligence. The high-performance themes of the day are "respect," "participation," "empowerment," "involvement," "teamwork," "self-management," and more.

Undoubtedly, too, the new economy is performance driven. Expectations of organizations and their members are very high. Success must be earned in a society that demands nothing less than the best from all its institutions. Organizations are expected to continuously excel on performance criteria that include concerns for innovativeness, employee development, and social responsibility, as well as more traditional measures of profitability and investment value. When they fail, customers, investors and employees are quick to let them know. For individuals, there are no guarantees of long-term employment. Jobs are increasingly earned and re-earned every day through one's performance accomplishments. Careers are being redefined in terms of "flexibility," "free agency," "skill portfolios," and "entrepreneurship." Today, it takes initiative and discipline and continuous learning to stay in charge of your own career destiny. Tomorrow's challenges are likely to be even greater.

Just what are the challenges ahead?

INTELLECTUAL CAPITAL

The dynamic pathways into the future are evident among new benchmarks being set in and by progressive organizations everywhere. Many will be introduced throughout *Management 7/e* and on its special student web_site. You should follow developments at companies like General Electric, for example, where former CEO Jack Welch has been viewed by some as one of the great corporate leaders of our time. In a highly competitive, fast-paced, and high-technology business environment, he claims that the essential dimension of organizational success rests with the talents of people. "We have to get everybody in the organization involved," Welch says about GE. "If you do that right, the best ideas rise to the top."[7]

Welch isn't alone in his views on executive leadership. At Herman Miller, the innovative manufacturer of designer furniture, respect for employees is a rule of thumb. The firm's core values include the statement: "Our greatest assets as a corporation are the gifts, talents and abilities of our employee-owners. . . . When we as a corporation invest in developing people, we are investing in our future." Former CEO Max DePree says, "At Herman Miller, we talk about the difference between being successful and being exceptional. Being successful is meeting goals in a good way—being exceptional is reaching your potential."[8]

The point of these examples is clear. People—what they know, what they learn, and what they do with it—are the ultimate foundations of organizational performance. They represent an **intellectual capital** defined as the collective brainpower or shared knowledge of a workforce that can be used to create value.[9] Indeed, the ultimate elegance of the new workplace may well be its ability to combine the talents of many people, sometimes thousands of them, to achieve unique and significant results.

This is the new age of the **knowledge worker**—someone whose mind is a critical asset to employers and who adds to the intellectual capital of the organization.[10] If you want a successful career in the new economy you must be willing to reach for the heights of personal competency and

www.volunteermatch.org

Not all work is "for-pay work." In today's complex society nonprofit organizations fulfill important roles, and they depend on volunteers to make it all possible. VolunteerMatch of San Francisco helps match volunteers across America with nonprofits needing their services. It is owned by ImpactOnline, Inc., a firm dedicated to increasing volunteerism through the Internet.

○ **Intellectual capital** is the collective brainpower or shared knowledge of a workforce.

○ A **knowledge worker** is someone whose knowledge is a critical asset to employers.

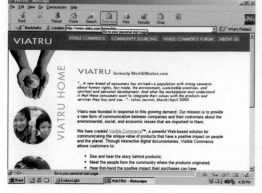

Old world artisan skills mix with the new economy's Internet to offer new business opportunities to impoverished areas around the globe. With the assistance of Viatru, handicraft industries in Nepal formerly threatened with extinction are finding new outlets for their goods. With the help of the Association of Craft Producers, a nongovernmental organization in Katmandu that supplies the goods through Viatru, the local copper craft guild is experiencing a rebirth. Gopi Ram, a local artisan, works long days, but his 7,500 rupees per month is double what he was earning before Viatru came along. Its new designs, market information and connections to the Museum of Fine Arts-Boston, Starbucks, The Body Shop, and other national retailers boost sales and the flow of money to needy villages. Viatru coordinates sales of products from emerging-economy firms that support child-education, retirement benefits, and improved labor conditions. Michelle Long, founder of Viatru states, "More work for more people is really what it is all about."[11]

accomplishment. You must be a self-starter willing to continuously learn from experience even in an environment that grows daily more complex and challenging.

GLOBALIZATION

Japanese management consultant Kenichi Ohmae suggests that the national boundaries of world business have largely disappeared.[12] At the very least we can say that they are fast disappearing. Who can state with confidence where their favorite athletic shoes or the parts for their personal computer were manufactured? More and more products are designed in one country, while their component parts are made in others and the assembly of the final product takes place in still another. Top managers at Ford, IBM, Sony, and other global corporations, for example, have no real need for the word "overseas" in everyday business vocabulary. They operate as global businesses that view themselves as equidistant from customers and suppliers, wherever in the world they may be located.

○ **Globalization** is the worldwide interdependence of resource flows, product markets, and business competition.

This is part of the force of **globalization,** the worldwide interdependence of resource flows, product markets, and business competition that characterizes our new economy.[13] In a globalized world, countries and peoples are increasingly interconnected through the news, in travel and lifestyles, in labor markets and employment patterns, and in business dealings. Government leaders now worry about the competitiveness of nations just as corporate leaders worry about business competitiveness.[14] The world is increasingly arranged in regional economic blocs, with Asia, North and Latin America, and Europe as key anchors, and with Africa fast emerging to claim its economic potential. Like any informed citizen, you too must understand the forces of globalization and be prepared to participate in them.

TECHNOLOGY

The global economy isn't the only beneficiary of developments with new technology. Who hasn't been affected by the Internet and the World Wide Web? It's part of the theme of *Management 7/e*—"Getting Connected"—

and the Internet support for the book greatly enriches your learning opportunities. Just join in and follow the links, get connected . . . the paths are endless, ever changing, and exciting to explore. If you aren't willing to become a participant in the still-exploding world of the information superhighway, you'll be left behind. It's not an option anymore; it's an entry requirement in the new workplace.

"With computers and high technology," someone once said, "work will never be the same." It has already changed and you had better be ready. For better or worse, we now live in a technology-driven world increasingly dominated by bar codes, automatic tellers, computerized telemarketing campaigns, electronic mail, Internet resources, electronic commerce, and more. Computers and information technology help organizations of all types and sizes, locally and internationally, to speed transactions and improve decision making.[15] From the small retail store to the large multinational firm, technology is an indispensable part of everyday operations—whether one is checking inventory, making a sales transaction, ordering supplies, or analyzing customer preferences.

These lessons of "e-business" are also being transferred to "e-government," as local and national governments rush to take advantage of the Internet revolution. And when it comes to communication, within the many parts of an organization or between the organization and its suppliers, customers, and external constituents, geographical distances hardly matter anymore. Computer networking can bring together almost anyone from anywhere in the world at the mere touch of a keyboard. In "virtual space" people in remote locations can hold meetings, access common databases, share information and files, make plans, and solve problems together—all without ever meeting face-to-face.

As the pace and complexities of technological change accelerate, the demand for knowledge workers with the skills to utilize technology to full advantage is increasing. The shift to an information-based economy is dramatically changing employment. By 2005, for example, less than 20 percent of American workers are projected to be in industry; the lowest percentage since 1850.[16] The fastest-growing occupations are computer related. Skilled help is in demand; low-skill workers displaced from declining industries find it difficult to find new jobs offering adequate pay. In a world where technological change is occurring at an accelerating rate, computer literacy must be mastered and continuously developed as a foundation for career success.

CAREER CONNECTION

Technology

**ServiceArizona E-Government
A Model for Web Services?**

The stereotypes of long lines and poor service are being tested by moving many government service activities to the Internet. One interesting experiment is ServiceArizona. The Arizona motor vehicle department supports registration renewals, applications for new ID cards, ordering personalized license plates, and other services 24 hours every day through their web site. The site has saved the state over $1.7 million per year compared to counter transactions. Even more impressive is the level of service and the customer approval ratings the site receives. In a recent survey, the motor vehicle department received an 80 percent approval rating for its service, far and away the best of any department in the state.

While the initial interest in most government web sites is to lower costs, the very nature of the relationship between a government and its constituents can be altered. The savings are not trivial—if governments can replicate the 20 percent savings on supply chain management that private firms record, that is a savings of $110 billion/year in the United State alone. On-line voting has been tried in a few areas, and many candidates for public office are experimenting with on-line campaigning and promotion. As a result of this and other attempts, the next Internet revolution will be e-government.

QUESTION: How will the Internet alter the relationship between government and the governed? What changes can be expected in the next five years? Is there a career for you in government service?

DIVERSITY

When published by the Hudson Institute, the report *Workforce 2000: Work and Workers for the 21st Century* created an immediate stir in business circles, among government policymakers, and in the public eye.[17] It called

○ **Workforce diversity** describes differences among workers in gender, race, age, ethnic culture, able-bodiness, religious affiliation, and sexual orientation.

attention to demographic trends their presence felt in the American workplace: the slow growth of the workforce, fewer younger workers entering the labor pool, the higher average age of the workforce, more women entering the workforce, and the increased proportions of minorities and immigrants in the workforce. A follow-up report, *Workforce 2020,* focusing on diversity themes and trends, was referred to as "a wake-up call for American workers, corporations, educators, parents, and government officials."[18] That wake-up call continues to ring, perhaps louder and clearer than ever before.

The term **workforce diversity,** discussed further in Chapter 2, is used to describe the composition of a workforce in terms of differences among the members.[19] These differences include gender, age, race, ethnicity, religion, sexual orientation, and ablebodiness. In the United States the legal context of human resource management, described in Chapter 12, is very strict in prohibiting the use of demographic characteristics for staffing decisions such as hiring and promotion. Executives at Microsoft know this only too well. The firm started 2001 facing a racial discrimination lawsuit in which current and former African-American employees claimed they were discriminated against in compensation and promotions.[20]

REALITY Check 1.1

Barriers to Advancement for Women of Color A comprehensive three-year study reported by Catalyst identified the four most commonly identified barriers cited by women of color that limit their paths upward in business. Lack of high-visibility assignments was one of the barriers. Take the on-line "Reality Check" to learn more about the results of this survey.

The issues of managing workforce diversity, however, extend beyond legal considerations alone. Today's increasingly diverse and multicultural workforce offers great opportunities with respect to potential performance gains.[21] By "valuing diversity" organizations can tap a rich talent pool and help everyone work to their full potential. But what does this really mean? According to one consultant, it has to mean more than simply "white males doing good deeds for minorities and women." It should mean "enabling every member of your workforce to perform to his or her potential." A female vice president at Avon once posed the challenge of managing diversity this way: "consciously creating an environment where everyone has an equal shot at contributing, participating, and most of all advancing."[22]

Although easy to say, meeting societal responsibilities to truly value diversity has proven harder to accomplish. Even though progress in equal opportunity continues to be made, lingering inequalities remain in the workplace. A study by Catalyst, a nonprofit research group focusing on corporate women, reports that among *Fortune* 500 companies the number of women corporate officers rose some 50 percent between 1995 and 2000. That's quite an increase. But overall, the gains were from 8.7 percent of these top positions in 1995 to 12.5 percent in 2000. That still leaves a lot of room for future progress. In 2000, furthermore, there were only two women CEOs in the *Fortune* 500. In terms of wage comparisons, for each $1 earned by white male managers, minority male managers earn 73 cents, minority women earn 57 cents and white women earn 59 cents. Catalyst also found that 66 percent of minority women in management are dissatisfied with their career advancement opportunities.[23]

○ **Prejudice** is the display of negative, irrational attitudes toward women or minorities.

○ **Discrimination** actively denies women and minorities the full benefits of organizational membership.

The fact is that diversity bias can still be a limiting factor in too many work settings. In respect to race relations in the workplace, for example, a *Fortune* magazine article concludes: "The good news is, there's plenty of progress for companies and employees to talk about . . . But what often doesn't get said, especially in mixed-race settings, is how much remains to get done."[24] **Prejudice,** or the holding of negative, irrational opinions and attitudes regarding members of diverse populations, sets the stage for diversity bias in the workplace. This bias can take the form of **discrimination** that actively disadvantages them by treating them unfairly and denying them the full benefits of organizational membership. It can also take the form of what some call the **glass ceiling effect**—the existence of an invisible barrier or "ceiling" that prevents women and minorities from rising above a certain level of organizational responsibility.[25] Scholar Judith Rosener suggests that the organization's loss is "undervalued and underutilized human capital."[26]

○ The **glass ceiling effect** is an invisible barrier limiting the advancement of women and minorities.

ETHICS

When a well-known business executive goes to jail for some misdeed, we notice. When a major environmental catastrophe occurs because of a business misdeed, we notice. Increasingly, too, we notice the "moral" aspects of the everyday behavior by organizations, their executives, and employees.[27] Society is becoming strict in its expectation that social institutions conduct their affairs according to high moral standards. Executives and employees at Bridgestone/Firestone and Ford Motor Company know this for sure. Both firms suffered serious breaches of customer confidence when some 6.5 million Firestone tires were recalled in August 2000. Many of these had been installed as original equipment on Ford vehicles. Tire failures were blamed in some 88 deaths and 250 injuries.[28] Among the concerns leading up to a Congressional inquiry of the situation were (1) how much did company executives know about the problem with the tires, and (2) just when did they first learn about it? While these questions were raised and debated, stock prices of both companies declined substantially and customers defected to their competitors. Ford's CEO came under pressure; Firestone's lost his job. His replacement, John Lamb, posted this message on the corporate web site: "I want my first act as the CEO of Bridgestone/Firestone to be an apology to those who suffered personal losses or have had problems with our products. The burden is on us to earn your trust all over again."[29]

The pressure for ethical and socially responsible conduct is on, and justifiably so. Organizations and their managers are responding. They have to. As John Lamb's apology for Firestone's missteps points out, you can't keep your customers if you don't treat them right and act in ways that are consistent with society's values. The expectations characteristic of this new century include sustainable development and protection of the natural environment, protection of consumers through product safety and fair practices, and the protection of human rights in all aspects of society, including employment.[30] Workplace concerns include equal employment opportunity, equity of compensation and benefits, participation and employee involvement, privacy and due process, freedom from sexual harassment, job security, and occupational health and safety. Employees are demanding more self-determination on the job—they want to be part of everyday decisions on how and when to do their jobs, and they expect real opportunities to participate in job-related decisions. Job security is a concern at a time when many organizations are cutting back their full-time workers and hiring more part-time or "contingency" workers.

Ethical and social responsibility issues involve all aspects of organizations, the behavior of their members, and their impact on society. You must be ready to understand the ethical context of working in the new economy and you must be prepared to perform in ways that fulfill your ethical commitments as well as those of your employer. Consider, for example, the ethical framework set by this statement from the credo of Johnson & Johnson:[31]

www.hudson.org

A Global Perspective

Become familiar with the work of the Hudson Institute, an internationally recognized public policy research organization based in Indianapolis, Indiana. Concerns for the digital future, global food issues, and workforce development are active themes in the institute's policy centers.

We are responsible to the communities in which we live and work and to the world community as well. We must be good citizens—support good works and charities and bear our fair share of taxes. We must encourage civic improvements and better health and education. We must maintain in good order the property we are privileged to use, protecting the environment and natural resources.

CAREERS

@

Get Connected!

Take a look ahead. Familiarize yourself with the *Management 7/e* Outcome Assessment Template.

The nature of work has changed in the new economy and the challenges of change make personal initiative and self-renewal hallmarks of the day. The career implications of the new employment patterns characteristic of this dynamic environment are extremely significant. British scholar Charles Handy suggests the analogy of the Irish shamrock to describe and understand them.[32]

Picture an organization as a shamrock with three leaves. Each leaf has a different career implication. In one leaf are the core workers. These full-time employees pursue traditional career paths. With success and the maintenance of critical skills, core employees can advance within the organization and may remain employed for a long time. In the second leaf of the shamrock organization are contract workers. They perform specific tasks as needed by the organization and are compensated on a contract or fee-for-services basis rather than by a continuing wage or salary. Contract workers sell a skill or service to employers; they will likely service many different employers over time. In the third leaf are the part-time workers who are hired only as needed and for only the number of hours needed. Employers expand and reduce their part-time staffs as business needs rise and fall. Part-time work can be a training ground for full-time work in the first leaf, when openings are available.

You must be prepared to prosper in any of the shamrock's three leaves. The typical career of the 21st century won't be uniformly full-time and limited to a single large employer. It is more likely to unfold opportunistically and involve several employment options over time. "Free agency" is a term increasingly used to describe career management in the new workplace.[33] What it means is that not only must you be prepared to change jobs and employers over time, but your skills must be portable and of current value in the employment markets. Skills aren't gained once and then forgotten; they must be carefully maintained and upgraded all the time. One career

HIGH PERFORMANCE Ohiou.edu
www.ohiou.edu **Electronic Student Portfolios Get the Job Done**

While a student at Ohio University, Ronald Larimer developed a very professional Electronic Student Portfolio. It includes his resume documenting leadership activities in student affairs, student work providing computer support for an instructor, and his summer work experience. The portfolio also gives examples of Ron's skills at computer programming, use of spreadsheet and database software, writing skills in the form of a one-page executive memorandum and a research report, as well as a sample PowerPoint presentation. Using his electronic portfolio as the lead, Ron was able to obtain a summer internship between his junior and senior years and compete for his first choice of jobs after graduation.[35]

consultant suggests that you approach this career scenario with the analogy of a surfer: "You're always moving. You can expect to fall into the water any number of times, and you have to get back up to catch the next wave."[34]

Handy's advice is that you maintain a "portfolio of skills" that are always up-to-date and valuable to potential employers. The end-of-text *Career Readiness Workbook* includes templates for you to build a personal Career Advancement Portfolio® that directly responds to Handy's challenge. By following the instructions provided you can build either a paper or electronic portfolio that includes a professional resume and work samples that demonstrate your critical managerial skills and competencies. A well-constructed student portfolio can be an important source of advantage in competitive markets as you search for internships and jobs. Consider what a Career Advancement Portfolio can do for you!

ORGANIZATIONS IN THE NEW WORKPLACE

The new world of work is a "wired" world, one tied to the connectivity made possible by information technology. Management consultant Tom Peters described work in new organizations this way:[36]

In the next few years, whether at a tiny company or behemoth, we will be working with an eclectic mix of contract teammates from around the globe, many of whom we'll never meet face-to-face. Every project will call for a new team, composed of specially tailored skills. . . . Every player on this team will be evaluated—pass-by-pass, at-bat by at-bat, for the quality and uniqueness and timeliness and passion of her or his contribution.

Organizations in the new workplace are challenging settings, but exciting for their great opportunities and possibilities. Peters calls it a "wired, wild new age of work." Whether these organizations are large or small, business or nonprofit, each should make real and positive contributions to society. We each have a stake in making sure that they perform up to expectations. For individuals, organizations are also the principal source of careers and one's economic livelihood. In his article "The Company of the Future" (see end-of-text *Fast Company* Collection), Harvard Professor Robert Reich says: "Everybody works for somebody or something—be it a board of directors, a pension fund, a venture capitalist, or a traditional boss. Sooner or later you're going to have to decide who you want to work for."[37]

In order to make good employment choices and perform well in a career, you must have a fundamental understanding of the nature of organizations in the new workplace. *Manager's Notepad 1.1* provides a first look at some of the critical survival skills that you should acquire to work well in the organizations of today . . . and tomorrow.[38]

WHAT IS AN ORGANIZATION?

Formally stated, an **organization** is a collection of people working together to achieve a *common purpose*.[39] It is a unique social phenomenon that enables its members to perform tasks far beyond the reach of individual accomplishment. This description applies to organizations of all sizes and types, from businesses such as Sears and eBay, to nonprofit organizations such as a government agency or community hospital. From society's perspective they all share a broad purpose—providing useful goods or

○ An **organization** is a collection of people working together in a division of labor to achieve a common purpose.

MANAGER'S NOTEPAD 1.1

Critical survival skills for the new workplace

- *Mastery:* You need be good at something; you need to be able to contribute something of value to your employer.
- *Contacts:* You need to know people; links with peers and others within and outside the organization are essential to get things done.
- *Entrepreneurship:* You must act as if you are running your own business, spotting ideas and opportunities, and stepping out to embrace them.
- *Love of technology:* You have to embrace technology; you don't have to be a technician, but you must be willing and able to fully utilize IT.
- *Marketing:* You need to be able to communicate your successes and progress, both yours personally and those of your work group.
- *Passion for renewal:* You need to be continuously learning and changing and updating yourself to best meet future demands.

---

services. Each in its own way should return value to society and satisfy customers' needs in order to justify continued existence.

Having a clear sense of purpose that is tied to "quality products" and "customer satisfaction" is increasingly viewed as a source of organizational strength and performance advantage. Belief in a strong and compelling organizational purpose is one of the reasons given by employees who remain very loyal to their employers. At Medtronics, a large Minnesota-based medical products company, for example, employees are noted for innovation and their commitment to a clear and singular corporate mission—helping sick people get well. The sense of common purpose centers attention and focuses their collective talents on accomplishing a compelling goal: improving the health and well-being of those who use Medtronics products.[40]

ORGANIZATIONS AS SYSTEMS

○ An **open system** transforms resource inputs from the environment into product outputs.

Organizations are systems composed of interrelated parts that function together to achieve a common purpose.[41] It is helpful to view them as **open systems** that interact with their environments in the continual process of transforming resource inputs into product outputs in the form of finished goods and/or services. As shown in *Figure 1.1*, the external environment

Figure 1.1 Organizations as open systems.

is a critical element in the open systems view of organizations. It is both a supplier of resources and the source of customers, and it has a significant impact on operations and outcomes. Both the boundaries of any organization—the supply side and the customer side—and its internal operations must be well managed for performance success.

In the open-systems view of organizations, the customer truly reigns supreme. Feedback from the environment tells an organization how well it is doing. Without customer willingness to use the organization's products, it is difficult to operate or stay in business over the long run. We have already discussed how quality failures in Firestone tires have cost the company severly in lost customers. Consider Medtronics and its corporate purpose again. The ultimate test for this firm also rests with the marketplace: Once someone uses a Medtronics product, the question becomes "Will they do so again . . . and will they recommend that others do the same?"

ORGANIZATIONAL PERFORMANCE

Resources and customers are two critical elements in the open-systems view of organizations. For an organization to perform well, resources must be well utilized and customers well served. The notion of *value creation* is very important in this context. If operations add value to the original cost of resource inputs, then (1) a business organization can earn a profit—that is, sell a product for more than the cost of making it (e.g., fast-food restaurant meals), or (2) a nonprofit organization can add wealth to society—that is, provide a public service that is worth more than its cost (e.g., fire protection in a community). Value is created when an organization's resources are utilized in the right way and at the right time and at minimum cost to create for customers high-quality goods and services.

The best organizations utilize a variety of performance measures. On the customer side, high performing firms measure customer satisfaction and loyalty, as well as market share. On the employee side, they measure retention, career development, job satisfaction, and related issues.[42] One of the most common indicators of overall organizational performance is **productivity**, a summary measure of the quantity and quality of work performance with resource utilization taken into account. Productivity can be measured at the individual and group as well as organizational levels.

Figure 1.2 links productivity with two terms commonly used in management, effectiveness and efficiency. **Performance effectiveness** is a measure of task output or goal accomplishment. If you are working in the manufacturing area of a computer firm, for example, performance effectiveness may mean that you meet a daily production target in terms of the quantity and quality of keyboards assembled. By so doing, you allow the

○ **Productivity** is the quantity and quality of work performance, with resource utilization considered.

○ **Performance effectiveness** is an output measure of task or goal accomplishment.

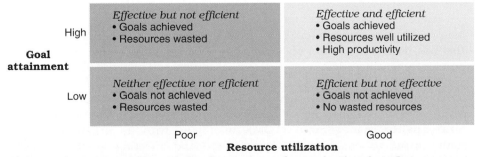

Figure 1.2 Productivity and the dimensions of organizational performance.

○ **Performance efficiency** is a measure of resource cost associated with goal accomplishment.

company as a whole to maintain its production schedule and meet customer demands for timely delivery and high-quality products.

Performance efficiency is a measure of the resource cost associated with goal accomplishment. Cost of labor is a common efficiency measure. Others include equipment utilization, facilities maintenance, and returns on capital investment. Returning to the example of computer assembly, the most efficient production is that accomplished at a minimum cost in materials and labor. If you were producing fewer computer keyboards in a day than you were capable of this would contribute to inefficiency in organizational performance; likewise, if you made a lot of mistakes or wasted materials in the assembly process this is also inefficient work that raises costs for the organization.

CHANGING NATURE OF ORGANIZATIONS

Change will be a continuing theme of this book, and organizations are certainly undergoing dramatic changes today. Among the many forces and trends in the new workplace, the following organizational transitions set an important context for the study of management:[43]

How organizations are changing →

- *Preeminence of technology:* New opportunities appear with each new development in computer and information technology; they continually change the way organizations operate, and how people work.

- *Demise of "command-and-control":* Traditional hierarchical structures with "do as I say" bosses are proving too slow, conservative, and costly to do well in today's competitive environments.

- *Focus on speed:* Everything moves fast today; in business those who get products to market first have an advantage, and in any organization work is expected to be both well done and timely.

- *Embrace of networking:* Organizations are networked for intense real-time communication and coordination, internally among parts and externally with partners, contractors, suppliers, and customers.

- *Belief in empowerment:* Demands of the new economy place premiums on high-involvement and participatory work settings that rally the knowledge, experience, and commitment of all members.

- *Emphasis on teamwork:* Today's organizations are less vertical and more horizontal in focus; they are increasingly driven by teamwork that pools talents for creative problem solving.

- *New workforce expectations:* A new generation of workers brings to the workplace less tolerance for hierarchy, more informality, and more attention to performance merit than to status and seniority.

- *Concern for work-life balance:* As society increases in complexity, workers are forcing organizations to pay more attention to balance in the often-conflicting demands of work and personal affairs.

○ **TQM** is managing with commitment to continuous improvement, product quality, and customer satisfaction.

There are many forces driving these changes in organizations. Along with the pressures of competition, globalization, and emerging technologies, there also has been a revolution of sorts among modern-day consumers. They are unrelenting in their demand for quality products and services. Organizations that fail to listen to their customers and fail to deliver quality goods and services at reasonable prices will be left struggling in a highly competitive environment. References will be made throughout this book to the concept of **total quality management (TQM)**—managing with an organization-wide commitment to continuous improvement and meeting customer needs completely.[44] For the moment, the quality commitment can be recognized as a hallmark of enlightened productivity management in any organization.

TAKE IT TO THE CASE!

Apple Computer Inc.
Where People and Design Create the Future

Innovative design is a mainstay of Apple's business model. But there's more to the company than that. Under the renewed leadership of co-founder Steve Jobs, Apple is considered a model of operating efficiency and marketing savvy. He claims we are entering the third and "golden age" of personal computing. What's the leadership effect of a vision like that? There's no doubt that Jobs brings passion, inventiveness, and a great eye for customer markets to the firm. But the execution comes from people and the team-driven, technology-rich, and talent-based high-performance enviroment that represents life within Apple. If you want to study a company that operates in the world of the new economy, the new workforce, and the new organization, take a look at Apple. Even in the intensely competitive computer industry the wizardry of Apple sets a benchmark for the rest of the pack.[45]

MANAGERS IN THE NEW WORKPLACE

In an article entitled "Putting People First for Organizational Success," Jeffrey Pfeffer and John F. Veiga argue forcefully that organizations perform better when they treat their members better. However, they also point out that too many organizations fail to operate in this manner and, as a consequence, suffer performance failures. Pfeffer uses the term "toxic workplaces" to describe organizations that treat their employees mainly as costs to be reduced. True high-performing organizations, he points out, treat people as valuable strategic assets that should be carefully nurtured.[46] The themes and concepts set forth in *Management 7/e* support this view that high-performing organizations operate with a commitment to people as their most important assets. Importantly, in the day-to-day flow of events in any workplace, those who serve in managerial roles have a special responsibility for ensuring that this commitment is fulfilled.

WHAT IS A MANAGER?

You find them in all organizations. They work with a wide variety of job titles—such as team leader, department head, project manager, unit supervisor, senior executive, administrator, and more. They also always work directly with other persons who are dependent on them for critical support and assistance in their own jobs. We call them **managers**, persons in organizations who directly support and help activate the work efforts and performance accomplishments of others.

○ A **manager** is a person who supports and is responsible for the work of others.

For those serving as managers, the responsibility is challenging and substantial. Any manager is responsible not just for his or her own work, but for the overall performance accomplishments of a team, work group, department, or even organization as a whole. Research conducted in 970 companies by the Saratoga Institute reports that the average manager oversees the work of 10.75 other people.[47] Whether they are called direct reports, team members, work associates, subordinates, or something else, these are the essential human resources whose tasks represent the real work of the organization. Those persons working with and reporting to managers are, in short, the critical human capital upon whose intellects and efforts the performance of any organization is ultimately buit. How well the manager performs in supporting them makes a critical difference in their performance and that of the organization.

Every manager's job thus entails a key responsibility—to help other people achieve high performance. As pointed out by management theorist Henry Mintzberg, being a manager in this sense is a most important and socially responsible job:[48]

> *No job is more vital to our society than that of the manager. It is the manager who determines whether our social institutions serve us well or whether they squander our talents and resources. It is time to strip away the folklore about managerial work, and time to study it realistically so that we can begin the difficult task of making significant improvement in its performance.*

LEVELS AND TYPES OF MANAGERS

The nature of managerial work is evolving as organizations change and develop with time. A *Wall Street Journal* report describes the transition as follows: "Not so long ago they may have supervised 10 people sitting outside their offices. Today they must win the support of scores more—employees of different backgrounds, job titles, and even cultures." The report goes on to say that "these new managers are expected to be skilled at organizing complex subjects, solving problems, communicating ideas, and making swift decisions."[49]

Levels of managers

At the highest levels of organizations, common job titles are chief executive officer, chief operating officer, president, and vice president. These **top managers** are responsible for the performance of an organization as a whole or for one of its larger parts. They pay special attention to the external environment, are alert to potential long-run problems and opportunities, and develop appropriate ways of dealing with them. The best top managers are future-oriented strategic thinkers who make many decisions under highly competitive and uncertain conditions. Top managers scan the environment, create and communicate long-term vision, and ensure that strategies and performance objectives are consistent with the organization's purpose and mission. Before retiring as Medtronics' CEO, Bill George crafted "Vision 2010" to position the firm as a client-centered deliverer of medical services. During his tenure sales increased fivefold and profits doubled. The hours were long and the work demanding. But George also loved his job, saying: "I always dreamed . . . of being head of a major corporation where the values of the company and my own values were congruent, where a company could become kind of a symbol for others, where the product that you represent is doing good for people."[50]

Middle managers are in charge of relatively large departments or divisions consisting of several smaller work units. Examples are clinic directors in hospitals; deans in universities; and division managers, plant managers, and branch sales managers in businesses. Middle managers work with top managers and coordinate with peers to develop and implement action plans consistent with organizational objectives. They should be team oriented and able to work well with people from all parts of an organization to get work accomplished. An important example is the job of **project manager**, someone who coordinates complex projects with task dead-

○ **Top managers** guide the performance of the organization as a whole or of one of its major parts.

○ **Middle managers** oversee the work of large departments or divisions.

○ **Project managers** coordinate complex projects with task deadlines and people with many areas of expertise.

MANAGER'S NOTEPAD 1.2

Nine responsibilities of team leaders

1. Plan meetings and work schedules.
2. Clarify goals and tasks, and gather ideas for improvement.
3. Appraise performance and counsel team members.
4. Recommend pay increases and new assignments.
5. Recruit, train, and develop team to meet performance goals.
6. Encourage high performance and teamwork.
7. Inform team members about organizational goals and expectations.
8. Inform higher levels of team needs and accomplishments.
9. Coordinate with other teams and support the rest of the organization.

lines while working with many persons of different expertise both within and outside the organization. At General Electric, for example, corporate troubleshooters or "black belts" have been organized to manage groups that solve problems and create change across divisions and geographic boundaries within the company. One of them, Wendell Barr, recruited a cross-functional team from marketing, human resources, and field operations staff to design a new compensation system.[51]

A first job in management typically occurs as an assignment as **team leader** or **supervisor**—someone in charge of a small work group composed of nonmanagerial workers. Even though most people enter the workforce as technical specialists, sooner or later they advance to positions of initial managerial responsibility. Job titles for these *first-line managers* vary greatly but include such designations as department head, group leader, and unit manager. For example, the leader of an auditing team is considered a first-line manager, as is the head of an academic department in a university. Managers at this level of responsibility ensure that their work teams or units meet performance objectives that are consistent with higher-level organizational goals. At Medtronics, for example, Justine Fritz led a 12-member team to launch a new product. "I've just never worked on anything that so visibly, so dramatically changes the quality of someone's life," she says, while noting that the demands are also great. "Some days you wake up, and if you think about all the work you have to do it's so overwhelming, you could be paralyzed." That's the challenge of managerial work at any level. Justine says: "You just have to get it done."[52] *Manager's Notepad 1.2* offers advice on the performance responsibilities of team leaders and supervisors.[53]

○ **Team leaders** or **supervisors** report to middle managers and directly supervise nonmanagerial workers.

Types of managers

In addition to serving at different levels of authority, managers work in different capacities within organizations. **Line managers** are responsible for work activities that make a direct contribution to the organization's outputs. For example, the president, retail manager, and department supervisors of a local department store all have line responsibilities. Their jobs in one way or another are directly related to the sales operations of the store. **Staff managers**, by contrast, use special technical expertise to advise and support the efforts of line workers. In a department store, the director of human resources and the chief financial officer would have staff responsibilities.

○ **Line managers** directly contribute to the production of the organization's basic goods or services.

○ **Staff managers** use special technical expertise to advise and support line workers.

Functional managers
are responsible for one area
of activity, such as finance,
marketing, production,
personnel, accounting, or
sales.

General managers are
responsible for complex
organizational units that
include many areas of
functional activity.

An **administrator** is
a manager who works
in a public or nonprofit
organization.

Accountability is the
requirement to show performance results to a supervisor.

Quality of work life is
the overall quality of human
experiences in the work-
place.

In business, **functional managers** have responsibility for a single area of activity, such as finance, marketing, production, personnel, accounting, or sales. **General managers** are responsible for more complex units that include many functional areas. An example is a plant manager who oversees many separate functions, including purchasing, manufacturing, warehousing, sales, personnel, and accounting. It is common for managers working in public or nonprofit organizations to be called **administrators.** Examples include hospital administrator, public administrator, city administrator, and human-service administrator.

MANAGERIAL PERFORMANCE

Managers everywhere face a common problem. They must all set the conditions through which others, working individually and in groups, can contribute their talents to the accomplishment of organizational goals. Furthermore, managers must do this while being held personally "accountable" for results achieved. The team leader reports to a middle manager, the middle manager reports to a top manager, and even the most senior top manager typically reports to a board of directors. In these reporting relationships, **accountability** exists as the requirement of one person to answer to a higher authority for performance results achieved in his or her area of work responsibility. These results will typically be measured in terms of team or work unit productivity, including the accomplishment of both performance effectiveness and performance efficiency.

But the concept of performance accountability alone does not tell the whole story. Managerial performance is multidimensional. Effective managers help others to *both* achieve high performance outcomes *and* experience satisfaction in their work. This dual concern for performance and satisfaction is a central theme in the new workplace, and it runs throughout *Management 7/e.*

The emphasis on satisfaction helps focus attention on **quality of work life** issues as an indicator of the overall quality of human experiences in the workplace. A "high-QWL" workplace expresses a true respect for people at work by offering such things as fair pay, safe working conditions, opportunities to learn and use new skills, room to grow and progress in a career, protection of individual rights, and pride in the work itself and in the organization. Part of any manager's accountability is to achieve high-performance outcomes while maintaining a high-quality work life environment.[54] Simply put, in the new workplace, performance, satisfaction, and a high-quality work life can and should go hand in hand.

CHANGING NATURE OF MANAGERIAL WORK

Managerial work in the organizations of today is also changing. The words "coordinator," "coach," and "team leader" are heard as often as "supervisor" or "manager." The work they perform is less directive and more supportive than in the past. It has to be in a world where high performance comes only to those who truly value and sustain human capital. There is little tolerance or need in today's organizations for those who simply sit back and tell others what to do. The best managers are well informed regarding the needs of those reporting to or dependent upon them. They can often be found working alongside those they supervise. They will always be found providing advice and developing the support needed for others to perform to the best of their abilities. High-performing managers are good at building working relationships with others, helping others develop their skills and performance competencies, fostering teamwork, and otherwise creating a work environment that is both performance driven and satisfying to those who do the required work.

An emphasis on customers increasingly drives managerial work in these new settings. Among the many changes taking place, the concept of the "upside-down pyramid" is one of the most descriptive. As shown in *Figure 1.3*, it offers an alternative and suggestive way of viewing organizations and the role played by managers within them. The operating workers are at the top of the upside-down pyramid, just below the customers and clients they serve. They are supported in their work efforts by managers located at the bottom. These managers aren't just order-givers, they are there to mobilize and deliver the support others require to best serve customer needs. The implications of this notion are dramatic, and they are consistent with the adage that people are an organization's most important asset. Each member of the upside-down pyramid is a value-added worker—someone who creates eventual value for the organization's customers or clients. The whole organization is devoted to serving the customer, and this is made possible with the support of managers.

Many trends and emerging practices in organizations, such as the upside-down pyramid, require new thinking from people who serve as managers. As noted earlier, we are in a time when the best managers are known more for "helping" and "supporting" than for "directing" and "order-giving." Even in an age of high technology and "smart" machines, the human resource is indispensable. Worker involvement and empowerment are critical building blocks of organizational success. Full human resource utilization increasingly means changing the way work gets done in organizations by pushing decision-making authority to the point where the best information and expertise exist—with the operating workers.[55]

Are Students Ready for Work? In a survey reported by USA Today, 66 percent of students said they were well prepared to work in diverse teams. Only 13 percent of employers agreed. Take the on-line "Reality Check" to further examine differences in student and employer perceptions.

Figure 1.3 The organization as an "upside-down pyramid."

THE MANAGEMENT PROCESS

The ultimate "bottom line" in every manager's job is to succeed in helping an organization achieve high performance by well utilizing all of its human and material resources. If productivity in the form of high levels of performance effectiveness and efficiency is a measure of organizational success, managers are largely responsible for ensuring its achievement. It is their job to successfully mobilize technology and talent by creating work environments within which others work hard and perform to the best of their abilities.[57]

FUNCTIONS OF MANAGEMENT

○ **Management** is the process of planning, organizing, leading, and controlling the use of resources to accomplish performance goals.

All managers in daily events must have the capabilities to recognize performance problems and opportunities, make good decisions, and take appropriate action. They do this through the process of **management**— planning, organizing, leading, and controlling the use of resources to accomplish performance goals. These four functions of management and their interrelationships are shown in *Figure 1.4*. All managers, regardless of title, level, type, and organizational setting, are responsible for the four functions.[58] However, it is important to know that they most often do not accomplish these functions in linear step-by-step fashion. Rather, the reality of managerial work is that the functions are being continually engaged as a manager moves from task to task and opportunity to opportunity in the process of mobilizing resources to accomplish goals.

Planning

○ **Planning** is the process of setting objectives and determining what should be done to accomplish them.

In management, **planning** is the process of setting performance objectives and determining what actions should be taken to accomplish them. Through planning, a manager identifies desired work results and identifies the means to achieve them. Take, for example, an Ernst & Young initiative that was developed to better meet the needs of the firm's female professionals.[59] Top management grew concerned about the firm's retention rates for women and by a critical report by the independent research

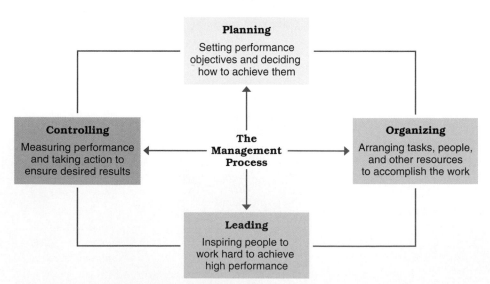

Figure 1.4 Four functions of management.

DIVERSITY Kraft Inc. www.kraft.com
Betsy Holden Breaks Glass Celling in Corporate Leadership

When Betsy Holden became the president and CEO of Kraft Foods, Inc., she had earned her way to the top. With a graduate degree from North-western's Kellogg School, she rose from Division Brand Manager to CEO in just 16 years. Praised for earning her many promotions with "a lot of hard work, focus and creativity," Holden's management style is in tune with the times. She calls it "positive, upbeat, enthusiastic, collaborative, and team-oriented." "I think I'm good at inspiring, setting a vision of what we need to go and do—and then engaging the team and putting together the game plan to get there," she says. Career development is important to her. When helping others, she asks them: "What skills do you need, what experiences do you need, what development do you need?" Perhaps the most impor-tant testimony to her management style is the next question: "How do we help you make that happen?"[56]

group Catalyst. Chairman Philip A. Laskawy, who personally chairs Ernst & Young's Diversity Task Force, responded by setting a planning objective to reduce turnover rates for women. Rates at the time were running some 22 percent per year and costing the firm about 150 percent of each per-son's annual salary to hire and train new staff.

Organizing

At Ernst & Young, Phil Laskawy believes that the best plans will fail with-out strong implementation. This begins with **organizing**, the process of assigning tasks, allocating resources, and arranging the coordinated activ-ities of individuals and groups to implement plans. Through organizing, managers turn plans into actions by defining jobs, assigning personnel, and supporting them with technology and other resources. Continuing with the example, Laskawy prepared to meet his planning objective by first organizing a new Office of Retention and hiring Deborah K. Holmes as a director to head it. As retention problems were identified in various parts of the firm, Holmes further convened special task forces to tackle them and recommend location-specific solutions. A Woman's Access Program was started to give women access to senior people for mentoring and career development.

○ **Organizing** is the process of assigning tasks, allocating resources, and arranging activities to im-plement plans.

Leading

Speaking at a forum of corporate leaders, Phil Laskawy said: "At Ernst & Young, the firm has been focused on the need to attract and retain the best by building a leadership and family culture. The firm wants all of our people to be committed to the same goal." In management, **leading** is the process of arousing people's enthusiasm to work hard and direct their ef-forts to fulfill plans and accomplish objectives. Through leading, managers build commitments to a common vision, encourage activities that support goals, and influence others to do their best work in the organization's behalf. In respect to the goals of Ernst & Young's Office of Retention, Deb-orah Holmes identified a core issue—work at the firm was extremely intense and women often felt strain because their spouses also worked. She became a champion for improved work-life balance and pursued it

○ **Leading** is the process of arousing enthusiasm and directing efforts toward or-ganizational goals.

through the special task forces. Although admitting that "there's no silver bullet" in the form of a universal solution, new initiatives from the Office included "call-free holidays" where professionals do not check voice mail or e-mail on weekends and holidays and "travel sanity" that limits staffers' travel to four days a week so they can get home for weekends.

Controlling

○ **Controlling** is the process of measuring performance and taking action to ensure desired results.

Phil Laskawy recognizes that a key issue in how well plans get implemented is how well the organization adapts to rapid change. In today's dynamic times, things don't always go as anticipated and plans must be modified and redefined with the passage of time. The management function of **controlling** is the process of measuring work performance, comparing results to objectives, and taking corrective action as needed. Through controlling, managers maintain active contact with people in the course of their work, gather and interpret reports on performance, and use this information to plan constructive action and change. At Ernst & Young, Laskawy and Holmes knew what the retention rates were when they started the new program, and they have been able to note improvements as the program's work progresses. Through measurement they were able to track progress against objectives. Yearly results indicate that retention is up at all levels. The initiative remains alive at the firm and Laskawy's original planning objectives are being accomplished. Lasting and significant change is contributing to improved work-life balance and better retention rates.

MANAGERIAL ACTIVITIES AND ROLES

Although the management process may seem straightforward, things are more complicated than they appear at first glance. In his classic book, *The Nature of Managerial Work,* Henry Mintzberg offers this observation on the daily activities of corporate chief executives: "There was no break in the pace of activity during office hours. The mail, . . . telephone calls, . . . and meetings . . . accounted for almost every minute from the moment these executives entered their offices in the morning until they departed in the evenings."[60] Today we would have to add ever-present e-mail to Mintzberg's list of executive preoccupations.[61]

In trying to systematically describe the nature of managerial work and the demands placed on those who do it, Mintzberg offers the set of 10 roles depicted in *Figure 1.5.* The roles involve managing information, people, and action. They are interconnected, and all managers must be prepared to perform them.[62] In Mintzberg's framework, a manager's *informational roles* involve the giving, receiving, and analyzing of information. The *interpersonal roles* involve interactions with people inside and outside the work unit. The *decisional roles* involve using information to make decisions to solve problems or address opportunities.

Mintzberg is also careful to note that the manager's day is unforgiving in intensity and pace of these role requirements. The managers he observed had little free time because unexpected problems and continuing requests for meetings consumed almost all the time that became available. Importantly, the responsibility of executive work was all-encompassing in the pressure it placed on the executives for continuously improving performance results. Says Mintzberg: "The manager can never be free to forget the job, and never has the pleasure of knowing, even temporarily, that there is nothing else to do. . . . Managers always carry the nagging suspicion that they might be able to contribute just a little bit more. Hence they assume an unrelenting pace in their work."[63]

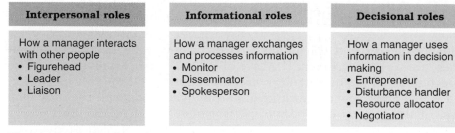

Interpersonal roles	Informational roles	Decisional roles
How a manager interacts with other people • Figurehead • Leader • Liaison	How a manager exchanges and processes information • Monitor • Disseminator • Spokesperson	How a manager uses information in decision making • Entrepreneur • Disturbance handler • Resource allocator • Negotiator

Figure 1.5 Mintzberg's ten managerial roles.

Managerial work is busy, demanding, and stressful not just for chief executives but for managers at all levels of responsibility in any work setting. A summary of research on the nature of managerial work offers this important reminder.[61] Managers work long hours. They work at an intense pace. They work at fragmented and varied tasks. They work with many communication media. And, they accomplish their work largely through interpersonal relationships.

MANAGERIAL AGENDAS AND NETWORKS

It is not only the complexity and pace of managerial work that makes it challenging. There are subtle intricacies in the day-to-day flow of events and interactions that must also be mastered. Consider this description of a brief incident in the day of the general manager of a business.[65]

> On his way to a meeting, a GM bumped into a staff member who did not report to him. Using this opportunity, in a two-minute conversation he: (a) asked two questions and received the information he needed; (b) reinforced their good relationship by sincerely complimenting the staff member on something he had recently done; and (c) got the staff member to agree to do something that the GM needed done.

The description provides a glimpse of an effective general manager in action. It portrays two activities that management consultant and scholar John Kotter considers critical to a general manager's success in mastering two critical challenges—agenda setting and networking. Through *agenda setting,* good managers develop action priorities for their jobs that include goals and plans that span long and short time frames. These agendas are usually incomplete and loosely connected in the beginning, but become more specific as the manager utilizes information that is continually gleaned from many different sources. The agendas are kept always in mind and are "played out" whenever an opportunity arises, as in the preceding quotation.

Good managers implement their agendas by working with a variety of people inside and outside the organization. In Kotter's example, the GM was getting things done through a staff member who did not report directly to him. This is made possible by *networking,* the process of building and maintaining positive relationships with people whose help may be needed to implement one's work agendas. Since networks are indispensable to managerial success in today's complex work environments, excellent managers devote much time and effort to network development. In the case of this general manager, for example, the networks included relationships with peers, boss and higher-level executives, subordinates and members of their work teams, as well as with external customers, suppliers, and community representatives.

www.ey.com

Find out more about Ernst & Young and the firm's initiative on retention of women, including women's networks—action-oriented groups created with leadership support to enhance women's affiliation with the firm. The networks include informal socials, dinners, retreats, and structured monthly meetings with steering committees.

MANAGERIAL LEARNING

British educator and consultant Charles Handy calls today's turbulent times "the age of unreason."[66] Above all, it is an era of high performance expectations for organizations and their members. Change is a way of life, and it demands new organizational and individual responses. And along with all this, the quest for high performance is relentless. Everywhere new workers are expected to use new ways to achieve high productivity under new and dynamic conditions. They are expected to become involved, fully participate, demonstrate creativity, and find self-fulfillment in their work. They are expected to be team players who understand the needs and goals of the total organization and who use new technologies to their full advantage.

○ **Lifelong learning** is continuous learning from daily experiences and opportunities.

All of this, of course, places a premium on your commitment to learning—not just formal learning in the classroom, but also **lifelong learning.** This is the process of continuously learning from our daily experiences and opportunities. Especially in a dynamic and ever-changing environment, a commitment to lifelong learning helps us build portfolios of skills that are always up to date and valuable in the labor markets. A critical part of job-related learning, furthermore, comes from "learning by doing." This means that you must always look for good job opportunities that make such learning possible.

ESSENTIAL MANAGERIAL SKILLS

○ A **skill** is the ability to translate knowledge into action that results in desired performance.

A **skill** is an ability to translate knowledge into action that results in desired performance. Obviously, many skills are required to master the challenging nature of managerial work. The most important ones are those that allow managers to help others become more productive in their work. Harvard scholar Robert L. Katz has classified the essential skills of managers into three categories: technical, human, and conceptual.[67] Although all three skills are essential for managers, he suggests that their relative importance tends to vary by level of managerial responsibility as shown in *Figure 1.6.*

○ A **technical skill** is the ability to use a special proficiency or expertise in one's work.

A **technical skill** is the ability to use a special proficiency or expertise to perform particular tasks. Accountants, engineers, market researchers, business planners, and computer scientists, for example, possess technical skills. These are initially acquired through formal education and are further developed by training and job experience. Technical skill in the new network economy is also increasingly tied to computer literacy and utilization of the latest information technology. Figure 1.6 shows that technical skills are very important at career entry levels. The critical question to be asked and positively answered by you in this respect and in preparation for any job interview comes down to this simple test: "What can you really do for an employer?"

○ A **human skill** is the ability to work well in cooperation with other people.

○ **Emotional intelligence** is the ability to manage ourselves and our relationships effectively.

The ability to work well in cooperation with other persons is a **human skill.** It emerges in the workplace as a spirit of trust, enthusiasm, and genuine involvement in interpersonal relationships. A manager with good human skills will have a high degree of self-awareness and a capacity to understand or empathize with the feelings of others. An important component of the essential human skills is **emotional intelligence.**[68] Discussed in Chapter 13 for its leadership implications, "EI" is defined by scholar and consultant Daniel Goleman as the "ability to manage

Lower level managers	Middle level managers	Top level managers

Conceptual skills—The ability to think analytically and achieve integrative problem solving

Human skills—The ability to work well in cooperation with other persons

Technical skills—The ability to apply expertise and perform a special task with proficiency

Figure 1.6 Essential managerial skills.

ourselves and our relationships effectively."[69] Given the highly interpersonal nature of managerial work, human skills are critical for all managers. Figure 1.6 shows that they are consistently important across all the managerial levels. Again a straightforward question puts you to the test of interpersonal skills and emotional intelligence: "How well do you work with others?"

All good managers ultimately have the ability to view situations broadly and to solve problems to the benefit of everyone concerned. This ability to think critically and analytically is a **conceptual skill.** It involves the ability to break down problems into smaller parts, to see the relations between the parts, and to recognize the implications of any one problem for others. As we assume ever-higher responsibilities in organizations, we are called upon to deal with more ambiguous problems that have many complications and longer-term consequences. Figure 1.6 shows that conceptual skills gain in relative importance for top managers. At this point, you should ask: "Am I developing critical thinking and problem-solving capabilities for long-term career success?"

○ A **conceptual skill** is the ability to think analytically and solve complex problems.

SKILL AND OUTCOME ASSESSMENT

Business and management educators are increasingly interested in helping people acquire the essential skills and develop specific competencies that can help them achieve managerial success. A **managerial competency** is a skill-based capability that contributes to high performance in a management job.[70] A number of these competencies have been implied in the previous discussion of the management process, including those related to planning, organizing, leading, and controlling. Competencies are also implicit in the information, interpersonal, and decision-making demands of managerial roles, as well as agenda setting and networking as managerial activities.

○ A **managerial competency** is a skill-based capability for high performance in a management job.

Manager's Notepad 1.3 further highlights some of the skills and personal characteristics business schools emphasize in helping students develop the foundations for continued professional development and career success. You can use this notepad as a preliminary checklist for assessing your career readiness in terms of professional skills and competencies. A format for more formally including this skill and outcome assessment template as part of your study of management is provided in the end-of-text *Career Readiness Workbook*.

> ### MANAGER'S NOTEPAD 1.3
>
> ## Mgt. 7/e skill and outcome assessment template: competencies for managerial success
>
> - Communication—demonstrates ability to share ideas and findings clearly in written and oral expression. This includes competencies in writing, oral presentation, giving/receiving feedback, and technology utilization.
> - Teamwork—demonstrates ability to work effectively as a team member and team leader. This includes competencies in team contribution, team leadership, conflict management, negotiation, and consensus building.
> - *Self-management*—demonstrates ability to evaluate oneself, modify behavior, and meet performance obligations. This includes competencies in ethical understanding/behavior, personal flexibility, tolerance for ambiguity, and performance responsibility.
> - Leadership—demonstrates ability to influence and support others to perform complex and sometimes ambiguous tasks. This includes competencies in diversity awareness, global awareness, project management, and strategic action.
> - Critical thinking—demonstrates ability to gather and analyze information for creative problem solving. This includes competencies in problem solving, judgment and decision making, information gathering and interpretation, and creativity/innovation.
> - Professionalism—demonstrates ability to sustain a positive impression, instill confidence, and maintain career advancement. This includes competencies in personal presence, personal initiative, and career management.

GETTING CONNECTED WITH *MANAGEMENT*

Management 7/e is designed to facilitate your learning about management, organizations, and the new workplace. When the chapter discussions are combined with the activities and resources in the *Career Readiness Workbook,* the book offers a unique opportunity to establish your career readiness.

Management 7/E Chapter organization

As described in *Figure 1.7,* the chapters are divided into five parts:

Chapter organization of
Management 7/e

- *Part 1: Management Today* focuses on the new workplace, environment, and diversity, as well as information and decision making. Chapters on these topics introduce important developments and forces that impact the emergence of the new management in this age of globalization and the new economy.

- *Part 2: Context* describes the historical and contemporary context for modern management. The chapters examine the historical foundations of management, the global economy, cultural dimensions, ethics, and social responsibility.

- *Part 3: Mission* addresses the purpose and goals of organizations and the action foundations for their accomplishment. The chapters focus on management functions of planning and controlling, with special emphasis on strategic management, entrepreneurship and new ventures.

- *Part 4: Organization* examines the nature of organizations as work systems and processes. The chapters describe approaches to organization structures, high-performance designs, and the all-important human resource management systems.

- *Part 5: Leadership* introduces the great opportunities of leadership in organizations, with special emphasis on understanding the personal skills and competencies requisite to leadership success. Chapter topics include motivation and rewards, individual performance, stress communication, teamwork and group performance, and the processes of innovation and change leadership.

Career Readiness Workbook

Management 7/e includes a unique and exciting end-of-text Career Readiness Workbook that provides resources to extend your learning in relevant career directions. Components in this workbook are also provided in enhanced electronic versions on the *Management 7/e* web site. They include:

- Career Advancement Portfolio®—a template for you to build a personal electronic student portfolio and/or paper portfolio with a professional resume for use in internship and job searches; includes the *Management 7/e* Skill and Outcome Assessment Template for documenting your accomplishments for academic and professional review.

Features in the Career Readiness Workbook

Figure 1.7 *Management 7/e*—A Learning Framework.

- Cases for Critical Thinking—contains cases presenting you with real-life situations faced by e-commerce companies, global corporations, family-owned and small enterprises, nonprofit and voluntary organizations.

- Integrative Learning Activities—a rich set of unique activities to help consolidate your learning about management through Internet research and presentation projects, and integrative multi-functional case studies.

- Exercises in Teamwork—30 exercises designed to improve your familiarity with real management situations and help you gain insight into your skills and capabilities in interpersonal relations and teamwork.

- Self-Assessments—30 self-assessment inventories designed to help identify your strengths and developmental needs in the essential managerial skills and competencies.

- The *Fast Company* Collection—readings selected from recent *Fast Company* magazine articles to further introduce you to the realities and fast-changing nature of organizations and management in today's workplace.

When this book declares *@GET CONNECTED!,* you should take notice. If you read and study the chapters in *Management 7/e*, explore and utilize the accompanying on-line learning resources, and take full advantage of your class discussions and activities, you will surely benefit by strengthening your foundations for career success. In the changing world of work today and with all the challenges of a new economy, the premium is on continuous learning and professional development. *Management 7/e* and its on-line resources were designed to help you gain advantage through improved career readiness. Go for it. Get connected!

STUDY Guide

The Chapter 1 Study Guide will help you review chapter content, prepare for examinations, and further build your career readiness. The *Summary* briefly highlights answers to questions first posed in the chapter opening Planning Ahead section. The list of *Key Terms* allows you to double check your familiarity with basic concepts and definitions. *Self-Test 1* gives you the opportunity to test your basic comprehension of chapter content using sample test questions. Suggestions offered as *Career Readiness Activities* direct your attention to relevant sections of the end-of-text Career Readiness Workbook, as well as to special Electronic Resources on the *Management 7/e* web site.

SUMMARY

What are the challenges of working in the new economy?

- Today's turbulent environment challenges everyone to understand and embrace continuous change and developments in a new information-driven and global economy.
- Work in the new economy is increasingly knowledge based, and people, with their capacity to bring valuable intellectual capital to the workplace, are the ultimate foundation of organizational performance.
- The forces of globalization are bringing increased interdependencies among nations and economies as customer markets and resource flows create intense business competition.
- Ever-present developments in information technology and the continued expansion of the Internet are reshaping organizations, changing the nature of work, and increasing the value of people capable of performing as knowledge workers.
- Organizations must value the talents and capabilities of a workforce whose members are increasingly diverse with respect to gender, age, race and ethnicity, able-bodiedness, and lifestyles.
- Society has high expectations for organizations and their members to perform with commitment to high ethical standards and in socially responsible ways, including protection of the natural environment and human rights.
- Careers in the new economy require great personal initiative to build and maintain skill "portfolios" that are always up-to-date and valuable to employers challenged by intense competition and opportunities of the information age.

What are organizations like in the new workplace?

- Organizations are collections of people working together to achieve a common purpose.
- As open systems, organizations interact with their environments in the process of transforming resource inputs into product outputs.
- Productivity is a measure of the quantity and quality of work performance, with resource utilization taken into account.
- High-performing organizations are both effective, in terms of goal accomplishment, and efficient, in terms of resource utilization.
- Organizations today continue to emphasize total quality management in a context of technology utilization, more empowerment and teamwork, and concern for work-life balance, among other trends.

Who are managers and what do they do?

- Managers directly support and facilitate the work efforts of other people in organizations.
- Top managers scan the environment, create vision, and emphasize long-term performance goals; middle managers coordinate activities in large departments or divisions; team leaders and supervisors support performance at the team or work-unit level.
- Functional managers work in specific areas such as finance or marketing; general managers are responsible for larger multifunctional units; administrators are managers in nonprofit organizations.
- A key aspect of managerial work is accountability to higher levels for performance results that the manager depends on other persons to accomplish.
- The upside-down pyramid view of organizations shows operating workers at the top and responsible for meeting customer needs while being supported from below by various levels of management.
- A key aspect in the changing nature of managerial work is emphasis on being good at "coaching" and "supporting" others, rather than simply "directing" and "order-giving."

What is the management process?

- The management process consists of the four functions of planning, organizing, leading, and controlling.
- Planning sets the direction; organizing assembles the human and material resources; leading provides the enthusiasm and direction; controlling ensures results.
- Managers implement the four functions in daily work that is intense and stressful, involving long hours and continuous performance pressures.
- Managerial success in this demanding context requires the ability to perform well in interpersonal, informational, and decision-making roles.
- Managerial success in this demanding context also requires the ability to utilize interpersonal networks to accomplish well-selected task agendas.

How do you learn the essential managerial skills and competencies?

- Career success in the new economy requires continual attention to the process of lifelong learning from all aspects of daily experience and job opportunities.
- Skills considered essential to managerial success are broadly described as technical—ability to utilize knowledge and technology; human—ability to work well with other people; and conceptual—ability to analyze and solve complex problems.
- *Management 7/e* offers skill and outcome assessment activities considered by business schools and employers as basic foundations for managerial success—communication, teamwork, self-management, leadership, critical thinking, and professionalism.
- *Management 7/e* focuses attention on your career potential through a special end-of-text Career Readiness Workbook, including a template for building print and electronic versions of your personal Career Advancement Portfolio®.
- *Management 7/e* enriches your learning experience with an On-line Study Guide and E-Resource Center for each chapter.

KEY TERMS

Accountability (p. 18)

Administrators (p. 18)

Conceptual skill (p. 25)

Controlling (p. 22)

Discrimination (p. 8)

Emotional intelligence (p. 24)

Functional managers (p. 18)

General managers (p. 18)

Glass ceiling effect (p. 9)

Globalization (p. 6)

Human skill (p. 24)

Intellectual capital (p. 5)

Knowledge worker (p. 5)

Leading (p. 21)

Lifelong learning (p. 24)

Line managers (p. 17)

Management (p. 20)

Manager (p. 15)

Managerial competency (p. 25)

Middle managers (p. 16)

Open system (p. 12)

Organization (p. 11)

Organizing (p. 21)

Performance effectiveness (p. 13)

Performance efficiency (p. 14)

Planning (p. 20)

Prejudice (p. 8)

Productivity (p. 13)

Project managers (p. 16)

Quality of work life (p. 18)

Skill (p. 24)

Staff managers (p. 17)

Supervisor (p. 17)

Team leader (p. 17)

Technical skill (p.24)

Top managers (p. 16)

Total quality management (p. 14)

Workforce diversity (p. 8)

SELF-TEST 1

Take this test here or on-line much as you would in a normal classroom situation. It is a good way to check your basic comprehension of chapter material. Answers may be found at the end of the book.

MULTIPLE-CHOICE QUESTIONS:

1. The process of management involves the functions of planning, _____ , leading, and controlling.
   (a) accounting (b) creating (c) innovating (d) organizing

2. An effective manager achieves both high-performance outcomes and high _____ among people doing the required work.
   (a) turnover (b) effectiveness (c) satisfaction (d) stress

3. Performance efficiency is a measure of the _____ associated with task accomplishment.
   (a) resource cost (b) goal specificity (c) product quality (d) product quantity

4. The requirement that a manager answer to a higher-level boss for results achieved by the manager's work team is called _____.
   (a) dependency (b) accountability (c) authority (d) empowerment

5. Productivity is a measure of the quantity and _____ of work produced, with resource utilization taken into account.
   (a) quality (b) cost
   (c) timeliness (d) duration

6. _____ managers in organizations should pay special attention to the external environment, looking for problems and opportunities, and finding ways to deal with them.
   (a) Top (b) Middle (c) Lower (d) First-line

6. The accounting manager for a local newspaper would be considered a _____ manager, whereas the production manager would be considered a _____ manager.
   (a) general, functional (b) middle, top (c) staff, line (d) senior, junior

8. When a supervisor clarifies desired work targets and deadlines for her work team, she is fulfilling the management function of _____.
   (a) planning (b) delegating (c) controlling (d) supervising

9. The process of building and maintaining good working relationships with others who may help implement a manager's work agenda is called _____.

   (a) interaction (b) networking (c) politicking
   (d) entrepreneurship

10. In Katz's framework, top managers tend to rely more on their _____ skills than do first-line managers.
(a) human (b) conceptual (c) decision making (d) technical

TRUE-FALSE QUESTIONS:

11. Managers usually work at a slow and leisurely pace.   T   F

12. Continuous improvement is a key element in total quality management. T   F

13. A clear organizational purpose can be a source of performance advantage. T   F

14. Someone with the title of "team leader" is working as a first-line manager. T   F

15. Prejudice involves the display of negative attitudes toward members of minority groups.   T   F

16. Managers in nonprofit organizations may be called administrators.   T   F

17. The new workplace expects managers to give more attention to "directing" and "order giving" in their daily work.   T   F

18. Human skills are not important for middle managers.   T   F

19. Managers are at the top of the organization when it is described as an up-side-down pyramid.   T   F

20. Demographic trends show that the workforce is expected to get increasingly diverse.   T   F

SHORT-RESPONSE QUESTIONS:

21. List and explain the importance of three pressures in the areas of ethics and social responsibility that managers must be prepared to face in the future.

22. Explain how "accountability" would operate in the relationships between (a) a manager and her subordinates and (b) the same manager and her boss.

23. Explain how the "glass ceiling effect" may work to the disadvantage of African-American middle managers in a large corporation.

24. What is "globalization" and how does it relate to Kenichi Ohmae's notion of the borderless world?

APPLICATION QUESTION:

25. You have just been hired as the new supervisor of an audit team for a national accounting firm. With eight years of experience, you feel technically well prepared for the assignment. However, this is your first formal appointment as a "manager." Things are complicated at the moment since the team should have 12 members, but there are five vacancies to be filled. Your boss wants the new team to be as "diverse" as possible. How will this situation challenge you to use and develop managerial skills and related competencies so that you can successfully manage diversity on the audit team?

CAREER readiness ACTIVITIES

Recommended activities from the end-of-text Career Readiness Workbook for this chapter include:

Case for Critical Thinking
- Apple Computer, Inc.—Passion, design, and the future

Integrative Learning Activities
- Research Project 1–Diversity Lessons
- Integrative Case–Outback Steakhouse, Inc.
- Integrative Case–Richard Branson Meets the New Economy

Exercises in Teamwork
- My Best Manager (#1)
- What Managers Do (#2)
- Defining Quality (#3)
- The Future Workplace (#13)

Self-Assessments
- A 21st-Century Manager (#1)
- Organizational Culture Preferences (#2)
- Diversity Awareness (#7)
- Are You Cosmopolitan? (#23)

The Fast Company Collection On-Line
- Robert Reich, "The Company of the Future"
- Alan Weber, "Danger: Toxic Company"
- Tom Peters, "The Brand Called 'You'"

ELECTRONIC RESOURCES

@ GET CONNECTED! Don't forget to take full advantage of the on-line support for Management 7/e.
- Chapter 1 On-line Study Guide
- Chapter 1 Self-test Answers
- Chapter 1 E-Resource Center

www.wiley.com/college/schermerhorn

2

Environment and diversity

Planning ahead

GETTING CONNECTED

Herman Miller—Core Values Drive High Performance

At Herman Miller, the innovative and award-winning manufacturer of designer furniture, the idea of the corporation goes well beyond its existence as a legal entity. The firm embraces its entire list of stakeholders, including employees, suppliers, customers, and community. Core values drive a unique and high-performance system.

Central to Herman Miller's values is a belief in "participation." Go to the web site and you'll find the firm self-described this way: "For 50 years participation has been central to Herman Miller. It still is. We believe in participation because we value and benefit from the richness of ideas and opinions of thousands of people. Participation enables employee-owners to contribute their unique gifts and abilities to the corporate community."

Herman Miller calls itself "a high-performance, values-driven community of people tied together by a common purpose." What are these core values? Together, they constitute what is called the "Herman Miller way."

- Making a meaningful contribution to our customers
- Cultivating community, participation, and people development
- Creating economic value for shareholders and employee-owners
- Responding to change through design and innovation
- Living with integrity and respecting the environment

The firm is a values-driven company that finds high performance through everyday respect for people. It utilizes a performance measurement and compensation system called "Economic Value Added" (EVA). EVA is an internal measurement of operating and financial performance linked to incentive compensation for every employee. The interest is to encourage short- and long-term continuous improvements that create economic value. The innovative SQA division, "Simple-Quick-Affordable," runs the highly efficient furniture plant which uses the latest in information technology to build furniture to order in Internet time.

Herman Miller stays on course even as it reinvents itself in face of highly competitive demands and a changing environment. Although business initiatives and strategies change, the core values remain the same. That's the beauty of a values-driven company.[1]

@ Get Connected!

Find out more about how Herman Miller's core values set the stage for high performance. Examine the firm's concept of corporate community. Take a look at the corporate background. Start to think more about the roles leaders play in building high-performing organizations. Get connected!

Once a benchmark for science fiction writers, the dawning of the 21st century is now presenting unrelenting new demands on organizations and their members. Managers today are learning to operate in a world that places a premium on information, technology utilization, quality, customer service, and speed. They are learning how to succeed in a world of intense competition, continued globalization of markets and business activities, and rapid technological change. This chapter introduces the external and internal environments of organizations as two important considerations in the quest for high performance in demanding and dynamic times. The chapter opening example of Herman Miller sets the stage. It introduces the importance of core values and the belief in people. It raises the question: What must organizations do to remain successful in the dynamic, complex, and ever-changing environment of today?

ENVIRONMENT AND COMPETITIVE ADVANTAGE

In his book, *The Future of Success*, former U.S. Secretary of Labor Robert Reich says: "The emerging economy is offering unprecedented opportunities, an ever-expanding choice of terrific deals, fabulous products, good investments, and great jobs for people with the right talents and skills. Never before in human history have so many had access to so much so easily."[2] On these terms, things couldn't be better for organizations and career seekers. But there are also major challenges to be faced. When looking at things from a business vantage point, IBM's CEO Louis V. Gerstner, Jr., once described the challenge this way: "We believe very strongly that the age-old levers of competition—labor, capital, and land, are being supplemented by knowledge, and that most successful companies in the future will be those that learn how to exploit knowledge—knowledge about customer behavior, markets, economies, technology—faster than their competitors."[3] Knowledge and speed are indispensable to success in this new economy. Even as Gerstner and other executives strive to lead their organizations toward a high-performance edge, they cannot afford for a minute to rest on past laurels. The world is too uncertain and the competition too intense for that. "In order to survive," Reich points out, "all organizations must dramatically and continuously improve—cutting costs, adding value, creating new products."[4]

WHAT IS COMPETITIVE ADVANTAGE?

○ A **competitive advantage** allows an organization to deal with market and environmental forces better than its competitors.

Astute executives understand the management implications in the prior observations. They are ever-alert to environmental trends that require adjustments in the ways their organizations operate and that offer opportunities to achieve **competitive advantage**.[5] This term refers to the utilization of a core competency that clearly sets an organization apart from its competitors and gives it an advantage over them in the marketplace. Simply put, competitive advantage comes from an ability to do things better than one's competitors. An organization may achieve competitive advantage in many ways, including through its products, pricing, customer service, cost efficiency, and quality, among other aspects of operating excellence. But regardless of how the advantage is achieved, the key result is the same—an ability to consistently do something of high value that one's competitors cannot replicate quickly or do as well.

The Bears That Mean Business John Sortino heard the call to competitive advantage. He also followed the pathways of entrepreneurship. He started Vermont Teddy Bear Company in Burlington, Vermont, after adding sunglasses to liven up his son's favorite teddy bear. The firm has grown into a substantial local employer, maker of over 300,000 bears a year, and winner of the prestigious Heritage of New England Award for commitment to exceptional quality. Vermont Teddy Bear's products are backed with lifetime and no-questions-asked guarantees. Sortino credits the award to the workers. Says he: "It is everyone working together which creates a successful customer service program."[6]

THE GENERAL ENVIRONMENT

Some years ago, at a time when American industry was first coming to grips with fierce competition from Japanese products, American quality pioneer J. M. Juran challenged an audience of Japanese executives with a prediction. He warned them against complacency, suggesting that America would bounce back in business competitiveness and that the words "Made in America" would once again symbolize world-class quality.[7] There seems little doubt today that Juran's prediction was accurate. Business excellence did resurge in America, with part of the reason coming from better understanding by business leaders of the interdependencies of their organizations with the external environment. Competitive advantage in the demanding global economy can be achieved only by continuously scanning the environment for opportunities, and taking effective action based on what is learned.[8] The ability to do this begins with the answer to a basic question: What is in the external environment of organizations?

The **general environment** consists of all the background conditions in the external environment of an organization. This portion of the environment forms a general context for managerial decision making. The major external environmental issues of our day include factors such as the following:

- *Economic conditions*—general state of the economy in terms of inflation, income levels, gross domestic product, unemployment, and related indicators of economic health.

- *Social-cultural conditions*—general state of prevailing social values on such matters as human rights, trends in education and related social institutions, as well as demographic patterns.

- *Legal-political conditions*—general state of the prevailing philosophy and objectives of the political party or parties running the government, as well as laws and government regulations.

- *Technological conditions*—general state of the development and availability of technology, including scientific advancements.

- *Natural environment conditions*—general state of nature and conditions of the natural environment, including levels of public concern expressed through environmentalism.

If we take the natural environment as an example, Japanese automakers seem to be finding the potential for competitive advantage. Both Honda and Toyota have received awards from the Sierra Club for excellence in

○ The **general environment** is comprised of cultural, economic, legal-political, and educational conditions.

← Elements in the general environment.

environmental engineering.[9] The two firms are on the leading edge by offering hybrid cars that combine gas and electric power. While America's automakers were betting that customers would stay loyal to large gas-fueled and often gas-hungry vehicles, their Japanese competitors saw the potential for competitive advantage. They are now gaining experience and reputation from being first to market with the more environmentally friendly hybrid vehicles.

Manager's Notepad 2.1 highlights important diversity trends in the sociocultural environment of organizations.[10] It is also important to note that differences in any and all general environment factors are especially noticeable when organizations operate internationally. External conditions vary significantly from one country and culture to the next. Managers of successful international operations understand these differences and help their organizations make the operating adjustments needed to perform within them. Like many large firms, the pharmaceutical giant Merck derives a substantial portion of its business from overseas operations. In a drive to further increase its global market share, Merck executives recognize the need to be well informed about and responsive to differing local conditions. In Europe, for example, they have entered into cooperative agreements with local companies, conducted research with local partners, and worked with local governments on legal matters.

THE SPECIFIC ENVIRONMENT

○ The **specific environment** includes the people and groups with whom an organization interacts.

The **specific environment** consists of the actual organizations, groups, and persons with whom an organization interacts and conducts business. These are environmental elements of direct consequence to the organization as it operates on a day-to-day basis. The specific environment is often described in terms of **stakeholders**—the persons, groups, and institutions who are affected in one way or another by the organization's performance. *Figure 2.1,* shows multiple stakeholders as they may exist in the external environment of a typical business firm.

○ **Stakeholders** are the persons, groups, and institutions directly affected by an organization's performance.

Sometimes called the *task environment*, the specific environment and the stakeholders are distinct for each organization. They can also change over time according to the company's unique customer base, operating

---

MANAGER'S NOTEPAD 2.1

Diversity trends in the sociocultural environment

- People of color are an increasing percentage of the workforce.
- More women are working.
- People with disabilities are gaining more access to the workplace.
- Workers are increasingly from nontraditional families (eg. single parents, dual wage earners).
- Average age of workers is increasing.
- Religious diversity of workers is increasing.

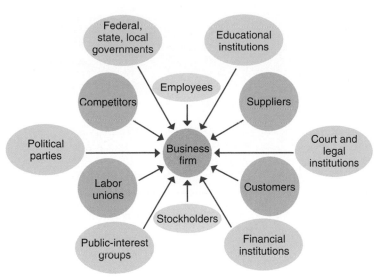

Figure 2.1 Multiple stakeholders in the environment of organizations.

needs, and circumstances. Important stakeholders common to the specific environment of most organizations include:

- *Customers*—specific consumer or client groups, individuals, and organizations that purchase the organization's goods and/or use its services.
- *Suppliers*—specific providers of the human, information, and financial resources and raw materials needed by the organization to operate.
- *Competitors*—specific organizations that offer the same or similar goods and services to the same consumer or client groups.
- *Regulators*—specific government agencies and representatives, at the local, state, and national levels, that enforce laws and regulations affecting the organization's operations.

← Components of the specific or task environment.

ENVIRONMENTAL UNCERTAINTY

The fact is that many organizations today face great uncertainty in their external environments. In this sense, **environmental uncertainty** means that there is a lack of complete information regarding what developments will occur in the external environment. This makes it difficult to predict future states of affairs and to understand their potential implications for the organization. *Figure 2.2* describes environmental uncertainty along two dimensions: (1) complexity, or the number of different factors in the environment and (2) the rate of change in these factors.[11]

In general, the greater the environmental uncertainty, the more attention that management in an organization must direct toward the external environment. It has to be continually studied and monitored to spot emerging trends. Also, the greater the environmental uncertainty the more need there is for flexibility and adaptability in organizational designs and work practices. Because of this uncertainty, organizations must be able to respond quickly as new circumstances arise and information becomes available. Throughout this book you will find many examples of how organizations are becoming more flexible in the attempt to better deal with the high amounts of environmental uncertainty that so often prevail in today's dynamic times.

○ **Environmental uncertainty** is a lack of complete information about the environment.

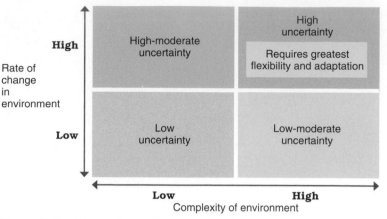

Figure 2.2 Dimensions of uncertainty in organizational environments.

CUSTOMER-DRIVEN ORGANIZATIONS

Question: What's your job?
Answer: I run the cash register and sack groceries.
Question: But isn't it your job to serve the customer?
Answer: I guess, but it's not in my job description.

This conversation illustrates what often becomes the missing link in the quest for total quality and competitive advantage: customer service.[12] Contrast this conversation with the following report from a customer of the Vermont Teddy Bear Company, who called to report that her new mail-order teddy bear had a problem. The company responded promptly, she said, and arranged to have the bear picked up and replaced. She wrote the firm to say "thank you for the great service and courtesy you gave me."[13]

WHO ARE THE CUSTOMERS?

Figure 2.3 expands the open-systems view of organizations introduced in Chapter 1 to now depict the complex internal operations of the organization as well as its interdependence with the external environment. In this figure the organization's *external customers* purchase the goods produced or utilize the services provided. They may be industrial customers, that is, other firms that buy a company's products for use in their own operations; or they may

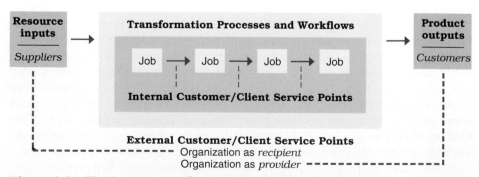
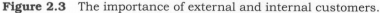

Figure 2.3 The importance of external and internal customers.

be retail customers or clients who purchase or use the goods and services directly. *Internal customers*, by contrast, are found within the organization. They are the individuals and groups who use or otherwise depend on the results of others' work in order to do their own jobs well. Any job or function is both a supplier and a customer. Customers have the right to expect high-quality and on-time inputs from the earlier points in the workflow; suppliers, in turn, have the responsibility to deliver high-quality and on-time inputs to the next point. The notion of customer service applies equally well to workflows within the organization as well as to the relationship between the organization and its ultimate consumers in the external environment.

WHAT CUSTOMERS WANT

Customers sit at the top when organizations are viewed as the upside-down pyramids described in Chapter 1. And without any doubt, customers put today's organizations to a very stiff test. They primarily want three things in the goods and services they buy: (1) high-quality, (2) low-cost, and (3) on-time delivery. Offering them anything less is unacceptable.

Organizations that can't meet these customer expectations suffer the market consequences; they lose competitive advantage. Some time ago, for example, Intel Corporation faced a crisis in customer confidence when a defect was found in one of its Pentium chips. At first top management of this highly regarded company balked at replacing the chips, suggesting that the defect wasn't really important. But customers were angry and unrelenting in their complaints. Eventually the customers won, as they should. Intel agreed to replace the chips without any questions asked. The company also learned two important lessons of successful businesses today: (1) always protect your reputation for quality products—it is hard to get and easy to lose, and (2) always treat your customers right—they, too, are hard to get and easy to lose.

CUSTOMER RELATIONSHIP MANAGEMENT

When pursued relentlessly as a goal, customer service can be an important source of competitive advantage. Just imagine the ramifications if every customer or client contact for an organization was positive. Not only would they return again as members of a loyal customer base, but they would also tell others and expand the size of that base. Progressive managers understand this concept and work hard to establish and maintain high standards of customer service. They try to provide every customer with goods and services that are high in quality and low in cost, meet their needs, and require only short waiting times. Operating a business or other type of organization with a customer-centered focus that strategically tries to build relationships and add value to customers is known as **customer relationship management**.

The utilization of "CRM" in pursuit of competitive advantage is rapidly evolving with the support of information technology that allows organizations to maintain intense communication with customers as well as to gather and utilize data regarding their needs and desires. At Marriott International, for example, CRM is supported by special customer management software that tracks information on customer preferences. When you check in, the likelihood is that your past requests for things like a king-size bed, no smoking room, and computer modem access will already be entered in your record. Says Marriott's chairman: "It's a big competitive advantage."[14]

www.dell.com

The customer is "captain" of the supply chain for Dell Computer. Founder and chairman Michael Dell firmly believes that competitive advantage can be found by focusing supply chain management on meeting customer preferences. The firm is a leader in using information technology to create operating efficiencies that deliver products and services meeting customer preferences.

○ **Customer relationship management** strategically tries to build lasting relationships and add value to customers.

Customer relationship management clearly belongs on the list of any manager's top strategic priorities. A *Harvard Business Review* survey reports that American business leaders rank customer service and product quality as the first and second most important goals in the success of their organizations, respectively.[15] In a survey by the market research firm Michelson & Associates, poor service and product dissatisfaction were also ranked #1 and #2 as reasons why customers abandon a retail store.[16] But reaching the goals of providing good service and quality products isn't guaranteed, and it isn't always easy. To meet the challenge, organizations must first find out what customers want and then give it to them. This simple prescription is at the heart of a comprehensive strategy for CRM.

○ **Supply chain management** strategically links all operations dealing with resource supplies.

Just as organizations need to manage customers on the output side, they are also customers of their suppliers. Supplier relationships must be well-managed too. The concept of **supply chain management** involves strategic management of all operations relating an organization to the suppliers of its resources—including purchasing, manufacturing, transportation, and distribution.[17] The goals of SCM are straightforward: achieve efficiency in all aspects of the chain while ensuring the necessary flow and on-time availability of quality resources for customer-driven operations.[18]

QUALITY-DRIVEN ORGANIZATIONS

If managing for high performance and competitive advantage is the theme of the day, "quality" is one of its most important watchwords. Customers want quality whether they are buying a consumer product or receiving a service. The achievement of quality objectives in all aspects of operations is a universal criterion of organizational performance in manufacturing and service industries alike. The competitive demands of a global economy are an important force in this race toward total quality operations. **ISO standards** set by the International Standards Organization in Geneva, Switzerland, have been adopted by many countries of the world as quality benchmarks. Businesses that want to compete as "world-class companies" in delivering consistent quality are increasingly expected to have **ISO 9000** certification at various levels. To gain certification in this family of standards, they must refine and upgrade quality in all operations and then undergo a rigorous assessment by outside auditors to determine whether they meet ISO requirements. Increasingly, the ISO "stamp of approval" is viewed as a necessity in international business; the ISO certification provides customers with assurance that a set of solid quality standards and processes are in place. In respect to quality of environmental management systems, for example, the new ISO 14000 series is now setting international standards.

○ **ISO certification** indicates conformance with a rigorous set of international quality standards.

TOTAL QUALITY MANAGEMENT

○ **Total quality management** is managing with an organization-wide commitment to continuous improvement, product quality, and customer needs.

The term **total quality management** (TQM) was introduced in Chapter 1. It describes the process of making quality principles part of the organization's strategic objectives, applying them to all aspects of operations, committing to continuous improvement, and striving to meet customers' needs by doing things right the first time. The quality movement around the world has been strongly influenced by the pioneering work of W. Edwards Deming and Joseph M. Juran. Interestingly, their ideas became popular in Japan starting in the early 1950s and only gained prominence in the United States after the Japanese became so successful in world markets by competing with a product quality advantage.[19] The commitment to total quality operations is now a way of life in world-class firms everywhere. In the United States, the Malcolm Baldrige National Quality Awards were established to benchmark excellence in quality achievements. In business, the award criteria focus on these performance areas: (1) customer-focused results, (2) financial and market results, (3) human resource results, (4) supplier and partner results, and (5) organizational effectiveness.[20]

There are many quality improvement approaches being tested and used around the world. Most begin with an insistence that the total quality commitment applies to everyone in an organization and to all aspects of operations, right from resource acquisition through to the production and distribution of finished goods and services.[21] One well-known consultant, Philip Crosby, became quite famous for offering these "four absolutes" of management for total quality control: (1) *quality means conformance to standards*—workers must know exactly what performance standards they are expected to meet; (2) *quality comes from defect prevention, not defect correction*—leadership, training, and discipline must prevent defects in the first place; (3) *quality as a performance standard must mean defect-free work*—the only acceptable quality standard is perfect work; and, (4) *quality saves money*—doing things right the first time saves the cost of correcting poor work.[22]

QUALITY AND CONTINUOUS IMPROVEMENT

Among the many approaches to quality commitment, the work of W. Edwards Deming is another useful benchmark. The story begins in 1951 when he was invited to Japan to explain quality control techniques that had been developed in the United States. The result was a lifelong relationship epitomized in the Deming prize, which is still annually awarded in Japan for excellence in quality. "When Deming spoke," we might say, "the Japanese listened." The principles he taught the Japanese were straightforward . . . and they worked: tally defects, analyze and trace them to the source, make corrections, and keep a record of what happens afterward.[23] Deming's "14 points to quality" emphasize constant innovation, use of statistical methods, and commitment to training in the fundamentals of quality assurance.[24]

The search for quality is closely tied to the emphasis on **continuous improvement**—always looking for new ways to improve on current performance.[25] A basic philosophy of total quality management is that one can never be satisfied; something always can and should be improved on. Continuous improvement must be a way of life. Another important aspect of total quality operations is cycle time—the elapsed time between receipt of an order and delivery of the finished product. The quality objective here is to reduce cycle time by finding ways to serve customer needs more quickly.

One way to combine employee involvement and continuous improvement is through the popular **quality circle** concept.[26] This is a group of workers (usually no more than 10) who meet regularly to discuss ways of improving the quality of their products or services. Their objective is to assume responsibility for quality and apply every member's full creative potential to ensure that it is achieved. Such worker empowerment can result in cost savings from improved quality and greater customer

Get Connected!

Learn more about Deming's 14 Points of Quality.

○ **Continuous improvement** involves always searching for new ways to improve operations quality and performance.

○ A **quality circle** is a group of employees who periodically meet to discuss ways of improving the quality of their products or services.

satisfaction. It can also improve morale and commitment, as the following remarks from quality circle members indicate: "This is the best thing the company has done in 15 years." . . . "The program proves that supervisors have no monopoly on brains." . . . "It gives me more pride in my work."[27]

CAREER CONNECTION

Diversity

Quality and Diversity Help Make Supply Chain Management Work

Solectron Corporation is a world leader in supply-chain facilitation for customized electronics technology, manufacturing, and service solutions. With an emphasis on quality, as a differentiating factor, the firm uses ISO 9000 and the Malcolm Baldrige National Quality Award to guide its activities. It has received the Baldrige award twice and a copy of its Baldrige Award Application Summary is available on its web site.

Solectron benchmarks Japanese manufacturing companies and combines American innovation with Japanese techniques in order to meet its quality goals. The firm has a strong organizational culture that uses a Japanese-based "Five S" system to insure that its vision for excellence is achieved. The Five Ss include: (1) *Seiri*—Organization; (2) *Seiton*—Orderliness; (3) *Seiso*—Cleanliness; (4) *Seiketsu*—Standardized Cleanup; (5) *Shitsuke*—Discipline. All this is done from a global platform, with 56,000 associates working out of 49 worldwide locations, including the Americas, Europe, and Asia/Pacific.

Solectron's vision and values drive the common purpose of the organization and create value for its customers. Managing diversity is a pathway to competitive advantage. In an employee survey, the firm once identified workers from 30 nationalities, speaking 40 native languages and dialects. To help them better understand each other and work together more productively, a cultural awareness program was started to help employees be more open in expressing opinions.

QUESTION: Are you ready for a career working in and helping to lead truly multicultural organizations? How can managing diversity lead to competitive advantage?

QUALITY, TECHNOLOGY AND DESIGN

This is the age of technology, and technology utilization has a major role to play in the quality aspects of operations. In retailing, for example, Levi Strauss & Company has a program called "Personal Pair" which uses flexible manufacturing systems to offer jeans made to someone's personal measurements. In the building supplies industry, Andersen Windows lets customers design their own windows to specification using the firm's special computer software. And at Reflect.com, customers can go on-line to custom design cosmetics and perfumes right from the formulations to the packaging.[28]

These are all examples of how new technologies are changing the nature of manufacturing and improving both quality and efficiency of operations. Among the terms describing these developments, *lean production* uses new technologies to streamline systems and allow work to be performed with fewer workers and smaller inventories. The use of *flexible manufacturing* allows processes to be changed quickly and efficiently to produce different products or modifications to existing ones. Through such techniques as *agile manufacturing* and *mass customization* organizations are able to make individualized products quickly and with production efficiencies once only associated with the mass production of uniform products.[29] All such systems utilize computer-based technologies to better integrate the various aspects of manufacturing with customer preferences. They allow modifications to be made quickly, with high quality and in cost-efficient fashion.

Another timely and important contribution to quality management is found in product design. We are all aware of design differences among products, be they cars, computers, cell phones, stereos, watches, clothes, or whatever. But what may not be recognized is that design makes a difference in how things are produced and at what level of cost and quality. A "good" design has eye appeal to the customer and is easy to manufacture with productivity. In today's competitive global economy, such designs are strategic weapons. "Design is it," says consultant Tom Peters, arguing that it will be the key to competitive advantage in the future.[30]

Progressive manufacturers now emphasize *design for manufacturing.* This means that products are styled to lower production costs and smooth the way toward high-quality results in all aspects of the manufacturing processes.[31] Styling is now often developed on the computer and then tested via simulation for its manufacturing implications. Teamwork among engineering, production, marketing, and other functional areas is also improving the design process. A manufacturing approach that shows respect for the natural environment is *design for disassembly.* The goal is to design products taking into account how their component parts will be reused at the end of product life. For example, automakers are using more parts that can be recycled; computer makers are now more willing to take back obsolete machines, disassemble them, and recycle the parts.

INTERNAL ENVIRONMENT AND ORGANIZATIONAL CULTURE

Culture is a popular word in management these days. Important differences in national cultures will be discussed in Chapter 5 on the global dimensions of management. Now it is time to talk about cultural differences in the internal environments of organizations. **Organizational culture** is defined by noted scholar and consultant Edgar Schein as the system of shared beliefs and values that develops within an organization and guides the behavior of its members.[32] Sometimes called the *corporate culture,* it is a key aspect of any organization and work setting. Whenever someone, for example, speaks of "the way we do things here," they are talking about the culture.

○ **Organizational culture** is the system of shared beliefs and values that develops within an organization and guides the behavior of its members.

WHAT STRONG CULTURES DO

Although it is clear that culture is not the sole determinant of what happens in organizations, it is an important influence on what they accomplish . . . and how. The internal culture has the potential to shape attitudes, reinforce common beliefs, direct behavior, and establish performance expectations and the motivation to fulfill them. A widely discussed study of successful businesses concluded that organizational culture made a major contribution to their long-term performance records.[33] Importantly, the cultures in these organizations provided for a clear vision of what the organization was attempting to accomplish, allowing individuals to rally around the vision and work hard to support and accomplish it. In these and related ways organizational culture is a bond that further mobilizes resources for action.[34]

Strong cultures, ones that are clear and well defined and widely shared among members, discourage dysfunctional work behaviors and encourage positive ones. They commit members to do things for and with one another that are in the best interests of the organization, and then they reinforce these habits. The best organizations have strong cultures that show respect for members and encourage adaptability and continuous improvement in all areas of operations. They are likely to have cultures that are performance oriented, emphasize teamwork, allow for risk taking, encourage innovation, and make the well-being of people a top management priority.[35] Honda is a good example. The firm's culture is tightly focused

www.patagonia.com

The new generation of workers is quite a test for empowerment and corporate culture. Patagonia, Inc., maker of quality outdoor wear and equipment, actively supports new values and workforce diversity. Casual is in; formal is out. Talent and commitment are in.

Elements in the observable culture of organizations.

around what is known as "The Honda Way"—a set of principles emphasizing ambition, respect for ideas, open communication, work enjoyment, harmony, and hard work.

LEVELS OF ORGANIZATIONAL CULTURE

Organizational culture is usually described from the perspective of the two levels shown in *Figure 2.4*—the "observable" culture and the "core" culture.[36] The *observable culture* is visible; it is what one sees and hears when walking around an organization as a visitor, a customer, or an employee. In strong culture organizations the observable culture will be readily apparent. It can be seen in the way people dress at work, how they arrange their offices, how they speak to and behave toward one another, the nature of their conversations, and how they talk about and treat their customers. More formally stated, the observable culture includes the following elements of daily organizational life—through them, new members learn the organization's culture and all members share and reinforce its special aspects over time:

- *Stories*—oral histories and tales, told and retold among members, about dramatic sagas and incidents in the life of the organization.
- *Heroes*—the people singled out for special attention and whose accomplishments are recognized with praise and admiration among members; they include founders and role models.
- *Rites and rituals*—the ceremonies and meetings, planned and spontaneous, that celebrate important occasions and performance accomplishments.
- *Symbols*—the special use of language and other nonverbal expressions to communicate important themes of organizational life.

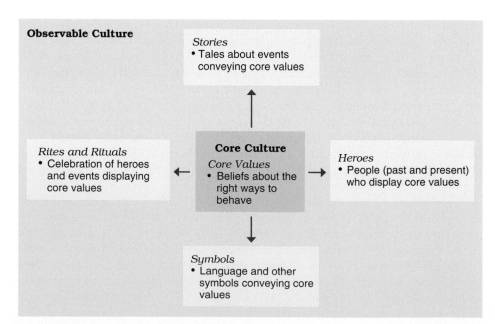

Figure 2.4 Levels of organizational culture—observable culture and core culture.

Standing at the foundation of what one directly observes in the daily life of an organization is a second and deeper level of culture. This is the **core culture**, and it determines why things are this way. It consists of *core values* or underlying assumptions and beliefs that influence behavior and actually give rise to the aspects of observable culture just described. Values are essential to strong culture organizations and are often widely publicized in formal statements of corporate mission and purpose. Strong culture organizations operate with a small but enduring set of core values. Researchers point out that the enduring commitment to core values is a major ingredient of organizations that achieve long-term success. Highly successful companies typically emphasize the values of performance excellence, innovation, social responsibility, integrity, worker involvement, customer service, and teamwork. Examples of core values that drive the best companies include "service above all else" at Nordstrom; "science-based innovation" at Merck; "encouraging individual initiative and creativity" at Sony; "fanatical attention to consistency and detail" at Disney.[37]

○ **Core values** are underlying beliefs shared by members of the organization and that influence their behavior.

LEADERSHIP AND ORGANIZATIONAL CULTURE

Leadership of the organizational culture involves establishing and maintaining appropriate core values. Whereas this is most often considered a top management job, the same definition holds for any manager or team leader at any level of responsibility. Just like the organization as a whole, any work team or group will have a culture. How well this culture operates to support the group and its performance objectives will depend in part on the strength of the core values. At any level, these values should meet the test of these three criteria: (1) *relevance*—core values should support key performance objectives; (2) *pervasiveness*—core values should be known by all members of the organization or group; and (3) *strength*—core values should be accepted by everyone involved.[38]

Attention is now being increasingly given to the concept of a **symbolic leader**, someone who uses symbols well to establish and maintain a desired organizational culture. Symbolic managers and leaders talk the "language" of the organization. They are always careful to use spoken and written words to describe people, events, and even the competition in ways that reinforce and communicate core values. *Language metaphors*—the use of positive examples from another context—are very powerful in this regard. For example, newly hired workers at Disney World and Disneyland are counseled to always think of themselves as more than employees; they are key "members of the cast," and they work "on stage." After all, they are told, Disney isn't just any business, it is an "entertainment" business.

○ A **symbolic leader** uses symbols to establish and maintain a desired organizational culture.

Good symbolic leaders highlight the observable culture. They tell key *stories* over and over again, and they encourage others to tell them. They often refer to the "founding story" about the entrepreneur whose personal values set a key tone for the enterprise. They often tell about organizational *heroes*, past and present, whose performances exemplify core values. They often use symbolic rites and rituals that glorify the performance of the organization and its members. At Mary Kay Cosmetics, gala events at which top sales performers share their tales of success are legendary. So to are the lavish incentive awards presented at these ceremonies, especially the pink luxury cars given to the most successful salespeople.[39]

DIVERSITY AND MULTICULTURAL ORGANIZATIONS

At the very time that we talk about the culture of an organization as a whole, we must also recognize the presence of diversity. Organizations are made up of people, each of whom comes as a unique individual. An important key to competitive advantage is respecting this diversity and allowing everyone's talents to be fully utilized.

○ The term **diversity** describes race, gender, age, and other individual differences.

As first introduced in Chapter 1, **diversity** is a term used to describe differences among people at work. Primary dimensions of diversity include age, race, ethinicity, gender, physical ability, and sexual orientation. But workplace diversity is a broader issue still, including also such things as religious beliefs, education, experience, and family status, among others.[40] In his book, *Beyond Race and Gender,* consultant R. Roosevelt Thomas, Jr. makes the point that "diversity includes everyone." He says: "In this expanded context, white males are as diverse as their colleagues."[41] Thomas also links diversity and organizational culture, believing that the way people are treated at work—with respect and inclusion, or with disrespect and exclusion—is a direct reflection of the organization's culture.

Thomas's diversity message to those who lead and manage organizations is straight to the point. Diversity is a potential source of competitive advantage, offering organizations a mixture of talents and perspectives that is ready and able to deal with the complexities and uncertainty in the every-changing 21st century environment. If you do the right things in organizational leadership, in other words, you'll gain competitive advantage through diversity. If you don't, you'll lose it.

○ **Multiculturalism** involves pluralism and respect for diversity.

○ A **multicultural organization** is based on pluralism and operates with respect for diversity.

WHAT IS A MULTICULTURAL ORGANIZATION?

A key issue in the culture of any organization is *inclusivity*—the degree to which the organization is open to anyone who can perform a job, regardless of their race, sexual preference, gender, or other diversity attribute.[42] The term **multiculturalism** refers to pluralism and respect for diversity in the workplace. There is no reason why organizational cultures cannot communicate core values and encourage common work directions that respect and empower the full demographic and cultural diversity that is now characteristic of our workforces. The "best" organizational cultures in this sense are inclusive. They value the talents, ideas, and creative potential of all members. The model in this regard is the truly **multicultural organization** with these characteristics:[43]

Characteristics of multicultural organizations.

- *Pluralism*—Members of both minority cultures and majority cultures are influential in setting key values and policies.
- *Structural integration*—Minority-culture members are well represented in jobs at all levels and in all functional responsibilities.
- *Informal network integration*—Various forms of mentoring and support groups assist in the career development of minority-culture members.
- *Absence of prejudice and discrimination*—A variety of training and task force activities continually address the need to eliminate culture-group biases.
- *Minimum intergroup conflict*—Diversity does not lead to destructive conflicts between members of majority and minority cultures.

ORGANIZATIONAL SUBCULTURES

Like society as a whole, organizations contain a mixture of **subcultures**, that is, cultures common to groups of people with similar values and beliefs based on shared work responsibilities and personal characteristics. There are *occupational cultures* in organizations, and they must be understood for their work and managerial implications.[44] For example, salaried professionals such as lawyers, scientists, engineers, and accountants have been described as having special needs for work autonomy and empowerment that may conflict with traditional management methods of top-down direction and control.[45] Unless these needs are recognized and properly dealt with, salaried professionals may prove difficult to integrate into the culture of the larger organization.

There are also *functional subcultures* in organizations, and people from different functions often have difficulty understanding and working well with one another. For example, employees of a business may consider themselves "systems people" or "marketing people" or "manufacturing people" or "finance people." When such identities are overemphasized, there is a tendency to separate in-group members from the rest of the organization. Members of the functional groups may spend most of their time with each other, develop a "jargon" or technical language that is shared among themselves, and view their role in the organization as more important than the contributions of the other functions.

Differences in *ethnic or national cultures* will be discussed in Chapter 5 on the global dimensions of management.[46] Although it is relatively easy to recognize that people from various countries and regions of the world may represent different cultural backgrounds, it is far harder to turn this awareness into the ability to work well with persons whose ethnic cultures differ from our own. The best understanding is most likely gained through direct contact and a personal commitment to remain open-minded when working with persons from different ethnic backgrounds. As imprecise as our understanding of ethnic subcultures may be, things seem even less clear on matters of race. Although one may speak in everyday conversations about "African American" and "Latino" or "Caucasian" cultures, one has to wonder what we really know about these *racial subcultures*.[47] Importantly, a key question remains largely unanswered: Where can we find frameworks for understanding them? If improved cross-cultural understandings can help people work better across national boundaries, why can't improved cross-cultural understandings help people from different racial subcultures work better together?

We live at a time when the influence of *generational subcultures* at work is of growing importance. But the issues are more subtle than young-old issues alone. It is possible to identify "generational gaps" among "Baby Boomers" now in their 50s, "Generation Xers" now in their 30s and early 40s, "Nexters" now in their 20s, and the "Millennial Generation" in high school at the turn of the century. Members of these generations grew up and are growing up in quite different worlds; they have been and are being influenced by different values and opportunities. Their work preferences and attitudes tend to reflect the influence of those differences. Someone who is 60 years old today, a common age for senior managers, was 15 in the 1950s. They may have difficulty understanding, supervising, and working with younger managers who were teenagers during the 1970s, 1980s, and even the 1990s. And if you are one of the latter

○ **Subcultures** are common to groups of people with similar values and beliefs based on shared work responsibilities and personal characteristics.

How Minority Employees View Their Work
In a study by Korn/Ferry International, the reported job satisfaction by black (64%) and white (62%) employees was quite comparable. But, things were far less similar when questions turned to issues of fairness and pay. Take the on-line "Reality Check" to learn more about the results of this survey.

Workforce projections can be found at the U.S. Bureau of Labor Statistics.

generations—perhaps the Millennial Generation, you'll need to ponder how well you will do in the future when working with colleagues who grew up in the early years of the 21st century.[48]

Issues of gender relationships and gender discrimination also continue to complicate the workplace. Some research shows that when men work together, a group culture forms around a competitive atmosphere, in which the games and stories deal with winning and losing in various situations. It also often involves the use of sports metaphors.[49] When women work together, a rather different culture may form, with more emphasis on personal relationships and collaboration. One can reasonably ask: What happens when *gender subcultures* mix in the organization?

CHALLENGES FACED BY MINORITIES AND WOMEN

The very term *diversity* basically means the presence of differences. But what does it mean when those differences are distributed unequally across organizational levels or among work functions? What difference does it make when one subculture is in "majority" status while others become "minorities" in respect to representation with the organization? Even though organizations are changing today, for example, most senior executives in large organizations are older, white, and male. There is still likely to be more workforce diversity at lower and middle levels of most organizations than at the top. Take a look at the situation described by *Figure 2.5*. What are the implications for minority members, such as women or persons of color, in organizations traditionally dominated by a majority culture, such as white males? Consider also the case of Jesse Spaulding, a regional manager for a restaurant chain owned by Shoney's. He says that the firm used to operate on the "buddy system" that "left people of color by the wayside" when it came to promotions. Things have changed now under Shoney's new leadership, and Spaulding is delighted with the opportunity—the firm has been ranked among Fortune magazine's list of America's 50 Best Companies for Minorities.[50]

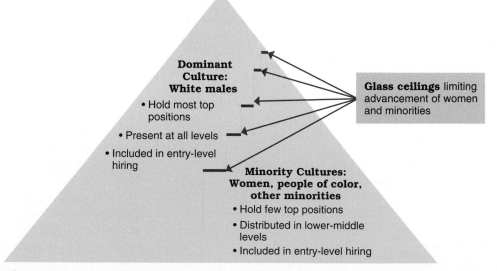

Figure 2.5 Glass ceilings as barriers to women and minority cultures in traditional organizations.

The daily work challenges faced by minority cultures or populations in organizations can range from having to deal with misunderstandings and lack of sensitivity on the one hand to suffering harassment and discrimination, active or subtle, on the other. *Sexual harassment* in the form of unwanted sexual advances, requests for sexual favors, and sexually laced communications is a problem female employees in particular may face. Minority workers can also be targets of cultural jokes; one survey reports some 45 percent of respondents had been the targets of such abuse. *Pay discrimination* is also an issue. One senior executive in the computer industry reported her surprise at finding out that the top performer in her work group, an African American male, was paid 25 percent less than anyone else. This wasn't because his pay had been cut to that level, she said, but because his pay increases over time had always trailed those given to his white coworkers. The differences added up significantly over time, but no one noticed or stepped forward to make the appropriate adjustment.[51] Minority members may also face *job discrimination*. Microsoft, for example, has been criticized as treating the firm's 5,000 or more temporary workers unfairly in terms of access to benefits and work assignments. Some temporaries (who wear orange identification badges at work) claim that they are treated as second-class citizens by the permanent employees (who wear blue badges).[52]

Sometimes the adaptation of minorities to organizations dominated by a majority culture takes the form of tendencies toward *biculturalism*—the display by members of minority cultures of characteristics of the majority culture that seem necessary to success in the organizational environment. For example, one might find gays and lesbians hiding their sexual orientation from coworkers out of fear of prejudice or discrimination; similarly, one might find an African American carefully training herself to not use at work certain words or phrases that might be considered by white coworkers as part of a cultural slang.

The special economic and work challenges faced by minorities are not always highly visible. We all know, for example, that the last decade was one of economic expansion; most Americans benefited from a growth in jobs and employment opportunities. But how many of us know that disabled workers largely failed to share in the gains? At the same time that demand for workers in general rose, the employment rate of the disabled fell over 10 percent for men and 5 percent for women.[53] While debate continues on the causes of the decline, the need to do more to improve work opportunities for the disabled is indisputable.

REALITY Check 2.2

How Does Age Affect Attitude?
Data collected from 4,000 executives show correlations between age and personality traits related to work effectiveness. Patience improves with age, blossoming (the data say) after the age of 45. Take the on-line "Reality Check" to learn more about age and attitude.

MANAGING DIVERSITY

There's no doubt today what minority workers want.[55] They want the same thing everyone wants. They want respect for their talents and a work setting that allows them to achieve to their full potential. It takes the best in diversity leadership at all levels of organizational management to meet these expectations. R. Roosevelt Thomas defines **managing diversity** as the process of comprehensively developing a work environment that is for everyone. He says that it involves creating an internal environment that allows "all kinds of people to reach their full potential" in the pursuit of organizational objectives.

○ **Managing diversity** is building an inclusive work environment that allows everyone to reach their full potential.

TAKE IT TO THE CASE!

The Coca-Cola Company
Coke Finds that Diversity Means Business

Coke didn't make *Fortune's* year-2000 list of best companies for minorities, but it plans to in the future. Senior executives at the firm were shocked when it became public knowledge that some employees of the firm considered it a biased place to work. Under direction of new CEO Doug Daft, the company has fought its way back from devastating publicity surrounding the dissatisfactions of its minority employees, including a $1.5 billion lawsuit filed by eight black employees. What were the complaints? Discrimination in promotions, performance evaluations, and pay, among others. And to make matters worse, the early complainants felt that their concerns were not taken seriously when raised with management. Daft has committed to reinventing Coke's corporate culture around respect for diversity. Although admitting that the company has its work cut out, the goals are in place. Compensation of top managers is now tied to how well they meet diversity goals.[54]

○ An **affirmative action** program commits the organization to hiring and advancing minorities and women.

Figure 2.6 describes managing diversity as the most comprehensive of three leadership approaches to diversity. The first is **affirmative action**, in which leadership commits the organization to hiring and advancing minorities and women. The second is *valuing diversity,* in which leadership commits the organization to education and training programs designed to help people better understand and respect individual differences. The third is *managing diversity,* in which leadership commits to changing the organizational culture to empower and include all people. For Thomas, managing diversity offers the most value in respect to competitive advantage.[56] A diverse workforce offers a rich pool of talents, ideas, and viewpoints useful for solving the complex problems of highly competitive and often-uncertain environments. When well managed this diversity becomes a major asset. A diverse workforce is best aligned with the needs and expectations of a diverse customer and supplier base, including those increasingly distributed around the world and among its cultures. Bell South CEO Duane Ackerman says: "Our customers come from diverse markets throughout the United States and the world. To help understand

Affirmative Action
Create upward mobility for minorities and women

Valuing Differences
Build quality relationships with respect for diversity

Managing Diversity
Achieve full utilization of diverse human resources

Figure 2.6 Multicultural organizations—from affirmative action to managing diversity.
Source: Developed from R. Roosevelt Thomas, Jr., *Beyond Race and Gender* (New York: AMACOM, 1991), p. 28.

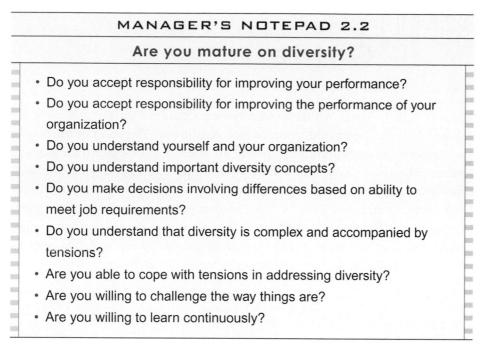

MANAGER'S NOTEPAD 2.2

Are you mature on diversity?

- Do you accept responsibility for improving your performance?
- Do you accept responsibility for improving the performance of your organization?
- Do you understand yourself and your organization?
- Do you understand important diversity concepts?
- Do you make decisions involving differences based on ability to meet job requirements?
- Do you understand that diversity is complex and accompanied by tensions?
- Are you able to cope with tensions in addressing diversity?
- Are you willing to challenge the way things are?
- Are you willing to learn continuously?

the needs of the global marketplace, Bell South has developed a workforce that reflects that diversity through all areas of its business."[57]

Organizations that Thomas calls "diversity mature" are well positioned to derive these and other sources of competitive advantage. In these organizations there is a diversity mission as well as an organizational mission; diversity is viewed as a strategic imperative and the members understand diversity concepts.[58] Ultimately, however, he considers the basic building block of a diversity-mature organization to be the *diversity-mature individual.* This is someone who can positively and honestly answer questions such as those posed in *Manager's Notepad 2.2.*[59]

Managing diversity is both a personal and organizational challenge. On a personal level, it means accepting the goal of diversity maturity as described in the accompanying notepad. As an organization, it means committing leadership to making fundamental changes in the organizational culture and its guiding mission and practices. Managers and people working at all levels of responsibility must benefit from a strong organizational culture based on true participation, involvement, and empowerment. Such cultures value the talents, ideas, and creative potential of all members, not just the majority members.

Perhaps the most important word in human resource management today is "inclusiveness." By valuing diversity and building multicultural organizations that include everyone, we can strengthen organizations and bring them into better alignment with the challenges and opportunities of today's environment. Importantly, the foundations of future success will be built on the foundations of diversity. As Michael R. Losey, president of the Society for Human Resource Management (SHRM) says: "Companies must realize that the talent pool includes people of all types, including older workers; persons with disabilities; persons of various religious, cultural and national backgrounds; persons who are not heterosexual; minorities; and women."[60]

@ Get Connected!

Visit Window on the World for business tips on diversity among the world's cultures.

STUDY Guide

The Chapter 2 Study Guide will help you review chapter content, prepare for examinations, and further build your career readiness. The *Summary* briefly highlights answers to questions first posed in the chapter opening Planning Ahead section. The list of *Key Terms* allows you to double-check your familiarity with basic concepts and definitions. *Self-Test 2* gives you the opportunity to test your basic comprehension of chapter content using sample test questions. Suggestions offered as *Career Readiness Activities* direct your attention to relevant sections of the end-of-text Career Readiness Workbook, as well as to special Electronic Resources on the *Management 7/e* web site.

SUMMARY

What is the external environment of organizations?

- Competitive advantage and distinctive competency can only be achieved by organizations that deal successfully with dynamic and complex environments.
- The external environment of organizations consists of both general and specific components.
- The general environment includes background conditions that influence the organization, including economic, sociocultural, legal-political, technological, and natural environment conditions.
- The specific or task environment consists of the actual organizations, groups, and persons an organization deals with; these include suppliers, customers, competitors, regulators, and pressure groups.
- Environmental uncertainty challenges organizations and their management to be flexible and responsive to new and changing conditions.

What is a customer-driven organization?

- Any organization must develop and maintain a base of loyal customers or clients, and a customer-driven organization recognizes customer service and product quality as foundations of competitive advantage.
- Customer service is a core ingredient of total quality operations, and it includes concerns for both internal customers and external customers.
- The "upside-down pyramid" is a symbol of how organizations of today are refocusing on customers and on the role of managers to support work efforts to continually improve quality and customer service.
- Operations management is specifically concerned with activities and decisions through which organizations transform resource inputs into product outputs.

- Today, operations management is increasingly viewed in a strategic perspective and with close attention to the demands of productivity, quality, and competitive advantage.

What is a quality-driven organization?

- To compete in the global economy organizations are increasingly expected to meet ISO 9000 certification standards of quality.
- Total quality management involves making quality a strategic objective of the organization and supporting it by continuous improvement efforts.
- The commitment to total quality operations requires meeting customers' needs—on time, the first time, and all the time.
- The use of quality circles—groups of employees working to solve quality problems—is a form of employee involvement in quality management.

What is the internal environment and organizational culture?

- The internal environment of organizations includes organizational culture, which establishes a personality for the organization as a whole and has a strong influence on the behavior of its members.
- The observable culture is found in the rites, rituals, stories, heroes, and symbols of the organization.
- The core culture consists of the core values and fundamental beliefs on which the organization is based.
- In organizations with strong cultures, members behave with shared understandings that support the accomplishment of key organizational objectives.
- Symbolic managers are good at building shared values and using stories, ceremonies, heroes, and language to reinforce these values in daily affairs.

How is diversity managed in a multicultural organization?

- The organizational culture should display a positive ethical climate, or shared set of understandings about what is considered ethically correct behavior.
- Multicultural organizations operate through a culture that values pluralism and respects diversity.
- Organizational cultures typically include the existence of many subcultures, including those based on occupational, functional, ethnic, racial, age, and gender differences in a diverse workforce.
- Challenges faced by organizational minorities include sexual harassment, pay discrimination, job discrimination and the glass ceiling effect.
- Managing diversity is the process of developing a work environment that is inclusive and allows everyone to reach their full work potential.
- Diversity leadership helps mobilize the full talents of an organization to achieve and sustain competitive advantage.

KEY TERMS

Affirmative action (p. 54)

Competitive advantage (p. 38)

Continuous improvement (p. 45)

Core values (p. 49)

Customer relationship management
(p. 43)

Diversity (p. 50)

Environmental uncertainty (p. 41)

General environment (p. 39)

ISO certification (p. 44)

ISO 9000 (p. 44)

Managing diversity (p. 53)

Multiculturalism (p. 50)

Multicultural organization (p. 50)

Organizational culture (p. 47)

Quality circle (p. 45)

Specific environment (p. 40)

Stakeholders (p. 40)

Subcultures (p. 51)

Supply chain management (p. 44)

Symbolic leader (p. 49)

Total quality management (p. 44)

SELF-TEST 2

Take this test here or on-line much as you would in a normal classroom situation. It is a good way to check your basic comprehension of chapter material. Answers may be found at the end of the book.

MULTIPLE-CHOICE QUESTIONS:

1. The general environment of an organization would include _____.
   (a) population demographics (b) activist groups (c) competitors
   (d) customers

2. Those persons and groups directly affected by an organization's performance are considered its _____.
   (a) core beneficiaries (b) cultural heroes (c) performance monitors
   (d) stakeholders

3. Two dimensions used in determining the level of perceived environmental uncertainty are the number of factors in the external environment and the _____ of these factors.
   (a) location (b) rate of change (c) independence (d) interdependence

4. Organizational practices like use of benchmarking, continuous improvement, and reduced cycle times indicate a commitment to _____.
   (a) affirmative action (b) total quality management (c) cost containment
   (d) supply chain management

5. The common quality standard for world-class companies is _____.
   (a) Deming prize (b) Baldrige award (c) TQM certification
   (d) ISO certification

6. New computer technologies have made possible _____, which produces individualized products quickly and efficiently for customers.
   (a) lean production (b) mass production (c) mass customization
   (d) robust design

7. Planned and spontaneous ceremonies and celebrations in the workplace illustrate the use of _____ to help to build strong corporate cultures.
   (a) rewards (b) heroes (c) rites and rituals (d) values

8. A _____ leader excels in the use of language metaphors, rites, and rituals to reinforce and build a desired organizational culture.
   (a) symbolic (b) bureaucratic (c) competitive (d) total quality

9. Pluralism and the absence of discrimination and prejudice are two important foundations of the _____.
   (a) glass ceiling effect (b) multicultural organization (c) quality circle
   (d) supply chain

10. When members of minority cultures behave in a way that takes on characteristics of the majority cultures this is called _____.
    (a) biculturalism (b) symbolic leadership (c) the glass ceiling effect
    (d) inclusivity

TRUE-FALSE QUESTIONS:

11. The specific environment of an organization might include its labor unions, customers, and government regulators.   T   F

12. The greater the environmental uncertainty the greater the attention senior managers should give to the external environment.   T   F

13. In a customer-driven organization, the only "customers" that count are those outside of the organization.   T   F

14. Although customer relationship management is a top strategic priority for businesses, supply chain management is considered a thing of the past.   T   F

15. Robust product designs are ones that minimize the risk of errors in production; that is, they are relatively "production proof."   T   F

16. Workforce diversity includes race and ethnicity, but does not include things like religious beliefs and sexual orientation.   T   F

17. In organizations with strong cultures one would not expect to find any subcultures.   T   F

18. Strong cultures can help organizations by encouraging positive work behaviors.   T   F

19. The ethical climate of a business firm is not an important part of its corporate culture.   T   F

20. According to consultant Roosevelt Thomas, the most comprehensive diversity approach is affirmative action.   T   F

SHORT-RESPONSE QUESTIONS:

21. What operating objectives are appropriate for an organization seeking competitive advantage through improved customer service?

22. What is the difference between an organization's external customers and its internal customers?

23. What is the difference between the observable and core cultures of an organization?

24. Why is it important for managers to understand subcultures in organizations?

APPLICATION QUESTION:

25. Two businesswomen, former college roommates, are discussing their jobs and careers over lunch. You overhear one saying to the other, "I work for a large corporation, while you own a small retail business. In my company there is strong corporate culture and everyone feels its influence. In fact, we are always expected to act in ways that support the culture and serve as role models for others to do so as well. This includes a commitment to diversity and multiculturalism. Because of the small size of your firm, things like corporate culture, diversity, and multiculturalism are not so important to worry about." Do you agree or disagree with this statement? Why?

CAREER readiness ACTIVITIES

Recommended learning activities from the end-of-text Career Readiness Workbook for this chapter include:

Career Advancement Portfolio
- Individual writing and group projects for any of the following activities.

Case for Critical Thinking
- The Coca-Cola Company: Diversity and a Global Presence

Integrative Learning Activities
- Research Project 1—Diversity Lessons
- Research Project 2—Changing Corporate Cultures
- Integrative Case—Outback Steakhouse

Exercises in Teamwork
- Defining Quality (# 3)
- Gender Differences in Management (# 20)
- Contingency Workforce (# 22)

Self-Assessments
- Organizational Culture Preferences (# 2)
- Cultural Attitudes Inventory (# 5)
- Diversity Awareness (# 7)

The Fast Company Collection On-Line
- Alan Weber, "Danger: Toxic Company"

ELECTRONIC RESOURCES

@ GET CONNECTED! Don't forget to take full advantage of the on-line support for Management 7/e.
- Chapter 2 On-line Study Guide
- Chapter 2 Self-test Answers
- Chapter 2 E-Resource Center

www.wiley.com/college/schermerhorn

3

Information and decision making

Planning ahead

CHAPTER 3 study questions

○ **How is information technology changing the workplace?**

○ **What are the current directions in information systems?**

○ **How is information used for decision making?**

○ **How do managers make decisions?**

○ **Why are knowledge management and organizational learning important?**

GETTING CONNECTED

Ford Motor Company—*Smart Companies Pursue E-Futures*

Ford isn't just your traditional carmaker anymore. It also isn't just another of the world's largest global companies. Like smart companies everywhere, Ford is getting connected. It's leading the automakers onto the Web.

E-commerce, or business on the Web, stands right up there with quality as "Job 1" at the firm. Ford's goal is no less than to reinvent the auto industry, from manufacturing to distribution.

By bringing the best of information technology to bear on the supply chain, Ford estimates that streamlining suppliers and distribution has the potential to save 25 percent of the retail price of a car. Working closely with technology experts Cisco Systems and Oracle, Ford developed an on-line trading mart for Ford's 30,000 suppliers. It allowed them to more quickly communicate, obtain better prices,

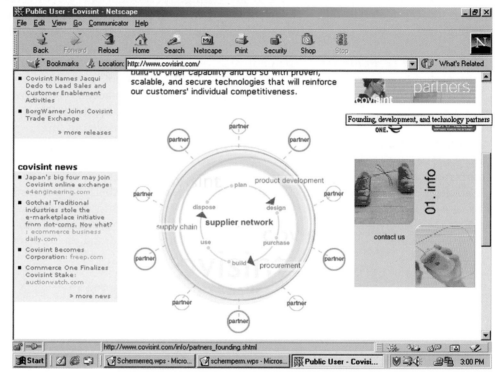

and get faster delivery. Ford has since joined with DaimlerChrysler and General Motors to launch COVISINT, a common electronic exchange intended to improve original equipment manufacturing.

Many Ford executives envision Ford as the "Dell Computer" of the future, with customers coming on-line at any time to order custom-configured automobiles with loads of Internet gadgets included. The ultimate value for Ford from its ventures onto the Web may well be increased services and better customer relationships. Who wouldn't want to custom-configure their car and order it by computer from home? That is where the real promise is to Ford. Customization via on-line services changes the auto industry from its historical "push" or seller-driven model to a more efficient "pull" or customer-driven model. Customers order what they want; Ford produces what they want, saving billions in inventory costs.

Ford's e-commerce strategy is not without risks. The level of complexity for automakers is daunting, with over 10,000 parts and 1 million possible variations. In addition, traditional dealer networks are entrenched and protected by a maze of state laws. Ford CEO Jacques Nasser, however, believes the automaker has no choice: "We're going to turn the old ways on their ears," he says. "It might not happen right away, but change is inevitable."[1]

@ Get Connected!

Ford hopes to see results from its e-commerce ventures within five years. What do you see? Search the Internet to find out if Ford is ahead of the pack. What are its competitors doing? How is IT changing the automobile industry? Get connected!

Just as technology is changing business in the automobile industry, it is also dramatically and continually changing the nature of work and organizations themselves. We are in what futurist Alvin Toffler calls the third wave of development, characterized by an information-driven society that is digital, networked, and continuously evolving.[2] The key to performance in this new world is **information** and the way it flows and is utilized by people in organizations. We live and work at a time when more information about more things is being made available to more people more quickly than ever before. The question is: How well do we individually and as organizations take full advantage of it?[3]

Our increasingly networked and global economy has been described by Peter Drucker as one in which "the productivity of knowledge and knowledge workers" will become the decisive competitive factor.[4] In this era of information, there is no doubt that **intellectual capital** is a major source of competitive advantage. As first defined in Chapter 1, it is the collective brainpower or shared knowledge of a workforce that can be used to create wealth.[5] Knowledge is an irreplaceable organizational resource, and the goal should always be to grow and create it. The information from which knowledge is created increasingly moves at high speed through electronic computer and telecommunication networks that link each of us to the world at large with an access and intensity never before possible. Thus, the foundations for knowledge building increasingly rest with two core competencies: (1) **computer competency**—ability to understand computers and use them to best advantage personally and professionally; and (2) **Information competency**—ability to utilize computers and information technology to locate, retrieve, evaluate, organize, and analyze information for decision making.

○ **Information** is data made useful for decision making.

○ **Intellectual capital** is the collective brainpower or shared knowledge of a workforce.

○ **Computer competency** is the ability to understand and use computers to advantage.

○ **Information competency** is the ability to utilize computers and information technology to locate, retrieve, evaluate, organize, and analyze information for decision making.

INFORMATION TECHNOLOGY AND THE NEW WORKPLACE

○ **Information technology** is computer hardware, software, networks, and databases supporting information utilization.

The future is now when it comes to the rapidly evolving state of **information technology**, the combination of computer hardware, software, networks, and databases that allows information to be shared, stored, and manipulated. Organizations are changing as continuing new developments in "IT" exert their influence. Information departments or centers are appearing on organization charts. The number and variety of information career fields is rapidly expanding. Job titles such as Chief Information Officer and Chief Knowledge Officer are appearing in the senior ranks of organizations. All of this, and more, is characteristic of the great opportunities of our new age of information. At the software firm PeopleSoft, for example, a vice president once faced the problem of trying to meet expectations for an early release of a sophisticated software package. His team used Web-based tools and a Lotus Notes database to facilitate a process that could have taken months if done any other way. The PeopleSoft team consolidated information from employees around the world and provided the needed feedback within two weeks. "It was really amazing," said the vice president, who added, "Then again, it's how we do things around here."[6]

WORK AND THE ELECTRONIC OFFICE

That's the way things are done at any progressive workplace these days. A good example of the everyday impact of information technology (IT) on work is the *electronic office*. This term refers to the use of computers and related technologies to electronically facilitate operations in an office environment. The electronic office that you may soon enter may well look like this.

People work at "smart" stations supported by computers that allow sophisticated voice, image, text, and other data-handling operations. Many of these stations are temporary spaces that telecommuters "visit" during those times when they are in the main office; otherwise they work from virtual offices—on the road, anywhere. Voice messaging utilizes the voice recognition capabilities of computers to take dictation, answer the telephone, and relay messages. Databases are easily accessed and shared to solve problems, and prepare and analyze reports. Documents drafted via word processing are stored for later retrieval and/or sent via electronic mail or facsimile transmission to other persons. Filing cabinets are few, and little paper is found. Meeting notes are written on electronic pads or jotted in palm-held electronic diaries. All are easily up-loaded into computer files. Mail arrives and is routed to its destination via computer, where it is electronically prioritized according to its importance and linked to relevant databases to speed problem solving. Computer conferencing and videoconferencing are commonplace. E-meetings allow people separated by great distances—perhaps distributed even around the world—to work together on projects every day without meeting personally face to face.

Are you ready to become a knowledge professional? Go on-line with the Ernst & Young Center for Business Knowledge and learn more about how professionals turn information into knowledge and knowledge into power.

This is not fantasy. It's real. Progressive organizations are doing all they can to utilize computers and information technology to streamline work, improve operating efficiencies, and make overall performance improvements. Such work settings are designed for high performance in a workplace dominated by concerns for speed—of decision making and action. Organizations exist in dynamic and turbulent environments where "speed to market," "quick response," "fast cycle time," and "time-based competition" are priority topics in any executive suite. They are continually investing in IT in the quest for competitive advantage through lower costs, better quality, and improved customer services.

HOW INFORMATION TECHNOLOGY IS CHANGING ORGANIZATIONS

Without a doubt, the most significant way in which IT is changing organizations today can be summed up in one sentence. *Information technology is breaking down barriers.*[7] It breaks barriers by making communication easy, immediate, inexpensive, and important. The benefits are important and the impact far reaching. As indicated in *Figure 3.1*, IT utilization is breaking down barriers within organizations and it is breaking down barriers between the organization and its environment. It is making the organizations more efficient and effective, and much more competitive in the process.[8]

Within organizations the increasing use of IT means that individuals and teams, working in different departments, levels, and physical locations, can more easily communicate and electronically share information with one another. It also means that the organization can operate with fewer middle managers whose jobs otherwise would be to facilitate these information flows. Instead of people moving information among

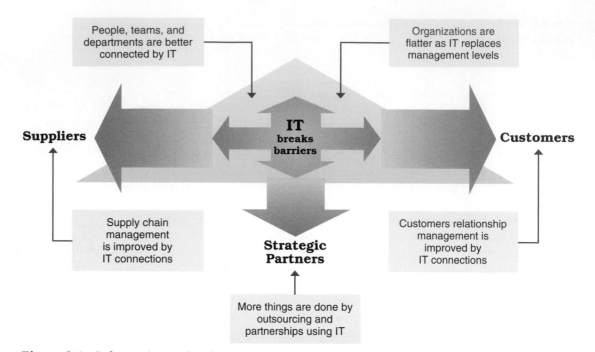

Figure 3.1 Information technology is breaking barriers and changing organizations.

and across levels, computers do the job for them. This means that IT-intensive organizations are "flatter" and operate with fewer levels than their more traditional organizational counterparts. It brings them opportunities for competitive advantage in increased speed of decision making, use of better and more timely information for decision making, and more coordination of decision making and action among relevant components. It also offers the advantage of increasing flexibility in reconfiguring operations and organizing special projects in response to competitive needs and opportunities.

The best organizations also take advantage of IT in managing their relationships with key elements in the external environment. IT plays an important role in customer relationship management by quickly and accurately providing information for decision makers regarding customer needs, preferences, and satisfactions. IT helps manage and control costs in all aspects of the supply chain from initiation of purchase to logistics and transportation to point of delivery and ultimate use. IT also helps build and manage relationships with strategic partners. It enables business contracts to be continuously maintained and efficiently fulfilled regardless of physical location.

Insights into the Digital Divide This won't surprise you: whites are more likely than minorities to have Internet access. But who uses the Web the most among those Americans who do have Internet access? Take the on-line "Reality Check" to learn more about the results of a "digital divide" survey by Forrester Research.

HOW INFORMATION TECHNOLOGY IS CHANGING BUSINESS

○ **Electronic commerce** is buying and selling goods and services through use of the Internet.

Welcome to the world of one of the most significant business developments of all time—**electronic commerce**, or "e-commerce." This is the process of buying and selling goods and services electronically through use of the Internet and related information technologies.[9] Business transactions between buyers and sellers are completed on-line rather

GLOBALIZATION Amazon.com (www.amazon.com) **In the Information Age, "Dot-Com" Means Business**

Amazon invites you to shop in their bookstore any time you want, day or night, 365 days a year. After all, it's on-line; e-business with a capital "E." It has established a new level and form of competition in the bookstore industry. And the growth goes on. Log onto Amazon.com today and you can also buy everything from health and beauty aids to tools and hardware, to toys and videogames, and more. You can shop Amazon.com in Japan, France, Germany, other countries. What began as a firm advertising "Your next book is only a click away," may now be the world's biggest consumer marketplace.

than face-to-face. In *business-to-consumer e-commerce*, or "B2C," businesses like Amazon.com and Dell.com sell directly to customers over the Internet. In *business-to-business e-commerce*, or "B2B," businesses use the Internet to collaborate and make transactions with one another. The chapter opening example of Ford shows how the automaker uses B2B to streamline buyer-seller relationships and gain productivity in its complex supply chains.

Companies that pursue e-commerce models are often called "dot-coms," due to the presence of the ".com" designation in their Web site addresses. One of the prominent companies in Web site registrations, Network Solutions, describes the stages of development in the "Dot-Com Lifecycle" as follows.[10]

1. *Secure an on-line identity:* Firms at this stage have a web address and most likely a posted home page.
2. *Establish a Web presence:* Firms at this stage use their homepage for advertising or promotional purposes; it offers company and/or product information, but does not allow visitors on-line queries or ordering.
3. *Enable e-commerce:* Firms at this stage are viable e-commerce businesses whose web sites allow visitors to order products on-line.
4. *Provide e-commerce and customer relationship management:* Firms at this stage use their web sites to develop and maintain relationships with customers by serving key processes, such as checking status of orders or inventory levels on-line.
5. *Utilize a service application model:* Firms at this stage use advanced web site capabilities to fully serve business functions and processes such as financial management and human resources.

◀ Steps in developing an e-business

The domain of electronic commerce is developing rapidly, and it is one of the forces of globalization that opens the world at large to competition and business opportunity. An emerging force in Asia and Europe that will make a major worldwide impact is known as *m-commerce*—the use of mobile phones to act as electronic wallets that allow users to perform banking transactions, purchase goods and services, and pay bills. In Britain, for example, Virgin Mobile customers use their cell phones to browse the Virgin Group web site to buy everything from wine to CDs to washing machines.[11]

INFORMATION AND INFORMATION SYSTEMS

Formally defined, *information* is data in the form of raw facts or descriptions that are meaningful and useful for decision making. People in any work setting, large or small, must have available to them the right information at the right time and in the right place if they are to perform effectively. This is made possible by **information systems** that use the latest in information technology to collect, organize, and distribute data in such a way that they become meaningful as information.

○ **Information systems** use IT to collect, organize, and distribute data for use in decision making.

WHAT IS USEFUL INFORMATION?

IT and the information systems that support work and decision making in organizations must provide information that is truly useful. The five essential characteristics of useful information are:

Characteristics of useful information

1. *Timeliness:* The information is available when needed; it meets deadlines for decision making and action.
2. *Quality:* The information is accurate and it is reliable; it can be used with confidence.
3. *Completeness:* The information is complete and sufficient for the task at hand; it is as current and up-to-date as possible.
4. *Relevance:* The information is appropriate for the task at hand; it is free from extraneous or irrelevant materials.
5. *Understandability:* The information is presented in proper form easily understood by the user; it is free from unnecessary detail.

INFORMATION NEEDS OF ORGANIZATIONS

The availability of advanced IT has made information more readily available and useful than ever before. This information serves the variety of needs described in *Figure 3.2*. At the organization's boundaries, information in the external environment must be accessed and used to successfully manage relationships with key stakeholders. Managers need this *intelligence information* to deal effectively with such outside parties as competitors, government agencies, creditors, suppliers, and stockholders. As Peter Drucker says about the information age, "a winning strategy will require information about events and conditions outside the institution." He goes on to add that organizations must have "rigorous methods for gathering and analyzing outside information."[12] In addition to the gathering of intelligence information, organizations also provide to the external environment many types of *public information.* This serves a variety of purposes ranging from image building to product advertising to financial reporting for taxes.

Within organizations, people need vast amounts of information to make decisions and solve problems in their daily work. These vertical and horizontal information flows are shown also in Figure 3.2. Higher-level managers tend to emphasize information utilization in strategic planning, whereas middle and lower managers focus more on operational considerations involving the implementation of these plans. The information needs of workers center on accomplishing tasks. This involves gathering, storing, sharing, and utilizing information to solve operating problems in order to best meet the needs of internal and

Information flows vertically and horizontally within an organization to facilitate problem solving and decision making.

Figure 3.2 External and internal information needs of organizations.

external customers. Organizations that are best able to facilitate the fast and easy sharing of information internally are well positioned for competitive advantage.

One of the greatest advantages of IT utilization within organizations, is its contribution to empowerment. The ability to gather and move information quickly and from top to bottom allows top levels to stay in control while freeing lower levels to make speedy decisions and take the actions they need to best perform their jobs. This helps build competitive and customer-responsive organizations. Silicon valley pioneer and Cisco Systems CEO John Chambers, for example, points out that he always has the information he needs to be in control from the top—be it earnings, expenses, profitability, gross margins, and more. He also says, importantly: "Because I have my data in that format, every one of my employees can make decisions that might have had to come all the way to the president. . . . Quicker decision making at lower levels will translate into higher profit margins. . . . Companies that don't do that will be noncompetitive."[13]

www.cisco.com

Network solutions are mainstream business at Cisco Systems. So are strategic alliances. The firm owns only two of the 38 plants that assemble its products.

DEVELOPMENTS IN INFORMATION SYSTEMS

You will encounter many types of information systems in your career. At times you may be the designer of a new system and you may serve on an information steering committee, but you will always be an end user. In this sense, your task will be to utilize information systems well to make good decisions, to master the performance requirements of complex projects, and more generally to contribute regularly to enhanced organizational productivity. As you look ahead, keep in mind the advice in *Manager's Notepad 3.1*.

Decision Support Systems

A **decision support system** (DSS) allows users to interact directly with a computer to organize and analyze data for solving complex and sometimes unstructured problems. Decision support systems are now available to

○ **Decision support systems** allow computers to help organize and analyze data for problem solving.

MANAGER'S NOTEPAD 3.1

Avoiding common information systems mistakes

- Don't assume more information is always better.
- Don't assume that computers eliminate human judgment.
- Don't assume the newest technology is always best.
- Don't assume nothing will ever go wrong with your computer.
- Don't assume that everyone understands how the system works.

---

assist in such business decisions as mergers and acquisitions, plant expansions, new product developments, and stock portfolio management, among many others.

A fast-growing technology involves group decision support systems (GDSSs), which are interactive computer-based information systems that facilitate group efforts to solve complex and unstructured problems. GDSS software, called *groupware*, allows several people to simultaneously work on a file or database and work together on computer networks. It facilitates information exchange, group decision making, work scheduling, and other forms of group activity without the requirement of face-to-face meetings. Groupware is especially useful in facilitating work by team members who work different shifts or are spread over large geographic distances, even globally. The willingness and skills needed to participate effectively in these *virtual teams* are increasingly essential to one's personal career portfolio. The Lotus Development Corporation offers a variety of groupware products that are popular in the business setting; WebCT or Blackboard offer additional versions popular in many universities.

Expert Systems

○ **Expert systems** allow computers to mimic the thinking of human experts for applied problem solving.

Another developing area of information technology is *artificial intelligence* (AI), a field of study that is concerned with building computer systems with the capacity to reason the way people do, even to the point of dealing with ambiguities and difficult issues of judgment. These **expert systems** mimic the thinking of human experts and, in so doing, offer consistent and "expert" decision-making advice to the user. Some expert systems are rule-based and use a complicated set of "if . . . then" rules to analyze problems. These rules are determined by specialists who work with actual human experts in a certain problem area and then build their problem-solving rules into a computer program. One complaint about the technology is that the use of expert systems "de-skills" work by requiring the employee to know less because the computer does more.[14] Advocates, however, point out that expert systems make it easier to concentrate one's attention and problem-solving skills on the most complex matters.

Intranets and Extranets

○ **Intranets** are computer networks used for communication and data sharing within an organization.

Central to the electronic office is the integration of computers and software into *networks* that allow users to easily transfer and share information through computer-to-computer linkages. **Intranets** are networks of computers that use special software such as Lotus Notes to allow persons working in various locations for the same organization to share databases and communicate electronically. The goal is to promote more integration across the organization and improve operations efficiency and quality. At Ford, for example, more than 120,000 workstations scattered in company offices around the world are linked by an intranet. Using a technology called the Concentric Network, moreover, Ford integrates voice, data, and video in a single network that allows employees to share information and work together in real time.[15]

A related trend is the emergence of fully integrated **enterprise-wide networks** that move information quickly and accurately from one point to another within an organization. For example, a field salesperson may pass on a customer's suggestion for a product modification via electronic mail. This mail arrives at the computer used by a product designer at company headquarters. After creating a computer-assisted design for the product, the designer passes it on simultaneously to engineering, manufacturing, finance, and marketing experts for their preliminary analysis. Working as a virtual team, everyone including the field salesperson may then further consider the design and agree on its business potential.

○ **Enterprise-wide networks** use IT to move information quickly and accurately within an organization.

Extranets are computer networks that use the public Internet to allow communication between the organization and elements in its external environment. IT that allows information transfers between two or more organizations is a basic foundation for the fast-paced developments occurring in electronic commerce. Through electronic data interchange (EDI), companies communicate electronically with one another to move and share documents such as purchase orders, bills, receipt confirmations, and even payments for services rendered.

○ **Extranets** are computer networks for communication between the organization and its environment.

INFORMATION SYSTEMS AND THE MANAGER'S JOB

Specific to the management context, a **management information system** (MIS) is specifically designed to use information technology to meet the information needs of managers as they make a variety of decisions on a day-to-day basis. For example, at C. R. England, Inc., a long-haul refrigerated trucking company in Salt Lake City, a computerized MIS monitors over 500 aspects of organizational performance. The system tracks everything from billing accuracy to arrival times to driver satisfaction with company maintenance on their vehicles. Pay bonuses and extra vacation days are awarded based on driver performance on such goals as safety and fuel consumption. Says CEO Dan England: "Our view was, if we could measure it, we could manage it."[16]

○ **Management information systems** use IT to meet the information needs of managers in daily decisions.

All of the critical managerial roles identified by Henry Mintzberg and discussed in Chapter 1 (see *Figure 3.3*) involve communication and information processing.[17] To be effective, any manager must act as a nerve center of information flows—gathering, giving, and receiving information from many sources. Today's developments in IT support all aspects of the management process, making possible performance levels that are truly extraordinary. Among the advantages of appropriate MIS utilization in the manager's job are:

- *Planning advantages*—MIS utilization allows for better and more timely access to useful information, as well as for the involvement of many people in the planning process.

← Advantages of appropriate MIS utilization in the management process

- *Organizing advantages*—MIS utilization allows for more ongoing and informed communication among all parts of the organization, helping ensure better coordination and integration.

Figure 3.3 Information systems and the nature of managerial work.

- *Leading advantages*—MIS utilization allows for better and more frequent communication with all organization members and key environmental stakeholders.

- *Controlling advantages*—MIS utilization allows for more immediate and complete measurement of performance results and real-time solutions to performance problems.

INFORMATION AND DECISION MAKING

Information sets the foundations for management and organizational success. The work of managers can be described as engaging in planning, organizing, leading, and controlling in the process of solving a continous stream of daily problems. The most obvious problem situation is a *performance deficiency*, that is, when actual performance is less than desired. For example, a manager faces a possible problem when turnover or absenteeism suddenly increases in the work unit, when a subordinate's daily output decreases, or when a higher executive complains about something that has been said or done. However, another important problem situation emerges as a *performance opportunity* when an actual situation either turns out better than anticipated or offers the potential to be so. The challenge in dealing with a performance deficiency or performance opportunity is to proceed with effective **problem solving**—the process of identifying a discrepancy between an actual and desired state of affairs and then taking action to resolve the deficiency or take advantage of the opportunity.

The entire problem-solving process is dependent on the right information being available to the right people at the right times so that they can make good problem-solving decisions. A **decision**, to be precise, is a choice among alternative possible courses of action. The process of decision making is

○ **Problem solving** involves identifying and taking action to resolve problems.

○ A **decision** is a choice among possible alternative courses of action.

driven in part by the quality of information available. Information systems assist managers to gather data, turn them into useful information, and utilize that information to make effective problem-solving decisions.

TYPES OF MANAGERIAL DECISIONS

Managers resolve problems by making different types of decisions in their day-to-day work. Some are **programmed decisions**, that is, solutions already available from past experience to solve problems that are familiar, straightforward, and clear with respect to information needs. These decisions apply best to problems that are matters of routine; although perhaps not predictable, they can at least be anticipated. This means that decisions can be planned or programmed in advance to be implemented as needed. In human resource management, for example, problems are common whenever decisions are made on pay raises and promotions, vacation requests, committee assignments, and the like. Knowing this, proactive or forward-looking managers plan ahead on how to make decisions on such complaints and conflicts when and if they should arise.

○ A **programmed decision** applies a solution from past experience to a routine problem.

Managers must also deal with new or unexpected situations that present unstructured problems full of ambiguities and information deficiencies. These problems are typically unanticipated and must be addressed as they occur. Unstructured problems require **nonprogrammed decisions** that specifically craft novel solutions to meet the demands of the unique situation at hand. Most problems faced by higher-level managers are of this type, with the problems often involving choice of strategies and objectives in situations of some uncertainty.

○ A **nonprogrammed decision** applies a specific solution crafted for a unique problem.

An extreme type of nonprogrammed decision must be made in times of **crisis**—the occurrence of an unexpected problem that can lead to disaster if not resolved quickly and appropriately. The growing dependence of organizations on technology raises many such opportunities. Any organization maintaining a web site, for example, may face occasional crisis shutdowns due to server failures. "Hacker" attacks on web sites are also increasingly common, as firms like Microsoft, eBay, and Amazon know only too well.[18]

○ A **crisis** is an unexpected problem that can lead to disaster if not resolved quickly and appropriately.

The ability to handle crises may be the ultimate test of a manager's problem-solving capabilities. Unfortunately, research indicates that managers may react to crises by isolating themselves and trying to solve the problem alone or in a small "closed" group.[19] This tendency actually denies them access to crucial information and assistance at the very time they are most needed. The crisis may even be accentuated if more problems are created because critical decisions are made with poor or inadequate information and from a limited perspective. Managers in progressive organizations anticipate that crises will occur and plan ahead on how to deal with them. Consider growing concerns about workplace violence in America. The U.S. Department of Labor offers guidelines for employers on how to recognize situations that are prone to violence and how to prepare for such crises.

DECISION CONDITIONS

People in organizations make decisions under each of the three conditions described in *Figure 3.4*—decisions in environments of certainty, risk, and uncertainty. Although managers make decisions in each environment,

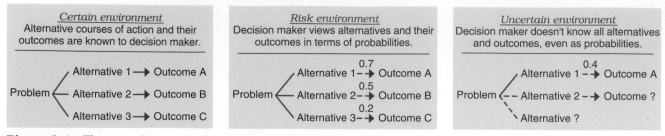

Figure 3.4 Three environments for managerial decision making and problem solving.

○ A **certain environment** offers complete information on possible action alternatives and their consequences.

○ A **risk environment** lacks complete information, but offers "probabilities" of the likely outcomes for possible action alternatives.

○ An **uncertain environment** lacks so much information that it is difficult to assign probabilities to the likely outcomes of alternatives.

the conditions of risk and uncertainty are common at higher management levels where problems are more complex and unstructured. Former Coca-Cola CEO Roberto Goizueta, for example, was known as a risk taker. Among his risky moves were introducing Diet Coke to the market, changing the formula of Coca-Cola to create New Coke, and then reversing direction after New Coke flopped.[20] More recently top management at H. J. Heinz Company took an unusual risk with the introduction of EZ Squirt, a "green" ketchup.

The decisions to market New Coke and green ketchup are quite different from the relative predictability of those made in a certain environment, one where sufficient information is available about possible alternative courses of action and their outcomes. This is an ideal decision condition where the task is simply to study the alternatives and choose the best solution.

Very few managerial problems occur in **certain environments**, but steps can sometimes be taken to reduce uncertainty. In the case of Heinz's green ketchup, for example, the firm made the go-ahead decision only after receiving favorable reports from kids participating in special focus groups testing the new product. However, this still left the firm with a **risk environment**, one where information on action alternatives and their consequences is incomplete, but some estimates of "probabilities" can be made. A *probability,* in turn, is the degree of likelihood (e.g., 4 chances out of 10) that an event will occur. Risk is a common decision condition for managers. It is especially typical for entrepreneurs and organizations that depend on ideas and continued innovation for their success.

When information is so poor that managers are unable even to assign probabilities to the likely outcomes of alternatives that are known, an **uncertain environment** exists. This is the most difficult decision condition.[21] The high level of uncertainty forces managers to rely heavily on creativity in solving problems; it requires unique, novel, and often totally innovative alternatives to existing patterns of behavior. Groups are frequently used for problem solving in such situations. In all cases, the responses to uncertainty depend greatly on intuition, judgment, informed guessing, and hunches—all of which leave considerable room for error.

HOW MANAGERS APPROACH DECISIONS

In practice, people display three quite different approaches or "styles" in the way they deal with problem situations. Some are *problem avoiders* who ignore information that would otherwise signal the presence of an opportunity or performance deficiency. Such persons are *inactive* and do not want to make decisions and deal with problems. *Problem solvers* by contrast are willing to make decisions and try to solve problems, but only when forced to by the situation. They are *reactive* in gathering information and responding to problems after they occur. As a result they may deal reasonably well with performance deficiencies, but they miss many performance opportunities. *Problem seekers* actively process information and constantly look for problems to solve or opportunities to explore. True problem seekers are *proactive* and forward thinking; they anticipate problems and opportunities and take appropriate action to gain the advantage. Success at problem seeking is one of the ways exceptional managers distinguish themselves from the merely good ones.

Another distinction in the way managers approach decisions contrasts tendencies toward "systematic" and "intuitive" thinking. In **systematic thinking** a person approaches problems in a rational, step-by-step, and analytical fashion. This type of thinking involves breaking a complex problem into smaller components and then addressing them in a logical and integrated fashion. Managers who are systematic can be expected to make a plan before taking action and then to search for information to facilitate problem solving in a step-by-step fashion.

Someone using **intuitive thinking**, by contrast, is more flexible and spontaneous and also may be quite creative.[22] This type of thinking allows us to respond imaginatively to a problem based on a quick and broad evaluation of the situation and the possible alternative courses of action. Managers who are intuitive can be expected to deal with many aspects of a problem at once, jump quickly from one issue to another, and consider "hunches" based on experience or spontaneous ideas. This approach tends to work best in situations of high uncertainty where facts are limited and few decision precedents exist.[23]

Managers should feel confident in approaching decisions from the perspectives of both systematic and intuitive thinking. Senior managers, in particular, must deal with portfolios of problems and opportunities that consist of multiple and interrelated issues. This requires *multidimensional thinking,* or the ability to view many problems at once, in relationship to one another, and across long and short time horizons.[24] The best managers also "map" multiple problems into a network that can be actively managed over time as priorities, events, and demands continuously change. And importantly, they are able to make decisions and take actions in the short run that benefit longer-run objectives. It is important not to be sidetracked from long-run goals while making decisions and sorting through a shifting mix of daily problems. Somehow a consistent long-term direction must be retained, even as each short-term problem is being resolved. This requires skill at **strategic opportunism**—the ability to remain focused on long-term objectives while being flexible enough to resolve short-term problems and opportunities in a timely manner.[25]

○ **Systematic thinking** approaches problems in a rational and analytical fashion.

○ **Intuitive thinking** approaches problems in a flexible and spontaneous fashion.

○ **Strategic opportunism** focuses on long-term objectives while being flexible in dealing with short-term problems.

CAREER CONNECTION

Entrepreneurship

D'Artagnan, Inc.   Where Specialty Foods Match Specialty Talents

Ariane Daguin and George Faison know the concept of risk quite well. In their former jobs as sales manager and general manager for a New York paté producer, they located a foie gras supplier as good as any in France. When their boss balked at contracting for all the farmer's output, they took a risk. Betting that there was a market, they quit their jobs, invested $15,000 to start D'Artagnan, Inc., and signed the supplier. Their company now far outshines their former employer. D'Artagnan is America's leading purveyor of foie gras, pates, sausages, smoked delicacies, and organic game and poultry. Its products are used by the world's top restaurants, hotels, retailers, cruise ships, and airlines.

QUESTION: D'Artagnan's founders found a market niche for their special talents. Do a personal "talent" inventory. In what entrepreneurship directions might your special talents lead you?

THE DECISION-MAKING PROCESS

○ The **decision-making process** begins with identification of a problem and ends with evaluation of implemented solutions.

The specific act of decision making involves making a choice among alternative courses of action. However, the **decision-making process** involves a cycle of activities and events that begin with identification of a problem and end with the evaluation of implemented solutions.[26]

STEPS IN DECISION MAKING

The common steps in a rational approach to decision making are described in *Figure 3.5.* They are (1) identify and define the problem, (2) generate and evaluate possible solutions, (3) choose a preferred solution and conduct the "ethics double check," (4) implement the solution, and (5) evaluate results. Importantly, Step 3 in this model includes a built-in "checkpoint" as a way to verify the ethical aspects of a decision before any action is taken. Working with the following short-but-true case will help put all five steps into perspective.

> *The Ajax Case.* On December 31, the Ajax Aluminum Company decided to close down its Murphysboro plant. Market conditions were forcing layoffs, and the company could not find a buyer for the plant. Of 172 employees, some had been with the company as long as 18 years, others as little as 6 months. All were to be terminated. Under company policy, they would be given severance pay equal to one week's pay per year of service. Ajax's top management faced a difficult problem: how to minimize the negative impact of the plant closing on these employees, their families, and the small town of Murphysboro itself.

This case reflects how competition, changing times, and the forces of globalization can take their toll on organizations, the people that work for them, and the communities in which they operate. Think about how you would feel as one of the affected employees. Think about how you would feel as the mayor of this small town. Think how you would feel as a corporate executive having to make the required decisions.

Decision-Making Step 1: Identify and Define the Problem

The first step in decision making is to find and define the problem. This is a stage of information gathering, information processing, and deliberation.[27]

The way a problem is originally defined can have a major impact on how it is eventually resolved. Three common mistakes may occur at this critical first step in decision making. *Mistake number 1* is defining the problem too broadly or too narrowly. To take a classic example, the problem stated as "Build a better mousetrap" might be better defined as "Get rid of the mice." That is, managers should define problems so as to give themselves the best possible range of problem-solving options. *Mistake number 2* is focusing on symptoms instead of causes. Symptoms are indicators that problems may exist, but they shouldn't be mistaken for the problems themselves. Managers should be able to spot problem symptoms (e.g., a drop in performance). But instead of treating symptoms (such as simply encouraging higher performance), managers should address their root causes (such as discovering the worker's need for training

E-tailers Can Learn from Their Customers Customers are a ready source of information that can be used to improve organizations. But, often they're never asked. When Greenfield Online, Inc., asked people why they are wary of on-line shopping, "shipping charges" topped the list. Wouldn't an on-line retailer want to know this? What else do you think causes on-line shopping worries? Take the on-line "Reality Check" to learn more about the results of this survey

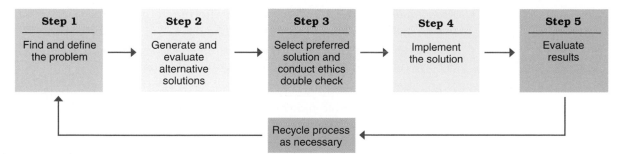

Figure 3.5 Steps in decision making and problem solving.

in the use of a complex new computer system). *Mistake number 3* is choosing the wrong problem to deal with. Managers should set priorities and deal with the most important problems first. They should also give priority to problems that are truly solvable.

> *Back to the Ajax Case.* Closing the Ajax plant will put a substantial number of people from this small community of Murphysboro out of work. The unemployment created will have a negative impact on individuals, their families, and the community as a whole. The loss of the Ajax tax base will further hurt the community. The local financial implications of the plant closure will be great. The problem for Ajax management is how to minimize the adverse impact of the plant closing on the employees, their families, and the community.

Decision-Making Step 2: Generate and Evaluate Possible Solutions

Once the problem is defined, it is possible to formulate one or several potential solutions. At this stage, more information is gathered, data are analyzed, and the pros and cons of possible alternative courses of action are identified. This effort to locate, clarify, and evaluate alternative solutions is critical to successful problem solving. The involvement of other persons is very important here in order to maximize information and build commitment. The end result can only be as good as the quality of the alternative solutions generated in this step. The better the pool of alternatives, the more likely a good solution will be achieved.

Common errors in this stage include selecting a particular solution too quickly and choosing an alternative that, although convenient, has damaging side effects or is not as good as others that might be discovered with extra effort. The analysis of alternatives should determine how well each possible course of action deals with the problem while taking into account the environment within which the problem exists. A very basic evaluation involves **cost-benefit analysis**, the comparison of what an alternative will cost in relation to the expected benefits. At a minimum, the benefits of a chosen alternative should be greater than its costs. Typical criteria for evaluating alternatives include the following:

○ **Cost-benefit analysis** involves comparing the costs and benefits of each potential course of action.

* *Benefits:* What are the "benefits" of using the alternative to solve a performance deficiency or take advantage of an opportunity?

* *Costs:* What are the "costs" of implementing the alternative, including resource investments as well as potential negative side effects?

* *Timeliness:* How fast will the benefits occur and a positive impact be achieved?

◄

Criteria for evaluating alternatives

- *Acceptability:* To what extent will the alternative be accepted and supported by those who must work with it?
- *Ethical soundness:* How well does the alternative meet acceptable ethical criteria in the eyes of the various stakeholders?

> *Back to the Ajax Case.* The Ajax plant is going to be closed. Among the possible alternatives that can be considered are (1) close the plant on schedule and be done with it; (2) delay the plant closing until all efforts have been made to sell it to another firm; (3) offer to sell the plant to the employees and/or local interests; (4) close the plant and offer transfers to other Ajax plant locations; or (5) close the plant, offer transfers, and help the employees find new jobs in and around Murphysboro.

Decision-Making Step 3: Choose a Solution

○ The **classical decision model** describes decision making with complete information.

At this point in the decision-making process an actual decision is made to select a particular course of action. Just how this is done and by whom must be successfully resolved in each problem situation. Management theory recognizes differences between the classical model and the behavioral model of decision making, as shown in *Figure 3.6.* The **classical decision model** views the manager as acting in a certain world. Here, the manager faces a clearly defined problem and knows all possible action alternatives as well as their consequences. As a result, he or she makes an **optimizing decision** that gives the absolute best solution to the problem. The classical approach is a very rational model that assumes perfect information is available for decision making.

○ An **optimizing decision** chooses the alternative giving the absolute best solution to a problem.

Behavioral scientists question these assumptions. Perhaps best represented by the work of Herbert Simon, they recognize the existence of *cognitive limitations,* or limits to our human information-processing capabilities.[28] These limitations make it hard for managers to become fully informed and make perfectly rational decisions. They create a *bounded rationality* such that managerial decisions are rational only within the boundaries defined by the available information. The *administrative* or **behavioral decision model**, accordingly, assumes that people act only in terms of what they perceive about a given situation. Because such perceptions are frequently imperfect, the decision maker has only partial knowledge about the available action alternatives and their consequences. Consequently, the first alternative that appears to give a satisfactory resolution of the problem is likely to be chosen. Simon, who won a Nobel Prize for his work, calls this the tendency toward **satisficing decisions**—choos-

○ The **behavioral decision model** describes decision making with limited information and bounded rationality.

○ A **satisficing decision** chooses the first satisfactory alternative that comes to attention.

Classical model Views manager as acting with complete information in a certain environment	**Behavioral model** Views manager as having cognitive limitations and acting with incomplete information in risk and uncertain environments	**Judgmental heuristics approach** Heuristics are adopted to simplify managerial decision making
• Clearly defined problem • Knowledge of all possible alternatives and their consequences • Optimizing decision—choice of the "optimum" alternative	• Problem not clearly defined • Knowledge is limited on possible alternatives and their consequences • Satisficing decision—choice of "satisfactory" alternative	Decisions are influenced by: • Information readily available in memory—the availability heuristic • Comparisons with similar circumstances—the representativeness heuristic • Current situation—The anchoring and adjustment heuristic

Figure 3.6 Classical, behavioral, and judgmental heuristics approaches in decision making.

ing the first satisfactory alternative that comes to your attention. This model seems especially accurate in describing how people make decisions about ambiguous problems in risky and uncertain conditions.

Back to the Ajax Case. Management at Ajax decided to follow alternative 5 as described in Step 2 of the decision-making process. They would close the plant, offer transfers to company plants in another state, and offer to help displaced employees find new jobs in and around Murphysboro.

Decision-Making Step 4: Implement the Solution

Given the choice of preferred solution, appropriate actions must be taken to fully implement it. This is the stage at which directions are finally set and problem-solving actions are initiated. Nothing new can or will happen according to plan unless action is taken. Managers not only need the determination and creativity to arrive at a decision, they also need the ability and willingness to implement it.

The "ways" in which previous steps have been accomplished can have an additional and powerful impact at this stage of implementation. Difficulties at this stage often trace to the *lack-of-participation error,* or the failure to adequately involve those persons whose support is necessary to ensure a decision's complete implementation. Managers who use participation wisely get the right people involved in decisions and problem solving from the beginning. When they do, implementation typically follows quickly, smoothly, and to everyone's satisfaction. Involvement not only makes everyone better informed, it also builds the commitments needed for implementation.

Back to the Ajax Case. Ajax ran an ad in the local and regional newspapers for several days. The ad called attention to an "Ajax skill bank" composed of "qualified, dedicated, and well-motivated employees with a variety of skills and experiences." Interested employers were urged to contact Ajax for further information.

Decision-Making Step 5: Evaluate Results

The decision-making process is not complete until results are evaluated. If the desired results are not achieved, the process must be renewed to allow for corrective actions. In this sense, evaluation is a form of managerial control. It involves a continuing commitment to gather information on performance results. Both the positive and negative consequences of the chosen course of action should be examined. If the original solution appears inadequate, a return to earlier steps in problem-solving may be required to generate a modified or new solution. In this way, problem solving becomes a dynamic and ongoing activity within the management process. Evaluation is also made easier if the solution involves clear objectives that include measurable targets and timetables.

Back to the Ajax Case. The advertisement ran for some 15 days. The plant's industrial relations manager commented, "I've been very pleased with the results." That's all we know. You can look back on the case and problem-solving process just described and judge for yourself how well Ajax management did in dealing with this very difficult problem. Perhaps you would have approached the situation and the five steps in decision making somewhat differently.

BEHAVIORAL INFLUENCES ON DECISION MAKING

○ **Heuristics** are strategies for simplifying decision making.

The manager's decision-making world is most often imperfect, subject to the influences of cognitive limitations, risk, and uncertainty. As a result, the behavioral model is more common in decision-making practice than the rational model. Faced with complex environments, limited information, and cognitive limitations, people also tend to use simplifying strategies for decision making. These strategies, shown in Figure 3.6, are called **heuristics**, and their use can cause decision errors. An awareness of judgmental heuristics and their potential biases can help improve your decision-making capabilities.[29]

The *availability heuristic* occurs when people use information "readily available" from memory as a basis for assessing a current event or situation. An example is deciding not to invest in a new product based on your recollection of how well a similar new product performed in the recent past. The potential bias is that the readily available information may be fallible and represent irrelevant factors. The new product that recently failed may have been a good idea that was released to market at the wrong time of year.

The *representativeness heuristic* occurs when people assess the likelihood of something occurring based on its similarity to a stereotyped set of occurrences. An example is deciding to hire someone for a job vacancy simply because he or she graduated from the same school attended by your last and most successful new hire. The potential bias is that the representative stereotype may fail to discriminate important and unique factors relevant to the decision. For instance, the abilities and career expectations of the newly hired person may not fit the job requirements.

The *anchoring and adjustment heuristic* involves making decisions based on adjustments to a previously existing value or starting point. An example is setting a new salary level for an employee by simply raising the prior year's salary by a reasonable percentage. The potential bias is that this may inappropriately bias a decision toward only incremental movement from the starting point. For instance, the individual's market value may be substantially higher than the existing salary. A simple adjustment won't keep this person from looking for another job.

○ **Escalating commitment** is the continuation of a course of action even though it is not working.

Good managers are also aware of another behavioral tendency and source of potential decision-making error called **escalating commitment**. This is a decision to increase effort and perhaps apply more resources to pursue a course of action that is not working.[30] In such cases, managers let the momentum of the situation overwhelm them. They are unable to decide to "call it quits," even when experience otherwise indicates that this is the most appropriate thing to do. *Manager's Notepad 3.2* offers advice on avoiding this tendency.

INDIVIDUAL AND GROUP DECISION MAKING

One of the important issues in decision making is the choice of whether to make the decision individually or with the participation of a group. The best managers and team leaders don't limit themselves to just one way. Instead, they switch back and forth among individual and group decision making to best fit the problems at hand. A managerial skill is the ability to choose the "right" decision method—one that provides for a timely and quality decision, and one to which people involved in the implementation

MANAGER'S NOTEPAD 3.2

How to avoid the escalation trap

- Set advance limits on your involvement and commitment to a particular course of action; stick with these limits.
- Make your own decisions; don't follow the lead of others since they are also prone to escalation.
- Carefully determine just why you are continuing a course of action; if there are insufficient reasons to continue, don't.
- Remind yourself of what a course of action is costing; consider the saving of such costs as a reason to discontinue.
- Watch for escalation tendencies; be on guard against their influence on both you and others involved in the course of action.

will be highly committed. To do this well, however, managers must understand both the potential assets and potential liabilities of moving from individual to more group-oriented decision making.[31]

The potential *advantages of group decision making* are highly significant, and they should be actively sought whenever time and other circumstances permit. Team decisions make greater amounts of information, knowledge, and expertise available to solve problems. They expand the number of action alternatives that are examined; they help to avoid tunnel vision and consideration of only limited options. Team decisions increase the understanding and acceptance of outcomes by members. And importantly, team decisions increase the commitments of members to work hard to implement final plans.

The *potential disadvantages of group decision making* trace largely to the difficulties that can be experienced in group process. In a team decision there may be social pressure to conform. That is, individual members may feel intimidated or compelled to go along with the apparent wishes of others. There may be minority domination, where some members feel forced or "railroaded" to accept a decision advocated by one vocal individual or small coalition. Also, there is no doubt that the time required to make team decisions can sometimes be a disadvantage. As more people are involved in the dialogue and discussion, decision making takes longer. This added time may be costly, even prohibitively so, in certain circumstances.[32]

ETHICAL DECISION MAKING

Chapter 6 is entirely devoted to ethics and social responsibility issues in management. For the present, however, it is important to recognize that any decision should be ethical. It should meet the test described in step 3 of decision making as the "ethics double check." This involves asking and answering two straightforward but powerful questions: (1) "How would I feel if my family found out about this decision?" (2) "How would I feel if this decision were published in the local newspaper?"

Although it adds time to decision making, the ethics double check is increasingly necessary to ensure that the ethical aspects of a problem are

TAKE IT TO THE CASE!

Sun Microsystems, Inc. (www.sun.com)
Company Listens to Customers "Wake-up" Calls

The call from eBay's CEO Margaret Whitham took Sun's president Edward Zander by surprise. Just at the time when the reliability of alternative Linux-based servers was in the news, eBay's web site went down for 22 hours due to a problem with its Sun servers. There had been early warning signs; eBay had had smaller computer crashes in the past. However, Sun hadn't realized the real problem. Sun's systems were sophisticated and users—that is, customers—needed more support in running them properly. With Sun's 40 percent share of the web server market at stake, Zander and CEO Scott McNealy swung into action. Says McNealy of the wake-up call from eBay: "That's when we realized it wasn't eBay's fault. It was our fault." Now the two are re-focusing Sun around customer service and product reliability. The firm's consultants don't just supply the hardware anymore; they help and teach customers to use it step-by-step.[35]

properly considered in the complex, fast-paced, and often-uncertain decision conditions so common in today's organizations. It is also consistent with the demanding moral standards of modern society. A willingness to pause to examine the ethics of a proposed decision may well result in both better decisions and the prevention of costly litigation. Again, Chapter 6 will explore these and related issues in depth. For now, consider whether an "ethics double check" could improve decision making in the earlier Ajax company case.

KNOWLEDGE MANAGEMENT AND ORGANIZATIONAL LEARNING

Management theorist Peter Drucker considers knowledge the principal resource of a competitive society and warns that "knowledge constantly makes itself obsolete."[33] This is an age in which intellectual capital counts highly, and knowledge workers—the people who have the knowledge—are critical assets. It is an age of transformation that places increasing value on learning and knowledge management.[34]

WHAT IS KNOWLEDGE MANAGEMENT?

○ **Knowledge management** is the processes using intellectual capital for competitive advantage.

A new term is earning a significant place in management theory and practice. The concept of **knowledge management** is used to describe the processes though which organizations develop, organize, and share knowledge to achieve competitive advantage.[36] It is a mobilization of intellectual capital. The significance of knowledge management as a strategic and integrating force in organizations is represented by the emergence of a new executive job title—*chief knowledge officer* (CKO). This position of CKO is responsible for energizing learning processes and making sure that an organization's portfolio of intellectual assets and pool of knowledge are well managed and continually enhanced. The intellectual assets, furthermore, include such things as patents, intellectual property rights, trade secrets, and special processes and methods, as well as the accumulated knowledge and understanding of the entire workforce. John Peetz, chief knowledge officer at Ernst & Young, considers knowledge management one of four core processes—"sell work, do work, manage people, and manage knowledge."[37]

Knowledge management involves the understanding of and commitment to the information technology described in this chapter. It requires the creation of an organizational culture in which information sharing, learning, and knowledge creation are part of the norm. It requires a special form of organizational leadership that recognizes that intellectual capital is an invaluable asset in this age of transformation. And at the bottom of it all, knowledge management requires managerial and leadership respect for people and their wonderful creative potential in organizations. According to Jack Welch, former CEO, General Electric:

> *All we are talking about is human dignity and voice—giving people a chance to speak, to have their best idea. That is a global desire of all people who breathe. . . . My job is allocating capital, human and financial, and transferring best practice. That's all. It's transferring ideas, constantly pushing ideas, putting the right people in the right job and giving them the resources to win."*[38]

Get Connected!

Check Network Solutions; learn how to register a domain name for your own dot-com business.

ORGANIZATIONAL LEARNING

"Learning," says BP Amoco's CEO John Browne, "is at the heart of a company's ability to adapt to a rapidly changing environment." He goes on to add, "In order to generate extraordinary value for its shareholders, a company must learn better than its competitors and apply that knowledge throughout its businesses faster and more widely than they do."[39] Like other progressive organizations today, BP is striving to build the foundations of a true **learning organization**. This is an organization that "by virtue of people, values, and systems is able to continuously change and improve its performance based upon the lessons of experience."[40] Consultant Peter Senge, author of the popular book, *The Fifth Discipline,* identifies the following core ingredients of learning organizations:[41]

○ A **learning organization** continuously changes and improves using the lessons of experience.

1. *Mental models:* Everyone sets aside old ways of thinking.
2. *Personal mastery:* Everyone becomes self-aware and open to others.
3. *Systems thinking:* Everyone learns how the organization works.
4. *Share vision:* Everyone understands and agrees to a plan of action.
5. *Team learning:* Everyone works together to accomplish the plan.

← Ingredients of learning organizations

Senge's concept of the learning organization places high value on developing the ability to learn and then make that learning continuously available to all organizational members. BP's CEO Browne says that organizations can learn from many sources. They can learn from their own experience. They can learn from the experiences of their contractors, suppliers, partners, and customers. And they can learn from firms in unrelated businesses.[42] All of this, of course, depends on a willingness to seek out learning opportunities from these sources and to make information sharing an expected and valued work behavior. In addressing the challenges of competing in a global economy, for example, General Electric's former CEO Jack Welch says: "The aim in a global business is to get the best ideas from everywhere. . . . Our culture is designed around making a hero out of those who translate ideas from one place to another, who help somebody else." During his leadership GE was transformed into a learning organization in which information and ideas are quickly shared across its many diverse components. By combining a strong culture with the support of the latest in information technology, Welch pursued his goal of creating a truly "boundaryless" company that values knowledge as a critical resource for competitive advantage.[43]

STUDY Guide

The Chapter 3 Study Guide will help you review chapter content, prepare for examinations, and further build your career readiness. The *Summary* briefly highlights answers to questions first posed in the chapter opening Planning Ahead section. The list of *Key Terms* allows you to double check your familiarity with basic concepts and definitions. *Self-Test 3* gives you the opportunity to test your basic comprehension of chapter content using sample test questions. Suggestions offered as *Career Readiness Activities* direct your attention to relevant sections of the end-of-text Career Readiness Workbook, as well as to special Electronic Resources on the Management 7/e web site.

SUMMARY

How is information technology changing the workplace?

- Continuing advances in computers and information technology (IT) bring many opportunities for improving the workplace by better utilizing information.
- Anyone entering the modern workplace, with its premium on intellectual capital and knowledge workers, must possess both computer competency and information competency.
- Today's "electronic" offices with e-mail, voice messaging, and networked computer systems are changing the way work is accomplished in and by organizations.
- A major and rapidly growing force in the economy are e-businesses, which use the Internet and computer networking to engage in business-to-consumer and business-to-business electronic commerce.

What are the current directions in information systems?

- A management information system (MIS) collects, organizes, stores, and distributes data in a way that meets the information needs of managers.
- Decision-support systems (DSSs) provide information and help managers make decisions to solve complex problems.
- Group decision-support systems utilize groupware to allow the computer-mediated exchange of information and decision making by group members.
- Intranets and computer networks allow persons within an organization to share databases and communicate electronically; extranets and the Internet allow for communication between the organization and its environment.

How is information used for decision making?

- Information is data that are made useful for decision making and problem solving.
- A problem is a discrepancy between an actual and a desired state of affairs.
- Managers face structured and unstructured problems in environments of certainty, risk, and uncertainty.
- The most threatening type of problem is the crisis, which occurs unexpectedly and can lead to disaster if it is not handled quickly and properly.

How do managers make decisions?

- The steps in the decision-making process are find and define the problem, generate and evaluate alternatives, choose the preferred solution, implement the solution, and evaluate the results.
- An optimizing decision, following the classical model, chooses the absolute best solution from a known set of alternatives.
- A satisficing decision, following the administrative model, chooses the first satisfactory alternative to come to attention.
- Judgmental heuristics, such as the availability heuristic, the anchoring and adjustment heuristic, and the representativeness heuristic, can bias decision making.
- Group decisions offer the potential advantages of greater information and expanded commitment, but they are often slower than individual decisions.

Why are knowledge management and organizational learning important?

- The old ways of management aren't good enough anymore; an age of transformation demands that the best of the past be combined with new thinking so organizations can be competitive in the 21st century.
- Knowledge management is the process of capturing, developing, and utilizing the knowledge of an organization to achieve competitive advantage.
- A learning organization is one in which people, values, and systems support continuous change and improvement based on the lessons of experience.

KEY TERMS

Behavioral decision model (p. 78)

Certain environment (p. 74)

Classical decision model (p. 78)

Computer competency (p. 64)

Cost-benefit analysis (p. 77)

Crisis (p. 73)

Decision (p. 72)

Decision-making process (p. 76)

Decision support system (p. 69)

Electronic commerce (p. 66)

Escalating commitment (p. 80)

Expert system (p. 70)

SELF-TEST 3

Take this test here or on-line much as you would in a normal classroom situation. It should offer you a good way to check your basic comprehension of chapter material. Answers may be found at the end of the book.

MULTIPLE-CHOICE QUESTIONS:

1. _____ is the collective brainpower or shared knowledge of an organization and its workforce.
   (a) Artificial intelligence (b) Groupware (c) Intellectual capital
   (d) Intelligence information

2. _____ are special computer programs with a series of "if . . . then" rules to help users analyze and solve problems.
   (a) Expert systems (b) Virtual systems (c) Intranets (d) Extranets

3. The computer software programs that support virtual teamwork in organizations are known as _____.
   (a) expert systems (b) heuristics (c) groupware (d) virtual systems

4. When Amazon.com and Dell.com use the Internet to sell products directly to customers, they are pursuing a form of e-commerce known as _____.
   (a) optimizing (b) B2B (c) B2C (d) networking

5. A problem is a discrepancy between a(n) _____ and a desired situation.
   (a) future (b) past (c) actual (d) desired

6. A(n) _____ thinker approaches problems in a rational and analytic fashion.
   (a) systematic (b) intuitive (c) internal (d) external

7. The first step in the problem-solving process is to _____.
   (a) identify alternatives (b) evaluate results (c) find and define the problem
   (d) choose a solution

8. Being asked to develop a plan for increased international sales is an example of the _____ problems that managers must be prepared to deal with.
   (a) expected (b) unstructured (c) crisis (d) structured

9. Costs, timeliness, and _____ are among the criteria recommended in this chapter for evaluating alternative courses of action.
   (a) ethical soundness (b) competitiveness (c) self-interest
   (d) past experience

10. The _____ decision model views managers as making optimizing decisions, whereas the _____ decision model views them as making satisficing decisions.
    (a) behavioral, human relations (b) classical, behavioral
    (c) heuristic, humanistic (d) quantitative, behavioral

TRUE-FALSE QUESTIONS:

11. The chief information officer is typically a middle manager in an organization.   T   F

12. The "electronic office" described in this chapter is interesting, but it is a long way from reality.   T   F

13. A field salesperson might interact directly with manufacturing schedulers through an enterprise-wide computer network.   T   F

14. Problems may be either performance deficiencies or performance opportunities. T   F

15. The final step in the problem-solving process is to choose a preferred solution.   T   F

16. Systematic thinking is more flexible and spontaneous than intuitive thinking.   T   F

17. The least common problem-solving environment faced by managers is risk.   T   F

18. The escalation trap is an unwillingness to allow the participation of others in the decision-making process.   T   F

19. Managers should always conduct an "ethics double check" of decisions made during the problem-solving process.   T   F

20. Knowledge management is an essential part of the competitive advantage gained by true learning organizations.   T   F

SHORT-RESPONSE QUESTIONS:

21. In any organization, what is the purpose of an information system?

22. What three factors are most important to the success of an information system and what are three common information system mistakes that managers should avoid?

23. What is the difference between problem solving and decision making?

24. How would a manager use systematic thinking and intuitive thinking in problem solving?

APPLICATION QUESTION:

25. As a participant in a new "mentoring" program between your university and a local high school, you have volunteered to give a presentation to a class of sophomores on the challenges in the new "electronic workplace." The goal is to sensitize them to developments in office automation and motivate them to take the best advantage of their high school program so as to prepare themselves for the workplace of the future. What will you say to them?

CAREER readiness ACTIVITIES

Recommended learning activities from the end-of-text Career Readiness Workbook for this chapter include:

Career Advancement Portfolio
- Individual writing and group presentation assignments based on any of the following activities.

Case for Critical Thinking
- Sun Microsystems—Will Sun Rule the Web? (# 3)

Integrative Learning Activities
- Research Project 3—Changing Corporate Cultures
- Integrative Case—Richard Branson Meets the New Economy

Exercises in Teamwork
- The Future Workplace (#13)
- Dots and Squares Puzzle (#14)
- Lost at Sea (#28)
- Creative Solutions (#29)

Self-Assessments
- Decision-Making Biases (#3)
- Your Intuitive Ability (#8)
- Facts and Inferences (#20)

The *Fast Company* Collection On-Line
- Scott Kirsner, "Collision Course"

ELECTRONIC RESOURCES

@ GET CONNECTED! Don't forget to take full advantage of the on-line support for *Management 7/e.*
- Chapter 3 On-line Study Guide
- Chapter 3 Self-test Answers
- Chapter 3 E-Resource Center

4

Historical foundations of management

Planning
ahead

CHAPTER 4 study questions

- ○ **What can be learned from classical management thinking?**

- ○ **What ideas were introduced by the human resource approaches?**

- ○ **What is the role of quantitative analysis in management?**

- ○ **What is unique about the systems view and contingency thinking?**

- ○ **What are continuing management themes of the 21st century?**

GETTING CONNECTED

SubmitOrder—What Is the "Newest" Old Thing?

Things don't just happen by magic when you go to an Internet web site, decide you'd like to order a product such as a new digital camera or the latest in fashion footwear, and hit "submit order." Did you ever wonder just what happens next to bring that new purchase to your doorstep, often in just one or two days' time?

Welcome to the new world of one of business's oldest fundamentals—taking and fulfilling a customer's order. Submit Order is a fast-growing entrepreneurial startup in Columbus, Ohio. Founded by executives in a local computer distributor, the idea for the business really took off when it attracted $75 million in venture-capital investment. CEO Dennis Spina took $55 million to build a massive warehouse and another $60 million to build a sophisticated information technology system linking the firm with its customers. Now, when you hit "submit order" on the web sites of Kmart, Estee Lauder, Zainy Brainy, and others, the likelihood is that Submit Order will be behind the delivery.

Welcome again to the new world of electronic commerce. A toy order submitted to Zainy Brainy will be transmitted electronically to SubmitOrder's warehouse. Labels and paperwork are electronically created, and the items are then "picked" from massive storage bins. They are electronically sorted and then packaged for delivery by UPS, FedEx, and other carriers.

It sounds easy—as on-line retailers expand their businesses someone has to ship their products. But CEO Spina says: "Putting all this together is much more complicated than I thought . . . I'm not only dealing with my customer but also their customers and their inventory. We basically have their franchise."

SubmitOrder is one of just a few competitors in this new arena of "e-fulfillment companies." CEO Spina is strategically positioning the firm as being the best at using information technology to fully integrate with customers' business systems.[1]

@ Get Connected!

Visit *SubmitOrder.com* and see how the company works. Compare it to emerging competitors like iFULfillment, Copera, and Sameday.com. Consider the opportunities for new business ventures in the world of e-business. Get connected!

SubmitOrder is a good example of the many new opportunities that are emerging for fast, radical transformation of traditional businesses by technology-driven innovations. But even in the rush to an exciting future, one shouldn't sell history short. Knowledge gained through past experience can and should be used as a foundation for future success.

When Harvard University Press released *Mary Parker Follett—Prophet of Management: A Celebration of Writings from the 1920s,* it clearly reminded us of the wisdom of history.[2] Although writing in a different day and age, Follett's ideas are rich with foresight. She advocated cooperation and better horizontal relationships in organizations, taught respect for the experience and knowledge of workers, warned against the dangers of too much hierarchy, and called for visionary leadership. Today we pursue similar themes while using terms like empowerment, involvement, flexibility, and self-management. Rather than naively believe that we are reinventing management practice, it may be better to recognize the historical roots of many modern ideas and admit that we are still trying to perfect them.[3]

In *The Evolution of Management Thought,* professor Daniel Wren traces management as far back as 5000 B.C., when ancient Sumerians used written records to assist in governmental and commercial activities.[4] Management was important to the construction of the Egyptian pyramids, the rise of the Roman Empire, and the commercial success of 14th-century Venice. By the time of the Industrial Revolution in the 1700s great social changes helped prompt a great leap forward in the manufacture of basic staples and consumer goods. Industrial change was accelerated by Adam Smith's ideas of efficient production through specialized tasks and the division of labor. By the turn of the 20th century, Henry Ford and others were making mass production a mainstay of the modern economy. Since then, the science and practices of management have been on a rapid and continuing path of development.

The legacies of this rich history of management must be understood as we move rapidly into the new conditions and challenges of 21st-century management.[5] The historical context of management thinking can be understood in the following framework. The *classical management approaches* focus on developing universal principles for use in various management situations. The *behavioral management approaches* focus on human needs, the work group, and the role of social factors in the workplace. The *quantitative management approaches* focus on applying mathematical techniques for management of problem solving. The *modern approaches* focus on the systems view of organizations and contingency thinking in a dynamic and complex environment. *Continuing themes* build from an emphasis on quality and performance excellence to embrace diversity and global awareness, and describe new leadership roles for a new era of management.

www.fourseasons.com

The Toronto-based Four Seasons Hotels and Resorts is careful to find employees who are sufficiently friendly and capable of teamwork to satisfy high-performance expectations. People are a priority in the firm's core beliefs: "Our greatest asset, and the key to our success, is our people. We believe that each of us needs a sense of dignity, pride and satisfaction in what we do."

CLASSICAL APPROACHES TO MANAGEMENT

There are three major branches within the classical approach to management: (1) scientific management, (2) administrative principles, and (3) bureaucratic organization. *Figure 4.1* associates each with a prominent person in the history of management thought. These names are important to know since they are still widely used in management conversations today. Also, the figure shows that the branches all share a common assumption:

people at work act in a rational manner that is primarily driven by economic concerns. Workers are expected to rationally consider opportunities made available to them and do whatever is necessary to achieve the greatest personal and monetary gain.[6]

SCIENTIFIC MANAGEMENT

In 1911 Frederick W. Taylor published *The Principles of Scientific Management,* in which he makes the following statement: "The principal object of management should be to secure maximum prosperity for the employer, coupled with the maximum prosperity for the employee."[7] Taylor, often called the "father of scientific management," noticed that many workers did their jobs their own way and without clear and uniform specifications. He believed that this caused them to loose efficiency and perform below their true capacities. He also believed that this problem could be corrected if workers were taught and then helped by supervisors to always perform their jobs in the right way.

○ **Scientific management** emphasizes careful selection and training of workers, and supervisory support.

Taylor used the concept of "time study" to analyze the motions and tasks required in any job and to develop the most efficient ways to perform them.[8] He then linked these job requirements with both training for the worker and support from supervisors in the form of proper direction, work assistance, and monetary incentives. This approach is known as **scientific management** and includes these four guiding action principles.

1. Develop for every job a "science" that includes rules of motion, standardized work implements, and proper working conditions.
2. Carefully select workers with the right abilities for the job.
3. Carefully train workers to do the job and give them the proper incentives to cooperate with the job "science."
4. Support workers by carefully planning their work and by smoothing the way as they go about their jobs.

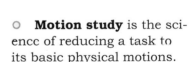

Principles of scientific management

Taylor tried to use scientific techniques to improve the productivity of people at work. The implications of his efforts, if not his exact scientific management principles, are found in many management settings today. A number of these are summarized in *Manager's Notepad 4.1.*

Mentioned in Taylor's first principle, **motion study** is the science of reducing a job or task to its basic physical motions. As contemporaries of Taylor, Frank and Lillian Gilbreth pioneered motion studies as

○ **Motion study** is the science of reducing a task to its basic physical motions.

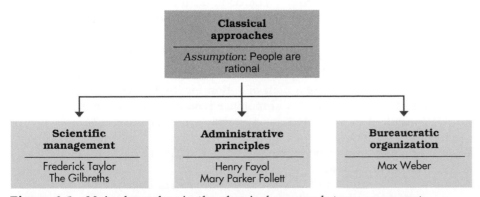

Figure 4.1 Major branches in the classical approach to management.

MANAGER'S NOTEPAD 4.1

Practical lessons from scientific management

- Make results-based compensation a performance incentive.
- Carefully design jobs with efficient work methods.
- Carefully select workers with the abilities to do these jobs.
- Train workers to perform jobs to the best of their abilities.
- Train supervisors to support workers so they can perform jobs to the best of their abilities.

---

www.maids.com

Taylor's insights are at work at the franchise home-cleaning service The Maids International. When faced with the problem of high labor turnover, the firm conducted systematic studies to show how employees worked. Tasks were redesigned and downtime was provided for relaxation. CEO Dan Bishop says: "Fatigue and boredom are what burn people out. We tried to eliminate them."

a management tool. In one famous study, they reduced the number of motions used by bricklayers and tripled their productivity.[9] The Gilbreths' work established the foundation for later advances in the areas of job simplification, work standards, and incentive wage plans—all techniques still used in the modern workplace.

The ideas of Taylor and the Gilbreths are evident at United Parcel Service, where workers are guided by carefully calibrated productivity standards. At regional sorting centers, sorters are timed according to strict task requirements and are expected to load vans at a set number of packages per hour. Delivery stops on regular van routes are studied and carefully timed, and supervisors generally know within a few minutes how long a driver's pickups and deliveries will take. Industrial engineers devise precise routines for drivers, who are trained to knock on customers' doors rather than spend even a few seconds looking for the doorbell. Handheld computers further enhance delivery efficiencies. At UPS, savings of seconds on individual stops add up to significant increases in productivity.

ADMINISTRATIVE PRINCIPLES

A second branch in the classical approach to management is based on attempts to document and understand the experiences of successful managers. Two prominent writers in this school of thought are Henri Fayol and Mary Parker Follett.

Henri Fayol

In 1916, after a career in French industry, Henri Fayol published *Administration Industrielle et Générale*.[10] The book outlines his views on the proper management of organizations and the people within them. It identifies the following five "rules" or "duties" of management, which closely resemble the four functions of management—planning, organizing, leading, and controlling—that we talk about today:

Fayol's rules of management →

1. *Foresight*—to complete a plan of action for the future.
2. *Organization*—to provide and mobilize resources to implement the plan.
3. *Command*—to lead, select, and evaluate workers to get the best work toward the plan.
4. *Coordination*—to fit diverse efforts together, and ensure information is shared and problems solved.
5. *Control*—to make sure things happen according to plan and to take necessary corrective action.

TAKE IT TO THE CASE!

United Parcel Service (www.ups.com)
Where Technology Rules the Road

Named Company of the Year by *Forbes* magazine, UPS is the world's largest package delivery company. It's also a leader in technology utilization for competitive advantage. Log on to the UPS web site and the company literally takes you around the world of package delivery. Operating efficiency and customer service are rules of the day, every day at UPS. The company claims "a technology infrastructure second to none, enabling customers to link product shipments, services and information throughout the transaction value chain." Customers find IT working for them through an efficient on-line package tracking system and transit and delivery times. Operations are streamlined through the firm's seamless supply chain. New directions are found in UPS e-Commerce Solutions. [11]

Most importantly, Fayol believed that management could be taught. He was very concerned about improving the quality of management and set forth a number of "principles" to guide managerial action. A number of them are still part of the management vocabulary. They include Fayol's *scalar chain principle*—there should be a clear and unbroken line of communication from the top to the bottom in the organization; the *unity of command principle*—each person should receive orders from only one boss; and, the *unity of direction principle*—one person should be in charge of all activities that have the same performance objective.

Mary Parker Follett

Another contributor to the administrative principles school was Mary Parker Follett, who was eulogized at her death in 1933 as "one of the most important women America has yet produced in the fields of civics and sociology."[12] In her writings about businesses and other organizations, Follett displayed an understanding of groups and a deep commitment to human cooperation—ideas that are highly relevant today. For her, groups were mechanisms through which diverse individuals could combine their talents for a greater good. She viewed organizations as "communities" in which managers and workers should labor in harmony, without one party dominating the other and with the freedom to talk over and truly reconcile conflicts and differences. She believed it was the manager's job to help people in organizations cooperate with one another and achieve an integration of interests.

Desired Competencies for Graduates
College graduates and prospective employers don't always agree on the desired competencies for management success. An employer survey ranked business knowledge as the number-1 desired competency. Take the on-line "Reality Check" to learn more about employer preferences when hiring college graduates.

A review of *Dynamic Administration: The Collected Papers of Mary Parker Follett* helps to illustrate the modern applications of her management insights.[13] Follett believed that making every employee an owner in the business would create feelings of collective responsibility. *Today,* we address the same issues under such labels as "employee ownership," "profit sharing," and "gain-sharing plans." Follet believed that business problems involve a wide variety of factors that must be considered in relationship to one another. *Today,* we talk about "systems" when describing the same phenomenon. Follett believed that businesses were services and that private profits should always be considered vis-a-vis the public good. *Today,* we pursue the same issues under the labels of "managerial ethics" and "corporate social responsibility."

BUREAUCRATIC ORGANIZATION

Max Weber was a late-19th-century German intellectual whose insights have had a major impact on the field of management and the sociology of organizations. His ideas developed somewhat in reaction to what he considered to be performance deficiencies in the organizations of his day. Among other things, Weber was concerned that people were in positions of authority not because of their job-related capabilities, but because of their social standing or "privileged" status in German society. For this and other reasons he believed that organizations largely failed to reach their performance potential.

⊙ A **bureaucracy** is a rational and efficient form of organization founded on logic, order, and legitimate authority.

At the heart of Weber's thinking was a specific form of organization he believed could correct the problems just described—a **bureaucracy**.[14] This is an ideal, intentionally rational, and very efficient form of organization founded on principles of logic, order, and legitimate authority. The defining characteristics of Weber's bureaucratic organization are as follows:

→ Characteristics of Weber's bureaucracy

- *Clear division of labor:* Jobs are well defined, and workers become highly skilled at performing them.
- *Clear hierarchy of authority:* Authority and responsibility are well defined for each position, and each position reports to a higher-level one.
- *Formal rules and procedures:* Written guidelines direct behavior and decisions in jobs, and written files are kept for historical record.
- *Impersonality:* Rules and procedures are impartially and uniformly applied with no one receiving preferential treatment.
- *Careers based on merit:* Workers are selected and promoted on ability and performance, and managers are career employees of the organization.

Weber believed that organizations would perform well as bureaucracies. They would have the advantages of efficiency in utilizing resources, and of fairness or equity in the treatment of employees and clients. In his words:

> *The purely bureaucratic type of administrative organization . . . is, from a purely technical point of view, capable of attaining the highest degree of efficiency. . . . It is superior to any other form in precision, in stability, in the stringency of its discipline, and in its reliability. It thus makes possible a particularly high degree of calculability of results for the heads of the organization and for those acting in relation to it. It is finally superior both in intensive efficiency and in the scope of its operations and is formally capable of application to all kinds of administrative tasks.*[15]

This is the ideal side of bureaucracy. However, the terms *bureaucracy* and *bureaucrat* are now often used with negative connotations. The *possible disadvantages of bureaucracy* include: excessive paperwork or "red tape," slowness in handling problems, rigidity in the face of shifting customer or client needs, resistance to change, and employee apathy. These disadvantages are most likely to cause problems for organizations that must be flexible and quick in adapting to changing circumstances—a characteristic of challenges in today's dynamic organizational environments. Researchers now try to determine when and under what conditions bureaucratic features work best. They also want to identify alternatives to the bureaucratic form. Indeed, current trends in management include many innovations that seek the same goals as Weber but with different approaches to how organizations can be structured.

BEHAVIORAL APPROACHES TO MANAGEMENT

During the 1920s, an emphasis on the human side of the workplace began to establish its influence on management thinking. Major branches that emerged in this behavioral or human resource approach to management are shown in *Figure 4.2*. They include the famous Hawthorne studies and Maslow's theory of human needs, as well as theories generated from these foundations by Douglas McGregor, Chris Argyris, and others. The behavioral approaches maintain that people are social and self-actualizing. People at work are assumed to seek satisfying social relationships, respond to group pressures, and search for personal fulfillment.

THE HAWTHORNE STUDIES AND HUMAN RELATIONS

In 1924, the Western Electric Company (predecessor to today's Lucent Technologies) commissioned a research program to study individual productivity at the Hawthorne Works of the firm's Chicago plant.[16] The initial "Hawthorne studies" had a scientific management perspective and sought to determine how economic incentives and the physical conditions of the workplace affected the output of workers. An initial focus was on the level of illumination in the manufacturing facilities; it seemed reasonable to expect that better lighting would improve performance. After failing to find this relationship, however, the researchers concluded that unforeseen "psychological factors" somehow interfered with their illumination experiments. This finding and later Hawthorne studies directed attention toward human interactions in the workplace and ultimately had a major influence on the field of management.

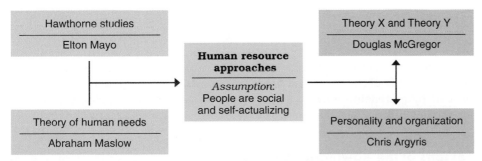

Figure 4.2 Foundations in the behavioral or human resource approaches to management.

Relay Assembly Test-Room Studies

In 1927, a team led by Harvard's Elton Mayo began more research to examine the effect of worker fatigue on output. Care was taken to design a scientific test that would be free of the psychological effects thought to have confounded the earlier illumination studies. Six workers who assembled relays were isolated for intensive study in a special test room. They were given various rest pauses, and workdays and workweeks of various lengths, and production was regularly measured. Once again, researchers failed to find any direct relationship between changes in physical working conditions and output. Productivity increased regardless of the changes made.

Mayo and his colleagues concluded that the new "social setting" created for workers in the test room accounted for the increased productivity. Two factors were singled out as having special importance. One was the *group atmosphere;* the workers shared pleasant social relations with one another and wanted to do a good job. The other was more *participative supervision.* Test-room workers were made to feel important, were given a lot of information, and were frequently asked for their opinions. This was not the case in their, or in the other workers', regular jobs elsewhere in the plant.

Employee Attitudes, Interpersonal Relations, and Group Processes

Mayo's studies continued to examine these factors until the worsening economic conditions of the Depression forced their termination in 1932. Until then, interest focused on employee attitudes, interpersonal relations, and group relations. In one study, over 21,000 employees were interviewed to learn what they liked and disliked about their work environment. "Complex" and "baffling" results led the researchers to conclude that the same things (e.g., work conditions or wages) could be sources of satisfaction for some workers and of dissatisfaction for others. The final Hawthorne study was conducted in the bank wiring room and centered on the role of the work group. A surprise finding here was that people would restrict their output in order to avoid the displeasure of the group, even if it meant sacrificing pay that could otherwise be earned by increasing output. Thus, it was recognized that groups can have strong negative, as well as positive, influences on individual productivity.

Lessons of the Hawthorne Studies

As scholars now look back, the Hawthorne studies are criticized for poor research design, weak empirical support for the conclusions drawn, and

---

the tendency of researchers to overgeneralize their findings.[17] Yet the significance of these studies as a turning point in the evolution of management thought remains intact. The Hawthorne studies helped shift the attention of managers and management researchers away from the technical and structural concerns of the classical approach and toward social and human concerns as keys to productivity. They showed that people's feelings, attitudes, and relationships with coworkers should be important to management, and they recognized the importance of the work group. They also identified the **Hawthorne effect**—the tendency of people who are singled out for special attention to perform as anticipated merely because of expectations created by the situation.

The Hawthorne studies contributed to the emergence of the **human relations movement** as an important influence on management thought during the 1950s and 1960s. This movement was largely based on the viewpoint that managers who used good human relations in the workplace would achieve productivity. Furthermore, the insights of the human relations movement set the stage for what has now evolved as the field of **organizational behavior,** the study of individuals and groups in organizations.

MASLOW'S THEORY OF HUMAN NEEDS

Among the insights of the human relations movement, the work of Abraham Maslow in the area of human "needs" is a key foundation. A **need** is a physiological or psychological deficiency a person feels the compulsion to satisfy. This is a significant concept for managers because needs create tensions that can influence a person's work attitudes and behaviors.

Maslow identified the five levels of human needs, shown in *Figure 4.3.* From lowest to highest in order they are: physiological, safety, social, esteem, and self-actualization needs. Maslow's theory is based on two

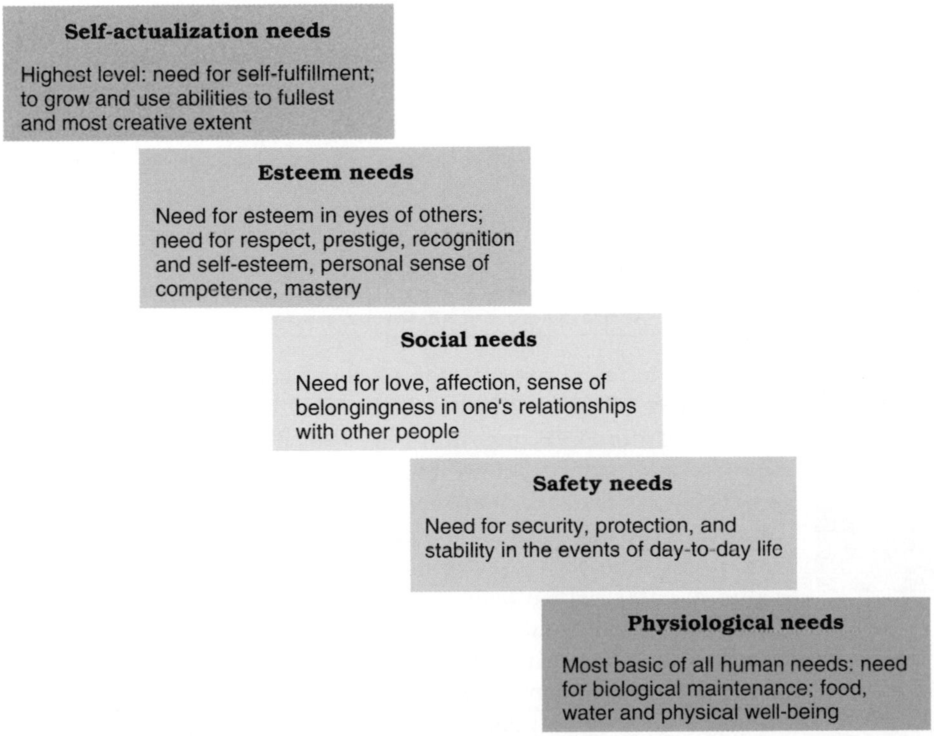

○ The **Hawthorne effect** is the tendency of persons singled out for special attention to perform as expected.

○ The **human relations movement** suggests that managers using good human relations will achieve productivity.

○ **Organizational behavior** is the study of individuals and groups in organizations.

○ A **need** is a physiological or psychological deficiency that a person wants to satisfy.

Self-actualization needs

Highest level: need for self-fulfillment; to grow and use abilities to fullest and most creative extent

Esteem needs

Need for esteem in eyes of others; need for respect, prestige, recognition and self-esteem, personal sense of competence, mastery

Social needs

Need for love, affection, sense of belongingness in one's relationships with other people

Safety needs

Need for security, protection, and stability in the events of day-to-day life

Physiological needs

Most basic of all human needs: need for biological maintenance; food, water and physical well-being

Figure 4.3 Maslow's hierarchy of human needs.

underlying principles.[18] The first is the *deficit principle*—a satisfied need is not a motivator of behavior. People act to satisfy "deprived" needs, those for which a satisfaction "deficit" exists. The second is the *progression principle*—the five needs exist in a hierarchy of "prepotency." A need at any level only becomes activated once the next-lower-level need has been satisfied.

According to Maslow, people try to satisfy the five needs in sequence. They progress step by step from the lowest level in the hierarchy to the highest. Along the way, a deprived need dominates individual attention and determines behavior until it is satisfied. Then, the next-higher-level need is activated and progression up the hierarchy occurs. At the level of self-actualization, the deficit and progression principles cease to operate. The more this need is satisfied, the stronger it grows.

Consistent with the human relations thinking, Maslow's theory implies that managers who can help people satisfy their important needs at work will achieve productivity. Although scholars now recognize that things are more complicated than this, as will be discussed in Chapter 14 on motivation and rewards, Maslow's ideas are still relevant to everyday management. Consider, for example, the case of dealing with volunteer workers who do not receive any monetary compensation. Managers in nonprofit organizations have to create jobs and work environments that satisfy the needs of volunteers. If the work isn't fulfilling, the volunteers will redirect their energies and volunteer to work somewhere else.

Get Connected!

Assess your managerial assumptions on-line or in the Career Readiness Workbook.

McGREGOR'S THEORY X AND THEORY Y

Douglas McGregor was heavily influenced by both the Hawthorne studies and Maslow. His classic book *The Human Side of Enterprise* advances the thesis that managers should give more attention to the social and self-actualizing needs of people at work.[19] McGregor called upon managers to shift their view of human nature away from a set of assumptions he called "Theory X" and toward ones he called "Theory Y." If you complete the Managerial Assumptions self-assessment in the end-of-text Career Readiness Workbook, it will offer insight into your tendencies with respect to these two sets of assumptions.

According to McGregor, managers holding **Theory X** assumptions approach their jobs believing that those who work for them generally dislike

○ **Theory X** assumes people dislike work, lack ambition, are irresponsible, and prefer to be led.

DIVERSITY (www.aimd.org) **American Institute for Managing Diversity Helping Others Understand Diversity**

At the American Institute for Managing Diversity, diversity is considered a business imperative. The institute founded by diversity author and consultant R. Roosevelt Thomas. Jr., was the first nonprofit national organization for the study of diversity issues. College students join the institute as AIMD interns and have the opportunity to learn about the field of diversity at the same time that they apply their developing skills. A core value of AIMD is the belief that the human potential is unlimited. Says AIMD's web site: "We envision societies that embrace diversity and in which diversity reinvigorates institutions at all levels; where a sense of community endures and is nurtured; and where barriers between people are overcome."[20]

work, lack ambition, are irresponsible, are resistant to change, and prefer to be led rather than to lead. McGregor considers such thinking inappropriate. He argues instead for the value of **Theory Y** assumptions in which the manager believes people are willing to work, are capable of self-control, are willing to accept responsibility, are imaginative and creative, and are capable of self-direction.

An important aspect of McGregor's ideas is his belief that managers who hold either set of assumptions can create **self-fulfilling prophecies**— that is, through their behavior they create situations where subordinates act in ways that confirm the original expectations. *Managers with Theory X assumptions* act in a very directive "command-and-control" fashion that gives people little personal say over their work. These supervisory behaviors often create passive, dependent, and reluctant subordinates who tend to do only what they are told to or required to do. This reinforces the original Theory X viewpoint. In contrast, *managers with Theory Y perspectives* behave in "participative" ways that allow subordinates more job involvement, freedom, and responsibility. This creates opportunities to satisfy esteem and self-actualization needs and causes workers to perform as expected with initiative and high performance. This time the self-fulfilling prophecy is a positive one.

Theory Y thinking is very consistent with developments in the new workplace and its emphasis on valuing workforce diversity. It is also central to the popular notions of employee participation, involvement, empowerment, and self-management.[21]

○ **Theory Y** assumes people are willing to work, accept responsibility, are self-directed and creative.

○ A **self-fulfilling prophecy** occurs when a person acts in ways that confirm another's expectations.

ARGYRIS'S THEORY OF ADULT PERSONALITY

Ideas set forth by the well-regarded scholar and consultant Chris Argyris also reflect a belief in the higher order of human nature advanced by Maslow and McGregor. In his book *Personality and Organization*, Argyris contrasts the management practices found in traditional and hierarchical organizations with the needs and capabilities of mature adults.[22] He concludes that some practices, especially those influenced by the classical management approaches, are inconsistent with the mature adult personality.

Consider these examples. In scientific management, the principle of specialization assumes that people will work more efficiently as tasks become better defined. Argyris believes that this may inhibit self-actualization in the workplace. In Weber's bureaucracy, people work in a clear hierarchy of authority with top-level managers directing and controlling lower levels. Argyris worries that this creates dependent, passive workers who feel they have little control over their work environments. In Fayol's administrative principles, the concept of unity of direction assumes that efficiency will increase when a person's work is planned and directed by a supervisor. Argyris suggests that this may create conditions for psychological failure; psychological success occurs when people define their own goals.

Like McGregor, the belief that managers who treat people positively and as responsible adults will achieve productivity is central to Argyris's thinking. His advice is to expand job responsibilities, allow more task variety, and adjust supervisory styles to allow more participation and promote better human relations. He believes that the common problems of employee absenteeism, turnover, apathy, alienation, and the like may be signs of a mismatch between workers' mature personalities and outdated management practices.

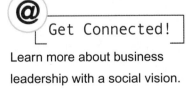

Get Connected!

Learn more about business leadership with a social vision. Go on-line with Business Enterprise Trust.

QUANTITATIVE APPROACHES TO MANAGEMENT

About the same time that some scholars were developing human resource approaches to management, others were investigating how quantitative techniques could improve managerial decision making. The foundation of the quantitative approaches to management is the assumption that mathematical techniques can be used to improve managerial decision making and problem solving. Today these applications are increasingly driven by computer technology and software programs.

MANAGEMENT SCIENCE

○ **Management science** uses mathematical techniques to analyze and solve management problems.

The terms **management science** and *operations research* are often used interchangeably to describe the scientific applications of mathematical techniques to management problems. A typical approach proceeds as follows. A problem is encountered, it is systematically analyzed, appropriate mathematical models and computations are applied, and an optimum solution is identified. In this process, a number of management science applications are commonly used. *Mathematical forecasting* helps make future projections that are useful in the planning process. *Inventory modeling* helps control inventories by mathematically establishing how much to order and when. *Linear programming* is used to calculate how best to allocate scarce resources among competing uses. *Queuing theory* helps allocate service personnel or workstations to minimize customer waiting time and service cost. *Network models* break large tasks into smaller components to allow for better analysis, planning, and control of complex projects. And *simulation* makes models of problems so different solutions under various assumptions can be tested.

Regardless of the specific technique used, the essence of the quantitative management approach includes these characteristics. There is a focus on decision making that has clear implications for management action. The techniques use "economic" decision criteria, such as costs, revenues, and return on investment. They also involve mathematical models that follow sophisticated rules and formulas.

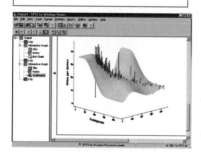

A popular and easy-to-use software program for statistical analysis is SPSS, available from SPSS Inc. From historical roots with the software being a tool for scholars and social science researchers, the firm has grown into a major provider of support data—based business problem solving, with special applications to customer relationship management and business intelligence. SPSS Inc. has been described as one of America's top small companies.

QUANTITATIVE ANALYSIS TODAY

University courses in management science, operations research, and quantitative business analysis provide a good introduction to these quantitative management foundations. Courses in operations management apply them to the physical production of goods and services. Since many of the techniques are highly sophisticated, organizations often employ staff specialists to help managers take advantage of them effectively. But software developments are making these techniques more readily available through easy-to-use applications for desktop and even handheld personal computers. This availability greatly expands their use throughout the workplace and makes it even more important for managers to understand the value of each technique. In all cases, of course, mathematical solutions to problems must be supported by good managerial judgment and an appreciation of the human factor.

MODERN APPROACHES TO MANAGEMENT

The modern approaches to management grew directly from foundations established by the classical, human resource, and quantitative schools of thought. Importantly, they also recognize that no one model or theory applies universally in all situations or to the exclusion of the others.

According to the modern management approaches, people are complex and variable. They have many varied needs that can change over time. They possess a range of talents and capabilities that can be developed. Organizations and managers, therefore, should respond to individual differences with a wide variety of managerial strategies and job opportunities. Key foundations of the modern management approaches include the systems view of organizations and contingency thinking.

SYSTEMS THINKING

Formally defined, a **system** is a collection of interrelated parts that function together to achieve a common purpose. A **subsystem** is a smaller component of a larger system.[23] One of the earliest management writers to adopt a systems perspective was Chester Barnard. His 1938 ground-breaking book *Functions of the Executive* was based on years of experience as a telephone company executive.[24] Barnard described organizations as cooperative systems in which the contributions of individuals are integrated for a common purpose. Importantly, Barnard considered this cooperation "conscious, deliberate, and purposeful." It was the job of the executives, or managers, through communication to make this cooperation happen.

Systems thinking continues to influence management theory and practice today.[25] One application is described in *Figure 4.4*. This figure first depicts the larger organization as an **open system** that interacts with its environment in the continual process of transforming inputs from suppliers into outputs for customers. Within the organization any

○ A **system** is a collection of interrelated parts working together for a purpose.

○ A **subsystem** is a smaller component of a larger system.

○ An **open system** interacts with its environment and transforms resource inputs into outputs.

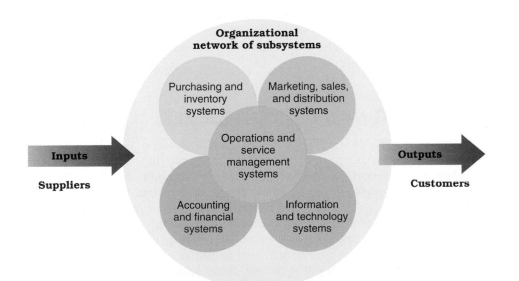

Figure 4.4 Organizations as complex networks of interacting subsystems.

number of critical subsystems can be described. In the figure, the operations and service management systems are a central point. They provide the integration among other subsystems, such as purchasing, accounting, sales, and information, that are essential to the work of the organization. Importantly, and as suggested by Barnard, high performance by the organization as a whole occurs only when each subsystem both performs its tasks well and works well in cooperation with the other subsystems. It is the job of managers throughout the organization to make this coordinated action possible.

CONTINGENCY THINKING

○ **Contingency thinking** tries to match management practices with situational demands.

Modern management is situational in orientation, that is, it attempts to identify management practices that are the best fit with the unique demands of a situation. It utilizes **contingency thinking** that tries to match managerial responses with the problems and opportunities specific to different settings, particularly those posed by individual and environmental differences. In the modern management approach, there is no expectation that one can or should find the "one best way" to manage in all circumstances. Rather, the contingency perspective tries to help managers understand situational differences and respond to them in appropriate ways.[26]

Contingency thinking is an important theme in this book, and its implications extend to all of the management functions—from planning and controlling for diverse environmental conditions, to organizing for different environments and strategies, to leading in different performance situations. For example, consider again the concept of bureaucracy—something Weber offered as an ideal form of organization. From a contingency perspective the strict bureaucratic form is only one possible way of organizing things. What turns out to be the "best" structure in any given situation will depend on many factors, including environmental uncertainty, an organization's primary technology, and the strategy being pursued. Only when the environment is relatively stable and operations are predictable does the bureaucracy work best; in other situations, alternative structures may be needed. Contingency thinking recognizes that what is a good structure for one organization may not work well for another, and what works well at one time may not work as well in the future as circumstances change.[27] This contingency approach to organization structure and design will be examined further in Chapters 10 and 11.

Mobility in American Society
Management theories and practices should keep pace with changes in society at large. Did you know that some 17 percent of Americans change their residences each year? Take the on-line "Reality Check" to learn more about mobility in American society. You may be surprised!

CONTINUING MANAGEMENT THEMES

The many accumulating insights into management practice have set the foundation for important trends and directions in management thought that are well in evidence as we begin the 21st century. Among the most important is the recognition that we live and work in a dynamic and ever-changing environment that puts unique and never-ending competitive pressures on organizations. Key themes reflected in discussions throughout *Management 7/e* include continuing pressures for quality and performance excellence, an expanding global awareness, and the importance of new leadership in an age of information, knowledge workers, and highly competitive business environments.

Figure 4.5 The organizational value chain.

QUALITY AND PERFORMANCE EXCELLENCE

The quality theme was first introduced in Chapter 1 and will continue throughout this book.[28] It remains a very important direction in management today. Managers and workers in truly progressive organizations are quality conscious. They understand the basic link between competitive advantage and the ability to always deliver quality goods and services to their customers. The best organizational cultures include quality as a core value and reinforce the quality commitment in all aspects of the work environment.

Every effort is made in total quality management (TQM) to build quality into all aspects of operations from initial acquisition of resources, through the transformation processes and work systems, all the way to ultimate product delivery to customers or clients. *Figure 4.5* describes the systems context for TQM in respect to the **value chain**—a specific sequence of activities that transform raw materials into a finished good or service.[29] Quality must be maintained at each point in the value chain, whether it is performed directly by the organization or is part of its network of relationships with suppliers and contractors.

○ A **value chain** is the sequence of activities that transform materials into finished products.

Closely aligned with the pursuit of quality is management commitment to performance excellence, a theme that became prominent when the book *In Search of Excellence: Lessons from America's Best-Run Companies* was published by Tom Peters and Robert Waterman.[30] Based on case investigations of successful companies, they identified the eight attributes of performance excellence shown in *Manager's Notepad 4.2.* These attributes are further representative of many themes and directions that are now common practice in organizations today.

GLOBAL AWARENESS

We are just emerging from a decade in which the quality and performance excellence themes have been reflected in the rise of "process reengineering," "virtual organizations," "agile factories," "network firms," and other new concepts reviewed in this book. But while the best formulas for success continue to be tested and debated, an important fact remains: much of the pressure for quality and performance excellence is created by a highly competitive global economy. Nowhere is this challenge more evident than in the continuing efforts of businesses around the globe to transform themselves into truly world-class operations.

GLOBALIZATION (www.daimler chrysler.com) DaimlerChrysler Can Quality Practices Travel the World?

When Mercedes Benz set up manufacturing in the United States, the best of its German management practices came too. In fact, evidence of Taylor's scientific management principles are at work now that Mercedes's popular M-class sport utility vehicles are "Made in Alabama." The German automaker expects its American workers to follow precise standards known as SMPs (standard methods and procedures). The SMPs are created by German engineers and specify everything right down to the way a lug nut should be tightened and where a tool should be placed when not in use.[31]

Like the lessons of performance excellence, current trends and directions in global awareness have ties back to the 1980s. That was a time when the success of Japanese industry caught worldwide attention and both scholars and consultants rushed to identify what could be learned from Japanese management practices. The books *Theory Z*, by *William Ouchi*, and *The Art of Japanese Management*, by Richard Tanner Pascale and Anthony G. Athos, were among the first that called attention to the possible link between unique Japanese practices and business success.[32] Ouchi used the term "Theory Z" to describe a management framework that incorporates into North American practices a variety of insights found in the Japanese models.[33] Prominent in the **Theory Z** management approach are such things as long-term employment, slower promotions and more lateral job movements, attention to career planning and development, use

○ **Theory Z** describes a management framework emphasizing long-term employment and teamwork.

MANAGER'S NOTEPAD 4.2

Eight attributes of performance excellence

- *Bias toward action*—making decisions and making sure that things get done.
- *Closeness to the customers*—knowing their needs and valuing customer satisfaction.
- *Autonomy and entrepreneurship*—supporting innovation, change, and risk taking.
- *Productivity through people*—valuing human resources as keys to quality and performance.
- *Hands-on and value-driven*—having a clear sense of organizational purpose.
- *Sticking to the knitting*—focusing resources and attention on what the organization does best.
- *Simple form and lean staff*—minimizing management levels and staff personnel.
- *Simultaneous loose-tight properties*—allowing flexibility while staying in control.

of consensus decision making, and emphasis on use of teamwork and employee involvement. And even though the Japanese economy and management systems face pressures of their own today, these early insights into the Japanese business experience helped to establish a global awareness that continues to enrich management thinking today. This international dimension of management will be examined thoroughly in the next chapter, with special attention on understanding cultural influences on management practices.

LEARNING ORGANIZATIONS

This remains the age of the **learning organization,** described in Chapter 3 as an organization that operates with values and systems that result in "continuous change and improvement based on the lessons of experience."[34] Learning organizations require for their success a value-driven organizational culture that emphasizes information, teamwork, empowerment, participation, and leadership. Learning organizations also depend for their success on special leadership qualities. This topic is so important that Part 5 of this book is entirely devoted to it, with special emphasis on motivation and rewards, communication, conflict and negotiation, teamwork, and change leadership. And when it comes to leadership, perhaps no other management theme is more influenced by directions in the new economy. Once again, history sets the stage for the future. In his book, *No Easy Victories,* John Gardner speaks of leadership as a special challenge and his words are well worth considering today.

○ A **learning organization** continuously changes and improves using the lessons of experience.

> Leaders have a significant role in creating the state of mind that is the society. They can serve as symbols of the moral unity of the society. They can express the values that hold the society together. Most important, they can conceive and articulate goals that lift people out of their petty preoccupations, carry them above the conflicts that tear a society apart, and unite them in the pursuit of objectives worthy of their best efforts.[35]

Leadership and the new directions of learning organizations will be singled out again and again in *Management 7/e* as important keys to personal and organizational performance. And performance by people and organizations, in turn, is the key to any society's economic development and growth. Managers of the 21st century will have to excel as never before to meet the expectations held of them and of the organizations they lead. Importantly, we must all recognize that new managerial outlooks and new managerial competencies appropriate to the new workplace are requirements for future leadership success. At the very least, the *21st-century manager* must be a:

← Characteristics of the 21st-century executive

- *Global strategist*—understands interconnections among nations, cultures, and economies; plans and acts with due consideration of them.
- *Master of technology*—comfortable with information technology; understands technological trends and their implications; able to use technology to best advantage.
- *Effective politician*—understands growing complexity of government regulations and the legal environment; able to relate them with the interests of the organization.
- *Inspiring leader*—attracts highly motivated workers and inspires them with a high-performance culture where individuals and teams can do their best work.

In Chapter 3 on information and decision making we discussed the special challenges of this age of information. It is an age in which Peter Drucker considers knowledge the principle resource of a competitive society. Drucker, you should recall, also cautions that knowledge constantly makes itself obsolete.[36] In a society where knowledge workers are increasingly important, new managers must be well educated . . . and they must continue that education throughout their careers. Success in turbulent times comes only through continuous improvement. The new economy requires everyone to be unrelenting in efforts to develop, refine, and maintain job-relevant skills and competencies. It requires leaders with strong people skills, ones attuned to the nature of an information/service society, ones who understand the international dimensions, and ones who establish commitments to work-life balance. And, the new economy places a premium on personal leadership qualities. Consider, for example, this comment by former corporate CEO and college president Ralph Sorenson: "It is the *ability to make things happen* that most distinguishes the successful manager from the mediocre or unsuccessful one. . . . The most cherished manager is the one who says 'I can do it,' and then does."[37]

"Do it," advises Sorenson. "Of course," you may quickly answer. But don't forget that the 21st-century manager must also do the "right" things—the things that really count, the things that add value to the organization's goods and/or services, the things that make a real difference in performance results and competitive advantage, and the ethical things. Those are challenging directions for leadership, learning organizations, and career success in the new economy.

@

Get Connected!

Ralph Sorenson is a board member of Bright Horizons Family Solutions, a firm specializing in work-site child care and work-life consulting services.

STUDY Guide

The Chapter 4 Study Guide will help you review chapter content, prepare for examinations, and further build your career readiness. The *Summary* briefly highlights answers to questions first posed in the chapter opening Planning Ahead section. The list of *Key Terms* allows you to double check your familiarity with basic concepts and definitions. *Self-Test 4* gives you the opportunity to test your basic comprehension of chapter content using sample test questions. Suggestions offered as *Career Readiness Activities* direct your attention to relevant sections of the end-of-text Career Readiness Workbook, as well as to special Electronic Resources on the *Management 7/e* web site.

SUMMARY

What can be learned from classical management thinking?

- Frederick Taylor's four principles of scientific management focused on the need to carefully select, train, and support workers for individual task performance.
- Henri Fayol suggested that managers should learn what are now known as the management functions of planning, organizing, leading, and controlling.
- Max Weber described bureaucracy with its clear hierarchy, formal rules, and well-defined jobs as an ideal form of organization.

What ideas were introduced by the human resource approaches?

- The human resource approaches shifted attention toward the human factor as a key element in organizational performance.
- The historic Hawthorne studies suggested that work behavior is influenced by social and psychological forces and that work performance may be improved by better "human relations."
- Abraham Maslow's hierarchy of human needs introduced the concept of self-actualization and the potential for people to experience self-fulfillment in their work.
- Douglas McGregor urged managers to shift away from Theory X and toward Theory Y thinking, which views people as independent, responsible, and capable of self-direction in their work.
- Chris Argyris pointed out that people in the workplace are adults and may react negatively when constrained by strict management practices and rigid organizational structures.

What is the role of quantitative analysis in management?

- The availability of high-power desktop computing provides new opportunities for mathematical methods to be used for problem solving.

- Many organizations employ staff specialists in quantitative management science and operations research to solve problems.
- Quantitative techniques in common use include various approaches to forecasting, linear programming, and simulation, among others.

What is unique about the systems view and contingency thinking?

- Organizations are complex open systems that interact with their external environments to transform resource inputs into product outputs.
- Resource acquisition and customer satisfaction are important requirements in the organization-environment relationship.
- Organizations are composed of many internal subsystems that must work together in a coordinated way to support the organization's overall success.
- Contingency thinking avoids "one best way" arguments, and recognizes the need to understand situational differences and respond appropriately to them.

What are continuing management themes of the 21st century?

- The commitment to meet customer needs 100 percent of the time guides organizations toward total quality management and continuous improvement of operations.
- The global economy is a dramatic influence on organizations today, and opportunities abound to learn new ways of managing from practices in other countries.
- This is the age of information in which knowledge and knowledge workers are major resources of modern society.
- New managers must accept and excel at leadership responsibilities to perform as global strategists, technology masters, consummate politicians, and leader/motivators.

KEY TERMS

Bureaucracy (p. 96)	Organizational behavior (p. 99)
Contingency thinking (p. 104)	Scientific management (p. 93)
Hawthorne effect (p. 99)	Self-fulfilling prophecies (p. 101)
Human relations movement (p. 99)	System (p. 103)
Learning organization (p. 107)	Subsystem (p. 103)
Management science (p. 102)	Theory X (p. 100)
Motion study (p. 97)	Theory Y (p. 101)
Need (p. 99)	Theory Z (p. 106)
Open system (p. 103)	Value chain (p. 105)

SELF-TEST 4

Take this test here or on-line much as you would in a normal classroom situation. It should offer you a good way to check your basic comprehension of chapter material. Answers may be found at the end of the book.

MULTIPLE-CHOICE QUESTIONS:

1. The assumption that people are complex with widely varying needs is most associated with the _____ management approaches.
   (a) classical (b) neoclassical (c) behavioral (d) modern

2. The father of scientific management is _____ .
   (a) Weber (b) Taylor (c) Mintzberg (d) Katz

3. The Hawthorne studies are an important foundation of the _____ approaches to management thinking.
   (a) classical (b) human resource (c) administrative (d) quantitative

4. Advice to study a job and carefully train workers to do that job with financial incentives tied to job performance would most likely come from _____ in the classical school of management thought.
   (a) scientific management (b) contingency management (c) Henri Fayol
   (d) Abraham Maslow

5. The highest level of need in Maslow's hierarchy is the level of _____ needs.
   (a) safety (b) esteem (c) self-actualization (d) physiological

6. Conflict between the mature adult personality and a rigid organization was a concern of the human relations theorist _____ .
   (a) Argyris (b) Follett (c) Gantt (d) Fuller

7. When people perform in a situation as they are expected to, this may be due to the _____ effect.
   (a) Hawthorne (b) Mayo (c) contingency (d) open-systems

8. Linear programming and queuing theory are examples of techniques found in the _____ approach to management.
   (a) classical (b) quantitative (c) bureaucratic organization (d) modern

9. Resource acquisition and customer satisfaction are important when an organization is viewed as a(n) _____ .
   (a) bureaucracy (b) closed system (c) open system (d) pyramid

10. Long-term employment and consensus decision making are characteristic of the _____ management framework.
    (a) Theory X (b) Theory Y (c) Theory Z (d) contingency

TRUE-FALSE QUESTIONS:

11. In contingency management thinking there is always one "best way" to manage.   T   F

12. The bureaucracy was described as an ideal form of organization by Max Weber.   T   F

13. Maslow's hierarchy of needs is part of contingency thinking.   T   F

14. Organizations consist of subsystems whose activities must be integrated and coordinated.   T   F

15. The role of quantitative analysis is not important in management today.   T   F

16. "Sticking to the knitting" is one of the eight attributes of performance excellence in organizations.   T   F

17. Theory Z is based on insights from Japanese management practices.   T   F

18. Modern management theory now rejects all of the insights of the classical approaches.   T   F

19. The human relations movement is a forerunner to the field of organizational behavior as we know it today.   T   F

20. Mary Parker Follett was an important contributor to the classical approach to management.   T   F

SHORT-RESPONSE QUESTIONS:

21. List three of McGregor's Theory Y assumptions that are consistent with the current emphasis on participation and involvement in the workplace.

22. How do the deficit and progression principles operate in Maslow's hierarchy-of-needs theory?

23. Define contingency thinking and give an example of how it might apply to management.

24. Explain why the external environment is so important in the open-systems view of organizations.

APPLICATION QUESTION:

25. Enrique Temoltzin has just been appointed the new manager of your local college bookstore. Enrique would like to make sure the store operates according to Weber's bureaucracy. Is this a good management approach for Enrique to follow? Why or why not?

CAREER readiness ACTIVITIES

Recommended learning activities from the end-of-text Career Readiness Workbook for this chapter include:

Career Advancement Portfolio
- Individual writing and group presentation assignments based on any of the following activities.

Case for Critical Thinking
- UPS–Information Technology Hits the Road (#2)

Integrative Learning Activities
- Research Project 2—Changing Corporate Cultures
- Integrative Case—Outback Steakhouse, Inc.
- Integrative Case—Richard Branson Meets the New Economy

Exercises in Teamwork
- What Would the Classics Say? (#5)
- The Great Management History Debate (#6)
- What Do You Value in Work? (#7)

Self-Assessments
- A 21st-Century Manager? (#1)
- Managerial Assumptions (#4)
- Work Values (#25)

The *Fast Company* Collection On-Line
- Scott Kirsner, "Collision Course"
- Robert Reich, "The Company of the Future"

ELECTRONIC RESOURCES

@ GET CONNECTED! Don't forget to take full advantage of the on-line support for *Management 7/e.*
- Chapter 4 On-line Study Guide
- Chapter 4 Self-test Answers
- Chapter 4 E-Resource Center

 www.wiley.com/college/schermerhorn

5

Global dimensions of management

Planning ahead

GETTING CONNECTED

NTT DoCoMo — Welcome to the "Wireless" World

Japan is leading the way, again. Of course, that's no surprise to those familiar with the world of international business. For years the major corporations of the Western world have studied Japanese management and organizational practices. Now they're studying again. The object of attention this time is NTT DoCoMo, an innovative and fast-growing powerhouse in the field of wireless communications.

The firm is guided by what it calls Vision 2010: "There are three words that characterize the business of DoCoMo—mobile, wireless, and personal. Our aim is to make the most of these features and pursue evolution of the mobile communications market." NTT DoCoMo energized the wireless world with its i-mode service for cell phones. With close to 1 million new subscribers each month, this allows users to access e-mail and the Internet including sites offering banking, weather, and ticketing. Says President Dr. Keiji Tachikawa: "We knew that if we could get the vast amount of information already on the Internet into our phones, we would attract large numbers of users." Succeed they did; the firm now has over 30 million cell phone customers and is rapidly expanding worldwide.

At the heart of NTT DoCoMo's operating success is a corporate culture that guides employees with what is called the DREAM. "D" is for *dynamics*—to change and grow continuously. "R" is for *relationship*—to accept and collaborate with each other. "E" is for *ecology*—to be aware of and to create a better natural environment. "A" is for *action*—to start and to accomplish things others haven't accomplished. "M" is for *multiview*—to keep a wide perspective and follow long-term thinking.

Is NTT DoCoMo coming your way? Most probably. The firm has momentum. It is embarked on an ambitious plan for strategic partnerships around the globe. Already a player in Europe's wireless competition, DoCoMo is the biggest investor in AT&T Wireless. Says Dr. Tachikawa: "Our policy is to create alliances in regions around the world . . . we want 'win–win' partnerships for everyone."[1]

@ **Get Connected!**

Look into the wireless industry, at home and around the world. Is NTT DoCoMo on the advantage? Someday soon the firm's partnerships may even bring HDTV to your cell phone. In the meantime, there's no doubt the world is going wireless. Get connected!

Get Connected!

Browse the country listings of Colossus, the international directory of country search engines.

There is no doubt about it. We live and work in a global community, one that grows smaller and more immediately accessible by the day. Led by CNN, network television brings on-the-spot news from around the world into our homes, 24 hours a day. The world's newspapers from *The New York Times* to *El Financiero* (Mexico) to *Le Monde* (France) to *The Japan Times* can be read from the Internet at the touch of a keyboard on your desktop PC; headlines may even be reached from your cell phone. It is possible to board a plane in Minneapolis and fly nonstop to Beijing; it is sometimes less expensive to fly from Columbus, Ohio, to Paris than to Albany, New York. Colleges and universities offer an increasing variety of study-abroad programs. E-mail and on-line chat rooms link us to friends and work partners around the world and at low cost.

This world of opportunities isn't just for tourists and travelers. It is time to recognize the emergence and implications of a global workplace. When Germany's Daimler-Benz announced a merger with America's Chrysler, the world noticed and we wondered about future consolidation of the global automobile industry. When Daimler later announced a planned layoff of 26,000 jobs in the United States, local ramifications became all too clear. But this is just one example of a business world in which national boundaries are increasingly blurred. It is already difficult to buy a car that is really "made in America," since so many components are manufactured in other countries. The gas station with the green-and-white "BP" logo is operated by British Petroleum, now known as BPAmoco; the familiar "Shell" station is brought to you courtesy of Royal-Dutch/Shell. And did you know that the majority of McDonald's sales are now coming from outside of the United States, and that some of its most profitable restaurants are located in places like Moscow, Budapest, Beijing, and elsewhere? Astute business investors know all this and more. They buy and sell only with awareness of the latest financial news from Hong Kong, London, Tokyo, New York, Johannesburg, and other of the world's financial centers. In this time of high technology, furthermore, they don't even have to leave home to do it—the latest information is readily available on the Internet.

Yes, we live and work today in a truly global village. You, like the rest of us, must get connected with the world's opportunities.

INTERNATIONAL MANAGEMENT AND GLOBALIZATION

○ In the **global economy** resources, markets, and competition are worldwide in scope.

○ **Globalization** is the process of growing interdependence among elements of the global economy.

This is the age of the **global economy** in which resource supplies, product markets, and business competition are worldwide rather than purely local or national in scope.[2] It is also a time heavily influenced by the forces of **globalization**, the process of growing interdependence among these components in the global economy. Harvard scholar and consultant Rosabeth Moss Kanter describes it as: "one of the most powerful and pervasive influences on nations, businesses, workplaces, communities, and lives . . ."[3]

The global economy offers great opportunities of worldwide sourcing, production, and sales capabilities.[4] But as businesses spread their reach around the world, the processes of globalization also bring many adjustments to traditional patterns. Large multinational businesses are increasingly adopting transnational or "global" identities, rather than being identified with a singular home. The growing strength and penetration of these businesses worldwide is viewed by some as a potential threat to national economies, and their local business systems, labor markets, and cultures.[5] All this adds up to great uncertainty as executives move into new and uncharted competitive territories. AOL Time Warner's Chairman Stephen M. Case describes the scene this way: "I sometimes feel like I'm behind the wheel of a race car. One of the biggest challenges is there are no road signs to help navigate. And in fact . . . no one has yet determined which side of the road we're supposed to be on."[6]

The term used to describe management in organizations with business interests in more than one country is **international management**. There is no denying its importance. Procter & Gamble, for example, pursues a global strategy with a presence in more than 70 countries; some 43 percent of Johnson & Johnson's business comes from outside the United States. As the leaders of these and other companies press forward with global initiatives, the international management challenges and opportunities of working across borders—national and cultural—must be mastered. New tests of managerial skills and viewpoints are emerging. A new breed of manager, the **global manager**, is increasingly sought after. This is someone informed about international developments, transnational in outlook, competent in working with people from different cultures, and always aware of regional developments in a changing world.

What about you? Are you prepared for the challenges of international management? Are you informed about the world and the forces of globalization?

EUROPE

The new Europe is a place of dramatic political and economic developments.[7] The **European Union** (EU) is a grouping of 15 countries who agreed to support mutual economic growth by removing barriers that previously limited cross-border trade and business development. Expectations are that the EU will expand to include at least 25 members in the near future. At present only Switzerland and Norway from Western Europe remain outside the group. At least a dozen countries, including several new republics of the former Soviet Union, have applied to join or expressed interest in joining.

As an economic union, the EU is putting the rest of the world on notice that European business is a global force to be reckoned with. Members are linked through favorable trade and customs laws intended to facilitate the free flow of workers, goods and services, and investments across national boundaries. Businesses in each member country have access to a market of over 375 million consumers, compared to 220 million in the United States and 120 million in Japan. Among the important business and economic developments in the EU are agreements to eliminate frontier controls and trade barriers, create uniform minimum technical product standards, open government procurement to businesses from all member countries, unify financial regulations, lift competitive barriers in banking and insurance, and even offer a common currency—the **Euro.** The emergence of the Euro as a new common currency set the stage for what *Business Week* referred to as "an unstoppable market process that will sweep away structures Old Europe held so dear—national corporations and banks, rigid work rules, generous work rules."[8] The impact of the Euro is being watched carefully as Europe marches into the 21st century. Although there is still political and economic risk, the expected benefits include higher productivity, lower inflation, and steady growth.

Get Connected!

Get fully informed. Learn about the case against globalization and the WTO. Check Global Trade Watch.

○ **International management** involves managing operations in more than one country.

○ A **global manager** is culturally aware and well informed on international affairs.

○ The **EU** is a political and economic alliance of European countries.

○ The **Euro** is the new common European currency.

All of this must also be considered in context with another dynamic element in the European scene—continuing legacies of the collapse of communism in the former Soviet Union and in nations formerly dominated by it. The traumas and tragedies of divisive civil and ethnic strife in the region of the former Yugoslavia are still in the news. Changes in political systems and governments add to the risk for foreign investors. Yet western businesses are responding to opportunities not only in Russia, but in such diverse places as Belarus, Latvia, and the Ukraine. For Eastern and Central Europe as a whole, the themes are social progress and economic growth. Business continues to make strong gains in the Czech Republic, Poland, and Hungary, in particular, and world-class standards are emerging as managers in this region learn the demands of competitive and free markets.

THE AMERICAS

○ **NAFTA** is the North American Free Trade Agreement linking Canada, the United States, and Mexico in a regional economic alliance.

Turning now to the Americas, the United States, Canada, and Mexico have joined together in the **North American Free Trade Agreement** (NAFTA). This agreement largely frees the flow of goods and services, workers, and investments within a region that has more potential consumers than its European rival, the EU. Getting approval of NAFTA from all three governments was not easy. Whereas Canadian firms worried about domination by U.S. manufacturers, American politicians were concerned about the potential loss of jobs to Mexico. Some calls were made for more government legislation and support to protect domestic industries from foreign competition. While Mexicans feared that free trade would bring a further intrusion of U.S. culture and values into their country, Americans complained that Mexican businesses did not operate by the same social standards—particularly with respect to environmental protection and the use of child labor.

○ *Maquiladoras* are foreign manufacturing plants that operate in Mexico with special privileges.

Often at issue in NAFTA controversies are the operations of *maquiladoras*, foreign manufacturing plants allowed to operate in Mexico with special privileges in return for employing Mexican labor.[9] *Maquiladora* firms are allowed to import materials, components, and equipment duty free. They employ lower-cost Mexican labor to assemble these materials into finished products, which can be exported with duty paid only on the "value added" in Mexico. Critics of *maquiladoras* accuse them of exploiting the availability of lower-cost Mexican labor and giving away jobs that would otherwise go to Americans. They also point to high "social costs" as a continuing influx of workers overburdens services in Mexican border towns and the region becomes increasingly "Americanized."

Advocates argue that *maquiladoras* bring increased employment and prosperity and help develop more highly skilled local workers. Reports indicate that they are flourishing, gaining in productivity, and creating jobs. General Motors, Ford, Philips, and United Technologies are just a few of the multinationals that have increased their *maquiladora* operations.[10] The utilization of Mexican labor force skills and the global reach of these operations are also growing. At General Motors of Mexico, for example, Mexican engineers developed a right-hand drive car for markets in Australia and South Africa.

Optimism regarding business and economic potential extends throughout Central and South America as well. Many countries of the region are cutting tariffs, updating their economic policies, and welcoming foreign investors. Chile is discussed as the next NAFTA partner, and other countries may soon follow. Some even seek the creation of a Free Trade Area of the

Americas (FTAA), a proposed free-trade zone that would stretch from Point Barrow, Alaska, all the way to Tierra del Fuego, Chile. In addition to NAFTA, other pieces of this potential pan-American economic union are already in place. The MERCOSUR agreement links Bolivia, Brazil, Paraguay, Uruguay, and Argentina; the Andean Pact links Venezuela, Colombia, Ecuador, Peru, and Bolivia; and the Caribbean Community, CARICOM, is also growing as an economic linkage. The possibility of a single monetary unit, along the EURO model, is being discussed within Mercosur. Clearly, the great significance of Latin America to world trade is a message being heard by many North American business and government leaders.

ASIA AND THE PACIFIC RIM

Although the region's recent financial problems have taken some of the luster off, Asia must still be respected for what has been called a "mega-market." McDonald's, for example, already has over 4,500 outlets in the region and the number is still growing. Asia is not only still gaining as a power in the world economy, it has already achieved superpower status. And this respect must not be limited to just Japan, China, and what have become known as the "Tigers" of South Korea, Taiwan, and Singapore. It must be more broadly accorded in the region as a whole. In Southeast Asia the long-term potential of the economies of Malaysia and Thailand is already significant, the Philippines is gaining attention, and Vietnam is more frequently in the news. Of course, Japan's economic power is an ever-present theme in Asia and in the global economy as a whole. Japanese companies, like NTT DoCoMo as featured in the chapter opener, are well evidenced in the world's largest Asian firms. Also included are a number of emerging world-class competitors from other Asian countries: Samsung (South Korea), Sime-Darby (Malaysia), and Siam Cement (Thailand), to name just three.

> ## CAREER CONNECTION
> ### *Global Entrepreneurship*
>
> **International Trade Administration**
> **Find Trade Information and More at Your Fingertips**
> There are many international trade resources available on the Web. Start with a visit to the United States Department of Commerce site of the International Trade Commission. Here you'll find "Country Commercial Guides" prepared by U.S. Embassy staff around the world. Published once a year, they contain information on the business and economic situation of foreign countries, including the political climate, marketing, trade regulations, investment climate, and business travel.
>
> Wander more; there is a lot of international trade information available at your desktop. The Kelley School of Business at Indiana University maintains a comprehensive list of international business resources on the Web. Search engine Colossus will help you find search engines in various countries of the world. Just start browsing, and you'll be surprised at the wealth of information available.
>
> Go to the Web and check out My Customs, Inc. Started by two entrepreneurs, this firm tries to make it as easy as possible for other entrepreneurs to buy and sell goods around the world. The firm's web site states its mission as helping to "eliminate the barriers to global e-commerce that are created by worldwide trade regulations."
>
> **QUESTION:** Does global entrepreneurship sound interesting to you? Are you familiar with the many resources that can help you plan an international business initiative? What countries might you choose to do business with?

Wherever you travel or do business in the Asian region, "opportunity" is the watchword of the day. Even with the recent economic crisis taken into account, the Asian and the Pacific Rim economies are soon expected to be larger than those of the current EU. The forum for Asia-Pacific Economic Cooperation (APEC) is gaining prominence as the platform for a regional economic alliance. Member countries already represent a third of the global marketplace, and APEC countries rank as the world's top market for cars and telecommunications equipment. It is not just "low-cost" labor that attracts businesses to Asia; the growing availability of highly skilled "brainpower" is increasingly high on its list of advantages.

India, the world's second-most populated country, is in the midst of economic expansion, with a high literacy rate and relatively inexpensive skilled labor. It is emerging as a world-class base for technology

@

Get Connected!

Find out more on the business potential of Africa. Consult the on-line Africa trade and investment resources.

development and software engineering. The Indian firm Wipro Ltd., for example, was the choice when Texas-based VideoDotCom needed help in software design. Says President John Tuder: "Their extensive e-commerce experience, development skills, pricing, and overall quality have made them my primary engineering team."[11]

China is the world's largest single-country marketplace (estimated at 1.3 billion consumers). It is also controversial as a business destination.[12] The country's relations with the global economy remain complicated by human rights concerns and poor protection of foreign copyrights and intellectual property, among other issues. Still, China is a major export power whose manufacturing plants supply major foreign retailers. Many outside firms—including RJR Nabisco, Coca-Cola, Procter & Gamble, and H. J. Heinz—are trying hard to penetrate China's vast markets with products manufactured there. The country's importance in the global economy will surely increase in the future. Executives at Salient Systems, an Ohio manufacturer of railway weighting systems, recognize the potential and the complications in this opportunity. They are working with China's Ministry of Railways on a $4 million project, and expect a long-term market for their products. But they've also had to learn how to protect their intellectual capital and manage the financial details. Says Chief Financial Officer, Sharron Harrison, "in China, the language barrier and the great distance are extremely difficult."[13]

AFRICA

Look at the map in *Figure 5.1*. Africa is a continent increasingly featured in the news.[14] Although often the focus of reports on ethnic turmoil and civil strife in countries struggling along pathways to peace and development, Africa also stands as a region that beckons international business. Whereas foreign businesses tend to avoid the risk of trouble spots, they are giving increased attention to stable countries with growing economies. A *Wall Street Journal* analysis singles out Uganda, the Ivory Coast, Botswana, South Africa, and Ghana for their positive business prospects.[15] The same report also notes that the Congo, Nigeria, and Angola are especially rich in natural resources. On the discouraging side, the rates of economic growth

Figure 5.1 Africa, continent of opportunity.

There is a turnaround underway in the East African nation of Mozambique. This former Portuguese colony is emerging from years of civil war that began with its independence in 1975. A local entrepreneur now says, "Mozambicans, sick of war, want a working society." And economics plays an important role. The country is now home to billion-dollar infrastructure projects financed by development agencies. A railroad corridor from the capital of Maputo to Johannesburg, South Africa, is under construction. McDonald's, as you might expect, is already checking locations for possible restaurant sites.[16]

in sub-Saharan Africa are among the lowest in the world. Many parts of the region suffer from terrible problems of poverty and the ravishment of a continuing AIDS epidemic. Africa's need for sustained assistance from the industrialized countries, including business investments and foreign aid, is well established.

The Southern Africa Development Community (SADC) links 14 countries of southern Africa in trade and economic development efforts. The objectives of SADC include harmonizing and rationalizing strategies for sustainable development among member countries.[17] More generally, a report by two Harvard professors recently analyzed the foreign investment environment of Africa and concluded that the region's contextual problems are manageable.[18] "In fact they should be viewed as opportunities," says James A. Austin, one of the co-authors. He adds: "If a company has the managerial and organizational capabilities to deal with the region's unique business challenges, then it will be able to enter a promising market."[19]

Post-apartheid South Africa, in particular, has benefited from political revival. A country of 44 million people and great natural resources, South Africa is experiencing economic recovery and attracting outside investors. It already accounts for half the continent's purchasing power.[20] Foreign investments in the country increased sharply after minority white rule ended and Nobel-prize winner Nelson Mandela became the nation's first black president. The U.S.–South Africa Binational Commission has been established to strengthen trade ties and promote investments in the country. Coca-Cola is among the firms responding to the call. In announcing a $200 million investment package, the company's then-chairman Douglas Daft said after a meeting with South African President Thabo Mbeki: "We are very optimistic about this country's future and the economic development of African nations."[21]

INTERNATIONAL BUSINESS CHALLENGES

John Chambers, CEO of Cisco Systems, Inc., a major networking technology firm with a worldwide reach, says: "I will put my jobs anywhere in the world where the right infrastructure is, with the right educated workforce, with the right supportive government."[22] Cisco and other firms like it are **international businesses**. They conduct for-profit transactions of goods and services across national boundaries. International businesses of all types and sizes are the foundations of world trade. They are the engines

○ An **international business** conducts commercial transactions across national boundaries.

for moving raw materials, finished products, and specialized services from one country to another in the global economy. The *reasons for international business*, the forces that drive companies to the marketplaces of the world, include the search for:

→ Reasons for engaging in international business

- *Profits*—Global operations offer profit potential.
- *Customers*—Global operations offer new markets to sell products.
- *Suppliers*—Global operations offer access to needed raw materials.
- *Capital*—Global operations offer access to financial resources.
- *Labor*—global operations offer access to lower labor costs.

COMPETITIVE GLOBAL BUSINESS ENVIRONMENT

The global environment of international business is complex and dynamic—and highly competitive. Percy Barnevik, when chairman of the global corporation ABB, once said: "Too many people think you can succeed in the long run just by exporting from America to Europe. But you need to establish yourself locally and become, for example, a Chinese, Indonesian, or Indian citizen."[23]

At the level of the task environment, global business executives must master the demands of operating with worldwide suppliers, distributors, customers, and competitors. They must also understand and deal successfully with general environment conditions that present many differences in economic, legal-political, and educational systems, among other aspects of business infrastructure.

Regional economic cooperation is increasing, but differences in *economic systems* around the world must still be recognized. Countries like Russia, Poland, Estonia, and others of the former Soviet Union used to operate with *central-planning economies*. That is, the central government made basic economic decisions for an entire nation. Such decisions largely determined the allocations of raw materials, set product or service output quotas, regulated wages and prices, and even distributed qualified personnel among alternative employers. Now these countries are trying to establish viable *free-market economies* such as those common to Germany, Canada, the United States, and other industrialized nations. Although they may vary in exact form, free-market economies operate under capitalism and the laws of market supply and demand. As economies transform from central planning to free markets they often face controversies over rising prices, unemployment, business competition, and the challenges of **privatization**—the selling of state-owned enterprises into private ownership. Foreign investment is crucial to the success of these developments.[24]

○ **Privatization** is the selling of state-owned enterprises into private ownership.

○ In the **WTO** member nations agree to negotitate and resolve disputes about tariffs and trade restrictions.

○ **Protectionism** is a call for tariffs and favorable treatments to protect domestic firms from foreign competition.

Among the chief worldwide economic issues, the **World Trade Organization** (WTO) deserves special attention. The WTO is organized around an international accord setting up a mechanism for monitoring international trade and resolving disputes among countries. Member nations agree to ongoing negotiations and the reduction of tariffs and trade restrictions, but trading relationships are often complicated. **Protectionism** in the form of political calls for tariffs and favorable treatments to help protect domestic businesses from foreign competition is a common and complicating theme. Government leaders, such as the president of the United States, face internal political dilemmas involving the often-conflicting goals of seeking freer international trade while still protecting domestic industries. These dilemmas can make it difficult to reach international agreement on trade matters.

TAKE IT TO THE CASE!

Harley Davidson Motor Company
(www.harley–davidson.com)
Where Style and Strategy Travel the Globe

Harley Davidson motorcycles rule the road these days. Along with the popular "Harley"-branded clothing and accessories, the company is on a roll. It wasn't always that way. During the late 1970s, the firm's sales suffered in face of new and stiff competition from Japan. The U.S. International Trade Commission granted Harley short-term tariff protection from Japanese motorcycles in 1983; the firm regrouped, put its house in order, and hasn't looked back since. The Harley Owner's Group has over a half-million members worldwide. Harley has a solid market in Japan, where its bikes are a mark of prestige for their owners. Harley is secure in pursuing its mission with a clear sense of its market: "We fulfill dreams through the experience of motorcycling."[25]

Legal environments vary widely from place to place, and organizations are expected to abide by the laws of the host country in which they are operating. The more home and host-country laws differ, the more difficult and complex it is for international businesses to adapt to local ways. Common legal problems in international business involve incorporation practices and business ownership; negotiating and implementing contracts with foreign parties; protecting patents, trademarks, and copyrights; and handling foreign exchange restrictions. In the United States, executives of foreign-owned companies must worry about antitrust issues that prevent competitors from regularly talking to one another. They also must deal with a variety of special laws regarding occupational health and safety, equal employment opportunity, sexual harassment, and other matters—all constraints potentially different from those they find at home. Mitsubishi Motors, the Japanese auto manufacturer, came face-to-face with this in the form of sexual harassment and discrimination claims pursued by the U.S. Equal Employment Opportunity Commission on behalf of female employees at the firm's Normal, Illinois plant. [26]

People are essential resources of organizations, and as *educational systems* vary from one country to the next so too does the availability of labor. A survey of business leaders around the world reports that many are worried about actual or potential "human resource deficits."[27] They recognize that problems of illiteracy and the absence of appropriate skills in the available workforce can compromise operations. They also increasingly recognize the broader social challenge of becoming more actively involved in education and training to help build supplies of qualified labor in a host country.

REALITY Check 5.1

Deciding on Overseas Locations In a Deloitte & Touche Fantus survey, executives ranked access to a skilled and educated workforce as the number-1 criterion when evaluating overseas business locations. Take the on-line "Reality Check" to learn more about the criteria used in international location decisions.

FORMS OF INTERNATIONAL BUSINESS

The common forms of international business are shown in *Figure 5.2*. When a business is just getting started internationally, global sourcing, exporting/importing, and licensing and franchising are the usual ways to begin. These are *market entry strategies* that involve the sale of goods or services to foreign markets but do not require expensive capital

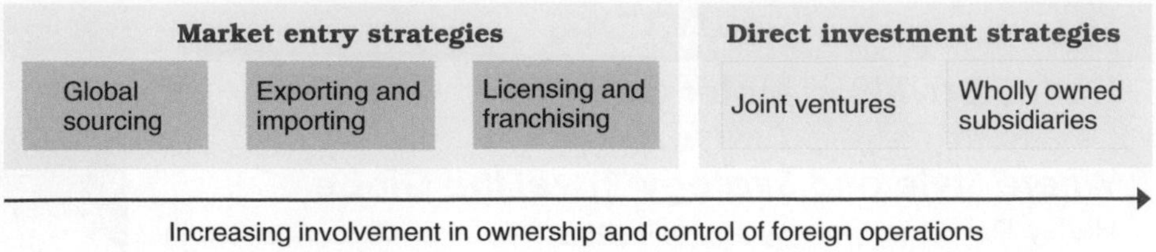

Market entry strategies			Direct investment strategies	
Global sourcing	Exporting and importing	Licensing and franchising	Joint ventures	Wholly owned subsidiaries

Increasing involvement in ownership and control of foreign operations

Figure 5.2 Common forms of international business—from market entry to direct investment strategies.

investments. Joint ventures and wholly owned subsidiaries are *direct investment strategies*. They require major capital commitments but create rights of ownership and control over operations in the foreign country.

Market Entry Strategies

○ In **global sourcing** materials or services are purchased around the world for local use.

A common first step into international business, **global sourcing** is the process of purchasing on a contract basis manufacturing components and/or services from points around the world. It is an international division of labor in which activities are performed in countries where they can be done well at the lowest cost. In manufacturing, global sourcing for cars assembled in the United States may mean purchasing windshields, instrument panels, seats, and fuel tanks from Mexico as well as electronics for antilock braking systems from Germany. In services, global sourcing is rapidly expanding in a variety of white-collar fields ranging from accounting and customer support to science research and technology development, and more. In all cases the global sourcing opportunity is to take advantage of international wage gaps and the availability of skilled labor by dispersing more and more work to foreign locations.

○ In **exporting** local products are sold abroad.

○ **Importing** is the process of acquiring products abroad and selling them in domestic markets.

A second form of international business involves **exporting**, selling locally made products in foreign markets, and/or **importing**, buying foreign-made products and selling them in domestic markets. Because the growth of export industries creates local jobs, governments often offer special advice and assistance to businesses that are trying to develop or expand their export markets. Many U.S. policymakers look to export industries, large and small, as one way to correct trade imbalances. One example is an export initiative that came by chance for Franklin Jacobs, founder of St. Louis–based Falcon Products, Inc., a commercial furniture company. While on a tour through Europe, he says, "I discovered that my products were a lot better and a lot cheaper" than those on the market there. An opportunist, Jacobs rented exposition space at the U.S. Embassy in London, shipped a container load of his furniture, received over US$200,000 in orders, and embarked on a new export initiative. The firm since grew to employ over 4,000 workers.[28]

○ A **licensing agreement** occurs when a firm pays a fee for the rights to make or sell another company's products.

○ **Franchising** provides the complete "package" of support needed to open a particular business.

A foreign firm may pay a fee and enter into a **licensing agreement** giving it the rights to make or sell another company's products. This international business approach typically grants access to a unique manufacturing technology, special patent, or trademark rights held by the licensor. It is one way to transfer technology from one country to another. **Franchising** is a form of licensing in which the licensee buys the complete "package" of support needed to open a particular business. As in domestic franchising agreements, firms like McDonald's, Wendy's, Subway, and others sell facility designs, equipment, product ingredients and recipes, and management systems to foreign investors, while retaining certain product and operating controls.

Direct Investment Strategies

To establish a direct investment presence in a foreign country, many firms enter into **joint ventures** or co-ownership arrangements that pool resources and share risks and control for business operations. This form of international business may be established by equity purchases and/or direct investments by a foreign partner in a local operation; it may also involve the creation of an entirely new business by a foreign and local partner. International joint ventures are "strategic alliances" that help participants to gain things through cooperation that otherwise would be difficult to achieve independently. This is a popular and expanding form of international business. In return for its investment in a local operation, for example, the outside or foreign partner often gains new markets and the assistance of a local partner who understands them. In return for its investment, the local partner often gains new technology as well as opportunities for its employees to learn new skills by working in joint operations. *Manager's Notepad 5.1* offers a checklist for choosing joint venture partners.[29]

○ A **joint venture** establishes operations in a foreign country through joint ownership with local partners.

A **wholly owned subsidiary** is a local operation completely owned and controlled by a foreign firm. Like joint ventures, foreign subsidiaries may be formed through direct investment in startup operations or through equity purchases in existing ones. When making such investments, foreign firms are clearly taking a business risk. They must be confident that they possess the expertise needed to manage and conduct business affairs successfully in the new environment. This is where prior experience gained through joint ventures can prove very beneficial.

○ A **wholly owned subsidiary** is a local operation completely owned by a foreign firm.

MULTINATIONAL CORPORATIONS

Many companies participate in international business in one form or another. A true **multinational corporation** (MNC) is a business firm with extensive international operations in more than one foreign country. Premier MNCs found in annual listings such as *Fortune* magazine's Global 500 include such global giants as General Electric, Exxon, and Wal-Mart from the United States; Mitsubishi, Toyota, and NTT DoCoMo of Japan; and DaimlerChrysler of Germany and Royal Dutch/Shell Group of the Netherlands and Great Britain. Also important on the

○ An **MNC** is a business with extensive international operations in more than one foreign country.

MANAGER'S NOTEPAD 5.1

Checklist for joint ventures

- Choose a partner familiar with your firm's major business.
- Choose a partner with a strong local workforce.
- Choose a partner with future expansion possibilities.
- Choose a partner with a strong local market for its own products.
- Choose a partner with shared interests in meeting customer needs.
- Choose a partner with good profit potential.
- Choose a partner in sound financial standing.

world scene are *multinational organizations* (MNOs)—like the International Federation of Red Cross and Red Crescent Societies, the United Nations, and the World Bank—whose nonprofit missions and operations span the globe.

TYPES OF MULTINATIONAL CORPORATIONS

A typical MNC operates in many countries but has corporate headquarters in one home or host country. Microsoft, Apple Computer, and McDonald's are among the ready examples. Although deriving substantial sales and profits from international sources, they and others like them typically also have strong national identifications. Yet, as the global economy grows more competitive, many multinationals are acting more like **transnational corporations**. They increasingly operate worldwide without being identified with one national home.[30] Executives with transnationals view the entire world as the domain for acquiring resources, locating production facilities, marketing goods and services, and for brand image. They seek total integration of global operations, try to operate across borders without home-based prejudices, make major decisions from a global perspective, distribute work among worldwide points of excellence, and employ senior executives from many different countries.[31] Nestlé is a good example in foods; Asea Brown Boveri (ABB) is another in diversified conglomerates. When one buys a Nestlé product in Brazil or has a neighbor working for ABB in Columbus, Ohio, who would know that both are actually registered Swiss companies?

○ A **transnational corporation** is an MNC that operates worldwide on a borderless basis.

PROS AND CONS OF MULTINATIONAL CORPORATIONS

In this time when consumer demand, resource supplies, product flows, and labor markets increasingly span national boundaries, the actions of MNCs are increasingly influential in the global economy. The United Nations has reported that MNCs hold one-third of the world's productive assets and control 70 percent of world trade. Furthermore, more than 90 percent of these MNCs are based in the Northern Hemisphere. While this may bring a sense of both accomplishment and future opportunity to business leaders, it can also be very threatening to countries and their domestic industries.

Host Country Issues

Both the global corporations and the countries that "host" their foreign operations should mutually benefit from any business relationship. *Figure 5.3* shows how things can and do go both right and wrong in MNC–host country relationships. The *potential host-country benefits* include larger tax bases, increased employment opportunities, technology transfers, the introduction of new industries, and the development of local resources. In respect to *potential host-country costs*, they sometimes complain that MNCs extract excessive profits, dominate the local economy, interfere with the local government, do not respect local customs and laws, fail to help domestic firms develop, hire the most talented of local personnel, and do not transfer their most advanced technologies.[32]

Of course executives of MNCs sometimes feel exploited as well in their relations with host countries. Consider China, for example, where major cultural, political, and economic differences confront the outsider.[33] Profits have proved elusive for some foreign investors; some have faced

The town of Shelby, North Carolina, knows just how cutthroat the global economy can be. The announcement that Kemet Electronics would lay off some 500 local employees and shift their jobs to Mexico hurt. Says Nancy Blackburn, a Kemet employee: "I worked all this time to get what I've got, and now it's gone. I thought I had found security."

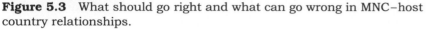

Figure 5.3 What should go right and what can go wrong in MNC–host country relationships.

government restrictions making it difficult to take profits out of the country; some have struggled to get needed raw materials, both domestically and from abroad.[34] The protection of intellectual property is an ongoing concern of foreign manufacturers, and managing relationships with government agencies can be very complicated. Although Motorola runs the largest foreign-owned operations inside China, for example, it must still negotiate business plans with the government. Says the firm's chief country representative K. P. To: "Even if you're wholly owned, you still need strong support from the government."[35]

Home Country Issues

MNCs may also encounter difficulties in the country where their headquarters are located. Even as many MNCs try to operate more globally, home-country governments and citizens tend to identify them with local and national interests. When an MNC outsources, cuts back, or closes a domestic operation to shift work to lower-cost international destinations, the loss of local jobs is controversial. Corporate decision makers are likely to be engaged by government and community leaders in critical debate about a firm's domestic social responsibilities. Home-country criticisms of MNCs include complaints about transferring jobs out of the country, shifting capital investments abroad, and engaging in corrupt practices in foreign settings.

ETHICAL ISSUES FOR MULTINATIONAL OPERATIONS

The ethical aspects of international business deserve special attention, and will be discussed further in Chapter 6 on managerial ethics and social responsibility. However, the issue of questionable practices must be raised in the international business context.

Corruption, engaging in illegal practice to further one's business interests, is a source of continuing controversy in the United States and for the managers of its MNCs. In 1977, the Foreign Corrupt Practices Act made it illegal for firms and their managers to engage in a variety of corrupt practices overseas, including giving bribes and excessive commissions to foreign officials in return for business favors. This law specifically bans payoffs to foreign officials to obtain or keep business, provides punishments for executives who know about or are involved in such activities, and requires detailed accounting records for international business transactions. Critics believe the law fails to recognize the "reality" of business as practiced in many foreign nations. They complain that American companies are at a competitive disadvantage because they can't offer the same

○ **Corruption** involves illegal practices to further one's business interests.

"deals" as competitors from other nations—deals that locals may regard as standard business practice.

○ **Sweatshops** employ workers at very low wages, for long hours, and in poor working conditions.

Sweatshops, business operations that employ workers at low wages for long hours and in poor working conditions, are another concern in the global business arena. Networks of outsourcing contracts are now common as manufacturers follow the world's low-cost labor supplies—countries like the Philippines, Sri Lanka, and Vietnam are popular destinations. Yet Nike, Inc., has learned from problems in Asia that a global company will be held publicly accountable for the work standards and employment practices of its foreign subcontractors. Facing activist criticism, the company revised its labor practices with recommendations from a review by the consulting firm Goodworks International. The firm now offers a special web site, Transparency 101, offering reports and audit results on its international labor practices. Chairman and CEO Phil Knight has pledged to extend its monitoring efforts to more than 750 manufacturing sites and contractors in 50 countries.[36]

○ **Child labor** is the full-time employment of children for work otherwise done by adults.

Child labor, the full-time employment of children for work otherwise done by adults, is another controversial issue. It has been made especially visible by activist concerns regarding the manufacture of handmade carpets in countries like Pakistan. Initiatives to eliminate child labor include an effort by the Rugmark Foundation to discourage purchases of carpets that do not carry its label. The "Rugmark" label is earned by a certification process to guarantee that a carpet manufacturer does not use illegal child labor.[37]

○ **Sustainable development** meets the needs of the present without hurting future generations.

Yet another ethical issue in international business relates to global concerns for environmental protection. Not only is the world's citizenry worried about disasters such as the pollution aftermath of the Gulf War, but more generally it expects global corporations to always respect the natural environment and pursue safe industrial practices. Industrial pollution of cities, hazardous waste, depletion of natural resources, and related concerns are now worldwide issues. The concept of **sustainable development** is a popular guideline advanced by activist groups. It is "development that meets the needs of the present without compromising the ability of future generations to meet their own needs."[38] As global corporate citizens, MNCs are increasingly expected to uphold high standards in dealing with sustainable development and protection of the natural

○ **ISO 14000** offers a set of certification standards for responsible environmental policies.

evironment—whenever and wherever they operate. The available guidelines for responsible environmental policies include **ISO 14000**, a set of certification standards developed by the International Standards Organization and recognized worldwide.

CULTURE AND GLOBAL DIVERSITY

○ **Culture** is a shared set of beliefs, values, and patterns of behavior common to a group of people.

Culture is the shared set of beliefs, values, and patterns of behavior common to a group of people. Anyone who has visited another country knows that cultural differences exist. **Culture shock**, the confusion and discomfort a person experiences when in an unfamiliar culture, is a reminder that many of these differences must be mastered just to travel comfortably around the world. But the important business and managerial implications of sociocultural differences must also be understood. An American exporter, for example, once went to see a Saudi Arabian official. He sat in the office with crossed legs and the sole of his shoe exposed—an unintentional sign of disrespect in the local culture. He passed documents to the host using his left hand, which Muslims

○ **Culture shock** is the confusion and discomfort a person experiences when in an unfamiliar culture.

consider unclean, and he refused to accept coffee when it was offered, suggesting criticism of the Saudi's hospitality. What was the price for these cultural miscues? He lost a $10 million contract to a Korean executive better versed in Arab ways.[39]

Ethnocentrism is the tendency to view one's culture as superior to others. It is surprisingly common international business, but it must be avoided. Local customs vary in too many ways for most of us to become true experts in the many cultures of our diverse world. Yet there are things we can do to respect differences, successfully conduct business abroad, and minimize culture shock. Self-awareness and reasonable sensitivity are the basic building blocks of cultural awareness, as suggested in *Manager's Notepad 5.2*.[40]

○ **Ethnocentrism** is the tendency to consider one's culture as superior to others.

POPULAR DIMENSIONS OF CULTURE

The first impressions of a traveler often include recognition and even "shock" over cultural differences. Among the popular dimensions of culture that should be understood are those relating to language, use of space, time orientation, religion, and the role of contracts.[41] When executives at British Airways surveyed international customers, for example, a simple lesson emerged—don't assume people from different cultures will have the same dining habits and preferences. Japanese, for example, commented that BA's food was "not bad for Westerners." They also pointed out that the white china dishes were similar to those used in Japanese hospitals and prisons. "The further away from our Western culture we go, the less satisfied our customers are," said one BA marketing manager; "people from other cultures have felt looked down upon." A major overhaul was undertaken to give the carrier a more truly global identity.[42]

Language

Language is a medium of culture. It provides access to the type of cultural understanding needed to conduct business and develop relationships. Not only do languages vary around the world; the same language (such as

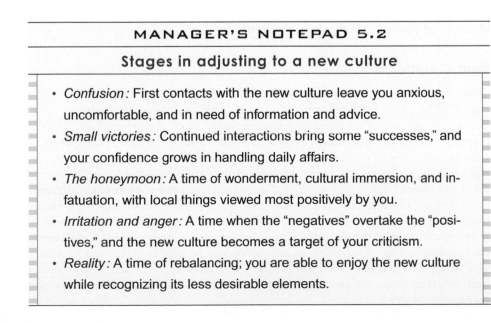

MANAGER'S NOTEPAD 5.2

Stages in adjusting to a new culture

- *Confusion:* First contacts with the new culture leave you anxious, uncomfortable, and in need of information and advice.
- *Small victories:* Continued interactions bring some "successes," and your confidence grows in handling daily affairs.
- *The honeymoon:* A time of wonderment, cultural immersion, and infatuation, with local things viewed most positively by you.
- *Irritation and anger:* A time when the "negatives" overtake the "positives," and the new culture becomes a target of your criticism.
- *Reality:* A time of rebalancing; you are able to enjoy the new culture while recognizing its less desirable elements.

English) can vary in usage from one country to the next (as it does from America to England to Australia). Although it isn't always possible to know a local language, such as Hungarian, it is increasingly usual in business dealings to find some common second language in which to communicate, such as English, French, German, or Spanish. The importance of good foreign language training is critical for the truly global manager. When Larry Johnston arrived in Paris to head up GE's medical equipment operations in Europe, the Middle East, and Africa, the first thing he did was study intensive French for a month. "I went from 7 A.M. to 8 P.M. and learned enough to converse," he says.[43]

○ **Low-context cultures** emphasize communication via spoken or written words.

According to anthropologist Edward T. Hall, there are systematic and important differences in the way cultures utilize language in communication.[44] He describes **low-context cultures** as those in which most communication takes place via the written or spoken word. In places like the United States, Canada, and Germany, for example, the message is delivered in very precise wording. One has to listen and read carefully to best understand what the message sender intends. Things are quite different in **high-context cultures**, where much communication takes place through nonverbal and situational cues, in addition to the written or spoken word. In such settings the words communicate only a (sometimes small) part of the message. The rest must be interpreted from the situational "context"—body language, physical setting, and even the past relationships among those involved. This process is often time consuming and very deliberate. In high-context Japan, for example, much emphasis is given to social settings in which potential partners develop a relationship and get to know one another; once this is accomplished, future business dealings can then be formed.

○ **High-context cultures** rely on nonverbal and situational cues as well as spoken or written words in communication.

Interpersonal Space

Hall considers the use of interpersonal space as one of the important "silent languages" of culture.[45] Arabs and many Latin Americans, for example, prefer to communicate at much closer distances than is standard in American practice. Misunderstandings are possible if one businessperson moves back as another moves forward to close the interpersonal distance between them. Some cultures of the world also value space more highly than others. Americans tend to value large and private office space. The Japanese are highly efficient in using space; even executive offices are likely to be shared in major corporations.

Time Orientation

Time orientation is another dimension of the silent language of culture.[46] The way people approach and deal with time tends to vary widely. Mexicans, for example, may specify *hora Americana* on invitations if they want guests to appear at the appointed time; otherwise, it may be impolite to arrive punctually for a scheduled appointment. When working in Vietnam, by contrast, punctuality is important and communicates respect for one's host.[47] Hall describes **monochronic cultures** in which people tend to do one thing at a time, such as schedule a meeting and give the visitor one's undivided attention for the allotted time.[48] This is standard American business practice. In **polychronic cultures**, by contrast, time is used to accomplish many different things at once. The American visitor to an Egyptian client may be frustrated by continued interruptions as people flow in and out of the office and various transactions are made.

○ In **monochronic cultures** people tend to do one thing at a time.

○ In **polychronic cultures** time is used to accomplish many different things at once.

Religion

Religion is also important as a cultural variable, and one should always be aware of religious traditions when visiting and working in other cultures. Religion is a major influence on many people's lives, and its impact may extend to practices regarding dress, food, and interpersonal behavior. It is a source of ethical and moral teaching, with associated personal and institutional implications. "Islamic banks" in the Middle East, for example, service their customers without any interest charges to remain consistent with teachings of the *Koran*. The traveler and businessperson should be sensitive to the rituals, holy days, and other expectations associated with religions in foreign countries. When working with Muslims in Malaysia, for example, it is polite to schedule business dinners after 8 P.M. This allows them to complete the evening prayer before dining. Similarly, it should be remembered that the Islamic holy month of Ramadan is a dawn-to-dusk time of fasting.

Democracy, private enterprise, and rural development are contributing to a turnaround in many of Africa's national economies. SBC Communications and Telekom Malaysia are joint investors in Telkom South Africa. Says a Senegalese aid worker, "Our societies are rich with boundless energy and systems that work."

Role of Agreements

Cultures vary in their use of contracts and agreements. In the United States a contract is viewed as a final and binding statement of agreements. This tends to hold true in general with low-context cultures. In other parts of the world with high-context cultures, such as China, the written contract may be viewed as more of a starting point. Once in place, it will continue to emerge and be modified as the parties work together over time. McDonald's found this out when the Chinese government ignored the firm's lease on a restaurant site in downtown Beijing and tore down the building to make room for a development project. In the United States, contracts are expected to be in writing; requesting a written agreement from an Indonesian who has given his "word" may be quite disrespectful.

VALUES AND NATIONAL CULTURES

As companies go global, their managers must become more global in viewpoints, experiences, and cultural appreciation. A German sales manager who travels frequently in the United States on business, for example, told a *Wall Street Journal* reporter that it took him a long time to understand the American culture. Speaking five languages, he was surprised at how few of his American counterparts had traveled abroad and at how generally "nonglobal" they were. But, he enjoyed the "friendliness and openness" of his American counterparts, as well as their tendency to "make quick decisions." Similarly, when Bob Hendry was sent to Germany to head General Motors' Adam Opel Division, he encountered work-style differences. The American emphasis on short-term monthly and quarterly performance, for example, clashed with the German focus on one-year and longer results.[49]

It is helpful to have a framework for understanding how basic cultural differences can influence management and organizational practices. Geert Hofstede, a Dutch scholar and international management consultant, studied personnel from a U.S.-based MNC operating in 40 countries. First published in his book *Culture's Consequences: International Differences in Work-Related Values*, his research offers one framework for understanding the management implications of broad differences in national cultures.[50] *Figure 5.4* shows how selected countries rank on the five dimensions Hofstede now uses in his model.

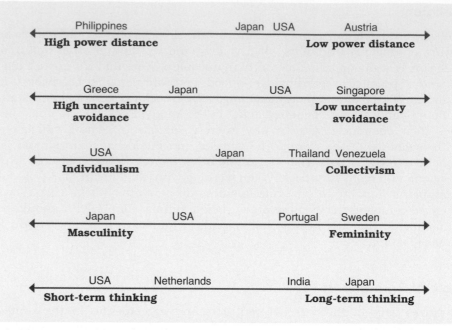

Figure 5.4 How countries compare on Hofstede's dimensions of national culture.

Hofstede's dimensions of national cultures →

1. *Power distance*—the degree to which a society accepts or rejects the unequal distribution of power in organizations and the institutions of society.
2. *Uncertainty avoidance*—the degree to which a society tolerates risk and situational uncertainties.
3. *Individualism-collectivism*—the degree to which a society emphasizes individual accomplishment and self-interests, versus collective accomplishments and the good of groups.
4. *Masculinity-femininity*—the degree to which a society values assertiveness and material success, versus feelings and concern for relationships.
5. *Time orientation*—the degree to which a society emphasizes short-term considerations versus greater concern for the future.[51]

Hofstede's framework helps identify useful managerial implications from these potential cultural differences. For example, workers from high power-distance cultures, such as Singapore, can be expected to show great respect to seniors and those in authority. In high uncertainty-avoidance cultures, employment practices that increase job security are likely to be favored. In highly individualistic societies (the United States ranked as the most individualistic in Hofstede's sample), workers may be expected to emphasize self-interests more than group loyalty. Outsiders may find that the workplace in more masculine societies, such as Japan, displays more rigid gender stereotypes. Also, corporate strategies in more long-term cultures are likely to be just that—more long-term oriented.

UNDERSTANDING CULTURAL DIVERSITY

Consider this scene.[52] Interbrew SA of Belgium purchased 50 percent ownership in Oriental Brewery of South Korea, bringing four western senior managers into the Korean operation. "It was a new experience," said

Ms. Park, one of Oriental's local staff. It was also a clash of two different business cultures. The newcomers wanted locals to express their ideas and work toward clear objectives; the locals were used to following orders and working through relationships. Some two years into the process of learning how to work together, Ms. Park finally agreed that the western and local staff were making progress toward building Oriental Brewery up to its performance potential.

Stepping into cross-cultural work and managerial situations of any sort is complicated; those associated with mergers and acquisitions are especially so. It takes all of one's understanding and skills to best deal with the challenges. In addition to the descriptions of popular and national cultures already discussed, the integrative framework of management scholar Fons Trompenaars can be helpful. In research with some 15,000 respondents from 47 countries, he identifies systematic cultural differences in the ways relationships are handled among people, attitudes toward time, and attitudes toward the environment.[53] By better understanding these patterns of difference, he suggests we can improve our cross-cultural work effectiveness.

Relationships with People

According to Trompenaars's framework, there are five ways in which people differ culturally in how they handle relationships with one another. They include the individualism-collectivism notion just discussed, as well as additional considerations:

1. *Universalism vs. particularism*—the degree to which a culture emphasizes rules and consistency in relationships or accepts flexibility and the bending of rules to fit circumstances.
2. *Individualism vs. collectivism*—the degree to which a culture emphasizes individual freedoms and responsibilities in relationships or focuses more on group interests and consensus.
3. *Neutral vs. affective*—the degree to which a culture emphasizes objectivity and reserved detachment in relationships or allows more emotionality and expressed feelings.
4. *Specific vs. diffuse*—the degree to which a culture emphasizes focused and in-depth relationships or broader and more superficial ones.
5. *Achievement vs. prescription*—the degree to which a culture emphasizes an earned or performance-based status in relationships or awards status based on social standing and nonperformance factors.

Attitudes Toward Time

Attitudes toward time in the Trompenaars framework differ in the relative emphasis given to the present versus the past and future. In cultures that take a *sequential view*, time is considered a continuous and passing series of events. This somewhat casual view of time may be represented by a circle and the notion that time is recycling, in the sense that a moment passed will return again. In cultures that take a *synchronic view*, by contrast, time takes on a greater sense of urgency. It is more linear, with an interrelated past, present, and future. Pressures to resolve problems quickly so that time won't be "lost" are more likely in synchronic than sequential cultures.

www.quicksilver aircraft.com

Quicksilver Enterprises, Inc., a California maker of popular ultra-light airplanes, decided to license a Brazilian distributor to build and sell the planes in that country. But six months after the Brazilians had learned how to build, fly, and fix the planes, royalty payments to Quicksilver stopped. The Brazilian company claimed it had changed the design and created a new plane. Quicksilver took a financial loss on the deal.

Attitudes Toward the Environment

Trompenaars also recognizes that cultures vary in their approach to the environment. In cultures that are *inner-directed*, people tend to view themselves as quite separate from nature. They are likely to consider the environment as something to be controlled or used for personal advantage. In cultures that are *outer-directed*, people tend to view themselves as part of nature. They are more likely to try and blend with or go along with the environment than to try to control it.

MANAGEMENT ACROSS CULTURES

○ **Comparative management** studies how management practices differ among countries and cultures.

The management process—planning, organizing, leading, and controlling—is as relevant to international operations as to domestic ones. Yet, as the preceding discussion of culture should suggest, these functions must be applied appropriately from one country and culture to the next. **Comparative management** is the study of how management systematically differs among countries and/or cultures. Today we recognize the importance of learning about how management is practiced around the world. Competition and the global economy have given rise to *global managers*, defined earlier as managers comfortable with cultural diversity, quick to find opportunities in unfamiliar settings, and able to marshal economic, social, technological, and other forces for the benefit of the organization.[54] Says Robin Willett, Group Deputy Chairman of Willett Systems, Ltd. of the United Kingdom: "Our aim has always been to be a truly global company, not simply an exporter. We work very hard at developing and maintaining an international mindset that is shared by everyone—from senior management to staff."[55] Global managers, simply put, apply the management functions successfully across national and cultural borders.

PLANNING AND CONTROLLING

The complexity of the international operating environment makes global planning and controlling especially challenging. Picture a home office somewhere in the United States, say Chicago. Foreign operations are scattered in Asia, Africa, South America, and Europe. Planning must somehow link the home office and foreign affiliates, while taking into account different environments, cultures, and needs. Increasingly, new technology facilitates the planning and control of global operations through vastly improved communications systems. Computer-based global networks allow home and field offices to share databases, electronically transfer documents, and even hold conferences and make group decisions through computer links and video conferencing.

○ **Political risk** is the possible loss of investment or control over a foreign asset because of political changes in the host country.

Firms with investments in foreign countries must also factor into their planning the risks of doing business across political and economic borders. One risk is *currency* risk. Companies like McDonald's, for example, must eventually convert their foreign currency earnings into dollars. But, the value of the dollar against other currencies varies over time and is not always easy to predict. McDonald's earnings fell by 5 percent in 2000, as the dollar's value relative to the Euro declined dramatically in just a few months' time. Another risk is **political risk**, the potential loss of one's investment in or managerial control over a foreign asset because of political changes in the host country. In general, the major threats of political risk come from social instabilities as a result of ethnic or other differences, armed conflicts and military disruptions, shifting government systems through elections or forced takeovers, and new laws and economic policies.

Political-risk analysis is a planning process that forecasts the probability of these and other political events that can threaten the security of a foreign investment. The stakes can be quite high. It is obvious, for example, that foreign investors suffered in the political turmoil of Iraq's invasion of Kuwait. It may be less obvious that in a single day it was possible for a U.S. firm in Mexico to lose close to one-third of its foreign assets overnight. How? Because the Mexican government decided to allow its currency, the peso, to float in the international money markets. The net result was a loss in the value of Mexican assets valued in U.S. dollars. Not all multinationals were caught totally by surprise. Firms that had done their political-risk analysis well took protective measures ahead of time.

○ **Political risk analysis** forecasts how political events may impact foreign investments.

ORGANIZING AND LEADING

The same factors that challenge the planning and controlling functions in the international arena also affect managerial efforts to organize and lead. The forces of globalization are complex indeed. For Caltex, it has meant closing a corporate headquarters in Dallas, Texas, and moving to Singapore. It has meant setting up a web site development division in South Africa and an accounting division in the Philippines. The general manager of the firm's new Manila operation says: "As technology and communication improve, we are scattering centers of excellence around the world."[56]

A rule of thumb for staffing international operations can be stated this way: "Hire competent locals, use competent locals, and listen to competent locals." But in addition, global success also frequently depends on the work of **expatriates**, employees who live and work in foreign countries on short-term or long-term assignments. For progressive firms, assigning home office personnel to foreign operations is increasingly viewed as a strategic opportunity.[57] Not only does this offer the individuals challenging work experiences, it also helps bring into the executive suite culturally

○ An **expatriate** lives and works in a foreign country.

DIVERSITY (www.Wal-Mart Stores, Inc.)
American Executive Finds the Way to China

Wal-Mart has gone international. In just over ten years, the firm has gone from America's #1 retailer to a presence on the world stage. Operating over 1,000 stores in ten countries, Wal-Mart's international division is a source of new career opportunities. Joe Hatfield, a 26-year Wal-Mart veteran heads the firm's push into China. Some 4,000 associates staff five Super Centers and a Sam's Club in China, and more are in the works. In China, Hatfield has had to learn how to deal with both China's markets (he spends a lot of time wandering the local shops to check preferences) and the Chinese government (he leads efforts to contribute to community projects). Says Hatfield: "We are not just going to march all over China."[58]

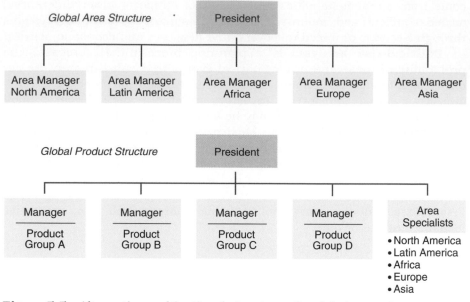

Figure 5.5 Alternative multinational structures for global operations.

aware managers with truly global horizons and interpersonal networks of global contacts. Of course, not everyone performs well in an overseas assignment. Among the foundations for success are such personal attributes as a high degree of cultural awareness and sensitivity, a real desire to live and work abroad, family flexibility and support, as well as technical competence in one's job.

A common organizing approach for organizations just getting started in international business is to appoint a vice president or other senior manger to oversee all foreign operations. This may be fine for limited international activity, but as global involvement expands it usually requires a more complex arrangement. The global area *structure* shown in *Figure 5.5* arranges production and sales functions into separate geographical units. This allows activities in major areas of the world to be given special executive attention. Another organizing option is the global *product structure*, also shown in the figure. It gives worldwide responsibilities to product group mangers, who are assisted by area specialists on the corporate staff. These specialists provide expert guidance on the unique needs of various countries or regions. When Carly Fiorina became CEO of Hewlett-Packard, for example, she found the firm losing touch with its international customers. Wanting to make it easier for them to buy HP products from anywhere in the world, she reorganized the firm into global sales and marketing groups to better match global services with local needs.[59]

ARE MANAGEMENT THEORIES UNIVERSAL?

Management practices in North America and Western Europe frequently have been used as models around the world. Increasingly, however, a significant question is asked—"Are management theories universal?" Geert Hofstede, whose framework for understanding national cultures was introduced earlier, believes they should *not* be applied universally.[60] He worries that many of these theories are ethnocentric and fail to take into account cultural differences. For example, he argues that the

American emphasis on participation in leadership reflects the culture's moderate stance on power distance. National cultures with lower scores, such as Sweden and Israel, are characterized by even more "democratic" leadership initiatives. France and some Asian countries with higher power-distance scores seem less concerned with participative leadership.

Hofstede also points out that the motivation theories of American scholars are value laden, with an emphasis on individual performance. He considers this viewpoint consistent with the high individualism found in Anglo-American countries such as the United States, Canada, and the United Kingdom. Elsewhere, where values are more collectivist, the theories may be less applicable. Even a common value, such as the desire for increased humanization of work, may lead in different management directions. Until recently, practices in the United States largely emphasized designing jobs for individuals. Elsewhere in the world, such as in Sweden, the emphasis has been on designing jobs to be performed by groups of workers.

Consider as well the implications of transferring to the United States and other Western countries some of the Japanese management practices that have attracted great interest over the years.[61] These include lifetime employment, gradual career advancement, collective decision making, and quality emphasis. All have been associated in one way or another with past successes in Japanese industry.[62] But as interesting as the practices may be, any transfers of practice must factor into account the distinctive Japanese cultural traditions in which they emerged—such as long-term orientation, collectivism, and high power distance.[63] It should be noted also that management and organizational practices are changing in Japan, some argue toward the Western models, as its businesses adjust to the demands of a new economy and shifting trends in social values.[64]

Context also counts in evaluating management and organizational practices. In Japan, *keiretsu* have been part of the success stories. They are long-term industry alliances or business groups that link together various businesses—manufacturers, suppliers, and finance companies—to attain common interests. The companies involved often own stock in one another; their boards of directors often overlap; they often do business with one another on a preferential basis. Not only must the influence of *keiretsu* on Japanese business success be recognized, it may be considered an unfair business practice in other countries such as the antitrust-conscious United States.

What Happens When the Expatriate Comes Home? International experience is supposed to be a big plus in today's corporations. But in research by the center for Global Assignments, 60 percent of returning American expatriates reported that the adjustment to coming home was harder than going overseas. Take the on-line "Reality Check" to learn more about executive experiences with international assignments.

○ A *keiretsu* is a group of Japanese manufacturers, suppliers, and finance firms with common interests.

GLOBAL ORGANIZATIONAL LEARNING

In the dynamic and ever-expanding global economy, cultural awareness is helping to facilitate more informed transfers of management and organizational practices. We live at a fortunate time when managers around the world are realizing they have much to share with and learn from one another. Global organizational learning is a timely and relevant theme. This point is evident in the following words of Kenichi Ohmae, noted Japanese management consultant and author of *The Borderless World*:

Companies can learn from one another, particularly from other excellent companies, both at home and abroad. The industrialized world is becoming increasingly homogeneous in terms of customer needs and social infrastructure, and only truly excellent companies can compete effectively in the global marketplace.[65]

Yes, we do have a lot to learn from one another. Yet it must be learned with full appreciation of the constraints and opportunities of different cultures and country environments. Like the American management practices before them, Japanese approaches and those from other cultures must be studied and adapted for local use very carefully. This applies to the way management is practiced in Mexico, Korea, Indonesia, Hungary, or any other part of the world. As Hofstede states, "Disregard of other cultures is a luxury only the strong can afford. . . . [The] consequent increase in cultural awareness represents an intellectual and spiritual gain. And as far as management theories go, cultural relativism is an idea whose time has come."[66]

The best approach to comparative management and global management learning is an alert, open, inquiring, and always cautious one. It is important to identify both the potential merits of management practices found in other countries *and* the ways cultural variables may affect their success or failure when applied elsewhere. We can and should be looking for new ideas to stimulate change and innovation. But we should hesitate to accept any practice, no matter how well it appears to work somewhere else, as a universal prescription to action. Indeed, the goal of comparative management studies is not to provide definitive answers but to help develop creative and critical thinking about the way managers around the world do things, and about whether they can and should be doing them better.

@
Get Connected!

Read the Universal Declaration of Human Rights adopted by the United Nations General Assembly on December 10, 1948.

STUDY Guide

The Chapter 5 Study Guide will help you review chapter content, prepare for examinations, and further build your career readiness. The *Summary* briefly highlights answers to questions first posed in the chapter opening Planning Ahead section. The list of *Key Terms* allows you to double check your familiarity with basic concepts and definitions. *Self-Test 5* gives you the opportunity to test your basic comprehension of chapter content using sample test questions. Suggestions offered as *Career Readiness Activities* direct your attention to relevant sections of the end-of-text Career Readiness Workbook, as well as to special Electronic Resources on the *Management 7e* web site.

SUMMARY

What are international management challenges of globalization?

- International management is practiced in organizations that conduct business in more than one country.
- Global managers are informed about international developments, transnational in outlook, competent in working with people from different cultures, and always aware of regional developments in a changing world.
- The global economy is making the diverse countries of the world increasingly interdependent regarding resource supplies, product markets, and business competition.
- The global economy is now strongly influenced by regional developments that involve growing economic integration in Europe, the Americas, and Asia, and the economic emergence of Africa.

What are the forms and opportunities of international business?

- Five forms of international business are global sourcing, exporting and importing, licensing and franchising, joint ventures, and wholly owned subsidiaries.
- The market entry strategies of global sourcing, exporting/importing, and licensing are common for firms wanting to get started internationally.
- Direct investment strategies to establish joint ventures or wholly owned subsidiaries in foreign countries represent substantial commitments to international operations.

What are multinational corporations and what do they do?

- Global operations are influenced by important environmental differences among the economic, legal-political, and educational systems of countries.

139

- A multinational corporation (MNC) is a business with extensive operations in more than one foreign country.
- True MNCs are global firms with worldwide missions and strategies that earn a substantial part of their revenues abroad.
- MNCs offer potential benefits to host countries in broader tax bases, new technologies, employment opportunities; MNCs can also disadvantage host countries if they interfere in local government, extract excessive profits, and dominate the local economy.
- The Foreign Corrupt Practices Act prohibits American MNCs from engaging in corrupt practices in their global operations.

What is culture and how does it relate to global diversity?

- Management and global operations are affected by the dimensions of popular culture, including language, space perception, time perception, religion, and the nature of contracts.
- Management and global operations are affected by differences in national cultures, including Hofstede's dimensions of power distance, uncertainty avoidance, individualism-collectivism, masculinity-femininity, and time orientation.
- Differences among the world's cultures may be understood in respect to how people handle relationships with one another, their attitudes toward time, and their attitudes toward the environment.

How do management practices and learning transfer across cultures?

- The management process must be used appropriately and applied with sensitivity to local cultures and situations.
- The field of comparative management studies how management is practiced around the world and how management ideas are transferred from one country or culture to the next.
- Cultural values and management practices should be consistent with one another; practices that are successful in one culture may work less well in others.
- The concept of global management learning has much to offer as the "borderless" world begins to emerge and as the management practices of diverse countries and cultures become more visible.

KEY TERMS

Child labor (p. 128)

Comparative management (p. 134)

Corruption (p. 127)

Culture (p. 128)

Culture shock (p. 128)

Ethnocentrism (p. 129)

Euro (p. 117)

European Union (p. 117)

Expatriates (p. 135)

Exporting (p. 124)

Franchising (p. 124)

Global economy (p. 116)

Global manager (p. 117)

Global sourcing (p. 124)

Globalization (p. 116)

High-context culture (p. 130)

Importing (p. 124)

International business (p. 121)

International management (p. 117)

ISO 14000 (p. 128)

Joint ventures (p. 125)

Keiretsu (p. 137)

Licensing agreement (p. 124)

Low-context culture (p. 130)

Maquiladora (p. 118)

Monochronic cultures (p. 130)

Multinational corporation (p. 125)

NAFTA (p. 118)

Political risk (p. 134)

Political-risk analysis (p. 135)

Polychronic cultures (p. 130)

Privatization (p. 122)

Protectionism (p. 122)

Sustainable development (p. 128)

Sweatshops (p. 128)

Transnational corporation (p. 126)

Wholly owned subsidiary (p. 125)

World Trade Organization (p. 122)

SELF-TEST 5

Take this test here or on-line much as you would in a normal classroom situation. It should offer you a good way to check your basic comprehension of chapter material. Answers may be found at the end of the book.

MULTIPLE-CHOICE QUESTIONS:

1. In addition to new markets, the possible business reasons for going international include the search for _____.
   (a) political risk (b) protectionism (c) lower labor costs (d) corrupt practices

2. A _____ is a foreign firm that operates with special privileges in Mexico in return for agreeing to employ Mexican labor.
   (a) *keiretsu* (b) *maquiladora* (c) *jacaranda* (d) *zapatista*

3. A common international direct investment strategy is _____.
   (a) exporting (b) joint venture (c) licensing (d) global sourcing

4. A government making decisions such as the distribution of labor and other resources to businesses is operating a _____ economy.
   (a) free-market (b) competitive (c) central-planning (d) supply-side

5. If a new government seizes all foreign assets in the country, the loss to foreign firms is a _____ risk of international business.
   (a) multinational (b) political (c) competitive (d) social

6. In _____ cultures, members tend to do one thing at a time; in _____ cultures, members tend to do many things at once.
   (a) monochronic, polychronic (b) ethnocentric, geocentric
   (c) collectivist, individualist (d) totalitarian, democratic

7. _____ is the process of selling government-owned assets, such as a state-owned company, to private buyers.
(a) Privatization (b) Capitalization (c) Incorporation (d) Licensing

8. A firm operating with individual vice presidents for Asia, Africa, and Europe would be using a global _____ structure.
(a) product (b) functional (c) area (d) matrix

9. In Hofstede's study of national cultures, America was found to be the most _____ among the 40 countries in his sample.
(a) individualist (b) collectivist (c) masculine (d) long term

10. A visitor who takes offense at a foreign custom and considers it inferior to his or her own culture is acting in a(n) way _____.
(a) individualistic (b) high-context (c) monochronic (d) enthnocentric

TRUE-FALSE QUESTIONS:

11. International business is something only large businesses pursue.   T   F

12. Businesses from countries within the EU benefit from agreements to remove barriers to cross-border trade among member nations.   T   F

13. The only Asian countries of economic importance are Japan and China.   T   F

14. Joint ventures are primarily designed to help the local partner gain technology and expertise from the foreign partner.   T   F

15. A company that moves away from a national identity and seeks total integration of global operations is a transnational company.   T   F

16. Religion is one aspect of culture that should not be considered in global business dealings.   T   F

17. American management theories have been found to be universally applicable around the world.   T   F

18. The notion of sustainable development means that a business stays profitable in a foreign country by following corrupt practices.   T   F

19. In a low-context culture like that of the United States, words tend to communicate the whole meaning of a message.   T   F

20. *Keiretsu* are long-term alliances that link Japanese businesses to one another.   T   F

SHORT-RESPONSE QUESTIONS:

21. Why is NAFTA important for American businesses?

22. Why do host countries sometimes complain about the operations of MNCs within their borders?

23. Why is the "power-distance" dimension of national culture important in management?

24. Choose a region of the world (Europe, the Americas, Africa, Asia) and describe its significance in the global economy.

APPLICATION QUESTION:

25. Kim has just returned from her first business trip to Japan. While there, she was impressed with the use of quality circles and work teams. Now back in Iowa, she would like to start the same practices in her canoe manufacturing company of 75 employees. Based on the discussion of culture and management in this chapter, what advice would you offer Kim?

CAREER readiness ACTIVITIES

Recommended learning activities from the end-of-text Career Readiness Workbook for this chapter include:

Career Advancement Portfolio
- Individual writing and group presentation assignments based on any of the following activities:

Case for Critical Thinking
- Harley Davidson—Making a Case for Protection

Intergrative Learning Activities
- Research Project 3—Foreign Investment in America
- Integrative Case—Outback Steakhouse, Inc.
- Integrative Case—Richard Branson Meets the New Economy

Exercises in Teamwork
- What Do You Value in Work? (#7)
- Gender Differences in Management (#20)
- The Best Job Design (#23)

Self-Assessments
- Cultural Attitudes Inventory (#5)
- Global Readiness Index (#6)
- Time Orientation (#24)

ELECTRONIC RESOURCES

@ GET CONNECTED! Don't forget to take full advantage of the on-line support for *Management 7/e.*
- Chapter 5 On-line Study Guide
- Chapter 5 Self-test Answers
- Chapter 5 E-Resource Center

6

Ethical behavior and social responsibility

Planning
ahead

GETTING CONNECTED

Goldman Environmental Prize—*Help Make this World a Better Place*
Each year six "environmental heroes" from the world's continental regions receive prestigious awards from the Goldman Environmental Foundation for their outstanding work as grassroots environmentalists. The foundation annually contributes $750,000 to fund the Goldman Environmental Prize for these heroes. Recent recipients have included:

- A Mexican peasant leader whose struggles against one of the world's largest lumber giants resulted in his imprisonment and torture—his prize had to be received in jail.
- A Russian lawyer who is breaking new legal ground as she pleads precedent-setting environmental cases in Russia.
- An ethnobotanist from Madagascar who is fighting to save the island's forests, which are rich with potentially life-saving drugs.
- A writer in China who publicly criticizes the Three Gorges Dam project now under construction—she was banned from free movement around the country.

The list of past winners goes on—an aboriginal woman fighting an Australian uranium mine; a Cameroonian lawyer protecting regional rainforests; a Burmese exposing environmental and human rights abuses. Each winner receives a "no strings attached" award of $125,000.

At a renunion, 42 recipients pledged to join forces in fighting what they called "the destructive impacts of economic globalization." Goldman activists are concerned about harmful effects on health and living conditions, as well as the environment. They pledge to put more pressure on local governments and to continue campaigning publicly against multinational corporations to explain their activities.

Foundation president Richard Goldman says: "During the past ten years, the recipients of the prize have opened our eyes to the obstacles and risks faced by individuals pursuing environmental interests worldwide. We believe that bringing attention to their issues raises the credibility of these individuals and offers them personal protection."

Nominations for the Goldman Environmental Prize are submitted anonymously from a network of 21 environmental organizations spanning 50 nations. The awards are recognized by 113 heads of state worldwide.[1]

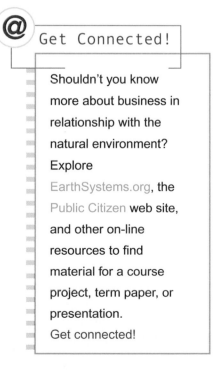

@ **Get Connected!**

Shouldn't you know more about business in relationship with the natural environment? Explore EarthSystems.org, the Public Citizen web site, and other on-line resources to find material for a course project, term paper, or presentation.
Get connected!

www.manhattan.edu

Manhattan College is committed to ethics, ethical behavior, and ethics training. Through its Center for Professional Ethics, the college offers training in the recognition of ethical problems, development of skills for dealing with them, and the building of ethical climates in organizational cultures.

The good news is that some organizations have added a new job title—Vice President of the Environment—to their executive suites. These senior managers work on everything from a company's recycling program to long-term corporate environmental policies. Global warming, global sustainability, and environmental protection are all on the agenda as organizations pursue what some call "the greening of the bottom line."[2] More and more companies are engaging in social outreach and including environmental issues and social concerns among top corporate goals.[3] Says the CEO of one large firm: "A lot of the blue-chip multinationals have a long tradition of charitable and community programs that date back to their foundation. What is new is that corporate responsibility is being written into the business model."[4] Quad/Graphics, Inc. founded by Harry V. Quadrucci, is a good example. The company values state: "It is our duty to conserve the resources of the planet and our privilege to contribute to our communities through philanthropic activities and charitable contributions."[5]

The bad news is that not all from the corporate world are always as positive examples. Consider these actual reports from past news stories. *Item:* Firm admits lowering phone contract bid after receiving confidential information from an insider that an initial bid "was not good enough to win." *Item:* Company admits overcharging consumers and insurers more than $13 million for repairs to damaged rental cars. *Item:* Executives get prison terms for selling adulterated apple juice; the juice labeled "100% fruit juice" was actually a blend of synthetic ingredients.

And that's not all. Consider these words from a commencement address delivered a few years ago at a well-known school of business administration. "Greed is all right," the speaker said. "Greed is healthy. You can be greedy and still feel good about yourself." The students, it is reported, greeted these remarks with laughter and applause. The speaker was Ivan Boesky, once considered the "king of the arbitragers."[6] It wasn't long after his commencement speech that Boesky was arrested, tried, convicted, and sentenced to prison for trading on inside information.

It is time to get serious about the moral aspects and social implications of decision making in organizations. In your career and in the work of any manager the ultimate task must be considered to be more than simply meeting performance expectations. Performance goals must always be achieved through ethically and socially responsible action. The following reminder from Desmond Tutu, archbishop of Capetown, South Africa, and former winner of the Nobel Peace Prize, is applicable to managers everywhere:

○ **Ethics** sets standards as to what is good or bad, or right or wrong in one's conduct.

You are powerful people. You can make this world a better place where business decisions and methods take account of right and wrong as well as profitability. . . . You must take a stand on important issues: the environment and ecology, affirmative action, sexual harassment, racism and sexism, the arms race, poverty, the obligations of the affluent West to its less-well-off sisters and brothers elsewhere.[7]

WHAT IS ETHICAL BEHAVIOR?

○ **Ethical behavior** is accepted as "right" or "good" in the context of a governing moral code.

For our purposes, **ethics** can be defined as the code of moral principles that sets standards of good or bad, or right or wrong, in one's conduct and thereby guides the behavior of a person or group.[8] Ethics provide principles to guide behavior and help people make moral choices among alternative courses of action. In practice, **ethical behavior** is that which is accepted to be "good" and "right" as opposed to "bad" or "wrong" in the context of the governing moral code.

LAW, VALUES, AND ETHICAL BEHAVIOR

It makes sense that there should be a legal component to ethical behavior; that is, one would expect that any legal behavior should be considered ethical. Yet slavery was once legal in the United States and laws once permitted only men to vote. That doesn't mean the practices were ethical; rather, we consider these laws unethical today. Furthermore, just because an action is not strictly illegal doesn't make it ethical. Living up to the "letter of the law" is not sufficient to guarantee that one's actions will or should be considered ethical.[9] Is it truly ethical, for example, for an employee to take longer than necessary to do a job? To make personal telephone calls on company time? To call in sick to take a day off for leisure? To fail to report rule violations by a coworker? None of these acts are strictly illegal, but many people would consider any one or more of them to be unethical.

Most ethical problems in the workplace arise when people are asked to do or find themselves about to do something that violates their personal conscience. For some, if the act is legal they proceed with confidence. For others, the ethical test goes beyond the legality of the act alone. The ethical question extends to personal **values**—the underlying beliefs and attitudes that help determine individual behavior. To the extent that values vary among people, we can expect different interpretations of what behavior is ethical or unethical in a given situation.

○ **Values** are broad beliefs about what is or is not appropriate behavior.

ALTERNATIVE VIEWS OF ETHICAL BEHAVIOR

There are many different interpretations of what constitutes ethical behavior. *Figure 6.1* shows four views of ethical behavior that philosophers have discussed over the years.[11] The first is the **utilitarian view**. Behavior that would be considered ethical from this perspective delivers the greatest good to the greatest number of people. Founded in the work of 19th-century philosopher John Stuart Mill, this is a results-oriented point of view that tries to assess the moral implications of decisions in terms of their

○ The **utilitarian view** considers ethical behavior that which delivers greatest good to the most people.

TAKE IT TO THE CASE!

Tom's of Maine
—Where "Doing Business" Means "Doing Good"

Values drive the natural-products firm Tom's of Maine. Founded by Tom Chappell and his wife Kate, the company was described by the Council of Economic Priorities as one of the "saints of social responsibility." Tom's products cost more, but customers know they support a company whose products don't pollute. Tom says, "I believe we have been able to expand upon the historical point of view that business is just for making money to a broader view that business is about doing good for others in the process of getting financial gain. The mission statement says—"We believe our company can be profitable and successful while acting in a socially and environmentally responsible manner."[10]

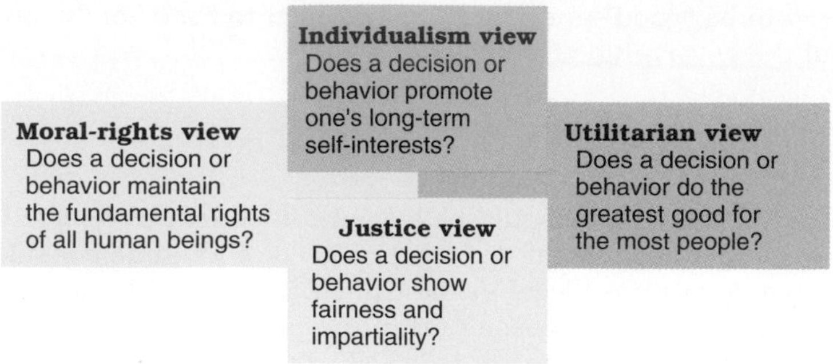

Individualism view
Does a decision or behavior promote one's long-term self-interests?

Moral-rights view
Does a decision or behavior maintain the fundamental rights of all human beings?

Utilitarian view
Does a decision or behavior do the greatest good for the most people?

Justice view
Does a decision or behavior show fairness and impartiality?

Figure 6.1   Four views of ethical behavior.

○ The **individualism view** considers ethical behavior as that which advances long-term self-interests.

○ The **moral-rights view** considers ethical behavior as that which respects and protects fundamental rights.

○ The **justice view** considers ethical behavior as that which treats people impartially and fairly according to guiding rules and standards.

○ **Procedural justice** is concerned that policies and rules are fairly administered.

○ **Distributive justice** is concerned that people are treated the same regardless of individual characteristics.

○ **Interactional justice** is the degree to which others are treated with dignity and respect.

consequences. Business decision makers, for example, are inclined to use profits, efficiency, and other performance criteria to judge what is best for the most people. A manager may make a utilitarian decision to cut 30 percent of a plant's workforce in order to keep the plant profitable and save jobs for the remaining 70 percent.

The **individualism view** of ethical behavior is based on the belief that one's primary commitment is to the advancement of long-term self-interests. When people pursue individual self-interests, they supposedly become self-regulating. For example, such things as lying and cheating for short-term gain should not be tolerated. If one person does it, everyone will do it, and no one's long-term interests will be served. The individualism view is supposed to promote honesty and integrity. But in business practice it may result in a pecuniary ethic, described by one business executive as the tendency to "push the law to its outer limits" and "run roughshod over other individuals to achieve one's objectives."[12]

Ethical behavior under a **moral-rights view** is that which respects and protects the fundamental rights of people. From the teachings of John Locke and Thomas Jefferson, for example, the rights of all people to life, liberty, and fair treatment under the law are considered inviolate. In organizations today, this concept extends to ensuring that employees are always protected in their rights to privacy, due process, free speech, free consent, health and safety, and freedom of conscience. The issue of *human rights* so characteristic of ethical concerns in the international business environment is central to this perspective. The United Nations stands by the Universal Declaration of Human Rights passed by the General Assembly in 1948.

Finally, the **justice view** of moral behavior is based on the belief that ethical decisions treat people impartially and fairly according to guiding rules and standards. This approach evaluates the ethical aspects of any decision on the basis of whether it is "equitable" for everyone affected.[13] One justice issue in organizations is **procedural justice**—the degree to which policies and rules are fairly administered. For example, does a sexual harassment charge levied against a senior executive receive the same full hearing as one made against a first-level supervisor? A second issue is **distributive justice**—the degree to which outcomes are allocated without respect to individual characteristics based on ethnicity, race, gender, age, or other particularistic criteria. For example, does a woman with the same qualifications and experience as a man receive the same consideration for hiring or promotion? A third issue is **interactional justice**—the degree to which others are treated with dignity and respect. For example, does a bank loan officer take the time to fully explain to an applicant why he or she was turned down for a loan?[14]

CULTURAL ISSUES IN ETHICAL BEHAVIOR

The influence of culture on ethical behavior is increasingly at issue as businesses and individuals travel the world. Corporate leaders must master difficult challenges when operating across borders that are cultural as well as national. Former Levi CEO Robert Haas once said that addressing ethical dilemmas as a corporate executive "becomes even more difficult when you overlay the complexities of different cultures and values systems that exist throughout the world."[15]

Those who believe that behavior in foreign settings should be guided by the classic rule of "When in Rome, do as the Romans do" reflect an ethical position of **cultural relativism**.[16] This is the notion that there is no one right way to behave and that ethical behavior is always determined by its cultural context. When it comes to international business, for example, an American executive guided by rules of cultural relativism would argue that the use of child labor is okay if it is consistent with local laws and customs. *Figure 6.2,* however, contrasts this position with the alternative of **universalism**. This ethical position suggests if a behavior or practice is not okay in one's home environment, it shouldn't be acceptable practice anywhere else. In other words, ethical standards are universal and should apply absolutely across cultures and national boundaries. Critics of such a universal approach claim that it is a form of **ethical imperialism**, or the attempt to externally impose one's ethical standards on others.

Business ethicist Thomas Donaldson discusses the debate between cultural relativism and ethical imperialism. Although there is no simple answer, he finds fault with both extremes. He argues instead that certain fundamental rights and ethical standards can be preserved while values and traditions of a given culture are respected.[17] The core values or "hyper-norms" that should transcend cultural boundaries focus on human dignity, basic rights, and good citizenship. With a commitment to core values creating a transcultural ethical umbrella, Donaldson believes international business behaviors can be tailored to local and regional cultural contexts. In the case of child labor, for example, the American executive might ensure that any children working in a factory under contract to his or her business would be provided schooling as well as employment. See *Manager's Notepad 6.1* for Donaldson's suggestions on how corporations can respect the core or universal values.[18]

○ **Cultural relativism** suggests there is no one right way to behave; ethical behavior is determined by its cultural context.

○ **Universalism** suggests ethical standards apply across all cultures.

○ **Ethical imperialism** is an attempt to impose one's ethical standards on other cultures.

ETHICS IN THE WORKPLACE

A classic quotation states: "Ethical business is good business." The same can be said for all persons and institutions throughout society. But the real test is when a manager or worker encounters a situation that challenges

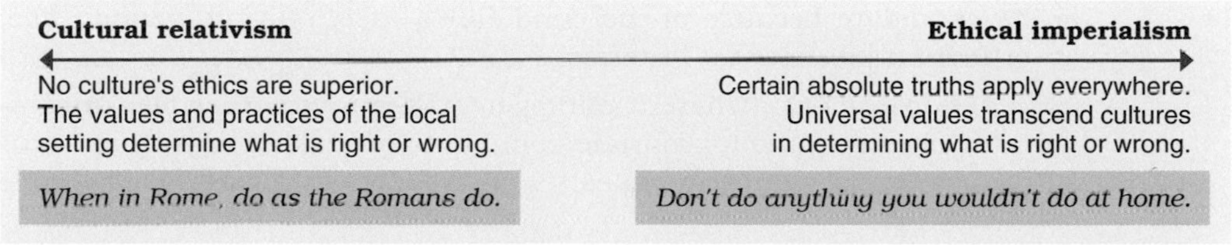

Cultural relativism	Ethical imperialism
No culture's ethics are superior. The values and practices of the local setting determine what is right or wrong.	Certain absolute truths apply everywhere. Universal values transcend cultures in determining what is right or wrong.
When in Rome, do as the Romans do.	*Don't do anything you wouldn't do at home.*

Figure 6.2 The extremes of cultural relativism and ethical imperialism.

Source: Developed from Thomas Donaldson, "Values *in Tension:* Ethics Away from Home," *Harvard Business Review,* vol. 74 (September–October 1996), pp. 48–62.

MANAGER'S NOTEPAD 6.1

How multinationals can respect universal values

Respect for Human Dignity
- Create a culture valuing employees, customers, and suppliers.
- Keep a safe workplace.
- Produce safe products and services.

Respect for Basic Rights
- Protect rights of employees, customers, and communities.
- Avoid any threats to safety, health, education, living standards.

Be Good Citizens
- Support social institutions, economic and educational systems.
- Work with governments and institutions to protect environment.

---

one's ethical beliefs and standards. Often ambiguous and unexpected, these "ethical dilemmas" are part of the challenge of modern society.

WHAT IS AN ETHICAL DILEMMA?

○ An **ethical dilemma** is a situation that although offering potential benefit or gain is also unethical.

An **ethical dilemma** is a situation that requires a choice regarding a possible course of action that, although offering the potential for personal or organizational benefit or both, may be considered unethical. It is often a situation in which action must be taken but for which there is no clear consensus on what is "right" and "wrong." The burden is on the individual to make good choices. An engineering manager speaking from experience sums it up this way: "I define an unethical situation as one in which I have to do something I don't feel good about."[19]

ETHICAL PROBLEMS FACED BY MANAGERS

There are many potential sources of discomfort in managerial decision making, many of them with ethical overtones. Some of the problem areas where managers can get caught in ethical dilemmas, along with sample situations, include:[20]

Ethical problem areas for managers

- *Discrimination*—where a manager denies promotion or appointment to a job candidate because of the candidate's race, religion, gender, age, or other non-job-relevant criterion.
- *Sexual harassment*—where a manager makes a coworker feel uncomfortable because of inappropriate comments or actions regarding sexuality; or where a manager requests sexual favors in return for favorable job treatment.
- *Conflicts of interest*—where a manager takes a bribe or kickback or extraordinary gift in return for making a decision favorable to the gift giver.

- *Customer confidence*—where a manager has privileged information regarding the activities of a customer and shares that information with another party.
- *Organizational resources*—where a manager uses official stationery or a company e-mail account to communicate personal opinions or requests to community organizations.

In a survey of *Harvard Business Review* subscribers, many of the ethical dilemmas reported by managers involved conflicts with superiors, customers, and subordinates.[21] The most frequent issues involved dishonesty in advertising and communications with top management, clients, and government agencies. Problems in dealing with special gifts, entertainment, and kickbacks were also reported. Significantly, the managers' bosses were singled out as sometimes pressuring their subordinates to engage in such unethical activities as supporting incorrect viewpoints, signing false documents, overlooking the boss's wrongdoings, and doing business with the boss's friends.

RATIONALIZATIONS FOR UNETHICAL BEHAVIOR

Why might otherwise reasonable people act unethically? Think back to the earlier examples and to those from your experiences. Consider the possibility of being asked to place a bid for a business contract using insider information, paying bribes to obtain foreign business, falsifying expense account bills, and so on. "Why," you should be asking, "do people do things like this?" In fact, there are at least four common rationalizations that may be used to justify misconduct in these and other ethical dilemmas.[22]

- Convincing yourself that the behavior is not really illegal.
- Convincing yourself that the behavior is really in everyone's best interests.
- Convincing yourself that nobody will ever find out what you've done.
- Convincing yourself that the organization will "protect" you.

After doing something that might be considered unethical, a rationalizer says, *"It's not really illegal."* This expresses a mistaken belief that one's behavior is acceptable, especially in ambiguous situations. When dealing with shady or borderline situations in which you are having a hard time precisely defining right from wrong, the advice is quite simple: When in doubt about a decision to be made or an action to be taken, don't do it.

Another common statement by a rationalizer is: *"It's in everyone's best interests."* This response involves the mistaken belief that because someone can be found to benefit from the behavior, the behavior is also in the individual's or the organization's best interests. Overcoming this rationalization depends in part on the ability to look beyond short-run results to address longer-term implications, and to look beyond results in general to the ways in which they are obtained. For example, in response to the question, "How far can I push matters to obtain this performance goal?" the recommended answer is often, "Don't try to find out."

Sometimes rationalizers tell themselves, *"No one will ever know about it."* They mistakenly believe that a questionable behavior is really "safe"

← Four ways of thinking about ethical behavior

Can Unethical Behavior Be Controlled?
In a survey by the accounting and consulting firm KPMG LLP, some 75 percent of respondents said they had witnessed unethical acts at work in the last 12 months. The next question is: What did they do about it? Take the on-line "Reality Check" to learn more.

The Council on Economic Priorities is part of an initiative called Social Accountability 8000, or SA8000. It proposes labor standards and a certification system to show that firms do not use child or forced labor, offer safe working conditions, pay sufficient wages for workers' basic needs, respect rights to organize, and don't regularly require more than 48-hour workweeks.

and will never be found out or made public. Unless it is discovered, the argument implies, no crime was really committed. Lack of accountability, unrealistic pressures to perform, and a boss who prefers "not to know" can all reinforce such thinking. In this case, the best deterrent is to make sure that everyone knows that wrongdoing will be punished whenever it is discovered.

Finally, rationalizers may proceed with a questionable action because of a mistaken belief that *the organization will stand behind me.* This is misperceived loyalty. The individual believes that the organization's best interests stand above all others. In return, the individual believes that top managers will condone the behavior and protect the individual from harm. But loyalty to the organization is not an acceptable excuse for misconduct; organizational loyalty should not stand above the law and social morality.

FACTORS INFLUENCING ETHICAL BEHAVIOR

It is almost too easy to confront ethical dilemmas from the safety of a textbook or a college classroom. In practice, people are often challenged to choose ethical courses of action in situations where the pressures may be contradictory and great. Increased awareness of the factors influencing ethical behavior can help you better deal with them in the future. *Figure 6.3* shows these influences emanating from the person, the organization, and the environment.

The Person

Family influences, religious values, personal standards, and personal needs, financial and otherwise, will help determine a person's ethical conduct in any given circumstance. Managers who lack a strong and consistent set of personal ethics will find that their decisions vary from situation to situation as they strive to maximize self-interests. Those who operate with strong *ethical frameworks*, personal rules or strategies for ethical decision making, will be more consistent and confident since choices are made against a stable set of ethical standards.

The Organization

The organization is another important influence on ethics in the workplace. We noted earlier that a person's immediate supervisor can have an important effect on the employee's behavior. Just exactly what a

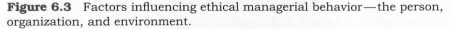

Figure 6.3 Factors influencing ethical managerial behavior—the person, organization, and environment.

supervisor requests, and which actions are rewarded or punished, can certainly affect an individual's decisions and actions. The expectations and reinforcement provided by peers and group norms are likely to have a similar impact. Formal policy statements and written rules are also very important in establishing an ethical climate for the organization as a whole. They support and reinforce the organizational culture, which can have a strong influence on members' ethical behavior.

At the Body Shop, founder Anita Roddick created an 11-point charter to guide the company's employees: "Honesty, integrity and caring form the foundations of the company and should flow through everything we do—we will demonstrate our care for the world in which we live by respecting fellow human beings, by not harming animals, by preserving our forests." The fact that the Body Shop still has to respond to occasional criticisms about its operations demonstrates the inadequacy of formal policies alone to guarantee consistent ethical behavior. A visit to the Body Shop web site, however, shows the firm's ongoing ethical commitments and provides answers to frequently asked questions regarding such controversial issues as animal testing in the cosmetics industry.[24]

The Environment

Organizations operate in external environments composed of competitors, government laws and regulations, and social norms and values, among other influences. Laws interpret social values to define appropriate behaviors for organizations and their members; regulations help governments monitor these behaviors and keep them within acceptable standards. The Foreign Corrupt Practices Act discussed in the previous chapter is one example. It sets standards for American companies that prohibit bribery practices abroad. Although complex, the law guides the firms away from making payments to foreign political parties or government officials in attempting to induce them to make special decisions favoring the company.

The climate of competition in an industry also sets a standard of behavior for those who hope to prosper within it. Sometimes the pressures of competition contribute further to the ethical dilemmas of managers. Former American Airlines president Robert Crandall once telephoned Howard Putnam, then president of now-defunct Braniff Airlines. Both companies were suffering from money-losing competition on routes from their home base of Dallas. A portion of their conversation follows:[25]

ETHICS AND SOCIAL RESPONSIBILITY
(www.polartec.com) **Living by Personal Values and "Common Sense"**

Many people said that Aaron Feurstein was crazy when he kept some 1,000 workers on the payroll after his apparel factory burned down. Today Malden Mills of Lawrence, Massachusetts, is back in business producing Polartec and Polarfleece knits. CEO Feurstein couldn't be prouder. He paid his jobless employees over $15 million. Now he is reaping the gains of a loyal workforce dedicated to their customers. Feurstein calls his decision just "common sense." Admired for his corporate decency, he hopes other CEOs believe "that there's a moral imperative that they must answer to as well."[23]

Putnam:	Do you have a suggestion for me?
Crandall:	Yes. . . . Raise your fares 20 percent. I'll raise mine the next morning.
Putnam:	Robert, we—
Crandall:	You'll make more money and I will, too.
Putnam:	We can't talk about pricing.
Crandall:	Oh, Howard. We can talk about anything we want to talk about.

The U.S. Justice Department disagreed. It alleged that Crandall's suggestion of a 20 percent fare increase amounted to an illegal attempt to monopolize airline routes. The suit was later settled when Crandall agreed to curtail future discussions with competitors about fares.

MAINTAINING HIGH ETHICAL STANDARDS

Progressive organizations support a variety of methods for maintaining high ethical standards in workplace affairs. Some of the most important efforts in this area involve ethics training, whistleblower protection, top management support, formal codes of ethics, and strong ethical cultures.

ETHICS TRAINING

○ **Ethics training** seeks to help people understand the ethical aspects of decision making and to incorporate high ethical standards into their daily behavior.

Ethics training, in the form of structured programs to help participants understand the ethical aspects of decision making, is designed to help people incorporate high ethical standards into their daily behaviors. An increasing number of college curricula now include courses on ethics, and seminars on this topic are popular in the corporate world. But it is important to keep the purpose of ethics training in perspective. An executive at Chemical Bank once put it this way: "We aren't teaching people right from wrong—we assume they know that. We aren't giving people moral courage to do what is right—they should be able to do that anyhow. We focus on dilemmas."[26] Many ethical dilemmas arise as a result of the time pressures of decisions. Ethics training is designed to help people deal with ethical issues while under pressure.

Manager's Notepad 6.2 presents a seven-step checklist for making ethical decisions when confronting an ethical dilemma. It offers a convenient reminder that the decision-making process includes responsibility for double checking a decision *before* taking action. The key issue in the checklist may well be Step 6—the risk of public disclosure of your action and your willingness to bear it. This is a strong way to test whether a decision is consistent with one's personal ethical standards.

WHISTLEBLOWER PROTECTION

Agnes Connolly pressed her employer to report two toxic chemical accidents, as she believed the law required; Dave Jones reported that his company was using unqualified suppliers in the construction of a nuclear power plant; Margaret Newsham revealed that her firm was allowing workers to do personal business while on government contracts; Herman Cohen charged that the ASPCA in New York was mistreating animals; Barry Adams complained that his hospital followed unsafe

Get Connected!

The National Whistleblower Center offers advice and support for U.S. federal workers and those in environmentally sensitive industries; the Government Accountability Project offers survival tips for whistleblowers.

MANAGER'S NOTEPAD 6.2

Checklist for making ethical decisions

Step 1. Recognize the ethical dilemma.

Step 2. Get the facts.

Step 3. Identify your options.

Step 4. Test each option: Is it legal? Is it right? Is it beneficial?

Step 5. Decide which option to follow.

Step 6. Double check decision by asking follow-up questions:

"How would I feel if my family found out about my decision?"

"How would I feel about this if my decision were printed in the local newspaper?"

Step 7. Take action.

---

practices.[27] They were **whistleblowers**, persons who expose the misdeeds of others in organizations in order to preserve ethical standards and protect against wasteful, harmful, or illegal acts.[28] All were fired from their jobs. Indeed, whistleblowers face the risks of impaired career progress and other forms of organizational retaliation, up to and including termination.

Today, federal and state laws increasingly offer whistleblowers some defense against "retaliatory discharge." But although signs indicate that the courts are growing supportive of whistleblowers, legal protection for whistleblowers can still be inadequate. Laws vary from state to state, and federal laws mainly protect government workers. Furthermore, even with legal protection, potential whistleblowers may find it hard to expose unethical behavior in the workplace. Some organizational barriers to whistleblowing include a *strict chain of command* that makes it hard to bypass the boss; *strong work group identities* that encourage loyalty and self-censorship; and *ambiguous priorities* that make it hard to distinguish right from wrong.[29]

In the attempt to remove these and other blocks to the exposure of unethical behaviors, some organizations have formally appointed staff members to serve as "ethics advisors." Others have set up formal staff units to process reported infractions. One novel proposal goes so far as to suggest the convening of *moral quality circles* to help create shared commitments for everyone to work at their moral best.[30]

○ A **whistleblower** exposes the misdeeds of others in organizations.

ETHICAL ROLE MODELS

Gabrielle Melchionda, a young entrepreneur in Portland, Maine, started Mad Gab's Inc., an all-natural skin-care business, while a college student in 1991. By 2000, sales had risen to over $300,000. That's when an exporter offered her a deal—sell $2 million of her products abroad. She turned it down. Why? The exporter also sold weapons, and that was against her values. Melchionda sets an ethical standard for her seven employees. Her values guide all business decisions, right from having an employee profit-sharing plan to hiring disabled adults to using only packaging designs that minimize waste.[31]

www.ci.sf.ca.us

The City of San Francisco is a social activist. Like a growing number of employers, San Francisco now requires companies that do business with it to offer benefits to domestic partners of their employees, the same benefits that spouses would enjoy.

Top managers, in large and small enterprises, have the power to shape an organization's policies and set its moral tone. They also have a major responsibility to use this power well. They can and should serve as role models of appropriate ethical behavior for the entire organization. Not only must their day-to-day behavior be the epitome of high ethical conduct, but top managers must also communicate similar expectations throughout the organization . . . and reinforce positive results. Unfortunately, communication from the top may subtly suggest that top management does not want to know about deceptive or illegal practices by employees, or simply doesn't care.

Even though top managers bear a special responsibility for setting the ethical tone of an organization, every manager is also in a position to influence the ethical behavior of the people who work for and with them. This means that all managers must act as ethical role models and set an ethical tone in their areas of responsibility. Care must be taken to do this in a positive and informed manner. The important supervisory act of setting goals and communicating performance expectations is a good case in point. A surprising 64 percent of 238 executives in one study, for example, reported feeling under pressure to compromise personal standards to achieve company goals. A *Fortune* survey also reported that 34 percent of its respondents felt a company president can create an ethical climate by setting *reasonable* goals "so that subordinates are not pressured into unethical actions."[32] Clearly, any manager in his or her relationships with subordinates may unknowingly encourage unethical practices by exerting *too* much pressure for them to accomplish goals that are *too* difficult. Part of the manager's ethical responsibility is to be realistic in setting performance goals for others.

CODES OF ETHICS

○ A **code of ethics** is a written document that states values and ethical standards intended to guide the behavior of employees.

Formal **codes of ethics** are official written guidelines on how to behave in situations susceptible to the creation of ethical dilemmas. They are found in organizations and in professions such as engineering, medicine, law, and public accounting. In the professions such as accounting and engineering, ethical codes try to ensure that individual behavior is consistent with the historical and shared norms of the professional group. Most codes of ethical conduct identify expected behaviors in terms of general organizational citizenship, the avoidance of illegal or improper acts in one's work, and good relationships with customers. In a related survey of companies with written codes, the items most frequently addressed included workforce diversity, bribes and kickbacks, political contributions, the honesty of books or records, customer–supplier relationships, and the confidentiality of corporate information.[33]

In the increasingly complex world of international business, codes of conduct for manufacturers and contractors are becoming more prevalent.[34] At Gap, Inc., global manufacturing is governed by a formal Code of Vendor Conduct.[35] Among the many areas covered, the document specifically deals with *discrimination*—stating "Factories shall employ workers on the basis of their ability to do the job, not on the basis of their personal characteristics or beliefs"; *forced labor*—stating "Factories shall not use any prison, indentured or forced labor"; *working conditions*—stating "Factories must treat all workers with respect and dignity and provide them with a safe and healthy environment"; and *freeedom of association*—stating "Factories must not interfere with workers who wish to lawfully and peacefully associate, organize or bargain collectively."

Although interest in codes of ethical conduct is growing, it must be remembered that the codes have limits. They cannot cover all situations, and they are not automatic insurance for universal ethical conduct. But they do play important roles in setting the ethical tone and expectations in organizations. When fully integrated into the organizational culture, furthermore, the moral fabric created has a strong influence on day-to-day behavior. Ultimately, of course, the value of any formal code of ethics still rests on the underlying human resource foundations of the organization—its managers and other employees. There is no replacement for effective hiring practices that staff organizations with honest and moral people. And there is no replacement for leadership by committed managers who are willing to set examples and act as positive ethical role models to ensure desired results.

REALITY Check 6.2

What the World Thinks about Social Responsibility In a survey of 25,000 people from 23 countries, Environics International Ltd. found that 90 percent wanted businesses to focus on more than profitability. Take the on-line "Reality Check" to learn more about how citizens of the world view dimensions of corporate social responsibility.

SOCIAL RESPONSIBILITY

It is now time to shift our interest in ethical behavior from the level of the individual to that of the organization. To begin, it is important to remember that all organizations exist in complex relationship with elements in their external environment. In Chapter 2, in fact, we described the environment of a business firm as composed of a network of other organizations and institutions with which it must interact. An important frame of reference is the field of **organizational stakeholders**, those persons, groups, and other organizations directly affected by the behavior of the organization and holding a stake in its performance.[36] In this context, **corporate social responsibility** is defined as an obligation of the organization to act in ways that serve both its own interests and the interests of its many external stakeholders.[37]

○ **Organizational stakeholders** are directly affected by the behavior of the organization and hold a stake in its performance.

○ **Corporate social responsibility** is the obligation of an organization to act in ways that serve the interests of its stakeholders.

STAKEHOLDER ISSUES AND PRACTICES

The positive examples are there. You just have to look for them. Ben & Jerry's Homemade, Inc. has long been considered an example of a firm committed to "linked prosperity"—sharing prosperity with its employees and the communities in which it operates. Each year 7.5 percent of the firm's pre-tax earnings go into a charitable foundation. Timberland Company provides each full-time employee 40 hours of paid time per year for community volunteer work. It also supports City Year, an organization that promotes community service. Hewlett-Packard started the e-Inclusion program to help rural villagers around the world gain access to technology and its advantages. The on-line auctioneer ebay, Inc. gave 100,000 of its pre-IPO shares to charity and another 100,000-plus after going public.[38]

The stakeholder pressures are there, too. Consumers, activist groups, nonprofit organizations, and governments are increasingly vocal and influential in directing organizations toward socially responsible practices. In today's information age business activities are increasingly transparent. Irresponsible practices are difficult to hide, wherever in the world they take place. Not only do news organizations find and disseminate the information, well-known activist organizations lobby, campaign, and actively pressure organizations to respect and protect everything from human

Get Connected!

The organization Human Rights Watch is dedicated to protecting the human rights of people around the world. Check its web site for current concerns and controversies.

rights to the natural environment. Prominent among them are Amnesty International, Greenpeace International, World Wildlife Fund, and Friends of the Earth, among many others. Increasingly important also are investor groups such as the Interfaith Council for Corporate Responsibility that publicize and lobby for social causes through share ownership. The groups pool resources, buy shares in companies, and then advance proxy resolutions and lobby corporate leadership to ensure the businesses perform in socially responsible ways.

Ultimately, organizational leadership is a critical influence on behavior by organizations and their members. The leadership beliefs that guide socially responsible organizational practices have been described as follows:[39]

→ **Leadership beliefs guiding socially responsible practices**

- *People*—belief that people do their best in healthy work environments with a balance of work and family life.
- *Communities*—belief that organizations perform best when located in healthy communities.
- *Natural environment*—belief that organizations gain by treating the natural environment with respect.
- *Long term*—belief that organizations must be managed and led for long-term success.
- *Reputation*—belief that one's reputation must be protected to ensure consumer and stakeholder support.

Perspectives on Social Responsibility

In academic and public-policy circles, two contrasting views of corporate social responsibility have stimulated debate with one side arguing against it and the other arguing for it.[40] The *classical view* holds that management's only responsibility in running a business is to maximize profits. In other words—the business of business is business and the principal concern of management should always be to maximize shareholder value. This narrow "shareholder" and "profit-driven" model is supported by Milton Friedman, a respected freemarket economist and Nobel Laureate. He says, "Few trends could so thoroughly undermine the very foundations of our free society as the acceptance by corporate officials of social responsibility other than to make as much money for their stockholders as possible."[41] The *arguments against corporate social responsibility* include fears that the pursuit of this goal will reduce business profits, raise business costs, dilute business purpose, give business too much social power, and do so without business accountability to the public.

By contrast, the *socioeconomic view* holds that management of any organization must be concerned for the broader social welfare and not just for corporate profits. This broad-based and stakeholder model is supported by Paul Samuelson, another distinguished economist and Nobel Laureate. He states, "A large corporation these days not only may engage in social responsibility, it had damn well better try to do so."[42] Among the *arguments in favor of corporate social responsibility* are that it will add long-run profits for businesses, improve the public image of businesses, and help them to avoid more government regulation. Businesses have the resources and ethical obligation to act responsibly.

Today, there is little doubt that the public at large wants businesses and other organizations to act with genuine social responsibility. Stakeholder expectations are increasingly well voiced and include demands that organizations integrate social responsibility into their core values and daily activities.

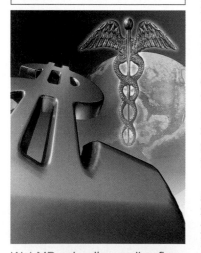

www.webmd.com

WebMD, a leading on-line firm offering connectivity and a full suite of healthcare services, is also a global citizen. The firm is using the Internet to spearhead a plan to deliver instant medical assistance to people in the world's least-developed nations.

As Tom's of Maine founders Tom and Kate Chappell clearly state: "When we founded the company, it was our goal to make a different kind of business, one where people, the environment and animals are seen as inherently worthy and deserving of respect. We remain committed to this mission, now more than ever."[43]

On the research side, there is increasing evidence that high performance in social responsibility can be associated with strong financial performance and, at worst, has no adverse financial impact. The argument that acting with a commitment to social responsibility will negatively affect the "bottom line" is hard to defend. Indeed, recent evidence suggests the existence of a *virtuous circle* in which corporate social responsibility leads to improved financial performance for the firm and this in turn leads to more socially responsible actions in the future.[44] There seems little reason to believe that businesses cannot serve the public good while advancing the financial interests of their shareholders. Even as the research and debate continues on this important concept, these historical comments by management theorist Keith Davis may still best sum up the corporate social responsibility debate.

> *Society wants business as well as all other major institutions to assume significant social responsibility. Social responsibility has become the hallmark of a mature, global organization. . . . The business which vacillates or chooses not to enter the arena of social responsibility may find that it gradually will sink into customer and public disfavor.*[45]

CAREER CONNECTION
Social Responsibility

Business for Social Responsibility
The Business Importance of Social Responsibility
Business for Social Responsibility is a strong advocate of responsible business practices. The web site reports *studies* showing a positive link between social responsibility and business performance.

- *Improved bottom line:* Companies making a public commitment to rely on their ethics codes outperformed others in *market value added.*

- *Reduced operating costs:* Environmental initiatives can reduce costs; reducing emissions of gases that contribute to global climate change can increase energy efficiency and reduce utility bills.

- *Increased sales and customer loyalty:* Markets are growing for products of firms customers perceive to be socially responsible; in one study 76 percent of consumers would switch brands to buy from a firm associated with a good cause.

- *Access to capital:* In the United States there is more than $2 trillion in assets managed in portfolios that screen investments on criteria including ethics, the environment, and corporate social responsibility.

- *Employee hiring and retention:* A study of MBA students found that over 50 percent were willing to accept lower salaries to work for socially responsible employers.

QUESTION: Would you prefer to work for a socially responsible employer? Who are they? Talk to executives in your community and do the research to find out.

EVALUATING SOCIAL PERFORMANCE

There are many action domains in which social responsibility can be pursued by business firms and other organizations. These include concerns for ecology and environmental quality, truth in lending and consumer protection, and aid to education. They also include service to community needs, employment practices, diversity practices, progressive labor relations and employee assistance, and general corporate philanthropy, among other possibilities. At the organizational level, a **social audit** can be used at regular intervals to report on and systematically assess an organization's resource commitments and action accomplishments in these and other areas. You might think of social audits as attempts to assess the social performance of organizations, much as accounting audits assess their financial performance.

○ A **social audit** is a systematic assessment of an organization's accomplishments in areas of social responsibility.

A formal assessment of corporate social performance might include questions posed at these four levels: (1) Is the organization's *economic responsibility* met—is it profitable? (2) Is the organization's *legal responsibility* met—does it obey the law? (3) Is the organization's *ethical responsibility* met—is it doing the "right" things? (4) Is the organization's *discretionary responsibility* met—does it contribute to the broader community?[46]

As you move up these levels, the assessment inquires into ever-greater demonstrations of social performance. An organization is meeting its economic responsibility when it earns a profit through the provision of goods and services desired by customers. Legal responsibility is fulfilled when an organization operates within the law and according to the requirements of various external regulations. An organization meets its ethical responsibility when its actions voluntarily conform not only to legal expectations but also to the broader values and moral expectations of society. The highest level of social performance comes through the satisfaction of an organization's discretionary responsibility. Here, the organization voluntarily moves beyond basic economic, legal, and ethical expectations to provide leadership in advancing the well-being of individuals, communities, and society as a whole.

SOCIAL RESPONSIBILITY STRATEGIES

○ An **obstructionist strategy** avoids social responsibility and reflects mainly economic priorities.

○ A **defensive strategy** seeks to protect the organization by doing the minimum legally required to satify social expectations.

○ An **accommodative strategy** accepts social responsibility and tries to satify prevailing economic, legal, and ethical performance critera.

Figure 6.4 describes four strategies of corporate social responsibility. The continuum shows a desirable shift in emphasis from acting obstructionist, at the lowest level, to displaying progressive citizenship, at the highest.[47] An **obstructionist strategy** ("Fight the social demands") reflects mainly economic priorities; social demands lying outside the organization's perceived self-interests are resisted. If the organization is criticized for wrongdoing, it can be expected to deny the claims. A **defensive strategy** ("Do the minimum legally required") seeks to protect the organization by doing the minimum legally necessary to satisfy expectations. Corporate behavior at this level conforms only to legal requirements, competitive market pressure, and perhaps activist voices. If criticized, intentional wrongdoing is likely to be denied.

Organizations pursuing an **accommodative strategy** ("Do the minimum ethically required") accept their social responsibilities. They try to satisfy economic, legal, and ethical criteria. Corporate behavior at this

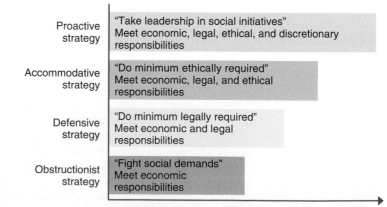

Figure 6.4 Four strategies of corporate social responsibility—from "obstructionist" to "proactive" behavior.

level is congruent with society's prevailing norms, values, and expectations, but at times it may be so only because of outside pressures. An oil firm, for example, may be willing to "accommodate" with cleanup activities when a spill occurs, but remain quite slow in taking actions to prevent them in the first place. Finally, the **proactive strategy** ("Take leadership in social initiatives") is designed to meet all the criteria of social performance, including discretionary performance. Corporate behavior at this level takes preventive action to avoid adverse social impacts from company activities, and it even anticipates or takes the lead in identifying and responding to emerging social issues.

○ A **proactive strategy** meets all the criteria of social responsibility, including discretionary performance.

ORGANIZATIONS AND SOCIETY

The fact remains, not all managers and not all organizations accept the challenge of committing to a proactive social responsibility strategy. Some may accept it, but have difficulty meeting the challenge. In this action, arena government, as the voice or instrument of the people, is often called upon to act in the public behalf.

HOW GOVERNMENT INFLUENCES ORGANIZATIONS

Governments often pass laws and establish regulating agencies to control and direct the behavior of organizations. It may not be too farfetched to say that behind every piece of legislation—national, state, or local—is a government agency charged with the responsibility of monitoring and ensuring compliance with its mandates. You know these agencies best by their acronyms: FAA (Federal Aviation Administration), EPA (Environmental Protection Agency), OSHA (Occupational Safety and Health Administration), and FDA (Food and Drug Administration), among many others.

Get Connected!

Learn more about business leadership with a social vision. Go on-line with Business Enterprise Trust.

Many themes already discussed as being key areas of social responsibility are backed by major laws. Business executives often complain many laws and regulations are overly burdensome.[48] Public outcries to "dismantle the bureaucracy" and/or "deregulate business" reflect concerns that specific agencies and their supportive legislation are not functional. But, the reality is that the legal environment is both complex and constantly changing. Managers must stay informed about new and pending laws as well as existing ones. As a reminder of the positive side of legislation, consider four areas in which the U.S. government takes an active role in regulating business affairs.

The first area is *occupational safety and health*. The Occupational Safety and Health Act of 1970 firmly established that the federal government was concerned about worker health and safety on the job. Even though some complain that the regulations are still not strong enough, the act continues to influence the concerns of employers and government policymakers for worker safety. Second is the area of *fair labor practices*. Legislation and regulations that prohibit discrimination in labor practices are discussed in Chapter 12 on human resource management. The Equal Employment Opportunity Act of 1972 and related regulations are designed to reduce barriers to employment based on race, gender, age, national origin, and marital status. Third is *consumer protection*. The Consumer Product Safety Act of 1972 gives government authority to examine and force a business to withdraw from sale any product that it feels is hazardous to the consumer. Children's toys and flammable fabrics are within the great range of products affected by such regulation. The fourth area concerns *environmental protection.* Several antipollution acts, beginning with the Air Pollution Control Act of 1962, are designed to eliminate careless pollution of the air, water, and land.

HOW ORGANIZATIONS INFLUENCE GOVERNMENT

The line of influence between government and organizations is not one way, with the government simply passing legislation and acting as a regulator. Just as governments take a variety of actions to influence organizations, so do the leaders and representatives of organizations take action to influence government. There are a number of ways in which businesses in particular attempt to influence government to adopt and pursue policies favorable to them.

○ **Lobbying** expresses opinions and preferences to government officials.

○ **Political action committees** collect money for donation to political campaigns.

Through *personal contacts and networks* executives get to know important people in government. These contacts can be used for persuasion. Through *public relations campaigns* executives can communicate positive images of their organizations to the public at large, with the potential for them to speak positively in the business's behalf. Through **lobbying**, often with the assistance of professional lobbying consultants or firms, executives can have their positions and preferences communicated directly to government officials. Executives also seek influence through financial contributions to legal organizations, called **political action committees** (PACs), that collect money and donate it to support favored political candidates. Finally, it must also be admitted that *illegal acts* sometimes occur. Executives can unfortunately resort to use of bribes or illegal financial campaign contributions in the attempt to gain influence over public officials.

WHY MANAGERS MAKE THE DIFFERENCE

Trends in the evolution of social values point to ever-increasing demands from governments and other organizational stakeholders that managerial decisions reflect ethical as well as high-performance standards. Today's workers and managers, as well as tomorrow's, must accept personal responsibility for doing the "right" things. Broad social and moral criteria must be used to examine the interests of multiple stakeholders in a dynamic and complex environment. Decisions must always be made and

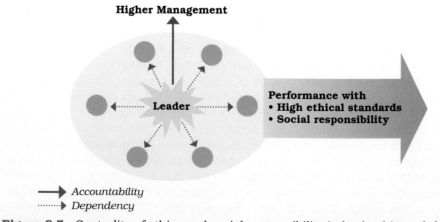

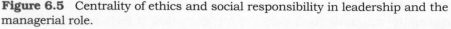

Figure 6.5 Centrality of ethics and social responsibility in leadership and the managerial role.

problems solved with ethical considerations standing side by side with high-performance objectives, be they individual, group, or organizational. Indeed, the point that profits and social responsibility can go hand in hand is being confirmed in new and creative ways.

As public demands grow for organizations to be accountable for ethical and social performance as well as economic performance, the manager stands once again in the middle. It is the manager whose decisions affect "quality-of-life" outcomes in the critical boundaries between people and organizations and between organizations and their environments. Everyone must be more willing to increase the weight given to ethical and social responsibility considerations when making these decisions. *Management 7/e* focuses your attention throughout on the demands depicted in *Figure 6.5*. It presents the manager's or team leader's challenge this way: to fulfill an accountability for achieving performance objectives, while always doing so in an ethical and socially responsible manner. The full weight of this responsibility holds in every organizational setting—small to large, and private or nonprofit—and at every managerial level, from bottom to top. There is no escaping the ultimate reality—being a manager is a very socially responsible job!

STUDY Guide

The Chapter 6 Study Guide will help you review chapter content, prepare for examinations, and further build your career readiness. The *Summary* briefly highlights answers to questions first posed in the chapter opening Planning Ahead section. The list of *Key Terms* allows you to double check your familiarity with basic concepts and definitions. *Self-Test 6* gives you the opportunity to test your basic comprehension of chapter content using sample test questions. Suggestions offered as *Career Readiness Activities* direct your attention to relevant sections of the end-of-text Career Readiness Workbook, as well as special Electronic Resources on the *Management 7/e* web site.

SUMMARY

What is ethical behavior?

- Ethical behavior is that which is accepted as "good" or "right" as opposed to "bad" or "wrong."
- Simply because an action is not illegal does not necessarily make it ethical in a given situation.
- Because values vary, the question of "What is ethical behavior?" may be answered differently by different people.
- Four ways of thinking about ethical behavior are the utilitarian, individualism, moral-rights, and justice views.
- Cultural relativism argues that no culture is ethically superior to any other.

How do ethical dilemmas complicate the workplace?

- When managers act ethically they have a positive impact on other people in the workplace and on the social good performed by organizations.
- An ethical dilemma occurs when someone must decide whether to pursue a course of action that, although offering the potential for personal or organizational benefit or both, may be considered potentially unethical.
- Managers report that their ethical dilemmas often involve conflicts with superiors, customers, and subordinates over such matters as

dishonesty in advertising and communications as well as pressure from their bosses to do unethical things.

- Common rationalizations for unethical behavior include believing the behavior is not illegal, is in everyone's best interests, will never be noticed, or will be supported by the organization.

How can high ethical standards be maintained?

- Ethics training in the form of courses and training programs helps people better deal with ethical dilemmas in the workplace.
- Whistleblowers expose the unethical acts of others in organizations, even while facing career risks for doing so.
- Top management sets an ethical tone for the organization as a whole, and all managers are responsible for acting as positive models of appropriate ethical behavior.
- Written codes of ethical conduct formally state what an organization expects of its employees regarding ethical conduct at work.

What is organizational social responsibility?

- Corporate social responsibility is an obligation of the organization to act in ways that serve both its own interests and the interests of its many external publics, often called stakeholders.
- Criteria for evaluating corporate social performance include economic, legal, ethical, and discretionary responsibilities.
- Corporate strategies in response to social demands include obstruction, defense, accommodation, and proaction, with more progressive organizations taking proactive stances.

How do organizations and government work together in society?

- Government agencies are charged with monitoring and ensuring compliance with the mandates of law.
- Managers must be well informed about existing and pending legislation in a variety of social responsibility areas, including environmental protection and other quality-of-life concerns.
- Organizations exert their influence on government in many ways, including interpersonal contacts of executives, use of lobbyists, and financial contributions to PACs.
- All managerial decisions and actions in every workplace should fulfill performance accountability with commitments to high ethical standards and socially responsible means.

KEY TERMS

Accommodative strategy (p. 160)

Codes of ethics (p. 156)

Corporate social responsibility (p. 157)

Cultural relativism (p. 149)

Defensive strategy (p. 160)

Distributive justice (p. 148)

Ethical behavior (p. 146)

Ethical dilemma (p. 150)

Ethical imperialism (p. 149)

Ethics (p. 146)

Ethics training (p. 154)

Individualism view (p. 148)

Interactional justice (p. 148)

Justice view (p.148)

Lobbying (p. 162)

Moral-rights view (p. 148)

Obstructionist strategy (p. 160)

Organizational stakeholders (p. 157)

Political action committees (p. 162)

Proactive strategy (p. 161)

Procedural justice (p. 148)

Social audit (p. 159)

Universalism (p. 149)

Utilitarian view (p. 147)

Values (p. 147)

Whistleblowers (p. 155)

SELF-TEST 6

Take this test here or on-line much as you would in a normal classroom situation. It should offer you a good way to check your basic comprehension of chapter material. Answers may be found at the end of the book.

MULTIPLE-CHOICE QUESTIONS:

1. _____ are personal beliefs that help determine whether a behavior will be considered ethical or unethical.
   (a) Values (b) Attitudes (c) Motives (d) Needs

2. Under the _____ view of ethical behavior, a businesswoman would be considered ethical if she reduced a plant's workforce by 10 percent in order to cut costs and save jobs for the other 90 percent.
   (a) utilitarian (b) individualism (c) justice (d) moral rights

3. A manager's failure to administer a late-to-work policy the same way for everyone is an ethical violation of _____ justice.
   (a) ethical (b) moral (c) distributive (d) procedural

4. Influences on a person's ethical behavior at work may come from _____ sources.
   (a) environmental (b) organizational (c) personal (d) all of these

5. A(n) _____ is someone who exposes the ethical misdeeds of others.
   (a) whistleblower (b) realist (c) ombudsman (d) stakeholder

6. Behavioral guidelines on matters such as _____ are often found in an organization's formal code of ethics.
(a) bribes (b) political contributions (c) relationships (d) all of these

7. The U.S. Equal Opportunity Act of 1972 is an example of government regulation of business with respect to _____.
(a) fair labor practices (b) consumer protection
(c) environmental protection (d) occupational safety and health

8. In the final analysis, high-performance goals in organizations should be achieved by _____ means.
(a) any possible (b) cultural relativism
(c) ethical imperialism (d) ethical and socially responsible

9. The most progressive organizational response to its corporate social responsibility is a(n) _____ strategy.
(a) accommodative (b) defensive (c) proactive (d) defensive

10. Two questions for conducting the ethics double check of a decision are: (a) "How would I feel if my family found out about this?" and (b) "How would I feel if _____?"
(a) my boss found out about this
(b) my subordinates found out about this
(c) this was printed in the local newspaper
(d) this went into my personnel file

TRUE-FALSE QUESTIONS:

11. A behavior that is legal will always be considered ethical.   T   F

12. The moral-rights view of ethical behavior emphasizes respect for fundamental human rights shared by everyone.   T   F

13. Treating everyone the same regardless of race or gender is an issue of distributive justice.   T   F

14. Cultural relativism argues for core values that absolutely apply anywhere in the world.   T   F

15. Convincing yourself that a behavior is not really illegal is one way to rationalize unethical behavior.   T   F

16. Strong work group identities are among the organizational barriers to whistleblowing.   T   F

17. The only managers who must act as ethical role models in an organization are the very top managers.   T   F

18. The classical view of corporate social responsibility holds that a firm's only responsibility is to maximize profits.   T   F

19. In a social audit, a firm meeting its legal responsibilities is satisfying the highest-level criterion of social responsibility.　　T　　F

20. Ethical dilemmas faced by practicing managers sometimes involve excessive pressure from their bosses.　　T　　F

SHORT-RESPONSE QUESTIONS:

21. Explain the difference between the individualism and justice views of ethical behavior.

22. List four common rationalizations for unethical managerial behavior.

23. What are the major elements in the socioeconomic view of corporate social responsibility?

24. What role do government agencies play in regulating the socially responsible behavior of businesses?

APPLICATION QUESTION:

25. A small outdoor clothing company has just received an attractive offer from a business in Bangladesh to manufacture its work gloves. The offer would allow for substantial cost savings over the current supplier. The company manager, however, has read reports that some Bangladesh businesses break their own laws and operate with child labor. How would differences in the following corporate responsibility strategies affect the manager's decision regarding whether to accept the offer: obstruction, defense, accommodation, and proaction?

CAREER readiness ACTIVITIES

Recommended learning activities from the end-of-text Career Readiness Workbook for this chapter include:

Career Advancement Portfolio
- Individual writing and group presentation assignments based on any of the following activities.

Case for Critical Thinking
- Tom's of Maine—Doing Good While Doing Business

Integrative Learning Activities
- Research Project 4—Corporate Social Responsibility
- Research Project 5—Affirmative Action Directions
- Integrative Case—Outback Steakhouse, Inc.

Exercises in Teamwork
- Confronting ethical dilemmas (#8)
- Interviewing job candidates (#15)
- Contingency workforce (#22)

Self-Assessments
- Cultural Attitudes Inventory (#5)
- Diversity Awareness (#7)
- Internal/External Control (#11)

The *Fast Company* Collection On-Line
- Scott Kirsner, "Collision Course"

ELECTRONIC RESOURCES

@ GET CONNECTED! Don't forget to take full advantage of the on-line support for *Management 7/e.*
- Chapter 6 On-line Study Guide
- Chapter 6 Self-test Answers
- Chapter 6 E-Resource Center

www.wiley.com/college/schermerhorn

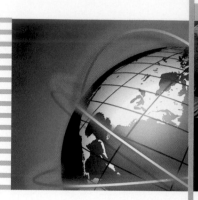

7

Planning and controlling

P l a n n i n g

ahead

CHAPTER 7 study questions

○ **How do managers plan?**

○ **What types of plans do managers use?**

○ **What are the useful planning tools and techniques?**

○ **What is the control process?**

○ **What control systems are used in organizations?**

GETTING CONNECTED!

Manheim.Com—*Know What You Want to Accomplish*

The environment of business is changing and technology is driving more firms to the Internet. But, what's the plan? Is it better to go from bricks-and-mortar to the Internet, or to go from the Internet to the necessary supporting bricks-and-mortar? The story of Manheim Auctions Inc. is of an old-fashioned business finding new ways to grow by also pursuing an Internet strategy. Already the world's largest used-car auctioning service, Manheim is striving to also become the world's largest wholesale seller of used cars on the Net. With over 80,000 dealers and manufacturers linked together, it's now moving hundreds of millions of dollars' worth of cars through the Internet and expects to hit the billion-dollar range before long.

What is the competitive edge? Manheim credits its success to two major factors: (1) it established enduring relationships with dealers—90 percent of all used-car dealers attend Manheim auctions, and (2) there are some 65 auction locations located across North America. Rob Leathern, an analyst with Jupiter Media Metrix, explains: "Anyone can build a web site to sell cars, but the notion of a zero-gravity player in this market—a pure dot com with no physical infrastructure or preexisting relationships—is naive. Manheim already owns the sweet spot. It's got loyal customers as well as the infrastructure that's needed to store, ship, repair, and recondition used cars. That will be a difficult edge for others to replicate."

Manheim is testing real-time Internet auctions that allow dealers to bid for cars from any location. Dealers who wish to sell to consumers may post the car on Manheim's consumer site—Autotrader.com—with one click. Dennis Berry, President and CEO of Manheim, says: "Our mission has always been to help used-car dealers succeed. A lot of dot coms say, 'We're going to bypass dealers. . . . We felt confident that if we built our on-line business on helping dealers succeed, we would win."

Manheim offers an interesting look into how firms in today's business environment are moving from an emphasis on products to an emphasis on service. Auctioning the used car is just the first step in the sales process; Manheim provides bodywork and engine repairs on all its automobiles. Post-auction sales reports provide information on prices and model availability to dealers. In addition, Manheim's web site offers market reports with used-car values based on millions of actual sales from Manheim Auctions. Information becomes the valuable commodity.[1]

@ **Get Connected!**

You, too, can build a business on the Internet. Take a demonstration tour of the Manheim site. Talk to your friends. Create an idea for an on-line business that could utilize insights from an e-business model. Get Connected!

Strategic management consultant Gary Hamel believes many of today's companies aren't going to make it for the long run. Why? "Organizations that succeed in this new century will be as different from industrial-era organizations as those companies themselves were different from craft-based industries," he says. "Companies are going to have to reinvent themselves much more frequently than before."[2] Quite fittingly, the title of his new book is *Leading the Revolution*.[3]

The chapter opening example of *Manheim Auctions* shows an "old economy" company stepping forward to implement plans designed to meet the challenges of the emerging "new economy." Rather than bask in past successes, Manheim executives are acting today in order to best prepare the firm for future opportunities. In its business and industry context, the changes unfolding at Manheim might be considered revolutionary. Hamel, at least, would view them as part of a process that is essential to success in an environment of continuous change and frequent uncertainty—"reinvention."

In management, one needs the ability to look ahead, make good plans, and then help others work effectively to best meet the challenges of the future. With the future uncertain, however, the likelihood is that even the best of plans made today may have to be changed tomorrow. Thus, managers also need the courage to be flexible in response to new circumstances, and the discipline to maintain control even as situations become hectic and the performance pressures stay unrelenting. In the ever-changing technology industry, for example, CEO T. J. Rodgers of Cypress Semiconductor Corp. is known for valuing both performance goals and accountability. Cypress employees work with clear and quantified work goals, which they typically set by themselves. Rogers emphasizes that the system is designed to find problems before they interfere with performance. He says: "Managers monitor the goals, look for problems, and expect people who fall behind to ask for help before they lose control of or damage a major project."[4]

HOW AND WHY MANAGERS PLAN

○ **Planning** is the process of setting objectives and determining how to accomplish them.

In Chapter 1 the management process was described as planning, organizing, leading, and controlling the use of resources to achieve performance objectives. The first of these functions, **planning**, sets the stage for the others. It is a process of setting objectives and determining how to best accomplish them. Said a bit differently, planning involves deciding exactly what you want to accomplish and how to best go about it.

IMPORTANCE OF PLANNING

When planning is done well, it creates a solid platform for further managerial efforts at *organizing*—allocating and arranging resources to accomplish essential tasks; *leading*—guiding the efforts of human resources to ensure high levels of task accomplishment; and *controlling*—monitoring task accomplishments and taking necessary corrective action.

The centrality of planning in management, as shown in *Figure 7.1*, is important to understand. In today's demanding organizational and career environments it is essential to always stay one step ahead of the competi-

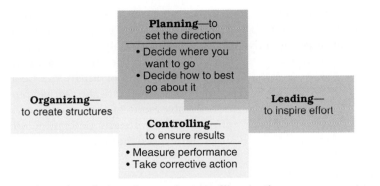

Figure 7.1 The roles of planning and controlling in the management process.

tion. This involves striving always to become better and better at what you are doing, and to be action oriented. An Eaton Corporation annual report, for example, once stated: "Planning at Eaton means taking the hard decisions before events force them upon you, and anticipating the future needs of the market before the demand asserts itself."[5] One way managers in progressive organizations try to get a "jump" on the future is with a total quality approach to planning that involves listening to their customers and then using this information for better planning.

○ **Objectives** are specific results that one wishes to achieve.

○ A **plan** is a statement of intended means for accomplishing objectives.

THE PLANNING PROCESS

In the planning process, **objectives** identify the specific results or desired outcomes that one intends to achieve. The **plan** is a statement of action steps to be taken in order to accomplish the objectives. The steps in the systematic planning process include the following:

1. *Define your objectives:* Identify desired outcomes or results in very specific ways. Know where you want to go; be specific enough that you will know you have arrived when you get there or know how far off the mark you are at various points along the way.
2. *Determine where you stand vis-á-vis objectives:* Evaluate current accomplishments relative to the desired results. Know where you stand in reaching the objectives; know what strengths work in your favor and what weaknesses may hold you back.
3. *Develop premises regarding future conditions:* Try to anticipate future events. Generate alternative "scenarios" for what may happen; identify for each scenario things that may help or hinder progress toward your objectives.
4. *Analyze and choose among action alternatives:* List and carefully evaluate the possible actions that may be taken. Choose the alternative(s) most likely to accomplish your objectives; describe step by step what must be done to follow the chosen course of action.
5. *Implement the plan and evaluate results:* Take action and carefully measure your progress toward objectives. Do what the plan requires; evaluate results; take corrective action, and revise plans as needed.

← Five steps in the planning process

The planning process just described is an application of the decision-making process introduced in Chapter 3. It is a systematic way to approach two important tasks: (1) setting performance objectives, and (2) deciding how to best achieve them. Importantly, in the complex setting of the modern workplace this is not a process that managers do while working alone in quiet rooms, free from distractions, and at scheduled times. Rather, planning should be part of a manager's everyday work routines. It should be an ongoing activity that is continuously done even while dealing with an otherwise hectic and demanding work setting.[6] Importantly, the best planning is always done with the active participation and involvement of those people whose work efforts will eventually determine whether the objectives are accomplished.

CAREER CONNECTION

Technology

Bureau of Labor Statistics
Where Will the Jobs Be?
Have you thought about where the job market is headed? One of the issues in career planning is to prepare yourself for the future job market, not just the present one. Take a look at information made available by the U.S. Bureau of Labor Statistics. The first thing you'll notice are the latest figures on unemployment, consumer price index, productivity, and more. There is current information on the U.S. economy, and the economies of states, regions, and major metropolitan areas.

Take a look at the up-to-date Career Guide to Industries, including manufacturing, finance and banking, and services. Did you know that the top five occupations projected as the fastest growing for a ten-year period are in the technology field? Computer engineers top the list, followed by computer support specialists, systems analysts, database administrators, and desktop publishing specialists. Health care is another growth industry; and retail service occupations are also expected to grow substantially.

Remember, no forecast is a guarantee of the future. The Bureau of Labor Statistics updates its forecasts regularly. Just like any good manager in any organization, however, you need to stay informed about developments in the labor markets. The U.S. Bureau of Labor Statistics web site is a good place to start.

QUESTION: Have you considered the career implications of job market trends? Are you heading toward a high-demand or low-demand occupation? Does your career planning recognize the need to prepare for a job market that values technology, skills, and knowledge?

BENEFITS OF PLANNING

Organizations in today's dynamic times are facing pressures from many sources. Externally, these include greater government regulations, ever-more-complex technologies, the uncertainties of a global economy, changing technologies, and the sheer cost of investments in labor, capital, and other supporting resources. Internally, they include the quest for operating efficiencies, new structures and technologies, alternative work arrangements, greater diversity in the workplace, and related managerial challenges. As you would expect, planning in such conditions offers a number of benefits.

Planning Improves Focus and Flexibility

Good planning improves focus and flexibility, both of which are important to the performance success of people and organizations in highly competitive and dynamic environments. An *organization with focus* knows what it does best, knows the needs of its customers, and knows how to serve them well. An *individual with focus* knows where he or she wants to go in a career or situation and is able to retain that objective even when difficulties arise. An *organization with flexibility* is willing and able to change and adapt to shifting circumstances, and operates with an orientation toward the future rather than the past or present. An *individual with flexibility* factors into career plans the problems and opportunities posed by new and developing situations—personal and organizational.

Planning Improves Action Orientation

Planning is a way for people and organizations to stay ahead of the competition and always become better at what they are doing. It helps avoid the complacency trap of simply being carried along by the flow of events or being distracted by successes or failures of the moment. It keeps the future visible as a performance target and reminds us that the best decisions are often made before events force them upon us. Management consultant Stephen R. Covey points out that the most successful executives "zero in on what they do that 'adds value' to an organization." Instead of working on too many things, Covey advises us to step back and identify the most important things to be doing.[7] Indeed, planning helps us to stay proactive rather than reactive in our approach to things. It does so because it makes us more (1) *results oriented*—creating a performance-oriented sense of direction; (2) *priority oriented*—making sure the most important things get first attention; (3) *advantage oriented*—ensuring that all resources are used to best advantage; and, (4) *change oriented*—anticipating problems and opportunities so they can be best dealt with.[8]

www.army.mil/

Continuous improvement is in with the U.S. Army. In the After-Action Review program, training exercises are videotaped and results are peer reviewed, with participants commenting on one another's performances. Expert observer-controllers give immediate feedback.

Planning Improves Coordination

Planning improves coordination. The many different individuals, groups, and subsystems in organizations are each doing many different things at the same time. But even as they pursue their specific tasks and objectives, their accomplishments must add up to meaningful contributions toward the needs of the organization as a whole. Good planning throughout an organization creates a *hierarchy of objectives* in which objectives at each level of work are linked together in means-ends fashion. Higher-level objectives as *ends* are directly tied to lower-level objectives as the *means* for their accomplishment.

Figure 7.2 uses the example of quality management to show how a hierarchy of objectives can guide and integrate efforts within a large manufacturing firm. The corporate-level quality objective is "Deliver error-free products that meet customer requirements 100 percent of the time." This translates down the hierarchy in means-ends fashion as a series of supporting objectives at each level. For one of the team leaders, it finally becomes a formal commitment to "assess capabilities of machine operators and provide/arrange appropriate training." Good planning helps ensure that the team leader's hard work in this example will make a positive contribution to the corporate-level quality objective.

Planning Improves Time Management

One of the side benefits that planning offers is better time management. Lewis Platt, former chairman of Hewlett-Packard, says: "Basically, the whole day is a series of choices."[9] These choices have to be made in ways that allocate your time to the most important priorities. Platt says that he is "ruthless about priorities" and that you "have to continually work to optimize your time."

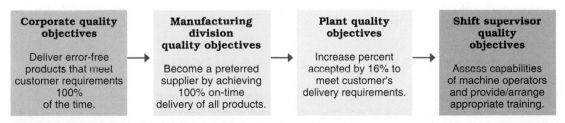

Corporate quality objectives	**Manufacturing division quality objectives**	**Plant quality objectives**	**Shift supervisor quality objectives**
Deliver error-free products that meet customer requirements 100% of the time.	Become a preferred supplier by achieving 100% on-time delivery of all products.	Increase percent accepted by 16% to meet customer's delivery requirements.	Assess capabilities of machine operators and provide/arrange appropriate training.

Figure 7.2 A sample hierarchy of objectives for total quality management.

MANAGER'S NOTEPAD 7.1

Tips on how to manage your time

- *Do* say "No" to requests that divert you from work you should be doing.
- *Don't* get bogged down in details that should be left to others.
- *Do* establish a system for screening telephone calls and e-mail.
- *Don't* let "drop-in" visitors use too much of your time.
- *Do* prioritize work tasks in order of importance and urgency.
- *Don't* become "calendar bound" by losing control of your schedule.
- *Do* work tasks in priority order.

Most of us have experienced the difficulties of balancing available time with the many commitments and opportunities we would like to fulfill. Each day, we are bombarded by a multitude of tasks and demands in a setting of frequent interruptions, crises, and unexpected events—the manager's job is especially subject to such complications. It is easy to lose track of time and fall prey to what consultants identify as "time wasters." In the process, too many of us allow our time to be dominated by other people and/or by what can be considered nonessential activities.[10] "To do" lists can help, but it is important to determine which "to dos" are the priorities, and then address them.[11] Some additional tips on how to manage your time are included in *Manager's Notepad 7.1*.

Planning Improves Control

When planning is done well, it is easier to exercise control by measuring performance results and taking action to improve things as necessary. Planning helps make this possible by defining the objectives along with the specific actions through which they are to be pursued. If results are less than expected, either the objectives or the action being taken, or both, can be evaluated and then adjusted in the control process. In this way planning and controlling work closely together in the management process. Without planning, control lacks a framework for measuring how well things are going and what could be done to make them go better. Without control, planning lacks the follow-through needed to ensure that things work out as intended.

TYPES OF PLANS USED BY MANAGERS

Managers face different planning challenges in the flow of activity in organizations. In some cases the planning environment is stable and quite predictable; in others it is more dynamic and uncertain. In all cases managers must understand the different types of plans and be able to use them effectively.

SHORT-RANGE AND LONG-RANGE PLANS

Organizations require plans that cover different time horizons. A rule of thumb is that *short-range plans* cover one year or less, *intermediate-range plans* cover one to two years, and *long-range plans* look three or more years

ENTREPRENEURSHIP
(www.volantsports.com) Volant Skis Inc.
A Tale of Two Brothers and Professional
Management

Colorado ski maker Volant Skis, Inc., founded by Hank and Bucky Kashiwa, was in trouble when consultant Mark Soderberg was hired. Half-finished skis were stacked everywhere; up to 40 percent of a day's production was being scrapped; dissatisfied customers left with unfilled orders. His approach? Admit the facts, stop production, analyze systems, and address quality problems. Within two years, orders were flowing again and production was smooth and efficient. As quality went up, costs went down. And with the ski business under control, management was able to consider strategic moves to counter the seasonality of skis, such as entering the golf or biking markets.[12]

into the future. Top management is most likely to be involved in setting long-range plans and directions for the organization as a whole, while lower management levels focus more on short-run plans that serve the long-term objectives. Importantly, all levels should understand the organization's long-term plans. In the absence of an integrated hierarchy of objectives and a long-range plan, there is always risk that the pressures of daily events may create confusion and divert attention from important tasks. In other words, we may be working hard but without achieving sustainable and clear long-term results.

Management researcher Elliot Jaques suggests that people vary in their capability to think out, organize, and work through events of different time horizons.[13] In fact, he believes that most people work comfortably with only three-month time spans; a smaller group works well with a one-year span; and only about one person in several million can handle a 20-year time frame. These are provocative ideas. Although a team leader's planning challenges may rest mainly in the weekly or monthly range, a chief executive is expected to have a vision extending five or more years into the future. Career progress to higher management levels requires the conceptual skills to work well with longer-range time frames.[14]

Complexities and uncertainties in today's environments are putting pressure on these planning horizons. In an increasingly global economy, planning opportunities and challenges are often worldwide in scope, not just local. And, of course, the information age is ever present in its planning implications. We now talk about planning in *Internet time*, where businesses are continually changing and updating plans. Even top managers must now face the reality that Internet time keeps making the "long" range of planning shorter and shorter.

STRATEGIC AND OPERATIONAL PLANS

Plans differ not only in time horizons but also in scope. **Strategic plans** address long-term needs and set comprehensive action directions for an organization or subunit. Top management planning of this scope involves determining objectives for the entire organization and then deciding on the actions and resource allocations to achieve them. There was a time, for example, when many large businesses sought to diversify into unrelated

○ A **strategic plan** comprehensively addresses long-term directions for the organization.

Consumer Spending on "E-tailing"
On-line retailing is surging, especially the travel industry. That's the report from Shop.org, the trade association for on-line retailers. What other areas do you think top the charts in on-line consumer spending? Take the on-line "Reality Check" to learn more about the results of this survey.

○　An **operational plan** addresses specific activities to implement strategic plans.

areas. A successful oil firm might have acquired an office products company or a successful cereal manufacturer might have acquired an apparel company. These decisions represent strategic choices regarding future directions for these companies and their use of scarce resources. Instead of reinvesting in areas of core competency, they were spending available monies on unrelated and probably unfamiliar areas of business activity. In the next chapter on strategic management we will examine the process through which such strategic choices are made and how they can be analyzed. For now, suffice it to say that diversification strategies haven't always proved successful. Many companies following them have since reversed course and followed the alternative strategy of divesting of unrelated businesses to focus on their core areas of expertise.

Operational plans define what needs to be done in specific areas to implement strategic plans and achieve strategic objectives. Typical operational plans in a business firm include *production plans*—dealing with the methods and technology needed by people in their work; *financial plans*—dealing with the money required to support various operations; *facilities plans*—dealing with the facilities and work layouts required to support task activities; *marketing plans*—dealing with the requirements of selling and distributing goods or services; and *human resource plans*—dealing with the recruitment, selection, and placement of people into various jobs.

POLICIES AND PROCEDURES

○　A **policy** is a standing plan that communicates broad guidelines for decisions and action.

Among the many plans in organizations, *standing plans* in the form of organizational policies and procedures are designed for use over and over again. They set guidelines that direct behavior in uniform directions for certain types of situations regardless of where or when they occur in an organization. A **policy** communicates broad guidelines for making decisions and taking action in specific circumstances. In matters relating to the workforce, for example, typical human resource policies address such matters as employee hiring, termination, performance appraisals, pay increases, and discipline.

Policies should focus attention on matters of special organizational consequence and then guide people in how they are supposed to deal with them. Consider the issue of *sexual harassment*. Enlightened employers take great pains to clearly spell out their policies on sexual harassment and the methods for implementing them. When Judith Nitsch started her own engineering consulting business, for example, she remembered the lessons of her corporate experience.[15] Nitsch defined a sexual harassment policy, took a hard line in its enforcement, and appointed both a male and a female employee for others to talk with about their sexual harassment concerns.

○　A **procedure** or **rule** precisely describes actions that are to be taken in specific situations.

Rules or **procedures** are plans that describe exactly what actions are to be taken in specific situations. They are often found stated in employee handbooks or manuals as "SOPs"—standard operating procedures. Whereas a sexual harassment policy, like Judith Nitsch's in the last example, sets a broad guideline for action, sexual harassment procedures define precise guidelines to be followed when someone believes they have been subjected to such harassment on the job. Under the policy, Nitsch will want to ensure that everyone receives fair, equal, and nondiscriminatory treatment should an alleged violation occur. One way to do this is to establish clear procedures regarding how a sexual harassment complaint is handled.

BUDGETS AND PROJECT SCHEDULES

In contrast to standing plans, which remain in place for extended periods of time, *single-use plans* are each used once to meet the needs of well-defined situations in a timely manner. **Budgets** are single-use plans that commit resources to activities, projects, or programs. They are powerful tools that allocate scarce resources among multiple and often competing uses. Good managers are able to bargain for and obtain adequate budgets to support the needs of their work units or teams. They are also able to achieve performance objectives while keeping resource expenditures within the allocated budget.

○ A **budget** is a plan that commits resources to projects or activities.

A *fixed budget* allocates resources on the basis of a single estimate of costs. The estimate establishes a fixed pool of resources that can be used, but not exceeded, in support of the specified purpose. For example, a manager may have a $25,000 budget for equipment purchases in a given year. A *flexible budget*, by contrast, allows the allocation of resources to vary in proportion with various levels of activity. Managers operating under flexible budgets can expect additional resource allocations when activity increases from one estimated level to the next. For example, a manager may have a budget allowance for hiring temporary workers if production orders exceed a certain volume.

In a **zero-based budget**, a project or activity is budgeted as if it were brand new. There is no assumption that resources previously allocated to a project or activity will simply be continued in the future. Instead, all projects compete anew for available funds. The intent is to totally reconsider priorities, objectives, and activities at the start of each new budget cycle. Using zero-based budgeting in a major division of Campbell Soups, for example, managers once discovered that 10 percent of the marketing budget was going to sales promotions no longer relevant to current product lines. Businesses, government agencies, and other types of organizations use zero-based budgeting to make sure that only the most desirable and timely programs receive funding.

○ A **zero-based budget** allocates resources to a project or activity as if it were brand new.

Project schedules are single-use plans that identify the activities required to accomplish a specific major project—for example, the completion of a new student activities building on a campus, the development of a new computer software program, or the implementation of a new advertising campaign for a sports team. In each case, the project schedule would define specific task objectives, activities to be accomplished, due dates and timetables for the activities, and resource requirements. Importantly, a good project schedule sets priorities so that everyone involved knows not only what needs to be done but also in what order so that the entire project gets finished on time.

○ A **project schedule** is a single-use plan for accomplishing a specific set of tasks.

PLANNING TOOLS AND TECHNIQUES

Planning is clearly essential to the success of the management process. The benefits, however, are most often realized when the planning approaches are comprehensive and the foundations are well established. In the latter regard, the useful planning tools and techniques include forecasting, contingency planning, the use of scenarios, benchmarking, participative planning, and the use of staff planners.

FORECASTING

○ A **forecast** is an attempt to predict future outcomes.

A **forecast** is a vision of the future. Forecasting is the process of making assumptions about what will happen in the future.[16] All good plans involve forecasts, either implicit or explicit. Periodicals such as *Business Week*, *Fortune*, and the *Economist* regularly report a variety of forecasts as a service to their readers—forecasts of economic conditions, interest rates, unemployment, and trade deficits, among other issues. Some are based on *qualitative forecasting*, which uses expert opinions to predict the future. In this case, a single person of special expertise or reputation or a panel of experts may be consulted. Others involve *quantitative forecasting* that uses mathematical and statistical analysis of data banks to predict future events. Time-series analysis makes predictions by using statistical routines such as regression analysis to project past trends into the future. General economic trends are often forecasted by econometric models that simulate events and make predictions based on relationships discovered among variables in the models. Statistical analysis of opinion polls and attitude surveys, such as those reported in newspapers and on television, are typically used to predict future consumer tastes, employee preferences, and political choices, among other issues.

Get Connected!

Visit *Fortune* or *Business Week* or the *Economist* on-line to find a current business or economic forecast.

In the final analysis forecasting always relies on human judgment. Even the results of highly sophisticated quantitative approaches still require interpretation. Forecasts should always be viewed as subject to error and therefore treated cautiously. Managers should remember that forecasting is not planning; planning is a more comprehensive activity that involves deciding what to do about the implications of forecasts once they are made. At GE Appliances, for example, no detail is neglected as the firm's planners study new international markets. Investment plans are made only after each country's unique points are carefully studied so that a mix of products and marketing approaches can be tailored to its needs.[17]

CONTINGENCY PLANNING

Planning, by definition, involves thinking ahead. But the more uncertain the planning environment, the more likely that one's original assumptions, predictions, and intentions may prove to be in error. Even the most carefully prepared projections may prove inadequate as experience develops. Unexpected problems and events frequently occur. When they do, plans may have to be changed. It is best to anticipate during the planning process that things might not go as expected. Alternatives to the existing plan can then be developed and readied for use when and if circumstances make them appropriate.

○ **Contingency planning** identifies alternative courses of action for use if and when circumstances change with time.

This is the process of **contingency planning**, identifying alternative courses of action that can be implemented if and when an original plan proves inadequate because of changing circumstances. Of course, changes in the planning environment must be detected as early as possible. "Trigger points" that indicate that an existing plan is no longer desirable must be preselected and then monitored. Sometimes this is accomplished simply by good forward thinking on the part of managers and staff planners. At other times, it can be assisted by a "devil's advocate" method, in which planners are formally assigned to develop worst-case forecasts of future events.

SCENARIO PLANNING

A long-term version of contingency planning, called **scenario planning**, involves identifying several alternative future scenarios or states of affairs that may occur. Plans are then made to deal with each should it actually occur.[18] Identifying different possible scenarios ahead of time helps organizations operate more flexibly in dynamic environments. Royal Dutch/Shell, for example, has been doing scenario planning for many years. The process began some 15 years ago when top managers asked themselves a perplexing question: "What would Shell do after its oil supplies ran out?" The question was answered by creating alternative future scenarios while remaining sensitive to the nature of growing environmental changes. Although recognizing that planning scenarios can never be inclusive of all future possibilities, a planning coordinator once said that scenarios help "condition the organization to think" and remain better prepared than its competitors for "future shocks." Among the issues and concerns for scenario planning today, the firm includes climate change, sustainable development, human rights, and biodiversity, among others.[19]

○ **Scenario planning** identifies alternative future scenarios and makes plans to deal with each.

BENCHMARKING

Another important influence on the success or failure of planning involves the frame of reference used as a starting point. All too often planners have only a limited awareness of what is happening outside the immediate work setting. Successful planning must challenge the status quo; it cannot simply accept things the way they are. One way to do this is through **benchmarking**, a technique that makes use of external comparisons to better evaluate one's current performance and identify possible actions for the future.[20] The purpose of benchmarking is to find out what other people and organizations are doing very well and to then plan how to incorporate these ideas into one's own operations. This powerful planning technique is increasingly popular in today's competitive business world. It is a way for progressive companies to learn from other "excellent" companies, not just competitors. It allows them to analyze and thoroughly compare all systems and processes for efficiencies and opportunities for innovation.

○ **Benchmarking** uses external comparisons to gain insights for planning.

USE OF STAFF PLANNERS

As the planning needs of organizations grow, there is a corresponding need to increase the sophistication of the overall planning system itself. In some cases, staff planners are employed to help coordinate planning for the organization as a whole or for one of its major components. These planners should be skilled in all steps of the formal planning process, including the benchmarking and scenario-planning approaches just discussed. They should also understand the staff, or advisory, nature of their roles. Given clear responsibilities and their special planning expertise, staff planners can bring focus to efforts to accomplish important, often strategic, planning tasks. But one risk is a tendency for a communication "gap" to develop between staff planners and line managers. This can cause a great deal of difficulty. Resulting plans may lack relevance, and line personnel may lack commitment to implement them

Get Connected!

Interested in technology? Check George Washington University's tech-forecast web site.

even if they are relevant. One trend in organizations today is to deemphasize the role of large staff planning groups and to place much greater emphasis on the participation and involvement of line managers in the planning process.

PARTICIPATION AND INVOLVEMENT

○ **Participatory planning** includes the people who will be affected by plans and/or whose help is needed to implement them.

Participation is a key word in the planning process. The concept of **participatory planning** requires that the process include people who will be affected by the resulting plans and/or will be asked to help implement them. This brings to the organization many benefits. Participation can increase the creativity and information available for planning. It can also increase the understanding, acceptance, and commitment of people to final plans. Indeed, planning should be organized and accomplished in a participatory manner that includes the contributions of many people representing diverse responsibilities and vantage points. This includes the level of strategic planning, once considered only the province of top management. The more aware all levels are of strategic plans and the more they are involved in helping to establish them, the greater the commitment throughout the organization to their accomplishment.

The centrality of participation in the planning process is highlighted in *Figure 7.3*. To create and implement the best plans, proper attention must always be given to genuinely involving others during all planning steps. Even though this process may mean that planning takes more time, it can improve results by improving implementation. When 7-Eleven executives planned for a dramatic overhaul of the firm—including a new information system and the introduction of new "upscale" products and services such as selling fancy meals-to-go—they learned a hard lesson on the value of participation in planning. Although their ideas sounded good at the top, franchisees balked at the

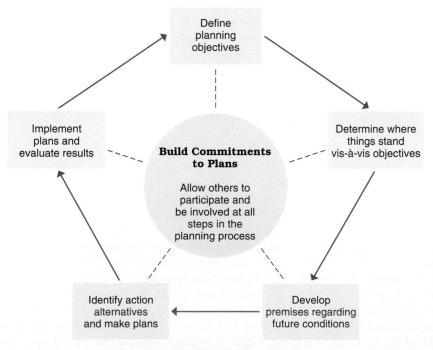

Formal Planning Process

Figure 7.3 How participation and involvement help build commitments to plans.

level of operations. The executives found that they needed to take time to sell the franchise owners before the advantages of their new corporate strategies could be realized. Now "University 7-Eleven" acts as a training hub to prepare workers for the new economy. The firm is planning a V.com service that allows videos and books to be ordered on-line and delivered to the local 7-Eleven store.[21]

THE CONTROL PROCESS

"Keeping in touch . . . Staying informed . . . Being in control." In addition to planning, these are important responsibilities for every manager. But *control* is a word like *power*; if you aren't careful when it is used, it leaves a negative connotation. Yet control plays a positive and necessary role in the management process. To have things "under control" is good; for things to be "out of control" generally is bad. As part of the management process, **controlling** is defined as a process of measuring performance and taking action to ensure desired results.

○ **Controlling** is the process of measuring performance and taking action to ensure desired results.

IMPORTANCE OF CONTROLLING

The purpose of controlling is straightforward—to make sure that plans are fulfilled and that actual performance meets or surpasses objectives. The foundation of control is information. Henry Schacht, former CEO of Cummins Engine Company, once discussed control in terms of what he called "friendly facts." He stated, "Facts that reinforce what you are doing . . . are nice, because they help in terms of psychic reward. Facts that raise alarms are equally friendly, because they give you clues about how to respond, how to change, where to spend the resources."[22]

If you refer back to Figure 7.1, it shows how controlling fits in with the rest of the management process. Planning sets the directions and allocates resources. Organizing brings people and material resources together in working combinations. Leading inspires people to best utilize these resources. Controlling sees to it that the right things happen, in the right way, and at the right time. It helps ensure that the performance contributions of individuals and groups are consistent with organizational plans. It helps ensure that performance accomplishments throughout an organization are consistent with one another in means-ends fashion. And it helps ensure that people comply with organizational policies and procedures.

STEPS IN THE CONTROL PROCESS

The classic example of the control process operating in its purest form is a home thermostat. We set the thermostat to a desired temperature. When the room gets too cold or hot, the thermostat senses the deviation and takes corrective action by turning on the heater or air conditioner. Once the desired temperature is achieved, the furnace or air conditioner is automatically turned off. This illustrates a **cybernetic control system**—one that is self-contained in its performance-monitoring and correction capabilities. The control process as practiced in organizations is not cybernetic, but it does follow similar principles.

○ A **cybernetic control system** is self-contained in its performance-monitoring and correction capabilities.

DIVERSITY (www.projectequality.org)
Project Equality Control Helps Promote
Fairness in Service and Employment

When the U. S. Department of Justice needed a Compliance Officer to monitor a settlement reached in an $8 million discrimination suit with the Adam's Mark hotel and resort chain, Project Equality was the choice. Project Equality will monitor Adam's Mark policies on customer service, employee training, and complaint investigation procedures, as well as conduct diversity training for the firm. It will also hire "discrimination testers" who will travel to Adam's Mark hotels and report on their treatment.[23]

As shown in *Figure 7.4*, the management control process involves four steps: (1) establish objectives and standards; (2) measure actual performance; (3) compare results with objectives and standards; and (4) take corrective action as needed. While essential to management, the process and its implications apply equally well to personal career planning. Think about it. Without career objectives, how do you know where you really want to go? How can you allocate your time and other resources to take best advantage of available opportunities? Without measurement standards, how can you assess any progress being made? How can you adjust current behavior to improve the prospects for future results?

Step 1: Establish Objectives and Standards

The control process starts with planning, when performance objectives and standards for measuring them are set. It can't begin without them. Performance objectives, furthermore, should represent key results that one wants to accomplish. The word "key" in the prior sentence is important. The focus in planning should be on describing "critical" or "essential" results that will make a substantial difference in the success of the organization. The standards are important, too, and they must also be considered right from the beginning. As key results are identified, one also has to specify the standards or specific measures that will be taken to indicate success or failure in their accomplishment. At Allstate Corporation, for example, a "diversity index" is used to quantify performance results on diversity issues. The firm surveys employees on how well it is doing in meeting its goals of bias-free customer service and respect for all. Employees rate their managers on a diversity index to show how well their behavior matches expectations. The diversity index scores help determine pay bonuses.[24]

○ An **output standard** measures performance results in terms of quantity, quality, cost, or time.

○ An **input standard** measures work efforts that go into a performance task.

Two types of standards are common to the organizational control process. **Output standards** measure performance results in terms of outcomes like quantity, quality, cost, or time of accomplished work. Allstate's use of the diversity index to rate managerial behavior is one example; others include percentage error rate, dollar deviation from budgeted expenditures, and the number of units produced or customers serviced in a time period. **Input standards**, by contrast, measure effort in terms of the amount of work expended in task performance. They are used in situations where outputs are difficult or expensive to measure. Examples of input standards include conformance to rules and procedures, efficiency in the use of resources, and work attendance or punctuality.

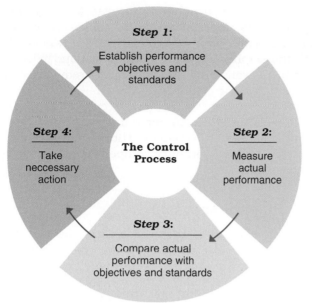

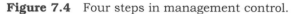

Figure 7.4 Four steps in management control.

Step 2: Measure Actual Performance

The second step of the control process is to measure actual performance. The goal here is to accurately measure the performance results (output standards) and/or the performance efforts (input standards). In both cases, the measurement must be accurate enough to spot significant differences between what is really taking place and what was originally planned. A common management failure in this regard is an unwillingness or inability to measure the performance of people at work. Yet without measurement, effective control is not possible.

Managers need to get comfortable with the act of measurement. When Linda Sanford was appointed head of IBM's sales force, she came with an admirable performance record during a 22-year career with the company. Notably, Sanford grew up on a family farm where she developed an appreciation for both teamwork and measuring results. "At the end of the day, you saw what you did, knew how many rows of strawberries you picked." At IBM she was known for walking around the factory just to see "at the end of the day how many machines were going out of the back dock."[25]

Step 3: Compare Results with Objectives and Standards

Step 3 in the control process is to compare measured performance with objectives and standards to establish the need for action. This step can be expressed as the following *control equation:* Need for Action = Desired Performance − Actual Performance.

There are different ways of comparing desired and actual performance. A *historical comparison* uses past performance as a benchmark for evaluating current performance. A *relative comparison* uses the performance achievements of other persons, work units, or organizations as the evaluation standard. An *engineering comparison* uses engineered standards set scientifically through such methods as time and motion studies. The delivery routines of drivers for UPS, for example, are carefully measured in terms of expected minutes per delivery on various routes.

www.shrm.org/

Are you familiar with the Society for Human Resource Management? SHRM reports that up to 25 percent of job applications and resumés contain errors. It is always important to check the references of job applicants to make sure that you get the right person to fill openings.

Earlier, the concept of benchmarking was formally introduced as a planning approach. Its importance to the control process is also clear. Benchmarking is rapidly gaining popularity as a means of identifying best practices, with the emphasis always on the question: "What can I or we do better?" Without rigorous and regular measurement comparisons—be they historical, relative, or engineering driven—answers to this question are difficult to get. In an Ernst & Young survey of fast-growing small businesses, for example, more than 80 percent were found to be using benchmarking to improve their performances. The comparisons were most likely to involve industry norms, a primary competitor, the industry leader, and similar world-class firms.[26]

Step 4: Take Corrective Action

○ **Management by exception** focuses managerial attention on substantial differences between actual and desired performance.

The control equation indicates that the greater the measured difference between desired and actual performance, the greater the need for action. The final step in the control process, accordingly, is taking any action necessary to correct or improve things. This allows for a judicious use of **management by exception**—the practice of giving priority attention to situations that show the greatest need for action. This approach can save valuable time, energy, and other resources, while allowing all efforts to be concentrated on the areas of greatest need.

Two types of exceptions may be encountered. The first is a *problem situation* in which actual performance is below the standard. The reasons for this performance deficiency must be understood. Corrective action is required to restore performance to the desired level. The second exception is an *opportunity situation* in which actual performance is above the standard. The reasons for this extraordinary performance must also be understood. Action should then be taken to continue this higher level of accomplishment in the future. The original plan, objectives, and standards can also be reviewed to determine whether they should be updated.

Measurement is certainly an important key to the control process. But so too is the willingness to confront the implications of the measurements, to learn from experience, and to actively plan to improve future performance. Consider, for example, the program of **after-action review** pioneered by the U.S. Army and now utilized in many corporate settings. This is a structured review of lessons learned and results accomplished on a completed project, task force, or special operation. Participants are asked to answer questions like: "What was the intent?" "What actually happened?" "What did we learn?"[27] The review focuses on team and individual learning, and focuses this learning on ways to improve performance in the future. It helps make continuous improvement a part of the organizational culture, and it encourages the people involved to take responsibility for their performance efforts and accomplishments.

○ An **after-action review** formally reviews results to identify lessons learned in a completed project, task force, or special operation.

TYPES OF CONTROLS

There are three major types of managerial controls—feedforward, concurrent, and feedback controls, as shown in *Figure 7.5*.[28] Each is relevant to a different phase of the organization's input-throughput-output cycle of activities. Each offers significant opportunities for actions to be taken that advance organizational productivity and high performance. And importantly, each offers the opportunity for performance-oriented organizational and personal learning through systematic assessment of actions and results.

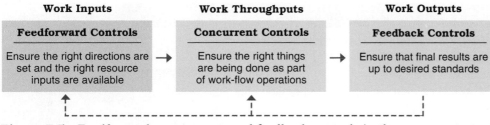

Figure 7.5 Feedforward, concurrent, and feedback controls in the management process.

Feedforward Controls

Feedforward controls, also called *preliminary controls*, are accomplished before a work activity begins. They ensure that objectives are clear, that proper directions are established, and that the right resources are available to accomplish them. By making sure that the stage is properly set for high performance, feedforward controls are preventive in nature. They are designed to eliminate the potential for problems later on in the process by asking an important but often-neglected question: "What needs to be done before we begin?" This is a forward-thinking and proactive approach to control rather than a reactive and defensive one.

The quality of resources is a key concern of feedback controls. At McDonald's, for example, preliminary control of food ingredients plays an important role in the firm's quality program. The company requires that suppliers of its hamburger buns produce them to exact specifications, covering everything from texture to uniformity of color. Even in overseas markets, the firm works hard to develop local suppliers that can offer dependable quality.[29]

○ A **feedforward control** ensures that directions and resources are right before the work begins.

Concurrent Controls

Concurrent controls focus on what happens during the work process. Sometimes called *steering controls*, they monitor ongoing operations and activities to make sure things are being done according to plan. Ideally, concurrent controls allow corrective actions to be taken before a task is completed. The key question is "What can we do to improve things before we finish?" Here, the focus is on quality of task activities during the work process. This approach to control can reduce waste in the form of unacceptable finished products or services.

Taking McDonald's again as an example, ever-present shift leaders provide concurrent control through direct supervision. They constantly observe what is taking place even while helping out with the work. They are trained to intervene immediately when something is not done right and to correct things on the spot. Detailed instruction manuals also "steer" workers in the right directions as their jobs are performed.

○ A **concurrent control** focuses on what happens during the work process.

Feedback Controls

Feedback controls, also called *postaction controls*, take place after work is completed. They focus on the quality of end results rather than on inputs and activities. They ask the question "Now that we are finished, how well did we do?" Restaurants, for example, ask how you liked a meal . . . after it is eaten; a final exam grade tells you how well you performed . . . after the course is over; a budget summary informs managers of any cost overruns . . . after a project is completed. In these and

○ A **feedback control** takes place after an action is completed.

TAKE IT TO THE CASE!

Wal-Mart Stores, Inc. *(www.walmart.com)*
Self-Management Counts at the #1 Retailer

Numbers count at Wal-Mart, a firm that takes its financial performance very seriously. Considered a model of management and operations for other retailers to follow, top management at the firm founded by Sam Walton has to take its performance seriously. That's part of the deal when you're #1 in a global industry. Work isn't always easy at Wal-Mart Stores, but it can be fulfilling. Nancy Handley once supervised the men's department at a suburban St. Louis store. She put in long hours, but liked the responsibility and recognition that came with the job. "I'm proud of who I've made myself into, and the department I've created," she said. Her daily decisions ranged from display changes to ordering merchandise and even some pricing. With experience came confidence and success. "I used to be scared" with the responsibility, Nancy said, but that grew into confidence that she made "pretty good decisions."[30]

other circumstances the feedback provided by the control process is useful information for improving things in the future. It also provides formal documentation of accomplishments that may be used for allocating performance-based rewards.

Employees at a McDonald's restaurant never know when a corporate evaluator may stop in to sample the food and the service. When this happens, however, the evaluator provides feedback with the goal of improving future operations.

INTERNAL AND EXTERNAL CONTROL

○ **Internal control** occurs through self-discipline and self-control.

○ **External control** occurs through direct supervision or administrative systems such as rules and procedures.

Managers have two broad options with respect to control. They can rely on people to exercise self-control over their own behavior. This strategy of **internal control** allows motivated individuals and groups to exercise self-discipline in fulfilling job expectations. Alternatively, managers can take direct action to control the behavior of others. This is a strategy of **external control** that occurs through personal supervision and the use of formal administrative systems. Organizations with effective control typically use both strategies to good advantage. However, the trend today is to increase the emphasis on internal or self-control. This is consistent with the renewed emphasis on participation, empowerment, and involvement in the workplace.

Internal control is exercised by people who are motivated to take charge of their own behavior on the job, and who are given the chance to do so. Douglas McGregor's Theory Y perspective, introduced in Chapter 4, recognizes the willingness of people to exercise self-control in their work.[31] Of course, McGregor also recognized that people are most likely to do this when they participate in setting performance objectives and standards. Reliance on an internal control strategy also requires a high degree of trust. When people are expected to work on their own and exercise self-control, managers must give them a chance to meet performance expectations.

The potential for self-control is increased when capable people have a clear sense of organizational mission, know their performance objectives, and have the resources necessary to do their jobs well. It is also enhanced by participative organizational cultures in which people are expected to treat each other with respect and consideration, are allowed to exercise personal initiative, and are given ample opportunities to experience satisfaction through job performance.

ORGANIZATIONAL CONTROL SYSTEMS

Each component in an organization's control systems should contribute to maintaining predictably high levels of performance. Internal control should be encouraged and supported; external control should be appropriate and rigorous. The management process provides for a certain amount of control when planning, organizing, and leading are well done. Additional and comprehensive control is provided by appropriate systems such as those dealing with compensation and benefits, employee discipline, financial information, and operations management.

COMPENSATION AND BENEFITS

Base compensation plays an important role in attracting a highly qualified workforce to the organization. If compensation is attractive and competitive in the prevailing labor markets, it can make the organization highly desirable as a place of employment. And if you get the right people into jobs, you can reduce costs and boost productivity over the long run. After all, the more capable a person is, the more self-control one can expect that person to exercise. When the wage and salary structure of an organization is unattractive and uncompetitive, however, it will be difficult to attract and retain a staff of highly competent workers. The less capable the workforce, the greater the burden on external controls to ensure that desired levels of performance are achieved and maintained.

The use of incentive compensation systems, discussed in Chapter 14 on motivation and rewards, also helps. When properly implemented, "pay-for-performance" and "merit pay" plans serve as control systems. They can be strong influences on individual and group behavior. The logic is quite straightforward, as described this way by a corporate executive: "Pay very poorly for poor performance; pay poorly for average performance; pay well for above-average performance; pay obscenely well for outstanding performance."[32]

Percentage of Women as Corporate Officers
Catalyst reports that 50 of the Fortune 500 companies had women holding a quarter or more of the top jobs in 2000; a 100 percent increase since 1995. But 90 companies from the list had none. Take the on-line "Reality Check" to learn more about women at the top ranks of corporations.

Because of the growing importance of a worker's total compensation package, fringe benefits also have control implications. Their attractiveness can also affect an organization's ability to recruit and retain a qualified workforce. In today's environment of rising costs and workforce diversity, fringe benefits—from health insurance to pension plans to child and elder care and more—can be very expensive. Many employers are now trying to provide individuals with more choice in selecting benefits that suit their diverse needs. At the same time, employers are seeking ways to reduce expenditures by asking employees to pay more of the fringe benefits' cost—an unpopular move with employees and labor unions alike.

EMPLOYEE DISCIPLINE SYSTEMS

Absenteeism . . . tardiness . . . sloppy work . . . the list of undesirable conduct can go on to even more extreme actions: falsifying records . . . sexual harassment . . . embezzlement. All are examples of behaviors that

Get Connected!

Do you know what you are worth? Check out where you're at and where you could be at Salary.com.

○ **Discipline** is the act of influencing behavior through reprimand.

○ **Progressive discipline** is the process of tying reprimands to the severity and frequency of misbehavior.

can and should be formally addressed in employee discipline systems. **Discipline** is the act of influencing behavior through reprimand. Ideally, this form of managerial control is handled in a fair, consistent, and systematic way.

Progressive discipline ties reprimands to the severity and frequency of the employee's infractions. Under such a system, penalties vary according to how significant a disruptive behavior is and how often it occurs. For example, the progressive discipline guidelines of one university state: "The level of disciplinary action shall increase with the level of severity of behavior engaged in and based on whether the conduct is of a repetitive nature." In this particular case, the ultimate penalty of "discharge" is reserved for the most severe behaviors (e.g., any felony crime) or for continual infractions of a less severe nature (e.g., being continually late for work and failing to respond to a series of written reprimands and/or suspensions).

The goal of a progressive discipline system is to achieve compliance with organizational expectations through the least extreme reprimand possible. But even this type of control can have unpleasant consequences. Sometimes the relationships between managers and disciplined workers take on an adversarial character. Sometimes managers wait too long and fail to take disciplinary action until a problem is very severe. And sometimes, poor attitudes form among persons who can't seem to change and keep receiving ever-harsher punishments.[33]

One way to develop a consistent personal approach to disciplinary situations is to remember the analogy of the "hot stove rules" of discipline. They begin with a simple rule: "When a stove is hot, don't touch it." We also know that when this rule is violated, you get burned—immediately, consistently, but usually not beyond the possibility of repair. Six "hot stove rules" for using reprimands in disciplinary action are described in *Manager's Notepad 7.2*.[34]

MANAGER'S NOTEPAD 7.2

"Hot stove rules" of employee discipline

- A reprimand should be immediate; a hot stove burns the first time you touch it.
- A reprimand should be directed toward someone's actions, not the individual's personality; a hot stove doesn't hold grudges, doesn't try to humiliate people, and doesn't accept excuses.
- A reprimand should be consistently applied; a hot stove burns anyone who touches it, and it does so every time.
- A reprimand should be informative; a hot stove lets a person know what to do to avoid getting burned in the future—"Don't touch."
- A reprimand should occur in a supportive setting; a hot stove conveys warmth but with an inflexible rule—"Don't touch."
- A reprimand should support realistic rules; the don't-touch-a-hot-stove rule isn't a power play, a whim, or an emotion of the moment; it is a necessary rule of reason.

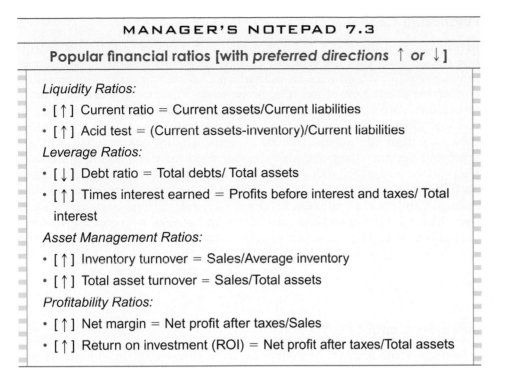

MANAGER'S NOTEPAD 7.3

Popular financial ratios [with *preferred directions* ↑ or ↓]

Liquidity Ratios:
- [↑] Current ratio = Current assets/Current liabilities
- [↑] Acid test = (Current assets-inventory)/Current liabilities

Leverage Ratios:
- [↓] Debt ratio = Total debts/ Total assets
- [↑] Times interest earned = Profits before interest and taxes/ Total interest

Asset Management Ratios:
- [↑] Inventory turnover = Sales/Average inventory
- [↑] Total asset turnover = Sales/Total assets

Profitability Ratios:
- [↑] Net margin = Net profit after taxes/Sales
- [↑] Return on investment (ROI) = Net profit after taxes/Total assets

INFORMATION AND FINANCIAL CONTROLS

The pressure is ever present today for all organizations to use their resources well and to perform with maximum efficiency. The use of information in financial analysis of firm or organizational performance is critical in managerial control. At a minimum, managers should be able to understand and assess for control purposes the following important financial aspects of organizational performance: (1) *Liquidity*—ability to generate cash to pay bills; (2) *Leverage*—ability to earn more in returns than the cost of debt; (3) *Asset management*—ability to use resources efficiently and operate at minimum cost; and, (4) *Profitability*—ability to earn revenues greater than costs.

These financial performance indicators can be assessed using a variety of financial ratios, including those shown in *Manager's Notepad 7.3*. Such ratios provide a framework for historical comparisons within the firm and external benchmarking relative to industry performance. They can also be used to set financial targets or goals to be shared with employees and tracked to indicate success or failure in their accomplishment. At Civco Medical Instruments, for example, a financial scorecard is shared with all employees. It shows the firm's financial performance on various key ratios on a monthly and annual basis. Employees always know factually how well the firm is doing. This helps them focus on what they can do differently and better, and strengthens personal commitments to future improvements in the firm's "bottom line."[35]

OPERATIONS MANAGEMENT AND CONTROL

Control is integral to operations management, where the emphasis is always on utilizing people, resources, and technology to best advantage. The areas of purchasing control, inventory control, and statistical quality control are all receiving current managerial attention.

Purchasing Control

Rising costs of materials are a fact of life in today's economy. Controlling these costs through efficient purchasing management is an important productivity tool. Like an individual, a thrifty organization must be concerned about how much it pays for what it buys. To leverage buying power more organizations are centralizing purchasing to allow buying in volume. They are committing to a small number of suppliers with whom they can negotiate special contracts, gain quality assurances, and get preferred service. They are also finding ways to work together in supplier-purchaser partnerships so they can operate in ways that allow each partner to better contain its costs. It is now more common, for example, that parts suppliers keep warehouses in their customer's facilities. The supplier maintains inventory and stocks it according to forecasted demand. The customer provides the space; the supplier does the rest. The benefits to the customer are lower purchasing costs and preferred service; the supplier gains an exclusive customer contract and more sales volume.

Inventory Control

Inventory is the amount of materials or products kept in storage. Organizations maintain inventories of raw materials, work in process, and/or finished goods. The goal of inventory control is to make sure that an inventory is just the right size to meet performance needs, thus minimizing the cost. The **economic order quantity** (EOQ) method of inventory control involves ordering a fixed number of items every time an inventory level falls to a predetermined point. When this point is reached, a decision is automatically made (typically by computer) to place a standard order to replenish the stock. Standard order sizes are mathematically calculated to minimize costs of inventory. The best example is the local supermarket, where hundreds of daily orders are routinely made on this basis.

○ Inventory control by **economic order quantity** orders replacements whenever inventory level falls to a predetermined point.

Another approach to inventory control is **just-in-time scheduling** (JIT). Made popular by the productivity of Japanese industry, JIT systems try to reduce costs and improve workflow by scheduling materials to arrive at a work station or facility "just in time" to be used. This minimizes carrying costs since almost no inventories are maintained—materials are ordered or components produced only as needed. The just-in-time approach is an important productivity-enhancing management innovation. The system allows production and purchasing to be done in small quantities and no earlier than necessary for use.

○ **Just-in-time scheduling** minimizes inventory by routing materials to work stations "just in time" to be used.

Statistical Quality Control

Consistent with the total quality management theme in today's workplace, the practice of **quality control** involves checking processes, materials, products, and services to ensure that they meet high standards. This responsibility applies to all aspects of operations, from the selection of raw materials and supplies right down to the last task performed to deliver the finished good or service. In *statistical quality control*, the process is supported by rigorous statistical analysis. Typically this means taking samples of work, measuring quality in the samples, and then determining the acceptability of results. Unacceptable results in a sample call attention to the need for investigation and corrective action to bring operations back up to standard. The power of statistics allows the sampling to be

○ **Quality control** checks processes, materials, products, and services to ensure that they meet high standards.

efficiently used as the basis for decision making. At General Electric, for example, a Six Sigma program drives the quest for competitive advantage. This means that statistically the firm's quality performance will tolerate no more than 3.4 defects per million—a perfection rate of 99.9997 percent! As tough as it sounds, "Six Sigma" is a common quality standard for the new workplace.

MBO: INTEGRATED PLANNING AND CONTROLLING

As shown throughout this chapter, planning and controlling must work together. A useful technique for integrating them in day-to-day practice is **management by objectives (MBO).** This is a structured process of regular communication in which a supervisor/team leader and subordinate/team member jointly set performance objectives and review results accomplished.[36] In its simplest terms, MBO requires a formal agreement between the supervisor and subordinate concerning (1) the subordinate's performance objectives for a given time period, (2) the plans through which they will be accomplished, (3) standards for measuring whether they have been accomplished, and (4) procedures for reviewing performance results.

> ○ **MBO** is a process of joint objective setting between a superior and subordinate.

MBO Process

The MBO process is illustrated in *Figure 7.6*. Note that the supervisor and subordinate *jointly* establish plans and *jointly* control results in any good MBO action framework. They agree on the high-priority performance objectives for the subordinate along with a timetable for their accomplishment and the criteria to be used in evaluating results.

Performance objectives are essential parts of the MBO. The way objectives are specified and how they are established will influence the success of the MBO process. Three types of objectives may be specified in an MBO contract. *Improvement objectives* document intentions for improving performance in a specific way and with respect to a specific factor. An example is "to reduce quality rejects by 10 percent." *Personal development objectives* pertain to personal growth activities, often those resulting in expanded job knowledge or skills. An example is "to learn the latest version of a computer spreadsheet package." Some MBO contracts also include *maintenance objectives*, which formally express intentions to maintain performance at an existing level. In all cases, performance objectives are written and formally agreed to by both the superior and subordinate. They also meet the following four *criteria of a good performance objective*:

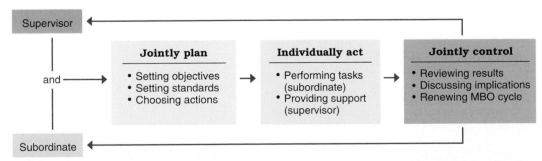

Figure 7.6 Management by objectives—an integrated planning and control framework.

Criteria of a good
performance objective

$\longrightarrow$

1. *Specific*—targets a key result to be accomplished.
2. *Time defined*—identifies a date for achieving results.
3. *Challenging*—offers a realistic and attainable challenge.
4. *Measurable*—is as specific and quantitative as possible.

One of the more difficult aspects of MBO relates to the last criterion—the need to state performance objectives as specifically and quantitatively as possible. Ideally, this occurs as agreement on a *measurable end product*, for example, "to reduce housekeeping supply costs by 5 percent by the end of the fiscal year." But some jobs, particularly managerial ones, involve performance areas that are hard to quantify. Rather than abandon MBO in such cases, it is often possible to agree on performance objectives that are stated as *verifiable work activities*. The accomplishment of the activities can then serve as an indicator of progress under the performance objective. An example is "to improve communications with my subordinates in the next three months by holding weekly group meetings." Whereas it can be difficult to measure "improved communications," it is easy to document whether the "weekly group meetings" have been held.

MBO Pros and Cons

MBO is one of the most talked about and debated management concepts of the past 25 years, and it has many advocates and critics.[37] As a result, good advice is available on what to do and what not to do if MBO is to be used to maximum advantage. Things to avoid doing in MBO include tying it to pay, focusing too much attention on easy objectives, requiring excessive paperwork, and having supervisors simply *tell* subordinates their objectives.

A major advantage of MBO is that it clearly focuses the subordinate's work efforts on the most important tasks and objectives; another is that it focuses the supervisor's work efforts on areas of support that can truly help the subordinate meet the agreed-upon objectives. Because the process involves direct face-to-face communication between supervisor and subordinate, MBO contributes to relationship building. It also gives the subordinate a structured opportunity to participate in decisions that affect his or her work. This encourages self-management rather than external control.[38] The motivational value of goal setting, to be discussed in Chapter 14, further suggests that participation in the MBO process can create a powerful enthusiasm to fulfill one's performance obligations.[39]

None of this potential is lost on many of today's best managers. Although they may describe what they are doing by different names, it has a common thread that is consistent with the MBO concept: if you want high performance from individual contributors, you must hire the best people, work with them to set challenging performance objectives, give them the best possible support, and hold them accountable for results.

STUDY Guide

The Chapter 7 Study Guide will help you review chapter content, prepare for examinations, and further build your career readiness. The *Summary* briefly highlights answers to questions first posed in the chapter opening Planning Ahead section. The list of *Key Terms* allows you to double check your familiarity with basic concepts and definitions. *Self-Test 7* gives you the opportunity to test your basic comprehension of chapter content using sample test questions. Suggestions offered as *Career Readiness Activities* direct your attention to relevant sections of the Career Readiness Workbook, as well as to special Electronic Resources on the *Management 7/e* web site.

SUMMARY

How do managers plan?

- Planning is the process of setting performance objectives and determining what should be done to accomplish them.
- A plan is a set of intended actions for accomplishing important objectives.
- Planning sets the stage for the other management functions—organizing, leading, and controlling.
- The steps in the planning process are (1) define your objectives, (2) determine where you stand vis-á-vis objectives, (3) develop your premises regarding future conditions, (4) identify and choose among alternative ways of accomplishing objectives, and (5) implement action plans and evaluate results.
- The benefits of planning include better focus and flexibility, action orientation, coordination, control, and time management.

What types of plans do managers use?

- Short-range plans tend to cover a year or less, while long-range plans extend up to five years or more.
- Strategic plans set critical long-range directions; operational plans are designed to implement strategic plans.
- Organizational policies, such as a sexual harassment policy, are plans that set guidelines for the behavior of organizational members.
- Organizational procedures and rules are plans that describe actions to be taken in specific situations, such as the steps to be taken when someone believes they have been sexually harassed.
- Organizational budgets are plans that allocate resources to activities, projects, or programs.

What are the useful planning tools and techniques?

- Forecasting, which attempts to predict what might happen in the future, is a planning aid but not a planning substitute.
- Contingency planning identifies alternative courses of action that can be implemented if and when circumstances change in certain ways over time.
- Scenario planning through the use of alternative versions of the future is a useful form of contingency planning
- Planning through benchmarking utilizes external comparisons to identify desirable action directions.
- Participation and involvement open the planning process to valuable inputs from people whose efforts are essential to the effective implementation of plans.

What is the control process?

- Controlling is the process of monitoring performance and taking corrective action as needed.
- The four steps in the control process are (1) establish performance objectives, (2) measure actual performance, (3) compare results with objectives, and (4) take necessary action to resolve problems or explore opportunities.
- Feedforward controls are accomplished before a work activity begins; they ensure that directions are clear and that the right resources are available to accomplish them.
- Concurrent controls monitor ongoing operations and activities to make sure that things are being done correctly; they allow corrective actions to be taken while the work is being done.
- Feedback controls take place after an action is completed and focus on end results; they address the question "Now that we are finished, how well did we do and what did we learn for the future?"
- External control is accomplished through personal supervision and the use of formal administrative systems.
- Internal control is self-control and occurs as people exercise self-management and take personal responsibility for their work.

What control systems are used in organizations?

- An appropriate compensation and benefits system assists in organizational control by helping to attract and retain a high-quality workforce.
- Discipline, the process of influencing behavior through reprimand, must be handled in a fair and systematic way.
- Use of financial information and the analysis of financial ratios, such as those dealing with liquidity, assets, and profitability, are important aspects of organizational control systems.
- Operations management contributes to the control process with a focus on efficiencies in such areas as purchasing and inventory control, as well as in the utilization of statistical approaches to quality control.
- Management by objectives is a process through which supervisors work with their subordinates to "jointly" set performance objectives and review performance results.

• The MBO process is highly participatory and should clarify performance objectives for a subordinate while identifying support that should be provided by a supervisor.

KEY TERMS

After-action review (p. 186)

Benchmarking (p. 181)

Budget (p. 179)

Concurrent control (p. 187)

Contingency planning (p. 180)

Controlling (p. 183)

Cybernetic control system (p. 183)

Discipline (p. 190)

Economic order quantity (p. 192)

External control (p. 188)

Feedback control (p. 187)

Feedforward control (p. 187)

Forecast (p. 180)

Input standards (p. 184)

Internal control (p. 188)

Just-in-time scheduling (p. 192)

Management by exception (p. 186)

Management by objectives (MBO) (p. 193)

Objectives (p. 173)

Operational plan (p. 178)

Output standards (p. 184)

Participatory planning (p. 182)

Plan (p. 173)

Planning (p. 172)

Policy (p. 178)

Procedures or rules (p. 178)

Progressive discipline (p. 190)

Project schedule (p. 179)

Quality control (p. 192)

Scenario planning (p. 181)

Strategic plan (p. 177)

Zero-based budget (p. 179)

SELF-TEST 7

Take this test here or on-line much as you would in a normal classroom situation. It should offer you a good way to check your basic comprehension of chapter material. Answers may be found at the end of the book.

MULTIPLE-CHOICE QUESTIONS:

1. Planning is defined as the process of _____ and _____ .
   (a) developing premises about the future, evaluating them
   (b) taking action, evaluating outcomes
   (c) measuring past performance, targeting future performance
   (d) setting objectives, deciding how to accomplish them

2. The benefits of planning include _____.
   (a) improved focus and flexibility (b) lower labor costs
   (c) reduced organizational control (d) guaranteed cost efficiency

3. In order to help implement its strategy, a business firm would likely develop an operational plan such as a _____.
   (a) benchmark (b) future scenario (c) forecast (d) marketing plan

4. _____ planning identifies alternative courses of action that can be taken if and when certain situations arise.
   (a) Benchmarking (b) Participative (c) Tactical (d) Contingency

5. The first step in the control process is to _____.
   (a) measure actual performance (b) establish objectives and standards
   (c) compare results with objectives and standards (d) take necessary action

6. The practice of giving attention to situations showing the greatest need for action is called management by _____.
   (a) objectives (b) results (c) efficiency (d) exception

7. Compensation and benefits systems that bring highly capable people to work for an organization _____.
   (a) increase the potential for self-control (b) increase the need for external control (c) eliminate the need for financial controls (d) make progressive discipline systems difficult to implement

8. A manager following the "hot stove rules" of progressive discipline would _____.
   (a) avoid giving the employee too much information about what he or she did wrong (b) stay flexible, reprimanding only at random (c) focus the reprimand on actions, not personality (d) delay reprimands until something positive can also be discussed

9. Review of an employee's performance accomplishments in an MBO system is done by _____.
   (a) the employee (b) the employee's supervisor (c) the employee and the supervisor (d) the employee, the supervisor, and a lawyer

10. A good performance objective is written in such a way that it is _____.
    (a) time defined (b) general rather than too specific (c) impossible to accomplish (d) difficult to measure results in precise terms

TRUE-FALSE QUESTIONS:

11. Good planning helps managers with the controlling process.   T   F

12. Planning is a form of time management.   T   F

13. A policy on organizational treatment of employees with the HIV virus is an example of a single-use plan.   T   F

14. Top managers spend most of their time dealing with strategic plans.   T   F

15. If forecasting is done well it is not necessary for managers to plan.   T   F

16. Planning is one aspect of the management process in which participation and involvement are not important.   T   F

17. It can be said that the management function of controlling sees to it that the right things happen in the right way and at the right time.   T   F

18. Examples of input standards of control include the percentage error rate and the number of customers serviced in a time period.   T   F

19. At McDonald's, the ever-present shift leaders exercise concurrent control through direct supervision of workers.   T   F

20. The best objectives in MBO are those set by supervisors for their subordinates.   T   F

SHORT-RESPONSE QUESTIONS:

21. List the five steps in the planning process.

22. How might planning through benchmarking be used by the owner/manager of a local bookstore?

23. How does Douglas McGregor's Theory Y relate to the concept of internal control?

24. How does a progressive discipline system work?

APPLICATION QUESTION:

25. Put yourself in the position of a management trainer. You are asked to make a short presentation to the local Small Business Enterprise Association at their biweekly luncheon. The topic you are to speak on is "How Each of You Can Use Management by Objectives for Better Planning and Control." What will you tell them and why?

CAREER readiness ACTIVITIES

Recommended learning activities from the end-of-text *Career Readiness Workbook* for this chapter include:

Case for Critical Thinking
- Wal-Mart Stores, Inc.—E-tailing in a World of Super Stores

Integrative Learning Activities
- Research Project 5—Affirmative Action Directions
- Research Project 6—Controversies in CEO Pay
- Integrative Case—Outback Steakhouse, Inc.
- Integrative Case—Richard Branson Meets the New Economy

Exercises in Teamwork
- Personal Career Planning (#10)
- The MBO Contract (#12)
- Force-Field Analysis (#30)

Self-Assessments
- Time Management Profile (#9)
- Internal/External Control (#11)
- Turbulence Tolerance Test (#23)

ELECTRONIC RESOURCES

@ GET CONNECTED! Don't forget to take full advantage of the on-line support for *Management 7/e.*
- Chapter 7 On-line Study Guide
- Chapter 7 Self-test Answers
- Chapter 7 E-Resource Center

8

Strategic management

Planning ahead

GETTING CONNECTED

Starbucks Coffee Company–*Get (and Stay) Ahead with Strategy*
Coffee just might be the most popular drink in the world. And, the well-known Starbucks may hold claim to the most valuable brand name in the industry. The strategic question is, How long can Starbucks keep brewing a better cup of coffee?

"Forever," might answer Howard Schultz, who in 2000 stepped down as CEO to become Chairman and Chief Global Strategist for the company. When he joined Starbucks in 1982 as director of retail operations, the firm was a small coffee retailer in Seattle. But Schultz saw more potential than this in the firm's future. After a trip to Italy, Schultz returned with the idea to build a coffee bar culture with Starbucks at its center. He sold the owners on the idea and the rest is history, Starbucks history, that is.

What drove Schultz in the early years was the vision of Starbucks' becoming a national chain of stores offering the finest coffee drinks and "educating consumers everywhere about fine coffee." The stores would be staffed by expert brewers who explained coffees as they were served. These employees would be given stock options to provide a sense of ownership in the company. Not only has Starbucks fulfilled this vision on the national scene, it has stuck to its values in the process. Employees are still center-stage in its mission statement, with two guiding principles at the top of the list: (1) "Provide a great work environment and treat each other with respect and dignity. (2) Embrace diversity as an essential component in the way we do business." You'll also find a strong commitment to the natural environment, the community, and coffee origin countries.

Today Starbucks is more than just another coffee bar retailer. Visit a store or go on-line and you'll find it now selling tea, chocolates, a variety of gift items, and even music. It's all part of a global strategy for growth. Schultz says: "Moving forward, we will continue to pursue opportunities that increase long-term value for our shareholders and our partners, provide unique experiences for our customers, and bring us ever closer to our goal of becoming the most recognized and respected brand of coffee in the world." At last count the firm already had over 3,300 outlets around the globe, and was still rapidly expanding. How far are you from a cup of Starbucks coffee?[1]

@ Get Connected!

Can Starbucks maintain its success? What are the risks of an aggressive growth strategy? Look at Starbucks financial reports; check its competitors. Enter the world of the corporate strategist. Get connected!

Let's change industries for a moment and move from Starbucks Coffee to the retailing world. Surely you are familiar with Wal-Mart, America's largest retailer and the recommended case study for Chapter 7. Wal-Mart's master plan is elegant in its simplicity: to deliver consistently low prices and high customer service. An important foundation is use of the latest technology. A sophisticated corporate satellite system and computer network keeps the home office in touch with operations at all stores. Inventories are monitored around the clock and a world-class distribution system ensures that stores are rarely out of the items customers are seeking. At Wal-Mart, all organizational systems are rallied around the goals—low prices, high customer service. Given the firm's impressive track record and strength, the competitors are asking, "How can we keep up?" Of course, the strategic visionaries at Wal-Mart are asking another question: "How can we stay ahead?"

Wal-Mart can't rest on past laurels. Success today is no guarantee of success tomorrow. We will surely see many changes in competitive retailing in the years ahead; we're already seeing many today. The industry is being challenged by the growth of electronic commerce. Success in a redefined market that includes both traditional "retailing" and the new "e-tailing" will come only to those with a sense of future opportunities and clear visions about what needs to be done.

This story can be told and retold for any organization operating in any industry. Similar forces and challenges confront managers in all settings, Starbucks among them. Today's environment places a great premium on effective "strategy" and "strategic management" as prerequisites for organizational success. "If you want to make a difference as a leader," says *Fast Company* magazine, "you've got to make time for strategy."[2]

STRATEGIC COMPETITIVENESS

○ A **competitive advantage** comes from operating in successful ways that are difficult to imitate.

An organization with **competitive advantage** operates with an attribute or combination of attributes that allows it to outperform its rivals. At Wal-Mart, for example, one source of such advantage is information technology that allows the retailer to quickly track sales and monitor inventories. In other industries, Dell Computer eliminates wholesale supplier markups by marketing direct to consumers; Toyota's shorter cycle times allow it to carry smaller amounts of work-in-process inventory. The goal for any organization, however, is not just to achieve competitive advantage. It is to make it sustainable, even as rivals attempt to duplicate and copy a success story. A *sustainable competitive advantage* is one that is difficult for competitors to imitate. At Wal-Mart again, the firm's use of IT is continuously improved. Competitors have trouble catching up, let alone getting ahead.

The task of achieving and sustaining competitive advantage can be daunting in any setting, with the retailing industry serving as a good example. Wal-Mart, Kmart, and Target each began operating in 1962. Of the top competitors they faced in that year, none exists today. All were killed by competition. Consider also Amazon.com, eToys.com, Garden.com, and Pets.com, firms that once shared the spotlight as darlings of "e-tailing" in the new economy. Only Amazon remains as of this writing, and its future is questioned by many skeptics. As you look around to other industries and organizations, which of today's big names will remain stars in the future? Which ones will be the dropouts or also-rans? In other words, who has the right strategy?

WHAT IS STRATEGY?

A **strategy** is a comprehensive action plan that identifies long-term direction for an organization and guides resource utilization to accomplish goals with sustainable competitive advantage. It focuses attention on the competitive environment and represents a "best guess" about what must be done to ensure future success in the face of rivalry and even as conditions change. Importantly, a strategy provides the plan for allocating and using resources with consistent **strategic intent**—that is, with all organizational energies directed toward a unifying and compelling target or goal.[3] At Coca-Cola, for example, strategic intent has been described as "To put a Coke within 'arm's reach' of every consumer in the world." Given the focus provided by this strategic intent, we would not expect Coca-Cola to be diversifying by investing in snack foods, as does its arch-rival PepsiCo.

In our fast-paced world of globalization and changing technologies, the "long-term" aspect of strategy is becoming ever shorter. As it does so, the challenges to the strategist become even greater. It used to be that companies could count on traditional "build-and-sell" business models that put them in control. In the early days of the automobile industry, for example, Henry Ford once said: "The customer can have any color he wants as long as it's black." His firm, quite literally, was in the driver's seat. Today things have changed and strategy is increasingly driven by customers and flexibility. Says John M. Jordan, Director of e-commerce research for Ernst & Young: "Customers are calling the shots, telling companies what they want, and companies have to respond to those desires or lose out." Stephen Haeckel, director of strategic studies at IBM's Advanced Business Institute, describes the shift in approach this way: "It's a difference between a bus, which follows a set route, and a taxi, which goes where customers tell it to go."[4]

○ A **strategy** is a comprehensive plan guiding resource allocation to achieve long-term organization goals.

○ **Strategic intent** focuses and applies organizational energies on a unifying and compelling goal.

STRATEGIC MANAGEMENT

In the case of Starbucks and Wal-Mart, crafting strategy may seem a deceptively simple task: find out what customers want, then provide it for them at the best prices and service. In practice, this task is made complex and risky by the forces and uncertainties of competitive environments.[5] Every strategist must remember that at the same time one is trying to create competitive advantage for an organization, competitors are always attempting to do the same. This gives rise to demands for strategies that can be called "bold," "aggressive," "fast-moving," and "innovative." But call them what you will, strategies don't just happen. They must be created. And strategies alone don't automatically bring success. They must be both well chosen and well implemented.

Strategic management is the process of formulating and implementing strategies to accomplish long-term goals and sustain competitive advantage. The essence of strategic management is looking ahead, understanding the environment and the organization, and effectively positioning the organization for competitive advantage in changing times. Chief executives must think strategically as they try to position their firms for new 21st-century markets. They must think strategically in deciding how to use new technologies to maximum advantage. They must think strategically in deciding how to take advantage of the global economy. And, they must think strategically where it really counts—in respect to what customers and clients really want.

○ **Strategic management** is the process of formulating and implementing strategies.

STRATEGIC MANAGEMENT GOALS

○ **Above-average returns** exceed what could be earned from alternative investments of equivalent risk.

Michael Porter, Harvard scholar and strategy consultant, says that "sound strategy starts with having the right goal."[6] He argues that the ultimate goal for any business should be superior profitability. This creates value for investors in the form of **above-average returns**, returns that exceed what an investor could earn by investing in alternative opportunities of equivalent risk.[7] At PepsiCo, this goal is stated as: "To increase the value of our shareholder's investment."

The ability to earn above-average returns is based in part on the competitive nature of organizational environments. Businesses compete in environments that vary in the following ways.[8] In a *monopoly environment*, there is only one player and no competition. This creates absolute competitive advantage that delivers sustainable and most likely excessive business profits. The U.S. Justice Department's antitrust lawsuit against Microsoft Corporation argued that the firm achieved actual or close to monopoly status in respect to the market on computer operating systems. An *oligopoly environment* contains a few players who do not directly compete against one another. Firms within an oligopoly sustain long-term competitive advantages within defined market segments. In the absence of competition within these segments, they can also reap excessive business profits. This describes conditions in the breakfast cereals market, for example. The industry is dominated by large players—Kellogg's, General Mills, and Quaker Oats—that control much of the market. It is difficult for new players to break in. From the customer's standpoint, both monopoly and oligopoly are disadvantageous. The lack of competition may keep prices high and product/service innovations low.

B2B Changes the World of Outsourcing
It is reported that businesses purchasing supplies in on-line auctions save as much as 20 percent. To date the biggest users are found in the computer and electronics industry. Take the on-line "Reality Check" to learn more about the use of B2B auctions.

The global economy has helped to create for many businesses today an *environment of hypercompetition*.[9] This is an environment in which there are at least several players who directly compete with one another. An example is the fast-food industry where McDonald's, Burger King, Wendy's, and many other restaurant chains all compete for largely the same customers. Because the competition is direct and intense, any competitive advantage that is realized is temporary. Successful strategies are often copied and firms must continue to find new strategies that deliver new sources of competitive advantage, even while trying to defend existing ones. McDonald's, for example, had to mount an aggressive campaign to defend its french fries—advertised as "America's Favorite Fries"—from a copycat attack by Burger King.[10] In hypercompetition, there are always some winners and losers. Business profits can be attractive but intermittent. The customer generally gains in this environment through lower prices and more product/service innovation.

THE STRATEGIC MANAGEMENT PROCESS

Strategic management is successful when organizations, even those operating in environments of hypercompetition, achieve sustainable competitive advantage and earn above-average returns. Successful strategies are crafted from insightful understandings of the competitive environment as well as intimate knowledge of the organization. And they are implemented with commitment and resolution. *Figure 8.1* describes a series of steps involved in fulfilling the two major responsibilities of the strategic management process—strategy formulation and strategy implementation.

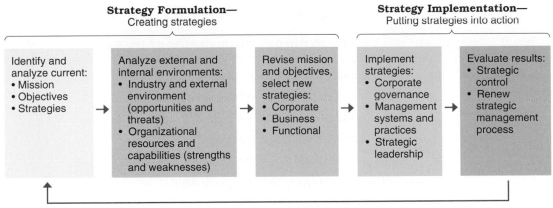

Figure 8.1 Strategy formulation and implementation in the strategic management process.

The first strategic management responsibility is **strategy formulation**, the process of creating strategy. This involves assessing existing strategies, organization, and environment to develop new strategies and strategic plans capable of delivering future competitive advantage. Peter Drucker associates this process with a set of five strategic questions: (1) *What is our business mission?* (2) *Who are our customers?* (3) *What do our customers consider value?* (4) *What have been our results?* (5) *What is our plan?*[11]

The second strategic management responsibility is **strategy implementation**, the process of allocating resources and putting strategies into action. Once strategies are created, they must be successfully acted upon to achieve the desired results. As Drucker says, "The future will not just happen if one wishes hard enough. It requires decision—now. It imposes risk—now. It requires action—now. It demands allocation of resources, and above all, of human resources—now. It requires work—now."[12] This is the responsibility for putting strategies and strategic plans into action. Every organizational and management system must be mobilized to support and reinforce the accomplishment of strategies. Scarce resources must be utilized for maximum impact on performance. All of this, in turn, requires a commitment to mastering the full range of strategic management tasks posed in *Manager's Notepad 8.1*.[13]

○ **Strategy formulation** is the process of creating strategies.

○ **Strategy implementation** is the process of putting strategies into action.

ANALYSIS OF MISSION, VALUES, AND OBJECTIVES

The strategic management process begins with a careful assessment and clarification of organizational mission, values, and objectives.[14] A clear sense of mission and objectives sets the stage for critically assessing the organization's resources and capabilities as well as competitive opportunities and threats in the external environment.

Mission

As first discussed in Chapter 1, the **mission** or purpose of an organization may be described as its reason for existence in society. Strategy consultant Michael Hammer believes that a mission should represent what the strategy or underlying business model is trying to accomplish. He suggests asking: "What are we moving to?" "What is our dream?" "What kind of a difference do we want to make in the world?"[15]

The best organizations have a clear sense of mission, and they utilize resources with clear strategic intent in respect to its fulfillment. At Mary

○ **The mission** is the organization's reason for existence in society.

MANAGER'S NOTEPAD 8.1

Five strategic management tasks

1. Identify organizational mission and objectives.
   Ask: "What business are we in? Where do we want to go?"
2. Assess current performance vis-à-vis mission and objectives.
   Ask: "How well are we currently doing?"
3. Create strategic plans to accomplish purpose and objectives.
   Ask: "How can we get where we really want to be?"
4. Implement the strategic plans.
   Ask: "Has everything been done that needs to be done?"
5. Evaluate results; change strategic plans and/or implementation processes as necessary.
   Ask: "Are things working out as planned? What can be improved?"

Kay, Inc., for example, the firm's mission is defined as "To enrich women's lives." Starbucks' mission is to be "the premier purveyor of the finest coffee in the world while maintaining our uncompromising principles as we grow." Intel's mission is to "do a great job for our customers, employees and stockholders by being the preeminent building block supplier to the worldwide Internet economy." The mission of the American Red Cross is to "provide relief to victims of disasters and help people prevent, prepare for, and respond to emergencies."

A good *mission statement* identifies the *domain* in which the organization intends to operate—including the *customers* it intends to serve, the *products* and/or *services* it intends to provide, and the *location* in which it intends to operate. The mission statement should also communicate the underlying philosophy that will guide employees in these operations. Consider the mission statement for Merck, one of the world's leading pharmaceutical companies: "To provide society with superior products and services—innovations and solutions that improve the quality of life and satisfy customer needs; to provide employees with meaningful work and advancement opportunities, and investors with a superior rate of return."[16]

An important test of corporate purpose and mission is how well it serves the organization's **stakeholders**. You should recall that these are individuals and groups—including customers, shareholders, suppliers, creditors, community groups, and others, who are directly affected by the organization and its strategic accomplishments. In the strategic management process, the stakeholder test can be done as a strategic constituencies analysis. Here, the specific interests of each stakeholder are assessed along with the organization's record in responding to them. *Figure 8.2* gives an example of how stakeholder interests can be reflected in a mission statement.

○ **Stakeholders** are individuals and groups directly affected by an organization and its accomplishments.

Core Values

○ **Organizational culture** is the predominant value system for the organization as a whole.

Behavior in and by organizations will always be affected in part by *values*, which are broad beliefs about what is or is not appropriate. **Organizational culture** was first defined in Chapter 2 as the predominant value system of the organization as a whole.[17] Through organizational cultures, the values

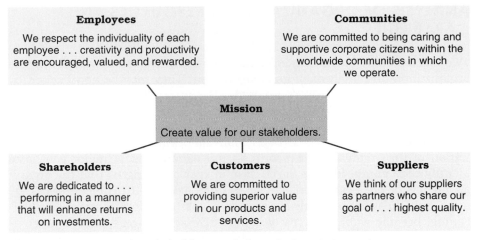

Figure 8.2 External stakeholders and the mission statement.

of managers and other members are shaped and pointed in common directions. In strategic management, the presence of strong core values for an organization helps build institutional identity. It gives character to an organization in the eyes of its employees and external stakeholders, and it backs up the mission statement. Shared values also help guide the behavior of organization members in meaningful and consistent ways. For example, Merck backs up its mission with a public commitment to core values that include preservation and improvement of human life, scientific excellence, ethics and integrity, and profits from work that benefits humanity. Intel backs up its mission by stating values such as: customer orientation, results orientation, risk taking, great place to work, quality, and discipline. At Nordstrom, the firm's commitment to valuing diversity is evidenced by the presence of a separate and very specific diversity mission statement.[18]

Objectives

Whereas a mission statement sets forth an official purpose for the organization and the core values describe appropriate standards of behavior for its accomplishment, **operating objectives** direct activities toward key and specific performance results. These objectives are shorter-term targets against which actual performance results can be measured as indicators of progress and continuous improvement. Any and all operating objectives should have clear means–end linkages to the mission and purpose. Any and all strategies should, in turn, offer clear and demonstrable opportunities to accomplish operating objectives. According to Peter Drucker, the *operating objectives of a business* might include the following:[19]

- *Profitability*—producing at a net profit in business.
- *Market share*—gaining and holding a specific market share.
- *Human talent*—recruiting and maintaining a high-quality workforce.
- *Financial health*—acquiring capital; earning positive returns.
- *Cost efficiency*—using resources well to operate at low cost.
- *Product quality*—producing high-quality goods or services.
- *Innovation*—developing new products and/or processes.
- *Social responsibility*—making a positive contribution to society.

○ **Operating objectives** are specific results that organizations try to accomplish.

← Operating objectives of a business

ANALYSIS OF ORGANIZATIONAL RESOURCES AND CAPABILITIES

○ A **SWOT analysis** examines organizational strengths and weaknesses and environmental opportunities and threats.

○ A **core competency** is a special strength that gives an organization a competitive advantage.

Two critical steps in the strategic management process are analysis of the organization and analysis of its environment. They may be approached by a technique known as **SWOT analysis**: the internal analysis of organizational Strengths and Weaknesses as well as the external analysis of environmental Opportunities and Threats.

As shown in *Figure 8.3*, a SWOT analysis begins with a systematic evaluation of the organization's resources and capabilities. A major goal is to identify **core competencies** in the form of special strengths that the organization has or does exceptionally well in comparison with competitors. They are capabilities that by virtue of being rare, costly to imitate, and nonsubstitutable become viable sources of competitive advantage.[20] Core competencies may be found in special knowledge or expertise, superior technologies, efficient manufacturing technologies, or unique product distribution systems, among many other possibilities. But always, and as with the notion of strategy itself, they must be viewed relative to the competition. Simply put, organizations need core competencies that do important things better than the competition and that are very difficult for competitors to duplicate.

Figure 8.3 highlights several reference points for the internal analysis of organizational strengths. Organizational weaknesses, of course, are the other side of the picture. They can also be found in the same or related areas and must be identified to gain a realistic perspective on the formulation of strategies. The goal in strategy formulation is to create strategies that leverage core competencies for competitive advantage by building upon organizational strengths and minimizing the impact of weaknesses.

ANALYSIS OF INDUSTRY AND ENVIRONMENT

A SWOT analysis is not complete until opportunities and threats in the external environment are also analyzed. They can be found among *macroenvironment* factors such as technology, government, social structures, and

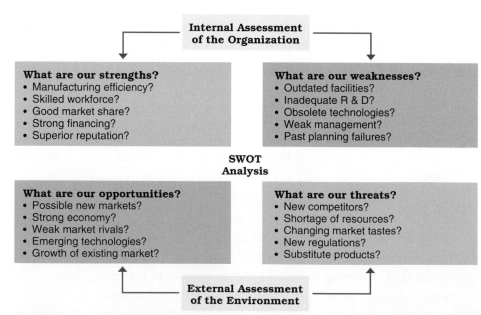

Figure 8.3 SWOT analysis of strengths, weaknesses, opportunities, and threats.

population demographics, the global economy, and the natural environment. They can also include developments in the *industry environment* of resource suppliers, competitors, and customers. As shown in Figure 8.3, opportunities may exist as possible new markets, a strong economy, weaknesses in competitors, and emerging technologies. Weaknesses may be identified in such things as the emergence of new competitors, resource scarcities, changing customer tastes, and new government regulations, among other possibilities.

In respect to the external environmental as a whole, the more stable and predictable it is, the more likely that a good strategy can be implemented with success for a longer period of time. But when the environment is composed of many dynamic elements that create uncertainties, more flexible strategies that change with time are needed. Given the nature of competitive environments today, strategic management must be considered an ongoing process in which strategies are formulated, implemented, revised, and implemented again in a continuous manner.

Michael Porter offers the five forces model shown in *Figure 8.4* as a way of adding sophistication to this analysis of the environment.[21] His framework for competitive industry analysis directs attention toward understanding the following forces:

1. *Industry competitors*—intensity of rivalry among firms in the industry. ← Porter's five competitive
2. *New entrants*—threats of new competitors entering the market. forces
3. *Suppliers*—bargaining power of suppliers.
4. *Customers*—bargaining power of buyers.
5. *Substitutes*—threats of substitute products or services.

From Porter's perspective, the foundations for any successful strategy rest with a clear understanding of these competitive environmental forces. He calls this the "industry structure." The strategic management challenge is to position an organization strategically within its industry, taking into account the implications of forces that make it more or less attractive. In general, an *unattractive industry* is one in which rivalry among competitors is intense, substantial threats exist in the form of possible new entrants and substitute products, and suppliers and buyers are very powerful in bargaining over such things as prices and quality. An *attractive industry*, by contrast, has less existing competition,

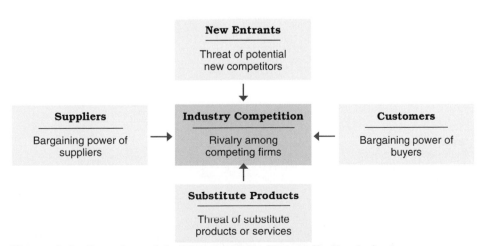

Figure 8.4 Porter's model of five strategic forces affecting industry competition.

Source: Developed from Michael E. Porter, *Competitive Strategy* (New York: Free Press, 1980).

few threats from new entrants or substitutes, and low bargaining power among suppliers and buyers.[22] By systematically analyzing industry attractiveness in respect to the five forces, Porter believes that strategies can be chosen to give the organization a competitive advantage relative to its rivals.

STRATEGIES USED BY ORGANIZATIONS

The strategic management process encompasses the three levels of strategy shown in *Figure 8.5*. Strategies are formulated and implemented at the organizational or corporate level, business level, and functional level. All should be integrated in means–end fashion to accomplish objectives and create sustainable competitive advantage.

LEVELS OF STRATEGY

○ A **corporate strategy** sets long-term direction for the total enterprise.

The level of **corporate strategy** directs the organization as a whole toward sustainable competitive advantage. For a business it describes the scope of operations by answering the following *strategic question*: "In what industries and markets should we compete?" The purpose of corporate strategy is to set direction and guide resource allocations for the entire enterprise. In large, complex organizations like General Electric, corporate strategy identifies the different areas of business in which a company intends to compete. The firm presently pursues business interests in aircraft engines, appliances, capital services, lighting, medical systems, broadcasting, plastics, and power systems, for example. Typical strategic decisions at the corporate level relate to the allocation of resources for acquisitions, new business development, divestitures, and the like across this business portfolio. Increasingly, corporate strategies for many businesses include an important role for global operations such as international joint ventures and strategic alliances.

○ A **business strategy** identifies how a division or strategic business unit will compete in its product or service domain.

Business strategy is the strategy for a single business unit or product line. It describes strategic intent to compete within a specific industry or market. Large conglomerates like General Electric are composed of many businesses, with many differences among them in product lines and even

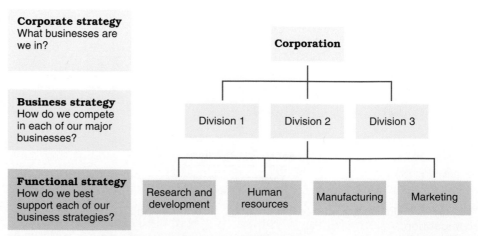

Figure 8.5 Levels of strategy in organizations.

industries. The term **strategic business unit (SBU)** is often used to describe a single business firm or a component that operates with a separate mission within a larger enterprise. The selection of strategy at the business level involves answering the *strategic question*: "How are we going to compete for customers in this industry and market?" Typical business strategy decisions include choices about product/service mix, facilities locations, new technologies, and the like. In single-business enterprises, business strategy is the corporate strategy.

> ○ An **SBU** is a major business area that operates with some autonomy.

Functional strategy guides the use of organizational resources to implement business strategy. This level of strategy focuses on activities within a specific functional area of operations. Looking again at Figure 8.5, the standard business functions of marketing, manufacturing, finance, and research and development illustrate this level of strategy. The *strategic question* to be answered in selecting functional strategies becomes "How can we best utilize resources to implement our business strategy?" Answers to this question typically involve the choice of progressive management and organizational practices that improve operating efficiency, product or service quality, customer service, or innovativeness.

> ○ A **functional strategy** guides activities within one specific area of operations.

GROWTH AND DIVERSIFICATION STRATEGIES

Traditionally one of the most common and popular of the grand or master strategies pursued by organizations at the corporate or business levels is growth.[23] **Growth strategies** pursue an increase in size and the expansion of current operations. They are popular in part because growth is viewed as necessary for long-run survival in some industries. One approach to growth is through **concentration**, where expansion is within the same business area. Coca-Cola, for example, pursues a highly aggressive and global growth strategy; Wal-Mart also pursues aggressive growth nationally and is embarked upon an international one.

> ○ A **growth strategy** involves expansion of the organization's current operations.
>
> ○ Growth through **concentration** is within the same business area.

Another approach to growth is through **diversification**, where expansion takes place through the acquisition of or investment in new and sometimes different business areas. A strategy of *related diversification* involves growth by acquiring new businesses or entering business areas that are related to what one already does. This strategy seeks the advantages of growth in areas that utilize core competencies and existing skills. An example is the acquisition of Tropicana by PepsiCo. Although Tropicana specializes in fruit juices, the business is related to PepsiCo's expertise in the beverages industry. A strategy of *unrelated diversification* involves growth by acquiring businesses or entering business areas that are different from what one already does. An example is the acquisition of Hughes Electronics Corporation by General Motors. Although GM is a big user of technology, the company did not have a mainstream core competency in high-technology electronics areas.

> ○ Growth through **diversification** is by acquisition of or investment in new and different business areas.

Diversification can also take the form of **vertical integration**, where a business seeks added value creation by acquiring suppliers (*backward vertical integration*) or distributors (*forward vertical integration*). In the automobile industry, backward vertical integration has been common as firms purchased suppliers of key parts to ensure quality and control over their availability. In beverages, both Coca-Cola and PepsiCo have pursued forward vertical integration by purchasing some of their major bottlers.

> ○ Growth through **vertical integration** is by acquiring suppliers or distributors.

There is a tendency to equate growth with effectiveness, but that is not necessarily true. Any growth strategy, whether by concentration or some form of diversification, must be well planned and well managed to achieve the desired results. Increased size of operation in any form adds challenge to the management process. Diversification, in particular, brings the difficulties of complexity and the need to manage and integrate very dissimilar operations. Research indicates that business performance may decline with too much unrelated diversification.[24]

RESTRUCTURING AND DIVESTITURE STRATEGIES

○ A **retrenchment strategy** involves reducing the scale of current operations.

○ **Restructuring** changes the scale and/or mix of operations to gain efficiency and improve performance.

○ **Downsizing** decreases the size of operations in the intent to become more streamlined.

○ **Divestiture** sells off parts of the organization to focus attention and resources on core business areas.

When organizations experience performance problems, perhaps due to unsuccessful diversification, retrenchment of some sort often takes place. The most extreme **retrenchment strategy** is *liquidation*, when operations cease due to the complete sale of assets or the declaration of bankruptcy. Less extreme but still of potential dramatic performance impact is **restructuring**. This changes the scale and/or mix of operations in order to gain efficiency and improve performance. The decision to restructure can be difficult for managers to make because, at least on the surface, it seems to be an admission of failure. But in today's era of challenging economic conditions and environmental uncertainty, restructuring is used frequently and with new respect.

Restructuring is sometimes accomplished by **downsizing**, which decreases the size of operations with the intent to become more streamlined.[25] The expected benefits are reduced costs and improved operating efficiency. A common way to downsize is cutting the size of the workforce. Research has shown that such downsizing is most successful when the workforce is reduced strategically, or in a way that allows for better focusing of resources on key performance objectives.[26] Downsizing with a strategic focus is sometimes referred to as *rightsizing*. This contrasts with the less-well-regarded approach of simply cutting staff "across the board."

Restructuring by **divestiture** involves selling off parts of the organization to refocus on core competencies, cut costs, and improve operating efficiency. This is a common strategy for organizations that find they have become overdiversified and are encountering problems managing the complexity of diverse operations. It is also a way for organizations to take advantage of the value of internal assets by "spinning off" or selling to shareholders a component that can stand on its own as an independent business. General Motors, as indicated earlier, has diversified over time from its core automobile manufacturing business. At one time it purchased Electronic Data Systems and operated it as part of the company. Later, EDS was spun off and now operates independently again as a large and prominent computer services company. Similarly, GM's former Delphi division was spun off and now operates independently as Delphi Automotive Systems.

COOPERATIVE STRATEGIES

○ In a **strategic alliance** organizations join together in partnership to pursue an area of mutual interest.

One of the trends today is toward more cooperation among organizations. In Chapter 5 on global dimensions of management, *international joint ventures* were discussed as a common form of international business. They are one among many forms of **strategic alliances** in which two or more organizations join together in partnership to pursue an area of mutual interest. One way to cooperate strategically is through *outsourcing alliances*, contracting to purchase important services from another organization. Many organizations today, for example, are outsourcing their IT function to firms like EDS in the belief that these services are better provided by a firm that specializes and maintains its expertise in this area. Cooperation in the supply chain also takes the form of *supplier alliances,* in which preferred supplier relationships guarantee a smooth and timely flow of quality supplies among alliance partners. Another common approach today is cooperation in *distribution alliances,* in which firms join together to accomplish product or services sales and distribution. An example is the alliance strategy of telecommunications giant AT&T. Facing a dynamic and highly competitive environment, and seeking to strategically refocus its business, AT&T leadership is pursuing alliances with a number of firms. With Cisco Systems it has an alliance to cooperate in marketing Internet solutions to businesses; with Hewlett Packard another sales channel alliance markets networking management services.

E-BUSINESS STRATEGIES

Without a doubt, one of the most frequently asked questions these days for the business executive is: "What is your **e-business strategy**?" This is the strategic use of the Internet to gain competitive advantage.

Popular e-business strategies involve B2B (business-to-business) and B2C (business-to-customer) applications. *B2B business strategies* involve the use of IT and the Internet to vertically link organizations with members of their supply chains. One of the interesting developments in this area involves the use of on-line auctions as a replacement for preferred supplier relationships and outsourcing alliances. Organizations can now go to the Internet to participate in auction bidding for supplies of many types. Whether small or large in size they immediately have access to potential suppliers competing for their attention from around the world. One of the largest of the on-line auctioneers is Freemarkets.com. Participants in its auctions save an average of 20 percent over their normal purchase prices.

B2C business strategies use IT and the Internet to link organizations with their customers. A common B2C strategy has already been illustrated several times in this chapter—*e-tailing* or the sale of goods directly to customers via the Internet. For some firms, e-tailing is all that they do; these are "new economy" firms and the business strategy is focused entirely on Internet sales—examples include Amazon.com, priceline.com, and Dell.com. For others, part of the traditional or "old economy," e-tailing has been added as a component in their business strategy mix—including

○ An **e-business strategy** strategically uses the Internet to gain competitive advantage.

TAKE IT TO THE CASE!

Procter & Gamble
You're Never Too Big for a Web-Based Turnaround
It's no secret that Procter & Gamble has some of the best brands in the global consumer goods industry. But like other old economy success stories, P&G has struggled with the new economy. The firm's new CEO, A. G. Lafly, is trying to integrate the firm with the Web. Use of the Internet may cut the firm's marketing research costs as much as 70 percent; web-based communications are improving supply chain management and customer relationship management. Says a senior executive: "We're at an inflection point in history. The challenge for all of us is either to change or die."[27]

MANAGER'S NOTEPAD 8.2

Web-based business models

- *Brokerage*—bringing buyers and sellers together to make transactions (e.g., CarsDirect.com).
- *Advertising*—providing information or services while generating revenue from advertising (e.g., Yahoo!).
- *Merchant model*—selling products wholesale and retail through the Web, e-tailing (e.g., Bluelight.com).
- *Subscription model*—selling access to the site through subscription (e.g., *Wall street Journal* Interactive).
- *Infomediary model*—collecting information on users and selling to other businesses (e.g., ePinions.com).
- *Community model*—supporting site by donations from community of users (e.g., National Public Radio Online).

Wal-Mart.com, ToysRUs.com, and IBM.com. By way of further introduction, *Manager's Notepad 8.2* lists some of the web-based business models now being tried.[28]

STRATEGY FORMULATION

Michael Porter says: "The company without a strategy is willing to try anything."[29] With a good strategy in place, by contrast, the resources of the entire organization can be focused on the overall goal—superior profitability or above-average returns. Whether one is talking about building e-business strategies for the new economy or crafting strategies for more traditional operations, it is always important to remember this goal and the need for sustainable competitive advantage. The major *opportunities for competitive advantage* are found in the following areas, which should always be considered in the strategy formulation process:[30]

Opportunities for sustainable competitive advantage

- *Cost and quality*—where strategy drives an emphasis on operating efficiency and/or product or service quality.
- *Knowledge and speed*—where strategy drives an emphasis on innovation and speed of delivery to market for new ideas.
- *Barriers to entry*—where strategy drives an emphasis on creating a market stronghold that is protected from entry by others.
- *Financial resources*—where strategy drives an emphasis on investments and/or loss sustainment that competitors can't match.

Importantly, any advantage gained in today's global and information-age economy of intense competition must always be considered temporary, at best. Things change too fast. Any advantage of the moment will sooner or later be eroded as new market demands, copycat strategies, and innovations by rivals take their competitive toll over time.[31] The challenge of achieving sustainable competitive advantage is thus a dynamic one. Strategies must be continually revisited, modified, and changed if the organization is to keep pace with changing circumstances. Formulating strategy to provide overall direction for the organization thus becomes an ongoing leadership responsibility.[32]

Fortunately, a number of strategic planning models or approaches are available to help executives in the strategy formulation process. At the business-level, one should understand Porter's generic strategies model and product life cycle planning. At the corporate level, it is helpful to understand portfolio planning, adaptive strategies, and incrementalism and emergent strategies.

PORTER'S GENERIC STRATEGIES

Michael Porter's five forces model for industry analysis was introduced earlier. Use of the model helps answer the question: Is this an attractive industry for us to compete in? Within an industry, however, the initial strategic challenge becomes positioning one's firm and products relative to competitors. The strategy question becomes: "How can we best compete for customers in this industry?"[33] Porter advises managers to answer this question by using his generic strategies framework shown in *Figure 8.6*.

According to Porter, business-level strategic decisions are driven by two basic factors: (1) *market scope*—ask: "How broad or narrow is your market target?" (2) *source of competitive advantage*—ask: "How will you compete for competitive advantage, by lower price or product uniqueness?" As shown in the figure, these factors combine to create the following four generic strategies that organizations can pursue. The examples in the figure and shown here are of competitive positions within the soft-drink industry.

1. **Differentiation**—where the organization's resources and attention are directed toward distinguishing its products from those of the competition (*example*: Coke, Pepsi).
2. **Cost leadership**—where the organization's resources and attention are directed toward minimizing costs to operate more efficiently than the competition (*example*: Big K Kola, discounter cola brands).
3. **Focused differentiation**—where the organization concentrates on one special market segment and tries to offer customers in that segment a unique product (*example*: A&W Root Beer, YooHoo).
4. **Focused cost leadership**—where the organization concentrates on one special market segment and tries in that segment to be the provider with lowest costs (*example*: Cherokee Red Pop).

www.americawest.com

America West Airlines is a low-cost, full-service airline. The firm is committed to sustaining financial strength and profitability, providing stability for employees, and creating shareholder value.

Porter's generic business strategies

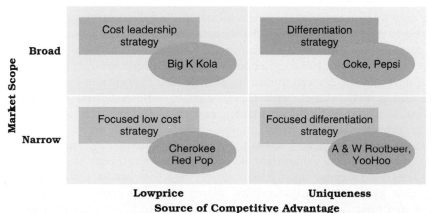

Figure 8.6   Porter's generic strategies framework: soft-drink industry examples.

○ A **differentiation strategy** offers products that are unique and different from the competition.

Organizations pursuing a **differentiation strategy** seek competitive advantage through uniqueness. They try to develop goods and services that are clearly different from those made available by the competition. The objective is to attract customers who become loyal to the organization's products and lose interest in those of competitors. This strategy requires organizational strengths in marketing, research and development, technological leadership, and creativity. It is highly dependent for its success on continuing customer perceptions of product quality and uniqueness. An example in the apparel industry is Polo Ralph Lauren, retailer of upscale classic fashions and accessories. In Ralph Lauren's words, Polo "redefined how American style and quality is perceived. Polo has always been about selling quality products by creating worlds and inviting our customers to be part of our dream."[34]

○ A **cost leadership strategy** seeks to operate with lower costs than competitors.

Organizations pursuing a **cost leadership strategy** try to continuously improve the operating efficiencies of production, distribution, and other organizational systems. The objective is to have lower costs than competitors and therefore achieve higher profits. This requires tight cost and managerial controls as well as products that are easy to manufacture and distribute. Of course, quality must not be sacrificed in the process. In retailing, Wal-Mart aims to keep its costs so low that it can always offer customers the lowest prices and still make a reasonable profit. Most discounters operate with 18 to 20 percent gross margins. Wal-Mart can accept less and still make the same or higher returns. In financial services, Vanguard Group has succeeded with a strategy based on keeping its costs low and therefore offering mutual funds to customers with minimum fees. Its web site proudly proclaims that Vanguard is the industry leader in having the lowest average expense ratios.

○ A **focused differentiation strategy** offers a unique product to a special market segment.

○ A **focused cost leadership strategy** seeks the lowest costs of operations within a special market segment.

Organizations pursuing **focus strategies** concentrate attention on a special market segment with the objective of serving its needs better than anyone else. The strategies focus organizational resources and expertise on a particular customer group, geographical region, or product or service line. They seek to gain competitive advantage in product differentiation or cost leadership. Importantly, focus strategies require willingness to concentrate and the ability to use resources to special advantage in a single area. Cathay Pacific Airlines, based in Hong Kong and long one of Asia's leading airlines, refocused on the tourist trade to bolster lagging revenues during the region's economic crisis. The firm offers dramatic discounts and special travel packages in attempting to lure customers from its rivals.

PRODUCT LIFE CYCLE PLANNING

○ **Product life cycle** is the series of stages a product or service goes through in the "life" of its marketability.

Another way to consider the dynamic nature of business strategy formulation is in terms of **product life cycle**. This is a series of stages a product or service goes through in the "life" of its marketability. In terms of planning, different business strategies are needed to support products in the life cycle stages of *introduction, growth, maturity,* and *decline.*[35] Products in the introduction and growth stages lend themselves to differentiation strategies. They require investments in advertising and market research to establish a market presence and build a customer base. In the maturity stage, the strategic emphasis shifts toward keeping customers and gaining production efficiencies. They may involve focus and an attempt at cost leadership. These strategies may hold initially as the product moves into decline. But at some point, strategic planners must seek new ways to extend product life.

QUALITY Endres Floral Company Where Selling a Better Rose Makes the Difference

A family-owned company in New Philadelphia, Ohio, Endres Floral Company has found its niche by selling "a better rose." And sell it does, shipping millions of roses per year to wholesalers. With 50 employees and 6 acres of greenhouses, the firm grows 170,000 rose bushes and harvests twice each day. To compete with lower-cost producers from South America, the firm differentiates itself on quality. Endres red roses are supposed to last 10 days to 2 weeks without drooping. They are stored in computer-controlled coolers and shipped in special containers. No Endres rose is out of water more than 10 minutes after cutting. A genuine Endres rose can be in a customer's home within 24 hours. The company was founded by Eugene V. Endres, now in the Ohio Agricultural Hall of Fame.[36]

Understanding product life cycles and adjusting strategy accordingly is an important business skill. Especially in dynamic times, managers need to recognize when a product life cycle is maturing. They should have contingency plans for dealing with potential decline, and they should be developing alternative products with growth potential. Consider what happened at IBM, a firm that dominated the market for large mainframe computers for years. As customers began to use ever-more-powerful PCs, the mainframe became less important to their operating systems. When the cellular phone industry was starting to use new digital technologies, Motorola continued to emphasize its successful, but older, analog products. Both IBM's and Motorola's top managers failed to properly address industry trends. Their companies lost momentum to very aggressive competitors.

PORTFOLIO PLANNING

In a single-product or single-business firm the strategic context is one industry. Corporate strategy and business strategy are the same, and resources are allocated on that basis. When firms move into different industries, resulting in multiple product or service offerings, they become internally more complex and often larger in size. This makes resource allocation a more challenging strategic management task, since the mix of businesses must be well managed. The strategy problem is similar to that faced by an individual with limited money who must choose among alternative stocks, bonds, and real estate in a personal investment portfolio. In multibusiness situations, strategy formulation also involves **portfolio planning** to allocate scarce resources among competing uses.[37]

○ A **portfolio planning** approach seeks the best mix of investments among alternative business opportunities.

BCG Matrix

Figure 8.7 summarizes an approach to business portfolio planning developed by the Boston Consulting Group and known as the **BCG matrix**. This framework ties strategy formulation to an analysis of business opportunities according to industry or market growth rate and market share.[38]

○ The **BCG matrix** analyzes business opportunities according to market growth rate and market share.

Market Growth Rate for SBU Products/Services

High

"Question Marks"—poor competitive position in a growing industry

Recommended strategy = growth or retrenchment; apply resources to accomplish positive turnaround or pull back if outlook poor

"Stars"—dominant competitive position in a growing industry

Recommended strategy = growth; add resources and build the business further based upon market projections

"Dogs"—poor competitive position in low-growth industry

Recommended strategy = retrenchment; divest, sell, liquidate the business to eliminate resource drain

"Cash Cows"—dominant position in low-growth industry

Recommended strategy = stability or modest growth; maintain benefits of strong cash flow while keeping resource investments minimum

Low

Low ← → High

Market Share of SBU Products/Services

"SBU" = Strategic Business Unit

Figure 8.7 The BCG matrix approach to corporate strategy formulation.

As shown in the figure, this comparison results in the following four possible business conditions, with each being associated with a strategic implication: (1) *stars*—high market share/high-growth businesses; (2) *cash cows*—high market share/low-growth businesses; (3) *question marks*—low market share/high-growth businesses; and (4) *dogs*—low market share/low-growth businesses.

Stars are high-market-share businesses in high-growth markets. They produce large profits through substantial penetration of expanding markets. The preferred strategy for stars is growth, and further resource investments in them are recommended. *Question marks* are low-market-share businesses in high-growth markets. They do not produce much profit but compete in rapidly growing markets. They are the source of difficult strategic decisions. The preferred strategy is growth, but the risk exists that further investments will not result in improved market share. Only the most promising question marks should be targeted for growth; others are restructuring or divestiture candidates.

Cash cows are high-market-share businesses in low-growth markets. They produce large profits and a strong cash flow. Because the markets offer little growth opportunity, the preferred strategy is stability or modest growth. "Cows" should be "milked" to generate cash that can be used to support needed investments in stars and question marks. *Dogs* are low-market-share businesses in low-growth-markets. They do not produce much profit, and they show little potential for future improvement. The preferred strategy for dogs is retrenchment by divestiture.

GE Business Screen

The appeal of portfolio planning is its ability to help managers focus attention on the comparative strengths and weaknesses of multiple businesses and/or products. Although the BCG matrix is easy to understand and use, it is criticized for limiting attention to only market share and business growth. Business situations are more complex than that. At GE, for example, corporate strategy must achieve the best allocation of resources among the mix of some 150-plus businesses owned by the conglomerate at any point in time. The businesses operate in very different environments, use different business models, and have different competitive advantages. What is known as the *GE Business Screen*, shown in *Figure 8.8*, was developed as an alternative portfolio planning framework. In fact, GE became famous under the leadership of CEO Jack Welch for following a rigorous de-

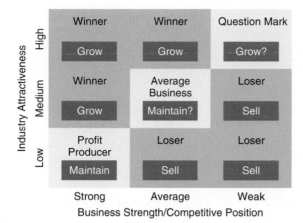

Figure 8.8 The GE Business Screen as a portfolio planning framework.

cision rule in strategic planning—either a business is or has the potential to be #1 or #2 in its industry, or it is removed from the GE portfolio.

In the **GE Business Screen**, the key planning dimensions are business strength and industry attractiveness.[39] Each is analyzed on multiple factors similar to a SWOT analysis. Industry attractiveness is considered in terms of market size and growth, capital requirements, and competitive intensity. Business strength or competitive position is assessed not only on market share but also on things like technological advantage, product quality, operating costs, and price competitiveness. The resulting nine-cell matrix allows for a finer classification of business units as "winners," "question marks," "average businesses," "profit producers," or "losers." The recommended strategic directions are to invest for growth in winners and question marks, maintain or stabilize average businesses and profit producers, and retrench or sell losers.

○ The **GE Business Screen** analyzes business strength and industry attractiveness for strategy formulation.

ADAPTIVE STRATEGIES

The Miles and Snow adaptive model of strategy formulation suggests that organizations should pursue product/market strategies congruent with their external environments.[40] A well-chosen strategy, in this sense, allows an organization to successfully adapt to environmental challenges. The *prospector strategy* involves pursuing innovation and new opportunities in the face of risk and with prospects for growth. This is best suited to a dynamic and high-potential environment. A prospector "leads" an industry by using existing technology to new advantage and creating new products to which competitors must respond. Fred Smith's original idea for Federal Express, the company he founded, was based on this strategic approach. This contrasts with a *defender strategy*, in which an organization avoids change by emphasizing existing products and current market share without seeking growth. Defense as a strategy is suited only for a stable environment and perhaps declining industries. Defenders, as do many small local retailers, try to maintain their operating domains with only slight changes over time. As a result, many suffer long-term decline in the face of competition.

The *analyzer strategy* seeks to maintain the stability of a core business while exploring selective opportunities for innovation and change. This strategy lies between the prospector and reactor strategies. It is a "follow-the-leader-when-things-look-good" approach. Many of the "clone" makers in the personal computer industry are analyzers; that is, they wait to see

www.worthington industries.com

Worthington Industries pursues a human resource strategy based on trust. There are no time clocks. All full-time employees are on salaries. The firm provides free coffee, in-plant barbershops, and medical-wellness centers.

eToys, Inc.
Making Sure the Business Strategy Has a Career Payoff

It's easy these days to start an on-line business, right? No, "wrong." The hot careers are all in dot-coms, right? No, "wrong."

There was a time when eToys, Inc.'s CEO Edward "Toby" Lenk could sit back and enjoy with satisfaction the success of his high-flying Internet company. Started with a vision "to make buying children's toys fun again," eToys topped $150 million in sales within four years, stocked over 100,000 items, and employed some 1,000 persons. It offered a user-friendly web site that kept the "store" open 24 hours a day, 7 days a week, every week of the year. For a time it seemed that Lenk was well ahead of the old economy stalwart, ToysRUs.

eToys, Inc., is gone now, a casualty of the great dot-com shakeout. ToysRUs is still around, with its own dot-com component. What was eToys' problem? Profits. At the same time that it was selling $150 million worth of toys on the Web it was losing over $180 million. Distribution costs were high. Investors lost confidence. The stock price tanked. Employees lost their jobs.

There are winning e-business strategies out there, and more will follow. These firms should be in your career horizons. But there will be a lot of "dot-bombs" too. That means not only business risk for investors, but also career risk for those who join the startup Internet companies.

QUESTION: Are you ready to make good career decisions in the new economy? Do you understand what it takes to have a winning e-business strategy? What is your competitive advantage in today's job markets?

what the industry leaders do and how well it works out before modifying their own operations. Organizations pursuing a *reactor strategy* are primarily responding to competitive pressures in order to survive. This is a "follow-as-last-resort" approach. Reactors do not have long-term and coherent strategies. Some public utilities and other organizations operating under government regulation may use this strategy to some extent.

INCREMENTALISM AND EMERGENT STRATEGY

Not all strategies are clearly formulated at one point in time and then implemented step by step. Not all strategies are created in systematic and deliberate fashion and then implemented as dramatic changes in direction. Instead, strategies sometimes take shape, change, and develop over time as modest adjustments to past patterns. James Brian Quinn calls this a process of *incrementalism*, whereby modest and incremental changes in strategy occur as managers learn from experience and make adjustments.[41] This approach has much in common with Henry Mintzberg's and John Kotter's descriptions of managerial behavior, as described in Chapter 1.[42] They view managers as planning and acting in complex interpersonal networks and in hectic, fast-paced work settings. Given these challenges, effective managers must have the capacity to stay focused on long-term objectives while still remaining flexible enough to master short-run problems and opportunities as they occur.

Such reasoning has led Mintzberg to identify what he calls **emergent strate-**

○ An **emergent strategy** develops over time as managers learn from and respond to experience.

gies.[43] These are strategies that develop progressively over time as "streams" of decisions made by managers as they learn from and respond to work situations. There is an important element of "craftsmanship" here that Mintzberg worries may be overlooked by managers who choose and discard strategies in rapid succession while using the formal planning models. He also believes that incremental or emergent strategic planning allows managers and organizations to become really good at implementing strategies, not just formulating them.

STRATEGY IMPLEMENTATION

No strategy, no matter how well formulated, can achieve longer-term success if it is not properly implemented. This includes the willingness to exercise control and make modifications as required to meet the needs of changing conditions. More specifically, current issues in strategy implementation include reemphasis on excellence in all management systems and practices, the responsibilities of corporate governance, and the importance of strategic leadership.

MANAGEMENT PRACTICES AND SYSTEMS

The rest of *Management 7/e* is all about strategy implementation. In order to successfully put strategies into action the entire organization and all of its resources must be mobilized in support of them. This, in effect, involves the complete management process from planning and controlling through organizing and leading. No matter how well or elegantly selected, a strategy requires supporting structures, the right technology, a good allocation of tasks and workflow designs, and the right people to staff all aspects of operations. The strategy needs to be enthusiastically supported by leaders who are capable of motivating everyone, building individual performance commitments, and utilizing teams and teamwork to best advantage. And, the strategy needs to be well and continually communicated to all relevant persons and parties. Only with such total systems support can strategies succeed through implementation in today's environments of change and innovation.

Common strategic planning pitfalls that can hinder implementation include both failures of substance and failures of process. *Failures of substance* reflect inadequate attention to the major strategic planning elements—analysis of mission and purpose, core values and corporate culture, organizational strengths and weaknesses, and environmental opportunities and threats. *Failures of process* reflect poor handling of the ways in which the various aspects of strategic planning were accomplished. An important process failure is the *lack of participation error*. This is failure to include key persons in the strategic planning effort.[44] As a result, their lack of commitment to all-important action follow-through may severely hurt strategy implementation. Process failure also occurs with too much centralization of planning in top management or too much delegation of planning activities to staff planners or separate planning departments. Another process failure is the tendency to get so bogged down in details that the planning process becomes an end in itself instead of a means to an end. This is sometimes called "goal displacement."

CORPORATE GOVERNANCE

Organizations today are experiencing new pressures at the level of **corporate governance**. This is the system of control and performance monitoring of top management that is maintained by boards of directors and other major stakeholder representatives. In businesses, for example, corporate governance is enacted by boards, institutional investors in a firm's assets, and other ownership interests. Each in its own way is a point of accountability for top management.[45]

Boards of directors are formally charged with ensuring that an organization operates in the best interests of its owners and/or the representative public in the case of nonprofit organizations. Controversies often arise over the role of *inside directors*, who are chosen from the senior management of the organization, and *outside directors*, who are chosen from other organizations and positions external to the organization. In the past corporate boards may have been viewed as largely endorsing or confirming

Freemarkets.com has been called the granddaddy of online auction sites. All auctions are conducted on the firm's web site with buyers and sellers able to bid and watch the auction's progress from their personal computers.

○ **Corporate governance** is the system of control and performance monitoring of top management.

the strategic initiatives of top management. Today they are increasingly expected to exercise control and take active roles in ensuring that the strategic management of an enterprise is successful.

If anything, the current trend is toward greater emphasis on the responsibilities of corporate governance. Top managers probably feel more accountability for performance than ever before to boards of directors and other stakeholder interest groups. Furthermore, this accountability relates not only to financial performance but also to broader social responsibility concerns. As discussed in Chapter 6 on ethics and social responsibility, for example, institutional investors such as the Interfaith Center for Corporate Social Responsibility purposely buy stock in a company to gain a voice in shareholder meetings. They do this to bring pressure on organizations to behave in socially responsible ways. Such pressure has been felt by PepsiCo and Texaco for their controversial involvements in Burma, a country whose totalitarian rulers were accused of human rights abuses. Under pressure, both PepsiCo and Texaco terminated their business interests in that country.

STRATEGIC LEADERSHIP

Strategic management is a leadership responsibility. Effective strategy implementation and control depends on the full commitment of all managers to supporting and leading strategic initiatives within their areas of supervisory responsibility. To successfully put strategies into action the entire organization and all of its resources must be mobilized in support of them. In our dynamic and often-uncertain environment, the premium is on **strategic leadership**—the capability to enthuse people to successfully engage in a process of continuous change, performance enhancement, and implementation of organizational strategies.[46] The broad issues associated with strategic leadership are so important that Part 5 of *Management 7/e* is devoted in its entirety to leadership and issues related to leadership development—including leadership models, motivation, communication, interpersonal dynamics, and teamwork.

Porter argues that the CEO of a business has to be the chief strategist, someone who provides strategic leadership.[47] He describes the task in the following way. A strategic leader has to be the *guardian of trade-offs*. It is the leader's job to make sure that the organization's resources are allocated in ways consistent with the strategy. This requires the discipline to sort through many competing ideas and alternatives to stay on course and not get sidetracked. A strategic leader also needs to *create a sense of urgency*, not allowing the organization and its members to grow slow and complacent. Even when doing well, the leader keeps the focus on getting better, and being alert to conditions that require adjustments to the strategy. A strategic leader needs to *make sure that everyone understands the strategy*. Unless strategies are understood, the daily tasks and contributions of people lose context and purpose. Everyone might work very hard, but without alignment to strategy the impact is dispersed rather than advancing in a common direction to accomplish the goals. Importantly, a strategic leader must *be a teacher*. It is the leader's job to teach the strategy and make it a "cause," says Porter. In order for strategy to work it must become an ever-present commitment throughout the organization. Everyone must understand the strategy that makes their organization different from others. This means that a strategic leader must *be a great*

○ **Strategic leadership** enthuses people to continuously change, refine, and improve strategies and their implementation.

Importance of Leadership Qualities
Fast Company magazine and Digital Marketing Services asked 1,000 college graduates to think about success and business leadership in the future. At the top of their list of very important leadership capabilities was "technology smarts." Take the on-line "Reality Check" to learn more about the qualities that make a difference in strategic leadership.

communicator. Philip M. Condit, Chairman and CEO of Boeing Co., keeps the message simple and focused on his firm's strategic priorities. "Every single Boeing group I talk to," he says, "that's in the speech, every single one. And I try to do it with exactly the same words every time . . . you've got to say the same thing over and over and over."[48]

Finally, it is important to note that the challenges faced by organizations today are so complex that it is often difficult for one individual to fulfill all strategic leadership needs. Strategic management in large firms is increasingly viewed as a team leadership responsibility. When Michael Dell founded Dell Computer, he did it in his dormitory room at college. Now the firm operates globally with $30 billion in sales. Dell is still Chairman and CEO, but he has two vice-chairmen to help with top management tasks. He observes: "I don't think you could do it with one person . . . there's way too much to be done."[49] As discussed in Chapter 17 on teams and teamwork, it takes hard work and special circumstances to create a real team—at the top or anywhere else in the organization.[50] Top management teams must work up to their full potential in order to bring the full advantages of teamwork to strategic leadership. Dell believes that his top management team has mastered the challenge. "We bounce ideas off each other," he says, "and at the end of the day if we say who did this, the only right answer is that we all did. Three heads are better than one."[51]

STUDY Guide

The Chapter 8 Study Guide will help you review chapter content, prepare for examinations, and further build your career readiness. The *Summary* briefly highlights answers to questions first posed in the chapter opening Planning Ahead section. The list of *Key Terms* allows you to double check your familiarity with basic concepts and definitions. *Self-Test 8* gives you the opportunity to test your basic comprehension of chapter content using sample test questions. Suggestions offered as *Career Readiness Activities* direct your attention to relevant sections of the end-of-text Career Readiness Workbook, as well as to special Electronic Resources on the *Management 7/e* web site.

SUMMARY

What are the foundations of strategic competitiveness?

- Competitive advantage is achieved by operating in ways that are difficult for competitors to imitate.
- A strategy is a comprehensive plan that sets long-term direction and guides resource allocation to achieve sustainable competitive advantage.
- The strategic goals of a business should include superior profitability and the generation of above-average returns for investors.
- Strategic thinking involves the ability to understand the different challenges of monopoly, oligopoly, and hypercompetition environments.

What is strategic management?

- Strategic management is the process of formulating and implementing strategies that achieve organizational goals in a competitive environment.
- The strategic management process begins with analysis of mission, clarification of core values, and identification of objectives.
- A SWOT analysis systematically assesses organizational resources and capabilities and industry/environmental opportunities and threats.
- Porter's five forces model analyzes industry attractiveness in terms of competititors, new entrants, substitute products, and the bargaining power of suppliers and buyers.

What types of strategies are used by organizations?

- Corporate strategy sets direction for an entire organization; business strategy sets direction for a business division or product/service line; functional strategy sets direction for the operational support of business and corporate strategies.

- The grand or master strategies used by organizations include growth—pursuing expansion; retrenchment—pursuing ways to scale back operations; stability—pursuing ways to maintain the status quo; and combination—pursuing the strategies in combination.

How are strategies formulated?

- The three options in Porter's model of competitive strategy are: differentiation—distinguishing one's products from the competition; cost leadership—minimizing costs relative to the competition; and focus—concentrating on a special market segment.
- The product life-cycle model focuses on different strategic needs at the introduction, growth, maturity, and decline stages of a product's life.
- The BCG matrix is a portfolio planning approach that classifies businesses or product lines as "stars," "cash cows," "question marks," or "dogs."
- The adaptive model focuses on the congruence of prospector, defender, analyzer, or reactor strategies with demands of the external environment.
- The incremental or emergent model recognizes that many strategies are formulated and implemented incrementally over time.

What are current issues in strategy Implementation?

- Management practices and systems—including the functions of planning, organizing, leading, and controlling—must be mobilized to support strategy implementation.
- Among the pitfalls that inhibit strategy implementation are failures of substance, such as poor analysis of the environment, and failures of process, such as lack of participation in the planning process.
- Corporate governance, involving the role of boards of directors in the performance monitoring of organizations, is being addressed as an important element in strategic management today.
- Strategic leadership involves the ability to manage trade-offs in resource allocations, maintain a sense of urgency in strategy implementation, and effectively communicate the strategy to key constituencies.
- Increasingly, organizations utilize top management teams to energize and direct the strategic management process.

KEY TERMS

Above-average returns (p. 204)

BCG matrix (p. 217)

Business strategy (p. 210)

Competitive advantage (p. 202)

Concentration (p. 211)

Core competencies (p. 208)

Corporate governance (p. 221)

Corporate strategy (p. 210)

Cost leadership strategy (p. 216)

Differentiation strategy (p. 216)

Diversification (p. 211)

Divestiture (p. 212)

Downsizing (p. 212)

E-business strategy (p. 213)

Emergent strategy (p. 220)

Focused differentiation strategy (p. 216)

Focused cost leadership strategy (p. 216)

Functional strategy (p. 211)

GE Business Screen (p. 219)

Growth strategy (p. 211)

Mission (p. 205)

Operating objectives (p. 207)

Organizational culture (p. 206)

Portfolio planning (p. 217)

Product life cycle (p. 216)

Restructuring (p. 212)

Retrenchment strategy (p. 212)

Stakeholders (p. 206)

Strategic alliance (p. 212)

Strategic business unit (p. 211)

Strategic intent (p. 203)

Strategic leadership (p. 222)

Strategic management (p. 203)

Strategy (p. 203)

Strategy formulation (p. 205)

Strategy implementation (p. 205)

SWOT analysis (p. 208)

Vertical integration (p. 211)

SELF-TEST 8

Take this test here or on-line much as you would in a normal classroom situation. It should offer you a good way to check your basic comprehension of chapter material. Answers may be found at the end of the book.

MULTIPLE-CHOICE QUESTIONS:

1. The most appropriate first question to ask in strategic planning is _____

   (a) "Where do we want to be in the future?"
   (b) "How well are we currently doing?"
   (c) "How can we get where we want to be?"
   (d) "Why aren't we doing better?"

2. An important purpose of strategic planning is to give an organization a _____ in the marketplace.
   (a) clear structure (b) sustainable competitive advantage (c) cash cow (d) strategic alliance

3. In a complex business such as the conglomerate General Electric, a(n) _____ -level strategy sets strategic direction for a strategic business unit or product division.
   (a) institutional (b) corporate (c) business (d) functional

4. An organization that is downsizing to reduce costs is implementing a grand strategy of _____.
   (a) growth (b) cost differentiation (c) retrenchment (d) stability

5. The _____ is a predominant value system for an organization as a whole.
   (a) code of ethics (b) organizational climate (c) institutional personality (d) corporate culture

6. A _____ in the BCG matrix would have a high market share in a low-growth market.
   (a) dog (b) cash cow (c) question mark (d) star

7. In Porter's five forces framework, which is a preferred condition for the firm?
   (a) many rivals (b) many substitutes (c) low bargaining power of suppliers (d) few barriers to entry

8. When PepsiCo acquired Tropicana, a maker of orange juice, the firm's strategy was one of _____.
   (a) related diversification (b) concentration (c) vertical integration (d) cooperation

9. Cost efficiency and product quality are two examples of _____ objectives of organizations.
   (a) official (b) operating (c) informal (d) institutional

10. The customer generally gains through lower prices and greater innovation in _____ environments.
    (a) monopoly (b) oligopoly (c) hypercompetition (d) central planning

TRUE-FALSE QUESTIONS:

11. A business can pursue growth through both concentration and diversification strategies.   T   F

12. An organization pursuing a stability strategy is always going to lose competitive advantage.   T   F

13. Core competencies can be identified in the analysis of organizational strengths and weaknesses.   T   F

14. In the adaptive model, a prospector strategy responds to events without having an overall guiding strategy.   T   F

15. Whether or not a CEO uses a top management team is an issue of corporate governance.   T   F

16. When an organization concentrates on one market segment and offers customers in that segment a unique product, this is considered a focused differentiation strategy.   T   F

17. The last stage in product life-cycle planning is maturity.   T   F

18. Portfolio planning like the GE Business Screen is considered most useful at the level of functional strategy.   T   F

19. Lack of participation is a failure of process in strategic planning.   T   F

20. One of the most important tasks of a strategic leader is to communicate the strategy.   T   F

SHORT-RESPONSE QUESTIONS:

21. What is the difference between corporate strategy and functional strategy?

22. How would a manager perform a SWOT analysis?

23. What is the difference between the BCG matrix and GE Business Screen as portfolio planning approaches?

24. What is strategic leadership?

APPLICATION QUESTION:

25. Kim Harris owns and operates a retail store selling the outdoor clothing of an American manufacturer to a predominately college student market. Lately, a large department store has opened a similar department and is selling similar clothing manufactured in China, Thailand, and Bangladesh at lower prices. Kim believes he is starting to lose business to this store. Assume you are part of a student team assigned to do a management class project for Kim. Kim's question for the team is "How can I apply Porter's generic strategies to better deal with my strategic planning challenges in this situation?" How will you reply?

readiness
CAREER | ACTIVITIES

Recommended learning activities from the end-of-text Career Readiness Workbook for Chapter 8 include:

Career Advancement Portfolio
- Individual writing and group presentation assignments based on any of the following activities.

Case for Critical Thinking
- Procter & Gamble—A Web-based Turnaround?

Integrative Learning Activities
- Research Project 2—Changing Corporate Cultures
- Integrative Case—Outback Steakhouse, Inc.
- Integrative Case—Richard Branson Meets the New Economy

Exercises in Teamwork
- What Managers Do (#2)
- Strategic Scenarios (#11)
- The Future Workplace (#13)
- Empowering Others (#19)

Self-Assessments
- A 21st-Century Manager? (#1)
- Organizational Culture Preferences (#2)
- Turbulence Tolerance Test (#24)

The *Fast Company* Collection On-Line
- Scott Kirsner, "Collision Course"

ELECTRONIC RESOURCES

@ GET CONNECTED! Don't forget to take full advantage of the on-line support for *Management 7/e.*
- Chapter 8 On-line Study Guide
- Chapter 8 Self-test Answers
- Chapter 8 E-Resource Center

---

www.wiley.com/college/schermerhorn

9

Entrepreneurship and new ventures

Planning ahead

CHAPTER 9 study questions

○ **What is entrepreneurship?**

○ **What is special about small businesses?**

○ **How does one start a new venture?**

○ **What resources support entrepreneurship and business development?**

GETTING CONNECTED

Count Me In for Women's Economic Independence—*Invest in People and Ideas*

Each year people with good ideas don't get the chance to turn them into reality. A good percentage of them are women. Count Me In for Women's Economic Independence is out to turn the tables and give female entrepreneurs a chance to get started. Co-founded by Nell Merlino, also founder and president of Strategy Community Action, Ltd. and creator of *Take Our Daughters to Work Day*, and Iris Burnett, former Professor at American University and Senior Vice President for the Sci-Fi Channel and USA Network, Count Me In uses the Internet to raise money for loans to female entrepreneurs.

Through their web site, www.count-me-in.org, Merlino and Burnett solicit contributions as small as $5 that are put into a revolving loan fund. The fund is then tapped to provide "microcredit" loans in amounts from $500 to $10,000 to help women start and expand small businesses. Women qualify for the loans by a unique credit scoring system that doesn't hold against them things like a divorce, time off to raise a family, or age, which might discourage conventional lenders.

Geneva Francais got a $1,500 loan to build storage shelves for her special cooking sauce, "Geneva's Splash," brewed and bottled in her kitchen. Francais is a 65-year-old widow. She says: "A bank would not loan a woman money when she is 65 years old. It's as simple as that." With Count Me In's loan she hopes to be able to double the $400-a-month Social Security income that she presently lives on. Heather McCartney is married to a high school principal in New York. She received a $5,000 loan to expand "Ethnic Edibles," her line of cookies and cookie cutters designed on traditional African motifs. The money will be used for packaging and marketing.

Merlino says: "Women own 38 percent of all businesses in this country, but still have far less access to capital than men because of today's process." Count Me In is out to change all that. The organization's loan fund is already over $1 million and growing daily. What's the average size of contribution? Just $15.[1]

@ Get Connected!

What do you think about this approach to "microcredit"? Just imagine what people can do just given the chance. And it often doesn't take a lot of money, either. Check out the resources for entrepreneurship in your community. Creating a plan to fill any gaps that might exist would make a great course project. Get connected!

Count Me In is an innovative organization. Its founders have done their homework. They've spotted a market niche missed or ignored by conventional lenders—small credit requests by women wanting to start or expand a small business. They've designed an Internet-driven way to address this niche and play an important social role. In short, they're in the business of doing good. Count Me In has the strategic focus, organization, and leadership that appear capable of bringing to it long-term success. It is an interesting example of what one can do with creativity and initiative in the world of work today. In fact, this is a chapter of examples. The goal is not only to inform, to better familiarize you with the nature of entrepreneurship and new venture creation. It's also to enthuse, to stimulate you to consider starting your own business, being your own boss, and making your own special contribution to society.

Consider Count Me In again. Not only is it an interesting enterprise. The name itself is enlightening. It suggests both hope and inclusion, the desire to bring everyone and anyone to the point of benefitting from the pursuit of their business ideas. This should be motivating to you, suggesting that there shouldn't be any excuses for not trying . . . for not giving your ideas a chance. What about it? Can we count you in to the world of entrepreneurship and new ventures?

THE NATURE OF ENTREPRENEURSHIP

○ **Entrepreneurship** is dynamic, risk-taking, creative, and growth-oriented behavior.

Today's dynamic environment demands that organizations and their managers adapt and renew themselves continually to succeed over time. People and organizations must change frequently and at a rapidly accelerating pace. Success in the highly competitive business environments, in particular, depends on **entrepreneurship**. This term is used to describe strategic thinking and risk-taking behavior that results in the creation of new opportunities for individuals and/or organizations. H. Wayne Huizenga, featured below, and a member of The Entrepreneur's Hall of Fame, describes it this way: "An important part of being an entrepreneur is a gut instinct that allows you to believe in your heart that something will work even though everyone else says it will not." You say, "I am going to make sure it works. I am going to go out there and make it happen."[2] These opportunities are illustrated in the success stories of business ventures that grew into large companies, such as the now-familiar Domino's Pizza and Federal Express, or of great new products like the popular Post-It Notes from large organizations such as 3M.

WHO ARE THE ENTREPRENEURS?

○ An **entrepreneur** is willing to pursue opportunities in situations others view as problems or threats.

An **entrepreneur** is a risk-taking individual who takes action to pursue opportunities others may fail to recognize or may even view as problems or threats. In the business context, an entrepreneur starts new ventures that bring to life new product or service ideas. Researchers are interested in the characteristics of entrepreneurs. They want to know whether and how entrepreneurs are different, and what it takes to achieve entrepreneurial success.

Before examining the findings, though, let's meet some real, high-profile entrepreneurs. Their stories are rich with ideas for all of us to consider. Although the people and what was accomplished are all different, they share something in common. These entrepreneurs built successful long-term businesses from good ideas and hard work.[3]

Mary Kay Ash—After a career in sales, Mary Kay "retired" for a month. The year was 1963. When starting to write a book to help women compete in the male-dominated business world she realized she was writing a business plan. From that plan arose Mary Kay Cosmetics. Launched on $5,000, the company now operates worldwide and has been named one of the best companies to work for in America. Mary Kay's goal from the beginning has been "to help women everywhere reach their full potential."

Richard Branson—Want to start an airline? Richard Branson did, but he started first in his native England with a student literary magazine and small mail-order record business. Since, he's built Virgin into one of the world's most recognized brand names. The business conglomerate now employs some 25,000 people around the globe in over 200 companies, including Virgin Airlines, Virgin Records, and even Virgin Cola. It's all very creative and ambitious. But that's Branson. "I love to learn things I know little about," he says.

Earl Graves—With a vision and a $175,000 loan, Earl Graves started *Black Enterprise* magazine in 1970. That success grew into the diversified business information company, Earl G. Graves, Ltd., including BlackEnterprise.com. Growing up in Brooklyn, New York, at the age of 6 he was selling Christmas cards to neighbors. Today the business school at his college alma mater, Baltimore's Morgan State University, is named after him. Graves says: "I feel that a large part of my role as publisher of *Black Enterprise* is to be a catalyst for black economic development in this country."

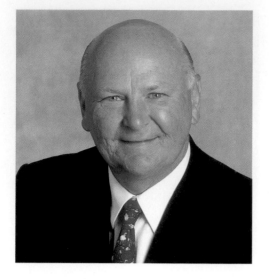

H. Wayne Huizenga—**What do** Waste Management, Inc., the Miami Dolphins **football team,** AutoNation, Inc., **and** Blockbuster Video **have in common?** They have all at one time been owned by entrepreneur Wayne Huizenga. How did it all start? In 1962, aged 25, he borrowed $5,000 from his father-in-law, got a used truck, and acquired a few trash-hauling accounts. He then built the world's largest waste disposal company, Waste Management. He's been buying, building, and selling businesses ever since . . . and reaping the benefits. Huizenga says: "Success depends on seizing the moment and sometimes creating your own opportunity."

Anita Roddick—In 1973 Anita Roddick was a 33-year-old housewife looking for a way to support herself and her two children. She spotted a niche for natural-based skin and health care products, and started mixing and selling her own from a small shop in Brighton, England. The Body Shop PLC has grown to some 1500 outlets in 47 countries with 24 languages, selling a product every half-second to one of its 86+ million customers. Known for building the firm with a commitment to human rights, the environment, and economic development, Roddick believes in business social responsibility. She says: "If you think you're too small to have an impact, try going to bed with a mosquito."

CHARACTERISTICS OF ENTREPRENEURS

Do you sense any common patterns in the prior examples? Hopefully you've taken advantage of the web links to find out more about each person. A common image of an entrepreneur is as the founder of a new business enterprise that achieves large-scale success, like the ones just mentioned. In today's world of e-business Jeff Bezos of Amazon.com is another dramatic example; he is headed for entrepreneurship hall of fame status some day. But, entrepreneurs also operate on a smaller and less-public scale. Those who take the risk of buying a local McDonald's or Subway Sandwich franchise, opening a small retail shop, or going into a self-employed service business are also entrepreneurs. Similarly, anyone who assumes responsibility for introducing a new product or change in operations within an organization is also demonstrating the qualities of entrepreneurship.

Obviously there's a lot to learn about entrepreneurs and entrepreneurship. Starting with the individual, however, indications are that entrepreneurs tend to share certain attitudes and behavioral tendencies. The general profile is of an individual that is very self-confident, determined, resilient, adaptable, and driven to excel.[4] You should be able to identify these attributes in the prior examples. In addition, typical *characteristics of entrepreneurs* include the following: [5]

- *Internal locus of control*: Entrepreneurs believe that they are in control of their own destiny; they are self-directing and like autonomy.
- *High energy level*: Entrepreneurs are persistent, hard working, and willing to exert extraordinary efforts to succeed.
- *High need for achievement*: Entrepreneurs are motivated to accomplish challenging goals; they thrive on performance feedback.
- *Tolerance for ambiguity*: Entrepreneurs are risk takers; they tolerate situations with high degrees of uncertainty.
- *Self-confidence*: Entrepreneurs feel competent, believe in themselves, and are willing to make decisions.
- *Action oriented*: Entrepreneurs try to act ahead of problems; they want to get things done quickly and do not want to waste valuable time.
- *Desire for independence*: Entrepreneurs want independence; they are self-reliant and want to be their own boss, not work for others.

← Characteristics of entrepreneurs

Entrepreneurs are sometimes distinguishable in terms of background and experiences, not just the prior personal characteristics.[6] *Childhood experiences and family environment* seem to make a difference. Evidence links entrepreneurs with parents who were entrepreneurial and self-employed. Similarly, entrepreneurs tend to be raised in families that encourage responsibility, initiative, and independence. Another issue is *career or work history*. Entrepreneurs who try one venture often go on to others. Prior career or personal experience in the business area or industry is also helpful. It also appears that entrepreneurs tend to emerge during certain *windows of career opportunity*. Most entrepreneurs start their businesses between the ages of 22 and 45. This appears to be an age spread that allows for risk taking. However, age is no barrier. When Tony DeSio was 50 he founded the Mail Boxes Etc. chain. He sold it for $300 million when he was 67 and suffering heart problems. Within a year he launched PixArts, another franchise chain based on photography and art.[7]

Get Connected!

If your community had its version of The Entrepreneur's Hall of Fame, who would you recommend for membership?

Finally, a recent report in the *Harvard Business Review* suggests that entrepreneurs may have unique and *deeply embedded life interests*. The article describes entrepreneurs as having strong interests in creative production—enjoying project initiation, working with the unknown, and creating unconventional solutions. They also have strong interests in enterprise control—described as finding enjoyment from running things. The combination of creative production and enterprise control is characteristic of people who want to start things and move things toward a goal.[8]

Undoubtedly, entrepreneurs seek independence and the sense of mastery that comes with success. That seems to keep driving Tony DeSio, in the example above. When asked by a reporter what he liked most about entrepreneurship, he replied: "Being able to make decisions without having to go through layers of corporate hierarchy—just being a master of your own destiny."[9] See *Manager's Notepad 9.1* for some additional thoughts on the nature of entrepreneurs and entrepreneurship.[10]

DIVERSITY AND ENTREPRENEURSHIP

Entrepreneurship is rich with diversity. And it grows richer by the day with the efforts of Count Me In and other organizations like it. The National Foundation for Women Business Owners (NFWBO) reports there are over 9 million businesses in the United States that are owned by women and creating jobs for 27.5 million people. This represents about 38 percent of all U.S. businesses. Its web site offers substantial web-based support for and facts about female entrepreneurs.[11] The NFWBO also reports a study to determine why women are starting new businesses at twice the rate of the national average. Most indicate being motivated by a new idea, or realizing that they could do for themselves what they were already doing for other employers. But among those leaving private sector employment to strike out on their own, 33 percent said they were not being taken seriously by their prior employer; 29 percent said they experienced "glass ceiling" issues.

Clearly, entrepreneurship offers women opportunities of striking out on their own; it is also a pathway to opportunity that may be blocked in other employment. In *Women Business Owners of Color: Challenges and Accomplishments*, the NFWBO discusses the motivations of women of color to pursue entrepreneurship because of glass ceiling problems. These include not being recognized or valued by their prior employers, not being taken seriously, and seeing others promoted ahead of them.[12]

Data reported by the Small Business Administration show that entrepreneurship is opening business doors for minorities. Minority-owned businesses are one of the fastest-growing sectors of the economy.[13] Businesses created by minority entrepreneurs employ over 4 million American workers and generate over $500 billion in annual revenues, and the numbers are growing daily. SBA data on businesses' growth rates for 1987–1997 also show the number of African-American-owned businesses growing 103 percent, Asian and other minority-owned firms growing 180 percent, and Hispanic-owned firms growing 232 percent.[14]

CAREER CONNECTION

High Performance

Wendy's International, Inc.
The Quest Is Always to Be the Very Best
Have you had your Wendy's today?

A lot of people have, and there's *quite a story* behind it. The first Wendy's restaurant opened in Columbus, Ohio, in November 1969. It's still there; there are also about 5,000 others now operating around the world. What began as founder David Thomas's dream to own his own restaurant has grown into a global enterprise. He has become one of the world's best-known entrepreneurs. Some call him "The world's most famous hamburger cook."

Now merged with the Canadian coffee and bakery Tim Horton's, Wendy's ranks a strong third behind fast-food leader McDonald's and #2 Burger King in the highly competitive restaurant industry. But there's more to Wendy's than profits and business performance alone. Social responsibility counts too.

Wendy's strives to be in touch with its communities, with a special focus on helping schools and school children. Dave founded the Dave Thomas Foundation for Adoption. Its goals are to "generate awareness about the thousands of children in America who are waiting for permanent homes and loving families; to educate prospective parents about the adoption process; and to streamline the adoption process by making it easier and more affordable."

QUESTION: Where does entrepreneurship fit into your career plans? Do you see a role for yourself in advancing "caring capitalism"? Look around your community; what are the opportunities to do good business while doing good?

ENTREPRENEURSHIP AND SMALL BUSINESS

The U.S. Small Business Administration defines a **small business** as one with 500 or fewer employees, with the definition varying a bit by industry. The SBA also states that a small business is one that is independently

---

MANAGER'S NOTEPAD 9.1

Challenging the myths about entrepreneurs

- *Entrepreneurs are born, not made:* Not true! Talent gained and enhanced by experience is a foundation for entrepreneurial success.
- *Entrepreneurs are gamblers:* Note true! Entrepreneurs are risk takers, but the risks are informed and calculated.
- *Money is the key to entrepreneurial success:* Not true! Just having money is no guarantee of success: there's a lot more to it than that; many entrepreneurs start with very little.
- *You have to be young to be an entrepreneur:* Not true! Age alone is no barrier to entrepreneurship; with age often comes experience, contacts, and other useful resources.
- *You have to have a degree in business to be an entrepreneur:* Not true! You may not need a degree at all; you don't need a business degree in preference to other majors; you can benefit from learning about business fundamentals.

---

owned and operated and that does not dominate its industry.[15] Almost 99 percent of American businesses meet this definition, and the small business sector is very important in most nations of the world. Among other things, small businesses offer major economic advantages. In the United States, for example, they employ some 52 percent of private workers, provide 51 percent of private sector output, receive 35 percent of federal government contract dollars, and provide almost all of the new jobs in the economy.[17]

The most common ways for an entrepreneur to get involved in a small business are to (1) start one, (2) buy an existing one, or (3) buy and run a **franchise**—where a business owner sells to another the right to operate the same business in another location. A franchise runs under the original owner's business name and guidance. In return the franchise parent receives a share of income or a flat fee from the franchisee.

○ A **small business** has fewer than 500 employees, is independently owned and operated, and does not dominate its industry.

○ A **franchise** is when one business owner sells to another the right to operate the same business in another location.

DIVERSITY www.anitasantiago.com
Anita Santiago Advertising, Inc.
Hispanic Ad Agency Helps Others Bridge the Gap

After moving to the United States from Venezuela some 20 years ago, Anita Santiago said, "I'll never be able to land a job." But she did, in the advertising business. Four years later she started her own ad agency to focus on the Latin community and help communicate her culture to large companies. *Que gran idioma tengo,* reads the front page of her web site, quoting Chilean poet Pablo Neruda: "What a great language I have." Says Santiago: "I can see culture from both sides. You can't learn that from a book." What's Anita's advice to the about-to-be entrepreneur? "Be the expert—as we are in biculturalism. . . . Be creative," she says, adding: "Lastly, hire the best people."[16]

ENTREPRENEURSHIP AND THE INTERNET

Have you started a "dot-com" today? The question is light, but the implications are heavy. The Internet has opened a whole new array of entrepreneurial possibilities. Just take a look at the action on eBay and imagine how many people are now running small trading businesses from their homes. Based upon current trends, the SBA is predicting that over 85 percent of small firms will be conducting business over the Internet by 2002.[18] Many of these firms will be existing ones that pursue new Internet-driven opportunities. For some of these, the old ways of operating from a bricks-and-mortar retail establishment will give way to entirely on-line business activities. That's what happened to Rod Spencer and his S&S Sportscards store in Worthington, Ohio. He closed the store. But he didn't do it because business was bad; business was really good, but the nature of the business had changed. It turned to cyberspace, with sales over the Internet eventually becoming so much greater than in-store sales that Spencer decided to follow the world of e-commerce. He now works from his own home with a computer and high-speed Internet connection; he saves the cost of renting retail space and hiring store employees. "I can do less business overall," he says, "to make a higher profit."[19]

Internet entrepreneurship isn't limited to trading through eBay or trying to create the next Amazon.com. The opportunities are truly limitless. You just need to let your creativity go to work. Consider entrepreneurship by what some call *.Com Moms*.[20] After time as an investment banker, Ginger Thomson wanted more flexible work. She says: "It wasn't the hours; it was whether I could go home if I needed to." While helping friends with an on-line magazine for teens, she hit upon an idea: helping teach her children, all preteens, and others how to be financially responsible—using the Web, of course. Thomson started doughNet.com, a site for 13- to 18-year-olds that lets them open a bank account, learn about investing, and even donate to charity.

Another area for Internet entrepreneurship is B2B, specialized business-to-business web sites that link buyers and sellers. Some entrepreneurial startups trying to crack this relatively new small business arena are: buzzsaw.com (construction industry), c-storematrix.com (convenience stores), and produceonline.com (grocery produce). With the allure of cost savings to users, the market for the on-line exchange industry at large is estimated as high as $6 trillion dollars by the year 2004. But as with all entrepreneurship, B2B in the small business sector is considered risky. Analysts are cautious on its future, questioning (1) whether they can garner enough users to withstand early startup costs, (2) whether enough small businesses are sufficiently automated to take advantage of the services, and (3) whether smaller businesses are willing to give up their traditional distributor relationships for the on-line exchange.[21]

INTERNATIONAL BUSINESS ENTREPRENEURSHIP

In Chapter 5 on the global dimensions of management the reasons why businesses go international were discussed. The same ones apply to the strategic opportunities for smaller businesses. They also often find that international business brings opportunities for expanded markets, additional financing, access to quality and possibly lower-cost resources, access to labor and technical expertise, and on-site locations for low-cost

How Entrepreneurs Get Started
In a survey of 448 business owners, some 18 percent indicated they began while working for a larger company. How did the rest of the entrepreneurs get started? Take the on-line "Reality Check" to learn more.

@ Get Connected!

Want to know more about Hispanic businesses? Check out Hispanic Business on-line.

manufacturing or outsourcing. The Internet now makes selling abroad relatively easy; today's advanced distribution firms also make product delivery quick and easy. Additionally, smaller businesses can find alliance opportunities in strategic ventures with foreign partners.

As the economies of the world's countries improve and the overall standards of living rise, consumer demand for goods and services grows as well. With this comes greater international business opportunities for exporting and importing in particular. Governments, federal and state, encourage exporting and try to support the growth of small businesses through exporting. Like most states, the Ohio State government, for example, offers export development assistance to entrepreneurs through its International Trade Division. At the national level, the International Trade Administration of the U.S. Department of Commerce provides similar services. The Small Business Administration reports a steady growth in loan guarantees for small business exporters, growing 600 percent over a recent five-year period.[22] Many smaller technology companies are seeking diversification opportunities abroad. With diversification comes some insurance against the risk of economic slowdown in any one area; if domestic business declines, the hope is that international business will take up the slack.

Of course, it takes an investment to move any business, small or large, toward international opportunities. One has to invest in travel, communication, and time to build relationships and gain expertise. But there is considerable support available; small manufacturers seeking to attract foreign customers may begin, for example, by joining the Thomas Register of American Companies. It provides an Internet search engine for prospective customers to locate potential American business suppliers. Through its Trade Net Export Advisor service, the SBA offers potential exporters everything from expert advice on getting started to actual trade leads around the world. Many other resources are available to those trying to get started in international business. You just have to look.

How Small Businesses Meet Their Financial Needs In a survey by Arthur Andersen, 19 percent of family business owners said that they relied on personal or home equity bank loans to meet their capital needs in the preceeding 12 months. How did the rest handle their day-to-day financial needs? Take the on-line "Reality Check" to learn more.

FAMILY BUSINESSES

Family businesses, ones owned and financially controlled by family members, represent the largest percentage of businesses operating worldwide. Facts reported by The Family Firm Institute indicate that family businesses account for 78 percent of new jobs created in the United States and provide 60 percent of the nation's employment.[23] Family businesses must solve the same problems of other small or large businesses—meeting the challenges of strategy, competitive advantage, and operational excellence. When everything goes right, the family firm is almost an ideal situation—everyone working together, sharing values and a common goal, and knowing that what they do benefits the family. But it doesn't always work out this way or stay this way over time and successive generations. Family businesses face problems that are quite unique to their situation.

"Okay, Dad, so he's your brother. But does that mean we have to put up with inferior work and an erratic schedule that we would never tolerate from anyone else in the business?"[24] This conversation introduces a problem that can all too often set the stage for failure in a family business—the *family business feud*. Simply put, members of the controlling family get into disagreements about work responsibilities, business strategy, operating approaches, finances, or other matters. The example

○ A **family business** is owned and controlled by members of a family.

is indicative of an intergenerational problem, but the feud can be between spouses, among siblings, between parents and children; it really doesn't matter. The key point is that unless the disagreements are resolved satisfactorily among the members and to the benefit of the business itself, the firm will have difficulty surviving, especially in a highly competitive environment.

○ The **succession problem** is the issue of who will run the business when the current head leaves.

Another significant problem faced by family businesses is the **succession problem**—transferring leadership from one generation to the next. A survey of small and midsized family businesses by Arthur Andersen indicated that 66 percent planned on keeping the business within the family.[25] The management question is: How will the assets be distributed and who will run the business when the current head leaves? Although this problem is not specific to the small firm, it is especially significant in the family business context, and particularly in those cases where the current head of the firm is the founder—the entrepreneur who started the business and built it into what it is today. The data on succession are eye-opening. About 30 percent of family firms survive to the second generation; only 12 percent survive to the third; only 3 percent are expected to survive beyond that.[26]

○ A **succession plan** describes how the leadership transition and related financial matters will be handled.

A family business that has been in operation for some time is a source of both business momentum and financial wealth. Both must be maintained in the process of succession. Business advisors recommend that this problem be addressed ahead of time through a **succession plan**—a formal statement that describes how the leadership transition and related financial matters will be handled when the time for changeover arrives. Operational considerations of the plan should include, among other possibilities: procedures for choosing or designating the firm's new leadership, legal aspects of any ownership transfer, and any financial and estate plans relating to the transfer. Ideally, the foundations for effective implementation of a succession plan are set up well ahead of the need to use it. The plan should be shared and understood among all affected by it. Ideally the leadership successor is identified ahead of time, and then well prepared through experience and training to perform the new role when needed.

GLOBALIZATION www.usmcoc.org
The United States–Mexico Chamber of Commerce Connecting Businesses Across Borders

Through a special program called "Wiring the Border," the U.S.–Mexico Chamber of Commerce is helping border companies to tap the e-commerce marketplace. The Chamber's president Albert C. Zapanta says: "This initiative will help small businesses reach the international marketplace and compete effectively around the world." Major U.S. and Mexican corporations, including IBM and TelMex, are helping to sponsor the program. The partners are contributing web-enabling components. The member small businesses will be joined in a virtual network that will utilize e-commerce to increase sales, profits, and employment. Zapanta says: "Communities along the border have not shared in the economic growth enjoyed by most Americans the past several years, but they have borne a disproportionate share of the burden." Through Wiring the Border, the Chamber and its partners hope to bring positive change to both sides of the border.[27]

WHY SMALL BUSINESSES FAIL

Small businesses have a high failure rate; one high enough to be scary. As many as 60 to 80 percent of new businesses fail in their first five years of operation. Succession problems account for part of the failures. But a large part comes from management mistakes. Business failures are largely due to poor decision making by the original entrepreneurs and owners on matters of consequence. Often, the entrepreneur is unable to successfully make the transition from entrepreneur to strategic leader and manager. Among the *reasons for new business failures* are:[28]

- *Lack of experience*—not having sufficient know-how to run a business in the chosen market or area.
- *Lack of expertise*—not having expertise in the essentials of business operations, including finance, purchasing, selling, and production.
- *Lack of strategy and strategic leadership*—not taking the time to craft a vision and mission, and formulate and properly implement strategy.
- *Poor financial control*—not keeping track of the numbers and failure to control business finances.
- *Growing too fast*—not taking the time to consolidate a position, fine tune the organization, and systematically meet the challenges of growth.
- *Lack of commitment*—not devoting enough time to the requirements of running a competitive business.
- *Ethical failure*—falling prey to the temptations of fraud, deception, and embezzlement.

← Reasons for new business failures

NEW VENTURE CREATION

Now that the reasons for business failure have been described, let's talk about doing it right. Whether your interest is low-tech or high-tech, on-line or off-line, opportunities for new ventures are always there for the true entrepreneur.[29] To pursue the entrepreneurship process and start a new venture, you just need good ideas and the courage to give them a chance. You must also be prepared to meet and master the test of strategy and competitive advantage. Can you identify a *market niche* that is being missed by other established firms? Can you identify a *new market* that has not yet been discovered by existing firms? Can you generate **first-mover advantage** by exploiting a niche or entering a market before competitors? These are the questions that entrepreneurs ask and answer in the process of beginning a new venture. A focus on the customer is critical, as suggested by the guidelines in *Manager's Notepad 9.2*.[30]

○ A **first-mover advantage** comes from being first to exploit a niche or enter a market.

LIFE CYCLES OF ENTREPRENEURIAL FIRMS

Figure 9.1 describes the stages common to the life cycles of entrepreneurial companies. It shows the relatively predictable progression of the small business.[31] The firm begins with the *birth stage*—where the entrepreneur struggles to get the new venture established and survive long enough to test the viability of the underlying business model in the marketplace. The firm then passes into the *breakthough stage*—where the business model

---

MANAGER'S NOTEPAD 9.2

Questions that keep a new venture customer focused

- Who is your customer?
- How will you reach key customer market segments?
- What determines customer choices to buy your product/service?
- Why is your product/service a compelling choice for the customer?
- How will you price your product/service for the customer?
- How much does it cost to make and deliver your product/service?
- How much does it cost to attract a customer?
- How much does it cost to support and retain a customer?

---

begins to work well, growth is experienced, and the complexity of managing the business operation expands significantly. Next comes the *maturity stage*—where the entrepreneur experiences the advantages of market success and financial stability, while also facing continuing challenges of meeting the needs for professional management skills.

Entrepreneurs often face control and management dilemmas when their firms experience growth, including possible diversification or global expansion. These are very challenging in terms of the management and strategic leadership skills required to maintain success. It is here that entrepreneurs encounter a variation of the succession problem described earlier for family businesses. This time the problem is succession from entrepreneurial leadership to professional strategic leadership. The former brings the venture into being and sees it through the early stages of life; the latter manages and leads the venture into maturity as an ever-evolving and perhaps still-growing corporate enterprise. If the entrepreneur is incapable or unwilling to meet the firm's needs in later life-cycle stages, continued business survival and success may well depend on the business being sold or management control being passed to professionals.

○ A **business plan** describes the direction for a new business and the financing needed to operate it.

WRITING THE BUSINESS PLAN

When people start new businesses, either independent ones or as new components of larger organizations, they can greatly benefit from having a good **business plan**. This is a plan that describes the details needed to

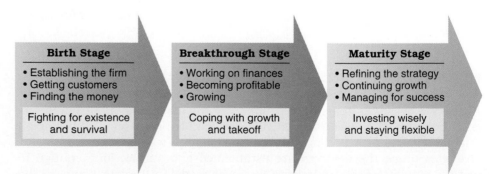

Figure 9.1 Stages in the life cycle of an entrepreneurial firm.

obtain startup financing and operate a new business. When well done, a business plan offers clear direction to an enterprise.[32] Says Ed Federkcil, who founded a small business called California Custom Sport Trucks: "It gives you direction instead of haphazardly sticking your key in the door every day and saying—'What are we going to do?'"[33] Banks and other financiers want to see a business plan before they loan money or invest in a new venture; senior managers want to see a business plan before they allocate scarce organizational resources to a new project. Importantly, the detail thinking required to prepare a business plan can contribute to the success of the new initiative.[34] For Federkeil and his business, that plan is now leading toward expansion through franchising.

Although there is no single template for a successful business plan, there is general agreement that a plan should have an executive summary, cover certain business fundamentals, be well-organized with headings, be easy to read, and be no more than about 20 pages in length. Basic items that should be included in a business plan are summarized in *Manager's Notepad 9.3*.[35] One of the great advantages of such a plan, of course, is forcing the entrepreneur to think through all of these issues and challenges before starting out.

In addition to what you will find in books and magazines, there are many on-line resources now available to assist in the development of a business plan. Among the alternatives are American Express Small Business Services, BusinessTown.com, and BizPlanIt.com. Many examples of

www.fambiz.com

Many universities have centers that specialize in family businesses. The University of Massachusetts, Montana State University, and Saint Louis University are examples. They offer research results, information, and special advice on operating family-owned businesses. The web site fambiz.com is a good source of information on family businesses, as is The Family Firm Institute.

MANAGER'S NOTEPAD 9.3

What to include in a business plan

- *Executive summary*—overview of business purpose and highlight of key elements of the plan.
- *Industry analysis*—nature of the industry, including economic trends, important legal or regulatory issues, and potential risks.
- *Company description*—mission, owners, and legal form.
- *Products and services description*—major goods or services, with special focus on uniqueness vis-á-vis competition.
- *Market description*—size of market, competitor strengths and weaknesses, five-year sales goals.
- *Marketing strategy*—product characteristics, distribution, promotion, pricing, and market research.
- *Operations description*—manufacturing or service methods, supplies and suppliers, and control procedures.
- *Staffing description*—management and staffing skills needed and available, compensation, human resource systems.
- *Financial projection*—cash flow projections for 1–5 years, break-even points, and phased investment capital.
- *Capital needs*—amount of funds needed to run the business, amount available, amount requested from new sources.

successful business plans are published on the Internet by the Moot Corp. The examples include plans from annual competitions in which MBA students present business plans to panels of potential investors in quest of actual financing for their startup ideas.

CHOOSING THE FORM OF OWNERSHIP

One of the important choices that must be made in starting a new venture is the legal form of ownership. There are a number of alternatives, and the choice among them involves careful consideration of their respective advantages and disadvantages. Briefly, the ownership forms include the following.

○ A **sole proprietorship** is an individual pursuing business for a profit.

A **sole proprietorship** is simply an individual or a married couple pursuing business for a profit. This does not involve incorporation; it is simple to start, run, and terminate. However, the business owner is personally liable for business debts and claims. This is the most common form of small business ownership in the United States.

○ A **partnership** is when two or more people agree to contribute resources to start and operate a business together.

A **partnership** is formed when two or more people agree to contribute resources to start and operate a business together. Most typically it is backed by a legal and written partnership agreement. Business partners agree on the contribution of resources and skills to the new venture, and on the sharing of profits, losses, and management responsibilities. The *general partnership* just described is the simplest and most common form. A *limited partnership* consists of a general partner and one or more "limited" partners who do not participate in day-to-day business management. They share in profits, but their losses are limited to the amount of their investment. *A limited liability partnership*, common among professionals such as accountants and attorneys, limits the liability of one partner for the negligence of another.

○ A **corporation** is a legal entity that exists separately from its owners.

A **corporation**, commonly identified by the "Inc." designation in a name, is a legal entity that exists separately from its owners. The corporation can be for profit, such as Microsoft, Inc., or not for profit, such as Count Me In, Inc. The corporate form grants the organization certain legal rights (e.g., to engage in contracts), and is also responsible for its own liabilities. This separates the owners from personal liability and gives the firm a life of its own that can extend beyond that of its owners. Both are important advantages. The disadvantage of incorporation rests largely with the cost of incorporating and the complexity of the documentation required to operate as an incorporated business.

FINANCING THE NEW VENTURE

○ **Debt financing** involves borrowing money that must be repaid over time with interest.

○ **Equity financing** involves exchanging ownership shares for outside investment monies.

Starting a new venture takes money, and that money often must be raised. Most likely, the cost of startup will exceed the amount available from personal sources. In these instances, there are two major sources from which the entrepreneur can obtain outside financing for the new venture. **Debt financing** involves going into debt by borrowing money from another person, a bank, or financial institution. This loan must be paid back over time with interest. A loan also requires collateral that pledges assets of the business or personal assets such as a home to secure the loan in case of default. **Equity financing** involves exchanging ownership shares in the business in return for outside investment monies. This money does not need to be paid back. It is an investment on the part of the provider, who assumes the risk for the outcomes of that investment. In return for taking that risk, the equity investor assumes some proportionate ownership control.

TAKE IT TO THE CASE!

Domino's Pizza
IT, CRM, and SCM Bring the Pizzas to Your Door

"Hello, Domino's Pizza, may I have your telephone number?" So begins a typical conversation when you telephone an order for a home delivery from Domino's Pizza. Within minutes, it seems, the pizza is at your door. Behind this seemingly simple transaction stands a customer-driven strategy and sophisticated use of technology. Domino's franchise stores depend upon quality and timely service from a complex chain of suppliers and distribution points. Over 6,600 stores, including those in 64 international markets, must be kept in stock with hundreds of products, ranging from food items to pizza boxes to business forms to cleaning supplies. Domino's is committed to customer relationship management and supply chain management to best support its franchise stores and better serve customers.[36]

Equity financing is usually obtained from **venture capitalists**, companies that pool capital and make investments in new ventures in return for an equity stake in the business. Typically, venture capitalists finance only a very small proportion of new ventures. They tend to focus on relatively large investments, such as $1 million or more, and they usually take a management role in order to grow the business and add value as soon as possible. Sometimes that value is returned in a fast-growing firm that gains a solid market base and becomes a candidate for an **initial public offering**, commonly known as an **IPO**. This is when shares of stock in the business are sold to the public and begin trading on a major stock exchange. When an IPO is successful and the share prices are bid up by the market, the original investments of the venture capitalist and entrepreneur rise in value. The anticipation of such return on investment is a large part of the venture capitalist's motivation; indeed, it is the nature of the venture capital business.

A recent report identified 1,237 venture capital firms in the United States.[37] Only nine of them, including Capital Across America and Women's Growth Capital Fund, specifically seek investments in women-owned companies. It's an accepted fact that even though women are starting more new businesses than ever before, they don't get as much of the available venture capital as men. When venture capital isn't available to the entrepreneur, male or female, another important financing option is the **angel investor**. This is a wealthy individual who is willing to invest a portion of this wealth in return for equity in a new venture. Angel investors are especially common and helpful in the very early startup stage. The presence of angel investment can help raise the confidence of venture capitalists and attract additional venture funding that would otherwise not be available. For example, when Liz Cobb wanted to start her sales compensation firm, Incentive Systems, she contacted 15 to 20 venture capital firms, was interviewed by 10, and was turned down by all of them. After she located $250,000 from two businessmen, the venture capital firms got interested again. She was able to obtain her first $2 million in financing, and has since built the firm into a 70-plus employee business.[38]

○ **Venture capitalists** make large investments in new ventures in return for an equity stake in the business.

○ An **IPO** is an initial selling of shares of stock to the public and for trading on a stock exchange.

○ An **angel investor** is a wealthy individual willing to invest in return for equity in a new venture.

ENTREPRENEURSHIP AND BUSINESS DEVELOPMENT

Entrepreneurship and the creative spark to launch new ventures is indispensable to the economy at large. It drives the formation of small businesses and new ventures that are so important to job creation and economic development. Larger enterprises need the same spark. Even as they operate more flexibly, in networks and with the advantages of IT, they too depend on entrepreneurship within the system to drive innovation for sustained competitive advantage.

INTRAPRENEURSHIP AND LARGE ENTERPRISES

○ **Intrapreneurship** is entrepreneurial behavior displayed by people or subunits within large organizations.

Just like their smaller counterparts, large organizations depend on the entrepreneurial spirit. High performance is increasingly based upon the contributions of workers who are willing to assume risk and encourage the creativity and innovation so important to continued success in dynamic and competitive environments. Yet this task is especially challenging in very large and complex systems whose natural tendencies may be toward stability, rigidity, and avoidance of risk. The concept of **intrapreneurship**—described as entrepreneurial behavior on the part of people and subunits operating within large organizations—brings deserved attention to this situation.[39] Through the efforts of *intrapreneurs* large organizations are able to turn new ideas into profitable new products, services, and business ventures. At Trilogy Software, Inc., for example, in Austin, Texas, talented engineers are hired directly from college. They attend Trilogy University for three months, learning about the company, and its mission, executives, and expectations. They are told that within two years they should be responsible for creating at least 20 percent of the company's new revenues. The "university" is designed to start the creative process and build the networks for venturing. So far Trilogy has created from within itself six successful new ventures.[40]

○ **Skunkworks** are teams allowed to work creatively together, free of constraints from the larger organization.

To enhance their competitive edge through intrapreneurship, however, managers often find that success depends on the ability of large organizations to act like small ones. To do this, some large organizations create small subunits, often called **skunkworks**, in which teams are allowed to work together in a unique setting that is highly creative and free of operating restrictions in the larger parent organization. A classic example

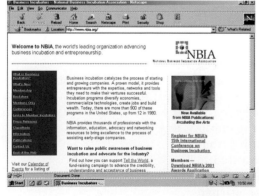

A large number of North America's 800 or so incubators belong to the National Business Incubation Association (NBIA). The nonprofit organization, located on the campus of Ohio University, is devoted to advancing business incubation and entrepreneurship. As the network hub of business incubation professionals, it provides information, education, advocacy, and networking resources to those who manage and operate business incubators offering assistance to early-stage companies. The NBIA conducts research and compiles statistics on business incubation, as well as producing informative publications, and tracking relevant legislation. For those interested in international business, it offers links to *business incubation sites around the world.*

occurred at Apple Computer, Inc., where a small group of enthusiastic employees was once sent off to a separate facility in Cupertino, California. Their mandate was straightforward: to create a state-of-the-art, user-friendly personal computer. The group operated free of the firm's normal product development bureaucracy, set its own norms, and worked together without outside interference. The "Jolly Roger" was even raised over their building as a symbol of independence. It worked. This is the team that brought the now-famous Macintosh computer into being.

BUSINESS INCUBATION

One of the advantages of intrapreneurship is that it takes place in a larger organizational environment that can be highly supportive in terms of money and other startup resources. Individual entrepreneurs who must start on their own face quite a different set of challenges. Even though entrepreneurship and new venture creation are creative and exciting prospects, they are also potentially daunting in complexity and required resources. One way that the motivation toward entrepreneurship can be maintained without suffering the discouragement of startup requirements is through the support of a **business incubator**. This is a special facility that offers space, a variety of shared administrative services, and management advice to help small businesses get started. Some ideas are focused on specific areas such as technology, manufacturing, or services; some are in more rural areas, others are city based. But regardless of focus and location, incubators share the common goal of helping to build successful new businesses that create jobs and improve economic development. They pursue this goal by nurturing startup businesses in the incubators to improve the chances for them to grow more quickly and become healthy enough to survive on their own. And, of course, with survival the economic benefits of job creation and new members joining the local business community are expected.

○ **Business incubators** offer space, shared services, and advice to help small businesses get started.

SMALL BUSINESS DEVELOPMENT CENTERS

With small business playing an important role in the economy, a variety of resources are available to promote the development of small- and medium-scale enterprises. At the level of the federal government, the United States Small Business Administration works with state and local agencies to support a network of over 1,000 **Small Business Development Centers** nationwide. These SBDCs offer guidance to entrepreneurs and small business owners—actual and prospective—in how to set up and successfully run a business operation. Often these centers are associated with universities or colleges and offer opportunities for students to learn first-hand the nature of small business and entrepreneurship.

○ **Small Business Development Centers** offer guidance and support to small business owners in how to set up and run a business operation.

As we said at the beginning, this is a chapter of *examples*. Other than by doing it, the best way to learn about entrepreneurship and venturing is to study and ponder the experiences of others. Here's a final example for you. When they joined the Silicon Valley Small Business Development Center, Jean Jaffess and her partners in Mambo Design & Consulting were able to find assistance in writing a business plan, understanding financial reports, and tax requirements. The decision to join in the incubator helped Mambo get started. Since then the firm has grown in sophistication and independence. It now offers a wide variety of Web design and consulting services. . . .[41] This is a success story. What better way to end a chapter on entrepreneurship and new ventures?

STUDY Guide

The Chapter 9 Study Guide will help you review chapter content, prepare for examinations, and further build your career readiness. The *Summary* briefly highlights answers to questions first posed in the chapter opening Planning Ahead section. The list of *Key Terms* allows you to double check your familiarity with basic concepts and definitions. *Self-Test 9* gives you the opportunity to test your basic comprehension of chapter content using sample test questions. Suggestions offered as *Career Readiness Activities* direct your attention to relevant sections of the end-of-text Career Readiness Workbook, as well as to special Electronic Resources on the *Management 7/e* web site.

SUMMARY

What is entrepreneurship?

- Entrepreneurship is risk-taking behavior that results in the creation of new opportunities for individuals and/or organizations.
- An entrepreneur is someone who takes strategic risks to pursue opportunities in situations others may view as problems or threats.
- There are many examples of entrepreneurs worldwide like Mary Kay Ash, Richard Branson, Earl Graves, and Anita Roddick whose experiences can be a source of learning and inspiration for others.
- Entrepreneurs tend to be creative people who are very self-confident, determined, resilient, adaptable, and driven to excel; they like to be masters of their own destinies.
- Entrepreneurship is rich with diversity, with women and minority-owned business startups increasing in numbers.

What is special about small businesses?

- Entrepreneurship results in the founding of many small business enterprises that offer job creation and other benefits to economies.
- The Internet has opened a whole new array of entrepreneurial possibilities, including on-line buying and selling and the more formal pursuit of new "dot-com" businesses.
- Smaller businesses are pursuing more global opportunities in the quest for expanded markets, access to labor and technical expertise, and locations for low-cost manufacturing or outsourcing.

- Family businesses that are owned and financially controlled by family members represent the largest percentage of businesses operating worldwide.
- A significant problem faced by family businesses is the succession problem of transferring leadership from one generation to the next.
- Small businesses have a high failure rate; as many as 60 to 80 percent of new businesses fail in their first five years of operation.
- Small business failures are largely due to poor management, when owners make bad decisions on matters of major business consequence.

How does one start a new venture?

- Entrepreneurial firms tend to follow the life-cycle stages of acceptance, breakthrough, and maturity, with each stage offering different management challenges to the entrepreneur.
- New startups should be guided by a good business plan that describes the intended nature of the business, how it will operate, and how financing will be obtained to operate it.
- An important issue is choice of the form of business ownership, with the proprietorship and corporate forms offering different advantages and disadvantages.
- Two basic ways of financing a new venture are through debt financing, by taking loans, and equity financing, which involves exchanging ownership shares in return for outside investment.
- Venture capitalists are companies that pool capital and make investments in new ventures in return for an equity stake in the business.
- The angel investor is a wealthy individual who is willing to invest a portion of his wealth in return for equity in a new venture.

What resources support entrepreneurship and business development?

- Intrapreneurship, or entrepreneurial behavior within larger organizations, is important in today's competitive environments.
- Business incubators offer space, shared services, and advice to small businesses in the startup stages.
- In the United States, small businesses can get a variety of forms of support and assistance from Small Business Development Centers funded by government sources.

KEY TERMS

Angel investor (p. 245)

Business incubator (p. 247)

Business plan (p. 242)

Corporation (p. 244)

Debt financing (p. 244)

Entrepreneur (p. 232)

Entrepreneurship (p. 232)

Equity financing (p. 244)

Family business (p. 239)

First-mover advantage (p. 241)

Franchise (p. 237)

IPO (p. 245)

Intrapreneurship (p. 246)

Partnership (p. 244)

Skunkworks (p. 246)

Small business (p. 237)

Small Business Development Center (p. 247)

Sole proprietorship (p. 244)

Succession plan (p. 240)

Succession problem (p. 240)

Venture capitalists (p. 245)

SELF-TEST 9

Take this test here or on-line much as you would in a normal classroom situation. It should offer you a good way to check your basic comprehension of chapter material. Answers may be found at the end of the book.

MULTIPLE-CHOICE QUESTIONS:

1. _____ is among the characteristics commonly associated with entrepreneurs.
   (a) Low tolerance for ambiguity (b) External locus of control
   (c) Low need for achievement (d) Self-confidence

2. When an entrepreneur is comfortable with uncertainty and willing to take risks, these are indicators of someone with _____.
   (a) high tolerance for ambiguity (b) internal locus of control
   (c) self-confidence (d) action orientation

3. Almost _____ percent of American businesses meet the definition of "small business" used by the Small Business Administration.
   (a) 40 (b) 99 (c) 75 (d) 81

4. When a business owner sells to another person the right to operate that business in another location, this is a _____.
   (a) conglomerate (b) franchise (c) joint venture (d) limited partnership

5. When a small business owner is concerned about passing the business on to heirs after retirement or death, he or she should prepare a formal _____ plan.
   (a) retirement (b) succession (c) franchising (d) liquidation

6. New small business startups often fail because of _____.
   (a) lack of business expertise (b) strict financial controls (c) slow growth
   (d) high ethical standards

7. When a new business is quick to exploit a market niche before competitors, this is called _____.
   (a) entrepreneurial behavior (b) tolerance for ambiguity
   (c) succession planning (d) first-mover advantage

8. In the first stage in the life cycle of an entrepreneurial new firm, the business owner is typically struggling to _____.
   (a) gain acceptance in the marketplace (b) find alliance partners for expansion (c) experience significant growth (d) bring professional management skills into the leadership team

9. When an outside investor receives an ownership share in a new business in return for her investment, she is providing _____ financing.
   (a) debt (b) equity (c) sole proprietorship (d) first-mover

10. A _____ is a term used to describe a small group of people operating with independence and in the expectation of being highly creative within a large organization.
    (a) skunkworks (b) product team (c) focus group (d) leadership council

TRUE-FALSE QUESTIONS:

11. Childhood experiences and family environment often make a difference in one's tendencies toward entrepreneurial behavior.   T   F

12. Data indicate that woman- and minority-owned businesses are declining in importance in the American economy.   T   F

13. Family-owned businesses provide over 75 percent of new jobs created in the United States.   T   F

14. A good business plan begins with an executive summary.   T   F

15. Cash flow projections are part of a good business plan.   T   F

16. Among the forms of business ownership, a sole proprietorship is a legal entity existing separately from its owners.   T   F

17. Venture capitalists typically prefer to provide debt financing to new-venture startups.   T   F

18. An angel investor is someone who buys 100 percent of an IPO.   T   F

19. The difference between entrepreneurship and intrapreneurship is that the latter takes place within the context of a large corporation.   T   F

20. In a business incubator, one would expect to find businesses that are "sick" and are being nurtured back to "health."   T   F

SHORT-RESPONSE QUESTIONS:

21. What is the relationship between diversity and entrepreneurship?

22. In what ways can the Internet be a driving force for entrepreneurship?

23. What are the advantages of choosing a limited partnership form of small business ownership?

24. How can a large corporation stimulate entrepreneurship within itself?

APPLICATION QUESTION:

25. Assume for the moment that you have a great idea for a potential Internet-based startup business. In discussing the idea with a friend, she advises you to be very careful in tying your business idea to potential customers and then describing it well in a business plan. "After all," she says, "you won't succeed without customers and you'll never get a chance to succeed if you can't attract financial backers through a good business plan." With these words to the wise, you proceed. What questions will you ask and answer to ensure that you are customer-focused in this business? What are the major areas that you would address in writing your initial business plan?

CAREER readiness ACTIVITIES

Recommended learning activities from the end-of-text *Career Readiness Workbook* for Chapter 9 include:

Career Advancement Portfolio
- Individual writing and group presentation assignments based on any of the following activities.

Case for Critical Thinking
- Domino's Pizza—Could You Do It?

Integrative Learning Activities
- Integrative Case—Outback Steakhouse. Inc.
- Integrative Case—Richard Branson Meets the New Economy

Exercises in Teamwork
- Strategic Scenarios (#11)
- Work vs. Family (#16)
- Why Do We Work? (#21)
- Creative Solutions (#29)

Self-Assessments
- Decision-Making Biases (#3)
- Entrepreneurship Orientation (#10)
- Internal/External Control (#11)
- Turbulence Tolerance Test (#23)

The *Fast Company* Collection On-Line
- Tom Peters, "The Brand Called 'You'"

ELECTRONIC RESOURCES

@ GET CONNECTED! Don't forget to take full advantage of the on-line support for *Management 7/e.*
- Chapter 9 On-line Study Guide
- Chapter 9 Self-test Answers
- Chapter 9 E-Resource Center

www.wiley.com/college/schermerhorn

10

Organizing

Planning ahead

GETTING CONNECTED

Edward Jones—*Structures Must Support Strategies*

Management scholar and consultant Peter Drucker once called brokerage firm Edward Jones "the Wal-Mart of Wall Street." He describes the firm as having a clear strategy and an innovative structure that directly supports it.

Like Wal-Mart, Edward Jones established itself in rural America. The structure is unique, with a strong core surrounded by largely independent satellite units. Drucker likens it to a "confederation of highly autonomous entrepreneurial units bound together by a highly centralized core of values and services."

The St. Louis-based firm has been called the "last 'not-com' brokerage." Managing partner John Bachman believes the firm succeeds by being different and he is not interested in becoming an online broker. If you visit the firm's modest web site, you can't trade on-line. But you can easily locate one of Edward Jones's 6000+ nearby branches.

A values-driven commitment to the customer is a common bond among the entrepreneurial Edward Jones brokers, as is a focus on long-term investing and a safety-first orientation. The business strategy is face-to-face and customer-oriented brokerage. Given that, the brokers have the freedom to deal with customers in their own way and in their local setting. Bachman says: "I'm comfortable with our strategy. There's a difference between being part of a market and being the total market. We're the leader in what we do."

Edward Jones has ranked as high as #7 on *Fortune* magazine's list of the best companies to work for in America; it has also been ranked highly on *Working Mother* magazine's list of the best firms for working mothers. Fast growing, the firm has expanded into Canada and the United Kingdom. The firm established itself in rural America and still keeps to its roots. Even with expansion into large cities, a third of its employees still work in single-broker offices in small towns.

Of course, it's a competitive business. Brokerage giant Merrill Lynch has a push of its own—to open small brokerage offices in small rural towns.[1]

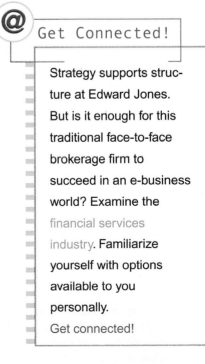

@ Get Connected!

Strategy supports structure at Edward Jones. But is it enough for this traditional face-to-face brokerage firm to succeed in an e-business world? Examine the financial services industry. Familiarize yourself with options available to you personally. Get connected!

Management scholar and consultant Henry Mintzberg is well-known for his work in the area of strategy and structure. Writing with a colleague in the *Harvard Business Review*, he points out both that organizations are changing very fast in today's world and that people within them are struggling to find their place.[2] The point is, people need to understand how their organizations work if they are to work well within them. Mintzberg notes some common questions: "What parts connect to one another?" "How should processes and people come together?" "Whose ideas have to flow where?" These and related questions raise critical issues about organization structures and how well they meet an organization's performance needs.

The organizing approach of Edward Jones—management through a strong central core surrounded by small and autonomous units—is one entrepreneurial benchmark. By building a well-focused yet market-responsive structure, the firm has established and sustained a niche in the highly competitive financial services industry. But this is only one of the many possible ways to structure for success. There are many options as organizations in all industries try new forms in the quest for sustained competitive advantage. Some are using designs that we will discuss as team, network, or even "boundaryless" and "virtual" organizations. Others involve restructuring in the form of management initiatives that involve downsizing, rightsizing, and delayering organizations in the search for productivity gains.

Among the vanguard organizations, those that consistently deliver above-average returns and outperform their competitors, one does find consistent themes. Regardless of the specific approaches taken, they all emphasize empowerment, support for employees, responsiveness to client or customer needs, flexibility in dealing with a dynamic environment, and continual attention to quality improvements. They also strive for positive cultures and high-quality-of-work-life experiences for members and employees. Importantly, nothing is constant; at least not for long. Change is always a possibility. Managers in progressive organizations are always seeking new ways to better organize the workplace to support strategies and achieve high-performance goals.

ORGANIZING AS A MANAGEMENT FUNCTION

○ **Organizing** arranges people and resources to work toward a goal.

Formally defined, **organizing** is the process of arranging people and other resources to work together to accomplish a goal. As one of the basic functions of management it involves both creating a division of labor for tasks to be performed and then coordinating results to achieve a common purpose. *Figure 10.1* shows the central role organizing plays in the management process. Once plans are created, the manager's task is to see to it that they are carried out. Given a clear mission, core values, objectives, and strategy, organizing begins the process of implementation by clarifying jobs and working relationships. It identifies who is to do what, who is in charge of whom, and how different people and parts of the organization relate to and work with one another. All of this, of course, can be done in different ways. This is where an understanding of situational contingencies becomes important. The strategic leadership challenge is to choose the best organizational form to fit the strategy and other situational demands.

WHAT IS ORGANIZATION STRUCTURE?

○ **Organization structure** is a system of tasks, reporting relationships, and communication linkages.

The way in which the various parts of an organization are formally arranged is usually referred to as the **organization structure**. It is the system of tasks, workflows, reporting relationships, and communication

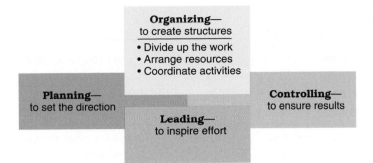

Figure 10.1 Organizing viewed in relationship with the other management functions.

channels that link together the work of diverse individuals and groups. Any structure should both allocate task assignments through a division of labor and provide for the coordination of performance results. A good structure that does both of these things well can be an important asset to an organization.[3] Unfortunately, it is easier to talk about good structures than it is to actually create them. This is why you often read and hear about organizations *restructuring*, or changing their structures in an attempt to improve performance. There is no one best structure that meets the needs of all circumstances. Structure must be addressed in a contingency fashion; as environments and situations change, structures must often be changed too. To make good choices, a manager must know the alternatives and be familiar with current trends and developments.

FORMAL STRUCTURE

You may know the concept of structure best in the form of an **organization chart**. This is a diagram that shows reporting relationships and the formal arrangement of work positions within an organization.[4] A typical organization chart identifies various positions and job titles as well as the lines of authority and communication between them. This is the **formal structure**, or the structure of the organization in its official state. It represents the way the organization is intended to function. *Manager's Notepad 10.1* identifies some of the things that you can learn by reviewing an organization chart.

○ An **organization chart** describes the arrangement of work positions within an organization.

○ **Formal structure** is the official structure of the organization.

INFORMAL STRUCTURE

Behind every formal structure typically lies an **informal structure**. This is a "shadow" organization made up of the unofficial, but often critical, working relationships between organizational members. If the informal

○ **Informal structure** is the set of unofficial relationships among an organization's members.

MANAGER'S NOTEPAD 10.1

What you can learn from an organization chart

- *Division of work:* Positions and titles show work responsibilities.
- *Supervisory relationships:* Lines show who reports to whom.
- *Communication channels:* Lines show formal communication flows.
- *Major subunits:* Positions reporting to a common manager are shown.
- *Levels of management:* Vertical layers of management are shown.

BEST PRACTICES www.siemens.com
Siemens, U.S.A. You Can Design
for Informal Learning

When the Center for Workforce Development conducted a study at a Siemens factory in North Carolina, the focus was on informal learning. What they found was that the cafeteria was a "hotbed" of learning as workers shared ideas, problems, and solutions with one another over snacks and meals. The Director of Training for Siemens said: "The assumption was made that this was chitchat, talking about the golf game. But there was a whole lot of work activity." For Seimens and other organizations the lesson is to mobilize informal learning opportunities as a resource for continuous organizational improvement.[5]

REALITY ✓
Check 10.1

Structural Changes for Global Businesses
An *IndustryWeek* survey of 175 CEOs and corporate officers focused on structural changes needed to survive in the tough global economy. They ranked #1 as restructuring to focus on core business areas. Take the on-line "Reality Check" to learn more about what executives say about changing organizational structures.

structure could be drawn, it would show who talks to and interacts regularly with whom regardless of their formal titles and relationships. The lines of the informal structure would cut across levels and move from side to side. They would show people meeting for coffee, in exercise groups, and in friendship cliques, among other possibilities. Importantly, no organization can be fully understood without gaining insight into the informal structure as well as the formal one.[6]

Informal structures can be very helpful in getting needed work accomplished in any organization. Indeed, they may be considered essential in many ways to organizational success. This is especially true during times of change when out-of-date formal structures may simply not provide the support people need to deal with new or unusual situations. Because it takes time to change or modify formal structures, this is a common occurrence. Through the emergent and spontaneous relationships of informal structures, people benefit by gaining access to interpersonal networks of emotional support and friendship that satisfy important social needs. They also benefit in task performance by being in personal contact with others who can help them get things done when necessary. In fact, what is known as *informal learning* is increasingly recognized as an important resource for organizational development. This is learning that takes place as people interact informally throughout the work day and in a wide variety of unstructured situations.

Of course, informal structures also have potential disadvantages. Because they exist outside the formal authority system, the activities of informal structures can sometimes work against the best interests of the organization as a whole. They can also be susceptible to rumor, carry inaccurate information, breed resistance to change, and even divert work efforts from important objectives. Also, "outsiders" or people who are left out of informal groupings may feel less a part of daily activities and suffer a loss of satisfaction. Some American managers of Japanese firms, for example, at times complain about being excluded from the "shadow cabinet." This is an informal group of Japanese executives who hold the real power to get things done in the firm and sometimes do so without the participation of others.[7]

TRADITIONAL ORGANIZATION STRUCTURES

A traditional principle of organizing is that performance gains are possible when people are allowed to specialize and become expert in specific jobs or tasks. Given this division of labor, however, decisions must then be made on how to group work positions into formal teams or departments and then link them together in a coordinated fashion within the larger organization. These decisions involve a process called **departmentalization** and it has traditionally resulted in three major types of organizational structures—the functional, divisional, and matrix structures.[8]

○ **Departmentalization** is the process of grouping together people and jobs into work units.

FUNCTIONAL STRUCTURES

In **functional structures**, people with similar skills and performing similar tasks are formally grouped together into work units. Members of functional departments share technical expertise, interests, and responsibilities. The first example in *Figure 10.2* shows a common functional structure in a business firm. In this case senior management is arranged by the functions of marketing, finance, production, and human resources. In this functional structure, manufacturing problems are the responsibility of the production vice president, marketing problems are the province of the marketing vice president, and so on. The key point is that members of each function work within their areas of expertise. If each function does its jobs properly, the expectation is that the business will operate successfully.

○ A **functional structure** groups together people with similar skills who perform similar tasks.

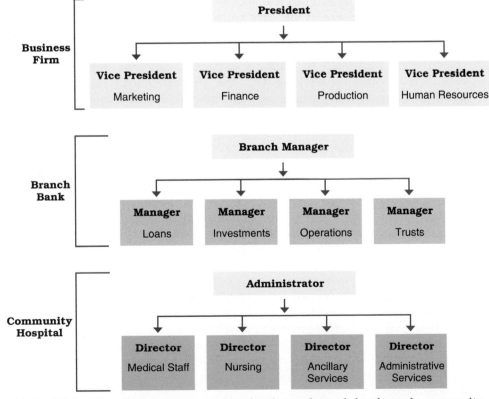

Figure 10.2 Functional structures in a business, branch bank, and community hospital.

Functional structures are not limited to businesses. The figure also shows how this form of departmentalization can be used in other types of organizations such as banks and hospitals. These types of structures typically work well for small organizations that produce only one or a few products or services. They also tend to work best in relatively stable environments where problems are predictable and the demands for change and innovation are limited. The major *advantages of a functional structure* include the following:

○ **Advantages of functional structures**

- Economies of scale with efficient use of resources.
- Task assignments consistent with expertise and training.
- High-quality technical problem solving.
- In-depth training and skill development within functions.
- Clear career paths within functions.

There are also potential *disadvantages of functional structures.* Common problems with functional structures involve difficulties in pinpointing responsibilities for things like cost containment, product or service quality, timeliness, and innovation in response to environmental changes. Such problems with functional structures become magnified as organizations grow in size and environments begin to change.

○ The **functional chimneys problem** is a lack of communication and coordination across functions.

Another significant concern is often called the **functional chimneys problem**. This refers to the lack of communication, coordination, and problem solving across functions. Because the functions become formalized not only on an organization chart but also in the mindsets of people, the sense of cooperation and common purpose breaks down. When functional units develop self-centered and narrow viewpoints they lose the total system perspective. When problems occur with another unit, they are too often referred up to higher levels for resolution rather than being addressed by people at the same level. This slows decision making and problem solving and can result in a loss of advantage in competitive situations. For example, when Ford took over as the new owner of Jaguar, it had to resolve many quality problems. The quality turnaround took longer than anticipated, in part because of what Jaguar's chairman called "excessive compartmentalization." In building cars, the different departments did very little talking and working with one another. Ford's response was to push for more interdepartmental coordination, consensus decision making, and cost controls, an approach that is now paying off.[9]

DIVISIONAL STRUCTURES

○ A **divisional structure** groups together people working on the same product, in the same area, with similar customers, or on the same processes.

A second organizational alternative is the **divisional structure**. It groups together people who work on the same product or process, serve similar customers, and/or are located in the same area or geographical region. As illustrated in *Figure 10.3*, divisional structures are common in complex organizations that have multiple and differentiated products and services, serve diverse customers, pursue diversified strategies, and/or operate in various and different competitive environments. The three major types of divisional approaches are the product, geographical, and process structures.

Divisional structures attempt to avoid problems common to functional structures. They are especially popular among organizations with diverse operations that extend across many products, territories, customers, and work processes.[10] The potential *advantages of divisional structures* include the following:

○ **Advantages of divisional structures**

- More flexibility in responding to environmental changes.
- Improved coordination across functional departments.

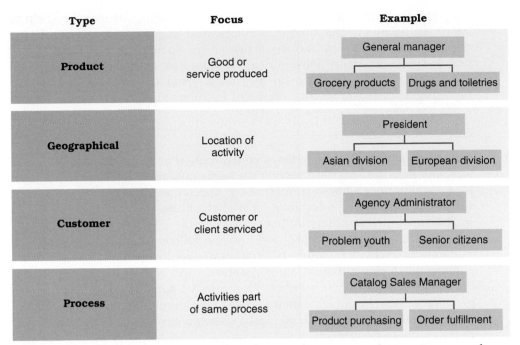

Type	Focus	Example
Product	Good or service produced	General manager — Grocery products / Drugs and toiletries
Geographical	Location of activity	President — Asian division / European division
Customer	Customer or client serviced	Agency Administrator — Problem youth / Senior citizens
Process	Activities part of same process	Catalog Sales Manager — Product purchasing / Order fulfillment

Figure 10.3 Divisional structures based on product, geography, customer, and process.

- Clear points of responsibility for product or service delivery.
- Expertise focused on specific customers, products, and regions.
- Greater ease in changing size by adding or deleting divisions.

As with other alternatives, there are potential *disadvantages of divisional structures*. They can reduce economies of scale and increase costs through the duplication of resources and efforts across divisions. They can also create unhealthy rivalries as divisions compete for resources and attention, and as they emphasize division needs and goals to the detriment of the goals of the organization as a whole.

Product Structures

Product structures, sometimes called *market structures*, group together jobs and activities working on a single product or service. They clearly identify costs, profits, problems, and successes in a market area with a central point of accountability. Consequently, managers are encouraged to be responsive to changing market demands and customer tastes. Common in large organizations, product structures may even extend into global operations. When taking over as H. J. Heinz's new CEO, William R. Johnson became concerned about the company's international performance. He decided a change in structure could help improve performance. The existing structure that emphasized countries and regions was changed to global product divisions. The choice was based on his belief that a product structure would bring the best brand management to all countries and increase cooperation around the world within product businesses.

○ A **product structure** groups together people and jobs working on a single product or service.

Geographical Structures

Geographical structures, sometimes called *area structures*, group together jobs and activities being performed in the same location or geographical region. They are typically used when there is a need to differentiate products or services in various locations, such as in different regions of a country.

○ A **geographical structure** groups together people and jobs performed in the same location.

They are also quite common in international operations, where they help to focus attention on the unique cultures and requirements of particular regions. For example at 3M, the firm's global operations are grouped into four areas: Latin America and Africa, Canada, Asia Pacific, and Europe and Middle East. Each geographical division is headed by a senior executive reporting to an Executive Vice President for International Operations.

Customer Structures

○ A **customer structure** groups together people and jobs that serve the same customers or clients.

Customer structures, sometimes called *market structures*, group together jobs and activities that are serving the same customers or clients. The major appeal is the ability to best serve the special needs of the different customer groups. This is a common form of structure for complex businesses in the consumer products industries—such as 3M. The firm is organized to focus attention around the world on the following markets—consumer and office, speciality materials, industrial, health care, electronics and communications, transportation, graphics, and safety. Customer structures are also useful in services, for example, where banks use them to give separate attention to consumer and commercial customers for loans. The example used in Figure 10.3 also shows a government agency serving different client populations.

Process Structures

○ A **process structure** groups jobs and activities that are part of the same processes.

A *work process* is a group of tasks related to one another that collectively create something of value to a customer.[11] An example is order fulfillment, as when you telephone a catalog retailer and request a particular item. The process of order fulfillment takes the order from point of initiation by the customer to point of fulfillment by a delivered order. A **process structure** groups together jobs and activities that are part of the same processes. In the example of Figure 10.3, this might take the form of product-purchasing teams, order-fulfillment teams, and systems-support teams for the mail-order catalog business. The importance of understanding work processes and designing process-driven organizations has been popularized by management consultant and author Michael Hammer.[12] The essentials of Hammer's ideas on work process design are discussed in the next chapter.

MATRIX STRUCTURES

○ A **matrix structure** combines functional and divisional approaches to emphasize project or program teams.

The **matrix structure**, often called the *matrix organization*, combines the functional and divisional structures just described. In effect, it is an attempt to gain the advantages and minimize the disadvantages of each. This is accomplished in the matrix by using permanent cross-functional teams to integrate functional expertise in support of a clear divisional focus on a product, project, or program.[13] As shown in *Figure 10.4*, workers in a matrix structure belong to at least two formal groups at the same time—a functional group and a product, program, or project team. They also report to two bosses—one within the function and the other within the team.

The matrix organization has gained a strong foothold in the workplace, with applications in such diverse settings as manufacturing (e.g., aerospace, electronics, pharmaceuticals), service industries (e.g., banking, brokerage, retailing), professional fields (e.g., accounting, advertising, law), and the nonprofit sector (e.g., city, state, and federal agencies, hospitals, universities). Matrix structures are also found in multinational

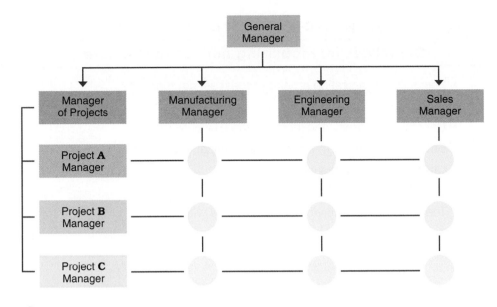

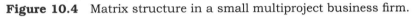

Functional personnel assigned to both projects and functional departments

Figure 10.4 Matrix structure in a small multiproject business firm.

corporations, where they offer the flexibility to deal with regional differences as well as multiple product, program, or project needs. Matrix structures are common in organizations pursuing growth strategies in dynamic and complex environments.

The main contribution of matrix structures to organizational performance lies in the use of permanent cross-functional teams. Team members work closely together to share expertise and information in a timely manner to solve problems. The potential *advantages of matrix structures* include the following:

- Better interfunctional cooperation in operations and problem solving.
- Increased flexibility in adding, removing, and/or changing operations to meet changing demands.
- Better customer service, since there is always a program, product, or project manager informed and available to answer questions.
- Better performance accountability through the program, product, or project managers.
- Improved decision making as problem solving takes place at the team level, where the best information is available.
- Improved strategic management, since top managers are freed from unnecessary problem solving to focus time on strategic issues.

← Advantages of a matrix structure

Predictably, there are also potential *disadvantages of matrix structures.* The two-boss system is susceptible to power struggles, as functional supervisors and team leaders vie with one another to exercise authority. The two-boss system can also be frustrating for matrix members if it creates task confusion and conflicts in work priorities. Team meetings in the matrix are also time consuming. Teams may develop "groupitis," or strong team loyalties that cause a loss of focus on larger organizational goals. And the requirements of adding the team leaders to a matrix structure can result in increased costs.[14]

MANAGER'S NOTEPAD 10.2

Guidelines for mobilizing horizontal structures

- Focus the organization around processes, not functions.
- Put people in charge of core processes.
- Decrease hierarchy and increase the use of teams.
- Empower people to make decisions critical to performance.
- Utilize information technology.
- Emphasize multiskilling and multiple competencies.
- Teach people how to work in partnership with others.
- Build a culture of openness, collaboration, performance commitment.

DEVELOPMENTS IN ORGANIZATION STRUCTURES

The realities of a global economy and the demands of strategies driven by hypercompetition are putting increasing pressures on organization structures. The performance demands are for more speed to market, greater customer orientation, constant productivity improvements, better technology utilization, and more. The environment is unrelenting in such demands. As a result, managers are continually searching for new ways to better structure their organizations to meet the demands of situations rife with complexity and constant pressure.

Structural innovation is always important in the search for productivity improvement and competitive advantage. The right structure becomes a performance asset; the wrong one becomes a liability—one that inhibits rather than facilitates people as they try to work with technologies and processes, and work well together.[15] Today, the vertical and control-oriented structures of the past are proving less and less sufficient to master the tasks at hand. The matrix structure is a first step toward improving flexibility and problem solving through better cross-functional integration. It is now part of a broader movement toward more horizontal structures that decrease hierarchy, increase empowerment, and more fully mobilize the talents of people to drive organizational performance. When combined with the ever-increasing power of information technologies, the new horizontal structures become much more responsive to environmental demands and much better aligned with organizational strategies. *Manager's Notepad 10.2* offers guidelines for mobilizing the opportunities of horizontal structures.[16]

TEAM STRUCTURES

Teams and teamwork are in as organizations are being restructured for greater internal integration. As the traditional vertical structures give way to more horizontal ones, teams are serving as the basic building blocks.[17] Organizations using **team structures** mobilize both permanent and temporary teams extensively to solve problems, complete special projects, and accomplish day-to-day tasks.[18]

○ A **team structure** uses permanent and temporary cross-functional teams to improve lateral relations.

As illustrated in *Figure 10.5*, a team structure involves teams of various types working together as needed to solve problems and explore opportunities, either on a full-time or part-time basis. These are often **cross-functional teams** composed of members from different areas of work responsibility.[19] The intention is to break down the functional chimneys or barriers inside the organization and create more effective lateral relations for ongoing problem solving and work performance. They are also often **project teams** that are convened for a particular task or "project" and that disband once it is completed. The intention here is to quickly convene people with the needed talents and focus their efforts intensely to solve a problem or take advantage of a special opportunity.

○ A **cross-functional team** brings together members from different functional departments.

○ **Project teams** are convened for a particular task or project and disband once it is completed.

There are many potential *advantages of team structures*. They are frequently tried when an organization experiences difficulties with communication and decision making due to the functional chimneys problem described earlier. At the same time that team assignments help to break down barriers between operating departments, they can also boost morale as people from different parts of an organization get to know more about one another. Because the teams focus shared knowledge and expertise on specific problems, they can also improve the speed and quality of decisions in many situations. People working in teams can experience a greater sense of involvement and identification, increasing their enthusiasm for the job.

All organizational structures should harness the full talents of the workforce. However, in team structures this goal is pursued relentlessly and with full recognition of the value of group as well as individual contributions. Within teams and under the guidance of formal and informal leaders, individuals are expected to work together through cooperation, shared commitments to a common purpose, and consensus.[20] After a research team at Polaroid Corporation developed a new medical imaging system in three years, when most had predicted it would take six, a senior executive said, "Our researchers are not any smarter, but by working together they get the value of each other's intelligence almost instantaneously."[21]

The complexities of teams and teamwork are discussed in Chapter 17. They contribute to the potential *disadvantages of team structures*. These include conflicting loyalties among members to both team and functional assignments. They also include issues of time management and group process. By their very nature, teams spend a lot of time in meetings. Not all of this time is productive. How well team members spend their time together often depends on the quality of interpersonal relations, group

www.kpmgcampus.com

The accounting and consulting giant KPMG abandoned a functional organization for an integrated team approach. Within industry-focused lines of business, regional areas have their own teams that draw upon both local and national information technology resources to serve customer needs.

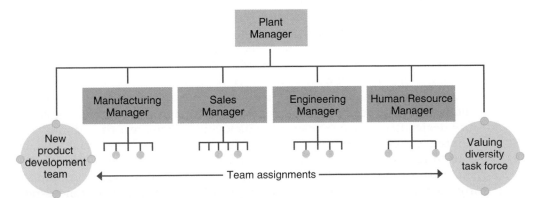

Figure 10.5 How a team structure uses cross-functional teams for improved lateral relations.

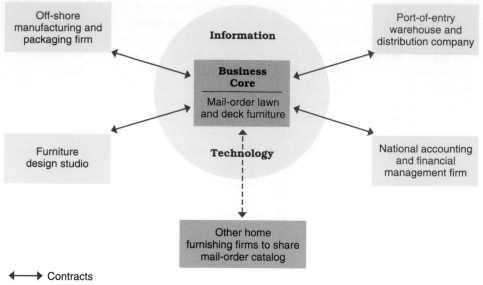

Figure 10.6 A network structure for a catalog-based retail business.

dynamics, and team management. All of these concerns, as described in Chapter 17, are manageable. There is no doubt about it. Teams and teamwork are hard work. But with good leadership and a committed membership, they are also invaluable organizational resources.

NETWORK STRUCTURES

○ A **network structure** uses IT to link with networks of outside suppliers and service contractors.

Organizations using variations of the **network structure** operate with a central core that is linked through "networks" of relationships with outside contractors and suppliers of essential services. With the great advantages offered by communications and information technology today, new emphasis is being given to strategically employing them to simplify and streamline organizational structures. Network structures accomplish this by engaging in a shifting variety of strategic alliances and business contracts that sustain operations. The old model was for organizations to own everything. The new model is to network and operate without the costs of owning all supporting functions or directly employing persons with all needed expertise. Network organizations own only the most essential or "core" components. They are able to do this by employing information technology now available to support aggressive outsourcing strategies.[22]

Figure 10.6 illustrates a network structure as it might work for a mail-order company selling lawn and deck furniture through a catalog. The firm itself is very small, consisting of a relatively few full-time employees working from a central headquarters. Beyond that, it is structured as a series of business relationships, maintained operationally using the latest in information technology. Merchandise is designed on contract with a furniture design firm—which responds quickly as designs are shared and customized via computer networking; it is manufactured and packaged by subcontractors located around the world—wherever materials, quality, and cost are found at best advantage; stock is maintained and shipped from a contract warehouse—ensuring quality storage and on-time expert shipping; and all of the accounting and financial details are managed on contract with an outside firm—providing better technical expertise than the firm could afford to employ on a full-time basis; and the quarterly catalog is designed, printed, and mailed cooperatively as a strategic alliance with two other firms that sell different home furnishings with a related price appeal. All of this, of course, is supported by a company web site maintained also by an outside contractor.

The creative use of information technology adds to the potential *advantages of network structures*. With the technological edge the mail-order company in the prior example can operate with fewer full-time employees and less complex internal systems. Network structures are very lean and streamlined. They help organizations stay cost competitive through reduced overhead and increased operating efficiency. Network concepts allow organizations to internally employ outsourcing strategies and contract out specialized business functions rather than maintain full-time staff to do them. A bank may contract with local firms to provide mailroom, cafeteria, and legal services; an airline might contract out customer service jobs at various airports. Information technology also allows the business relationships of networks to operate across great distances rather than face to face. Such arrangements are increasingly common in the international arena, where the Internet, e-mail, net meetings, and other computer networks bring the advantages of global operations into easy reach at minimum cost.

Within the operating core of a network structure, a variety of interesting jobs are created for those who must coordinate the entire system of relationships. In fact, the potential *disadvantages of network structures* largely lie with the demands of this responsibility. The more complex the business or mission of the organization, the more complicated the network of contracts and relationships that must be maintained. It may be difficult to control and coordinate among them. If one part of the network breaks down or fails to deliver, the entire system suffers the consequences. Also, there is the potential for loss of control over activities contracted out, and for a lack of loyalty to develop among contractors who are used infrequently rather than on a long-term basis.

As information technology continues to develop and as the concept of network structures becomes better understood, there is no doubt that they will grow in number and range of applications in the future. They are great for smaller businesses and organizations, including entrepreneurial ones. They are also valuable for larger organizations like Cisco Systems, where the network approach offers great advantages of efficiency of operations, speed to market, and customer orientation.

CAREER CONNECTION

Social Responsibility

ACEnet

Harnessing the Power of Networks for Economic Development

June Holley, president of the Appalachian Center for Economic Networks (ACEnet), uses network organization concepts to support economic development in rural America. The Athens, Ohio, center serves as a *networking hub for small businesses*, microenterprises that come together to share expertise and connections in order to develop new business initiatives.

ACEnet offers information and business incubator support, including the facilities of a large community kitchen. Over 100 area farmers and entrepreneurs have so far rented kitchen space to test new products. As they cook, they rub elbows with one another. When Chris Chmiel started experimenting with a wild local fruit, pawpaws, he ended up talking with someone from the local Casa Nueva restaurant. Now the restaurant serves "pawpaw coladas."

Holley began ACEnet with the goal of tapping local ingenuity and resources for economic development. The pathway to progress was connection—bringing people into contact with one another. By finding one another and combining skills and products, Holley believed an engine for economic growth could be unlocked. ACEnet was to become the networking hub that fueled the engine.

Networking performs for ACEnet. Holley says that "poverty is due to isolation." By breaking the isolation ACEnet provides a valuable community service. "Put two people together in a room," Holley says, "and they'll figure out how to come out ahead together."

Why can't we have more organizations like this?

QUESTION: What's the status of economic development in your community or region? Are there any organizations like ACEnet addressing rural and/or urban development needs? Is there a role for you in harnessing the power of networks for social good?

For a company that considers its mission to help "shape the future of the Internet," Cisco Systems, Inc. certainly stays on course. The firm uses a network structure that harnesses the powers of information technology and the Internet to best business advantage. It is part of a vast array of strategic alliances with firms like KPMG Consulting, EDS, and others. Over 30 plants produce its products from locations around the world; it owns only two. Some 90 percent of its orders arrive electronically; 52 percent of its orders are filled without a Cisco employee involved in the transaction. CEO John Chambers says: "To my customers it looks like one big virtual plant where my suppliers and inventory systems are directly tied into an ecosystem." He considers this the way of the future where everything inside and outside a company is interconnected. "The people who get that," he says, "will have a huge competitive advantage."[23]

BOUNDARYLESS ORGANIZATIONS

○ A **boundaryless organization** eliminates internal boundaries among parts and external boundaries with the external environment.

It is increasingly popular today to speak about creating a **boundaryless organization** that eliminates internal boundaries linking component parts and external boundaries linking with the external environment.[24] The boundaryless organization can be viewed as a combination of the team and network structures just described, with the addition of "temporariness." In the internal context, teamwork and communication—spontaneous, as needed, and intense—replace formal lines of authority. There is an absence of boundaries that traditionally and structurally separate organizational members from one another. In the external context, organizational needs are met by a shifting mix of outsourcing contracts and operating alliances that form and disband with changing circumstances. A "photograph" that documents an organization's configuration of external relationships today will look different from one taken tomorrow, as the form naturally adjusts to new pressures and circumstances. *Figure 10.7* shows how the absence of internal and external barriers helps people work in ways that bring speed and flexibility to the boundaryless firm.

Key requirements of boundaryless organizations are the absence of hierarchy, empowerment of team members, technology utilization, and acceptance of impermanence. Work is accomplished by empowered people who come together voluntarily and temporarily to apply their expertise to a task, gather additional expertise from whatever sources may be required to perform it successfully, and stay together only as long as the task is a work in process. The focus in the boundaryless form is on talent for task. The assumption is that empowered people working together without bureaucratic restrictions can accomplish great things. Such a work setting is supposed to encourage creativity, quality, timeliness, and flexibility, while reducing inefficiencies and increasing speed. At General Electric, for example, the drive toward boundaryless operations is supported in part by aggressive "digitization." The firm is moving more and more administrative work onto the Web—where it can be done faster and among persons directly involved. Intermediaries in the form of support personnel are not needed. Welch

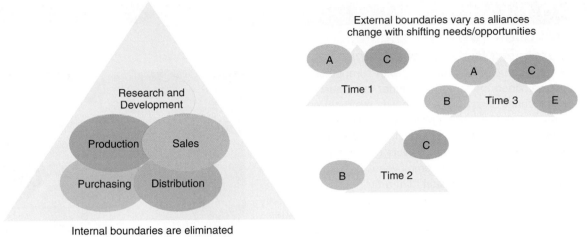

Figure 10.7 The boundaryless organization eliminates internal and external barriers.

expects that digitization can save GE $1.6 billion in just a year's time, with the elimination of 11,000 jobs made uneccesary in the new boundaryless environment.[25]

Knowledge sharing is an essential component of the boundaryless organization. One way to think of this is in the context of a very small organization, perhaps a startup. In the small firm, everyone pitches in to help out as needed and when appropriate to get things done. There are no formal assignments and there are no job titles or job descriptions standing in the way. People with talent work together as needed to get the job done. The boundaryless organization, in its pure form, is just like that. Even in the larger organizational context, meetings and spontaneous sharing are happening continuously perhaps involving thousands of people working together in hundreds of teams that form and disband as needed. Again, the great opportunities of information technology help make all of this possible. At consulting giant PricewaterhouseCoopers, for example, knowledge sharing brings together 160,000 partners spread across 150 countries in a vast virtual learning and problem-solving network. Partners collaborate electronically through on-line databases where information is stored, problems posted, and questions asked and answered in real time by those with experience and knowledge relevant to the problem at hand. Technology makes collaboration instantaneously and always possible, breaking down boundaries that might otherwise slow or impede the firm's performance.[26]

In the organization/environment interface, boundaryless operations emerge in a special form that is sometimes called the **virtual organization**.[27] This is an organization that operates in a shifting network of external alliances that are engaged as needed, and with the support of extensive technology utilization. The boundaries that traditionally separate a firm from its suppliers, customers, and even competitors are largely eliminated, temporarily and in respect to a given transaction or business purpose. Virtual organizations come into being "as needed" when alliances are called into action to meet specific operating needs and objectives. When mobilized, alliance members contribute for mutual benefit their special expertise and competencies. When the work is complete, the alliance rests until next called into action. Importantly, the virtual organization operates in this manner with the mix of mobilized alliances continuously shifting and with an expansive pool of potential alliances always ready to be called upon as needed.

@ **Get Connected!**

Do a Web search of virtual organizations. Use Lexis-Nexis if you can. How "virtual" are we getting?

○ A **virtual organization** is a shifting network of strategic alliances that are engaged as needed.

TAKE IT TO THE CASE!

Nucor Corporation (www.nucor.com)
Where Streamlining Is a Matter of Principle

Nucor Corp. is a "mini-mill" steel company with a reputation for cost efficiency and streamlined management. Under the leadership of former Chairman F. Kenneth Iverson, the firm was restructured to operate with a minimum of staff. Iverson's philosophy was to put daily decision making into the hands of operating people. Larger steel companies typically have eight or nine levels of management. Even though Nucor itself has over 7,000 employees, he had only three management levels in a typical division. "I'm a firm believer in having the fewest number of management levels and in delegating authority to the lowest level possible," said Iverson. This included an emphasis on decentralization, with plant managers given substantial operating autonomy. Iverson didn't believe in corporate jets, company cars, reserved parking spaces, or executive dining rooms either, saying "We're trying to get our employees to feel they're a real part of the company and that what they do makes the company successful. . . . We've tried to eliminate any differences between management and the rest of our employees."[28]

ORGANIZING TRENDS

○ The **upside-down pyramid** puts customers at the top, served by workers whose managers support them.

Change is part of organizational life. Even as traditional structures are modified, refined, and abandoned in the search for new ones, the organizing practices that create and implement them must change too. In Chapter 1 the concept of the **upside-down pyramid** was introduced as an example of the new directions in management. By putting customers on top, served by workers in the middle, who are in turn supported by managers at the bottom, this notion tries to refocus attention on the marketplace and customer needs. Although more of a concept than a depiction of an actual structure, such thinking is representative of forces shaping new directions in how the modern workplace is organized. Among the organizing trends to be discussed next, a common theme runs throughout—making the adjustments needed to streamline operations for cost efficiency, higher performance, and increased participation by workers.

SHORTER CHAINS OF COMMAND

○ The **chain of command** links all persons with successively higher levels of authority.

A typical organization chart shows the **chain of command**, or the line of authority that vertically links each position with successively higher levels of management. The classical school of management suggested that the chain of command should operate according to the *scalar principle*: There should be a clear and unbroken chain of command linking every person in the organization with successively higher levels of authority up to and including the top manager.

When organizations grow in size they tend to get taller, as more and more levels of management are added to the chain of command. This increases overhead costs; it tends to decrease communication and access between top and bottom levels; it can greatly slow decision making; and it can lead to a loss of contact with the client or customer. These are all reasons why "tall" organizations with many levels of management are often criticized for inefficiencies and poor productivity. The current trend in organizing seeks to address this problem directly.

Trend. Organizations are being "streamlined" by cutting unnecessary levels of management; flatter and more horizontal structures are viewed as a competitive advantage.

LESS UNITY OF COMMAND

Another classical management principle describes how the chain of command should operate in daily practice. The *unity-of-command principle* states that each person in an organization should report to one and only one supervisor. This notion of "one person–one boss" is a foundation of the traditional pyramid form of organization. It is intended to avoid the confusion potentially created when a person gets work directions from more than one source. Unity of command is supposed to ensure that everyone clearly understands assignments and does not get conflicting instructions. It is violated, for example, when a senior manager bypasses someone's immediate supervisor to give him or her orders. This can create confusion for the subordinate and also undermine the supervisor's authority.

The "two-boss" system of matrix structure is a clear violation of unity of command. Whereas the classical advice is to avoid creating multiple reporting relationships, the matrix concept creates them by design. It does so in an attempt to improve lateral relations and teamwork in special programs or projects. Unity of command is also less predominant in the team structure and in other arrangements that emphasize the use of cross-functional teams or task forces. Clearly, the current trend is for less, not more, unity of command in organizations.

Trend. Organizations are using more cross-functional teams, task forces, and horizontal structures, and they are becoming more customer conscious; as they do so, employees often find themselves working for more than one "boss."

WIDER SPANS OF CONTROL

The **span of control** is the number of persons directly reporting to a manager. When span of control is "narrow," only a few people are under a manager's immediate supervision; a "wide" span of control indicates that the manager supervises many people. There was a time in the history of management thought when people searched for the ideal span of control. Although the magic number was never found, this *span-of-control principle* evolved: there is a limit to the number of people one manager can effectively supervise; care should be exercised to keep the span of control within manageable limits.

Figure 10.8 shows the relationship between span of control and the number of levels in the hierarchy of authority. *Flat structures* have wider spans of control—they have few levels of management; *tall structures* have narrow spans of control—they have many levels of management. Because tall organizations have more managers, they are more costly. They are also generally viewed as less efficient, less flexible, and less customer sensitive than flat organizations. Before making spans of control smaller, therefore, serious thought should always be given to both the cost of the added management overhead and the potential disadvantages of a taller chain of command. When spans of control are increased, by contrast, overhead

www.intel.com

Intel is a major player in the dynamic computer chip industry. It is a fast-moving company, and it operates in a fast-moving environment. To stay ahead of its competitors, Intel relies heavily on a team organization. Hierarchy takes a back seat to teamwork. Says one team member, "We report to each other."

○ **Span of control** is the number of subordinates directly reporting to a manager.

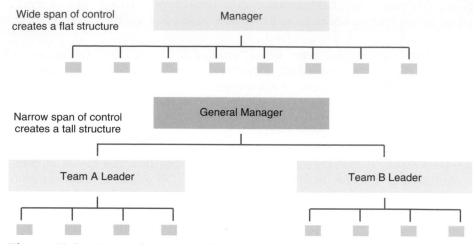

Figure 10.8 Spans of control in "flat" versus "tall" structures.

costs are reduced, and workers with less direct supervision in the flatter structure may benefit from more independence.[29]

> *Trend.* Many organizations are shifting to wider spans of control as levels of management are eliminated and empowerment gains prominence; individual managers are taking responsibility for larger numbers of subordinates who operate with less direct supervision.

MORE DELEGATION AND EMPOWERMENT

○ **Delegation** is the process of distributing and entrusting work to other persons.

All managers must decide what work they should do themselves and what should be left for others. At issue here is **delegation**—the process of entrusting work to others by giving them the right to make decisions and take action. There are three steps to delegation. In *step 1, the manager assigns responsibility* by carefully explaining the work or duties someone else is expected to do. This *responsibility* is an expectation for the other person to perform assigned tasks. In *step 2, the manager grants authority to act.* Along with the assigned task, the right to take necessary actions (for example, to spend money, direct the work of others, use resources) is given to the other person. *Authority* is a right to act in ways needed to carry out the assigned tasks. In *step 3, the manager creates accountability.* By accepting an assignment, the person takes on a direct obligation to the manager to complete the job as agreed upon. *Accountability*, originally defined in Chapter 1, is the requirement to answer to a supervisor for performance results.

A classical principle of organization warns managers not to delegate without giving the subordinate sufficient authority to perform. When insufficient authority is delegated, it will be very hard for someone to live up to performance expectations. They simply don't have the authority needed to get the job done. The *authority-and-responsibility principle* states: authority should equal responsibility when work is delegated from a supervisor to a subordinate. Useful guidelines for delegating are offered in *Manager's Notepad 10.3.*[30]

A common management failure is unwillingness to delegate. Whether due to a lack of trust in others or to a manager's inflexibility in the way things get done, failure to delegate can be damaging. It overloads the manager with work that could be done by others; it also denies others many opportunities to fully utilize their talents on the job. When well done, by

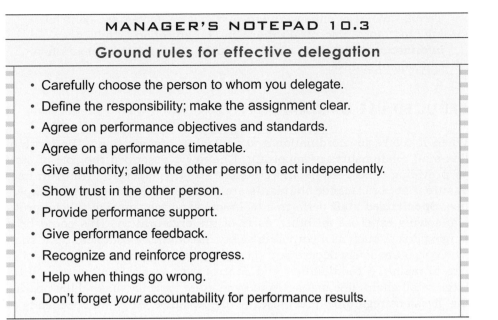

MANAGER'S NOTEPAD 10.3

Ground rules for effective delegation

- Carefully choose the person to whom you delegate.
- Define the responsibility; make the assignment clear.
- Agree on performance objectives and standards.
- Agree on a performance timetable.
- Give authority; allow the other person to act independently.
- Show trust in the other person.
- Provide performance support.
- Give performance feedback.
- Recognize and reinforce progress.
- Help when things go wrong.
- Don't forget *your* accountability for performance results.

contrast, delegation leads to empowerment, in that people have the freedom to contribute ideas and do their jobs in the best possible ways. This involvement can increase job satisfaction for the individual and frequently results in better job performance.

> *Trend.* Managers in progressive organizations are delegating more; they are finding more ways to empower people at all levels to make more decisions affecting themselves and their work.

DECENTRALIZATION WITH CENTRALIZATION

A question frequently asked by managers is: "Should most decisions be made at the top levels of an organization, or should they be dispersed by extensive delegation throughout all levels of management?" The former approach is referred to as **centralization**; the latter is called **decentralization**. There is no classical principle on centralization and decentralization. The traditional pyramid form of organization may give the impression of being a highly centralized structure, while decentralization is characteristic of newer structures and many recent organizing trends. But the issue doesn't have to be framed as an either/or choice. Today's organizations can operate with greater decentralization without giving up centralized control. This is facilitated by developments in information technology.

With computer networks and advanced information systems managers at higher levels can more easily stay informed about a wide range of day-to-day performance matters. Because they have information on results readily available, they can allow more decentralization in decision making.[31] If something goes wrong, presumably the information systems will sound an alarm and allow corrective action to be taken quickly. At BancOne, Inc., for example, the demands of growth and an expanding geographical base have not blurred the lines of authority and accountability. Individual banks in geographically dispersed locations are closely monitored for performance results. With the guiding theme of "centralizing paper and decentralizing people," BancOne has decentralized its branch bank operations while retaining central control.

○ **Centralization** is the concentration of authority for most decisions at the top level of an organization.

○ **Decentralization** is the dispersion of authority to make decisions throughout all levels of the organization.

Trend. Whereas empowerment and related forces are contributing to more decentralization in organizations, advances in information technology simultaneously allow for the retention of centralized control.

REDUCED USE OF STAFF

○ **Specialized staff** provide technical expertise for other parts of the organization.

When it comes to coordination and control in organizations, the issue of line-staff relationships is important. Chapter 1 described the role of staff as providing expert advice and guidance to line personnel. This can help ensure that performance standards are maintained in areas of staff expertise. **Specialized staff** perform a technical service or provide special problem-solving expertise for other parts of the organization. This could be a single person, such as a corporate safety director, or a complete unit, such as a corporate safety department. Many organizations rely on staff specialists to maintain coordination and control over a variety of matters. In a large retail chain, line managers in each store typically make daily operating decisions regarding direct sales of merchandise. But staff specialists at the corporate or regional levels provide direction and support so that all the stores operate with the same credit, purchasing, employment, and advertising procedures.

○ **Personal staff** are "assistant-to" positions that support senior managers.

Organizations may also employ **personal staff**, individuals appointed in "assistant-to" positions with the purpose of providing special support to higher-level managers. Such assistants help by following up on administrative details and performing other duties as assigned. They can benefit also in terms of career development through the mentoring relationships that such assignments offer. An organization, for example, might select promising junior managers as temporary administrative assistants to senior managers. This helps them gain valuable experience at the same time that they are facilitating the work of executives.

Problems in line-staff distinctions can and do arise. In too many cases, organizations find that the staff grows to the point where it costs more in administrative overhead than it is worth. This is why staff cutbacks are common in downsizing and other turnaround efforts. There are also cases where conflicts in line-staff relationships cause difficulties. This often occurs when line and staff managers disagree over the extent of staff authority. At the one extreme, staff has purely *advisory authority* and can "suggest" but not "dictate." At the other extreme, it has *functional authority* to actually "require" that others do as requested within the boundaries of staff expertise. For example, a human resource department may advise line managers on the desired qualifications of new workers being hired (advisory authority); the department will likely require the managers to follow equal-employment-opportunity guidelines in the hiring process (functional authority).

Growth Drivers in Business Strategy
A survey by Mercer Management Consulting identified new product development as the #1 growth driver behind business strategies. Take the on-line "Reality Check" to learn more about what executives say about strategies for growing their businesses.

There is no one best solution to the problem of how to divide work between line and staff responsibilities. What is best for any organization will be a cost-effective staff component that satisfies, but doesn't overreact to, needs for specialized technical assistance to line operations. The current trend is to reduce staff as organizations are being restructured to increase productivity and lower costs.

Trend. Organizations are reducing the size of staff; they are seeking increased operating efficiency by employing fewer staff personnel and using smaller staff units.

STUDY Guide

The Chapter 10 Study Guide will help you review chapter content, prepare for examinations, and further build your career readiness. The *Summary* briefly highlights answers to questions first posed in the chapter opening Planning Ahead section. The list of *Key Terms* allows you to double check your familiarity with basic concepts and definitions. *Self-Test 10* gives you the opportunity to test your basic comprehension of chapter content using sample test questions. Suggestions offered as *Career Readiness Activities* direct your attention to relevant sections of the end-of-text Career Readiness Workbook, as well as to special Electronic Resources on the *Management 7/e* web site.

SUMMARY

What is organizing as a management function?

- Organizing is the process of creating work arrangements of people and re-sources, be it for a small unit, a large division, or an entire enterprise.
- To organize a work setting, decisions must be made about how to divide up the work that needs to be done, allocate people and resources to do it, and coordinate results to achieve productivity.
- Structure is the system of tasks, reporting relationships, and communica-tion that links together the people and positions within an organization.
- Formal structure, such as shown on an organization chart, describes how an organization is supposed to work.
- The informal structure of organization consists of the unofficial working re-lationships among members.

What are the major types of organization structures?

- Departmentalization is the process of creating structure by grouping people together in formal work units or teams.
- In functional structures, people with similar skills who perform similar ac-tivities work together under a common manager.
- In divisional structures, people who work on a similar product, work in the same geographical region, serve the same customers, or participate in the same work process are grouped together under common managers.
- A matrix structure combines the functional and divisional approaches to create permanent cross-functional project teams.

What are the new developments in organization structures?

- Increasing complexity and greater rates of change in the environment are challenging the performance capabilities of traditional organization structures.
- New developments include the growing use of team structures that create horizontal organizations using cross-functional teams and task forces to improve lateral relations and improve problem solving at all levels.
- New developments are also underway in respect to network structures that cluster systems of contracted services and strategic alliances around a core business or organizational center.
- Boundaryless organizations eliminate internal and external organizational boundaries to utilize a shifting mix of internal teams and teamwork to accomplish temporary tasks and projects.
- Virtual organizations eliminate external organizational boundaries and mobilize a shifting mix of strategic alliances to accomplish specific tasks and projects.

What organizing trends are changing the workplace?

- Traditional vertical command-and-control structures are giving way to more horizontal structures strong on employee involvement and flexibility.
- Many organizations today are operating with shorter chains of command and less unity of command.
- Many organizations today are operating with wider spans of control and fewer levels of management.
- The emphasis in more organizations today is on effective delegation and empowerment.
- Advances in information technology are making it possible to operate with decentralization while still maintaining centralized control.
- Reduction in the size of staff is a trend in organizations seeking greater efficiency and productivity.

KEY TERMS

Boundaryless organization (p. 268)

Centralization (p. 273)

Chain of command (p. 270)

Cross-functional teams (p. 265)

Customer structure (p. 262)

Decentralization (p. 273)

Delegation (p. 272)

Departmentalization (p. 259)

Divisional structure (p. 260)

Formal structure (p. 257)

Functional chimneys problem (p. 260)

Functional structure (p. 259)

Geographical structure (p. 261)

Informal structure (p. 257)

Matrix structure (p. 262)

Network structure (p. 266)

Organization chart (p. 257)

Organization structure (p. 256)

Organizing (p. 256)

Personal staff (p. 274)

SELF-TEST 10

Take this test here or on-line much as you would in a normal classroom situation. It is a good way to check your basic comprehension of chapter material. Answers may be found at the end of the book.

MULTIPLE-CHOICE QUESTIONS:

1. _____ is the system of communication and authority that links together the various parts of an organization.
   (a) Structure (b) Empowerment (c) Decentralization (d) Differentiation

2. An organization chart shows the _____ structure of an organization.
   (a) personal (b) impersonal (c) formal (d) informal

3. Good organizing _____.
   (a) clarifies who does what (b) identifies who is in charge of whom
   (c) establishes official channels of communication (d) all of these

4. An organization chart showing vice presidents of marketing, finance, manufacturing, and purchasing all reporting to the president is depicting a _____ structure.
   (a) functional (b) matrix (c) network (d) product

5. The "two-boss" system of reporting relationships is found in the _____ structure.
   (a) functional (b) matrix (c) geographical (d) product

6. A manufacturing business with a functional structure has recently developed two new product lines. The president of the company might consider shifting to a _____ structure to gain a stronger product focus for operations.
   (a) functional (b) matrix (c) divisional (d) network

7. Better lower-level teamwork and more top-level strategic management are among the expected advantages in a _____ structure.
   (a) divisional (b) matrix (c) geographical (d) product

8. "Tall" organizations tend to have long chains of command and _____ spans of control.
   (a) wide (b) narrow (c) informal (d) centralized

9. The unity-of-command principle is intentionally violated in the
   _____ structure.
   (a) divisional (b) matrix (c) geographical (d) product

10. In delegation, _____ is the right of a subordinate to act in ways
    needed to carry out the assigned tasks.
    (a) authority (b) responsibility (c) accountability (d) centrality

TRUE-FALSE QUESTIONS:

11. A boundaryless organization utilizes elements of the team and network
    structures.   T   F

12. Managers should not waste their time trying to understand informal
    structures in their organizations.   T   F

13. A matrix structure is a combination of the functional and divisional
    structures.   T   F

14. Vertical structures are proving more popular as organizations try to deal
    with change and uncertainty.   T   F

15. A potential disadvantage of the divisional structure is that divisions will
    become self-centered and lose focus on organizationwide goals.   T   F

16. The functional chimneys problem is a typical problem encountered by
    organizations using team structures.   T   F

17. Organizations cannot operate with both centralization and decentraliza-
    tion.   T   F

18. Many organizations today are finding that a large staff component in-
    creases productivity.   T   F

19. Empowerment is a desired outcome of delegation.   T   F

20. A wider span of control for the manager can mean greater job autonomy
    for the subordinates.   T   F

SHORT-RESPONSE QUESTIONS:

21. What is the difference between a product divisional structure and a geo-
    graphical or area divisional structure?

22. What are some of the symptoms that might indicate a functional struc-
    ture is causing problems for the organization?

23. Explain by example the concept of a network organization structure.

24. What positive results might be expected when levels of management are
    reduced and the chain of command shortened in an organization?

APPLICATION QUESTION:

25. Faisal Sham supervises a group of seven project engineers. His unit is experiencing a heavy workload as the demand for different versions of one of his firm's computer components is growing. Faisal finds that he doesn't have time to follow up on all design details for each version. Up until now he has tried to do this all by himself. Two of the engineers have shown interest in helping him coordinate work on the various designs. As a consultant, what would you advise Faisal in terms of delegating work to them?

CAREER readiness ACTIVITIES

Recommended learning activities from the end-of-text *Career Readiness Workbook* for this chapter include:

Career Advancement Portfolio
- Individual writing and group presentation assignments based on any of the following activities.

Case for Critical Thinking
- Nucor Corporation—Structuring for Efficiency and Effectiveness

Integrative Learning Activities
- Research Project 2—Changing Corporate Cultures
- Integrative Case—Outback Steakhouse, Inc.
- Integrative Case—Richard Branson Meets the New Economy

Exercises in Teamwork
- The Future Workplace (#13)
- Empowering Others (#19)

Self-Assessments
- Organizational Culture Preference (#2)
- Managerial Assumptions (#4)
- Organizational Design Preference (#12)

The *Fast Company* Collection On-Line
- Robert Reich, "The Company of the Future"

ELECTRONIC RESOURCES

@ GET CONNECTED! Don't forget to take full advantage of the on-line support for *Management 7/e*.
- Chapter 10 On-line Study Guide
- Chapter 10 Self-test Answers
- Chapter 10 E-Resource Center

www.wiley.com/college/schermerhorn

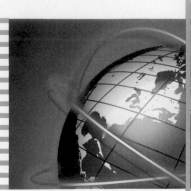

11

Organizational design and work processes

Planning
ahead

GETTING CONNECTED

MobShop, Inc.—*Design for Integration, Empowerment, and Speed*
It began as an idea shared among three guys on their mountain bikes. How fast can an idea be turned into a company? Well, it took

Jim Rose, Salim Teja, and Jonathan Ehrlich only about three months to start a firm first known as Accompany, Inc. In that time they wrote the business, found startup money, and launched the first web site.

That's fast! It's also characteristic of the speed with which organizations must be prepared to invent and reinvent themselves to compete in an Internet-driven economy.

Time moves fast for Rose, Teja, and Ehrlich. Their idea was to create an on-line buying club in which large numbers of people could join purchases to save money. Accompany, Inc. worked and the firm is now called MobShop, Inc.—a name described by the founders as "more memorable and not quite as confusing" as their first choice.

MobShop pools orders from customers to strike preferred purchasing deals with suppliers. It is designed to give individuals and small organizations access to the same purchasing power and volume discounts that larger organizations gain.

The business model of demand aggregation is proving very successful, but MobShop must keep moving for the competitive edge. As a startup, it was three friends, their ideas, and spontaneous enthusiasm that was shared by others who began working with them. There weren't a lot of people involved. You might say, it was easy to work together and work fast.

That was the beginning. Now, with the second-fastest-growing e-commerce web site, strategic leadership faces new demands as MobShop grows in size and complexity. The challenge is to keep up the pace even as the scale of operations grows and the number of people involved gets larger and larger. And then, of course, there's a world out there. MobShop is expanding into Europe and has aspirations for keeping what CEO Rose describes as a "leadership position in the global market for demand aggregation services and technology."[1]

@ **Get Connected!**

Why hasn't anyone created a "MobShop" on your campus? Could the business model work by pooling students' buying needs? Consider the possibilities. Give MobShop a good look. Talk to your friends and do some market research.
Get connected!

It's one thing to start fresh and start small, as did MobShop. Organizations like that should be quick and nimble, and their members should have little trouble creatively working together. It can be quite a different story for organizations that are already large and complex, and that must also meet the demands of competitive environments and changing times. Consider Nestle, a firm once called by *Fortune* magazine a "Swiss powerhouse . . . racing across the developing world, building roads, farms, factories, and whatever else it needs to capture new markets."[2] MobShop is just starting to branch out internationally; Nestle is already the largest branded food company in the world. But it too must keep looking for and responding to opportunities around the globe. Strategic leadership at Nestle tries to position the firm for growth while adapting its strategies to fit regional conditions and by allowing local managers autonomy to pursue opportunities specific to their countries. It also transfers managers around regions and continuously shares among them new ideas for improved operations. In Nestle's competitive environment just as with MobShop's, success depends on the ability to continuously achieve integration, empowerment, and speed.

Organizations everywhere are changing and adapting their structures to best meet competitive demands in the new economy. Traditional structures are being flattened, networks are being developed, IT is being utilized, and decision making is decentralized to the point where knowledge exists. The goals are clear: improved teamwork, more creativity, shorter product development cycles, better customer service, and higher productivity overall. Changing times require more flexible and well-integrated organizations that can deliver high-quality products and services while still innovating for sustained future performance. We already know that team structures and network organizations are gaining in popularity.[3] Yet organizations face widely varying problems and opportunities, and there is no one best way to structure and manage them. The key to success is finding the best design to master the unique situational needs and challenges for each organization.[4]

ORGANIZATIONAL DESIGN ESSENTIALS

A variety of organizational structures were examined in the previous chapter. The point was made that managers must be ever alert to prospects for improving performance through adjustments in structure. Change is the ever-present fact of life in organizations today. The various trends in organization and management practices that were described in Chapter 10 are resulting in fundamental changes in the way people work and organizations operate. Today, one finds more sharing of tasks, reduced emphasis on hierarchy, greater emphasis on lateral communication, more teamwork, and more decentralization of decision making and empowerment.

WHAT IS ORGANIZATIONAL DESIGN?

○ **Organizational design** is the process of creating structures that best serve mission and objectives.

Organizational design is the process of choosing and implementing structures that best arrange resources to serve the organization's mission and objectives.[5] The ultimate purpose of organizational design is to create an alignment between supporting structures and situational challenges. As shown in *Figure 11.1*, this includes taking into consideration the impli-

No it's not a church. It's an advertising agency. But it's a unique one, offering an example of changing directions in organizations. If you look at the stationery of the London-based advertising agency, St. Luke's, you'll find everyone's name listed—from the creative director to the receptionist. The focus is on achieving creativity and work space is designed so that everyone shares common areas to maximize interaction and connectivity. The culture is informal; every employee is a part owner; a six-member board elected by staff members oversees the company. Everyone focuses on great service to customers. One member of the firm describes working there as like "the difference between going to grade school and going to the university. At school the bell goes 'ding' and tells you what to do. We have no bell. Like the university, as long as you create great stuff, we don't care how you do it."[7]

cations of environment, strategies, people, technology, and size.[6] Importantly, the process of organizational design is a problem-solving activity that should be approached in a contingency fashion that takes all of these factors into account. There is no universal design that applies in all circumstances. The goal is to achieve a best fit among structure and the unique situation faced by each organization.

As suggested in the example of St. Luke's, key directions for changes in organizations today involve a basic shift in attention away from a traditional emphasis on more vertical or authority-driven structures to ones that are more horizontal and task-driven. In management theory, these developments are framed by an important distinction between bureaucratic designs that are mechanistic and vertical in nature, and adaptive designs that are more organic and horizontal in nature. This distinction itself is viewed from the *contingency position* that there is no one best way to organize, and that the choice of organizational design should always be made to achieve the best fit with situational needs.

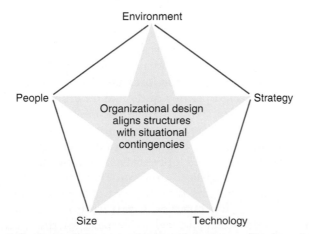

Figure 11.1 A framework for organizational design—aligning structures with situational contingencies.

BUREAUCRATIC DESIGNS

As first introduced in the discussion on historical foundations of management in Chapter 4, a *bureaucracy* was described as a form of organization based on logic, order, and the legitimate use of formal authority. Its distinguishing features include a clear-cut division of labor, strict hierarchy of authority, formal rules and procedures, and promotion based on competency. According to sociologist Max Weber, bureaucracies were supposed to be orderly, fair, and highly efficient.[8] In short, they were a model form of organization. Yet if you use the term "bureaucracy" today, it may well be interpreted with a negative connotation. If you call someone a "bureaucrat," it may well be considered an insult. Instead of operating efficiency, the bureaucracies that we know are often associated with "red tape"; instead of being orderly and fair, they are often seen as cumbersome and impersonal to the point of insensitivity to customer or client needs. And the bureaucrats? Don't we assume that they work only according to rules, diligently following procedures and avoiding any opportunities to take initiative or demonstrate creativity?

Management researchers recognize that there are limits to bureaucracy, particularly in their tendencies to become unwieldy and rigid.[9] Instead of viewing all bureaucratic structures as inevitably flawed, however, management theory takes a contingency perspective. The critical contingency questions to be asked and answered are: (1) When is a bureaucratic form a good choice for an organization? (2) What alternatives exist when it is not a good choice?

A basis for answering these questions lies in pioneering research conducted in England during the early 1960s by Tom Burns and George Stalker.[10] After investigating 20 manufacturing firms, Burns and Stalker concluded that two quite different organizational forms could be successful, with the choice among them depending upon the nature of a firm's external environment. A more bureaucratic form, which Burns and Stalker called a *mechanistic approach*, thrived when the environment was stable. But it experienced difficulty when the environment was rapidly changing and uncertain. In these dynamic situations, a much less bureaucratic form, called an *organic approach*, performed best. *Figure 11.2* portrays these two approaches as opposite extremes on a continuum of organizational design alternatives.

Organizations that operate with more **mechanistic designs** are highly bureaucratic in nature. As shown in the figure, they typically operate with more centralized authority, many rules and procedures, a precise division of labor, narrow spans of control, and formal means of coordination. Mechanistic designs are described as "tight" structures of the traditional vertical or pyramid form.[11] An example is your local fast-food restaurant. A relatively small operation, each store operates quite like others in the franchise chain and according to rules established by the corporate management. You will notice that service personnel work in orderly and disciplined ways, guided by training, rules and procedures, and close supervision by crew leaders who work alongside them. Even their appearances are carefully regulated, with everyone working in a standardized uniform. These restaurants perform well as they repetitively deliver items that are part of their standard menus. You quickly encounter the limits, however, if you try to order something not on the menu. The servers aren't allowed to prepare anything out of the ordinary. The chains also encounter difficulty when consumer tastes change or take on regional preferences that are different from what the corporate menu provides. Adjustments to the system are typically a long time coming.

REALITY
Check 11.1

Reasons for Unscheduled Absences
People can't contribute if they don't come to work. A survey of absence patterns experienced by 305 employers by CCH International showed that absences due to work stress increased 14 percent in a five-year period. Take the on-line "Reality Check" to learn more about absence patterns in the workforce.

○ A **mechanistic design** is centralized with many rules and procedures, a clear-cut division of labor, narrow spans of control, and formal coordination.

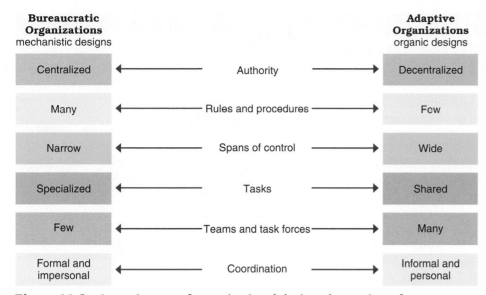

Bureaucratic Organizations mechanistic designs		Adaptive Organizations organic designs
Centralized	Authority	Decentralized
Many	Rules and procedures	Few
Narrow	Spans of control	Wide
Specialized	Tasks	Shared
Few	Teams and task forces	Many
Formal and impersonal	Coordination	Informal and personal

Figure 11.2 A continuum of organizational design alternatives: from bureaucratic to adaptive organizations.

ADAPTIVE DESIGNS

The limits of bureaucracy are especially apparent in organizations that must operate in the highly competitive environments created by the forces of globalization and ever-changing technologies. It's hard, for example, to find a technology company, consumer products firm, financial services business, or "dot-com retailer" these days that isn't making continual adjustments in operations and organizational design. Things keep changing on them, and many of the changes are very difficult to predict.

"It's a millennial change," says Dee Hock, the founder of Visa International. "We can't run 21st-century society with 17th-century notions of organization."[12] Enlightened managers are helping organizations reconfigure into new forms that emphasize flexibility and speed without losing sight of important performance objectives. Harvard scholar and consultant Rosabeth Moss Kanter notes that the ability to respond quickly to shifting environmental challenges often distinguishes successful organizations from less successful ones. Specifically, Kanter states,

> The organizations now emerging as successful will be, above all, flexible; they will need to be able to bring particular resources together quickly, on the basis of short-term recognition of new requirements and the necessary capacities to deal with them. . . . The balance between static plans—which appear to reduce the need for effective reaction— and structural flexibility needs to shift toward the latter.[13]

The organizational design trend is now toward more **adaptive organizations** that operate with a minimum of bureaucratic features and with cultures that encourage worker empowerment and participation. They display features of the **organic designs** portrayed in Figure 11.2, including more decentralized authority, fewer rules and procedures, less precise division of labor, wider spans of control, and more personal means of coordination. They are described as relatively loose systems in which a lot of work gets done through informal structures and networks of interpersonal contacts.[14] Organic designs recognize and legitimate these linkages and

○ An **adaptive organization** operates with a minimum of bureaucratic features and encourages worker empowerment and teamwork.

○ An **organic design** is decentralized with fewer rules and procedures, open divisions of labor, wide spans of control, and more personal coordination.

TAKE IT TO THE CASE!

PricewaterhouseCoopers *(www.pwcglobal.com)*
Restructuring for Client Service in a Global Economy

It wasn't that long ago that PricewaterhouseCoopers was created from the merger of two giants in the accounting/consulting industry—Price Waterhouse and Coopers & Lybrand. Reflecting consolidation of firms in a competitive industry, the immediate management challenges were creating one company from the former two—blending cultures, goals, people, and structures into a competitive whole. But the restructuring goes on. PWC's latest reorganization tries to unlock its increasingly complex operations. PricewaterhouseCoopers will retain the audit, business advisory, and tax services. The firm's management consulting, business process outsourcing, and corporate finance and human resource consulting services will function as independent entities, free to seek external strategic alliances. In announcing the reorganization, the firm stated: "In essence, we have become an organization trying to follow two missions at the same time. . . . Our restructuring plan will allow each of our businesses to grow and prosper free of the constraints which one can inadvertently impose on the other."[15]

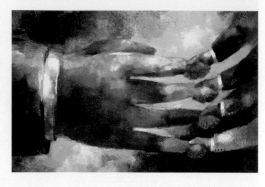

give them the resources they need to operate best. This works well for organizations facing dynamic environments that demand flexibility in dealing with changing conditions. They are also increasingly popular in the new workplace, where the demands of total quality management and competitive advantage place more emphasis on internal teamwork and responsiveness to customers.

Above all, adaptive organizations are built upon trusting that people will do the right things on their own initiative. They move organizational design in the direction of what some might call *self-organization*, where the focus is on freeing otherwise capable people from unnecessarily centralized control and restrictions. Moving toward the adaptive form means letting workers take over production scheduling and problem solving; it means letting workers set up their own control techniques; it means letting workers use their ideas to improve customer service. In the ultimately adaptive organizations, it means that members are given the freedom to do what they can do best—get the job done. This creates what has been described in earlier chapters as a **learning organization**, one designed for continuous adaptation through problem solving, innovation, and learning.[16]

○ A **learning organization** is designed for continuous adaptation through problem solving, innovation, and learning.

CONTINGENCIES IN ORGANIZATIONAL DESIGN

Good organizational design decisions should result in supportive structures that satisfy situational demands and allow all resources to be used to best advantage. This is true contingency thinking. Among the contingency factors in the organizational design checklist featured in *Manager's Notepad 11.1* are the environment, strategy, technology, size and life cycle, and human resources.

MANAGER'S NOTEPAD 11.1

Organizational design checklist

Check 1: Does the design fit well with the major problems and opportunities of the external environment?

Check 2: Does the design support the implementation of strategies and the accomplishment of key operating objectives?

Check 3: Does the design support core technologies and allow them to be used to best advantage?

Check 4: Can the design handle changes in organizational size and different stages in the organizational life cycle?

Check 5: Does the design support and empower workers and allow their talents to be used to best advantage?

ENVIRONMENT

The organization's external environment and the degree of uncertainty it offers are of undeniable importance in organizational design.[17] A *certain environment* is composed of relatively stable and predictable elements. As a result, an organization can succeed with relatively few changes in the goods or services produced or in the manner of production over time. Bureaucratic organizations and mechanistic designs are quite adequate under such conditions. An *uncertain environment* will have more dynamic and less predictable elements. Changes occur frequently and may catch decision makers by surprise. As a result, organizations must be flexible and responsive over relatively short time horizons. This requires more adaptive organizations and organic designs. *Figure 11.3* summarizes these relationships, showing how increasing uncertainty in organizational environments calls for more horizontal and adaptive designs.

STRATEGY

The nature of organizational strategies and objectives should influence the choice of structure. Research on these contingency relationships is often traced to the pioneering work of Alfred Chandler Jr., who analyzed the histories of DuPont, General Motors, Sears, and Standard Oil of New

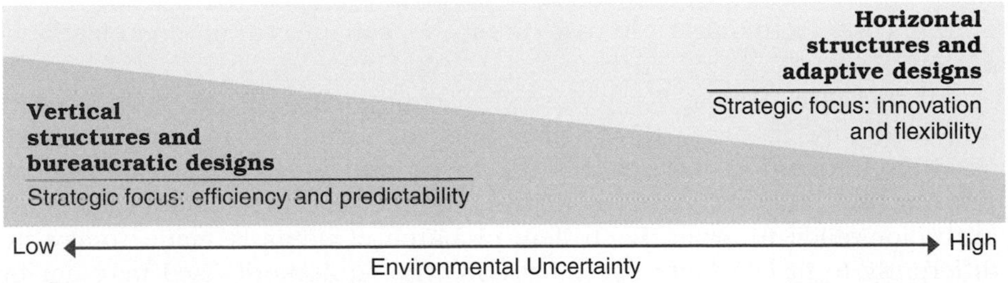

Horizontal structures and adaptive designs
Strategic focus: innovation and flexibility

Vertical structures and bureaucratic designs
Strategic focus: efficiency and predictability

Low ⟵ ⟶ High
Environmental Uncertainty

Figure 11.3 Environmental uncertainty and the performance of vertical and horizontal designs.

Magnum Machine & Fab, Inc.

How to Keep a Job Shop Afloat

Running a small business is hard in the best of circumstances. But it takes a master manager to keep things on course through an economic downturn. At Magnum Machine & Fab, Inc., the 11 workers know the meaning of hard work. They build to order metal parts crafted to specifications provided by the firm's customers. It's a classic "job shop" where each order becomes a new job to be tackled and completed by skilled craft workers.

When times are good at this Washington, Pa., firm owned by Carl Bogatay, there are pallets of raw steel stacked up waiting to be used. They represent orders waiting to be filled on the big metal cutting machines. When there are few pallets around, like now, you know things are getting bad.

With a downturn at hand, Carl is worried he may have to lay off some workers. These, like Neil Jenkins, are highly skilled. In good times their skills are in high demand. If they left Magnum, they would have had numerous other job opportunities. Neil is taking a cautious approach to his personal finances, choosing to delay a planned home remodeling project. He says: "I don't want to start it, because I want to be sure I have the money to finish it."

Carl Bogatay runs more than a metal working shop; he runs a firm that is an important part of the life of each and every one of his workers. Part of his responsibility is to keep things running well for them. Right now, when things are tight, he says his dream is to "get out of debt and have enough to get the parking lot paved." Through it all, however, his entrepreneurial side remains strong. He just bought another small metalworking firm.

QUESTION: What types of small job shops exist in your community? Have you ever spoken to an owner or to workers? Do you understand the challenges and responsibilities of running small businesses in challenging times?

Jersey in depth[18] Chandler's conclusion that "structure follows strategy" is an important premise of organizational design. An organization's structure must support its strategy if the desired results are to be achieved.[19]

When strategy is stability oriented, the choice of organizational design should be based on the premise that little significant change will be occurring in the external environment. This means that plans can be set and operations programmed to be routinely implemented. To best support this strategic approach, the organization should be structured to operate in well-defined and predictable ways. This is most characteristic of bureaucratic organizations that use more mechanistic design alternatives.

When strategy is growth oriented and when strategy is likely to change frequently, the situation as a whole becomes more complex, fluid, and uncertain. Operating objectives are likely to include the need for innovation and flexible responses to changing competition in the environment. Operations and plans are likely to have short life spans, and require frequent and even continuous modification over time. The most appropriate structure is one that allows for internal flexibility and freedom to create new ways of doing things. This is most characteristic of the empowerment found in adaptive organizations using more organic design alternatives.

TECHNOLOGY

Technology is the combination of knowledge, skills, equipment, computers, and work methods used to transform resource inputs into organizational outputs. It is the way tasks are accomplished using tools, machines, techniques, and human know-how. The availability of appropriate technology is a cornerstone of productivity, and the nature

○ **Technology** includes equipment, knowledge, and work methods that transform inputs into outputs.

○ **Small-batch production** manufactures a variety of products crafted to fit customer specifications.

of the core technologies in use must be considered in organizational design.

In the early 1960s, Joan Woodward conducted a study of technology and structure in over 100 English manufacturing firms. She classified core *manufacturing technology* into three categories.[20] In **small-batch production**, such as a racing bicycle shop, a variety of custom products are tailor-made to order. Each item or batch of items is made somewhat differently to fit customer specifications. The equipment used may not be elaborate, but a high level of worker skill often is needed. In **mass production**, the organization produces a large number of uniform products in an assembly-line system. Workers are highly dependent on one another, as the product passes from stage to stage until completion. Equipment may be sophisticated, and workers often follow detailed instructions while performing simplified jobs. Organizations using **continuous-process production** are highly automated. They produce a few products by continuously feeding raw materials—such as liquids, solids, and gases—through a highly automated production system with largely computerized controls. Such systems are equipment intensive but can often be operated by a relatively small labor force. Classic examples are automated chemical plants, steel mills, oil refineries, and power plants.

Woodward found that the right combination of structure and technology was critical to organizational success. The best small-batch and continuous-process plants in her study had more flexible organic structures; the best mass-production operations had more rigid mechanistic structures. The implications of this research have become known as the **technological imperative**: technology is a major influence on organizational structure.

The importance of technology for organizational design applies in services as well as manufacturing, although the core *service technologies* are slightly different.[21] In health care, education, and related services, an **intensive technology** focuses the efforts of many people with special expertise on the needs of patients or clients. In banks, real estate firms, insurance companies, employment agencies, and others like them, a **mediating technology** links together parties seeking a mutually beneficial exchange of values—typically a buyer and seller. Finally, a **long-linked technology** can function like mass production, where a client is passed from point to point for various aspects of service delivery.

SIZE AND LIFE CYCLE

Typically measured by number of employees, *organizational size* is another contingency factor in organizational design.[22] Although research indicates that larger organizations tend to have more mechanistic structures than smaller ones, it is clear that this is not always best for them.[23] In fact, a perplexing managerial concern is that organizations tend to become more bureaucratic as they grow in size and consequently have more difficulty adapting to changing environments.

It is especially important to understand the design implications of the **organizational life cycle**, or the evolution of an organization over time through different stages of growth. The *stages in the organizational life cycle* can be described as:

1. *Birth stage*—when the organization is founded by an entrepreneur.
2. *Youth stage*—when the organization starts to grow rapidly.
3. *Midlife stage*—when the organization has grown large with success.
4. *Maturity stage*—when the organization stabilizes at a large size.[24]

In its *birth stage* the founder usually runs the organization. It stays relatively small, and the structure is quite simple. The organization starts to grow rapidly during the *youth stage* and management responsibilities extend among more people. Here, the simple structure begins to exhibit the stresses of change. An organization in the *midlife stage* is even larger, with a more complex and increasingly formal structure. More levels appear in the chain of command, and the founder may have difficulty remaining in control. In the *maturity stage*, the organization stabilizes in size, typically with a mechanistic structure. It runs the risk of becoming complacent and slow in competitive markets. Bureaucratic tendencies

○ **Mass production** manufactures a large number of uniform products with an assembly-line type of system.

○ In **continuous-process production** raw materials are continuously transformed by an automated system.

○ The **technological imperative** states that technology is a major influence on organizational structure.

○ **Intensive technology** focuses the efforts and talents of many people to serve clients.

○ **Mediating technology** links together people in a beneficial exchange of values.

○ In **long-linked technology** a client moves from point to point during service delivery.

○ In the **organizational life cycle** an organization passes through different stages from birth to maturity.

← Stages in the organizational life cycle

toward stability may lead an organization at this stage toward decline. Steps must be taken to counteract these tendencies and allow for needed creativity and innovation.

One way of coping with the disadvantages of bigness is *downsizing*, that is, taking actions to reduce the scope of operations and number of employees. This response is often used when top management is challenged to reduce costs quickly and increase productivity.[25] But, perhaps more significantly, good managers in many organizations find unique ways to overcome the disadvantages of large size before the crisis of downsizing hits. They are creative in fostering **intrapreneurship**, described in Chapter 9 as the pursuit of entrepreneurial behavior by individuals and subunits within large organizations.[26] They also find ways for smaller entrepreneurial units to operate with freedom and autonomy within the larger organizational framework. **Simultaneous systems**, for example, are organizations that utilize both mechanistic and organic designs to meet the need for production efficiency and continued innovation. This "loose-tight" concept in organizational design is depicted in *Figure 11.4*.

○ **Intrapreneurship** is entrepreneurial behavior by individuals and subunits within large organizations.

○ **Simultaneous systems** operate when mechanistic and organic designs operate together in an organization.

HUMAN RESOURCES

Another contingency factor in organizational design is people—the human resources that staff the organization for action. A good organizational design provides people with the supporting structures they need to achieve both high performance and satisfaction in their work. Modern management theory views people-structure relationships in a contingency fashion. The prevailing argument is that there should be a good "fit" between organization structures and the human resources.[27]

An important human resource issue in organizational design is skill. Any design should allow the expertise and talents of organizational members to be unlocked and utilized to the fullest. Especially in the age of information and knowledge workers, high-involvement organic designs with their emphasis on empowerment are crucial. When IBM purchased the software firm Lotus, for example, the intention was to turn it into a building block for the firm's networking business. But Lotus was small and IBM was huge. The whole thing had to be carefully handled or IBM might lose many of the talented people who created the popular LotusNotes and related products. The solution was to adapt the design to fit the people. IBM gave Lotus the space it needed to retain the characteristics of a creative software house. Says the firm's head of software at the time: "You have to keep the people, so you have to ask yourself why it is they like working there."[28]

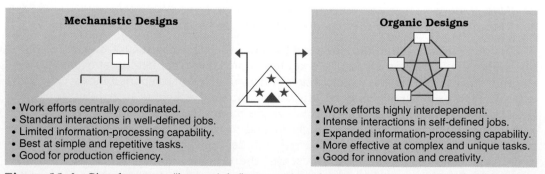

Figure 11.4 Simultaneous "loose-tight" properties of team structures support efficiency and innovation.

SUBSYSTEMS DESIGN AND INTEGRATION

Organizations are composed of **subsystems**, such as a department or work unit headed by a manager, that operate as smaller parts of a larger and total organizational system. Ideally, the work of subsystems serves the needs of the larger organization. Ideally, too, the work of each subsystem supports the work of others. Things don't always work out this way, however. Another challenge of organizational design is to create subsystems and coordinate relationships so that the entire organization's interests are best met.

> A **subsystem** is a work unit or smaller component within a larger organization.

Important research in this area was reported in 1967 by Paul Lawrence and Jay Lorsch of Harvard University.[29] They studied 10 firms in three different industries—plastics, consumer goods, and containers. The firms were chosen because they differed in performance. The industries were chosen because they faced different levels of environmental uncertainty. The plastics industry was uncertain; containers was more certain; consumer goods was moderately uncertain. The results of the Lawrence and Lorsch study can be summarized as follows.

First, the total system structures of successful firms in each industry matched their respective environmental challenges. Successful plastics firms in uncertain environments had more organic designs; successful container firms in certain environments had more mechanistic designs. This result was consistent with the earlier research by Burns and Stalker already discussed in this chapter.[30] Second, Lawrence and Lorsch found that subsystem structures in the successful firms matched the challenges of their respective subenvironments. Subsystems within the successful firms assumed different structures to accommodate the special problems and opportunities of their operating situations. Third, the researchers found that subsystems in the successful firms worked well with one another, even though they were very different from one another.

Americans Working Longer

The United Nations' International Labor Organization (ILO) reports that the average American adult works some 2000 hours per year for pay. Take the on-line "Reality Check" to learn how this compares with workers in other parts the world.

SUBSYSTEM DIFFERENCES

Figure 11.5 depicts operating differences between three divisions in one of the firms studied by Lawrence and Lorsch. The illustration shows how research and development, manufacturing, and sales subunits may operate differently in response to unique needs. This illustrates **differentiation**, which is the degree of difference that exists between the internal components of the organization.

> **Differentiation** is the degree of difference between subsystems in an organization.

There are four common *sources of subsystems differentiation*. First, the planning and action horizons of managers vary from short term to long term. Sometimes *differences in time orientation* become characteristic of work units themselves. In a business firm, for example, the manufacturing subsystem may have a shorter-term outlook than does the research and development group. These differences can make it difficult for personnel from the two units to work well together. Second, the different tasks assigned to work units may also result in *differences in objectives*. For example, cost-conscious production managers and volume-conscious marketing managers may have difficulty agreeing on solutions to common problems.

Third, *differences in interpersonal orientation* can affect subsystem relations. To the extent that patterns of communication, decision making,

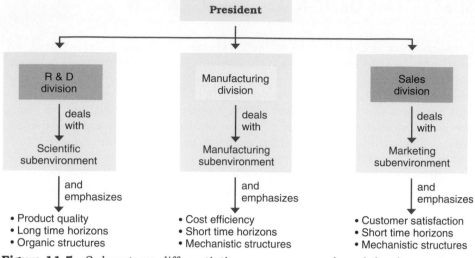

Figure 11.5 Subsystems differentiation among research and development (R&D), manufacturing, and sales divisions.

and social interaction vary, it may be harder for personnel from different subsystems to work together. And fourth, *differences in formal structure* can also affect subsystem behaviors. Someone who is used to flexible problem solving in an organic setting may find it very frustrating to work with a manager from a mechanistic setting who is used to strict rules.

HOW TO ACHIEVE INTEGRATION

○ **Integration** is the level of coordination achieved between subsystems in an organization.

The term **integration** in organization theory refers to the level of coordination achieved among an organization's internal components. Organizational design involves the creation of both differentiated structures and appropriate integrating mechanisms. A basic *organizational design* paradox, however, makes this a particularly challenging managerial task. Increased differentiation among organizational subsystems creates the need for greater integration; however, integration becomes harder to achieve as differentiation increases.

Manager's Notepad 11.2 identifies several mechanisms for achieving subsystem integration.[31] The first integrating mechanisms listed in the notepad rely more on vertical coordination and the use of authority relationships in the chain of command. The use of rules and procedures, hierarchical referral, and planning work best when differentiation is low. Integrating mechanisms that emphasize horizontal coordination and improved lateral relations work better when differentiation is high.[32] They include the use of direct contact between managers, liaison roles, task forces, teams, and matrix structures.

WORK PROCESS DESIGN

○ **Process reengineering** systematically analyzes work processes to design new and better ones.

From the emphasis on subsystems integration and more cross-functional collaboration in organizational design has come a popular development known as business **process reengineering**.[33] This is defined by consultant Michael Hammer as the systematic and complete analysis of work processes and the design of new and better ones.[34] The goal of a

MANAGER'S NOTEPAD 11.2

How to improve subsystems integration

- *Rules and procedures:* Clearly specify required activities.
- *Hierarchical referral:* Refer problems upward to a common superior.
- *Planning:* Set targets that keep everyone headed in the same direction.
- *Direct contact:* Have subunit managers coordinate directly.
- *Liaison roles:* Assign formal coordinators to link subunits together.
- *Task forces:* Form temporary task forces to coordinate activities and solve problems on a timetable.
- *Teams:* Form permanent teams with the authority to coordinate and solve problems over time.
- *Matrix organizations:* Create a matrix structure to improve coordination on specific programs.

reengineering effort is to focus attention on the future, on customers, and on improved ways of doing things. It tries to break people and mindsets away from habits, preoccupation with past accomplishments, and tendencies to continue implementing old and outmoded ways of doing things. Simply put, reengineering is a radical and disciplined approach to changing the way work is carried out in organizations.

WHAT IS A WORK PROCESS?

In his book *Beyond Reengineering*, Michael Hammer defines a **work process** as "a related group of tasks that together create a result of value for the customer."[35] They are the things people do to turn resource inputs into goods or services for customers. Hammer goes further to highlight the following key words in this definition and their implications: (1) *group*—tasks are viewed as part of a group rather than in isolation; (2) *together*—everyone must share a common goal; (3) *result*—the focus is on what is accomplished, not on activities; (4) *customer*—processes serve customers and their perspectives are the ones that really count.

○ A **work process** is a related group of tasks that together create a value for the customer.

The concept of **workflow**, or the movement of work from one point to another in the manufacturing or service delivery processes, is central to the understanding of processes.[36] The various aspects of a work process must all be completed to achieve the desired results, and they must typically be completed in a given order. An important starting point for a reengineering effort is to diagram or map these workflows as they actually take place. Then each step can be systematically analyzed to determine whether it is adding value and to consider ways of streamlining to improve efficiency. Since some form of computer support is typically integral to organizational workflows today, special attention should be given to maximizing the contribution of new technology to the reengineering of processes. At PeopleSoft, for example, paper forms are definitely out; the goal is to eliminate them as much as possible. Employees are even able to order their own supplies through a direct web link to

○ **Workflow** is the movement of work from one point to another in a system.

Office Depot. The firm's chief information officer once said: "Nobody jumps out of bed in the morning and says, 'I want to go to work and fill out forms.' We create systems that let people be brilliant rather than push paper."[37]

HOW TO REENGINEER CORE PROCESSES

Given the mission, objectives, and strategies of an organization, business process reengineering can be used to regularly assess and fine-tune work processes to ensure that they directly add value to operations. Each process is viewed as a "black box" with inputs and outputs. The process is what turns the inputs into outputs, and the outputs should have greater value coming out than did the inputs as they went in. Through a technique called **process value analysis**, core processes are identified and carefully evaluated for their performance contributions. Each step in a workflow is examined. Unless a step is found to be important, useful, and contributing to the value added, it is eliminated. Process value analysis typically involves the following steps.[38]

○ **Process value analysis** identifies and evaluates core processes for their performance contributions.

Steps in process value analysis →

1. Identify the core processes.
2. Map the core processes in respect to workflows.
3. Evaluate all tasks for the core processes.
4. Search for ways to eliminate unnecessary tasks or work.
5. Search for ways to eliminate delays, errors, and misunderstandings.
6. Search for efficiencies in how work is shared and transferred among people and departments.

Figure 11.6 shows an example of how reengineering and better use of computer technology can streamline a purchasing operation. A purchase order should result in at least three value-added outcomes: order fulfill-

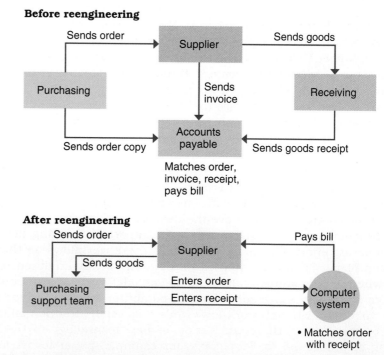

Figure 11.6 How reengineering can streamline core business processes.

ment, a paid bill, and a satisfied supplier. Work to be successfully accomplished includes such things as ordering, shipping, receiving, billing, and payment. A traditional business system might have purchasing, receiving, and accounts payable as separate functions, with each communicating with each other and the supplier. Alternatively, reengineering might design a new purchasing support team whose members handle the same work more efficiently and with the support of the latest computer technology.[39]

PROCESS-DRIVEN ORGANIZATIONS

Customers, teamwork, and efficiency are central to Hammer's notion of process reengineering. He describes the case of Aetna Life & Casualty Company where a complex system of tasks and processes once took as much as 28 days to accomplish.[40] Customer service requests were handled in step-by-step fashion by many different persons. After an analysis of workflows, the process was redesigned into a "one and done" format where a single customer service provider handled each request from start to finish. One of Aetna's customer account managers said after the change was made: "Now we can see the customers as individual people. It's no longer 'us' and 'them.'"[41]

Hammer also describes reengineering at GTE, now a unit of the new Verizon Communications. Before reengineering, customer inquiries for telephone service and repairs required extensive consultation between technicians and their supervisors. After process value analysis, technicians were formed into geographical teams that handled their own scheduling, service delivery, and reporting. They were given cellular telephones and laptop computers to assist in managing their work, resulting in the elimination of a number of costly supervisory jobs. The technicians enthusiastically responded to the changes and opportunities. "The fact that you've got four or five people zoned in a certain geographical area," said one, "means that we get personally familiar with our customers' equipment and problems."[42]

The prior examples describe the essence of process reengineering. The approach tries to redesign processes to center control for them with an identifiable group of people, and to focus each person and the entire system on meeting customer needs and expectations. It tries to eliminate duplication of work and systems bottlenecks, and in so doing tries to reduce costs and increase efficiency while creating an ever-present capacity for change. As Hammer says in describing the ultimate *process-driven organization*:

Traditional organizations were designed for execution, not for change; they lacked the mechanisms for recognizing and responding to change, and their rigid structures made accommodating change a traumatic event. Not so with a process enterprise. Its intrinsic customer focus and its commitment to outcome measurement make it vigilant and proactive in perceiving the need for change; the process owner, freed from other responsibilities and wielding the power of process design, is an institutionalized agent of change; and employees who have an appreciation for customers and who are measured on outcomes are flexible and adaptable.[43]

www.psgroup.com

At Patricia Seybold Group of Boston, senior vice president Ronni Marshak specializes in work group products. To improve a process she determines how it works, the sequence of activities or tasks involved, the responsibilities of the people involved, and the rules of the process or conditions under which it might change. This is often done with the assistance of consultants and special software tools.

STUDY Guide

The Chapter 11 Study Guide will help you review chapter content, prepare for examinations, and further build your career readiness. The *Summary* briefly highlights answers to questions first posed in the chapter opening Planning Ahead section. The list of *Key Terms* allows you to double check your familiarity with basic concepts and definitions. *Self-Test 11* gives you the opportunity to test your basic comprehension of chapter content using sample test questions. Suggestions offered as *Career Readiness Activities* direct your attention to relevant sections of the end-of-text Career Readiness Workbook as well as to special Electronic Resources on the *Management 7/e* web site.

SUMMARY

What are the essentials of organizational design?

- Organizational design is the process of choosing and implementing structures that best arrange resources to serve mission and purpose.
- Bureaucratic or mechanistic organizational designs are vertical in nature and perform best for routine and predictable tasks.
- Adaptive or organic organizational designs are horizontal in nature and perform best in conditions requiring change and flexibility.

How do contingency factors influence organizational design?

- Environment, strategy, technology, size, and people are all contingency factors influencing organizational design.
- Certain environments lend themselves to more vertical and mechanistic organizational designs. Uncertain environments require more horizontal and adaptive organizational designs.
- Technology—including the use of knowledge, equipment, and work methods in the transformation process—is an important consideration in organizational design.
- Although organizations tend to become more mechanistic as they grow in size, designs must be used to allow for innovation and creativity in changing environments.

What are the major issues in subsystems design?

- Organizations are composed of subsystems that must work well together.
- Differentiation is the degree of difference that exists between various subsystems; integration is the level of coordination achieved among them.

- As organizations become more highly differentiated they have a greater need for integration, but as differentiation increases integration is harder to accomplish.
- Low levels of differentiation can be handled through authority relationships and more vertical organizational designs.
- Greater differentiation requires more intense coordination through horizontal organizational designs, with an emphasis on cross-functional teams and lateral relations.

How can work processes be reengineered?

- A work process is a related group of tasks that together create value for a customer.
- Business process engineering is the systematic and complete analysis of work processes and the design of new and better ones.
- In reengineering the workflows of an organization are diagrammed to identify how work moves from one point to another throughout a system.
- In process value analysis all elements of a process and its workflows are examined to identify their exact contributions to key performance results.

KEY TERMS

Adaptive organization (p. 285)

Continuous-process production (p. 289)

Differentiation (p. 291)

Integration (p. 292)

Intensive technology (p. 289)

Intrapreneurship (p. 290)

Learning organization (p. 286)

Long-linked technology (p. 289)

Mass production (p. 289)

Mechanistic design (p. 284)

Mediating technology (p. 289)

Organic design (p. 285)

Organizational design (p. 282)

Organizational life cycle (p. 289)

Process reengineering (p. 292)

Process value analysis (p. 294)

Simultaneous systems (p. 290)

Small-batch production (p. 288)

Subsystem (p. 291)

Technology (p. 288)

Technological imperative (p. 289)

Work process (p. 293)

Workflow (p. 293)

SELF-TEST 11

Take this test here or on-line much as you would in a normal classroom situation. It is a good way to check your basic comprehension of chapter material. Answers may be found at the end of the book.

MULTIPLE-CHOICE QUESTIONS:

1. The bureaucratic organization described by Max Weber is similar in nature to the _____ organization described by Burns and Stalker.
   (a) adaptive (b) mechanistic (c) organic (d) adhocracy

2. Teamwork, less emphasis on hierarchy, and wide spans of control are typical in _____.
   (a) mechanistic structures (b) bureaucracies (c) centralized structures
   (d) adaptive organizations

3. The production method characteristic of an oil refinery is a good example of what Woodward referred to as the _____ technology.
   (a) intensive (b) continuous-process (c) mass-production
   (d) small-batch

4. As organizations grow in size, they tend to become more _____ in design, although this is not always best for them.
   (a) mechanistic (b) organic (c) adaptive (d) flexible

5. A basic paradox in subsystem design is that as differentiation increases the need for _____ also increases, but it is harder to accomplish.
   (a) cost efficiency (b) innovation (c) integration (d) transformation

6. A(n) _____ organizational design works best in _____ environments.
   (a) flexible, stable (b) organic, uncertain
   (c) mechanistic, dynamic (d) adaptive, certain

7. The important contingency factors in organizational design include _____.
   (a) organizational strategy (b) organizational size and life cycle
   (c) human resources of the organization (d) all of these

8. When the members of a marketing department pursue sales volume objectives and those in manufacturing pursue cost efficiency objectives, this is an example of _____.
   (a) simultaneous systems (b) subsystems differentiation
   (c) subsystems integration (d) small batch production

9. A work process is defined as a related group of tasks that together create a result of value for _____.
   (a) shareholders (b) customers (c) workers (d) society

10. The first step in process value analysis is to _____.
    (a) look for ways to eliminate unnecessary tasks
    (b) map or diagram the workflows (c) identify core processes
    (d) look for efficiencies in transferring work among people and departments

TRUE-FALSE QUESTIONS:

11. A key trend in organizations today is the emphasis on horizontal integration and teamwork.   T   F

12. Organizations should never use simultaneous structures involving both mechanistic and organic designs.   T   F

13. A small machine shop making racing engines for cars operates with what Woodward would call a small-batch technology.   T   F

14. In organizational design, a basic principle is that strategy should always follow and support structure.   T   F

15. In complex organizations, subunit differences in structure and time orientation may cause integration problems.   T   F

16. The use of teams and task forces is achieving integration by emphasizing vertical aspects of organizational design.   T   F

17. Once a new organization gets an effective structure, it should use this structure through all stages of its life cycle.   T   F

18. Short-term horizons for a manufacturing unit and long-term horizons for an R&D unit illustrate differentiation among subsystems.   T   F

19. Business process reengineering focuses on customers and improved ways of doing things.   T   F

20. The process reengineering approach is not a good fit with current organizational interests in teamwork.   T   F

SHORT-RESPONSE QUESTIONS:

21. "Organizational design should always be addressed in contingency fashion." Explain this statement.

22. What difference does environment make in organizational design?

23. Describe the relationship between differentiation and integration as issues in subsystems design.

24. If you were a reengineering consultant, how would you describe the steps in a typical approach to process value analysis?

APPLICATION QUESTION:

25. Two business women, former college roommates, are discussing their jobs and careers over lunch. You overhear one saying to the other: "I work for a large corporation. It is bureaucratic and very authority driven. However, I have to say that it is also very successful. I like working there." Her friend commented somewhat differently. She said: "My, I wouldn't like working there at all. In my organization things are very flexible and the structures are loose. We have a lot of freedom and the focus on operations is much more horizontal than vertical. And, we too are very successful." After listening to the conversation and using insights from management theory, how can these two very different "success stories" be explained?

CAREER readiness ACTIVITIES

Recommended learning activities from the end-of-text Career Readiness Workbook for this chapter include:

Career Advancement Portfolio
- Individual writing and group presentation assignments based on any of the following activities.

Case for Critical Thinking
- PricewaterhouseCoopers—Changing Economy, Changing Mission, Changing Design

Integrative Learning Activities
- Research Project 4—Corporate Social Responsibilities
- Integrative Case—Outback Steakhouse, Inc.

Exercises in Teamwork
- Defining Quality (#3)
- What Would the Classics Say? (#5)
- The Best Job Design (#23)

Self Assessments
- Organizational Culture Preferences (#2)
- Organizational Design Preferences (#12)
- Two-Factor Profile (#17)

The *Fast Company* Collection On-Line
- Robert Reich, "The Company of the Future"

ELECTRONIC RESOURCES

@ GET CONNECTED! Don't forget to take full advantage of the on-line support for *Management 7/e.*
- Chapter 11 On-line Study Guide
- Chapter 11 Self-test Answers
- Chapter 11 E-Resource Center

12

Human resource management

Planning ahead

GETTING CONNECTED

WetFeet.Com—*Make People Your Top Priority*

Isn't it time to get your feet wet? Visit WetFeet.Com and find lots of information on careers, career readiness, and even potential employers.

The firm was founded by Gary Alpert and Steve Pollock when they were MBA students at Stanford University. Why? They thought there should be a better way for college students and other job seekers to research potential employers and find the best jobs for themselves. The result is a leading career information web site—one that has won consumer awards for its architecture.

Hit the careers link and you'll have access to sound advice on setting up a job search. There's expert advice available on creating a resumé, preparing for job interviews, and finding internships. Browse the site for further information on compensation packages; learn how to negotiate for salary and perks. Need to know more about diversity issues, sexual harassment, and more? Just read the latest reports or join a discussion group on the topic.

Wet Feet's extensive resources help you get to know a potential employer at the right time—before, not after, accepting a job. Go to the companies link and you can access their research on hundreds of firms, culled from public information and also from in-depth interviews with company recruiting staff and people working for the company.

If you're interested in management consulting, for example, visit the information site on the innovative Monitor Company; heading into financial services, check out Vanguard; interested in telecommunications, look up Nextel; going toward information systems, find out more on RedHat Software and the linux movement; want retailing, see what reports say about the Limited.

They're all there, along with an ever-expanding list of many more possible employers. You just have to look for them.

Part of WetFeet's business strategy is use of strategic alliances. One recent move was to join with WorkExchange Global Network, the largest global exchange that matches people with projects. It offers an efficient way for employers to source and recruit professional talent in real time for project-specific work. Craig Norris, CEO of WorkExchange, says: "Together, WetFeet.Com and WorkExchange can power effective recruiting in the tightest labor market in history."[1]

@ Get Connected!

WetFeet.Com offers a great place to explore different career fields and plan a job search. Take a look; follow the links; use the resources at WetFeet.Com to prepare an initial job search strategy for yourself. If you're not ready for full-time employment, turn it into an internship search. Get connected!

Today, perhaps more than ever before, the pressures of global competition and social change are influencing not just the organizations in which we work, but the very nature of employment itself. Almost a decade ago, *Fortune* magazine hailed the onset of a human resources "revolution."[2] Well, the revolution continues in full swing and its developments are affecting organizations of all types and sizes. The watchwords and buzzwords of changing times are all around—reengineering, rightsizing, digitizing, outsourcing, networking, empowering, and the like. You should be reading and thinking seriously about them. They have important implications for those of us who seek satisfying and successful careers in the new economy. In his book, *The Future of Success*, Robert Reich calls this "the age of the terrific deal" and describes it as follows:[3]

> *Combine the Internet, wireless satellites, and fiber optics, great leaps in computing power . . . a quantum expansion of broadband connection . . . a map of the human genome and tools to select and combine genes and even molecules—and you've got a giant, real-time, global bazaar of almost infinite choice and possibility.*

Get Connected!

Lots of organizations post job vacancies on-line; see Starbucks, for example. Stay informed about opportunities. Check out web sites for employers of interest to you.

The choices and possibilities in the new economy are already bringing about fundamental changes in the employer-employee relationship. Reich, for example, points to a shift away from a system in which people work loyally as traditional "employees" for "employers" who provide them career-long job and employment security. He sees the shift toward a system where we become sellers of our services (talents) to those buyers (employers) who are willing to pay for them. Those who do "buy" are looking for the very best people, whose capabilities and motivations match the demands of high-performance organizations. At Cisco Systems, CEO John Chambers says: "We realized early on that a world-class engineer with 5 peers can outproduce 200 regular engineers. . . . So your success is dependent on your ability to attract the very best talent and then get out of the way and empower them."[4]

All of this, of course, is changing the terms of your future career. "Create a brand called 'You,'" "Build a portfolio of skills," "Protect your mobility," "Take charge of your destiny," "Add value to your organization," advise the modern career gurus.[5] That advice is on target. But let's turn to the really tough question: "Are you ready?" Test yourself by asking and answering these *career readiness questions*: Who am I? What do I want? What have I done? What do I know? What can I do? Why should someone hire me?

DIVERSITY AND THE PRIMACY OF PEOPLE

We know that organizations are changing rapidly.[6] Structures are moving from the vertical to the more horizontal; teams and teamwork are increasingly essential to strategic advantage; working across functions, in networks, in virtual links, and in real time are part and parcel of today's high-performance work settings. Developments in information technology are making communication increasingly intense while information itself becomes more rich, abundant, and timely than ever before. Everywhere, people are expected to work with emphasis on serving customers and performing core processes as needed, in the best ways, and with freedom to make the necessary choices while doing so. But what also stands out in this new workplace with all of its technological advantages and structural changes is one undeniable fact. People still drive the system.

WHY PEOPLE MAKE THE DIFFERENCE

Human resource development has to be a top priority in any organization with high performance aspirations. Testimonials like these say it all: "*People are our most important asset*"; "It's *people* who make the difference"; "It's the *people* who work for us who . . . determine whether our company thrives or languishes."[7] Found on web sites, in annual reports, and in executive speeches, they communicate a very specific understanding. Even with the guidance of the best strategies and supported by the best designs, an organization must be well staffed with capable and committed people if it is to fully achieve its objectives.

There is ample research available to support this viewpoint. In an *Academy of Management Executive* article entitled "Putting People First for Organizational Success," Jeffrey Pfeffer and John F. Veiga state: "There is a substantial and rapidly expanding body of evidence . . . that speaks to the strong connection between how firms manage their people and the economic results achieved."[8] They forcefully argue that organizations perform better when they treat their members better. The management practices associated with successful organizations are employment security, decentralization, use of teams, good compensation, extensive training, and information sharing. However, Pfeffer also points out that too many organizations fail to operate in this manner, and calls them "toxic workplaces" that treat their employees poorly.[9]

Additional backup for the primacy of people is offered by James Baron and David Kreps in their book, *Strategic Human Resources: Frameworks for General Managers*.[10] Stating that "human resources are key to organizational success or failure," they summarize empirical research showing a positive relationship between human resource policies and organizational performance.[11] A study of 170 firms in the high-technology sector shows that the founders' initial decisions on human resource policies and practices had long-term impact on company performance. Those startups whose founders showed strong and early commitments to a positive human resource philosophy were able to operate in the future with fewer managers and with greater reliance on self-management by their employees.

A competitive marketplace places a primacy on being able to hire and retain talented people who have the abilities, knowledge, and ideas to match the demands of a challenging 21st-century environment. No one's talents can be wasted. Consider the strategic leadership implications of these comments made by Jeffrey Pfeffer in his book, *The Human Equation: Building Profits by Putting People First*.[12]

> *The key to managing people in ways that lead to profit, productivity, innovation, and real organizational learning ultimately lies in how you think about your organization and its people. . . . When you look at your people, do you see costs to be reduced? . . . Or, when you look at your people do you see intelligent, motivated, trustworthy individuals—the most critical and valuable strategic assets your organization can have?*

REALITY ✓
Check 12.1

Graduating Students' Expectations for Work A WetFeet.Com study of some 1600 undergraduate and graduate students shows men expecting almost $7,000 per year more in salary than women. Take the on-line "Reality Check" to learn more about gender differences in work expectations.

The popular musician Stevie Wonder, blind since birth, has joined with SAP America, an enterprise-integration software company, to offer the Stevie Wonder Vision Awards. These will go to companies that promote employment opportunities for the visually impaired.

THE DIVERSITY ADVANTAGE

Throughout this book diversity has been linked with competitive advantage. It brings to problem-solving and strategy formulation an array of talents, perspectives, experiences, and world views that broaden any organization's repertoire of skills and capabilities.

That's one side of the diversity story—finding the best talent available. The other side of the story is tapping it—finding ways to allow diversity to work its advantages to help create high-performing organizations.[13] To do this, the diversity advantage not only must be recognized, it must be fully unlocked. Diversity consultant and author R. Roosevelt Thomas puts the challenge this way: "Managers must find ways to get the highest level of contribution from their workers. And they will not be able to do that unless they are aware of the many ways that their understanding of diversity relates to how well, or how poorly, people contribute." Thomas goes further to identify what he calls the *diversity rationale* that must drive organizations today:

> *To thrive in an increasingly unfriendly marketplace, companies must make it a priority to create the kind of environment that will attract the best new talent and will make it possible for employees to make their fullest contribution.*[14]

Respect for talent in all of its forms is a major theme in the book *Proversity: Getting Past Face Value and Finding the Soul of People*, by author and consultant Lawrence Otis Graham.[15] He suggests that managers committed to building high-performance work environments take a simple test. The question is: Which of the following qualities would you look for in anyone who works for you—work ethic, ambition and energy, knowledge, creativity, motivation, sincerity, outlook, collegiality and collaborativeness, curiosity, judgment and maturity, and integrity? In answering, you most likely selected all of these qualities; at least you should have. The next question to consider is: "Where can you find people with these workplace qualities?" The answer is "everywhere." That's the point made by Graham and by others who advise people and organizations on diversity issues in human resource management.[16]

Job-relevant talent is not restricted because of anyone's race, gender, religion, marital or parental status, sexual orientation, ethnicity, or other diversity characteristics. If one lets these characteristics interfere with finding, hiring, and developing the best job talents available, the loss will be someone else's gain. The best employers and the best managers know that. They know that to succeed in building high-performing organizations with sustainable competitive advantage in today's challenging times, they must place a primacy on people. This includes all people with the talent and desire to do good work.

HUMAN RESOURCE MANAGEMENT

○ **HRM** is the process of attracting, developing, and maintaining a quality workforce.

The process of **human resource management (HRM)** involves attracting, developing, and maintaining a talented and energetic workforce to support organizational mission, objectives, and strategies. In order for strategies to be well implemented, workers with relevant skills and enthusiasm are needed. The task of human resource management is to make them avail-

Pick up any copy of *Working Mother* magazine or browse the on-line version. You can learn about the 100 Best Companies for Working Mothers and stay up to date on opportunities for female entrepreneurship. You'll also find informative articles dealing with the challenges and opportunities faced by working mothers. One featured Maria Hinojosa, a correspondent for CNN and mother of a son and daughter. As a professional, she brings to her audience a perspective on multiculturalism and a penchant for putting inner-city issues in the public eye. She is proud of her role as a mother as well as her professional accomplishments. Hinojosa cites a Spanish saying: *Los niños traen muchos regalos*—"Children bring many gifts."[17]

able. A marketing manager at Ideo, a Palo-Alto-based industrial design firm, says, for example: "If you hire the right people . . . if you've got the right fit . . . then everything will take care of itself."[18]

LAWS AGAINST EMPLOYMENT DISCRIMINATION

Discrimination in employment occurs when someone is denied a job or a job assignment for reasons that are not job relevant. It is against federal law in the United States to discriminate in employment. A sample of major U.S. laws prohibiting job discrimination is provided in *Figure 12.1.*

An important cornerstone of legal protection for employee rights to fair treatment is found in *Title VII of the Civil Rights Act of 1964*, as amended by the *Equal Employment Opportunity Act of 1972* and the *Civil Rights Act (EEOA) of 1991*. These Acts provide for **equal employment opportunity (EEO)**—the right to employment without regard to race, color, national origin, religion, gender, age, or physical and mental ability. The intent is to ensure all citizens have a right to gain and keep employment based only on their ability to do the job and their performance once on the job. EEO is federally enforced by the Equal Employment Opportunity Commission (EEOC), which has the power to file civil lawsuits against organizations that do not provide timely resolution of any discrimination charges lodged against them. These laws generally apply to all public and private organizations employing 15 or more people.

Under Title VII, organizations are also expected to show **affirmative action** in giving preference in hiring and promotion to women and minorities, including veterans, the aged, and the disabled. This is to ensure that women and minorities are represented in the workforce in proportion to their actual availability in the area labor market.[19] *Affirmative Action Plans* may also be adopted by or required of organizations to show that they are correcting previous patterns of discriminatory activity and/or are actively preventing its future occurrence. The pros and cons of affirmative action are debated at both the federal and state levels, and controversies sometimes make the news. Criticisms tend to focus on the use of group membership (e.g., female or minority) instead of individual performance in employment decisions.[20] The issues raised include the potential for members of majority populations to claim *reverse discrimination*. White males, for

○ **Discrimination** occurs when someone is denied a job or a job assignment for reasons not job relevant.

○ **Equal employment opportunity** is the right to employment and advancement without regard to race, sex, religion, color, or national origin.

○ **Affirmative action** is an effort to give preference in employment to women and minority group members.

Equal Pay Act of 1963	Requires equal pay for men and women performing equal work in an organization.
Title VII of the Civil Rights Act of 1964 (as amended)	Prohibits discrimination in employment based on race, color, religion, sex, or national origin.
Age Discrimination in Employment Act of 1967	Prohibits discrimination against persons over 40; restricts mandatory retirement.
Occupational Health and Safety Act of 1970	Establishes mandatory health and safety standards in workplaces.
Pregnancy Discrimination Act of 1978	Prohibits employment discrimination against pregnant workers.
Americans With Disabilities Act of 1990	Prohibits discrimination against a qualified individual on the basis of disability.
Civil Rights Act of 1991	Reaffirms Title VII of the 1964 Civil Rights Act; reinstates burden of proof by employer, and allows for punitive and compensatory damages.
Family and Medical Leave Act of 1993	Allows employees up to 12 weeks of unpaid leave with job guarantees for childbirth, adoption, or family illness.

Figure 12.1   A sample of U.S. laws influencing human resource management.

example, may claim that preferential treatment given to minorities in a particular situation interferes with their individual rights.

As a general rule EEO legal protections do not restrict an employer's right to establish **bona fide occupational qualifications**. These are criteria for employment that can be clearly justified as being related to a person's capacity to perform a job. The use of bona fide occupational qualifications based on race and color is not allowed under any circumstances; those based on sex, religion, and age are very difficult to support. Years ago, for example, airlines tried to use customer preferences to justify the hiring of only female flight attendants. It didn't work; today men and women serve in this capacity.[21]

In addition to race and gender, which get a lot of attention in the news, there are other areas of legal protection against discrimination that deserve a manager's concern. Listed below are four examples and brief summaries of their supporting laws. Complexities in the laws would require further research in the context of any possible case to which they might be applied.

○ **Bona fide occupational qualifications** are EEO exceptions justified by individual capacity to perform a job.

U.S. laws protecting against job discrimination

→ • *Disabilities:* The *Americans With Disabilities Act of 1990* prevents discrimination against people with disabilities. The law forces employers to focus on abilities and what a person can do. Increasingly, persons with disabilities are gaining in employment opportunities.

• *Age:* The *Age Discrimination in Employment Act of 1967 as amended in 1978 and 1986* protects workers against mandatory retirement ages. Age discrimination occurs when a qualified individual is adversely affected by a job action that replaces him or her with a younger worker.

• *Pregnancy:* The *Pregnancy Discrimination Act of 1978* protects female workers from discrimination because of pregnancy. A pregnant em-

MANAGER'S NOTEPAD 12.1

Illegal (and legal) questions when interviewing a job candidate

- National Origin—Are you a U.S. citizen? [*Legal:* Are you authorized to work in the United States?]
- Family—Are you married? [*Legal:* Would you be willing to relocate?]
- Family—Do you plan to have children? [*Legal:* Are you willing to travel as needed?]
- Family—Who lives with you? [*Legal:* This job requires occasional overtime, is that okay?]
- Age—How old are you? [*Legal:* Are you over 18?]
- Arrest Record—Have you ever been arrested? [*Legal:* Have you ever been convicted of (crime relevant to job performance)?]
- Military Service—Were you honorably discharged from the military? [*Legal*: What type of training did you receive in the military?]
- Disability—Do you have any disabilities? [*Legal:* Can you perform (described in detail) as an essential part of the job?]

ployee is protected against termination or adverse job action because of the pregnancy, and is entitled to reasonable time off work.

- *Family matters:* The *Family and Medical Leave Act of 1993* protects workers who take unpaid leaves for family matters from losing their jobs or employment status. Workers are allowed up to 12 weeks' leave for childbirth, adoption, personal illness, or illness of a family member.

CURRENT LEGAL ISSUES IN HRM

Human resource management must be accomplished within the framework of government regulations and laws. All managers are expected to act within the law and follow equal opportunity principles. Failure to do so is not only unjustified in a free society, it can also be a very expensive mistake resulting in fines and penalties. The American legal and regulatory environment covers human resource management activities related to pay, employment rights, occupational health and safety, retirement, privacy, vocational rehabilitation, and related areas. It is also constantly changing as old laws are modified and new ones are added. As a reminder of the legal context of human resource management, for example, *Manager's Notepad 12.1* identifies questions that under U.S. laws are considered illegal for an interviewer to ask you during a job interview.[22]

Legal issues in human resource management are continually before the courts. The more prominent among them are frequently in the news. A committed manager or human resource professional would want to stay informed on the following and other management issues of current

○ **Sexual harassment** occurs as behavior of a sexual nature that affects a person's employment situation.

legal and ethical consequence.[23] **Sexual harassment** occurs when a person experiences conduct or language of a sexual nature that affects their employment situation. According to the EEOC, sexual harassment is behavior that creates a hostile work environment, interferes with their ability to do a job, or interferes with their promotion potential. As discussed in Chapter 7 on planning, organizations should have clear sexual harassment policies in place along with the procedures for implementing them.

The *Equal Pay Act of 1963* provides that men and women in the same organization should be paid equally for doing equal work in terms of required skills, responsibilities, and working conditions. But a lingering issue involving gender disparities in pay involves **comparable worth**, the notion that persons performing jobs of similar importance should be paid at comparable levels. Why should a long-distance truck driver, for example, be paid more than an elementary teacher in a public school? Does it make any difference that the former is a traditionally male occupation and the latter a traditionally female occupation? Advocates of comparable worth argue that such historical disparities are due to gender bias. They would like to have the issue legally resolved.

○ **Comparable worth** holds that persons performing jobs of similar importance should be paid at comparable levels.

○ **Independent contractors** are hired on temporary contracts and are not part of the organization's official workforce.

The legal status and employee entitlements of *part-time workers* and **independent contractors** are also being debated. In today's era of downsizing, outsourcing, and projects, more and more persons are hired as temporary workers who work under contract to an organization and do not become part of its official workforce. They work only "as needed." The problem occurs when they are engaged regularly by the same organization and become what many now call *permatemps*. Even though regularly employed by one organization, they work without benefits such as health insurance and pension eligibilities. If they were legally considered employees, these independent contractors would be eligible for benefits, and the implications for their employers would be costly. A number of legal cases are now before the courts seeking resolution of this issue.

Another area where legal influences on human resource management are often in the news is *labor–management relations*. Labor contracts between large unions, such as the United Auto Workers, and large companies, such as Ford and General Motors, are often controversial. We also read and hear about labor unions complaining about unfair practices by employers of their members, and about employers complaining about unfair practices by the unions to which their employees belong. These issues and their legal foundations are discussed later in this chapter in a special section on labor–management relations.

HUMAN RESOURCE MANAGEMENT PROCESS

The human resource management process involves attracting, developing, and maintaining a quality workforce. The first responsibility of *attracting a quality workforce* includes human resource planning, recruitment, and selection. The second responsibility of *developing a quality workforce* includes employee orientation, training and development, and career planning and development. The third responsibility of *maintaining a quality workforce* includes management of employee retention and turnover, performance appraisal, and compensation and benefits.

Human resource specialists often assist line managers in fulfilling these three responsibilities. A human resource department appears on many organization charts and is often headed by a senior executive

Get Connected!

There are student chapters of SHRM on many college campuses. Should you consider joining?

reporting directly to the chief executive officer. It is also increasingly common to find organizations outsourcing various technical aspects of the human resource management process. There are a growing number of career opportunities with consulting firms that provide such specialized services as recruiting, compensation planning, outplacement, and the like. In a dynamic environment complicated by legal issues, labor shortages, economic turmoil, changing corporate strategies, new organization and job designs, high technology, and changing personal values and expectations, human resource specialists become ever-more important. Many belong to the Society for Human Resource Management (SHRM), a professional organization dedicated to keeping its membership up-to-date in all aspects of HRM and its complex legal environment.

STRATEGIC HUMAN RESOURCE MANAGEMENT

Any organization should at all times have the right people available to do the work required to achieve and sustain competitive advantage. **Strategic human resource management** applies the HRM process to ensure the effective accomplishment of organizational mission.[24] Strategic HRM mobilizes human resources to implement strategies and sustain competitive advantage. This requires a top-level commitment to **human resource planning**, a process of analyzing staffing needs and planning how to satisfy these needs in a way that best serves organizational mission, objectives, and strategies.[25]

The major elements in strategic human resource planning are shown in *Figure 12.2.* The process begins with a review of organizational mission, objectives, and strategies. This establishes a frame of reference for forecasting human resource needs and labor supplies, both within and outside the organization. Ultimately, the planning process should help managers identify staffing requirements, assess the existing

○ **Strategic HRM** involves attracting, developing, and maintaining a quality workforce to implement organizational strategies.

○ **Human resource planning** analyzes staffing needs and identifies actions to fill those needs.

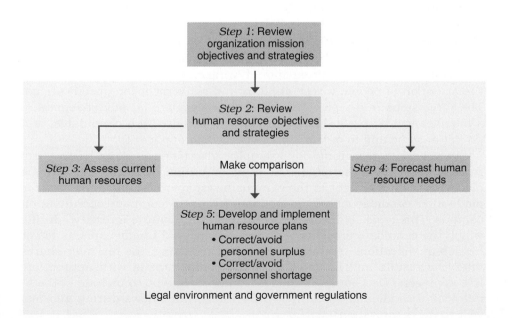

Figure 12.2 Steps in strategic human resource planning.

workforce, and determine what additions and/or replacements are required to meet future needs. It is no secret, for example, that high-tech workers are in great demand today and many organizations are experiencing or are anticipating difficulty in meeting their staffing needs. At GE Medical Systems, a multigenerational staffing plan is used to help resolve the problem. For every new product plan there is a human resource plan associated with it—one that covers all generations of the product's anticipated life.[26]

○ **Job analysis** studies job requirements and facets that can influence performance.

○ A **job description** details the duties and responsibilities of a job holder.

○ A **job specification** lists the qualifications required of a job holder.

To plan successfully to meet strategic human resource requirements managers must not only understand the mission and strategies, they must also understand the jobs that need to be done. The foundations for human resource planning are set by **job analysis**—the orderly study of job facts to determine just what is done, when, where, how, why, and by whom in existing or potential new jobs.[27] The job analysis provides useful information that can then be used to write and/or update **job descriptions**. These are written statements of job duties and responsibilities. The information in a job analysis can also be used to create **job specifications**. These are lists of the qualifications—such as education, prior experience, and skill requirements—needed by any person hired for or placed in a given job.

ATTRACTING A QUALITY WORKFORCE

With a human resource plan prepared, the process of attracting a quality workforce begins. An advertisement once run by the Motorola Corporation identified the goal this way: "Productivity is learning how to hire the person who is *right* for the job." To attract the right people to its workforce, an organization must first know exactly what it is looking for—it must have a clear understanding of the jobs to be done and the talents required to do them well. Then it must have the systems in place to excel at employee recruitment and selection.

THE RECRUITING PROCESS

○ **Recruitment** is a set of activities designed to attract a qualified pool of job applicants.

Recruitment is a set of activities designed to attract a *qualified* pool of job applicants to an organization. Emphasis on the word "qualified" is important. Effective recruiting should bring employment opportunities to the attention of people whose abilities and skills meet job specifications. The three steps in a typical recruitment process are (1) advertisement of a job vacancy, (2) preliminary contact with potential job candidates, and (3) initial screening to create a pool of qualified applicants.

In collegiate recruiting, for example, advertising is done by the firm posting short job descriptions in print or on-line through the campus placement center and/or in the campus newspaper. Preliminary contact is made after candidates register for interviews with company recruiters on campus. This typically involves a short 20- to 30-minute interview, during which the candidate presents a written resume and briefly explains his or her job qualifications. As part of the initial screening, the recruiter shares interview results and resumes from the campus visits with appropriate line managers. Decisions will then be made about who to include in the final pool of candidates to be invited for further interviews during a formal visit to the organization.

External and Internal Recruitment

The collegiate recruiting example is one of *external recruitment* in which job candidates are sought from outside the hiring organization. Web sites like HotJobs.com and America's Job Bank, newspapers, employment agencies, colleges, technical training centers, personal contacts, walk-ins, employee referrals, and even persons in competing organizations are all sources of external recruits. Competition is especially tough in the very tight labor markets characteristic of the new economy. When Nokia, the Finnish mobile-phone maker, needed high-tech talent it went global with its recruiting process. Nokia posted all job openings on a web site and received thousands of resumes from all over the world. In just two years, the percentage of non-Finns in the company workforce rose some 10 percent. The head of Nokia's recruiting strategy says: "There are no geographical boundaries anymore."[28]

Internal recruitment seeks applicants from inside the organization. Most organizations have a procedure for announcing vacancies through newsletters, electronic bulletin boards, and the like. They also rely on managers to recommend subordinates as candidates for advancement. Internal recruitment creates opportunities for long-term career paths. Consider the story of Robert Goizueta. As CEO of Coca-Cola when he died, Goizueta owned over $1 billion of the company's stock. He made his way to the top over a 43-year career in the firm, an example of how loyalty and hard work can pay off.[29]

Both recruitment strategies offer potential advantages and disadvantages. External recruiting brings in outsiders with fresh perspectives. It also provides access to specialized expertise or work experience not otherwise available from insiders. Internal recruitment is usually less expensive. It also deals with persons whose performance records are well established. A history of serious internal recruitment can also be encouraging to employees. It builds loyalty and motivation, showing that one can advance in the organization by working hard and achieving high performance at each point of responsibility.

Of the many thousands of resumés received each year by Southwest Airlines, only about 3.5 percent of applicants are hired. The selection process is rigorous. Even humor counts; it goes with the corporate culture. An interviewee may be asked to "tell a joke." It's a serious requirement—you can't work for the company if you can't pass the levity test.

Realistic Job Previews

There is another important recruitment issue that must be considered—honesty and full information. In what may be called *traditional recruitment*, the emphasis is on selling the organization to job applicants. In this case, only the most positive features of the job and organization are communicated to potential candidates. Bias may even be introduced as these features are exaggerated while negative features are concealed. This form of recruitment is designed to attract as many candidates as possible. The problem is that it may create unrealistic expectations that result in costly turnover when new hires leave prematurely. The individual suffers a career disruption; the employer suffers lost productivity and the additional recruiting costs of finding another candidate.

The alternative is to provide **realistic job previews** that give the candidate *all* pertinent information about the job and organization without distortion and *before* the job is accepted.[30] Instead of "selling" only positive features of a job, this approach tries to be realistic and balanced in the information provided. It tries to be fair in depicting actual job and organizational features, both favorable and unfavorable. The interviewer providing a realistic job preview to a job candidate, for example, might be overheard to use phrases such as these: "Of course,

○ **Realistic job previews** provide job candidates with all pertinent information about a job organization.

there are some downsides. . . ." "Things don't always go the way we hope. . . ." "Something that you will want to be prepared for is. . . ." "We have found that some new hires had difficulty with. . . ."

When engaged in this type of conversation about the job and organization, the candidate gets a more complete and balanced view of the future employment possibility. This helps to establish more "realistic" job expectations when starting work as a new employee. With expectations more realistic, the individual is better prepared to handle the "ups and downs" of a new job. A better perspective on the employment relationship, higher levels of early job satisfaction, and less inclination to prematurely quit are among the benefits of this interview approach.

MAKING SELECTION DECISIONS

○ **Selection** is choosing from a pool of the best-qualified job applicants.

The process of **selection** involves choosing from a pool of applicants the person or persons who offer the greatest performance potential. Steps in a typical selection process are shown in *Figure 12.3*. They are (1) completion of a formal application form, (2) interviewing, (3) testing, (4) reference checks, (5) physical examination, and (6) final analysis and decision to hire or reject. As with all aspects of the human resource management process the best employers exercise extreme care in making selection decisions. At Federal Express, for example, psychological testing is used to identify what the firm calls "risk taking and courage of conviction."[31]

○ **Reliability** means a selection device measures consistently over repeated uses.

○ **Validity** means a selection device has a demonstrated link with future job performance.

In using any selection devices, including such testing, it is important to know that they meet the important criteria of reliability and validity. **Reliability** means that the device is consistent in measurement; it returns the same results time after time. **Validity** means that there is a demonstrable relationship between a person's score or rating on a selection device and their eventual job performance. In simple terms, validity means that a good score really does predict good performance. Many college students, for example, question the validity of employers using their grades as predictors of future job performance when screening job applicants.

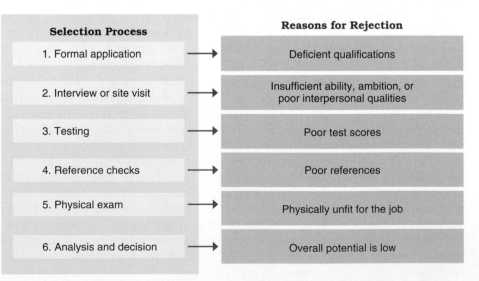

Selection Process	Reasons for Rejection
1. Formal application	Deficient qualifications
2. Interview or site visit	Insufficient ability, ambition, or poor interpersonal qualities
3. Testing	Poor test scores
4. Reference checks	Poor references
5. Physical exam	Physically unfit for the job
6. Analysis and decision	Overall potential is low

Figure 12.3 Steps in the selection process: the case of a rejected job applicant.

MANAGER'S NOTEPAD 12.2

How to conduct job interviews

- *Plan ahead:* Review the job specifications and job description as well as the candidate's application; allow sufficient time for a complete interview.
- *Create a good interview climate:* Allow sufficient time; choose a quiet place; be friendly and show interest; give the candidate your full attention.
- *Conduct a goal-oriented interview:* Know what information you need and get it; look for creativity, independence, and a high energy level.
- *Avoid questions that may imply discrimination:* Focus all questioning on the job applied for and the candidate's true qualifications for it.
- *Answer the questions asked of you, and others that may not be asked:* Do your part to create a realistic job preview.
- *Take notes:* Document details and impressions for later deliberation and decision making.

Are they just making excuses for not using their time well in college, or do they have a legitimate point?

Application Forms

The application form declares the individual to be a formal candidate for a job. It documents the applicant's personal history and qualifications. The personal resume is often included with the job application. This important document should accurately summarize an applicant's special qualifications. As a job applicant, you should exercise great care in preparing your resume for job searches. See the Career Advancement Portfolio® section in the end-of-text Career Readiness Workbook for advice on resume preparation. As a recruiter, you should also learn how to screen applications and resumes for insights that can help you make good selection decisions. Importantly, the application should request only information that is directly relevant to the job and the applicant's potential job success.

Interviews

Interviews are extremely important in the selection process because of the information exchange they allow.[32] It is a time when both the job applicant and potential employer can learn a lot about one another. However, interviews are also recognized as potential stumbling blocks in the selection process. Sometimes interviewers ask the wrong things, sometimes they talk too much, sometimes the wrong people do the interviewing. Other times, the interviewer falls prey to personal biases and makes a judgment that fails to fully consider the applicant's capabilities. Among the recommendations for how to interview a job applicant are those shown in *Manager's Notepad 12.2.*

www.jnj.com

Johnson & Johnson's ethics credo includes the importance of families: "We must be mindful of ways to help our employees fulfill their family responsibilities." J&J's managers have training in diversity and the needs of nontraditional families. The company offers family care leave, on-site day care, elder-care referral, and other services.

Employment Tests

Testing is often used in the screening of job applicants. Some common employment tests are designed to identify intelligence, aptitudes, personality, and interests; others ask the applicant to indicate how he or she would respond to a series of job-relevant situations. Whenever tests are used and in whatever forms, however, the goal should be to gather information that will help predict the applicant's eventual performance success. Like any selection device, an employment test should meet the criteria of *reliability* and *validity* described earlier. Any employment test, furthermore, should be legally defensible on the grounds that it actually measures an ability required to perform the job.

New developments in testing extend the process into actual demonstrations of job-relevant skills and personal characteristics. An **assessment center** evaluates a person's potential by observing his or her performance in experiential activities designed to simulate daily work. A related approach is *work sampling*, which asks applicants to work on actual job tasks while being graded by observers on their performance. When Mercedes opened its new plant in Alabama, it had over 45,000 applicants for 1,500 jobs. To help make its selection decisions the firm set up job-specific exercises to determine who had the best of the required skills and attitudes. One was a tire-changing test, with color-coded bolts and a set of instructions. As Charlene Paige took the test she went slow and carefully followed directions. Two men that went with her changed the tires really fast. She got the job because the firm wanted people who would follow directions and work for quality. Now Charlene has worked into the position of team leader in an assembly shop.[33]

CAREER CONNECTION

Human Resources

Saratoga Institute

What's a Worker Worth, Anyway?

Here's a human resource management question for you. Assume you run a service firm. It has $1 million in revenues and earns $500,000 in profits before taxes. Operating expenses total $200,000; payroll and benefits costs are an additional $300,000. The question is: *What is your return on human capital?*

This example is from the Saratoga Institute. The firm states its goal as helping "companies around the world leverage Human Capital Intelligence to attract, retain, manage, and develop their people, helping them maximize the value of their human assets." Part of Saratoga's strength is measuring human capital. The firm specializes in helping managers understand financial metrics and then leverage them to make better decisions in human resource management.

Did you analyze the figures? You should have arrived at a human capital return on investment of 1.67. That means per $1 of investment in payroll and benefits, the human resources of the firm returned $1.67 in value. Not bad.

To get the answer, deduct operating expenses plus payroll and benefits expenses from total revenue to get adjusted profit (result = $500,000). Then divide adjusted profit by payroll and benefits costs (result = 1.67).

QUESTION: Employers today are increasingly diligent in getting maximum return from investments in human capital. What value can you add to an employer of choice? Are you competitive in the marketplace for talent?

Reference and Background Checks

○ An **assessment center** examines how job candidates handle simulated work situations.

Reference checks are inquiries to previous employers, academic advisors, coworkers, and/or acquaintances regarding the qualifications, experience, and past work records of a job applicant. Although they may be biased if friends are prearranged "to say the right things if called," reference checks can be helpful in revealing important information not discovered elsewhere in the selection process. The Society for Human Resources Management, for example, estimates that 25 percent of job applications and resumes contain errors.[34] The references given by a job applicant can also add credibility to an application if they include a legitimate and even prestigious list of persons.

Physical Examinations

Many organizations ask job applicants to take a physical examination. This health check helps ensure that the person is physically capable of fulfilling job requirements. It may also be used as a basis for enrolling the applicant in health-related fringe benefits such as life, health, and disability insurance programs. A recent and controversial development in this area is the emerging use of drug testing. This has become part of preemployment health screening and a basis for continued employment at some organizations. At a minimum, care must be exercised that any required test is job relevant and does not discriminate in any way against the applicant.

Final Decisions to Hire or Reject

The best selection decisions are most likely to be those involving extensive consultation among the manager or team leader, potential coworkers, and human resource staff. Importantly, the emphasis in selection must always be comprehensive and focus on all aspects of the person's capacity to perform in a given job. After all, the selection decision poses major consequences for organizational performance and for the internal environment or work climate. Just as a "good fit" can produce long-term advantage, a "bad fit" can be the source of many and perhaps long-term problems. Sometimes the people who know this lesson best are those who run small businesses. Says one dairy store owner who knew the importance of customer service in retail sales, "If applicants have a good attitude, we can do the rest . . . but if they have a bad attitude to start with, everything we do seems to fail."[35]

DEVELOPING A QUALITY WORKFORCE

When people join an organization, they must "learn the ropes" and become familiar with "the way things are done." It is important that newcomers be helped to fit into the work environment in a way that furthers their development and performance potential. **Socialization** is the process of influencing the expectations, behavior, and attitudes of a new employee in a way considered desirable by the organization.[36] The intent of socialization in human resource management is to help achieve the best possible fit between the individual, the job, and the organization.

○ **Socialization** systematically changes the expectations, behavior, and attitudes of new employees.

EMPLOYEE ORIENTATION

Socialization of newcomers begins with **orientation**—a set of activities designed to familiarize new employees with their jobs, coworkers, and key aspects of the organization as a whole. This includes clarifying mission and culture, explaining operating objectives and job expectations, communicating policies and procedures, and identifying key personnel.

○ **Orientation** familiarizes new employees with jobs, coworkers, and organizational policies and services.

The first six months of employment are often crucial in determining how well someone is going to perform over the long run. It is a time when the original expectations are tested, and patterns are set for future relationships between an individual and employer. Unfortunately, orientation is sometimes neglected and newcomers are often left to fend for themselves. They may learn job and organizational routines on their own or through casual interactions with coworkers, and they may acquire job attitudes the same way.[37] The result is that otherwise well-intentioned and capable persons may learn inappropriate attitudes and/or behaviors. Good orientation, by contrast, enhances a person's understanding of the organization and adds purpose to his or her daily job activities. Increased performance, greater job satisfaction, and greater work commitment are the desired results.

At the Disney World Resort in Buena Vista, Florida, a large percentage of the workforce has direct customer service responsibilities. Each employee is carefully selected and trained to provide high-quality customer service as a "cast member." During orientation, newly hired employees are taught the corporate culture. They learn that everyone employed by the company, regardless of her or his specific job—be it entertainer, ticket seller, or groundskeeper—is there "to make the customer happy." The company's interviewers say that they place a premium on personality. "We can train for skills," says an HRM specialist. "We want people who are enthusiastic, who have pride in their work, who can take charge of a situation without supervision."[38]

Threats to Employee Retention

A survey of employers by the Society for Human Resource Management revealed that higher salaries offered by others was the biggest threat to employee retention. Take the on-line "Reality Check" to learn more about the factors that can make it difficult to retain talented workers.

TRAINING AND DEVELOPMENT

○ **Training** provides learning opportunities to acquire and improve job-related skills.

Training is a set of activities that provides the opportunity to acquire and improve job-related skills. This applies both to the initial training of an employee and to upgrading or improving someone's skills to meet changing job requirements. A major concern of American employers is the lack of educational preparation of some workers for jobs, often high-technology jobs, in the new workplace. These concerns even extend to the basic skills of reading, writing, and arithmetic, as well as to computer skills. Progressive organizations offer extensive training programs to ensure that their workers always have the skills and computer literacy needed to perform well.

On-the-Job Training

○ **Coaching** involves an experienced person offering performance advice to a less-experienced person.

On-the-job training takes place in the work setting while someone is doing a job. A common approach is job rotation that allows people to spend time working in different jobs and thus expand the range of their job capabilities. Another is **coaching**, in which an experienced person provides performance advice to someone else. One form of coaching is **mentoring**, in which early-career employees are formally assigned as protégés to senior persons. The mentoring relationship gives them regular access to advice on developing skills and getting a good start in their careers. An informal type of coaching involves **modeling**. This occurs when someone demonstrates through day-to-day personal behavior that which is expected of others. One way to learn managerial skills, for example, is to observe and practice the techniques displayed by good managers. Modeling is a very important influence on behavior in organizations. A good

○ **Mentoring** assigns early career employees as protégés to more senior ones.

○ **Modeling** demonstrates through personal behavior the job performance expected of others.

example is how the behaviors of senior managers help set the ethical culture and standards for other employees.

Off-the-Job Training

Off-the-job training is accomplished outside the work setting. It may be done within the organization at a separate training room or facility or at an off-site location. Examples of the latter include attendance at special training programs sponsored by universities, trade or professional associations, or consultants. The willingness of organizations to invest in training is a good indicator of their commitment to the people they hire. Intel, for example, allocates a percent of its annual payroll to spend on training through the firm's in-house university.[39]

An important form of off-the-job training involves **management development**, designed to improve a person's knowledge and skill in the fundamentals of management. For example, *beginning managers* often benefit from training that emphasizes delegating duties; *middle managers* may benefit from training to better understand multifunctional viewpoints; *top managers* may benefit from advanced management training to sharpen their decision-making and negotiating skills and to expand their awareness of corporate strategy and direction. At the Center for Creative Leadership, managers learn by participating in the Looking Glass simulation that models the pressures of daily work. The simulation is followed by extensive debriefings and discussion in which participants give feedback to one another. One participant commented, "You can look in the mirror but you don't see yourself. People have to say how you look."[40]

○ **Management development** is training to improve knowledge and skills in the management process.

PERFORMANCE MANAGEMENT SYSTEMS

Performance has to be measured. The rule holds whether you are talking about a hospital's contribution to the community, a business's quarterly financial results, a work team's project accomplishment, or an individual's job performance. With measurement comes the opportunity to not only document results but to also take steps toward their future improvement. Part of the human resource management responsibility is design and implementation of a successful **performance management system**. This is a system that ensures that performance standards and objectives are set, that performance is regularly assessed for accomplishments, and that actions are taken to improve performance potential in the future.

○ A **performance management system** sets standards, assesses results, and plans for performance improvements.

Purpose of Performance Appraisal

The process of formally assessing someone's work accomplishments and providing feedback is **performance appraisal**. It serves two basic purposes in the maintenance of a quality workforce: (1) evaluation, and (2) development. The *evaluation purpose* is intended to let people know where they stand relative to performance objectives and standards. The *development purpose* is intended to assist in their training and continued personal development.[41]

The evaluation purpose of performance appraisal focuses on past performance and measures results against standards. Performance is

○ **Performance appraisal** is the process of formally evaluating performance and providing feedback to a job holder.

documented for the record and to establish a basis for allocating rewards. The manager acts in a *judgmental role* in which he or she gives a direct evaluation of another person's accomplishments. The development purpose of performance appraisal, by contrast, focuses on future performance and the clarification of success standards. It is a way of discovering performance obstacles and identifying training and development opportunities. Here the manager acts in a *counseling role*, focusing on a subordinate's developmental needs.

Like employment tests, any performance appraisal method can fulfill these purposes only when the criteria of *reliability* and *validity* are met. To be reliable, the method should consistently yield the same result over time and/or for different raters; to be valid, it should be unbiased and measure only factors directly relevant to job performance. Both these criteria are especially important in today's complex legal environment. A manager who hires, fires, or promotes someone is increasingly called upon to defend such actions—sometimes in specific response to lawsuits alleging that the actions were discriminatory. At a minimum, written documentation of performance appraisals and a record of consistent past actions will be required to back up any contested evaluations.

Performance Appraisal Methods

○ A **graphic rating scale** uses a checklist of traits or characteristics to evaluate performance.

Organizations use a variety of performance appraisal methods. One of the simplest is a **graphic rating scale**, such as the example in *Figure 12.4*. Such scales offer the appraisers checklists of traits or characteristics thought to be related to high performance outcomes in a given job. A manager rates the individual on each trait using a numerical score. The primary appeal of graphic rating scales is that they are relatively quick and easy to complete. Their reliability and validity are questionable, however, because the categories and scores are subject to varying interpretations.

○ A **BARS** uses specific descriptions of actual behaviors to rate various levels of performance.

A more advanced approach is the **behaviorally anchored rating scale** (BARS), which offers an appraiser rating scales for actual behaviors that exemplify various levels of performance achievement in a job. Look at the case of a customer service representative illustrated in *Figure 12.5*. "Extremely poor" performance is clearly defined as rude or disrespectful treatment of a customer. Because performance assessments are anchored to specific descriptions of work behavior, a BARS is more reliable and valid than the graphic rating scale. The behavioral anchors can also be helpful in training people to master job skills of demonstrated performance importance. The city of Irving, Texas, used a BARS approach in redesigning its performance appraisal system. Many examples of different levels of job performance were written so that appraisers could just pick the ones most representative of city workers' job behaviors.[42]

○ The **critical-incident technique** keeps a log of someone's effective and ineffective job behaviors.

The **critical-incident technique** involves keeping a running log or inventory of effective and ineffective job behaviors. By creating a written record of positive and negative performance examples, this method documents success or failure patterns that can be specifically discussed with the individual. Using the case of the customer service representative again, a critical-incidents log might contain the following types of entries: *Positive example*—"Took extraordinary care of a customer who had purchased a defective item from a company store in another city"; *negative example*—"Acted rudely in dismissing the complaint of a customer who felt that a sale item was erroneously advertised."

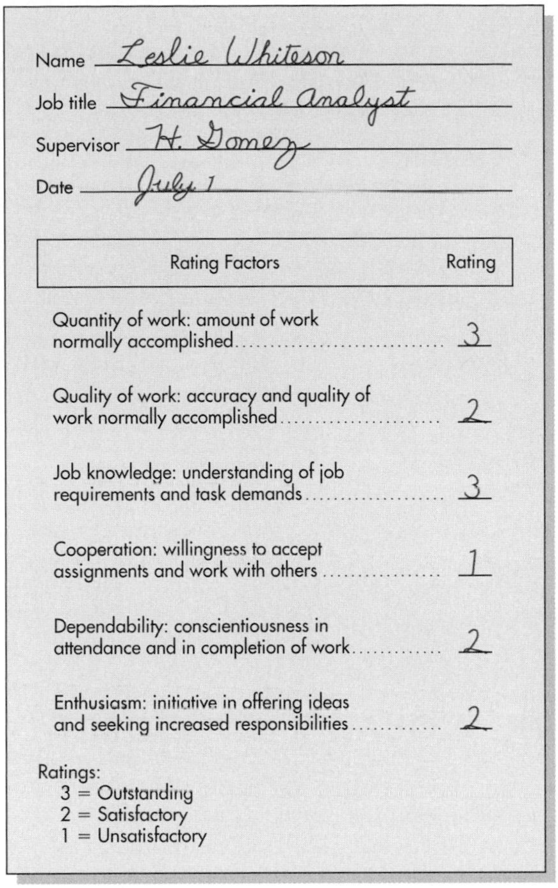
Name Leslie Whiteson
Job title Financial Analyst
Supervisor H. Gomez
Date July 1

Rating Factors	Rating
Quantity of work: amount of work normally accomplished	3
Quality of work: accuracy and quality of work normally accomplished	2
Job knowledge: understanding of job requirements and task demands	3
Cooperation: willingness to accept assignments and work with others	1
Dependability: conscientiousness in attendance and in completion of work	2
Enthusiasm: initiative in offering ideas and seeking increased responsibilities	2

Ratings:
3 = Outstanding
2 = Satisfactory
1 = Unsatisfactory

Figure 12.4 Sample graphic rating scale for performance appraisal.

Some performance management systems use **multiperson comparisons**, which formally compare one person's performance with that of one or more others. Such comparisons can be used on their own or in combination with some other method. They can also be done in different ways. In *rank ordering*, all persons being rated are arranged in order of performance achievement. The best performer goes at the top of the list, the worst performer at the bottom; no ties are allowed. In *paired comparisons*, each person is formally compared with every other person and rated as either the superior or the weaker member of the pair. After all paired comparisons are made, each person is assigned a summary ranking based on the number of superior scores achieved. In *forced distribution*, each person is placed into a frequency distribution that requires that a certain percentage fall into specific performance classifications, such as top 10 percent, next 40 percent, next 40 percent, and bottom 10 percent.

○ A **multiperson comparison** compares one person's performance with that of others.

Not all performance appraisals are completed only by one's immediate boss. It is increasingly popular today to expand the role of a job's stakeholders in the appraisal process. The new workplace often involves use of *peer appraisal*, including in the process others who work regularly and directly with a job holder, and *upward appraisal*, including in the process subordinates reporting to the job holder. An even broader stakeholder approach is known as **360° feedback**, where superiors, subordinates, peers, and even internal and external customers are involved in the appraisal of a job holder's performance.[43]

○ **360° feedback** includes in the appraisal process superiors, subordinates, peers, and even customers.

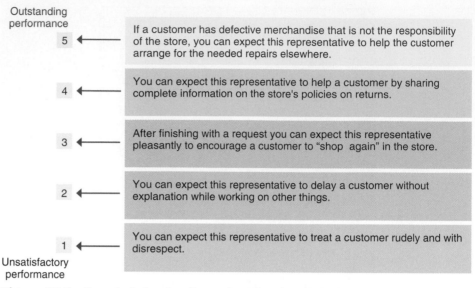

Outstanding performance

5 ← If a customer has defective merchandise that is not the responsibility of the store, you can expect this representative to help the customer arrange for the needed repairs elsewhere.

4 ← You can expect this representative to help a customer by sharing complete information on the store's policies on returns.

3 ← After finishing with a request you can expect this representative pleasantly to encourage a customer to "shop again" in the store.

2 ← You can expect this representative to delay a customer without explanation while working on other things.

1 ← You can expect this representative to treat a customer rudely and with disrespect.

Unsatisfactory performance

Figure 12.5 Sample behaviorally anchored rating scale for performance appraisal.

MAINTAINING A QUALITY WORKFORCE

An important goal of human resource management is to maintain a qualified workforce, even in a dynamic environment with constantly shifting work demands and labor markets. It is not enough to attract and develop workers with the talents to achieve high-performance results for the short term only. They must be successfully retained, nurtured, and managed for long-term effectiveness. When adverse turnover occurs and talented workers leave to pursue other opportunities, the resulting costs for the employer can be staggering. The best employers commit themselves to progressive human resource systems that support the retention of those workers who count most—the talented ones.

Recently, the Society for Human Resource Management surveyed employers to identify the tools they found most effective in retaining talented employees.[45] The results ranked the most effective retention practices as good benefits—especially health care, competitive salaries, flexible work schedules and personal time off, and opportunities for training and development.

CAREER DEVELOPMENT

In his book *The Age of Unreason*, British scholar and consultant Charles Handy discusses dramatic new developments in the world of work and careers. Specifically, Handy says: "The times are changing and we must change with them."[46] Each of us should take this advice and take charge of our careers. The Career Advancement Portfolio® section of the end-of-text Career Readiness Workbook is a useful resource in helping you to meet this challenge.

○ A **career** is a sequence of jobs that constitute what a person does for a living.

Formally defined, a **career** is a sequence of jobs and work pursuits that constitute what a person does for a living. For many of us, a career begins on an anticipatory basis with our formal education. From there it progresses into an initial job choice and any number of subsequent

TAKE IT TO THE CASE!

BET Holdings II, Inc. *(www.bet.com)*
World-Class Entrepreneur Places His "BET" on the Future

It takes an entrepreneur to start a business, but it takes quality people to keep it running . . . and growing. Robert Johnson, founder and CEO of BET Holdings, knows that for sure. BET Holdings is the first African-American-owned and -operated media and entertainment company to provide quality television programming, entertainment products, publishing and Internet services specifically designed to appeal to African-American interests. The company owns and operates four television networks (including BET Cable network), owns Arabesque Books (a leading African-American line of romance novels), and is an investor in four magazines, among them *Savoy* and *IMPACT*. After a successful debut, BET.com quickly became the highest-trafficked African-American portal on the Internet. Don't count on Johnson stopping there. He's still building strength for the future. If you've got the talent, you too might BET on it.[44]

choices that may involve changes in task assignments, employing organizations, and even occupations. A *career path* is a sequence of jobs held over time during a career. Career paths vary between those that are pursued internally with the same employers and those pursued externally among various employers. Whereas many organizations place great emphasis on making long-term career opportunities available to their employees, Handy's view of the future is that external career paths will be increasingly important.

Career planning is the process of systematically matching career goals and individual capabilities with opportunities for their fulfillment. It involves answering such questions as "Who am I?," "Where do I want to go?," "How do I get there?" While some suggest that a career should be allowed to progress in a somewhat random but always opportunistic way, others view a career as something to be rationally planned and pursued in a logical step-by-step fashion. In fact, a well-managed career will probably include elements of each. The carefully thought-out plan can point you in a general career direction; an eye for opportunity can fill in the details along the way.

○ **Career planning** is the process of systematically matching career goals and individual capabilities with opportunities for their fulfillment.

When you think about adult life stages or transitions, you should note that sooner or later most people's careers level off. A **career plateau** is a position from which someone is unlikely to move to a higher level of work responsibility.[47] Three common reasons for career plateaus are personal choice, limited abilities, and limited opportunities. For some, the plateau may occur at a point in life when it suits their individual needs; for others, the plateau may be unwanted and frustrating.

○ A **career plateau** is a position from which someone is unlikely to move to a higher level of work responsibility.

WORK-LIFE BALANCE

"Hiring good people is tough," starts an article in the *Harvard Business Review*. The sentence finishes with "keeping them can be even tougher."[48] A very important issue in maintaining a quality workforce

○ **Work-life balance** involves balancing career demands with personal and family needs.

relates to today's fast-paced and complicated life styles that bring with them inevitable pressures on the balance between work and personal time. This issue of **work-life balance** deals with how people balance the demands of careers with their personal and family needs. "Family" in this context includes not just children, but also elderly parents and other relatives in need of care. Among progressive employers, human resource policies and practices that support a healthy work-life balance are increasingly viewed as positive investments. Benchmarks are available and they are growing in number. At First Union Bank in Charlotte, North Carolina, for example, employees have access to on-site day care as well as such additional services as medical and dental offices, dry cleaning, and even video rentals. All of this is aimed at improving employee welfare and productivity.[49]

Included among work-life balance concerns are the unique needs of *single parents*, who must balance complete parenting responsibilities with a job, and *dual-career couples*, who must balance the career needs and opportunities of each partner. The special needs of both working mothers and working fathers are also being recognized.[50] Not surprisingly, the "family-friendliness" of an employer is now frequently and justifiably used as a screening criterion by job candidates. *Business Week, Working Mother*, and *Fortune* are among the magazines annually reporting surveys on the issue.

COMPENSATION AND BENEFITS

○ **Base compensation** is a salary or hourly wage paid to an individual.

Chapter 7 pointed out that good compensation and benefit systems improve control by attracting qualified people to the organization, and helping to retain them. **Base compensation** in the form of salary or hourly wages can make the organization a desirable place of employment. It can help get the right people into jobs to begin with; by making outside opportunities less attractive it can also help keep them there. Unless an organization's prevailing wage and salary structure is competitive in the relevant labor markets, it will be difficult to attract and retain a staff of highly competent workers. A basic rule of thumb is to carefully study the labor market and pay at least as much as, and perhaps a bit more than, what competitors are offering. The additional area of *incentive pay* is discussed in detail in Chapter 14 on motivation and rewards.

○ **Fringe benefits** are nonmonetary compensation in the form of health insurance, retirement plans, etc.

The organization's employee-benefit program also plays a role in attracting and retaining capable workers. **Fringe benefits** are the additional nonwage or nonsalary forms of compensation provided to an organization's workforce. They can now constitute some 30 percent or more of a typical worker's earnings. Benefit packages usually include various options on disability protection, health and life insurance, and retirement plans. At the executive level, these benefits may extend into such additional "perks" as company cars and expenses, deferred compensation, supplemental retirement benefits, and personal tax and financial planning.

○ **Flexible benefits** programs allow employees to choose from a range of benefit options.

The ever-rising cost of fringe benefits, particularly employee medical benefits, is a major worry for employers. Some are attempting to gain control over health-care costs by becoming more active in their employees' choices of health-care providers and by encouraging healthy lifestyles. An increasingly common approach overall is **flexible benefits**, sometimes known as *cafeteria benefits*, which let the employee choose a set of benefits within a certain dollar amount. The employee gains when such plans are better able to meet individual needs; the employer gains from being more responsive to a wider range of needs in a diverse workforce.

RETENTION AND TURNOVER

The several steps in the human resource management process both conclude and recycle with *replacement* decisions, that is, with the management of promotions, transfers, terminations, layoffs, and retirements. Any replacement situation should be approached as an opportunity to review human resource plans, update job analyses, rewrite job descriptions and job specifications, and ensure that the best people are selected to perform the required tasks.

Some replacement decisions shift people between positions within the organization. *Promotion* is movement to a higher-level position; *transfer* is movement to a different job at a similar level of responsibility. Another set of replacement decisions relates to *retirement*, something most people look forward to . . . until it is close at hand. Then the prospect of being retired often raises fears and apprehensions. Many organizations offer special counseling and other forms of support for retiring employees, including advice on company benefits, money management, estate planning, and use of leisure time. Downsizing is sometimes accompanied by special offers of early retirement, that is, retirement before formal retirement age but with special financial incentives. Where this is not possible, organizations may provide outplacement services to help terminated employees find other jobs.

The most extreme replacement decisions involve *termination*, the involuntary and permanent dismissal of an employee. In some cases the termination is based on performance problems. The person involved is not meeting the requirements of the job or has violated key organizational policy. In other cases the termination may be due to financial conditions of the employer, such as those requiring downsizing or restructuring. The persons involved may be performing well, but are being terminated as part of a workforce reduction. In any case, it may be hard for the person being dismissed to accept the decision. Especially in the case of workforce reduction, the termination notice may come by surprise and without the benefit of advance preparation for either the personal or the financial shock. The experts' advice to the employee is to ask at least three tough questions of the ex-boss: "Why am I being released?" "What are my termination benefits?" "Can I have a good reference?" Advice for the manager who must handle a termination is offered in *Manager's Notepad 12.3*.

LABOR–MANAGEMENT RELATIONS

A final aspect of human resource management involves the role of organized labor. **Labor unions** are organizations to which workers belong that deal with employers on the workers' behalf.[51] Although they used to be associated primarily with industrial and business occupations, labor unions increasingly represent such public-sector employees as teachers, college professors, police officers, and government workers. They are important forces in the modern workplace both in the United States and around the world. Today, about 13.5 percent of American workers belong to a union; the figures are over 30 percent for Canada and some 25 percent for Great Britain.[52]

Labor unions act as a collective "voice" in dealing with employers of their members. They serve as bargaining agents that negotiate legal contracts affecting many aspects of the employment relationship. These

○ A **labor union** is an organization of workers that deals with employers on the workers' collective behalf.

MANAGER'S NOTEPAD 12.3

Things to remember when handling a dismissal

- Dismissal can be as personally devastating as a divorce or the death of a loved one.
- Dismissal should always be legally defensible and done in complete compliance with organizational policies.
- Dismissal should not be delayed unnecessarily; it is best done as soon as the inevitability of the dismissal is known.
- Dismissal of good performers should include offers of assistance to help them reenter the labor market.

○ A **labor contract** is a formal agreement between a union and employer about the terms of work for union members.

○ **Collective bargaining** is the process of negotiating, administering, and interpreting a labor contract.

labor contracts, for example, typically specify the rights and obligations of employees and management with respect to wages, work hours, work rules, seniority, hiring, grievances, and other conditions of employment. All of this has implications for management. In a unionized work setting, the labor contract and its legal implications must be considered when making human resource management decisions.

The foundation of any labor and management relationship is **collective bargaining**, which is the process of negotiating, administering, and interpreting labor contracts. Labor contracts and the collective bargaining process—from negotiating a new contract to resolving disputes under an existing one—are major influences on human resource management in unionized work settings. They are also governed closely in the United States by a strict legal framework with three important foundations. The *National Labor Relations Act of 1935* (known as the *Wagner Act*) protects employees by recognizing their right to join unions and engage in union activities. It is enforced by the National Labor Relations Board (NLRB). The *Taft-Hartley Act of 1947* protects employers from unfair labor practices by unions and allows workers to decertify unions. And the *Civil Service Reform Act Title VII of 1978* clarifies the right of government employees to join and be represented by labor unions.

The collective bargaining process typically occurs in face-to-face meetings between labor and management representatives. During this time, a variety of demands, proposals, and counterproposals are exchanged. Several rounds of bargaining may be required before a contract is reached or a dispute over a contract issue is resolved. And, as you might expect, the process can lead to problems.

In *Figure 12.6*, labor and management are viewed as "win-lose" adversaries, destined to be in opposition and possessed of certain weapons with which to fight one another. If labor–management relations take this form, a lot of energy on both sides can be expended in prolonged conflict. For years, the bargaining between U.S. automakers on the one hand, and the strong, demanding leadership of the United Auto Workers on the other, had an adversarial character. Unions perceived management as aloof and uncaring in dealing with the needs of auto workers. The resulting labor contracts tried to protect worker interests through complex work rules and expensive compensation packages. While all this was happening, the competitiveness of the automakers was eroding. Many layoffs and plant closings occurred.

Get Connected!

Go global in your understanding about unions. Look at the Internet guide to Labor Unions around the World.

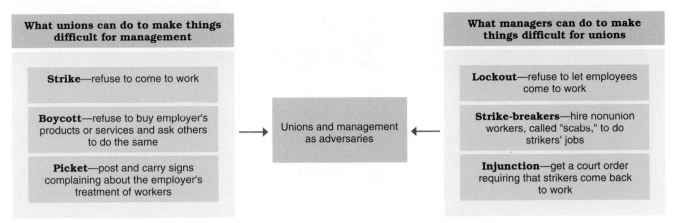

Figure 12.6 The traditional adversarial view of labor–management relations.

The traditional adversarial model of labor–management relations is, to some extent, giving way to a new and more progressive era of greater cooperation. Even the automakers and the UAW have tried to work more closely together to reduce production costs while maintaining basic worker rights and benefits. Each side seems more willing to understand that the productivity and future survival of the industry depend on cooperation and mutual adjustment to new and challenging times. In today's competitive and challenging global economy, cooperation between unions and employers seems to be gaining headway.

CHAPTER 12 STUDY Guide

The Chapter 12 Study Guide will help you review chapter content, prepare for examinations, and further build your career readiness. The *Summary* briefly highlights answers to questions first posed in the chapter opening Planning Ahead section. The list of *Key Terms* allows you to doublecheck your familiarity with basic concepts and definitions. *Self-Test 12* gives you the opportunity to test your basic comprehension of chapter content using sample test questions. Suggestions offered as *Career Readiness Activities* direct your attention to relevant sections of the end-of-text Career Readiness Workbook as well as to special Electronic Resources on the *Management 7/e* web site.

SUMMARY

Why do people make the difference?

- Even in this age of information, high technology, and globalization, people still drive the system; they make organizations work.
- Organizations with positive human resource policies and practices are gaining significant performance advantages in such areas as lower turnover, more sales, higher profits, and increased shareholder wealth.
- The commitment to human resources made by founders of startups has long-term consequences for organizational performance.
- The challenges of complexity and uncertainty in highly competitive environments are best met by a diverse and talented workforce.
- The diversity advantage is gained only when the talents of all persons, regardless of personal characteristics, are unlocked and given the opportunity to perform.

What is strategic human resource management?

- The human resource management process is the process of attracting, developing, and maintaining a quality workforce.
- A complex legal environment influences human resource management, giving special attention to equal employment opportunity.
- Human resource planning is the process of analyzing staffing needs and identifying actions to satisfy these needs over time.
- The purpose of human resource planning is to make sure the organization always has people with the right abilities available to do the required work.

How do organizations attract a quality workforce?

- Recruitment is the process of attracting qualified job candidates to fill vacant positions.
- Recruitment can be both external and internal to the organization.
- Recruitment should involve realistic job previews that provide job candidates with accurate information on the job and organization.
- Managers typically use interviews, employment tests, and references to help make selection decisions; the use of assessment centers and work sampling is becoming more common.

How do organizations develop a quality workforce?

- Orientation is the process of formally introducing new hires to their jobs, performance requirements, and the organization.
- On-the-job training may include job rotation, coaching, apprenticeship, modeling, and mentoring.
- Off-the-job training may include a range of formal courses and programs, as well as simulations and other training specifically tailored to job needs.
- Performance management systems focus on the establishment of work standards and the assessment of results through performance appraisal.
- Common performance appraisal methods are graphic rating scales, narratives, behaviorally anchored rating scales, and multiperson comparisons.

How do organizations maintain a quality workforce?

- Career planning systematically matches individual career goals and capabilities with opportunities for their fulfillment.
- Programs that address work-life balance and the complex demands of job and family responsibilities are increasingly important in human resource management.
- Compensation and benefits packages must be continually updated so the organization maintains a competitive position in external labor markets.
- Whenever workers must be replaced over time because of promotions, transfers, retirements, and terminations, the goal should be to treat everyone fairly while ensuring that jobs are filled with the best personnel available.
- Where labor unions exist, labor–management relations should be positively approached and handled with all due consideration of applicable laws.

KEY TERMS

Affirmative action (p. 307)

Assessment center (p. 316)

Base compensation (p. 324)

Behaviorally anchored rating scale (p. 320)

Bona fide occupational qualifications (p. 308)

Career (p. 322)

Career planning (p. 323)

Career plateau (p. 323)

Coaching (p. 318)

Collective bargaining (p. 326)

Comparable worth (p. 310)

Critical incident technique (p. 320)

Discrimination (p. 307)

Equal employment opportunity (p. 307)

Flexible benefits (p. 324)

Fringe benefits (p. 324)

Graphic rating scale (p. 320)

Human resource management (p. 306)

Human resource planning (p. 311)

Independent contractors (p. 310)

Job analysis (p. 312)

Job description (p. 312)

Job specification (p. 312)

Labor contract (p. 326)

Labor union (p. 325)

Management development (p. 319)

Mentoring (p. 318)

Modeling (p. 318)

Multiperson comparison (p. 321)

Orientation (p. 317)

Performance appraisal (p. 319)

Performance management system (p. 319)

Realistic job preview (p. 313)

Recruitment (p. 312)

Reliability (p. 314)

Selection (p. 314)

Sexual harassment (p. 310)

Socialization (p. 317)

Strategic human resource management (p. 311)

360° feedback (p. 321)

Training (p. 318)

Validity (p. 314)

Work-life balance (p. 324)

SELF-TEST 12

Take this test here or on-line much as you would in a normal classroom situation. It is a good way to check your basic comprehension of chapter material. Answers may be found at the end of the book.

MULTIPLE-CHOICE QUESTIONS:

1. Human resource management is defined as the process of _____, developing, and maintaining a high-quality workforce.
   (a) attracting (b) compensating (c) appraising (d) testing

2. A(n) _____ is a criterion that can be legally justified for use in screening candidates for employment.
(a) job description (b) bona fide occupational qualification
(c) job evaluation (d) occupational benchmark

3. _____ programs are designed to improve employment opportunities for minorities.
(a) Realistic recruiting (b) External recruiting (c) Affirmative action
(d) Labor–management cooperation

4. An employment test that fails to yield similar results over time when taken by the same person would be considered _____.
(a) nonspecific (b) unstable (c) contradictory (d) unreliable

5. The assessment center approach to employee selection relies heavily on _____.
(a) pencil-and-paper tests (b) simulations and experiential exercises
(c) the review of written resumes (d) formal one-on-one interviews

6. _____ is a form of on-the-job training wherein an individual learns by observing others who demonstrate desirable job behaviors.
(a) Case study (b) Work sampling (c) Modeling (d) Simulation

7. The first step in human resource planning is to _____.
(a) forecast human resource needs (b) forecast labor supplies
(c) assess the existing workforce (d) review organizational mission, objectives, and strategies

8. In the American legal environment, the _____ Act of 1947 protects employers from unfair labor practices by unions.
(a) Wagner (b) Taft-Hartley (c) Labor Union (d) Hawley-Smoot

9. Socialization of newcomers occurs during the _____ step of the staffing process.
(a) recruiting (b) orientation (c) selecting (d) training

10. Performance appraisal should _____.
(a) serve only evaluation purposes (b) not be done through forced comparisons (c) use reliable and valid methods (d) result in at least 10 percent "poor performance" ratings

TRUE-FALSE QUESTIONS:

11. In the United States, the legal environment affecting the staffing process is not very complex.   T   F

12. In human resource planning, a job analysis determines exactly what is done in existing jobs.   T   F

13. The job specification identifies the qualifications required for someone to fill a job successfully.   T   F

14. External recruitment is always better than internal recruitment.   T   F

15. In a realistic job preview, a job applicant is provided with accurate information about a job and/or organization, even if it has negative aspects.   T   F

16. Collective bargaining is the process of negotiating, administering, and interpreting a labor contract.   T   F

17. The evaluation purpose of performance appraisal is served by managers acting in counseling roles.   T   F

18. An adversarial relationship in labor–management relations always improves productivity in unionized work settings.   T   F

19. Flexible benefit programs are becoming less important today.   T   F

20. Career plateaus can create problems as organizations try to maintain a quality workforce.   T   F

SHORT-RESPONSE QUESTIONS:

21. How do internal recruitment and external recruitment compare in terms of advantages and disadvantages for the employer?

22. Why is orientation an important part of the staffing process?

23. What is the difference between the graphic rating scale and the BARS as performance appraisal methods?

24. How does mentoring work as a form of on-the-job training?

APPLICATION QUESTION:

25. Sy Smith is not doing well in his job. The problems began to appear shortly after Sy's job was changed from a manual to a computer-based operation. He has tried but is just not doing well in terms of learning to use the computer and meet the performance expectations. As a 55-year-old employee with over 30 years with the company, Sy is both popular and influential among his work peers. Along with his performance problems you have also noticed the appearance of some negative attitudes—a tendency for Sy to "badmouth" the firm. As Sy's manager, what options would you consider in terms of dealing with the issue of his retention in the job and in the company? What would you do and why?

readiness
CAREER ACTIVITIES

Recommended learning activities from the end-of-text Career Readiness Workbook for this chapter include:

Career Advancement Portfolio
- Individual writing and group presentation assignments based on any of the following activities.

Case for Critical Thinking
- BET Holdings II, Inc.—Building the Best African-American Internet Portal

Integrative Learning Activities
- Research Project 5—Affirmative Action Directions
- Integrative Case—Outback Steakhouse. Inc.

Exercises in Teamwork
- Interviewing Job Candidates (#15)
- Work vs. Family (#16)
- Compensation and Benefits Debate (#17)

Self-Assessments
- Decision-Making Biases (#3)
- Diversity Awareness (#7)
- Performance Appraisal Assumptions (#13)

The *Fast Company* Collection On-Line
- Tom Peters, "The Brand Called 'You'"
- Robert Reich, "The Company of the Future"
- Alan Weber, "Danger: Toxic Company"

ELECTRONIC RESOURCES

@ GET CONNECTED! Don't forget to take full advantage of the on-line support for *Management 7/e.*
- Chapter 12 On-line Study Guide
- Chapter 12 Self-test Answers
- Chapter 12 E-Resource Center

www.wiley.com/college/schermerhorn

13

Leading

Planning ahead

GETTING CONNECTED

Butcher Company—You Have to Believe in People

Even as the "dot-com" and "new economy" companies make most of the news, there is still a lot of the "old economy" around. And if we take the time to look at the Butcher Company, there's still a lot to learn about leadership from them as well.

This maker of floor care products made headlines when its founder Charlie Butcher, at the age of 83 and with his wife and seven children, sold the firm to family-owned S.C. Johnson Company. Not a bad deal for Charlie and family, you might say.

Well yes, but the story is much deeper than that. You see, after Charlie sold the company he shared $18 million of the proceeds with the firm's 325 employees. Not only that, he chose to sell to another family-owned firm so he could do it. Says Charlie: "I knew if I went public I would be able to give out $18 million. Investors are very tight with their money."

The day after the sale Charlie was at the plant handing out bonus checks. The firm's president Paul P. McClaughlin said the employees "just filled up with tears. They would just throw their arms around Charlie and give him a hug." But this wasn't anything new in terms of Charlie Butcher's leadership style; he's been a believer in people all along. This was a chance to confirm what he'd been practicing for years—a belief that treating talented people well will create business success. "When people are happy in their jobs, they are at least twice as productive," he says.

Charlie Butcher's people-oriented approach to business meant that his workers received high starting salaries, flexible hours, and freedom to change jobs if unhappy. As a result, he believes the firm benefited by having workers who made fewer mistakes and produced more. The end result for Charlie was an innovative and successful company that still had a future even when he decided to call it quits.

What did the $18 million add up to for Charlie's loyal Butcher Company workers? An average of $55,000 per person was the net return; each received about $1.50 for every hour they worked for the firm over the years. Was it worth it for Charlie? Of course. He says: "The most important reward you can receive from business is the happiness you feel when you are able to make an important difference in the lives of the people who helped you succeed. Our hope and belief is that the S.C. Johnson Company will continue to grow Butcher's and assure that it will always be a great place for our employees to work."[1]

@ Get Connected!

Charlie Butcher demonstrated that every one of his employees was part "owner" of the firm's success. His final act confirmed what Charlie's leadership style had been saying all along—everyone at the Butcher Company had a stake in the business. Use the opportunities in the *Career Readiness Workbook* to analyze your leadership style; take charge of your continued professional development. Get connected!

What is great leadership, you ask? At Herman Miller, Inc., the innovative Michigan-based maker of office furniture, the answer lies in a belief in people. Max DePree, the firm's former chairperson and the son of its founder, tells the story of a millwright who worked for his father.[2] The millwright held an important job in the plant. He was responsible for keeping all of the machines supplied with power from a central boiler. When the man died, DePree's father, wishing to express his sympathy to the family, went to their home. There he listened as the widow read some beautiful poems, which, he was surprised to learn, had been written by the millwright. To this day, DePree says, he and his father still wonder, "Was he a poet who did millwright's work, or was he a millwright who wrote poetry?"

Max DePree summarizes the lesson of the story this way: "It is fundamental that leaders endorse a concept of persons. This begins with an understanding of the diversity of people's gifts, talents, and skills." According to DePree, when we recognize the unique qualities of others, we become less inclined to believe that we alone know what is best. By valuing diversity, not only do we learn what may be needed to provide others with meaningful work and opportunities, we also benefit by allowing everyone's contribution to have an influence on the organization.

Under DePree's leadership, and using techniques such as participative ownership and teamwork, Herman Miller achieved the rank of one of *Fortune*'s "most admired" American corporations. The leadership lessons extend to all types and sizes of organizations. Great leaders everywhere are able to bring out the best in other people. In the words of management consultant Tom Peters: "Leaders get their kicks from orchestrating the work of others—not from doing it themselves."[3] He goes on to say that the leader is "rarely—possibly never?—the best performer." They don't have to be; they thrive through and by the successes of others.

THE NATURE OF LEADERSHIP

It is time for you to seriously think about the many demands made on those who serve as leaders in the new workplace. One theme in this chapter relates to the distinction between management and leadership.[4] Warren Bennis, a respected leadership scholar and consultant, claims that too many American corporations are "over-managed and under-led."[5] The late Grace Hooper, another management expert and the first female admiral in the U.S. Navy, said, "You manage things; you lead people."[6]

○ **Leadership** is the process of inspiring others to work hard to accomplish important tasks.

A glance at the shelves in your local bookstore will quickly confirm that **leadership**—the process of inspiring others to work hard to accomplish important tasks—is one of the most popular management topics. As shown in *Figure 13.1*, it is also one of the four functions that constitute the management process. Planning sets the direction and objectives; organizing brings the resources together to turn plans into action; leading builds the commitments and enthusiasm needed for people to apply their talents fully to help accomplish plans; and controlling makes sure things turn out right.

Today's leaders are being challenged in new and demanding ways. The time frames for getting things accomplished are becoming shorter; leaders are expected to get things right the first time, with second chances few and far between; the problems to be resolved through leadership are complex, ambiguous, and multidimensional; leaders are expected to be long-

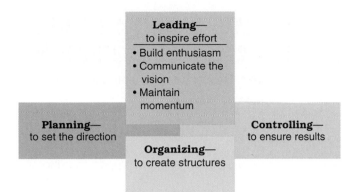

Figure 13.1 Leading viewed in relationship to the other management functions.

term oriented even while meeting demands for short-term performance results.[7] Anyone aspiring to career success in leadership must rise to these challenges, and more.[8] To succeed as a leader in our new workplace, one must be good at dealing with all aspects of communication, interpersonal relations, motivation, job design, teamwork, and change—all topics covered in this final part of *Management 7/e*.

LEADERSHIP AND VISION

"Great leaders," it is said, "get extraordinary things done in organizations by inspiring and motivating others toward a common purpose."[9] Frequently today, leadership is associated with **vision**—a future that one hopes to create or achieve in order to improve upon the present state of affairs. The term **visionary leadership** describes a leader who brings to the situation a clear and compelling sense of the future as well as understanding of the actions needed to get there successfully.[10] But there is more to it than that—simply having the vision of a desirable future is not enough. Truly great leaders are extraordinarily good at turning their visions into concrete results. Importantly, this involves the essential ability to communicate one's vision in such a way that others commit their hard work to its fulfillment. Visionary leaders, simply put, inspire others to take the actions necessary to turn vision into reality. At General Electric, for example, an "A" leader is considered to be someone "... with vision and the ability to articulate that vision to the team, so vividly and powerfully that it also becomes their vision."[11]

The accompanying *Manager's Notepad 13.1* offers five principles for meeting the challenges of visionary leadership.[12] Recognize that the suggestions go beyond a manager's responsibilities for making long-term plans and drafting budgets. They go beyond putting structures in place and assigning people to jobs. And, they go beyond making sure that results are consistent with the original plan. Leadership with vision means doing all these things and more. It means beginning with a clear vision; it means communicating that vision to all concerned; and it means getting people motivated and inspired to pursue the vision in their daily work. It means bringing meaning to the work that people do—making what they do worthy and valuable. Visionary leadership was the ultimate test for Max DePree at Herman Miller; it is a cornerstone of managerial success in dynamic leadership settings around the world.

○ **Vision** is a term used to describe a clear sense of the future.

○ **Visionary leadership** brings to the situation a clear sense of the future and an understanding of how to get there.

MANAGER'S NOTEPAD 13.1

Five principles of visionary leadership

- *Challenge the process:* Be a pioneer; encourage innovation and support people who have ideas.
- *Show enthusiasm:* Inspire others through personal enthusiasm to share in a common vision.
- *Help others to act:* Be a team player and support the efforts and talents of others.
- *Set the example:* Provide a consistent role model of how others can and should act.
- *Celebrate achievements:* Bring emotion into the workplace and rally "hearts" as well as "minds."

POWER AND INFLUENCE

○ **Power** is the ability to get someone else to do something you want done or to make things happen the way you want.

The foundations of effective leadership lie in the way a manager uses power to influence the behavior of other people. **Power** is the ability to get someone else to do something you want done. It is the ability to make things happen the way you want them to.[13] Research recognizes that a need for power is essential to executive success.[14] But this need for power is not a desire to control for the sake of personal satisfaction; it is a desire to influence and control others for the good of the group or organization as a whole. This "positive" face of power is the foundation of effective leadership. *Figure 13.2* shows one set of power sources that is based in the position a person holds and a second set that is based in one's personal qualities.[15]

Sources of Position Power

One important source of power is a manager's official status, or position, in the organization's hierarchy of authority. Whereas anyone holding a managerial position theoretically has this power, how well it is used will vary from one person to the next. Consequently, leadership success will vary as well. The three bases of *position power* are reward power, coercive power, and legitimate power.

○ **Reward power** is the capacity to offer something of value as a means of influencing other people.

Reward power is the ability to influence through rewards. It is the capability to offer something of value—a positive outcome—as a means of influencing the behavior of other people. This involves the control of re-

Sources of power...

Power of the POSITION: Based on things managers can offer to others.	Power of the PERSON: Based on the ways managers are viewed by others.
Rewards: "If you do what I ask, I'll give you a reward."	**Expertise**—as a source of special knowledge and information.
Coercion: "If you don't do what I ask, I'll punish you."	**Reference**—as a person with whom others like to identify.
Legitimacy: "Because I am the boss; you *must* do as I ask."	

Figure 13.2 Sources of position power and personal power used by managers.

High Performance The School Leadership Academy Where Leadership Is About Making Vision Happen

At the School Leadership Academy in New York City, founder Lorraine Monroe brings leadership to life in the Monroe Doctrine—leadership principles that include what she calls the "heart of the matter": "We can reform society only if every place we live—every school, workplace, church, and family—becomes a site of reform." Monroe has held a variety of responsible positions in New York City public schools, and previously founded an experimental public high school in Harlem, the Frederick Douglas Academy. Monroe says: "Leadership is about making a vision happen. . . . The job of a good leader is to articulate a vision that others are inspired to follow. . . . That leader makes everybody in an organization understand how to make the vision active." Her book "Nothing's Impossible: Leadership Lessons from the Front Lines," was praised by *Ms. Magazine* as offering inspiration on every page.[16]

---

wards or resources such as pay raises, bonuses, promotions, special assignments, and verbal or written compliments. To mobilize reward power, a manager says, in effect, "If you do what I ask, I'll give you a reward."

Coercive power is the ability to influence through punishment. It is the capacity to punish or withhold positive outcomes as a way to influence the behavior of other people. A manager may attempt to coerce someone by threatening him or her with verbal reprimands, pay penalties, and even termination. To mobilize coercive power, a manager says, in effect, "If you don't do what I want, I'll punish you."

> ○ **Coercive power** is the capacity to punish or withhold positive outcomes as a means of influencing other people.

Legitimate power is the ability to influence through authority—the right by virtue of one's organizational position or status to exercise control over persons in subordinate positions. It is the capacity to influence the behavior of other people by virtue of the rights of office. To mobilize legitimate power, a manager says, in effect, "I am the boss and therefore you are supposed to do as I ask."

> ○ **Legitimate power** is the capacity to influence other people by virtue of formal authority, or the rights of office.

Sources of Personal Power

Another source of power lies in the individual manager and the unique personal qualities she or he brings to a leadership situation. This is a very important source of power that a truly successful leader cannot do without. Two bases of *personal power* are expert power and referent power.

Expert power is the ability to influence through special expertise. It is the capacity to influence the behavior of other people because of one's knowledge, understanding, and skills. Expertise derives from the possession of technical know-how or information pertinent to the issue at hand. This is developed by acquiring relevant skills or competencies or by gaining a central position in relevant information networks. It is maintained by protecting one's credibility and not overstepping the boundaries of true understanding. When a manager uses expert power, the implied message is, "You should do what I want because of my special expertise or information."

> ○ **Expert power** is the capacity to influence other people because of specialized knowledge.

Referent power is the ability to influence through identification. It is the capacity to influence the behavior of other people because they admire you and want to identify positively with you. Reference is a power derived from charisma or interpersonal attractiveness. It is developed and main-

> ○ **Referent power** is the capacity to influence other people because of their desire to identify personally with you.

tained through good interpersonal relations that encourage the admiration and respect of others. When a manager uses referent power, the implied message is, "You should do what I want in order to maintain a positive self-defined relationship with me."

Turning Power into Influence

To succeed at leadership, anyone must be able to both acquire all types of power and appropriately use them to achieve goals and pursue a shared vision.[17] To begin, the best leaders and managers understand that different outcomes are associated with use of the various power bases. When one relies on rewards and legitimacy to influence others, the likely outcome is temporary compliance. The follower will do what the leader requests, but only so long as the reward continues and/or the legitimacy persists. Inability to continue the reward or attempting to influence outside the range of one's legitimacy will result in a loss of compliance. When one relies on coercion to gain influence, compliance is also dependent upon the continued threat of punishment. In this case, however, the compliance is very temporary and often accompanied by resistance. Use of expert and reference power creates the most enduring influence; they create commitment. Followers respond positively because of internalized understanding or beliefs that create their own long-lasting effects on behavior.

Position power alone is often insufficient to achieve and sustain needed influence. Personal power and the bases of expert and reference power often make the difference between leadership success and mediocrity. This is particularly true in one's ability to influence the behavior of peers and superiors in the organization. Four points to keep in mind are (1) there is no substitute for expertise, (2) likable personal qualities are very important, (3) effort and hard work breed respect, and (4) personal behavior must support expressed values.[18]

How Culture Influences Views of the "Ideal" Leader Researchers Charles Hampton Turner and Fons Trompenaars asked workers across cultures if they preferred a *specifics* leader, focused on getting the job done, or an *integrated-whole leader*, focused on getting subordinates to work well together. Workers from Canada ranked the highest in preferring a specifics leader, while Singapore ranked the lowest. Take the on-line "Reality Check" to learn the leadership preferences of workers from other countries.

In organizations, power and influence are also linked to where one fits and how one acts in the structures and networks of the workplace. *Centrality* is important. Managers, for example, must establish a broad network of interpersonal contacts and get involved in the important information flows within them. They must avoid becoming isolated. *Criticality* is important. To gain power, managers must take good care of others who are dependent on them. They should take care to support them exceptionally well by doing things that add value to the work setting. *Visibility* is also important. It helps to become known as an influential person in the organization. Good managers don't hesitate to make formal presentations, participate in key task forces or committees, and pursue special assignments that can display their leadership talents and capabilities.

ETHICS AND THE LIMITS TO POWER

Barnard's acceptance theory of authority

On the issue of ethics and the limits to power, it is always helpful to remember Chester Barnard's *acceptance theory of authority*. He identifies four conditions that determine whether a leader's directives will be followed and true influence achieved:[19] (1) The other person must truly understand the directive. (2) The other person must feel capable of carrying out the directive. (3) The other person must believe that the directive is in the organization's best interests. (4) The other person must believe that the directive is consistent with personal values.

When the complexities of ethical dilemmas were discussed in Chapter 6, it was noted that many such dilemmas begin when leaders and managers pressure followers to do questionable things. Using the acceptance theory of authority as a starting point, the ethical question a follower must always be prepared to ask is "Where do I (or will I) draw the line; at what point do I (or will I) refuse to comply with requests?" Someday you may face a situation in which you are asked by someone in authority to do something that violates personal ethics and/or even the law. Can you . . . will you . . . when will you say "no"? After all, as Barnard said, it is "acceptance" that establishes the limits of managerial power.

LEADERSHIP AND EMPOWERMENT

At many points in this book we have talked about **empowerment**, the process through which managers enable and help others to gain power and achieve influence within the organization. Effective leaders empower others by providing them with the information, responsibility, authority, and trust to make decisions and act independently within their areas of expertise. They know that when people feel empowered to act, they tend to follow through with commitment and high-quality work. They also realize that power in organizations is not a "zero-sum" quantity. That is, in order for someone to gain power, it isn't necessary for someone else to give it up. Indeed, today's high-performance organizations are masters at mobilizing power and commitment to the vision throughout all ranks of employees.

○ **Empowerment** distributes decision-making power throughout an organization.

Max DePree of Herman Miller, for example, praises leaders who are willing to focus on what is best for the organization and "permit others to share ownership of problems—to take possession of the situation."[20] Lorraine Monroe of The School Leadership Academy says: ". . . a really great boss is not afraid to hire smart people. You want people who are smart about things you are not smart about."[21] Both are talking about *leadership through empowerment*—allowing and helping people to use their experience, knowledge and judgment to make a real difference in daily workplace affairs. Doing so requires respect for the talents and creativity of others. And, it requires the confidence to let people work with initiative in responsible jobs, participate in decisions affecting their work, and make reasonable choices regarding work-life balance.

Manager's Notepad 13.2 offers tips on how leaders can empower others.[22] There are many benefits for managers who are successful at doing so. On the one hand, empowerment allows people to act independently and feel more "adult" in their work activities. On the other hand, a manager who empowers others tends to gain power too. Having a high-performing work unit certainly helps establish the criticality, centrality, and visibility of one's position. The very act of empowering others may create a positive relationship and build referent power.[23] And, what better way to demonstrate expertise than to show that one's team does a great job?

LEADERSHIP TRAITS AND BEHAVIORS

For centuries, people have recognized that some persons perform very well as leaders, whereas others do not. The question still debated is "Why?" Historically, the issue of leadership success has been studied from the perspective of the trait, behavioral, and contingency

MANAGER'S NOTEPAD 13.2

How to empower others

- Get others involved in selecting their work assignments and the methods for accomplishing tasks.
- Create an environment of cooperation, information sharing, discussion, and shared ownership of goals.
- Encourage others to take initiative, make decisions, and use their knowledge.
- When problems arise, find out what others think and let them help design the solutions.
- Stay out of the way; give others the freedom to put their ideas and solutions into practice.
- Maintain high morale and confidence by recognizing successes and encouraging high performance.

approaches to be discussed here. Each takes a slightly different tack in attempting to explain both leadership effectiveness and identify the pathways to leadership development.

SEARCH FOR LEADERSHIP TRAITS

An early direction in leadership research involved the search for universal traits or distinguishing personal characteristics that would separate effective and ineffective leaders.[24] Sometimes called the *great person theory*, the notion was to identify successful leaders and then determine what made them great. If a listing of definitive universal leadership traits could be made, it would then be easy to select for leadership positions only those people with the requisite characteristics. Those wanting to become leaders or those seeking to improve their leadership success could set personal development goals for aquiring them.

Historically, researchers struggled with their inability to find consistent patterns of leadership traits. More recent research indicates that certain personal traits may be important, but that they must be considered along with other situational factors. Briefly, the results of many years of research in this direction can be summarized as follows. Physical characteristics such as a person's height, weight, and physique make no difference in determining leadership success. On the other hand, certain personal traits do seem to differentiate leaders. A study of over 3,400 managers, for example, found that followers rather consistently admired certain things about leaders.[25] The most respected leaders were described by their followers as honest, competent, forward-looking, inspiring, and credible. Such positive feelings may enhance a leader's effectiveness, particularly with respect to creating vision and a sense of empowerment. In a comprehensive review of research to date, Shelley Kirkpatrick and

Edwin Locke further identify these personal traits as being common among successful leaders.[26]

- *Drive:* Successful leaders have high energy, display initiative, and are tenacious.
- *Self-confidence:* Successful leaders trust themselves and have confidence in their abilities.
- *Creativity:* Successful leaders are creative and original in their thinking.
- *Cognitive ability:* Successful leaders have the intelligence to integrate and interpret information.
- *Business knowledge:* Successful leaders know their industry and its technical foundations.
- *Motivation:* Successful leaders enjoy influencing others to achieve shared goals.
- *Flexibility:* Successful leaders adapt to fit the needs of followers and demands of situations.
- *Honesty and integrity:* Successful leaders are trustworthy; they are honest, predictable, and dependable.

Personal traits of successful leaders

FOCUS ON LEADERSHIP BEHAVIORS

Recognizing that the possession of certain traits alone is not a guarantee of leadership success, researchers next turned their attention to examine how leaders behave when working with followers. In effect this shifted attention from a focus on *who* leaders are toward concern for *what* leaders do. Generally known as *behavioral theories of leadership*, work in this tradition sought to determine which **leadership style**—the recurring pattern of behaviors exhibited by a leader—worked best.[27] If the preferred style could be identified, the implications were straightforward and practical: train leaders to become skilled at using the ideal style to best advantage.

Leadership style is the recurring pattern of behaviors exhibited by a leader.

Most research in the leader behavior tradition focused on two dimensions of leadership style: (1) concern for the task to be accomplished and (2) concern for the people doing the work. The terminology used to describe these dimensions varies among many studies. Concern for task is sometimes called *initiating structure, job-centeredness*, and *task orientation*; concern for people is sometimes called *consideration, employee-centeredness,* and *relationship orientation*. But regardless of the terminology, the behaviors characteristic of each dimension are quite clear. A *leader high in concern for task* plans and defines work to be done, assigns task responsibilities, sets clear work standards, urges task completion, and monitors performance results. By contrast, a *leader high in concern for people* acts warm and supportive toward followers, maintains good social relations with them, respects their feelings, is sensitive to their needs, and shows trust in them.

Behaviors of task- and people-oriented leaders

The results of leader behavior research at first suggested that followers of people-oriented leaders would be more productive and satisfied than those working for more task-oriented leaders.[28] Later results, however, suggested that truly effective leaders were high in both concern for people and concern for task. *Figure 13.3* describes one of the popular versions of this conclusion—the Leadership Grid® of Robert Blake and Jane Mouton.[29] This grid is designed not only to describe alternative leadership styles and identify a preferred one, but also to assist in the process of leadership development. The approach uses assessments to

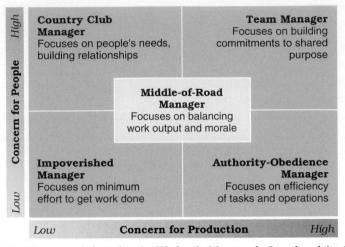

Figure 13.3   Managerial styles in Blake & Mouton's Leadership Grid.

Get Connected!

Get your Task-People leadership score on-line and in the *Career Readiness Workbook* (assessment #14).

first determine where someone falls with respect to people and task concerns. Then a training program is designed to help shift the person's style in the preferred direction of becoming strong on both dimensions. Blake and Mouton called this preferred style *team management*. This leader shares decisions with subordinates, encourages participation, and supports the teamwork needed for high levels of task accomplishment. In today's terminology, this could also be a manager who "empowers" others.

An important personal question in leadership development is, of course: "Which type of leader are you?" Is your style most typically perceived by others as one of team management? Or, is it one of the following styles that are considered by Blake and Mouton to be much less effective? *Impoverished management* displays low concern for both people and tasks. Leaders with this style turn most decisions over to the work group and show little interest in the work process or its results. *Authority-obedience management* shows high concern for the task and low concern for people. Leaders with this style make most of the decisions for the work group, give directions, and expect their orders to be followed. *Country club management* shows high concern for people and low concern for tasks. Leaders with this style are warm in interpersonal relationships, avoid conflict, and seek harmony in decision making. *Middle-of-the-road management* is noncommital in emphasizing both task and people concerns. This leader puts forth minimum required effort in balancing the task and people needs of the group to maintain adequate but not exemplary performance.

CONTINGENCY APPROACHES TO LEADERSHIP

As leadership research continued to develop, scholars recognized the need to probe still further beyond leader behaviors alone and examine them in relationship to situational attributes. Interest thus turned to yet another question: "When and under what circumstances is a particular leadership style preferable to others?" This is the essence of the following *contingency approaches*, which share the goal of understanding the conditions for leadership success in widely varying situations.

FIEDLER'S CONTINGENCY MODEL

An early contingency leadership model developed by Fred Fiedler was based on the premise that good leadership depends on a match between leadership style and situational demands.[30] Leadership style is measured on what Fiedler calls the *least-preferred coworker scale*. Known as the LPC scale, it is available as self-assessment #16 in the end-of-text *Career Readiness Workbook*. According to Fiedler, a person's LPC score describes tendencies to behave either as a task-motivated or relationship-motivated leader. This either/or concept is important. Fiedler believes that leadership style is part of one's personality; therefore, it is relatively enduring and difficult to change. Instead of trying to train a task-motivated leader to behave in a relationship-motivated manner, or vice versa, Fiedler suggests that the key to leadership success is putting the existing styles to work in situations for which they are the best "fit." This is true contingency leadership thinking with the goal of successfully matching one's style with situational demands.

Get Connected!

Get your LPC leadership score on-line and in the *Career Readiness Workbook* (assessment #16).

Understanding Leadership Situations

In Fiedler's theory, the amount of control a situation allows the leader is a critical issue in determining the correct style-situation fit. Three contingency variables are used to diagnose situational control. The *quality of leader-member relations* (good or poor) measures the degree to which the group supports the leader. The *degree of task structure* (high or low) measures the extent to which task goals, procedures, and guidelines are clearly spelled out. The *amount of position power* (strong or weak) measures the degree to which the position gives the leader power to reward and punish subordinates. *Figure 13.4* shows eight leadership situations that result from different combinations of these variables. They range from the most favorable situation of high control (good leader-member relations, high task structure, strong position power), to the least favorable situation of low control (poor leader-member relations, low task structure, weak position power).

Matching Leadership Style and Situation

Figure 13.4 also summarizes Fiedler's extensive research on the contingency relationships between situation control, leadership style, and leader effectiveness. Neither the task-oriented nor the relationship-oriented leadership style is effective all the time. Instead, each style appears to work

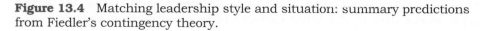

Leader–member relations	**Combinations of situational characteristics**							
	Good	Good	Good	Good	Poor	Poor	Poor	Poor
Task structure	High	High	Low	Low	High	High	Low	Low
Position power	Strong	Weak	Strong	Weak	Strong	Weak	Strong	Weak
Situational control	Very high ←							→ Very low
Preferred leadership styles	Task oriented			Relationship oriented			Task oriented	

Figure 13.4 Matching leadership style and situation: summary predictions from Fiedler's contingency theory.

www.gore.com

Empowerment is in at W. L. Gore & Associates, of Newark, Delaware. Product development specialists create teams to develop new high-quality products and manufacture them in small plants. Everyone is an "associate" at Gore, and leaders achieve their positions by accomplishment and the support of others. "Leadership," says late founder Bill Gore, "is defined by what you do, not who you are."

best when used in the right situation. The results can be stated as two propositions. *Proposition 1* is that a task-oriented leader will be most successful in either very favorable (high-control) or very unfavorable (low-control) situations. *Proposition 2* is that a relationship-oriented leader will be most successful in situations of moderate control.

Fiedler believes that leadership success depends on a good leader–situation match. This means that prospective leaders should actively seek situations for which their predominant style is most appropriate. Assume, for example, that you are the leader of a team of bank tellers. The tellers seem highly supportive of you, and their job is clearly defined regarding what needs to be done. You have the authority to evaluate their performance and to make pay and promotion recommendations. This is a high-control situation consisting of good leader-member relations, high task structure, and high position power. Figure 13.4 shows that a task-motivated leader would be most effective in this situation.

Now take another example. Suppose that you are chairperson of a committee asked to improve labor–management relations in a manufacturing plant. Although the goal is clear, no one can say for sure how to accomplish it. Task structure is low. Because committee members are free to quit any time they want, the chairperson has little position power. Because not all members believe the committee is necessary, poor leader-member relations are apparent. According to Figure 13.4, this low-control situation also calls for a task-motivated leader.

Finally, assume that you are the new head of a retail section in a large department store. Because you were selected over one of the popular sales clerks you now supervise, leader-member relations are poor. Task structure is high since the clerk's job is well defined. Your position power is low because the clerks work under a seniority system and fixed wage schedule. Figure 13.4 shows that this moderate-control situation requires a relationship-motivated leader.

HERSEY-BLANCHARD SITUATIONAL LEADERSHIP MODEL

The Hersey-Blanchard situational leadership model suggests that successful leaders adjust their styles depending on the *maturity* of followers, indicated by their readiness to perform in a given situation.[31] "Readiness," in this sense, is based on how able and willing or confident followers are to perform required tasks. As shown in *Figure 13.5*, the possible leadership styles that result from different combinations of task-oriented and relationship-oriented behaviors are as follows:

Leadership styles in the situational model →

- *Delegating*—allowing the group to make and take responsibility for task decisions; a low-task, low-relationship style.
- *Participating*—emphasizing shared ideas and participative decisions on task directions; a low-task, high-relationship style.
- *Selling*—explaining task directions in a supportive and persuasive way; a high-task, high-relationship style.
- *Telling*—giving specific task directions and closely supervising work; a high-task, low-relationship style.

Managers using this model must be able to implement the alternative leadership styles as needed. The *delegating style* works best in high-readiness situations of able and willing or confident followers; the *telling style* works best at the other extreme of low readiness, where followers

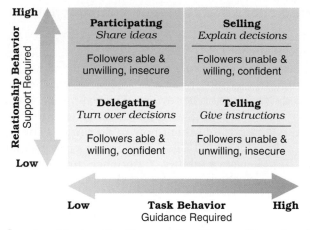

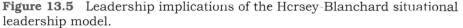

Figure 13.5 Leadership implications of the Hersey-Blanchard situational leadership model.

are unable and unwilling or insecure. The *participating style* is recommended for low-to-moderate readiness (followers able but unwilling or insecure) and the *selling style* for moderate-to-high readiness (followers unable but willing or confident). Hersey and Blanchard further believe that leadership styles should be adjusted as followers change over time. The model also implies that if the correct styles are used in lower-readiness situations, followers will "mature" and grow in ability, willingness, and confidence. This allows the leader to become less directive as followers mature. Although the Hersey-Blanchard model is intuitively appealing, limited research has been accomplished on it to date.[32]

HOUSE'S PATH-GOAL LEADERSHIP THEORY

A third contingency leadership approach is the *path-goal theory* advanced by Robert House.[33] This theory suggests that an effective leader is one who clarifies paths through which followers can achieve both task-related and personal goals. The best leaders help people progress along these paths, remove any barriers that stand in their way, and provide appropriate rewards for task accomplishment. House identifies four leadership styles that may be used in this "path-goal" sense:

* *Directive leadership*—letting subordinates know what is expected; giving directions on what to do and how; scheduling work to be done; maintaining definite standards of performance; clarifying the leader's role in the group.

* *Supportive leadership*—doing things to make work more pleasant; treating group members as equals; being friendly and approachable; showing concern for the well-being of subordinates.

* *Achievement-oriented leadership*—setting challenging goals; expecting the highest levels of performance; emphasizing continuous improvement in performance; displaying confidence in meeting high standards.

* *Participative leadership*—involving subordinates in decision making; consulting with subordinates; asking for suggestions from subordinates; using these suggestions when making a decision.

Leadership styles in the path-goal theory

Path-Goal Predictions and Managerial Implications

The path-goal leadership theory is summarized in *Figure 13.6*. It advises a manager to always use leadership styles that complement situational needs. This means that the leader adds value by contributing things that are missing from the situation or that need strengthening; she or he specifically avoids redundant behaviors. For example, when team members are expert and competent at their tasks it is unnecessary and not functional for the leader to tell them how to do things. The important contingencies for making good path-goal leadership choices include subordinate personal characteristics (ability, experience, and locus of control) and the work environment characteristics (task structure, authority system, and work group).

In path-goal theory, for example, the match of leader behaviors and situation might take the following forms.[34] When *job assignments* are unclear, directive leadership is appropriate to clarify task objectives and expected rewards. When *worker self-confidence* is low, supportive leadership is appropriate to increase confidence by emphasizing individual abilities and offering needed assistance. When *performance incentives* are poor, participative leadership is appropriate to clarify individual needs and identify appropriate rewards. When *task challenge* is insufficient in a job, achievement-oriented leadership is appropriate to set goals and raise performance aspirations. In all these examples, the value added by the choice of leadership style is expected to lead to greater effort by the subordinate and improve satisfaction and performance.

Substitutes for Leadership

○ **Substitutes for leadership** are factors in the work setting that direct work efforts without the involvement of a leader.

Path-goal theory has also contributed to the recognition of what some theorists call **substitutes for leadership**.[35] These are aspects of the work setting and the people involved that can reduce the need for a leader's personal involvement. In effect, they make leadership from the "outside" unnecessary because leadership is already built into the situation. Possible substitutes for leadership include *subordinate characteristics* such as ability, experience, and independence; *task characteristics* such as routineness and availability of feedback; and *organizational characteristics* such as clarity of plans and formalization of rules and procedures. When substitutes are present, managers should avoid redundant leadership behaviors and concentrate on things that truly require outside attention.

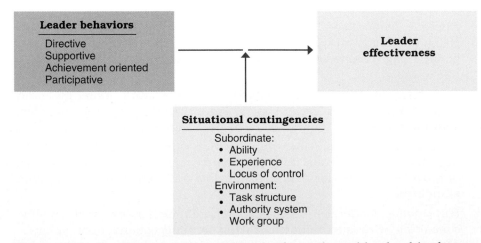

Figure 13.6 Contingency relationships in the path-goal leadership theory.

VROOM-JAGO LEADER-PARTICIPATION MODEL

The Vroom-Jago leader-participation model is designed to help a leader choose the method of decision making that best fits the nature of the problem being faced. In this approach, an effective leader is someone able to consistently choose and implement from the following alternatives the most appropriate decision methods.[36]

An **authority decision** is one made by the leader and then communicated to the group. Participation is minimized. No input is asked of group members other than to provide specific information on request. A **consultative decision** is made by the leader after asking group members for information, advice, or opinions. In some cases, group members are consulted individually; in others, the consultation occurs during a meeting of the group as a whole. In a **group decision**, all members participate in making a decision and work together to achieve a consensus regarding the preferred course of action. This approach to decision making is a form of empowerment, and it is successful to the extent that each member is ultimately able to accept the logic and feasibility of the final group decision.[37]

For a manager who wants to be successful at leading through participation, the challenge in effectively managing the decision process is twofold. First, the leader must know when each decision method is the preferred approach. Second, the leader must be able to properly implement each when needed. As shown in *Figure 13.7*, Vroom-Jago's normative model of leadership effectiveness recommends using more group-oriented and participative decision methods when:

- Leaders lack sufficient information to solve a problem by themselves.
- The problem is unclear and help is needed to clarify the situation.
- Acceptance of the decision by others is necessary for implementation.
- Adequate time is available to allow for true participation.

In true contingency fashion, no one decision method is considered by the Vroom-Jago model as universally superior to any others. Rather, leadership success results when the decision method used correctly matches the characteristics of the problem to be solved. Each of the three decision methods is appropriate in certain situations, and each has its advantages and disadvantages. The key rules guiding the choice relate to: (1) *decision quality*—based on the location of information needed for problem solving; and, (2) *decision acceptance*—based on the importance of subordinate acceptance to eventual solution implementation. You may think of these in the context of an equation: Decision Effectiveness = Decision Quality × Decision Acceptance.

Use of participative decision methods offers important benefits to the leader.[38] They help improve decision quality by bringing more information to bear on the problem. They help improve decision acceptance as participants gain understanding and become committed to the process. And, they also contribute to the development of leadership potential in others through the experience of active participation in the problem-solving process. However, there is also a cost to be considered. The greater the participation, the more time required for the decision process. Leaders do not always have sufficient time available; some problems must be resolved immediately. In such cases, the authority decision may be the only option. As shown in Figure 13.7, the more authority-oriented decisions work best when leaders personally have the expertise needed to solve the problem, they are confident and capable of

○ An **authority decision** is a decision made by the leader and then communicated to the group.

○ A **consultative decision** is a decision made by a leader after receiving information, advice, or opinions from group members.

○ A **group decision** is a decision made with the full participation of all group members.

←

When participation works best

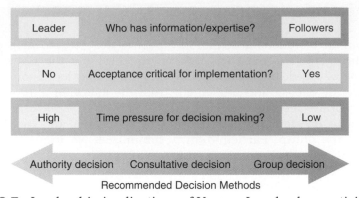

Leader	Who has information/expertise?	Followers
No	Acceptance critical for implementation?	Yes
High	Time pressure for decision making?	Low

Authority decision   Consultative decision   Group decision

Recommended Decision Methods

Figure 13.7 Leadership implications of Vroom-Jago leader-participation model.

acting alone, others are likely to accept the decision they make, and little or no time is available for discussion.

ISSUES IN LEADERSHIP DEVELOPMENT

○ A **charismatic leader** is a leader who develops special leader-follower relationships and inspires followers in extraordinary ways.

Current trends in leadership thinking seek to integrate and extend the insights discussed so far in this chapter.[39] This is the era of "superleaders" who, through vision and strength of personality, have a truly inspirational impact on others.[40] Their leadership efforts result in followers not only meeting performance expectations but performing above and beyond them. These are **charismatic leaders** who develop special leader-follower relationships and inspire others in extraordinary ways. The presence of charismatic leadership is reflected in followers who are enthusiastic about the leader and his or her ideas, who work very hard to support them, who remain loyal and devoted, and who seek superior performance accomplishments.[41]

TAKE IT TO THE CASE!

Southwest Airlines
It Takes a Leader to Make the Leadership Difference

Herb Kelleher has led Southwest Airlines from a small startup in 1971 to one of America's premier airlines. And he's done it with a difference—low fares, on-time performance, and . . . fun! It wasn't just a winning airline industry strategy—finding a market niche and sticking with it—that Kelleher's leadership has brought to the firm. It's also a leadership style focused on building and sustaining a positive organizational culture. Kelleher's personal style has been described as "dynamic" and based on "humor and friendliness." He expects the same from Southwest's employees. Those that fit the model tend to stay; the firm is a model for maintaining employee loyalty. What is his advice to other would-be leaders? "Ask your employees what's important to them. Ask your customers what is important to them. Then do it."[42]

TRANSFORMATIONAL LEADERSHIP

The term **transformational leadership** describes someone who is truly inspirational as a leader and who arouses others to seek extraordinary performance accomplishments. A transformational leader uses charisma and related qualities to raise aspirations and shift people and organizational systems into new high-performance patterns. Scholars differentiate this from **transactional leadership**, which describes someone who is more methodical in keeping others focused on progress toward goal accomplishment. A transactional leader adjusts tasks, rewards, and structures to move followers toward accomplishing organizational objectives.[43]

Importantly, these are not mutually exclusive leadership approaches. Transactional leadership is a foundation or building block that helps support transformational leadership. On its own, however, transactional leadership is acknowledged to be insufficient to meet the leadership challenges and demands of today's dynamic work environments. In settings where continuous and often large-scale change is often a high priority, the additional inspirational impact of transformational leadership is essential to achieve sustainable high-performance results.

The notion of transformational leadership offers a distinct management challenge, with important personal development implications. It is not enough to possess leadership traits, know the leadership behaviors, and understand leadership contingencies to act effectively from a transactional perspective. Any manager must also be prepared to lead in an inspirational way and with a compelling personality. The transformational leader provides a strong aura of vision and contagious enthusiasm that substantially raises the confidence, aspirations, and commitments of followers to meet high-performance demands. The special qualities that are often characteristic of such transformational leaders include the following:[44]

- *Vision*—having ideas and a clear sense of direction; communicating them to others; developing excitement about accomplishing shared "dreams."
- *Charisma*—arousing others' enthusiasm, faith, loyalty, pride, and trust in themselves through the power of personal reference and appeals to emotion.
- *Symbolism*—identifying "heroes," offering special rewards, and holding spontaneous and planned ceremonies to celebrate excellence and high achievement.
- *Empowerment*—helping others develop, removing performance obstacles, sharing responsibilities, and delegating truly challenging work.
- *Intellectual stimulation*—gaining the involvement of others by creating awareness of problems and stirring their imagination to create high-quality solutions.
- *Integrity*—being honest and credible, acting consistently out of personal conviction, and following through commitments.

> ○ **Transformational leadership** is inspirational leadership that gets people to do more in achieving high performance.

> ○ **Transactional leadership** is leadership that directs the efforts of others through tasks, rewards, and structures.

← Attributes of transformational leaders

EMOTIONAL INTELLIGENCE

An area of leadership development that is currently very popular is **emotional intelligence**, first discussed in Chapter 1 as an element of the essential human skills of managers. As popularized by the work of Daniel Goleman, "EI" is defined as "the ability to manage ourselves and our relationships effectively."[45] According to his research, a leader's emotional

> ○ **Emotional intelligence** is the ability to manage ourselves and our relationships effectively.

intelligence is an important influence on his or her effectiveness, especially in more senior management positions. In Goleman's words: "the higher the rank of the person considered to be a star performer, the more emotional intelligence capabilities showed up as the reason for his or her effectiveness."[46] This is a strong endorsement, indeed, for consideration of one's emotional intelligence in a developing portfolio of comprehensive leadership capabilities. Important too is Goleman's belief that emotional intelligence skills can be learned at any age—it's never too late.

For purposes of research and training, Goleman breaks emotional intelligence down into five critical components.[47] He argues that each of us should strive to build competencies in each component and thereby maximize our ability to utilize emotional intelligence and build better relationships with others. The critical components of EI are the following. *Self-awareness* is an ability to understand our own moods and emotions, and understand their impact on our work and on others. *Self-regulation* is the ability to think before we act, and to control otherwise disruptive impulses. *Motivation* is the ability to work hard with persistence, and for reasons other than money and status. *Empathy* is the ability to understand the emotions of others, and to use this understanding to better relate to them. *Social skill* is the ability to establish rapport with others, and to build good relationships and networks.

According to Goleman, these skills in emotional intelligence are necessary for leadership success. A person lacking in EI, for example, might fail to recognize how excessive stress is contributing to bad attitudes and negative behavior among team members. As a team leader, he or she might push too hard for performance results and further complicate the situation. A leader high in EI would be quicker to notice that emotions were running high due to stress and thus take action to help the team members better deal with the stressful conditions. Team performance would likely improve as a result of this more "emotionally intelligent" leadership response to a problem situation.

GENDER AND LEADERSHIP

One of the leadership themes of continuing interest deals with the question of whether gender influences leadership styles and/or effectiveness. Sara Levinson, President of NFL Properties, Inc., of New York, for example, explored the question directly in a conversation with the all-male members of her management team. "Is my leadership style different from a man's?" she asked. "Yes," they replied, suggesting that the very fact that she was asking the question of them helped to demonstrate the difference. They also indicated that her leadership style emphasized communication and gathering ideas and opinions from others. When Levinson probed further by asking the team members "Is this a distinctly 'female' trait?," they said that they thought it was.[48]

The evidence clearly supports that both women and men can be effective leaders.[49] As suggested by the prior example, however, they may tend toward somewhat different styles.[50] Victor Vroom and his colleagues have investigated gender differences in respect to the leader-participation model discussed earlier.[51] They find women managers to be significantly more participative than their male counterparts. Although followers in their studies value participation by all leaders, they tend to value participation by female leaders more highly than by men. Women may tend toward a style sometimes

Dimensions of emotional intelligence

@

Get Connected!

Get your EI score on-line and in the *Career Readiness Workbook* (assessment #26).

REALITY Check 13.2

How Do Women Lead? A study of the performance evaluations of 425 managers by Hagberg Consulting Group found women managers significantly outscoring men on their ability to motivate others. Take the on-line "Reality Check" to learn more about gender differences in this study of male and female executives.

referred to as *interactive leadership*.[52] This style focuses on the building of consensus and good interpersonal relations through communication and involvement. Leaders of this style display behaviors typically considered democratic and participative—such as showing respect for others, caring for others, and sharing power and information with others. This interactive style also has qualities in common with the transformational leadership just discussed.[53] Men, by contrast, may tend toward more of a transactional approach to leadership—relying more on directive and assertive behaviors, and using authority in a traditional "command and control" sense.

Given the emphasis on shared power, communication, cooperation, and participation in the new-form organizations of today, these results are provocative. Gender issues aside, the interactive leadership style seems to be an excellent fit with the demands of a diverse workforce and the new workplace. As Harvard Professor and consultant Rosabeth Moss Kanter says: "Women get high ratings on exactly those skills required to succeed in the Global Information Age, where teamwork and partnering are so important."[54] Regardless of whether the relevant behaviors are displayed by women or men, it seems clear that future leadership success will rest more often on one's capacity to lead through positive relationships and empowerment than through aloofness and formal authority. The chapters that follow on leading through motivation, communication, interpersonal relations, group dynamics and teamwork, and change leadership are highly relevant to this issue.

DRUCKER'S "OLD-FASHIONED" LEADERSHIP

Peter Drucker offers another very pragmatic approach to leadership in the new workplace. It is based on what he refers to as a "good old-fashioned" view of the plain hard work it takes to be a successful leader. Consider, for example, Drucker's description of a telephone conversation with a potential consulting client who was the human resources vice president of a big bank: "We'd want you to run a seminar for us on how one acquires charisma," she said. Drucker's response was not what she expected. He advised her that there's more to leadership than the popular emphasis on personal qualities that offer a sense of personal "dash" or charisma. In fact, he said that "leadership . . . is work."[55]

Drucker's observations on leadership offer a useful complement to the transformational leadership ideas just discussed. He identifies the following three essentials of leadership. First, Drucker believes that the foundation of effective leadership is *defining and establishing a sense of mission*. A good leader sets the goals, priorities, and standards. A good leader keeps them all clear and visible, and maintains them. In Drucker's words, "The leader's first task is to be the trumpet that sounds a clear sound." Second, he believes in *accepting leadership as a responsibility rather than a rank*. Good leaders surround themselves with talented people. They are not afraid to develop strong and capable subordinates. And they do not blame others when things go wrong. As Drucker says, "The buck stops here" is still a good adage to remember. Third, Drucker stresses the importance of *earning and keeping the trust of others*. The key here is the leader's personal integrity. The followers of good leaders trust them. This means that they believe the leader means what he or she says and that his or her actions will be consistent with what is said. In Drucker's words again, "Effective leadership . . . is not based on being clever; it is based primarily on being consistent."

ETHICAL ASPECTS OF LEADERSHIP

○ **Integrity** in leadership is honesty, credibility, and consistency in putting values into action.

Firmly embedded in the concept of transformational leadership and good old-fashioned leadership is **integrity**—the leader's honesty, credibility, and consistency in putting values into action. Leaders have an undeniable responsibility to set high ethical standards to guide the behavior of followers. For managers, the ethical aspects of leadership are important and everyday concerns. At General Electric, for example, the "A" leader is described as someone with "the instinct and courage to make the tough calls." This leader also does so "decisively, but with fairness and absolute integrity."[56]

Concerned about what he perceives as a lack of momentum in organizational life, John W. Gardner talks about the "moral aspects" of leadership.[57] "Most people in most organizations most of the time," he writes, "are more stale than they know, more bored than they care to admit." Leaders, according to Gardner, have a moral obligation to supply the necessary spark to awaken the potential of each individual—to urge each person "to take the initiative in performing leader-like acts." He points out that high expectations tend to generate high performance. It is the leader's job to remove "obstacles to our effective functioning—to help individuals see and pursue shared purposes."

Gardner's premise is that people with a sense of ownership of their jobs will naturally outperform those who feel they are outsiders. Moral leaders instill ownership by truly respecting others and helping them to do their best. By doing so they build organizations that consistently perform to society's expectations.[58] Moral leadership, therefore, must be clearly and strongly anchored in a true commitment to people. This wisdom is evident in the following leadership advice from two exemplars featured in our early chapter examples, Max DePree of Herman Miller and Lorraine Monroe of The School Leadership Academy.[59]

"Nobody is common. Everybody has a right to be an insider."

Max DePree

"The real leader is a servant of the people she leads."

Lorraine Monroe

The Chapter 13 Study Guide will help you review chapter content, prepare for examinations, and further build your career readiness. The *Summary* briefly highlights answers to questions first posed in the chapter opening Planning Ahead section. The list of *Key Terms* allows you to double check your familiarity with basic concepts and definitions. *Self-Test 13* gives you the opportunity to test your basic comprehension of chapter content using sample test questions. Suggestions offered as *Career Readiness Activities* direct your attention to relevant sections of the end-of-text Career Readiness Workbook, as well as to special Electronic Resources on The *Management 7/e* web site.

SUMMARY

What is the nature of leadership?

- Leadership is the process of inspiring others to work hard to accomplish important tasks.
- Vision, or a clear sense of the future, is increasingly considered to be an essential ingredient of effective leadership.
- Visionary leaders are able to communicate their vision to others and build the commitments needed to perform the required work.
- Power, the ability to get others to do what you want them to do, is an essential ingredient of effective leadership.
- Managerial power may be gained through the formal position in the organization and/or through personal sources of influence.
- Sources of position power include rewards, coercion, and legitimacy or formal authority; sources of personal power include expertise and reference.
- Effective leaders empower others—that is, they help and allow others to take action and make job-related decisions on their own.

What are the important leadership traits and behaviors?

- Early leadership research searched unsuccessfully for a definitive set of personal traits that differentiated successful and unsuccessful leaders.
- Traits that seem to have a positive impact on leadership include drive, integrity, and self-confidence, among others.
- Research on leader behaviors focused on alternative leadership styles that involved concerns for task and concerns for people.
- One suggestion of leader-behavior researchers is that effective leaders will be good at team-based or participative leadership that is high in both task and people concerns.

355

What are the contingency theories of leadership?

- Contingency leadership approaches point out that no one leadership style always works best; rather, the best style is one that properly matches the demands of each unique situation.
- Fiedler's contingency theory describes how situational differences in task structure, position power, and leader-member relations may influence which leadership style works best.
- House's path-goal theory points out that leaders should add value to situations by responding with supportive, directive, achievement-oriented, and/or participative styles as needed.
- The Hersey-Blanchard situational model recommends using task-oriented and people-oriented behaviors, depending on the "maturity" of the group a manager is attempting to lead.
- The Vroom-Jago leader-participation theory advises leaders to choose decision-making methods—individual, consultative, group—that best fit the problems they are trying to resolve.

What are current issues in leadership development?

- Transactional leadership focuses on tasks, rewards, and structures to influence follower behavior.
- Charismatic leadership creates a truly inspirational relationship between leader and followers.
- Transformational leaders use charisma and related qualities to inspire extraordinary efforts in support of innovation and large-scale change.
- Emotional intelligence, the ability to manage our relationships and ourselves effectively, is an important dimension of leadership capability.
- The interactive leadership style seems consistent with the demands of the new workplace and the emphasis on communication, involvement, and interpersonal respect.
- All leadership is "hard work" that always requires a personal commitment to meeting the highest ethical and moral standards.

KEY TERMS

SELF-TEST 13

Take this test here or on-line much as you would in a normal classroom situation. It is a good way to check your basic comprehension of chapter material. Answers may be found at the end of the book.

MULTIPLE-CHOICE QUESTIONS:

1. Someone with a clear sense of the future and the actions needed to get there is considered a _____ leader.
   (a) task-oriented (b) people-oriented (c) transactional (d) visionary

2. Managerial power = _____ power × _____ power.
   (a) reward, punishment (b) reward, expert (c) legitimate, position
   (d) position, personal

3. A manager who says "Because I am the boss, you must do what I ask" is relying on _____ power.
   (a) reward (b) legitimate (c) expert (d) referent

4. Among the personal traits now considered important for managerial success is _____ .
   (a) self-confidence (b) gender (c) age (d) height

5. According to research into leader behaviors, the most successful leader is one who acts with a _____ .
   (a) high initiating structure (b) high consideration
   (c) high concern for task and high concern for people
   (d) low job centeredness and high employee centeredness

6. In Fiedler's contingency theory, both highly favorable and highly unfavorable leadership situations are best dealt with by a _____ leader.
   (a) task-oriented (b) democratic (c) participative (d) relationship-oriented

7. Directive leadership and achievement-oriented leadership are among the options in House's _____ theory of leadership.
   (a) trait (b) path-goal (c) transformational (d) life-cycle

8. Vision, charisma, integrity, and symbolism are all on the list of attributes typically associated with _____ leaders.
   (a) contingency (b) informal (c) transformational (d) transactional

9. _____ leadership theory suggests that leadership success is achieved by correctly matching leadership style with situations.
   (a) Path-goal (b) Fiedler's (c) Transformational (d) Blake and Mouton's

10. In the leader-behavior approaches to leadership, someone who does a very good job of planning work, setting standards, and monitoring results would be considered a _____ leader.
    (a) task-oriented (b) control-oriented (c) achievement-oriented
    (d) employee-centered

TRUE-FALSE QUESTIONS:

11. A good leader will always be a good manager.   T   F

12. Possession of so-called leadership traits guarantees that a person will be a successful leader.   T   F

13. Referent power is developed and maintained in part through good interpersonal skills.   T   F

14. One outcome of the leader-behavior approach is the belief that people can be trained to acquire and utilize a successful leadership style.   T   F

15. In Fiedler's contingency leadership approach, a person's leadership style is considered very flexible and easy to modify from one situation to the next.   T   F

16. A major point of path-goal theory is that a leader's contributions should complement or "add value" to a situation.   T   F

17. In the Vroom-Jago leader-participation model, all decisions should be made by group consensus.   T   F

18. A charismatic leader is someone who is very successful with the transactional aspects of leadership.   T   F

19. Managers who empower their subordinates to make more decisions are losing power themselves.   T   F

20. The only leadership theory now considered correct is the Hershey-Blanchard situational theory.   T   F

SHORT-RESPONSE QUESTIONS:

21. Why does a person need both position power and personal power to achieve long-term managerial effectiveness?

22. What is the major insight offered by the Vroom-Jago leader-participation model?

23. What are the three variables that Fiedler's contingency theory uses to diagnose the favorability of leadership situations, and what does each mean?

24. How does Peter Drucker's view of "good old-fashioned leadership" differ from the popular concept of transformational leadership?

APPLICATION QUESTION:

25. When Marcel Henry took over as leader of a new product development team, he was both excited and apprehensive. "I wonder," he said to himself on the first day in his new assignment, "if I can meet the challenges of leadership." Later that day, Marcel shares this concern with you during a coffee break. Based on the insights of this chapter, how would you describe to him the essential implications for his personal leadership development of the current thinking on charismatic or transformational leadership?

CAREER readiness ACTIVITIES

Recommended learning activities from the end-of-text *Career Readiness Workbook* for this chapter include:

Career Advancement Portfolio
- Individual writing and group presentation assignments based on any of the following activities.

Case for Critical Thinking
- Southwest Airlines—How Herb Kelleher Led the Way

Integrative Learning Activities
- Research Project 1 – Diversity Lessons
- Research Project 2 – Changing Corporate Cultures
- Integrative Case – Outback Steakhouse. Inc.
- Integrative Case – Richard Branson Meets the New Economy

Exercises in Teamwork
- What Managers Do (#2)
- Sources and Uses of Power (#18)
- Empowering Others (#20)
- Gender Differences in Management (#21)

Self-Assessments
- Managerial Assumptions (#4)
- "T-P" Leadership Questionnaire (#14)
- "T-T" Leadership Style (#15)
- Least-Preferred Co-worker Scale (#16)
- Emotional Intelligence (#26)

The *Fast Company* Collection On-Line
- Tony Schwartz, "How Do You Feel?"

ELECTRONIC RESOURCES

@ GET CONNECTED! Don't forget to take full advantage of the on-line support for *Management 7/e*.
- Chapter 13 On-line Study Guide
- Chapter 13 Self-test Answers
- Chapter 13 E-Resource Center

14

Motivation and rewards

Planning ahead

GETTING CONNECTED

Ipswitch, Inc. — *Value Diversity and Individual Differences*
How would you like to work for a company that cares enough to not want you to burn yourself out through overworking? Take a look at Ipswitch, Inc., a small privately held software firm specializing in software solutions for Internet and intranet applications.

Founded in 1991 by Roger Greene, Ipswitch is a firm with a mission. As Greene says: "I set out to build a company where I could set ambitious goals, achieve them, enjoy working there for a long time to come, and make money."

That's not all to the Ipswitch story. Greene regularly reminds employees about the need to take time for personal affairs—not missing vacation time, using their personal days, for example. He has also just increased the amount of paid time off to five weeks from the previous three. Why?

Greene felt personally refreshed after a long trip to India, and decided all employees should have enough time for rejuvenating vacations.

In an industry where employee turnover is very high, the Ipswitch culture pays off with turnover under 9 percent. It's a caring company, where employees get to know each other and provide a support system—at work and personally.

When technical support administrator Mary Lawlor's boyfriend died, almost all the employees went to the wake and funeral. The firm hired a bereavement counselor to help. Mary was overwhelmed by her co-workers' support, saying: "There aren't words to describe what that did for me."

Greene's philosophy is firmly embedded in the corporate culture, even as Ipswitch grows. Ipswitch pays higher salaries to keep attracting the best talent, rather than relying on the more risky stock options. It invests heavily in research and development to maintain a progressive and creative environment. But still, Ipswitch remains committed to the individual and work-life balance.

Chief Financial Officer Art Beals says: "We downgrade the idea of being a workaholic." As for the tendency of many people to work hard for 30 to 40 years and then retire to "have fun," Greene, says: "I'd much rather live life as it goes along and do neat things while you're working and enjoy every year of your life."

Not long ago Ipswitch employees celebrated the firm's tenth-year anniversary. As you might expect, they did it in style—with a four-day cruise to the Bahamas![1]

@ Get Connected!

What do you want from work? There's a lot of firms like Ipswitch out there, but you have to go looking. Don't settle for anything less than the best fit between the work environment and opportunities and your personal goals. Build a portfolio of skills that is always marketable. Stay informed on where the best jobs are.
Get connected!

Why do some people work enthusiastically, often doing more than required to turn out extraordinary performance? Why do others hold back and do the minimum needed to avoid reprimand or termination? How can a team leader or manager build a high-performance work setting? What can be done to ensure that the highest possible performance is achieved by every person in every job on every workday? These questions are, or should be, asked by managers in all work settings. Good answers begin with a true respect for people, with all of their talents and diversity, as the human capital of organizations. The best managers already know this. Like the opening example of Ipswitch, Inc. and Roger Greene's leadership, the work cultures they create invariably reflect an awareness that "productivity through people" is an irreplaceable ingredient for long-term organizational success. Consider these comments by those who know what it means to lead a high-performance organization.[2]

When people feel connected to something with a purpose greater than themselves, it inspires them to reach for levels they might not otherwise obtain. . . . Our business is based on human potential.
George Zimmer, founder and CEO of Men's Warehouse

No business goal is worth sacrificing your values. If you have to treat people poorly, or cut corners in your dealings with customers, forget it. . . . You can build an organization based on mutual loyalty . . . but you can't do it if you treat people as disposable.
Patrick Kelly, CEO of PSS World Medical

It's part of a soundly designed strategy. . . . If you hire adults and treat them like adults, then they'll behave like adults.
Jim Goodnight, CEO of SAS Institute

It is easy to say as a leader or in a mission statement that "people are our most important asset." But the proof comes with backing such a statement up with actions that support it. This means consistently demonstrating that one's organization is committed to people, that it offers a truly "motivational" work environment. In this sense, however, human nature is always both fascinating and challenging. The human side of the workplace becomes complicated as the intricacies of human psychology come into play with daily events and situations. At a packaging plant in California, for example, senior executive Kevin Kelley learned that a supervisor was starting to retire on the job. The man had worked his 20 years and felt it was time to slow down. He was unresponsive to gentle "nudging" from co-workers and managers. But when Kelley politely confronted him with the facts, saying, "We need your talent, your knowledge of those machines," the supervisor responded with new vigor in his work and earned the praise of his peers. For his part, Kelley believes in employee involvement and claims that one of the best motivators is information on the firm's competitive environment. With information, so to speak, comes the motivation to work hard and keep the company competitive.[3]

WHAT IS MOTIVATION?

○ **Motivation** accounts for the level, direction, and persistence of effort expended at work.

This chapter contains many ideas on how managers exercise leadership in ways that encourage other people to work hard in their jobs. The concept of **motivation** is central to this goal. The term is used in management theory to describe forces within the individual that account for the level, direction, and persistence of effort expended at work. Simply put, a highly motivated person works hard at a job; an unmotivated person does not. A manager who leads through motivation does so by creating conditions under which other people feel consistently inspired to work hard. Obviously, a highly motivated workforce is indispensable to the achievement of sustained high-performance results.

MOTIVATION AND REWARDS

A *reward* is a work outcome of positive value to the individual. A motivational work setting is rich in rewards for people whose performance accomplishments help meet organizational objectives. In management, it is useful to distinguish between two types of rewards, extrinsic and intrinsic. **Extrinsic rewards** are externally administered. They are valued outcomes given to someone by another person, typically, a supervisor or higher-level manager. Common workplace examples are pay bonuses, promotions, time off, special assignments, office fixtures, awards, verbal praise, and the like. In all cases, the motivational stimulus of extrinsic rewards originates outside of the individual; the rewards are made available by another person or by the organizational system.[4]

> ○ An **extrinsic reward** is provided by someone else.

Intrinsic rewards, by contrast, are self-administered. They occur "naturally" as a person performs a task and are, in this sense, built directly into the job itself. The major sources of intrinsic rewards are the feelings of competency, personal development, and self-control people experience in their work.[5] In contrast to extrinsic rewards, the motivational stimulus of intrinsic rewards is internal and does not depend on the actions of some other person. Being self-administered, they offer the great advantage and power of "motivating from within." An air traffic controller, for example, says, "I don't know of anything I'd rather be doing. I love working the airplanes."[6] At a small copper kettle manufacturer in northern Ohio, 50-year-old Steve Schifer makes timpani drum bowls. He says: "It gets in your blood and you can't get rid of it. It's something you can create with your hands and no one else can."[7]

> ○ An **intrinsic reward** occurs naturally during job performance.

REWARDS AND PERFORMANCE

Starbucks, the popular coffee house chain, seems to have the recipe right—not just for coffee, but also for rewards and performance. The company offers a stock option plan to all its employees. Called "bean stock," the incentive plan offers employees stock options linked to their base pay. This means they can buy the company's stock at a fixed price in the future; if the market value is higher than the price of their option, they gain. CEO Howard Schulz says the plan had an immediate impact on attitudes and performance. The phrase "bean-stocking it" came to be used by employees when they found ways to reduce costs or increase sales. Schulz is committed to the motivational value of the innovative reward plan.[8]

There are many possible ways to creatively link rewards and performance in the new workplace, that is, to establish performance-contingent rewards. To take full advantage of the possibilities, however, managers must (1) respect diversity and individual differences, (2) clearly understand what people want from work, and (3) allocate rewards to satisfy the interests of both individuals and the organization. Among the insights into this

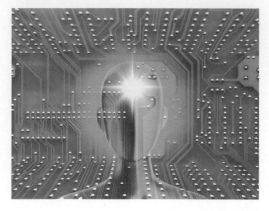

ENTREPRENEURSHIP (www.saba.com)
Saba Software, Inc. Investing in Human
Capital Pays for Itself

For organizations dedicated to innovation and customer service there's no substitute for human capital in the form of knowledge, skills, and experience. At Saba Software, Inc., getting and keeping the best talent is essential in the highly competitive information technology industry. The firm is proud of Chris Hegleson, an innovator with two patents to his credit. Hegleson could work just about anywhere. Why does he stay with Saba? Because it's a good place to work. He says that the firm is committed to employee training, staffed with workers who like and help one another, and is a far cry from the "ruthless" work environments he experienced at other companies. While quick to leave less-favored employers, at Saba he doesn't return the calls of headhunters.[9]

complex process that are available, the *content theories of motivation* help us to understand human needs and how people with different needs may respond to different work situations. The *process theories of motivation* offer additional insights into how people give meaning to rewards and then respond with various work-related behaviors. The *reinforcement theory of motivation* focuses attention on the environment as a major source of rewards and influence on human behavior.

CONTENT THEORIES OF MOTIVATION

○ A **need** is an unfulfilled physiological or psychological desire.

Most discussions of motivation begin with the concept of individual **needs**—the unfulfilled physiological or psychological desires of an individual. Content theories of motivation use individual needs to explain the behaviors and attitudes of people at work. The basic logic is straightforward. People have needs; these needs result in behaviors to satisfy them by obtaining extrinsic and intrinsic rewards. Although each of the following theories discusses a slightly different set of needs, all agree that needs cause tensions that influence attitudes and behavior. Good managers and leaders establish conditions in which people are able to satisfy important needs through their work. They also take action to eliminate work obstacles that interfere with the satisfaction of important needs.

HIERARCHY OF NEEDS THEORY

○ **Lower-order needs** are physiological, safety, and social needs in Maslow's hierarchy.

○ **Higher-order needs** are esteem and self-actualization needs in Maslow's hierarchy.

The theory of human needs developed by Abraham Maslow was introduced in Chapter 4 as an important foundation of the history of management thought. Recall that according to his hierarchy of human needs, **lower-order needs** include physiological, safety, and social concerns, and **higher-order needs** include esteem and self-actualization concerns.[10] Whereas lower-order needs are desires for social and physical well-being, the higher-order needs represent a person's desires for psychological development and growth.

Maslow offers two principles to describe how these needs affect human behavior. The *deficit principle* states that a satisfied need is not a motivator of behavior. People are expected to act in ways that satisfy deprived needs—that is, needs for which a "deficit" exists. The *progression principle* states that a need at one level does not become activated until the next-lower-level need is already satisfied. People are expected to advance step by step up the hierarchy in their search for need satisfactions. At the level of self-actualization, the more these needs are satisfied, the stronger they are supposed to grow. According to Maslow, a person should continue to be motivated by opportunities for self-fulfillment as long as the other needs remain satisfied.

Benefits that Attract the Best Workers
Compensation and benefits are important sources of need satisfaction. Take the on-line "Reality Check" to learn more about benefit priorities in the American workforce.

Although research has not verified the strict deficit and progression principles just presented, Maslow's ideas are very helpful for understanding the needs of people at work and for determining what can be done to satisfy them. His theory advises managers to recognize that deprived needs may negatively influence attitudes and behaviors. By the same token, providing opportunities for need satisfaction may have positive motivational consequences. *Figure 14.1* illustrates how managers can use Maslow's ideas to better meet the needs of the people with whom they work. Notice that the higher-order self-actualization needs are served entirely by intrinsic rewards. The esteem needs are served by both intrinsic and extrinsic rewards. Lower-order needs are served solely by extrinsic rewards.

ERG THEORY

One of the most promising efforts to build on Maslow's work is the ERG theory proposed by Clayton Alderfer.[11] This theory collapses Maslow's five needs categories into three. *Existence needs* are desires for physiological and material well-being. *Relatedness needs* are desires for satisfying interpersonal relationships. *Growth needs* are desires for continued psychological growth and development. Alderfer's ERG theory also differs from Maslow's theory in other respects. This theory does not assume that lower-level needs must be satisfied before higher-level needs become activated. According to ERG theory, any or all of these three types of needs can influence individual

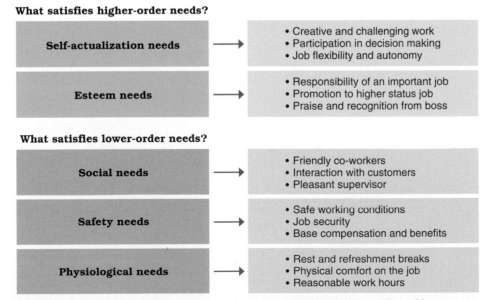

What satisfies higher-order needs?

| Self-actualization needs | → | • Creative and challenging work
• Participation in decision making
• Job flexibility and autonomy |
| Esteem needs | → | • Responsibility of an important job
• Promotion to higher status job
• Praise and recognition from boss |

What satisfies lower-order needs?

Social needs	→	• Friendly co-workers • Interaction with customers • Pleasant supervisor
Safety needs	→	• Safe working conditions • Job security • Base compensation and benefits
Physiological needs	→	• Rest and refreshment breaks • Physical comfort on the job • Reasonable work hours

Figure 14.1 Opportunities for satisfaction in Maslow's hierarchy of human needs.

behavior at a given time. Alderfer also does not assume that satisfied needs lose their motivational impact. ERG theory thus contains a unique *frustration-regression principle*, according to which an already-satisfied lower-level need can become reactivated and influence behavior when a higher-level need cannot be satisfied. Alderfer's approach offers an additional means for understanding human needs and their influence on people at work.

TWO-FACTOR THEORY

Another framework for understanding the motivational implications of work environments is the two-factor theory of Frederick Herzberg.[12] The theory was developed from a pattern identified in the responses of almost 4,000 people to questions about their work. When questioned about what "turned them on," they tended to identify things relating to the nature of the job itself. Herzberg calls these **satisfier factors**. When questioned about what "turned them off," they tended to identify things relating more to the work setting. Herzberg calls these **hygiene factors**.

As shown in *Figure 14.2*, the two-factor theory associates hygiene factors, or sources of job *dis*satisfaction, with aspects of *job context*. That is, "dissatisfiers" are considered more likely to be a part of the work setting than of the nature of the work itself. The *hygiene factors* include such things as working conditions, interpersonal relations, organizational policies and administration, technical quality of supervision, and base wage or salary. It is important to remember that Herzberg's two-factor theory would argue that improving the hygiene factors, such as by adding piped-in music or implementing a no-smoking policy, can make people less dissatisfied with these aspects of their work. But they would not in themselves contribute to increases in satisfaction. That requires attention to an entirely different set of factors and managerial initiatives.

To really improve motivation, Herzberg advises managers to give proper attention to the satisfier factors. As part of *job content* the satisfier factors deal with what people actually do in their work. By making improvements in what people are asked to do in their jobs, Herzberg suggests that job satisfaction and performance can be raised. The important *satisfier factors* include such things as a sense of achievement, feelings of recognition, a sense of responsibility, the opportunity for advancement, and feelings of personal growth.

Scholars have criticized Herzberg's theory as being method-bound and difficult to replicate.[13] For his part, Herzberg reports confirming studies in

○ A **satisfier factor** is found in job content, such as a sense of achievement, recognition, responsibility, advancement, or personal growth.

○ A **hygiene factor** is found in the job context, such as working conditions, interpersonal relations, organizational policies, and salary.

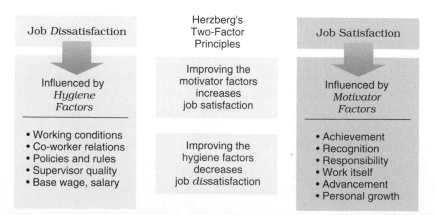

Figure 14.2 Herzberg's two-factor theory.

countries located in Europe, Africa, the Middle East, and Asia.[14] At the very least, the two-factor theory remains a useful reminder that there are two important aspects of all jobs: *job content*, what people do in terms of job tasks; and *job context*, the work setting in which they do it. Herzberg's advice to managers is still timely: (1) always correct poor context to eliminate actual or potential sources of job dissatisfaction; and (2) be sure to build satisfier factors into job content to maximize opportunities for job satisfaction. The two-factor theory also cautions managers not to expect too much by way of motivational improvements from investments in such things as special office fixtures, attractive lounges for breaks, and even high base salaries. Instead, it focuses on the nature of the job itself and directs attention toward such things as responsibility and opportunity for personal growth and development. These directions are very consistent with themes in the new workplace.

ACQUIRED NEEDS THEORY

In the late 1940s, David McClelland and his colleagues began experimenting with the Thematic Apperception Test (TAT) as a way of examining human needs. The TAT asks people to view pictures and write stories about what they see. The stories are then content analyzed for themes that display individual needs.[15] From this research, McClelland identified three needs that are central to his approach to motivation. **Need for Achievement (nAch)** is the desire to do something better or more efficiently, to solve problems, or to master complex tasks. **Need for Power (nPower)** is the desire to control other people, to influence their behavior, or to be responsible for them. **Need for Affiliation (nAff)** is the desire to establish and maintain friendly and warm relations with other people.

According to McClelland, people acquire or develop these needs over time as a result of individual life experiences. In addition, he associates each need with a distinct set of work preferences. Managers are encouraged to recognize the strength of each need in themselves and in other people. Attempts can then be made to create work environments responsive to them. People high in the need for achievement, for example, like to put their competencies to work, they take moderate risks in competitive situations, and they are willing to work alone. As a result, the work preferences of high-need achievers include (1) individual responsibility for results, (2) achievable but challenging goals, and (3) feedback on performance.

Through his research McClelland concludes that success in top management is not based on a concern for individual achievement alone. It requires broader interests that also relate to the needs for power and affiliation. People high in the need for power are motivated to behave in ways that have a clear impact on other people and events. They enjoy being in control of a situation and being recognized for this responsibility. A person with high need for power prefers work that involves control over other persons, has an impact on people and events, and brings public recognition and attention.

Importantly, McClelland distinguishes between two forms of the power need. *The need for "personal" power* is exploitative and involves manipulation for the pure sake of personal gratification. This type of power need is not successful in management. By contrast, the *need for "social" power* is the positive face of power. It involves the use of power in a socially responsible way, one that is directed toward group or organizational objectives rather than personal ones. This need for social power is essential to managerial leadership.

@ Get Connected!

Check your two-factor profile on-line and in the Career Readiness Workbook (assessment #17).

○ **Need for Achievement (nAch)** is the desire to do something better, to solve problems, or to master complex tasks.

○ **Need for Power (nPower)** is the desire to control, influence, or be responsible for other people.

○ **Need for Affiliation (nAff)** is the desire to establish and maintain good relations with people.

At SGI, formerly known as Silicon Graphics, employees can receive "spirit" awards for things like "encouraging creativity" and "seeking solutions rather than blame." Fifty awards are given annually. Winners get trips to Hawaii for two and a year-long appointment to the management advisory group.

People high in the need for affiliation seek companionship, social approval, and satisfying interpersonal relationships. They take a special interest in work that involves interpersonal relationships, work that provides for companionship, and work that brings social approval. McClelland believes that people very high in the need for affiliation alone may not make the best managers. For these managers, the desire for social approval and friendship may complicate managerial decision making. There are times when managers and leaders must decide and act in ways that other persons may disagree with. To the extent that the need for affiliation interferes with someone's ability to make these decisions, managerial effectiveness will be sacrificed. Thus, the successful executive, in McClelland's view, is likely to possess a high need for social power that is greater than an otherwise strong need for affiliation.

QUESTIONS AND ANSWERS ON CONTENT THEORIES

Figure 14.3 shows how the human needs identified by Maslow, Alderfer, Herzberg, and McClelland compare with one another. Although the terminology varies, there is a lot of common ground. The insights of the theories can and should be used together to add to our understanding of human needs in the workplace. By way of summary, the following questions and answers further clarify the content theories and their managerial implications.[16]

"How many different individual needs are there?" Research has not yet identified a perfect list of individual needs at work. But, as a manager, you can use the ideas of Maslow, Alderfer, Herzberg, and McClelland to better understand the various needs that people may bring with them to the work setting.

"Can a work outcome or reward satisfy more than one need?" Yes, work outcomes or rewards can satisfy more than one need. Pay is a good example. It is a source of performance feedback for the high need achiever. It can be a source of personal security for someone with strong existence needs. It can also be used indirectly to obtain things that satisfy social and ego needs.

"Is there a hierarchy of needs?" Research does not support the precise five-step hierarchy of needs postulated by Maslow. It seems more legitimate to view human needs as operating in a flexible hierarchy, such as the one in Alderfer's ERG theory. However, it is useful to distinguish between the motivational properties of lower-order and higher-order needs.

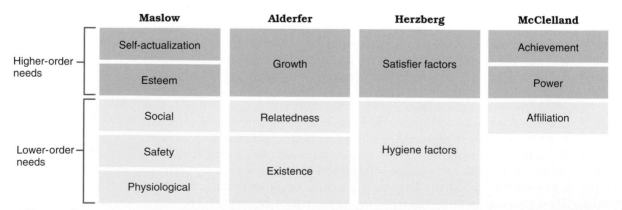

	Maslow	Alderfer	Herzberg	McClelland
Higher-order needs	Self-actualization	Growth	Satisfier factors	Achievement
	Esteem			Power
Lower-order needs	Social	Relatedness	Hygiene factors	Affiliation
	Safety	Existence		
	Physiological			

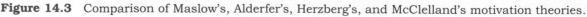

Figure 14.3 Comparison of Maslow's, Alderfer's, Herzberg's, and McClelland's motivation theories.

"How important are the various needs?" Research is inconclusive as to the importance of different needs. Individuals vary widely in this regard. They may also value needs differently at different times and at different ages or career stages. This is another reason that managers should use the insights of all the content theories to understand the differing needs of people at work.

PROCESS THEORIES OF MOTIVATION

Although the details vary, each of the content theories described in the last section can help managers better understand individual differences and deal positively with workforce diversity. Another set of theories, the process theories, add to this understanding. The equity, expectancy, and goal-setting theories each offer advice and insight on how people actually make choices to work hard or not, based on their individual preferences, the available rewards, and possible work outcomes.

EQUITY THEORY

The equity theory of motivation is best known through the work of J. Stacy Adams.[17] It is based on the logic of social comparisons and the notion that perceived inequity is a motivating state. That is, when people believe that they have been unfairly treated in comparison to others, they will be motivated to eliminate the discomfort and restore a perceived sense of equity to the situation. The classic example is pay. The equity question is: "In comparison with others, how fairly am I being compensated for the work that I do?" According to Adam's equity theory, an individual who perceives that she or he is being treated unfairly in comparison to others will be motivated to act in ways that reduce the perceived inequity.

Figure 14.4 shows how the equity dynamic works in the form of input-to-outcome comparisons. Equity comparisons are especially common whenever managers allocate extrinsic rewards, things like compensation, benefits, preferred job assignments, and work privileges. The comparison points may be coworkers in the group, workers elsewhere in the organization, and even persons employed by other organizations. Perceived inequities occur whenever people feel that the rewards received for their work efforts are unfair given the rewards others appear to be getting for their work efforts. Adams predicts that people will try to deal with perceived negative inequity, the case where the individual feels disadvantaged in comparison with others, by:

- Changing their work inputs by putting less effort into their jobs.
- Changing the rewards received by asking for better treatment.
- Changing the comparison points to make things seem better.
- Changing the situation by leaving the job.

← Possible responses to perceived inequity

The research on equity theory has largely been accomplished in the laboratory. It is most conclusive with respect to perceived negative inequity. People who feel underpaid, for example, experience a sense of anger. This causes them to try and restore perceived equity to the situation by pursuing one or more of the actions described in the prior list, such as reducing current work efforts to compensate for the missing rewards or even quitting the job.[18] By the same token there is evidence that the equity dynamic occurs

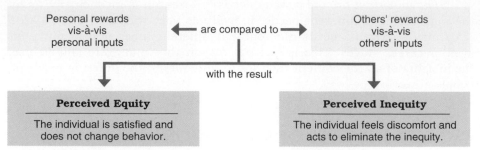

Figure 14.4 Equity theory and the role of social comparison.

among people who feel overpaid. This time the perceived inequity is associated with a sense of guilt. The attempt to restore perceived equity may involve, for example, increasing the quantity or quality of work, taking on more difficult assignments, or working overtime.

Equity theory is another good reminder of a key point to be discussed in Chapter 17—people behave according to their perceptions. Here, the issue is the way rewards are perceived by their recipients. What influences individual behavior is not the reward's absolute value or the manager's intentions. The recipient's perceptions of the reward in its social context determines the motivational outcomes. Rewards perceived as equitable should have a positive result on satisfaction and performance; those perceived as inequitable may create dissatisfaction and cause performance problems.

It is every manager's responsibility to ensure that any negative consequences of the equity comparison are avoided, or at least minimized, when rewards are allocated. Informed managers anticipate perceived negative inequities whenever especially visible rewards such as pay or promotions are allocated. Instead of letting equity concerns get out of hand, they carefully communicate the intended value of rewards being given, clarify the performance appraisals upon which they are based, and suggest appropriate comparison points.

As mentioned earlier, pay is a common source of equity controversies in the workplace and its significance should never be underestimated. In addition to the general equity issues involved, two additional equity situations deserve special consideration. First is the issue of *gender equity*. It is well established that women on the average only earn about 78 percent as much as men.[19] This difference is most evident in occupations traditionally dominated by men, such as the legal professions, but it also includes ones where females have traditionally held most jobs, such as teaching. Second is the issue of *comparable worth*. This is the concept that people doing jobs of similar value based on required education, training, and skills (such as nursing and accounting) should receive similar pay. Advocates of comparable worth claim that it corrects historical pay inequities and is a natural extension of the "equal-pay-for-equal-work" concept. Critics claim that "similar value" is too difficult to define and that the dramatic restructuring of wage scales would have a negative economic impact on society as a whole.

How Do Employers Treat Their Employees? It's no surprise that a *Business Week* survey reported 73 percent of workers believe that senior executives in large companies are paid too much. Take the on-line "Reality Check" to learn more about how employers are perceived by their employees.

EXPECTANCY THEORY

Victor Vroom introduced to the management literature another process theory of work motivation that has made an important contribution.[20] The expectancy theory of motivation asks a central question: What determines the willingness of an individual to work hard at tasks important to the organization? In response to this question, expectancy theory suggests that "people will do what they can do when they want to do it." More specifically, Vroom suggests that the motivation to work depends on the relationships between the *three expectancy factors*, depicted in *Figure 14.5* and described here:

- **Expectancy**—a person's belief that working hard will result in a desired level of task performance being achieved (this is sometimes called effort-performance expectancy).

- **Instrumentality**—a person's belief that successful performance will be followed by rewards and other potential outcomes (this is sometimes called performance-outcome expectancy).

- **Valence**—the value a person assigns to the possible rewards and other work-related outcomes.

← Three expectancy factors

Expectancy theory posits that motivation (*M*), expectancy (*E*), instrumentality (*I*), and valence (*V*) are related to one another in a multiplicative fashion: $M = E \times I \times V$. In other words, motivation is determined by expectancy times instrumentality times valence. This multiplier effect among the expectancy factors has important managerial implications. Mathematically speaking, a zero at any location on the right side of the equation (that is, for *E*, *I*, or *V*) will result in zero motivation. Managers are thus advised to act in ways that maximize all three components of the equation—expectancy (people must believe that if they try they can perform), instrumentality (people must perceive that high performance will be followed by certain outcomes), and valence (people must value the outcomes). Not one of these factors can be left unattended.

Suppose, for example, that a manager is wondering whether the prospect of earning a promotion will be motivational to a subordinate. A typical assumption is that people will be motivated to work hard to earn a promotion. But is this necessarily true? Expectancy theory predicts that a person's motivation to work hard for a promotion will be low if any one or more of the following three conditions apply. First, *if expectancy is low motivation will suffer*. The person may feel that he or she cannot achieve the performance level necessary to get promoted. So why try? Second, *if instrumentality is low motivation will suffer*. The person may lack confidence that a high level of task performance will result in being promoted. So why try? Third, *if valence is low motivation will suffer*. The person may place little value on receiving a promotion. It simply isn't much of a reward. So, once again, why try?

Expectancy theory makes managers aware of such issues. It can help them better understand and respond to different points of view in the workplace. As shown in *Figure 14.6*, the management implications include being willing to work with each individual to maximize his or her expectancies,

○ **Expectancy** is a person's belief that working hard will result in high task performance.

○ **Instrumentality** is a person's belief that various outcomes will occur as a result of task performance.

○ **Valence** is the value a person assigns to work-related outcomes.

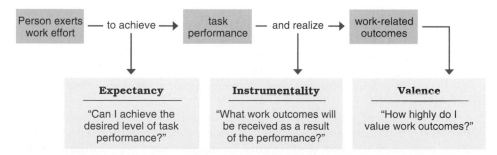

Figure 14.5 Elements in the expectancy theory of motivation.

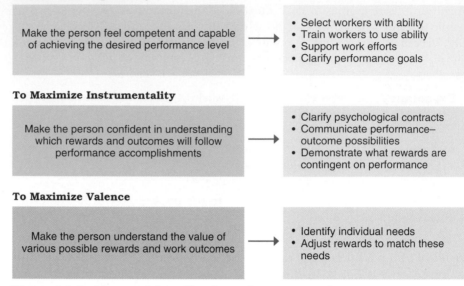

Figure 14.6 Managerial implications of expectancy theory.

instrumentalities, and valences in ways that support organizational objectives. Stated a bit differently, a manager should work with others to clearly link effort and performance, confirm performance-outcome relationships, and reward performance with valued work outcomes.

GOAL-SETTING THEORY

Another process theory, as described by Edwin Locke, focuses on the motivational properties of task goals.[21] The basic premise of this goal-setting theory is that task goals can be highly motivating—*if* they are properly set and *if* they are well managed. Goals give direction to people in their work. Goals clarify the performance expectations between a supervisor and subordinate, between co-workers, and across subunits in an organization. Goals establish a frame of reference for task feedback. Goals also provide a foundation for behavioral self-management.[22] In these and related ways, Locke believes goal setting can enhance individual work performance and job satisfaction.

To achieve the motivational benefits of goal setting, research by Locke and his associates indicates that managers and team leaders must work with others to set the right goals in the right ways. The key issues and principles in managing this goal-setting process are described in *Manager's Notepad 14.1*, and "participation" is an important element. The degree to which the person expected to do the work is involved in setting the performance goals can influence his or her satisfaction and performance. Research indicates that a positive impact is most likely to occur when the participation (1) allows for increased understanding of specific and difficult goals and (2) provides for greater acceptance and commitment to them. Along with participation, the opportunity to receive feedback on goal accomplishment is also essential to motivation.

The concept of *management by objectives* (MBO), first introduced in Chapter 7 on planning and controlling, is a good illustration of a participative approach to joint goal setting by supervisors and subordinates. The MBO process helps to unlock and apply the motivational power of

MANAGER'S NOTEPAD 14.1

How to make goal setting work for you

- *Set specific goals:* They lead to higher performance than more generally stated ones, such as "Do your best."
- *Set challenging goals:* When viewed as realistic and attainable, more difficult goals lead to higher performance than do easy goals.
- *Build goal acceptance and commitment:* People work harder for goals they accept and believe in; they resist goals forced on them.
- *Clarify goal priorities:* Make sure that expectations are clear as to which goals should be accomplished first and why.
- *Provide feedback on goal accomplishment:* Make sure that people know how well they are doing in respect to goal accomplishment.
- *Reward goal accomplishment:* Don't let positive accomplishments pass unnoticed; reward people for doing what they set out to do.

goal-setting theory. In addition to MBO, managers should also be aware of the participation options. It may not always be possible to allow participation when selecting exactly which goals need to be pursued, but it may be possible to allow participation in the decisions about how to best pursue them. Furthermore, the constraints of time and other factors operating in some situations may not allow for participation. In these settings, research suggests that workers will respond positively to externally imposed goals if the supervisors assigning them are trusted and if the workers believe they will be adequately supported in their attempts to achieve them.

REINFORCEMENT THEORY OF MOTIVATION

The content and process theories described so far use cognitive explanations of behavior. They are concerned with explaining "why" people do things in terms of satisfying needs, resolving felt inequities, and/or pursuing positive expectancies and task goals. Reinforcement theory, by contrast, views human behavior as determined by its environmental consequences. Instead of looking within the individual to explain motivation and behavior, it focuses on the external environment and the consequences it holds for the individual. The basic premises of the theory are based on what E. L. Thorndike called the **law of effect**: Behavior that results in a pleasant outcome is likely to be repeated; behavior that results in an unpleasant outcome is not likely to be repeated.[23]

○ The **law of effect** states that behavior followed by pleasant consequences is likely to be repeated; behavior followed by unpleasant consequences is not.

○ **Operant conditioning** is the control of behavior by manipulating its consequences.

REINFORCEMENT STRATEGIES

Psychologist B. F. Skinner popularized the concept of **operant conditioning** as the process of applying the law of effect to control behavior by manipulating its consequences.[24] You may think of operant conditioning

○ **Organizational behavior modification** is the application of operant conditioning to influence human behavior at work.

○ **Positive reinforcement** strengthens a behavior by making a desirable consequence contingent on its occurrence.

○ **Negative reinforcement** strengthens a behavior by making the avoidance of an undesirable consequence contingent on its occurrence.

○ **Punishment** discourages a behavior by making an unpleasant consequence contingent on its occurrence.

○ **Extinction** discourages a behavior by making the removal of a desirable consequence contingent on its occurrence.

as learning by reinforcement. In management the term is often discussed in respect to **organizational behavior modification (OB Mod)**, the application of operant conditioning techniques to influence human behavior in the workplace.[25] The goal of OB Mod is to use reinforcement principles to systematically reinforce desirable work behavior and discourage undesirable work behavior.

Four strategies of reinforcement are used in operant conditioning. **Positive reinforcement** strengthens or increases the frequency of desirable behavior by making a pleasant consequence contingent on its occurrence. *Example*: A manager nods to express approval to someone who makes a useful comment during a staff meeting. **Negative reinforcement** increases the frequency of or strengthens desirable behavior by making the avoidance of an unpleasant consequence contingent on its occurrence. *Example*: A manager who has been nagging a worker every day about tardiness does not nag when the worker comes to work on time one day. **Punishment** decreases the frequency of or eliminates an undesirable behavior by making an unpleasant consequence contingent on its occurrence. *Example*: A manager issues a written reprimand to an employee who reports late for work one day. **Extinction** decreases the frequency of or eliminates an undesirable behavior by making the removal of a pleasant consequence contingent on its occurrence. *Example*: A manager observes that a disruptive employee is receiving social approval from coworkers; the manager counsels co-workers to stop giving this approval.

An example of how these four reinforcement strategies can be applied in management is shown in *Figure 14.7*. The supervisor's goal in the example is to improve work quality as part of a TQM program. Note how the supervisor can use each of the strategies to influence continuous improvement practices among employees. Note, too, that the strategies of both positive and negative reinforcement strengthen desirable behavior when it occurs. The punishment and extinction strategies weaken or eliminate undesirable behaviors.

POSITIVE REINFORCEMENT

Among the reinforcement strategies, positive reinforcement deserves special attention. It should be a central part of any manager's motivational strategy. One of the best examples of how this approach has been used

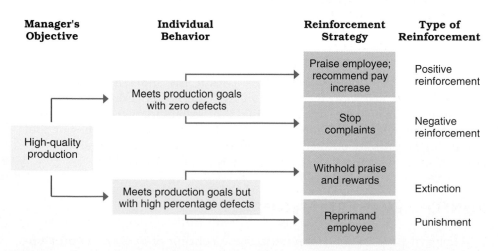

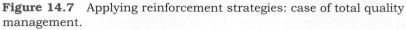

Figure 14.7 Applying reinforcement strategies: case of total quality management.

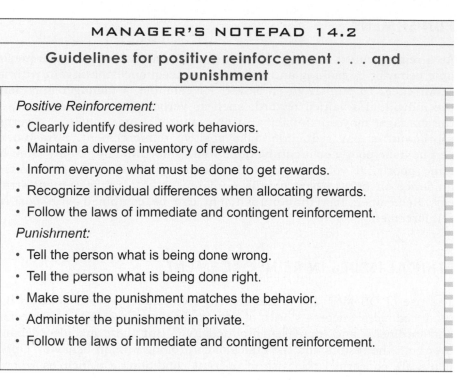

MANAGER'S NOTEPAD 14.2

Guidelines for positive reinforcement . . . and punishment

Positive Reinforcement:

- Clearly identify desired work behaviors.
- Maintain a diverse inventory of rewards.
- Inform everyone what must be done to get rewards.
- Recognize individual differences when allocating rewards.
- Follow the laws of immediate and contingent reinforcement.

Punishment:

- Tell the person what is being done wrong.
- Tell the person what is being done right.
- Make sure the punishment matches the behavior.
- Administer the punishment in private.
- Follow the laws of immediate and contingent reinforcement.

with great success is the classic story of Mary Kay Cosmetics. Most everyone knows that the legendary pink Cadillac has been a sought-after prize by top sellers for many years. More recently and to keep pace with changing times, founder Mary Kay Ash has added the Grand Prix, Grand Am, and a sport vehicle, the white GMC Jimmy, as North American options. Of course, all the cars are awarded with great ceremony at a gala celebration.[26]

All managers would do well to understand two important laws of positive reinforcement. First, the *law of contingent reinforcement* states: For a reward to have maximum reinforcing value, it must be delivered only if the desired behavior is exhibited. Second, the *law of immediate reinforcement* states: The more immediate the delivery of a reward after the occurrence of a desirable behavior, the greater the reinforcing value of the reward. Managers should use these laws to full advantage in the everyday pursuit of the benefits of positive reinforcement. Several useful guidelines are presented in *Manager's Notepad 14.2*.

The power of positive reinforcement can be mobilized through a process known as **shaping**. This is the creation of a new behavior by the positive reinforcement of successive approximations to it. The timing of positive reinforcement can also make a difference in its impact. A *continuous reinforcement schedule* administers a reward each time a desired behavior occurs. An *intermittent reinforcement schedule* rewards behavior only periodically. In general, a manager can expect that continuous reinforcement will elicit a desired behavior more quickly than will intermittent reinforcement. Also, behavior acquired under an intermittent schedule will be more permanent than will behavior acquired under a continuous schedule. One way to succeed with a shaping strategy, for example, is to give reinforcement on a continuous basis until the desired behavior is achieved. Then an intermittent schedule can be used to maintain the behavior at the new level.

○ **Shaping** is positive reinforcement of successive approximations to the desired behavior.

www.rockyboots.com

Workers at Rocky Shoes & Boots in Nelsonville, Ohio, know the goals. A goal clock prominently displays actual performance versus the daily goal for the factory's production of shoes and boots. With new modular technologies and a focus on teams, plant efficiency and profitability have increased.

PUNISHMENT

As a reinforcement strategy, punishment attempts to eliminate undesirable behavior by making an unpleasant consequence contingent with its occurrence. To punish an employee, for example, a manager may deny the individual a valued reward, such as verbal praise or merit pay, or the manager may administer an unpleasant outcome, such as a verbal reprimand or pay reduction. Like positive reinforcement, punishment can be done poorly or it can be done well. Unfortunately, it may often be done poorly. If you look back to Manager's Notepad 14.2, it offers guidance on how to best handle punishment as a reinforcement strategy. Remember, too, that punishment can be combined with positive reinforcement.

ETHICAL ISSUES IN REINFORCEMENT

The use of OB Mod and reinforcement techniques in work settings has produced many success stories of improved safety, decreased absenteeism and tardiness, and increased productivity.[27] But there are also debates over both the results and the ethics of controlling human behavior. Opponents are concerned that use of operant conditioning principles ignores the individuality of people, restricts their freedom of choice, and ignores the fact that people can be motivated by things other than externally administered rewards. Advocates attack the criticisms straight on. They agree that reinforcement involves the control of behavior, but they argue that control is part of every manager's job. The real question may be not whether it is ethical to control behavior but whether it is ethical not to control behavior well enough so that the goals of both the organization and the individual are well served. Even as research continues, the value of reinforcement techniques seems confirmed. This is especially true when they are combined with the insights of the other motivation theories discussed in this chapter.[28]

MOTIVATION AND COMPENSATION

By way of summary, *Figure 14.8* offers an integrative view of motivation that takes advantage of insights from each of the theoretical perspectives discussed so far. It shows how they can be combined into one model of motivational dynamics in the workplace. In this figure motivation leads to effort that, when combined with appropriate individual abilities and organizational support, leads to performance. The motivational impact of any rewards received for this performance depends on equity and reinforcement considerations. Ultimately, satisfaction with rewards should lead to increased motivation to work hard in the future.

Of the motivation issues that can be addressed within this framework, perhaps none receives as much attention as the special case of compensation.[29] There are many advantages, both individual and organizational, to be gained from a truly motivational compensation scheme. In general, the success of any such system lies in its ability to apply the alternative motivation theories in positive and credible ways. In practice, however, the link between motivation and compensation is usually very complicated.

TAKE IT TO THE CASE!

Saturn, Inc.
A Different Kind of Car Company

Saturn, Inc., a wholly owned subsidiary of General Motors, was designed to be different. It is self-described as follows: "We think a company that treats employees and customers better will build cars that are better, too." Like other world-class manufacturers, the firm actively pursues continuous improvement and strategic operations management. But the firm is also known for innovative and employee-centered manufacturing in a team-driven work setting. "Partnership" is an important company theme. A risk/reward compensation system is integral to the team-focused operation. The philosophy is that employees want to share in the success of their performance efforts; operationally, the program is designed to focus everyone's performance on achieving company goals.[30]

PAY FOR PERFORMANCE

The notion of paying people for their performance is consistent with the equity, expectancy, and reinforcement theories.[31] Formally defined, **merit pay** is a compensation system that awards pay increases in proportion to individual performance contributions. By allocating pay increases in this way managers are attempting to recognize and positively reinforce high performers and to encourage them to work hard for similar accomplishments in the future. They are also attempting to remind low performers of their lack of achievement and send a signal that they must do better in the future.

○ **Merit pay** awards pay increases in proportion to performance contributions.

The concept of merit pay is a logical extension of the motivation theories. In principle at least, it makes sense to reward people in proportion to their work contributions. Because of the difficulty of actually linking pay with performance in a truly contingent and equitable manner, however, merit pay does not always achieve the desired results. A successful merit pay system must have a solid foundation in

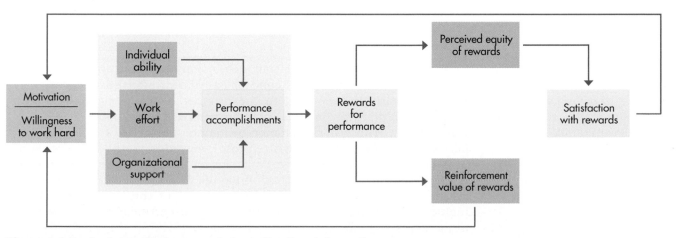

Figure 14.8 An integrated approach to motivational dynamics.

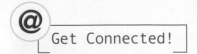

Get Connected!

Visit the AFL-CIO web site to learn about labor's criticisms of executive pay.

agreed-upon and well-defined "performance measures." Any weakness in the performance appraisal methods can undermine a merit pay system. And, lack of consistency in applying merit pay at all levels of the organization can jeopardize its credibility. There is concern today, for example, that CEO pay isn't adequately linked to performance. Magazines like *Business Week* and *Fortune* regularly report on the issues. The impression of some is that CEOs are well rewarded no matter how well the company performs. A critical report by *Responsible Wealth* cites Honeywell CEO Michael Bonsignore as an example. The year he made some $54 million in total compensation his firm was laying off 11,600 workers worldwide.[32]

For these and related reasons, not everyone believes in merit pay. John Whitney, author of *The Trust Factor*, suggests that pay-for-performance may not work very well. While pointing out that market forces should determine base pay, Whitney believes that organizations can benefit by making the annual merit increase an equal percentage of base. This communicates a universal sense of importance and helps to avoid frustrations and complaints when merit increases are tied to performance differences. Says Whitney: "Quibbling over whether someone should get a 4.7% raise or 5.1% is a colossal waste of time."[33]

INCENTIVE COMPENSATION SYSTEMS

Today, employees at all levels in more and more organizations are benefiting from special incentive compensation systems of many forms. Examples include pay for knowledge, bonus pay plans, profit-sharing plans, gain-sharing plans, and employee stock ownership plans.[34] As you consider the descriptions that follow, however, remember that any incentive compensation system will work only as well as its implementation. The well-known compensation scholar and consultant Edward Lawler, for example, tells of this experience.[35] While consulting with a furniture manufacturing plant, he became convinced that a "gain sharing" incentive plan would be helpful and thus advised the plant manager on starting one. The manager proceeded only reluctantly, claiming: "These guys are already paid enough . . . they should be happy to have a job." Says Lawler: "Although the program was somewhat successful, the plant manager's continuing tendency to call it an 'employee bribe program' definitely limited its success."

Pay for Knowledge

○ **Skills-based pay** is a system of paying workers according to the number of job-relevant skills they master.

In addition to paying for performance, some organizations now emphasize paying for knowledge. A concept called **skills-based pay**, for example, pays workers according to the number of job-relevant skills they master. Federal Express uses this approach in its pay-for-knowledge reward system. The firm's customer-contact employees, for example, must periodically take and pass written job knowledge tests. Test scores are incorporated into the employee's performance appraisals, and pay can be increased for employees scoring highly. Skills-based pay systems are common in self-managing teams where part of the "self-management" includes responsibilities for the training and certification of co-workers in job skills.

Bonus Pay

Bonus pay plans provide onetime or lump-sum payments to employees based on the accomplishment of specific performance targets or some other extraordinary contribution, such as an idea for a work improvement. They typically do not increase base salary or wages. Bonuses have been most common at the executive level, but they are now being used more extensively. Corning, for example, has tried rewarding individual achievements with on-the-spot bonuses of 3 to 6 percent of someone's pay. As director of risk management and prevention for the firm, for example, Peter Maier gave about 40 percent of his subordinates individual bonuses in a year. He says, "If someone has done a spiffy job, you need to recognize them."[36]

Profit Sharing

Profit-sharing plans distribute to some or all employees a proportion of net profits earned by the organization during a stated performance period. The exact amount typically varies according to the level of profits and each person's base compensation. At the marketing services firm Valassis Communications Inc., a member of *Fortune*'s 100 Best Companies to Work for, every employee from the press operator right up to CEO is eligible for profit sharing that runs from 10 to 25 percent of pay. At Vatex America, a T-shirt and sweatshirt manufacturing firm, CEO Jerry Gorde started a profit-sharing program to help "democratize" the work environment. The program distributes 10 percent of pretax profits to employees each month and an additional amount at the end of the year. The exact share depends on an individual's monthly attendance, tardiness, and performance as rated by supervisors.[37]

CAREER CONNECTION

High Performance

Lincoln Electric

A History of Making Pay-for-Performance Pay Off

Lincoln Electric is known for its innovative approach to employee compensation. Founded in 1895, the firm uses a "pay-for-performance" system that has become a benchmark for other businesses. The system includes a low base salary that is supplemented by bonuses tied to company profitability and individual performance ratings.

Employees are held accountable for each piece of work they produce. Pieces are "signed," or marked, so that defective ones are easily traced back to the worker. Rejects and returns are noted on employees' merit ratings that impact year-end bonuses.

Lincoln's system isn't for everyone. And, it's not problem free. When Lincoln embarked on international expansion that affected its profitability, domestic workers complained. They felt their bonuses were being threatened by things beyond their control—the costs of the firm's globalization drive. Former CEO Donald Hastings described the problem this way: "We did it too fast, paid too much; we didn't understand foreign markets and cultures."

QUESTION: Are you ready to work in a strong performance-driven compensation system? How do you feel about linking pay directly to individual performance? As a manager, will you be able to make difficult decisions that affect the pay of those working for you?

Gain Sharing

Gain-sharing plans extend the profit-sharing concept by allowing groups of employees to share in any savings or "gains" realized through their efforts to reduce costs and increase productivity. Specific formulas are used to calculate both the performance contributions and gain-sharing awards. The classic example is the Scanlon plan, which usually results in 75 percent of gains being distributed to workers and 25 percent being kept by the company. At East Alabama Medical Center, another of *Fortune*'s 100 Best Companies, the mission focuses everyone's attention on caring for people. A gain-sharing plan directly supports that mission. Designed with employee participation, the program rewards employees with gain-sharing compensation for meeting patient satisfaction and financial goals. The CEO distributes the checks at a special annual ceremony.[38]

Employee Stock Ownership

Employee stock ownership plans involve employees in ownership through the purchase of stock in the companies that employ them. Whereas formal "ESOP" plans are often used as financing schemes to save jobs and prevent business closings, stock ownership by employees is an important performance incentive. It can be motivating to have an ownership share in one's place of employment. An approach to employee ownership through stock options gives the option holder the right to buy shares of stock at a future date at a fixed price. This links ownership directly with a performance incentive, since employees holding stock options presumably are motivated to work hard to raise the price of the firm's stock. When the price has risen they can exercise their option and buy the stock at a discount, thus realizing a financial gain. Stock options are most common in senior executive compensation, but their use is spreading to include lower-level employees.

The Hay Group reports that the most admired companies in America are also ones that offer stock options to a greater proportion of their work forces. Intel, Merck, and Kimberly-Clark are examples of global firms that allow all of their employees to have access to options.[39] One of the issues to be considered with stock options, however, relates to their risk. If and when a company's shares perform poorly, the options it is offering as a performance incentive are worth less; their motivational value is largely eliminated. When the technology companies experienced a downturn in the stock market, for example, many employees were disappointed with incentive pay that was tied to stock options. Many firms experienced turnover problems as talented employees resigned to pursue other and more promising opportunities. As a result, there was a resurgence of interest in adding cash bonuses to the incentive compensation packages. In an industry where human capital is paramount to success, the most progressive employers responded. How would you like to someday receive a letter like this one sent to two top executives by Amazon.com's chairman Jeff Bezos? "In recognition and appreciation of your contributions," his letter read, "Amazon.com will pay you a special bonus in the amount of $1,000,000 (1 million dollars)."[40] Not bad for a performance incentive!

Get Connected!

Looking for need satisfaction? Check *Fortune*'s list of the 100 Best Companies to Work for.

S T U D Y
Guide

The Chapter 14 Study Guide will help you review chapter content, prepare for examinations, and further build your career readiness. The *Summary* briefly highlights answers to questions first posed in the chapter opening Planning Ahead section. The list of *Key Terms* allows you to double check your familiarity with basic concepts and definitions. *Self-Test 14* gives you the opportunity to test your basic comprehension of chapter content using sample test questions. Suggestions offered as *Career Readiness Activities* direct your attention to relevant sections of the end-of-text Career Readiness Workbook, as well as to special Electronic Resources on the *Management 7/e* web site.

SUMMARY

What is motivation?

- Motivation involves the level, direction, and persistence of effort expended at work; simply put, a highly motivated person works hard.
- Extrinsic rewards are given by another person; intrinsic rewards derive naturally from the work itself.
- To maximize the motivational impact of rewards, they should be allocated in ways that respond to both individual and organizational needs.
- The three major types of motivation theories are the content, process, and reinforcement theories.

What are the different types of individual needs?

- Maslow's hierarchy of human needs suggests a progression from lower-order physiological, safety, and social needs to higher-order ego and self-actualization needs.
- Alderfer's ERG theory identifies existence, relatedness, and growth needs.
- Herzberg's two-factor theory points out the importance of both job content and job context factors in satisfying human needs.
- McClelland's acquired needs theory identifies the needs for achievement, affiliation, and power, all of which may influence what a person desires from work.
- Managers should respect individual differences and diversity to create motivating work environments.

What are the insights of process theories of motivation?

- Adams's equity theory recognizes that social comparisons take place when rewards are distributed in the workplace.
- People who feel inequitably treated are motivated to act in ways that reduce the sense of inequity; perceived negative inequity may result in someone working less hard in the future.
- Vroom's expectancy theory states that Motivation = Expectancy × Instrumentality × Valence.
- Expectancy theory encourages managers to make sure that any rewards offered for motivational purposes are both achievable and individually valued.
- Locke's goal-setting theory emphasizes the motivational power of goals; people tend to be highly motivated when task goals are specific rather than ambiguous, difficult but achievable, and set through participatory means.

What role does reinforcement play in motivation?

- Reinforcement theory recognizes that human behavior is influenced by its environmental consequences.
- The law of effect states that behavior followed by a pleasant consequence is likely to be repeated; behavior followed by an unpleasant consequence is unlikely to be repeated.
- Reinforcement strategies used by managers include positive reinforcement, negative reinforcement, punishment, and extinction.
- Positive reinforcement works best when applied according to the laws of contingent and immediate reinforcement.

What are the trends in motivation and compensation?

- The area of compensation provides a good test of a manager's ability to integrate and apply the insights of all motivation theories.
- Pay for performance in the form of merit pay plans ties pay increases to performance increases.
- Various incentive compensation programs, such as bonuses, gain sharing, and profit sharing, allow workers to benefit materially from improvements in profits and productivity.
- Pay-for-knowledge systems typically link pay to the mastery of job-relevant skills.

KEY TERMS

Expectancy (p. 371)

Extinction (p. 374)

Extrinsic reward (p. 363)

Higher-order needs (p. 364)

Hygiene factor (p. 366)

Instrumentality (p. 371)

Intrinsic reward (p. 363)

Law of effect (p. 373)

Lower-order needs (p. 364)

Merit pay (p. 377)

Motivation (p. 362)

Need (p. 364)

Need for achievement (p. 367)

Need for affiliation (p. 367)

Need for power (p. 367)

Negative reinforcement (p. 374)

Operant conditioning (p. 373)

OB Mod (p. 374)

Positive reinforcement (p. 374)

Punishment (p. 374)

Satisfier factors (p. 366)

Shaping (p. 375)

Skills-based pay (p. 378)

Valence (p. 371)

SELF-TEST 14

Take this test here or on-line much as you would in a normal classroom situation. It is a good way to check your basic comprehension of chapter material. Answers may be found at the end of the book.

MULTIPLE-CHOICE QUESTIONS:

1. Lower-order needs in Maslow's hierarchy correspond to _____ needs in ERG theory.
   (a) growth (b) affiliation (c) existence (d) achievement
2. A worker high in need for _____ power in McClelland's theory tries to use power for the good of the organization.
   (a) position (b) expert (c) referent (d) social
3. In the _____ theory of motivation, an individual who feels under-rewarded relative to a co-worker might be expected to reduce his or her performance in the future.
   (a) ERG (b) acquired needs (c) two-factor (d) equity
4. Which of the following is a correct match?
   (a) McClelland—ERG theory (b) Skinner—reinforcement theory
   (c) Vroom—equity theory (d) Locke—expectancy theory
5. The expectancy theory of motivation says that: motivation = expectancy × _____ × _____.
   (a) rewards, valence (b) instrumentality, valence (c) equity, instrumentality (d) rewards, valence
6. The law of _____ states that behavior followed by a positive consequence is likely to be repeated, whereas behavior followed by an undesirable consequence is not likely to be repeated.
   (a) reinforcement (b) contingency (c) goal setting (d) effect

7. _____ is a positive reinforcement strategy that rewards successive approximations to a desirable behavior.
   (a) Extinction (b) Negative reinforcement (c) Shaping (d) Merit pay

8. A(n) _____ pay plan gives bonuses based on the savings in costs or increases in productivity workers help to generate.
   (a) merit (b) gain-sharing (c) entrepreneurial (d) skills-based

9. In Herzberg's two-factor theory, base pay is considered a(n) _____ factor.
   (a) valence (b) satisfier (c) equity (d) hygiene

10. Jobs high in _____ rewards naturally provide workers with higher-order need satisfactions.
    (a) intrinsic (b) extrinsic (c) monetary (d) profit-sharing

TRUE-FALSE QUESTIONS:

11. By definition, a highly motivated worker will always be a high-performing worker.   T   F

12. The ego need is the highest-level need in Maslow's needs hierarchy.   T   F

13. Pay is an example of a work outcome that can satisfy more than one type of need.   T   F

14. In goal-setting theory, goals that are easy to accomplish have the strongest motivational impact.   T   F

15. Reinforcement theory uses cognitive explanations of behavior.   T   F

16. Pay and praise are examples of intrinsic rewards.   T   F

17. A person with a high expectancy believes that she or he can perform a task at a desired high level.   T   F

18. Someone high in need for achievement would have strong social needs in Maslow's hierarchy.   T   F

19. Research has confirmed the existence of the hierarchy of needs first described by Abraham Maslow.   T   F

20. Punishment should not be used with positive reinforcement.   T   F

SHORT-RESPONSE QUESTIONS:

21. What types of preferences does a person high in the need for achievement bring with him or her to the workplace?

22. Why is participation important to goal-setting theory?

23. What is motivation to work?

24. What is the managerial significance of Herzberg's distinction between factors in the job content and job context?

APPLICATION QUESTION:

25. How can a manager combine the powers of goal setting and positive reinforcement to create a highly motivational work environment for a group of workers with high needs for achievement?

CAREER readiness ACTIVITIES

Recommended learning activities from the end-of-text Career Readiness Workbook for this chapter include:

Career Advancement Portfolio
- Individual writing and group presentation assignments based on any of the following activities.

Case for Critical Thinking
- Saturn, Inc. — Making Pay for Performance Pay Off

Integrative Learning Activities
- Research Project 6—Controversies in CEO Pay
- Integrative Case—Outback Steakhouse. Inc.
- Integrative Case—Richard Branson Meets the New Economy

Exercises in Teamwork
- What Do You Value in Work? (#7)
- Work vs. Family (#16)
- Compensation and Benefits Debate (#17)
- Why Do We Work? (#21)

Self-Assessments
- Organizational Design Preference (#12)
- Two-Factor Profile (#17)

The *Fast Company* Collection On-Line
- Alan Weber, "Danger: Toxic Company"

ELECTRONIC RESOURCES

@ GET CONNECTED! Don't forget to take full advantage of the on-line support for *Management 7/e.*
- Chapter 14 On-line Study Guide
- Chapter 14 Self-test Answers
- Chapter 14 E-Resource Center

www.wiley.com/college/schermerhorn

15

Individuals, job design, and stress

Planning
ahead

GETTING CONNECTED

Monitor Company—*Unlock Everyone's Performance Potential*

The Monitor Company isn't just another of the world's top strategic management consulting firms. It's a firm with a difference, and a major part of that difference is a genuine respect for knowledge.

Where is the knowledge located? In the minds of each and every one of the firm's 1,000+ employees, as well as with their clients. And, of course, the firm must actively recruit and retain the best consulting talent if it is to stay on top of this highly competitive industry.

Essential to Monitor's talent development strategy is to provide people with a work environment that meets their needs, doesn't inhibit them with performance obstacles, and is full of learning opportunities.

Says Alan Kantrow, chief knowledge officer for Monitor: "The employees we are trying to attract expect to have a series of careers. If Monitor can't provide outlets for their ambitions, they'll go elsewhere. So by design, all the roles, titles and clusters of activities are transitory."

Consulting jobs at Monitor are complex and the deadlines are often tight. No one ever knows for sure who is the expert. Everyone has to work together, while depending upon each other to do their best.

The team that successfully helped Bermuda turn around its flagging tourism industry was headed by project coordinator Joseph Babiec. About the experience he says: "We were a team of equals. It didn't matter who was in Bermuda the longest. I worked for you. Then you worked for me."

It had to be that way. The team was dealing with different and sometimes warring government units, labor unions, outside investors, and industry representatives. Whereas strictly defined roles and rigid hierarchy of team authority would have made the task almost impossible, the knowledge-based approach of Monitor's consulting team worked wonders for the client, and did so quickly. Labor agreements are now signed, new investments are flowing back into the country, and the number of cruise visitors is soaring again.

Not bad for a bunch of young Americans from a Boston-based consulting firm.

But then again, they work for a firm that is dedicated to talent, a firm that states that part of its mission is "creating personal competitive advantage—in the form of unique skills and insights—for each of our employees."[1]

@ Get Connected!

How well do you fit in this new world of knowledge and knowledge management? Are you looking for an employer who truly respects individual talents, as does Monitor? Make sure that any employer you choose has the job design, culture, and learning environment that is the best fit for you. Get connected!

For managers in organizations of all types and sizes, both for-profit and not-for-profit, a critical pathway toward performance improvement is better mobilizing and better unlocking the great potential of human talent.[2] The ideal situation is a loyal and talented workforce that is committed to organizational goals and highly motivated to work hard in their behalf. But saying this is one thing; achieving it is quite another. Even in the best of circumstances the management of human resources is a challenging task. It becomes even more complicated when organizations aggressively seek operating efficiencies by outsourcing more work, restructuring operations, downsizing payrolls, and the like.[3]

No one doubts that every employer must attract, develop, and maintain a talented pool of human resources. This is, however, just the starting point. In order for the talent to have an impact on organizational performance, it must be supported, nurtured, and allowed to work to its best advantage. All too often it is not, observe scholars Jeffrey Pfeffer and Charles O'Reilly. They believe that too many organizations underperform because they operate with great untapped "hidden value" in human resources; they fail to take full advantage of the talent they already have available.[4] O'Reilly and Pfeffer criticize organizations "with smart, motivated, hard-working, decent people who nevertheless don't perform very well because the company doesn't let them shine and doesn't really capitalize on their talent and motivation." They also praise true high-performance organizations as ones able to "produce extraordinary results from almost everybody."

This praise frames our inquiry into the topics of this chapter and the next: to learn how to design jobs and build work settings so that almost everybody can produce extraordinary work results. The present chapter addresses this challenge in terms of individuals, job design, and work stress; the next one focuses on teams and teamwork. A central premise of both chapters, consistent with all of *Management 7/e*, is that when the work experience is well designed, people—the essential and irreplaceable human resources of organizations—can both achieve high-performance results and experience a high-quality work life.

THE MEANING OF WORK

Get Connected!

Visit the web site of the Working Women's Department of the AFL-CIO, developed under the leadership of Karen Nussbaum.

What do you think about when you see or hear the word *work*? Is it a "turn-on" or a "turn-off"? When Dolly Parton sang "Working 9 to 5; what a way to make a living," she reminded us of an unfortunate reality—that work is not a positive experience for everyone. Dolly's song continued: "Barely getting by; it's all taking and no giving. They just use your mind, and they never give you credit. It's enough to drive you crazy if you let it."[5] Isn't it a shame when this is what work really means to someone? Some years ago, Karen Nussbaum founded an organization called "9 to 5" that was devoted to improving women's salaries and promotion opportunities in the workplace. She started the business after leaving her job as a secretary at Harvard University. Describing what she calls "the incident that put her over the edge," Nussbaum says, "One day . . . I was sitting at my desk at lunchtime, when most of the professors were out. A student walked into the office and looked me dead in the eye and said, 'Isn't *anyone* here?'"[6] Nussbaum founded 9 to 5 to support her personal commitment to "remake the system so that it does not produce these individuals."

Although in different ways and through different media, Parton and Nussbaum direct our attention toward an unfortunate fact of life in the

DIVERSITY (www.ey.com) Ernst & Young
Finding the Best Talent Requires a Family-Friendly Workplace

As the top accounting firms vie for first place in their industry, they are also battling for reputation as the most family-friendly employers. A growing economy challenges everyone with problems of finding and retaining the best-skilled professionals. Among the recruiting and retention tools that work well are flexible work arrangements that allow employees more choice in scheduling their job duties. At Ernst & Young, an Office of Retention was created to oversee the new push toward flexibility in work and career management, and a computer database was developed to help employees choose work schedules that are best for them. These trends in worker empowerment and involvement are indicative of efforts to help all employees find opportunities for respect and self-fulfillment at work.[7]

modern workplace—that some people, too many people, work under conditions that fail to provide them with respect and satisfaction. It does not have to be this way. More and more employers are coming to the same conclusion: People, individuals like you and me, are the foundation for high performance in the workplace. When managers value people and create jobs and work environments that respect people's needs and potential, everyone gains.

PSYCHOLOGICAL CONTRACTS

Work should involve a positive give and take, or exchange of values, between the individual and the organization. This sense of mutual benefit is expressed in the concept of a **psychological contract**, which is defined as an informal understanding about what an individual gives to and receives from an organization as part of the employment relationship.[8] The ideal work situation is one in which the exchange of values in the psychological contract is considered fair. When the psychological contract is broken, however, morale problems easily develop. This problem surfaced in Japan where workers historically enjoyed high job security and, in return, put in long work hours at great personal sacrifice. But when the Japanese economy experienced difficulty and companies cut back on job protections, worker morale declined. The psychological contract shared between worker and employer had been damaged.[9]

> ○ A **psychological contract** is the set of expectations held by an individual about working relationships with the organization.

As shown in *Figure 15.1*, a healthy psychological contract offers a balance between contributions made to the organization and inducements received in return. A person offers *contributions*, or valued work activities, such as effort, time, creativity, and loyalty. These are among the things that make the individual a desirable resource. *Inducements* are things of value that the organization gives to the individual in exchange for these contributions. Typical inducements include pay, fringe benefits, training, and opportunities for personal growth and advancement. Such inducements should be valued by employees and should make it worthwhile for them to work hard for the organization.

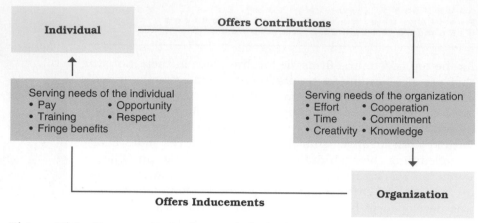

Figure 15.1 Components in the psychological contract.

WORK AND THE QUALITY OF LIFE

The term *quality of work life* (QWL) was first used in Chapter 1 to describe the overall quality of human experiences in the workplace. Most people spend many hours a week, and many years of their lives, at work. What happens to them at work, how they are treated, and what their work is like can all have an influence on their overall lives. Simply put, the quality of work is an important component in the quality of life for most of us.[10] Anyone who serves as a manager, therefore, must accept that this job carries a high level of social responsibility. The way managers treat people at work may have consequences extending far beyond the confines of the actual work setting. Our experiences at work can and often do spill over to affect our nonwork activities and lives, just as our nonwork experiences sometimes affect our attitudes and performance at work.

Poor management practices can diminish a person's overall quality of life, not just the quality of work life; good management, by contrast, has the potential to enhance both. And if you think the preceding comments are an overstatement, consider the implications of this steelworker's compelling words once shared with the noted American author Studs Terkel:[11]

When I come home, know what I do for the first twenty minutes? Fake it. I put on a smile. I got a kid three years old. Sometimes she says, "Daddy, where've you been?" I say, "Work." I could have told her I'd been in Disneyland. What's work to a three-year-old kid? If I feel bad, I can't take it out on the kid. Kids are born innocent of everything but birth. You can't take it out on your wife either. That is why you go to a tavern. You want to release it there rather than do it at home. What does an actor do when he's got a bad movie? I got a bad movie every day.

Today's managers are increasingly expected to focus their attention on creating work environments within which people can have positive experiences while performing to high levels of expectation. A term relevant in this respect is *work-life balance*, described earlier in this book as the fit between one's job or work responsibilities and personal or family needs. When job demands get to the point of interfering with personal responsibilities and vice-versa, stress and performance problems are likely results. The goal, of course, is to achieve a productive and satisfying balance of

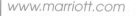
www.marriott.com

When Marriott Hotels redesigned the job of doorman to improve customer service, many tasks were rolled into one job description—bellman, doorman, front-desk clerk, and concierge. One worker commented: "I have more responsibilities. I feel better about my job, and the guests get better service."

career and family pursuits. The themes of this chapter all relate in one way or another to this goal, with many examples of how progressive employers can increase employee involvement through better job designs and become more family friendly through alternative work schedules and stress management assistance. Recognition for the importance of people, for example, is a core value at Deloitte & Touche. The firm stands behind this value with a commitment to work-life balance described in this way: "Talented, creative people need control over where, how, and when they work, and, at times, they need help managing and coping with the responsibilities, opportunities, and challenges life can present."[12]

SATISFACTION, PERFORMANCE, AND JOB DESIGN

A **job** is a collection of tasks performed in support of organizational objectives. The process of **job design** is one of creating or defining jobs by assigning specific work tasks to individuals and groups. Job design uses the insights of motivation theories discussed in the last chapter to help accomplish two major goals—high levels of both job satisfaction and job performance. Jobs can and should be designed so that satisfaction and performance go hand in hand. One without the other is simply insufficient to meet the high standards expected of today's workplace. There is no reason why you or anyone else cannot experience personal satisfaction while making high-performance work contributions.

○ A **job** is the collection of tasks a person performs in support of organizational objectives.

○ **Job design** is the allocation of specific work tasks to individuals and groups.

JOB SATISFACTION

One measure of quality of work life is **job satisfaction**.[13] This is the degree to which an individual feels positively or negatively about various aspects of the job. We have all heard someone criticized for having a "bad attitude." In the present context, job satisfaction is an important attitude that can and does influence behavior at work. The question becomes: How can we develop job satisfaction and positive work attitudes? In answering this question, satisfaction with such things as pay, tasks, supervision, coworkers, work setting, and advancement opportunities must be considered. These are all facets of job satisfaction that can be addressed through job design in the attempt to improve attitudes and raise the quality of work life.

Researchers know that there is a strong relationship between job satisfaction and *absenteeism*. Workers who are more satisfied with their jobs attend more regularly; they are absent less often than those who are dissatisfied. There is also a relationship between job satisfaction and *turnover*. Satisfied workers are more likely to stay and dissatisfied workers are more likely to quit their jobs. Both of these findings are important since absenteeism and turnover are costly in terms of the additional recruitment and training that are needed to replace workers, as well as in the productivity lost while new workers are learning how to perform up to expectations.

Closely related to job satisfaction are two other concepts with quality of work life implications. **Job involvement** is defined as the extent to which an individual is dedicated to a job. Someone with high job involvement, for example, would be expected to work beyond expectations to complete a special project. **Organizational commitment** is defined as the loyalty of an individual to the organization itself. Someone with a high organizational commitment would identify strongly with the organization

○ **Job satisfaction** is the degree to which an individual feels positively or negatively about a job.

○ **Job involvement** is defined as the extent to which an individual is dedicated to a job.

○ **Organizational commitment** is defined as the loyalty of an individual to the organization.

and take pride in considering himself or herself a member. A survey of 55,000 American workers by the Gallup Organization, for example, found that attitudes reflecting job involvement and commitment correlated with higher profits for employers. The four attitudes that counted most were: believing one has the opportunity to do best every day, believing one's opinions count, believing fellow workers are committed to quality, and believing there is a connection between one's work and the company's mission.[14]

In another poll of American workers, *The Wall Street Journal* asked this question: How satisfied are you with your current job? What would you predict?[15] Interestingly, the survey indicated that a majority of workers were at least to some extent satisfied with their jobs. The responses are as follows: 37 percent, completely satisfied; 47 percent, somewhat satisfied; 10 percent, somewhat dissatisfied; 4 percent, completely dissatisfied; 2 percent, not sure. The same poll went on to identify some 36 percent of workers as "workbodies" who felt more fulfilled at work than at home, while another 34 percent were "homebodies" who felt just the opposite.[16] Into which category do you fall?

INDIVIDUAL PERFORMANCE

Somewhere in Michigan near a Ford Motor Company plant, the following sign once hung in a tavern: "I spend forty hours a week here—am I supposed to work too?" The message in these words is an important one in management: it is one thing for people to come to work; it is quite another for them to perform at high levels while they are on the job. Formally defined, **job performance** is the quantity and quality of tasks accomplished by an individual or group at work. Performance, as is commonly said, is the "bottom line" for people at work. It is a cornerstone of productivity, and it should contribute to the accomplishment of organizational objectives. As earlier examples have suggested, however, some workers achieve a sense of personal satisfaction from their jobs and others do not; some perform at high levels of accomplishment, while others do not. The test of a manager's skill is to discover what work means to other people and then to create job designs that help them to achieve satisfaction along with high performance.

○ **Job performance** is the quantity and quality of task accomplishment by an individual or group.

Individual Performance Equation →

Consider the insights of the *Individual Performance Equation:* Performance = Ability × Support × Effort. The logic of this equation is straightforward and very practical. If high performance is to be achieved in any work setting, the individual contributor must possess the right abilities (creating the *capacity* to perform), work hard at the task (showing the *willingness* to perform), and have the necessary support (creating the *opportunity* to perform).[17] All three factors are important and necessary; failure to provide for any one or more is likely to cause performance losses and establish limited performance ceilings.

Performance Begins with Ability

Ability counts. As the basic foundation of aptitudes and skills it establishes an individual's capacity to perform at a high level of accomplishment. This is the central issue in human resource management, as discussed in Chapter 12. Proper employee selection brings people with the right abilities to a job; poor selection does not. Good training and development keep peoples' skills up to date and their jobs relevant; poor or insufficient training does not.

The goal of maintaining and increasing the ability of workers in every job should be central to all human resource development initiatives and policies. The best managers never let a job vacancy or training opportunity pass without giving it serious attention. The best managers make sure every day that all jobs under their supervision are staffed up to the moment with talented people. By renewing and redoubling their commitments to the ability factor and best practices in human resource management, managers can make substantial contributions to performance development.

Performance Requires Support

The support factor in the individual performance equation can be easily neglected in day-to-day management practice. But such oversight comes at a high cost. Even the most capable and hard-working individual will not achieve the highest performance levels unless proper support is available. Support creates a work environment rich in opportunities to apply one's talents to maximum advantage. To fully utilize their abilities workers need sufficient resources, clear goals and directions, freedom from unnecessary rules and job constraints, appropriate technologies, and performance feedback. Providing these and other forms of direct work support is a basic managerial responsibility. Doing it right, however, requires a willingness to get to know the jobs to be done and the people doing them. The best information on the need for support, of course, comes from the workers themselves. Wouldn't it be nice to hear more managers speak the following words in everyday conversations with their subordinates: "How can I help you today?"

Job Satisfaction across Cultures In an international survey comparison, workers from Switzerland scored the highest, with 82 percent of respondents saying they liked their jobs. Take the on-line "Reality Check" to learn more about how workers from other countries, including the United States, responded.

Performance Involves Effort

Without any doubt, effort—the willingness to work hard at a task—is an irreplaceable component of the high-performance workplace. Even the most capable workers won't achieve consistent high performance unless they are willing to try hard enough. But the decision by anyone to work hard or not rests squarely on the shoulders of the individual alone. This is the ultimate test of the motivation theories discussed in Chapter 14.

All any manager (or teacher, or parent) can do is attempt to create the conditions under which the answer to the all-important question—"Should I work hard today?"—is more often "Yes!" than "No!" And quite frankly, the most powerful and enduring "Yes" is the one driven by forces within the individual—intrinsic motivation—rather than by outside initiatives such as supervisory appeals, offers of monetary reward, or threats of punishment. Good managers understand this reality as they design jobs for people in organizations.

JOB DESIGN ALTERNATIVES

Job design is in many ways an exercise in "fit." A good job design provides a good fit between the individual worker and the task requirements. To explore this notion further, consider a short case.[18] Datapoint Corporation manufactures a line of personal computers. Jackson White has just been employed by Datapoint. He is a competent person who enjoys interpersonal relationships. He also likes to feel helpful or stimulating to others. How do you think he will react to each of the following job designs?

@ Get Connected!

Check your job design preferences on-line and in the Career Readiness Workbook (assessment #18).

In *Job 1*, Jackson reports to a workstation on the computer assembly line. A partially assembled circuit board passes in front of him on a conveyor belt every 90 seconds. He adds two pieces to each board and lets the conveyor take the unit to the next workstation. Quality control is handled at a separate station at the end of the line. Everyone gets a 10-minute break in the morning and afternoon and a 30-minute lunch period. Jackson works by himself in a quiet setting.

In *Job 2*, Jackson works on the same assembly line. Now, however, a circuit board comes to his station every 12 minutes, and he performs a greater number of tasks. He adds several pieces to the board, adds a frame, and installs several electric switches. Periodically, Jackson changes stations with one of the other workers and does a different set of tasks on earlier or later stages of the same circuit board. In all other respects, the work setting is the same as in the first job described.

In *Job 3*, Jackson is part of a team responsible for completely assembling circuit boards for the computers. The team has a weekly production quota but makes its own plans for the speed and arrangement of the required assembly processes. The team is also responsible for inspecting the quality of the finished boards and for correcting any defective units. These duties are shared among the members and are discussed at team meetings. Jackson has been selected by the team as its plant liaison. In addition to his other duties, he works with people elsewhere in the plant to resolve any production problems and achieve plant-wide quality objectives.

These three job design alternatives are identified in *Figure 15.2* as job simplification, job enlargement and rotation, and job enrichment, respectively. Each varies in how specialized the division of labor becomes—that is, in how narrowly job tasks are defined. Although not every one of these designs may be a good choice to maximize Jackson White's performance and satisfaction, each has a role to play in the modern workplace.

Job Simplification

○ **Job simplification** employs people in clearly defined and very specialized tasks.

Job simplification involves standardizing work procedures and employing people in well-defined and highly specialized tasks. This is an extension of the scientific management approach discussed in Chapter 4. Simplified jobs are narrow in *job scope*—that is, the number and variety of different tasks a

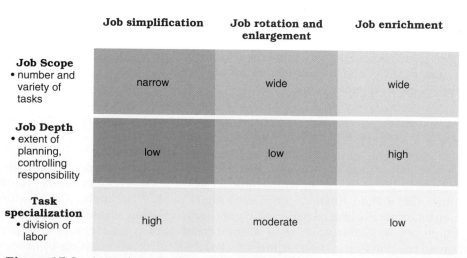

	Job simplification	Job rotation and enlargement	Job enrichment
Job Scope • number and variety of tasks	narrow	wide	wide
Job Depth • extent of planning, controlling responsibility	low	low	high
Task specialization • division of labor	high	moderate	low

Figure 15.2 A continuum of job-design alternatives.

person performs. Jackson White's first job on the assembly line was highly simplified. He isn't alone. Many employees around the world earn their livings working at highly simplified tasks. The most extreme form of job simplification is **automation**, or the total mechanization of a job.

The logic of job simplification is straightforward. Because the jobs don't require complex skills, workers should be easier and quicker to train, less difficult to supervise, and easy to replace if they leave. Furthermore, because tasks arc well defined, workers should become good at them while performing the same work over and over again. Consider the case of Cindy Vang, who works on an assembly line for Medtronics, Inc. She works in a dust-free room making a specialized medical component. She is certified on five of 14 job skills in her department. At any given time, however, she performs one of them, for example, feeding small devices by tweezers into special containers. It is tedious work without much challenge. But Vang says: "I like it." Importantly, she notes that the job doesn't interfere with her home life with a husband and three sons. Her economic needs are met in a low-stress job and comfortable work environment.[19]

Situations don't always work out this well in highly simplified jobs. Productivity can suffer as unhappy workers drive up costs through absenteeism and turnover, and through poor performance caused by boredom and alienation. Although simplified jobs appeal to some people, disadvantages can develop with the structured and repetitive tasks. For example, in the Datapoint case, Jackson White's social need is thwarted in Job 1 because the assembly line prevents interaction with co-workers. We would predict low satisfaction, occasional tardiness and absenteeism, and boredom, which may cause a high error rate. White's overall performance could be just adequate enough to prevent him from being fired. This is hardly sufficient for a computer maker trying to maintain a high-performance edge in today's competitive global economy.

Job Rotation and Job Enlargement

One way to move beyond simplification in job design is to broaden the scope through **job rotation**, increasing task variety by periodically shifting workers between jobs involving different task assignments. Job rotation can be done on a regular schedule; it can also be done periodically or occasionally. The latter approach is often used in training to broaden people's understanding of jobs performed by others. Another way to broaden scope is **job enlargement**, increasing task variety by combining two or more tasks that were previously assigned to separate workers. Often these are tasks done immediately before or after the work performed in the original job. *Figure 15.3* shows how such *horizontal loading*—pulling prework and/or later work stages into the job—can be used to enlarge jobs. In this job design strategy the old job is permanently changed through the addition of new tasks.

Jackson White's second job on the modified assembly line is an example of job enlargement with occasional job rotation. Instead of doing only one task, he now does three. Also, he occasionally switches jobs to work on a different part of the assembly. Because job enlargement and rotation can reduce some of the monotony in otherwise simplified jobs, we would expect an increase in White's satisfaction and performance. Satisfaction should remain only moderate, however, because the job still does not respond completely to his social needs. Although White's work quality should increase as boredom is reduced, some absenteeism is likely.

○ **Automation** is the total mechanization of a job.

○ **Job rotation** increases task variety by periodically shifting workers between jobs involving different tasks.

○ **Job enlargement** increases task variety by combining into one job two or more tasks previously assigned to separate workers.

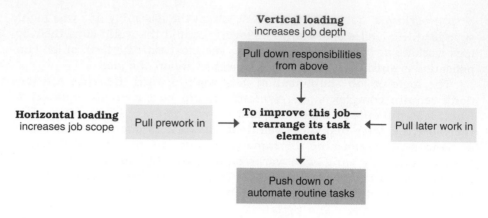

Figure 15.3 How to improve job design by horizontal and vertical loading.

Job Enrichment

Frederick Herzberg, whose two-factor theory of motivation was discussed in Chapter 14, questions the true value of horizontally loading jobs through enlargement and rotation. "Why," he asks, "should a worker become motivated when one or more meaningless tasks are added to previously existing ones or when work assignments are rotated among equally meaningless tasks?" By contrast, he says, "If you want people to do a good job, give them a good job to do."[20] He argues that this is best done through **job enrichment**, the practice of building more opportunities for satisfaction into a job by expanding its content.

In contrast to job enlargement and rotation, job enrichment focuses not just on job scope but also on *job depth*—that is, the extent to which task planning and evaluating duties are performed by the individual worker rather than the supervisor. As depicted in Figure 15.3, changes designed to increase job depth are sometimes referred to as *vertical loading*. Herzberg's recommendations for enriching jobs through vertical loading are found in *Manager's Notepad 15.1.*[21] There are some elements of job enrichment in Job 3 in the Datapoint case. Jackson White works in a team responsible for task planning and evaluation, as well as actual product assembly. The job provides opportunities to satisfy his social needs, and allows for added challenge from acting as the team's plant liaison. Higher performance and satisfaction are the predicted results.

○ **Job enrichment** increases job depth by adding work planning and evaluating duties normally performed by the supervisor.

DIRECTIONS IN JOB ENRICHMENT

Job enrichment is an important strategy with the potential to improve individual performance and satisfaction in the new workplace. But modern management theory takes job enrichment a step beyond the suggestions of Frederick Herzberg. Most importantly, it adopts a contingency perspective and recognizes that job enrichment may not be best for everyone. Among the directions in job design, the core characteristics model developed by J. Richard Hackman and his associates offers a way for managers to create jobs, enriched or otherwise, that best fit the needs of people and organizations.[22]

MANAGER'S NOTEPAD 15.1

Job enrichment checklist

Check 1: Remove controls that limit people's discretion in their work.

Check 2: Grant people authority to make decisions about their work.

Check 3: Make people understand their accountability for performance results.

Check 4: Allow people to do "whole" tasks or complete units of work.

Check 5: Make performance feedback available to those doing the work.

CORE CHARACTERISTICS MODEL

The model described in *Figure 15.4* offers a diagnostic approach to job enrichment. Five core job characteristics are identified as task attributes of special importance. A job that is high in the core characteristics is considered enriched; the lower a job scores on the core characteristics, the less enriched it is.

The *five core job characteristics* are as follows:

1. *Skill variety*—the degree to which a job requires a variety of different activities to carry out the work and involves the use of a number of different skills and talents of the individual.

2. *Task identity*—the degree to which the job requires completion of a "whole" and identifiable piece of work, that is, one that involves doing a job from beginning to end with a visible outcome.

3. *Task significance*—the degree to which the job has a substantial impact on the lives or work of other people elsewhere in the organization or in the external environment.

4. *Autonomy*—the degree to which the job gives the individual substantial freedom, independence, and discretion in scheduling the work and in determining the procedures to be used in carrying it out.

5. *Feedback from the job itself*—the degree to which carrying out the work activities required by the job results in the individual obtaining direct and clear information on the results of his or her performance.

← Five core job characteristics

According to Figure 15.4, this model of job design views job satisfaction and performance as being influenced by three critical psychological states of the individual: (1) experienced meaningfulness of the work; (2) experienced responsibility for the outcomes of the work; and (3) knowledge of actual results of work activities. These psychological states, in turn, are influenced by the presence or absence of the five core job characteristics. In true contingency fashion, however, the core characteristics will not affect all people in the same way. Generally speaking, people who respond most favorably to enriched jobs will have strong higher-order needs and appropriate job knowledge and skills. They will also be otherwise satisfied with job context. One of the key contingency or moderator variables in the model is **growth-need strength**, described in Alderfer's ERG theory

○ **Growth-need strength** is the desire to achieve psychological growth in one's work.

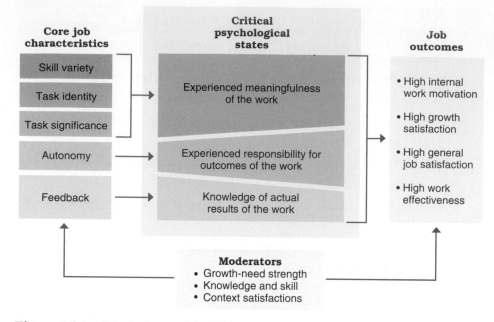

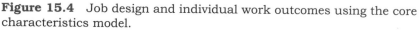

Figure 15.4 Job design and individual work outcomes using the core characteristics model.
Source: Reprinted by permission from J. Richard Hackman and Greg R. Oldham, *Work Redesign* (Reading, MA: Addison-Wesley, 1980), p. 90.

(see Chapter 14) as the degree to which an individual seeks psychological growth in his or her work. The expectation is that people with strong growth needs will respond most positively to enriched jobs.

When job enrichment is a good job design choice, Hackman and his colleagues recommend five ways to improve the core characteristics. First, you can *form natural units of work*. Make sure that the tasks people perform are logically related to one another and provide a clear and meaningful task identity. Second, try to *combine tasks*. Expand job responsibilities by pulling together into one larger job a number of smaller tasks previously done by others. Third, *establish client relationships*. Put people in contact with others who, as clients inside and/or outside the organization, use the results of their work. Fourth, *open feedback channels*. Provide opportunities for people to receive performance feedback as they work and to learn how performance changes over time. Fifth, *practice vertical loading*. Give people more control over their work by increasing their authority to perform the planning and controlling previously done by supervisors.

TECHNOLOGY AND JOB ENRICHMENT

An important issue of job enrichment involves the impact of technology on job design.[23] The managerial challenge is quite clear: job design should proceed with the goal of increasing productivity through integrated **sociotechnical systems**. These are job designs that use technology to best advantage while still treating people with respect and allowing their human talents to be applied to their fullest potential.[24] The continuing inroads made by computers into the workplace are changing structures, workflows, and the mix of skills needed in many settings. Consider the special case of *robotics*—the use of computer-controlled machines to completely automate work tasks previously performed by hand. Such automation of work is the most extreme form of job simplification and has both its limits and critics.

○ A **sociotechnical system** integrates technology and human resources in high-performance systems.

On the positive side, technology offers an opportunity to take over many routine tasks previously assigned to individuals and thereby frees human talents for more enriched job assignments. In this and other ways, technology utilization and job enrichment can be complementary strategies.

QUESTIONS AND ANSWERS ON JOB ENRICHMENT

"Is it expensive to implement job enrichment?" Job enrichment can be costly. The cost grows as the required changes in technology, workflow, and other facilities become more complex.

"Will people demand more pay for doing enriched jobs?" Herzberg believes that if people are being paid truly competitive wages (i.e., if pay dissatisfaction does not already exist), the satisfactions of performing enriched tasks will be adequate compensation for the increased work involved. But a manager must be cautious on this issue. Any job-enrichment program should be approached with recognition that pay may be an issue for the people involved.[25]

"Should everyone's job be enriched?" No, contingency counts. The people most likely to respond favorably to job enrichment are those seeking higher-order or growth-need satisfactions at work and who have the levels of training, education, and ability required to perform the enriched job.

"What do the unions say about job enrichment?" It is hard to speak for all unions. Suffice it to say that the following comments made some years ago by one union official are still worth consideration. "Better wages, shorter hours, vested pensions, a right to have a say in their working conditions, the right to be promoted on the basis of seniority, and all the rest. That's the kind of job enrichment that unions believe in."[27]

CAREER CONNECTION

Globalization

The Crafts Center
Meet the Craftswomen of the World
Did you know that one-quarter of the families in the world are totally supported by women? Did you know that another quarter of them are supported primarily by women? Paola Gianturco didn't, until she heard the news from the United Nations' Fourth World Conference on Women held in China. Since then she has traveled the world to learn more about the struggles of third-world women entrepreneurs. The result is a co-authored book, *In Her Hands: Craftswomen Changing the World*, and a revitalization of her consulting career.

Along with her colleague Toby Tuttle, Gianturco met Muslim mirror embroiderers in a poor Indian village in the state of Gujarat. They found women knitters in a Bolivian cooperative blessing loan money with confetti and beer. They watched Zulu women weave baskets in South Africa to be sold under a common brand name. What they found were craftswomen who were highly skilled in their work, and proud to be artisans as well as serve as the principal means of financial support for their families. In Turkey they observed carpet weavers taking turns to help out at each other's looms. One could pick up where the other left off and vice-versa. They had what Gianturco and Tuttle called a "shared knowledge base" that enabled them to share tasks and fill in for one another as needed.

Gianturco is on the Board of Directors of The Crafts Council in Washington, D.C., and also serves on the board of The Association for Women in Development.

QUESTION: The artisans of the world work with skill and commitment. What is the status of craftworkers in your community? Are there career or volunteer opportunities for you in helping them gain access to markets and economic prosperity?

ALTERNATIVE WORK ARRANGEMENTS

Not only is the content of jobs changing for people in today's workplace, the context is changing too. Among the more significant developments is the emergence of a number of alternative ways for people to schedule their work time.[28] This is especially important as employers deal with work-life balance issues affecting today's highly diverse workforce. Many are finding that alternative work schedules can help attract and retain the best workers. It is popular in this sense to talk about a new and more "flexible"

TAKE IT TO THE CASE!

Boeing Company (www.boeing.com)
Blending Technology and Talent to Create High-Performance Products

At Boeing Company, technology and people were keys to the development of the 777 aircraft. Designs for the 777 airplane utilized the latest computer-assisted techniques and were largely paperless. Engineers worked out problems on powerful computers, including all the coordinating details of over 130,000 engineered parts and more than 3 million rivets, screws, and fasteners. But technology didn't stand alone; people counted too. Engineers worked in a team structure where cross-functional "design-build" teams included representatives from all areas, whose contributions were essential. Design and manufacturing problems were solved by the teams before production started.[26]

workplace in which alternative work schedules such as the compressed workweek, flexible working hours, job sharing, telecommuting, and part-time work are more and more common.

THE COMPRESSED WORKWEEK

○ A **compressed work-week** allows a full-time, 40-hour-per-wek job to be completed in less than five days.

A **compressed workweek** is any work schedule that allows a full-time job to be completed in less than the standard 5 days of 8-hour shifts.[29] Its most common form is the "4–40," that is, accomplishing 40 hours of work in four 10-hour days. One advantage of the 4–40 schedule is that the employee receives 3 consecutive days off from work each week. This benefits the individual through more leisure time and lower commuting costs. The organization should also benefit through lower absenteeism and any improved performance that may result. Potential disadvantages include increased fatigue and family adjustment problems for the individual, as well as increased scheduling problems, possible customer complaints, and union objections for the organization.

Positive examples of this approach to work scheduling are available. At USAA, a diversified financial services company that has been listed among the 100 best companies to work for in America, nearly 75 percent of the firm's San Antonio workforce is on a four-day schedule, with some working Monday through Thursday and others working Tuesday through Friday. Company benefits include improved employee morale, lower overtime costs, less absenteeism, and less sick leave. At PNC Financial Services Group, a shift to a four-day week helped correct morale problems caused by longer commuting when a deposit-support department was moved to a new location. "I got such positive feedback that I was shocked," the supervisor said. Turnover in the department also fell, and productivity increased.[30]

FLEXIBLE WORKING HOURS

○ **Flexible working hours** give employees some choice in the pattern of daily work hours.

The term **flexible working hours**, also called *flexitime* or *flextime*, describes any work schedule that gives employees some choice in the pattern of their daily work hours. A sample flexible working schedule offers choices of starting and ending times, such as the program depicted in *Figure 15.5*. Employees in this example work 4 hours of "core" time, or the time they must be present at work. In this case, core time falls between 9 and 10 A.M. and 1 and 3 P.M. They are then free to choose another 4 work hours from "flextime" blocks. Such flexible schedules give employees greater autonomy while ensuring that they maintain work responsibility. Early risers may choose to come in earlier and leave earlier, while still completing an 8-hour day; late sleepers may choose to start later in the morning and leave later. In between these extremes are opportunities to attend to personal affairs, such as dental appointments, home emergencies, visits to children's schools, and so on.

The advantages of flexible working hours are especially important to members of a diverse workforce. By offering flexibility, organizations can attract and hold employees with special nonwork responsibilities. The work schedule is important to many dual-career couples who face the complications of managing careers and other responsibilities, including parenting. Single parents with young children and employees with elder-care responsibilities also find it very attractive to have the option of adjusting work schedules to allow for other obligations to be met. The added discretion flextime provides may also encourage workers to have more positive attitudes toward the organization. The global resource center at Business for Social Responsibility reports that companies are finding that flexible scheduling has performance benefits. At the women's sports apparel company Athleta, for example, turnover rates average less than one percent as compared to the industry average of 38 percent. The firm's CEO attributes its success to the use of flexible scheduling.[31]

JOB SHARING

Another important development for today's workforce is **job sharing**, whereby one full-time job is split between two or more persons. Job sharing often involves each person working one-half day, but it can also be done on weekly or monthly sharing arrangements. When it is feasible for jobs to be split and shared, organizations can benefit by employing talented people who would otherwise be unable to work. The qualified specialist who is also a parent may be unable to stay away from home for a full workday but may be able to work a half day. Job sharing allows two such persons to be employed as one. Although there are sometimes adjustment problems, the arrangement can be good for all concerned.

Job sharing is sometimes viewed skeptically by those who don't believe two workers can perform a shared job as productively as one person

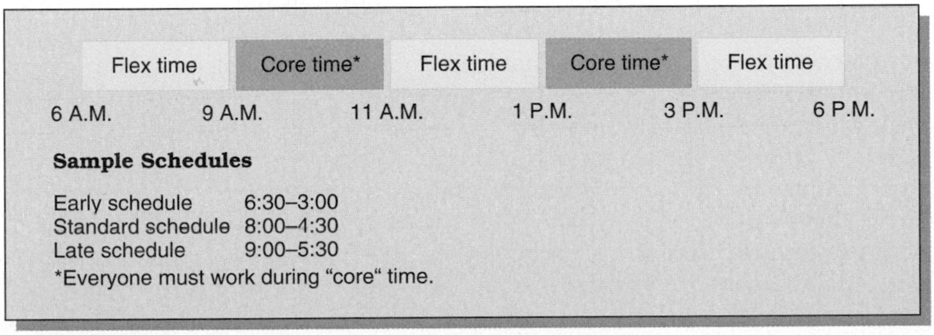

○ **Job sharing** splits one job between two people.

Flex time	Core time*	Flex time	Core time*	Flex time
6 A.M.	9 A.M. 11 A.M.		1 P.M. 3 P.M.	6 P.M.

Sample Schedules

Early schedule 6:30–3:00
Standard schedule 8:00–4:30
Late schedule 9:00–5:30
*Everyone must work during "core" time.

Figure 15.5 A sample flexible working hours schedule.

www.catalystwomen.org

Catalyst, a New York–based research organization, reports that both men and women support more flexible working schedules. They want the freedom to "come in early, leave late, go to the school play or a soccer game," and to do so without fear of damaging their careers. Many people now use the availability of flexible hours as a screening criterion in searching for employment.

○   **Telecommuting** or flexiplace involves working at home or other places using computer links to the office.

alone. However, when such concerns were investigated at Lotus Development Corporation early in the life of its job-sharing program, the results turned out to be just the opposite. When performance was studied, none of the initial nine teams of job sharers had to apologize to anybody. They were among the top performers in annual merit pay appraisals.[32]

Job sharing should not be confused with a more controversial concept called *work-sharing*. This involves an agreement between employees who face layoffs or terminations to cut back their work hours so they can all keep their jobs. Instead of losing 20 percent of a firm's workforce to temporary layoffs in an unexpected business downturn, for example, a work-sharing program would cut everyone's hours by 20 percent to keep them all employed. This allows employers to retain trained and loyal workers even when forced to temporarily economize by reducing labor costs. For employees whose seniority might otherwise protect them from layoff, the disadvantage is lost earnings. For those who would otherwise be terminated, however, it provides continued work—albeit with reduced earnings—and with a preferred employer. Some unions endorse this concept, and it is now legal in many states. It is prohibited in others, however, because of legal complications relating to unemployment compensation and benefits.

TELECOMMUTING

Another significant development in work scheduling is the growing popularity of a variety of ways for people to work away from a fixed office location. This includes alternatives ranging from self-employment and entrepreneurship based at home, to utilizing the latest in computer and information technology to maintain a "virtual" office that travels from point-to-point with you. **Telecommuting**, sometimes called *flexiplace*, is a work arrangement that allows at least a portion of scheduled work hours to be completed outside of the office, with *work-from-home* one of the options. Often this is facilitated by computer linkages to clients or customers and a central office. The number of telecommuters is rising rapidly, with some 24 million Americans telecommuting at least occasionally.[33]

Telecommuting frees the jobholder from the normal constraints of commuting, fixed hours, special work attire, and even direct contact with supervisors. It is popular, for example, among computer programmers and is found increasingly in such diverse areas as marketing, financial analysis, and administrative support. New terms are becoming associated with telecommuting practices. We speak of *hoteling* when telecommuters come to the central office and use temporary office facilities; we are immersed in a world of *telemarketing* where customers are contacted and orders taken by service personnel working in diverse locations; and we often refer to *virtual offices* that include everything from an office at home to mobile workspace in automobiles.

Overall, there is no doubt that telecommuting is with us to stay as an important aspect of the continually developing new workplace.[34] Along with it, predictably, come potential advantages and disadvantages from a job design and management perspective. When asked what they like about these alternatives, telecommuters tend to report increased productivity, fewer distractions, the freedom to be your own boss, and the benefit of having more time for themselves. On the negative side, they cite working too much, having less time to themselves, difficulty separating work and personal life, and having less time for family.[35] Other considerations for

---

MANAGER'S NOTEPAD 15.2

How to make telecommuting work for you

- Treat telecommuting like any work day; keep regular hours.
- Limit nonwork distractions; set up private space dedicated to work.
- Establish positive routines and work habits; be disciplined.
- Report regularly to your boss and main office; don't lose touch.
- Seek out human contact; don't become isolated.
- Use technology: instant messaging, intranet links, net meetings.
- Keep your freedoms and responsibilities in balance.
- Reward yourself with time off; let flexibility be an advantage.

---

the individual include feelings of isolation and loss of visibility for promotion. Managers, in turn, may be required to change their routines and procedures to accommodate the challenges of supervising people from a distance. Such problems tend to be magnified in situations where employees feel forced into these work arrangements rather than opting for them voluntarily.[36] One telecommuter's advice to others is: "You have to have self-discipline and pride in what you do, but you also have to have a boss that trusts you enough to get out of the way."[37] *Manager's Notepad 15.2* offers several guidelines for how to make telecommuting work for you.[38]

PART-TIME WORK

The growing use of temporary workers is another striking employment trend, and it has a controversial side.[39] **Part-time work** is done on any schedule less than the standard 40-hour work week and that does not qualify the individual as a full-time employee. Many employers rely on part-time **contingency workers** who supplement the full-time workforce, often on a long-term basis. *Permatemps*, for example, are important at the Lamson & Sessions Company's plastics plant in Bowling Green, Ohio. The firm is in continuous operation and operates with a core group of full-time employees who comprise about 50 percent of the total workforce. The other 50 percent consists of temporaries and independent contractors who work for the firm as needed.[40]

Contingency workers now constitute some 30 percent of the American workforce; over 90 percent of firms surveyed by the American Management Association use them.[41] No longer limited to the traditional areas of clerical services, sales personnel, and unskilled labor, these workers serve an increasingly broad range of employer needs. It is now possible to hire on a part-time basis everything from executive support, such as a chief financial officer, to such special expertise as engineering, computer programming, and market research.

Because part-time or contingency workers can be easily hired, contracted with, and/or terminated in response to changing needs, many employers like the flexibility they offer in controlling labor costs and dealing with cyclical demand. On the other hand, some worry that temporaries

○ **Part-time work** is temporary and requires less than the standard 40-hour workweek.

○ **Contingency workers** are employed on a part-time and temporary basis to supplement a permanent workforce.

lack the commitment of permanent workers and may lower productivity. Perhaps the most controversial issue of the part-time work trend relates to the different treatment part-timers may receive from employers. They may be paid less than their full-time counterparts, and many do not receive important benefits, such as health care, life insurance, pension plans, and paid vacations.

There is no doubt that many part-timers would like to achieve full-time status with their employers. On the other hand, the Families and Work Institute reports that 33 percent of women and 28 percent of men would work part-time if they could afford it; the AARP reports that 58 percent of baby boomers entering retirement would like to work part time. Clearly, human resource management practices that support part-timers can pay off by responding to these interests. At Pfizer, for example, a special sales force called Vista Rx is made up entirely of part-timers. They work 60 percent of full-time and receive proportionate benefits. The group outperforms other sales units, and there is a waiting list of internal applicants for the available positions. Some of Pfizer's most talented veterans have chosen to join the program rather than opting for early retirement. Both the individuals and the firm have gained in the process.[42]

JOB STRESS

○ **Stress** is a state of tension experienced by individuals facing extraordinary demands, constraints, or opportunities.

Flexibility in work scheduling can go a long way toward assisting with the pressures and tensions of achieving a satisfactory work-life balance. However, it is also necessary to recognize and consider an important fact of working life. The jobs that people are asked to perform, and the relationships and circumstances under which they have to do them, are often causes of significant stress. Formally defined, **stress** is a state of tension experienced by individuals facing extraordinary demands, constraints, or opportunities.[43] Any look toward your future work career would be incomplete without considering stress as a challenge that you are sure to encounter along the way—and a challenge you must be prepared to help others learn to deal with.

With the ever-present and ever-changing demands of working in the new economy, it is not surprising that people are experiencing more stress in their daily lives. In his book *The Future of Success*, for example, Robert Reich says that even though the new economy gives us much to celebrate, its "rewards are coming at the price of lives that are more frenzied, less secure, more economically divergent, more socially stratified."[44] At center stage in this milieu stand job stress and its implications for the managerial role. Consider this statement by a psychologist working with top-level managers who have alcohol abuse problems: "All executives deal with stress. They wouldn't be executives if they didn't. Some handle it well, others handle it poorly."[45]

SOURCES OF STRESS

○ A **stressor** is anything that causes stress.

The things that cause stress are called **stressors**. Whether they originate directly in the work setting or emerge in personal and nonwork situations, they all have the potential to influence one's work attitudes, behavior, and job performance.

Work factors have an obvious potential to create job stress. Some 46 percent of workers in one survey reported that their jobs were highly stressful; 34 percent said that their jobs were so stressful that they were thinking of quitting.[46] Today, we often experience such stress in long hours of work, excessive e-mails, unrealistic work deadlines, difficult bosses or co-workers, and unwelcome or unfamiliar work.[47] It is associated with excessively high or low task demands, role conflicts or ambiguities, poor interpersonal relations, or career progress that is too slow or too fast. Stress tends to be high during periods of work overload, when office politics are common, and among persons working for organizations undergoing staff cutbacks and downsizing. This latter situation and lack of "corporate loyalty" to the employee can be especially stressful to employees who view themselves as "career" employees and who are close to retirement age. Two of the common work-related stress syndromes are: (1) *set up to fail*—where the performance expectations are impossible or the support is totally inadequate to the task; and (2) *mistaken identity*—where the individual ends up in a job that doesn't at all match talents or that he or she simply doesn't like.[48]

A variety of *personal factors* are also sources of potential stress for people at work. Such individual characteristics as needs, capabilities, and personality can influence how one perceives and responds to the work situation. Researchers, for example, identify a **Type A personality** that is high in achievement orientation, impatience, and perfectionism. Type A persons are likely to create stress in circumstances that others find relatively stress-free. Type A's, in this sense, bring stress on themselves. The stressful behavior patterns of *Type A personalities* include the following:[49]

○ A **Type A personality** is a person oriented toward extreme achievement, impatience, and perfectionism.

← Characteristics of Type A personalities

- Always moving, walking, and eating rapidly.
- Acting impatient, hurrying others, disliking waiting.
- Doing, or trying to do, several things at once.
- Feeling guilty when relaxing.
- Trying to schedule more in less time.
- Using nervous gestures such as a clenched fist.
- Hurrying or interrupting the speech of others.

Finally, stress from *nonwork factors* can have spillover effects that affect the individual at work. Stressful life situations including such things as family events (e.g., the birth of a new child), economics (e.g., a sudden loss of extra income), and personal affairs (e.g., a preoccupation with a bad relationship) are often sources of emotional strain. Depending on the individual and his or her ability to deal with them, preoccupation with such situations can affect one's work and add to the stress of work-life conflicts.

CONSEQUENCES OF STRESS

The discussion of stress so far may give the impression that it always acts as a negative influence on our lives. Stress actually has two faces—one constructive and one destructive.[50] Consider the analogy of a violin.[51] When a violin string is too loose, the sound produced by even the most skilled player is weak and raspy. When the string is too tight, however, the sound gets shrill and the string might even snap. But when the tension on the string is just right, neither too loose or too tight, a most beautiful sound is created. With just enough stress, in other words, performance is optimized. The same argument tends to hold in the workplace. **Constructive stress**—sometimes called *eustress*, acts in a positive way for the individual

○ **Constructive stress** acts in a positive way to increase effort, stimulate creativity, and encourage diligence in one's work.

and/or the organization. It occurs in moderation and proves energizing and performance enhancing.[52] The stress is sufficient to encourage increased effort, stimulate creativity, and enhance diligence in one's work, while not overwhelming the individual and causing negative outcomes. Individuals with a Type A personality, for example, are likely to work long hours and to be less satisfied with poor performance. For them, challenging task demands imposed by a supervisor may elicit higher levels of task accomplishment. Even nonwork stressors such as new family responsibilities may cause them to work harder in anticipation of greater financial rewards.

○ **Destructive stress** impairs the performance of an individual.

Just like tuning the violin string, however, achieving the right balance of stress for each person and situation is difficult. The question is, "When is a little stress too much stress?" **Destructive stress**, or *distress*, is dysfunctional for the individual and/or the organization. It occurs as intense or long-term stress that, as shown in *Figure 15.6*, overloads and breaks down a person's physical and mental systems. Destructive stress can lead to **job burnout**—a form of physical and mental exhaustion that can be incapacitating both personally and in respect to one's work. Productivity can suffer as people react to very intense stress through turnover, absenteeism, errors, accidents, dissatisfaction, and reduced performance. Today as well, there is increased concern for another job consequence of excessive stress, **workplace rage**—overtly aggressive behavior toward co-workers and the work setting in general. Lost tempers are a common example; the unfortunate extremes are tragedies involving physical harm to others.[53]

○ **Job burnout** is physical and mental exhaustion that can be incapacitating personally and in respect to work.

○ **Workplace rage** is overtly aggressive behavior toward co-workers or the work setting.

Medical research is also concerned that too much stress can reduce resistance to disease and increase the likelihood of physical and/or mental illness. It may contribute to health problems such as hypertension, ulcers, substance abuse, overeating, depression, and muscle aches, among others.[54] Also important to understand is that excessive work stress can have spillover effects on one's personal life. A study of dual-career couples found that one partner's work experiences can have psychological consequences for the other; as one's work stress increases the partner is likely to experience stress too.[55] The bottom line here is that any stress we experience at work is contagious; it can affect one's spouse, family, and friends. The wife of a company controller, for example, went through a time when her husband was stressed by a boss who was overly critical. "He was angry, really angry when he came home," she says. His mood affected her and their young child and created what she called "one of the worst times in our seven-year marriage."[56]

Get Connected!

Take the stress self-test on-line and in the Career Readiness Workbook (assessment #21).

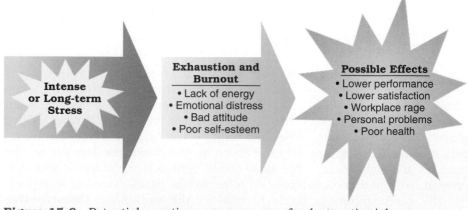

Figure 15.6 Potential negative consequences of a destructive job stress–burnout cycle.

STRESS MANAGEMENT STRATEGIES

There are at least four reasons that managers should also be skilled at dealing with workplace stress.[57] The first is humanitarianism. To the extent that managerial awareness and action can enhance employee health, managers have a humanitarian responsibility to do so. The second is productivity. Healthy employees are absent less often, make fewer errors, and must be replaced less frequently than less healthy ones. The third is creativity. Persons in poor health tend to be less creative and are less likely to take reasonable risks than their healthy counterparts. The fourth is return on investment. When poor health reduces or removes the individual's contribution to the organization, return on the time and money invested in human resources is lost.

Managers should obviously be alert to signs of excessive stress in themselves and the people with whom they work. The multiple and varied symptoms of excessive stress include changes in work attitudes and performance as well as personal restlessness, irritability, and stomach upset. The best stress management alternative is to prevent it from ever reaching excessive levels in the first place. Stressors emerging from personal and nonwork factors must be recognized so that action can be taken to prevent them from adversely affecting the work experience. Family difficulties may be relieved by a change of work schedule, or the anxiety they cause may be reduced by an understanding supervisor.

Among the work factors with the greatest potential to cause excessive stress are role ambiguities, conflicts, and overloads. *Role clarification* through a management-by-objectives (MBO) approach can work to good advantage here. By bringing the supervisor and subordinate together in face-to-face task-oriented communications, MBO offers an opportunity to spot stressors and take action to reduce or eliminate them. Another issue is often a poor fit between individual abilities and aspirations and job demands. In this case job redesign may be helpful to better configure task requirements. Alternatively, changing jobs altogether can help achieve the desired person-job fit. People can also be encouraged to maintain adequate self-awareness and take a realistic approach to their responsibilities.

Sometimes others need help to combat the tendency of "working too much." They need to be reminded not to forgo vacations, or not to work excessive overtime, for example. Many organizations provide special help in the form of *employee assistance programs*. These programs help employees deal with special problems that may be adding excessive stress to their lives, such as personal financial problems, difficulties with child care or elder care, substance abuse, and so forth. In organizations undergoing downsizing, layoffs, or cutbacks, it is important to understand the *survivor syndrome*—stress experienced by persons who remain but fear for their jobs in the future. As more organizations experience this phenomenon, they are responding with programs to help those employees who remain employed to better cope after major staff cutbacks have occurred.

Personal wellness is a term used to describe the pursuit of one's physical and mental potential through a personal health-promotion program.[58] This form of *preventative stress management* recognizes the individual's responsibility to enhance his or her personal health through a disciplined approach to such things as smoking, alcohol use, maintaining a nutritious diet, and engaging in a regular exercise and physical-fitness program. The essence of personal wellness is a lifestyle that reflects a true commitment to health.

○ **Personal wellness** is the pursuit of one's full potential through a personal-health promotion program.

MANAGER'S NOTEPAD 15.3

Six ways to cope with workplace stress

1. *Take control of the situation:* Do your best, know your limits, and avoid unrealistic deadlines.
2. *Pace yourself:* Plan your day to do high-priority things first, but stay flexible and try to slow down.
3. *Open up to others:* Discuss your problems, fears, and frustrations with those who care about you.
4. *Do things for others:* Think about someone else's needs, and try to help satisfy those needs.
5. *Exercise:* Engage in regular physical activity as recommended by your physician.
6. *Balance work and recreation:* Schedule time for recreation, including vacations from your work.

Personal wellness makes a great deal of sense as a personal stress-management strategy. Those who aggressively maintain their personal wellness are better prepared to deal with the inevitable stresses of work and work-life conflicts. They may be able to deal with levels of workplace stress that are higher than others can tolerate; they may also have more insight into the personal wellness needs of their subordinates. Indeed, many organizations are now formally sponsoring wellness programs for employees. Among the health-promotion activities typically offered are smoking control, health risk appraisals, back care, stress management, exercise/physical fitness, nutrition education, high blood pressure control, and weight control. The expectations are that investments in such programs benefit both the organization and its employees.

Ultimately the keys to personal stress management throughout a career rest with knowing how to help yourself. It is fitting, therefore, to end this discussion with *Manager's Notepad 15.3* and its useful guidelines for coping with workplace stress.[59]

The Chapter 15 Study Guide will help you review chapter content, prepare for examinations, and further build your career readiness. The *Summary* briefly highlights answers to questions first posed in the chapter opening Planning Ahead section. The list of *Key Terms* allows you to double check your familiarity with basic concepts and definitions. *Self-Test 15* gives you the opportunity to test your basic comprehension of chapter content using sample test questions. Suggestions offered as *Career Readiness Activities* direct your attention to relevant sections of the end-of-text Career Readiness Workbook, as well as to special Electronic Resources on the *Management 7/e* web site.

SUMMARY

What is the meaning of work?

- Work is an activity that produces value for people; it is something people do to "earn a living."
- Work is an exchange of values between individuals who offer contributions such as time and effort to organizations that offer monetary and other inducements in return.
- A healthy psychological contract occurs when a person believes that his or her contributions and inducements are in balance; it is one component in a high quality of work life.
- Quality of work life (QWL) is an important issue in creating opportunities for positive work-life balance.

What are the issues in satisfaction, performance, and job design?

- Job design is the process of creating or defining jobs by assigning specific work tasks to individuals and groups.
- Jobs should be designed so workers enjoy high levels of both job performance and job satisfaction.
- The high-performance equation states: Performance = Ability × Support × Effort.
- Job simplification creates narrow and repetitive jobs consisting of well-defined tasks with many routine operations, such as the typical assembly-line job.
- Job enlargement allows individuals to perform a broader range of simplified tasks; job rotation allows individuals to transfer between different jobs of similar skill levels on a rotating basis.
- Job enrichment results in more meaningful jobs that involve more autonomy in decision making and broader task responsibilities.

409

How can jobs be enriched?

- The diagnostic approach to job enrichment involves analyzing jobs according to five core characteristics: skill variety, task identity, task significance, autonomy, and feedback.
- Jobs deficient in one or more of these core characteristics can be redesigned to improve their level of enrichment.
- Jobs can be enriched by forming natural work units, combining tasks, establishing client relationships, opening feedback channels, and vertically loading to give workers more planning and controlling responsibilities.
- Job enrichment does not work for everyone; it works best for people with a high growth-need strength—the desire to achieve psychological growth in their work.

What are alternative work arrangements?

- Alternative work schedules can make work hours less inconvenient and enable organizations to respond better to individual needs and personal responsibilities.
- The compressed workweek allows 40 hours of work to be completed in only 4 days' time.
- Flexible working hours allow people to adjust the starting and ending times of their daily schedules.
- Job sharing allows two people to share one job.
- Telecommuting allows people to work at home or in mobile offices through computer links with their employers and/or customers.
- An increasing number of people work on part-time schedules; more and more organizations are employing part-timers or contingency workers to reduce their commitments to full-time positions.

How can job and workplace stress be managed?

- Stress occurs as the tension accompanying extraordinary demands, constraints, or opportunities.
- Stress can be destructive or constructive; a moderate level of stress typically has a positive impact on performance.
- Stressors are found in a variety of work, personal, and nonwork situations.
- For some people, having a Type A personality creates stress as a result of continual feelings of impatience and pressure.
- Stress can be effectively managed through both prevention and coping strategies, including a commitment to personal wellness.

KEY TERMS

Automation (p. 395)   Contingency workers (p. 403)

Compressed workweek (p. 400)   Destructive stress (p. 406)

Constructive stress (p. 405)   Flexible working hours (p. 400)

SELF-TEST 15

Take this test here or on-line much as you would in a normal classroom situation. It is a good way to check your basic comprehension of chapter material. Answers may be found at the end of the book.

MULTIPLE-CHOICE QUESTIONS:

1. Which statement about QWL is incorrect?
   (a) QWL can influence work-life balance.
   (b) Managers should create high-QWL environments.
   (c) QWL is related to the worker's overall quality of life.
   (d) QWL is the only important job design consideration.
2. A manager's job design goals should be to establish the conditions for workers to achieve high levels of both task performance and _____.
   (a) financial gain (b) social interaction (c) job satisfaction
   (d) job security
3. Vertical loading of a job is most associated with _____.
   (a) bringing prework into the job
   (b) bringing later work stages into the job
   (c) bringing higher-level or managerial work into the job
   (d) increasing the quantity of output expected from a job
4. The _____ strategy of job design allows workers to shift regularly between a variety of jobs requiring essentially the same skills.
   (a) job simplification (b) job enlargement (c) job rotation (d) job sharing
5. The addition of more planning and evaluating responsibilities to a job is an example of the _____ job design strategy.
   (a) job enrichment (b) job enlargement (c) job rotation (d) job sharing
6. _____ is one of the core characteristics that should be improved upon in order to enrich a job.
   (a) Work-life balance (b) Task significance (c) Growth-need strength
   (d) Automation

7. Workers in a compressed workweek typically work 40 hours in
_____ days.
(a) 3 (b) 4 (c) 5 (d) a flexible number of

8. Another term used to describe part-time workers is _____.
(a) contingency workers (b) virtual workers (c) flexible workers
(d) secondary workers

9. _____ is where two workers split one job on an arranged work
schedule; _____ is where a group of workers accept reduced individual work hours in order to avoid layoffs.
(a) Job rotation, job sharing (b) Job sharing, work sharing
(c) Job enrichment, job sharing (d) Job splitting, job reduction

10. Hoteling is a development associated with the growing importance of
_____ in the new workplace.
(a) personal wellness (b) telecommuting (c) compressed workweeks
(d) Type A personalities

TRUE-FALSE QUESTIONS:

11. It is not a manager's responsibility to deal with the psychological contracts of people at work.   T   F

12. It is safe to say that improvements in job satisfaction should result in
lower absenteeism.   T   F

13. The contingency approach to job design rules out any use of job simplification.   T   F

14. Job enlargement is a good example of job enrichment for an individual
worker.   T   F

15. The basic idea of sociotechnical systems is to replace all human effort
with machines.   T   F

16. Job enrichment is good for everyone.   T   F

17. Part-time work is increasing in importance in the American
economy.   T   F

18. Flexible working hours are proving useful in "family-friendly" companies
trying to meet the needs of diverse workforces.   T   F

19. Stress can have positive as well as negative effects on work
performance.   T   F

20. The "spillover effect" helps explain how stressful life situations can adversely affect one's work.   T   F

SHORT-RESPONSE QUESTIONS:

21. What is a "healthy" psychological contract?

22. What difference does growth-need strength make in the job enrichment
process?

23. Why is it important for a manager to understand the Type A personality?

24. Why might an employer not be interested in offering employees the option
of working on a compressed workweek schedule?

APPLICATION QUESTION:

25. Kurt Swenson has just attended a management development program in which the following "high-performance equation" was discussed: Performance = Ability × Support × Effort. As a plant manager, he is interested in implementing the concept. He plans to hold a meeting for all of his team leaders to explain the implications of this equation. If you were Kurt, how would you explain the importance of each performance factor—ability, support, effort—and how would you explain the significance of the multiplication signs in the equation?

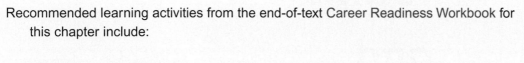

CAREER readiness ACTIVITIES

Recommended learning activities from the end-of-text Career Readiness Workbook for this chapter include:

Career Advancement Portfolio
  • Individual writing and group presentation assignments based on any of the following activities.
Case for Critical Thinking
  • Boeing Company—Talent Builds a Better Plane
Integrative Learning Activities
  • Research Project 6—Controversies in CEO Pay
  • Integrative Case—Outback Steakhouse, Inc.
Exercises in Teamwork
  • What Do You Value in Work? (#7)
  • The Future Workplace (#13)
  • Work vs. Family (#16)
  • The "Best" Job Design (#23)
Self-Assessments
  • Two-Factor Profile (#17)
  • Job Design Choices (#18)
  • Stress Self-Test (#21)
The *Fast Company* Collection On-Line
  • Robert Reich, "The Company of the Future"
  • Alan Weber, "Danger: Toxic Company"

ELECTRONIC RESOURCES

@ GET CONNECTED! Don't forget to take full advantage of the on-line support for *Management 7/e.*
• Chapter 15 On-line Study Guide
• Chapter 15 Self-test Answers
• Chapter 15 E-Resource Center

16

Teams and teamwork

Planning ahead

GETTING CONNECTED

Motorola, Inc. — *Teams Are Worth the Hard Work*

Teams of all types are in at Motorola, Inc., a major global player in the highly competitive technology sector. You can find teams working in Motorola plants around the world. At its Plantation, Florida, facility, new applicants are carefully screened for their attitudes toward teamwork. A quality team at the Florida plant suggested ways to streamline workflow and increased output by 150 percent.

Enthusiasm and high-performance norms rule the day at Motorola's Penang, Malaysia, operation. A team spirit rallies the plant's workers, who in one year alone submitted 41,000 suggestions for improvement and saved the firm some $2 million. The Malaysian plant sets a high benchmark. Says one manager who recently spent three years working there, "The whole plant in Penang had this craving for learning."

At Motorola Australia, team skills top the list of qualities sought in new employees. The company web site states: "If you can demonstrate personal attributes such as teamwork, initiative, adaptability, excellent communication skills and strong analysis and problem-solving skills, then Motorola is for you."

For creativity and problem solving, Motorola utilizes Total Customer Satisfaction Teams. These are groups that bring together diverse members to address a specific goal, such as cycle-time reduction, quality improvement, profit improvement, environmental leadership, and process improvement. TCS teams with cross-functional memberships, have advanced the firm's environmental mission by helping to improve water conservation, clean up waste discharge, and reduce packaging waste.

Teams also are critical to outreach and community. Says Barbara Clark of Motorola's Southwest Workforce & Education Team in Arizona: "As a technology company, Motorola is in continuous renewal. To maintain our competitive edge and sustain success, we know we must reach beyond today to prepare our next generation of employees and consumers. In order to do that, Motorola is making a strategic investment in education."

Clark is part of a team that links Motorola with educators in the community in an attempt to strengthen the educational system so that graduates have the skills and capabilities needed to compete in tomorrow's workplace. The corporate mission supported by the team is: "To proactively collaborate with the K–16 educational system to cultivate the talent needed to sustain company growth."[1]

@ **Get Connected!**

There's no doubt that you'll have to be good at teamwork in the new workplace. Are you prepared to lead teams? . . . to participate well as a member of teams? Just how good are your team skills? Take advantage of the opportunities for skill building in the Career Readiness Workbook. Get connected!

People have the need to work in teams. There is a desire to work with others and enjoy the benefits of your work and your successes together... these satisfactions are as important today as they have ever been.
                                                    Andy Grove, Chairman of Intel, Inc.

I learned a long time ago that in team sports or in business, a group working together can always defeat a team of individuals even if the individuals, by themselves, are better than your team... If you're going to empower people and you don't have teamwork, you're dead.
                                                    John Chambers, CEO of Cisco Systems

As these opening quotes from leaders of two of the world's powerhouse technology firms suggest, the new workplace is rich in teams and teamwork.[2] In building high-performance organizations driven by speed, innovation, efficiency, spontaneity, and continuous change, harnessing the great potential of teams and teamwork is a part of the process. The overarching goal is always to create work environments within which the full talents of people are enthusiastically mobilized in support of organizational goals. This critical human capital of organizations must be nurtured and developed both at the level of the individual contributor, the subject of the last chapter, and at the level of the work group or team, our present concern. But even as we recognize that finding the best ways to utilize teams as performance resources is an increasingly important managerial task, the ability to successfully lead through teamwork is not always easy to achieve.

Just the words *group* and *team* elicit both positive and negative reactions in the minds of many people. Although it is said that "two heads are better than one," we are also warned that "too many cooks spoil the broth." The true skeptic can be heard to say, "A camel is a horse put together by a committee." Against this somewhat humorous background lies a most important point. Teams are rich in performance potential; they are also very complex in the way they work and very challenging to lead for high-performance results.[3] Consider, too, these realities: Many people prefer to work in teams rather than independently; over 60 percent of the average worker's time is spent in a team environment. Yet even though most workers spend at least some time in teams, less than half receive team training.[4]

TEAMS IN ORGANIZATIONS

Most tasks in organizations are well beyond the capabilities of individuals alone; they can only be accomplished by people working together in teams. Especially in this age of intellectual capital and knowledge work, true managerial success will be earned in substantial part through success at mobilizing, leading, and supporting high-performing teams. The new organizational designs and cultures require it, as does any true commitment to empowerment and employee involvement.[5] There is no doubt that teams are indispensable to the new workplace. The question for managers and team leaders, and the guiding theme of this chapter, thus becomes: How do we make sure that teams and teamwork are utilized to everyone's best advantage?

Before proceeding, let's be specific about the terminology. A **team** is a small group of people with complementary skills, who work together to accomplish shared goals while holding themselves mutually accountable for performance results.[6] **Teamwork** is the process of people working together to accomplish these goals.

○ A **team** is a collection of people who regularly interact to pursue common goals.

○ **Teamwork** is the process of people actively working together to accomplish common goals.

CHALLENGES OF TEAMWORK

Figure 16.1 shows four important roles that managers must perform in order to fully master the challenges of teams and teamwork. These roles, along with examples, are: (1) *supervisor*—serving as the appointed head of a formal work unit; (2) *facilitator*—serving as the peer leader and networking hub for a special task force; (3) *participant*—serving as a helpful contributing member of a project team; and (4) *coach*—serving as the external convenor or sponsor of a problem-solving team staffed by others. In all of these settings, performance results will depend on both the understanding of how teams operate and actively helping them succeed.

Experience has taught all of us that teams and teamwork are not problem free. Who hasn't heard people complain about having to attend what they consider to be another "time-wasting" meeting?[7] And, who hasn't encountered **social loafing**—the presence of "free-riders" who slack off because responsibility is diffused in teams and others are present to do the work?[8] Things don't have to be this way. The time we spend in groups can be productive and satisfying, but to make it so we must understand the complex nature of groups and their internal dynamics.[9]

An important skill is knowing *when* a team is the best choice for a task. Another is knowing *how* to work with and manage the team to best accomplish that task. Take social loafing as an example. What can a leader or other concerned team member do when someone is free riding? It's not easy, but the problem can be addressed. Actions can be taken to make individual contributions more visible, reward individuals for their contributions, make task assignments more interesting, and keep group size small so that free riders are more visible and subject to peer pressure and leader evaluation.[10]

As we proceed, keep in mind other problems encountered when we work in teams. Personality conflicts are commonplace. Individual differences in personality and work style can disrupt the team. Tasks are not always clear. Ambiguous agendas and/or ill-defined problems can cause teams to work too long on the wrong things. Not everyone is always ready to work. Sometimes the issue is motivation, but it may be due to conflicts with other work deadlines and priorities. It may also be caused by a lack of team organization and/or progress. Time is wasted when meetings lack purpose and when members come unprepared. These and other difficulties can turn the great potential of teams into frustration and failure.

Clearly, teams are hard work. But, they are also worth it!

○ **Social loafing** is the tendency of some people to avoid responsibility by "free-riding" in groups.

Meeting Patterns Around the World
Cultures vary and so do their approaches to meetings. In the United States, it is common for meetings to open informally, with a brief introduction, perhaps a cup of coffee, and even a light joke. Take the on-line "Reality Check" to learn more about meeting practices in other parts of the world.

Supervisor   Network facilitator   Helpful participant   External coach

How managers get involved with teams and teamwork

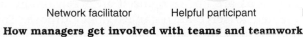

Figure 16.1 Team and teamwork roles for managers.

SYNERGY AND THE USEFULNESS OF TEAMS

○ **Synergy** is the creation of a whole greater than the sum of its individual parts.

A major reason why teams are worth the effort is **synergy**—the creation of a whole that is greater than the sum of its parts. Teamwork in our society makes available everything from aircraft to the Internet to music videos. It all happens because of synergy, the bringing together of individual talents and efforts to create extraordinary things. Synergy occurs when a team uses its membership resources to the fullest and thereby achieves through collective action far more than could otherwise be achieved. This is obviously an important advantage for organizations facing the uncertainties and demands of increasingly complex operating environments.

Teams are also useful in other ways. They can be very beneficial for their members. Being part of a team can have a strong influence on individual attitudes and behaviors. When the experience is positive, working in and being part of a team helps satisfy important individual needs. Sometimes these are needs that may be difficult to meet in the regular work setting. Thus, teams can be very good for both organizations and their members. They are an indispensable human resource whose usefulness in the work setting includes the following:[11]

Usefulness of teams →

- More resources for problem solving.
- Improved creativity and innovation.
- Improved quality of decision making.
- Greater commitments to tasks.
- Higher motivation through collective action.
- Better control and work discipline.
- More individual need satisfaction.

FORMAL AND INFORMAL GROUPS

○ A **formal group** is officially recognized and supported by the organization.

The teams officially recognized and supported by the organization for specific purposes are **formal groups**. They are part of the formal structure and are created to fulfill a variety of essential operations. A good example is the work group consisting of a manager and subordinates, and responsible for the continuing performance of tasks important to the organization. Work groups exist in various sizes and go by different labels. They may be called *departments* (e.g., market research department), *units* (e.g., product assembly unit), *teams* (e.g., customer service team), or *divisions* (e.g., office products division), among other possibilities. In all cases, they are the building blocks of organization structures. Indeed, in Rensis Likert's classic view of organizations, they are interlocking networks of groups in which managers and leaders serve important "linking pin" roles.[12] Each manager or leader serves both as a superior in one functional group and as a subordinate in the next-higher-level one. When the resulting vertical and horizontal linkages are well managed, they help integrate the diverse activities and accomplishments of teams throughout an organization.

○ An **informal group** is unofficial and emerges from relationships and shared interests among members.

Standing in contrast to the formal groups just described are the **informal groups** that are also present and important in every organization. These informal groups are not recognized on organization charts and are not officially created to serve an organizational purpose. They emerge as part of the informal structure and from natural or spontaneous relationships among people. You might recognize these as *interest groups* in which workers band together to pursue a common cause or special position, such as a concern for poor working conditions. Some emerge as *friendship groups* that develop for a wide variety of personal reasons, including shared nonwork interests. Others emerge as *support groups* in which the members basically help one another do their jobs.

Two points about informal groups are especially important for managers to understand. First, informal groups are not necessarily bad. Indeed, they can have a positive impact on work performance. In particular, the relationships and connections made possible by informal groups may actually help speed the workflow or allow people to "get things done" in ways not possible within the formal structure. Second, informal groups can help satisfy social needs that members find otherwise thwarted or left unmet in the formal work setting. Among other things, members of informal groups often find that the groups offer social satisfactions, security, support, and a sense of belonging.

TRENDS IN THE USE OF TEAMS

The trend toward greater empowerment in organizations is associated with new developments that extend the use of teams beyond the formal group or work team described earlier.[13] In previous chapters, for example, we noted the growing use of cross-functional teams to improve integration. A variety of employee involvement teams, including quality circles, are also increasingly more commonplace as managers seek to expand opportunities for broadbased participation in workplace affairs. Developments in information technology are also creating further opportunities for people to work together in computer-mediated or virtual teams.

COMMITTEES

A **committee** brings people together outside of their daily job assignments to work in a small team for a specific purpose. The task agenda is typically narrow, focused, and ongoing. Membership changes over time as the committee remains in existence. Committees are led by a designated head or chairperson, who is held accountable for performance results. Organizations usually have a variety of permanent or standing committees dedicated to a wide variety of concerns—diversity and compensation are two common examples.[14] At Marriott International, a committee of top executives meets several times each year to focus on human capital. The group reviews progress in hiring and retaining the best talent, and makes suggestions for future improvements.[15]

○ A **committee** is a formal team designated to work on a special task on a continuing basis.

PROJECT TEAMS AND TASK FORCES

Project teams or **task forces** perform important work for the organization, but exist only temporarily. Importantly, the task assignments for project teams and task forces are very specific; completion deadlines are also clearly defined. Once the project or task is completed the team disbands; on long-running projects, the membership of the team may change over time. Creativity and innovation are very important. Project teams, for example, might be formed to develop a new product or

○ A **task force** is a formal team convened for a specific purpose and expected to disband when that purpose is achieved.

service, redesign an office layout, or provide specialized consulting for a client.[16] Like committees, project teams and task forces bring together people from various parts of an organization to work on common problems. They bring to the team special skills and expertise critical to its purpose. In order to achieve the desired results, any project team or task force must be carefully established and then well run. Some guidelines for managing projects and task forces are found in *Manager's Notepad 16.1*.[17]

CROSS-FUNCTIONAL TEAMS

○ A **cross-functional team** is a formally designated work team with a manager or team leader, whose members come from different functional units of an organization.

Organizational design today emphasizes adaptation and horizontal integration.[18] It emphasizes problem solving and information sharing. It also tries to eliminate the functional chimneys problem, described in Chapter 10 as the tendency of workers to remain within their functions and restrict communication with other parts of an organization. The **cross-functional team**, whose members come from different functional units and parts of an organization, is indispensable to fulfillment of these design goals.

Typically, the members of a cross-functional team come together to work on a specific problem or task and to do so with the needs of the whole organization in mind. They are expected to share information, explore new ideas, seek creative solutions, and meet project deadlines. Importantly, they are expected to not be limited by narrow functional concerns and demands. Rather, the team members collectively and individually are to think and act cross-functionally and in the best interests of the total system. At ABB Industrial Systems, Inc., cross-functional teams are specifically created to knock down the "walls" separating departments within the firm. Representation on a team might consist, for example, of engineers, buyers, assemblers, and shipping clerks.[19]

EMPLOYEE INVOLVEMENT TEAMS

○ An **employee involvement team** meets on a regular basis to use its talents to help solve problems and achieve continuous improvement.

Another development in today's organizations is use of many types of **employee involvement teams**. These are groups of workers who meet on a regular basis outside of their formal assignments, with the goal of applying their expertise and attention to important workplace matters. The general purpose of employee involvement teams is continuous improvement. Using a problem-solving framework, the teams try to bring the benefits of employee participation to bear on a wide variety of performance issues and concerns. The Total Customer Satisfaction Teams at Motorola, featured in the chapter opener, are examples.

○ A **quality circle** is a team of employees who meet periodically to discuss ways of improving work quality.

Another popular form of employee involvement team is the **quality circle**, a group of workers that meets regularly to discuss and plan specific ways to improve work quality.[20] Usually it consists of 6 to 12 members from a work area. After receiving special training in problem solving, team processes, and quality issues, members of the quality circle try to come up with suggestions that can be implemented to raise productivity through quality improvements. Quality circles became popular in U.S. industry in part because of their place in Japanese management. Along with other types of involvement teams, they are now found in organizations where empowerment and participation are valued as keys to high performance.

VIRTUAL TEAMS

A newer form of group that is increasingly common in today's organizations is the **virtual team**, sometimes called a *computer-mediated group* or *electronic group network*.[21] This is a team of people who work together and solve problems largely through computer-mediated rather than face-to-face interactions. Chapter 3, on information and decision making, highlighted the role of new technology in today's organizations. Among the many developments, the sophistication of networking technologies and groupware programs is highly significant. As organizations become increasingly global in their operations and perspectives, the opportunity to utilize virtual teams whose members are physically dispersed, even among locations around the world, is highly advantageous.

○ Members of a **virtual team** work together and solve problems through computer-based interactions.

GLOBALIZATION (www.ford.com)
Ford Motor Company Teams Help Drive a Greener Company

Recycling car parts is the goal of the RAT pack at Ford Motor Company. The firm's Recycle Action Team meets once a week to find new ways to use recycled materials and to recycle as much as possible of the firm's products. Take scrap tires, for example. Ford vehicles now are incorporating parts made from recycled tires, soda bottles, and even used carpeting from homes. A special project of Ford's environmental outreach and strategy program, RAT is a good example of applying team creativity and initiative to solve important problems. The E-RAT or European version of the teams has recently been implemented. Ford also purchased a vehicle reclying facility in Florida, and plans to expand the activity as part of its goal of reducing the amount of old auto parts that end up in landfills.[22]

Recycling gives autos "new life"

The automobile is one of the most highly recycled durable goods – second only to auto batteries. More than 75 percent of a vehicle is recycled after its useful life – including all metals, catalytic converters, batteries and many fluids. In addition, some familiar consumer products are finding a second life in today's cars and trucks. Recycled products now being used by Ford Motor Company include:

SODA BOTTLES · LUGGAGE RACKS · OLD BUMPERS · NEW TAILLAMPS · GRILLE REINFORCEMENTS · DOOR PADDING · USED TIRES · BRAKE PEDAL PADS · BATTERY HOUSINGS · SPLASH SHIELDS

Source: Ford Motor Company

The use of intranets and special software support for computerized meetings is changing the way many committees, task forces, and other problem-solving teams function.[23] Working in virtual environments, team members address problems and seek consensus on how to best deal with them. This is just like any team in respect to *what* gets done. *How* things get done, however, is different for virtual teams. This can be a source of both potential problems and advantages, which should be understood by managers considering the utilization of virtual teams in daily affairs.

Problems in virtual teamwork can occur when the members have difficulty establishing good working relationships. Relations among team members can become depersonalized as the lack of face-to-face interaction limits the role of emotions and nonverbal cues in the communication process.[24] But virtual teams also have many potential advantages. They can save time and travel expenses. They can allow members to work collectively in a time-efficient fashion, and without interpersonal difficulties that might otherwise occur—especially when the issues are controversial. A vice president for human resources at Marriott, for example, once called electronic meetings "the quietest, least stressful, most productive meetings you've ever had."[25] Virtual teams can also be easily expanded to include additional experts as needed, and the discussions and information shared among team members can be stored on-line for continuous updating and access.

Developing insights on virtual teams suggests that following some basic guidelines can help ensure that the advantages outweigh the disadvantages. The critical ingredients relate to the creation of positive impressions and the development of trust among team members who lack face-to-face meeting opportunities. First, virtual teams should begin with social messaging that allows the exchange of information about themselves to personalize the process. Second, virtual team members should be assigned clear roles so that they can focus while working alone and also know what others are doing. Third, virtual team members must join and engage the team with positive attitudes that support a willingness to work hard to meet team goals.[26]

SELF-MANAGING WORK TEAMS

In a growing number of organizations the *functional team* consisting of a first-level supervisor and his or her immediate subordinates is disappearing. It is being replaced with a new organizational form built from the foundation of **self-managing work teams**. Sometimes called *autonomous work groups*, these are teams of workers whose jobs have been redesigned to create a high degree of task interdependence and who have been given authority to make many decisions about how they go about doing the required work.[27]

○ Members of a **self-managing work team** have the authority to make decisions about how they share and complete their work.

Self-managing teams operate with participative decision making, shared tasks, and the responsibility for many of the managerial tasks performed by supervisors in more traditional settings. The "self-management" responsibilities include planning and scheduling work, training members in various tasks, sharing tasks, meeting performance goals, ensuring high quality, and solving day-to-day operating problems. In some settings, the team's authority may even extend to "hiring" and "firing" its members when necessary. A key feature is *multitasking*, in which team members each have the skills to perform several different jobs. As shown in *Figure 16.2*, typical characteristics of self-managing teams are as follows:

Characteristics of self-managing teams →

- Members are held collectively accountable for performance results.
- Members have discretion in distributing tasks within the team.
- Members have discretion in scheduling work within the team.

- Members are able to perform more than one job on the team.
- Members train one another to develop multiple job skills.
- Members evaluate one another's performance contributions.
- Members are responsible for the total quality of team products.

The structural implications of self-managing teams are also depicted in Figure 16.2. Members of a self-managing team report to higher management through a team leader rather than a formal supervisor, making the role of first-line supervisor unnecessary. This is an important change in the traditional structure. Each self-managing team handles the supervisory duties on its own, and each team leader handles the upward reporting relationships. High-level managers to whom self-managing teams report must learn to work with teams rather than individual subordinates. This can be a difficult challenge for some managers who are used to more traditional operating methods. As the concept of self-managing teams spreads globally, researchers are also examining the receptivity of different cultures to self-management concepts.[28] Such cultural dimensions as high-power distance and individualism, for example, may generate resistance that must be considered when implementing this and other team-based organizational practices.

Within a self-managing team the emphasis is always on participation. The leader and members are expected to work together not only to do the required work but also to make the decisions that determine how it gets done. A true self-managing team emphasizes team decision making, shared tasks, high involvement, and collective responsibility for accomplished results. The expected advantages include better performance, decreased costs, and higher morale. Of course, these results are not guaranteed. Managing the transition to self-managing teams from more traditional work

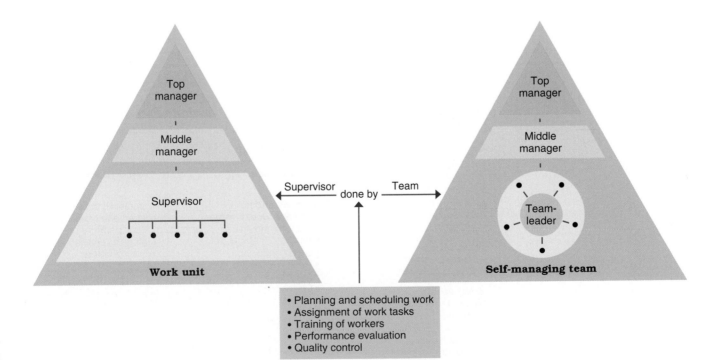

Figure 16.2 Organizational and management implications of self-managing work teams.

settings isn't always easy; the process requires leadership committed to both empowerment and a lot of support.

TEAM PROCESSES AND DIVERSITY

Regardless of its form and purpose, any team must achieve three key results—perform tasks, satisfy members, and remain viable for the future.[29] On the *performance* side, a work group or team is expected to transform resource inputs (such as ideas, materials, and objects) into product outputs (such as a report, decision, service, or commodity) that have some value to the organization. The members of a team should also be able to experience *satisfaction* from both these performance results and their participation in the process. And, in respect to *future viability*, the team should have a social and work climate that makes members willing and able to work well together in the future, again and again as needed.

WHAT IS AN EFFECTIVE TEAM?

○ An **effective team** achieves high levels of both task performance and membership satisfaction.

An **effective team** is one that achieves and maintains high levels of both task performance and member satisfaction, and retains its viability for future action.[30] *Figure 16.3* shows how any team can be viewed as an open system that transforms various resource inputs into these outcomes. Among the important inputs are such things as the organizational setting, the nature of the task, the team size, and the membership characteristics.[31] Each of these factors plays a role in setting the stage for group performance.

Group Inputs

The *nature of the task* is always important. It affects how well a team can focus its efforts and how intense the group process needs to be to get the job done. Clearly defined tasks make it easier for team members

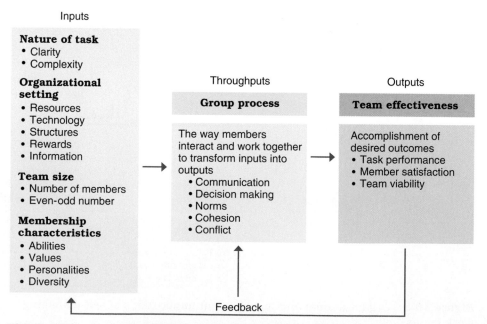

Figure 16.3 An open systems model of work team effectiveness.

to focus their work efforts. Complex tasks require more information exchange and intense interaction than do simpler tasks. The *organizational setting* can also affect how team members relate to one another and apply their skills toward task accomplishment. A key issue is the amount of support provided in terms of information, material resources, technology, organization structures, available rewards, and spatial arrangements. Increasingly, for example, organizations are being architecturally designed to directly facilitate teamwork. At SEI Investments, the office design makes it difficult for the 150-odd employees to avoid their co-workers. They all work in a large, open space without cubicles or dividers; each has a private set of office furniture and fixtures—but all on wheels; all technology easily plugs and unplugs from suspended power beams that run overhead. Project teams convene and disband as needed, and people easily meet and converse intensely with the ebb and flow of work all day.[32]

Team size affects how members work together, handle disagreements, and reach agreements. The number of potential interactions increases geometrically as teams increase in size, and communications become more congested. Teams larger than about six on seven members can be difficult to manage for the purpose of creative problem solving. When voting is required, teams with odd numbers of members are often preferred so as to prevent "ties." In all teams, the *membership characteristics* are important. Teams must have members with the right abilities, or skill mix, to master and perform tasks well. They must also have values, personalities, and diversity appropriate to the task and that are sufficiently compatible for everyone to work well together.

Group Process

Although having the right inputs available to a team is important, it is not a guarantee of effectiveness. What is called **group process** counts too. It is the way the members of any team actually work together as they transform inputs into outputs. The process aspects of any group or team include how well members communicate with one another, make decisions, and handle conflicts, among other things. When process breaks down and the internal dynamics fail in any way, team effectiveness can suffer. This Team Effectiveness Equation is a helpful reminder: Team effectiveness = quality of inputs + (process gains − process losses).

○ **Group process** is the way team members work together to accomplish tasks.

← Team effectiveness equation

Team Diversity

Team diversity, in the form of different values, personalities, experiences, demographics, and cultures among the membership, can present significant group process challenges. The more homogeneous the team—the more similar the members are to one another—the easier it is to manage relationships. As team diversity increases, so too does the complexity of interpersonal relationships among members. But with the complications also come special opportunities. The more heterogeneous the team—the more diversity among members—the greater the variety of available ideas, perspectives, and experiences that can add value to problem solving and task performance.

In teamwork, as with organizations at large, the diversity lesson is very clear. There is a lot to gain when membership diversity is valued and well managed. The process challenge is to maximize the advantages of team diversity while minimizing its potential disadvantages. In the international arena, for example, research indicates that culturally diverse work teams have more difficulty learning how to work well together than do culturally homogeneous teams.[33] That is, they tend to struggle more in the early stages of working together. However, once the process challenges are successfully mastered the diverse teams eventually prove to be more creative than the homogeneous ones.

STAGES OF TEAM DEVELOPMENT

A synthesis of research on small groups suggests that there are five distinct phases in the life cycle of any team:[34]

→ Stages of team development

1. *Forming*—a stage of initial orientation and interpersonal testing.
2. *Storming*—a stage of conflict over tasks and working as a team.
3. *Norming*—a stage of consolidation around task and operating agendas.
4. *Performing*—a stage of teamwork and focused task performance.
5. *Adjourning*—a stage of task completion and disengagement.

Forming Stage

The forming stage involves the first entry of individual members into a team. This is a stage of initial task orientation and interpersonal testing. As individuals come together for the first time or two, they ask a number of questions: "What can or does the team offer me?" "What will I be asked to contribute?" "Can my needs be met while my efforts serve the task needs of the team?"

In the forming stage, people begin to identify with other members and with the team itself. They are concerned about getting acquainted, establishing interpersonal relationships, discovering what is considered acceptable behavior, and learning how others perceive the team's task. This may also be a time when some members rely on or become temporarily dependent on another member who appears "powerful" or especially "knowledgeable." Such things as prior experience with team members in other contexts and individual impressions of organization philosophies, goals, and policies may also affect member relationships in new work teams. Difficulties in the forming stage tend to be greater in more culturally and demographically diverse teams.

Storming Stage

The storming stage of team development is a period of high emotionality. Tension often emerges between members over tasks and interpersonal concerns. There may be periods of outright hostility and infighting. Coalitions or cliques may form around personalities or interests. Subteams form around areas of agreement and disagreement involving group tasks and/or the manner of operations. Conflict may develop as individuals compete to impose their preferences on others and to become influential in the group's status structure.

Important changes occur in the storming stage as task agendas become clarified and members begin to understand one another's interpersonal styles. Here attention begins to shift toward obstacles that may stand in the way of task accomplishment. Efforts are made to find ways to meet team goals while also satisfying individual needs. Failure in the storming stage can be a lasting liability, whereas success in the storming stage can set a strong foundation for later team effectiveness.

www.rockport.com

When Angel Martinez was CEO of Rockport Co he expanded the top management team to implement change and new performance norms. Says Martinez, "The easiest thing is getting rid of everyone, but that can create many more problems in the long run."

Norming Stage

Cooperation is an important issue for teams in the norming stage. At this point, members of the team begin to become coordinated as a working unit and tend to operate with shared rules of conduct. The team feels a sense of leadership, with each member starting to play useful roles. Most interpersonal hostilities give way to a precarious balancing of forces as norming builds initial integration. Harmony is emphasized, but minority viewpoints may be discouraged.

In the norming stage, members are likely to develop initial feelings of closeness, a division of labor, and a sense of shared expectations. This helps protect the team from disintegration. Holding the team together may become even more important than successful task accomplishment.

Performing Stage

Teams in the performing stage are more mature, organized, and well functioning. This is a stage of total integration in which team members are able to deal in creative ways with both complex tasks and any interpersonal conflicts. The team operates with a clear and stable structure, and members are motivated by team goals.

The primary challenges of teams in the performing stage are to continue refining the operations and relationships essential to working together as an integrated unit. Such teams need to remain coordinated with the larger organization and adapt successfully to changing conditions over time. A team that has achieved total integration will score high on the criteria of team maturity, such as those on the checklist in *Figure 16.4*.[35]

Adjourning Stage

The final stage of team development is adjourning, when team members prepare to achieve closure and disband. It is especially common for temporary groups that operate in the form of committees, task forces, and projects. Ideally, the team disbands with a sense that important goals have been accomplished. Members are acknowledged for their contributions and the group's overall success. This may be an emotional time, and disbandment should be managed with this possibility in mind. For members who have worked together intensely for a period of time, breaking up the close relationships may be painful. In all cases, the team would like to disband with members feeling they would work with one another again sometime in the future.

CAREER CONNECTION

Technology

Broadwing, Inc.
Fast Teams Get Creative in Tough Workouts
You can't be slow in the rapidly developing, and changing, communication industry. When Cinncinnati Bell acquired IXC Communications, the firm changed its name to Broadwing, Inc. CEO Richard Ellenberger says the firm is implementing a growth strategy. He also calls it a "disruptive force" in the industry. "We are on the attack," he says.

Ellenberger takes a creative approach to team development. He once gave small teams cardboard and tape, and had them build boats to race one another in a swimming pool. His point? Get the workers thinking creatively and as a team.

Another time, Ellenberger sent 25 employees to NASCAR legend Richard Petty's racing school in Florida. They all learned to drive stock cars at over 120 mph. Says Tom Osha: "It was an incredibly invigorating experience, but it was quite a nervous one." That's part of the point, says Ellenberger: "The element of speed is something most people have a fear of until they experience it. And once they experience it, they can't get enough of it."

Speed is essential to Broadwing's competitive strategy, and he wants it to become part of the corporate culture. He also wants to be sure everyone has the competitive spirit. At a company retreat held at an aquarium, he had sushi delivered for everyone. Again, what was the point? Ellenberger had them eat the sushi while staring at the live fish swimming in the aquarium. This was supposed to inspire them to be more aggressive in attacking and trying to devour Broadwing's competition.

QUESTION: This is a unique approach to team development. But it may be in tune with the fast-paced communication industry. Will Broadwing, Inc. be a winner? How about you—are you ready for speed, competition, and teamwork in your career?

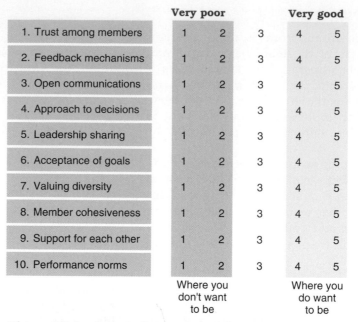

	Very poor			Very good	
1. Trust among members	1	2	3	4	5
2. Feedback mechanisms	1	2	3	4	5
3. Open communications	1	2	3	4	5
4. Approach to decisions	1	2	3	4	5
5. Leadership sharing	1	2	3	4	5
6. Acceptance of goals	1	2	3	4	5
7. Valuing diversity	1	2	3	4	5
8. Member cohesiveness	1	2	3	4	5
9. Support for each other	1	2	3	4	5
10. Performance norms	1	2	3	4	5
	Where you don't want to be			Where you do want to be	

Figure 16.4 Criteria for assessing the maturity of a team.

NORMS AND COHESIVENESS

○ A **norm** is a behavior, rule, or standard expected to be followed by team members.

A **norm** is a behavior expected of team members.[36] It is a "rule" or "standard" that guides their behavior. When violated, a norm may be enforced with reprimands and other sanctions. In the extreme, violation of a norm can result in a member being expelled from a team or socially ostracized by other members. The *performance norm*, which defines the level of work effort and performance that team members are expected to contribute, is extremely important. It can have positive or negative implications for team performance and organizational productivity. In general, work groups and teams with positive performance norms are more successful in accomplishing task objectives than are teams with negative performance norms. Other important team norms relate to such things as helpfulness, participation, timeliness, quality, and innovation.

Because a team's norms are largely determined by the collective will of its members, it is difficult for a manager or designated leader simply to dictate which norms will be adopted. Instead, the concerned manager or team leader must help and encourage members to develop norms that support organizational objectives. During forming and storming steps of development, for example, norms relating to membership issues such as expected attendance and levels of commitment are important. By the time the stage of performing is reached, norms relating to adaptability and change become most relevant. Guidelines for *how to build positive norms* are as follows.[37]

How to build positive norms →

- Act as a positive role model.
- Reinforce the desired behaviors with rewards.
- Control results by performance reviews and regular feedback.
- Train and orient new members to adopt desired behaviors.
- Recruit and select new members who exhibit the desired behaviors.

TAKE IT TO THE CASE!

Steinway & Sons
Craftwork Plus Teamwork Builds Famous Pianos

Stop in at Steinway & Sons on-line and take their factory tour. You'll see how the finest in individual craftwork, the ingenuity of patented designs and methods, and the very best of teamwork combine to still build what may be the world's most famous pianos. The firm remains true to its history, dating to its founding in 1853 by Henry Englehard Steinway. Over half the firm's 114 patents were in place before 1900. The traditions of skilled craftspeople building handmade pianos continues. Today, however, through teamwork and modern organization, the firm produces some 5,000 pianos a year worldwide.[38]

- Hold regular meetings to discuss progress and ways of improving.
- Use team decision-making methods to reach agreement.

Norms vary in the degree to which they are accepted and adhered to by team members. Conformity to norms is largely determined by the strength of **cohesiveness**, defined as the degree to which members are attracted to and motivated to remain part of a team.[39] Persons in a highly cohesive team value their membership and strive to maintain positive relationships with other team members. They experience satisfaction from team identification and interpersonal relationships. Because of this, highly cohesive teams are good for their members. They can also be very good for organizations, but not always. It all depends on the performance norm that the cohesiveness is paired with.

A <u>basic rule of group dynamics</u> is: The more cohesive the team, the greater the conformity of members to team norms. This has important implications for team performance. Look at *Figure 16.5*. When the performance norm of a team is positive, high cohesion and the resulting conformity to norms has a beneficial effect on overall team performance. This is a "best-case" scenario for both the manager and the organization. Competent team members work hard and reinforce one another's task accomplishments while experiencing satisfaction with the team. But when the performance norm is negative in a cohesive team, high conformity to the norm can have undesirable results. The figure shows this as a "worst-case" scenario where team performance suffers from restricted work efforts by members. Between these two extremes are mixed situations of moderate to low performance.

○ **Cohesiveness** is the degree to which members are attracted to and motivated to remain part of a team.

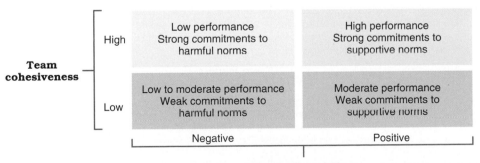

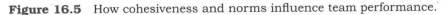

Figure 16.5 How cohesiveness and norms influence team performance.

To achieve and maintain the best-case scenario shown in Figure 16.5, managers should be skilled at influencing both the norms and cohesiveness of any team. They will want to build and maintain high cohesiveness in teams whose performance norms are positive. Guidelines on *how to increase cohesion* include the following:

How to increase team cohesiveness →

- Induce agreement on team goals.
- Increase membership homogeneity.
- Increase interactions among members.
- Decrease team size.
- Introduce competition with other teams.
- Reward team rather than individual results.
- Provide physical isolation from other teams.

TASK AND MAINTENANCE NEEDS

○ A **task activity** is an action taken by a team member that directly contributes to the group's performance purpose.

○ A **maintenance activity** is an action taken by a team member that supports the emotional life of the group.

Research on the social psychology of groups identifies two types of activities that are essential if team members are to work well together over time.[40] **Task activities** contribute directly to the team's performance purpose, whereas **maintenance activities** support the emotional life of the team as an ongoing social system. Although a person with formal authority, such as a chairperson or supervisor, will often handle them, the responsibility for both types of activities should be shared and distributed among all team members. Any member can help lead a team by taking actions that help satisfy its task and maintenance needs. This concept of *distributed leadership in teams* thus makes every member continually responsible for recognizing when task and/or maintenance activities are needed and then stepping in to provide them.

Figure 16.6 offers useful insights on distributed leadership in teams. Leading through task activities involves making an effort to define and solve problems and apply work efforts in support of accomplishing tasks. Without relevant task activities, such as initiating agendas, sharing information, and others listed in the figure, teams will have difficulty accomplishing their objectives. Leading through maintenance activities, by contrast, helps strengthen and perpetuate the team as a social system. When the maintenance activities such as encouraging

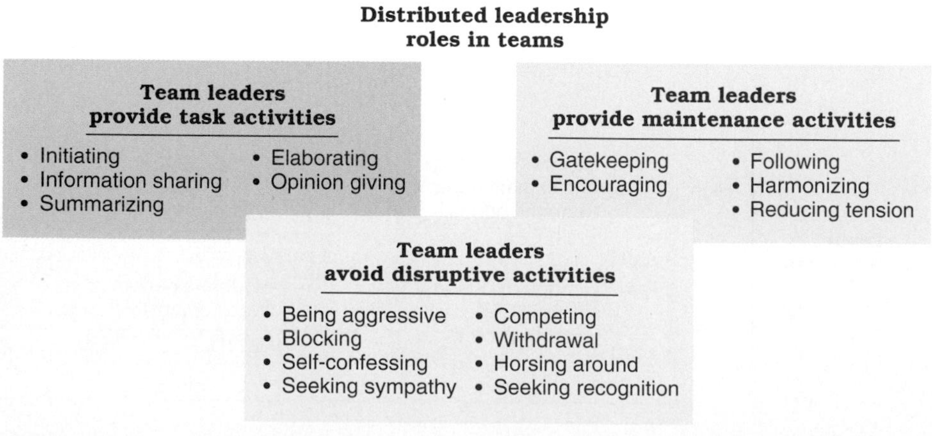

Distributed leadership roles in teams

Team leaders provide task activities
- Initiating
- Information sharing
- Summarizing
- Elaborating
- Opinion giving

Team leaders provide maintenance activities
- Gatekeeping
- Encouraging
- Following
- Harmonizing
- Reducing tension

Team leaders avoid disruptive activities
- Being aggressive
- Blocking
- Self-confessing
- Seeking sympathy
- Competing
- Withdrawal
- Horsing around
- Seeking recognition

Figure 16.6 Distributed leadership helps teams meet task and maintenance needs.

others and reducing tensions are performed well, good interpersonal relationships are achieved and the ability of the team to stay together over the longer term is ensured.

Both team task and maintenance activities stand in distinct contrast to the *dysfunctional activities* also described in Figure 16.6. Activities such as withdrawing and horsing around are usually self-serving to the individual member. They detract from, rather than enhance, team effectiveness. Unfortunately, very few teams are immune to dysfunctional behavior by members. Everyone shares in the responsibility for minimizing its occurrence and meeting the distributed leadership needs of a team by contributing functional task and maintenance behaviors.

COMMUNICATION NETWORKS

Figure 16.7 depicts three interaction patterns and communication networks that are common in teams.[41] When teams are interacting intensively and their members are working closely together on tasks, close coordination of activities is needed. This need is best met by a **decentralized communication network** in which all members communicate directly with one another. Sometimes this is called the *all-channel* or *star communication network*. At other times and in other situations team members work on tasks independently, with the required work being divided up among them. Activities are coordinated and results pooled by a central point of control. Most communication flows back and forth between individual members and this hub or center point. This creates a **centralized communication network** as shown in the

○ A **decentralized communication network** allows all members to communicate directly with one another.

○ In a **centralized communication network**, communication flows only between individual members and a hub or center point.

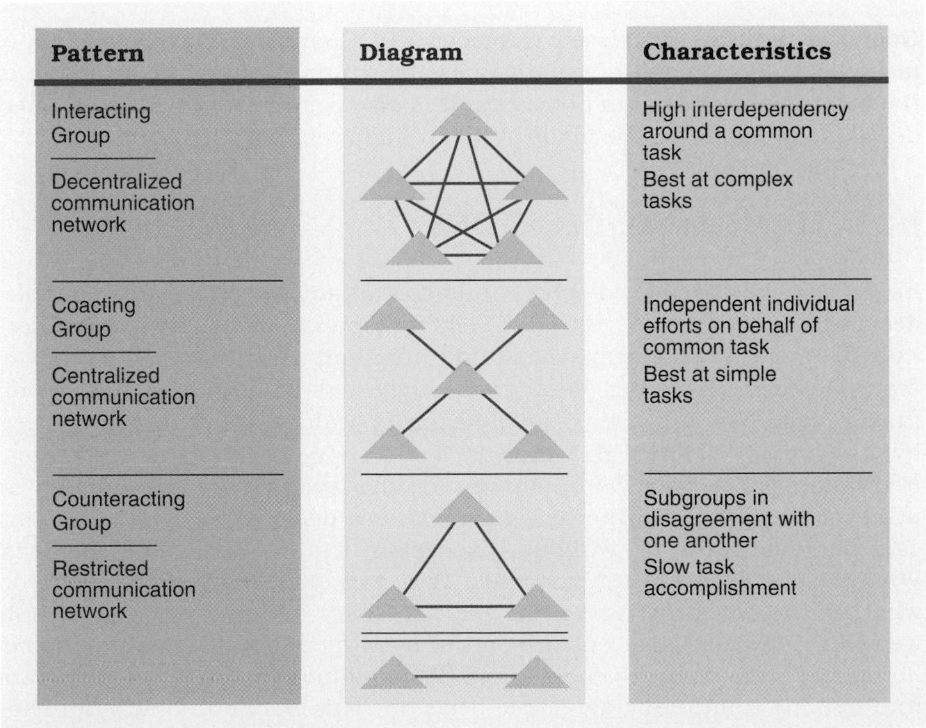

Pattern	Diagram	Characteristics
Interacting Group Decentralized communication network		High interdependency around a common task Best at complex tasks
Coacting Group Centralized communication network		Independent individual efforts on behalf of common task Best at simple tasks
Counteracting Group Restricted communication network		Subgroups in disagreement with one another Slow task accomplishment

Figure 16.7 Interaction patterns and communication networks in teams.
Source: John R. Schermerhorn, Jr., James G. Hunt and Richard N. Osborn, *Organizational Behavior*, 6th ed. (New York: Wiley, 1997), p. 351. Used by permission.

figure. Sometimes this particular network is called a *wheel* or *chain communication structure*.

When teams are composed of subgroups experiencing issue-specific disagreements, such as a temporary debate over the best means to achieve a goal, the resulting interaction pattern involves a *restricted communication network*. Here, the polarized subgroups contest one another and engage in sometimes-antagonistic relations. Communication between the subgroups is often limited and biased, with the result that problems can easily occur.

The best teams use communication networks in the right ways, at the right times, and for the right tasks. In general, centralized communication networks seem to work better on simple tasks.[42] These tasks require little creativity, information processing, and problem solving and lend themselves to more centralized control. They tend to be performed faster and more accurately by coacting groups. The reverse is true for more complex tasks, where interacting groups do better. Here, the decentralized networks work well since they are able to support the more intense interactions and information sharing required to perform under such task conditions. Interacting groups tend to be the top performers when tasks get complicated. When subgroups have difficulty communicating with one another, task accomplishment typically suffers for the short run at least. If the team is able to restore good communication between subgroups, it can benefit from the creativity and critical evaluation that typically accompanies conflict. If the subgroups drift further and further apart, negative dynamics set in and the team may suffer long-term damage.

DECISION MAKING IN TEAMS

○ **Decision making** is the process of making choices among alternative courses of action.

Decision making, discussed extensively in Chapter 2, is the process of making choices among alternative possible courses of action. It is one of the most important group processes. It is also complicated by the fact that decisions in teams can be made in several different ways.

HOW TEAMS MAKE DECISIONS

Edgar Schein, a respected scholar and consultant, notes that teams make decisions by at least six methods: lack of response, authority rule, minority rule, majority rule, consensus, and unanimity.[43] In *decision by lack of response*, one idea after another is suggested without any discussion taking place. When the team finally accepts an idea, all others have been bypassed and discarded by simple lack of response rather than by critical evaluation. In *decision by authority rule*, the leader, manager, committee head, or some other authority figure makes a decision for the team. This can be done with or without discussion and is very time efficient. Whether the decision is a good one or a bad one, however, depends on whether the authority figure has the necessary information and on how well this approach is accepted by other team members. In *decision by minority rule*, two or three people are able to dominate or "railroad" the team into making a mutually agreeable decision. This is often done by providing a suggestion and then forcing quick agreement by challenging the team with such statements as "Does anyone object? . . . Let's go ahead, then."

One of the most common ways teams make decisions, especially when early signs of disagreement arise, is *decision by majority rule*. Here, formal voting may take place, or members may be polled to find the majority viewpoint. This method parallels the democratic political system and is often used without awareness of its potential problems. The very process of voting can create coalitions; that is, some people will be "winners" and others will be "losers" when the final vote is tallied. Those in the minority—the "losers"—may feel left out or discarded without having had a fair say. They may be unenthusiastic about implementing the decision of the "majority," and lingering resentments may impair team effectiveness in the future. There is no better example of the dynamics associated with close voting than the American presidential elections of 2000, and the great controversy over Bush/Gore vote tallies in Florida.

Teams are often encouraged to follow *decision by consensus*. This is a state of affairs whereby discussion leads to one alternative being favored by most members and the other members agree to support it. When a consensus is reached, even those who may have opposed the chosen course of action know that they have been heard and have had an opportunity to influence the decision outcome. Consensus, therefore, does not require unanimity. But it does require that team members be able to argue, engage in reasonable conflict, and yet still get along with and respect one another.[44] And, it requires that there be the opportunity for any dissenting members to feel they have been able to speak—and that they have been listened to.

A *decision by unanimity* may be the ideal state of affairs. Here, all team members agree on the course of action to be taken. This is a "logically perfect" method for decision making in teams, but it is also extremely difficult to attain in actual practice. One of the reasons that teams sometimes turn to authority decisions, majority voting, or even minority decisions, in fact, is the difficulty of managing the team process to achieve consensus or unanimity.

Getting to Group Consensus
Everyone talks about group consensus, but we are often disappointed in our abilities to reach it. The truth of the matter is that consensus is only possible when the members of a team do the right things to make it possible. Do you know how to help move a team toward consensus? Take the on-line "Reality Check" to learn more about guidelines for reaching consensus.

ASSETS AND LIABILITIES OF GROUP DECISIONS

The best teams don't limit themselves to just one decision-making method. Instead, they vary methods to best fit the problems at hand, in true contingency management fashion. A very important team leadership skill is the ability to help a team choose the "best" decision method—one that provides for a timely and quality decision and one to which the members are highly committed. This reasoning is consistent with the Vroom–Jago leader-participation model discussed in Chapter 13.[45] You should recall that this model describes how leaders should utilize the full range of individual, consultative, and group decision methods as they resolve daily problems. To do this well, however, team leaders must understand the potential assets and potential liabilities of group decisions.[46]

The potential *advantages of group decision making* are significant. Because of this, the general argument is that team decisions should be sought whenever time and other circumstances permit. Team decisions make greater amounts of information, knowledge, and expertise available to solve problems. They expand the number of action alternatives that are examined; they help groups to avoid tunnel vision and tendencies to consider only a limited range of options. Team decisions increase the understanding and acceptance of outcomes by members. And importantly, team decisions increase the commitments of members to follow through to implement the decision once made. Simply put, team decisions can result in quality decisions that all members work hard to make successful.

The potential *disadvantages of group decision making* largely trace to the difficulties that can be experienced in group process. In a team decision there may be social pressure to conform. Individual members may feel intimidated or compelled to go along with the apparent wishes of others. There may be minority domination, where some members feel forced or "railroaded" to accept a decision advocated by one vocal individual or small coalition. Also, the time required to make team decisions can sometimes be a disadvantage. As more people are involved in the dialogue and discussion, decision making takes longer. This added time may be costly, even prohibitively so, in certain circumstances.[47]

GROUPTHINK

A high level of cohesiveness can sometimes be a disadvantage during decision making. Members of very cohesive teams feel so strongly about the group that they may not want to do anything that might detract from feelings of goodwill. This may cause them to publicly agree with actual or suggested courses of action, while privately having serious doubts about them. Strong feelings of team loyalty can make it hard for members to criticize and evaluate one another's ideas and suggestions. Unfortunately, there are times when desires to hold the team together at all costs and avoid disagreements may result in poor decisions.

○ **Groupthink** is a tendency for highly cohesive teams to lose their evaluative capabilities.

Psychologist Irving Janis calls this phenomenon **groupthink**, the tendency for highly cohesive groups to lose their critical evaluative capabilities.[48] You should be alert to spot the following *symptoms of groupthink* when they occur in your decision-making teams:

Symptoms of groupthink →

- *Illusions of invulnerability:* Members assume the team is too good for criticism or beyond attack.
- *Rationalizing unpleasant and disconfirming data:* Members refuse to accept contradictory data or to thoroughly consider alternatives.
- *Belief in inherent group morality:* Members act as though the group is inherently right and above reproach.
- *Stereotyping competitors as weak, evil, and stupid:* Members refuse to look realistically at other groups.
- *Applying direct pressure to deviants to conform to group wishes:* Members refuse to tolerate anyone who suggests the team may be wrong.
- *Self-censorship by members:* Members refuse to communicate personal concerns to the whole team.
- *Illusions of unanimity:* Members accept consensus prematurely, without testing its completeness.
- *Mind guarding:* Members protect the team from hearing disturbing ideas or outside viewpoints.

Groupthink can occur anywhere. In fact, Janis ties a variety of well-known historical blunders to the phenomenon, including the lack of preparedness of the United States' naval forces for the Japanese attack on Pearl Harbor, the Bay of Pigs invasion under President Kennedy, and the

MANAGER'S NOTEPAD 16.2

How to avoid groupthink

- Assign the role of critical evaluator to each team member; encourage a sharing of viewpoints.
- Don't, as a leader, seem partial to one course of action; do absent yourself from meetings at times to allow free discussion.
- Create subteams to work on the same problems and then share their proposed solutions.
- Have team members discuss issues with outsiders and report back on their reactions.
- Invite outside experts to observe team activities and react to team processes and decisions.
- Assign one member to play a "devil's advocate" role at each team meeting.
- Hold a "second-chance" meeting after consensus is apparently achieved to review the decision.

many roads that led to the United States' involvement in Vietnam. When and if you encounter groupthink, Janis suggests taking action along the lines shown in *Manager's Notepad 16.2.*

CREATIVITY IN TEAM DECISION MAKING

Among the potential benefits that teams can bring to organizations is increased creativity. Two techniques that are particularly helpful for creativity in decision making are brainstorming and the nominal team technique.[49] Both can now be pursued in computer-mediated or virtual team discussions, as well as in face-to-face formats.[50]

In *brainstorming*, teams of 5 to 10 members meet to generate ideas. Brainstorming teams typically operate within these guidelines. *All criticism is ruled out*—judgment or evaluation of ideas must be withheld until the idea-generation process has been completed. *"Freewheeling" is welcomed*—the wilder or more radical the idea, the better. *Quantity is important*—the greater the number of ideas, the greater the likelihood of obtaining a superior idea. *Building on one another's ideas is encouraged*—participants should suggest how ideas of others can be turned into better ideas, or how two or more ideas can be joined into still another hybrid idea.

<- Rules for brainstorming

By prohibiting criticism, the brainstorming method reduces fears of ridicule or failure on the part of individuals. Ideally, this results in more enthusiasm, involvement, and a freer flow of ideas among members. But there are times when team members have very different opinions and goals. The differences may be so extreme that a brainstorming meeting might deteriorate-into antagonistic arguments and harmful conflicts. In such cases, a *nominal group technique* could help. This approach uses a highly structured meeting agenda to allow everyone to contribute ideas without the interference of evaluative comments by others. It allows for many alternatives to be generated and evaluated without risk of inhibitions or hostilities.

How to run a nominal group →

The basic steps for running a nominal group session are easy to implement. Participants are first asked to work alone and respond in writing with possible solutions to a stated problem. Ideas are then shared in round-robin fashion without any criticism or discussion; all ideas are recorded as they are presented. Ideas are next discussed and clarified in round-robin sequence, with no evaluative comments allowed. Next, members individually and silently follow a written voting procedure that allows for all alternatives to be rated or ranked in priority order. Finally, the last two steps are repeated as needed to further clarify the process.

LEADING HIGH-PERFORMANCE TEAMS

When we think of the word "team," sporting teams often come to mind. And we know these teams certainly have their share of problems. Members slack off or become disgruntled; even world-champion teams have losing streaks; and, the most highly talented players sometimes lose motivation, quibble with other team members, and lapse into performance slumps. When these things happen, the owners, managers, and players are apt to take corrective action to "rebuild the team" and restore what we have called team effectiveness. Work teams are teams in a similar sense. Even the most mature work team is likely to experience problems over time. When such difficulties arise, structured efforts at team building can help.

THE TEAM-BUILDING PROCESS

○ **Team building** is a sequence of collaborative activities to gather and analyze data on a team and make changes to increase its effectiveness.

Team building is a sequence of planned activities used to gather and analyze data on the functioning of a team and to implement constructive changes to increase its operating effectiveness.[51] Most systematic approaches to team building follow the steps described in *Figure 16.8*. The cycle begins with the awareness that a problem may exist or may develop within the team. Members then work together to gather and analyze data so that the problem is finally understood. Action plans are made by members and collectively implemented. Results are evaluated in similar fashion by team members working together. Any difficulties or new problems that are discovered serve to recycle the team-building process. Consider this added detail in the case featured in Figure 16.8.

The consultant received a call from the hospital's director of personnel. He indicated that a new hospital president felt the top management team lacked cohesiveness and was not working well together as a team. The consultant agreed to facilitate a team-building activity that would include a day-long retreat at a nearby resort hotel. The process began when the consultant conducted interviews with the president and other members of the executive team. During the retreat, the consultant reported these results to the team as a whole. He indicated that the hospital's goals were generally understood by all but that they weren't clear enough to allow agreement on action priorities. Furthermore, he reported that interpersonal problems between the director of nursing services and the director of administration were making it difficult for

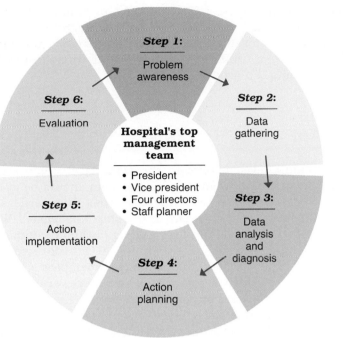

Figure 16.8 Steps in the team-building process: case of the hospital top management team.

the team to work together comfortably. These and other issues were addressed by the team at the retreat. Working sometimes in small subteams, and at other times together as a whole, they agreed first of all that action should be taken to clarify the hospital's overall mission and create a priority list of objectives for the current year. Led by the president, activity on this task would involve all team members and was targeted for completion within a month. The president asked that progress on the action plans be reviewed at each of the next three monthly executive staff meetings. Everyone agreed.

This actual example from the author's experience introduces team building as a way to assess a work team's functioning and take corrective action to improve its effectiveness. It can and should become a regular work routine. There are many ways to gather data on team functioning, including structured and unstructured interviews, questionnaires, and team meetings. Regardless of the method used, the basic principle of team building remains the same. The process requires that a careful and collaborative assessment of the team's inputs, processes, and results be made. All members should participate in data gathering, assist in data analysis, and collectively decide on actions to be taken.

Sometimes teamwork can be improved when people share the challenges of unusual and even physically demanding experiences. On a fall day, for example, a team of employees from American Electric Power (AEP) went to an outdoor camp for a day of team-building activities. They worked on problems like how to get six members through a spider-web maze of bungee cords strung two feet above the ground. When her colleagues lifted Judy Gallo into their hands to pass her over the obstacle, she was nervous. But a trainer told the team this was just like solving a problem together at the office. The spider web was just another

www. worthington industries.com

At Worthington Industries, the innovative Ohio steelmaker, applicants for new positions must pass the team test. They interview with members of their potential teams and then must serve a 90-day probation period before being voted on by an employee council of co-workers.

performance constraint like difficult policies or financial limits they might face at work. After "high-fives" for making it through the Web, Judy's team jumped tree stumps together, passed hula hoops while holding hands, and more. Says one team trainer, "We throw clients into situations to try and bring out the traits of a good team."[52]

TEAM LEADERSHIP CHALLENGES

Among the many developments in the workplace today, the continuing effort to refine and apply creative team concepts should be at the forefront of any progressive manager's action agendas. But harnessing the full potential of teams involves special leadership challenges. We know, for example, that high-performance teams generally share common characteristics. These include a clear and elevating goal, a task-driven and results-oriented structure, competent and committed members who work hard, a collaborative climate, high standards of excellence, external support and recognition, and strong and principled leadership.[53]

The last point on this list—the need for strong and principled leadership—may be the key to them all. In their book, *Teamwork: What Can Go Right/What Can Go Wrong,* Carl Larson and Frank LaFasto state: "The right person in a leadership role can add tremendous value to any collective effort, even to the point of sparking the outcome with an intangible kind of magic."[54] They further point out that leaders of high-performing teams share many characteristics with the "transformational leader," examined in Chapter 13.

What successful team leaders do →

Successful team leaders *establish a clear vision of the future.* This vision serves as a goal that inspires hard work and the quest for performance excellence; it creates a sense of shared purpose. Successful team leaders help to *create change.* They are dissatisfied with the status quo, influence team members toward similar dissatisfaction, and infuse the team with the motivation to change in order to become better. Finally, successful team leaders *unleash talent.* They make sure the team is staffed with members who have the right skills and abilities. And they make sure these people are highly motivated to use their talents to achieve the group's performance objectives. Included in this responsibility is developing future leaders for the team. Joe Liemandt, founder and CEO of the software firm Trilogy, Inc., says: As Trilogy grew, one of the most important lessons we learned is that hiring for raw talent isn't enough. We had to build leaders. I believe you should always work to replace yourself."[55]

You don't get a high-performing team by just bringing a group of people together and giving them a shared name or title. Leaders of high-performance teams create supportive climates in which team members know what to expect from the leader and each other, and know what the leader expects from them. They empower team members. By personal example they demonstrate the importance of setting aside self-interests to support the team's goals. And, they view team building as an ongoing leadership responsibility. As said before, teams are hard work. But they are worth it.[56]

STUDY Guide

The Chapter 16 Study Guide will help you review chapter content, prepare for examinations, and further build your career readiness. The *Summary* briefly highlights answers to questions first posed in the chapter opening Planning Ahead section. The list of *Key Terms* allows you to double check your familiarity with basic concepts and definitions. *Self-Test 16* gives you the opportunity to test your basic comprehension of chapter content using sample test questions. Suggestions offered as *Career Readiness Activities* direct your attention to relevant sections of the end-of-text Career Readiness Workbook, as well as to special Electronic Resources on the *Management 7/e* web site.

SUMMARY

How do teams contribute to organizations?

- A team is a collection of people who work together to accomplish a common goal.
- Organizations operate as interlocking networks of formal work teams, which offer many benefits to the organizations and to their members.
- Teams help organizations through synergy in task performance, the creation of a whole that is greater than the sum of its parts.
- Teams help satisfy important needs for their members, providing various types of support and social satisfactions.
- Social loafing and other problems can limit the performance of teams.

What are current trends in the use of teams?

- Teams are important mechanisms of empowerment and participation in the workplace.
- Committees and task forces are used to facilitate operations and allow special projects to be completed with creativity.
- Cross-functional teams bring members together from different departments and help improve lateral relations and integration in organizations.
- Employee involvement teams, such as the quality circle, allow employees to provide important insights into daily problem solving.
- New developments in information technology are making virtual teams, or computer-mediated teams, more commonplace.
- Self-managing teams are changing organizations by allowing team members to perform many tasks previously reserved for their supervisors.

How do teams work?

- An effective team achieves high levels of task performance, member satisfaction, and team viability.

- Important team input factors include the organizational setting, nature of the task, size, and membership characteristics.
- A team matures through various stages of development, including forming, storming, norming, performing, and adjourning.
- Norms are the standards or rules of conduct that influence the behavior of team members; cohesion is the attractiveness of the team to its members.
- In highly cohesive teams, members tend to conform to norms; the best situation for a manager or leader is a team with positive performance norms and high cohesiveness.
- Distributed leadership in serving a team's task and maintenance needs helps in achieving long-term effectiveness.
- Effective teams make use of alternative communication networks to best complete tasks.

How do teams make decisions?

- Teams can make decisions by lack of response, authority rule, minority rule, majority rule, consensus, and unanimity.
- The potential advantages of more team decision making include having more information available and generating more understanding and commitment.
- The potential liabilities to team decision making include social pressures to conform and greater time requirements.
- Groupthink is a tendency of members of highly cohesive teams to lose their critical evaluative capabilities and make poor decisions.
- Techniques for improving creativity in team decision making include brainstorming and the nominal group technique.

What are the challenges of high-performance team leadership?

- Team building helps team members develop action plans for improving the way they work together and the results they accomplish.
- The team-building process should be data based and collaborative, involving a high level of participation by all team members.
- High-performance work teams have a clear and shared sense of purpose as well as strong internal commitment to its accomplishment.

KEY TERMS

Centralized communication network (p. 431)

Cohesiveness (p. 429)

Committee (p. 419)

Cross-functional team (p. 420)

Decentralized communication network (p. 431)

Decision making (p. 432)

Effective team (p. 424)

Employee involvement team (p. 420)

Formal group (p. 418)

Group process (p. 425)

Groupthink (p. 434)

Informal group (p. 418)

Maintenance activity (p. 430)   Task activity (p. 430)

Norm (p. 428)   Task force (p. 419)

Quality circle (p. 420)   Team (p. 416)

Self-managing work teams (p. 422)   Team building (p. 436)

Social loafing (p. 417)   Teamwork (p. 416)

Synergy (p. 418)   Virtual team (p. 421)

SELF-TEST 16

Take this test here or on-line much as you would in a normal classroom situation. It is a good way to check your basic comprehension of chapter material. Answers may be found at the end of the book.

MULTIPLE-CHOICE QUESTIONS:

1. Teams can be good for organizations because they may _____.
   (a) increase creativity in problem solving
   (b) help control and discipline members
   (c) satisfy individual needs (d) all of these

2. In an organization operating with self-managing teams, the traditional role of _____ is replaced by the role of team leader.
   (a) chief executive officer (b) first-line supervisor
   (c) middle manager (d) general manager

3. An effective team is defined as one that achieves high levels of task performance, member satisfaction, and _____.
   (a) resource efficiency (b) team viability (c) consensus (d) creativity

4. In the open-systems model of teams, the _____ is an important input factor.
   (a) communication network (b) decision-making method
   (c) performance norm (d) set of membership characteristics

5. A basic rule of team dynamics states that the greater the _____ in a team, the greater the conformity to norms.
   (a) membership diversity (b) cohesiveness (c) task structure
   (d) competition among members

6. Groupthink is most likely to occur in teams that are _____.
   (a) large in size (b) diverse in membership (c) high performing
   (d) highly cohesive

7. Gatekeeping is an example of a _____ activity that can help teams work effectively over time.
   (a) task (b) maintenance (c) team-building (d) decision-making

8. Members of a team tend to become more motivated and able to deal with conflict during the _____ stage of team development.
(a) forming (b) norming (c) performing (d) adjourning

9. One way for a manager to build positive norms within a team is to _____.
(a) act as a positive role model (b) adjourn the team
(c) introduce groupthink (d) isolate the team from others

10. When teams are highly cohesive _____.
(a) members are high performers
(b) members tend to be satisfied with their team membership
(c) members have positive norms (d) all of these

TRUE-FALSE QUESTIONS:

11. Informal groups should be eliminated because they create problems for organizations.   T   F

12. Cross-functional committees and task forces can be used to improve lateral coordination.   T   F

13. Teams larger than 7 or so members may have difficulty solving problems together.   T   F

14. The only important norm in a work team is the performance norm.   T   F

15. A work team with a negative performance norm and low cohesiveness is the worst case for managers.   T   F

16. Self-censorship by members during team discussions is an indicator that groupthink may be operating.   T   F

17. Team building occurs when a manager tells a team what to do to improve performance.   T   F

18. Teams that are required to document decisions by voting are better off with an odd number of members.   T   F

19. Increasing the homogeneity of team membership is likely to increase team cohesiveness.   T   F

20. Multiskilling is a typical characteristic of self-managing teams.   T   F

SHORT-RESPONSE QUESTIONS:

21. How can a manager improve team effectiveness by modifying inputs?

22. What is the relationship between a team's cohesiveness, performance norm, and performance results?

23. How would a manager know that her team was suffering from groupthink (give two symptoms) and what could she do about it (give two responses)?

24. What makes a self-managing team different from a traditional work team?

APPLICATION QUESTION:

25. Marcos Martinez has just been appointed manager of a production team operating the 11 P.M. to 7 A.M. shift in a large manufacturing firm. An experienced manager, Marcos is concerned that the team members really like and get along well with one another but they also appear to be restricting their task outputs to the minimum acceptable levels. What could Marcos do to improve things in this situation and why should he do them?

CAREER *readiness* ACTIVITIES

Recommended learning activities from the end-of-text *Career Readiness Workbook* for this chapter include:

Career Advancement Portfolio
- Individual writing and group presentation assignments based on any of the following activities.

Case for Critical Thinking
- Steinway & Sons—Combining Craftwork and Teamwork

Integrative Learning Activities
- **Integrative Case**—Outback Steakhouse. Inc.
- **Integrative Case**—Richard Branson Meets the New Economy

Exercises in Teamwork
- **Leading through Participation (#4)**
- **Work Team Dynamics (#27)**
- **Lost at Sea (#28)**
- **Creative Solution (#29)**

Self-Assessments
- Decision-Making Biases (#3)
- Facts and Inferences (#20)
- Team Leader Skills (#22)
- Emotional Intelligence (#26)

The *Fast Company* Collection On-Line
- **Tony Schwartz,** "How Do You Feel?"

ELECTRONIC RESOURCES

@ GET CONNECTED! Don't forget to take full advantage of the on-line support for *Management 7/e.*
- Chapter 16 On-line Study Guide
- Chapter 16 Self-test Answers
- Chapter 16 E-Resource Center

17

Communication and interpersonal skills

Planning ahead

GETTING CONNECTED

Center for Creative Leadership—*Lead the Way with Communication*
The importance of communication and interpersonal skills in leadership development is mainstream at the internationally regarded Center for Creative Leadership. Headquartered in Greensboro, North Carolina, and with three other U.S. locations, the center's mission is stated as: "to advance the understanding, practice and development of leadership for the benefit of society worldwide." A new branch in Brussels, Belgium, expands the center's reach to European managers.

We all know that leaders need to be able to effectively communicate with diverse audiences and that they require the interpersonal skills to engage and enthuse others in their work. But, the fact remains that a substantial percentage of managers report having difficulties in dealing with communication and interpersonal relations.

Through a variety of intensive programs, emphasizing assessments and simulations, the Center for Creative Leadership is committed to helping managers in all settings to gain better insight into their interpersonal styles and build the leadership skills needed for personal and organizational success. The center has achieved a global reputation for excellence and innovation in leadership

development programs. *Business Week* has ranked it #1 for executive education in leadership.

Coaching for leadership development is an important initiative within the center. "People used to think, and some still do," states the center's web site, "that leadership development can be learned in a single event. It has always been the Center's view that just the opposite is true. Leadership development is an ongoing and highly personal process, and it must include ongoing support."

Supporting in a variety of ways the personal efforts of managers who want to better develop themselves as leaders is what the Center for Creative Leadership is all about. When Richard S. Herlich came to the Center he had been recently promoted to director of marketing for his firm. "I thought I had the perfect style," he said. He learned through role-playing that others viewed him as an aloof and poor communicator. After returning to his job and meeting with his subordinates to discuss his style, Herlich became more involved in their work projects.

Another participant, Robert Siddall, received feedback that he was too structured and domineering. Center instructors worked with him to develop more positive relationships and to display a more "coaching" style of management. After returning to his job Siddall's performance ratings went up, and his relationships with coworkers improved. He says, "If I start screaming and yelling, they say—'Old Bob, old Bob.'"[1]

@ Get Connected!

Are you fully prepared to meet the leadership challenges of the future? Just how good are your communication skills? Are you comfortable dealing with conflict and negotiations? Take a further look at your career readiness. Don't waste time. Get connected!

Anyone heading into the new workplace must understand that the work of managers and team leaders is highly interpersonal and communication intensive. Whether you work at the top of the organization communicating strategies and building support for organizational goals or at a lower level interacting with others to support their work efforts and your own, communication and interpersonal skills are essential to your personal toolkit. Think back to the descriptions of managerial work by Henry Mintzberg, John Kotter, and others as discussed in Chapter 1. For Mintzberg, managerial success involves performing well as an information "nerve center," gathering information from and disseminating information to internal and external sources.[2] For Kotter, it depends largely on one's ability to build and maintain a complex web of interpersonal networks with insiders and outsiders, so as to implement work priorities and agendas.[3] Says Pam Alexander, CEO of Ogilvy Public Relations Worldwide: "Relationships are the most powerful form of media. Ideas will only get you so far these days. Count on personal relationships to carry you further."[4]

The ability to communicate well both orally and in writing is a critical managerial skill and the foundation of effective leadership.[5] Through communication people exchange and share information with one another, and influence one another's attitudes, behaviors, and understandings. Communication allows managers to establish and maintain interpersonal relationships, listen to others, and otherwise gain the information needed to create an inspirational workplace. No manager can handle conflict, negotiate successfully, and succeed at leadership without being a good communicator. It is no wonder that "communication skills" often top the list of attributes employers look for in job candidates. Any career portfolio should include adequate testimony to one's abilities to communicate well in interpersonal relationships, in various forms of public speaking, and increasingly through the electronic medium of the computer. At Intel, Inc., for example, as many as 3 million e-mail messages a day move through the firm's computer networks. Some workers personally process as many as 300 per day; the average worker spends 2.5 hours per day "communicating" with others via her or his computer.[6]

Get Connected!

Visit Monster.com for advice on how to negotiate salary and other terms with an employer.

THE COMMUNICATION PROCESS

○ **Communication** is the process of sending and receiving symbols with meanings attached.

Communication is an interpersonal process of sending and receiving symbols with messages attached to them. In more practical terms, the key elements in the communication process are shown in *Figure 17.1*. They include a *sender*, who is responsible for encoding an intended *message* into meaningful symbols, both verbal and nonverbal. The message is sent through a *communication channel* to a *receiver*, who then decodes or interprets its *meaning*. This interpretation, importantly, may or may not match the sender's original intentions. *Feedback*, when present, reverses the process and conveys the receiver's response back to the sender. Another way to view the communication process is as a series of questions. "Who?" (sender) "says what?" (message) "in what way?" (channel) "to whom?" (receiver) "with what result?" (interpreted meaning).

WHAT IS EFFECTIVE COMMUNICATION?

○ In **effective communication** the intended meaning of the source and the perceived meaning of the receiver are identical.

Effective communication occurs when the intended message of the sender and the interpreted meaning of the receiver are one and the same. Although this should be the goal in any communication attempt, it is not

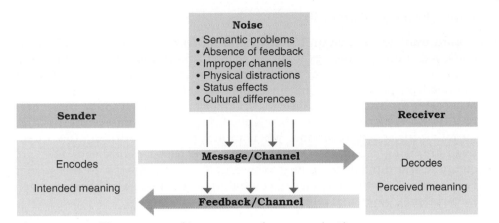

Figure 17.1 The process of interpersonal communication.

always achieved. **Efficient communication** occurs at minimum cost in terms of resources expended. Time, in particular, is an important resource in the communication process. Picture your instructor taking the time to communicate individually with each student about this chapter. It would be virtually impossible. Even if it were possible, it would be costly. This is why managers often leave voice-mail messages and interact by e-mail rather than visit their subordinates personally. Simply put, these alternatives are more efficient ways to communicate than through one-on-one and face-to-face communications.

○ **Efficient communication** occurs at minimum cost.

One problem is that efficient communications are not always effective. A low-cost approach such as an e-mail note to a distribution list may save time, but it does not always result in everyone getting the same meaning from the message. Without opportunities to ask questions and clarify the message, erroneous interpretations are possible. By the same token, an effective communication may not always be efficient. If a work team leader visits each team member individually to explain a new change in procedures, this may guarantee that everyone truly understands the change. But it may also be very costly in the demands it makes on the leader's time. A team meeting would be more efficient. In these and other ways, potential trade-offs between effectiveness and efficiency must be recognized in communication.

BARRIERS TO EFFECTIVE COMMUNICATION

Effective communication is a two-way process that requires effort and skill on the part of both the sender and the receiver. **Noise**, as Figure 17.1 shows, is anything that interferes with the effectiveness of the communication process. For example, Mazda Corporation president Yoshihiro Wada once met with representatives of the firm's American joint venture partner, Ford. But he had to use an interpreter. He estimated that 20 percent of his intended meaning was lost in the exchange between himself and the interpreter; another 20 percent was lost between the interpreter and the Americans, with whom he was ultimately trying to communicate.[7] In addition to these obvious problems when different languages are involved in a communication attempt, common sources of noise include poor choice of channels, poor written or oral expression, failure to recognize nonverbal signals, physical distractions, and status effects.

○ **Noise** is anything that interferes with communication effectiveness.

Poor Choice of Channels

○ A **communication channel** is the medium through which a message is sent.

A **communication channel** is the medium through which a message is conveyed from sender to receiver. Good managers choose the right communication channel, or combination of channels, to accomplish their intended purpose in a given situation.[8] In general, *written channels* are acceptable for simple messages that are easy to convey and for those that require extensive dissemination quickly. They are also important, at least as follow-up communications, when formal policy or authoritative directives are being conveyed. *Oral channels* work best for messages that are complex and difficult to convey, where immediate feedback to the sender is valuable. They are also more personal and can create a supportive, even inspirational, emotional climate.

Poor Written or Oral Expression

Communication will be effective only to the extent that the sender expresses a message in a way that can be clearly understood by the receiver. This means that words must be well chosen and properly used to express the sender's intentions. When they are not, semantic barriers to communication occur as encoding and decoding errors and as mixed messages. Consider the following "bafflegab" found among some executive communications.

> *A business report said:* "Consumer elements are continuing to stress the fundamental necessity of a stabilization of the price structure at a lower level than exists at the present time." (*Translation:* Consumers keep saying that prices must go down and stay down.)

> *A manager said:* "Substantial economies were effected in this division by increasing the time interval between distribution of data-eliciting forms to business entities." (*Translation:* The division was saving money by sending fewer questionnaires to suppliers.)

Both written and oral communication require skill. It isn't easy, for example, to write a concise letter or to express one's thoughts in a computer e-mail report. Any such message can easily be misunderstood. It takes

Entrepreneurship (www.walmart.com) **Wal-Mart, Inc.** Nobody Communicated Better than "Mr. Sam"

The late Sam Walton, Wal-Mart's founder, was a master communicator. Stopping once to visit a Memphis store, he called everyone to the front, saying, "Northeast Memphis, you're the largest store in Memphis, and you must have the best floor-cleaning crew in America. This floor is so clean, let's sit down on it." Kneeling casually and wearing his Wal-Mart baseball cap, Walton congratulated them on their fine work. "I thank you," he said. "The company is so proud of you we can hardly stand it," he said, reminding them of bonus checks recently given out. "But," he added, "you know that confounded Kmart is getting better, and so is Target. So what's our challenge?" Walton asked. "Customer service," he replied in answer to his own question. Walton's quality message was clear to everyone.[9]

practice and hard work to express yourself well. The same holds true for oral communication that takes place via the spoken word in telephone calls, face-to-face meetings, formal briefings, video conferences, and the like. *Manager's Notepad 17.1* identifies guidelines for an important oral communication situation faced by managers—the executive briefing or formal presentation.[10]

Failure to Recognize Nonverbal Signals

Nonverbal communication takes place through such things as hand movements, facial expressions, body posture, eye contact, and the use of interpersonal space. It can be a powerful means of transmitting messages. Eye contact or voice intonation can be used intentionally to accent special parts of an oral communication. The astute observer notes the "body language" expressed by other persons. At times our body may be "talking" for us even as we otherwise maintain silence. And when we do speak, our body may sometimes "say" different things than our words convey. A **mixed message** occurs when a person's words communicate one message while his or her actions, body language, appearance, or situational use of interpersonal space communicate something else. Watch how people behave in a meeting. A person who feels under attack may move back in a chair or lean away from the presumed antagonist, even while expressing verbal agreement. All of this is done quite unconsciously, but it sends a message to those alert enough to pick it up.

○ **Nonverbal communication** takes place through gestures and body language.

○ A **mixed message** results when words communicate one message while actions, body language, or appearance communicate something else.

MANAGER'S NOTEPAD 17.1

How to make a successful presentation

- *Be prepared:* Know what you want to say; know how you want to say it; and rehearse saying it.
- *Set the right tone:* Act audience centered; make eye contact; be pleasant and confident.
- *Sequence points:* State your purpose; make important points; follow with details; then summarize.
- *Support your points:* Give specific reasons for your points; state them in understandable terms.
- *Accent the presentation:* Use good visual aids and provide supporting "handouts" when possible.
- *Add the right amount of polish:* Attend to details; have room, materials, and arrangements ready to go.
- *Check your technology:* Check everything ahead of time; make sure it works and know how to use it.
- *Don't bet on the Internet:* Beware of plans to make real-time Internet visits; save sites on a disk and use a browser to open the file.
- *Be professional:* Be on time; wear appropriate attire; and act organized, confident, and enthusiastic.

Faster decision making is one of the goals behind Alcoa's new-form executive suites. Senior executives work in "cockpit offices" with special furniture and short, movable walls. This is designed to promote interaction and spontaneous association. The new executive offices include a common "coffee kitchen" complete with chalkboards for jotting down ideas that pop up in informal conversations.

Nonverbal channels probably play a more important part in communication than most people recognize. One researcher indicates that gestures alone may make up as much as 70 percent of communication.[11] In fact, a potential side effect of the growing use of electronic mail, computer networking, and other communication technologies is that gestures and other nonverbal signals that may add important meaning to the communication event are lost.

Physical Distractions

Any number of physical distractions can interfere with the effectiveness of a communication attempt. Some of these distractions, such as telephone interruptions, drop-in visitors, and lack of privacy, are evident in the following conversation between an employee, George, and his manager:

> Okay, George, let's hear your problem [phone rings, boss picks it up, promises to deliver a report "just as soon as I can get it done"]. Uh, now, where were we—oh, you're having a problem with your technician. She's [manager's secretary brings in some papers that need his immediate signature; secretary leaves] . . . you say she's overstressed lately, wants to leave. . . . I tell you what, George, why don't you [phone rings again, lunch partner drops by] . . . uh, take a stab at handling it yourself. . . . I've got to go now.[12]

Besides what may have been poor intentions in the first place, the manager in this example did not do a good job of communicating with George. This problem could be easily corrected. If George has something important to say, he should set aside adequate time for the meeting. Additional interruptions such as telephone calls and drop-in visitors could be eliminated by issuing appropriate instructions to the secretary. Many communication distractions can be avoided or at least minimized through proper planning.

Status Effects

"Criticize my boss? I don't have the right to." "I'd get fired." "It's her company, not mine." As suggested in these comments, the hierarchy of authority in organizations creates another potential barrier to effective communications. Consider the "corporate cover-up" once discovered at an electronics company. Product shipments were being predated and papers falsified to meet unrealistic sales targets set by the president. His managers knew the targets were impossible to attain, but at least 20 persons in the organization cooperated in the deception. It was months before the top found out. What happened in this case is **filtering**—the intentional distortion of information to make it appear favorable to the recipient.

○ **Filtering** is the intentional distortion of information to make it appear most favorable to the recipient.

The presence of such information filtering is often found in communications between lower and higher levels in organizations. Tom Peters, the popular management author and consultant, has called such information distortion "Management Enemy Number 1."[13] Simply put, it most often involves someone "telling the boss what he or she wants to hear." Whether the reason behind this is a fear of retribution for bringing bad news, an unwillingness to identify personal mistakes, or just a general desire to please, the end result is the same. The person receiving filtered communications can end up making poor decisions because of a biased and inaccurate information base.

IMPROVING COMMUNICATION

A number of things can be done to overcome barriers and improve the process of communication. They include active listening, making constructive use of feedback, opening upward communication channels, understanding proxemics and the use of space, utilizing technology, and valuing diversity.

ACTIVE LISTENING

Managers must be very sensitive to their listening responsibility. When people "talk," they are trying to communicate something. That "something" may or may not be what they are saying. **Active listening** is the process of taking action to help the source of a message say exactly what he or she really means. There are five rules for becoming an active listener:[14]

1. *Listen for message content:* Try to hear exactly what content is being conveyed in the message.
2. *Listen for feelings:* Try to identify how the source feels about the content in the message.
3. *Respond to feelings:* Let the source know that her or his feelings are being recognized.
4. *Note all cues:* Be sensitive to nonverbal and verbal messages; be alert for mixed messages.
5. *Paraphrase and restate:* State back to the source what you think you are hearing.

Different responses to the following two questions contrast how a "passive" listener and an "active" listener might act in real workplace conversations. Put yourself in the position of the questioner in each case; then consider how you would react to each listener's response. Question 1: "Don't you think employees should be promoted on the basis of seniority?" *Passive listener's response*: "No, I don't!" *Active listener's response*: "It seems to you that they should, I take it?" Question 2: "What does the supervisor expect us to do about these out-of-date computers?" *Passive listener's response*: "Do the best you can, I guess." *Active listener's response*: "You're pretty disgusted with those machines, aren't you?"

The prior examples should give you a sense of how the active listening approach can facilitate and encourage communication in difficult circumstances, rather than discourage it. *Manager's Notepad 17.2* offers an additional set of useful guidelines for good listening.

CONSTRUCTIVE FEEDBACK

The process of telling other people how you feel about something they did or said, or about the situation in general, is called **feedback**. The art of giving feedback is an indispensable skill, particularly for managers who must regularly give feedback to other people. Often this takes the form of performance feedback given as evaluations and appraisals. When poorly done, such feedback can be threatening to the recipient and cause resentment. When properly done, feedback—even performance criticism—can be listened to, accepted, and used to good advantage by the receiver.[15] Managers at General Electric, for example, are evaluated on how they give

○ **Active listening** helps the source of a message say what he or she really means.

← Rules for active listening

○ **Feedback** is the process of telling someone else how you feel about something that person did or said.

MANAGER'S NOTEPAD 17.2

Ten steps to good listening

1. Stop talking.
2. Put the other person at ease.
3. Show that you want to listen.
4. Remove any potential distractions.
5. Empathize with the other person.
6. Don't respond too quickly; be patient.
7. Don't get mad; hold your temper.
8. Go easy on argument and criticism.
9. Ask questions.
10. Stop talking.

---

performance feedback to employees. Each subordinate must be annually rated by the manager on a low-high performance curve; the weakest are advised to find jobs elsewhere. By the same token, GE managers are also evaluated on how well they receive feedback. Employees are encouraged to let their bosses know how they are performing, and they can do so anonymously if they prefer.[16]

There are ways to help ensure that feedback is useful and constructive rather than harmful. To begin with, the sender must learn to recognize when the feedback he or she is about to offer will really benefit the receiver and when it will mainly satisfy some personal need. A supervisor who berates a computer operator for data analysis errors, for example, actually may be angry about personally failing to give clear instructions in the first place. Also, a manager should make sure that any feedback is considered from the recipient's point of view as understandable, acceptable, and plausible. Usefully accepted *guidelines for giving "constructive" feedback* include:[17]

Constructive feedback ⟶ guidelines

- Give feedback directly and with real feeling, based on trust between you and the receiver.

- Make sure that feedback is specific rather than general; use good, clear, and preferably recent examples to make your points.

- Give feedback at a time when the receiver seems most willing or able to accept it.

- Make sure the feedback is valid and limit it to things the receiver can be expected to do something about.

- Give feedback in small doses; never give more than the receiver can handle at any particular time.

USE OF COMMUNICATION CHANNELS

○ **Channel richness** is the capacity of a communication channel to effectively carry information.

Channel richness is the capacity of a channel or communication medium to carry information in an effective manner.[18] *Figure 17.2* shows that face-to-face communication, for example, is very high in richness,

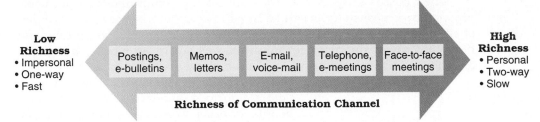

| Low Richness
• Impersonal
• One-way
• Fast | Postings, e-bulletins | Memos, letters | E-mail, voice-mail | Telephone, e-meetings | Face-to-face meetings | High Richness
• Personal
• Two-way
• Slow |

Richness of Communication Channel

Figure 17.2 Channel richness and the use of communication media.

enabling personal two-way interaction and real-time feedback. At the other end of the continuum, posted e-mail or hard-copy bulletins are very low in richness, representing impersonal one-way interaction and largely insulated from quick feedback. In between, you can see how the other common channels of electronic and traditional letters and memos, as well as telephone conversations and voice-mail messages array themselves. Obviously managers need to understand the limits of a channel and choose wisely when using them to communicate various types of messages.

There are a number of steps that can be taken to keep communication channels open to reduce the harmful effects of status effects and filtering, described earlier. A popular approach is called **management by wandering around (MBWA)**. This means dealing directly with subordinates by regularly spending time walking around and talking with them about a variety of work-related matters. Instead of relying on less rich and more formal channels to bring information to your attention, MBWA involves finding out for yourself what is going on in a rich face-to-face communication channel. The basic objectives are to break down status barriers, increase the frequency of interpersonal contact, and get more and better information from lower-level sources. Of course, this requires a trusting relationship. Patricia Gallup, CEO of PC Connection, is well known for her interactive style of leadership and emphasis on communication. She makes herself available by e-mail and greets employees by name as she walks the hallways. MBWA is clearly part of her style. She spends as much time as possible out of her office and on the floor where she can be close to workers in the various departments.[19]

Management practices designed to open channels and improve upward communications have traditionally involved *open office hours*, whereby busy senior executives like Gallup set aside time in their calendars to welcome walk-in visits during certain hours each week. Today this approach can be expanded to include *on-line discussion forums* and "chat rooms" that are open at certain hours. Programs of regular *employee group meetings* are also helpful. Here, a rotating schedule of "shirtsleeve" meetings brings top managers into face-to-face contact with mixed employee groups throughout an organization. In some cases, a comprehensive communications program includes an *employee advisory council* composed of members elected by their fellow employees. Such a council may meet with top management on a regular schedule to discuss and react to new policies and programs that will affect employees. Again, the face-to-face groups can be supplemented with a variety of *computer-mediated meetings* that serve similar purposes, overcoming the time and distance limitations that might otherwise make communication less frequent or intense.

○ In **MBWA** managers spend time outside of their offices to meet and talk with workers at all levels.

www.scotts.com

The Scotts Company holds large meetings to thank employees for their work, tell them the results of the firm's financial performance, and celebrate teamwork. The food is good and plentiful, there is music and entertainment, and a lot of information is shared.

When bosses suspect that they are having communication problems, *communication consultants* can be hired to conduct interviews and surveys of employees on their behalf. Marc Brownstein, president of a public relations and advertising firm, for example, was surprised when managers in an anonymous survey complained that he was a poor listener and gave them insufficient feedback. They also felt poorly informed about the firm's financial health. In other words, poor communication was hurting staff morale. With help from consultants, Brownstein now holds more meetings and works more aggressively to share information and communicate regularly with the firm's employees.[20]

Another communication approach that seeks to broaden the awareness of "bosses" regarding the feelings and perceptions of other people that they work closely with is 360-degree feedback discussed in chapter 12.[21] This typically involves upward appraisals done by a manager's subordinates as well as additional feedback from peers, internal and external customers, and higher-ups. A self-assessment is also part of the process. Often this feedback is gathered through questionnaires in which respondents can remain anonymous. The goal of 360-degree feedback is to provide the manager with information that can be used for constructive improvement. Managers who have participated in the process often express surprise at what they learn. Some have found themselves perceived as lacking vision, having bad tempers, being bad listeners, lacking flexibility, and the like.[22]

PROXEMICS AND SPACE DESIGN

An important but sometimes neglected part of communication involves proxemics, or the use of interpersonal space.[23] The distance between people conveys varying intentions in terms of intimacy, openness, and status. And, the proxemics or physical layout of an office is an often-overlooked form of nonverbal communication. Check it out. Offices with two or more chairs available for side-by-side seating, for example, convey different messages from those where the manager's chair sits behind the desk and those for visitors sit facing in front.

Office or workspace architecture is becoming increasingly recognized for its important influence on communication and behavior. If you visit Sun Microsystems in San Jose, California, for example, you will see many public spaces designed to encourage communication among persons from different departments. Many meeting areas have no walls and most of the walls that exist are glass. Ann Bamesberger, manager of planning and research, says: "We were creating a way to get these people to communicate

---

CAREER CONNECTION
Service Organizations

Mayo Clinic Communication Is the Lifeblood of Quality Health Care

In health care the Mayo Clinic stands in a class all by itself. Founded some 100 years ago by Dr. Charles and Dr. Will Mayo, the clinic is still guided by the original vision: "thorough diagnosis, accurate answers and effective treatment through the application of collective wisdom to the problems of each patient."

Over 25,000 employees of Mayo rely on the open flow of communication and continual sharing of ideas to meet the commitment to excellence. They are assisted by the latest in information technology, including visual media. An up-to-date visual media department teaches clinic members how to use the latest tools and techniques. Says Mary Mitchell, head of the media support services: "We consult with them to help them understand how to use the tools to make their presentation more dynamic."

Communication is integral to a clinic devoted to teamwork, patient information, and the very best in medical care. The more than 400,000 patients who visit the clinics in three states are testimony to both the success of the model and the value of harnessing communication as a pathway to excellence.

QUESTION: Communication and information sharing help Mayo's staff serve patient needs. Do service organizations in your community do as well? Talk to people, ask questions as you go about your daily business. Think about how communication improves organizations. Get connected!

with each other more." Importantly, the Sun project involved not only the assistance of expert architectural consultants, but also extensive inputs and suggestions from the employees themselves. The results seem to justify the effort. A senior technical writer, Terry Davidson, says: "This is the most productive workspace I have ever been in."[24]

TECHNOLOGY UTILIZATION

Prerequisites to entry into just about any workplace with career value are basic computer literacy and a willingness to use the new technologies to maximum advantage. The new age of communication is one of e-mail, voice mail, on-line discussions, videoconferencing, virtual or computer-mediated meetings, and more. A related and important development is the growing use of in-house or corporate intranets to provide opportunities for increased communication and collaboration. Progressive organizations use database programs such as Lotus Domino to host continuous on-line forums for internal communication and knowledge sharing among employees. The purpose is to encourage fast and regular communication, and to provide a source of up-to-date information for problem solving and work implementation. When IBM surveyed its employees to find out how they learned what was going on at the company, executives were not surprised that co-workers were perceived as credible and useful sources. But they were surprised that the firm's intranet ranked equally high. IBM's internal web sites were ranked higher than news briefs, company memos, and information from managers.[25]

Technology offers the power of the *electronic grapevine*, speeding messages and information from person-to-person. When the members of a sixth-grade class in Taylorsville, North Carolina (population 1566) sent out the e-mail message "Hi! . . . We are curious to see where in the world our e-mail will travel," they were surprised. Over a half-million replies flooded in, overwhelming not only the students but the school's computer system.[26] Messages fly with equal speed and intensity around organizations. The results can be both functional—when the information is accurate and useful—and dysfunctional—when the information is false, distorted, or simply based on rumor. Managers should be quick to correct misimpressions and inaccuracies; they should also utilize the grapevines as a means to quickly transfer factual and relevant information among organizational members.

How Private Is Office Communication? For most workers there is an increasing chance that their employers are monitoring their communication and performance. Electronic monitoring was up 45 percent in a survey by the American Management Association. Take the on-line "Reality Check" to learn more about the ways in which employers monitor employee communications.

VALUING CULTURE AND DIVERSITY

Workforce diversity and globalization are two of the most talked-about trends in modern society. Communicating under conditions of diversity, where the sender and receiver are part of different cultures, is certainly a significant challenge. Cross-cultural communication challenges were first discussed in Chapter 5 on the global dimensions of management. Now, it is useful to recall that a major source of difficulty is **ethnocentrism**, the tendency to consider one's culture superior to any and all others. Ethnocentrism can adversely affect communication in at least three major ways: (1) it may cause someone to *not* listen well to what others have to say; (2) it may cause someone to address or speak with others in ways that alienate them; and (3) it may lead to the use of inappropriate stereotypes when dealing with persons from another culture.[27]

○ **Ethnocentrism** is the tendency to consider one's culture superior to any and all others.

For years, cultural challenges have been recognized by international travelers and executives. But as we know, you don't have to travel abroad to come face to face with communication and cultural diversity. Just going to work is a cross-cultural journey for most of us today. The workplace abounds with subcultures based on gender, age, ethnicity, race, and other factors. As a result, the importance of cross-cultural communication skills applies at home just as well as it does in a foreign country. Remember, too, that cultural skills are gained by reaching out, crossing cultural boundaries, and embracing differences.

PERCEPTION

Perception is the process through which people receive, organize, and interpret information from the environment.

The process through which people receive and interpret information from the environment is called **perception**. It is the way we form impressions about ourselves, other people, and daily life experiences and the way we process information into the decisions that ultimately guide our actions.[28]

As shown in *Figure 17.3*, perception acts as a screen or filter through which information must pass before it has an impact on communication, decision making, and action. The results of this screening process vary because individual perceptions are influenced by such things as values, cultural background, and other circumstances of the moment. Simply put, people can and do perceive the same things or situations very differently. And importantly, people behave according to their perceptions. Unless the potential for alternative perceptions is recognized and understood, this influence on individual behavior may be neglected.

PERCEPTION AND ATTRIBUTION

It is natural for people to try to explain what they observe and the things that happen to them. This process of developing explanations for events is called *attribution*. The fact that people can perceive the same things quite differently has an important influence on attributions and their ultimate influence on behavior. In social psychology, attribution theory describes how people try to explain the behavior of themselves and other people.[29] One of its significant applications is in the context of people's performance at work.

Fundamental **attribution error** overestimates internal factors and underestimates external factors as influences on someone's behavior.

Fundamental **attribution error** occurs when observers blame another person's performance failures more on internal factors relating to the individual than on external factors relating to the environment. In the case of someone who is producing poor-quality work, for example,

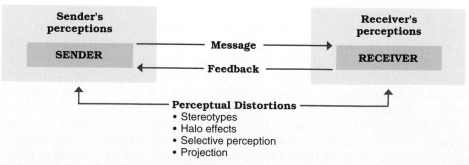

Figure 17.3 Perception and communication.

a supervisor might blame a lack of job skills or laziness—an unwillingness to work hard enough. These internal explanations of the performance deficiency, moreover, are likely to lead the supervisor to try to resolve the problem through training, motivation, or even replacement. The attribution error leads to the neglect of possible external explanations. They might suggest, for example, that the poor-quality work was caused by unrealistic time pressures or substandard technology. Opportunities to improve upon these factors through managerial action will thus be missed.

Another confounding aspect of perception and attribution is the **self-serving bias**. This occurs because individuals tend to blame their personal failures or problems on external causes, and attribute their successes to internal causes. In this instance, the individual may give insufficient attention to the need for personal change and development. Instead, he or she may be prone to take credit for successes and focus on the environment to explain away failures.

> ○ **Self-serving bias** explains personal success by internal causes and personal failures by external causes.

PERCEPTUAL TENDENCIES AND DISTORTIONS

In addition to the attribution errors just discussed, a variety of perceptual distortions can also influence human behavior in the workplace. Of particular interest are the use of stereotypes, halo effects, selectivity, and projection.

Stereotypes

A **stereotype** occurs when someone is identified with a group or category, and then oversimplified attributes associated with the group or category are linked back to the individual. Common stereotypes are those of young people, old people, teachers, students, union members, males, and females, among others. The phenomenon, in each case, is the same: a person is classified into a group on the basis of one piece of information, such as age, for example. Characteristics commonly associated with the group are then assigned to the individual. What is generalized about the group (e.g., "Young people dislike authority") may or may not be true about the individual.

> ○ A **stereotype** is when attributes commonly associated with a group are assigned to an individual.

Stereotypes based on such factors as gender, age, and race can, and unfortunately still do, bias the perceptions of people in some work settings. The *glass ceiling*, mentioned in Chapter 1 as an invisible barrier to career advancement, still exists in some places. Legitimate questions can be asked about *racial and ethnic stereotypes* and about the slow progress of minority managers into America's corporate mainstream.[30] Their numbers in the executive ranks remain disappointingly low, despite clear advances in the recent past; of the 7,000+ board members at *Fortune* 1000 companies in 1999, only 220 were African American, 82 Hispanic, and 37 Asian.[31]

In the world of international business, only about 13 percent of American managers sent abroad by their employers on work assignments are women. Why? A Catalyst study of opportunities for women in global business points to *gender stereotypes* that place women at a disadvantage to men for these types of opportunities. The tendency is to assume they lack the ability and/or willingness for working abroad.[32] Although employment barriers caused by gender stereotypes are falling, women may still suffer from false impressions and biases imposed on them. Even everyday behavior may be misconstrued based upon inaccurate perceptions. Consider this example: *Case—"He's* talking with coworkers." (*Interpretation:* He's discussing a new deal.); "*She's* talking with coworkers." (*Interpretation:* She's gossiping.)[33]

Finally, *ability stereotypes* and *age stereotypes* also exist in the workplace. Their inappropriate use may place disabled and older workers at a disadvantage in various work situations. A worker with a disability may be overlooked in the hiring process because the recruiter assumes that someone with a disability would have a difficult time meeting a normal work schedule. A talented older worker may not be promoted to fill an important and challenging job, because a manager assumes older workers lack creativity, are cautious, and tend to avoid risk. On the other hand, for those who break through the stereotypes to find the true value in people, the rewards are there. When Jess Bell, former CEO of family-run Bonne Bell, the maker of popular cosmetics such as Lip Shake, needed workers he didn't hesitate to value age. He set up a special production department to fit the needs of senior workers. They now number 20 percent of the firm's workforce. The average age of the workers is 70, and the oldest is 90. They are loyal and productive, with about half saying they really need the work to pay their bills—their social security checks don't go far enough.[34]

Halo Effects

○ A **halo effect** occurs when one attribute is used to develop an overall impression of a person or situation.

A **halo effect** occurs when one attribute is used to develop an overall impression of a person or situation. When meeting someone new, for example, the halo effect may cause one trait, such as a pleasant smile, to result in a positive first impression. By contrast, a particular hairstyle or manner of dressing may create a negative reaction. Halo effects cause the same problem for managers as do stereotypes; that is, individual differences become obscured. This is especially significant with respect to a manager's view of subordinates' work performance. One factor, such as a person's punctuality, may become the "halo" for a positive overall performance evaluation. Even though the general conclusion seems to make sense, it may or may not be true in a given circumstance.

Selectivity

○ **Selective perception** is the tendency to define problems from one's own point of view.

Selective perception is the tendency to single out for attention those aspects of a situation or person that reinforce or appear consistent with one's existing beliefs, values, or needs.[35] What this often means in an organization is that people from different departments or functions—such as marketing and manufacturing—tend to see things from their own points of view and tend not to recognize other points of view. Like the other perceptual distortions just discussed, selective perception can bias a manager's view of situations and individuals. One way to reduce its impact is to gather additional opinions from other people.

Projection

○ **Projection** is the assignment of personal attributes to other individuals.

Projection is the assignment of personal attributes to other individuals. A classic projection error is to assume that other persons share our needs, desires, and values. Suppose, for example, that you enjoy a lot of responsibility and challenge in your work. Suppose, too, that you are the newly appointed supervisor for people whose work you consider dull and routine. You might move quickly to start a program of job enrichment to help them experience more responsibility and challenge. This may not be a good decision. Instead of designing jobs to best fit their needs, you have designed their jobs to fit *yours*. In fact, your subordinates may be quite satisfied and productive doing jobs that, to you, seem routine. Such projection errors can be controlled through self-awareness and a willingness to communicate and empathize with other persons, that is, to try to see things through their eyes.

COMMUNICATION AND CONFLICT MANAGEMENT

Communication and related interpersonal skills must be at the forefront of any attempt to develop managerial and leadership expertise. The former CEO of Arthur Andersen, Lawrence A. Weinback, says, "Pure technical knowledge is only going to get you to a point. Beyond that, interpersonal skills become critical."[36] Among these essential skills, the ability to deal with interpersonal conflicts is critical. Formally defined, **conflict** is a disagreement between people on substantive or emotional issues.[37] Managers and leaders spend a lot of time dealing with conflicts of various forms. **Substantive conflicts** involve disagreements over such things as goals; the allocation of resources; the distribution of rewards, policies, and procedures; and job assignments. **Emotional conflicts** result from feelings of anger, distrust, dislike, fear, and resentment, as well as from personality clashes. Both forms of conflict can cause problems in the workplace. But when managed well, they can be helpful in promoting high performance, creativity, and innovation.

○ **Conflict** is a disagreement over issues of substance and/or an emotional antagonism.

○ **Substantive conflict** involves disagreements over goals, resources, rewards, policies, procedures, and job assignments.

○ **Emotional conflict** results from feelings of anger, distrust, dislike, fear, and resentment as well as from personality clashes.

CONSEQUENCES OF CONFLICT

Whether or not conflict benefits people and organizations depends on two factors: (1) the intensity of the conflict and (2) how well the conflict is managed. The inverted "U" curve depicted in *Figure 17.4* shows that conflict of moderate intensity can be good for performance. This **functional conflict**, or *constructive conflict*, stimulates people toward greater work efforts, cooperation, and creativity. At very low or very high intensities **dysfunctional conflict**, or *destructive conflict*, occurs. Too much conflict is distracting and interferes with other more task-relevant activities; too little conflict may promote complacency and the loss of a creative, high-performance edge.

○ **Functional conflict** is constructive and helps task performance.

○ **Dysfunctional conflict** is destructive and hurts task performance.

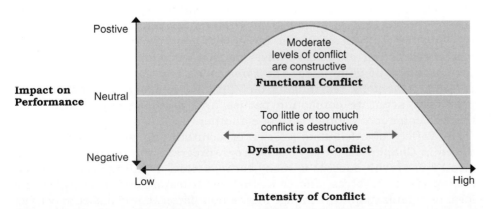

Figure 17.4 The relationship between conflict and performance.

www.pwc.com

Differences in perception are evident in a PricewaterhouseCoopers/ McGraw-Hill study of 6,800 senior managers and 450,000 employees. Although some 75 percent of managers agreed that company management is interested in workers' well-being, only 52 percent of employees believed this was the case.

CAUSES OF CONFLICT

Conflict in organizations may arise for a variety of reasons. Indeed, the following antecedent conditions can make the eventual emergence of conflict very likely. *Role ambiguities* set the stage for conflict. Unclear job expectations and other task uncertainties increase the probability that some people will be working at cross-purposes, at least some of the time. *Resource scarcities* cause conflict. Having to share resources with others and/or compete directly with them for resource allocations creates a potential situation conflict, especially when resources are scarce. *Task interdependencies* cause conflict. When individuals or groups must depend on what others do to perform well themselves, conflicts often occur. *Competing objectives* are opportunities for conflict. When objectives are poorly set or reward systems are poorly designed, individuals and groups may come into conflict by working to one another's disadvantage. *Structural differentiation* breeds conflict. Differences in organization structures and in the characteristics of the people staffing them may foster conflict because of incompatible approaches toward work. And *unresolved prior conflicts* tend to erupt in later conflicts. Unless a conflict is fully resolved, it may remain latent in the situation as a lingering basis for future conflicts over the same or related matters.

HOW TO DEAL WITH CONFLICT

When any one or more of these antecedent conditions is present, an informed manager expects conflicts to occur. And when they do, the conflicts then can either be "resolved," in the sense that the sources are corrected, or "suppressed," in that the sources remain but the conflict behaviors are controlled. Suppressed conflicts tend to fester and recur at a later time. They can also contribute to other conflicts over the same or related issues. True **conflict resolution** eliminates the underlying causes of conflict and reduces the potential for similar conflicts in the future.

○ **Conflict resolution** is the removal of the substantial and/or emotional reasons for a conflict.

Managers can try several approaches to restructure situations in order to resolve conflicts between individuals or groups. There are times when *appealing to superordinate goals* can focus the attention of conflicting parties on one mutually desirable end state. The appeal to higher-level goals offers all parties a common frame of reference against which to analyze differences and reconcile disagreements. Conflicts whose antecedents lie in the competition for scarce resources can also be resolved by *making more resources available* to everyone. Although costly, this technique removes the reasons for the continuing conflict. By *changing the people*, that is, by replacing or transferring one or more of the conflicting parties, conflicts caused by poor interpersonal relationships can be eliminated. The same holds true for *altering the physical environment* by rearranging facilities, work space, or workflows to physically separate conflicting parties and decrease opportunities for them to come into contact with one another.

A variety of *integrating devices* or coordinating mechanisms, introduced in Chapter 11 as ways to improve integration in organizations, can also be used with success in many settings. Implementing liaison personnel, special task forces, and cross-functional teams, and even the matrix form of organization, can change interaction patterns and assist in conflict management. *Changing reward systems* may reduce the competition be-

Get Connected!

Assess your conflict management style on-line and in the Career Readiness Workbook.

tween individuals and groups for rewards. Creating systems that reward cooperation can encourage behaviors and attitudes that promote teamwork and keep conflict within more constructive limits. *Changing policies and procedures* may redirect behavior in ways that minimize the likelihood of unfortunate conflict situations. Finally, *training in interpersonal skills* can help prepare people to communicate and work more effectively in situations that are conflict prone.

CONFLICT MANAGEMENT STYLES

Interpersonally, people respond to conflict through different combinations of cooperative and assertive behaviors.[38] *Cooperativeness* is the desire to satisfy another party's needs and concerns; *assertiveness* is the desire to satisfy one's own needs and concerns. *Figure 17.5* shows five interpersonal styles of conflict management that result from various combinations of the two. Briefly stated, these conflict management styles involve the following behaviors:

- **Avoidance**—being uncooperative and unassertive; downplaying disagreement, withdrawing from the situation, and/or staying neutral at all costs.
- **Accommodation** or *smoothing*—being cooperative but unassertive; letting the wishes of others rule; smoothing over or overlooking differences to maintain harmony.
- **Competition** or *authoritative command*—being uncooperative but assertive; working against the wishes of the other party, engaging in win-lose competition, and/or forcing through the exercise of authority.
- **Compromise**—being moderately cooperative and assertive, bargaining for "acceptable" solutions in which each party wins a bit and loses a bit.
- **Collaboration** or *problem solving*—being both cooperative and assertive; trying to fully satisfy everyone's concerns by working through differences; finding and solving problems so that everyone gains.[39]

The various conflict management styles can have quite different outcomes.[40] Thus they should be selected and used with caution, and with the requirements of each unique conflict situation carefully considered. Conflict management by *avoiding* or *accommodating* often creates **lose-lose conflict**. No one achieves her or his true desires and the underlying reasons for conflict often remain unaffected. Although a lose-lose conflict may appear settled or may even disappear for a while, it tends to recur in the future. Avoidance is an extreme form of nonattention. Everyone pretends that conflict doesn't really exist and hopes that it will simply go away. Accommodation plays down differences and highlights similarities and areas of agreement. Peaceful coexistence through a recognition of common interests is the goal. In reality, such smoothing may ignore the real essence of a conflict.

Competing and *compromising* tend to create **win-lose conflict**. Here, each party strives to gain at the other's expense. In extreme cases, one party achieves its desires to the complete exclusion of the other party's desires. Because win-lose methods fail to address the root causes of conflict, future conflicts of the same or a similar nature are likely to occur. In competition, one party wins, as superior skill or outright domination allows his or her desires to be forced on the other. This occurs in the form of authoritative command, where the forcing is accomplished by a higher-level

← Five conflict management styles

○ **Avoidance** pretends that a conflict doesn't really exist.

○ **Accommodation** or smoothing plays down differences and highlights similarities to reduce conflict.

○ **Competition** or authoritative command uses force, superior skill, or domination to "win" a conflict.

○ **Compromise** occurs when each party to the conflict gives up something of value to the other.

○ **Collaboration** or problem solving involves working through conflict differences and solving problems so everyone wins.

○ In **lose-lose conflict** no one achieves his or her true desires and the underlying reasons for conflict remain unaffected.

○ In **win-lose conflict** one party achieves its desires and the other party does not.

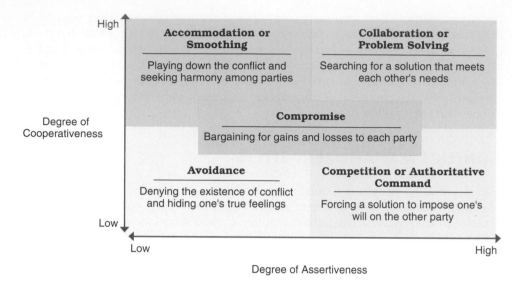

Figure 17.5 Alternative conflict management styles.

supervisor who simply dictates a solution to subordinates. Compromise occurs when trade-offs are made such that each party to the conflict gives up and gains something of value. As a result, neither party is completely satisfied, and antecedents for future conflicts are established.

○ In **win-win conflict** the conflict is resolved to everyone's benefit.

Collaborating in true problem solving tries to reconcile underlying differences and is often the most effective conflict management style. It is a form of **win-win conflict** whereby issues are resolved to the mutual benefit of all conflicting parties. This is typically achieved by confronting the issues and through the willingness of those involved to recognize that something is wrong and needs attention. Win-win conditions are created by eliminating the underlying causes of the conflict. All relevant issues are raised and discussed openly. Win-win methods are clearly the most preferred of the interpersonal styles of conflict management.

TAKE IT TO THE CASE!

The United Nations
Conflict and Negotiation Are Center Stage When Nations Meet

On any given day, United Nations Secretary General Kofi A. Annan can be counted on to have his hands full. Full of conflict, that is. The UN, committed by mission to preserving peace through international cooperation and collective security, is often center stage when members of the community of 189 nations have disagreements with one another. Part of Annan's task is to help them peacefully resolve conficts and together advance harmony and progress throughout the world. One of Annan's current priorities is to gain endorsement by world business and labor leaders of a Global Compact supporting human rights, labor, and the environment. The compact is designed to unite them in practices "enabling all the world's people to share the benefits of globalization and embedding the global market in values and practices that are fundamental to meeting socio-economic needs."[41]

NEGOTIATION

Put yourself in the following situations. How would you behave, and what would you do? (1) You have been offered a promotion and would really like to take it. However, the pay raise being offered is less than you hoped. (2) You have enough money to order one new computer for your department. Two of your subordinates have each requested a new computer for their individual jobs.[42] These are but two examples of the many negotiation situations that involve managers and other people in the typical workplace.

Negotiation is the process of making joint decisions when the parties involved have different preferences. Stated a bit differently, it is a way of reaching agreement when decisions involve more than one person or group. People negotiate over such diverse matters as salary, merit raises and performance evaluations, job assignments, work schedules, work locations, special privileges, and many other considerations. All such situations are susceptible to conflict and require exceptional communication skills.

○ **Negotiation** is the process of making joint decisions when the parties involved have different preferences.

NEGOTIATION GOALS AND APPROACHES

There are two important goals in negotiation. *Substance goals* are concerned with outcomes; they are tied to the "content" issues of the negotiation. *Relationship goals* are concerned with processes; they are tied to the way people work together while negotiating and how they (and any constituencies they represent) will be able to work together again in the future.

Effective negotiation occurs when issues of substance are resolved and working relationships among the negotiating parties are maintained or even improved in the process. The three criteria of effective negotiation are (1) *quality*—negotiating a "wise" agreement that is truly satisfactory to all sides; (2) *cost*—negotiating efficiently, using up minimum resources and time; and (3) *harmony*—negotiating in a way that fosters, rather than inhibits, interpersonal relationships.[43] The way each party approaches a negotiation can have a major impact on these outcomes.[44]

Distributive negotiation focuses on "claims" made by each party for certain preferred outcomes. This can take a competitive form in which one party can gain only if the other loses. In such "win-lose" conditions, relationships are often sacrificed as the negotiating parties focus only on their respective self-interests. It may also become accommodative if the parties defer to one another's wishes simply "to get it over with."

○ **Distributive negotiation** focuses on "win-lose" claims made by each party for certain preferred outcomes.

Principled negotiation, often called **integrative negotiation**, is based on a "win-win" orientation. The focus on substance is still important, but the interests of all parties are considered. The goal is to base the final outcome on the merits of individual claims and to try to find a way for all claims to be satisfied if at all possible. No one should "lose," and relationships should be maintained in the process.

○ **Principled/integrative negotiation** uses a "win-win" orientation to reach solutions acceptable to each party.

GAINING INTEGRATIVE AGREEMENTS

In their book *Getting to Yes*, Roger Fisher and William Ury point out that truly integrative agreements are obtained by following four negotiation rules:[45]

1. Separate the people from the problem.
2. Focus on interests, not on positions.
3. Generate many alternatives before deciding what to do.
4. Insist that results are based on some objective standard.

← Four rules of principled negotiation

Proper attitudes and good information are important foundations for such integrative agreements. The attitudinal foundations of integrative agreements involve the willingness of each negotiating party to trust, share information with, and ask reasonable questions of the other party. The informational foundations of integrative agreements involve each party knowing what is really important to them and finding out what is really important to the other party. In addition, each should understand his or her personal **best alternative to a negotiated agreement (BATNA)**. This is an answer to the question "What will I do if an agreement can't be reached?"

Figure 17.6 introduces a typical case of labor–management negotiations over a new contract and salary increase. This helps to illustrate elements of classic two-party negotiation as they occur in many contexts.[46] To begin, look at the figure and case from the labor union's perspective. The union negotiator has told her management counterpart that the union wants a new wage of $12.00 per hour. This expressed preference is the union's *initial offer*. However, she also has in mind a *minimum reservation point* of $10.75 per hour. This is the lowest wage rate that she is willing to accept for the union. But the management negotiator has a different perspective. His *initial offer* is $9.75 per hour, and his *maximum reservation point*, the highest wage he is prepared eventually to offer to the union, is $11.25 per hour.

In classic two-party negotiation of this type, the **bargaining zone** is defined as the zone between one party's minimum reservation point and the other party's maximum reservation point. The bargaining zone of $10.75 per hour to $11.25 per hour in this case is a "positive" one since the reservation points of the two parties overlap. If the union's minimum reservation point were greater than management's maximum reservation point, no room would exist for bargaining. Whenever a positive bargaining zone exists, there is room for true negotiation.

A key task for any negotiator is to discover the other party's reservation point. Until this is known and each party becomes aware that a positive bargaining zone exists, it is difficult to proceed effectively. When negotiation does move forward, each negotiator typically tries to achieve an agreement that is as close as possible to the other party's reservation point. Returning to Figure 17.6, the union negotiator would like to get an offer as close to $12.00 per hour as possible. The management negotiator would like to get a contract for as close to $9.75 per hour as possible.

AVOIDING NEGOTIATION PITFALLS

The negotiation process is admittedly complex, and negotiators must guard against common mistakes. Four negotiator pitfalls that can be avoided by proper discipline and personal attention should be recognized. The first is the tendency of *falling prey to the myth of the "fixed pie."* This involves acting

○ **BATNA** is the best alternative to a negotiated agreement.

○ A **bargaining zone** is the area between one party's minimum reservation point and the other party's maximum reservation point.

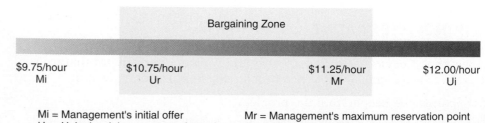

	Bargaining Zone		
$9.75/hour Mi	$10.75/hour Ur	$11.25/hour Mr	$12.00/hour Ui

Mi = Management's initial offer   Mr = Management's maximum reservation point
Ur = Union's minimum reservation point   Ui = Union's initial offer

Figure 17.6 The bargaining zone in classic two-party negotiation.

on the distributive assumption that in order for you to gain, the other person must give something up. Negotiating this way fails to recognize the integrative assumption that the "pie" can sometimes be expanded and/or utilized to everyone's advantage. A second negotiation error is the *nonrational escalation of conflict*. The negotiator in this case becomes committed to previously stated "demands" and allows concerns for "ego" and "face saving" to increase the perceived importance of satisfying these demands. The third error is *overconfidence and ignoring the other's needs*. The error here is becoming overconfident that your position is the only correct one and failing to see the needs of the other party and the merits in its position. The fourth error is the tendency to do *too much "telling" and too little "hearing."* When committing the "telling" problem, parties to a negotiation don't really make themselves understood to each other. When committing the "hearing" problem neither party listens sufficiently to understand what the other is saying.[47]

It may not always be possible to achieve integrative agreements. When disputes reach the point of impasse, mediation and arbitration can be useful. **Mediation** involves a neutral third party who tries to improve communication between negotiating parties and keep them focused on relevant issues. The *mediator* does not issue a ruling or make a decision, but can take an active role in discussions. This may include making suggestions in an attempt to move the parties toward agreement. **Arbitration**, such as salary arbitration in professional sports, is a stronger form of dispute resolution. It involves a neutral third party, the *arbitrator*, who acts as a "judge" and issues a binding decision. This usually includes a formal hearing in which the arbitrator listens to both sides and reviews all facets of the case before making a ruling. Some organizations formally provide for a process called *alternative dispute resolution*. This approach utilizes mediation and/or arbitration but only after direct attempts to negotiate agreements between the conflicting parties have failed. Often an *ombudsperson*, or designated neutral third party who listens to complaints and disputes, plays a key role in the process.

○ In **mediation** a neutral party tries to help conflicting parties improve communication to resolve their dispute.

○ In **arbitration** a neutral third party issues a binding decision to resolve a dispute.

ETHICAL ISSUES IN NEGOTIATION

Managers, and anyone else involved in negotiation, should maintain high standards of ethical conduct even when they are personally engaged in a dynamic and challenging situation. The motivation to behave unethically sometimes arises from an undue emphasis on the profit motive. This may be experienced as a desire to "get just a bit more" or to "get as much as you can" from a negotiation. The motivation to behave unethically may also result from a sense of competition. This may be experienced as a desire to "win" a negotiation just for the sake of it or as a misguided belief that someone else must "lose" in order for you to gain.

When unethical behavior occurs in negotiation, the persons involved sometimes attempt to rationalize or explain it away. We first discussed such rationalizations for unethical conduct in Chapter 6. In a negotiation situation, the following comments may be indicative of inappropriate rationalizing: "It was really unavoidable," "Oh, it's harmless," "The results justify the means," or "It's really quite fair and appropriate."[48] Moral issues aside, tendencies to use or accept such explanations can be challenged by the possibility that any short-run gains may be accompanied by long-run losses. Unethical parties should also realize that they may be targeted for later "revenge" from those disadvantaged by their tactics. Furthermore, once people behave unethically in one situation, they may consider such behavior acceptable in similar circumstances in the future.

Get Connected!

Visit the Center for International Development and Conflict Management to learn about conflict resolution in the global context.

STUDY Guide

The Chapter 17 Study Guide will help you review chapter content, prepare for examinations, and further build your career readiness. The *Summary* briefly highlights answers to questions first posed in the chapter opening Planning Ahead section. The list of *Key Terms* allows you to double check your familiarity with basic concepts and definitions. *Self-Test 17* gives you the opportunity to test your basic comprehension of chapter content using sample test questions. Suggestions offered as *Career Readiness Activities* direct your attention to relevant sections of the end-of-text Career Readiness Workbook, as well as to special Electronic Resources on the *Management 7/e* web site.

SUMMARY

What is the communication process?

- Communication is the interpersonal process of sending and receiving symbols with messages attached to them.
- Effective communication occurs when the sender and the receiver of a message both interpret it in the same way; efficient communication occurs when the message is sent at low cost for the sender.
- Noise is anything that interferes with the effectiveness of communication; it occurs in the form of poor utilization of channels, poor written or oral expression, physical distractions, and status effects, among other possibilities.

How can communication be improved?

- Active listening, through reflecting back and paraphrasing, can help overcome communication barriers.
- Upward communication may be improved through MBWA (managing by wandering around), and by the use of structured meetings, suggestion systems, advisory councils, and the like.
- Space can be used and designed to improve communication in organizations.
- The appropriate use of information technology, such as e-mail and intranets, can improve communication in organizations.
- Greater cross-cultural awareness and sensitivity can help reduce the difficulties of communication and diversity.

How does perception influence communication?

- Perception acts as a filter through which all communication passes as it travels from one person to the next.
- Because people tend to perceive things differently, the same message may be interpreted quite differently by different people.
- Attribution is the process of assigning explanations to events.
- Attribution theory identifies tendencies toward fundamental attribution errors when judging the performance of others and self-serving bias when judging our own performance.
- Common perceptual distortions that may reduce communication effectiveness include stereotypes, projections, halo effects, and selective perception.

How can we deal positively with conflict?

- Conflict occurs as disagreements over substantive or emotional issues.
- Managers should support functional conflict that facilitates a high-performance edge and creativity; they should avoid the harmful effects of too little or too much conflict that becomes dysfunctional.
- Conflict may be managed through structural approaches that involve changing people, goals, resources, or work arrangements.
- Personal conflict management styles include avoidance, accommodation, compromise, competition, and collaboration.
- True conflict resolution involves problem solving through a win-win collaborative approach.

How can we negotiate successful agreements?

- Negotiation is the process of making decisions in situations in which the participants have different preferences.
- Both substance goals, those concerned with outcomes, and relationship goals, those concerned with processes, are important in successful negotiation.
- Effective negotiation occurs when issues of substance are resolved and the process results in good working relationships.
- Distributive approaches to negotiation emphasize win-lose outcomes and are usually harmful to relationships.
- Integrative approaches to negotiation emphasize win-win outcomes and the interests of all parties.

KEY TERMS

Accommodation (p. 461)

Active listening (p. 451)

Arbitration (p. 465)

Attribution error (p. 456)

Avoidance (p. 461)

Bargaining zone (p. 464)

BATNA (p. 464)

Channel richness (p. 452)

Collaboration (p. 461)

Communication (p. 446)

Communication channel (p. 448)

Competition (p. 461)

Compromise (p. 461)

Conflict (p. 459)

Conflict resolution (p. 460)

Distributive negotiation (p. 463)

Dysfunctional conflict (p. 459)

Effective communication (p. 446)

Efficient communication (p. 447)

Emotional conflict (p. 459)

Ethnocentrism (p. 455)

Feedback (p. 451)

Filtering (p. 450)

Functional conflict (p. 459)

Halo effect (p. 458)

Integrative negotiation (p. 463)

Lose-lose conflict (p. 461)

MBWA (p. 453)

Mediation (p. 465)

Mixed message (p. 449)

Negotiation (p. 463)

Noise (p. 447)

Nonverbal communication (p. 449)

Perception (p. 456)

Principled negotiation (p. 463)

Projection (p. 458)

Selective perception (p. 458)

Self-serving bias (p. 457)

Stereotype (p. 457)

Substantive conflict (p. 459)

Win-lose conflict (p. 461)

Win-win conflict (p. 462)

SELF-TEST 17

Take this test here or on-line much as you would in a normal classroom situation. It is a good way to check your basic comprehension of chapter material. Answers may be found at the end of the book.

MULTIPLE-CHOICE QUESTIONS:

1. The use of paraphrasing and reflecting back in communication is characteristic of _____.
   (a) mixed messages (b) active listening (c) passive listening
   (d) ethnocentrism

2. When the intended meaning of the sender and the interpreted meaning of the receiver are the same, communication is _____.
   (a) effective (b) perceived (c) selective (d) efficient

3. Constructive feedback is _____.
(a) general rather than specific (b) indirect rather than direct
(c) given in small doses (d) given any time the sender is ready

4. When a manager uses e-mail to send a message that is better delivered in person, the communication process suffers from _____.
(a) semantic problems (b) a poor choice of communication channels
(c) physical distractions (d) status effects

5. _____ can help minimize the risk of status effects limiting upward communication.
(a) Projection (b) One-way communication (c) MBWA
(d) Impression management

6. Cross-cultural communication may run into difficulties because of _____, or the tendency to consider one's culture superior to others.
(a) multiculturalism (b) ethnocentrism (c) mixed messages (d) projection

7. An appeal to superordinate goals is an example of a(n) _____ approach to conflict management.
(a) avoidance (b) structural (c) assertiveness (d) compromise

8. The conflict management style with the greatest potential for true conflict resolution involves _____.
(a) compromise (b) competition (c) smoothing (d) collaboration

9. When a person is highly cooperative but not very assertive in approaching conflict, the conflict management style is referred to as _____.
(a) avoidance (b) authoritative (c) smoothing (d) collaboration

10. The three criteria of an effective negotiation are quality, cost, and _____.

(a) harmony (b) timeliness (c) acceptability (d) durability

TRUE-FALSE QUESTIONS:

11. Effective communication is always efficient.   T   F

12. Of the 10 rules for good listening described in the chapter, "stop talking" is the first and the tenth.   T   F

13. Semantic problems in communication may involve a poor choice of words in a written message.   T   F

14. Senior managers can be highly confident that information received from lower levels is unbiased.   T   F

15. Proxemics deals with how communication involves the use of space.   T   F

16. One-way communications such as e-mail messages are often efficient, but they are not always effective.   T   F

17. The best conflict management style is one of high assertiveness and low cooperativeness.   T   F

18. Substantive conflicts are of managerial concern, but emotional conflicts are not.   T   F

19. Win-lose claims are common among parties engaged in distributive negotiation.   T   F

20. Arbitration involves a neutral third party acting as a judge to resolve a negotiation.   T   F

SHORT-RESPONSE QUESTIONS:

21. Briefly describe what a manager would do to be an "active listener" when communicating with subordinates.

22. What is the difference between the halo effect and selective perception?

23. How do tendencies toward assertiveness and cooperativeness in conflict management result in win-lose, lose-lose, and win-win outcomes?

24. What is the difference between substance and relationship goals in negotiation?

APPLICATION QUESTION:

25. After being promoted to store manager for a new branch of a large department store chain, Harold Welsch was concerned about communication in the store. Six department heads reported directly to him, and 50 full-time and part-time sales associates reported to them. Given this structure, Harold worried about staying informed about all store operations, not just those coming to his attention as senior manager. What steps might Harold take to establish and maintain an effective system of upward communication in his store?

CAREER readiness ACTIVITIES

Recommended learning activities from the *Career Readiness Workbook* for this chapter include:

Career Advancement Portfolio
- Individual writing and group presentation assignments based on any of the following activities.

Case for Critical Thinking
- The United Nations—How Nations Work (or Don't Work) Together

Integrative Learning Activities
- Research Project 1—Diversity Lessons
- Research Project 5—Affirmative Action Directions
- Integrative Case—Outback Steakhouse, Inc.
- Integrative Case—Richard Branson Meets the New Economy

Exercises in Teamwork
- What Managers Do (#2)
- Upward Appraisal (#24)
- Feedback and Assertiveness (#25)
- How to Give, Take Criticism (#26)

Self-Assessments
- Cultural Attitudes Inventory (#5)
- Diversity Awareness (#7)
- Assertiveness (#25)
- Emotional Intelligence (#26)

The *Fast Company* Collection On-Line
- Tony Schwartz, "How Do You Feel?"

ELECTRONIC RESOURCES

@ GET CONNECTED! Don't forget to take full advantage of the on-line support for *Management 7/e.*
- Chapter 17 On-line Study Guide
- Chapter 17 Self-test Answers
- Chapter 17 E-Resource Center

www.wiley.com/college/schermerhorn

18

Change
leadership

Planning
ahead

GETTING CONNECTED

ZF Micro Devices—Continuous Innovation = Competitive Advantage

Talk about great ideas! What about a complete "PC on a chip"? Better yet, make it a complete PC that is crash proof and virus resistant. Possible? Of course, just about anything is possible in today's rapidly advancing high-tech society. But, it takes a real innovator to create a raw concept and then turn it into reality. That's just what David L. Feldman, founder and CEO of ZF Micro Devices Inc., did. And, he did it the hard way.

Feldman's career began as a social worker. When budget cuts put pressure on his future he enrolled in a night course to learn circuit board design. In 1983 he started his first company. He has never looked back.

In 1995 he took $100,000 to start ZF Micro. Five years later it was a 63-person company pushing a great idea—a PC on a chip. The MachZ chip has the power of an early Pentium desktop and works on the Linux operating system. It is specifically designed for smaller appliances and Internet-enabled devices. Many firms are designing products around it—applications range from medical devices to vending machines.

What is ZF Linux's advantage in a market that is highly competitive? It begins with the idea itself. The MachZ isn't just a chip, or a processor that must be coupled with a motherboard. It really is a computer, and the operating system is built in. Thus, it's tiny (1.4 inches square), it's crash proof (the system is embedded in the chip), and it's cheap—just over $50.

But now that Feldman is finding a market for his PC on a chip, a whole host of leadership and management challenges are setting in. By the time you read this he may have taken the firm public with an IPO. He expects orders for as many as 3.5 million MachZs before long. The firm is working on many new product applications, and sales offices have been opened in Europe and South America. And as the market grows, so too will ZF Micro.

Feldman, like other entrepreneurs and innovators, will have to learn how to successfully master the challenges of change leadership to maintain the success of his innovative product and new company. He says: "In bringing the first true PC System-on-a-Chip to the market we were determined to provide world-class software tools to our customers." Now he'll need to build ZF Micro Devices as a competitive world-class company to boot.[1]

@ Get Connected!

Are you ready to participate in an innovation-driven and highly competitive global economy? Do you have good ideas? Can you help others to put their ideas into action? Build your plan for continued personal and professional development. Get connected!

www.clorox.com

Top management at Clorox tries to avoid chasing new management fads. "You need to be fairly selective and consistent over time so you're not upsetting your organization over the tool of the month," says the Vice President of Strategy and Planning. "When top management is linked to fads, confidence is easily undermined in the employee ranks."

When a group of Japanese students drove out of Tokyo one day, the event wouldn't have seemed remarkable to bystanders. But when they arrived some 900 kilometers later on the northern island of Hokkaido, Mitsubishi's president was sure pleased. The students' car, powered by a new engine technology, had made the trip without refueling! In fact, there was fuel to spare in the gas tank. It was an important breakthrough for the company. For a long time engineers had known the feat was technically possible, but they didn't know just how to do it. Finally, through hard work, a lot of information sharing and problem solving, and through learning, they found the answer.[2]

It is answers to problems that move people, organizations, and societies continuously ahead in our dynamic and very challenging world. We are living and working at a time when intellectual capital, knowledge management, and learning organizations are taking center stage. Rightfully so. Harvard scholars Michael Beer and Nitin Nohria observe: "The new economy has ushered in great business opportunities and great turmoil. Not since the Industrial Revolution have the stakes of dealing with change been so high. Most traditional organizations have accepted, in theory at least, that they must either change or die."[3] Speaking from the vantage point of a corporate leader always looking toward the future, John Chambers, CEO of Cisco Systems, would no doubt agree. "Companies that are successful will have cultures that thrive on change," he says, "even though change makes most people uncomfortable."[4]

Unfortunately and even though the watchwords of today continue to be *change, change,* and *change,* many organizations and too many leaders are slow in responding to the challenge. Creating positive change in organizations, as suggested by Chambers, is not an easy task. Change involves complexity, uncertainty, anxiety, and risk. Leading organizations on the pathways of change takes great understanding, discipline, and commitment to creativity and human ingenuity.[5] In his book *The Circle of Innovation,* consultant Tom Peters further warns that we must refocus the attention of managers and leaders away from past accomplishments and toward the role of innovation as the primary source of competitive advantage. Doing well in the past, simply put, is no guarantee of future success.[6]

The future is the issue in this final chapter of *Management 7/e*—organizational futures, managerial futures, and your future. It is time to inquire once more into your managerial abilities to master the challenges of change and career readiness in the evolving new workplace. Take the opportunity to expand your portfolio of career skills to include the capacity for change leadership and self-renewal. As always, get connected!

CHALLENGES OF CHANGE

The World Economic Forum is a famous and futuristic think tank for global business, government, and civic leaders. At the 2001 forum held in Davos, Switzerland, the popular buzzwords were "business Webs," "value networks," "molecular organizations," and more. The following trends and possibilities were prominent among observations about the changing nature of business in the new economy.[7]

Companies that design and brand their own products, build and package them, and then deliver them to customers will soon no longer exist.

Companies (now) have the ability to strip down their business to its essence, to focus on where the greatest value creation (and profits) lies.

Extraneous functions can be eliminated through partnerships and newly supercharged forms of outsourcing.

Instead of one big monolithic entity, companies start to look like clusters of distributed capabilities.

There are those who might go so far as to say that the corporation as we have traditionally known it is dead, or at least dying.[8] For sure the traditional forms, practices, and systems of the past are being replaced by dramatic new developments driven by the forces of information technology and the relentless pressures of global competitiveness. And, this is all happening very fast. No leader in any organization, no matter how big or small and whether operating for-profit or not-for-profit, can fail to take notice. What lies ahead in the emerging digital and networked world of the 21st century is far too challenging for that.

STRATEGIC COMPETITIVENESS

Although the points and details may differ, the conclusion reached by futurists is the same. The years ahead will be radically different from those past. We and our organizations must be prepared not only to change, but to change continuously and in the face of ever-present uncertainties. In earlier chapters we discussed the implications of this prospect to the benefits of **learning organizations**—ones that mobilize people, values, and systems to achieve continuous change and performance improvements driven by the lessons of experience.[9] Scholar and consultant Peter Senge, author of the popular book *The Fifth Discipline,* advises managers to stimulate and lead change in ways that create true learning organizations in which everyone: (1) sets aside old ways of thinking, (2) becomes self-aware and open to others, (3) learns how the whole organization works, (4) understands and agrees to action plans, and (5) works together to accomplish the plans.[10]

○ A **learning organization** utilizes people, values, and systems to continuously change and improve its performance.

ENTREPRENEURSHIP (www.kinkos.com)
Kinko's There's a Lot of Creativity Around a College Campus

What better source of creativity than a college campus? Ideas are all around, there for the taking. But it takes courage to put them to the market test. Some years ago, Paul Orfeala noticed his college student peers lining up repeatedly to use photocopy machines in the library—putting coins in page-by-page. Surely, he thought, there must be a better way. After graduation he opened a photocopy shop near his university. He could have called it "Paul's." Instead he used the nickname given to him in college—Kinko's. Now Kinko's is the world's leading provider of visual communications services and document copying. It is a still-growing global network of over 1,100 digitally connected locations and over 25,000 employees in nine countries.[11]

Senge's learning organization is the ideal; it is the target. It is what change leaders should strive for as they move organizations forward into the complicated world of tomorrow. Consider the boxed example of Kinko's—a success story, to this point in time. But, the real Kinko's story is not the one just told; it's the one that lies ahead. Paul Orfeala cannot allow Kinko's to rest on past laurels. His firm, like others, will survive and prosper in the future only by sustaining its competitive advantage—that is, by creating a combination of attributes that allows the firm to consistently outperform its rivals and that is difficult for them to imitate.

○ **Strategic leadership** creates the capacity for on-going strategic change.

This is a challenge of **strategic leadership**, defined by scholars Duane Ireland and Michael Hitt as the "ability to anticipate, envision, maintain flexibility, think strategically, and work with others to initiate changes that will create a viable future for the organization."[12] Strategic leaders are change leaders that build learning organizations and keep them competitive even in difficult and uncertain times. The goal is to institutionalize as a core competency the ability to successfully and continuously change. Dawn Lepore, Vice chairman and CIO of the financial services firm Charles Schwab, points out that this isn't just pushing change for the sake of change. The change must have a strategic and customer-driven purpose. She says: "What we must have—and I do mean 'must'—is a core competence in reinventing ourselves as the needs of our customers change with the marketplace." *Manager's Notepad 18.1* highlights strategic leadership components that best prepare managers to meet this challenge.[13]

CONTINUOUS INNOVATION

○ **Innovation** is the process of taking a new idea and putting it into practice.

The 21st century world of organizations will be driven by **innovation**, the process of creating new ideas and putting them into practice.[14] Management consultant Peter Drucker calls innovation "an effort to create purposeful, focused change in an enterprise's economic or social potential."[15] Said a bit differently, it is the act of converting new ideas into usable applications that ideally have the positive economic or social consequences. Consider two very different examples.

Groove Neworks, Inc. The firm has been described as "Napster for business" and founder Ray Ozzie is sometimes called the "wizard of peer-to-peer computing." After watching his son play multiplayer games on the Web and his daughter send instant messages, Ozzie realized the potential for new software devoted to "P2P" collaboration in business. The innovative new Groove software, is attracting lots of interest. It should. Ozzie created Lotus Notes, now owned by IBM and selling more than 68 million licenses at last count.[16]

Grammeen Phone What happens when the digital age meets the developing world? Progress, at least if you are part of the Grammeen Bank network in Bangladesh. Most of the country's 68,000 villages have no phone service; the average annual income is about $200. That is changing through an innovative program. The bank makes loans to women entrepreneurs to allow them to buy and operate a cellular telephone, each typically serving an entire village. The bank's goal is twofold: to receive an economic return on its investment and to contribute to economic development. The Canadian International Development Agency praises the social impact, suggesting the model spread to serve the rural poor in other nations.[17]

Innovation in and by organizations occurs in two broad forms: (1) *process innovations*, which result in better ways of doing things; and (2) *product innovations*, which result in the creation of new or improved goods and services. The management of both requires active encouragement and support for *invention*—the act of discovery, and for *application*—the act of use. Invention relates to the development of new ideas. Managers need to be concerned about building new work environments that stimulate creativity and an ongoing stream of new ideas. Application, on the other hand, deals with the utilization of inventions to take the best advantage of ideas. Here, managers must make sure that good ideas for new or modified work processes are actually implemented. They must also make sure that the commercial potential of ideas for new products or services is fully realized.

One way to describe the full set of leadership responsibilities for the innovation process is in these five steps, constituting what consultant Gary Hamel calls the *wheel of innovation*.[18]

1. *Imagining*—thinking about new possibilities; making discoveries by ingenuity or communication with others; extending existing ways. ← Hamel's wheel of innovation
2. *Designing*—testing ideas in concept; discussing them with peers, customers, clients, or technical experts; building initial models, prototypes, or samples.
3. *Experimenting*—examining practicality and financial value through experiments and feasibility studies.
4. *Assessing*—identifying strengths and weaknesses, potential costs and benefits, and potential markets or applications, and making constructive changes.
5. *Scaling*—gearing up and implementing new processes; putting to work what has been learned; commercializing new products or services.

One of the major features of organizational innovation is that the entire process must be related to the needs of the organization and its marketplace. New ideas alone are not sufficient to guarantee success in this setting; they must be implemented effectively in order to contribute to organizational performance.

Figure 18.1 uses the example of new product development to further highlight how the various steps of the innovation process contribute to something of great business significance, **commercializing innova-**

○ **Commercializing innovation** turns ideas into economic value added.

MANAGER'S NOTEPAD 18.1

Six components of strategic leadership

1. Determining the organization's purpose or vision.
2. Exploiting and maintaining the organization's core competencies.
3. Developing the organization's human capital.
4. Sustaining an effective organizational culture.
5. Emphasizing and displaying ethical practices.
6. Establishing balanced organizational controls.

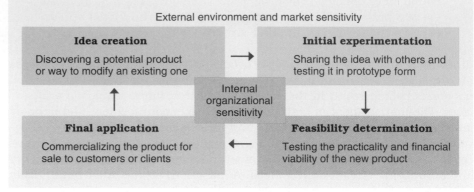

Figure 18.1 Process of innovation in organizations: the case of new product development.

tion.[19] This is the process of turning new ideas into products or processes that can make an economic difference in increased profits through higher sales or reduced costs. For example, 3M Corporation generates over one-third of its revenues from products that didn't exist four years ago. The firm, for whom product innovation is a way of life, owes its success to the imagination of employees like Art Fry. He's the person whose creativity turned an adhesive that "wasn't sticky enough" into the blockbuster product known worldwide today as Post-It Notes.®

CHARACTERISTICS OF INNOVATIVE ORGANIZATIONS

How Employees Rate Corporate Change Programs Companies supposedly live with constant change. A recent survey reports that cost reduction is high on the list of change goals; increasing revenues has a lower priority. These are important goals, but are they being realized? Take the on-line "Reality Check" to learn more about how employees view corporate change initiatives.

Innovative organizations like 3M, Johnson & Johnson, Apple Computer, and others mobilize talent and intellectual capital to support creativity and entrepreneurship. Their managers at all levels are masters at actively leading the innovative process.[20] In highly innovative organizations, the *corporate strategy and culture support innovation*. The strategies of the organization, the visions and values of senior management, and the framework of policies and expectations emphasize an entrepreneurial spirit. Innovation is expected, failure is accepted, and the organization is willing to take risks. For example, Johnson & Johnson's former CEO James Burke once said: "I try to give people the feeling that it's okay to fail, that it's important to fail." The key here is for managers to eliminate risk-averse climates and replace them with organizational cultures in which innovation is expected and failure is accepted.

In highly innovative organizations, *organization structures support innovation*. More and more large organizations are trying to capture the structural flexibility of smaller ones. That is, they are striving for more organic operations with a strong emphasis on lateral communications and cross-functional teams and task forces. In particular, research and development, historically a separate and isolated function, is being integrated into a team setting. As Peter Drucker points out, "Successful innovations . . . are now being turned out by cross-functional teams with people from marketing, manufacturing, and finance participating in research work from the very beginning."[21] Innovative organizations are also reorganizing to create many smaller divisions that allow creative teams or "skunkworks" to operate and to encourage "intrapreneurial" new ventures.

In highly innovative organizations, *top management supports innovation*. In the case of 3M, for example, many top managers have been the innovators and product champions of the company's past. They understand the innovation process, are tolerant of criticisms and differences of opinion, and take all possible steps to keep the goals clear and the pressure on. The key, once again, is to allow the creative potential of people to operate fully.[22]

In highly innovative organizations, *the organization's staffing supports innovation* well. Organizations need different kinds of people to succeed in all stages of the innovation process. The *critical innovation roles* to be filled include the following:[23]

- *Idea generators*—people who create new insights from internal discovery or external awareness, or both.

← Innovation roles in organizations

- *Information gatekeepers*—people who serve as links between people and groups within the organization and with external sources.

- *Product champions*—people who advocate and push for change and innovation in general and for the adoption of specific product or process ideas in particular.

- *Project managers*—people who perform the technical functions needed to keep an innovative project on track with all the necessary resource support.

- *Innovation leaders*—people who encourage, sponsor, and coach others to keep the innovation values and goals in place and channel energies in the right directions.

ORGANIZATIONAL CHANGE

Change is intertwined with the processes of creativity and organizational innovation. Creativity fosters innovation and, according to Drucker, purposeful innovation should result in changes of positive economic or social consequence.[24] This all sounds quite positive and not very controversial. But what about the realities of trying to systematically change organizations and the behaviors of people within them? Is there more to the story? When Angel Martinez became CEO of Rockport Company, for example, he sought to change traditional ways that were not aligned with future competition. Rather than embrace the changes he sponsored, employees resisted. Martinez said they "gave lip service to my ideas and hoped I'd go away."[25] With persistance he was able to bring positive change to the firm. Rockport has since become an important part of Reebok International. Consider also what once happened at Bank of America. After the company announced a large quarterly operating loss, its new CEO at the time, Samuel Armacost, complained about the lack of "agents of change" among his top managers. Claiming that the managers seemed more interested in taking orders than initiating change, Armacost said, "I came away quite distressed from my first couple of management meetings. Not only couldn't I get conflict, I couldn't even get comment. They were all waiting to see which way the wind blew."[26]

CHANGE LEADERSHIP

A **change agent** is a person or group who takes leadership responsibility for changing the existing pattern of behavior of another person or social system. Change agents make things happen, and part of every manager's job is to act as a change agent in the work setting. This requires being alert to sit-

○ A **change agent** tries to change the behavior of another person or social system.

uations or to people needing change, being open to good ideas, and being able to support the implementation of new ideas in actual practice. *Figure 18.2* contrasts a *change leader* with a "status quo manager." The former is forward-looking, proactive, and embraces new ideas; the latter is backward-looking, reactive, and comfortable with habit. Obviously, the new workplace demands change leadership at all levels of management.

MODELS OF CHANGE LEADERSHIP

In Chapter 16 on teams and teamwork, we discussed the concept of distributed leadership in teams. The point was that every team member has the potential to lead by serving group needs for task and maintenance activities. The same notion applies when it comes to change leadership in organizations. The responsibilities for change leadership are ideally distributed and shared top to bottom.

Top-Down Change

○ In **top-down change**, the change initiatives come from senior management.

In **top-down change**, strategic and comprehensive changes are initiated with the goal of comprehensive impact on the organization and its performance capabilities. This is the domain of strategic leadership as discussed earlier in the chapter. Importantly, however, reports indicate that some 70 percent or more of large-scale change efforts actually fail.[27] The most common reason is poor implementation. The success of top-down change is usually determined by the willingness of middle-level and lower-level workers to actively support top-management initiatives. Change programs have little chance of success without the support of those who must implement them. Any change that is driven from the top runs the risk of being perceived as insensitive to the needs of lower-level personnel. It can easily fail if implementation suffers from excessive resistance and insufficient commitments to change. Thus, it is not enough to simply mandate change from the top—it must be supported by effective change leadership. Listed in *Manager's Notepad 18.2* are several lessons learned from the study of successful large-scale transformational change in organizations.[28]

○ **Theory E change** is based on activities that increase shareholder or economic value.

A version of top-down change in business is called **Theory E change**, or change based on activities that increase shareholder or economic value as soon as possible.[29] Managers who pursue Theory E change utilize economic incentives, major restructuring and downsizing, and similar activities in the attempt to improve a firm's financial performance. The approach is very much top-down in nature and may carry heavy costs for employees and even corporate traditions. An example was the major restructuring of General Dynamics, led by new CEO William A. Anders, which resulted in divestiture of seven businesses and workforce reduction of some 71,000 people. But, economic value was improved to the delight of

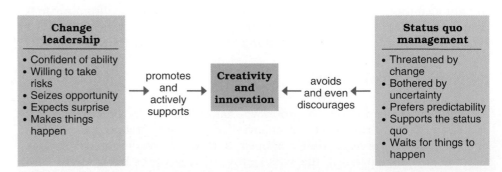

Figure 18.2 Change leadership versus status quo management.

MANAGER'S NOTEPAD 18.2

How to lead transformational change

- Establish a sense of urgency for change.
- Form a powerful coalition to lead the change.
- Create and communicate a change vision.
- Empower others to move change forward.
- Celebrate short-term "wins" and recognize those who help.
- Build on success; align people and systems with new ways.
- Stay with it; keep the message consistent; champion the vision.

---

the financial markets. Theory E change of this type is driven from the top, emphasizes changes in structures and systems, and tries to gain employee support through financial incentives.

Bottom-up Change

Bottom-up change is also important in organizations. In such cases, the initiatives for change come from persons throughout an organization and are supported by the efforts of middle-level and lower-level managers acting as change agents. Bottom-up change is essential to organizational innovation and is very useful in terms of adapting operations and technologies to the changing requirements of work. It is made possible by empowerment, involvement, and participation as discussed in earlier chapters. For example, at Johnson Controls, Inc., Jason Moncer was given the nickname "Mr. Kaizen" by his co-workers.[30] The nickname refers to a Japanese practice of continuous improvement. Moncer earned it by offering many ideas for changes in his work area. At his plant, workers contributed over 200 suggestions that were implemented in just one year alone. The company is committed to the belief that workers should be encouraged to use their job knowledge and common sense to improve things. In other words, when the workers talk, managers listen.

○ In **bottom-up change**, change initiatives come from all levels in the organization.

A version of bottom-up change in business is called **Theory O change**, or change based on activities that increase organizational performance capabilities.[31] Change leaders pursuing the Theory O model try various approaches to improve organizational culture and develop human capital to improve performance capabilities. A historical example is Hewlett-Packard, famous for the "HP Way" and for focusing organizational improvements around building employee commitment to new directions. Theory O change encourages participation from the bottom up, values employee attitudes, progresses step by step through experimentation and evolution, and tries to inspire support through employee involvement.

○ **Theory O change** is based on activities that increase organizational performance capabilities.

Integrated Change Leadership

The most successful and enduring change leadership is that which can harness the advantages of both top-down and bottom-up change. Top-down initiatives may be needed to break traditional patterns and implement difficult economic adjustments; bottom-up initiatives are necessary to build institutional capability for sustainable change and organizational learning. An example is the two-decade-long transformation efforts of Jack Welch at Gen-

eral Electric. When first taking over as CEO in 1981, he began an aggressive top-down E-type restructuring that led to major workforce cuts and a trimmer organization structure. Once underway, however, this evolved into O-type change focusing on employee involvement.

Why Large-Scale Change Efforts Often Fail
Most large-scale change efforts fail because senior executives fail to establish a sense of urgency throughout the organization. Take the on-line "Reality Check" to learn more about reasons for change failure.

A widely benchmarked program called Work-Out is a good example. It actively involves all levels in a process of continuous reassessment and planned change.[32] In Work-Out sessions employees confront their managers in a "town meeting" format, with the manager in front listening to suggestions for removing performance obstacles and improving operations. The managers are expected to respond immediately to the suggestions and support positive change initiatives raised during the session. The ability of the Work-Out design to stimulate bottom-up change has been widely praised as part of GE's efforts at continuous improvement.

PLANNED AND UNPLANNED CHANGE

Planned change occurs as a result of specific efforts by a change agent.

A **performance gap** is a discrepancy between the desired and actual state of affairs.

Unplanned change occurs spontaneously and without a change agent's direction.

We are particularly interested in **planned change** that occurs as a result of the specific efforts of a change agent. Planned change is a direct response to a person's perception of a **performance gap**, or a discrepancy between the desired and actual state of affairs. Performance gaps may represent problems to be resolved or opportunities to be explored. In each case, managers as change agents should be ever alert to performance gaps and take action to initiate planned changes to deal with them.

But, **unplanned changes** are important too. They occur spontaneously or randomly and without the benefit of a change agent's attention. Unplanned changes may be disruptive, such as a wildcat strike that results in a plant closure, or beneficial, such as an interpersonal conflict that results in a new procedure on interdepartmental relations. The appropriate goal in managing unplanned change is to act immediately once it is recognized in order to minimize negative consequences and maximize possible benefits.

FORCES AND TARGETS FOR CHANGE

The impetus for organizational change can arise from a variety of external forces.[33] These include the global economy and market competition, local economic conditions, government laws and regulations, technological developments, market trends, and social forces, among others. As an organi-

High Performance Toro Company
Mistakes Can Be Turned into Successes

Since its founding in 1914, Toro has created many innovative products for the landscaping and lawn-care markets. But success doesn't always come in a straight line. Once, when a new molding technique didn't work, Toro lost mower sales. Members of the engineering team responsible for the technique were called to the CEO's office. But instead of "pink slips," they were met with a party that included balloons and a cake. The celebration was in honor of the risk they had taken. Later, it was found that the technique could be used successfully in the production of other Toro products.[34]

zation's general and specific environments develop and change over time, the organization must adapt as well. Internal forces for change are important too. Indeed, any change in one part of the organization as a complex system—perhaps a change initiated in response to one or more of the external forces just identified—can often create the need for change in another part of the system.

The many targets for planned change are found among all the aspects of organizations already discussed in this book. All of them, including the following common *organizational targets for change*—tasks, people, culture, technology, and structure—are highly interrelated:[35]

- *Tasks*—the nature of work as represented by organizational mission, objectives, and strategy, and the job designs for individuals and groups.

←
Organizational targets for change

- *People*—the attitudes and competencies of the employees and the human resource systems that support them.

- *Culture*—the value system for the organization as a whole and the norms guiding individual and group behavior.

- *Technology*—the operations and information technology used to support job designs, arrange workflows, and integrate people and machines in systems.

- *Structure*—the configuration of the organization as a complex system, including its design features and lines of authority and communications.

MANAGING PLANNED CHANGE

Change is a complicated phenomenon in any setting, and human nature always stands at the heart of it. People tend to act habitually and in stable ways over time. They may not want to change even when circumstances require it. As a manager and change agent, you will need to recognize and deal with such tendencies in order to successfully lead planned change.

PHASES OF PLANNED CHANGE

Kurt Lewin, a noted psychologist, recommends that any planned-change effort be viewed as the three-phase process shown in *Figure 18.3*.[36] Lewin's three phases of planned change are (1) *unfreezing*—preparing a system for change; (2) *changing*—making actual changes in the system; and (3) *refreezing*—stabilizing the system after change.

Unfreezing

In order for change to be successful, people must be ready for it. Planned change has little chance for long-term success unless people are open to doing things differently. **Unfreezing** is the stage in which a situation is prepared for change and felt needs for change are developed. It can be facilitated in several ways: through environmental pressures for change, declining performance, the recognition that problems or opportunities exist, and through the observation of behavioral models that display alternative approaches. When handled well, conflict can be an important unfreezing force in organizations. It often helps people break old habits and recognize alternative ways of thinking about or doing things.

○ **Unfreezing** is the phase during which a situation is prepared for change.

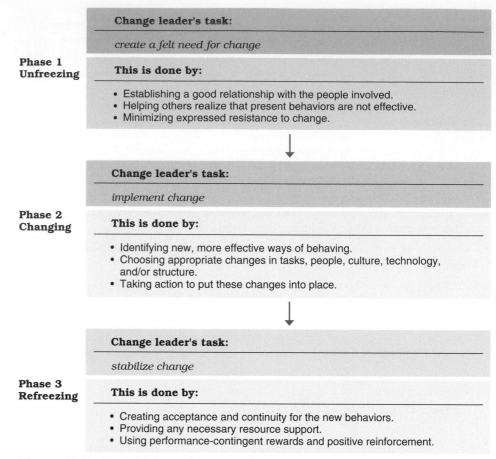

Figure 18.3 Lewin's three phases of planned organizational change.

Changing

○ **Changing** is the phase where a planned change actually takes place.

In the **changing** phase, something new takes place in a system, and change is actually implemented. This is the point at which managers initiate changes in such organizational targets as tasks, people, culture, technology, and structure. Ideally, all change is done in response to a good diagnosis of a problem and a careful examination of alternatives. However, Lewin believes that many change agents enter the changing phase prematurely, are too quick to change things, and therefore end up creating resistance to change. When managers implement change before people feel a need for it, consequently, there is an increased likelihood of failure.

Refreezing

○ **Refreezing** is the phase at which change is stabilized.

The final stage in the planned-change process is **refreezing.** Here, the manager is concerned about stabilizing the change and creating the conditions for its long-term continuity. Refreezing is accomplished by appropriate rewards for performance, positive reinforcement, and providing necessary resource support. It is also important to evaluate results carefully, provide feedback to the people involved, and make any required modifications in the original change. When refreezing is done poorly, changes are too easily forgotten or abandoned with the passage of time. When it is done well, change can be more long lasting.

CHOOSING A CHANGE STRATEGY

Managers use various approaches when trying to get others to adopt a desired change. *Figure 18.4* summarizes three common change strategies known as force-coercion, rational persuasion, and shared power.[37] Each can have very different consequences for change agent and change target alike.

Force-Coercion Strategies

A **force-coercion strategy** uses the power bases of legitimacy, rewards, and punishments as the primary inducements to change. A change agent that seeks to create change through force-coercion believes that people who run things are basically motivated by self-interest and by what the situation offers in terms of potential personal gains or losses.[38] This change agent believes that people change only in response to such motives, tries to find out where their vested interests lie, and then puts the pressure on. Once a weakness is found, it is exploited. The change agent is always quick to work "politically" by building supporting alliances wherever possible. If the change agent has formal authority, she or he uses it along with whatever rewards and punishments are available. As Figure 18.4 shows, the likely outcomes of force-coercion are immediate compliance but little commitment.

> A **force-coercion strategy** pursues change through formal authority and/or the use of rewards or punishments.

Force-coercion can be pursued in at least two ways, both of which can be commonly observed in organizations. In a *direct forcing* strategy, the change agent takes direct and unilateral action to "command" that change take place. This involves the exercise of formal authority or legitimate power, offering special rewards, and/or threatening punishment. In *political maneuvering,* the change agent works indirectly to gain special advantage over other persons and thereby make them change. This involves bargaining, obtaining control of important resources, or granting small favors.

Regardless of the exact approach taken, the force-coercion strategy on its own produces limited results. Although it can be implemented rather quickly, most people respond to this strategy out of fear of punishment or hope for a reward. This usually results in only temporary compliance with the change agent's desires. The new behavior continues only so long as the opportunity for rewards and punishments is present. For this reason, force-coercion is most useful as an unfreezing device that helps people break old patterns of behavior and gain initial impetus to try new ones. The example of General Electric's Work-Out program, noted earlier, applies here.[39] Jack

Change Strategy	Power Bases	Managerial Behavior	Likely Results	
Force–Coercion Using position power to create change by decree and formal authority	Legitimacy Rewards Punishments	*Direct forcing* and unilateral action *Political maneuvering* and indirect action	Fast	Temporary compliance
Rational Persuasion Creating change through rational persuasion and empirical argument	Expertise	*Informational efforts* using credible knowledge, demonstrated facts, and logical argument		
Shared power Developing support for change through personal values and commitments	Reference	*Participative efforts* to share power and involve others in planning and implementing change	Slow	Longer term Internalization

Figure 18.4 Alternative change strategies and their leadership implications.

Welch started Work-Out to create a forum for active employee empowerment of continuous change. But, he didn't make the program optional. Like others of Welch's change initiatives at the firm, participation in Work-Out was mandatory from the start. Welch used his authority as leader to initiate a new program that he felt confident would survive and prosper on its own—once it was experienced. Part of his commitment to change leadership was a willingness to use authority as needed to get things started.

Rational Persuasion Strategies

○ A **rational persuasion strategy** pursues change through empirical data and rational argument.

Change agents using a **rational persuasion strategy** attempt to bring about change through persuasion backed by special knowledge, empirical data, and rational argument. A change agent following this strategy believes that people are inherently rational and are guided by reason in their actions and decision making.[40] Once a specific course of action is demonstrated to be in a person's self-interest, the change agent assumes that reason and rationality will cause the person to adopt it. Thus, he or she uses information and facts to communicate the essential desirability of change.

The likely outcome of rational persuasion is eventual compliance with reasonable commitment. When successful, a rational persuasion strategy helps both unfreeze and refreeze a change situation. Although slower than force-coercion, it tends to result in longer lasting and internalized change. To be successful, a manager using rational persuasion must convince others that the cost–benefit value of a planned change is high and that it will leave them better off than before. This can come directly from the change agent if she or he has personal credibility as an "expert." If not, it can be obtained in the form of consultants and other outside experts, or from credible demonstration projects and benchmarks. The magic of Walt Disney World, for example, extends to more than family fun and holidays. Disney, the company, is widely respected for its business and management practices. Many firms use Disney to both benchmark and demonstrate to employees how change initiatives can improve their own operations. A Ford vice president says, "Disney's track record is one of the best in the country as far as dealing with customers." The firm sends managers to Disney to learn about customer loyalty, hoping to drive customer-service initiatives of their own.[41] In this sense the power of rational persuasion is straightforward: If it works for Disney, why can't it work for us?

Shared Power Strategies

○ A **shared power strategy** pursues change by participation in assessing values, needs, and goals.

A **shared power strategy** engages people in a collaborative process of identifying values, assumptions, and goals from which support for change will naturally emerge. The process is slow, but it is likely to yield high commitment. Sometimes called a *normative reeducative strategy,* this approach is based on empowerment and is highly participative in nature. It relies on involving others in examining personal needs and values, group norms, and operating goals as they relate to the issues at hand. Power is shared by the change agent and other persons as they work together to develop a new consensus to support needed change.

Managers using shared power as an approach to planned change need referent power and the skills to work effectively with other people in group situations. They must be comfortable allowing others to participate in making decisions that affect the planned change and the way it is implemented. Because it entails a high level of involvement, this strategy is often quite time consuming. But importantly, power sharing is likely to result in a longer-lasting and internalized change.

A change agent who shares power begins by recognizing that people have varied needs and complex motivations.[42] He or she believes people behave as they do because of sociocultural norms and commitments to the expectations of others. Changes in organizations are understood to inevitably involve changes in attitudes, values, skills, and significant relationships, not just changes in knowledge, information, or intellectual rationales for action and practice. Thus, when seeking to change others, this change agent is sensitive to the way group pressures can support or inhibit change. In working with people, every attempt is made to gather their opinions, identify their feelings and expectations, and incorporate them fully into the change process.

The great "power" of sharing power in the change process lies with unlocking the creativity and experience available from within the system, and often missed at the top. Unfortunately, many managers are hesitant to engage this process for fear of losing control of the strategic direction, or of having to compromise on important organizational goals. Harvard scholar Teresa M. Amabile, however, points out that managers and change leaders should have the confidence to share power regarding means and processes, but not overall goals. "People will be more creative," she says, "if you give them freedom to decide how to climb particular mountains. You needn't let them choose which mountains to climb."[43]

UNDERSTANDING RESISTANCE TO CHANGE

Change typically brings with it resistance. When people resist change, furthermore, they are defending something important and that appears to them as threatened by the attempted change. A change of work schedules for workers in ON Semiconductor's Rhode Island plant, for example, may not have seemed like much to top management. But to the workers it was significant enough to bring about an organizing attempt by the Teamster's Union. When management delved into the issues, they found that workers viewed changes in weekend work schedules as threatening to their personal lives. With inputs from the workers, the problem was resolved satisfactorily.[44]

There are any number of reasons why people in organizations may resist planned change. Some of the more common ones are shown in *Manager's Notepad 18.3.* Such resistance is often viewed by change agents and managers as something that must be "overcome" in order for change to be successful. This is not necessarily true. Resistance is better viewed as feedback that the informed change agent can use to constructively

---

modify a planned change to better fit situational needs and goals. When resistance appears, it usually means that something can be done to achieve a better "fit" between the planned change, the situation, and the people involved. Going back to the issue of work schedules once again, this conversation with a manager is reported by Jim Stam, a shift work consultant with Circadian Technologies. *Manager*—"Come on, Jim, there must be one schedule that's the right schedule for this industry." *Jim*— "Yes, it's the one the people in the plant pick."[45]

DEALING WITH RESISTANCE TO CHANGE

Once resistance to change is recognized and understood, it can be dealt with in various ways.[46] Among the alternatives for effectively managing resistance, the *education and communication* approach uses discussions, presentations, and demonstrations to educate people beforehand about a change. *Participation and involvement* allows others to contribute ideas and help design and implement the change. The *facilitation and support* approach involves providing encouragement and training, actively listening to problems and complaints, and helping to overcome performance pressures. *Facilitation and agreement* provides incentives that appeal to those who are actively resisting or ready to resist. This approach makes trade-offs in exchange for assurances that change will not be blocked. *Manipulation and co-optation* tries to covertly influence others by providing information selectively and structuring events in favor of the desired change. *Explicit and implicit coercion* forces people to accept change by

---

MANAGER'S NOTEPAD 18.3

Why people may resist change

- *Fear of the unknown*—not understanding what is happening or what comes next.
- *Disrupted habits*—feeling upset when old ways of doing things can't be followed.
- *Loss of confidence*—feeling incapable of performing well under the new ways of doing things.
- *Loss of control*—feeling that things are being done "to" you rather than "by" or "with" you.
- *Poor timing*—feeling overwhelmed by the situation or that things are moving too fast.
- *Work overload*—not having the physical or psychic energy to commit to the change.
- *Loss of face*—feeling inadequate or humiliated because it appears that the "old" ways weren't "good" ways.
- *Lack of purpose*—not seeing a reason for the change and/or not understanding its benefits.

threatening resistors with a variety of undesirable consequences if they do not go along as planned. Obviously, the last two approaches carry great risk and potential for negative side effects.

MANAGING TECHNOLOGICAL CHANGE

Technological change is common in today's organizations, but it also brings special challenges to change leaders. For the full advantages of new technologies to be realized, a good fit must be achieved with work needs, practices, and people. This, in turn, requires sensitivity to resistance and continual gathering of information so that appropriate adjustments can be made all during the time a new technology is being implemented. In this sense, the demands of managing technological change have been described using the analogy of contrasting styles between navigators from the Micronesian island of Truk and their European counterparts.[47]

The European navigator works from a plan, relates all moves during a voyage to the plan, and tries to always stay "on course." When something unexpected happens, the plan is revised systematically, and the new plan followed again until the navigator finds the ship to be off course. The Trukese navigator, by contrast, starts with an objective and moves off in its general direction. Always alert to information from waves, clouds, winds, etc., the navigator senses subtle changes in conditions and steers and alters the ship's course continually to reach the ultimate objective.

Like the navigators of Truk, technological change may best be approached as an ongoing process that will inevitably require improvisation as things are being implemented. New technologies are often designed external to the organization in which they are to be used. The implications of such a technology for a local application may be difficult to anticipate and plan for ahead of time. A technology that is attractive in concept may appear complicated to the new users; the full extent of its benefits and/or inadequacies may not become known until it is tried. This, in turn, means that the change leader and manager should be alert to resistance, should continually gather and process information relating to the change, and should be willing to customize the new technology to best meet the needs of the local situation.[48]

www.hyatt hotels.com

For many years Hyatt Hotels has used surveys to examine organizational climate and effectiveness. A questionnaire to all employees asks: "Tell us what you think of management." From this they create a General Morale Index that is closely watched by senior management.

ORGANIZATION DEVELOPMENT

Among consulting professionals, **organization development (OD)** is known as a comprehensive approach to planned organizational change that involves the application of behavioral science in a systematic and long-range effort to improve organizational effectiveness.[49] *Organization development* is supposed to help organizations cope with environmental and other pressures for change while also improving their internal problem-solving capabilities. OD, in this sense, brings the quest for continuous improvement to the planned-change process.

There will always be times when the members of organizations should sit together and systematically reflect on strengths and weaknesses

○ **Organization development** is a comprehensive effort to improve an organization's ability to deal with its environment and solve problems.

as well as performance accomplishments and failures. Organization development is one way to ensure that this happens in a supportive and action-oriented environment. OD is an important avenue through which leaders can advance planned-change agendas, foster creativity and innovation, and more generally assist people and systems to continuously improve organizational performance. It often involves the assistance of an external consultant or an internal staff person with special training. But importantly, all managers should have the skills and commitment to utilize the various elements of OD in their continuous-improvement agendas. The notion of organization development dovetails nicely with the popular concepts of total quality management (TQM) and employee involvement discussed throughout this book. In fact, the OD approach may offer added opportunities to utilize them to the best advantage.[50]

ORGANIZATION DEVELOPMENT GOALS

In organization development two goals are pursued simultaneously. The *outcome goals of OD* focus on task accomplishments, while the *process goals of OD* focus on the way people work together. It is this second goal that strongly differentiates OD from more general attempts at planned change in organizations. You may think of OD as a form of "planned change plus," with the "plus" meaning that change is accomplished in such a way that organization members develop a capacity for continued self-renewal. That is, OD tries to achieve change while helping organization members become more active and self-reliant in their ability to continue changing in the future. What also makes OD unique is its commitment to strong humanistic values and established principles of behavioral science. OD is committed to improving organizations through freedom of choice, shared power, and self-reliance, and by taking the best advantage of what we know about human behavior in organizations.

HOW ORGANIZATION DEVELOPMENT WORKS

Figure 18.5 presents a general model of OD and shows its relationship to Lewin's three phases of planned change. To begin the OD process successfully, any consultant or facilitator must first *establish a working relationship* with members of the client system. The next step is *diagnosis—* gathering and analyzing data to assess the situation and set appropriate change objectives. This helps with unfreezing as well as pinpointing

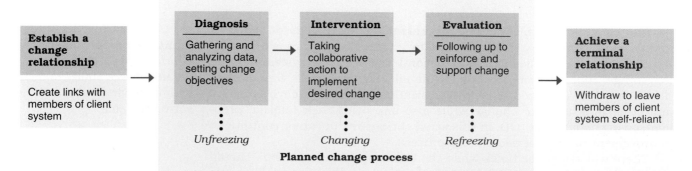

Figure 18.5 Organization development and the planned change process.

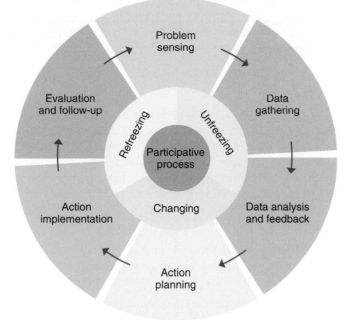

Figure 18.6 Action research is a foundation of organization development.

appropriate directions for action. Diagnosis leads to active *intervention,* wherein change objectives are pursued through a variety of specific interventions, a number of which will be discussed shortly.

Essential to any OD effort is *evaluation.* This is the examination of the process to determine whether things are proceeding as desired and whether further action is needed. Eventually, the OD consultant or facilitator should *achieve a terminal relationship* that leaves the client able to function on its own. If OD has been well done, the system and its members should be better prepared to manage their ongoing need for self-renewal and development.

The success or failure of any OD program lies in part in the strength of its methodological foundations. As shown in *Figure 18.6,* these foundations rest on **action research**—the process of systematically collecting data on an organization, feeding it back to the members for action planning, and evaluating results by collecting more data and repeating the process as necessary. Action research is initiated when someone senses a performance gap and decides to analyze the situation to understand its problems and opportunities. Data gathering can be done in several ways. Interviews are a common means of gathering data in action research. Formal written surveys of employee attitudes and needs are also growing in popularity. Many such "climate," "attitude," or "morale" questionnaires have been tested for reliability and validity. Some have even been used so extensively that norms are available so that one organization can compare its results with those from a broad sample of counterparts.

> **Action research** is a collaborative process of collecting data, using it for action planning, and evaluating the results.

ORGANIZATION DEVELOPMENT INTERVENTIONS

The foundations of organization development include respect for people and a commitment to their full participation in self-directed change processes. It is employee involvement in action. OD rallies an organization's human resources through teamwork and in support of constructive change. This process is evident in the variety of **OD interventions** or

> An **OD intervention** is a structured activity that helps create change in organization development.

activities that are initiated to directly facilitate the change processes. Importantly, these interventions are linked to concepts and ideas discussed elsewhere in this book and that are well represented in the practices and approaches of the new workplace.[51]

Individual Interventions

Concerning individuals, organization development practitioners generally recognize that the need for personal growth and development are most likely to be satisfied in a supportive and challenging work environment. They also accept the premise that most people are capable of assuming responsibility for their own actions and of making positive contributions to organizational performance. Based on these principles, some of the more popular OD interventions designed to help improve individual effectiveness include the following:

Individual OD interventions →

- *Sensitivity training*—unstructured sessions (T-groups) where participants learn interpersonal skills and increased sensitivity to other people.
- *Management training*—structured educational opportunities for developing important managerial skills and competencies.
- *Role negotiation*—structured interactions to clarify and negotiate role expectations among people who work together.
- *Job redesign*—realigning task components to better fit the needs and capabilities of the individual.
- *Career planning*—structured advice and discussion sessions to help individuals plan career paths and programs of personal development.

Team Interventions

The team plays a very important role in organization development (OD). OD practitioners recognize two principles in this respect. First, teams are viewed as important vehicles for helping people satisfy important needs. Second, it is believed that improved collaboration within and among teams can improve organizational performance. Selected OD interventions designed to improve team effectiveness include the following:

Team OD interventions →

- *Team building*—structured experiences to help team members set goals, improve interpersonal relations, and become a better functioning team.
- *Process consultation*—third-party observation and advice on critical team processes (e.g., communication, conflict, and decision making).
- *Intergroup team building*—structured experiences to help two or more teams set shared goals, improve intergroup relations, and become better coordinated.

Organization-Wide Interventions

At the level of the total organization, OD practitioners operate on the premise that any changes in one part of the system will also affect other parts. The organization's culture is considered to have an important impact on member attitudes and morale. And it is believed that structures and jobs can be designed to bring together people, technology, and systems in highly productive and satisfying working combinations. Some of the OD interventions often applied with an emphasis on organizational effectiveness include the following:

- *Survey feedback*—comprehensive and systematic data collection to identify attitudes and needs, analyze results, and plan for constructive action.
- *Confrontation meeting*—one-day intensive, structured meetings to gather data on workplace problems and plan for constructive actions.
- *Structural redesign*—realigning the organization structure to meet the needs of environmental and contextual forces.
- *Management by objectives*—Formalizing MBO throughout the organization to link individual, group, and organizational objectives.

← Organization-wide OD interventions

PERSONAL CHANGE AND CAREER READINESS

Now is the final chance for us to raise once again the issue of *you,* your continued personal and professional development and your career readiness. When it comes to career success during changing times, one thing without a doubt will remain true—*what happens is up to you.*

EARLY CAREER ADVICE

In times like ours where change is ever-present, fast-moving, and often unpredictable, the management of one's career and career development is extremely challenging. The challenges become even more magnified in the context of career entry, when one is beginning a new job with a new employer. In terms of early career advice, *lesson one* is clear: there is no substitute for performance. No matter what the assignment, you must work hard to quickly establish your credibility and value in any new job. The advice of *lesson two* is also undeniable: you must be and stay flexible. Don't hide from ambiguity; don't depend on structure. Instead, you must be always able and willing to adapt personally to new work demands, new situations and people, and new organizational forms. The demands of *lesson three* help keep the focus: you can't go forward without talent. You must commit to continuous learning and professional development. In order to get and stay ahead in a career during very competitive times, you must become a talent builder—someone who is always adding to and refining your talents to make them valuable to an employer. This requires discipline in continuously seeking the learning opportunities from your daily experiences, including the ones that present problems and prove difficult for you. The "ability" to learn can only benefit you personally when accompanied by the "willingness" to learn.

According to noted author and consultant Stephen Covey, the foundations for career success are within everyone's grasp. But, both the motivation and the effort required to succeed must come from within. Only you can make this commitment, and it is best made right from the beginning. Covey's advice is for you to take charge of your destiny, and to always move your career forward by: (1) behaving like an entrepreneur, (2) seeking feedback on your performance continually, (3) setting up your own mentoring systems, (4) getting comfortable with teamwork, (5) taking risks to gain experience and learn new skills, (6) being a problem solver, and (7) keeping your life in balance.[52]

www.motorola.com

Motorola's "internal readiness" program helps make sure women and minorities get the assistance they need for corporate success. A vice president says, "We're talking about competitive advantage. If everybody else is stuck in the muck and mire of sexism and racism and we can blow out of that, look at all the people who will be available to us who the competition can't get."

BUILDING THE BRAND CALLED "YOU"

The best career advice returns again and again to the same message—what happens is up to you. Don't let yourself down. Step forward and take charge of your continued learning and professional development. Build, refine, and market what author and consultant Tom Peters refers to as the "brand called 'you.'" Peters advises each of us to continually work hard to create and maintain a unique and timely package of skills and capabilities with career potential. In Peters words, your personal brand should be "remarkable, measurable, distinguished, and distinctive" relative to the competition—others like you.[53]

SUSTAINING CAREER ADVANTAGE

> ○ **Sustainable career advantage** is a combination of personal attributes that allows you to consistently outperform others in meeting needs of employers.

As with organizations that must innovate to achieve competitive advantage in their markets, you must be able to quickly adapt to the demands of an ever-changing workplace, economy, and career environment. As shown in *Figure 18.7*, this means that you must establish and maintain a **sustainable career advantage**. This is a combination of personal attributes—skills and capabilities—that allow you to consistently outperform others, that are continuously improving, and that are always timely and relevant to the needs of employers.

The following section in *Management 7/e* contains an extensive Career Readiness Workbook. It is designed to help you begin the process of brand building and to prepare your credentials for sustainable career advantage in a world of dynamic employment opportunities. Hopefully you have already taken advantage of many learning activities offered in the workbook. Its many options are well worth serious attention.

Don't neglect the opportunity to build your personal Career Advancement Portfolio to document your academic and personal accomplishments for external review. Of particular importance is a skill and outcome assessment that shows potential employers your capabilities in the important areas of professionalism, leadership, self-management,

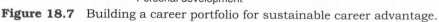

Figure 18.7 Building a career portfolio for sustainable career advantage.

TAKE IT TO THE CASE!

Walt Disney Company
Where Brand Building Is an Art Form

Yes, brand building is an art form at the company that Walt Disney built. He began in 1922 with a firm called Laugh-O-Gram Films. It failed in 1923. But Walt didn't give up. Later that year he and brother Roy launched Disney Brothers Studio on $3,000. The company has changed a lot since then, now a global giant and a benchmark in organizational practices. It's all built with human talent and an eye to the future. The firm's Professional Development Institute offers programs in leadership, service, and creativity that are highly valued within the firm and externally. "Join us," says the corporate electronic billboard advertising Disney careers. "We are a cast of thousands . . . our varied backgrounds, personalities and talents make us each an integral part of team Disney."[54]

communication, teamwork, and critical thinking. Talent that builds from these foundations is what today's employers are looking for, both among full-time employees and student interns.

Use your career portfolio to show important skills and outcomes gained from your management studies. Put the entire package on-line as a means of further distinguishing yourself from the competition. Once started, your **electronic career portfolio** can be easily maintained as a continuing resource for self-assessment and personal development, as well as to communicate your talents to potential employers.

Management 7/e has been rich with insights into the new workplace, the nature of managerial work, and the great challenges organizations face in a highly competitive global economy. As you move forward in this exciting world of work, you must continue the process of brand building and continue to strengthen your potential for a satisfying life-long career. You have to master the challenges of change without forgetting the goal: sustainable career advantage. Also, you can never forget that career development is a personal responsibility. Although many foundations have been set during your management course and other university studies, what happens next and in your career future is up to you.

There is no better time than the present to begin the process of career advancement. Make the commitment to move forward, right now. Get and stay connected!

○ An **electronic career portfolio** documents academic and personal accomplishments on-line for external review.

STUDY
Guide

The Chapter 18 Study Guide will help you review chapter content, prepare for examinations, and further build your career readiness. The *Summary* briefly highlights answers to questions first posed in the chapter opening Planning Ahead section. The list of *Key Terms* allows you to double check your familiarity with basic concepts and definitions. *Self-Test 18* gives you the opportunity to test your basic comprehension of chapter content using sample test questions. Suggestions offered as *Career Readiness Activities* direct your attention to relevant sections of the end-of-text Career Readiness Workbook, as well as to special Electronic Resources on the *Management 7/e* web site.

SUMMARY

What are the challenges of change?

- The future will be like our past; always unpredictable, very challenging, and full of continuous change.
- A learning organization is one in which people, values, and systems support innovation and continuous change based upon the lessons of experience.
- Organizations need strategic leaders who work with a strategic direction to initiate and successfully implement changes that help organizations perform well in changing environments.
- Innovation allows creative ideas to be turned into products and/or processes that benefit organizations and their customers.
- Highly innovative organizations tend to have supportive cultures, strategies, structures, staffing, and top management.
- The possible barriers to innovation in organizations include a lack of top management support, excessive bureaucracy, short time horizons, and vested interests.

What is the nature of organizational change?

- Change leaders are change agents who take responsibility for helping to change the behavior of people and organizational systems.
- Managers should be able to spot change opportunities and lead the process of planned change in their areas of work responsibilities.

- Although organizational change can proceed with a top-down emphasis, inputs from all levels of responsibility are essential to achieve successful implementation.
- Theory E change seeks to improve economic performance through restructuring; Theory O change seeks to build organizational capability through improved culture and human resource development.
- The many possible targets for change include organizational tasks, people, cultures, technologies, and structures.

How can planned organizational change be managed?

- Lewin identified three phases of planned change: unfreezing—preparing a system for change; changing—making a change; and refreezing—stabilizing the system with a new change in place.
- Good change agents understand the nature of force-coercion, rational persuasion, and shared power change strategies.
- People resist change for a variety of reasons, including fear of the unknown and force of habit.
- Good change agents deal with resistance positively and in a variety of ways, including education, participation, facilitation, manipulation, and coercion.
- The special case of technological change requires an openness to resistance and willingness to improvise as implementation proceeds.

What is organization development?

- Organization development (OD) is a comprehensive approach to planned organization change that uses principles of behavioral science to improve organizational effectiveness over the long term.
- OD has both outcome goals, with a focus on improved task accomplishment, and process goals, with a focus on improvements in the way people work together to accomplish important tasks.
- The OD process involves action research wherein people work together to collect and analyze data on system performance and decide what actions to take to improve things.
- OD interventions are structured activities that are used to help people work together to accomplish change; they may be implemented at the individual, group, and/or organizational levels.

How do you build career readiness in a change environment?

- What happens in your career is up to you; take responsibility for building and maintaining a competitive "brand called 'you.'"
- Take charge of your learning; create a career portfolio that documents at all times your career readiness by displaying critical skills and accomplishments.
- Use the insights, examples, and concepts from *Management 7/e* and your introductory management course as a strong foundation for lifelong personal development and career advancement.

KEY TERMS

Action research (p. 491)

Bottom-up change (p. 481)

Change agent (p. 479)

Changing (p. 484)

Commercializing innovation (p. 477)

Electronic career portfolio (p. 495)

Force-coercion strategy (p. 485)

Innovation (p. 476)

Learning organizations (p. 475)

OD interventions (p. 491)

Organization development (p. 489)

Performance gap (p. 482)

Planned change (p. 482)

Rational persuasion strategy (p. 486)

Refreezing (p. 484)

Shared power strategy (p. 486)

Sustained career advantage (p. 494)

Strategic leadership (p. 476)

Theory E change (p. 480)

Theory O change (p. 481)

Top-down change (p. 480)

Unfreezing (p. 483)

Unplanned change (p. 482)

SELF-TEST 18

Take this test here or on-line much as you would in a normal classroom situation. It should offer you a good way to check your basic comprehension of chapter material. Answers may be found at the end of the book.

MULTIPLE-CHOICE QUESTIONS:

1. In organizations, both product innovation, creating new goods or services, and _____ innovation, creating new ways of doing things, are important.
   (a) content (b) process (c) quality (d) task

2. The first step in Hamel's "wheel of innovation" is _____.
   (a) imagining (b) assessing (c) experimenting (d) scaling

3. In an innovative organization, _____ support(s) innovation.
   (a) strategy and culture (b) structure (c) top management (d) all of these.

4. A manager using a force-coercion strategy will rely on _____ to bring about change.
   (a) expertise (b) reference (c) rewards, punishments, or authority
   (d) information

5. The most participative of the planned change strategies is _____.
   (a) force-coercion (b) rational persuasion (c) shared power (d) command

6. Trying to covertly influence others, offering only selective information, and/or structuring events in favor of the desired change are ways of dealing with resistance by _____.
   (a) participation (b) manipulation and cooptation (c) force-coercion (d) facilitation

7. In organization development (OD), both _____ and _____ goals are important.
   (a) task, maintenance (b) management, labor (c) outcome, process (d) profit, market share

8. Sensitivity training and role negotiation are examples of organization development interventions at the _____ level.
   (a) individual (b) group (c) systemwide (d) organization

9. The concept of empowerment is most often associated with the _____ strategy of planned change.
   (a) market-driven (b) rational persuasion (c) direct forcing (d) normative-reeducative

10. Unfreezing occurs during the _____ step of organizational development.
    (a) diagnosis (b) intervention (c) evaluation (d) termination

TRUE-FALSE QUESTIONS:

11. According to consultant Peter Senge, today's leaders and managers should create "learning" organizations.   T   F

12. A good strategic leader is always a change leader.   T   F

13. Top management support is helpful but not essential to organizational innovation.   T   F

14. Successful change in organizations occurs only in bottom-up and never in top-down fashion.   T   F

15. Unplanned change can be good for organizations.   T   F

16. Successful technological change often involves improvisation and adjustments during the change process.   T   F

17. Organization development (OD) is a short-run approach to improving organizational effectiveness.   T   F

18. Organizations always require outside consultants in order to continue with organization development.   T   F

19. The confrontation meeting is an OD intervention to improve overall organizational effectiveness.   T   F

20. In a changing environment there is little anyone can do to maintain career readiness.   T   F

SHORT-RESPONSE QUESTIONS:

21. Identify and explain the importance of three internal targets for organizational change.

22. What are the three phases of change described by Lewin, and what do they mean?

23. What are the major differences in potential outcomes achieved by managers using the force-coercion, rational persuasion, and shared power strategies of planned change?

24. What does the statement "OD equals planned change plus" mean?

APPLICATION QUESTION:

25. As a newly appointed manager in any work setting, you are liable to identify things that "could be done better" and to have many "new ideas" that you would like to implement. Based on the ideas presented in this chapter, how should you go about effecting successful planned change in such situations?

CAREER readiness ACTIVITIES

Recommended learning activities from the end-of-text *Career Readiness Workbook* for this chapter include:

Career Advancement Portfolio
- Individual writing and group presentation assignments based on any of the following activities.

Case for Critical Thinking
- The Walt Disney Company—Walt's Legacy Keeps Growing

Integrative Learning Activities
- Research Project 2—Changing Corporate Cultures
- Integrative Case—Outback Steakhouse, Inc.
- Integrative Case—Richard Branson Meets the New Economy

Exercises in Teamwork
- My Best Manager (#1)
- Leading through Participation (#4)
- Personal Career Planning (#10)
- The Future Workplace (#13)
- Empowering Others (#19)

Self-Assessments
- A 21st-Century Manager? (#1)
- Turbulence Tolerance Test (#24)
- Internal/external Locus of Control (#11)

The *Fast Company* Collection On-Line
- Robert Reich, "The Company of the Future"
- Tom Peters, "The Brand Called 'You'"

ELECTRONIC RESOURCES

@ GET CONNECTED! Don't forget to take full advantage of the on-line support for *Management 7/e*.
- Chapter 18 On-line Study Guide
- Chapter 18 Self-test Answers
- Chapter 18 E-Resource Center

www.wiley.com/college/schermerhorn

CAREER READINESS
READINESS
W O R K B O O K

Career Advancement Portfolio®

What Is a Career Advancement Portfolio®?
Planning Your Career Advancement Portfolio®
Resume Writing Guide
Interview Preparation Guide
Skill and Outcome Assessment Template

Getting Started with Your Career Advancement Portfolio®
Paper Portfolio Format
Electronic Portfolio Builder
Career Development Plan
Sample Portfolio Components

Cases for Critical Thinking

1. **Apple Computer. Inc.**—Passion, design and the future

2. **The Coca-Cola Company**—Diversity and a global presence

3. **Sun Microsystems**—Will Sun rule the Web?

4. **United Parcel Service**—Information technology hits the road

5. **Harley Davidson**—Is there a case for protection?

6. **Tom's of Maine**—Doing good while doing business

7. **Wal-Mart**—E-tailing in a world of super stores

8. **Procter & Gamble**—A Web-based turnaround?

9. **Domino's Pizza**—Could you do it?

10. **Nucor Corporation**—Structuring for efficiency and effectiveness

11. **Pricewaterhouse Coopers**—Changing economy, mission, design

12. **BET Holdings II. Inc.**—Building the best African-American Internet portal

13. **Southwest Airlines**—How Herb Kelleher led the way

14. **Saturn Inc.**—Making pay-for-performance pay off

15. **Boeing Company**—Talent builds a better plane

16. **Steinway & Sons**—Combining craftwork and teamwork

17. **The United Nations**—Getting nations to work together

18. **The Walt Disney Company**—Walt's legacy keeps growing

Integrative Learning Activities

Research and Presentation Projects
1. **Diversity Lessons**
2. **Changing Corporate Cultures**
3. **Foreign Investment in America**
4. **Corporate Social Responsibility**
5. **Affirmative Action Directions**
6. **Controversies in CEO Pay**

*Additional Projects Are Available On-Line

Cross-Functional Integrative Cases
Outback Steakhouse, Inc.

Richard Branson Meets the New Economy

Exercises in Teamwork

1. **My Best Manager**
2. **What Managers Do**
3. **Defining Quality**
4. **Leading Through Participation**
5. **What Would the Classics Say?**
6. **The Great Management History Debate**
7. **What Do You Value in Work?**
8. **Confronting Ethical Dilemmas**
9. **Beating the Time Wasters**
10. **Personal Career Planning**
11. **Strategic Scenarios**
12. **The MBO Contract**
13. **The Future Workplace**
14. **Dots and Squares Puzzle**
15. **Interviewing Job Candidates**
16. **Work vs. Family**
17. **Compensation and Benefits Debate**
18. **Sources and Uses of Power**

@ GET CONNECTED! Don't forget to utilize the following at the *Management 7/E* Electronic Resources web site: www.wiley.com/college/schermerhorn.

- On-line updated Cases for Critical Thinking
- Extra on-line Research and Presentation Projects
- On-line Integrative Cross-functional Cases
- On-line Self-Assessments (workbook assessments and more)
- The *Fast Company* Collection on-line

@ *Fast Company* Collection On-Line!

Robert Reich, "The Company of the Future"
Alan Weber, "Danger: Toxic Company"
Scott Kirsner, "Collision Course"
Tony Schwartz, "How do You Feel?"
Tom Peters, "The Brand Called You"

Note: All case sources within this workbook section are readily available on our web site: www.wiley.com/college/schermerhorn.

Career Advancement Portfolio

David S. Chappell
John R. Schermerhorn, Jr.

OHIO UNIVERSITY

A *Career Advancement Portfolio*® (CAP) is a paper or electronic collection of documents that summarizes your academic and personal accomplishments in a way that effectively communicates with academic advisors and potential employers.[1]

At a minimum, your CAP should include the following:

Minimum components of a Career Advancement Portfolio

- an up-to-date professional resume.
- a listing of courses in your major and related fields of study.
- a listing of your extra-curricular activities and any leadership positions.
- documentation of your career readiness in terms of skills and learning outcomes.

The purpose of a CAP is twofold—academic assessment and career readiness.

1. *Academic Assessment Goal* The CAP serves as an ongoing academic assessment tool that documents your learning and career readiness throughout your university stay. As you progress through a curriculum, the portfolio depicts the progress you are making in acquiring the skills and competencies necessary to be successful in lifelong career pursuits. Over time, it will become increasingly sophisticated in

[1] See David S. Chappell and John R. Schermerhorn, Jr., "Using Electronic Student Portfolios in Management Education: A Stakeholder Perspective," *Journal of Management Education*, vol. 23 (1999), pp. 651–62.

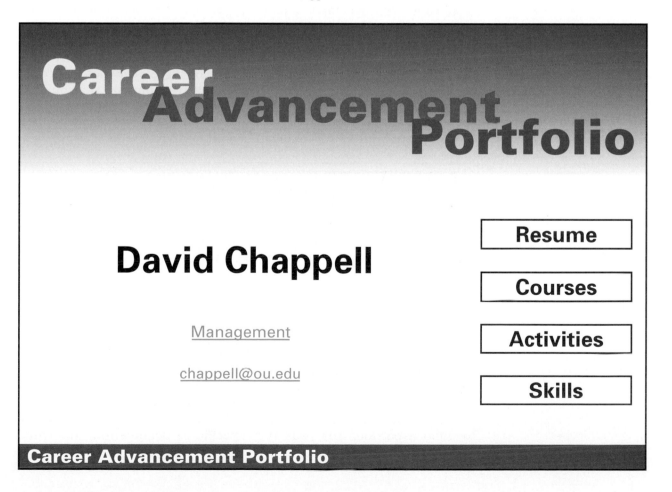

Career Advancement Portfolio

David Chappell

Management

chappell@ou.edu

Resume

Courses

Activities

Skills

Career Advancement Portfolio

the range and depth of capabilities and accomplishments that are documented. A well-documented CAP is a very effective way of summarizing your academic achievements in consultation with both faculty advisors and professors.

2. *Career Readiness Goal* The CAP serves as an important means of communicating your resume and credentials to potential employers as you search for internship and full-time job opportunities. Here, the portfolio evolves into an effective career tool that offers insight far beyond the standard resume. Potential employers can readily examine multiple aspects of your accomplishments and skill sets in order to make a desired match. A professional and complete CAP allows potential employers to easily review your background and range of skills and capabilities. It may convey your potential to a much greater depth and with a more positive impression than a traditional resume. There is no doubt that a professional and substantive CAP can help set you apart from the competition and attract the interest of employers.

Planning Your *Career Advancement Portfolio*®

Your CAP should document, in a progressive and developmental manner, your credentials and accomplishments as they build throughout your academic career. As you progress through the curriculum in your major and supplementary fields of study, the CAP should be refined and materials added to display your most up-to-date skills, competencies, and accomplishments. Use of the *Management 7/e* Skill and Outcome Assessment Framework, described shortly, will help you to do this. We ask our students to utilize the CAP as a portfolio for storing and assessing their written work in our courses, and for assessing their skills and accomplishments as part of our department's formal outcome assessment program.

The closer you get to graduation, the entries in your CAP should become more specific to your job and career goals. In this way, your personal CAP becomes a dynamic and evolving career tool with value far beyond that of the standard resume. We recommend that our students plan their CAPs to serve two immediate career purposes: (1) obtain a professional internship for the junior/senior year period, and (2) obtain their initial full-time job postgraduation.

> **@ GET CONNECTED!** Take the opportunity to interact with the on-line version of the *Career Advancement Portfolio*®. Visit the electronic career portfolio builder at www.wiley.com/college/schermerhorn.

A good example of what a CAP can do for you was introduced in Chapter 1 in the example of the electronic student portfolio created and maintained by Ronald Larimer while a student at Ohio University. Ron began his CAP early in his junior year and then used it successfully to obtain his desired internship and also his first choice of full-time job. Beginning with his resume, Ron continued to build the CAP and add materials that showed his developing skills and competencies over the course of his program of studies. By the time of graduation, his CAP included a very professional resume that documented his major courses and grades, leadership activities, part-time work experiences and internship, and his extensive computer skills.

Ron Larimer took advantage of his coursework and assignments to build a portfolio that was very specific in documenting his career readiness. He included for review by potential employers actual samples of his skills at computer programming, his use of spreadsheet and database software, his writing skills in the form of a one-page executive memorandum and a research report, an Excel data analysis, and a PowerPoint presentation.

These are just a few examples of the many different types of materials that you can include in your personal CAP as testimonies to your academic accomplishments and career readiness. Why don't you get started now by going on-line to build the front page for your electronic *Career Advancement Portfolio*®? Get connected!

Resume Writing Guide

The first thing that should go into your CAP is a professional resume. Don't worry about how sophisticated or complete it is at first. The important things are to (1) get it started and (2) continue to build it throughout your academic program of study. You'll be surprised at how complete it will become with systematic attention and a personal commitment to take full advantage of the professional development opportunities available to you.

We have provided a template, or resume builder, on the *Management 7/e* web site. It is in the format of the example that is also provided here. Take a look at the example—A. Gayle Hunter's resume. It shows both a professional format and the types of things that can and should be included. We have annotated the sample to show how an internship recruiter or potential employer might respond when reading the resume for the first time. Wouldn't you like to have such positive reactions to the accomplishments and experiences documented in your resume?

Interview Preparation Guide

You'll know that your CAP was worthwhile and successful when it helps you land a preferred internship or your first-choice job. But the CAP is just part of the process; it helps get you to the point of a formal interview. In order to help you prepare for this step in the recruiting process, consider the following tips on job interviewing.[2]

- *Research the organization*—Make sure you read their recent literature, including annual reports, scan current news reports, and examine the industry and their major competitors.

- *Prepare to answer common interview questions*—Sample questions include: What do you really want to do in life? What do you consider your greatest strengths and weaknesses? How can you immediately contribute to our organization? Why did you choose your college or university? What are your interests outside of work? What was your most rewarding college experience? How would one of your professors describe you? What do you see yourself doing five years from now?

- *Dress for success*—Remember that impressions count, and first impressions often count the most. If you aren't sure what to wear or how to look, get advice from your professors and from career counselors at your college or university.

[2] This section and the tips were recommended by our colleague Dr. Lenie Holbrook of Ohio University.

Sample Resume for Career Advancement Portfolio

■ Note: The annotations indicate positive reactions by a prospective employer to the information being provided.

■ [Web site support for building your personal resume is provided at www.wiley.com/college/schermerhorn.]

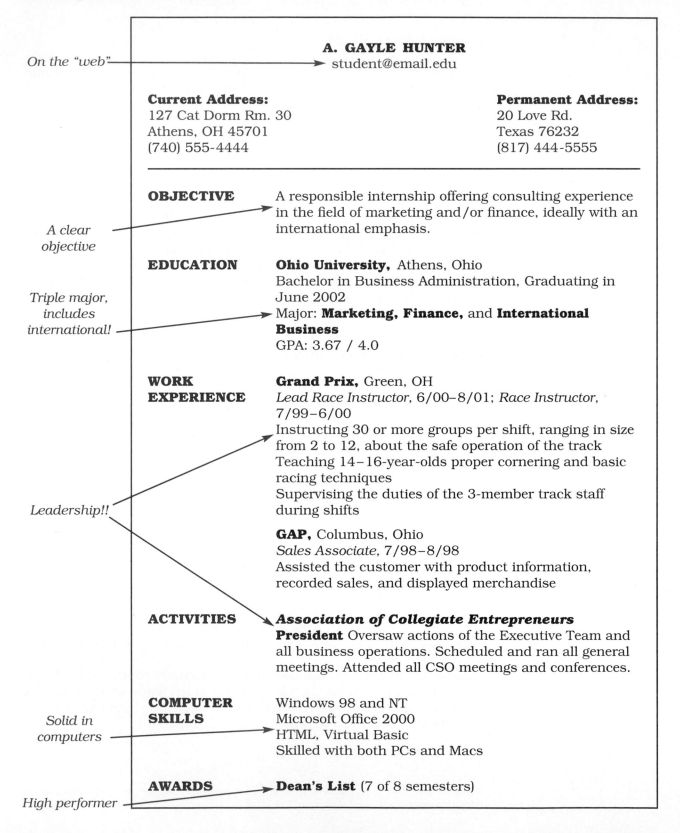

On the "web"

A clear objective

Triple major, includes international!

Leadership!!

Solid in computers

High performer

A. GAYLE HUNTER
student@email.edu

Current Address:
127 Cat Dorm Rm. 30
Athens, OH 45701
(740) 555-4444

Permanent Address:
20 Love Rd.
Texas 76232
(817) 444-5555

OBJECTIVE
A responsible internship offering consulting experience in the field of marketing and/or finance, ideally with an international emphasis.

EDUCATION
Ohio University, Athens, Ohio
Bachelor in Business Administration, Graduating in June 2002
Major: **Marketing, Finance,** and **International Business**
GPA: 3.67 / 4.0

WORK EXPERIENCE
Grand Prix, Green, OH
Lead Race Instructor, 6/00–8/01; Race Instructor, 7/99–6/00
Instructing 30 or more groups per shift, ranging in size from 2 to 12, about the safe operation of the track
Teaching 14–16-year-olds proper cornering and basic racing techniques
Supervising the duties of the 3-member track staff during shifts

GAP, Columbus, Ohio
Sales Associate, 7/98–8/98
Assisted the customer with product information, recorded sales, and displayed merchandise

ACTIVITIES
Association of Collegiate Entrepreneurs
President Oversaw actions of the Executive Team and all business operations. Scheduled and ran all general meetings. Attended all CSO meetings and conferences.

COMPUTER SKILLS
Windows 98 and NT
Microsoft Office 2000
HTML, Virtual Basic
Skilled with both PCs and Macs

AWARDS
Dean's List (7 of 8 semesters)

Skill and Outcome Assessment Framework

Communication - Demonstrates ability to share ideas and findings clearly in written and oral expression.

- Writing
- Oral presentation
- Giving and receiving feedback
- Technology utilization

Leading - Demonstrates ability to influence and support others to perform complex and ambiguous tasks.

- Diversity awareness
- Global awareness
- Project management
- Stragetic leadership

Teamwork - Demonstrates ability to work effectively as a team member and a team leader.

- Team contribution
- Team leadership
- Conflict management
- Negotiation and consensus building

Critical Thinking - Demonstrates ability to gather and analyze information for creative problem solving

- Problem solving
- Judgment and decision making
- Information gathering/interpretation
- Creativity and innovation

Self-Management - Demonstrates ability to evaluate oneself, modify behavior, and meet obligations.

- Ethical understanding/behavior
- Personal flexibility
- Tolerance for ambiguity
- Performance responsibility

Professionalism - Demonstrates ability to sustain a positive impression, instill confidence and advance in a career.

- Personal presence
- Personal initiative
- Career management
- Unique "value added"

- *Dine for success*—There are no inverview "time-outs" for refreshments or meals. The interview is always on. Make sure that you know how to dine in the presence of others. If you don't, get help before the interview.

- *Follow-up*—After the interview send a "thank you" letter, ideally no longer than a week later. In the letter be sure to mention specific things about the organization that were important/insightful to you, and take the opportunity to clarify again where and how you believe you would fit as a valuable employee. Be prompt in providing any additional information requested during the interview.

Skill and Outcome Assessment Framework

Skill and outcome assessment is an increasingly important part of management education. It allows you to document key academic accomplishments and career readiness for faculty review and for review by potential employers. Following the suggestions of the AACSB, International Association for Management Education, we have integrated with *Management 7/e* a Skill and Outcome Assessment Framework that focuses on the following six areas of professional development.

Six components of the professional Skill and Outcome Assessment Framework

1. *Communication*—Demonstrates ability to share ideas and findings clearly in written and oral expression, and with technology utilization.

2. *Leadership*—Demonstrates ability to influence and support others to perform complex and ambiguous tasks.

3. *Teamwork*—Demonstrates ability to work effectively as a team member and as a team leader.

4. *Critical Thinking*—Demonstrates ability to gather and analyze information for creative problem solving.

5. *Self-Management*—Demonstrates ability to evaluate oneself, modify behavior, and meet obligations.

6. *Professionalism*—Demonstrates ability to sustain a positive impression, instill confidence, and advance in a career.

Each of the learning resources and activities to follow in the *Management 7/e* Career Readiness Workbook—cases, projects, exercises, self-assessments, and professional readings—are linked with one or more of these skills and outcome assessment areas. There is no better time than the present to start participating in the learning experiences and documenting your results and accomplishments in your CAP. For convenience, the complete *Management 7/e* Skill and Outcome Assessment Framework is available on-line. Get Connected!

Getting Started with Your *Career Advancement Portfolio*®

The supplementary resource materials available with *Management 7/e* support the development of your personal CAP in either paper or electronic versions. In both cases, the basic portfolio consists of (1) a professional resume and (2) a compendium of coursework samples that display your career readiness skills and capabilities.

Paper Portfolio Format

The easiest way to organize a paper portfolio is with a three-ring binder. This binder should be professional in appearance and have an attractive cover page that clearly identifies it as your CAP. The binder should be indexed with dividers that allow a reader to easily browse the resume and other materials to gain a complete view of your special credentials. To help you get started with a paper portfolio, the following sections offer samples of coursework materials that our students have placed in their CAPs.

Electronic Portfolio Builder

In today's age of information technology and electronic communication, it is highly recommended that you develop an on-line or electronic *Career Advancement Portfolio*.® This format allows you to communicate easily and effectively through the Internet with employers offering potential internship and job placements. An on-line version of your CAP can be displayed either on your personal web site or on one provided by your university. Once you have created an electronic portfolio, it is easy to maintain. It is also something that will impress reviewers and help set you apart from the competition. At the very least, the use of an electronic CAP communicates to potential employers that you are a full participant in this age of information technology. Easy-to-use instructions and templates for building your personal and electronic CAP are available on the *Management 7/E web site.*

Career Development Plan—A Recommended Portfolio Project

A very good way to start your personal CAP is by completing the following project as part of your introductory management course, or on your own initiative. Called the "Career Development Plan," the objective of this project is to identify professional development opportunities that you can take advantage of while in college to advance your personal career readiness. Instructions for the project are available both here and in an on-line interactive version.

Deliverable: Write and file in your electronic or paper *Career Advancement Portfolio®* a two-part memorandum that is written in professional format and addressed to your instructor or to "prospective employer." The memorandum should do the following.

- *Part A.* Answer the question: What are my personal strengths and weaknesses as a potential manager?

    It is recommended that you utilize the *Management 7/e* Skill & Outcome Assessment Framework in structuring your analysis. It is also recommended that you support your answer in part by analysis of scores and results from a selection of teamwork exercises and self-assessments both in this workbook and on the *Management 7/e* web site. You can also supplement the analysis with other relevant personal insights.

- *Part B.* Answer the question: How can I best take advantage of opportunities remaining in my undergraduate experience to improve my managerial potential?

    Make this answer as specific as possible. Describe a clear plan of action that encompasses the time available to you between now and graduation. This plan should include summer and intercession activities, as well as academic and extracurricular experiences. Your goal should be to build a resume and career portfolio through these activities that will best present you as a skilled and valuable candidate for the entry-level job that you would like in your chosen career field.

Evaluation: Your career development memorandum should be professional and error-free, and meet the highest standards of effective written communication. It should be sufficiently analytical in Part A to show serious consideration of your personal strengths and weaknesses in managerial potential at this point in time. It should be sufficiently detailed and in-depth in Part B so that you can objectively evaluate your progress step-by-step between now and graduation. Overall, it should be a career development plan you can be proud to formally include in your CAP and share with potential employers interested in hiring you for a summer internship or for a full-time job.

Sample: What follows is an Excerpt from a Student's Career Development Plan submitted in one of the author's classes. Note that this student not only completed a set of self-assessments from the Career Readiness Workbook as part of the project, she also asked friends and relatives to assess her on the same instruments. She submitted the

The Objective

To analyze a person's managerial and leadership skills, there must first be a way to assess them. Dr. Schermerhorn has developed a web site complete with self-assessments for student use (Schermerhorn, 2001). For the purpose of this study, I have completed the following self-assessments.

Organizaitonal Design Preference	Least Preferred Coworker Score	T-T Leadership Results	Cultural Attitudes Inventory	Two-Factor Profile
Conflict Mgt. Styles	Theory X and Y	Personal Power Profile	My Skills Inventory	Classroom Ethics

Upon completion of each section, I could see how my personal views ranked toward certain qualities of managing and leadership techniques.

In addition, I have compiled graphics that compare my results with the averages of my female classmates, as well as the class as a whole. *(click here to view)* I also obtained additional assessments on my potential managing qualities from others who know me well and have compiled charts and explanations of those results. *(click here to view)*

Personal Strengths

As a potential manager, I found through the self-assessments and also how others assessed my views, that I do possess some strengths. I found that I am strong in both my transactional and transformational leadership methods. For successful future leaders, it is necessary to have great strength in both. I also found that I value job content a bit more than job context, but both are relatively close.

final report electronically, along with supporting Excel analyses and graphs to present the assessment results. This excerpt is from her on-line posting of the project.

Sample *Career Advancement Portfolio*® Components

The *Career Readiness Workbook* in *Management 7/e* is rich with resources that can help you fill in your CAP, and document accomplishments with the core skill and outcome assessment areas. We encourage you to take full advantage of the cases, research projects, team exercises, self-assessments, and professional readings as part of your course experience. The assignments that you produce while working with them can be included in your CAP—assuming that they meet the test of true professional quality.

The following samples are taken from the CAPs built by our students. They document a range of accomplishments and capabilities. As with the sample resume presented earlier, we have shown them here with illustrative comments (written in red) that show how a prospective employer might react when reading them in print or viewing them on-line. As you look at these samples, ask: "How can I take best advantage of my course accomplishments to document my career readiness?"

Executive Memorandum

MEMORANDUM

Professional format →

Date: September 10, 2001
To: Professor Chappell
From: Cherlene Hall
Re: MGT300 Internet Report on Novell, Inc.

**Novell:
The
Networking
Company**

Novell is the world's leading network software provider. Novell makes possible the connected enterprise, bringing structure to the Internet to make it a serious business tool. Novell empowers customers to take charge of the changes brought on by the proliferation of the Internet and intranets.

Clear, easy to understand

Good written expression! →

Novell software solutions include server-operating environments, network applications, and distributed network services. These solutions enable businesses of all sizes to integrate the diverse information resources within their organizations and to access the global Internet. Businesses deploy Novell networks to make more efficient use of information technology, improve customer service, and enhance communication and collaboration both internally and with customers, partners, and suppliers.

Incorporated in 1983, Novell helped create the local-area network (LAN) market by delivering the first server-based software products to connect personal computers.

Written Assignment in French

La Conception de L'Amour Pendant toute L'Histoire

La conception de l'amour pendant toute l'histoire est tres interresant de voir. Pendant l'histoire, les formes de l'amour ont change un peu, mais l'idee le plus de base reste la meme. Dans les ouvrages au XVIeme siecle, on peut trouver les idees de l'amour qui sont semblable a la conception de l'amour dans notre societe moderne. Avec un comparaison entre la poesie de Louise Labe et Ronsard au XVIeme siecle, et le film Indochine, que Regis Wargnier a realise a 1992, on peut voir la conception de l'amour pendant l'histoire.

Second language skill!! →

Pour bien comprendre la comparaison de l'amour entre le film moderne est les ouvrages au XVIeme siecle, on doit savoir un petit resume du film. La guerre a Indochine n'arretait pas pour le francais jusqu'a le mai, 1954. Pendant cette periode, une fille

International Virtual Teamwork Project

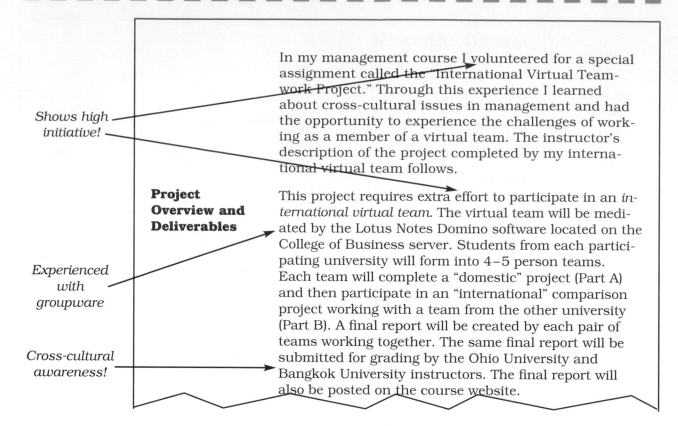

Shows high initiative!

In my management course I volunteered for a special assignment called the "International Virtual Teamwork Project." Through this experience I learned about cross-cultural issues in management and had the opportunity to experience the challenges of working as a member of a virtual team. The instructor's description of the project completed by my international virtual team follows.

Project Overview and Deliverables

Experienced with groupware

This project requires extra effort to participate in an *international virtual team*. The virtual team will be mediated by the Lotus Notes Domino software located on the College of Business server. Students from each participating university will form into 4–5 person teams. Each team will complete a "domestic" project (Part A) and then participate in an "international" comparison project working with a team from the other university (Part B). A final report will be created by each pair of teams working together. The same final report will be submitted for grading by the Ohio University and Bangkok University instructors. The final report will also be posted on the course website.

Cross-cultural awareness!

Slide from PowerPoint Presentation

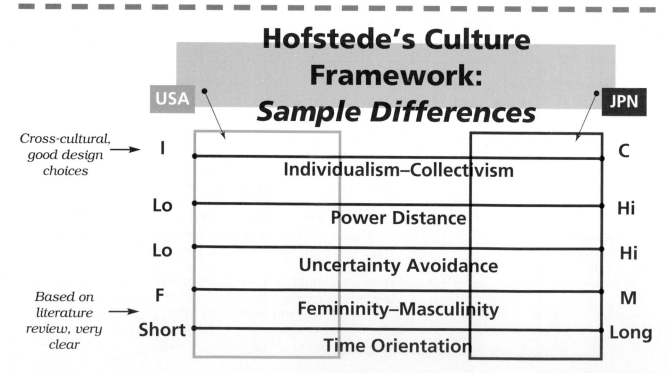

Hofstede's Culture Framework: *Sample Differences*

USA — JPN

Cross-cultural, good design choices → I — Individualism–Collectivism — C

Lo — Power Distance — Hi

Lo — Uncertainty Avoidance — Hi

F — Femininity–Masculinity — M

Based on literature review, very clear → Short — Time Orientation — Long

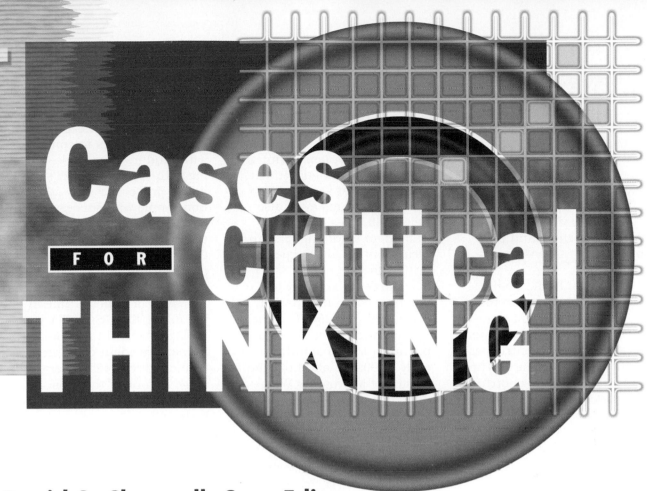

Cases FOR Critical THINKING

David S. Chappell, Case Editor

CASE 1

Apple Computer, Inc.: Passion, Design, and the Future

Apple Computer paradoxically exists as both one of America's greatest successes as well as one of its greatest failures. It single-handedly created the personal computer industry, bringing such behemoths as IBM and Digital Equipment almost to their knees. At the same time, Apple is an example of opportunities lost due to large personal egos and poor management decisions. It represents a fascinating microcosm of American business.

Corporate History

The history of Apple Computer is a history of passion among its founders, employees, and loyal users. Started by a pair of Stevens, Steven Wozniak and Steven Jobs, both had an interest in electronics at an early age, with Wozniak at Hewlett-Packard and Jobs at Atari. Wozniak constructed his first personal computer, the Apple I, and along with Jobs, created Ap-

Note: All cases are available in updated on-line versions. The blue underscored words/phrases in the cases indicate Internet links. See the *MANAGEMENT 7/e* web site at www.wiley.com/college/schermerhorn.

ple Computer on April 1, 1976.[1]

However, it wasn't until 1977 and the introduction of the Apple II, with its plastic case and color graphics, that things began to take off. The addition of a floppy drive in early 1978 added to the popularity of the new computer. By 1980, the release of the Apple III found the company with several thousand employees and Steven Jobs at the helm.

Early on Apple Computer exhibited an extreme emphasis on new and innovative styling in its computer offerings. Jobs' eccentric personality pervaded the culture of Apple and all the people who worked there. He took a personal interest in the development of new products, including the Lisa and the legendary MacIntosh, with its graphical interface and 3.5 inch floppy disk.

The passion Apple is so famous for was clearly evident in the design of the MacIntosh. Project teams worked around the clock to develop the machine, in addition to its innovative graphical user interface (GUI) operating system (Mac OS). Based loosely on a design developed by the Xerox Palo Alto Research Center, the use of graphical icons to create simplified user commands was immensely popular.[2]

With the entrance of IBM into the personal computer market in 1981, Jobs realized that it was time for Apple to "grow up." In early 1983, he was able to persuade John Sculley, then president of Pepsi-Cola, to join Apple as President. The two men clashed almost from the start, with Sculley eventually ousting Jobs from the company.

After struggling early,

the launch of the Mac II, with its increased speed with its Motorola chip and expandability, reinvigorated Apple's sales once again. The twin introductions of the LaserWriter, the first affordable PostScript laser printer for the Mac, and PageMaker, one of the first Desktop Publishing programs ever, also helped lift sales. These two in tandem made the Mac an ideal solution for inexpensive publishing.[3]

However, a saturated personal computer market, due largely to IBM PC-clones of every variety, caused Apple huge problems in the early 1990s. In addition, the launch of Microsoft's Windows 3.0, a greatly improved version of the Wintel operating system, proved a major obstacle for Apple.

A major turning point occurred in 1991, when Apple contemplated licensing its Mac operating system to other computer manufacturers and making it run on Intel-based machines. Had the firm chosen this strategy, it may well be that Apple would be the present-day Microsoft. However, Apple's COO at the time, Michael Spindler, nixed the idea, saying that it was "too late to license."[4]

Innovative Design to the Rescue

In the 1990s, Apple introduced the very popular Powerbooks notebook computer line, along with the unsuccessful Newton personal digital assistant. Sculley, having lost interest in the day-to-day operations of Apple, was eventually forced out and replaced with Michael Spindler.

Spindler oversaw a number of innovations, in-

cluding the PowerMac family, the first Macs to be based on the PowerPC chip, an extremely fast processor co-developed with IBM and Motorola. The PowerPC processor allowed Macs to compete with, and in many cases surpass, the speed of Intel's newer processors.[5] In addition, Apple was successful in licensing its operating system to a number of Mac-cloners, but never with the necessary numbers to extend its market share.

After a difficult time in the mid-1990s, Spindler was replaced with Gil Amelio, the former president of National Semiconductor. This set the stage for one of the most famous returns in corporate history.

After leaving Apple, Steven Jobs started NeXT computer, an advanced personal computer with a sleek, innovative design. However, with its proprietary software, the device never caught a large following. Jobs then cofounded Pixar computer-animation studios in the late 1980s. It has co-produced Toy Story, Toy Story 2, and A Bug's Life with Walt Disney Studios.[6]

Jobs' Return

In late 1996, Apple announced the purchase of NeXT, a computer firm that Steven Jobs had developed after leaving the firm. Jobs returned to Apple in an unofficial capacity as advisor to the President. However, with the resignation of Gil Amelio, Jobs eventually accepted the role of "interim CEO" (i CEO) of Apple Computer. He wasted no time in making his return felt.

Jobs announced an alliance with its former rival,

Microsoft. In exchange for $150 million in Apple Stock, Microsoft and Apple would have a 5-year patent cross-license for their graphical interface operating systems. He revoked licenses allowing the production of Mac clones, and started offering Macs over the web through the Apple Store.

In addition to a slew of new product offerings, Jobs introduced the iMac, with a revolutionary see-through design that has proved popular amongst consumers. This was followed shortly by the iBook, a similar-type portable computer. Apple once again was viewed as an industry innovator, with its revolutionary designs and innovations.[7]

Unfortunately, Apple remains a relatively small player in the computer industry. While its products are wildly popular among a dedicated set of users, it still commands a little over 5 percent of the total computer market. It remains locked in constant boom-or-bust cycles dependent on its ability to turn out a stream of new product hits.

What Does the Future Hold?

Apple is faced with a stark reality: Can it continue to offer both hardware and software solutions in a rapidly changing technology environment? Its decision early on to keep its technology proprietary, as opposed to IBM's decision to support an open architecture system, has proved to be a costly strategy to support in the long run.

There are those that argue that Apple should reinvent itself once again, and this time concentrate on

software. Apple is gradually admitting that it can no longer afford to fight the Wintel system, the combination of Microsoft's Windows operating system and the Intel processor. Apple's new product introductions fail to attract many present non-Mac users—just 15 per cent of its revenues come from Wintel customers.[8]

Apple is betting that its new operating system, the Mac OS X, will be a big hit with computer users. It is the largest update in the operating system since it was first released in the mid-1980s. Once again, will this attract new buyers, or just recycle present Apple enthusiasts?

Much of Apple's problems stem from a crowded computer market. In order to attract buyers from outside its core constituent group, the firm is forced to slash prices. In addition, it has failed to recognize the popularity of CD-ROM or DVD technology, just recently offering these options on Apple computers.

Part of Apple's new corporate strategy, developed in the face of a massive slowdown in the technology industry, involves taking advantage of the explosion of personal electronic devices—CD-players, MP3 players,

digital cameras, DVD-players, etc.—by building Mac-only applications that added value to those devices. Just as iMovie adds tremendous value to Digital Cameras, iDVD adds value to Digital Cameras and to DVD-players, and iTunes adds value to CD and MP3 players. It is Apple's hope that making the Mac the "Digital Hub" of the new "Digital Lifestyle" will revitalize Apple's sales and guarantee the long-term security of the company.[9]

You Do the Research

1. Can Apple continue as an independent concern with such a small share of the computer market?
2. Should the firm provide its operating system to run on both Apple and PC systems?
3. What would you suggest to Steven Jobs that he do to popularize the Apple computer line?

Review Questions

1. Why is Apple not a dominant provider of personal computers?
2. Can Apple Survive?
3. If you were advising Jobs, what would you suggest?
4. Locate five sources on the web that discuss Apple and the history of the personal computer market.

CASE 2

The Coca-Cola Company: Diversity and a Global Presence

As one of the world's best known brands, Coca Cola has endured some important changes in the latter half of the 1990s. The CEO for the last 17 years, Roberto Goizueta, passed away on October 18, 1997 of lung cancer. During Mr. Goizueta's tenure at Coca-Cola, the market value dramatically increased from $4 billion in 1981 to nearly $150 billion today (Click here for 1999 results). This makes him one of the greatest value creators in history. Former Chief Financial Officer, Douglas Ivester, was appointed as his replacement. The question on many investors' minds is can Coke continue its incredible pace in the global soft drink market?

Coca-Cola's Global Dominance

The larger a company is, the harder it is to continue to grow at a steady pace. This was the major challenge facing the Coca-Cola Company in the late 1990s. The U.S. market had already been well developed, with an average of 296 8-ounce servings of Coke products consumed by every man, woman, and child (1). But the Company had not introduced a major new product in nearly 10 years. Demand for diet drinks—the fastest growing soft drinks of the 1980s—had leveled off, and demand for cola-flavored drinks had begun to decrease (2). According to a former Coke executive: "The problem was that Diet Coke was driving the engine and everybody was living off that (3)."

Meanwhile, the competition had not been sleeping. Pepsi was test-marketing a colorless cola, Crystal Pepsi, in response to consumers' interest in clear flavored waters and seltzers. Pepsi had also come out with a new advertising campaign and slogan. Neither company appeared to be particularly concerned about competition from other soft drink manufacturers. However, consumers were drinking more and more new types of beverages, and traditional juice companies such as Very Fine and Ocean Spray had begun to package their products in single-serving cans, in addition to the traditional bottles or juice boxes. Snapple, once owned by Quaker Oats and now by Triarc Beverage Group, developed a new process for bottling tea that required no preservatives and expanded its product line from juices into seltzers and other natural sodas (4).

Roberto Goizueta, former Chief Executive Officer of Coca-Cola Company, recognized the problem. He challenged his new Chief Operating Officer, Company President Douglas Ivester, to rejuvenate the Coke brand. Under Ivester's direction, Coke's advertising agency was given the freedom to develop different messages and marketing campaigns aimed at different groups of consumers. Previously, Coke had been advertised with a single theme and image, intended to appeal to everyone. Ivester also rehired Sergio Zyman as head of marketing. This surprised many people, since Zyman had been largely responsible for "New Coke," a reformulation of Coca-Cola with a new taste designed to compete more closely with Pepsi but which had proved highly unpopular among Coke drinkers.

Zyman led the introduction of new packaging—the plastic contour bottle, based on Coke's traditional glass shape (5). He also emphasized the importance of marketing the product in ways other than just traditional advertising. One new idea was "fast-lane merchandisers"—coolers of coke at the end of check-out counters designed to attract people standing in line (6). The Company also signed an agreement with Rutgers University, in New Jersey, paying the school $10 million for 10-year rights to be the exclusive supplier of soft-drinks and juices, including vending machines, cafeterias, convenience stores, and student centers (7). A similar Pepsi contract with Pennsylvania State University was expected to earn Pepsi $14 million over 10 years. In addition to their sales, both companies valued these contracts because of their ability to reach and influence younger cola drinkers.

The Coca-Cola Company also began actively to develop new products (8). It introduced PowerAde, challenging Gatorade in the $1.2 billion sports drink market, and promoted it with free samples at the World Cup soccer matches throughout the United States. OK Soda, a lightly carbonated drink targeted at "Generation X," was targeted at consumers in their late teens and early twenties. The company also developed Fruitopia drinks, mixtures of fruit flavors such as cranberry lemonade, for the alternative beverage market.

CEO Goizueta and President Ivester were also concerned with expanding Coke's international base. In 1993, more than 6.3 billion unit cases of Coke and Coke Classic were sold worldwide, in more than 195 countries. Diet Coke, also known as Coke Light, was the number one low-calorie soda in the world, available in 117 countries. However 80 percent of the 1.3 billion unit cases was sold in only four markets, all English speaking. Fanta was the only global brand in orange sodas, available in 170 countries, and Sprite, available in 168 countries, was the fifth largest selling brand in the world. Coke was also the largest marketer of juice and juice-drink products in both the United States (with brands including Minute Maid and Hi-C) and the world. However, Goizueta felt that there was still room to grow.

To manage the scope of its business, the Coca-Cola Company is divided into two soft drink business sectors, the North America Business Sector and the International Business Sector. The North America Business Sector is made up of Coca-Cola USA, which operates in the United States, Coca-Cola Ltd., which is responsible for soft drink operations in Canada, and Houston-based Coca-Cola Foods, which produces and markets juices and juice drinks.

The International Business Sector is divided into four operating groups, each of which is responsible for a geographic region of the globe. The Greater Europe Group manages the countries of the European Union, Central and Eastern Europe, Scandinavia and the former Soviet Union. The Latin America Group oversees Mexico and Central and South America; the Middle and Far East Group manages the countries of the Pacific and the Middle East. The Africa Group is responsible for sub-Saharan Africa.

Traditionally, the Coca-Cola Company's main technique for entering and building foreign markets had been through independent bottlers, to whom it sold its "secret formula" in the form of syrup or concentrate. However, this meant relying on the local bottlers to distribute and market Coke products. Soon after he became

CEO, Goizueta was asked by John Hunter, his regional manager in the Philippines, to consider becoming an active partner in the Philippine bottler, which had been neglecting Coke and concentrating on the beer it bottled. Coke invested $13 million, becoming the controlling partner in a joint venture with the bottler. Goizueta and his managers made this their model for international expansion. When entering a new market, the Company would seek to establish distribution of Coke products in key population centers and develop relationships with the important retail channels. It would look for "well capitalized business partners with local know-how and visibility." The workforce would come from the local area and would be extensively trained and eligible for promotion.

These strong, experienced partner companies helped Coke move quickly into Eastern Europe in the 1990s. On one tour, Goizueta attended the opening of plants in Prague (with anchor bottler Coca-Cola Amatil of Australia), Warsaw (with anchor bottler Ringnes of Norway), and Bucharest. When the United States ended its ban with Vietnam in 1994, Coca-Cola had already signed a joint venture agreement for at least two plants and was prepared to start operations within weeks. Coke re-entered the market in India in late 1993, having left the country many years earlier when the Indian government pushed for local ownership. This time, Coke formed a strategic alliance with Parle Exports, a local company with its own soft drink brands and a network of 60 bottling plants. The company saw India's 896

million people and fast-growing middle class as a significant growth opportunity. Coke also began a joint venture with the Swiss Company, Nestle, to produce and market canned coffee and tea drinks.

Coke's Dominance

The Coca-Cola Company is the global soft drink industry leader. Every day in 1994, consumers enjoyed an average of more than 773 million servings of Coca-Cola (known as Coca-Cola classic in the United States. and Canada), diet Coke (known as Coca-Cola light in some countries), Sprite, Fanta, and other products of The Coca-Cola Company. Syrups, concentrates, and beverage bases for Coca-Cola, the Company's flagship brand, and other Company soft drinks are manufactured and sold by The Coca-Cola Company and its subsidiaries in more than 195 countries around the world (9; 10).

One of Ivester's first threats was the currency crisis across Southeast Asia in late 1997. Rather than viewing the situation as a setback, the new chairman saw it as an opportunity to bolster its business in these areas. The strength of the dollar against other major currencies is a primary concern, as Coke receives 80% of its profit from overseas—15% to 17% from Japan alone. Coca Cola learned from the peso crisis in Mexico in 1994 and used that situation to build its business there—with a market share much larger than it was in 1994. Ivester's decision to restructure Coca Cola's global bottling system by lashing together hundreds of small bottlers into a handful of well-capitalized "anchor" bottlers with strong local ties and distribution systems is paying off handsomely (11).

In a continued sign of its global emphasis, in December 1997, Coca Cola signed an agreement to purchase the Orangina brands and four bottling and concentrate plants in France from Pernod Ricard SA for a value of $700 million. However, both Pepsi and the French government have worked to overturn the agreement. With its addition of Surge and Citra, Coke is acknowledging the movement of the US market away from colas (72% in 1990 to 64% in 1996), with the fastest growing brands including Sprite, Mountain Dew, and Dr. Pepper (12).

With global opportunity also goes global risk. In the third quarter of 1998, Coke suffered a drop in its unit shipments from 11% to 3% growth compared to the previous year's quarter as a result of the Asian currency crisis and global recessionary effects. System-wide revenue slipped 4%, although Coke still showed a profit of $888 million (13). However, unit shipment growth remains slow in 1999, causing analysts to question whether Ivester can continue the fantastic growth of the Coca Cola franchise.

Coke's Unit Case Volume by Region

North America	30.4%
Latin America	25.7%
Europe	20.5%
Asia	16.4%
Africa and Middle East	7.0%

Source: Company Report

In addition, Coke experienced some embarrassing problems with its brands in Europe in June 1999, including a contamination scare that caused over 200 people to become sick in Belgium. Coke was forced to recall 14 million cases of its drinks at a loss of over $60 million (14). Coke was soundly criticized for its slow reaction to the crisis.

As a result of this and other problems, Douglas Ivester announced on December 6, 1999 that he would be stepping down as CEO of Coca-Cola in April of 2000. "After reflection and thought, I have concluded that it is time for me to move on to the next stage of my life." (15) Coke's board named Douglas Daft as Ivester's replacement.

Daft faces a host of problems, including slowing unit growth, an ugly class action racial discrimination suit which has resulted in a $195.2 million settlement offer from the firm to over 2000 of its employees, and an aborted takeover offer for Quaker Oats and its Gatorade Sport drink brand. Losing out to Pepsico in the Gatorade battle leaves Coke with a weakened strategy of beefing up its "fizzless" soft drinks products, which include the Nestea line of drinks and fruit drink Fruitopia, as well as introducing new products. (16)

But it is exactly these drinks on which Coke is pinning its hopes for a dramatic turnaround. Daft is attempting to change the highly bureaucratic, slow moving, centralized structure of Coke to promote a change to "thinking local, acting local". He was able to develop just such a strategy in his former post in Asia, where Coke now sells over 250 different drinks. (17) As one of his first acts in taking over as CEO, he axed 6000 employees, many of them middle and senior managers in Atlanta.

Coke plans to introduce its own energy drink, KMX. In addition, it will develop a bottled coffee drink, Planet Java. This gives Coke its first U.S. coffee brand and pits it against Frappuccino, a venture between Pepsi-Cola Co. and Starbucks Corp., which currently faces no significant competition in the category. "Planet Java is a great way for us to get into the market," said Susan McDermott, a spokeswoman for Coca-Cola North America. "It's got a distinctive brand personality and it's performing well in areas where it's available." (18)

You Do the Research

1. Can Coke stay up with changing tastes for non-cola drinks?
2. How has the discrimination suit hurt Coke?
3. Can the firm continue to grow with the pace reflected by Goizueta?

Review Questions

1. What are the management functions performed by Mr. Goizueta, Mr. Hunter, and Mr. Ivester? How do their responsibilities differ?
2. Describe the changes in Coca-Cola's environment since Mr. Goizueta became CEO and after his death.
3. How has the Coca-Cola Company changed to adapt to its environment?
4. Find five Internet sites discussing Coca-Cola or its competitors.

Sun Microsystems: Will Sun Rule the Web?

What does it take to foster a computer revolution? Bill Gates' Microsoft model, based on distributed personal computers with software (largely Microsoft's) loaded on each individual machine, may be slowly giving way to a networked system long championed by Scott McNealy's Sun Microsystems. In fact, McNealy has been one of the few computer industry leaders to take on Microsoft directly with a zeal and tenacity that is legendary. Steven M. Milunovich, an analyst with Merrill Lynch and Company, argues that "If you want to know where the computer industry is going, ask Sun." (1)

Corporate History

Sun Microsystems was founded by Andreas Bechtolsheim, Bill Joy, Vinod Khosla, and Scott McNealy in 1982. The first Sun system, the Sun-1, was a high-performance computer based on readily available, inexpensive components and the UNIX operating system largely developed by Joy while in graduate school at the University of California-Berkeley. From the very start, Sun resisted the so-called Microsoft Windows/Intel (Wintel) model and concentrated on high-end workstations, suitable for engineering, designers, Wall Street traders, and CAD/CAM applications.

Scott McNealy took over as President of Sun in 1984, and since then has waged a constant war with Bill Gates and Microsoft. At first, Sun's market niche of high-end workstations kept it from competing directly with personal computers. However, over time PCs acquired more and more computing power, putting them in more direct competition with workstations. As a consequence, Sun has branched out into other computer areas, with an emphasis on the Internet.

Sun is the only major company that builds an entire line of computers based exclusively on its own designs, its own chips, dubbed Sparc, and its own software, a version of the Unix operating system known as Solaris. As such, Sun stands alone as the "pure" alternative to the Wintel world. (2) This strategy is not without its detractors, who point out that Sun handicaps itself by requiring huge R&D expenses compared to those firms relying on Windows and Intel. Sun spends 10.4% of its sales on R&D, compared to 4.5% at Compaq and 1.6% at Dell, who rely on Intel and Microsoft for much of their research. (3)

McNealy boasts that "there are three technology companies left in the computer world. Intel, Microsoft and Sun." (4) "They [Sun] are beginning to be viewed as much more credible as an end-to-end solution provider," says Joe Ferlazzo, an analyst at Technology Business Research. Sun offers an attractive alternative with the same operating system on everything from a $2,500 workstation with a single Sparc chip to a $1 million server with 64 parallel chips delivering as much computing power as an IBM mainframe. "That's what's needed in the ISP environment and in corporate computing" he adds. In the opposite camp, Susan Whitney of IBM argues that "To believe that a single architecture will address all the business requirements is not a sound strategy." (5)

Undeterred, McNealy stays convinced of his mission, which is no less than to overthrow the personal computer. "The PC is just a blip. It's a big, bright blip," Says McNealy. "Fifty years from now, people are going to look back and say: 'Did you really have a computer on your desk? How weird.'" (6) Analyst C.B. Lee of Sutro and Company and a former Sun manager argues that "McNealy shoots off his mouth too much. At some point, you've gotta be more mature." (7)

Offsetting McNealy's brashness is Ed Zander, chief operating officer for Sun, who exhibits a more conservative aura. "I think McNealy and Zander are kind of like yin and yang," says Milunovich from Merrill Lynch. "McNealy is the high priest of the religion. Ed is much more pragmatic. Having both is very good for Sun." (8)

One thing McNealy has been able to accomplish is the constant reinvention of Sun as times and external conditions change. Starting with workstations and their various components, he has now positioned the firm to offer top-of-the-line servers that power the Internet. With the development of Java and Jini, Sun is evolving into a powerful software machine that serves to drive the Internet and future "information appliances."

To do this, Sun recognizes the need for talented people. Many observers rate Sun's employees among the most talented in Silicon Valley. To keep them in a competitive marketplace, Sun emphasizes perks:

Family care: Adoptive parents receive financial assistance of up to $ 2,000. Lactation rooms help new mothers return to work. In the San Francisco Bay Area, parents can take sick children to a special day-care center that cares for children with minor illnesses. Sun also offers a dependent-care spending account, a consultation and referral program, and an employee-assistance program providing short-term professional counseling.

Private workspace: When Sun designed its Menlo Park, Calif., campus,

the company asked employees for suggestions—and found that engineers prefer private offices over Dilbert-like cubicles. The engineers got the space they demanded for quiet development time.

Respecting employee time: Flexible hours and telecommuting help accommodate busy schedules and keep employees from wasting time on California freeways. Train travelers can catch a special shuttle to Sun facilities, and the company reimburses some commuting costs. (9)

Hard to Find Where the Sun Don't Shine

As early as 1987, Sun coined the phrase, "The network is the computer." (10) But it has only been recently, with the full advent of the Internet coupled with Sun's Java programming language, that all the pieces may actually be falling into place to make this vision a reality. "Microsoft's vision was to put a mainframe on everybody's desktop," claims McNealy. "We want to provide dial tone for the Internet. We couldn't have more different visions." (11)

In 1995, Java was introduced as the first universal software designed from the ground up for Internet and corporate intranet developers to write applications that run on any computer, regardless of the processor or operating system. (12) Most recently Sun has introduced Jini, a promising technology that lets computers and appliances connect to a network

as simply as a telephone plugs into the wall.
(13) Sun's objective is to make access to the Internet and computing as simple as picking up a phone and hearing a "Webtone."

Even Microsoft yielded to Java's appeal, licensing a version to develop its own line of software. Java'a appeal is its ability to lower companies' IT costs because it runs unchanged on any device with a computer chip, enabling everything from wallet-sized cards to trucks to communicate over a network. However, Microsoft and Sun immediately got into a battle when Microsoft made a proprietary version of Java to run only on Windows programs. Sun sued and has won an initial ruling against Microsoft.

Sun claims that network computing will herald a shift away from personal computers to more friendly appliances such as phones, digital assistants, and televisions. It hopes Java will provide the link to its powerful network servers with these new network devices. (14) Microsoft prefers its Windows CE operating system to provide this link. In addition, it views web appliances as "companions" rather than replacements to todays PCs.

The allure of a host of Internet devices is their ability to bring in more users. Their convenience and ease-of-use promotes a more ubiquitous presence for the Web and the information located there. Java goes after this "embedded" software market by powering the programs that run everything from phone switches to factory automation equipment.

Java-Powered Net "Appliances"

Network Computers TVs and Cable Set-Top Boxes	Stripped-down desktop computers run programs downloaded from the Internet TCI will distribute 20 million Java-equipped set-top boxes to encourage communication over cable.
Screenphones	Simple devices for straightforward services such as grocery ordering.
Cellular Phones and Pagers	Cellular phone manufacturers plan to use Java to offer new services through their cellular devices.
Smart Cards	Java smart cards program routine processes, such as airline ticket purchases, directly on the cards.
Cars	Navigation and diagnostic systems powered by Java programs.
Keys	Java-powered rings and pass cards. (15)

Sun claims Java is ideally suited for the "network computer" (NC)—a low-cost machine that has no hard drive, relying instead on a network that would supply it with small Java programs. Plummeting personal computer prices have stalled the takeoff of the NC, but McNealy and Sun remain committed to the idea. "Every day, 27,000 people (at Sun) get up and do one thing: network computing," claims Ed Zander. "That's a very, very powerful story." (16)

Sun Meets AOL/Netscape

In perhaps its greatest coup to date, on November 24, 1998, Sun signed an alliance agreement with America Online in association with its $4.2 billion purchase of Netscape Communications. Access to Netscape's E-commerce software allows Sun to hawk its servers and attract customers that want a more complete package. (17) In addition, Sun has access to one of the three largest portals on the Web. In exchange for providing $350 million in licensing, marketing, and advertising fees for the deal, AOL agrees to buy $500 million in Sun servers over the next three years. In addition, the firms cooperate on the iPlanet e-commerce enterprise.

Open system advocates were originally concerned about AOL's involvement in the deal. They felt that AOL might hinder the free distribution of Netscape's browser. However, Stephen Case, AOL founder, assures doubters that the partnership will continue to allow free access to Netscape's browser technology. He intends to depend on Sun Microsystems to develop systems to provide Internet access over next-generation devices.

As a partner with AOL and Netscape, Sun is now in position to challenge IBM, Hewlett-Packard, and others in developing the systems that will let corporations rebuild their businesses in cyberspace. The challenge for Sun CEO Scott G. McNealy will be to behave like the top-tier industry leader that this deal may finally make him. And he'll need to make sure that Sun not only talks like a good partner but behaves like one, too. (18)

A major factor in Sun's favor is a world in which companies will choose to outsource anything that's not a demonstrably clear competitive advantage. Things such as human resources, financials, e-mail and web hosting all will clearly follow in the steps of payroll and facility security—that is, they'll be outsourced. Sun's been saying that the network is the computer for at least a decade. Oracle has been talking the talk for about three years. SAP was founded on the principle of centralized control since the early 1970s. But so far, no vendor has been able to convince any company that it should put its technological assets into someone else's hands. This is starting to change. (19)

The firm most strategically positioned to take advantage of this shift is Sun or possibly IBM Global Services. Scott McNealy has stated several times that companies should never think about purchasing another server again. He means that companies should leave the costs of maintaining scalability and reliability of fundamental systems to someone that specializes in the technology. (20)

Even so, the Internet must continue to evolve in order for Sun to realize its vision. John McFarlane, head of Solaris software, puts it plainly. "We depend upon extreme reliability, availability and scalability as a market differentiator . . . I know from my seventeen years as a Nortel employee how much it hurts when there's a service failure of any kind, and how great it feels when the network would take a licking and keep on ticking. The same ethic applies at Sun. We run our own company systems on Sun, and our average downtime is about 22 minutes per-employee-per-year. Another way to put it is we experience about 99.96% uptime for every company user. We won a contract with the New York Stock Exchange because of our ability to deliver their required 99.99% uptime—and so far we're at 100%. If the Internet is truly to succeed as the next great communication medium for mainstream users, and the WebTone is to truly represent the same level of connectivity as the dial-tone, then that level of reliability must be our model for all users. We call it the utility model of computing." (21)

With all these changes going on, how does a company cope? McNealy sums up his strategy by arguing, "If everybody thought that what we were doing was the right thing, everybody would do what we are doing. If you are controversial and you are wrong, you've got a big problem. You have to be very controversial and very right to make lots of money." (22) Sun contends that "The Network is the Computer." Do you agree?

What Does the Future Hold?

1. Can Sun continue to be a leader in the server market with new competitors entering?
2. Is McNealy's vision of the Internet correct, or has something changed to alter it?
3. Who appears to be leading in the network appliance operating systems?

Review Questions

1. What has been Sun's impact on the Internet? Positive or negative?
2. With increased competition from Microsoft, will Sun continue to set standards for Internet connectivity?
3. How might the growth in Net appliances help or hurt Sun? How well positioned is Sun for future competitive advantage?

CASE 4

United Parcel Service: Information Technology Hits the Road

United Parcel Service (UPS), the world's largest package distribution company, transports more than 3.3 billion parcels and documents annually. With over 500 aircraft, 149,000 vehicles, and 1,700 facilities providing service in over 200 countries, the firm has a worldwide commitment to serving the needs of the global marketplace. How does the company control such a vast and extended enterprise?

Corporate History

In 1907 there was a great need in America for private messenger and delivery services. With few private home telephones, luggage, packages, and personal messages had to be carried by hand. The US Postal Service would not begin the parcel post system for another six years. To help meet this need, an enterprising 19-year-old, James E. ("Jim") Casey, borrowed $100 from a friend and established the American Messenger Company in Seattle, Washington. Despite stiff competition, the company did well, largely because of Jim Casey's strict policies: customer courtesy, reliability, round-the-clock service, and low rates. These principles, which guide UPS even today, are summarized by Jim's slogan: "Best Service and Lowest Rates." (1)

Obsessed with efficiency from the beginning, the company pioneered the concept of consolidated delivery—combining packages addressed to certain neighborhoods onto one delivery vehicle. In this way, manpower and motorized equipment could be used more efficiently. The 1930s brought more growth. By this time, UPS provided delivery services in all major West Coast cities, and a foothold was established on the other end of the country with a consolidated delivery service in the New York City area. Many innovations were adopted, including the first mechanical system for package sorting, and a 180-foot-long conveyor belt installed in Los Angeles. During this time, accountant George D. Smith joined the firm and helped make financial cost control the cornerstone of all planning decisions. The name United Parcel Service was adopted: "United" because shipments were consolidated and "Service" because, "Service is all we have to offer." All UPS vehicles were painted the now-familiar Pullman brown color because it was neat, dignified, and professional. (2)

In 1953, UPS resumed air service, which had been discontinued during the Depression, offering two-day service to major cities on the East and West Coasts. Packages flew in the cargo holds of regularly scheduled airlines. Called UPS Blue Label Air, the service grew, until by 1978 it was available in every state, including Alaska and Hawaii. The demand for air parcel delivery increased in the 1980s, and federal deregulation of the airline industry created new opportunities for UPS. But deregulation caused change, as established airlines reduced the number of flights or abandoned routes altogether. To ensure dependability, UPS began to assemble its own jet cargo fleet—the largest in the industry. With growing demand for faster service, UPS entered the overnight air delivery business, and by 1985 UPS Next Day Air service was available in all 48 states and Puerto Rico. Alaska and Hawaii were added later. That same year, UPS entered a new era with international air package and document service, linking the United States and six European nations.

UPS Today

In 1988 UPS received authorization from the FAA (Federal Aviation Administration) to operate its own aircraft, thus officially becoming an airline. Recruiting the best people available, UPS merged

a number of cultures and procedures into a seamless operation called UPS Airline. UPS Airline was the fastest-growing airline in FAA history, formed in little more than one year with all the necessary technology and support systems. Today, UPS Airline is among the ten largest airlines in the United States. UPS Airline features some of the most advanced information systems in the world, like the COMPASS (Computerized Operations Monitoring, Planning, and Scheduling System), which provides information for flight planning, scheduling, and load handling. The system, which can be used to plan optimum flight schedules up to six years in advance, is unique in the industry.

Today, the UPS system moves over 11.5 million packages and documents daily around the globe. From pickup at over 60,000 drop-off locations, packages are transported by 157,000 brown trucks to over 2,400 centralized "hubs" where a combined workforce of over 338,000 employees sorts and distributes packages around the world. A huge technology support system that supports over 1 million cellular calls per day allows UPS to track all its packages electronically. Over $1.5 billion has been invested in technology systems in the past five years alone. Nonetheless, analysts suggest that UPS trails rival Federal Express by over one year in technology applications. (3)

However, this drive for efficiency does not come without a cost. The Teamsters Union voted to strike UPS in early August 1997, stranding millions of packages across the U.S. The strike lasted approximately two weeks until a settlement was reached re-

garding the use of temporary workers and outside contractors. The ramifications of the action could have long-term, negative consequences for the company and dubious gains for the workers.

Innovations at UPS

Tom Weidemeyer, president and chief operating officer of UPS Airline, likes to say that UPS likes to take the really long-term view about investments in its infrastructure. Technology at UPS spans an incredible range, from specially designed package delivery vehicles to global computer and communications systems. For example, UPSnet is a global electronic data communications network that provides an information processing pipeline for international package processing and delivery. UPSnet, which has more than 500,000 miles of communications lines, including a UPS satellite, links more than 1,300 distribution sites in 46 countries. The system tracks 821,000 packages daily. (4)

Weidemeyer introduced three additional changes. First, the entire airfleet of over 231 aircraft has been raised to meet Stage 3 noise requirements, three years ahead of the 1999 U.S. compliance deadline, at a cost of over $500 million. Second, he has introduced heads-up displays (HUDs) on all of UPS's 61 Boeing 727s. "In this business, it goes almost beyond reliability to criticality. There is only one launch, and if you miss that then you miss it. The HUDs will help us get even higher reliability." (5) Third, Weidemeyer has UPS in the charter passenger service. UPS has five 727s that have been converted to a dual cargo/passenger configuration. On Fridays, in three hours the planes can be converted from freight to 113 passenger seats. Vacation Express, an Atlanta travel agency, charters the aircraft, complete with UPS pilots, for weekend flights. (6)

UPS's commitment to technology is reflected in the upgrades it undertook for its Louisville international hub. The Atlanta-based delivery giant spent $275 million to build a 2.7 million-square-foot facility that has been dubbed "Hub 2000." The name reflects the high-tech nature of the building and the $584 million UPS invested in equipment and furnishings to replace the existing 1 million-square-foot sorting center. The new building, with three peninsulas jutting out from the main section, has 42 bays where airplanes can pull up much as in truck docks at conventional factories and warehouses. Computerized overhead scanners read "smart labels" and determine the direction packages will take along conveyor belts en route to the airplanes. Rather than replace workers, UPS hired an additional 6,000 sorters as the hub has expanded. (7)

Three Trends Driving the Industry

Frederick Smith of FedEx identifies three trends driving the package business. *Globalization* will cause the world express-transportation market to explode from today's $12 billion to more than $150 billion. While DHL Worldwide Express is a major player in the international market, UPS and Fed Ex are expanding at a rapid

pace. The fastest-growing segments of UPS's business are the express and international markets, whose revenues leapt by almost 25 percent in 1997. Lee Hibbets of Air Cargo Management Group in Seattle states that "FedEx is seen as more aggressive, whereas UPS is a little bit more methodical and long-term." (8)

Cost cutting among firms—primarily by cutting inventory—fits into the package firms' delivery systems. Technology plays a part in every company's future, but FedEx has a distinct edge in this area. It has installed computer terminals for 100,000 customers and given proprietary software to another 650,000. As a result, shippers now label 60 percent of their own packages, with FedEx receiving electronic notifications for pickup and delivery. (9)

Internet commerce, rather than a threat to the shippers, turns out to be a vast opportunity. Electronic commerce generates a huge need for shipping, and the package deliverers hope to capture the lion's share of the business. FedEx's recent $2.7 merger with Caliber System, with its RPS trucking subsidiary comprising 13,000 trucks, puts it in even closer competition with UPS.

It remains to be seen who will win out in the package delivery wars, but FedEx and UPS are both leaders in the market. Their ability to track packages around the world is a testament to the value of technology in the workplace. With innovations generating higher productivity, the future for package delivery remains bright.

UPS, trading under the symbol (UPS), sold a 10 percent stake in the company

with the offering of 109.4 million shares, meaning the offering raised $5.47 billion. The underwriters, including most of the major investment banks on Wall Street, have an allotment of another 10.94 million shares that could push the IPO above $6 billion, a record for Wall Street. (10)

The UPS offering was 14 to 15 times oversubscribed, and after the IPO price of $50 per share on November 9, 1999, the price rose to over $67 the following day (Click here for recent stock price). UPS, with $2.6 billion cash on hand, used the IPO to create a market in its stock on behalf of its employees and retirees, in addition to providing funds for acquisitions. (11)

With UPS Logistics, the company is expanding its role in managing supply chain operations and logistics for corporations. In addition, UPS has launched e-Ventures to develop operations supporting e-commerce and Internet-based firms.

You Do the Research

1. Is UPS staying up with FedEx in the global package delivery race?
2. What unique risks face the firm in its attempts to gain more of a global presence?
3. How does going from a private to a publicly traded firm affect UPS's decision-making process?

Review Questions

1. How does performance appraisal assist control and how does it relate to UPS?
2. How has UPS implemented the use of the Internet and how does it apply to control?
3. The fourth management function is controlling; explain and relate to UPS.

Harley-Davidson: Is There a Case for Protection?

Brought back from near death, Harley-Davidson Motorcycles represents a true American success story. Reacting to global competition, Harley has been able to reestablish itself as the dominant maker of big bikes in the United States. However, success often breeds imitation, and Harley faces a mixture of domestic and foreign competitors encroaching on its market. Can it meet the challenge?

Harley-Davidson

When Harley-Davidson was founded in 1903, it was one of over 100 firms producing motorcycles in the United States. The U.S. government became an important customer for the company's high-powered, reliable bikes, using them in both world wars. By the 1950s, Harley-Davidson was the only remaining American manufacturer. (1)

But British competitors were beginning to enter the market with faster, lighterweight bikes. Honda Motor Company of Japan began marketing lightweight bikes in the United States, moving into middleweight vehicles in the 1960s. Harley initially tried to compete by manufacturing smaller bikes but had difficulty making them profitably. The company even purchased an Italian motorcycle firm, Aermacchi, but many of its dealers were reluctant to sell the small Aermacchi Harleys. (2) American Machine and Foundry Co. (AMF) took over Harley in 1969, expanding its portfolio of recreational products. AMF increased production from 14,000 bikes to 50,000 bikes per year. This rapid expansion led to significant problems with quality, how-

ever, and better-built Japanese motorcycles began to take over the market. Harley's share of its major U.S. market—heavyweight motorcycles—fell to 23 percent. (3)

In 1981, a group of 13 managers bought Harley-Davidson back from AMF and began to turn the company around. Richard Teerlink, CEO of Harley since 1987, joined the company that year as chief financial officer. He described the problem the new management faced: "The problem was us. The problem was the guys in the white shirts and ties." He explained that "our solution was to get back to detail. The key was to know the business, know the customer, and pay attention to detail." (4) The key comments in this process were increasing quality and improving service to customers and dealers. Management kept the classic Harley style and focused on the company's traditional strength—heavyweight and super-heavyweight bikes. Once Harley's quality image had been restored, the company slowly began to expand production. The company made only 280 bikes per day in January 1992, increasing output to 345 by the end of the year.

Despite increasing demand, production was scheduled to reach only 420 per day, approximately 100,000 per year, by 1996. (5)

The popularity of the motorcycles continued to increase throughout the 1980s. The average Harley purchaser was in his late thirties, with an average household income of over $40,000. Teerlink didn't like the description of his customers as "aging" baby boomers: "Our customers want the sense of adventure that they get on our bikes. . . . Harley-Davidson doesn't sell transportation, we sell transformation. We sell excitement, a way of life." (6) Managers participated in this lifestyle, many riding their bikes to work and participating in rallies. (7) The company built on the enthusiasm of its customers by creating the Harley Owners Group (H.O.G.). H.O.G. members receive a bimonthly magazine, emergency road service, Harley rental programs for trips, and opportunities to meet and ride with other Harley owners.

Although the company had been exporting motorcycles ever since it was founded, it wasn't until the late 1980s that Harley-Davidson management began to think seriously about international markets. Traditionally, the company's ads had been translated word for word into foreign languages. Now, ads were developed specifically for different markets, and rallies were adapted to fit local customs. In 1993, a branch office of H.O.G. was set up in Frankfurt, Germany, to serve European owners and fans. According to Wilke, "As the saying goes, we needed to think global but act local." (8)

The company also began to actively recruit and develop dealers in Europe and Japan. It purchased a Japanese distribution company and built a large parts warehouse in Germany to support its European operations. (9) The bikes proved to be as popular abroad as in the United States. Japanese owners ranged from middle-aged men who had first seen Harleys ridden by American soldiers just after World War II, to younger riders who were intrigued by the mechanics or the American image. It was an expensive interest, with bike prices overseas ranging up to $25,000. (10) Foreign dealers were just as enthusiastic as their customers. At the ninetieth birthday rally, the general manager of a chain of Harley-Davidson dealerships in Greece summed up his feelings about his product: "You can own a Suzuki or a Kawasaki, but you can only love a Harley. It's the only bike you can develop a relationship with." (11)

Harley-Davidson continued to look for ways to expand its activities. On a biking tour in Europe, Wilke realized that German motorcyclists rode at high speeds, often more than 100 mph. As a result, the company began to study ways to give Harleys a smoother ride. It also began to emphasize accessories that would give riders more protection. (12) The company also created a line of Harley Motor Accessories available through dealers or by catalog, all adorned with the Harley-Davidson logo. These jackets, caps, T-shirts, and other items became popular with nonbikers as well. In fact, the clothing and parts had a higher profit margin than the motorcycles; nonbike products made up as much as half of sales at some dealers.

Despite pressure from customers and dealers, Harley-Davidson's top management resisted the temptation to expand at a faster pace. Teerlink explained that, although the company had looked into manufacturing overseas, "our customers are buying a piece of the American dream. Overseas manufacturing just wouldn't work for them." (13) The company reaffirmed its long-term strategic objectives: to be number one in consumer satisfaction in the United States and abroad, to develop the ability to produce and market more than 100,000 units per year by 1996, and support those sales with parts, accessories, and merchandise. (14)

International Efforts

Harley continues to make inroads in overseas markets. Important events include a joint venture it has launched with Porsche AG of Stuttgart, Germany, in which they will "source and assemble powertrain components for use in potential new motorcycle products." (15) Also noteworthy is the June 23, 1997 announcement that Jeffrey L. Bleustein has taken over as Harley-Davidson's president and CEO. Richard Teerlink remained the chairman. (16)

One interesting area of development is Japan. Harley-Davidson Japan KK estimates that 51,000 of its bikes can be found on the roads and that that number is increasing rapidly. One event assisting in this rise is the government's removal of a restriction that required drivers to pass a stringent National Police Agency examination for bikes over 401 cc. Drivers now must pass only a local driving school test. The next step in promoting Harleys will be to persuade the police to permit two to ride on a bike on highways, a practice that is presently illegal. As a result of these initiatives, Harley-Davidson expects 50,000 new large motorbike licenses to be granted in 1997, almost double that of a year before. (17)

Harley motorcycles are among America's fastest-growing exports to Japan. Japanese bikers bought 4,387 Harleys from January through August 1997, up 27 percent from a year before. To rev up sales, Harley's Japanese subsidiary is obsessing over details by customizing its marketing approach to Japanese tastes. Harley also offers shinier and more complete tool kits than those offered in the United States. (18)

Harley bikes have long been considered symbols of prestige in Japan. Before World War II, they were built under a licensing arrangement by a small company called Rikuo. Toshiaki Iijima, 56, the president of a construction company, has shelled out $54,000 on his 1340 cc red Ultra Classic Electric Glide, including $28,000 for a sidecar to help him keep his balance. Consistent with their U.S. counterparts, many Japanese enthusiasts see themselves as rebels on wheels.

Success Breeds Imitation

A handful of new U.S. motorcycle manufacturers are trying to catch a ride with Harley-Davidson's "Made in America" craze. With Harley-Davidson's control of 47 percent of the domestic market for heavyweight machines (chrome-laden cruisers, aerodynamic rocket bikes mostly produced by the Japanese, and oversize touring motorcycles), its dominance remains secure. However, with manufacturers such as Big Dog Motorcycles, Polaris Industries, and Excelsior-Henderson starting to produce larger bikes, Harley's success is currently stimulating new ventures. (19)

Industry analyst Don Brown of DJB Associates estimates the U.S. retail sales of street bikes will exceed 231,000 in 1997, up 44 percent since 1991. Worldwide, heavyweight motorcycles represent a $4.8 billion market. Harley has been steadily increasing production, from 118,000 bikes in 1996 to 204,000 in 2000. (20)

Big Dog represents the high end, building customized bikes that run upwards of $22,000 each, compared to $16,000 for a Harley. Its 55 employees will turn out about 300 bikes in 1997. Polaris, a $1.2 billion snowmobile manufacturer, is aiming its $12,500 Victory at its present all-terrain vehicle and personal watercraft consumers. Excelsior is providing the Super X for between $16,000 and $20,000, with an annual capacity of 20,000 motorcycles produced in its Belle Plaine, Minnesota plant. (21)

A recent effort by Harley to expand its buyer base involves the development of its Blast motorcycle from its Buell division. 50 percent of Blast sales goes to women, raising the overall percentage of women buying Harleys from 2 percent to 9 percent. With 14 consecutive years of increased production, the future for Harley appears bright. (22)

You Do the Research

1. How successful have the new American competitors been against Harley?
2. Should Harley alter its "image" as the U.S. population ages?
3. Should businesses like Harley receive protection from overseas competition?

Review Questions

1. Describe Harley-Davidson's international business strategy. Would you consider Harley to be a multinational corporation?
2. If you were Harley's top management, in which regions of the world would you consider expanding?
3. Evaluate Harley-Davidson's decision not to produce overseas. What would be the advantages of overseas production?

What problems might the company encounter if it does manufacture abroad?
4. Describe how Harley's management style may have changed over time. Use optional classical, human relations, and modern approaches in your answer. Check Harley's Homepage for information.
5. Harley appears to have moved from providing a product (motorcycles) to providing a service (a way of life). Discuss how this movement from products to services may have affected the company.
6. What effect might Harley's movement overseas have on its potential management choice of Theory Z?
7. Locate five sources on the web that discuss early theories of management.

CASE 6

Tom's of Maine: Doing Good while Doing Business

Tom's of Maine represents one of the first natural health care companies to distribute their product beyond the normal channels of health food stores. While it continues to grow, the owners, Tom and Katie Chappell, continue to emphasize the values that got them started over 28 years ago. The question becomes, can a small firm stay true to its founding principles and continue to grow in a fiercely competitive environment?

Tom's of Maine

For its first 15 years, Tom's of Maine looked a lot like many other new businesses. It was started in 1970 by Tom and Katie Chappell, two people with an idea they believed in and felt others would also buy into, and financed by a small loan. Like many business startups, the company's first product was not successful. Its phosphate-free detergent was environmentally friendly but, according to founder Tom Chappell, "it didn't clean so well." (1) Consumers did appear to be interested in "green" or environmentally friendly products, however, and the fledgling company's next products, toothpaste and soap, were more successful.

All Tom's of Maine products were made with all-natural ingredients and packaged using recycled materials whenever possible. New personal care products, including shampoo and deodorant, were developed while avoiding the controversial practice of animal testing. (2) This refusal caused Tom's to wait seven years and shell out about 10 times the usual sum to get the American Dental Association's seal of approval for its fluoride toothpastes.

In 1992, Tom's deodorant accounted for 25 percent of its business. Chappell reformulated the product for ecological reasons (replacing petroleum with vegetable glycerin), but the new formulation "magnified the human bacteria that cause odor" in half its customers. After much agonizing, Chappell ordered the deodorant taken off the shelves at a cost of $400,000, or 30 percent of the firm's projected profits for the year. Dissatisfied consumers were sent refunds or the new product, along with a letter of apology.

Tom's of Maine recovered from this experience, but founder Tom Chappell was not happy. The company's products were a success in health food stores, and Chappell was beginning to think in terms of national distribution. He had hired a team of marketing people who had experience at major companies. At the same time, he felt that something was missing; he was "tired of creating new brands and making money." (3)

One pivotal event was the introduction of a baking soda toothpaste. The product was gritty and didn't have the sweet flavor typical of commercial toothpastes, and the marketing manager told Chappell, "In all candor I don't know how we're going to sell it." (4) Chappell insisted that the product be test marketed. It proved to be a best seller and was quickly copied by Arm and Hammer and Proctor and Gamble. (5) It also appeared that a new product's sales potential had become more important to the company than the qualities of the product itself. "We were working for the numbers, and we got the numbers. But I was confused by success, unhappy with success" said Chappell. (6) He later wrote, "I had made a real go of something I'd started. What more could I do in life except make more money? Where was the purpose and direction for the rest of my life?" (7) As a result of this line of thinking in the fall of 1986, the successful businessman Tom Chappell entered Harvard Divinity School. (8)

The years that Chappell spent as a part-time student at the Divinity School brought him to a new understanding of his role. "For the first time in my career, I had the language I needed to debate my bean-counters" he explained. (9) He realized that his company was his ministry. "I'm here to succeed. But there's a qualifier. It's not to succeed at all costs, it's to succeed according to my principles. (10)

One tangible result was a mission statement for the company. This document spelled out the values that would guide the company in the future. It covered the types of products ordered and the need for natural ingredients and high quality. It also included respect for employees and the need for meaningful work as well as fair pay. It pointed out the need to be concerned with the community and even the world. Finally, it called for Tom's of Maine "to be a profitable and successful company, while acting in a socially responsible manner." (11) Some of the company's programs were the result of decisions made by top management. The company began donating 10 percent of its pretax profits to charities ranging from art organizations to environmental groups. These included funds donated to state and local curbside recycling programs, and a pledge of $100,000 for the Rainforest Alliance.

The company also urged its employees to get involved in charitable causes. It set up a program that allowed employees to donate 5 percent of their work time to volunteer activities. Employees enthusiastically took advantage of the opportunity. When one employee began teaching art classes for emotionally disturbed children, others became interested, until almost all of the company's employees were involved. (12) One tangible result was a cardboard totem pole, which decorated the corporate hallways. (13) Other employees worked in soup kitchens and homeless shelters. Employees formed their own teams to work on projects or used the company's matching service. Tom's even created the position of "Vice President of Community Life."

The volunteer program did have its costs, however.

Other employees had to pitch in to cover volunteers' absences, which amounted to the equivalent of 20 days a month. However, Colleen Myers, the VP of Community Life, felt that the volunteer activities were valuable to the company as well as the community. "After spending a few hours at a soup kitchen or a shelter you're happy to have a job. It's a morale booster, and better morale translates pretty directly into better productivity." (14) Sometimes the company even benefited directly from these activities. Chappell explained, "The woman who headed up those art classes—she discovered she's a heck of a project manager. We found that out, too." (15)

Employee benefits were not strictly psychological. The company offered flexible four-day scheduling and subsidized day care. Even coffee breaks were designed with employee preferences in mind, providing them with fresh fruit. The company also worked with individual employees, helping them earn their high school equivalency degrees and develop skills for new positions. (16)

By 1993, Tom's of Maine was moving beyond health food stores and into supermarkets and drugstores, where 70 percent of toothpaste is purchased. Its products are widely distributed on the East Coast and are moving up the West Coast from California; the brand is carried in 30,000 mass market outlets nationwide, including Wal-Mart. Katie Sisler, vice president of marketing, felt that the company's marketing strategy was low key. "We just tell them our story. We tell them why we have such a loyal base of consumers who vote with their dollars ever day. A number of trade accounts appreciate our social responsibility and are willing to go out on a limb with us. (17) Tom Chappell agreed: "We're selling a lot more than toothpaste; we're selling a point of view—that nature is worth protecting." (18)

By the mid 1990s, Tom's of Maine was facing increasing competition. Its prices were similar to those of its national competitors for baking soda toothpaste, but 20 to 40 percent higher for deodorant and mouthwash. Tom Chappell did not appear worried, however. He felt that "You have to understand from the outset that they have more in the marketing war chest than you. That's not the way you're going to get market share, you're going to get it by being who you are." (19) He explained his philosophy. "A small business obviously needs to distinguish itself from the commodities. If we try to act like commodities, act like a toothpaste, we give up our souls. Instead, we have to be peculiarly authentic in everything we do." (20) This authenticity is applied to both ingredients and advertising decisions. "When you start doing that customers are very aware of your difference. And they like the difference." (21)

By 1997, total sales approached $20 million. Of its 250 all-natural products, including shampoo, deodorant, and mouthwash, toothpaste still provides the bulk of the sales with a contribution between $10 million and $12 million. While behemoth Proctor and Gamble produces 250 million tubes of toothpaste annually, Tom's produces 8 million tubes.

Nationally, Tom's has grabbed a 0.7 percent market share; in major markets such as New York, Boston, and the Rockies, the company claims the share is between 2 and 3 percent. (22)

In addition, Chappell's message is starting to draw the attention of several Fortune 500 companies. Ralph Larsen, chairman and CEO of Johnson and Johnson, a $20 billion company with 87,000 employees in 160 subsidiaries, says that Chappell is "charting a new course" and recently invited him to address his top management team at J&J's New Brunswick, New Jersey headquarters. (23) Robert Reich, former secretary of labor, says "The debate that sounds as if it's about maximizing shareholder returns versus being socially responsible usually comes down to whether a top manager is paying attention only to very short-term performance or is taking a longer-term view." (24) Arnold Hiatt, former president and CEO of Stride Rite, agrees with Chappell's brand of "common-good capitalism," particularly as it impacts employees. Hiatt now serves as cochair of Business for Social Responsibility, whose 900 member companies include Ben and Jerry's, Home Depot, Levi Strauss and Reebok. (25)

Chappell reinforces his message with his seven "intentions" for others seeking a values-profits balance:

1. Connect with goodness. Non-work discussions with an upbeat spin usually draw people to common ground, away from hierarchical titles.
2. Know thyself, be thyself. Discovering and tapping people's passions, gifts

and strengths generates creative energy.

3. Envision your destiny. The company is better served if its efforts are steered by strengths instead of following market whims.
4. Seek counsel. The journey is long, and assistance from others is absolutely necessary.
5. Venture out. The success of any business hinges on pushing value-enhanced products into the market.
6. Assess. Any idea must be regularly reviewed and refined if necessary.
7. Pass it on. Since developing and incorporating values is a trial-and-error and process, sharing ideas and soliciting feedback allows for future growth. (26)

Chappell's emphasis on his New Age philosophy does not overshadow his concern for profitable goals. The firm's recent purchase of an herbal-extract company has allowed it to grow 25–35 percent annually with its addition of a cough, cold, and wellness line of products. (27)

Interesting Facts:

- Chappell's name is pronounced "chapel"
- Tom's of Maine gives away 10% of its pretax profits to charities, gives 3 months maternity leave, provides child-care subsidies, and encourages employees to spend 5% of their paid work time doing volunteer service—with nearly 80% of the employees participating (9).
- The manufacturing plant is housed in an old converted railway station.
- Toothpaste is mixed in 3,000-pound batches.

- As an 11-year old, Tom served as a model for a Norman Rockwell portrait of a choirboy.

You Do the Research

1. Was Tom's correct to purchase the herbal-extract company—does it fit with his objectives?
2. Should Tom's stay independent—or should it merge with a larger firm?
3. Can Chappell's approach to ethical management work at larger firms?

Review Questions

1. Which way of thinking about ethical behavior best describes Tom's of Maine and its founder, Tom Chappell?
2. What potential dilemma did Tom Chappell face in the mid-1980s?
3. How important were Tom Chappell's personal views in helping Tom's of Maine to be successful?
4. Find five Internet sites that discuss ethics and social responsibility.

CASE 7

Wal-Mart: E-tailing in a World of Super Stores

Wal-Mart has grown to be the dominant discount merchandise retailer in the United States and is now branching out overseas. It accomplished this feat by locating in primarily small, rural communities—away from competitors. People who put $1,000 into Wal-Mart stock when it went public in 1970 saw that investment grow to nearly $2 million by 1993.[1] The question becomes, can Wal-Mart continue to expand and succeed in an increasingly hostile retail environment?

Out of Arkansas

Wal-Mart was first opened in 1962 by Sam Walton in Bentonville, Arkansas. Since then it has become the largest retailer in the United States, with over 3,300 Wal-Mart stores, and has become the largest online retailer. It has also experienced some of the best customer approval scores in retail history. Wal-Mart employs 728,000 individuals, and in 1996 reached sales of $105 billion dollars. Together Kmart, Target, and Wal-Mart hold over 85 percent of the

1996 Sales	% of Total
Hard goods (hardware, housewares)	25
Soft goods/domestics	25
Stationery and candy	11
Records and electronics	10
Pharmaceuticals	9
Sporting goods and toys	9
Health and beauty aids	7
Jewelry and shoes	4

Source: Hoovers, 1996

discount store market share. Despite the death of its founder Sam Walton, Wal-Mart continues to be successful. Under his successor, CEO David Glass, the little discount store chain started in Arkansas has become one of the largest corporations in the world. It is already on its way to achieving Sam Walton's 1991 prediction of $125 billion sales by the turn of the century.[2]

In his 1990 letter to Wal-Mart stockholders, CEO David Glass laid out the company's philosophy: "We approach this new exciting decade of the '90s much as we did in the '80s—focused on only two main objectives, (1) providing the customers what they want, when they want it, all at a value, and (2) treating each other as we would hope to be treated, acknowledging our total dependency on our associate-partners to sustain our success."[3]

He felt that the traditional format of organization, employee commitment, cost control, carefully planned locations for new stores, and attention to customer needs and desires would enable Wal-Mart to meet Sam's lofty prediction. In addition to its main objectives, Wal-Mart has stayed true to its basic values and beliefs. Its success originated in three fundamental principals: *Respect for the Individual, Service for our Customers,* and *Striving for Excellence.*

Wal-Mart has grown by paying careful attention to its market niche of customers looking for quality at a bargain price. Customers do not have to wait for a sale to realize savings. Many of its stores are located in smaller towns, primarily throughout the South and Midwest. Glass knew that although the traditional geographical markets served by Wal-Mart were not saturated, growth in these areas was limited and any strategy to achieve continuing growth would have to include expansion into the Northeast and the West Coast. It might also have to include new product lines and higher-priced products to allow existing stores to achieve year-to-year sales growth. By mid-1994, the company had a firm base in New England, and it was growing rapidly in the West. The geographical areas Wal-Mart has recently been expanding into have different demographics than those in which the company has traditionally grown. These were large urban areas where entrenched competition was offered by such companies as Kmart and Target.

In 1993, the company added the 91-store Pace Membership Warehouse chain, which it had purchased from Kmart.[4] Competition was increasing as smaller regional chains such as Costco and Price Club merged and opened stores in many of the same markets as Wal-Mart.[5] The company began to experiment with one-stop shopping in 1987, when it opened Hypermart* USA, a Wal-Mart/supermarket combination. Wal-Mart is now made up of five retail divisions: Wal-Marts, Wal-Mart Supercenters (Wal-Mart with grocery), SAM's Clubs (membership warehouse clubs), Bud's Discount City (discount warehouse outlets), and an International Division.

Wal-Mart has a lean corporate staff. Its buyers are known as tough negotiators who ascribe to the corporate policy "Buy American whenever possible." The company has set up an extensive control procedure based on a satellite communication system that links all stores with the Bentonville, Arkansas, headquarters. The satellite system is also used to transmit messages from headquarters, training materials, and communications between stores and can even be used to track the company's delivery trucks. In addition, Wal-Mart has an on-line system with its suppliers. This system has linked Wal-Mart's computer systems with its suppliers. The showroom employees also have "Magic Wands," which are small handheld computers linked by radio frequency to the store's computer terminals. Given that a typical Wal-Mart store contains more than 70,000 standard items in stock, these innovative devices help to keep up-to-the-minute track of inventory, deliveries, and backup merchandise in stock. Because of its innovative technology, Wal-Mart has gained a *competitive advantage* in the speed with which it delivers goods to the customer.

While each new Wal-Mart brings in new jobs, it can also bring detrimental effects to the community as well. A 1991 *Wall Street Journal* article noted that many small retailers are forced to close after Wal-Mart opens nearby.[6] In one Wisconsin town, even J.C. Penny lost 50 percent of its Christmas sales and closed down when Wal-Mart opened up. In an Iowa town, four clothing and shoe stores, a hardware store, a drug store, and a dime store all went out of business. In 1994, the voters in Greenfield, Massachusetts, forced Wal-Mart to withdraw its building plans by using a few simple rules of engagement. It also had to give up plans to build in Bath, Maine; Simi Valley, California; and two towns in Pennsylvania. Vermont successfully resisted all Wal-Mart plans to locate in that state.

Even Wal-Mart's "Bring it home to the USA" buying program produced controversy when an NBC news program found clothing that had been made abroad on racks under a "Made in the USA" sign in 11 stores. In addition, the program showed a tape of children sewing at a Wal-Mart supplier's factory in Bangladesh. Wal-Mart insisted that its supplier was obeying local labor laws, which allowed 14-year-olds to work. A company official had also paid a surprise visit to the factory and had not found any problems. CEO Glass stated that "I can't tell you today that illegal child labor] hasn't happened someplace, somewhere. All we can do is try our best to prevent it."[7]

Meanwhile, Wal-Mart began considering international expansion. In March 1994, the company bought 122 Canadian Woolco stores, formerly owned by Woolworth Corp., the largest single purchase Wal-Mart had ever made.[8] In 1997, Wal-Mart opened six stores abroad, bringing the number of international units to 207, with the largest concentration in Canada followed by Mexico. In addition, Wal-Mart has gone to places such as Brazil, Puerto Rico, San Luis Potosi, Asia, China, Indonesia, and South America. Even in a global economy the jobs are always local, and the products are "made right here" whenever possible. These international stores reported $5 billion in sales in 1996. Wal-Mart employees now show pride in their company by shouting the Wal-Mart Cheer, which can be heard in many different languages in the many different regions of the world.[9]

Wal-Mart is proud to have various philosophies, called Culture Stories. First, the Sundown Rule means Wal-Mart strives to answer requests by sundown on the day it receives them. Next, the Ten-Foot Attitude promises that if an employee comes within ten feet of a customer the employee must look the customer in the eye and ask if the person would like to be helped. Every Day Low Prices is another philosophy. Wal-Mart believes that by lowering markup, they will earn more because of increased volume, thereby bringing consumers added value for the dollar everyday. Also, customers have been known to send letters to individual associates for giving exceptional service. This is what Wal-Mart calls Exceeding Customer Expectations.

Wal-Mart believes in bringing people from diverse backgrounds together, which is the idea behind the Minority- and Women Owned Development Program. It helps minority- and women-owned businesses provide goods and services in the retail sector. Wal-Mart knows that cultural diversity translates into customer satisfaction. A key to Wal-Mart's popularity with customers is its hometown identity. People Greeters welcome shoppers at the entrance of each store.

Customer service and community support go hand in hand. Wal-Mart strives to enhance the quality of life in each town in which it operates by implementing community outreach programs, led by local associates living in the town. Also, Wal-Mart has created projects to help the national community as well with such efforts as the Competitive Edge Scholarship Fund, raising funds for the Children's Miracle Network Telethon., and raising money and providing manpower for fundraisers benefiting such organizations as the Boy and Girl Scouts, and donating funds from bake sales to benefit charities.

In the past few years, Wal-Mart has made a commitment to the environment in its communities. It recycles over 700,000 tons of cardboard, paper, and plastic each year. Wal-Mart has opened three "EcoStores," which serve as laboratories for ideas that can potentially be used in future stores. These stores are energy efficient and environmentally friendly. The chains' Green Coordinators are knowledgeable about environmental issues and share information with Wal-Mart associates and customers.

Increasing the shareholders' value is very important to the corporation. In their 1997 Annual Report Wal-Mart stated that it had generated over $3 billion in free cash flow, which enabled it to enhance shareholder value.[10] This cash flow increased the dividend by 29 percent while also increasing the size of its share repurchase program. It will also help the company to reach its targeted annual total shareholder return of 15 percent.[11]

This rate of return has been accomplished by cutting inventories by over $2 billion, thereby saving $150 million in interest costs. Overseas expansion added $9.5 billion in sales in 1997, with a profit of more than $100 million.[12] Wal-Mart has an extensive online-shopping site on the Web as well. And Glass has a prototype for a green and white Wal-Mart convenience store on his desk in Bentonville.

Still, the company faces stiff competition from old and new rivals alike. Privately owned Meijers is one of the 16 fastest-growing companies in the country and the nation's fifth-largest discount retailer. Having enjoyed double-digit annual growth for so long, Wal-Mart now seems ready to admit to a slower (15 percent, versus 25 percent in earlier days) but still profitable growth strategy.[13] Over 100 supercenters, totaling 180,000 square feet in floor space (and generating $65 million in sales on average), are replacing smaller 90,000 square feet ($25 million average sales) Wal-Mart stores, in addition to promoting Wal-Mart's entry into the $450 billion grocery business.[14]

As CEO, David Glass has to determine whether any changes to the organization's style, culture, and structure will be necessary to carry the company to a higher level. In essence, he must decide whether the company's past strategy will allow Wal-Mart to continue to dominate as a retailer into the 21st century. He put it best in the 1997 annual report: "So if anyone wonders where our next $100 billion will come from—it will come from customers who recognize value throughout the world and from our associates who deliver it with a smile."[15]

Review Questions

1. Who are Wal-Mart's major external stakeholders?
2. Do a SWOT analysis of Wal-Mart. What are the company's distinctive competencies?
3. How would you describe Wal-Mart's "Grand" strategy for the next decade? In terms of Porter's generic strategies? In terms of Miles and Snow's adaptive model (see Chapter 9)?

The P&G Story

With its impressive list of consumer products, including Tide, Crest, Pantene, Tampax, Pringles, Pampers, Oil of Olay, Folgers, Jif, Cover Girl, Downy, Dawn, Bounty, Charmin, and Iams pet foods, P&G represents worldwide sales of over $40 billion. Tide and its sister brand outside the U.S., Ariel, together have more sales than any other P&G brand. (2)

From the beginning, P&G has pioneered new ways of doing business, from new product innovations to new ways of reaching out to its consumers. It pioneered the use of radio and television advertising as new media to reach the mass market. It was one of the first firms to use profit-sharing, a company research lab, and mass advertising. With $3.5 billion in advertising, the firm remains one of the largest advertisers in the world.

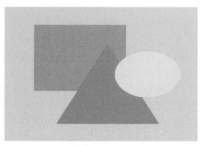

CASE 8

Procter and Gamble: A Web-based Turnaround?

A s one of the world's largest consumer products companies, Procter and Gamble markets more than 300 products to more than five billion consumers in 140 countries. (1) Having begun as a small soap and candle-making firm in Cincinnati, Ohio in 1837, it is widely recognized as a leading Old Economy story. The question becomes, can P&G learn to live with the New Economy Internet?

Recently, P&G has entered into a host of new product markets, including health care through the acquisition of Norwich Eaton Pharmaceuticals in 1982 and Richardson-Vicks in 1985, beauty care with Noxell, Max Factor, and Ellen Betrix in the late '80s and early '90s, and the $25 billion pet food industry with its purchase of Iams Pet Foods. The Company that began as a small Midwestern partnership had grown into one of America's largest multinational corporations. (3)

P&G exhibits a history of strong leaders, including John Smale, Edwin L. Artzt, and John Pepper (from 1995–1997) and Durk Jager, who took over in 1998 and began to shake up the normally conservative corporate culture. P&G suffered from a 1990s phenomenon of weakening brand identification among consumers, with the resulting effect of sluggish sales growth.

Artzt, known during his tenure as the "prince of darkness," had kept profits moving upwards by slashing 30 production plants and cutting 13,000 jobs. Pepper, with Jager as his chief operating officer, set the ambitious goal of doubling sales to $70 billion by 2006, through rapid product innovation and the exploitation of markets outside the United States. (4) Pepper eventually stepped aside in 1998 to allow his more aggressive subordinate to take over.

Jager took over a company that had become overly paternalistic, formula-driven, risk-averse, and inbred. The smallest decisions had to be referred to senior management and employees' adherence to strict rules and policies earned them the name of "Proctoids" by outside analysts. (5) Events in the 1990s, including lower-priced copycat products and big store chains such as Wal-Mart offering store brands of their own, served to pressure P&G's margins even more.

Jager brought in a new approach, represented by his motto that "If it ain't broke, break it." (6) He announced a reorganization that removed another 15,000 jobs and moved the company away from a country-based approach to that of product categories. It turned out to be too much in too short of a time. Failed takeover targets, including Gillette, Warner-Lambert, and American Home Products, along with disappointing sales and profit figures, doomed Jager's attempt at changing the corporate culture.

After only 18 months at the helm, Jager was replaced by Pepper's return to Chairman and Alan Lafley, known as a consensus builder, as chief executive. Lafley immediately made it clear that P&G intended to slow down the change process and restore a sagging employee morale by returning to the firm's core values. Its stock price, after dropping to $53.63 from $117.75, has recovered somewhat. (7) The question arises, where does P&G go from here?

P&G and the Internet

Lafley has made it clear that "We are making the Web a part of everything we do. We believe it multiplies the value of all of our strengths." He claims that P&G is "quietly transforming into a new-economy company" and that the "the biggest opportunity to leverage scale may be the Internet." (8)

Evidence of this transformation exists in a bevy of Web initiatives, including Reflect.com, Yet2.com, InnovationNet, Trasnora, and MorethanACard.com. These sites support one-to-one marketing initiatives and Internet-enabled personalization of products. Lafley intends to use the Net to remake the consumer products industry the same way P&G used the radio and television. (9)

From its main web site of www.pg.com, the firm wants to deepen the consumer's relationship with everything P&G. Early success is represented by 7 million hits a month on Pampers.com and 1.2 million/month on the firm's Mr-Clean.com location.

The firm is moving away from its reliance on "big bang" advertising campaigns in favor of "diffusing" a new brand into the culture gradually. Its new hair care product, Physique, was publicized heavily from its www.physique.com site. Result: 5 million hits on CLub Physique, allowing the firm to gather huge amounts of customer data in exchange for free samples.

The firm's prime site at www.pg.com acts as a portal to its other subordinate sites, packed with information and suggestions for a variety of uses for its long product list. The site is "transaction-enabled"—so P&G can both offer samples and sell products. This has some of P&G's retailers nervous about the firm reaching out to consumers directly. However, P&G's chief information officer, Steve David, states that "We are not going to be in the distribution business. First and foremost this is about trial. And it's good for our mainline retailers because it helps them create demand for new products." (10)

Individuals are invited to "help create new products" at the firm's homesite. "The whole Internet is enabling us to cut our marketing research costs by anywhere from half to 70 percent," claims Wade Miquelon, codirector of P&G's venture capital fund. Focus groups cannot match the speed of the Web—"Concept testing is going from weeks to days," states Miquelon. (11)

Its MorethanACard site is an attempt to enter the "gifting site." For $25, P&G has put together care packages of its products for different occasions. As an example, its New Arrivals package includes Pampers and Febreze, an odor neutralizer. P&G is attempting to enter into an arrangement with Target.com to carry MorethanACard.com gift bundles in order to provide better logistics.

At Reflect.com, the firm targets upscale women by designing unique cosmetic formulations for each woman and branding them with the name of her choice. (12) The increased cost of making "one-offs" is offset by the huge gross margins inherent to cosmetics. In addition, the firm learns firsthand about the preferences of its users, thereby providing invaluable feedback to its brand managers.

Yet2.com attempts to license the valuable patent rights from P&G's R&D practices. If the firm can license just 100 patents per year, "you're starting to talk real money," claims Conrad Langenhagen, director of strategic planning at Yet2.com. "And most of this is just pure profit—97 percent to 99 percent." (13)

Two internal intranet initiatives include InnovationNet and Transora. InnovationNet supports discussions from a database searchable by 18,000 employees from R&D, engineering, licensing, and purchasing. It provides a "virtual global lunchroom" to encourage product and process in-

novations. Transora is an online commodity auction site that supports B2B exchanges. CIO Steve David argues that P&G has the potential to save 10 to 15 percent on the cost of nonstrategic raw materials.

Its most ambitious foray involves MIT and technology known as "smart packaging." Also known as "auto-ID," the process involves embedding ultracheap microchips into packages, creating the ultimate in seamless, integrated supply-chain management through supermarket check-out. (14) When a shopper pulls a bottle of Tide off the shelf it would, via the Internet, charge the shopper's credit card and instantaneously inform the factory to produce more Tide.

Not everyone is as excited about the potential impact of the Web on P&G as Lafley. Merrill Lynch's

Heather Murren worries more about employee morale and long-term earnings than the Internet. "It's hard to envision it being important to a company like Procter and Gamble," she says. (15) Others are more supportive. "If not everything they're trying today works, that OK," argues securities analyst Daniel Peris. "Enough of these ventures will work that its going to benefit them. They don't have to win on all fronts, they just have to win a little bit." (16)

Review Questions

1. Can Lafley turn P&G's bureaucratic structure around in order to become more responsive to consumers?
2. Can P&G really become a New Economy company?
3. What might the "new" P&G look like because of the Internet?

CASE 9

Domino's Pizza: Could You Do It?

Domino's Pizza operates a network of over 6,600 owned and franchised stores in the United States and 64 international markets. With sales of over 360 million pizzas annually and revenues of $3.36 billion, corporate employment of over 15,000, and 105,000 additional associates including both full- and part-time, it represents an impressive success story. Starting in 1960 with one store in Ypsilanti, Michigan, Tom Monaghan redefined the pizza industry, and in so doing, built a corporate powerhouse. Could you do the same, given the chance?

The Domino Story

Tom Monaghan and brother James borrowed $500 in 1960 to purchase "DomiNick's," a pizza store, in Ypsilanti, Michigan. The fol-

lowing year Tom bought out his brother's half interest by trading him a used Volkswagen Beetle. In 1965 Tom changed the name of the establishment to "Domino's Pizza" and two years later opened the first franchise location in Ypsilanti. (1)

Having grown up in orphanages, Tom had a desire to succeed and do it in a large way. In his first 13 years in the business, he worked 100-hour work weeks, seven days a week. He only had one vacation, and that was for six days when he got married to his wife Margie. (2) The quote below exhibits his high need to be the best at whatever he does:

I was distracted by some of the rewards of success, which was hurting my business. I put all of these distractions aside, and focused solely on Domino's Pizza. I decided to take a 'millionaire's vow of poverty.' I am focusing on God, family and Domino's Pizza. (3)

The pizza industry is highly fragmented, with over 61,000 pizzerias in the United States. Over 3 billion pizzas are sold each year, with every man, woman, and child in America averaging 23 pounds annually. As an example, Pizza Hut uses 2.5 percent of all the milk produced in the United States (over 3.2 billion pounds) for cheese. (4) The problem becomes in how to create advantage and differentiate the product—is a pizza just a pizza?

Monaghan decided to concentrate only on pizzas and developed the strategy of delivering a hot pie in 30 minutes or less. He chose to locate his early franchises in college towns and near military bases, both high consumers of pizzas. This strategy proved to be very successful, and Domino's passed 200 locations in the late 1970s. (5) It is presently the second largest pizza chain after Pizza Hut.

Monaghan is credited with developing many of the pizza practices now taken for granted within the industry, including dough trays, the corrugated pizza box, insulated bags to transport pizzas, and a unique system of internal franchising. "Tom Monaghan made pizza delivery what it is today," says Eric Marcus, a 46-unit Domino's franchisee based in Dayton, Ohio. "The one thing about Tom is that he knew what he wanted, and he knew how to stay focused on what he wanted. He had a vision that pizza should be delivered in 30 minutes or less." (6)

The 1980s proved to be a huge time for growth for Domino's, as it closed out the decade with over 5,000 locations and $2 billion in sales. (7) During that time, Monaghan purchased the Detroit Tigers baseball team and developed significant philanthropic activities in various Donino's communities.

The Domino's Pizza story is not without challenges. In 1968 the firm's commissary and company headquarters were destroyed by fire. In 1976, Amstar Corp., maker of Domino Sugar, filed a trademark infringement lawsuit against the firm that was settled in Domino's favor in 1980. In 1993, in reaction to a $73 million lawsuit, the firm discontinued the "30 minute guarantee" and replaced it with the Total Satisfaction Guarantee:

If for any reason you are dissatisfied with your Domino's Pizza dining experience, we will re-make your pizza or refund your money. (8)

Monaghan himself has not been without controversy. In 1989 he took a hiatus from the business for 2-1/2 years to devote himself to Catholic philanthropy. A devoted Catholic, he supervised the construction of a cathedral near Managua, Nicaragua; built a mission in the Honduras mountain town of San Pedro Sula; and founded a group of 450 Catholic chief executives who travel to places of Catholic interest. (9) His outspoken opposition to abortion attracted a boycott of Domino's by the National Organization for Women (NOW).

In 1998, Monaghan sold "a significant" portion of his ownership in Domino's to Bain Capital Inc., a Massachusetts Investment firm. While he remained on the board of directors, he will not be engaged in the day-to-day activities of the firm. Instead, he wants to devote his time to his religious pursuits, including building a convent in Ann Arbor, Michigan. (10)

Taking over as President of Domino's was David Brandon, who managed the firm to a 4.4 percent growth in sales in his first full year. He was formerly employed with Procter and Gamble in Cincinnati and was most recently President and CEO of Valassis Communications, Inc., a leading sales promotion company. In addition to the franchise operations, he is responsible for overseeing 623 corporate-owned stores throughout the United States. (11)

Domino's Future

With a history of innovations in the pizza industry, Domino's constantly looks for new ways to enhance customer value. Domino's is presently working with Motorola in a test of its mobile electronic funds transfer point of sale (EFTPOS) device, the TransAKT(TM), providing customers the option to pay for their delivered pizza with credit and PIN-secured debit cards right on their doorstep. "As the vast majority of our business is transacted on the customers' door step, we are acutely aware of the importance of providing our customers with safe, reliable and convenient methods of payment at the point of delivery," said Bryan Dobb, President of Mad Pizza Company, whose 58 franchise locations in Canada and the U.S. will try out the technology. (12)

A new advertising campaign attempts to introduce what goes on behind the scenes at Domino's stores. "Bad Andy," a Muppetlike creature created by the Jim Henson Co., is "bad" because he tries to stop dedicated Domino's workers from their mission: producing and delivering hot, fresh pies to consumers. (13) The campaign has proved successful in increasing Domino's sales since the launch of the ads.

Domino's conducts an annual awards ceremony to honor its highest performers throughout its franchise system. Franchise operators are recognized for highest sales, safe driver awards, new managers, and a host of franchise innovations. (14)

Monaghan remains as a consultant to the pizza chain, but he prefers to spend his time on his philantropies, including a brotherhood organization for Catholic business leaders.

- Ave Maria School of Law, a Catholic venture in Ann Arbor.
- Owns a Catholic radio station in Ann Arbor and monthly Catholic newspaper called Credo.
- Spiritus Sanctus, a model Catholic school for grades kindergarten through eight in Ann Arbor. (15)

Monaghan displays the drive and determination representative of many entrepreneurs in today's dynamic market. Could *you* do what Tom Monaghan did?

You Do the Research

1. Do you have what it takes to be entrepreneurial in today's business environment?
2. What are the characteristics of pizza that make it particularly attractive as one of America's favorite takeout foods?
3. What are pizza parlors presently doing to differentiate their products?

Review Questions

1. What allowed Tom Monaghan to develop Domino's into a worldwide enterprise?
2. Why do you think Tom Monaghan has chosen to get out of the day-to-day operations of Domino's?
3. Do *you* have what it takes to be an entrepreneur?

CASE 10

Nucor Corporation: Structuring for Efficiency and Effectiveness

Nucor achieved its position as one of the largest steel producers in the United States by carefully monitoring costs and paying attention to the needs of its markets. This strategy of providing its customers with a competitive product at competitive prices has brought success and growth to Nucor, in sales, income, and stock price. Recently, however, the control of the organization has been brought into question. The recent announcement of a joint venture between Nucor and U.S. Steel to develop, test, and bring on-line a new method for turning iron ore into steel added to the concern over the ability of company management to maintain the entrepreneurial spirit for which the company is famous.

Background

Nucor is the second largest steel producer (2nd in assets, 1st in profits) in the United States. Its profits of $123 million have made it one of the most efficient firms in the steel industry. Nucor achieved that position by focusing on the manufacturing segment known as minimills—the relatively small, electrically powered mills that melt down scrap steel to manufacture products. This process saves on costly labor, raw materials, and the capital-intensive machinery necessary to produce steel from iron ore. A major concern of minimill steel manufacturers is maintaining quality, since their raw material consists of scrap steel of varying quality, containing a variety of alloys and impurities. Another concern is the recent rising price of scrap steel.

Nucor started out by manufacturing steel for the beams and posts produced in company-owned structural steel manufacturing plants and then expanded by selling its low-cost steel to other firms. Outside customers gradually became the primary outlet for sales by the minimills. Nucor was able to expand sales from the minimills by keeping costs below its competitors, both in the United States and abroad. Nucor has consistently sought ways to lower costs while broadening markets. During the latter part of the 1980s, much of the company's efforts were placed on developing technology for manufacturing sheet—flat-rolled steel of the type used by automotive and appliance manufacturers—which had traditionally been the sole domain of the big steel companies and foreign competitors. Ken Iverson, former CEO of Nucor, risked several hundred million dollars in adapting an untested German process for manufacturing this flat steel. Fortunately, the gamble paid off, increasing the company's growth in both sales and profits.

Iverson determined that one means of maintaining both quality control and costs was a highly decentralized organizational structure. Corporate staff was kept to a minimum. All decisions dealing with operations were delegated to the individual plants. Iverson believed that the managers closest to the action should be given the responsibility to develop plans to allow the plants, and the firm, to adapt to any changes in the environment. Iverson also gave plant-level mangers the authority to make and implement the decisions necessary to make these adaptations. Each plant manager gave a brief monthly report to headquarters and received a report comparing the divisions' performance. Major expenditures and changes were made by consensus at the periodic meetings of all plant and corporate managers.

Iverson took pride in the lean corporate structure. But the lack of corporate staff appeared to become a problem as Nucor expanded. By 1994 the company was operating 16 plants, and the flat-rolled steel plants increased the diversity of the operations reporting to the president. Nucor president, John Correnti, noted "My biggest fear is even though we're now a $3.3 billion company, we've still got to act, feel, and smell like a $300 million company (1)." Some steel industry analysis remained concerned over how Iverson would continue to control the growth of a company that was attempting to diversify its product line.

Iverson is not overly concerned with how Nucor will cope. He delights in highlighting Nucor's seeming incongruities:

- Nucor's 7,000 employees are the best-paid workers in our industry, yet Nucor has the lowest labor cost per ton of steel produced.
- Nucor is a Fortune 500 company with sales in excess of $3.6 billion, yet we have a total of just 22 people working at our corporate headquarters, and just four layers of management from the CEO to the front-line worker.
- Nucor operates in a "rust belt" industry that lost one out of two jobs over a 25-year span, yet Nucor has never laid off an employee or shut down a facility for lack of work, nor have we lost money in any business quarter for more than 30 consecutive years.
- We are in a labor-intensive and technology-intensive business, yet we've built most of our manufacturing facilities in areas that have more cows than people.
- We track and manage costs more closely than just about any business you can name, yet we anticipate and accept that roughly half of our investments in new ideas and new technologies will yield no usable results.
- Nucor pays hourly wages and salaries that run about 66 percent to 75 percent of the average for our industry—the rest of our employees' income comes from "at risk" bonuses—yet we regularly have large pools of qualified applicants for every job opening.
- Our company is broken up

into 21 independently operated businesses, each with almost complete local autonomy, yet we have an unusually active and free exchange of ideas and solutions across divisional, geographical, and functional boundaries.

- We have no R&D department or corporate engineering group, yet we were America's first major operator of "minimills," the first to demonstrate that minimills could make flat-rolled steel (a high-end steel product formerly made only by the Big Steel companies), the first to apply thin-slab casting (a technology Big Steel had written off as impractical), and the first to commercially produce iron carbide (an energy-efficient substitute for the scrap metal from which minimills make steel).

New Steel, November, 1997

Nucor replaces many control features common to most companies with an incentive program that focuses on productivity. As Ted Kuster of New Steel notes: "What Nucor management has been able to do is get workers to identify their own interests fundamentally with those of management, something managers have been attempting to do, not very successfully, since the dawn of industry (2)." Iverson stresses four clear-cut principles:

1. Management is obligated to manage the company in such a way that employees will have the opportunity to earn according to their productivity.
2. Employees should feel confident that if they do their jobs properly, they will have a job tomorrow.
3. Employees have the right to be treated fairly and must believe that they will be.
4. Employees must have an avenue of appeal when they believe they are being treated unfairly (2).

The question becomes: Can this management arrangement continue as the company grows?

Questions facing Nucor management revolved around issues of staffing, control, communications, and planning. As the span of control of top management increased, concern over whether operations were becoming unwieldy and uncomfortable became evident. Iverson was proud of the fact that there were only three layers between the President and workers on the floor. Managers were being rewarded for meeting short-term goals of increased sales, decreased costs, and quality maintenance. For example, Nucor managers would set standards for quality and output for groups of 25 to 30 employees and reward them with weekly bonuses.

Nucor top management maintained that this highly decentralized and lean organizational structure was necessary to meet foreign competition. According to top management, this structure would allow the firm to take advantage of those growth opportunities available in the environment. The risk was that the lower levels of management would follow short-term goals at the expense of long-term corporate objectives and coordination.

The Future

There was also concern that the joint venture with U.S.

Steel would hinder the quick decision making typical at Nucor. Iverson had gambled by committing to the first phase of the new process on his own, without first testing the process in a pilot plant on a small scale. The next stage was to complete the new process with a plant in the United States, relying on the high level of research and development skills at U.S. Steel and the ability of Nucor to pioneer new methods. Analysts wondered whether Nucor could coexist with U.S. Steel, with its large, hierarchical structure and strong union. This challenge was especially important since the new venture was felt to be the focal point for the continued growth of Nucor.

In the late 1990s, Iverson was fired by the Board of Directors of Nucor. His successor, John Correnti, who along with Iverson were the two major proponents of the minimill concept, was ushered out soon afterwards. Daniel R. DiMicco is the new President and CEO, but with years of experience at Nucor, the vision may or may not change. Will the new management attempt to rein in the general managers of the various operating entities of Nucor—a situation neither Iverson nor Correnti supported?

You Do the Research

1. Should Nucor stay with the minimill concept, or branch out into other technologies?
2. Why can't older, established steel mills compete against Nucor more effectively?
3. What happened to Nucor's attempt to exploit its iron carbide technology?

Review Questions

1. Evaluate Nucor's strategy using Porter's Competitive Strategy Framework.
2. Evaluate Nucor based on Miles and Snow's Adaptive Model.
3. Is Nucor capable of continuing its entrepreneurial spirit as it grows larger?

CASE 11

PricewaterhouseCoopers: Changing Economy, Mission, Design

Since the late 1980s, the national accounting/consulting industry has been dominated by the Big Six Firms of Arthur Andersen & Co., Coopers & Lybrand LLP, Deloitte & Touche, Ernst & Young, KPMG, and Price Waterhouse. Together, they charged more than $45 billion in fees 1996. In September 1997, Price Waterhouse and Coopers and Lybrand announced plans to merge their operations into what will represent the second-largest firm behind Andersen. What does this combination portend for both the firms and the industry in general?

From Six to Five

Mergers are not new to the accounting industry. Once known as the Big Eight, the mergers in the late 1980s of Deloitte Haskins & Sells with Touche Ross & Company to form Deloitte & Touche and Ernst & Whinney with Arthur Young & Company to form Ernst & Young, shrank the industry to the Big Six. (1) Price Waterhouse attempted to merge with Deloitte in 1984, but talks were canceled. In 1989, Price Waterhouse once again was set to merge, this time with Arthur Andersen, but the deal fell apart after quarrels over a new name. (2)

However, Price remained under pressure to combine with a larger player. In September of 1997, it announced that it intended to merge with Coopers & Lybrand in a deal that creates a firm with combined world-wide revenues of $12 billion, over 130,000 employees, and more than 8,500 partners. As the fifth- (Coopers) and sixth- (Price) largest players in the accounting/consulting market, their combination may have been inevitable. "Had Price Waterhouse not done this deal, they were in danger of fast becoming a niche player as the smallest of the Big Six," claimed Arthur Bowman, editor of *Bowman's Accounting Reports*. (3)

In addition to its U.S. operation, Price is active in Asia and South America. Price represents such industries as chemicals, entertainment and media, and energy. Coopers has a strong presence in Europe and specializes in consumer products, manufacturing, and communications on an international scale. The need to develop a larger presence in consulting appears to have been one of the main motivations for the merger. (4) In 1996, for the first time, the 100 biggest accountancy firms in the United States earned more from consulting ($8.3 billion) than they did from either auditing ($7.9 billion) or tax ($5 billion). (5)

While previous mergers in the industry have been motivated by the need to reduce the size of the firms and reduce overhead, the Price/Coopers union is motivated by the need for global support and seamless business consulting. Shortly after the Price/Coopers announcement, KPMG and Ernst & Young announced that they too would be merging. However, in early March of 1998, they announced they had abandoned their proposed $18 billion merger after four tumultuous months of negotiations.

The need for economies of scale is starkly evident when revenues per partner are compared across the firms in the industry. On average, Price Waterhouse's 3,300 partners generated $1.5 million apiece in 1996, with Coopers' 5,200 partners averaging $1.3 million. By comparison, Arthur Andersen's 2,611 partners generated an average of $3.6 miilion each.

A number of forces in the rapidly changing accounting/consulting industry are both supporting and aggravating such combinations. The market for professional business services is growing more rapidly overseas than it is in the United States. (6) Globalization of the industry is expected to become increasingly prevalent throughout this century and into the next. The *U.S. Industry and Trade Outlook* forecasts that demand for U.S. management, consulting, and public relations services overseas will continue to grow at 14 to 15 percent annually into the 21st century compared to a domestic growth rate averaging 5.4 per cent annually. (7)

Another cause for concern is legal liability. All Big Five accounting firms have become limited liability partnerships (LLP) in an effort to protect their partners from litigation. Especially now as the firms strengthen their global presence, partners in Britain, for example, do not wish to be sued for alleged errors of their colleagues in California. Even more pervasive is the conflict between accountants and consultants, which tends to pull the two major revenue sources in opposite directions. Indeed, many clients have problems with the new one-stop firms, as conflicts of interest arise when they are independently audited by the same firm providing professional business advice.

The Future: PricewaterhouseCoopers

One of the biggest problems with any merger as large as Price and Coopers is the potential for clashing cultures. A former Coopers & Lybrand partner likens Price Waterhouse to a Roman legion: pristine, well-equipped, and efficiently drilled. Alternatively, Coopers "are the Visigoths of the industry throwing stones from the tops of trees." (8) Price has a stong team culture; new business at Coopers is fought over "tooth and nail" internally. (9) Andersen Worldwide recently voted to split off its consulting and accounting arms.

Howard Schilit, an accounting professor who is president of the Center for Financial Research and Analysis, worries that "each of the firms has a very special culture and it will be difficult to merge the two together." (10) James Wadia, managing director and head of Arthur Andersen, the accounting arm of Andersen Worldwide, notes that "These megamergers are difficult to do. The firms get distracted, and there's tremendous opportunity in the turmoil." Andersen lost its top-ranked spot during the last merger wave, only to reclaim it a few years later. Wadia insists that internal growth, not mergers, is the way to grow and hopes to pick up disgruntled partners from the merged firms. (11)

Having been considered a merger partner with Hewlett-Packard, the deal was dropped at HP's request. (12) The new question becomes: will PricewaterhouseCoopers follow the lead of Accenture, the worldwide organization formerly known as Andersen Consulting, and KPMG Consulting in floating a public offering? PWC has remained topheavy since its merger, and needs to cut costs in order to stay competitive in the consulting arena. In addition, it needs the capital available from public financing in order to invest and grow in the increasingly competitive busines services market.

You Do the Research

1. Should PricewaterhouseCoopers go public with an IPO?
2. What effect might this change in business model have on the firm?
3. Will mergers continue in the public accounting arena?

Review Questions

1. Compare the cultures between Price and Coopers. Are there differences?
2. What pressure does this merger put on the rest of the industry?
3. Would you classify the accounting/consulting work design as small batch, mass production, or continuous process according to Joan Woodward's classification?

BET Holdings II, Inc.: Building the Best African-American Internet Portal

Robert Johnson, born the ninth of ten children in Hickory, Mississippi, is a true rags-to-riches success story. His father, Archie, chopped wood while his mother taught school, and their search for a better life led them to Freeport, Illinois, a predominantly white working-class neighborhood. Archie supplemented his factory jobs by operating his own junkyard on the predominantly black east side of town. Edna Johnson got a job at Burgess Battery, and although she eventually secured a job for her son Robert at the battery firm, he knew it wasn't for him. (1)

Bobby Johnson showed an enterprising nature at an early age, delivering papers, mowing lawns, and cleaning out tents at local fairs. At Freeport High School, Robert was an honors student and was able to enter the University of Illinois upon graduation. Virgil Hemphill, his freshman roommate, commented that "He was not overly slick, overly smooth. He was kind of innocent and naive. His strength was being able to talk to different types of people. I went to Freeport with him, and he could communicate with the regular people and with the suit-and-tie people." (2) Johnson did well at Illiniois, studying history, holding several work-study jobs, and participating at Kappa Alpha Psi, a black fraternity. After graduation in 1968, Johnson was admitted to Princeton University's Woodrow Wilson School of Public and International Affairs, a two-year program with a full scholarship plus expenses. However, he dropped out after the first semester to marry his college sweetheart, Sheila Crump, a former cheerleader and gifted violinist. He eventually returned to Princeton to earn his masters degree in public administration in 1972. (3)

He moved on to Washington to work at the Corporation for Public Broadcasting, followed by the Washington Urban League, where the director, Sterling Tucker, was leading the struggle for District home rule. Tucker appreciated Johnson's ability to think both "micro-ly and macro-ly" while still "thinking like a visionary" in pursuing larger goals. (4) Having moved on to the Congressional Black Caucus, Johnson became impressed with the possibilities for black power that lay in television and cable in particular. In 1976, he moved on to work as a lobbyist for the National Cable Television Association (NCTA), where he gained invaluable insight into the cable industry.

At the NCTA's 1979 convention, Johnson met Bob Rosencrans, president of UA-Columbia Cablevision. While Bob Johnson had a strong idea in providing cable programming to minority audiences, he had no satellite time; Rosencrans owned some unused slots on one of the three cable TV satellites, and was looking for programs to support his local franchises. "I just said, 'Bob, you're on. Let's go.' I don't think we even charged him. We knew he couldn't afford much, and for us, it was a plus because it gave us more ammunition to sell cable. The industry was not attracting minority customers." (5)

With $15,000 from a consulting contract that he received upon his departure from NCTA, Robert Johnson launched Black Entertainment Television (BET) at 11 P.M. on January 8, 1980. The first BET show was a 1974 African safari movie, "Visit to a Chief's Son." Initially, BET aired for only two hours on Friday nights. The first show bounced off an RCA satellite and into 3.8 million homes served by Rosencrans' franchises. Johnson received his first crucial financing from John Malone of TCI in the form of a $380,000 loan plus $120,000 to purchase 20 percent of BET. (6)

Johnson's original staff at BET included Vivian Goodier, who came over from NCTA and assisted Johnson with the original BET business plan. In addition, Johnson hired his secretary, Carol Coody, and his older sister Polly. The BET staff approached cable companies, subscribers, and others at industry shows, using a little 10-by-10 booth with a collapsible table and display. After a decade of learning the finer points of cable industry, Johnson went public with BET and raised $70 million.

However, this did not occur without controversy. In 1992, Goodier, Coody, and Polly Johnson all sued Robert Johnson, claiming that he had promised them shares of the company in exchange for their hard work. These claims were eventually settled, with $900,000 each going to Coody and Polly and more than $2 million for Goodier, who claimed a personal relationship with Bob Johnson. (7)

To raise capital in the 1980s, Johnson sold off pieces of BET to Time Inc. and Taft Broadcasting for over $10 million. However, controversy over programming has followed Johnson from the start, with his heavy reliance on music videos (60 percent of total programming), gospel and religious programs, infomercials, and reruns of older shows such as *Sanford and Son* and *227*. (8) Lydia Cole, BET vice-president for programming, does not let her young daughters watch BET, claiming "We don't watch BET. I'm concerned about the images portrayed of young girls." (9)

Johnson lives on a $4.3 million, 133-acre horse farm in Virginia, and while he supports a large number of black causes, he declines to be identified as a role model. "I don't want to be seen as a hero to younger people. I want to be seen as a good solid business guy who goes out and does a job, and the job is to build a business. . . . What are my responsibilities to black people at large? If I help my family get over and deal with the problems they might confront, then I have achieved that one goal that is my responsibility to society at large." (10)

Although Johnson professes to want to produce original programming, he continues to suffer from low fees compared to other cable offerings. Early in BET's existence, Johnson was earning only 2 cents per subscriber, while major networks such as TNT and USA were getting 15 to 20 cents. Johnson has won the battle for higher fees, which jumped from 2.5 cents to 5 cents in 1989, and eventually to 15.5 cents in the next five years. BET is watched by 52 million households, 142,000 in any given minute, and ranks nineteenth among 28 cable channels tracked by Nielsen data. (11) Subscriber fees generated $50.4 million in 1996, compared to $60 million through infomercials and advertising. (12)

The Future

Robert Johnson continues to have grand plans for BET, seeking to turn the enterprise into what marketers call an umbrella brand. (13) The firm publishes two national magazines that reach 250,000 readers: *Young Sisters and Brothers* for teens and *Emerge* for affluent adults, and it has interests in film production, electronic retailing, and radio. (14) The first BET SoundStage restaurant opened in suburban Washington, with another opening in Disney World in Orlando. With Hilton as a partner, Johnson hopes to open a casino in Las Vegas, Nevada. (15)

Johnson (audio livecast from NPR) wants to capture some of the black consumers' disposable income—valued at $425 billion annually. To do this, he partners primarily with such big names as Disney, Hilton, Blockbuster, Microsoft, and others. "You simply cannot get big anymore by being 100 percent black-owned anything" Johnson claims. (16) Reaching 98 percent of all black cable homes, his BET cable station, reaching 63.4 million households in the U.S., provides the perfect medium to influence this increasingly affluent black audience.

His most ambitious venture to date has been to create the largest African-American web portal in the world. His development of BET Interactive, with its BET.com and 360hiphop.com, represents a powerful force on the Web. Voted "Best African American Community Site 2001" by *Yahoo! Internet Life* magazine, BET.com provides a combination of online content and community tailored to the unique interests, preferences, and issues of African Americans aged 18-49. (17) 360hiphop.com offers users a compelling hip-hop experience, including culture, lifestyle, music, as well as news and politics. (18)

Consistent with Johnson's vision, BET Holdings II was purchased in whole by Viacom, Inc. for a price of $3 billion. BET founder Robert L. Johnson remains Chairman and CEO of the unit, reporting to Viacom President and Chief Operating Officer, Mel Karmazin. (19) Johnson becomes the second largest shareholder in Viacom behind Summer Redstone and boasts a personal wealth now estimated at $1.63 billion. (20)

Many compare the deal to Ted Turner selling his Turner broadcasting unit to Time Warner. "A couple of significant things have happened as a result of this," says Ken Smikle, president of Target Market News, a research firm that studies black consumer behavior.

"The deal has produced one of a few African American billionaires in America. We need to take pride in the idea that we are capable of playing with the big boys in the way that the big boys play." (21)

You Do the Research

1. Was Johnson correct in selling his BET Holdings II to Viacom?
2. Will BET Interactive become a major force on the Web?
3. What's next for Robert Johnson?

Review Questions

1. How does motivation influence performance and is this evident in BET?
2. What role does reinforcement play in motivation?
3. What is happening in the area of motivation and compensation?

CASE 13

Southwest Airlines: How Herb Kelleher Led the Way

The U.S. airline industry experienced problems in the early 1990s. From 1989 through 1993, the largest airlines, including American, United, Delta, and USAIR, lost billions of dollars. Only Southwest Airlines remained profitable throughout that period. CEO and cofounder Herb Kelleher pointed out that "We didn't make much for a while there. It was like being the tallest guy in a tribe of dwarfs." (1) Nevertheless, his company had sales of $3.8 billion in 1997, an increase over 1996 of 12 percent, and profits of $317 million. This is particularly noteworthy since Southwest is not a nationwide air carrier; 85 percent of its flights are under 500 miles. (2) How did a little airline get to be so big? Its success is due to its key values, developed by Kelleher and carried out daily by his 25,000 employees. These core values are humor, altruism, and "luv" (the company's stock ticker symbol). (3)

One of the things that makes Southwest so unique is its short-haul focus. The airline doesn't assign seats or sell tickets through the reservation systems used by travel agents. Many passengers buy tickets at the gate. The only food served is peanuts or crackers. But passengers don't seem to mind. In fact, serving Customers (at Southwest, always written with a capital "C") is the focus of the company's employees. As the Executive Vice President for Cutomers, Colleen Barrett, said, " We will never jump on employees for leaning too far toward the customer, but we come down on them hard for not using common sense." (4) As *Fortune* magazine summarized, "Treating the customer right is a lot easier when employees are treating one another that way." Southwest's core values produce employees who are highly motivated and who care about the customers and about one another.

One way in which Southwest carries out this philosophy is by treating employees and their ideas with respect. Executive Vice President Barrett formed a "culture committee," made up of employees from different functional areas and levels, who meet quarterly to come up with ideas for maintaining Southwest's corporate spirit and image. All managers, officer, and directors are expected to "get out in the field," meet and talk to employees, and understand their jobs. Employees are encouraged to use their creativity and sense of humor to make their jobs and the customers' experience more enjoyable. Gate agents, for example, are given a book of games to play with waiting passengers when a flight is delayed. Flight agents might do an imitation of Elvis or Mr. Rogers while making announcements. Other have jumped out of the overhead luggage bins to surprise boarding passengers. (5)

CEO Kelleher knows that not everyone would be happy as a Southwest employee, however: "What we are looking for, first and foremost, is a sense of humor. Then we are looking for people who have to excel to satisfy themselves and who work well in a collegial environment." He feels that the company can teach specific skills but a compatible attitude is most important. When asked to prove that she had a sense of humor Mary Ann Adams, hired in 1997 as a finance executive, recounted a practical joke in which she turned an unflattering picture of her boss into a screen saver for her department (6).

To encourage employees to treat one another as well

as they treat their customers, departments examine linkages within Southwest to see what their internal "customers" need. The provisioning department, for example, whose responsibility is to provide the snacks and drinks for each flight, selects a flight attendant as "customer of the month." The department's own board of directors makes the selection decision, as well as other managerial decisions, for the provisioning department. Kelleher and Barrett are invited to these board meetings, and both feel that it is important to attend. Other departments have sent their internal "customers" pizza and ice cream. Employees write letters commending the work of other employees or departments, and these letters are valued as much as those from customers. When problems do occur between departments, the employees work out solutions in supervised meetings.

Employees exhibit the same attitude of altruism and "luv" (Southwest's term for its relationship with its customers) to other groups as well. Nearly 25 percent of Southwest employees volunteered their time at Ronald McDonald Houses throughout Southwest's territory. When the company purchased a small regional airline, employees personally sent cards and company T-shirts to their new colleagues to welcome them to the Southwest family. They demonstrate similar caring to the company itself. As gasoline prices rose during the period of the Gulf War in the early 1990s, many of the employees created the "Fuel from the Heart Program," donating fuel to the company by deducting the cost of one or more gallons from their paychecks.

Acting in the company's best interests is also directly in the interest of its employees. Southwest has a profit-sharing plan in which approximately 15 percent of net profit is distributed to employees and unlike many of its competitors Southwest consistently has profits to share. Employees also own 13 percent of Southwest stock. Although 80 percent unionized, the company has a history of good labor relations. In fact, the firm and the pilots union have recently agreed to an unusual 10-year contract under which the pilots will receive stock options to buy millions of shares, as well as profit sharing, but will receive no wage increase during the first 5 years. (7)

According to Harvard University professor John Kotter, setting the standard for low costs in the airline industry does not mean Southwest is "cheap." "Cheap is trying to get your prices down by nibbling costs off everything . . . [firms like Southwest Airlines] are thinking 'efficient,' which is very different. . . . They recognize that you don't necessarily have to take a few pennies off of everything. Sometimes you might even spend more." (8) By buying one type of plane—the Boeing 737—Southwest saves both on pilot training and on maintenance costs. The "cheap" paradigm would favor used planes; Southwest's choice results in the youngest fleet of airplanes in the industry because the model favors high-productivity over lower expenses.

Southwest currently operates 346 Boeing 737 jets:

TYPE	NUMBER	SEATS
737-200	33	122
737-300	194	137
737-500	25	122
737-700	94	137

By utilizing its planes an average of 11 hours and 20 minutes each day, Southwest is able to make more trips with fewer planes than any other airline. Its ground turnaround time of 17 minutes is the best in the industry. Not serving meals and cooperation from its ground and flight crews make this amazing statistic possible.

Keeping labor costs low is one of the ways in which Southwest maintains its competitive advantage. Employees' productivity is higher than that of any other airline. As of 1994, the company had won its eleventh "Triple crown" for being number one in the industry in on-time performance, baggage handling, and customer satisfaction. However, management also worried about the effects on morale of limited opportunities for promotion. The company has created "job families" with different grade levels so that employees can work their way up within their job category. However, as Executive V.P. Barrett notes, "some jobs are worth only so much money," and after five or six years employees begin to hit the maximum for their job category.

Southwest's management has other concerns for the future. The addition of Baltimore, Chicago, and Cleveland has increased routes, personnel, and distance. As the company continues to grow, it is becoming more difficult for employees in outlying locations to get to meetings and events at its Dallas headquarters. Recently, problems with delivery of 737–700 aircraft from the Boeing Company hobbled some of Southwest's expansion plans.

Another issue is how to maintain the culture of caring and fun while expanding rapidly into new markets. Southwest's success has been built with the enthusiasm and hard work of its employees; as CEO Kelleher said, "The people who work here don't think of Southwest as a business. They think of it as a crusade." (9) Cultivating that crusading atmosphere must be a continuing priority for the company.

The major concern for investors is the succession plans for Herb Kelleher. So much of Southwest's success is attributable to Kelleher's unique management and leadership styles that questions remain as to how the firm can continue its dominance when the charismatic leader leaves.

1999 Fun Facts:

- Southwest received 216,000 resumes and hired 5,134 new Employees.
- Southwest booked 6.5 million reservations monthly.
- Southwest served 90.9 million bags of peanuts.
- Southwest served 7.3 million bags of raisins.
- Southwest uses about 74 million gallons of jet fuel per month.
- Southwest has 812 married couples. In other words, 1,624 Southwest Employees have spouses who also work for the Company.
- Southwest received requests for service from 148 destinations.

You Do the Research

1. What happens to Southwest when Herb leaves?
2. As Southwest continues to expand, can it hold onto its founding principles?
3. How does the merger activity in the airline industry impact Southwest?

Review Questions

1. What needs were Southwest's employees able to meet through their jobs?
2. How did Southwest motivate its employees?
3. What are the principal motivational problems facing Southwest as it continues to expand?

CASE 14

Saturn, Inc.: Making Pay-for-Performance Pay Off

- -

As one of the world's best known brands, Saturn, the General Motors car division that brought new production and marketing concepts to American car manufacturers, faces tough questions in an increasingly competitive global market. Its reliance on a limited offering of compact models hurts its performance in the face of declining sales. Can it continue to set the standards for customer satisfaction and reliability and depend on an innovative employee pay-for-performance package?

The Saturn Story

Jack Smith Jr., appointed CEO and President of General Motors Corporation in 1992 after a revolt of the outside members of the Board of Directors, noted that the firm had turned around its losing ways by focusing on its customers. In a speech to auto dealers in Michigan, he cited the success of the Saturn Division of GM for setting the standard for "hassle-free purchasing and services, and . . . exceeding customer expectations." Smith further noted that this success had led to the addition of a third shift at the Spring Hill,

Tennessee, complex that produced Saturns. Moreover, Saturn dealers continued to lead all dealer organizations in the United States in unit sales per outlet. (1)

The original plan, developed in 1982, was given to Richard LeFauve, who was named President of Saturn Corporation after its first president died shortly after the company was set up. The plan called for a $5 billion investment in a series of plants that would produce up to 350,000 cars per year. By 1988, when the plant was just about completed, the investment had been trimmed to approximately $3 billion.

The Saturn complex was comprised of a series of six interconnected buildings. Four of the six buildings were manufacturing and assembly plants. The remaining two were a maintenance and utilities facility and a training and administration building. The complex had a rated production capacity of 240,000 cars per year. This was to be expanded to 310,000 with the addition of a third shift in 1993.

The Saturn Corporation was the first new automotive division of General Motors since 1918. The purpose of developing a new division was to meet the competition of the Japanese, particularly at the lower end of the product line. (2) GM had seen its share of the U.S. market fall throughout the 1970s. This was especially true for lower-priced cars. U.S. auto consumers no longer had confidence in the ability of GM to be able to produce a low-priced, high-quality car. Roger Smith, then CEO of GM, felt that the only way to overcome this perception was to launch an entirely new line of cars. The technol-ogy, labor policies, work rules, and marketing of this new product were to be developed from scratch; there would be no preconceived notions concerning any of these areas brought in from the existing organization structure or culture. (3)

The initial phase of planning for the Saturn Corporation was carried out by bringing together managers and workers from 55 plants in 17 GM divisions. The "Group of 99"—so named because it consisted of 99 United Auto Workers (UAW) members, GM mangers, and staff personnel—started meeting in 1984. (4) The group quickly split into separate research teams to study all aspects of the new operation. One of the teams realized that labor relations would be a critical factor in the development and implementation of a successful new offering. GM entered into separate negotiations with the UAW to develop a new contract strictly for the Saturn Corporation.

The rest of GM was covered by a master contract with the United Auto Workers, which covered not only wages, benefits, and hours of work but also a complex series of work rules that restricted GM's ability to transfer workers from one task to another on the production line. GM felt that the effectiveness of the new Saturn Corporation would be dependent on more flexible work rules. Management wanted the ability to develop the kind of work flexibility found in most Swedish and Japanese auto plants. The UAW finally agreed to a system of self-governing work teams on the production line at the Saturn assembly plant. These teams would be de-signed to follow the construction of an automobile unit throughout the entire assembly line. Under the terms of the contact, workers would be cross-trained so that the members of each team could switch off on the various tasks required to complete the assembly of each individual unit.

Saturn uses a "risk and reward compensation system" that puts 12% of a worker's pay at risk, contingent on: (5)

1. 5% risk on quality—a threshold, measured in reduction of sample defects per vehicle, that must be met before the reward portion, which also contains a quality goal, can kick in;
2. 5% risk on training; and
3. 2% risk on team skills.

All Saturn workers are paid at a rate equal to 88 percent of average GM compensation. The 12 percent at risk brings pay "up to a line" roughly equal with industry averages, with the reward portion providing possibilities "above the line." (6) The basis for the reward portion contains provisions regarding schedules, productivity, and quality. Saturn uses the Uniform Vehicle Evaluation system, an international standard in which auditors enter the plant and select 20 to 25 cars at random and evaluate these for sample defects (4). With the American public's present loss of appetite for small cars, the system may need to be rvamped for cost reduction rather than output. In early 1998, the Saturn union voted to retain the innovative system, 4,052 in favor with 2,120 opposed. (7)

In many ways, this was similar to the assembly process employed by Volvo at some of its auto plants which had led to increased quality, decreased boredom, and increased job satisfaction on the part of its workers. Each member of the Saturn work team was put through an extensive training program before joining the assembly line. The 350 hours of training were designed to cover both technical and team-building aspects of the job.

Richard LeFauve was selected as the new president of Saturn Corporation because of his experience within GM. He had spent two years in charge of GM's Adam Opel unit in Germany, where he had supervised the development of a sporty new Kadett model. Moreover, LeFauve had gained experience with the German labor-management system. Under German co-determination laws, labor is required to have a say in decision making and management is required to grant labor a position on the board of directors. This, it was felt, would give LeFauve better insight into the problems that might develop as the new labor contract was implemented.

GM management sought and developed new technology and machinery consistent with the new labor agreement. A great many robots and other forms of automation were incorporated into the production line to help reduce employee boredom and fatigue and to help ensure high quality standards. Furthermore, company engineers developed a platform that was designed to move along with the car. In this manner, workers no longer needed to walk at a steady pace beside the car to be able to complete their tasks; instead, workers and the car moved together on the new platform.

The new organization was built around several key factors. They included:
- Quality as a top priority
- Ownership by all
- Equality of all
- Total trust
- People orientation
- Union/management partnership
- Authority commensurate with responsibility

These factors were put to the test in 1991. Unfortunately, the results of the first year of operation indicated that the Saturn plant would not meet its goals. Under the terms of the Saturn/UAW contract, workers could suffer penalties that would mean their salary would equal approximately 80 percent of the average GM worker's annual wages. There was concern that the workers would find this unacceptable since some of the failure was not their fault. Furthermore, there had been quality lapses in the initial products. While many had been caught and corrected before the autos left the plant, other cars had to be recalled. All of these factors led to lower production, productivity, and quality standards than had originally been planned for the first year.

Management decided to share the responsibility for falling short of the first-year goals. It relaxed the terms of the contact and essentially granted bonuses that brought Saturn salaries to approximately 95 percent of an hourly worker's average annual wage. Management hoped this would convince the workers that the company planned to live up to the seven key points outlined earlier.

It was still unclear, however, whether the Saturn cars being sold were replacing Japanese sales or cars that would have been sold by other GM units. Moreover, GM management realized that sales of Saturn cars could not possibly recoup the original $3 billion investment in the new unit. They would have to be able to transfer the ideas, technology, concepts, and labor relations developed for the Saturn plants to other parts of the GM organization to make the investment worthwhile.

To compound problems, the new workers that were being added to the Saturn workforce were being recruited from closed GM plants, under an agreement with the UAW. These new workers were being rushed onto the production line with only one-third the training time of the original Saturn workers. Many managers and original members of the Saturn union felt that these two factors might reduce morale at the Saturn complex and could lead to a decline in the quality standards that had contributed to the success of this unit. Both Smith and LeFauve knew that the continued growth and quality of the Saturn projects and service would be key factors in the success of GM as a whole.

Saturn's Future

The Saturn story has been one of alternating success and failure in the 1990s. IntelliChoice ranked the 1997 SL1, SL2, SC1, and SC2 models as the "Best Overall Values" in their respective classes. J.D. Power put Saturn in first place for sales satisfaction and seventh in customer satisfaction. (The top six were all luxury cars— Lexus, Infiniti, Acura, Mercedes-Benz, Cadillac, and Jaguar).

At the same time, the competition in the 1998 small-car market is increasing dramatically. Experts claim that Saturn's limited lineup is holding back sales, with the car company only offering a coupe, sedan, and wagon—all small cars based on the same architecture and looking pretty much the same. Saturn brought a new midsize car online in 1999, and added a sport-utility vehicle in 2001. (8) Saturn desperately needs to broaden its product line in order to stay competitive. (9)

New initiatives include an attempt to open foreign markets with Japan targeted with 80 dealerships. In addition, GM wants Saturn to market its electric vehicle, the EV-1. (10) Mike Bennett, head of the UAW Local 1853 at Saturn, states: "We're go-ing to be a 100-year car company, right? Well, if we're going to be a 100-year car company, we need to be a learning organization." (11)

You Do the Research

1. What other incentive plans can you find on the Web?
2. What would you want in order to increase your performance in college?
3. Is pay-for-performance for you?

Review Questions

1. Describe the changes that GM is trying to implement at Saturn Corp.
2. What are the critical factors in developing the management of the Saturn Corp. plants?
3. What problems might GM management face in trying to transplant the Saturn concept to other GM units?

CASE 15

Boeing Company: Talent Builds a Better Plane

Boeing, based in Seattle, Washington, has remained the world's #1 commercial aircraft manufacturer for more than 30 years, with more than 60 percent of the world market share. A major exporter, its aircraft, which range from the popular 737 to the Jumbo 747, are flown by every major airline in the world. However, even in the face of success, Boeing is under intense pressure to reinvent the way it develops and manufactures aircraft.

A Proud History

William Boeing built his first airplane in 1916 with navy officer Conrad Westervelt. His Seattle factory, originally named Pacific Aero Products, changed its name to Boeing Airplane Company the following year. The company produced training planes for the U.S. Navy in World War I. After the war, Boeing began the first international airmail service between Seattle and Victoria, British Columbia, with its B-1 flying boat. (1)

Between the wars, Boeing created the United Aircraft and Transport Corporation to facilitate its manufacturing and transportation concerns. The company introduced the first all-metal airliner in 1933. The following year, due to changes in airmail rules, the firm was forced to sell its airline operations (the predecessor of today's United Air-lines) and concentrate on aircraft manufacturing. (2)

Boeing has always been a leader in aircraft innovations, introducing the Model 314 Clipper (flying boats) used by Pan Am, the Model 307 Stratoliner (the first aircraft with a pressurized cabin), and the B-17 bomber during World War II. However, it was the introduction in 1954 of the Boeing 707 that redefined the aircraft industry as we know it today. For over the following 40 years, Boeing has added to its line of aircraft, including the Jumbo 747, its popular 737, and the more recent 777 to meet the increasing needs of airline travel both in the United States and around the world.

After recent mergers with McDonnell Douglas in 1997 and the space and defense divisions of Rockwell International in 1996, Boeing is suffering from the problems associated with such mergers. With orders for new aircraft at an all-time high, the firm faces problems keeping up with production demands. The situation got so bad that the company actually closed down its 737 and 747 production lines for a month in 1997 in order to gain control of its needs, problems that caused it to write off a $1.6 billion charge in the third quarter and face over $300 million in penalties from customers for late deliveries. As a result, Boeing has announced a radical new development strategy in early 1998.

The Need for Change

Boeing is an example of what can happen to a company that is overwhelmed by good fortune. Record orders required that Boeing ramp up its production from 18 jets a month in 1995 to 43 by early 1998. In an attempt to hire and train 41,000 new workers, the company often raided its own suppliers, aggravating an already strained supply chain. In May of 1997, the FAA warned Boeing about improper paperwork on its 737s, and as a result it stepped up its inspections of Boeing assembly lines. (3)

Meanwhile, Boeing faces stiff rivalry from Airbus Industrie, a European consortium that builds the A300 aircraft family. In early 1998, the four countries of France, Germany, Britain, and Spain agreed to a merger for the consortium to eliminate inefficient assembly methods and make the company more competitive with Boeing. (4) The European jet maker's market share edged up to 30 percent, as it booked record orders. Boeing's production delays and costly overhead structure makes it increasingly difficult to compete in a market dominated by a concern for cost. As Byron Callan, aerospace analyst for Merrill Lynch, emphasizes, ". . . the name of the game is cost." (5)

As a result of these and other problems, Boeing CEO Philip Condit formed a project team called the Aircraft Creation Process Strategy (ACPS), nicknamed by suppliers as "faster-better-cheaper."

(6) The goal is to curb the production time of aircraft from 60 months to 12 and cut the costs from around $6.5 billion to $1 billion. (7) Headed by Walter Gillette, the program is conducted in close association with Boeing's suppliers and airlines. Since 1960, the price per seat of transport aircraft has increased more than 140 percent, while yield per passenger mile has dropped by about half. Time-to-market for new aircraft during the same period increased from 3 to almost 4.5 years from the "first order." (8)

With no new airplanes on its drawing boards, Boeing has only one place to look for a competitive advantage—the factory floor. (9) The new scheme is intended to supplant a system of engineering, manufacturing, and parts procurement that dates back to the production of B-17 and B-29 bombers in the 1940s. Over the years, the system has grown more and more complex; it does not necessarily produce more airplanes, but definitely produces more paperwork. (10)

An additional problem is the extraordinary choice Boeing offers its customers on aircraft configurations. On the 747 alone, there are four bulkhead options that can result in the repositioning of 2,500 parts and the modification of 900 pages of drawings. Computers help track some of these problems, but every factory has its own computer system, and parts lists are maintained on over 400 different databases. Robert Hammer, VP of production process reform, observes that "You know the Baldrige prize for the best manufacturing processes? Well, if there was a prize for the opposite, this

system would win it hands down." So, can the system be fixed? No way, says Hammer. "We're going to kill it." (11)

ACPS envisions a number of improvements to the present system. Key strategies include reuse of existing components and reducing parts counts with integrated, monolithic structures. Common, modular, and integrated systems also would be employed. Aircraft catalog options will be reduced with financial incentives to limit aircraft customization. Production changes range from building multiple models of aircraft on a single production line, with the aircraft flyable almost immediately, to "last-stage customization" centers for interiors and paint application. (12)

Emphasis is also being placed on how workers actually do their jobs on the assembly line, a process Boeing calls "lean manufacturing." (13) To this end, the firm retained the consulting firm Shinijutsu, run by Yoshiki Iwata, a former Toyota engineer who speaks no English. Iwata's first step was to identify piles of unnecessary inventory. Boeing's factories turn their stocks only 2 to 3 times per year, while an efficient manufacturing operation might turn stock 12 times a year. Boeing holds about $18 billion in gross inventories, equivalent to about 35 percent of total revenues. If it can trim that figure to 25 percent, the average for American industry, it can free up $6 billion in free cash flow annually. (14)

Another minor but symbolic innovation involved ladders. Airline fuselages are curved, but to gain access to them on the factory floor a worker used a straight ladder. The closer the worker got to the top of the ladder, the farther he/she had to stretch to reach the fuselage. Iwata's conclusion was to use a ladder that's shaped like an upside-down J. (15) Indeed, Boeing is introducing many reforms American automobile manufacturers were forced to make 10 years ago because of competition from Japan. Employees contribute by huddling in five-day "accelerated improvement workshops" where they brainstorm on how to do their jobs more efficiently. (16)

Boeing's challenge is one it should be prepared for: for decades it has succeeded at designing, building, marketing, and servicing very big and very complex machines on a global scale. As Condit notes, "Large-scale systems integration is what we do. Airplanes, space stations, launch vehicles. Things with lots of parts." (17) What could be a more challenging test of Boeing than the integration of itself? (18)

However, doubts persist as to whether Boeing can accomplish all it intends with this new program. Gordon Bethune, chairman and CEO of Continental Airlines and a former Boeing executive, states that "This company is trying to do so much at the same time—increase production, make its manufacturing lean, and deal with mergers. It's like a guy who's juggling eggs, and then somebody tosses him an orange. It's easy to drop something." (19)

Continued Competition

Boeing faces an increased challenge from Airbus Industrie's announcement of its 650-seat Superjet, the A380. While Boeing has expressed skepticism that a market exists for a jetliner of this size, Airbus has been able to collect orders for 50 of the commercial jets. In addition, Airbus has been successful in gathering orders from UPS, FedEx, and Northwest Airlines. Airbus has actually overtaken Boeing in worldwide market share based on total orders.

In reaction to this competitive threat, Boeing has announced that it is moving its headquarters from its longtime home town of Seattle and instituting a broad plan to shift away from aircraft manufacturing into faster-growing services. These services include Internet for air travelers, aircraft servicing, and space communications. (20)

You Do the Research

1. What difficulties has Boeing experienced in integrating the purchases of McDonnell Douglas and Rockwell?
2. What options does Boeing have in order to meet the increased competitive threat of Airbus?
3. How does the airline industry trend toward smaller, regional jets impact Boeing?

Review Questions

1. Interpret Boeing's work design based on the core job characteristics of the Job Characteristics Model presented in this chapter.
2. Interpret "old" versus "new" trends in the workplace in regard to Boeing's shift away from 1940s methods to new, more modern work designs.
3. Do environmental conditions assist or hinder Boeing's attempts to restructure its work force?

CASE 16

Steinway & Sons: Combining Craftwork and Teamwork

- -

Steinway and Sons remains one of the best-known producers of concert pianos in the world. Throughout its great history the company has shown a distinctive talent at innovation and quality workmanship, as evidenced by its 114 patents. In an age of mass production, Steinway continues to manufacture a limited number of handmade pianos in a unique testament to individual craftsmanship. However, Steinway's dominance in the concert piano market is being challenged by several rivals. Can Steinway continue its cherished ways, or will it need to adjust to new circumstances?

A Long History

Steinway & Sons was founded in 1853 by German immigrant Henry Engelhard Steinway in a Manhattan loft on Varick Street. Henry was a master cabinet maker who built his first piano in the kitchen of his Seesen, Germany, home. By the time Henry established Steinway & Sons, he had built 482 pianos. The first piano produced by the company, number 483, was sold to a New York family for $500. It is now displayed at New York City's Metropolitan Museum of Art.

Steinway's unique quality became obvious early in the history of the firm, evidenced by its winning gold medals in several American and European exhibitions in 1855. The company gained international recognition in 1867 at the Paris Exhibition when it was awarded the prestigious "Grand Gold Medal of Honor" for excellence in manufacturing and engineering. (1) Henry Steinway developed his pianos with emerging technical and scientific research, including the acoustical theories of the renowned physicist Hermann von Helmhotz.

In the early 1890s, Steinway moved to its current location in the Astoria section of Queens, New York, and built Steinway Village. Virtually its own town, Steinway Village had its own foundries, factory, post office, parks, and housing for employees. Its factory today still uses many of the craftsmanship techniques handed down from previous generations. Steinway produces approximately 5,000 pianos annually, worldwide, with over 900 prominent concert artists bearing the title of Steinway Artist. (2)

New Competition

Yamaha Corporation of America has sold pianos in the United States since 1960 and remains the preferred brand for top jazz and pop artists. But in the late 1980s, Yamaha chose to enter the concert piano market in direct competition with Steinway. Developing grand pianos such as the CFIIIS provided Yamaha with the product offering to attack Steinway's 95 percent market share in concert sales. Yamaha created its Concert and Artist Service—similar to Steinway's—to supply pianos across the country.

Steinway was owned in the 1970s by CBS, and many concert artists complained that the quality had suffered as a result of that ownership. Pianists talked of the "Teflon controversy," when Steinway replaced some fabric innards with Teflon (it now coats the Teflon with fabric). Steinway was sold by CBS in 1985, and many experts voiced the opinion that Steinway's legendary quality was returning. Larry Fine, a piano expert, argues that "a Steinway has a kind of sustained, singing tone that a Yamaha doesn't have. Yamaha has a more brittle tone in the treble that some jazz pianists prefer." (3)

Even with increased competition, the Steinway Tradition continues. Every grand piano takes over a year to complete and incorporates over 1,000 details that set a Steinway apart from competitors. A tour of the Steinway factory is a trip back through time, as many of the manufacturing techniques have not changed since 1853.

Recently, Steinway developed Boston Piano in an attempt to broaden its market. Boston pianos—designed by Steinway & Sons with the latest computer technology—are manufactured in Japan by Kawai, the second-largest Japanese piano maker. At first, Boston intended to ship all of its pianos to markets outside of Japan, but when Kawai expressed interest in distributing them throughout Japan, Steinway took a different tack.

Boston's success in Japan is a result of an unorthodox method called "guerrilla marketing." This approach involved developing new dealers, referrals, and direct-mail programs. But the strategy also brought into play "selection events." With display space at a premium in Japan's cramped cities, displaying 65 grand pianos in one location was something quite new. Using telemarketing and direct mail, Boston's Japanese distributor attracted 260 people to a selection event in Osaka . . . and sold 100 pianos. Boston Piano now accounts for 10 percent of the Japanese market. (4)

By transferring its quality and knowledge of building pianos to Boston, Steinway is able to open up a whole new market to exploit. Its core competence of hand craftsmanship can be applied in a newer, high-technology manner to a lower-priced market niche.

A New Partnership

On May 25, 1995 Steinway & Sons merged with The Selmer Company, manufacturer of brasswind, woodwind, percussion, and stringed instruments, to form Steinway Musical Instruments, Inc. The new company's strategy strives to capitalize on its strong brand names and leading market positions. The company's net sales of $258 million for 1996 were split between Steinway piano sales (53 percent) and sales of Selmer band and orchestral instruments (47 percent). In addition, the purchase of William Lewis Violin and the Emerson Flute Company adds to the band and musical instrument line.

On August 1, 1996, an initial public offering (IPO) of common stock raised $63 million in new equity capital. This money allowed the firm to repay over $54 million of senior secured notes, thereby greatly improving the financial flexibility of the new company.

Steinway's piano sales are influenced by general economic conditions in the United States and Europe, demographic trends, and general interest in music and the arts. Steinway's operating results are primarily influenced by grand piano sales. Given the total number of grand pianos sold by Steinway in any year (3,066 in 1996), a decrease of a relatively small number of units sold by Steinway can have a material impact on its business and operating results.

Domestic grand piano unit sales have increased 32.2% from 1993 to 1996, largely attributable to the economic recovery in the United States and increased selling and marketing efforts. Grand piano unit sales to international markets have remained relatively flat over the same period primarily as a result of the weakness of the European economies. In 1996, approximately 54 percent of Steinway's net sales were in the United States, 33 percent in Europe, and the remaining 13 percent primarily in Asia. (5)

Unlike many of its competitors in the piano industry, Steinway does not provide extended financing arrangements to its dealers. To facilitate the long-term financing required by some dealers, Steinway has arranged for financing through a third-party provider which generally involves no guarantee by Steinway.

In early 2001, Steinway and sons introduced a third line of pianos, called the Essex, to complement its Steinway and Boston lines. The line offers two grand and two upright models ranging in price from $5,200 to

$17,800. With the Essex, Steinway now provides pianos for every level of musical ability and budget. (6)

The question remains, can Steinway continue to operate in the way that has proved successful over the past 140 years? The recent merger with The Selmer Company creates a stronger and more diversified firm.

Review Questions

1. How have group norms developed in Steinway?
2. How does Steinway's piano manufacturing process exhibit the need for teamwork?
3. Suggest how a new employee might work his or her way through the Stages of Group Development.

You Do the Research

1. How does Steinway continue its emphasis on craftsmanship in this age of mass production?
2. Can any of Steinway's processes be transferred to other companies?
3. What other consumer products appear to be using a Steinway approach to the market?

CASE 17

The United Nations: Getting Nations to Work Together

The United Nations is a historically unique organization that strives for communication and cooperation across nations of the world. UN members are sovereign nations—the organization is not a world government and does not make laws. Beginning on October 24, 1945 with 51 countries, it has grown into a collection of 189 countries (Tuvalu was admitted on September 5, 2000) who together accept the obligations of the UN Charter, an international treaty that sets out basic principles of international relations. It is an organization that truly embraces the concept of diversity and conflict resolution. (1)

A World Order

The failure of the League of Nations following World War I left individual governments with no formalized world body to work out conflicts between nations. As a result, World War II materialized into a global conflict. At the conclusion of the Second World War, some leading nations chose to develop a successor to the League, known as the United Nations. The UN was meant to give all nations—large or small, rich or poor, with differing political and economic systems—a voice and vote in the process of world politics.

The United Nations is made up of six main branches:

1. The General Assembly—a "parliament of nations" where each member has one vote.
2. The Security Council—is provided primary responsibility for maintaining international peace and security.
3. The Economic and Social Council—coordinates the economic and social work of the UN system.
4. The Trusteeship Council—responsible for international supervision of 11 Trust territories to promote their self-government. With this task completed in 1994, the body meets only when necessary.
5. The Secretariat—headed by the Secretary-General, it handles the administrative work of the United Nations.
6. The International Court of Justice—located in the Hague, this body, also known as the World Court, is responsible for deciding disputes between countries.

An organization chart of the UN shows how these various branches work together to further the Charter of the organization. (2) While best known for its peacekeeping and humanitarian assistance, the UN—in cooperation with more than 30 affiliated organizations known together as the UN system—promotes human rights, protects the environment, fights disease, fosters economic development, and reduces poverty. (3) Consistent with its Charter, the UN represents ". . . a centre for harmonizing the actions of nations. . . ." (4)

For the 2000–2001 session of the General Assembly, the body is considering over 170 differing topics, from globalization to the consolidation of new democracies. Its actions cannot be "forced" onto any state, but its recommendations are an important indication of world opinion.

The Security Council is composed of 15 members. Five of these are permanent, including the United States, the United Kingdom, France, the Russian Federation, and China. The other ten are elected for 2-year terms. Decisions require nine "yes" votes, and any permanent member can veto any decision. The Council has the power to enforce its decisions, including economic sanctions, arms embargos, or in rare occations, "all necessary means," which includes collective military force.

It is in its ability to marshall international public opinion where the UN offers the most opportunity. World conflicts are discussed on a world stage with a world audience. From the Cuban missle crisis in 1962 to restoring peace to the Balkins in the late 1990s,

the UN helps prevent conflicts and in post-conflict situations it lays the foundation for durable peace.

In one of its most inclusive experiences to date, the UN served as a focal point in arranging a coalition of nations to counter Iraq's invasion and occupation of Kuwait in the early 1990s. thirty-four nations, under the auspices of the Security Council, provided the military forces necessary to "Desert Storm" and drove Saddam Hussein's forces out. President George Bush's claim of a "New World Order" as a result of the outcome did not come to pass.

How Does It Work?

The UN General Assembly meets from September to December in regular session. All nations have an equal vote on a range of international issues. (5) When not in session, the Assembly's work is carried out by its comittees and the Secretariat.

The Security Council has the primary responsibility for maintaining international peace and security. The Council may convene any time it is felt necessary, and under the Charter, all member states are required to carry out the Security Council's mandates.

The United Nations has many subunits that do not attract the media attention of the General Assembly and

Security Council. The UN system attempts to pool resources with autonomous organizations joined with the UN by special agreements. These groups work with the UN to advance world peace and prosperity.

Numerous initiatives by the UN include:

- UN peacekeeping—recently involved in 15 operations—is staffed by 37,400 UN military and civilian personnel from 89 countries.
- The UN, along with the World Bank and the UN Development Programme, provides assistance worth more than $30 billion per year.
- Its World Food Programme provides about one-third of the world's food aid. Emergency food assistance helps feed more than 86 million people in 82 countries around the world. (6)
- A joint UNICEF–World Health Organization (WHO) initiative has immunized 80 percent of the world's children against 6 killer diseases.
- More international law has been developed through the UN in the past five decades than in all previous history.
- UN agencies aid and protect more than 25 million refugees and displaced persons around the world.

The UN's Universal Declaration of Human Rights, dating from 1948, argues that basic rights and freedoms exist for all men and women of the world. The High Commissioner for Human Rights coordinates all UN human rights activities, working with governments to promote their observance.

The UN provides an infrastructure system that transcends national borders, thereby encouraging international solutions to world problems. While many support its aims, the organization is not without its detractors. Many smaller countries argue against domination from the larger nations, particularly from the Security Council's permanent membership.

In reaction to pressure from a number of nations, including the United States, the UN launched a reform movement in the late 1990s. Discussions on financing, operations, and Security Council makeup continue, but many times to the frustration of the smaller countries.

"If reform of the [Security] Council is to be truly comprehensive and consistent with the spirit and realities of our time, then we must seek to remove—or at least, as a first step, restrict—the use of the veto power. Democracy in the United Nations is a mockery if the voice of the majority is rendered meaningless by the narrow interests of the dominant few." (Minister for Foreign Affairs of Malaysia, HE Dato' Seri Abdullah bin Haji Ahmad Badawi) (7)

Others argue that the UN is too liberal and supports nondemocratic regimes around the globe. The United States withheld its dues for a number of years in protest to UN policies and charges of administrative waste within its programs.

The Future

Yet, the UN still represents the world's best opportunity to create a climate of communication and dispute resolution across national borders. The UN is an ongoing forum for disarmament negotiations, contributing to both the Nuclear Non-Proliferation Treaty (1968) and the Comprehensive Nuclear-Test-Ban Treaty in 1996.

UN Secretary-General Mr. Kofi Annan states it best when he argues: "Let it be remembered as a time when all of us joined forces and seized the opportunities created by the new era to revitalize our United Nations—this unique and universal instrument for concerted action in pursuit of the betterment of humankind." (8)

Review Questions

1. Is the UN a viable "organization"?
2. How could you improve the UN?
3. What will the UN look like in 10 years?

The Walt Disney Company: Walt's Legacy Keeps Growing

The Walt Disney Company has evolved from a wholesome family-oriented entertainment company into a massive multimedia conglomerate. Its July 31, 1991 acquisition of ABC Network is the most recent of a number of changes in the organization. With this purchase, Disney moves beyond being a mere producer of media into the distribution of its and others' media products through a variety of channels. Has CEO Michael Eisner changed his mind from his earlier vision that "Content is King" to a realization that control of distribution may be where the new value lies?

Disney Through the Years

After his first film business failed, artist Walt Disney and his brother Roy started a film studio in Hollywood in 1923. The first Mickey Mouse cartoon, *Plane Crazy*, was completed in 1928, and the first cartoon with a soundtrack, *Steamboat Willie*, was the third production. The studio's first animated feature film was *Snow White* in 1937, followed by *Fantasia* and *Pinocchio* in the 1940s. Disneyland, the theme park developed largely by Walt, opened in 1955 in Anaheim, California. The television series, the *Mickey Mouse Club,* was produced from 1955 to 1959, and the Disney weekly television series (under different names, including *The Wonderful World of Disney*) ran for 29 straight years. (1)

Walt Disney died in 1966 of lung cancer. Disney World in Orlando, Florida, opened in 1971, the same year that Roy Disney died. His son, Roy E., took over the organization, but without the creative leadership of brothers Walt and Roy Disney, the firm fell on hard times. Walt's son-in-law, Ron Miller, became president in 1980. Many industry watchers felt that Disney had lost its creative energy and sense of direction because of lackluster corporate leadership. In 1984, the Bass family, in alliance with Roy E. Disney, bought a controlling interest in the company. Their decision to bring in new CEO Michael Eisner from Paramount and a new president, Frank Wells, from Warner Bros. ushered in a new era in the history of Disney. (2)

Work the Brand

Michael Eisner has been involved in the entertainment industry from the start of his career (interestingly, beginning at ABC Television in the 1960s). He exhibits a knack for moving organizations from last place to first through a combination of hard work and timely decisions. From ABC, Eisner moved on to Paramount Pictures in 1976, which at the time was dead last of the six major motion picture studios. During his reign as president, it moved to first with blockbusters such as *Raiders of the Lost Ark, Trad-*ing Places, Beverly Hills Cop, and *Airplane*, along with other megahits. By applying lessons he learned in television to keep costs down, the average cost of a Paramount picture during his tenure was $8.5 million, while the industry average was $12 million. (3)

Eisner viewed Disney as a greatly underutilized franchise identified by millions throughout the world. In addition to reenergizing film production, Eisner wanted to extend the brand recognition of Disney products through a number of new avenues. Examples of his efforts included the Disney Channel (cable), Tokyo Disneyland (Disney receives a management fee only), video distribution, Disney Stores, Broadway shows *(Beauty and the Beast),* and additional licensing arrangements for the Disney characters.

Disney represents movie production assets (Buena Vista Television, the Disney Channel, Miramax Film Company, and Touchstone Pictures), theme parks, publication companies (Disney Press, Mouse Works, Hyperion Press), and professional sports franchises (the Mighty Ducks hockey team and part of the California Angels baseball team).

However, in the early 1990s problems began emerging for Disney. An attempt to build a theme park in Virginia based on a Civil War theme was defeated by local political pressure. EuroDisney, the firm's theme park in Farnce resulted in over $500 million in losses for Disney due to miscalculations on attendance and concessions. In 1994, Eisner underwent emergency open heart bypass surgery and Frank Wells, long working in the shadows of his boss but increasingly viewed as integral for the success of Disney, died in a helicopter crash. Eisner's choice to succeed Wells, Michael Ovitz from Creative Artists Agency, did not work out and Ovitz soon left. Stories of Eisner's dictatorial management style brought succession worries to shareholders.

Capital Cities/ABC

Once again, Eisner ushered in a new era at Disney by announcing the $19 billion takeover of Capital Cities/ABC on July 31, 1995. The deal came in the same week as Westinghouse Electric Corporation's $5.4 billion offer for CBS Inc. Disney represents one of several consolidations of the media conglomerates that are increasingly controlling the distribution of entertainment programming in the United States. It ranks as the third largest media conglomerate behind AOL Time Warner and Viacom.

Eisner appreciated the importance of both programming content and the distribution assets needed to deliver it. (4) As a result of many of his decisions, Disney has transformed from a sleepy film production studio into a major entertainment giant, with its revenues of over $2 billion in 1987 increasing to $22 billion in 1997. (5) Its stock price has multiplied over 15 times, creating enormous wealth for both stockholders and executives of Disney.

One of the biggest questions arising from the ABC deal is whether Disney paid too dearly for declining network assets. Viewership among all the major networks continues to decline on a regular basis. Michael Jordan, the CEO of CBS, complains that "the pure network tlelevision business is basically a low-margin to breakeven business." (6) The networks are squeezed by having to pay extravagantly for programming and attracting an audience of older viewers who are scorned by advertisers.

However, another way to look at networks is as the lifeblood of the global, vertically integrated entertainment giants that own them as loss leaders that act to promote their parent's more lucrative operations. In this scenario, ABC acts as Disney's megaphone to tell the masses about Disney movies, theme parks, Disney-made shows, and toys. Indeed, rather than shrinking, Rupert Murdoch's Fox, Paramount's UPN, and Time Warner's WB are three of the newest networks, with Barry Diller and Lowell Paxson planning to launch networks of their own.

Synergy is one key in today's network economies. ABC is able to turn 50 percent profit margins on its 10 network-owned stations and will realize a profit of over $550 miilion, largely because of local news shows and syndicated shows like *Oprah* and *Wheel of Fortune*. The other big payday comes when networks own and syndicate a hit show, something they could not do before they were deregulated in the mid-1990s. By owning more of their own shows, the networks avoid increasing license fees from the production companies. (7)

One risk in this strategy is that a network will miss out on a hit by favoring its own shows. Disney has blocked out certain parts of the week for its own shows. Fox and Disney appear best situated to exploit their platforms, with Fox injecting new life into an old brand, and Disney providing diverse production assets to feed its network. (8) This strategy works as long as networks remain big; since 1992, ABC and CBS have lost 25 percent and 23 percent of their viewers respectively. The networks have cushioned this problem by investing more in their cable holdings.

However, not everything Disney touches turns to gold. In early 2001, the company was forced to downscalc its go.com Internet site as it continues to lose hundreds of millions of dollars. Its share price remains virtually unchanged since 1998. (9)

Eisner remains committed to integrating the ABC network into the greater Dis-

---

Mickey Meets ABC
Business Week, 8-14-95: 31

PRODUCTION	DISTRIBUTION
Walt Disney Pictures	11 company-owned TV stations
Touchstone Pictures	228 TV affiliates
ABC Productions	21 radio stations
CABLE	**PUBLISHING**
ESPN	Newspapers in 13 states
Lifetime	Fairchild Publications
A&E	Chilton Publications
Disney Channel	

ney picture. "It sounds funny, but I am thinking about the millennium change. I've got to protect the Disney brand well into the future." (10)

Review Questions

1. Examine the internal and external forces for change faced by Disney.
2. How have external forces in the entertainment industry affected Disney's need for change?
3. What changes do you foresee in the entertainment industry in the next five years?
4. Find 4 Internet sites discussing change management, stress management, or the entertainment industry.

You Do the Research

1. Can Disney turn its fortunes around?
2. Has the firm really moved past its reputation as a theme park provider?
3. Are media conglomerates headed for trouble?

INTEGRATIVE

LEARNING

ACTIVITIES

RESEARCH

AND

PRESENTATION

P R O J E C T S

PROJECT 1

Diversity Lessons—"What Have We Learned?"

There are many reports out there—*Workforce 2020, Workforce 2000,* and *Opportunity 2000,* among others. Diversity in the workplace is clearly the subject of significant attention. Managers and employers are being urged to recognize and value diversity, and many are pursuing active programs to improve the environment for diversity in the workplace. Yet "glass ceilings" remain obstacles to career and personal accomplishment for too many women and African Americans and other minorities.

QUESTION

What are the "facts" in terms of progress for minorities and women in the workplace? What lessons of diversity have been learned? What are the "best" employers doing?

Instructions

Use research sources at your disposal to complete a project report addressing the research question. Specific topics for consideration might include the following:

- Case studies of employers reported as having strong diversity programs. What do they have in common? What do they do differently? Is there a basic "model" that could be followed by managers in other settings?
- Investigation of diversity with specific reference to how well people of different racial, ethnic, gender, and generational groups work together. What do we know about this, if anything? What are the common problems, if any? What concerns do managers and workers have?
- Analysis of survey reports on how the "glass ceiling" may affect the careers of women and minorities in various occupational settings. Get specific data, analyze them, and develop the implications. Prepare a report that summarizes your research.
- A critical look at the substance of diversity training programs. What do these programs try to accomplish, and how? Are they working or not, and how do we know? Is there a good model for diversity training that may be used by others?
- Look at where we go from here. What diversity issues lie ahead to be successfully mastered by the new managers of tomorrow?

PROJECT 2

Changing Corporate Cultures

"Culture" is still a popular topic in management circles. Conventional wisdom holds that strong cultures can bond employees to a common sense of mission and reinforce work habits needed to serve customers well and maintain productivity. One aspect of organizational culture that is criticized today is lack of loyalty—loyalty of the organization to employees and of employees to the organization.

QUESTION

What do you think? Are organizational cultures changing? If so, are they changing for the better or for the worse?

Instructions

Use research sources at your disposal to complete a project report addressing this question. Specific topics for consideration might include the following:

- Look for the latest thinking of management scholars and consultants on the role of "corporate culture" in successful organizations.

Many case examples and reports should be available on this topic. Look for success stories and try to interpret them in the context of the research question.

- Give special attention in your research to issues relating to loyalty. Try to access surveys of employees commenting on how they feel about job security, commitment to their organization, etc.
- Make a list, from your research, of things that can be done to change the culture of an organization or work unit in a positive manner. Critically evaluate each of these items in terms of these action criteria: (a) feasibility of dealing with the item, (b) length of time needed to achieve impact on the item, and (c) the follow-up or reinforcement needed to maintain this impact. Review your entire analysis and answer this question: "Can the recommended things really be accomplished by (a) a CEO, (b) a middle manager, and (c) a team leader?"
- Place the issue of corporate culture in the context of the growing number of international mergers, joint ventures, and strategic alliances found in the global economy. What is the importance of differences in "corporate cultures" as organizations of different "national cultures" try to work with one another? What do management consultants and scholars know or have to say about managing the problems of culture in this specific arena of business activity?

PROJECT 3

Foreign Investment in America— "What Are the Implications?"

Foreign investment in the United States is high and growing. For example, there are more than 1,500 Japanese manufacturing companies in the United States. The number of Americans employed in these firms is over 300,000 and growing. In smaller communities like Marysville, Ohio, and Smyrna, Tennessee, the presence of a Honda or Nissan plant has substantial implications for the local economy and for the local way of life in general. Indeed, some Americans view the growing Japanese investment in the United States as a cause for concern, not jubilation.

QUESTION

Which is it? Is foreign investment in the United States a cause for concern, or is it something to be welcomed?

Instructions

Use research sources at your disposal to complete a project report on this question. Specific topics for consideration might include the following:

- The status of current foreign investment in the United States. How much is there, how fast is it growing, in what major industries is it found, and where is it located?

- The primary benefits and costs of this investment for the local communities and regions in which foreign firms operate. What do the communities gain from their presence? What price do they pay?
- The nature of Japanese investment in particular. What are the effects of Japanese *keiretsu?* Do these linkages within business groups spill over to influence how Japanese firms operate in America? Do the *keiretsu* work to the disadvantage of non-Japanese firms wanting to do business with them in the United States?
- How do Americans feel about working for foreign employers? Do the Americans have opportunities for career advancement in the foreign firms? Do these opportunities vary for men and women? Are foreign companies considered to be "good" employers? Why or why not?

PROJECT 4

Corporate Social Responsibility—"What's the Status?"

The average fast-food restaurant generates enormous waste each day. Actions taken to reduce this waste are applauded. The U.S. Food and Drug Administration monitors food labeling to guard the public against inappropriate claims. Firms sanctioned by the FDA often pay a price in negative publicity. Waste management and product labeling are but two of a growing range of business activities that are being publicly scrutinized for their social responsibility implications.

QUESTION

Where do businesses stand today with respect to the criteria for evaluating social responsibility discussed in the textbook?

Instructions

Use research sources at your disposal to complete a project report on this question. Specific topics for consideration might include the following:

- Research and evaluate the "status" of major organizations on a variety of social responsibility performance matters. How well are they doing? Would you use them as models of social responsibility for others to follow, or not?
- Conduct research to identify current examples of the "best" and the "worst" organizations in terms of performance or social responsibility criteria. Pursue this investigation on an (a) international, (b) national, and/or (c) local scale.
- Choose an issue such as environmental protection or product labeling. Conduct research to identify the "best" and the "worst" organizations in terms of performance in these specific areas. Again, consider looking at this issue on an (a) international, (b) national, and/or (c) local scale.
- Create a scale that could be used to measure the social responsibility performance of an organization. Review the scholarly research in this area but use your own judgment. Test your scale by applying it to two or three local organizations.

PROJECT 5

Affirmative Action Directions—"Where Do We Go from Here?"

In a *Harvard Business Review* article ("From Affirmative Action to Affirming Diversity," March–April 1990), R. Roosevelt Thomas makes the following statement: "Sooner or later, affirmative action will die a natural death." He goes on to praise its accomplishments but then argues that it is time to "move beyond affirmative action" and learn how to "manage diversity." There are a lot of issues that may be raised in this context—issues of equal employment opportunity, hiring quotas, reverse discrimination, and others.

QUESTION

What about it? What is the status of affirmative action today?

Instructions

Use research sources at your disposal to complete a project report addressing this question. Specific topics for consideration might include the following:

- Read the Thomas article. Make sure you are clear on the term *affirmative action* and its legal underpinnings. Research the topic, identify the relevant laws, and make a history line to chart its development over time.
- Examine current debates on affirmative action at the level of national policy. What are the issues? How are the "for" and "against" positions being argued?
- Consider "reverse discrimination." Is there any pattern to employment situations in which reverse discrimination emerges as a management concern? Identify cases where reverse discrimination has been charged. How have they been resolved and with what apparent human resource management implications?
- Examine current controversies over *hiring quotas*. Is this what affirmative action is all about? What are the arguments, pro and con? What do the "experts" say about it? Where do we seem to be headed in this area?
- Look at organizational policies that deal with diversity matters. Find what you consider to be the "best" examples. Analyze them and identify the common ground. Prepare a summary that could be used as a policy development guideline for human resource directors who want to make sure their organizations truly support and value diversity in the workforce.
- Try to look at all of these issues and controversies from different perspectives. Talk to people of different "majority" and "minority" groups in your college or university. Find out how they view these things—and why. What are the implications for human resource management today?

Controversies in CEO Pay—"Is It Too High?"

The high, sometimes extremely high, pay of CEOs in many American corporations has caught the public's eye. Many people aren't very happy with what they are discovering. One report states that CEOs take home, on average, 160 times the pay of their employees, and earn three to six times what their counterpart CEOs in Japanese and European companies earn. It is not only the magnitude of the pay that is bothersome. Controversial too is the belief that the pay of some CEOs goes up even when their firms' performance goes down.

QUESTION

What is happening in the area of executive compensation? Are CEOs paid too much? Are they paid for "performance," or are they paid for something else?

Instructions

Use research sources at your disposal to complete a project report addressing this question. Specific topics for consideration might include the following:

- Check the latest reports on CEO pay. Try to get the facts. Prepare a briefing report as if you were writing a short informative article for *Fortune* magazine. The title of your article should be "Status Report: Where We Stand Today on CEO Pay."
- Address the pay-for-performance issue. Do corporate CEOs get paid for performance or for something else? What do the researchers say? What do the business periodicals say? Find some examples to explain and defend your answers to these questions.
- Find some positive cases where you consider a CEO's pay to be justified. What criteria are you using to justify it?
- Take a position: Should a limit be set on CEO pay? If no, why not? If yes, what type of limit do we set? Should we deal with an absolute dollar limit, a multiple of what the lowest-paid worker in a firm earns, or some other guideline? Why? Who, if anyone, should set these limits—Congress, company boards of directors, or someone else?
- Take a poll on campus. What do other students think about CEO pay? Do they think limits should be set? Take a poll in your local community. What does the public at large think? How does the public feel about limits to CEO pay? How about you—what is your conclusion? Is the attack on CEO pay justified?

@ GET CONNECTED! Additional Research and Presentation Projects are available on-line at www.wiley.com/college/schermerhorn.

Cross-Functional
INTEGRATIVE
CASES

David S. Chappell, Case Editor

Outback Steakhouse, Inc.
Fueling the Fast-Growth Company

- - - - - - - - - - - - - - - - -

Marilyn L. Taylor, D.B.A., Gottlieb-Missouri, Distinguished Professor of
Business Strategy, Henry W. Bloch School of Business and Public
Administration, University of Missouri—Kansas City,
Kansas City, MO 64110

Krishnan Ramaya, Ph.D., Henry W. Bloch School of Business and
Public Administration, University of Missouri—Kansas City,
Kansas City, MO 64110

George M. Puia, Ph.D., School of Business,
Indiana State University, Terre Haute, IN 47809
Tel: (812) 237-2090

*Support for the development of this case and its accompanying video
were provided by*

Center for Entrepreneurial Leadership
Ewing Marion Kauffman Foundation
Kansas City, MO

Note: All cases are available in updated on-line versions. The blue underscored words/phrases in the cases indicate Internet links. See the *MANAGEMENT 7/e* web site at www.wiley.com/college/schermerhorn.

The authors express deep appreciation to the following individuals at the Ewing Marion Kauffman Foundation: Dr. Ray Smilor, vice president of the Center for Entrepreneurial Leadership Inc.; Ms. Pam Kearney, communications specialist, Communications Department; and Ms. Judith Cone, ETI professional with the Center for Entrepreneurial Leadership Inc. In addition, the authors wish also to express appreciation to Outback executives Chris Sullivan, chairman and CEO; Bob Basham, president and COO; Tim Gannon, sr. vice president; Bob Merritt, sr. vice president, CFO, and treasurer; Nancy Schneid, vice president of marketing; Ava Forney, assistant to the chairman and CEO; as well as the other Outback officers, executives, and employees who gave so enthusiastically and generously of their time, knowledge, and skills to make this case study possible.

Contact Person: George M. Puia, Ph.D.

Management cooperated in the field research for this case, which was written solely for the purpose of stimulating student discussion. Copyright © 1998 Case Research Journal, Marilyn Taylor, George Puia, Krishnan Ramaya.

Exhibits may be found in the Instructor's Manual.

Outback Steakhouse: Fueling the Fast-Growth Company

Since the company's initial public offering in June of 1991, Wall Street observers had continually predicted a downturn in the price of Outback's stock. Indeed, most analysts viewed Outback as just another fad in an intensely competitive industry where there are plenty of imitators. They continued to caution that Outback was in a saturated market and that the company could not continue growing at its existing pace. The December 1994 issue of *Inc.* magazine declared Outback's three founders as winners of the coveted Entrepreneur of the Year award. The company was profiled in 1994 and early 1995 by the business press as one of the biggest success stories in corporate America in recent years.[1]

At 5:00 P.M. on a Saturday in early 1995 in Brandon, a suburb outside Tampa, the lines had already begun to form in a strip mall outside Outback Steakhouse. Customers waited anywhere from half an hour to almost two hours for a table.

The firm's founders, Chris Sullivan, Bob Basham, and Tim Gannon, organized Outback in August 1987 with the expectation of building five restaurants and spending increased leisure time on the golf course and with their families. In 1988 the company had sales of $2.7 million from its two restaurants. By year-end 1994 the chain exceeded all of the founders' expectations, with over 200 restaurants and $549 million in systemwide sales (see Exhibits 1 and 2 for financial data) and had formed a joint venture partnership with Texas-based Carrabbas Italian Grill to enter the lucrative Italian restaurant segment, currently dominated by General Mills' Olive Garden. A 1994 national survey of the country's largest restaurant chains ranked Outback first in growth (52.9%), second by sales per unit ($3.3 million), sixth by market share (5.9%), and tenth by number of units (205), all of which was accomplished in less than six years (see Exhibit 3).[2]

The founders expected that Outback could grow into a 550–600-unit chain in the continental United States. During 1995 alone, the company expected to add 65 to 70 new restaurants, maintain overall sales growth comparable to 1994, and continue to increase its same-store sales. In spite of the company's past success and future plans, however, analysts and other industry observers questioned how long Outback could continue its astounding growth, whether the company could maintain its strong momentum while pursuing multiple major strategic thrusts to propel its growth, and whether and how the culture of the company could be maintained. Skepticism about Outback's continued growth was clearly evident in the way Wall Street analysts viewed the company. By the end of 1994, Outback's stock was one of the most widely held stocks on the short sellers' list.[3] Adjusted for stock splits, Outback's share price rose from $3.50 to almost $30 over a three-year period. Exhibits 4 and 5 provide information on Outback's stock performance as well as samples of analysts' perspectives on Outback's continued growth during 1994.

The French Restaurant Legacy

The French coined the term *restaurant*, meaning "a food that restores," and were the first to create a place that could be defined as a restaurant by modern standards.[4] Before the French Revolution most culinary experiences were the exclusive domain of the nobility. The French Revolution dispersed the nobility and their chefs. The chefs, denied the patronage of the nobles, scattered throughout Europe, taking the restaurant concept with them.

In contrast, American restaurants grew up in response to the need to serve the burgeoning 19th-century U.S. workforce. The rapid growth of U.S. cities, fueled by the influx of European immigrants, provided the initial impetus for the American restaurant industry. Initially, restaurants were single family-owned operations and consisted of two broad categories.[5] The first category, fine dining, had facilities that were affordable only to the wealthy and were located primarily in major cities. The second category catered primarily to industrial workers. This latter category included concepts such as lunch wagons and soda fountains, which later evolved into coffee shops and luncheonettes. These grew rapidly in response to the continuous expansion of urban areas. The American obsession with efficiency propelled yet another restaurant concept, the self-service restaurant, to become a central theme for 20th-century American restaurants.

Retail and theater chains emerged with the new century. The first large U.S. restaurant chain organization was the brainchild of Frederick Henry Harvey, an English immigrant.[6] After his Harvey House opened in 1876 in Topeka, Kansas, restaurant chains too quickly became part of the American scene.

The restaurant industry's $290 billion revenues in 1993 accounted for 4.3 percent of U.S. GDP.[7] The industry's 100 largest chains accounted for 40 percent of total industry sales. U.S. restaurants in the latter part of the twentieth century could broadly be classified into three segments—fast-food, casual dining, and fine dining. However, within these three broad categories were highly fragmented sub-segment markets. The fast-food segment was primarily catered to by major chains such as McDonald's, Wendy's, Burger King, Hardee's, and Kentucky Fried Chicken. Casual dining catered to the cost conscious and typically priced menu entrees between fastfood and fine dining restaurants. Fine dining establishments catered to affluent customers and were located primarily in major metropolitan areas. Fine dining establishments were mostly single-unit businesses. In the early 1990s 75 percent of all casual dining establishments were still mom-and-pop operations.[8] The industry was characterized by high failure rates. Approximately 75 percent of all establishments failed within the first year; 90 percent within five years. Failure in the restaurant industry was attributed to a plethora of factors, including undercapitalization, poor location, poor food quality, underestimation of the effort needed to be successful, the effect of changing demographics segments, and government regulations.[9]

Restaurant operations are highly labor-intensive businesses. However, aspiring restaurant owners often seriously underestimated their capitalization requirements, that is, the funds needed for leasehold improvements and equipment. Indeed, new restaurants are often seriously undercapitalized. The owners might also fail to plan for other startup funds such as the first year's working capital, preopening expenses, advertising, and inventory costs.

Location choice was another common error. A restaurant location had to attract sufficient traffic to sustain operations. The demographics required for appropriate fine dining restaurant sites were different from those required for casual dining establishments, which differed again from fast-food establishments such as McDonald's. The availability of suitable locations especially in major cities had become an important factor in the success or failure of restaurants.

Aspiring restaurant owners also often underestimated *the effort required* to make a restaurant successful. Running a restaurant was hard work and could easily involve 80 to 100 hours of work each week. *Changing demographics* affected not only location choices but also the theme and type of restaurant. What had once been easily definable segments had fundamentally changed. It had become increasingly difficult to clearly define targetable segments. *American Demographics* magazine referred to the current situation as "particle markets."[10] Examples of such particle markets included empty nesters, stepfamilies, the baby boomlet, immigrants, the disabled, savers, the affluent, the elderly, and others. The restaurant industry was also one of the country's most *regulated industries.* Myriad regulations on such issues as hygiene, fire safety, and the consumption of alcoholic beverages governed daily operations.

Still another requirement for a successful restaurant was the maintenance of consistent *food quality.* Maintaining a level of consistent food quality was challenging. Any variability in food quality was typically viewed as deficient.

Founding Outback Steakhouse—From Down Under to Where?

In March 1987 three friends—Chris Sullivan, Bob Basham, and Tim Gannon—opened their first two Outback restaurants in Tampa, Florida. Each of the three had started early in their careers in the restaurant industry—Chris as a busboy, Bob as a dishwasher, and Tim as a chef's assistant. Between them they had more than sixty years of restaurant experience, most in the casual dining segment. The three met when they went to work for Steak & Ale, a Pillsbury subsidiary, shortly after they completed college in the early 1970s. Chris and Bob went to executive roles in the Bennigan's restaurant group, part of the Steak & Ale group. The two men met their mentor and role model in casual dining legend Norman Brinker. Brinker had headed Pillsbury's restaurant subsidiary. When Brinker

left Pillsbury to form Brinker International, Chris and Bob followed him. Among Brinker International's casual dining chains was Chili's. Brinker helped the two men finance a chain of 17 Chili's restaurants in Florida and Georgia. Chris and Bob described their contribution as "sweat equity."[11] Brinker was considered a leading pioneer in the development of the causal dining industry.[12] Brinker International, the restaurant holding company that Brinker created, was widely considered an industry barometer for the casual dining segment.

Brinker International, the parent company, acquired Chris and Bob's interest in the Chili's franchise for $3 million in Brinker stock. With about $1.5 million each, Chris and Bob turned their attention to a long-standing dream—their own entrepreneurial venture. They considered several options, finally settling on the idea of a startup venture consisting of a small chain of casual dining restaurants. Each of the two men brought special skills to the table—Chris in his overall strategic sense and Bob in his strong skills in operations and real estate.

In early fall 1987 the two men asked Tim Gannon to join Outback as its chief chef. Tim had left Steak & Ale in 1978 to play a significant entrepreneurial role in several restaurant chains and single-establishment restaurants, primarily in the New Orleans area. His last venture was a restaurant with Pete Fountain at the New Orleans World's Fair. The venture at the World's Fair had experienced early success and then suddenly

encountered severe financial difficulties, leaving Tim with virtually no financial resources. In fact, when Gannon accepted Chris and Bob's invitation to join them, he had to sell his one remaining prized possession, a saddle, in order to buy gas money to travel from New Orleans to Tampa.

Tim brought with him recipes drawn from 25 years of experience. His first tutelage had been under a French chef in Aspen, Colorado. Concerning his initial teacher, Tim said:

I was an Art History major (who) found his way to Colorado to Aspen to ski. My first job was as a cook. That job became exciting because the man I worked for was a chef from Marseilles who had a passion for great foods. I grew to love the business. . . . I have made the restaurant industry my whole life.

Bob Basham especially wanted a restaurant concept that focused on steaks. The three men recognized that in the United States in-home consumption of beef had declined over the years, primarily because of health concerns. However, they also noted that the upscale steak houses and the budget steak houses were extremely popular in spite of all the concerns about red meat. That observation came from their market research, which Bob Basham described as follows:

We visited restaurants to see what people were eating. We talked to other people in the industry. Basically we observed and read trade magazines. That is the kind of research I am talking about. We did not hire a marketing research crew to go out and do a research project. It was more hands-on research. . . . the experts said people will eat less red meat, but we saw them lining up to get in. We believed in human behavior, not market research.

The partners concluded that people were cutting in-home red meat consumption but were still very interested in going out to a restaurant for a good steak. They saw an untapped opportunity between high-priced and budget steakhouses to serve quality steaks at an affordable price.

Outback operated in the dinner house category of the casual dining segment where 75 percent of all such establishments were family-owned and operated. The top fifteen dinner house chains accounted for approximately $9 billion dollars in total sales.[13] Dinner house chains usually had higher sales volumes than fast-food chains. However, dinner houses typically cost more to build and operate.[14]

The initial investment for Outback came from the sale of the Chili's restaurant franchise. Both men were able to forgo taking cash salaries from Outback for the company's first two years. Funding for the early restaurants came from their own resources, relatives, and the sale of limited partnerships. During 1990 the founders turned to venture capitalists for about $2.5 million. Just as the venture capital deal was materializing, Bob Merritt was hired as CFO. Trained as an accountant, Merrit had extensive experience with the financial side of the restaurant business.

Prior to joining Outback, Merritt served as the vice president of finance for JB's Restaurants. Merritt had IPO experience, and the founders later decided a public offering was warranted. The company went public in June 1991. The market had a general aversion toward restaurant stocks during the mid- and late 1980s. However, Outback's share offering, contrary to expectations, traded at premium. CFO Merritt recalled his efforts to borrow funds in 1990 even after the venture-capital infusion:

In November 1990, Outback was really taking off. . . . The most significant limitation was capital. . . . So, I shaved off my beard—because Tampa is a fairly conservative community—and went from bank to bank. I spent every day trying to borrow. I think we were asking for $1.5M so that we could finance that year's crop of equipment packages for the restaurants. We basically met with dead ends. . . . [It was] very frustrating. . . . So Chris and I started talking about where the market was. One strategy, I felt, was to sell a little bit of the company to finance maybe 18 months of growth, get a track record in the Street and come back with another offering with credibility. [So] we priced the transaction at about a 20 percent discount relative to the highest-flying restaurant stock we could find and, of course, the stock traded up from 15 to 22 on the first day. At that point we were trading at a premium for restaurant stocks.

Outback's continuing success made possible two addi-

tional stock offerings during the following eighteen months. All together, a total of $68 million was raised. By the end of 1994, the founders owned almost 24 percent of the company, which was valued at approximately $250 million.

Outback's Strategy and Structure—"No rules—just right"

The Theme—"Cheerful, comfortable, enjoyable, and fun!"

The three partners debated for some time about the appropriate theme and name for their restaurants. They wanted a casual theme but felt that the western theme was overused by budget steak houses. Ultimately, they focused on an Australian theme. None of the partners had ever been to Australia, but U.S. attention was focused there. Bob Basham explained:

In late 1987–88 when we started there was a lot of hype about Australia. We had just lost the Americas Cup not long before that. They were celebrating their bicentennial. The movie Crocodile Dundee had just come out. [So, there] was a lot of interest in Australia when we were looking for a theme . . . that was probably one of our hardest decisions . . . (we) wanted to stay away from a western theme. . . . [We] started talking about Australia [which] is perceived as very casual and we wanted to be a casual steakhouse. It is a good marketing niche tool and we continue to take advantage of it in our ads.

Bob's wife, Beth, ultimately wrote the name "Outback" with her lipstick on a mirror. As Tim Gannon put it, the name epitomized:

[what] we wanted to convey. We wanted to be a hearty good-fun atmosphere and [the name] represents our personalities too. The three of us live robust, fun lives.

The founders of Outback were convinced that any enduring concept must place a heavy emphasis upon fun, family, quality food, and community. Bob Basham explained:

I don't care what business you are in, if you aren't having fun, you shouldn't be in that business. . . . Chris, Tim, and I have a lot of fun doing what we are doing, and we want our people to have a lot of fun doing what they are doing. We try to set it up so they can do that.

Tim, whom the other two partners described as being the "hospitality" part of the team, elaborated on the entertainment aspect of the Outback theme:

We are in the business of entertainment and the way we entertain is through flavors. Service is a big component of that. We want our customers—someone who comes in at 7 P.M. and waits until 9 P.M. and leaves at 10:30 P.M.—to view us as their entertainment. We owe it to them!

Outback employees who waited on customers typically handled only three tables at a time, and this allowed closer customer attention.

Choosing the Menu— "Kookaburra Wings, Victoria's Filet, Chocolate Thunder Down Under"

The company gave Australian theme names to many of the menu items. For example, Buffalo chicken wings were called "Kookabura wings," a filet mignon was called "Victoria's Filet," and a rich chocolate sauce dessert was titled, "Chocolate Thunder Down Under." The menu also included a wide variety of beverages, including a full liquor service featuring Australian beer and wine. The menu for the trio's casual dining operation featured specially seasoned steaks and prime rib and also included chicken, ribs, fish, and pasta entrees. Tim explained the menu selections for Outback:

At Outback we don't look at other menus or trends. . . . [The] best things I learned in a lifetime I put in the menu.

The company's house specialties included its "'Aussie-Tizers'. . . and delectable desserts."[15] The company's signature trademark quickly became its best-selling "Aussie-Tizer," the "Bloomin' Onion." The idea for a large single-hearted onion cut to resemble a blooming flower, dipped in batter, and fried was originally developed by a New Orleans chef from a picture in a Japanese book. Tim added seasonings and enlarged it to "Outback size." The company expected to serve nine million "Bloomin' Onions" in 1995.

The menu, attention to quality from suppliers, and the emphasis on exceeding customer expectations all contributed to the high food quality. At about 40 percent of total costs, Outback's food costs were among the highest in the industry. "If we didn't have the highest food costs in the industry," explained Bob Basham, "we would be worried."

Outback's founders paid particular attention to the flavor profiles of the food. As Bob Merritt put it:

One of the important reasons for our success is that we took basic American meat and potatoes and enhanced the flavor profile so that it fit with the aging population. . . . Just look at what McDonald's and Burger King did in their market segment. They tried to add things to their menu that were more flavorful. McDonald's put the Big Mac on their menu because they found that as people aged, they wanted more flavor. McDonald's could not address that customer need with an old cheeseburger which tastes like cardboard. . . . That's why Tex Mex is such a great segment. That's why Italian is such a great segment because Italian food tends to have higher flavor profiles. It's not happenstance. It's a science. There's too much money at risk in this business not to know what's going on with customer taste preferences.

The founders knew that as people age, their taste buds also age. Thus, they recognized that their baby-boomer customers, those born in the 1946 to 1964 period, would demand more flavor in their food.

The 1995 menu remained essentially the same in character as originally envisioned in 1987. The price range of appetizers was about $2 to $6 with entrees ranging between $8 and $17. The average check per person was approximately $15 to $16.[16] The changing of menu items was done with care. For example, a new item planned for 1995 was the rack of lamb. As Tim Gannon explained, the menu was an issue to which all three founders turned their attention:

Where we all come together is on the menu. Bob comes to the plate thinking how the kitchen can put this out and how it can be stored. Chris will look at it from how the customer is going to view it. Is it of value? I come to it from a flavor point of view. Is it an exciting dish? We all add something to the final decision.

Tim and the staff at the company's original restaurant located on Henderson Avenue in Tampa, Florida, undertook most of the company's R&D. The founders approved any menu changes only after paying careful attention to development. For example, Tim and the Henderson staff had worked for a number of months on the rack of lamb entree. Tim explained:

We have been working with it [the rack of lamb entree] for some time on the operational side trying to get the cook times down. The flavors are there. Chris is excited although it [the rack] is not a mainstream product. It is an upscale product for us. . . . We are still fine-tuning the operational side to be sure it is in balance with other things we are doing. We are serving 800 dinners a night, and you can't have a menu item that throws the chemistry of the kitchen off.

Quality Fanatics— "We won't tolerate less than the best"

Outback executives and restaurant managers were staunchly committed to the principle that good food required outstanding ingredients. Tim explained the company's attention to the suppliers:

I have been to every onion grower from Oregon, Idaho, and all the way to Mexico looking for a continuous supply of single-hearted onions. I talk to the growers. . . . If it's a product you serve, you cannot rely on the words of a distributor to say, "This is what we have." I have to get into the fields and see what they have. If I am going to take 50 percent of the crop like that, I have to get into the fields to know, to see, how the crop is developed. So that took me into the fields of Idaho to see what makes onions get that big and what makes double hearts because they are hard for us to use. We do that with everything, the species of shrimp, which boats have the ice, what's the best safety standards. [I go] with the guys who purchase the cattle and learn to look for what they look for. . . . That's the only way you can produce great food.

Supplier relationships were long-standing. The company made beef purchases centrally for the entire Outback system. The company's original menu was designed by Tim Gannon with help from Warren LeRuth, one of New Orleans's premier chefs. LeRuth recommended Bruss, a Chicago-based meatpacking company, as a source of high-quality beef. Tim explained why Bruss was such a great partner as a supplier:

We couldn't even get samples [from the others]. We were on a low budget at the time. This company believed in us. They sent us samples after samples. . . . Their cutters were more like craftsmen; the sense of pride that the Chicago butchers have about their product is really what we wanted in our restaurants. Bruss was at about $37 million at the time. Today, they are at $100 million, and we represent $75 to $80 million of that. We've been a great partner for them as they have been for us.

In 1994 Outback had two major suppliers of beef, but Bruss continued to supply over half of the Outback restaurants. About 60 percent of Outback's menu items were red meat entrees, and its best-selling steak alone accounted for about 25 percent of entrees sold. The attention to quality extended, however, to all suppliers. Vanilla, used only for the whipped cream in just one dessert item, was the "real thing" from the island of Madagascar. Olive oil was imported from Tuscany and wheels of parmesan cheese from Italy. Tim explained the company policy:

. . . if any supplier replaces our order with a cheap imitation, I will know about it and they will not supply us anymore. . . . I will not tolerate anything less than the best.

The attention to quality and

detail was also evidenced at the individual restaurant level. For example, croutons were made daily at each restaurant with 17 different seasonings, including fresh garlic and butter, and cut by hand into irregular shapes so that customers would recognize they were handmade.

In addition to his oversight of supplier quality, Tim Gannon also focused on continual training of the restaurant staff throughout the Outback system. He held about ten meetings a year in various parts of the country with staff members from various regional restaurants. Typically, about 50 kitchen managers and other kitchen staff attended these meetings. There was a presentation from a special guest with half of the group in the front of the restaurant. In the meantime, the other half of the group worked on "the basics" in the kitchen. Then the two groups exchanged places. Tim felt these meetings were critical for generating new ideas, sometimes from very new kitchen staff employees. For example, one new employee had urged attention to the dessert sauces. Discussion of this issue ultimately resulted in a reformulation of the sauces so that they did not so easily crystallize as well as the installation of the warmers that held the sauces at a constant temperature. This innovation allowed the restaurants to serve desserts more quickly.

The restaurant general managers also emphasized food quality. This commitment was illustrated by Joe Cofer, manager of the Henderson Street restaurant in Tampa, when he said:

We watch the food as it comes out of the kitchen, touching every single plate to make sure every single plate is perfect—that's our commitment to this restaurant [i.e.,] to watch the food. We can take care of every single table by watching the food. If we have a problem at a table, we go to talk to them.

Designing a Restaurant—"Bob Basham's Memorial Kitchen"

Facility design was also a critical component in quality food preparation. Bob Basham especially paid attention to kitchen design, so much so that Chris and Tim termed Outback's kitchen design Bob's "Memorial Kitchen." Fully 45 percent of Outback's restaurant unit was generally dedicated to the kitchen. Analysts and other industry observers had pointed out that Outback could enlarge the dining area and reduce wait times for customers. However, Bob Basham explained the logic behind the company's restaurant design:

Restaurants get busy on a Friday night or a Saturday night when most people go out to eat. That's when you are trying to make the best impression on people. [But] physically, the kitchen cannot handle the demand. So if you have standards in your operation of a 12-minute cook time. . . . [it's] impossible to execute that way. We all decided we would not have it happening in our restaurant. So we underdesigned the front of the house and overdesigned the back of the house. That has worked very, very

well for us. To this day we limit the number [of tables]. Even in our busiest restaurants where people tell us we could be twice as big and do twice the sales, we still discipline ourselves to build our restaurants one size.

The interior design was a "subtle decor featuring blond woods, large booths and tables [with] Australian memorabilia—boomerangs, surfboards, maps, and flags."[17] A typical Outback occupied over 6,000 square feet, featuring a dining room and an island bar. The restaurant area had 30 to 35 tables and could seat about 160 patrons. The bar had about six to nine tables with seating for about 35.

Location Is Everything?—"You're going to put a restaurant where? For dinner only?!"

The company's first restaurant was located on a site that had held several restaurants before Bob and Chris leased it. Early Outback restaurants were all located in strip shopping centers or were retrofits of existing freestanding restaurant sites. When the company first started, lease costs for retrofits were lower than the cost of constructing and owning a building. Bob Basham explained the rationale behind Outback's location strategy:

. . . We call it our A-market B-location. . . . we didn't have enough money to go to the corner of Main and Main. So we felt that if we went to a great market [that] had great demographics that we needed, and got in what we

called a B-location, that typically most restaurant companies would think of as a B-location, we felt we could be successful there if we executed great, and that strategy continues today.

However, as the company expanded into other parts of the country, the cost structure shifted. In 1993 the company developed a prototype that was being constructed in most new locations. The company devoted significant effort to site evaluation efforts that focused on area demographics, target population density, household income levels, competition, and specific site characteristics such as visibility, accessibility, and traffic volume.

Conventional wisdom in the restaurant industry suggested that facilities should be utilized as long as possible during the day. However, Outback restaurants were open daily for seven hours from 4:30 to 11:30 P.M. This dinner-only approach had been highly successful. The dinner-only concept had led to the effective utilization of systems, staff, and management. By not offering lunch, Outback avoided restaurant sites in high-traffic, high-cost city centers. Furthermore, the dinner-only theme minimized the strain on staff. Tips were typically much higher for dinner than for lunch or breakfast service. Outback restaurants averaged 3,800 customers per week and were usually filled shortly after opening. In an industry where a sales-to-investment ratio of 1.2:1 was considered strong, Outback's restaurants generated $2.10 in sales for every $1 invested in the facility.

Operating Structure— "No organization charts here"

Management remained informal in 1995. Corporate headquarters were located on the second floor of an unpretentious office building near the Tampa airport. The headquarters offices were about two miles from the original store on Henderson Boulevard. Headquarters staff numbered approximately 80. Corporate existed as a service center. As Bob Merritt put it:

We exist here to service the restaurants. . . . There is nothing I can do from Tampa, Florida, to make sure the customer has a great experience in Kansas City, nothing except to put in management people who have great attitudes, who like to take care of people, who are highly motivated economically, and make sure they have hired the best and most highly motivated people, and trained them to get the job done. It is absolutely our point of differentiation. You can get at the food and all the other stuff, but in the end what makes this company work is its decentralized nature and our willingness, particularly Chris and Bob's willingness, to live with the mistakes of their subordinates and look at those mistakes as opportunities to teach, not opportunities to discipline. That is the pervasive element of our corporate culture that makes it work.

There was no human resources department at corporate. However, Trudy Cooper, vice president for training and development, had been involved in the hiring of asso-ciates at most new restaurants until 1994. In 1994 Cooper added two coordinators who helped with new restaurant openings. One of the coordinators supervised training in the front operations and the other supervised the kitchen. Each selected 15 other high-quality employees from restaurants throughout the system to work on a temporary, one to one basis with the new employees during an opening. The two coordinators and the special training staff all returned to their home restaurant assignments once an opening was completed.

Training at a new restaurant site took place over a two-week period. Outback absorbed all the costs related to an opening into the marketing/advertising budget. The restaurant staff had four practice nights. On the first night, a Friday, the guests were family members of the staff. On the second and third nights, Saturday and Sunday, the invited guests were community members, including construction workers, vendors, and other VIP guests. The fourth night, Monday, was charity night. Trudy Cooper described a new restaurant opening:

We have those people on site for about two weeks. We have classroom sessions, then a food show and a wine show. We do a mock night. We do two nights of role play. We do a night with the media followed by a charity function. All of the proceeds go to charity. It is $10 a person for heavy hors d'oeuvres and an open bar. We make quite a bit of money on that night for the charity chosen by the restaurant manager.

Local press representatives were invited to a special briefing session an hour in advance of the opening night. All the proceeds from opening night went to a charity of the restaurant manager's choice.

A typical Outback restaurant staff consisted of a general manager, one assistant manager, and a kitchen manager plus 50 to 70 hourly employees, many of whom worked part-time. Job candidates for the restaurant staff were required to pass an aptitude test that assessed basic skills such as making change at the till. Every applicant interviewed with two managers. A friendly and outgoing disposition was a critical job requirement. The company also used psychological profile tests to better understand an applicant's personality.

Outback placed a great degree of emphasis upon learning and personal growth throughout the company. Trudy Cooper called it "Our learn-teach-learn approach." Chris Sullivan further explained:

I was given the opportunity to make a lot of mistakes and learn, and we try to do that today. We try to give our people a lot of opportunity to make some mistakes, learn, and go on.

"Every worker an owner . . ."

The three founders keenly remembered their early desire to own their own restaurant. Consequently, Outback provided ownership opportunities at three levels in the organization: at the individual restaurant level; through multiple store arrangements (joint venture and franchise opportunities); and through the newly formed employee stock ownership plan.

Top management selected the joint venture partners and franchisees. As franchisee Hugh Connerty put it, "There is no middle management here. All franchisees report directly to the president." Franchisees and joint venture partners in turn hired the general managers at each restaurant. All of the operating partners and general managers were required to complete a comprehensive 12-week training course that emphasized the company's operating strategy, procedures, and standards.

From the beginning, the founders wanted ownership opportunities for each restaurant general manager and formed the limited partner arrangement. Each restaurant general manager committed to a five-year contract and invested $25,000 for a 10 percent stake in the restaurant. Initially, the arrangement was in the form of a limited partnership. However, the company was in the process of converting all agreements to general partnerships backed with liability insurance.

Under the program, the restaurant general manager received a base salary of $45,000 plus 10 percent of the pre-rent "cash flow" from the restaurant. "Pre-rent" cash flow for Outback restaurants was calculated monthly and defined as earnings before taxes, interest, and depreciation.[18] Each manager's name appeared over the restaurant door with the designation, "Proprietor." An average Outback generated $3.2 million in sales and a pre-rent "cash flow" of $736,000. Average total compensation for managing partners exceeded $100,000, including an average $73,600 share of the restaurant profits. If the manager chose to leave the company at the end of a five-year period, Outback bought out the manager's ownership. If managers chose to stay with Outback, they could sign up for five additional years at the same restaurant or invest another $25,000 in a new store. After the company went public in 1991, the company began to give restaurant managers nonqualified stock options at the time they became managing partners. The options vested at the end of five years. Each manager received about 4,000 shares of stock over the five-year period. Outback's attractive arrangements for restaurant general managers resulted in a 1994 management turnover of 5 percent compared to 30 percent to 40 percent industrywide.

By early 1995, eleven stores had celebrated their five-year anniversaries (see Exhibit 3). Of the eleven managers, two had left the company. One later returned. Four had gone on to new stores in which they invested $25,000 with the same repeat deal. Five stayed with their same stores, renewing their contract with additional options that would vest at the end of the second five-year period. Joe Cofer, manager of the Henderson Street Outback in Tampa, indicated how his position as general manager of the restaurant affected his life:

I have been with the Outback for about 4 1/2 years now. I

started out as a manager. Sixteen months ago I was offered a partnership in the Henderson store. I grew up in Tampa, right down the street, and have lived here nearly my whole life. So when they offered me this store, it was perfect. . . . If you walk in the restaurant and look at the name on the sign, some people I went to high school with say, "How in the heck did this happen?". . . . The other organization [I worked for] had long hours when you were open from 11:30 in the morning until 1 or 2 in the evening. Those hours have a tendency to burn people out. . . . At Outback, from the [supplier] level all the way down to the dishwasher level we all work as a team. That is another difference between Outback and the organization I used to work for. . . . Here at Outback we don't have those rules and regulations . . . Chris always claims he plays a lot of golf in the daytime and has a lot of fun. . . . He will come up to you and ask, "Are you having fun?" [We say] "Oh, we're having a great time." He says, "Okay, that's the way you need to run this stuff."

Multiple-store ownership occurred through franchises, joint venture partnership arrangements, and sometimes a combination. The founders' original plan did not include franchises. However, in 1990 a friend who owned several restaurants in Kentucky asked to put Outback franchises in two of his restaurants that had not done very well. The founders reluctantly awarded the KY franchise. The two franchised restaurants quickly became successful. Under a franchise arrangement, the franchisees paid 3 percent of gross revenues to Outback.

After the IPO the company began to form joint venture partnerships with individuals who had strong operating credentials but not a lot of funds to invest. Under a joint venture arrangement a joint venture partner invested $50,000 and in return received a $50,000 base salary, plus 10 percent of the "cash flow" generated by the restaurants in his/her group after the restaurant general managers were paid their 10 percent. Therefore, a joint venture partner who operated ten Outbacks generating $600,000 each would end up with $54,000 per unit or $540,000 total plus the $50,000 base. Since Outback's general managers were experienced restaurateurs, the joint venture partners focused primarily on area development, including site research for new locations and hiring and training new managers. The company instituted its employee stock ownership plan in 1993 for employees at the restaurant level. At the time the ESOP was established, all employees received stock proportional to their time in service. Each employee received a yearly statement. The stock ownership program required no investment from the employees and vested after five years.

Advertising and Promotion—"We have always established that Outback is quality product at a great value"

Vice president of marketing Nancy Schneid came to Outback in 1990. Before working for Outback, Schneid had been first a media buyer in a large advertising agency and then an advertising sales representative for Tampa's dominant radio station. She met Chris and Bob while she was at the radio station and they were running their Chili's franchise. Although Chili's advertising strategy did not usually include radio advertising, Chris and Bob chose to use a significant level of local radio advertising.

Nancy was well aware of Chris and Bob's success with Chili's. When they established Outback, she became an early investor in the form of a limited partnership. She explained how the radio station she worked with was able to help the three entrepreneurs with advertising:

When they first opened Outback they were struggling. Our radio station was expensive to advertise on. . . . So I made an opportunity for them to go on radio on a morning show that had a 35 percent share of the market and an afternoon show that had a 28 percent share of the market. That gave them the opportunity to tell the Tampa Bay community about the concept [which was] in a very B location on Henderson. Tim Gannon came at 5:00 A.M. and set up a cooking station downstairs. He cooked and ran food upstairs while Chris and Bob talked to the DJ. They basically owned the morning show.

Outback used very little print media. Print advertisements typically appeared only if a charity or sports event offered space as part of its package. Thus, Outback ads might appear in the American Cancer Magazine or a golf tournament program. Billboards were used to draw customers to specific restaurant locations. TV advertising began in 1991 after the local advertising agency, the West Group in Tampa, was selected. The company produced about three or four successful TV advertisements per year. Although not a company spokesman, well-known model Rachel Hunter had participated in several of the ads and had become identified with Outback. Hunter's New Zealand origin was generally interpreted by audiences to be Australian.

Except for the development of the TV advertisements, advertising and marketing efforts were decentralized. As VP Schneid put it:

We are very much micro-managers when it comes to the spending of our media dollars. . . . We are very responsive to the needs of the community, for example, Big Sisters and Brothers. . . . [Our advertising, marketing, and community involvement efforts] help us build friends and an image of great food at a great price.

Community Involvement— "We have been rewarded . . . out of proportion to our needs, and we want to give some of that back"

Central to Outback's operating strategy was a high degree of visibility and involvement in the community. Outback sponsored the Out-

back Bowl that first aired on ESPN on New Year's afternoon 1996. In addition, the company was involved in a number of charity golf tournaments with a unique format involving food preparation and service at each hole. Community involvement involved not only top management but everyone at Outback. Each new store opening involved community participation and community service to charities. Other community involvement took various forms. The Tampa-based corporate staff included a full-time special events person with a staff that catered to charity as well as for-profit events in the Tampa area. For many charity events Outback provided the food while staff donated their time.

For example, a black-tie dinner for 400 was scheduled for May 1995 at Tampa's Lowry Park Zoo, a special interest of Outback's three top executives.

Every local restaurant managing partner was likely to have a Little League or other sports sponsorship. Basham explained:

We are really involved in the community. . . . I think you have to give back. We have been very, very fortunate, we have been rewarded . . . out of proportion to our needs, and we want to give some of that back to the community. . . . I think if more people did that we would have a lot less problems in this country than we have right now. . . . I have certainly been rewarded out of proportion to any contribution I feel I have made, and I just feel I should give something back. That goes throughout our company.

The Founders' Relationship— "The three of us kind of stay on each other, challenging each other, kid each other a lot, but more than anything support each other to make this thing work"

The three founders contributed in different ways to running the company. Each shared his perspective on his own as well the others' roles. Chris gave his view of the trio:

. . . Bob and I became corporate-type restaurant people, and sometimes that is more systems-oriented and not so much hospitality-oriented. Tim really brought that to our success. But more than that, he is easy to get along with. He absolutely gets done what needs to get done. He needs a little prodding. Bob and I need a little prodding. So the three of us kind of stay on each other, kid each other a lot, but more than anything support each other to make this thing work.

Bob explained the synergy among the three:

We have been together eight years. I think we have a balance between our strengths and our weaknesses. There are some things Chris does extremely well that I don't do well. There are things that Tim puts into the formula that Chris and I could not do as well as he does, and hopefully there are some things that I do well that they would need. I think just the three of us have synergies together that have really worked very positively for us. We kind of all feed off of each other. . . . Right now, each one of us has a different role in the company. I concentrate on operations, the people side of the business, the day-to-day going-on of the business. I think Chris has a little more of the strategic overview of the company, keeps us going in the direction we need to be going. He is very good at seeing things long-term. Tim is our food guy. Tim makes sure that we can all have a lot of fun. He has a lot of fun in his work. So we have a balance there. We all contribute and it all works.

Tim gave his perspective on how he fit in:

. . . My challenge: How do I fit in? . . . Partnerships of three are always hard but it has worked very well. I now understand my role and have been treated well. . . . [There is] nothing in life greater than having a great partnership. . . . We meet all the time. I never make a menu decision without them, Chris has eyes for the guest and Bob has eyes for the employee. . . . A lot of organizations bust up at the top, not bottom! I only want to work with Outback.

Competition—"We have all we need of the greatest kind of flattery"

A number of competitors in casual dining's steak dinner house subsegment had begun to make their presence felt. The most formidable competition was the Wichita, Kansas-based Lone Star Steakhouse & Saloon. However, there was also a grow-ing set of players with a formula involving rustic buildings and beef value items that began operations in early 1990 and 1991. These included Sizzler International's Buffalo Ranch, Shoney's Barbwire, S&A Restaurant Corp.'s Montana Steak Co., and O'Charley Logan's Roadhouse. In addition, a number of chains had added or upgraded steak menu items in reaction to Outback.

Chris Sullivan explained his view of competition and what Outback had to do:

Our competitors—there are a lot . . . [We] can't run way from it—it's a fact. I think a lot of companies get in trouble because they start worrying about what the competitor is doing and they react to that. We really ask our people and we talk about—just go out and execute and do what you do best. The customers will decide . . . If we continue to do what we have been doing, we feel very, very confident that we will continue to be successful regardless of the number of competitors out there because with our situation, our setup, and the proprietors we have in our restaurants, I don't think there is anybody who can compete with us.

Outback's Future Outlook

The company as a whole was optimistic about its future. Wall Street analysts were skeptical, however. Citing the numerous entrants into the industry, they argued that casual dining operators such as Outback were close to saturation and questioned whether the firm could with-stand the intense competitive pressures characteristic of the industry. However, Outback's management was unperturbed by Wall Street concerns or by the increasing competition. Joe Cofer summarized the management attitude:

I've heard so many times, "I love coming to your restaurant because your staff is so upbeat, they are so happy." They are always great people to have work for you. People just love the people here. . . . I see us as a McDonald's of the future, but a step up. I don't think anybody can come close to our efficiency because it is so simplistic and everyone is so laid back about it from the owners on down. And we are having such fun, making so much money. No one wants to go anywhere. I will never work for another company as long as I live. . . . You have that feeling mixed with the great food. I don't think anyone is a threat. . . . You have a very good investment with the stock. The stock has split three times in the last three years. . . . This is just going to split more and more and more. I'm just going to hold on to it forever. Hopefully, it will be my retirement.

The company intended to drive its future growth through a four-pronged strategy: (1) continuous expansion within the United States with an additional 300 to 350 Outback concept stores, (2) the rollout of Carrabbas Italian franchise as its second system of restaurants, (3) development of additional restaurant themes, and (4) international franchising. Chris Sullivan explained:

. . . We can do 500 to 600 restaurants, and possibly more over the next five years. . . . Our Italian concept, Carrabbas, that is in its infancy stage right now. . . has the potential to have the same kind of growth pattern that we have had in Outback. . . . We will continue to focus on Outback and continue to build that because we have a lot of work left there. Develop Carrabbas and use that as our next growth vehicle and continue to look . . . for a third leg on that stool, and who knows what is going to be hot in a couple of years. . . . The world is becoming one big market, and we want to be in place so we don't miss that opportunity. There are some problems, some challenges with it, but at this point there have been some casual restaurants chains that have gone [outside the United States] and their average unit sales are way, way above the sales level they enjoyed in the United States. So the potential is there. . . . We are real excited about the future internationally.

In the face of the dire predictions from industry observers and analysts, Outback CEO Chris Sullivan put his organization's plans quite simply: "We want to be the major player in the casual dining segment."[19]

Richard Branson
Meets the New Economy

— — — — — — — — — — — — — — — — —

David S. Chappell, Ohio University

Sir Richard Branson represents one of the most charismatic entrepreneurs of the 21st century. His collection of companies under the umbrella brand of "Virgin" has confounded analysts with his ability to spot emerging trends and profit by them. One senior executive at *Virgin* describes it as a "branded venture-capital firm." (1) Branson has repeatedly redefined its business operations, keeping alive an enlivened entrepreneurial spirit. His latest venture moves the firm firmly onto the Net—was he right to try it?

History

I f nothing else, Richard Branson has been flamboyant. His objective from the start has been to be noticed, have fun, and make money by constantly starting new firms. (2) Virgin represents a 3 billion pound company that has created over 200 new businesses and employs over 25,000 people since its inception in 1970. (3) Virgin Group Limited presently represents 170 businesses and includes everything from planes, trains, finance, soft drinks, music, mobile phones, holidays, cars, wines, publishing, bridal wear—and more. (4)

> **I want Virgin to be as well-known around the world as Coca-Cola (2)**
>
> Sir Richard Branson

Virgin doesn't represent a business so much as it represents a business-making machine. (5) And the force that keeps this alive is 51-year-old Sir Richard Branson. Born in 1950, Branson's first venture was the publication of a magazine called *Student*. His headmaster at the Stowe School remarked after the first issue was released, "Congratulations Branson. I predict you will either go to prison or become a millionaire." (6)

In fact, Branson did relatively poorly as a student. As a dyslexic, nearsighted young man, he performed badly on standard IQ tests. What these tests failed to capture was the ambition and passion for success. Although he is often identified as a "hippie billionaire" in public, it masks a deep determination to succeed in business.

The magazine intended from the start to tie many schools together by focusing on the students and not the schools. The first edition appeared with a cover picture drawn by Peter Blake, who designed the Beatles' Sergeant Pepper album cover, in addition to an interview with Blake. This was to foreshadow Branson's unique ability to energize others with his business ideas. (7)

This was followed quickly in 1970 with a foray into discount records. Running ads in a mail-order catalog, an increasing number of individuals purchased discounted records from Branson and Company. His group from the magazine found an old shop, cleaned it up, and started a discount record store. Wanting to name their business, three options were identified: "Slipped Disc," "Student," and "Virgin." Since they were all virgins at business, the Virgin name was selected. (7) It quickly became the largest discount music megastore chain in the world.

In 1972 Branson branched out into the music recording business with Virgin Records. His first recording artist, Mike Oldfield, released "Tubular Bells" and went on to sell over 5 million copies. When punk rock became popular, Branson signed the Sex Pistols, a group no other recording studio would touch. Other groups included Genesis, Simple Minds, Culture Club, Phil Collins, and the Rolling Stones.

Others might have been content with their early success, but Richard Branson was not finished. Running his business interests out of a houseboat on the Thames river, he launched Virgin Airways in 1984 (now Virgin Atlantic) with a single jumbo jet. Taking on British Airways, he sued them for alleged dirty tricks and won. The airline is famous for its offbeat perks, including massages and premium first-class service.

Branson also refuses to follow the leaders in the industries. As many airlines drop fares and cut service in order to compete for passengers, Branson keeps Virgin Atlantic focused on customer services at reasonable fares, including ice cream with movies, private bedrooms, showers, and exercise facilities.

However, not everything touched by Branson turns to gold. He was forced in the early 1990s to sell his beloved Virgin Records to Thorn EMI to secure the survival of his Virgin Airlines. "I had to sell a company I loved," said Branson. (9)

As a result, Branson now uses a strategy of using wealthy partners to provide the bulk of the cash necessary to run a business, with Virgin providing the brand name recognition in exchange for a controlling interest in the venture.

Branson hasn't been shy about promoting himself, releasing books including "Losing My Virginity: How I Survived, Had Fun, and Made a Fortune Doing Business My Way" and "Richard Branson: The Authorized Biography." Outside of Branson himself, the firm's most visible asset is the stellar red-and-white Virgin logo. Splashed across everything he touches, it serves as a unifying presence and assurance of quality to its legion of consumers.

Dubbed as the "Barnum of British Business," Sir Richard is well known for his offbeat business stunts. He donned a wedding dress to launch Virgin Bride, and he drove and fired a World War II tank at a Coca Cola sign in Times Square to launch his Virgin Cola. (10) He sails and is a hot-air balloon enthusiast, engaging in several around-the-world attempts.

As a consummate promoter, Branson never misses a chance to gain valuable publicity. He promotes the Virgin brand at every opportunity. Branson kicked off his new mobile phone service by driving around central London on a flatbed truck with 20 nude female models holding mobile phones under the slogan, "What You See Is What You Get." A few months before, Branson went to New Delhi and rode a white elephant to Parliament to persuade the government to open India to Virgin Atlantic. It worked; Virgin Atlantic now services the country. (11)

Although he admits that he is a technophobe, Branson nonetheless identifies the Internet as the next big business. "I'm not that interested in the Net, personally," says Branson. (12) However, his goal is no less ambitious than to develop Virgin.com as one of the top 10 portals on the Internet, in competition with the likes of Yahoo! and AOL.

By aggregating a large number of services under one Net umbrella, he hopes to gain valuable economies of scale by cross-promoting his many businesses. By combining with experienced business partners, he gains valuable insights at reduced costs. The Internet may provide the unifying mechanism that draws all his businesses together. By collecting all his businesses under the Virgin.org website, he can cross-promote the various businesses in a more cost-efficient manner.

A Brave New World?

With a personal wealth valued at over $3 billion, Sir Richard continues to confound his rivals. Rather than mixing with investment bankers, he has a habit of keeping his companies private—preferring to sell off

---

We look for opportunities where we can offer something better, fresher and more valuable, and we seize them. We often move into areas where the customer has traditionally received a poor deal, and where the competition is complacent. (8)

Sir Richard Branson

---

chunks of his empire to fund new business startups. His sale of a 49 percent share of Virgin Atlantic to Singapore Airlines for $979 million provides him the needed cash to plow into his Internet ventures. (13)

Although Virgin represents a late arrival to the Internet, Branson has attacked

> A lot of people never thought Virgin was very logical because we didn't specialize in any one area. But then the Internet comes along, and I'm able to pretend that it was all a carefully crafted plan. (14)
>
> Sir Richard Branson

the venture with the same enthusiasm as his previous business startups.

Many of his business interests already had a presence on the Web, including Thetrainline.com, a joint venture with British transport company Stagecoach. The site sells tickets for Britain's 23 train operators, has over 1.8 million users, purchases of $2.5 million weekly, and is adding 55,000 new users each week. (15) By transferring an airline-type reservation system onto the Net, Virgin earns 9 percent of every ticket booked. And consistent with his Net strategy, Virgin will sell competitors' services right alongside its own. What Branson is hoping to do is leverage his presence into a "cyberbrand" with a premium presence on the Web.

"Virgin's approach to the Net has been very clever" claims Simon Knox, professor of brand marketing at the Cranfield University School of Management in Bedford. "Each launch of a new business builds upon the one before, rather than developing isolated branded businesses." (16) Others disagree, with Michael Arnbjerg of market researcher IDC in Copenhagen arguing that "Virgin can leverage its brand in certain market sectors, but that's not enough to become a major player." (17)

Virgin.com represents the 12th most popular Web destination in Britain with over 1.9 million visitors a month. The question remains, can Sir Richard leverage the hip, consumer-friendly image and exceptional service of Virgin across a wider offering? Others have tried and failed—can Virgin find the secret formula to success?

An E-Business Sampler

Virgin Atlantic Airways As Virgin's biggest online moneymaker, the airline uses the Net to sell tickets and to save inventory costs by ordering spare parts over the Web.

Virgintravelstore.com An online travel agency that can book everything from airline flights to hotel rooms to guided tours from a wide selection of travel companies, including Virgin.

Virgin Mobile A joint venture with Deutsche Telekom's cellular unit, One 2 One, that was launched in November 1999. Virgin Mobile has 548,000 customers in Britain and is expanding to Australia and Southeast Asia.

Virgin Money Similar to Charles Schwab, it provides online trading of securities and financial information on every financial product on the market—not just Virgin's.

Radiofreevirgin.com A free digital radio tuner gives listeners CD-quality music from 50 Net channels. It hopes to eventually go global.

Virgin Energy An Internet-based gas and electricity supplier; 25 percent owned by London Electricity, it has attracted 5,500 consumers and hopes to expand to Europe.

Virginwines.com Uses software to analyze buyers' purchase patterns to help guide them through a 17,500-wine listing. Sales average $58,000/week.

Virgin Direct Along with partners, this site sells insurance, mortgages, and investment funds. It has more than 1 million customers and $4 billion in assets.

Click here for a complete list. (18)

Virgin Auctions provides an online marketplace for off-line products. On its opening, Branson offered flights, cars, wine, and mobile phones from his various enterprises, with all bids starting at $1.50. Hoping to imitate the success of EBay.com, he hopes to attract new users who will stay to look over his other sites.

Branson intends to leverage his position as a major provider of mobile phone service in connection with his Web services. "Branson realizes the considerable potential for mobile phones as a distribution channel, and any of his businesses can benefit from this," argues Peter Richardson, analyst at the Gartner Group. (19) His foray into the wireless arena is supported by investor George Soros and Microsoft co-founder Paul Allen. Virgin Mobile provides him a direct link to customers without extra marketing costs. He believes that eventually most of the transactions on Virgin.com will be made through cell phones rather than over PCs.

In addition to new sources of revenue, Branson is using the Net to streamline the vast array of services offered by Virgin. The Net can improve the efficiency of Virgin's vast supply chain needs, resulting in huge savings in inventory costs. Virgin anticipates the Internet will boost its efficiencies and shave 15 percent off its overall costs.

V Shop represented a money-losing venture that offered a miniature version of the Virgin Megastore, with music, videos, entertainment gear, software, and mobile phones. V Shop now keeps only the most popular items on its shelves, with the remainder of 110,000 products available via in-store kiosks linked to the Net. Virgin is saving $300,000 a year at each of the 150 V Shops. "Technology has enabled us to put a dying business back on its feet and make a small store big," claims Virgin Entertainment Group CEO Simon Wright. (20)

Despite all its grand new services, Virgin is late to the Web. With most of its sales from Virgin.com available only in Britain, the company's online sales represent a rather puny $216 million. That is just a fraction of Virgin's total sales of $5.2 billion. Several analysts also question the wisdom of splashing the Virgin logo over such a disparate range of

businesses—will the strategy undermine the integrity of the brand? (21)

Virgin believes its strength lies in selling its own merchandise, something neither Yahoo! or AOL does, which gives it an advantage. "Being completely virtual and simply selling other peoples' products is a zero-sum game," argues Will Whitehorn, a Virgin director of e-commerce activities. Jamie Wood of J. P. Morgan and Company contends that "The Web works best when a brand aggregates a variety of services into one place with a guaranteed level of service." (22)

It's Virgin's reputation for superior service that ties all these efforts together. If Branson can create a one-stop shopping experience among the public, then the brand umbrella concept will work. His efforts also support the concept that the "clicks-and-bricks" approach provides the most appropriate business model for success on the Web. The Web acts as a central nervous sytem for his disparate businesses.

Branson remains convinced that the Web offers a new and exciting channel of access to worldwide customers at a fraction of the cost of normal channels. Yet, he remains committed to the people at Virgin as individuals. "It all comes down to people" he remarks. (23) He writes the Virgin employees a monthly letter from his paper notebook, and invites them to write or call him with their problems or dreams.

Not everyone is enamored with Sir Richard. Tom Bower has written a book that presents Branson in a much less flattering light. He points out the many disap-

pointments in the Virgin brand, including Virgin Cola, Virgin Express—the low-cost Belgian airline—and Virgin's Glasgow train service, which has seen some of the worst service since the railroads were privatized.

In addition, the meltdown of many dot.com businesses in America may portend a similar fate for his Internet conglomerate. Numerous business models, from Boo.com to Furniture.com, have failed and gone out of business while failing to have ever turned a profit. One of the closest rivals to Virgin's megabrand model—Amazon.com—continues to struggle, having lost over 80 percent of its market value in the last year.

> **I never went into business solely to make money.**
>
> Sir Richard Branson

Additionally, some analysts worry about Branson's high-profile and high-handed handling of Virgin. While he has a loyal following of top managers in the firm, no heir apparent exists in the event of a need for succession.

With most of his success in Britain, it remains to be seen if he can leverage his Web success to other markets, particularly the largest of them all—the United States. Virgin has decided to pull back from online music sales in the U.S. through its Virgin Megastore site due to slow sales.

Branson appears to be continuing to support his vision of having fun and making money. With no giant corporate office staff, and content to run his empire out of one of his four houses around London, his unique competence appears to be the ability to empower and fuel peoples' ideas around him. His goal remains to turn Virgin into the premier 21st-century global brand.

Did Virgin arrive on the Internet too late to take advantage of its opportunities? Does the Web offer the integration necessary for Branson to derive all the cross-selling efficiencies from his various products and services? It should be an interesting ride.

eXercises *in* TEAMWORK

My Best Manager

Preparation

Working alone, make a list of the *behavioral attributes* that describe the *best* manager you have ever worked for. This could be someone you worked for in a full-time or part-time job, summer job, volunteer job, student organization, or whatever. If you have trouble identifying an actual manager, make a list of behavioral attributes of the type of manager you would most like to work for in your next job.

Instructions

Form into groups as assigned by your instructor, or work with a nearby classmate. Share your list of attributes and listen to the lists of others. Be sure to ask questions and make comments on items of special interest. Work together to create a master list that combines the unique attributes of the "best" managers experienced by members of your group. Have a spokesperson share that list with the rest of the class.

Source: Adapted from John R. Schermerhorn, Jr., James G. Hunt, and Richard N. Osborn, *Managing Organizational Behavior*, 3rd ed. (New York: Wiley, 1988), pp. 32–33. Used by permission.

What Managers Do

Preparation

Think about the questions that follow. Record your answers in the spaces provided.

1. How much of a typical manager's time would you expect to be allocated to these relationships? (total should = 100%)

___% of time working with subordinates

___% of time working with boss

___% of time working with peers and outsiders

2. How many hours per week does the average manager work? ___ hours

3. What amount of a manager's time is typically spent in the following activities? (total should – 100%)

___% in scheduled meetings

___% in unscheduled meetings

___% doing desk work

___% talking on the telephone

___% walking around the organization/ work site

Instructions

Talk over your responses with a nearby classmate. Explore the similarities and differences in your answers. Be prepared to participate in class discussion led by your instructor.

Defining Quality

Preparation

Write your definition of the word *quality* here. QUALITY =

Instructions

Form groups as assigned by your instructor. (1) Have each group member present a definition of the word *quality*. After everyone has presented, come up with a consensus definition of *quality*. That is, determine and write down one definition of the word with which every member can agree. (2) Next, have the group assume the position of top manager in each of the following organizations. Use the group's *quality* definition to state for each a *quality objective* that can guide the behavior of members in producing high-"quality" goods and/or services for customers or clients. Elect a spokesperson to share group results with the class as a whole.

Organizations:

a. A college of business administration

b. A community hospital

c. A retail sporting goods store

d. A fast-food franchise restaurant

e. A United States post office

f. A full-service bank branch

g. A student-apartment rental company

h. A "tie-dye" T-shirt manufacturing company

i. A computer software manufacturing firm

Leading Through Participation

Preparation

Read each of the following vignettes. Write in the space to the left of each whether you think the leader should handle the situation with an individual decision (I), consultative decision (C), or group decision (G).

Vignette I

You are a general supervisor in charge of a large team laying an oil pipeline. It is now necessary to estimate your expected rate of progress in order to schedule material deliveries to the next field site. You know the nature of the terrain you will be traveling and have the historical data needed to compute the mean and variance in the rate of speed over that type of terrain. Given these two variables, it is a simple matter to calculate the earliest and latest times at which materials and support facilities will be needed at the next site. It is important that your estimate be reasonably accurate; underestimates result in idle supervisors and workers, and overestimates result in materials being tied up for a period of time before they are to be used. Progress has been good, and your 5 supervisors along with the other members of the gang stand to receive substantial bonuses if the project is completed ahead of schedule.

Vignette II

You are supervising the work of 12 engineers. Their formal training and work experience are very similar, permitting you to use them interchangeably on projects. Yesterday, your manager informed you that a request had been received from an overseas affiliate for 4 engineers to go abroad on extended loan for a period of 6 to 8 months. He argued and you agreed that for a number of reasons this request should be filled from your group. All your engineers are capable of handling this assignment, and from the standpoint of present and future projects there is no particular reason that any one should be retained over any other. The problem is complicated by the fact that the overseas assignment is in what is generally regarded in the company as an undesirable location.

Vignette III

You are the head of a staff unit reporting to the vice president of finance. He has asked you to provide a report on the firm's current portfolio including recommendations for changes in the *selection criteria* currently employed. Doubts have been raised about the efficiency of the existing system in the current market conditions, and there is considerable dissatisfaction with prevailing rates of return. You plan to write the report, but at the moment you are quite perplexed about the approach to take. Your own specialty is the bond market, and it is clear to you that a detailed knowledge of the equity market, which you lack, would greatly enhance the value of the report. Fortunately, 4 members of your staff are specialists in different segments of the equity market. Together, they possess a vast amount of knowledge about the intricacies of investment. However, they seldom agree on the best way to achieve anything when it comes to the stock market. Whereas they are obviously conscientious as well as knowledgeable, they have major differences when it comes to investment philosophy and strategy. The report is due in 6 weeks. You have already begun to familiarize yourself with the firm's current portfolio and have been provided by management with a specific set of constraints that any portfolio must satisfy. Your immediate problem is to come up with some alternatives to the firm's present practices and select the most promising ones for detailed analysis in your report.

Vignette IV

You are on the division manager's staff and work on a wide variety of problems of both an administrative and technical nature. You have been given the assignment of developing a universal method to be used in each of the 5 plants in the division for manually reading equipment registers, recording the readings, and transmitting the scoring to a centralized information system. All plants are located in a relatively small geographical region. Until now there has been a high error rate in the reading and/or transmittal of the data. Some locations have considerably higher error rates than others, and the methods used to record and transmit the data vary between plants. It is probable, therefore, that part of the error variance is a function of specific local conditions rather than anything else, and this will complicate the establishment of any system common to all plants. You have the information on error rates but no information on the local practices that generate these errors or on the local conditions that necessitate the different practices. Everyone would benefit from an improvement in the quality of the data because it is used in a number of important decisions. Your contacts with the plants are through the quality control supervisors responsible for collecting the data. They are a conscientious group committed to doing their jobs well but are highly sensitive to interference on the part of higher management in their own operations. Any solution that does not receive the active support of the various plant supervisors is unlikely to reduce the error rate significantly.

Instructions

Form groups as assigned by the instructor. Share your choices with other group members and try to achieve a consensus on how the leader should best handle each situation. Refer back to the discussion of the Vroom-Jago "leader-participation" theory presented in Chapter 13. Analyze each vignette according to their ideas. Do you come to any different conclusions? If so, why? Nominate a spokesperson to share your results in general class discussion.

Source: Victor H. Vroom and Arthur G. Jago, *The New Leadership* (Englewood Cliffs, NJ: Prentice Hall, 1988). Used by permission.

EXERCISE 5

What Would the Classics Say?

Preparation

Consider this situation:

Six months after being hired, Bob, a laboratory worker, is performing just well enough to avoid being fired. He was carefully selected and had the abilities required to do the job really well. At first Bob was enthusiastic about his new job, but now he isn't performing up to this high potential. Fran, his supervisor, is concerned and wonders what can be done to improve this situation.

Instructions

Assume the identity of one of the following persons: Frederick Taylor, Henri Fayol, Max Weber, Abraham Maslow, Chris Argyris. Assume that *as this person* you have been asked by Fran for advice on the management situation just described. Answer these questions as you think your assumed identity would respond. Be prepared to share your answers in class and to defend them based on the text's discussion of this person's views.

1. As (*your assumed identity*), what are your basic beliefs about good management and organizational practices?

2. As (*your assumed identity*), what do you perceive may be wrong in this situation that would account for Bob's low performance?

3. As (*your assumed identity*), what could be done to improve Bob's future job performance?

The Great Management History Debate

Preparation

Consider the question "What is the best thing a manager can do to improve productivity in her or his work unit?"

Instructions

The instructor will assign you, individually or in a group, to one of the following positions. Complete the missing information as if you were the management theorist referred to. Be prepared to argue and defend your position before the class.

- Position A: "Mary Parker Follett offers the best insight into the question. Her advice would be to . . . " (advice to be filled in by you or the group).

- Position B: "Max Weber's ideal bureaucracy offers the best insight into the question. His advice would be to . . . " (advice to be filled in by you or the group).

- Position C: "Henri Fayol offers the best insight into the question. His advice would be to . . . " (advice to be filled in by you or the group).

- Position D: "The Hawthorne studies offer the best insight into the question. Elton Mayo's advice would be to . . . " (advice to be filled in by you or the group).

What Do You Value in Work?

Preparation

The following 9 items are from a survey conducted by Nicholas J. Beutell and O. C. Brenner ("Sex Differences in Work Values," *Journal of Vocational Behavior*, vol. 28, 1986, pp. 29–41). Rank order the 9 items in terms of how important (9 = most important) they would be to you in a job.

How important is it to you to have a job that:
____ Is respected by other people?
____ Encourages continued development of knowledge and skills?
____ Provides job security?
____ Provides a feeling of accomplishment?
____ Provides the opportunity to earn a high income?
____ Is intellectually stimulating?
____ Rewards good performance with recognition?
____ Provides comfortable working conditions?
____ Permits advancement to high administrative responsibility?

Instructions

Form into groups as designated by your instructor. Within each group, the *men in the group* will meet to develop a consensus ranking of the items as they think the *women* in the Beutell and Brenner survey ranked them. The reasons for the rankings should be shared and discussed so they are clear to everyone. The *women in the group* should not participate in this ranking task. They should listen to the discussion and be prepared to comment later in class discussion. A spokesperson for the men in the group should share the group's rankings with the class.

Optional Instructions

Form into groups as designated by your instructor but with each group consisting entirely of men or women. Each group should meet and decide which of the work values members of the *opposite* sex ranked first in the Beutell and Brenner survey. Do this again for the work value ranked last. The reasons should be discussed, along with the reasons why each of the other values probably was not ranked first . . . or last. A spokesperson for each group should share group results with the rest of the class.

Source: Adapted from Roy J. Lewicki, Donald D. Bowen, Douglas T. Hall, and Francine S. Hall, *Experiences in Management and Organizational Behavior,* 3rd ed. (New York: Wiley, 1988), pp. 23–26. Used by permission.

EXERCISE 8

Confronting Ethical Dilemmas

Preparation

Read and indicate your response to each of the situations below.

a. Ron Jones, vice president of a large construction firm, receives in the mail a large envelope marked "personal." It contains a competitor's cost data for a project that both firms will be bidding on shortly. The data are accompanied by a note from one of Ron's subordinates saying: "This is the real thing!" Ron knows that the data could be a major advantage to his firm in preparing a bid that can win the contract. *What should he do?*

b. Kay Smith is one of your top-performing subordinates. She has shared with you her desire to apply for promotion to a new position just announced in a different division of the company. This will be tough on you since recent budget cuts mean you will be unable to replace anyone who leaves, at least for quite some time. Kay knows this and in all fairness has asked your permission before she submits an application. It is rumored that the son of a good friend of your boss is going to apply for the job. Although his credentials are less impressive than Kay's, the likelihood is that he will get the job if she doesn't apply. *What will you do?*

c. Marty Jose got caught in a bind. She was pleased to represent her firm as head of the local community development committee. In fact, her supervisor's boss once held this position and told her in a hallway conversation, "Do your best and give them every support possible." Going along with this, Marty agreed to pick up the bill (several hundred dollars) for a dinner meeting with local civic and business leaders. Shortly thereafter, her supervisor informed everyone that the entertainment budget was being eliminated in a cost-saving effort. Marty, not wanting to renege on supporting the community development committee, was able to charge the dinner bill to an advertising budget. Eventually, an internal auditor discovered the mistake and reported it to you, the personnel director. Marty is scheduled to meet with you in a few minutes. *What will you do?*

Instructions

Working alone, make the requested decisions in each of these incidents. Think carefully about your justification for the decision. Meet in a group assigned by your instructor. Share your decisions and justifications in each case with other group members. Listen to theirs. Try to reach a group consensus on what to do in each situation and why. Be prepared to share the group decisions, and any dissenting views, in general class discussion.

Beating the Time Wasters

Preparation

1. Make a list of all the things you need to do tomorrow. Prioritize each item in terms of *how important it is to create outcomes that you can really value.* Use this classification scheme:

(a) Most important, top priority
(b) Important, not top priority
(c) Least important, low priority

Look again at all activities you have classified as B. Reclassify any that are really A's or C's. Look at your list of A's. Reclassify any that are really B's or C's. Double-check to make sure you are comfortable with your list of C's.

2. Make a list of all the "time wasters" that often interfere with your ability to accomplish everything you want to on any given day.

Instructions

Form into groups as assigned by the instructor. Have all group members share their lists and their priority classifications. Members should politely "challenge" each other's classifications to make sure that only truly "high-priority" items receive an A rating. They might also suggest that some C items are of such little consequence that they might not be worth doing at all. After each member of the group revises his or her "to do" list based on this advice, go back and discuss the time wasters identified by group members. Develop a master list of time wasters and what to do about them. Have a group spokesperson be prepared to share discussion highlights and tips on beating common time wasters with the rest of the class.

Source: Developed from Roy J. Lewicki, Donald D. Bowen, Douglas T. Hall, and Francine S. Hall. *Experiences in Management and Organizational Behavior,* 3rd ed. (New York: John Wiley & Sons, 1988), pp. 314–16.

Personal Career Planning

Preparation

Complete the following three activities, and bring the results to class. Your work should be in a written form suitable for your instructor's review.

Step 1: *Strengths and Weaknesses Inventory* Different occupations require special talents, abilities, and skills if people are to excel in their work. Each of us, you included, has a repertoire of existing strengths and weaknesses that are "raw materials" we presently offer a potential employer. Of course, actions can (and should!) be taken over time to further develop current strengths and to turn weaknesses into strengths. Make a list identifying your most important strengths and weaknesses at the

moment in relation to the career direction you are most likely to pursue upon graduation. Place a * next to each item you consider most important to address in your courses and student activities *before* graduation.

Step 2: *Five-Year Career Objectives* Make a list of 3 to 5 career objectives that are appropriate given your list of personal strengths and weaknesses. Limit these objectives to ones that can be accomplished within 5 years of graduation.

Step 3: *Five-Year Career Action Plans* Write a specific action plan for accomplishing each of the 5 objectives. State exactly what you will do, and by when, in order to meet each objective. If you will need special support or assistance, identify it *and* state how you will obtain it. Remember, an outside observer should be able to read your action plan for each objective and end up feeling confident that (a) he or she knows exactly what you are going to do, and (b) why.

Instructions

Form into groups as assigned by the instructor. Share your career-planning analysis with the group; listen to those of others. Participate in a discussion that examines any common patterns and major differences among group members. Take advantage of any opportunities to gather feedback and advice from others. Have one group member be prepared to summarize the group discussion for the class as a whole. Await further class discussion led by the instructor.

Source: Developed in part from Roy J. Lewicki, Donald D. Bowen, Douglas T. Hall, and Francine S. Hall, *Experiences in Management and Organizational Behavior.* 3rd ed. (New York: John Wiley and Sons, 1988), pp. 261–67. Used by permission.

Strategic Scenarios

Preparation

In today's turbulent environments, it is no longer safe to assume that an organization that was highly successful yesterday will continue to be so tomorrow—or that it will even be in existence. Changing times exact the best from strategic planners. Think about the situations currently facing the following well-known organizations; think, too, about the futures they may face.

McDonald's
Texaco
Xerox
Harvard University
United Nations
National Public Radio

Instructions

Form into groups as assigned by your instructor. Choose one or more organizations from the prior list (as assigned) and answer for that organization the following questions:

1. What in the future might seriously threaten the success, perhaps the very existence, of this organization? (As a group develop at least three such *future scenarios.*)

2. Estimate the probability (0 to 100 percent) of each future scenario occurring.

3. Develop a strategy for each scenario that will enable the organization to successfully deal with it.

Thoroughly discuss these questions within the group and arrive at your best possible consensus answers. Be prepared to share and defend your answers in general class discussion.

Source: Suggested by an exercise in John F. Veiga and John N. Yanouzas, *The Dynamics of Organization Theory: Gaining a Macro Perspective* (St. Paul, MN: West, 1979), pp. 69–71.

The MBO Contract

Listed below are performance objectives from an MBO contract for a plant manager.

1. To increase deliveries to 98% of all scheduled delivery dates

2. To reduce waste and spoilage to 3% of all raw materials used

3. To reduce lost time due to accidents to 100 work days/year

4. To reduce operating cost to 10% below budget

5. To install a quality-control system at a cost of less than $53,000

6. To improve production scheduling and increase machine utilization time to 95% capacity

7. To complete a management development program this year

8. To teach a community college course in human resource management

1. Study this MBO contract. In the margin write one of the following symbols to identify each objective as an improvement, maintenance, or personal development objective.

I = Improvement objective
M = Maintenance objective
P = Personal development objective

2. Assume that this MBO contract was actually developed and implemented under the following circumstances. After each statement, write "yes" if the statement reflects proper MBO procedures and write "no" if it reflects poor MBO procedures.

(a) The president drafted the 8 objectives and submitted them to Atkins for review.

(b) The president and Atkins thoroughly discussed the 8 objectives in proposal form before they were finalized.

(c) The president and Atkins scheduled a meeting in 6 months to review Atkins's progress on the objectives.

(d) The president didn't discuss the objectives with Atkins again until the scheduled meeting was held.

(e) The president told Atkins his annual raise would depend entirely on the extent to which these objectives were achieved.

3. Share and discuss your responses to parts 1 and 2 of the exercise with a nearby classmate. Reconcile any differences of opinion by referring back to the chapter discussion of MBO. Await further class discussion.

The Future Workplace

Instructions

Form groups as assigned by the instructor. Brainstorm to develop a master list of the major characteristics you expect to find in the future workplace in the year 2010. Use this list as background for completing the following tasks:

1. Write a one-paragraph description of what the typical "Workplace 2010 *manager's*" workday will be like.

2. Draw a "picture" representing what the "Workplace 2010 organization" will look like.

Choose a spokesperson to share your results with the class as a whole *and* explain their implications for the class members.

Dots and Squares Puzzle

1. Shown here is a collection of 16 dots. Study the figure to determine how many "squares" can be created by connecting the dots.

2. Draw as many squares as you can find in the figure while making sure a dot is at every corner of every square. Count the squares and write this number in the margin to the right of the figure.

3. Share your results with those of a classmate sitting nearby. Indicate the location of squares missed by either one of you.

4. Based on this discussion, redraw your figure to show the maximum number of possible squares. Count them and write this number to the left of the figure.

5. Await further class discussion led by your instructor.

Interviewing Job Candidates

Preparation

Make a list of the "generic" questions you think any employment interviewer should ask any job candidate, regardless of the specific job or situation. Then, place an X next to those of the following items you think represent additional important questions to ask.

____ How old are you?
____ Where were you born?
____ Where are you from?
____ What religion are you?
____ Are you married, single, or divorced?
____ If not married, do you have a companion?
____ Do you have any dependent children or elderly parents?

Instructions

Form work groups as assigned by your instructor. Share your responses with other group members, and listen to theirs. Develop a group consensus on a list of "generic" interview questions you think any manager should be prepared to ask of job candidates. Also develop a group consensus on which of the items on the preceding list represent questions that an interviewer should ask. Elect a spokesperson to present the group's results to the class, along with the reasons for selecting these questions.

Work vs. Family—You Be the Judge

1. Read the following situation.

Joanna, a single parent, was hired to work 8:15 A.M. to 5:30 P.M. weekdays selling computers for a firm. Her employer extended her work day until 10 P.M. weekdays and from 8:15 A.M.–5:30 P.M. on Saturdays. Joanna refused to work the extra hours, saying that she had a six-year old son and that so many work hours would lead to neglect. The employer said this was a special request during a difficult period and that all employees needed to share in helping out during the "crunch." Still refusing to work the extra hours, Joanna was fired. She sued the employer.

2. You be the judge in this case. Take an individual position on the following questions:

Should Joanna be allowed to work only the hours agreed to when she was hired? Or, is the employer correct in asking all employees, regardless of family status, to work the extra hours? Why?

3. Form into groups as assigned by the instructor. Share your responses to the questions and try to develop a group consensus. Be sure to have a rationale for the position the group adopts. Appoint a spokesperson who can share results with the class. Be prepared to participate in open class discussion.

Source: This case scenario is from Sue Shellenbarger, "Employees Challenge Policies on Family and Get Hard Lessons," *The Wall Street Journal* (December 17, 1997), p. B1.

Compensation and Benefits Debate

Preparation

Consider the following quotations.

On compensation: "A basic rule of thumb should be—pay at least as much, and perhaps a bit more, in base wage or salary than what competitors are offering."

On benefits: "When benefits are attractive or at least adequate, the organization is in a better position to employ highly qualified people."

Instructions

Form groups as assigned by the instructor. Each will be given *either* one of the preceding position statements *or* one of the following alternatives.

On compensation: Given the importance of controlling costs, organizations can benefit by paying as little as possible for labor.

On benefits: Given the rising cost of health-care and other benefit programs and the increasing difficulty many organizations have staying in business, it is best to minimize paid benefits and let employees handle more of the cost on their own.

Each group should prepare to debate a counterpoint group on its assigned position. After time is allocated to prepare for the debate, each group will present its opening positions. Each will then be allowed one rebuttal period to respond to the other group. General class discussion on the role of compensation and benefits in the modern organization will follow.

Sources and Uses of Power

Preparation

Consider *the way you behaved* in each of the situations described below. They may be from a full-time or part-time job, student organization or class group, sports team, or whatever. If you do not have an experience of the type described, try to imagine yourself in one; think about how you would expect yourself to behave.

1. You needed to get a peer to do something you wanted that person to do but were worried he or she didn't want to do it.

2. You needed to get a subordinate to do something you wanted her or him to do but were worried the subordinate didn't want to do it.

3. You needed to get your boss to do something you wanted him or her to do but were worried the boss didn't want to do it.

Instructions

Form into groups as assigned by the instructor. Start with situation 1 and have all members of the group share their approaches. Determine what specific sources of power (see Chapter 13) were used. Note any patterns in group members' responses. Discuss what is required to be successful in this situation. Do the same for situations 2 and 3. Note any special differences in how situations 1, 2, and 3 should be or could be handled. Choose a spokesperson to share results in general class discussion.

Empowering Others

Instructions

Think of times when you have been in charge of a group—this could be a full-time or part-time work situation, a student work group, or whatever. Complete the following questionnaire by recording how you feel about each statement according to this scale:

1 = Strongly disagree   2 = Disagree
3 = Neutral   4 = Agree   5 = Strongly agree
When in charge of a group I find

____ **1.** Most of the time other people are too inexperienced to do things, so I prefer to do them myself.

____ **2.** It often takes more time to explain things to others than to just do them myself.

____ **3.** Mistakes made by others are costly, so I don't assign much work to them.

____ **4.** Some things simply should not be delegated to others.

____ **5.** I often get quicker action by doing a job myself.

____ **6.** Many people are good only at very specific tasks and so can't be assigned additional responsibilities.

____ **7.** Many people are too busy to take on additional work.

____ **8.** Most people just aren't ready to handle additional responsibilities.

____ **9.** In my position, I should be entitled to make my own decisions.

Scoring

Total your responses: enter the score here [____].

Interpretation

This instrument gives an impression of your *willingness to delegate*. Possible scores range from 9 to 45. The higher your score, the more willing you appear to be to delegate to others. Willingness to delegate is an important managerial characteristic: It is essential if you—as a manager—are to "empower" others and give them opportunities to assume responsibility and exercise self-control in their work. With the growing importance of empowerment in the new workplace, your willingness to delegate is worth thinking about seriously. Be prepared to share your results and participate in general class discussion.

Source: Questionnaire adapted from L. Steinmetz and R. Todd, *First Line Management,* 4th ed. (Homewood, IL: BPI/Irwin, 1986), pp. 64–67. Used by permission.

EXERCISE 20

Gender Differences in Management

1. The question is "Do women or men make better managers?"

2. A research study by the Foundation for Future Leadership examined the management abilities of 645 men and 270 women in terms of supervisor, peer, and self-evaluations. Among the management skills studied were those listed below.

Skills	Women Higher	Men Higher	No Difference
Problem solving	_____	_____	_____
Planning	_____	_____	_____
Controlling	_____	_____	_____
Managing self	_____	_____	_____
Managing relationships	_____	_____	_____
Leading	_____	_____	_____
Communicating	_____	_____	_____

3. Indicate in the space provided whether you believe women scored higher on the average than men for each skill, men scored higher than women, or no difference in scores was found.

4. Meet in your discussion groups to share results and the rationale for your choices. Try to arrive at a group consensus regarding the likelihood of differences between women and men. Ask questions of one another:
• What is your experience with men as bosses?
• What is your experience with women as bosses?
• Why exactly do you think women/men would score better on each dimension?
• Is it useful to try and identify gender differences in management?
• Why is gender even relevant when it comes to questions about management skills?

5. Be prepared to summarize your results and participate in further class discussion led by the instructor.

Why Do We Work?

Preparation

Read the following "ancient story."

In days of old a wandering youth happened upon a group of men working in a quarry. Stopping by the first man he said, "What are you doing?" The worker grimaced and groaned as he replied, "I am trying to shape this stone, and it is backbreaking work." Moving to the next man he repeated the question. This man showed little emotion as he answered, "I am shaping a stone for a building." Moving to the third man, our traveler heard him singing as he worked. "What are you doing?" asked the youth. "I am helping to build a cathedral," the man proudly replied.

Instructions

In groups assigned by your instructor, discuss this short story. Ask and answer the question: "What are the lessons of this ancient story for (a) workers and (b) managers of today?" Ask members of the group to role-play each of the stonecutters, respectively, while they answer a second question asked by the youth: "Why are you working?" Have someone in the group be prepared to report and share the group's responses with the class as a whole.

Source: Developed from Brian Dumaine, "Why Do We Work," _Fortune_ (December 26, 1994), pp. 196–204.

The Case of the Contingency Workforce

Preparation

Part-time and contingency work is a rising percentage of the total employment in the United States. Go to the library and read about the current use of part-time and contingency workers in business and industry. Ideally, go to the Internet, enter a government database, and locate some current statistics on the size of the contingent labor force, the proportion that is self-employed and part-time, and the proportion of part-timers who are voluntary and involuntary.

Instructions

In your assigned work group, pool the available information on the contingency workforce. Discuss the information. Discuss one another's viewpoints on the subject as well as its personal and social implications. Be prepared to participate in a classroom "dialog session" in which your group will be asked to role-play one of the following positions:

a. Vice president for human resources of a large discount retailer hiring contingency workers.

b. Owner of a local specialty music shop hiring contingency workers.

c. Recent graduate of your college or university working as a contingency employee at the discount retailer in (a).

d. Single parent with two children in elementary school, working as a contingency employee of the music shop in (b).

The question to be answered by the (a) and (b) groups is "What does the contingency workforce mean to me?" The question to be answered by the (c) and (d) groups is "What does being a contingency worker mean to me?"

The "Best" Job Design

Preparation

Use the left-hand column to rank the following job characteristics in the order most important *to you* (1 = highest to 10 = lowest). Then use the right-hand column to rank them in the order in which you think they are most important *to others*.

____ Variety of tasks ____
____ Performance feedback ____
____ Autonomy/freedom in work ____
____ Working on a team ____
____ Having responsibility ____
____ Making friends on the job ____
____ Doing all of a job, not part ____
____ Importance of job to others ____
____ Having resources to do well ____
____ Flexible work schedule ____

Instructions

Form work groups as assigned by your instructor. Share your rankings with other group members. Discuss where you have different individual preferences and where your impressions differ from the preferences of others. Are there any major patterns in your group—for either the "personal" or the "other" rankings? Develop group consensus rankings for each column. Designate a spokesperson to share the group rankings and results of any discussion with the rest of the class.

Source: Developed from John M. Ivancevich and Michael T. Matteson, *Organizational Behavior and Management,* 2nd ed. (Homewood, IL: BPI/Irwin, 1990), p. 500. Used by permission.

Upward Appraisal

Instructions

Form into work groups as assigned by the instructor. The instructor will then leave the room. As a group, complete the following tasks:

1. Within each group create a master list of comments, problems, issues, and concerns about the course experience to date that members would like to communicate with the instructor.

2. Select one person from the group to act as spokesperson and give your feedback to the instructor when he or she returns to the classroom.

3. The spokespersons from each group should meet to decide how the room should be physically arranged (placement of tables, chairs, etc.) for the feedback session. This should allow the spokespersons and instructor to communicate while they are being observed by other class members.

4. While the spokespersons are meeting, members remaining in the groups should discuss what they expect to observe during the feedback session.

5. The classroom should be rearranged. The instructor should be invited in.

6. Spokespersons should deliver feedback to the instructor while observers make notes.

7. After the feedback session is complete, the instructor will call on observers for comments, ask the spokespersons for their reactions, and engage the class in general discussion about the exercise and its implications.

Source: Developed from Eugene Owens, "Upward Appraisal: An Exercise in Subordinate's Critique of Superior's Performance," *Exchange: The Organizational Behavior Teaching Journal,* vol. 3 (1978), pp. 41–42.

Feedback and Assertiveness

Preparation

Indicate the degree of discomfort you would feel in each situation below by circling the appropriate number:

1, high discomfort
2, some discomfort
3, undecided
4, very little discomfort
5, no discomfort

1 2 3 4 5 **1.** Telling an employee who is also a friend that she or he must stop coming to work late.

1 2 3 4 5 **2.** Talking to an employee about his or her performance on the job.

1 2 3 4 5 **3.** Asking an employee if she or he has any comments about your rating of her or his performance.

1 2 3 4 5 **4.** Telling an employee who has problems in dealing with other employees that he or she should do something about it.

1 2 3 4 5 **5.** Responding to an employee who is upset over your rating of his or her performance.

1 2 3 4 5 **6.** An employee's becoming emotional and defensive when you tell her or him about mistakes on the job.

1 2 3 4 5 **7.** Giving a rating that indicates improvement is needed to an employee who has failed to meet minimum requirements of the job.

1 2 3 4 5 **8.** Letting a subordinate talk during an appraisal interview.

1 2 3 4 5 **9.** An employee's challenging you to justify your evaluation in the middle of an appraisal interview.

1 2 3 4 5 **10.** Recommending that an employee be discharged.

1 2 3 4 5 **11.** Telling an employee that you are uncomfortable with the role of having to judge his or her performance.

1 2 3 4 5 **12.** Telling an employee that her or his performance can be improved.

1 2 3 4 5 **13.** Telling an employee that you will not tolerate his or her taking extended coffee breaks.

1 2 3 4 5 **14.** Telling an employee that you will not tolerate her or his making personal telephone calls on company time.

Instructions

Form three-person teams as assigned by the instructor. Identify the 3 behaviors with which they indicate the most discomfort. Then each team member should practice performing these behaviors with another member, while the third member acts as an observer. Be direct, but try to perform the behavior in an appropriate way. Listen to feedback from the observer and try the behaviors again, perhaps with different members of the group. When finished, discuss the exercise overall. Be prepared to participate in further class discussion.

Source: Feedback questionnaire is from Judith R. Gordon, *A Diagnostic Approach to Organizational Behavior,* 3rd ed. (Boston: Allyn and Bacon, 1991), p. 298. Used by permission.

How to Give, and Take, Criticism

Preparation

The "criticism session" may well be the toughest test of a manager's communication skills. Picture Setting 1—you and a subordinate meeting to review a problem with the subordinate's performance. Now picture Setting 2—you and your boss, meeting to review a problem with *your* performance. Both situations require communication skills in giving and receiving feedback. Even the most experienced person can have difficulty, and the situations can end as futile gripe sessions that cause hard feelings. The question is "How can such 'criticism sessions' be handled in a positive manner that encourages improved performance . . . and good feelings?"

Instructions

Form into groups as assigned by the instructor. Focus on either Setting 1 or Setting 2, or both, as also assigned by the instructor. First, answer the question from the perspective assigned. Second, develop a series of action guidelines that could best be used to handle situations of this type. Third, prepare and present a mini-management training session to demonstrate the (a) unsuccessful and (b) successful use of these guidelines.

If time permits, outside of class prepare a more extensive management training session that includes a videotape demonstration of your assigned criticism setting being handled first poorly and then very well. Support the videotape with additional written handouts and an oral presentation to help your classmates better understand the communication skills needed to successfully give and take criticism in work settings.

Work Team Dynamics

Preparation

Think about your course work group, a work group you are involved in for another course, or any other group suggested by the instructor. Indicate how often each of the following statements accurately reflects your experience in the group. Use this scale:

1 = Always 2 = Frequently 3 = Sometimes
4 = Never

_____ **1.** My ideas get a fair hearing.
_____ **2.** I am encouraged to give innovative ideas and take risks.
_____ **3.** Diverse opinions within the group are encouraged.
_____ **4.** I have all the responsibility I want.
_____ **5.** There is a lot of favoritism shown in the group.
_____ **6.** Members trust one another to do their assigned work.
_____ **7.** The group sets high standards of performance excellence.
_____ **8.** People share and change jobs a lot in the group.
_____ **9.** You can make mistakes and learn from them in this group.
_____ **10.** This group has good operating rules.

Instructions

Form groups as assigned by your instructor. Ideally, this will be the group you have just rated. Have all group members share their ratings, and make one master rating for the group as a whole. Circle the items over which there are the biggest differences of opinion. Discuss those items and try to find out why they exist. In general, the better a group scores on this instrument, the higher its creative potential. If everyone has rated the same group, make a list of the five most important things members can do to improve its operations in the future. Nominate a spokesperson to summarize the group discussion for the class as a whole.

———————

Source: Adapted from William Dyer, *Team Building,* 2nd ed. (Reading, MA: Addison-Wesley, 1987), pp. 123–25.

Lost at Sea

Consider This Situation

You are adrift on a private yacht in the South Pacific when a fire of unknown origin destroys the yacht and most of its contents. You and a small group of survivors are now in a large raft with oars. Your location is unclear, but you estimate that you are about 1,000 miles south-southwest of the nearest land. One person has just found in her pockets 5 $1 bills and a packet of matches. Everyone else's pockets are empty. The following items are available to you on the raft.

	A	B	C
Sextant	_____	_____	_____
Shaving mirror	_____	_____	_____
5 gallons water	_____	_____	_____
Mosquito netting	_____	_____	_____
1 survival meal	_____	_____	_____
Maps of Pacific Ocean	_____	_____	_____
Flotable seat cushion	_____	_____	_____
2 gallons oil-gas mix	_____	_____	_____
Small transistor radio	_____	_____	_____
Shark repellent	_____	_____	_____
20 square feet black plastic	_____	_____	_____
1 quart 20-proof rum	_____	_____	_____
15 feet nylon rope	_____	_____	_____
24 chocolate bars	_____	_____	_____
Fishing kit	_____	_____	_____

Instructions

1. *Working alone,* rank in Column **A** the 15 items in order of their importance to your survival ("1" is most important and "15" is least important).

2. *Working in an assigned group,* arrive at a "team" ranking of the 15 items and record this ranking in Column **B.** Appoint one person as group spokesperson to report your group rankings to the class.

3. *Do not write in Column* **C** until further instructions are provided by your instructor.

———————

Source: Adapted from "Lost at Sea: A Consensus-Seeking Task," in *The 1975 Handbook for Group Facilitators.* Used with permission of University Associates, Inc.

Creative Solutions

Instructions

Complete these 5 tasks while working alone. Be prepared to present and explain your responses in class.

1. Divide the following shape into four pieces of exactly the same size.

2. Without lifting your pencil from the paper, draw no more than 4 lines that cross through all of the following dots.

```
.    .    .

.    .    .

.    .    .
```

3. Draw the design for a machine that will turn the pages of your textbook so you can eat a snack while studying.

4. Why would a wheelbarrow ever be designed this way?

5. Turn the following into words.

(a) ____ program

(b) r\e\a\d\i\n\g

(c) ECNALG

(d)   j
        u
    yousme
        t

(e) stand
        i

Optional Instructions

After working alone, share your responses with a nearby classmate or with a group. See if you can develop different and/or better solutions based on this exchange of ideas.

Source: Ideas 2 and 5 found in Russell L. Ackoff, *The Art of Problem Solving* (New York: Wiley, 1978); ideas 1 and 4 found in Edward De Bono, *Lateral Thinking: Creativity Step by Step* (New York: Harper & Row, 1970); source for 5 is unknown.

Force-Field Analysis

1. Form into your class discussion groups.

2. Review the concept of force-field analysis—the consideration of forces driving in support of a planned change and forces resisting the change.

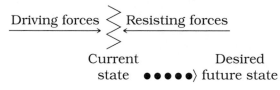

3. Use this force-field analysis worksheet in the assignment:

List of Driving Forces (those supporting the change)

_____
_____ . . . list as many as you can think of

List of Resisting Forces (those working against the change)

_____
_____ . . . list as many as you can think of

4. Apply force-field analysis and make your lists of driving and resisting forces for one of the following situations:
(a) Due to rapid advances in web-based computer technologies, the possibility exists that the course you are presently taking could be in part offered on-line. This would mean a reduction in the number of required class sessions, but an increase in students' responsibility for completing learning activities and assignments through computer mediation.
(b) A new owner has just taken over a small walk-in-and-buy-by-the-slice pizza shop in a college town. There are presently 8 employees, 3 of whom are full-time and 5 of whom are part-timers. The shop is presently open 7 days a week from 10:30 A.M. to 10:30 P.M. each day. The new owner believes there is a market niche available for late-night pizza and would like to stay open each night until 2 A.M.
(c) A situation assigned by the instructor.

5. Choose the 3 driving forces that are most significant to the proposed change. For each force develop ideas on how it could be further increased or mobilized in support of the change.

6. Choose the 3 resisting forces that are most significant to the proposed change. For each force develop ideas on how it could be reduced or turned into a driving force.

7. Be prepared to participate in class discussion led by the instructor.

Management Skills

Assessments

A 21st-Century Manager?

Instructions

Rate yourself on the following personal characteristics. Use this scale.

S = Strong, I am very confident with this one.
G = Good, but I still have room to grow.
W = Weak, I really need work on this one.
U = Unsure, I just don't know.

1. *Resistance to stress:* The ability to get work done even under stressful conditions.

2. *Tolerance for uncertainty:* The ability to get work done even under ambiguous and uncertain conditions.

3. *Social objectivity:* The ability to act free of racial, ethnic, gender, and other prejudices or biases.

4. *Inner work standards:* The ability to personally set and work to high performance standards.

5. *Stamina:* The ability to sustain long work hours.

6. *Adaptability:* The ability to be flexible and adapt to changes.

7. *Self-confidence:* The ability to be consistently decisive and display one's personal presence.

8. *Self-objectivity:* The ability to evaluate personal strengths and weaknesses and to understand one's motives and skills relative to a job.

9. *Introspection:* The ability to learn from experience, awareness, and self-study.

10. *Entrepreneurism:* The ability to address problems and take advantage of opportunities for constructive change.

Scoring

Give yourself 1 point for each S, and 1/2 point for each G. Do not give yourself points for W and U responses. Total your points and enter the result here [PMF = ___].

Interpretation

This assessment offers a self-described *profile of your management foundations (PMF).* Are you a perfect 10, or is your PMF score something less than that? There shouldn't be too many 10s around. Ask someone who knows you to assess you on this instrument. You may be surprised at the differences between your PMF score as you described it and your PMF score as described by someone else. Most of us, realistically speaking, must work hard to grow and develop continually in these and related management foundations. This list is a good starting point as you consider where and how to further pursue the development of your managerial skills and competencies. The items on the list are recommended by the American Assembly of Collegiate Schools of Business (AACSB) as the skills and personal characteristics that should be nurtured in college and university students of business administration. Their success—and yours—as 21st-century managers may well rest on (1) an initial awareness of the importance of these basic management foundations and (2) a willingness to strive continually to strengthen them throughout the work career.

Source: See *Outcome Measurement Project,* Phase I and Phase II Reports (St. Louis: American Assembly of Collegiate Schools of Business, 1986 and 1987).

ASSESSMENT 2

Which Organizational Culture Fits You?

Instructions

Indicate which one of the following organizational cultures you feel most comfortable working in.

1. A culture that values talent, entrepreneurial activity, and performance over commitment; one that offers large financial rewards and individual recognition.

2. A culture that stresses loyalty, working for the good of the group, and getting to know the right people; one that believes in "generalists" and step-by-step career progress.

3. A culture that offers little job security; one that operates with a survival mentality, stresses that every individual can make a difference, and focuses attention on "turn-around" opportunities.

4. A culture that values long-term relationships; one that emphasizes systematic career development, regular training, and advancement based on gaining functional expertise.

Scoring

These labels identify the four different cultures: 1 = "the baseball team," 2 = "the club," 3 = "the fortress," and 4 = "the academy."

Interpretation

To some extent, your future career success may depend on working for an organization in which there is a good fit between you and the prevailing corporate culture. This assessment can help you learn how to recognize various cultures, evaluate how well they can serve your needs, and recognize how they may change with time. A risk taker, for example, may be out of place in a "club" but fit right in with a "baseball team." Someone who wants to seek opportunities wherever they may occur may be out of place in an "academy" but fit right in with a "fortress."

Source: Developed from Carol Hymowitz, "Which Corporate Culture Fits You?" *Wall Street Journal* (July 17, 1989), p. B1.

ASSESSMENT 3

Decision-Making Biases

Instructions

How good are you at avoiding potential decision-making biases? Test yourself by answering the following questions:

1. Which is riskier:
(a) driving a car on a 400-mile trip?
(b) flying on a 400-mile commercial airline flight?

2. Are there more words in the English language:
(a) that begin with "r"?
(b) that have "r" as the third letter?

3. Mark is finishing his MBA at a prestigious university. He is very interested in the arts and at one time considered a career as a musician. Is Mark more likely to take a job:
(a) in the management of the arts?
(b) with a management consulting firm?

4. You are about to hire a new central-region sales director for the fifth time this year. You predict that the next director should work out reasonably well since the last four were "lemons" and the odds favor hiring at least one good sales director in five tries. Is this thinking
(a) correct?
(b) incorrect?

5. A newly hired engineer for a computer firm in the Boston metropolitan area has 4 years' experience and good all-around qualifications. When asked to estimate the starting salary for this employee, a chemist with very little knowledge about the profession or industry guessed an annual salary of $35,000. What is your estimate?
$____ per year

Scoring

Your instructor will provide answers and explanations for the assessment questions.

Interpretation

Each of the preceding questions examines your tendency to use a different judgmental heuristic. In his book *Judgment in Managerial Decision Making,* 3rd ed. (New York: John Wiley & Sons, 1994), pp. 6–7, Max Bazerman calls these heuristics "simplifying strategies, or rules of thumb" used in making decisions. He states, "In general, heuristics are helpful, but their use can sometimes lead to severe errors. . . . If we can make managers aware of the potential adverse impacts of using heuristics, they can then decide when and where to use them." This assessment offers an initial insight into your use of such heuristics. An informed decision maker understands the heuristics, is able to recognize when they appear, and eliminates any that may inappropriately bias decision making.

Test yourself further. Before hearing from your instructor, go back and write next to each item the name of the judgmental heuristic (see Chapter 3 text discussion) that you think applies.

Then write down a situation that you have experienced and in which some decision-making bias may have occurred. Be prepared to share and discuss this incident with the class.

Source: Incidents from Max H. Bazerman, *Judgment in Managerial Decision Making,* 3rd ed. (New York: Wiley, 1994), pp. 13–14. Used by permission.

What Are Your Managerial Assumptions?

Instructions

Read the following statements. Use the space to the left to write "Yes" if you agree with the statement, or "No" if you disagree with it. Force yourself to take a "yes" or "no" position. Do this for every statement.

1. Are good pay and a secure job enough to satisfy most workers?

2. Should a manager help and coach subordinates in their work?

3. Do most people like real responsibility in their jobs?

4. Are most people afraid to learn new things in their jobs?

5. Should managers let subordinates control the quality of their work?

6. Do most people dislike work?

7. Are most people creative?

8. Should a manager closely supervise and direct the work of subordinates?

9. Do most people tend to resist change?

10. Do most people work only as hard as they have to?

11. Should workers be allowed to set their own job goals?

12. Are most people happiest off the job?

13. Do most workers really care about the organization they work for?

14. Should a manager help subordinates advance and grow in their jobs?

Scoring

Count the number of "yes" responses to items 1, 4, 6, 8, 9, 10, 12; write that number here as [X = ____]. Count the number of "yes" responses to items 2, 3, 5, 7, 11, 13, 14; write that score here [Y = ____].

Interpretation

This assessment sheds insight into your orientation toward Douglas McGregor's Theory X (your "X" score) and Theory Y (your "Y" score) assumptions. You should review the discussion of McGregor's thinking in Chapter 4 and consider further the ways in which you are likely to behave toward other people at work. Think, in particular, about the types of "self-fulfilling prophecies" you are likely to create.

Cultural Attitudes Inventory

Instructions

Complete this inventory by circling the number that indicates the extent to which you agree or disagree with each of the following statements.

Strongly Disagree				Strongly Agree
1	2	3	4	5

1. Meetings are usually run more effectively when they are chaired by a man.

    1   2   3   4   5

2. It is more important for men to have a professional career than it is for women to have a professional career.

    1   2   3   4   5

3. Women do not value recognition and promotion in their work as much as men do.

1   2   3   4   5

4. Women value working in a friendly atmosphere more than men do.

1   2   3   4   5

5. Men usually solve problems with logical analysis; women usually solve problems with intuition.

1   2   3   4   5

6. Solving organizational problems usually requires the active, forcible approach that is typical of men.

1   2   3   4   5

7. It is preferable for a man to be in a high-level position rather than a woman.

1   2   3   4   5

8. There are some jobs in which a man can always do better than a woman.

1   2   3   4   5

9. Women are more concerned with the social aspects of their job than they are with getting ahead.

1   2   3   4   5

10. An individual should not pursue his or her own goals without considering the welfare of the group.

1   2   3   4   5

11. It is important for a manager to encourage loyalty and a sense of duty in the group.

1   2   3   4   5

12. Being accepted by the group is more important than working on your own.

1   2   3   4   5

13. Individual rewards are not as important as group welfare.

1   2   3   4   5

14. Group success is more important than individual success.

1   2   3   4   5

15. It is important to spell out job requirements and instructions in detail so that people always know what they are expected to do.

1   2   3   4   5

16. Managers expect workers to follow instructions and procedures closely.

1   2   3   4   5

17. Rules and regulations are important because they inform workers what the organization expects of them.

1   2   3   4   5

18. Standard operating procedures are helpful to workers on the job.

1   2   3   4   5

19. Operating instructions are important for workers on the job.

1   2   3   4   5

20. It is often necessary for a supervisor to emphasize his or her authority and power when dealing with subordinates.

1   2   3   4   5

21. Managers should be careful not to ask the opinions of subordinates too frequently.

1   2   3   4   5

22. A manager should avoid socializing with his or her subordinates off the job.

1   2   3   4   5

23. Subordinates should not disagree with their manager's decisions.

1   2   3   4   5

24. Managers should not delegate difficult and important tasks to their subordinates.

1   2   3   4   5

25. Managers should make most decisions without consulting subordinates.

1   2   3   4   5

Scoring

Add up your responses to items 1–9 and divide by 9; record the score here [MF = ____]. Add up your response to items 10–14 and divide by 5; record the score here [IC = ___]. Add up your responses to items 15–19 and divide by 5; record the score here [UA = ___]. Add up your responses to items 20–25 and divide by 6; record the score here [PD = ___].

Interpretation

Each of these scores corresponds to one of Hofstede's (see Chapter 5) dimensions of national culture: MF = masculinity-femininity; IC = individualism-collectivism; UA = uncertainty avoidance; PD = power distance. His research shows that various "national" cultures of the world score differently on these dimensions. Consider how closely *your* scores may represent *your* national culture. What are the implications of your score for your future work as a manager? Compare yourself to these scores from a sample of U.S. and Mexican students; MF: U.S. = 2.78 and Mexico = 2.75; IC: U.S. = 2.19 and Mexico = 3.33; UA: U.S. = 3.41 and Mexico = 4.15; PD: U.S. = 1.86 and Mexico = 2.22. Are there any surprises in this comparison?

Source: Items are part of a larger instrument developed by Peter W. Dorfman and Jon P. Howell, New Mexico State University. Used by permission. The comparative data are from Stephen P. Robbins, *Management,* 3rd ed. (Englewood Cliffs, NJ: Prentice Hall, 1990). p. 670.

ASSESSMENT 6

Global Readiness Index

Instructions

Rate yourself on each of the following items to establish a baseline measurement of your readiness to participate in the global work environment.

Rating Scale:

1 = Very Poor
2 = Poor
3 = Acceptable
4 = Good
5 = Very Good

____ **1.** I understand my own culture in terms of its expectations, values, and influence on communication and relationships.

____ **2.** When someone presents me with a different point of view, I try to understand it rather than attack it.

____ **3.** I am comfortable dealing with situations where the available information is incomplete and the outcomes unpredictable.

____ **4.** I am open to new situations and am always looking for new information and learning opportunities.

____ **5.** I have a good understanding of the attitudes and perceptions toward my culture as they are held by people from other cultures.

____ **6.** I am always gathering information about other countries and cultures and trying to learn from them.

____ **7.** I am well informed regarding the major differences in government, political, and economic systems around the world.

____ **8.** I work hard to increase my understanding of people from other cultures.

____ **9.** I am able to adjust my communication style to work effectively with people from different cultures.

____ **10.** I can recognize when cultural differences are influencing working relationships and adjust my attitudes and behavior accordingly.

Interpretation

To be successful in the 21st-century work environment, you must be comfortable with the global economy and the cultural diversity that it holds. This requires a *global mindset* that is receptive to and respectful of cultural differences, *global knowledge* that includes the continuing quest to know and learn more about other nations and cultures, and *global work skills* that allow you to work effectively across cultures.

Scoring

The goal is to score as close to a perfect "5" as possible on each of the three dimensions of global readiness. Develop your scores as follows.

Items $(1 + 2 + 3 + 4)/4$
= ____ Global Mind-set Score

Items $(5 + 6 + 7)/3$
= ____ Global Knowledge Score

Items $((8 + 9 + 10)/3$
= ____ Global Work Skills Score

_____

Source: Developed from "Is Your Company Really Global," *Business Week* (December 1, 1997).

ASSESSMENT 7

Diversity Awareness

Instructions

Complete the following questionnaire.

Diversity Awareness Checklist

Consider where you work or go to school as the setting for the following questions. Indicate "O" for often, "S" for sometimes, and "N" for never in response to each of the following questions as they pertain to the setting.

____ **1.** How often have you heard jokes or remarks about other people that you consider offensive?

____ **2.** How often do you hear men "talk down" to women in an attempt to keep them in an inferior status?

____ **3.** How often have you felt personal discomfort as the object of sexual harassment?

____ **4.** How often do you work or study with African Americans or Hispanics?

____ **5.** How often have you felt disadvantaged because members of ethnic groups other than yours were given special treatment?

____ **6.** How often have you seen a woman put in an uncomfortable situation because of unwelcome advances by a man?

____ **7.** How often does it seem that African Americans, Hispanics, Caucasians, women, men, and members of other minority demographic groups seem to "stick together" during work breaks or other leisure situations?

____ **8.** How often do you feel uncomfortable about something you did and/or said to someone of the opposite sex or a member of an ethnic or racial group other than yours?

____ **9.** How often do you feel efforts are made in this setting to raise the level of cross-cultural understanding among people who work and/or study together?

____ **10.** How often do you step in to communicate concerns to others when you feel actions and/or words are used to the disadvantage of minorities?

Scoring

There are no correct answers for the Diversity Awareness Checklist.

Interpretation

In the diversity checklist, the key issue is the extent to which you are "sensitive" to diversity issues in the workplace or university. Are you comfortable with your responses? How do you think others in your class responded? Why not share your responses with others and examine different viewpoints on this important issue?

_____

Source: Items for the WV Cultural Awareness Quiz selected from a longer version by James P. Morgan Jr., and published by University Associates, 1987. Used by permission.

Your Intuitive Ability

Instructions

Complete this survey as quickly as you can. Be honest with yourself. For each question, select the response that most appeals to you.

1. When working on a project, do you prefer to
(a) be told what the problem is but be left free to decide how to solve it?
(b) get very clear instructions about how to go about solving the problem before you start?

2. When working on a project, do you prefer to work with colleagues who are
(a) realistic?
(b) imaginative?

3. Do you most admire people who are
(a) creative?
(b) careful?

4. Do the friends you choose tend to be
(a) serious and hard working?
(b) exciting and often emotional?

5. When you ask a colleague for advice on a problem you have, do you
(a) seldom or never get upset if he or she questions your basic assumptions?
(b) often get upset if he or she questions your basic assumptions?

6. When you start your day, do you
(a) seldom make or follow a specific plan?
(b) usually first make a plan to follow?

7. When working with numbers do you find that you
(a) seldom or never make factual errors?
(b) often make factual errors?

8. Do you find that you
(a) seldom daydream during the day and really don't enjoy doing so when you do it?
(b) frequently daydream during the day and enjoy doing so?

9. When working on a problem, do you
(a) prefer to follow the instructions or rules when they are given to you?
(b) often enjoy circumventing the instructions or rules when they are given to you?

10. When you are trying to put something together, do you prefer to have
(a) step-by-step written instructions on how to assemble the item?
(b) a picture of how the item is supposed to look once assembled?

11. Do you find that the person who irritates you *the most* is the one who appears to be
(a) disorganized?
(b) organized?

12. When an unexpected crisis comes up that you have to deal with, do you
(a) feel anxious about the situation?
(b) feel excited by the challenge of the situation?

Scoring

Total the number of "a" responses circled for questions 1, 3, 5, 6, 11; enter the score here [A = ___]. Total the number of "b" responses for questions 2, 4, 7, 8, 9, 10, 12; enter the score here [B = ___]. Add your "a" and "b" scores and enter the sum here [A + B = ___]. This is your *intuitive score*. The highest possible intuitive score is 12; the lowest is 0.

Interpretation

In his book *Intuition in Organizations* (Newbury Park, CA: Sage, 1989), pp. 10–11, Weston H. Agor states, "Traditional analytical techniques . . . are not as useful as they once were for guiding major decisions. . . . If you hope to be better prepared for tomorrow, then it only seems logical to pay some attention to the use and development of intuitive skills for decision making." Agor developed the preceding survey to help people assess their tendencies to use intuition in decision making. Your score offers a general impression of your strength in this area. It may also suggest a need to further develop your skill and comfort with more intuitive decision approaches.

_____

Source: AIM Survey (El Paso, TX: ENFP Enterprises, 1989). Copyright © 1989 by Weston H. Agor. Used by permission.

Time Management Profile

Instructions

Complete the following questionnaire by indicating "Y" (yes) or "N" (no) for each item. Force yourself to respond yes or no. Be frank and allow your responses to create an accurate picture of how you tend to respond to these kinds of situations.

_____ **1.** When confronted with several items of similar urgency and importance, I tend to do the easiest one first.

_____ **2.** I do the most important things during that part of the day when I know I perform best.

_____ **3.** Most of the time I don't do things someone else can do; I delegate this type of work to others.

_____ **4.** Even though meetings without a clear and useful purpose upset me, I put up with them.

_____ **5.** I skim documents before reading them and don't complete any that offer a low return on my time investment.

_____ **6.** I don't worry much if I don't accomplish at least one significant task each day.

_____ **7.** I save the most trivial tasks for that time of day when my creative energy is lowest.

_____ **8.** My workspace is neat and organized.

_____ **9.** My office door is always "open"; I never work in complete privacy.

_____ **10.** I schedule my time completely from start to finish every workday.

_____ **11.** I don't like "to do" lists, preferring to respond to daily events as they occur.

_____ **12.** I "block" a certain amount of time each day or week that is dedicated to high-priority activities.

Scoring

Count the number of "Y" responses to items 2, 3, 5, 7, 8, 12. [Enter that score here _____.] Count the number of "N" responses to items 1, 4, 6, 9, 10, 11. [Enter that score here _____.] Add together the two scores.

Interpretation

The higher the total score, the closer your behavior matches recommended time management guidelines. Reread those items where your response did not match the desired one. Why don't they match? Do you have reasons why your behavior in this instance should be different from the recommended time management guideline? Think about what you can do (and how easily it can be done) to adjust your behavior to be more consistent with these guidelines. For further reading, see Alan Lakein, _How to Control Your Time and Your Life_ (New York: David McKay, no date), and William Oncken. _Managing Management Time_ (Englewood Cliffs, NJ: Prentice Hall, 1984).

Source: Suggested by a discussion in Robert E. Quinn, Sue R. Faerman, Michael P. Thompson, and Michael R. McGrath, _Becoming a Master Manager: A Contemporary Framework_ (New York: John Wiley & Sons, 1990), pp. 75–76.

Entrepreneurship Orientation

Instructions

Answer the following questions.

1. What portion of your college expenses did you earn (or are you earning)?
(a) 50 percent or more
(b) less than 50 percent
(c) none

2. In college, your academic performance was/is
(a) above average.
(b) average.
(c) below average.

3. What is your basic reason for considering opening a business?
(a) I want to make money.
(b) I want to control my own destiny.
(c) I hate the frustration of working for someone else.

4. Which phrase best describes your attitude toward work?
(a) I can keep going as long as I need to; I don't mind working for something I want.
(b) I can work hard for a while, but when I've had enough, I quit.
(c) Hard work really doesn't get you anywhere.

5. How would you rate your organizing skills?
(a) superorganized
(b) above average
(c) average
(d) I do well to find half the things I look for.

6. You are primarily a(n)
(a) optimist.
(b) pessimist.
(c) neither.

7. You are faced with a challenging problem. As you work, you realize you are stuck. You will most likely
(a) give up.
(b) ask for help.
(c) keep plugging; you'll figure it out.

8. You are playing a game with a group of friends. You are most interested in
(a) winning.
(b) playing well.
(c) making sure that everyone has a good time.
(d) cheating as much as possible.

9. How would you describe your feelings toward failure?
(a) Fear of failure paralyzes me.
(b) Failure can be a good learning experience.
(c) Knowing that I might fail motivates me to work even harder.
(d) "Damn the torpedoes! Full speed ahead."

10. Which phrase best describes you?
(a) I need constant encouragement to get anything done.
(b) If someone gets me started, I can keep going.
(c) I am energetic and hard-working—a self-starter.

11. Which bet would you most likely accept?
(a) a wager on a dog race
(b) a wager on a racquetball game in which you play an opponent
(c) Neither. I never make wagers.

12. At the Kentucky Derby, you would bet on
(a) the 100-to-1 long shot.
(b) the odds-on favorite.
(c) the 3-to-1 shot.
(d) none of the above.

Scoring

Give yourself 10 points for each of the following answers: 1a, 2a, 3c, 4a, 5a, 6a, 7c, 8a, 9c, 10c, 11b, 12c; total the scores and enter the results here [I = ___]. Give yourself 8 points for each of the following answers: 3b, 8b, 9b; total the scores and enter the results here [II =___]. Give yourself 6 points for each of the following answers; 2b, 5b; total the scores and enter the results here [III = ___]. Give yourself 5 points for this answer: 1b; enter the result here [IV = ___]. Give yourself 4 points for this answer: 5c; enter the result here [V = ___]. Give yourself 2 points for each of the following answers: 2c, 3a, 4b, 6c, 9d, 10b, 11a, 12b; total the scores and enter the results here [VI = ___]. Any other scores are worth 0 points. Total your summary scores for I + II + III + IV + V + VI and enter the result here [EP = ___].

Interpretation

This assessment offers an impression of your *entrepreneurial profile,* or EP. It compares your characteristics with those of typical entrepreneurs. Your instructor can provide further information on each question as well as some additional insights into the backgrounds of entrepreneurs. You may locate your EP score on the following grid.

100+ = Entrepreneur extraordinaire
80–99 = Entrepreneur
60–79 = Potential entrepreneur
0–59 = Entrepreneur in the rough

Source: Instrument adapted from Norman M. Scarborough and Thomas W. Zimmerer, *Effective Small Business Management,* 3rd ed. (Columbus: Merrill, 1991), pp. 26–27. Used by permission.

ASSESSMENT 11

Internal/External Control

Instructions

Circle either "a" or "b" to indicate the item you most agree with in each pair of the following statements.

1. (a) Promotions are earned through hard work and persistence.
(b) Making a lot of money is largely a matter of breaks.

2. (a) Many times the reactions of teachers seem haphazard to me.
(b) In my experience I have noticed that there is usually a direct connection between how hard I study and the grades I get.

3. (a) The number of divorces indicates that more and more people are not trying to make their marriages work.
(b) Marriage is largely a gamble.

4. (a) It is silly to think that one can really change another person's basic attitudes.
(b) When I am right I can convince others.

5. (a) Getting promoted is really a matter of being a little luckier than the next guy.
(b) In our society an individual's future earning power is dependent upon his or her ability.

6. (a) If one knows how to deal with people, they are really quite easily led.
(b) I have little influence over the way other people behave.

7. (a) In my case the grades I make are the results of my own efforts; luck has little or nothing to do with it.
(b) Sometimes I feel that I have little to do with the grades I get.

8. (a) People like me can change the course of world affairs if we make ourselves heard.
(b) It is only wishful thinking to believe that one can really influence what happens in society at large.

9. (a) Much of what happens to me is probably a matter of chance.
(b) I am the master of my fate.

10. (a) Getting along with people is a skill that must be practiced.
(b) It is almost impossible to figure out how to please some people.

Scoring

Give 1 point for 1b, 2a, 3a, 4b, 5b, 6a, 7a, 8a, 9b, 10a.

8–10 = high *internal* locus of control
6–7 = moderate *internal* locus of control
5 = mixed locus of control
3–4 = moderate *external* locus of control

Interpretation

This instrument offers an impression of your tendency toward an *internal locus of control* or *external locus of control.* Persons with a high internal locus of control tend to believe they have control over their own destinies. They may be most responsive to opportunities for greater self-control in the workplace. Persons with a high external locus of control tend to believe that what happens to them is largely in the hands of external people or forces. They may be less comfortable with self-control and more responsive to external controls in the workplace.

Source: Instrument from Julian P. Rotter, "External Control and Internal Control," *Psychology Today* (June 1971), p. 42. Used by permission.

Organizational Design Preference

Instructions

To the left of each item, write the number from the following scale that shows the extent to which the statement accurately describes your views.

5 = strongly agree
4 = agree somewhat
3 = undecided
2 = disagree somewhat
1 = strongly disagree

I prefer to work in an organization where

1. goals are defined by those in higher levels.

2. work methods and procedures are specified.

3. top management makes important decisions.

4. my loyalty counts as much as my ability to do the job.

5. clear lines of authority and responsibility are established.

6. top management is decisive and firm.

7. my career is pretty well planned out for me.

8. I can specialize.

9. my length of service is almost as important as my level of performance.

10. management is able to provide the information I need to do my job well.

11. a chain of command is well established.

12. rules and procedures are adhered to equally by everyone.

13. people accept the authority of a leader's position.

14. people are loyal to their boss.

15. people do as they have been instructed.

16. people clear things with their boss before going over his or her head.

Scoring

Total your scores for all questions. Enter the score here [_____].

Interpretation

This assessment measures your preference for working in an organization designed along "organic" or "mechanistic" lines (see Chapter 11). The higher your score (above 64), the more comfortable you are with a mechanistic design; the lower your score (below 48), the more comfortable you are with an organic design. Scores between 48 and 64 can go either way. This organizational design preference represents an important issue in the new workplace. Indications are that today's organizations are taking on more and more organic characteristics. Presumably, those of us who work in them will need to be comfortable with such designs.

Source: John F. Veiga and John N. Yanouzas. *The Dynamics of Organization Theory: Gaining a Macro Perspective* (St. Paul, MN: West, 1979), pp. 158–60. Used by permission.

Performance Appraisal Assumptions

Instructions

In each of the following pairs of statements, check off the statement that best reflects your assumptions about performance evaluation.

Performance evaluation is

1. (a) a formal process that is done annually.
   (b) an informal process done continuously.

2. (a) a process that is planned for subordinates.
   (b) a process that is planned with subordinates.

3. (a) a required organizational procedure.
   (b) a process done regardless of requirements.

4. (a) a time to evaluate subordinates' performance.
   (b) a time for subordinates to evaluate their manager.

5. (a) a time to clarify standards.
   (b) a time to clarify the subordinate's career needs.

6. (a) a time to confront poor performance.
   (b) a time to express appreciation.

7. (a) an opportunity to clarify issues and provide direction and control.
   (b) an opportunity to increase enthusiasm and commitment.

8. (a) only as good as the organization's forms.
   (b) only as good as the manager's coaching skills.

Scoring

There is no formal scoring for this assessment, but there may be a pattern to your responses. Check them again.

Interpretation

In general, the "a" responses represent a more traditional approach to performance appraisal that emphasizes its *evaluation* function. This role largely puts the supervisor in the role of documenting a subordinate's performance for control and administrative purposes. The "b" responses represent a more progressive approach that includes a strong emphasis on the *counseling* or *development* role. Here, the supervisor is concerned with helping the subordinate do better and with learning from the subordinate what he or she needs to be able to do better. There is more of an element of reciprocity in this role. It is quite consistent with new directions and values emerging in today's organizations.

Source: Developed in part from Robert E. Quinn, Sue R. Faerman, Michael P. Thompson, and Michael R. McGrath, *Becoming a Master Manager: A Contemporary Framework* (New York: John Wiley & Sons, 1990), p. 187. Used by permission.

"T-P" Leadership Questionnaire

Instructions

The following items describe aspects of leadership behavior. Respond to each item according to the way you would most likely act if you were the leader of a work group. Circle whether you would most likely behave in the described way: always (A), frequently (F), occasionally (O), seldom (S), or never (N).

A F O S N   1. I would most likely act as the spokesperson of the group.

A F O S N   **2.** I would encourage over-time work.

A F O S N   **3.** I would allow members complete freedom in their work.

A F O S N   **4.** I would encourage the use of uniform procedures.

A F O S N   **5.** I would permit the members to use their own judgment in solving problems.

A F O S N   **6.** I would stress being ahead of competing groups.

A F O S N   **7.** I would speak as a representative of the group.

A F O S N   **8.** I would push members for greater effort.

A F O S N   **9.** I would try out my ideas in the group.

A F O S N   **10.** I would let the members do their work the way they think best.

A F O S N   **11.** I would be working hard for a promotion.

A F O S N   **12.** I would tolerate postponement and uncertainty.

A F O S N   **13.** I would speak for the group if there were visitors present.

A F O S N   **14.** I would keep the work moving at a rapid pace.

A F O S N   **15.** I would turn the members loose on a job and let them go to it.

A F O S N   **16.** I would settle conflicts when they occur in the group.

A F O S N   **17.** I would get swamped by details.

A F O S N   **18.** I would represent the group at outside meetings.

A F O S N   **19.** I would be reluctant to allow the members any freedom of action.

A F O S N   **20.** I would decide what should be done and how it should be done.

A F O S N   **21.** I would push for increased performance.

A F O S N   **22.** I would let some members have authority which I could otherwise keep.

A F O S N   **23.** Things would usually turn out as I had predicted.

A F O S N   **24.** I would allow the group a high degree of initiative.

A F O S N   **25.** I would assign group members to particular tasks.

A F O S N   **26.** I would be willing to make changes.

A F O S N   **27.** I would ask the members to work harder.

A F O S N   **28.** I would trust the group members to exercise good judgment.

A F O S N   **29.** I would schedule the work to be done.

A F O S N   **30.** I would refuse to explain my actions.

A F O S N   **31.** I would persuade others that my ideas are to their advantage.

A F O S N   **32.** I would permit the group to set its own pace.

A F O S N   **33.** I would urge the group to beat its previous record.

A F O S N   **34.** I would act without consulting the group.

A F O S N   **35.** I would ask that group members follow standard rules and regulations.

Interpretation

Score the instrument as follows.

a. Write a "1" next to each of the following items if you scored them as S (seldom) or N (never).

8, 12, 17, 18, 19, 30, 34, 35

b. Write a "1" next to each of the following items if you scored them as A (always) or F (frequently).

1, 2, 3, 4, 5, 6, 7, 9, 10, 11, 13, 14, 15, 16, 20, 21, 22, 23, 24, 25, 26, 27, 28, 29, 31, 32, 33

c. Circle the "1" scores for the following items, and then add them up to get your TOTAL "P" SCORE = ____.

3, 5, 8, 10, 15, 18, 19, 22, 23, 26, 28, 30, 32, 34, 35

d. Circle the "1" scores for the following items, and then add them up to get your

TOTAL "T" SCORE = ____.

1, 2, 4, 6, 7, 9, 11, 12, 13, 14, 16, 17, 20, 21, 23, 25, 27, 29, 31, 33

e. Record your scores on the following graph to develop an indication of your ten-dencies toward task-oriented leadership, people-oriented leadership, and shared leadership. Mark your T and P scores on the appropriate lines, then draw a line be-tween these two points to determine your shared leadership score.

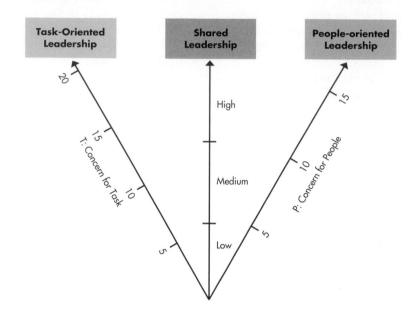

Source: Modified slightly from "T-P Leadership Questionnaire," University Associates, Inc., 1987. Used by permission.

ASSESSMENT 15

"T-T" Leadership Style

Instructions

For each of the following 10 pairs of state-ments, divide 5 points between the two ac-cording to your beliefs or perceptions of yourself or according to which of the two statements characterizes you better. The 5 points may be divided between the a and b statements in any one of the following ways: 5 for a, 0 for b; 4 for a, 1 for b; 3 for a, 2 for b; 1 for a, 4 for b; 0 for a, 5 for b, but not equally (2-1/2) between the two. Weigh your choices between the two ac-cording to which one characterizes you or your beliefs better.

1. (a) As leader I have a primary mission of maintaining stability.
(b) As leader I have a primary mission of change.

2. (a) As leader I must cause events.
(b) As leader I must facilitate events.

3. (a) I am concerned that my followers are rewarded equitably for their work.
(b) I am concerned about what my fol-lowers want in life.

4. (a) My preference is to think long range: What might be.
(b) My preference is to think short range: What is realistic.

5. (a) As a leader I spend considerable energy in managing separate but related goals.
(b) As a leader I spend considerable energy in arousing hopes, expectations, and aspirations among my followers.

6. (a) Although not in a formal classroom sense, I believe that a significant part of my leadership is that of teacher.
(b) I believe that a significant part of my leadership is that of facilitator.

7. (a) As leader I must engage with followers on an equal level of morality.
(b) As leader I must represent a higher morality.

8. (a) I enjoy stimulating followers to want to do more.
(b) I enjoy rewarding followers for a job well done.

9. (a) Leadership should be practical.
(b) Leadership should be inspirational.

10. (a) What power I have to influence others comes primarily from my ability to get people to identify with me and my ideas.
(b) What power I have to influence others comes primarily from my status and position.

Scoring

Circle your points for items 1b, 2a, 3b, 4a, 5b, 6a, 7b, 8a, 9b, 10a and add up the total points you allocated to these items; enter the score here [T = ____]. Next, add up the total points given to the uncircled items 1a, 2b, 3a, 4b, 5a, 6b, 7a, 8b, 9a, 10b; enter the score here [T = ____].

Interpretation

This instrument gives an impression of your tendencies toward "transformational" leadership (your T score) and "transactional" leadership (your T score). You may want to refer to the discussion of these concepts in Chapter 13. Today, a lot of attention is being given to the transformational aspects of leadership—those personal qualities that inspire a sense of vision and the desire for extraordinary accomplishment in followers. The most successful leaders of the future will most likely be strong in both "T"s.

_____

Source: Questionnaire by W. Warner Burke, Ph.D. Used by permission.

ASSESSMENT 16

Least-Preferred Co-worker Scale

Instructions

Think of all the different people with whom you have ever worked—in jobs, in social clubs, in student projects, or whatever. Next think of the *one person* with whom you could work *least* well—that is, the person with whom you had the most difficulty getting a job done. This is the one person—a peer, boss, or subordinate—with whom you would least want to work. Describe this person by circling numbers at the appropriate points on each of the following pairs of bipolar adjectives. Work rapidly. There are no right or wrong answers.

Pleasant	8 7 6 5 4 3 2 1	Unpleasant
Friendly	8 7 6 5 4 3 2 1	Unfriendly
Rejecting	1 2 3 4 5 6 7 8	Accepting
Tense	1 2 3 4 5 6 7 8	Relaxed
Distant	1 2 3 4 5 6 7 8	Close
Cold	1 2 3 4 5 6 7 8	Warm
Supportive	8 7 6 5 4 3 2 1	Hostile
Boring	1 2 3 4 5 6 7 8	Interesting
Quarrelsome	1 2 3 4 5 6 7 8	Harmonious
Gloomy	1 2 3 4 5 6 7 8	Cheerful
Open	8 7 6 5 4 3 2 1	Guarded
Backbiting	1 2 3 4 5 6 7 8	Loyal
Untrustworthy	1 2 3 4 5 6 7 8	Trustworthy
Considerate	8 7 6 5 4 3 2 1	Inconsiderate
Nasty	1 2 3 4 5 6 7 8	Nice
Agreeable	8 7 6 5 4 3 2 1	Disagreeable
Insincere	1 2 3 4 5 6 7 8	Sincere
Kind	8 7 6 5 4 3 2 1	Unkind

Scoring

This is called the "least-preferred coworker scale" (LPC). Compute your LPC score by totaling all the numbers you circled; enter that score here [LPC = ____].

Interpretation

The LPC scale is used by Fred Fiedler to identify a person's dominant leadership style (see Chapter 13). Fiedler believes that this style is a relatively fixed part of one's personality and is therefore difficult to change. This leads Fiedler to his contingency views, which suggest that the key to leadership success is finding (or creating) good "matches" between style and situation. If your score is 73 or above, Fiedler considers you a "relationship-motivated" leader; if your score is 64 and below, he considers you a "task-motivated" leader. If your score is between 65 and 72, Fiedler leaves it up to you to determine which leadership style is most like yours.

Source: Fred E. Fiedler and Martin M. Chemers. *Improving Leadership Effectiveness: The Leader Match Concept,* 2nd ed. (New York: John Wiley & Sons, 1984). Used by permission.

ASSESSMENT 17

Two-Factor Profile

Instructions

On each of the following dimensions, distribute a total of "10" points between the two options. For example:

Summer weather	(7)	(3)	Winter weather
1. Very responsible job	(___)	(___)	Job security
2. Recognition for work accomplishments	(___)	(___)	Good relations with coworkers
3. Advancement opportunities at work	(___)	(___)	A boss who knows his/her job well
4. Opportunities to grow and learn on the job	(___)	(___)	Good working conditions
5. A job that I can do well	(___)	(___)	Supportive rules, policies of employer
6. A prestigious or high status job	(___)	(___)	A high base wage or salary

Scoring

Summarize your total scores for all items in the *left-hand column* and write it here: MF = ____.

Summarize your total scores for all items in the *right-hand column* and write it here: HF = ____.

Interpretation

The "MF" score indicates the relative importance that you place on motivating or satisfier factors in Herzberg's two-factor theory. This shows how important job content is to you.

The "HF" score indicates the relative importance that you place on hygiene or dissatisfier factors in Herzberg's two-factor theory. This shows how important job context is to you.

ASSESSMENT 18

Job Design Preference

Instructions

People differ in what they like and dislike about their jobs. Listed below are 12 pairs of jobs. For each pair, indicate which job you would prefer. Assume that everything else about the jobs is the same—pay attention only to the characteristics actually listed for each pair of jobs. If you would prefer the job in Column A, indicate how much you prefer it by putting a check mark in a blank to the left of the Neutral point. If you prefer the job in Column B, check one of the blanks to the right of Neutral. Check the Neutral blank only if you find the two jobs equally attractive or unattractive. Try to use the Neutral blank sparingly.

Column A		**Column B**
1. A job that offers little or no challenge.	Strongly prefer A — Neutral — Strongly prefer B	A job that requires you to be completely isolated from coworkers.
2. A job that pays well.	Strongly prefer A — Neutral — Strongly prefer B	A job that allows considerable opportunity to be creative and innovative.
3. A job that often requires you to make important decisions.	Strongly prefer A — Neutral — Strongly prefer B	A job in which there are many pleasant people to work with.
4. A job with little security in a somewhat unstable organization.	Strongly prefer A — Neutral — Strongly prefer B	A job in which you have little or no opportunity to participate in decisions that affect your work.
5. A job in which greater responsibility is given to those who do the best work.	Strongly prefer A — Neutral — Strongly prefer B	A job in which greater responsibility is given to loyal employees who have the most *seniority.*
6. A job with a supervisor who sometimes is highly critical.	Strongly prefer A — Neutral — Strongly prefer B	A job that does not require you to use much of your talent.
7. A very routine job.	Strongly prefer A — Neutral — Strongly prefer B	A job in which your coworkers are not very friendly.

8. A job with a supervisor who respects you and treats you fairly.

Strongly Neutral Strongly
prefer A prefer B

A job that provides constant opportunities for you to learn new and interesting things.

9. A job that gives you a real chance to develop yourself personally.

Strongly Neutral Strongly
prefer A prefer B

A job with excellent vacation and fringe benefits.

10. A job in which there is a real chance you could be laid off.

Strongly Neutral Strongly
prefer A prefer B

A job that offers very little chance to do challenging work.

11. A job that gives you little freedom and independence to do your work in the way you think best.

Strongly Neutral Strongly
prefer A prefer B

A job with poor working conditions.

12. A job with very satisfying teamwork.

Strongly Neutral Strongly
prefer A prefer B

A job that allows you to use your skills and abilities to the fullest extent.

Interpretation

People differ in their need for psychological growth at work. This instrument measures the degree to which you seek growth need satisfaction. Score your responses as follows:

For items 1, 2, 7, 8, 11, and 12 give yourself the following points for each item:

1	2	3	4	5	6	7
Strongly Neutral Strongly
prefer A prefer B

For items 3, 4, 5, 6, 9, and 10 give yourself the following points for each item.

7	6	5	4	3	2	1
Strongly Neutral Strongly
prefer A prefer B

Add up all of your scores and divide by 12 to find the average. If you score above 4.0 your desire for growth need satisfaction through work tends to be high and you are likely to prefer an enriched job. If you score below 4.0 your desire for growth need satisfaction through work tends to be low and you are likely to not be satisfied or motivated with an enriched job.

Source: Reprinted by permission from J. R. Hackman and G. R. Oldham, *The Job Diagnostic Survey: An Instrument for the Diagnosis of Jobs and the Evaluation of Job Redesign Projects, Technical Report 4* (New Haven, CT: Yale University, Department of Administrative Sciences, 1974).

- - - - - ASSESSMENT 19 - - - - - - - - -

Conflict Management Styles

Instructions

Think of how you behave in conflict situations in which your wishes differ from those of one or more other persons. In the space to the left of each of the following statements, write the number from the following scale that indicates how likely you are to respond that way in a conflict situation.

1 = very unlikely   2 = unlikely
3 = likely   4 = very likely

____ **1.** I am usually firm in pursuing my goals.
____ **2.** I try to win my position.
____ **3.** I give up some points in exchange for others.
____ **4.** I feel that differences are not always worth worrying about.
____ **5.** I try to find a position that is intermediate between the other person's and mine.
____ **6.** In approaching negotiations, I try to be considerate of the other person's wishes.
____ **7.** I try to show the logic and benefits of my positions.
____ **8.** I always lean toward a direct discussion of the problem.
____ **9.** I try to find a fair combination of gains and losses for both of us.
____ **10.** I attempt to work through our differences immediately.
____ **11.** I try to avoid creating unpleasantness for myself.
____ **12.** I try to soothe the other person's feelings and preserve our relationships.
____ **13.** I attempt to get all concerns and issues immediately out in the open.
____ **14.** I sometimes avoid taking positions that would create controversy.

____ **15.** I try not to hurt others' feelings.

Scoring

Total your scores for items 1, 2, 7; enter that score here [*Competing* = ____]. Total your scores for items 8, 10, 13; enter that score here [*Collaborating* = ____]. Total your scores for items 3, 5, 9; enter that score here [*Compromising* = ____]. Total your scores for items 4, 11, 14; enter that score here [*Avoiding* = ____]. Total your scores for items 6, 12, 15; enter that score here [*Accommodating* = ____].

Interpretation

Each of the scores above corresponds to one of the conflict management styles discussed in Chapter 16. Research indicates that each style has a role to play in management but that the best overall conflict management approach is collaboration; only it can lead to problem solving and true conflict resolution. You should consider any patterns that may be evident in your scores and think about how to best handle the conflict situations in which you become involved.

Source: Adapted from Thomas-Kilmann, *Conflict Mode Instrument.* Copyright © 1974, Xicom, Inc., Tuxedo, NY 10987. Used by permission.

ASSESSMENT 20

Facts and Inferences

Preparation

Read the following report:

Often, when we listen or speak, we don't distinguish between statements of fact and those of inference. Yet, there are great differences between the two. We create barriers to clear thinking when we treat inferences (guesses, opinions) as if they are facts. You may wish at this point to test your ability to distinguish facts from inferences by taking the accompanying fact-inference test based on those by Haney (1973).

Instructions

Carefully read the following report and the observations based on it. Indicate whether you think the observations are true, false, or doubtful on the basis of the information presented in the report. Write T if the observation is definitely true, F if the observation is definitely false, and ? if the observation may be either true or false. Judge each observation in order. Do not reread the observations after you have indicated your judgment, and do not change any of your answers.

A well-liked college instructor had just completed making up the final examinations and had turned off the lights in the office. Just then a tall, broad figure with dark glasses appeared and demanded the examination. The professor opened the drawer. Everything in the drawer was picked up and the individual ran down the corridor. The president was notified immediately.

_____ **1.** The thief was tall, broad, and wore dark glasses.

_____ **2.** The professor turned off the lights.

_____ **3.** A tall figure demanded the examination.

_____ **4.** The examination was picked up by someone.

_____ **5.** The examination was picked up by the professor.

_____ **6.** A tall, broad figure appeared after the professor turned off the lights in the office.

_____ **7.** The man who opened the drawer was the professor.

_____ **8.** The professor ran down the corridor.

_____ **9.** The drawer was never actually opened.

_____ **10.** Three persons are referred to in this report.

When told to do so by your instructor, join a small work group. Now, help the group complete the same task by making a consensus decision on each item. Be sure to keep a separate record of the group's responses and your original individual responses.

Scoring

Your instructor will read the correct answers. Score both your individual and group responses.

Interpretation

To begin, ask yourself if there was a difference between your answers and those of the group for each item. If so, why? Why do you think people, individually or in groups, may answer these questions incorrectly? Good planning depends on good decision making by the people doing the planning. Being able to distinguish "facts" and understand one's "inferences" are important steps toward improving the planning process. Involving others to help do the same can frequently assist in this process.

———————

Source: Joseph A. Devito, _Messages: Building Interpersonal Communication Skills,_ 3rd ed. (New York: Harper-Collins, 1996), referencing William Haney, _Communicational Behavior: Text and Cases,_ 3rd ed. (Homewood, II.: Irwin, 1973). Reprinted by permission.

- - - - - - **ASSESSMENT 21** - - - - - - - - - - -

Stress Self-Test

Instructions

Complete the following questionnaire. Circle the number that best represents your tendency to behave on each bipolar dimension.

Am casual about appointments	1 2 3 4 5 6 7 8	Am never late
Am not competitive	1 2 3 4 5 6 7 8	Am very competitive
Never feel rushed	1 2 3 4 5 6 7 8	Always feel rushed
Take things one at a time	1 2 3 4 5 6 7 8	Try to do many things at once
Do things slowly	1 2 3 4 5 6 7 8	Do things fast
Express feelings	1 2 3 4 5 6 7 8	"Sit on" feelings
Have many interests	1 2 3 4 5 6 7 8	Have few interests but work

Scoring

Total the numbers circled for all items, and multiply this by 3; enter the result here [____].

Interpretation

This scale is designed to measure your personality tendency toward Type A or Type B behaviors. As described in Chapter 16, a Type A personality is associated with high stress. Persons who are Type A tend to bring stress on themselves even in situations where others are relatively stress-free. This is an important characteristic to be able to identify in yourself and in others.

Points	Personality
120+	A+
106–119	A
100–105	A–
90–99	B+
below 90	B

Source: Adapted from R. W. Bortner. "A Short Rating Scale as a Potential Measure of Type A Behavior." *Journal of Chronic Diseases*, vol. 22 (1966), pp. 87–91. Used by permission.

ASSESSMENT 22

Team Leader Skills

Instructions

Consider your experience in groups and work teams. Ask: "What skills do I bring to team leadership situations?" Then, complete the following inventory by rating yourself on each item using this scale.

1 = Almost Never
2 = Seldom
3 = Sometimes
4 = Usually
5 = Almost Always

1 2 3 4 5   **1.** I facilitate communications with and among team members between team meetings.

1 2 3 4 5   **2.** I provide feedback/coaching to individual team members on their performance.

1 2 3 4 5   **3.** I encourage creative and "out-of-the-box" thinking.

1 2 3 4 5   **4.** I continue to clarify stakeholder needs/expectations.

1 2 3 4 5   **5.** I keep team members' responsibilities and activities focused within the team's objectives and goals.

1 2 3 4 5   **6.** I organize and run effective and productive team meetings.

1 2 3 4 5   **7.** I demonstrate integrity and personal commitment.

1 2 3 4 5   **8.** I have excellent persuasive and influence skills.

1 2 3 4 5   **9.** I respect and leverage the team's cross-functional diversity.

1 2 3 4 5   **10.** I recognize and reward individual contributions to team performance.

1 2 3 4 5   **11.** I use the appropriate decision-making style for specific issues.

1 2 3 4 5   **12.** I facilitate and encourage

border management with the team's key stakeholders.

1 2 3 4 5 **13.** I ensure that the team meets its team commitments.

1 2 3 4 5 **14.** I bring team issues and problems to the team's attention and focus on constructive problem solving.

1 2 3 4 5 **15.** I provide a clear vision and direction for the team.

Scoring

The inventory measures seven dimensions of team leadership. Add your scores for the items listed next to each dimension below to get an indication of your potential strengths and weaknesses.

1,9	Building the Team
2,10	Developing People
3,11	Team Problem Solving/Decision Making
4,12	Stakeholder Relations
5,13	Team Performance
6,14	Team Process
7,8,15	Providing Personal Leadership

Interpretation

The higher the score, the more confident you are on the particular skill and leadership capability. When considering the score, ask yourself if others would rate you the same way. Consider giving this inventory to people who have worked with you in teams and have them rate you. Compare the results to your self-assessment. Also, remember that it is doubtful that any one team leader is capable of exhibiting all the skills listed above. More and more, organizations are emphasizing "top management teams" that blend a variety of skills, rather than depending upon the vision of the single, heroic leader figure. As long as the necessary leadership skills are represented within the membership it is more likely that the team will be healthy and achieve high performance. Of course, the more skills you bring with you to team leadership situations the better.

Source: Developed from Lynda McDermott, Nolan Brawley, and William Waite, *World-Class Teams: Working Across Borders* (New York: Wiley, 1998).

ASSESSMENT 23

Turbulence Tolerance Test

Instructions

The following statements were made by a 37-year-old manager in a large, successful corporation. How would you like to have a job with these characteristics? Using the following scale, choose your response to the left of each statement.

0 = This feature would be very unpleasant for me.

1 = This feature would be somewhat unpleasant for me.

2 = I'd have no reaction to this feature one way or another.

3 = This would be enjoyable and acceptable most of the time.

4 = I would enjoy this very much; it's completely acceptable.

_____ **1.** I regularly spend 30 to 40 percent of my time in meetings.

_____ **2.** Eighteen months ago my job did not exist, and I have been essentially inventing it as I go along.

_____ **3.** The responsibilities I either assume or am assigned consistently exceed the authority I have for discharging them.

_____ **4.** At any given moment in my job, I have on the average about a dozen phone calls to be returned.

_____ **5.** There seems to be very little relation in my job between the quality of my performance and my actual pay and fringe benefits.

_____ **6.** About 2 weeks a year of formal management training is needed in my job just to stay current.

7. Because we have very effective equal employment opportunity (EEO) in my company and because it is thoroughly multinational, my job consistently brings me into close working contact at a professional level with people of many races, ethnic groups and nationalities, and of both sexes.

8. There is no objective way to measure my effectiveness.

9. I report to three different bosses for different aspects of my job, and each has an equal say in my performance appraisal.

10. On average about a third of my time is spent dealing with unexpected emergencies that force all scheduled work to be postponed.

11. When I have to have a meeting of the people who report to me, it takes my secretary most of a day to find a time when we are all available, and even then, I have yet to have a meeting where everyone is present for the entire meeting.

12. The college degree I earned in preparation for this type of work is now obsolete, and I probably should go back for another degree.

13. My job requires that I absorb 100-200 pages of technical materials per week.

14. I am out of town overnight at least 1 night per week.

15. My department is so interdependent with several other departments in the company that all distinctions about which departments are responsible for which tasks are quite arbitrary.

16. In about a year I will probably get a promotion to a job in another division that has most of these same characteristics.

17. During the period of my employment here, either the entire company or the division I worked in has been reorganized every year or so.

18. While there are several possible promotions I can see ahead of me, I have no real career path in an objective sense.

19. While there are several possible promotions I can see ahead of me, I think I have no realistic chance of getting to the top levels of the company.

20. While I have many ideas about how to make things work better, I have no direct influence on either the business policies or the personnel policies that govern my division.

21. My company has recently put in an "assessment center" where I and all other managers will be required to go through an extensive battery of psychological tests to assess our potential.

22. My company is a defendant in an antitrust suit, and if the case comes to trial, I will probably have to testify about some decisions that were made a few years ago.

23. Advanced computer and other electronic office technology is continually being introduced into my division, necessitating constant learning on my part.

24. The computer terminal and screen I have in my office can be monitored in my bosses' offices without my knowledge.

Scoring

Add up all of your scores and then divide the total by 24. This is your "Turbulence Tolerance Test" (TTT) score.

Interpretation

This instrument gives an impression of your tolerance for managing in turbulent times—something likely to characterize the world of work well into the next century. In general, the higher your TTT score, the more comfortable you seem to be with turbulence and change—a positive sign.

For comparison purposes, the average TTT scores for some 500 MBA students and young managers was 1.5–1.6. The test's author suggests TTT scores may be interpreted much like a grade-point average in which 4.0 is a perfect "A". On this basis, a 1.5 is below a "C"! How did you do?

Source: Peter B. Vail, *Managing as a Performance Art: New Ideas for a World of Chaotic Change* (San Francisco: Jossey-Bass, 1989), pp. 8–9. Used by permission.

Time Orientation

Instructions

This instrument examines your tendencies to favor "monochronic" or "polychronic" time orientations. Rate your tendencies for each item below using the following scale.

Rating Scale:

1 = Almost never   2 = Seldom
3 = Sometimes   4 = Usually
      5 = Almost always

____ **1.** I like to do one thing at a time.

____ **2.** I have a strong tendency to build lifetime relationships.

____ **3.** I concentrate on the job at hand.

____ **4.** I base the level of promptness on the particular relationship.

____ **5.** I take time commitments (deadlines, schedules) seriously.

____ **6.** I borrow and lend things often and easily.

____ **7.** I am committed to the job.

____ **8.** Intimacy with family and friends is more important than respecting their privacy.

____ **9.** I adhere closely to plans.

____ **10.** I put obligations to family and friends before work concerns.

____ **11.** I am concerned about not disturbing others (follow rules of privacy).

____ **12.** I change plans often and easily.

____ **13.** I emphasize promptness in meetings.

____ **14.** I am committed to people and human relationships.

____ **15.** I show great respect for private property (seldom borrow or lend).

____ **16.** I am highly distractible and frequently interrupt what I am doing.

____ **17.** I am comfortable with short-term relationships.

____ **18.** I like to do many things at once.

Scoring

To obtain your *monochronic time orientation* score sum results for items 1, 3, 5, 7, 9, 11, 13, 15, 17. To obtain your *polychronic time orientation* score sum results for items 2, 4, 6, 8, 10, 12, 14, 16, 18.

Interpretation

A person high in monochronic time orientation approaches time in a linear fashion with things dealt with one at a time in an orderly fashion. Time is viewed as a precious commodity, not to be wasted; this person values punctuality and promptness.

A person high in polychronic time orientation tends to do a number of things at once, intertwining them together in a dynamic process that considers changing circumstances. Commitments are viewed as objectives, but capable of adjustment when necessary.

Cultural differences in orientations toward time can be observed. Tendencies toward monochronic time orientation are common to North America and northern European cultures. Tendencies toward polychronic time orientation are common in cultures of the Middle East, Asia, and Latin America.

Source: Adapted from J. Ned Seelye and Alan Seelye-James. *Culture Clash* (Lincolnwood, IL: NTC Business Books, 1996).

Assertiveness

Instructions

This instrument measures tendencies toward aggressive, passive, and assertive behaviors in work situations. For each statement below, decide which of the following answers best fits you.

1 = Never true
2 = Sometimes true
3 = Often true
4 = Always true

_____ **1.** I respond with more modesty than I really feel when my work is complimented.

_____ **2.** If people are rude, I will be rude right back.

_____ **3.** Other people find me interesting.

_____ **4.** I find it difficult to speak up in a group of strangers.

_____ **5.** I don't mind using sarcasm if it helps me make a point.

_____ **6.** I ask for a raise when I feel I really deserve it.

_____ **7.** If others interrupt me when I am talking, I suffer in silence.

_____ **8.** If people criticize my work, I find a way to make them back down.

_____ **9.** I can express pride in my accomplishments without being boastful.

_____ **10.** People take advantage of me.

_____ **11.** I tell people what they want to hear if it helps me get what I want.

_____ **12.** I find it easy to ask for help.

_____ **13.** I lend things to others even when I don't really want to.

_____ **14.** I win arguments by dominating the discussion.

_____ **15.** I can express my true feelings to someone I really care for.

_____ **16.** When I feel angry with other people, I bottle it up rather than express it.

_____ **17.** When I criticize someone else's work, they get mad.

_____ **18.** I feel confident in my ability to stand up for my rights.

Scoring

Obtain your scores as follows:

Aggressiveness tendency score—Add items 2, 5, 8, 11, 14, and 17
Passive tendency score—Add items 1, 4, 7, 10, 13, and 16
Assertiveness tendency score—Add items 3, 6, 9, 12, 15, and 18

Interpretation

The maximum score in any single area is 24. The minimum score is 6. Try to find someone who knows you well. Have this person complete the instrument also as it relates to you. Compare his or her impression of you with your own score. What is this telling you about your behavior tendencies in social situations?

Source: From Douglas T. Hall, Donald D. Bowen, Roy J. Lewicki, and Francine S. Hall, _Experiences in Management and Organizational Behavior_, 2d ed. (New York: Wiley, 1985). Used by permission.

Emotional Intelligence

Instructions

Rate yourself on how well you are able to display the abilities for each item listed below. As you score each item, try to think of actual situations in which you have been called upon to use the ability. Use the following scale.

1	2	3	4	5	6	7
Low Ability		Neutral			High Ability	

1 2 3 4 5 6 7 **1.** Identify changes in physiological arousal.

1 2 3 4 5 6 7 **2.** Relax when under pressure in situations.

1 2 3 4 5 6 7 **3.** Act productively when angry.

1 2 3 4 5 6 7 **4.** Act productively in situations that arouse anxiety.

1 2 3 4 5 6 7 **5.** Calm yourself quickly when angry.

1 2 3 4 5 6 7 **6.** Associate different physical cues with different emotions.

1 2 3 4 5 6 7 **7.** Use internal "talk" to affect your emotional states.

1 2 3 4 5 6 7 **8.** Communicate your feelings effectively.

1 2 3 4 5 6 7 **9.** Reflect on negative feelings without being distressed.

1 2 3 4 5 6 7 **10.** Stay calm when you are the target of anger from others.

1 2 3 4 5 6 7 **11.** Know when you are thinking negatively.

1 2 3 4 5 6 7 **12.** Know when your "self-talk" is instructional.

1 2 3 4 5 6 7 **13.** Know when you are becoming angry.

1 2 3 4 5 6 7 **14.** Know how you interpret events you encounter.

1 2 3 4 5 6 7 **15.** Know what senses you are currently using.

1 2 3 4 5 6 7 **16.** Accurately communicate what you experience.

1 2 3 4 5 6 7 **17.** Identify what information influences your interpretations.

1 2 3 4 5 6 7 **18.** Identify when you experience mood shifts.

1 2 3 4 5 6 7 **19.** Know when you become defensive.

1 2 3 4 5 6 7 **20.** Know the impact your behavior has on others.

1 2 3 4 5 6 7 **21.** Know when you communicate incongruently.

1 2 3 4 5 6 7 **22.** "Gear up" at will.

1 2 3 4 5 6 7 **23.** Regroup quickly after a setback.

1 2 3 4 5 6 7 **24.** Complete long-term tasks in designated time frames.

1 2 3 4 5 6 7 **25.** Produce high energy when doing uninteresting work.

1 2 3 4 5 6 7 **26.** Stop or change ineffective habits.

1 2 3 4 5 6 7 **27.** Develop new and more productive patterns of behavior.

1 2 3 4 5 6 7 **28.** Follow words with actions.

1 2 3 4 5 6 7 **29.** Work out conflicts.

1 2 3 4 5 6 7 **30.** Develop consensus with others.

1 2 3 4 5 6 7 **31.** Mediate conflict between others.

1 2 3 4 5 6 7 **32.** Exhibit effective interpersonal communication skills.

1 2 3 4 5 6 7 **33.** Articulate the thoughts of a group.

1 2 3 4 5 6 7 **34.** Influence others, directly or indirectly.

1 2 3 4 5 6 7 **35.** Build trust with others.

1 2 3 4 5 6 7 **36.** Build support teams.

1 2 3 4 5 6 7 **37.** Make others feel good.

1 2 3 4 5 6 7 **38.** Provide advice and support to others, as needed.

1 2 3 4 5 6 7 **39.** Accurately reflect people's feelings back to them.

1 2 3 4 5 6 7 **40.** Recognize when others are distressed.

1 2 3 4 5 6 7 **41.** Help others manage their emotions.

1 2 3 4 5 6 7 **42.** Show empathy to others.

1 2 3 4 5 6 7 **43.** Engage in intimate conversations with others.

1 2 3 4 5 6 7 **44.** Help a group to manage emotions.

1 2 3 4 5 6 7 **45.** Detect incongruence between others' emotions or feelings and their behaviors.

Scoring

This instrument measures six dimensions of your emotional intelligence. Find your scores as follows.

Self-awareness—Add scores for items 1, 6, 11, 12, 13, 14, 15, 17, 18, 19, 20, 21
Managing emotions—Add scores for items 1, 2, 3, 4, 5, 7, 9, 10, 13, 27
Self-motivation—Add scores for items 7, 22, 23, 25, 26, 27, 28
Relating well—Add scores for items 8, 10, 16, 19, 20, 29, 30, 31, 32, 33, 34, 35, 36, 37, 38, 39, 42, 43, 44, 45
Emotional mentoring—Add scores for items 8, 10, 16, 18, 34, 35, 37, 38, 39, 40, 41, 44, 45

Interpretation

The prior scoring indicates your self-perceived abilities in these dimensions of emotional intelligence. To further examine your tendencies, go back for each dimension and sum the number of responses you had that were 4 and lower (suggesting lower ability), and sum the number of responses you had that were 5 or better (suggesting higher ability). This gives you an indication by dimension of where you may have room to grow and develop your emotional intelligence abilities.

———————

Source: Scale from Hendrie Weisinger, *Emotional Intelligence at Work* (San Francisco: Jossey-Bass, 1998), pp. 214–15. Used by permission.

@ **GET CONNECTED!** Complete the on-line versions of these and additional self-assessments. See www.wiley.com/college/schermerhorn.

Glossary

A

Above-average returns exceed what could be earned from alternative investments of equivalent risk.

Accommodation or **smoothing** plays down differences and highlights similarities to reduce conflict.

An **accommodative strategy** accepts social responsibilities and tries to satisfy prevailing economic, legal, and ethical performance criteria.

Accountability is the requirement to show performance results to a supervisor.

Action research is a collaborative process of collecting data, using it for action planning, and evaluating the results.

Active listening involves taking action to help the source of a message say what he or she really means.

An **adaptive organization** operates with a minimum of bureaucratic features and encourages worker empowerment and teamwork.

The **administrative decision model** describes how managers act in situations of limited information and bounded rationality.

An **administrator** is a manager who works in a public or nonprofit organization.

An **affirmative action program** tries to increase employment opportunities for women and minorities.

An **after-action review** formally reviews results to identify lessons learned in a completed project, task force, or special operation.

An **analyzer strategy** seeks the stability of a core business while selectively responding to opportunities for innovation and change.

An **angel investor** is a wealthy individual willing to invest in return for equity in a new venture.

APEC, Asia-Pacific Economic Cooperation is a platform for regional economic alliances among Asian and Pacific Rim countries.

Applications software allows the user to perform a variety of information-based tasks without writing unique computer programs.

An **apprenticeship** is a special form of training that involves a formal assignment to serve as understudy or assistant to a person who already has the desired job skills.

Arbitration is the process by which parties to a dispute agree to abide by the decision of a neutral and independent third party, called an arbitrator.

In **arbitration** a neutral third party issues a binding decision to resolve a dispute.

The **Asian-Pacific Economic Forum (APEC)** is a platform for regional economic alliance among Asian and Pacific Rim countries.

An **assessment center** is a selection technique that engages job candidates in a series of experimental activities over a 1- or 2-day period.

Attribution error overestimates internal factors and underestimates external factors as influences on someone's behavior.

Authority is the right to assign tasks and direct the activities of subordinates in ways that support accomplishment of the organization's purpose.

An **authority decision** is a decision made by the leader and then communicated to the group.

Automation is the total mechanization of a job.

Avoidance involves pretending that a conflict doesn't really exist or hoping that a conflict will simply go away.

B

A **bargaining zone** is the area between one party's minimum reservation point and the other party's maximum reservation point.

Base compensation is a salary or hourly wage paid to an individual.

BATNA is the "best alternative to a negotiated agreement," or what can be done if an agreement cannot be reached.

The **BCG matrix** ties strategy formulation to an analysis of business opportunities according to market growth rate and market share.

The **behavioral decision model** describes decision making with limited information and bounded rationality.

A **behaviorally anchored rating scale (BARS)** is a performance appraisal method that uses specific descriptions of actual behaviors to rate various levels of performance.

Benchmarking is a process of comparing operations and performance with other organizations known for excellence.

Bona fide occupational qualifications are EEO exceptions justified by individual capacity to perform a job.

A **bonus pay plan** provides cash bonuses to employees based on the achievement of specific performance targets.

In **bottom-up change**, change initiatives come from all levels in the organization.

Bottom-up planning begins with ideas developed at lower management levels, which are modified as they are passed up the hierarchy to top management.

A **boundaryless organization** eliminates internal boundaries among parts and external boundaries with the external environment.

Brainstorming is a group technique for generating a large quantity of ideas by free-wheeling contributions made without criticism.

A **budget** is a plan that commits resources to projects or programs; a formalized way of allocating resources to specific activities.

Bureaucracy is a rational and efficient form of organization founded on logic, order, and legitimate authority.

Business incubators offer space, shared services, and advice to help small businesses get started.

A **business plan** describes the direction for a new business and the financing needed to operate it.

A **business strategy** identifies the intentions of a division or strategic business unit to compete in its special product and / or service domain.

C

A **career** is a sequence of jobs that constitute what a person does for a living.

Career planning is the process of systematically matching career goals and individual capabilities with opportunities for their fulfillment.

A **career plateau** is a position from which someone is unlikely to move to a higher level of work responsibility.

A **career portfolio** documents academic and personal accomplishments for external review.

Centralization is the concentration of authority for most decisions at the top level of an organization.

In a **centralized communication network** communication flows only between individual members and a hub or center point.

A **certain environment** offers complete information on possible action alternatives and their consequences.

The **chain of command** links all persons with successively higher levels of authority.

A **change agent** is a person or group that takes leadership responsibility for changing the existing pattern of behavior of another person or social system.

Changing is the central phase in the planned-change process in which a planned change actually takes place.

Channel richness is the capacity of a communication channel to effectively carry information.

A **charismatic leader** is a leader who develops special leader-follower relationships and inspires followers in extraordinary ways.

Child labor is the full-time employment of children for work otherwise done by adults.

A **CIO** is a senior executive responsible for IT and its utilization throughout an organization.

The **classical decision model** describes how managers ideally make decisions using complete information.

Coaching is the communication of specific technical advice to an individual.

A **code of ethics** is a written document that states values and ethical standards intended to guide the behavior of employees.

Coercive power is the capacity to punish or withhold positive outcomes as a means of influencing other people.

Cohesiveness is the degree to which members are attracted to and motivated to remain part of a team.

Collaboration or **problem solving** involves working through conflict differences and solving problems so everyone wins.

Collective bargaining is the process of negotiating, administering, and interpreting a labor contract.

A **combination strategy** involves stability, growth, and retrenchment in one or more combinations.

Commercializing innovation turns ideas into economic value added.

A **committee** is a formal team designated to work on a special task on a continuing basis.

Communication is the process of sending and receiving symbols with meanings attached.

A **communication channel** is the medium through which a message is sent.

Comparable worth holds that persons performing jobs of similar importance should be paid at comparable levels.

Comparative management is the study of how management practices differ systematically from one country and/or culture to the next.

Competition or **authoritative command** uses force, superior skill, or domination to "win" a conflict.

A **competitive advantage** is a special edge that allows an organization to deal with market and environmental forces better than its competitors.

A **compressed workweek** is any work schedule that allows a full-time job to be completed in less than the standard 5 days of 8-hour shifts.

Compromise occurs when each party to the conflict gives up something of value to the other.

Computer competency is the ability to understand and use computers to advantage.

Growth through **concentration** is within the same business area.

A **conceptual skill** is the ability to think analytically and solve complex problems to the benefit of everyone involved.

A **concurrent control** or *steering control* is a control that acts in anticipation of problems and focuses primarily on what happens during the work process.

Conflict is a disagreement over issues of substance and/or an emotional antagonism.

Conflict resolution is the removal of the reasons—substantial and/or emotional—for a conflict.

Constructive stress acts in a positive way to increase effort, stimulate creativity, and encourage diligence in one's work.

A **consultative decision** is a decision made by a leader after receiving information, advice, or opinions from group members.

Contingency planning identifies alternative courses of action that can be taken if and when circumstances change with time.

Contingency thinking maintains that there is no one best way to manage; what is best depends on the situation.

Contingency workers are employed on a part-time and temporary basis to supplement a permanent workforce.

Continuous improvement involves always searching for new ways to improve operations quality and performance.

In **continuous-process production** raw production materials continuously move through an automated system.

A **control chart** is a method for quality control in which work results are displayed on a graph that clearly delineates upper control limits and lower control limits.

Controlling is the process of measuring performance and taking action to ensure desired results.

A **control process** is the process of establishing performance objectives and standards, measuring actual performance, comparing actual performance with objectives and standards, and taking necessary action.

A **core competency** is a special strength that gives an organization a competitive advantage.

Core values are underlying beliefs shared by members of the organization and that influence their behavior.

Corporate culture is the predominant value system for the organization as a whole.

Corporate governance is the system of control and performance monitoring of top management.

Corporate social responsibility is an obligation of an organization to act in ways that serve both its own interests and the interests of its many external publics.

A **corporate strategy** sets long-term direction for the total enterprise.

A **corporation** is a legal entity that exists separately from its owners.

Corruption involves illegal practices to further one's business interests.

A **cost leadership strategy** is a corporate competitive strategy that seeks to achieve lower costs than competitors by improving efficiency of production, distribution, and other organizational systems.

Cost-benefit analysis involves comparing the costs and benefits of each potential course of action.

Creativity is ingenuity and imagination that results in a novel solution to a problem.

A **crisis** is an unexpected problem that can lead to disaster if not resolved quickly and appropriately.

A **critical incident technique** is a performance appraisal method that involves a running log of effective and ineffective job behaviors.

A **cross-functional team** is a team structure in which members from different functional departments work together as needed to solve problems and explore opportunities.

Cultural relativism suggests there is no one right way to behave; ethical behavior is determined by its cultural context.

Culture is a shared set of beliefs, values, and patterns of behavior common to a group of people.

Culture shock is the confusion and discomfort a person experiences when in an unfamiliar culture.

Customer relationship management strategically tries to build lasting relationships and add value to customers.

A **customer structure** is a divisional structure that groups together jobs and activities that serve the same customers or clients.

A **cybernetic control system** is a control system that is entirely self-contained in its performance monitoring and correction capabilities.

Cycle time is the elapsed time between the receipt of an order and the delivery of a finished good or service.

D

Decentralization is the dispersion of authority to make decisions throughout all levels of the organization.

A **decentralized communication network** allows all members to communicate directly with one another.

A **decision** is a choice among alternative courses of action for dealing with a "problem."

Decision making is the process of making choices among alternative possible courses of action.

The **decision-making process** begins with identification of a problem and ends with evaluation of implemented solutions.

A **decision-support system** allows managers to interact with the computer to utilize information for solving structured and semistructured problems.

Debt financing involves borrowing money that must be repaid over time with interest.

A **defender strategy** is a corporate competitive strategy that emphasizes existing products and current market share without seeking growth.

A **defensive strategy of social responsibility** seeks to protect the organization by doing the minimum legally required to satisfy social expectations.

Delegation is the process of distributing and entrusting work to other persons.

Departmentalization is the process of grouping together people and jobs under common supervisors to form various work units or departments.

Design for disassembly is the design of products with attention to how their component parts will be used when product life ends.

Design for manufacturing is creating a design that lowers production costs and improves quality in all stages of production.

Destructive stress impairs the performance of an individual.

Differentiation is the degree of differences that exist among people, departments, or other internal components of an organization.

A **differentiation strategy** is a corporate strategy that seeks competitive advantage through uniqueness, by developing goods and/or services that are clearly different from those offered by the competition.

Discipline is the act of influencing behavior through reprimand.

Discrimination is an active form of prejudice that disadvantages people by denying them full benefits of organizational membership.

A **distinctive competence** is a special strength that gives an organization a competitive advantage in its operating domain.

Distributive justice concerns the degree to which people are treated the same regardless of individual characteristics such as ethnicity, race, gender, or age.

Distributive negotiation focuses on "win-lose" claims made by each party for certain preferred outcomes.

The term **diversity** describes race, gender, age, and other individual differences.

Growth through **diversification** is by acquisition of or investment in new and different business areas.

Divestiture sells off parts of the organization to focus attention and resources on core business areas.

A **divisional structure** groups together people who work on the same product, work with similar customers, or work in the same area or processes.

Downsizing decreases the size of operations in the intent to become more streamlined.

A **dual-career couple** is one in which both adult partners are employed.

Dysfunctional conflict is destructive and hurts task performance.

E
___

An **e-business strategy** strategically uses the Internet to gain competitive advantage.

The **economic order quantity (EOQ)** method orders a fixed number of items every time an inventory level falls to a predetermined point.

Effective communication occurs when the intended meaning of the source and the perceived meaning of the receiver are identical.

An **effective group** is a group that achieves and maintains high levels of both task performance and membership satisfaction over time.

Effective negotiation occurs when issues of substance and working relationships among the negotiating parties are maintained or even improved in the process.

An **effective team** achieves high levels of both task performance and membership satisfaction.

Efficient communication is communication that occurs at minimum cost in terms of resources expended.

Electronic commerce or *e-business* uses information technology to support online commercial transactions.

An **emergent strategy** develops over time as managers learn from and respond to experience.

Emotional conflict results from feelings of anger, distrust, dislike, fear, and resentment as well as from personality clashes.

Emotional intelligence is the ability to manage ourselves and our relationships effectively.

An **employee involvement team** meets on a regular basis to use its talents to help solve problems and achieve continuous improvement.

An **employee stock ownership plan** (ESOP) allows employees to share ownership of their employing organization through the purchase of stock.

Employment discrimination occurs when non-job relevant criteria are used for hiring and job placements.

Empowerment distributes decision-making power throughout an organization.

An **enterprise-wide network** is a set of computer-communication links that connect a diverse set of activities throughout an organization.

An **entrepreneur** is willing to pursue opportunities in situations others view as problems or threats.

Entrepreneurial pay involves workers putting part of their compensation at risk in return for the right to pursue entrepreneurial ideas and share in any resulting profits.

Entrepreneurship is dynamic, risk taking, creative, and growth oriented behavior.

Environmental uncertainty is a lack of complete information about the environment.

Environmentalism is the expression and demonstration of public concern for conditions of the natural or physical environment.

Equal employment opportunity (EEO) is the right to employment and advancement without regard to race, sex, religion, color, or national origin.

Equity financing involves exchanging ownership shares for outside investment monies.

Escalating commitment is the tendency to continue to pursue a course of action even though it is not working.

Ethical behavior is accepted as "right" or "good" in the context of a governing moral code.

An **ethical dilemma** is a situation with a potential course of action that, although offering potential benefit or gain, is also unethical.

The attempt to externally impose one's ethical standards on other cultures is criticized as a form of **ethical imperialism**.

Ethics form the code of morals that set standards as to what is good or bad, or right or wrong in one's conduct.

Ethics training seeks to help people better understand the ethical aspects of decision making and to incorporate high ethical standards into their daily behavior.

Ethnocentrism is the tendency to consider one's culture as superior to all others.

The **Euro** is the new common European currency.

The **European Union (EU)** is a political and economic alliance of European countries that have agreed to support mutual economic growth and to lift barriers that previously limited cross-border trade and business development.

Eustress is stress that is constructive for an individual and helps her or him achieve a positive balance with the external environment.

An **executive information system** offers special support for top managers to access, process, and share information via computer to make a variety of operational and strategic decisions.

An **expatriate** lives and works in a foreign country.

Expectancy is a person's belief that working hard will result in high task performance.

Expert power is the capability to influence other people because of specialized knowledge.

An **expert system (EI)** is a computer program designed to analyze and solve problems at the level of the human expert.

Exporting is the process of producing products locally and selling them abroad in foreign markets.

External control is control that occurs through direct supervision or administrative systems, such as rules and procedures.

An **external customer** is the customer or client who buys or uses the organization's goods and/or services.

Extinction discourages a behavior by making the removal of a desirable consequence contingent on the occurrence of the behavior.

Extranets are computer networks that use the public Internet for communication between the organization and its environment.

An **extrinsic reward** is a reward given as a motivational stimulus to a person, usually by a superior.

F

A **family business** is owned and controlled by members of a family.

Feedback is the process of telling someone else how you feel about something that person did or said or about the situation in general.

A **feedback control** or *postaction control* is a control that takes place after an action is completed.

A **feedback control** or *preliminary control* ensures that proper directions are set and that the right resources are available to accomplish them before the work activity begins.

Filtering is the intentional distortion of information to make it appear most favorable to the recipient.

First-line managers oversee single units and pursue short-term performance objectives consistent with the plans of middle and top management levels.

A **first-mover advantage** comes from being first to exploit a niche or enter a market.

A **flexible benefits** program allows employees to choose from a range of benefit options within certain dollar limits.

A **flexible budget** allows the allocation of resources to vary in proportion with various levels of activity.

Flexible manufacturing involves the ability to change manufacturing processes quickly and efficiently to produce different products or modifications of existing ones.

Flexible working hours are work schedules that give employees some choice in the pattern of daily work hours.

A **focus strategy** is a corporate competitive strategy that concentrates attention on a special market segment to serve its needs better than the competition.

A **focused cost leadership strategy** seeks the lowest costs of operations within a special market segment.

A **focused differentiation strategy** offers a unique product to a special market segment.

A **force-coercion strategy** attempts to bring about change through formal authority and/or the use of rewards or punishments.

A **forecast** is an attempt to predict outcomes; it is a projection into the future based on historical data combined in some scientific manner.

A **formal group** is a group created by the formal authority within the organization.

Formal structure is the structure of the organization in its pure or ideal state.

A **formal team** is officially recognized and supported by the organization.

A **franchise** is when one business owner sells to another the right to operate the same business in another location.

Franchising is a form of licensing in which the licensee buys the complete "package" of support needed to open a particular business.

Fringe benefits are additional nonmonetary forms of compensation (e.g., health plans, retirement plans) provided to an organization's workforce.

The **functional chimneys problem** is a lack of communication and coordination across functions.

Functional conflict is constructive and helps task performance.

A **functional group** is a formally designated work group consisting of a manager and subordinates.

Functional managers are responsible for one area of activity, such as finance, marketing, production, personnel, accounting, or sales.

A **functional strategy** guides activities within one specific area of operations.

A **functional structure** is an organizational structure that groups together people with similar skills who perform similar tasks.

A **functional team** is a formally designated work team with a manager or team leader.

G

A **gain-sharing plan** allows employees to share in any savings or "gains" realized through their efforts to reduce costs and increase productivity.

The **GE Business Screen** analyzes business strength and industry attractiveness for strategy formulation.

In the **General Agreement on Tariffs and Trade (GATT)** and **World Trade Organization (WTO)** member nations agree to ongoing negotiations and reducing tariffs and trade restrictions.

The **general environment** is comprised of the cultural, economic, legal–political, and educational conditions in the locality in which an organizational operates.

General managers are responsible for complex organizational units that include many areas of functional activity.

A **geographical structure** is a divisional structure that groups together jobs and activities being performed in the same location or geographical region.

The **glass ceiling effect** is an invisible barrier that limits the advancement of women and minorities to higher-level responsibilities in organizations.

The **global economy** is an economic perspective based on worldwide interdependence of resource supplies, product markets, and business competition.

A **global manager** works successfully across international boundaries.

Global sourcing is a process of purchasing materials or components in various parts of the world and then assembling them at home into a final product.

Globalization is the worldwide interdependence of resource flows, product markets, and business competition.

A **grapevine** is a common informal communication network.

A **graphic rating scale** is a performance appraisal method that uses a checklist of traits or characteristics thought to be related to high-performance outcomes in a given job.

A **group** is a collection of people who regularly interact with one another over time in respect to the pursuit of one or more common goals.

Group cohesiveness is the degree to which members are attracted to and motivated to remain part of a group.

A **group decision** is a decision made with the full participation of all group members.

A **group decision-support system** facilitates group efforts at solving complex problems while utilizing computerized information systems.

Group dynamics are forces operating in groups that affect task performance and membership satisfaction.

A **group norm** is a behavior, rule, or standard expected to be followed by group members.

Group process is the way team members work together to accomplish tasks.

Groupthink is a tendency for highly cohesive teams to lose their evaluative capabilities.

Groupware is a software system that allows people from different locations to work together in computer-mediated collaboration.

A **growth strategy** involves expansion of the organization's current operations.

Growth-need strength is an individual's desire to achieve a sense of psychological growth in her or his work.

H

A **halo effect** occurs when one attribute is used to develop an overall impression of a person or situation.

The **Hawthorne effect** is the tendency of persons singled out for special attention to perform as expected.

Heuristics are strategies for simplifying decision making.

High-context cultures rely on nonverbal and situational cues as well as spoken or written words in communication.

Higher order needs, in Maslow's hierarchy, are esteem and self-actualization needs.

The **human relations movement** is based on the viewpoint that managers who use good human relations in the workplace will achieve productivity.

Human resource maintenance is a team's ability to maintain its social fabric so that members work well together.

Human resource management is the process of attracting, developing, and maintaining a talented and energetic workforce.

Human resource planning is the process of analyzing staffing needs and identifying actions to fill those needs over time.

Human resources are the people, individuals, and groups that help organizations produce goods or services.

A **human skill** is the ability to work well in cooperation with other people.

A **hygiene factor** is a factor in the work setting, such as working conditions, interpersonal relations, organizational policies, and administration, supervision, and salary.

I

Importing is the process of acquiring products abroad and selling them in domestic markets.

Independent contractors are hired on temporary contracts and are not part of the organization's official workforce.

An **individual decision** is made when a manager chooses a preferred course of action without consulting others.

The **individualism view** is a view of ethical behavior based on the belief that one's primary commitment is to the advancement of long-term self-interests.

An **informal group** is not offically created and emerges based on relationships and shared interests among members.

Informal learning occurs as people interact informally throughout the work day.

Informal structure is the undocumented and officially unrecognized structure that coexists with the formal structure of an organization.

Information is data made useful for decision making.

Information competency is the ability to utilize computers and information technology to locate, retrieve, evaluate, organize, and analyze information for decision making.

An **information system** collects, organizes, and distributes data regarding activities occurring inside and outside an organization.

Information technology is computer hardware, software, networks, and databases supporting information utilization.

Innovation is the process of taking a new idea and putting it into practice as part of the organization's normal operating routines.

An **input standard** is a standard that measures work efforts that go into a performance task.

Inside-out planning focuses planning on internal strengths and trying to do better than what one already does.

Instrumentality is a person's belief that various work-related outcomes will occur as a result of task performance.

Integration is the level of coordination achieved among subsystems in an organization.

Integrity in leadership is honesty, credibility, and consistency in putting values into action.

Intellectual capital is the collective brain-power or shared knowledge of a workforce.

Intensive technology focuses the efforts and talents of many people with high interdependence to serve clients.

Interactional justice is the degree to which others are treated with dignity and respect.

Internal control is self-control that occurs through self-discipline and the personal exercise of individual or group responsibility.

An **internal customer** is someone who uses or depends on the work of another person or group within the organization.

An **international business** conducts commercial transactions across national boundaries.

International management involves the conduct of business or other operations in foreign countries.

Interorganizational information systems facilitate information transfers among two or more organizations.

Intranets are computer networks that allow persons within an organization to share databases and communicate electronically.

Intrapreneurship is entrepreneurial behavior displayed by people or subunits within large organizations.

An **intrinsic** or **natural reward** is a reward that occurs naturally as a person performs a task or job.

Intuitive thinking occurs when someone approaches problems in a flexible and speontaneous fashion.

Inventory consists of materials or products kept in storage.

An **IPO** is an initial selling of shares of stock to the public and for trading on a stock exchange.

ISO 9000 certification is granted by the International Standards Organization to indicate that a business meets a rigorous set of quality standards.

ISO 14000 offers a set of certification standards for responsible environmental policies.

J

A **job** is the collection of tasks a person performs in support of organizational objectives.

Job analysis is an orderly study of job requirements and facets that can influence performance results.

Job burnout is physical and mental exhaustion that can be incapacitating personally and in respect to work.

A **job description** is a written statement that details the duties and responsibilities of any person holding a particular job.

Job design is the allocation of specific work tasks to individuals and groups.

Job enlargement is a job-design strategy that increases task variety by combining into one job two or more tasks that were previously assigned to separate workers.

Job enrichment is a job-design strategy that increases job depth by adding to a job some of the planning and evaluating duties normally performed by the supervisor.

Job involvement is defined as the extent to which an individual is dedicated to a job.

Job performance is the quantity and quality of task accomplishment by an individual or group.

Job rotation is a job-design strategy that increases task variety by periodically shifting workers among jobs involving different tasks.

Job satisfaction is the degree to which an individual feels positively or negatively about various aspects of the job, including assigned tasks, work setting, and relationships with coworkers.

Job scope is the number and combination of tasks an individual or group is asked to perform.

Job sharing is an arrangement that splits one job between two people.

Job simplification is a job-design strategy that involves standardizing work procedures and employing people in clearly defined and very specialized tasks.

A **job specification** is a list of the qualifications required of any job occupant.

A **joint venture** is a form of international business that establishes operations in a foreign country through joint ownership with local partners.

The **justice view** considers ethical behavior as that which treats people impartially and fairly according to guiding rules and standards.

Just-in-time scheduling (JIT) schedules materials to arrive at a work station or facility "just in time" to be used.

K

Keiretsu is a Japanese term describing alliances or business groups that link together manufacturers, suppliers, and finance companies with common interests.

Knowledge management is the processes utilizing organizational knowledge to achieve competitive advantage.

A **knowledge worker** is someone whose knowledge is a critical asset to employers.

L

A **labor contract** is a formal agreement between a union and the employing organization that specifies the rights and obligations of each party with respect to wages, work hours, work rules, and other conditions of employment.

A **labor union** is an organization to which workers belong and that deals with employers on their collective behalf.

Thorndike's **law of effect** states that behavior followed by unpleasant consequences is likely to be repeated, whereas behavior followed by unpleasant consequences is not likely to be repeated.

Leadership is the process of inspiring others to work hard to accomplish important tasks.

Leadership style is the recurring pattern of behaviors exhibited by a leader.

Leading is the process of arousing enthusiasm and directing human-resource efforts toward organizational goals.

Lean production involves streamlining systems and implementing new technologies to allow work to be performed with fewer workers and smaller inventories.

Learning is any change in behavior that occurs as a result of experience.

A **learning organization** utilizes people, values, and systems to continuously change and improve its performance based on the lessons of experience.

Legitimate power is the capability to influence other people by virtue of formal authority or the rights of office.

A **licensing agreement** occurs when a firm pays a fee for the rights to make or sell another company's products.

Lifelong learning is continuous learning from daily experiences and opportunities.

Line managers have direct responsibility for activities making direct contributions to the production of the organization's basic goods or services.

Lobbying expresses opinions and preferences to government officials.

In **long-linked technology** a client moves from point to point during service delivery.

In **lose-lose conflict** no one achieves his or her true desires and the underlying reasons for conflict remain unaffected.

Low-context cultures emphasize communication via spoken or written words.

Lower-order needs, in Maslow's hierarchy, are physiological, safety, and social needs.

M

A **maintenance activity** is an action taken by a team member that supports the emotional life of the group.

Management is the process of planning, organizing, leading, and controlling the use of resources to accomplish performance goals.

Management by exception focuses managerial attention on substantial differences between actual and desired performance.

Management by objectives (MBO) is a process of joint objective setting between a superior and subordinate.

In **management by wandering around (MBWA)** workers at all levels talk with bosses about a variety of work-related matters.

Management development is training to improve knowledge and skills in the fundamentals of management.

A **management information system (MIS)** collects, organizes, and distributes data in such a way that the information meets managers' needs.

Management science or operations research is a scientific approach to management that uses mathematical techniques to analyze and solve problems.

A **manager** is a person in an organization who is responsible for the work performance of one or more other persons.

Managerial competency is a skill or personal characteristic that contributes to high performance in a management job.

Managing diversity is building an inclusive work environment that allows everyone to reach their full potential.

Manufacturing resources planning (MRPII) is an operations planning and control system that extends MRP to include the control of all organizational resources.

Maquiladoras are foreign manufacturing plants that operate in Mexico with special privileges.

Mass customization involves manufacturing individualized products quickly and with the production efficiencies once only associated with mass production of uniform products.

Mass production is the production of a large number of one or a few products with an assembly-line type of system.

A **master budget** is a comprehensive short-term budget for an organization as a whole.

Materials requirements planning (MRP) is an operations planning and control system for ensuring that the right materials and parts are always available at each stage of production.

A **matrix structure** is an organizational form that combines functional and divisional departmentation to take best advantage of each.

A **mechanistic design** is highly bureaucratic, with centralized authority, many rules and procedures, a clearcut division of labor, narrow spans of controls, and formal coordination.

Mediating technology links together parties seeking a mutually beneficial exchange of values.

In **mediation** a neutral party engages in substantive discussions with conflicting parties in the hope that the dispute can be resolved.

Mentoring is the act of sharing experiences and insights between a seasoned and a junior manager.

Merit pay is a system of awarding pay increases in proportion to performance contributions.

Middle managers report to top-level management, oversee the work of several units, and implement plans consistent with higher level objectives.

The **mission** of an organization is its reason for existing as a supplier of goods and/or services to society.

A **mixed message** results when a person's words communicate one message while actions, body language, or appearance communicate something else.

Modeling demonstrates through personal behavior that which is expected of others.

In a **monochronic culture** people tend to do one thing at a time.

The **moral-rights view** is a view of ethical behavior that seeks to respect and protect the fundamental rights of people.

Motion study is the science of reducing a task to its basic physical motions.

Motivation is a term used in management theory to describe forces within the individual that account for the level, direction, and persistence of effort expended at work.

A **multicultural organization** is based on pluralism and operates with respect for diversity in the workplace.

Multidimensional thinking is the capacity to view many problems at once, in relationship to one another, and across long and short time horizons.

A **multinational corporation (MNC)** is a business firm with extensive international operations in more than one foreign country.

A **multiperson comparison** is a performance appraisal method that involves comparing one person's performance with that of one or more other persons.

N

NAFTA is the **North American Free Trade Agreement** linking Canada, the United States, and Mexico in a regional economic alliance.

A **narrative approach** to performance appraisal method uses a written essay description of a person's job performance.

A **need** is a physiological or psychological deficiency a person feels the compulsion to satisfy.

Need for Achievement (nAch) is the desire to do something better or more efficiently, to solve problems, or to master complex tasks.

Need for Affiliation (nAff) is the desire to establish and maintain good relations with people.

Need for Power (nPower) is the desire to control, influence, or be responsible for other people.

Negative reinforcement strengthens a behavior by making the avoidance of an undesirable consequence contingent on the occurrence of the behavior.

Negotiation is the process of making joint decisions when the parties involved have different preferences.

A **network** is a system of computers that are linked together to allow users to easily transfer and share information.

A **network structure** is an organizational structure that consists of a central core with "networks" of outside suppliers of essential business services.

Noise is anything that interferes with the effectiveness of the communication process.

The **nominal group technique** is a group technique for generating ideas by following a structured format of individual response, group sharing without criticism, and written balloting.

A **nonprogrammed decision** is unique and specifically tailored to a problem at hand.

Nonverbal communication is communication that takes place through channels such as body language and the use of interpersonal space.

A **norm** is a behavior, rule, or standard expected to be followed by team members.

O

Objectives are the specific results or desired end states that one wishes to achieve.

An **obstructionist strategy** avoids social responsibility and reflects mainly economic priorities.

An **OD intervention** is a structured activity initiated by consultants or managers that directly assists in a comprehensive organizational development program.

An **open system** interacts with its environment and transforms resource inputs into outputs.

Operant conditioning is the process of controlling behavior by manipulating its consequences.

An **operating budget** is a budget that assigns resources to a responsibility center on a short-term basis.

Operating objectives are specific results that organizations try to accomplish.

An **operational plan** is a plan of limited scope that addresses those activities and resources required to implement strategic plans.

Operations management is a branch of management theory that studies how organizations transform resource inputs into product and service outputs.

An **optimizing decision** results when a manager chooses an alternative that gives the absolute best solution to a problem.

An **organic design** is decentralized with fewer rules and procedures, more open divisions of labor, wide spans of control, and more personal coordination.

An **organization** is a collection of people working together in a division of labor to achieve a common purpose.

An **organization chart** is a diagram that describes the basic arrangement of work positions within an organization.

Organization development (OD) is the application of behavioral science knowledge in a long-range effort to improve an organization's ability to cope with change in its external environment and increase its internal problem-solving capabilities.

Organization structure is the system of tasks, reporting relationships, and communication that links people and groups together to accomplish tasks that serve the organizational purpose.

Organizational behavior is the study of individuals and groups in organizations.

Organizational behavior modification is the application of operant conditioning to influence human behavior at work.

Organizational commitment is defined as the loyalty of an individual to the organization.

Organizational communication is the process through which information is exchanged through interactions among people inside an organization.

Organizational culture is the system of shared beliefs and values that develops within an organization and guides the behavior of its members.

Organizational design is the process of creating structures that best organize resources to serve mission and objectives.

Organizational ecology is the study of how building design may influence communication and productivity.

The **organizational life cycle** is the evolution of an organization over time through different stages of growth.

Organizational stakeholders are directly affected by the behavior of the organization and hold a stake in its performance.

Organizing is the process of arranging people and resources to work toward a common purpose.

Orientation consists of activities through which new employees are made familiar with their jobs, their co-workers, and the policies, rules, objectives, and services of the organization as a whole.

An **output standard** is a standard that measures performance results in terms of quantity, quality, cost, or time.

Outside-in planning uses analysis of the external environment and makes plans to take advantage of opportunities and avoid problems.

P

Participatory planning is the inclusion in the planning process of as many people as possible from among those who will be affected by plans and/or asked to help implement them.

A **partnership** is when two or more people agree to contribute resources to start and operate a business together.

Part-time work is work done on a basis that classifies the employee as "temporary" and requires less than the standard 40-hour workweek.

Perception is the process through which people receive, organize, and interpret information from the environment.

Performance appraisal is a process of formally evaluating performance and providing feedback on which performance adjustments can be made.

Performance effectiveness is an output measure of a task or goal accomplishment.

Performance efficiency is a measure of the resource cost associated with goal accomplishment.

A **performance gap** is a discrepancy between the desired and actual state of affairs.

A **performance management system** sets standards, assesses results, and plans actions to improve future performance.

A **performance norm** identifies the level of work effort and performance expected of group members.

Personal staff are "assistant-to" positions that provide special administrative support to higher level positions.

Personal wellness is the pursuit of one's physical and mental potential through a personal-health promotion program.

A **plan** is a statement of intended means for accomplishing a desired result.

Planned change occurs as a result of specific efforts in its behalf by a change agent.

Planning is the process of setting objectives and determining what should be done to accomplish them.

A **policy** is a standing plan that communicates broad guidelines for making decisions and taking action.

Political action committees collect money for donation to political campaigns.

Political risk is the possible loss of investment or control over a foreign asset because of political changes in the host country.

Political risk analysis forecasts how political events may impact foreign investments.

In a **polychronic culture** time is used to accomplish many different things at once.

A **portfolio planning** approach seeks the best mix of investments among alternative business opportunities.

Positive reinforcement strengthens a behavior by making a desirable consequence contingent on the occurrence of the behavior.

Power is the ability to get someone else to do something you want done or to make things happen the way you want.

Prejudice is the holding of negative, irrational attitudes toward individuals because of their group identity.

Principled/integrative negotiation uses a "win-win" orientation to reach solutions acceptable to each party.

Privatization is the selling of state-owned enterprises into private ownership.

A **proactive strategy** meets all the criteria of social responsibility, including discretionary performance.

A **problem** is a difference between an actual situation and a desired situation.

Problem solving is the process of identifying a discrepancy between an actual and desired state of affairs and then taking action to resolve it.

A **problem symptom** is a sign of the presence of a performance deficiency or opportunity that should trigger a manager to act.

Procedural justice concerns the degree to which policies and rules are fairly administered.

A **procedure** or **rule** is a standing plan that precisely describes what actions are to be taken in specific situations.

A **process** is a group of related tasks creating something of value to a customer.

Process reengineering systematically analyzes work processes to design new and better ones.

A **process structure** groups jobs and activities that are part of the same processes.

Process value analysis identifies and evaluates core processes for their performance contributions.

Product life cycle is the series of stages a product or service goes through in the "life" of its marketability.

A **product structure** is an organizational structure that groups together jobs and activities working on a single product or service.

Productivity is a summary measure of the quantity and quality of work performance with resource utilization considered.

A **profit-sharing plan** distributes a proportion of net profits to employees during a stated performance period.

The **program evaluation and review technique (PERT)** is a means for identifying and controlling the many separate events involved in the completion of projects.

A **programmed decision** applies a solution from past experience to the problem at hand.

Progressive discipline is the process of tying reprimands in the form of penalties or punishments to the severity of the employee's infractions.

Project management is the responsibility for making sure that all activities in a project are completed on time, in the order specified, and with high quality.

Project managers coordinate complex projects with task deadlines and people with many areas of expertise.

A **project schedule** is a single-use plan for accomplishing a specific set of tasks.

Project teams are convened for a particular task or project and disband once it is completed.

Projection is the assignment of personal attributes to other individuals.

A **prospector strategy** is a corporate competitive strategy that involves pursuing innovation and new opportunities in the face of risk and with the prospects of growth.

Protectionism is a call for tariffs and favorable treatments to protect domestic firms from foreign competition.

Proxemics is the use of interpersonal space, such as in the process of interpersonal communication.

A **psychological contract** is the shared set of expectations held by an individual and the organization, specifying what each expects to give and receive from the other in the course of their working relationship.

Punishment discourages a behavior by making an unpleasant consequence contingent on the occurrence of that behavior.

Q

Quality is a degree of excellence, often defined as the ability to meet customer needs 100 percent of the time.

A **quality circle** is a group of employees who meet periodically to discuss ways of improving the quality of their products or services.

Quality control involves checking processes, material, products, or services to ensure that they meet high standards.

Quality of work life (QWL) is the overall quality of human experiences in the workplace.

R

A **rational persuasion strategy** attempts to bring about change through persuasion backed by special knowledge, empirical data, and rational argument.

A **reactor strategy** is a corporate competitive strategy that involves simply responding to competitive pressures in order to survive.

Realistic job previews are attempts by the job interviewer to provide the job candidate with all pertinent information about a prospective job and the employing organization, without distortion and before a job offer is accepted.

A **reason strategy** of influence relies on personal power and persuasion based on data, needs, and/or values.

A **reciprocity strategy** of influence involves the mutual exchange of values and a search for shared positive outcomes.

Recruitment is a set of activities designed to attract a qualified pool of job applicants to an organization.

Referent power is the capability to influence other people because of their desires to identify personally and positively with the power source.

Refreezing is the final stage in the planned-change process during which the manager is concerned with stabilizing the change and creating the conditions for its long-term continuity.

Reliability refers to the ability of an employment test to yield the same result over time if taken by the same person.

Replacement is the management of promotions, transfers, terminations, layoffs, and retirements.

Responsibility is the obligation to perform that results from accepting assigned tasks.

A **responsibility center** is a work unit formally charged with budgetary responsibility for carrying out various activities.

Restructuring changes the scale and/or mix of operations to gain efficiency and improve performance.

A **retrenchment strategy** involves slowing down, cutting back, and seeking performance improvement through greater efficiencies in operations.

A **retribution strategy** of influence relies on position power and results in feelings of coercion or intimidation.

A **reward** is a work outcome of positive value to the individual.

Reward power is the capability to offer something of value—a positive outcome—as a means of influencing other people.

A **risk environment** is a problem environment in which information is lacking, but some sense of the "probabilities" associated with action alternatives and their consequences exists.

Robotics is the use of computer-controlled machines to completely automate work tasks previously performed by hand.

A **role** is a set of activities expected of a person in a particular job or position within the organization.

Role ambiguity occurs when a person in a role is uncertain about what others expect in terms of his or her behavior.

Role conflict occurs when the person in a role is unable to respond to the expectations held by others.

Role overload occurs when too many role expectations are being communicated to a person at a given time.

Role underload occurs when a person is underutilized or asked to do too little and/or to do things that fail to challenge her or his talents and capabilities.

S

Satisficing involves choosing the first satisfactory alternative that comes to your attention.

A **satisfier factor** is a factor in job content, such as a sense of achievement, recognition, responsibility, advancement, or personal growth, experienced as a result of task performance.

Scenario planning identifies alternative future "scenarios" and makes plans to deal with each.

Scientific management involves developing a science for every job, including rules of motion and standardized work instruments, careful selection and training of workers, and proper supervisory support for workers.

Selection is the process of choosing from a pool of applicants the person or persons who best meet job specifications.

Selective perception is the tendency to define problems from one's own point of view or to single out for attention things consistent with one's existing beliefs, values, or needs.

A **self-fulfilling prophecy** occurs when a person acts in ways in order to confirm another's expectations.

A **self-managing work team,** sometimes called an autonomous work group, is a group of workers whose jobs have been redesigned to create a high degree of task interdependence and who have been given authority to make decisions about how they go about the required work.

Self-serving bias explains personal success by internal causes and personal failures by external causes.

Semantic barriers are verbal and nonverbal symbols that are poorly chosen and expressed, creating barriers to successful communication.

Sexual harassment occurs as behavior of a sexual nature that affects a person's employment situation.

Shaping is positive reinforcement of successive approximations to the desired behavior.

A **shared power strategy** is a participative change strategy that relies on involving others to examine values, needs, and goals in relationship to an issue at hand.

Simultaneous systems operate when mechanistic and organic designs operate together in an organization.

A **single-use plan** is used only once.

A **skill** is the ability to translate knowledge into action that results in the desired performance.

Skills-based pay is a system of paying workers according to the number of job-relevant skills they master.

Skunkworks are teams allowed to work creatively together, free of constraints from the larger organization.

Small-batch production is the production of a variety of custom products that are tailor-made, usually with considerable craftsmanship, to fit customer specifications.

A **small business** has fewer than 500 employees, is independently owned and operated, and does not dominate its industry.

Small Business Development Centers offer guidance and support to small business owners in how to set up and run a business operation.

A **social audit** is a systematic assessment and reporting of an organization's commitments and accomplishments in areas of social responsibility.

Social loafing is the tendency of some people to avoid responsibility by "free-riding" in groups.

Socialization is the process of systematically changing the expectations, behavior, and attitudes of a new employee in a manner considered desirable by the organization.

A **sociotechnical system** designs jobs so that technology and human resources are well integrated in high-performance systems with maximum opportunities for individual satisfaction.

A **sole proprietorship** is an individual pursuing business for a profit.

Span of control is the number of subordinates reporting directly to a manager.

Specialized staff are positions that perform a technical service or provide special problem-solving expertise for other parts of the organization.

A **specific environment** is comprised of the actual organizations and persons with whom the focal organization must interact in order to survive and prosper.

A **stability strategy** maintains the present course of action.

Staff managers use special technical expertise to advise and support the efforts of line workers.

Stakeholders are the persons, groups, and institutions directly affected by an organization's performance.

A **standing plan** is used more than once.

Statistical quality control is the use of statistical techniques to assist in the quality control process.

A **stereotype** results when an individual is assigned to a group or category and then the attributes commonly associated with the group or category are assigned to the individual in question.

In a **strategic alliance** organizations join together in partnership to pursue an area of mutual interest.

A **strategic business unit (SBU)** is a separate operating division that represents a major business area and operates with some autonomy vis-à-vis other similar units in the organization.

A **strategic constituencies analysis** is the review and analysis of the interests of external stakeholders of an organization.

Strategic human resource management involves attracting, developing, and maintaining a quality workforce to implement organizational strategies.

Strategic intent focuses and applies organizational energies on a unifying and compelling goal.

Strategic leadership enthuses people to continuously change, refine, and improve strategies and their implementation.

Strategic management is the managerial responsibility for leading the process of formulating and implementing strategies that lead to longer-term organizational success.

Strategic opportunism is the ability to remain focused on long-term objectives by being flexible in dealing with short-term problems and opportunities as they occur.

A **strategic plan** is comprehensive and addresses longer-term needs and directions of the organization.

A **strategy** is a comprehensive plan or action orientation that sets critical direction and guides the allocation of resources for an organization to achieve long-term objectives.

Strategy formulation is the process of creating strategies.

Strategy implementation is the process of putting strategies into action.

Stress is a state of tension experienced by individuals facing extraordinary demands, constraints, or opportunities.

A **stressor** is anything that causes stress.

A **structured problem** is familiar, straightforward, and clear in its information requirements.

Subcultures within organizations are common to groups of people with similar values and beliefs based upon shared personal characteristics.

Substantive conflict is disagreement over such things as goals, the allocation of resources, distribution of rewards, policies, and procedures, and job assignments.

Substitutes for leadership are factors in the work setting that move work efforts toward organizational objectives without the direct involvement of a leader.

A **subsystem** is a work unit or smaller component within a larger organization.

A **succession plan** describes how the leadership transition and related financial matters will be handled.

The **succession problem** is the issue of who will run the business when the current head leaves.

Supply chain management strategically links all operations dealing with resource supplies.

Survivor syndrome is the stress experienced by people who fear for their jobs after having "survived" large layoffs and staff cutbacks in an organization.

Sustainable career advantage is a combination of personal attributes that allows you to consistently outperform others in meeting needs of employers.

Sustainable development meets the needs of the present without hurting future generations.

Sweatshops employ workers at very low wages, for long hours, and in poor working conditions.

A **SWOT analysis** sets the stage for strategy formulation by analyzing organizational strengths and weaknesses and environmental opportunities and threats.

A **symbolic leader** uses symbols to establish and maintain a desired organizational culture.

Synergy is the creation of a whole that is greater than the sum of its individual parts.

A **system** is a collection of interrelated parts working together for a purpose.

Systematic thinking occurs when someone approaches problems in a rational and analytical fashion.

T

A **task activity** is an action taken by a group member that contributes directly to the group's performance purpose.

A **task force** is a formal team convened for a specific purpose and expected to disband when that purpose is achieved.

Task goals are performance targets for individuals and/or groups.

A **team** is a collection of people who regularly interact to pursue common goals.

Team building is a sequence of collaborative activities to gather and analyze data on a team and make changes to increase its effectiveness.

Team leaders or supervisors report to middle managers and directly supervise nonmanagerial workers.

A **team structure** is an organizational structure through which permanent and temporary teams are created to improve lateral relations and solve problems throughout an organization.

Teamwork is the process of people working together in groups to accomplish common goals.

A **technical skill** is the ability to use a special proficiency or expertise in one's work.

Technology is the combination of equipment, knowledge, and work methods that allows an organization to transform inputs into outputs.

The **technological imperative** states that technology is a major influence on organizational structure.

Telecommuting or **flexiplace** involves working at home or other places using computer links to the office.

Theory E change is based on activities that increase shareholder or economic value.

Theory O change is based on activities that increase organizational performance capabilities.

Theory X is a set of managerial assumptions that people in general dislike work, lack ambition, are irresponsible and resistant to change, and prefer to be led than to lead.

Theory Y is a set of managerial assumptions that people in general are willing to work and accept responsibility and are capable of self-direction, self-control, and creativity.

Theory Z is a term that describes a management framework used by American firms following Japanese examples.

In **top-down change**, the change initiatives come from senior management.

Top-down planning begins with broad objectives set by top management.

Top managers are the highest level managers and work to ensure that major plans and objectives are set and accomplished in accord with the organization's purpose.

Total quality management (TQM) is managing with an organization-wide commitment to continuous work improvement, product quality, and meeting customer needs completely.

Training involves a set of activities that provide learning opportunities through which people can acquire and improve job-related skills.

A **trait** is a relatively stable and enduring personal characteristic of an individual.

Transactional leadership is leadership that orchestrates and directs the efforts of others through tasks, rewards, and structures.

Transformational leadership is the ability of a leader to get people to do more than they originally expected to do in support of large-scale innovation and change.

A **transnational corporation** is an MNC that operates worldwide on a borderless basis.

A **type A personality** is a person oriented toward extreme achievement, impatience, and perfectionism and who may find stress in circumstances others find relatively stress-free.

360-degree feedback is an upward communication approach that involves upward appraisals done by a manager's subordinates, as well as additional feedback from peers, internal and external customers, and higher-ups.

U

An **uncertain environment** is a problem environment in which information is so poor that it is difficult even to assign probabilities to the likely outcomes of known alternatives.

Unfreezing is the initial phase in the planned-change process during which the manager prepares a situation for change.

Universalism suggests ethical standards apply across all cultures.

Unplanned change occurs spontaneously or at random and without a change agent's direction.

An **unstructured problem** involves ambiguities and information deficiencies.

The **upside-down pyramid** puts customers at the top, served by workers whose managers support them.

The **utilitarian view** considers ethical behavior as that which delivers the greatest good to the greatest number of people.

V

Valence is the value a person assigns to work-related outcomes.

Validity refers to the ability of an employment test to measure exactly what it is intended to relative to the job specification.

A **value chain** is the sequence of activities that transform materials into finished products.

Values are broad beliefs about what is or is not appropriate behavior.

Venture capitalists make large investments in new ventures in return for an equity stake in the business.

Growth through **vertical integration** is by acquiring suppliers or distributors.

A **virtual meeting** is a meeting conducted by a computer-mediated process of information sharing and decision making.

The **virtual office** enables workers to "commute" via computer networks, fax machines, and express mail delivery service.

A **virtual organization** is a shifting network of strategic alliances that are engaged as needed.

A **virtual team** is a group of people who work together and solve problems through computer-based rather than face-to-face interactions.

Vision is a term used to describe a clear sense of the future.

Visionary leadership brings to the situation a clear sense of the future and an understanding of how to get there.

W

A **whistleblower** exposes the misdeeds of others in organizations.

A **wholly owned subsidiary** is a local operation completely owned by a foreign firm.

A **win-lose conflict** occurs when one party achieves its desires at the expense and exclusion of the other party's desires.

A **win-win conflict** occurs when conflict is resolved to the mutual benefit of all concerned parties.

A **work process** is a related group of tasks that together create a value for the customer.

Work-at-home involves accomplishing a job while spending all or part of one's work time in the home.

Workflow is the movement of work from one point to another in a system.

Workforce diversity is a term used to describe demographic differences (age, gender, race and ethnicity, and ablebodiedness) among members of the workforce.

Work-life balance involves balancing career demands with personal and family needs.

Workplace rage is overtly aggressive behavior toward coworkers or the work setting.

In the **WTO** member nations agree to negotiate and resolve disputes about tariffs and trade restrictions.

Z

A **zero-based budget** allocates resources to a project or activity as if it were brand new.

Endnotes

Chapter 1 Notes

[1]"Monster.com Growth Continues With 8 Million Job Seeker Accounts; Monster.com Dominates The Online Career Space, Ranked #1 According to Media Metrix," *Business Wire* (June 20, 2000). See also www.monster.com.

[2]Information from the *Fast Company* web site: www.fastcompany.com.

[3]"The 100 Best Companies," *Fortune* (January 8, 2001), pp. 148ff.

[4]Charles O'Reilly III and Jeffrey Pfeffer, *Hidden Value: How Great Companies Achieve Extraordinary Results with Ordinary People* (Boston: Harvard Business School Press, 2000), p. 2.

[5]For a research perspective see Denise M. Rousseau, "Organizational Behavior in the New Organizational Era," *Annual Review of Psychology,* vol. 48 (1997), pp. 515–46; for a consultant's perspective see Tom Peters, *The Circle of Innovation* (New York: Knopf, 1997); and Joan Magretta, *Managing in the New Economy* (Boston: Harvard Business School Press, 1999).

[6]See Kevin Kelly, *New Rules for a New Economy: 10 Radical Strategies for a Connected World* (New York: Penguin, 1999).

[7]Information from Thomas A. Stewart, "Brain Power," *Fortune* (March 17, 1997), p. 107; John A. Byrne, "Jack: A Close-Up Look at How America's #1 Manager Runs GE," *Business Week* (June 8, 1998), pp. 91–111; Robert Slater, *Jack Welch and the G.E. Way: Management Insights and Leadership Secrets of the Legendary CEO* (New York: McGraw-Hill, 1998).

[8]Max DePree's books include *Leadership Is an Art* (New York: Dell, 1990) and *Leadership Jazz* (New York: Dell, 1993). See also Herman Miller's home page at www.hermanmiller.com.

[9]Thomas A. Stewart, *Intellectual Capital: The Wealth of Organizations* (New York: Bantam, 1998).

[10]See Peter F. Drucker, *The Changing World of the Executive* (New York: T.T. Times Books, 1982), and *The Profession of Management* (Cambridge, MA: Harvard Business School Press, 1997); and, Francis Horibe, *Managing Knowledge Workers: New Skills and Attitudes to Unlock the Intellectual Capital in Your Organization* (New York: Wiley, 1999).

[11]Kenichi Ohmae's books include *The Borderless World: Power and Strategy in the Interlinked Economy* (New York: Harper, 1989); *The End of the Nation State* (New York: Free Press, 1996); *The Invisible Continent: Four Strategic Imperatives of the New Economy* (New York: Harper, 1999).

[12]For a discussion of globalization see Thomas L. Friedman, *The Lexus and the Olive Tree: Understanding Globalization* (New York: Bantam Doubleday Dell, 2000); and John Micklethwait and Adrian Woolridge, *A Future Perfect: The Challenges and Hidden Promise of Globalization* (New York: Crown, 2000).

[13]Michael E. Porter, *The Competitive Advantage of Nations: With a New Introduction* (New York: Free Press, 1998).

[14]Miriam Jordan, "Web Sites Revive Fading Handicrafts," *Wall Street Journal* (June 12, 2000), pp. B1, B12. See also www.world2market.com.

[15]See for example, Carl Shapiro and Hal R. Varian, *Information Rules: A Strategic Guide to the Network Economy* (Cambridge, MA: Harvard Business School Press, 1998).

[16]Peter Coy, "The Creative Economy," *Business Week* (August 28, 2000), pp. 74–82.

[17]*Workforce 2000: Work and Workers for the 21st Century* (Indianapolis: Towers Perrin/Hudson Institute, 1987).

[18]Richard W. Judy and Carol D'Amico (editors), *Workforce 2020: Work and Workers for the 21st Century* (Indianapolis: Hudson Institute, 1997).

[19]See Richard D. Bucher, *Diversity Consciousness: Opening Our Minds to People, Cultures, and Opportunities* (Upper Saddle River, NJ: Prentice-Hall, 2000).

[20]See Yochi J. Dreazen and Jess Bravin, "Bias Suit Against Microsoft Aims at 'Flat' Workplace," *Wall Street Journal* (January 4, 2001), p. A10.

[21]For a discussion of diversity issues see R. Roosevelt Thomas, "From Affirmative Action to Affirming Diversity," *Harvard Business Review* (March–April

1990), pp. 107–17; and *Beyond Race and Gender: Unleashing the Power of Your Total Workforce by Managing Diversity* (New York: AMACOM, 1992).

[22]Quotations from Thomas, op cit. (1990); and, *Business Week* (August 8, 1990), p. 50, emphasis added.

[23]"Catalyst Survey Shows Women Comprise 12.5% of Total Fortune 500 Executives," Associated Press, New York (November 14, 2000). Leon E. Wynter, "Business & Race," *Wall Street Journal* (December 3, 1997), p. B1; and "Perforations in the Glass Ceiling," *Business Week* (December 22, 1997), pp. 23; 44. See also www.catalystwomen.org; and, *Fortune* magazine's annual report on "America's 50 Best Companies for Minorities."

[24]For background see Taylor Cox Jr., "The Multicultural Organization," *Academy of Management Executive*, vol. 5 (1991), pp. 34–47; and *Cultural Diversity in Organizations: Theory, Research and Practice* (San Francisco: Berrett-Koehler, 1993). For a recent survey and the quote, see Stephanie N. Mehta, "What Minority Employees Really Want," *Fortune* (July 10, 2000), pp. 181–86.

[25]For discussions of the glass ceiling effect see: Ann M. Morrison, Randall P. White, and Ellen Van Velso, *Breaking the Glass Ceiling* (Reading, MA: Addison-Wesley, 1987); Anne E. Weiss, *The Glass Ceiling: A Look at Women in the Workforce* (New York: Twenty First Century, 1999); Debra E. Meyerson and Joyce K. Fletcher, "A Modest Manifestor for Shattering the Glass Ceiling," *Harvard Business Review* (January–February 2000).

[26]Judith B. Rosener, "Women Make Good Managers, So What?" *Business Week* (December 11, 2000), p. 24.

[27]See, for example, Clarence Walton, *The Moral Manager* (New York: Harper Business, 1990).

[28]For information see the numerous news reports on this problem. One starting point is Matthew L. Wald, "Tread Failures Lead to Recall of 6.5 Million Firestone Tires," *New York Times* (August 10, 2000).

[29]Information from corporate web site, http://www.bridgestone-firestone.com, January 5, 2001.

[30]Hudson Institute, *Workforce 2020: Work and Workers for the 21st Century*, op cit.

[31]Credo selection from www.jnj.com.

[32]Charles Handy, *The Age of Unreason* (Cambridge, MA: Harvard Business School Press, 1990).

[33]See the issue feature "Free Agent Nation," *Fast Company* (December 1997).

[34]"Is Your Job Your Calling?" *Fast Company* (February–March 1998), p. 108.

[35]This material is provided courtesy of Ronald Larimer and is used with his permission.

[36]Tom Peters, "The New Wired World of Work," *Business Week* (August 28, 2000), pp. 172–73.

[37]Robert Reich, "The Company of the Future," *Fast Company* (November 1998), p. 124ff.

[38]Developed from Peters, op cit. (2000).

[39]For an overview of organizations and organization theory see W. Richard Scott, *Organizations: Rational, Natural and Open Systems* (Englewood Cliffs, NJ: Prentice-Hall, 1997).

[40]Ronald B. Lieber, "Why Employees Love These Companies," *Fortune* (January 12, 1998), pp. 72–74; and, David Whitford, "A Human Place to Work," *Fortune* (January 8, 2001), pp. 108–120. See also www. medtronic.com.

[41]For a discussion of organizations as systems, see Lane Tracy, *The Living Organization* (New York: Quorum Books, 1994).

[42]"Measuring People Power," *Fortune* (October 2, 2000), p. 186.

[43]Developed from Jay A. Conger, *Winning 'em Over: A New Model for Managing in the Age of Persuasion* (New York: Simon & Shuster, 1998), pp. 180–81; Stewart D. Friedman, Perry Christensen, and Jessica DeGroot, "Work and Life: The End of the Zero-Sum Game," *Harvard Business Review* (November–December 1998): 119–29; Chris Argyris, "Empowerment: The Emperor's New Clothes," *Harvard Business Review* (May–June 1998): 98–105; John A. Byrne, "Management by Web," *Business Week* (August 28, 2000), pp. 84–98.

[44]Philip B. Crosby, *Quality Is Still Free: Making Quality Certain in Uncertain Times* (New York: McGraw-Hill, 1995). For a comprehensive review see Robert E. Cole and W. Richard Scott (eds), *The Quality Movement & Organization Theory* (Thousand Oaks, CA: Sage, 2000).

[45]"Apple," *Business Week* (July 31, 2000), pp. 102–13; "Apple Wins with Design," *Business Week* (July 31, 2000); pp. 144; "Apple Putting Hopes on New MacIntosh Line," *New York Times* (January 10, 2001), p. C7.

[46]Jeffrey Pfeffer and John F. Veiga, "Putting People First for Organizational Success," *Academy of Management Executive*, vol. 13 (May 1999), pp. 37–48;

and Jeffrey Pfeffer, *The Human Equation: Building Profits by Putting People First* (Boston: Harvard Business School Press, 1998).

[47]"Workweek," *Wall Street Journal* (January 9, 2001), p. 1.

[48]Henry Mintzberg, "The Manager's Job: Folklore and Fact," *Harvard Business Review*, vol. 53 (July–August 1975), p. 61. See also his book *The Nature of Managerial Work* (New York: Harper & Row, 1973 and HarperCollins, 1997).

[49]Hal Lancaster, "Middle Managers Are Back—But Now They're 'High-Impact' Players," *Wall Street Journal* (April 14, 1998), p. B1.

[50]Information from David Whitford, "A Human Place to Work," *Fortune* (January 8, 2001), pp. 108–20.

[51]Lancaster, op cit.

[52]Whitford, op cit.

[53]For a perspective on the first-level manager's job, see Leonard A. Schlesinger and Janice A. Klein, "The First-Line Supervisor: Past, Present and Future," pp. 370–82, in Jay W. Lorsch (ed), *Handbook of Organizational Behavior* (Englewood Cliffs, NJ: Prentice-Hall, 1987). Research reported in "Remember Us?" *Economist* (February 1, 1992), p. 71.

[54]Stewart D. Friedman, Perry Christensen and Jessica De Groot, "Work and Life: The End of the Zero-Sum Game," *Harvard Business Review* (November–December 1998), pp. 119–29.

[55]See Anne Fisher, "Six Ways to Supercharge Your Career," *Fortune* (January 13, 1997), pp. 46–57.

[56]Information from Terry Stephan, "Honing Her Kraft," *Northwestern* (winter 2000), pp. 22–25.

[57]Information from Marc Weingarten, "The Next Napster," *Smart Business* (March 2001), pp. 48–49.

[58]For a classic study see Thomas A. Mahoney, Thomas H. Jerdee, and Stephen J. Carroll, "The Job(s) of Management," *Industrial Relations*, vol. 4 (February 1965), pp. 97–110.

[59]This running example is developed from information from "Accountants Have Lives, Too, You Know," *Business Week* (February 23, 1998), pp. 88–90, and the Ernst & Young web site: www.ey.com.

[60]Mintzberg, *The Nature of Managerial Work*, op cit. (1973), p. 30.

[61]See for example, John R. Veiga and Kathleen Dechant, "Wired World Woes: www.help," *Academy of Management Executive*, vol. 11 (August 1997), pp. 73–79.

[62]See Mintzberg, *The Nature of Managerial Work*, op cit.; and, Henry Mintzberg, "Covert Leadership: The Art of Managing Professionals," *Harvard Business Review* (November–December 1998), pp. 140–47.

[63]Mintzberg, op cit. (1973), p. 60.

[64]For research on managerial work see Morgan W. McCall Jr., Ann M. Morrison, and Robert L. Hannan, *Studies of Managerial Work: Results and Methods. Technical Report #9* (Greensboro, NC: Center for Creative Leadership, 1978), pp. 7–9. See also John P. Kotter, "What Effective General Managers Really Do," *Harvard Business Review* (November–December 1982), pp. 156–57.

[65]Kotter, "What Effective General Managers Really Do," p. 164. See also his book, *The General Managers* (New York: Free Press, 1986); and David Barry, Catherine Durnell Crampton, and Stephen J. Carroll, "Navigating the Garbage Can: How Agendas Help Managers Cope with Job Realities," *Academy of Management Executive*, vol. 11 (May 1997), pp. 43–56.

[66]See Handy, op cit., and *Beyond Certainty: The Changing Worlds of Organizations* (Cambridge, MA: Harvard Business School Press, 1997).

[67]Robert L. Katz, "Skills of an Effective Administrator," *Harvard Business Review*, (September–October 1974), p. 94.

[68]Hendrie Weisinger, *Emotional Intelligence at Work* (San Francisco: Jossey-Bass, 2000).

[69]See Daniel Goleman's books *Emotional Intelligence* (New York: Bantam, 1995) and *Working with Emotional Intelligence* (New York: Bantam, 1998); and his articles "What Makes a Leader," *Harvard Business Review* (November–December 1998), pp. 93–102, and "Leadership that Makes a Difference," *Harvard Business Review* (March–April 2000), pp. 79–90, quote from p. 80.

[70]Richard E. Boyatzis, *The Competent Manager: A Model for Effective Performance* (New York: Wiley, 1982).

ServiceArizona: Information from Matthew Symonds, "The Next Revolution," *The Economist* (June 24, 2000).

Chapter 2 Notes

[1]Information from David Rocks, "Reinventing Herman Miller," *Business Week e.biz* (April 3, 2000), pp. E88–E96; www.hermanmiller.com.

[2]Robert Reich, *The Future of Success* (New York: Knopf, 2001), p. 7.

[3]Quote from *The New Blue* (IBM Annual Report, 1997), p. 8.

[4]Reich, op cit.

[5]See Michael E. Porter, *Competitive Strategy: Techniques for Analyzing Industries and Competitors* (New York: Free Press, 1980) and *Competitive Advantage: Creating and Sustaining Superior Performance* (New York: Free Press, 1986); also, Richard A. D'Aveni, *Hyper-Competition: Managing the Dynamics of Strategic Maneuvering* (New York: Free Press, 1994).

[6]Information from *The Vermont Teddy Bear Company Gazette*, vol. 4 (summer 1993); and, corporate web site: http://www.vtbear.com/ar96history.html.

[7]Joseph M. Juran, "Made in U.S.A.: A Renaissance in Quality," *Harvard Business Review* (July–August 1993), pp. 42–50.

[8]Michael Porter, *The Competitive Advantage of Nations* (New York: Free Press, 1989).

[9]Information from Paul Raeburn, "The Japanese Are Making the Right Bet on Hybrids," *Business Week* (August 14, 2000), p. 70.

[10]See Richard D. Bucher, *Diversity Consciousness: Opening Our Minds to People, Cultures, and Opportunities* (Upper Saddle River, NJ: Prentice-Hall, 2000), p. 201.

[11]James D. Thompson, *Organizations in Action* (New York: McGraw-Hill, 1967), and Robert B. Duncan, "Characteristics of Organizational Environments and Perceived Environmental Uncertainty," *Administrative Science Quarterly*, vol. 17 (1972), pp. 313–27. For discussion of the implications of uncertainty see Hugh Courtney, Jane Kirkland and Patrick Viguerie, "Strategy Under Uncertainty," *Harvard Business Review* (November–December 1997), pp. 67–79.

[12]Quotation from a discussion by Richard J. Shonberger and Edward M. Knod Jr., Operations Management: Serving the Customer, 3d ed. (Plano, TX: Business Publications, 1988), p. 4.

[13]Quote from *The Vermont Teddy Bear Company Gazette*, op cit., p. 3.

[14]Information from "How Marriott Never Forgets a Guest," *Business Week* (February 21, 2000), p. 74.

[15]Rosabeth Moss Kanter, "Transcending Business Boundaries: 12,000 World Managers View Change," *Harvard Business Review* (May–June 1991), pp. 151–64.

[16]Reported in Jennifer Steinhauer, "The Undercover Shoppers," *New York Times* (February 4, 1998), pp. C1, C2.

[17]Roger D. Blackwell and Kristina Blackwell, "The Century of the Consumer: Converting Supply Chains into Demand Chains," *Supply Chain Management Review* (fall 1999).

[18]See Michael Dell, *Direct from Dell: Strategies that Revolutionized an Industry* (New York: Harper Business, 1999).

[19]See Joseph M. Juran, *Quality Control Handbook*, 3d ed. (New York: McGraw-Hill, 1979) and "The Quality Trilogy: A Universal Approach to Managing for Quality," in H. Costin (ed.), *Total Quality Management* (New York: Dryden, 1994); W. Edwards Deming, *Out of Crisis* (Cambridge, MA: MIT Press, 1986) and "Deming's Quality Manifesto," *Best of Business Quarterly*, vol. 12 (winter 1990–1991), pp. 6–10. See also Howard S. Gitlow and Shelly J. Gitlow, *The Deming Guide to Quality and Competitive Position* (Englewood Cliffs, NJ: Prentice-Hall, 1987); Juran, "Made in U.S.A.," op cit., 1993.

[20]Information from the Baldrige Award web site: http://www.quality.nist.gov/bcpg.pdf.htm; see also, "Does the Baldrige Award Really Work? *Harvard Business Review* (January–February 1992), pp. 126–47.

[21]Philip B. Crosby, *Quality is Free* (New York: McGraw-Hill, 1979); *The Eternally Successful Organization* (New York: McGraw-Hill, 1988); and, *Quality Is Still Free: Making Quality Certain in Uncertain Times* (New York: McGraw-Hill, 1995).

[22]Christopher Knowlton, "What America Makes Best," *Fortune* (March 28, 1988), pp. 40–54; Roger L. Hale, Douglas R. Hoelscher, and Ronald E. Kowal, *Quest for Quality* (Minneapolis, MN: Tennant Company, 1989); and Roger L. Hale, Donald D. Carlton, Ronald E. Kowal, and Tim K. Sehnert, *Made in the USA: How One American Company Helps Satisfy Customer Needs through Strategic Supplier Quality Management* (Minneapolis, MN: Tennant Company, 1991).

[23]Rafael Aguay, *Dr. Deming: The American Who Taught the Japanese about Quality* (New York: Free Press, 1997).

[24]See W. Edwards Deming, *Out of Crisis*, op cit.

[25]See Edward E. Lawler III, Susan Albers Mohrman, Gerald E. Ledford Jr., *Employee Involvement and Total Quality Management: Practices and Results in Fortune 1000 Companies* (San Francisco: Jossey-Bass, 1992).

[26]Edward E. Lawler III and Susan Albers Mohrman, "Quality Circles After the Fad," *Harvard Business Review*, January–February 1985), pp. 65–71.

[27]Quotes from Arnold Kanarick, "The

Far Side of Quality Circles," *Management Review*, vol. 70 (October 1981), pp. 16–17.

28John A. Byrne, "Management by Web," *Business Week* (August 28, 2000), pp. 84–96.

29See B. Joseph Pine II, Bart Victor, and Andrew C. Boynton, "Making Mass Customization Work," *Harvard Business Review*, (September–October 1993), pp. 108–19; and "The Agile Factory: Custom-made, Direct from the Plant," *Business Week*, Special report on "21st Century Capitalism" (January 23, 1995), pp. 158–59; and Justin Martin, "Give 'Em *Exactly* What They Want," *Fortune* (November 10, 1997), p. 283.

30Tom Peters, *The Circle of Innovation* (New York: Knopf, 1997), p. 429.

31Martin, op cit. (1997).

32Edgar H. Schein, "Organizational Culture," *American Psychologist*, vol. 45 (1990), pp. 109–19. See also Schein's *Organizational Culture and Leadership*, 2d ed. (San Francisco: Jossey-Bass, 1997); and, *The Corporate Culture Survival Guide* (San Francisco: Jossey-Bass, 1999).

33James Collins and Jerry Porras, *Built to Last* (New York: Harper Business, 1994).

34Schein, 1996; Terrence E. Deal and Alan A. Kennedy, *Corporate Cultures: The Rites and Rituals of Corporate Life* (Reading, MA: Addison-Wesley, 1982); Ralph Kilmann, Beyond the Quick Fix (San Francisco: Jossey-Bass, 1984).

35In their book *Corporate Culture and Performance* (New York: MacMillan, 1992), John P. Kotter and James L. Heskett make the point that strong cultures have the desired effects over the long term only if they encourage adaptation to a changing environment. See also Collins and Porras, *Built to Last*, op cit. (1994).

36This is a simplified model developed from Schein, *Organizational Culture and Leadership*, op cit. (1997).

37James C. Collins and Jerry I. Porras, "Building Your Company's Vision," *Harvard Business Review* (September–October 1996), pp. 65–77.

38Ralph H. Kilmann, Mary J. Saxton, and Roy Serpa, "Issues in Understanding and Changing Corporate Culture," *California Management Review*, vol. 28 (1986), pp. 87–94.

39See Mary Kay Ash, *Mary Kay: You Can Have It All* (New York: Roseville, CA: Prima Publishing, 1995).

40Lee Gardenswartz and Anita Rowe, *Managing Diversity: A Complete Desk Reference and Planning Guide* (Chicago: Irwin, 1993).

41R. Roosevelt Thomas, Jr., *Beyond Race and Gender* (New York: AMACOM, 1992), p. 10; see also R. Roosevelt Thomas, Jr. "From 'Affirmative Action' to 'Affirming Diversity,'" *Harvard Business Review*, (November–December 1990), pp. 107–17; R. Roosevelt Thomas, Jr. with Marjorie I. Woodruff, *Building a House for Diversity* (New York: AMACOM, 1999).

42Gardenswartz and Rowe, op cit. p. 220+.

43Taylor Cox Jr., *Cultural Diversity in Organizations* (San Francisco: Berrett-Koehler, 1994).

44Joseph A. Raelin, *Clash of Cultures* (Cambridge, MA: Harvard Business School Press, 1986).

45Geert Hofstede, *Culture's Consequences* (Beverly Hills: Sage, 1982).

46For examples of role model approaches see Anthony Robbins and Joseph McClendon III, *Unlimited Power: A Black Choice* (New York: Free Press, 1997) and Augusto Failde and William Doyle, *Latino Success: Insights from America's Most Powerful Latino Executives* (New York: Free Press, 1996).

47See, for example, the discussion in Ron Zembke, Claire Raines and Bob Filipczak, *Generations at Work: Managing the Clash of Veterans, Boomers, Xers, and Nexters in Your Workplace* (New York: AMACOM, 1999); and, Brian O'Reilly, "Meet the Future: It's Your Kids," *Fortune* (July 24, 2000), pp. 144–64.

48Barbara Benedict Bunker, "Appreciating Diversity and Modifying Organizational Cultures: Men and Women at Work," Chapter 5 in Suresh Srivastva and David L. Cooperrider, *Appreciative Management and Leadership* (San Francisco: Jossey-Bass, 1990).

49See Gary N. Powell, *Women & Men in Management* (Thousand Oaks, CA: Sage, 1993) and Cliff Cheng (ed.), *Masculinities in Organizations* (Thousand Oaks, CA: Sage, 1996). For added background, see also Sally Helgesen, *Everyday Revolutionaries: Working Women and the Transformation of American Life* (New York: Doubleday, 1998).

50Information from ibid., and Mehta, op cit., p. 183.

51Information from Stephanie N. Mehta, "What Minority Employees Really Want," *Fortune* (July 10, 2000), pp. 181–86.

52Information from "The Bugs in Microsoft Culture," *Fortune* (January 8, 2001), p. 128.

53Data reported in "How to Enable the Disabled," *Business Week* (November 6, 2000), p. 36.

54Information from Ann Harrington, "Coke Denied: Prevention Is the Best Defense," *Fortune* (July 10, 2000), p. 188.

55This section is based on ideas set forth by R. Roosevelt, Thomas, Jr., in *Beyond Race and Gender*, op cit., 1992; and, Thomas and Woodruff, *Building a House for Diversity*, op cit., 1999.

56Thomas, *Beyond Race and Gender*, op cit., p. 17.

57"Diversity Today: Corporate Recruiting Practices in Inclusive Workplaces," *Fortune* (June 12, 2000), p. S6.

58Thomas, Jr. and Woodruff, *Building a House for Diversity*, op cit. (1999), pp. 211–26.

59Based on ibid., pp. 11–12.

60"Diversity Today: Corporate Recruiting Practices in Inclusive Workplaces," *Fortune* (June 12, 2000), p. S4.

Information on Solectron from corporate web site: www.solectron.com (January 29, 2001).

Chapter 3 Notes

1Information from Kerwin, Kathleen; Stepanek, Marcia and Welch, David. "At Ford, E-Commerce Is Job 1," *Business Week* (February 28, 2000), pp. 74–78. See also the autoxchange web site at: https://www.autoxchange.com/US/home.jsp.

2See Alvin Toffler, *Powershift* (New York: Bantam Books, 1990), and http://www.tofflerassociates.com/index1.htm.

3Information from "E-Meetings Redefine Productivity," *Fortune*, Special Advertising Section (February 5, 2001), p. S2.

4Peter F. Drucker, "Looking Ahead: Implications of the Present," *Harvard Business Review*, (September–October 1997), pp. 18–32.

5Thomas A. Stewart, *Intellectual Capital: The Wealth of Organizations* (New York: Doubleday, 1997).

6Paul Roberts, "Humane Technology–PeopleSoft," *Fast Company* (April–May 1998), p. 122.

7See Susan G. Cohen and Don Mankin, "The Changing Nature of Work: Managing the Impact of Information Technology," Chapter 6 in Susan Albers Mohrman, Jay R. Galbraith, Edward E. Lawler III and Associates, *Tomorrow's Organization: Crafting Winning Capabilities in a Dynamic World* (San Francisco: Jossey-Bass, 1998), pp. 154–78.

8Information from example in "Management by Web," *Business Week* (August 28, 2000), p. 88.

9Efraim Turban, R. Kelly Rainer, Jr.,

and Richard E. Potter, *Introduction to Information Technology* (New York: Wiley, 2001).

[10]Information from Robert W. Bly, "Does Your 'Second Generation' Site Get a Passing Grade?" (September 8, 2000), http://www.dotcom.com.

[11]Gautam Naik and Almar Latour, "M-Commerce: Mobile and Multiplying," *Wall Street Journal* (August 18, 2000), p. B1.

[12]Drucker, "Looking Ahead" (1997), p. 22.

[13]Information from John A. Byrne, "Visionary vs. Visonary," *Business Week* (August 28, 2000), pp. 210–14.

[14]The article by Dorothy Leonard-Barton and John J. Sviokla, "Putting Expert Systems to Work," *Harvard Business Review*, (March–April 1988), 91–98, provides a practical overview of expert systems and their management applications. See also Barbara Garson, *The Electronic Sweatshop* (New York: Viking Penguin, 1989).

[15]Mary J. Cronin, "Ford's Intranet Success," *Fortune* (March 30, 1998), p. 158; and Steven V. Brull, "Networks That Do New Tricks," *Business Week* (April 6, 1998), p. 100.

[16]Jaclyn Fierman, "Winning Ideas from Maverick Managers," *Fortune* (February 6, 1995), pp. 66–80.

[17]Henry Mintzberg, *The Nature of Managerial Work* (New York: HarperCollins, 1997).

[18]Information from Peter Burrows, "Sun's Bid to Rule the Web," *Business Week* (July 24, 2000), pp. EB31–42.

[19]For scholarly reviews, see Dean Tjosvold, "Effects of Crisis Orientation on Managers' Approach to Controversy in Decision Making," *Academy of Management Journal*, vol. 27 (1984), pp. 130–38; and Ian I. Mitroff, Paul Shrivastava, and Firdaus E. Udwadia, "Effective Crisis Management," *Academy of Management Executive*, vol. 1 (1987), pp. 283–92.

[20]See David Greisling, *I'd Like to Buy the World a Coke: The Life and Leadership of Roberto Goizueta* (New York: Wiley, 1998).

[21]See Hugh Courtney, Jane Kirkland, and Patrick Viguerie, "Strategy Under Uncertainty," *Harvard Business Review*, (November–December 1997), pp. 67–79.

[22]For a good discussion, see Watson H. Agor, *Intuition in Organizations: Leading and Managing Productively* (Newbury Park, CA: Sage, 1989); Herbert A. Simon, "Making Management Decisions: The Role of Intuition and Emotion," *Academy of Management Executive*, vol.

1 (1987), pp. 57–64; Orlando Behling and Norman L. Eckel, "Making Sense Out of Intuition," *Academy of Management Executive*, vol. 5 (1991), pp. 46–54.

[23]Agor, (1989), p. 11.

[24]Daniel J. Isenberg, "How Senior Managers Think," *Harvard Business Review*, vol. 62 (November–December, 1984), pp. 81–90.

[25]Daniel J. Isenberg, "The Tactics of Strategic Opportunism," *Harvard Business Review*, vol. 65 (March–April 1987), pp. 92–97.

[26]See George P. Huber, *Managerial Decision Making* (Glenview, IL: Scott, Foresman 1975). For a comparison, see the steps in Xerox's problem-solving process as described in David A. Garvin, "Building a Learning Organization," *Harvard Business Review* (July–August 1993), pp. 78–91.

[27]Peter F. Drucker, *Innovation and Entrepreneurship: Practice and Principles* (New York: Harper & Row, 1985).

[28]For a sample of Simon's work, see Herbert A. Simon, *Administrative Behavior* (New York: Free Press, 1947); James G. March and Herbert A. Simon, *Organizations* (New York: Wiley, 1958); Herbert A. Simon, *The New Science of Management Decision* (New York: Harper, 1960).

[29]This presentation is based on the work of R. H. Hogarth, D. Kahneman, A. Tversky, and others, as discussed in Max H. Bazerman, *Judgment in Managerial Decision Making*, 3d ed. (New York: Wiley, 1994).

[30]Barry M. Staw, "The Escalation of Commitment to a Course of Action," *Academy of Management Review*, vol. 6 (1981): 577–87; Barry M. Staw and Jerry Ross, "Knowing When to Pull the Plug," *Harvard Business Review*, vol. 65 (March–April 1987): 68–74.

[31]The classic work is Norman R. Maier, "Assets and Liabilities in Group Problem Solving," *Psychological Review*, vol. 74 (1967), pp. 239–49.

[32]Ibid.

[33]Peter F. Drucker, "The Future That has Already Happened," *Harvard Business Review*, vol. 75 (September–October 1997), pp. 20–24.

[34]Peter F. Drucker, Esther Dyson, Charles Handy, Paul Daffo, and Peter M. Senge, "Looking Ahead: Implications of the Present," *Harvard Business Review*, vol. 75 (September–October, 1997).

[35]Information from Peter Burrows, "Sun's Bid to Rule the Web," *Business Week* (July 24, 2000), pp. EB31–42.

[36]See, for example, Thomas H. Davenport and Laurence Prusak, *Working*

Knowledge: How Organizations Manage What They Know (Cambridge, MA: Harvard Business School Press, 1997).

[37]Hal Lancaster, "Contributors to Pools of Company Know-How Are Valued Employees," *Wall Street Journal* (December 9, 1997), p. B1; Thomas A. Stewart, "Is This Job Really Necessary?" *Fortune* (January 12, 1998), pp. 154–55.

[38]Richard Waters, "Own Words: Jack Welch, General Electric," *Financial Times* (October 1, 1997).

[39]Steven E. Prokesch, "Unleashing the Power of Learning," *Harvard Business Review*, (September–October 1997), pp. 147–68.

[40]Peter Senge, *The Fifth Discipline* (New York: Harper, 1990).

[41]Ibid.

[42]Prokesch, op cit. (1997).

[43]Waters, op cit. (1997).

For information, see D'Artagnan story at company web site, www.d'artagnan.com.

Chapter 4 Notes

[1]Information from Mike Pramik, "Fulfilling the Promise of Internet Shopping," *Columbus Dispatch* (December 24, 2000), pp. F1, 2.

[2]Pauline Graham, *Mary Parker Follett— Prophet of Management: A Celebration of Writings from the 1920's* (Boston: Harvard Business School Press, 1995).

[3]For a timeline of twentieth-century management ideas see "75 Years of Management Ideas and Practices: 1922–1997," *Harvard Business Review*, supplement (September–October 1997).

[4]A thorough review and critique of the history of management thought, including management in ancient civilizations, is provided by Daniel A. Wren, *The Evolution of Management Thought*, 4th ed. (New York: Wiley, 1993).

[5]See "75 Years of Management Ideas & Practice," *Harvard Business Review* (September–October 1997), special supplement.

[6]For a sample of this work see Henry L. Gantt, *Industrial Leadership* (Easton, MD: Hive, 1921; Hive edition published in 1974); Henry C. Metcalfe and Lyndall Urwick (eds.), *Dynamic Administration: The Collected Papers of Mary Parker Follett* (New York: Harper & Brothers, 1940); James D. Mooney, *The Principles of Administration*, rev. ed. (New York: Harper & Brothers, 1947); Lyndall Urwick, *The Elements of Administration* (New York: Harper & Brothers,

1943) and *The Golden Book of Management* (London: N. Neame, 1956).

[7]References on Taylor's work are from Frederick W. Taylor, *The Principles of Scientific Management* (New York: W. W. Norton, 1967), originally published by Harper & Brothers in 1911. See Charles W. Wrege and Amedeo G. Perroni, "Taylor's Pig-Tale: A Historical Analysis of Frederick W. Taylor's Pig-Iron Experiments," *Academy of Management Journal*, vol. 17 (March 1974), pp. 6–27, for a criticism; see Edwin A. Lock, "The Ideas of Frederick W. Taylor: An Evaluation," *Academy of Management Review*, vol. 7 (1982), p. 14, for an examination of the contemporary significance of Taylor's work. See also the recent biography, Robert Kanigel, *The One Best Way* (New York: Viking, 1997).

[8]Kanigel, *One Best Way*, op cit.

[9]See Frank B. Gilbreth, *Motion Study* (New York: Van Nostrand, 1911).

[10]For information see UPS web site: www.ups.com.

[11]Available in the English language as Henri Fayol, *General and Industrial Administration* (London: Pitman, 1949); subsequent discussion is based on M. B. Brodie, *Fayol on Administration* (London: Pitman, 1949).

[12]M. P. Follett, *Freedom and Coordination* (London: Management Publications Trust, 1949).

[13]Judith Garwood, "A Review of *Dynamic Administration: The Collected Papers of Mary Parker Follett*," *New Management*, vol. 2 (1984), pp. 61–62; eulogy from Richard C. Cabot, *Encyclopedia of Social Work*, vol. 15, s.v., "Follett, Mary Parker," p. 351.

[14]A. M. Henderson and Talcott Parsons (eds. and trans.), *Max Weber: The Theory of Social Economic Organization* (New York: Free Press, 1947).

[15]Ibid., p. 337.

[16]The Hawthorne studies are described in detail in F. J. Roethlisberger and William J. Dickson, *Management and the Worker* (Cambridge: Harvard University Press, 1966) and G. Homans, *Fatigue of Workers* (New York: Reinhold, 1941). For an interview with three of the participants in the relay-assembly test-room studies, see R. G. Greenwood, A. A. Bolton, and R. A. Greenwood, "Hawthorne a Half Century Later: 'Relay Assembly Participants Remember'," *Journal of Management*, vol. 9 (1983), pp. 217–31.

[17]The criticisms of the Hawthorne studies are detailed in Alex Carey, "The Hawthorne Studies: A Radical Criticism," *American Sociological Review*, vol. 32 (1967); pp. 403–16; H. M. Parsons, "What Happened at Hawthorne?" *Science*, vol. 183 (1974), pp. 922–32; B. Rice, "The Hawthorne Defect: Persistence of a Flawed Theory," *Psychology Today*, vol. 16 (1982), pp. 70–74. See also Wren, *Evolution of Management Thought*, op cit.

[18]This discussion of Maslow's theory is based on Abraham H. Maslow, *Eupsychian Management* (Homewood, IL: Richard D. Irwin, 1965), and Abraham H. Maslow, *Motivation and Personality*, 2d ed. (New York: Harper & Row, 1970).

[19]Douglas McGregor, *The Human Side of Enterprise* (New York: McGraw-Hill, 1960).

[20]See Gary Heil, Deborah F. Stevens, and Warren G. Bennis, *Douglas McGregor on Management: Revisiting the Human Side of Enterprise* (New York: Wiley, 2000).

[21]Information from "About AIMD," American Institute for Managing Diversity web site: http://www.aimd.org/about_aimd.htm.

[22]Chris Argyris, *Personalitly and Organization* (New York: Harper & Row, 1957).

[23]The ideas of Ludwig von Bertalanffy contributed to the emergence of this systems perspective on organizations. See his article, "The History and Status of General Systems Theory," *Academy of Management Journal*, vol. 15 (1972), pp. 407–26. This viewpoint is further developed by Daniel Katz and Robert L. Kahn in their classic book, *The Social Psychology of Organizations* (New York: Wiley, 1978). For an integrated systems view, see Lane Tracy, *The Living Organization* (New York: Quorum Books, 1994). For an overview, see W. Richard Scott, *Organizations: Rational, Natural, and Open Systems*, 4th ed. (Upper Saddle River, NJ: Prentice-Hall, 1998).

[24]Chester I. Barnard, *Functions of the Executive* (Cambridge, MA: Harvard University Press, 1938).

[25]See discussion by Scott, op cit. (1998), pp. 66–68.

[26]Peter F. Drucker, "The Future That has Already Happened," *Harvard Business Review*, vol. 75 (September–October 1997): pp. 20–24.

[27]For an overview, see Scott, op cit. (1998), pp. 95–97.

[28]For the classics see: See W. Edwards Deming, *Quality, Productivity, and Competitive Position* (Cambridge, MA: MIT Press, 1982); Joseph M. Juran, *Quality Control Handbook*, 3d ed. (New York: McGraw-Hill 1979).

[29]Jay R. Gailbraith, "Designing the Networked Organization: Leveraging Size and Competencies" in Susan Albers Mohrman, Jay R. Galbraith, Edward E. Lawler III and Associates, *Tomorrow's Organization: Crafting Winning Capabilities in a Dynamic World* (San Francisco: Jossey-Bass, 1998), pp. 92–94.

[30]Thomas J. Peters and Robert H. Waterman Jr., *In Search of Excellence: Lessons from America's Best-Run Companies* (New York: Harper & Row, 1982).

[31]Information from Justin Martin, "Mercedes: Made in Alabama," *Fortune* (July 7, 1997), pp. 150–58; "A Plant Grows in Alabama," *Mercedes Momentum* (Spring, 1998), pp. 56–61.

[32]William Ouchi, *Theory Z: How American Businesses Can Meet the Japanese Challenge* (Reading, MA: Addison-Wesley, 1981) and Richard Tanner Pascale and Anthony G. Athos, *The Art of Japanese Management: Applications for American Executives* (New York: Simon & Schuster, 1981).

[33]Ouchi, op cit. (1981); see also the review by J. Bernard Keys, Luther Tray Denton, and Thomas R. Miller, "The Japanese Management Theory Jungle-Revisited," *Journal of Management*, vol. 20 (1994), pp. 373–402.

[34]The classic work is Peter Senge, *The Fifth Discipline* (New York: Harper, 1990).

[35]John Gardner, *No Easy Victories* (New York: Harper & Row, 1968).

[36]Peter F. Drucker, "Looking Ahead: Implications of the Present," *Harvard Business Review*, (September–October, 1997), pp. 18–32.

[37]Quote from Ralph Z. Sorenson, "A Lifetime of Learning to Manage Effectively," *Wall Street Journal* (February 28, 1983), p. 18.

See Kemba J. Dunham, "Dot-Commers Go Where Profits Truly Don't Matter," *Wall Street Journal* (December 5, 2000), pp. B1, B2.

Chapter 5 Notes

[1]Information from "NTT DoCoMo Flies Past the Milestones," *Fortune* (July 24, 2000), advertisement; and, corporate web site: http://www.nttdocomo.com.

[2]See Kenichi Ohmae, *The Evolving Global Economy* (Cambridge, MA: Harvard Business School Press, 1995).

[3]Rosabeth Moss Kanter, *World Class: Thinking Locally in the Global Economy* (New York: Simon & Schuster, 1995), preface.

[4]For a discussion of globalization see Thomas L. Friedman, *The Lexus and the Olive Tree: Understanding Globalization* (New York: Bantam Doubleday Dell, 2000); and John Micklethwait and

Adrian Woolridge, *A Future Perfect: The Challenges and Hidden Promise of Globalization* (New York: Crown, 2000).

[5]For a discussion of issues see James H. Mittleman, *The Globalization Syndrome* (Princeton, NJ: Princeton University Press, 2000).

[6]Quote from Jeffrey E. Garten, "The Mind of the CEO," *Business Week* (February 5, 2001), p. 106.

[7]The *Economist* is a good weekly source of information on Europe. See www.economist.com.

[8]For an overview see "Europe's Mid-Life Crisis," *The Economist: A Survey of the European Union* (May 31, 1997).

[9]A monthly publication that covers the *maquiladora* industries is the *Twin Plant News* (El Paso, Texas); see web site at: http://www.twin-plant-news.com/.

[10]Joel Millman, "High-Tech Jobs Transfer to Mexico with Surprising Speed," *Wall Street Journal* (April 9, 1998), p. A18.

[11]Information from Mark Clifford and Manjeet Kripalani, "Different Countries, Adjoining Cubicles," *Business Week* (August 28, 2000), pp. 182–84.

[12]For an overview of business in China see John Studdard and James G. Shiro, *The New Silk Road: Secrets of Business Success in China Today* (New York: Wiley, 2000).

[13]Mike Pramik, "Salient's Dealings in China Illustrate Need to Prepare for Different Practices," *Columbus Dispatch* (May 4, 1998), p. 3.

[14]The *Economist* is a good weekly source of information on Africa. See www.economist.com.

[15]Quotes from Mort Rosenblum, "Turnaround: Once a Basket Case, Mozambique Now a Free-Market Example," *Columbus Dispatch* (December 14, 1997), p. 4c.

[16]Michael M. Phillips, "Into Africa," *Wall Street Journal* (September 18, 1997), pp. R6, R20.

[17]Information from Africa information web site: http://www.mbendi.co.za/orsadc.htm.

[18]James A. Austin and John G. McLean, "Pathways to Business Success in Sub-Saharan Africa," *Journal of African Finance and Economic Development*, vol. 2 (1996), pp. 57–76.

[19]Information from "International Business: Consider Africa," *Harvard Business Review*, vol. 76 (January–February 1998), pp. 16–18.

[20]See "Inside View: South Africa," *New York Times* (September 18, 2000), pp. A15–A17.

[21]IPR Strategic Business Information Database (May 21, 2000).

[22]Quote from John A. Byrne, "Visionary vs. Visionary," *Business Week* (August 28, 2000), p. 210.

[23]Quoted from "Own Words: Percy Barnevik, ABB and Investor," *Financial Times Limited*, 1998.

[24]For research discussions of privatization and transitional economies see R. Duane Ireland, Shaker A. Zahra, Isabel Gutierrez, and Michael A. Hitt (special issue editors), "Special Topic Forum on Privatization and Entrepreneurial Transformation" *Academy of Management Review*, vol. 25 (July 2000), pp. 509–669.

[25]Information from Rich Teerlink, "Harley's Leadership U-Turn," *Harvard Business Review* (March–April 2000), pp. 3–4. See also Rich Teerlink and Lee Ozley, *More Than a Motorcycle: The Leadership Journey at Harley-Davidson* (Cambridge, MA: Harvard Business School Press 2000); and corporate web site: http://www.harley-davidson.com/company/company.asp.

[26]See "Slow Healing at Mitsubishi," *Business Week* (September 22, 1997), pp. 74–75; Ben Rand, "When Cultures Clash," *Rockland Journal-News* (October 26, 1997) p. E1; "EEOC Scores Major Victory in Mitsubishi Lawsuit," U.S. Equal Employment Opportunity Commission, press release (January 21, 1998).

[27]Sylvia Ann Hewlett, "The Boundaries of Business: The Human Resource Deficit," *Harvard Business Review*, (July–August 1991), pp. 131–33. See also William B. Johnston, "Global Workforce 2000: The New World Labor Market," *Harvard Business Review*, (March–April 1991), pp. 115–27.

[28]First reported in *Business Week* (February 29, 1988), pp. 63–66; further information on corporate web site http://www.falconproducts.com/.

[29]Developed from Anthony J. F. O'Reilly, "Establishing Successful Joint Ventures in Developing Nations: A CEO's Perspective," *Columbia Journal of World Business* (spring 1988), pp. 65–71; and "Best Practices for Global Competitiveness," *Fortune* (March 30, 1998), pp. S1–S3, special advertising section.

[30]See Peter F. Drucker, "The Global Economy and the Nation-State," *Foreign Affairs*, vol. 76 (September–October 1997): 159–71.

[31]This framework is introduced in David P. Rutenberg, *Multinational Management* (Boston: Little Brown, 1982).

[32]Adapted from R. Hall Mason, "Conflicts between Host Countries and Multinational Enterprise," *California Management Review*, vol. 17 (1974), pp. 6, 7.

[33]For a good overview, see Randall E. Stross, *Bulls in the China Shop and Other Sino-American Business Encounters* (New York: Pantheon, 1991); as well as Studdard and Shapiro, op cit. (2000).

[34]For an interesting discussion of one company's experience in China see Jim Mann, *Beijing Jeep: A Case Study of Western Business in China* (Boulder, CO: Westview Press, 1997).

[35]Craig Smith, "Foreign Investors Break Free From Chinese Partners," *Wall Street Journal* (June 11, 1998), p. A17.

[36]Information from corporate web site: http://www.nikeBiz.com/labor/toc_monitoring.shtml.

[37]*New York Times*, "An Industry Monitors Child Labor" (October 16, 1997), pp. B1, B9; and Rugmark International web site: http://www.rugmark.de/english/e_home.htm.

[38]Definition from World Commission on Environment and Development, *Our Common Future* (Oxford: Oxford University Press, 1987); reported on International Institute for Sustainable Development web site: http://iisd1.iisd.ca/about/sdoverview.htm.

[39]Examples reported in Neil Chesanow, *The World-Class Executive* (New York: Rawson Associates, 1985).

[40]Based on Barbara Benedict Bunker, "Appreciating Diversity and Modifying Organizational Cultures: Men and Women at Work," in Suresh Srivastiva and David L. Cooperrider, *Appreciative Management and Leadership: The Power of Positive Thought and Action in Organizations* (San Francisco: Jossey-Bass, 1990), pp. 127–49.

[41]For a good overview of the practical issues, see Philip R. Harris and Robert T. Moran, *Managing Cultural Differences*, 2d ed. (Houston: Gulf Publishing, 1987); and Martin J. Gannon, *Understanding Global Cultures* (Thousand Oaks, CA: Sage, 1994).

[42]Information from Ronald B. Lieber, "Flying High, Going Global," *Fortune* (July 7, 1997), pp. 195–97.

[43]See Gary P. Ferraro, "The Need for Linguistic Proficiency in Global Business," *Business Horizons* (May–June 1996), pp. 39–46; quote from Carol Hymowitz, "Companies Go Global, But Many Managers Just Don't Travel Well," *Wall Street Journal* (August 15, 2000), p. B1.

[44]Edward T. Hall, *Beyond Culture* (New York: Doubleday, 1976).

[45]Edward T. Hall, *The Silent Language* (New York: Anchor Books, 1959); *The Hidden Dimension* (New York: Anchor Books, 1969).

[46]Hall, op cit., *The Silent Language*.

[47]Lady Borton, "Learning to Work with Viet Nam," *The Academy of Management Executive*, vol. 14 (December 2000), pp. 20–31.

[48]Edward T. Hall, *Hidden Differences* (New York: Doubleday, 1990).

[49]Both examples from Carol Hymowitz, "Companies Go Global, But Many Managers Just Don't Travel Well," *Wall Street Journal* (August 15, 2000), p. B1.

[50]Geert Hofstede *Culture's Consequences* (Beverly Hills: Sage, 1984). Hofstede and Michael H. Bond further explore Eastern and Western perspectives on national culture in their article "The Confucius Connection: From Cultural Roots to Economic Growth," *Organizational Dynamics*, vol. 16 (1988), pp. 4–21, which presents comparative data from Bond's "Chinese Values Survey."

[51]For an introduction to the fifth dimension, see Hofstede and Bond, "The Confucious Connection."

[52]Michael Schuman, "How Interbew Blended Disparate Ingredients in Korean Beer Venture," *Wall Street Journal* (July 24, 2000), pp. A1, A6.

[53]Fons Trompenaars, *Riding the Waves of Culture: Understanding Cultural Diversity in Business* (London: Nicholas Brealey Publishing, 1993).

[54]See Robert B. Reich, "Who Is Them?" *Harvard Business Review*, (March–April 1991), pp. 77–88.

[55]"Going International: Willett Systems Limited," *Fortune* (February 16, 1998), p. S6, special advertising section.

[56]Mark Clifford and Majeet Kripalani, "Different Countries, Adjoining Cubicles," *Business Week* (August 28, 2000), pp. 182–84.

[57]For a perspective on the role of women in expatriate managerial assignments, see Marianne Jelinek and Nancy J. Adler, "Women: World-Class Managers for Global Competition," *Academy of Management Executive* (February 1988), pp. 11–19; for a discussion of the globalization of management careers, see Lancaster, op cit. (1998).

[58]Information from Peter Wonacott, "Wal-Mart Finds Market Footing in China," *Wall Street Journal* (July 17, 2000), p. A31; and corporate web site: http://www.walmartstores.com /corporate/coinfo_international.html.

[59]Information from Gail Edmondson, "See the World, Erase its Borders," *Business Week* (August 28, 2000), pp. 113–14.

[60]Geert Hofstede, "Motivation, Leadership, and Organization," p. 43. See also Hofstede's "Cultural Constraints in Management Theories," *Academy of Management Review*, vol. 7 (1993), pp. 81–94.

[61]The classics are William Ouchi, *Theory Z: How American Businesses Can Meet the Japanese Challenge* (Reading, MA: Addison-Wesley, 1981) and Richard Tanner Pascale and Anthony G. Athos, *The Art of Japanese Management: Applications for American Executives* (New York: Simon & Schuster, 1981).

[62]For a good discussion, see Chapters 4 and 5 in Miriam Erez and P. Christopher Early, *Culture, Self-Identity, and Work* (New York: Oxford University Press, 1993).

[63]J. Bernard Keys, Luther Tray Denton, and Thomas R. Miller, "The Japanese Management Theory Jungle—Revisited," *Journal of Management*, vol. 20 (1994), pp. 373–402.

[64]See Yumiko Ono and Bill Spindle, "Standing Alone: Japan's Long Decline Makes One Thing Rise—Individualism," *Wall Street Journal* (December 29, 2000), pp. A1, A4.

[65]Quote from Kenichi Ohmae, "Japan's Admiration for U.S. Methods Is an Open Book," *Wall Street Journal* (October 10, 1983), p. 21. See also his book *The Borderless World: Power and Strategy in the Interlinked Economy*, op cit. (1989).

[66]Geert Hofstede, "A Reply to Goodstein and Hunt," *Organizational Dynamics*, vol. 10 (summer 1981); pp. 68.

Chapter 6 Notes

[1]Information from *Philanthropy News Digest*, vol. 5 (April 21, 1999); Jim Carlton, "Environmentalists to Fight Globalization," *Wall Street Journal* (July 17, 2000), p. A2; and Goldman Foundation web site: http://www.goldmanprize .org/.

[2]See Joel Makower, *Beyond the Bottom Line: Putting Social Responsibility to Work for Your Business and the World* (New York: Simon & Schuster, 1994).

[3]See a variety of information at Business for Social Responsibility web site: http://www.bsr.org/resourcecenter /index.html.

[4]Information and quotes from "The Socially Correct Corporate," *Fortune* special advertising section (July 24, 2000), pp. S32–S34.

[5]See "Quad/Graphics's Environmental Philosophy," corporate document (Pewaukee, WI: Quad/Graphics, 1998); information on corporate web site: http://www.qg.com/.

[6]Reported in Adam Smith, "Wall Street's Outrageous Fortunes," *Esquire* (April 1987), p. 73.

[7]Desmond Tutu, "Do More Than Win," *Fortune* (December 30, 1991), p. 59.

[8]For an overview, see Francis Joseph Aguilar, *Managing Corporate Ethics: Learning from America's Ethical Companies How to Supercharge Business Performance* (New York: Oxford, 1994); and Linda K. Trevino and Katherine A. Nelson, *Managing Business Ethics* (New York: Wiley, 1995).

[9]Trevino and Nelson, op cit., p. 15.

[10]Tom Chappell, *The Soul of a Business: Managing for Profit and for the Common Good* (New York: Bantam Books, 1993); and information from corporate web site: http://www.tomsofmaine.com/mission/stewardship_content.htm.

[11]See Gerald F. Cavanagh, Dennis J. Moberg, and Manuel Velasquez, "The Ethics of Organizational Politics," *Academy of Management Review*, vol. 6 (1981), pp. 363–74; Justin G. Locknecker, Joseph A. McKinney, and Carlos W. Moore, "Egoism and Independence: Entrepreneurial Ethics," *Organizational Dynamics* (winter 1988), pp. 64–72; Justin G. Locknecker, Joseph A. McKinney, and Carlos W. Moore, "The Generation Gap in Business Ethics," *Business Horizons* (September–October 1989), pp. 9–14.

[12]Raymond L. Hilgert, "What Ever Happened to Ethics in Business and in Business Schools," *The Diary of Alpha Kappa Psi* (April 1989), pp. 4–8.

[13]Jerald Greenburg, "Organizational Justice: Yesterday, Today, and Tomorrow," vol. 16 *Journal of Management*, pp. 399–432; and Mary A. Konovsky, "Understanding Procedural Justice and its Impact on Business Organizations," vol. 26 (2000), *Journal of Management*, pp. 489–511.

[14]Interactional justice is described by Robert J. Bies, "The Predicament of Injustice: The Management of Moral Outrage," in L. L. Cummings & B. M. Staw (eds.), *Research in Organizational Behavior*, vol. 9 (Greenwich, CT: JAI Press, 1987), pp. 289–319. The example is from Carol T. Kulik & Robert L. Holbrook, "Demographics in Service Encounters: Effects of Racial and Gender Congruence on Perceived Fairness," *Social Justice Research* (in press).

[15]Robert D. Haas, "Ethics—A Global Business Challenge," *Vital Speeches of the Day* (June 1, 1996), pp. 506–9.

[16]Thomas Donaldson, "Values in Tension: Ethics Away from Home," *Harvard Business Review,* vol. 74 (September October 1996); pp. 48–62.

[17]Thomas Donaldson and Thomas W. Dunfee, "Towards a Unified Conception of Business Ethics: Integrative Social Contracts Theory," *Academy of Management Review,* vol. 19 (1994), pp. 252–85.

[18]Developed from Donaldson, op cit.

[19]Reported in Barbara Ley Toffler, "Tough Choices: Managers Talk Ethics," *New Management,* vol. 4 (1987), pp. 34–39. See also Barbara Ley Toffler, *Tough Choices: Managers Talk Ethics* (New York: Wiley, 1986).

[20]See discussion by Trevino and Nelson, op cit., pp. 47–62.

[21]Information and the following case from Steven N. Brenner and Earl A. Mollander, "Is the Ethics of Business Changing?" *Harvard Business Review,* vol. 55 (January–February 1977).

[22]Saul W. Gellerman, "Why 'Good' Managers Make Bad Ethical Choices," *Harvard Business Review,* vol. 64 (July–August, 1986), pp. 85–90.

[23]Information from Thomas Teal, "Not a Fool, Not a Saint," *Fortune* (November 11, 1996), pp. 201–4; quote from Shelley Donald Coolidge, *The Christian Science Monitor* (March 28, 1996).

[24]The Body Shop came under scrutiny over the degree to which its business practices actually live up to this charter and the company's self-promoted green image. See, for example, John Entine, "Shattered Image," *Business Ethics* (September–October 1994), pp. 23–28.

[25]Information on this case from William M. Carley, "Antitrust Chief Says CEOs Should Tape all Phone Calls to Each Other," *Wall Street Journal* (February 15, 1983), p. 23; "American Air, Chief End Antitrust Suit, Agree Not to Discuss Fares with Rivals," *Wall Street Journal* (July 15, 1985), p. 4; "American Airlines Loses Its Pilot," *Economist* (April 18, 1998), p. 58.

[26]Alan L. Otten, "Ethics on the Job: Companies Alert Employees to Potential Dilemmas," *Wall Street Journal* (July 14, 1986), p. 17; and "The Business Ethics Debate," *Newsweek* (May 25, 1987), p. 36.

[27]See "Whistle-Blowers on Trial," *Business Week* (March 24, 1997), pp. 172–78; "NLRB Judge Rules for Massachusetts Nurses in Whistle-Blowing Case," *American Nurse* (January–February 1998), p. 7.

[28]For a review of whistleblowing, see Marcia P. Micelli and Janet P. Near, *Blowing the Whistle* (Lexington, MA: Lexington Books, 1992); see also Micelli and Near, "Whistleblowing: Reaping the Benefits," *Academy of Management Executive,* vol. 8 (August 1994); pp. 65–72.

[29]Information from James A. Waters, "Catch 20.5: Mortality as an Organizational Phenomenon," *Organizational Dynamics,* vol. 6 (spring 1978), pp. 3–15.

[30]Robert D. Gilbreath, "The Hollow Executive," *New Management,* vol. 4 (1987); pp. 24–28.

[31]Information from "Gifts of Gab: A Start-up's Social Conscience Pays Off," *Business Week* (February 5, 2001), p. F38.

[32]Developed from recommendations of the Government Accountability Project reported in "Blowing the Whistle without Paying the Piper."

[33]All reported in Charles D. Pringle and Justin G. Longnecker, "The Ethics of MBO," *Academy of Management Review,* vol. 7 (April 1982), pp. 309. See also Barry Z. Posner and Warren H. Schmidt, "Values and the American Manager: An Update," *California Management Review,* vol. 26 (spring 1984), pp. 202–16.

[34]Information from corporate web site: http://www.gapinc.com/community /sourcing/vendor_conduct.htm.

[35]Information from the UN web site: http://www.un.org/partners/business /fs1.htm.

[36]See Thomas Donaldson and Lee Preston, "The Stakeholder Theory of the Corporation," *Academy of Management Review,* vol. 20 (January 1995), pp. 65–91.

[37]For a good review see Robert H. Miles, *Managing the Corporate Social Environment* (Englewood Cliffs, NJ: 1987).

[38]Information from "The Socially Correct Corporate," *Fortune* special advertising section (July 24, 2000), pp. S32–S34; David Kirkpatrick, "Looking for Profits in Poverty," *Fortune* (February 5, 2001), pp. 174–76.

[39]Developed from a discussion in Makower, *Beyond the Bottom Line,* pp. 17–18.

[40]The historical framework of this discussion is developed from Keith Davis, "The Case for and against Business Assumption of Social Responsibility," *Academy of Management Journal* (June 1973), pp. 312–22; Keith Davis and William Frederick, *Business and Society: Management: Public Policy, Ethics,* 5th ed. (New York: McGraw-Hill, 1984). The debate is also discussed by Makower, *Beyond the Bottom Line,* pp. 28–33. See also, "Civics 101," *Economist* (May 11, 1996), p. 61.

[41]The Friedman quotation is from Milton Friedman, *Capitalism and Freedom* (Chicago: University of Chicago Press, 1962); the Samuelson quotation is from Paul A. Samuelson, "Love That Corporation," *Mountain Bell Magazine* (spring 1971). Both are cited in Davis, "The Case for and Against."

[42]Davis and Frederick, *Business and Society.*

[43]Quote from corporate web site: http://www.tomsofmaine.com/.

[44]See Makower, op cit. (1994), pp. 71–75; and Sandra A. Waddock and Samuel B. Graves, "The Corporate Social Performance-Financial Performance Link," *Strategic Management Journal* (1997), pp. 303–19.

[45]Davis, op cit.

[46]Archie B. Carroll, "A Three-Dimensional Model of Corporate Performance," *Academy of Management Review,* vol. 4 (1979), pp. 497–505.

[47]Elizabeth Gatewood and Archie B. Carroll, "The Anatomy of Corporate Social Response," *Business Horizons,* vol. 24 (September–October 1981), pp. 9–16.

[48]For the other side of this issue and the support available through government sources for small businesses, see "When Bureaucrats Are a Boon," *Business Week,* Enterprise issue (September 1, 1997), pp. ENT 4–6.

Information from The Global Social Responsibility Resource Center, Business for Social Responsibility web site: http://www.bsr.org/resourcecenter /index.html.

Chapter 7 Notes

[1]Information and quotes from Cheryl Dahle, "Used Cars, New Model," *Fast Company* (July 2000), pp. 316–26. See also www.manheim.com.

[2]Quote from "Today's Companies Won't Make It, and Gary Hamel Knows Why," *Fortune* (September 4, 2000), p. 386–387.

[3]Gary Hamel, *Leading the Revolution* (Boston: Harvard Business School Press, 2000).

[4]Quotes in this section from T. J. Rodgers, with William Taylor and Rick Foreman, "No Excuses Management," *World Executive's Digest* (May 1994) pp. 26–30; see also corporate web site: http://www.cypress.com/corporate /index.html.

[5]Quote from 1985 Eaton Corporation Annual Report.

[6]Henry Mintzberg, "The Manager's Job: Folklore and Fact," *Harvard Business Review*, vol. 53 (July–August 1975), pp. 54–67; Henry Mintzberg, "Planning on the Left Side and Managing on the Right," *Harvard Business Review*, vol. 54 (July–August 1976), pp. 46–55.

[7]Quote from Stephen Covey and Roger Merrill, "New Ways to Get Organized at Work," *USA Weekend* (February 6–8, 1998), p. 18. Books by Stephen R. Covey include: *The 7 Habits of Highly Effective People: Powerful Lessons in Personal Change* (New York: Fireside, 1990), and Stephen R. Covey and Sandra Merril Covey, *The 7 Habits of Highly Effective Families: Building a Beautiful Family Culture in a Turbulent World* (New York: Golden Books, 1996).

[8]For a classic study, see Stanley Thune and Robert House, "Where Long-Range Planning Pays Off," *Business Horizons*, vol. 13 (1970), pp. 81–87. For a critical review of the literature, see Milton Leontiades and Ahmet Teel, "Planning Perceptions and Planning Results," *Strategic Management Journal*, vol. 1 (1980), pp. 65–75; J. Scott Armstrong, "The Value of Formal Planning for Strategic Decisions," *Strategic Management Journal*, vol. 3 (1982), pp. 197–211. For special attention to the small business setting, see Richard B. Robinson Jr., John A. Pearce II, George S. Vozikis, and Timothy S. Mescon, "The Relationship between Stage of Development and Small Firm Planning and Performance," *Journal of Small Business Management*, vol. 22 (1984), pp. 45–52; Christopher Orphen, "The Effects of Long-Range Planning on Small Business Performance: A Further Examination," *Journal of Small Business Management*, vol. 23 (1985), pp. 16–23. For an empirical study of large corporations, see Vasudevan Ramanujam and N. Venkatraman, "Planning and Performance: A New Look at an Old Question," *Business Horizons*, vol. 30 (1987), pp. 19–25.

[9]Quotes from *Business Week* (August 8, 1994), pp. 78–86.

[10]See William Oncken Jr. and Donald L. Wass, "Management Time: Who's Got the Monkey?" *Harvard Business Review*, vol. 52 (September–October 1974), 75–80, and featured as an HBR classic, *Harvard Business Review*, (November–December 1999).

[11]Covey and Merrill, "New Ways to Get Organized," op cit., p. 18.

[12]Information from Thomas Petzinger Jr., "How a Ski Maker on a Slippery Slope Regained Control," *Wall Street Journal* (October 3, 1997), p. 3; see also corporate web site: www.volantsports.com.

[13]See Elliot Jaques, *The Form of Time* (New York: Russak & Co., 1982). For an executive commentary on his research, see Walter Kiechel III, "How Executives Think," *Fortune* (December 21, 1987), pp. 139–44.

[14]See Henry Mintzberg, "Rounding Out the Manager's Job," *Sloan Management Review* (fall 1994), pp. 1–25.

[15]Information from "Avoiding a Time Bomb: Sexual Harassment," *Business Week*. Enterprise issue (October 13, 1997), pp. ENT20–21.

[16]For a thorough review of forecasting, see J. Scott Armstrong, *Long-Range Forecasting*, 2d ed. (New York: Wiley, 1985).

[17]Information from Linda Grant, "GE's 'Smart Bomb' Strategy," *Fortune* (July 21, 1997), pp. 109–10.

[18]The scenario-planning approach is described in Peter Schwartz, *The Art of the Long View* (New York: Doubleday/Currency, 1991); and Arie de Geus, *The Living Company: Habits for Survival in a Turbulent Business Environment* (Boston, MA: Harvard Business School Press, 1997).

[19]Information from Schwartz, *The Art of the Long View*, and de Geus, *The Living Company*, op cit.; see also corporate web site: http://www.shell.com/royal-en/directory/0,5029,25414,00.html.

[20]See, for example, Robert C. Camp, *Business Process Benchmarking* (Milwaukee: ASQ Quality Press 1994); Michael J. Spendolini, *The Benchmarking Book* (New York: AMACOM, 1992); and Christopher E. Bogan and Michael J. English, *Benchmarking for Best Practices: Winning Through Innovative Adaptation* (New York: McGraw-Hill, 1994).

[21]"How Classy Can 7-Eleven Get?" *Business Week* (September 1, 1997), pp. 74–75; and, Kellie B. Gormly, "7-Eleven Moving Up a Grade," *Columbus Dispatch* (August 3, 2000), pp. C1–C2.

[22]Information from Loirraine Kee, "Adam's Mark Report Stirs Controversy in Group that Made Study," *St. Louis Post Dispatch* (July 29, 2000), p. 8; and, "Department of Justice Asks Project Equality to Insure Adam's Mark's Compliance," Project Equality news release (March 22, 2000).

[23]"The Renewal Factor: Friendly Fact, Congenial Controls," *Business Week* (September 14, 1987), p. 105.

[24]Information from Leon E. Wynter, "Allstate Rates Managers on Handling Diversity," *Wall Street Journal* (October 1, 1997), p. B1.

[25]Information from Raju Narisetti, "For IBM, a Groundbreaking Sales Chief," *Wall Street Journal*, (January 19, 1998), pp. B1, B5.

[26]Toddi Gutner, "Better Your Business: Benchmark It," *Business Week*, Enterprise issue (April 27, 1998), pp. ENT4–6.

[27]Rob Cross and Lloyd Baird, "Technology Is Not Enough: Improving Performance by Building Institutional Memory," *Sloan Management Review* (Spring 2000), p. 73.

[28]Based on discussion by Harold Koontz and Cyril O'Donnell, *Essentials of Management* (New York: McGraw-Hill, 1974), pp. 362–65; see also Rob Cross and Lloyd Baird, "Technology is Not Enough: Improving Performance by Building Organizational Memory," *Sloan Management Review* (Spring 2000), pp. 69–78.

[29]See John F. Love, *McDonald's: Behind the Arches* (New York: Bantam Books, 1986); Ray Kroc and Robert Anderson, *Grinding It Out: The Making of McDonald's* (New York: St. Martin's Press, 1990).

[30]Information from Louis Lee, "I'm Proud of What I've Made Myself Into—What I've Created," *Wall Street Journal* (August 27, 1997), pp. B1, B5.

[31]Douglas McGregor, *The Human Side of Enterprise* (New York: McGraw-Hill, 1960).

[32]Cited in Peter F. Drucker, *Management: Tasks, Responsibilities, and Practices* (New York: Harper & Row, 1973), p. 797.

[33]Eric L. Harvey, "Discipline vs. Punishment," *Management Review*, vol. 76 (March 1987); pp. 25–29.

[34]The "hot stove rules" are developed from R. Bruch McAfee and William Poffenberger, *Productivity Strategies: Enhancing Employee Job Performance* (Englewood Cliffs, NJ: Prentice-Hall, 1982), pp. 54–55. They are originally attributed to Douglas McGregor, "Hot Stove Rules of Discipline," in *Personnel: The Human Problems of Management*, G. Strauss and L. Sayles, eds. (Englewood Cliffs, NJ: Prentice-Hall, 1967).

[35]Information from Karen Carney, "Successful Performance Measurement: A Checklist," *Harvard Management Update* (No. U9911B), 1999.

[36]See Dale D. McConkey, *How to Manage by Results*, 3d ed. (New York: AMACOM, 1976); Stephen J. Carroll Jr. and Henry J. Tosi Jr., *Management by Objectives: Applications and Research*

(New York: Macmillan, 1973); and Anthony P. Raia, *Managing by Objectives* (Glenview, IL: Scott, Foresman, 1974).

[37]Douglas McGregor, *The Human Side of Enterprise* (New York: McGraw-Hill, 1960).

[38]The work on goal setting and motivation is summarized in Edwin A. Locke and Gary P. Latham, *Goal Setting: A Motivational Technique That Works!* (Englewood Cliffs, NJ: Prentice-Hall, 1984).

[39]For a discussion of research, see Carroll and Tosi, *Management by Objectives* (1973); Raia, *Managing by Objectives* (1974); Steven Kerr, "Overcoming the Dysfunctions of MBO," *Management by Objectives*, vol. 5, no. 1 (1976). Information in part from Dylan Loeb McClain, "Job Forecast: Internet's Still Hot," *New York Times* (January 30, 2001), p. 9.

Chapter 8 Notes

[1]Information from "Starbucks: Making Values Pay," *Fortune* (September 29, 1997), pp. 261–72; Howard Schultz and Dori Jones Yang, *Pour Your Heart Into It* (San Francisco: Hyperion, 1997); and corporate web site: www.starbucks.com.

[2]Keith H. Hammond, "Michael Porter's Big Ideas," *Fast Company* (March 2001), pp. 150–56.

[3]Gary Hamel and C. K. Prahalad, "Strategic Intent," *Harvard Business Review* (May–June, 1989), pp. 63–76.

[4]Information and quotes from Marcia Stepanek, "How Fast Is Net Fast?" *Business Week E-Biz* (November 1, 1999), pp. EB52–EB54.

[5]For research support, see Daniel H. Gray, "Uses and Misuses of Strategic Planning," *Harvard Business Review*, vol. 64 (January–February 1986), pp. 89–97.

[6]Hammond, op cit., p. 153.

[7]Michael A. Hitt, R. Duane Ireland, and Robert E. Hoskisson, *Strategic Management: Competitiveness and Globalization* (Minneapolis: West, 1997), p. 5.

[8]See Michael E. Porter, *Competitive Strategy: Techniques for Analyzing Industries and Competitors* (New York: Free Press, 1980), and *Competitive Advantage: Creating and Sustaining Superior Performance* (New York: Free Press, 1986); and Richard A. D'Aveni, *Hyper Competition: Managing the Dynamics of Strategic Maneuvering* (New York: Free Press, 1994).

[9]D'Aveni, op cit.

[10]Example from "Memorable Memo: McDonald's Sends Operators to War on Fries," *Wall Street Journal*, (December 18, 1997), p. B1.

[11]Peter F. Drucker, "Five Questions," *Executive Excellence* (November 6, 1994), pp. 6–7.

[12]Peter F. Drucker, *Management: Tasks, Responsibilities, Practices* (New York: Harper & Row, 1973), p. 122.

[13]Ibid.

[14]See Laura Nash, "Mission Statements—Mirrors and Windows," *Harvard Business Review* (March–April 1988), pp. 155–56. James C. Collins and Jerry I. Porras, "Building Your Company's Vision," *Harvard Business Review* (September–October 1996), pp. 65–77; James C. Collins and Jerry I. Porras, *Built to Last: Successful Habits of Visionary Companies* (New York: Harper Business, 1997).

[15]Gary Hamel, *Leading the Revolution* (Boston, MA: Harvard Business School Press, 2000), pp. 72–73.

[16]Information from corporate web site: http://www.merck.com/overview /philosophy.html.

[17]Terrence E. Deal and Allen A. Kennedy, *Corporate Cultures: The Rites and Rituals of Corporate Life* (Reading, MA: Addison-Wesley, 1982), p. 22. For more on organizational culture see Edgar H. Schein, *Organizational Culture and Leadership*, 2d ed. (San Francisco: Jossey-Bass, 1997).

[18]Information from corporate web site: http://store.nordstrom.com/content /pub/aboutus/diversity/mission_ statement.asp.

[19]Peter F. Drucker's views on organizational objectives are expressed in his classic books, *The Practice of Management* (New York: Harper & Row, 1954); and *Management: Tasks, Responsibilities, Practices* (New York: Harper & Row, 1973). For a more recent commentary, see his article, "Management: The Problems of Success," *Academy of Management Executive*, vol. 1 (1987), pp. 13–19.

[20]C. K. Prahalad and Gary Hamel, "The Core Competencies of the Corporation," *Harvard Business Review* (May–June 1990), pp. 79–91; see also, Hitt, et al., op. cit., pp. 99–103.

[21]For a discussion of Michael Porter's approach to strategic planning, see his books *Competitive Strategy* and *Competitive Advantage*; his article, "What Is Strategy?" *Harvard Business Review* (November–December, 1996), pp. 61–78; and Richard M. Hodgetts' interview "A Conversation with Michael E. Porter: A Significant Extension Toward Operational Improvement and Positioning," *Organizational Dynamics* (summer 1999), pp. 24–33.

[22]See the discussion by Hitt, et al., op cit., pp. 66–67.

[23]The four grand strategies were originally described by William F. Glueck, *Business Policy: Strategy Formulation and Management Action*, 2d ed. (New York: McGraw-Hill, 1976).

[24]Hitt, et al., op. cit., p. 197.

[25]See William McKinley, Carol M. Sanchez and A.G. Schick, "Organizational Downsizing: Constraining, Cloning, Learning," *Academy of Management Executive*, vol. 9 (August 1995), pp. 32–44.

[26]Kim S. Cameron, Sara J. Freeman, and A. K. Mishra, "Best Practices in White-Collar Downsizing: Managing Contradictions," *Academy of Management Executive*, vol. 4 (August 1991), pp. 57–73.

[27]Kayte VanScoy, "Can the Internet Hot-Wire P & G?" *Smart Business* (January 2001), pp. 69–79; Matt Murray, "As Huge Companies Keep Growing, CEOs Struggle to Keep Pace," *Wall Street Journal* (February 8, 2001), pp. A1, A6.

[28]Information from Michael Rappa, *Business Models on the Web* (www.ecommerce.ncsu.edu/business_ models.html, February 6, 2001).

[29]D'Aveni, *Hyper-Competition*, op cit., pp. 13–16, 21–24.

[30]Ibid.

[31]Ibid.

[32]See the discussion in Thomas L. Wheelen and J. David Hunger, *Strategic Management & Business Policy*, 7th ed. (Upper Saddle River, NJ: Prentice-Hall, 2000), pp. 133–147.

[33]Porter, op cit., 1980, 1986, 1996.

[34]Information from www.polo.com.

[35]Information from Suzanne Steel, "Quality in Bloom," *Business Today* (August 22, 1994), pp. 1–2.

[36]See George V. Potts, "Exploit Your Product's Life Cycle," *Harvard Business Review* (September–October 1988), pp. 32–36.

[37]Richard G. Hammermesh, "Making Planning Strategic," *Harvard Business Review*, vol. 64 (July–August 1986), pp. 115–120; Richard G. Hammermesh, *Making Strategy Work* (New York: Wiley, 1986).

[38]See Gerald B. Allan, "A Note on the Boston Consulting Group Concept of Competitive Analysis and Corporate Strategy," Harvard Business School, Intercollegiate Case Clearing House, ICCH9-175-175 (Boston: Harvard Business School, June 1976).

[39]Hammermesh, op cit. (1986).

[40]The adaptive model is described in Raymond E. Miles and Charles C.

Snow's book, *Organizational Strategy, Structure, and Process* (New York: McGraw-Hill, 1978); and their articles, "Designing Strategic Human Resources Systems," *Organizational Dynamics*, vol. 13 (summer 1984), pp. 36–52, and "Fit, Failure, and the Hall of Fame," *California Management Review*, vol. 26 (spring 1984), pp. 10–28.

[41]James Brian Quinn, "Strategic Change: Logical Incrementalism," *Sloan Management Review*, vol. 20 (fall 1978), pp. 7–21.

[42]Henry Mintzberg, *The Nature of Managerial Work* (New York: Harper & Row, 1973); John R. P. Kotter, *The General Manager*s (New York: Free Press, 1982).

[43]Henry Mintzberg, "Planning on the Left Side and Managing on the Right," *Business Review*, vol. 54 (July–August 1976), pp. 46–55; Henry Mintzberg and James A. Waters, "Of Strategies, Deliberate and Emergent," *Strategic Management Journal*, vol. 6 (1985), pp. 257–72; Henry Mintzberg, "Crafting Strategy," *Harvard Business Review*, vol. 65 (July–August 1987), pp. 66–75.

[44]For research support, see Daniel H. Gray, "Uses and Misuses of Strategic Planning," *Harvard Business Review*, vol. 64 (January–February 1986), pp. 89–97.

[45]For a discussion of corporate governance issues, see Hugh Sherman and Rajeswararao Chaganti, *Corporate Governance and the Timeliness of Change* (Westport, CT: Quorum Books, 1998).

[46]See R. Duane Ireland and Michael A. Hitt, "Achieving and Maintaining Strategic Competitiveness in the 21st Century," *Academy of Management Executive*, vol. 13 (1999), pp. 43–57.

[47]Murray, op cit., p. A6.

[48]Jon R. Katzenbach, "The Myth of the Top Management Team," *Harvard Business Review* (November–December 1997), pp. 82–91.

[49]Murray, op cit., p. A6.

[50]Hammond, op cit.

[51]Murray, op cit., p. A6.

Information from Arlene Weintraub, "He's Not Playing," *Business Week E.Biz* (July 24, 2000), pp. E92–E96; Paul C. Judge, "Internet Strategies that Work," *Fast Company* (March 2001), pp. 169–78.

Chapter 9 Notes

[1]Information from "Women Business Owners Receive First-Ever Micro Loans Via the Internet," *Business Wire* (August 9, 2000); Jim Hopkins, "Non-Profit Loan Group Takes Risks on Women in Business," *USA Today* (August 9, 2000), p. 2B; "Women's Group Grants First Loans to Entrepreneurs," *The Columbus Dispatch* (August 10, 2000), p. B2.

[2]Speech at the Lloyd Greif Center for Entrepreneurial Studies, Marshall School of Business, University of Southern California, 1996.

[3]Information from the corporate web sites and from The Entrepreneur's Hall of Fame: http://www.ltbn.com/hallof fame.html.

[4]For a review and discussion of the entrepreneurial mind see Jeffry A. Timmons, *New Venture Creation: Entrepreneurship for the 21st Century* (New York: Irwin/McGraw-Hill, 1999), pp. 219–25.

[5]See the review by Robert D. Hisrich and Michael P. Peters, *Entrepreneurship*, 4th ed. (New York: Irwin/McGraw-Hill, 1998), pp. 67–70.

[6]Based on research summarized by Hisrich and Peters, op. cit. pp. 70–74.

[7]Information from Jim Hopkins, "Serial Entrepreneur Strikes Again at Age 70," *USA Today* (August 15, 2000).

[8]Timothy Butler and James Waldroop, "Job Sculpting: The Art of Retaining Your Best People," *Harvard Business Review* (September–October 1999), pp. 144–52.

[9]Hopkins, op cit.

[10]This list is developed from Timmons, op. cit, pp. 47–48; and Hisrich and Peters, op. cit., pp. 67–70.

[11]Data from *Paths to Entrepreneurship: New Directions for Women in Business* (New York: Catalyst, 1998) as summarized on the National Foundation for Women Business Owners web site: http://www.nfwbo.org/key.html.

[12]National Foundation for Women Business Owners, *Women Business Owners of Color: Challenges and Accomplishments* (1998).

[13]"New Report of Growth of Minority-Owned Businesses," news release SBA 99-16 *ADVO* (April 15, 1999).

[14]*The Facts About Small Business 1999* (Washington, DC: U.S. Small Business Administration, Office of Advocacy).

[15]Information from "Got Spanish?" *Business Week Frontier* (August 14, 2000), p. F12; and, "Cultivating Creativity," interview by National Association of Female Executives (August 2000): http://www.nafe.com/.

[16]See U.S. Small Business Administration web site: www.sba.gov.

[17]*SBA Business Answer Card 1998*, (Washington, DC: SBA Office of Advocacy).

[18]"Small Business Expansions in Electronic Commerce," U.S. Small Business Administration, Office of Advocacy (June 2000).

[19]Information from Will Christensen, "Rod Spencer's Sports-Card Business has Migrated Cyberspace Marketplace," *Columbus Dispatch* (July 24, 2000), p. F1.

[20]Information from Lisa Bertagnoli, ".Com Moms: Dream of Being Your Own Boss?" *Working Mother* (August 7, 2000).

[21]Information from Kevin Ferguson, "To B2B or Not B2B," *Business Week Frontier* (August 14, 2000), pp. F36–F42.

[22]Information from Joseph Pereira, "Leaving the Office," *Wall Street Journal* (July 17, 2000), p. R18; corporate web site: http://www.corporate.onvia.com/; and corporate communication (November 28, 2000).

[23]See "Join the Globetrotters: More Small Businesses are Hustling to Export," *Business Week Frontier* (November 8, 1999), p. F10.

[24]Information from Scott Williams, "Program to Help Firms Enter the Internet Marketplace," *Hispanic Business* (August 2000); and information on the program web site: http://www.usmcoc.org/wiringdescription.html.

[25]Data reported by The Family Firm Institute: http://ffi.org/looking/factsfb.html.

[26]Conversation from the case "Am I my Uncle's Keeper?" by Paul I. Karofsky (Northeastern University Center for Family Business) and published at: http://www.fambiz.com/contprov.cfm?ContProvCode=NECFB&ID=140.

[27]*Survey of Small and Mid-Sized Businesses: Trends for 2000* (Arthur Andersen, 2000).

[28]Ibid.

[29]Based on Norman M. Scarborough and Thomas W. Zimmerer, *Effective Small Business Management* (Englewood Cliffs, NJ: Prentice-Hall, 2000), pp. 25–30; and Scott Clark, "Most Small-Business Failures Tied to Poor Management," *Business Journal* (April 10, 2000).

[30]See, for example, John L. Nesheim, *High Tech Start Up* (New York: Free Press, 2000).

[31]Developed from William S. Sahlman, "How to Write a Great Business Plan," *Harvard Business Review*, (July–August 1997), pp. 98–108.

[32]Discussion based on "The Life Cycle of Entrepreneurial Firms," in Ricky Griffin, *Management*, 6th ed. (New York: Houghton Mifflin, 1999), pp. 309–310; and Neil C. Churchill and Virginia L. Lewis, "The Five Stages of Small Business Growth," *Harvard Busi-*

ness Review, (May–June 1993), pp. 30–50.

[33]See Ibid.; Linda Pinson and Jerry Jinnett, *Anatomy of a Business Plan: A Step-By-Step Guide to Starting Smart, Building the Business, and Securing Your Company's Future*, 4th ed. (Dearborn Trade, 1999).

[34]Marcia H. Pounds, "Business Plan Sets Course for Growth," *Columbus Dispatch* (March 16, 1998), p. 9; see also firm web site: http://www.calcustoms.com/.

[35]Paul Reynolds, "The Truth about Start-Ups," *Inc.* (February 1995), p. 23.

[36]Standard components of business plans are described in many text sources such as Pinson and Jinnett, op. cit. (1999), and Scarborough and Zimmerer, op. cit. (2000); and on web sites such as: American Express Small Business Services, Business Town .com, and BizPlanIt.com.

[37]See James D. Krasner and Michel Soignet, "Strategic Vision Drives Domino's Pizza Distribution," *Logistics Management* (Spring 1997) and available at http://www.manufacturing.net/ magazine/logistic/archives/1997/scmr/ 11pizza.htm; quotes from the corporate web site: www.dominos.com.

[38]"You've Come a Long Way Baby," *Business Week Frontier* (July 10, 2000).

[39]Information from Kevin Ferguson, "Nothing Ventured," *Business Week Frontier* (July 10, 2000), pp. F28–F34.

[40]Gifford Pinchot III, *Intrapreneuring, or Why You Don't Have to Leave the Corporation to Become an Entrepreneur* (New York: Harper & Row, 1985).

[41]Information from John A. Byrne, "Management by Web," *Business Week* (August 28, 2000), pp. 84–97.

[42]Story originally reported by Christopher Farrell, "When Bureaucrats Are a Boon," *Business Week*, Enterprise issue (September 1, 1997), pp. ENT4–6; for current progress see company web site: http://www.mambodesign.com/index .html.

For information see Wendy's corporate web site: www.wendys.com.

Chapter 10 Notes

[1]Information from Richard Teitelbaum, "The Wal-Mart of Wall Street," *Fortune* (October 13, 1997), pp. 128–30; and Edward Jones: The Last Not-Com Brokerage," *Industry Standard* (August 7, 2000); on-line: http://www.the standard.com/article/display/0,1151, 17432,000.html.

[2]Henry Mintzberg and Ludo Van der Heyden, "Organigraphs: Drawing How Companies Really Work," *Harvard Business Review* (September–October 1999), pp. 87–94.

[3]The classic work is Alfred D. Chandler, *Strategy and Structure* (Cambridge, MA: MIT Press, 1962).

[4]See Alfred D. Chandler Jr., "Origins of the Organization Chart," *Harvard Business Review* (March–April 1988), pp. 156–57.

[5]See David Krackhardt and Jeffrey R. Hanson, "Informal Networks: The Company behind the Chart," *Harvard Business Review* (July–August 1993), pp. 104–11.

[6]Information and quotes from Maggie Jackson, "Work's Lessons Occurring in Unexpected Places," *Rockland Journal-News* (January 7, 1998), pp. 4A, 4E.

[7]See Kenneth Noble, "A Clash of Styles: Japanese Companies in the U.S.," *New York Times* (January 25, 1988), p. 7.

[8]For a discussion of departmentalization, see H. I. Ansoff and R. G. Bradenburg, "A Language for Organization Design," *Management Science*, vol. 17 (August 1971), pp. B705–B731; Mariann Jelinek, "Organization Structure: The Basic Conformations," in Mariann Jelinek, Joseph A. Litterer, and Raymond E. Miles (eds.), *Organizations by Design: Theory and Practice* (Plano, TX: Business Publications, 1981), pp. 293–302; Henry Mintzberg, "The Structuring of Organizations," in James Brian Quinn, Henry Mintzberg, and Robert M. James (eds.), *The Strategy Process: Concepts, Contexts, and Cases* (Englewood Cliffs, NJ: Prentice-Hall, 1988), pp. 276–304.

[9]Robert L. Simison, "Jaguar Slowly Sheds Outmoded Habits," *Wall Street Journal* (July 26, 1991), p. A6; and Richard Stevenson, "Ford Helps Jaguar Get Back Old Sheen," *International Herald Tribune* (December 14, 1994), p. 11.

[10]These alternatives are well described by Mintzberg, "The Structuring of Organizations," op cit.

[11]The focus on process is described in Michael Hammer, *Beyond Reengineering* (New York: Harper Business, 1996).

[12]Ibid.

[13]Excellent reviews of matrix concepts are found in Stanley M. Davis and Paul R. Lawrence, *Matrix* (Reading, MA: Addison-Wesley, 1977); Paul R. Lawrence, Harvey F. Kolodny, and Stanley M. Davis, "The Human Side of the Matrix," *Organizational Dynamics*, vol. 6 (1977), pp. 43–61; Harvey F. Kolodny, "Evolution to a Matrix Organization," *Academy of Management Review*, vol. 4 (1979), pp. 543–53.

[14]Davis and Lawrence, *Matrix*, op cit.

[15]See Henry Mintzberg and Ludo Van der Heyden, "Organigraphs: Drawing How Companies Really Work," *Harvard Business Review* (September–October 1999), pp. 87–94.

[16]Developed from Frank Ostroff, *The Horizontal Organization: What the Organization of the Future Looks Like and How it Delivers Value to Customers* (New York: Oxford University Press, 1999).

[17]The nature of teams and teamwork is described in Jon R. Katzenbach and Douglas K. Smith, "The Discipline of Teams," *Harvard Business Review* (March–April 1993), pp. 111–20.

[18]Susan Albers Mohrman, Susan G. Cohen, and Allan M. Mohrman Jr., *Designing Team-Based Organizations* (San Francisco: Jossey-Bass, 1996).

[19]See Glenn M. Parker, *Cross-Functional Teams* (San Francisco: Jossey-Bass, 1995).

[20]See Ron Ashkenas, Dave Ulrich, Todd Jick, Steve Kerr, *The Boundaryless Organization: Breaking the Chains of Organizational Structure* (San Francisco: Jossey-Bass, 1996); Rupert F. Chisholm, *Developing Network Organizations: Learning from Practice and Theory* (Reading, MA: Addison-Wesley, 1998).

[21]Information from William Bridges, "The End of the Job," *Fortune* (September 19, 1994), pp. 62–74; Alan Deutschman, "The Managing Wisdom of High-Tech Superstars," *Fortune* (October 17, 1994), pp. 197–206.

[22]See the discussion by Jay R. Galbraith, "Designing the Networked Organization: Leveraging Size and Competencies," in Susan Albers Mohrman, Jay R. Galbraith, Edward E. Lawler, III, and Associates, *Tomorrow's Organizatoins: Crafting Winning Strategies in a Dynamic World* (San Francisco: Jossey-Bass, 1998), pp. 76–102.

[23]Information from John A. Byrne, "Management by Web," *Business Week* (August 28, 2000), pp. 84–97.

[24]Ashkenas, et al., *The Boundaryless Organization: Breaking the Chains of Organizational Structure*, op cit.

[25]Robert Slater, *Jack Welch and the GE Way: Management Insights and Leadership Secrets from the Legendary CEO* (New York: 1998); "Jack the Job-Killer Strikes Again," *Business Week* (February 12, 2001), p. 12.

[26]Information from ibid.

[27]See the collection of articles by Cary L. Cooper and Denise M. Rousseau (eds.), *The Virtual Organization: Vol. 6, Trends in Organizational Behavior* (New York: Wiley, 2000).

[28]See "The Odd Couple of Steel," *Business Week* (November 7, 1994), pp.

106–8; "Go-Go Goliaths," *Business Week* (February 13, 1995), pp. 64–70; and, corporate web site: http://www.nucor.com/.

[29]David Van Fleet, "Span of Management Research and Issues," *Academy of Management Journal*, vol. 26 (1983), pp. 546–52.

[30]Developed from Roger Fritz, *Rate Your Executive Potential* (New York: Wiley, 1988), pp. 185–86; Roy J. Lewicki, Donald D. Bowen, Douglas T. Hall, and Francine S. Hall, *Experiences in Management and Organizational Behavior*, 3d ed. (New York: Wiley, 1988), p. 144.

[31]See George P. Huber, "A Theory of Effects of Advanced Information Technologies on Organizational Design, Intelligence, and Decision Making," *Academy of Management Review*, vol. 15 (1990), pp. 67–71.

Thomas Petzinger, Jr., "June Holley Brings a Touch of Italy to Appalachian Effort," *Wall Street Journal* (October 24, 1997), p. B1; Thomas Petzinger, Jr., *The New Pioneers: The Men and Women Who Are Transforming the Workplace and Marketplace* (New York: Simon & Schuster, 1999).

Chapter 11 Notes

[1]Information from Marcia Stepanek, "How Fast is Net Fast?" *Business Week E.Biz* (November 1, 1999), pp. EB52–Eb54; and, corporate web site: www.mobshop.com.

[2]Carla Rapoport, "Nestle's Brand Building Machine," *Fortune* (September 19, 1994), pp. 147–56.

[3]Jessica Lipnack and Jeffrey Stamps, *The Age of the Network: Organizing Principles for the 21st Century* (Essex Junction, VT: Omneo, 1994).

[4]For a discussion of organization theory and design, see W. Richard Scott, *Organizations: Rational, Natural, and Open Systems*, 4th ed. (Upper Saddle River, NJ: Prentice-Hall, 1998).

[5]Andrew Ross Sorkin, "Gospel According to St. Luke's," *New York Times* (February 12, 1998), pp. C1, C7; see also corporate web site: www.stlukes.co.uk.

[6]For a classic work see Jay R. Galbraith, *Organizational Design* (Reading, MA: Addison Wesley, 1977).

[7]This framework is based on Harold J. Leavitt, "Applied Organizational Change in Industry," in James G. March, *Handbook of Organizations* (New York: Rand McNally, 1965), pp. 1144–70; and, Edward E. Lawler III, *From the Ground Up: Six Principles for the New Logic Corporation* (San Francisco: Jossey-Bass Publishers, 1996), pp. 44–50.

[8]Max Weber, *The Theory of Social and Economic Organization*, A. M. Henderson, trans., and H. T. Parsons (New York: Free Press, 1947).

[9]For classic treatments of bureaucracy, see Alvin Gouldner, *Patterns of Industrial Bureaucracy* (New York: Free Press, 1954); Robert K. Merton, *Social Theory and Social Structure* (New York: Free Press, 1957).

[10]Tom Burns and George M. Stalker, *The Management of Innovation* (London: Tavistock, 1961; republished by Oxford University Press, London, 1994).

[11]See Henry Mintzberg, *Structure in Fives: Designing Effective Organizations* (Englewood Cliffs, NJ: Prentice-Hall, 1983).

[12]Information from Thomas Petzinger Jr., "Self-Organization Will Free Employees to Act Like Bosses," *Wall Street Journal* (January 3, 1997), p. B1.

[13]See Rosabeth Moss Kanter, *The Changing Masters* (New York: Simon & Schuster, 1983). Quotation from Rosabeth Moss Kanter and John D. Buck, "Reorganizing Part of Honeywell: From Strategy to Structure," *Organizational Dynamics*, vol. 13 (winter 1985), pp. 6.

[14]See for example, Jay R. Galbraith, Edward E. Lawler III, and Associates, *Organizing for the Future* (San Francisco: Jossey-Bass Publishers, 1993); Susan Albers Mohrman, Jay R. Galbraith, Edward E. Lawler, III, and Associates, *Tomorrow's Organizations: Crafting Winning Strategies in a Dynamic World* (San Francisco: Jossey-Bass, 1998).

[15]Peter Senge, *The Fifth Discipline: The Art and Practice of the Learning Organization* (New York: Doubleday, 1994).

[16]Information from "The Reorganization of PriceWaterhouseCoopers, explained," corporate web site: http://www.pwcglobal.com/gx/eng/main/campaigns/next.html.

[17]A classic treatment of environment and organizational design is found in James D. Thompson, *Organizations in Action* (New York: McGraw-Hill, 1967). See also Scott, *Organizations*, pp. 264–69.

[18]Alfred D. Chandler Jr., *Strategy and Structure: Chapter in the History of American Industrial Enterprise* (Cambridge, MA: MIT Press, 1962).

[19]See, for example, Danny Miller, "Configurations of Strategy and Structure: Towards a Synthesis," *Strategic Management Journal*, vol. 7 (1986), pp. 233–49.

[20]Joan Woodward, *Industrial Organization: Theory and Practice* (London: Oxford University Press, 1965; republished by Oxford University Press, 1994).

[21]This classification is from Thompson, *Organizations in Action*, op. cit.

[22]See Peter M. Blau and Richard A. Schoennerr, *The Structure of Organizations* (New York: Basic Books, 1971); and Scott, *Organizations*, pp. 259–63.

[23]D. E. Gumpert, "The Joys of Keeping the Company Small," *Harvard Business Review* (July–August 1986); pp. 6–8, 12–14.

[24]John R. Kimberly, Robert H. Miles, *The Organizational Life Cycle* (San Francisco: Jossey-Bass, 1980).

[25]Kim Cameron, Sarah J. Freeman, and Naneil K. Mishra, "Best Practices in White-Collar Downsizing: Managing Contradictions," *Academy of Management Executive*, vol. 5 (August 1991), pp. 57–73.

[26]See Gifford Pinchot III, *Intrapreneuring: Or Why You Don't Have to Leave the Corporation to Become an Entrepreneur* (New York: Harper & Row, 1985).

[27]See Jay Lorsch and John Morse, *Organizations and Their Members: A Contingency Approach* (New York: Harper & Row, 1974); and, Scott, *Organizations*, pp. 263–64.

[28]"The Rebirth of IBM," *The Economist* (June 6, 1998), pp. 65–68.

[29]Paul R. Lawrence and Jay W. Lorsch, *Organizations and Environment* (Boston: Division of Research, Graduate School of Business Administration, Harvard University, 1967).

[30]Burns and Stalker, op cit.

[31]See Jay R. Galbraith, *Organizational Design* (Reading, MA: Addison-Wesley, 1977); and Susan Albers Mohrman, "Integrating Roles and Structure in the Lateral Organization," chapter 5 in Jay R. Galbraith, Edward E. Lawler III, and Associates, *Organizing for the Future* (San Francisco: Jossey-Bass Publishers, 1993).

[32]For a good discussion of coordination and integration approaches, see Scott, *Organizations*, pp. 231–39.

[33]Michael Hammer and James Champy, *Reengineering the Corporation: A Manifesto for Business Revolution*, rev. ed. (New York: Harper Business, 1999).

[34]Michael Hammer, *Beyond Reengineering* (New York: Harper Business, 1997).

[35]Hammer, *Beyond Reengineering*, op cit., p. 5; see also the discussion of processes in Gary Hamel, *Leading the Revolution* (Boston, MA: Harvard Business School Press, 2000).

[36]Thomas M. Koulopoulos, *The Workflow Imperative* (New York: Van Nostrand Reinhold, 1995); Hammer, *Beyond Reengineering*, op cit.

[37]Paul Roberts, "Humane Technology—PeopleSoft," *Fast Company*, vol. 14 (1998), p. 122.

[38]Ronni T. Marshak, "Workflow Business Process Reengineering," special advertising section, *Fortune* (1997).

[39]A similar example is found in Hammer, *Beyond Reengineering*, op cit., pp. 9, 10.

[40]Ibid., pp. 28–30.

[41]Ibid., p. 29.

[42]Ibid., p. 27.

[43]Quote from Hammer and Company web site: http://www.hammerandco.com/WhatIsAProcessOrgFrames.html.

Information from Timothy Aeppel, "At a Job Shop, It's the Year of Living Cautiously," *Wall Street Journal* (February 8, 2001), pp. B1, B4.

Chapter 12 Notes

[1]Information from corporate web site: www.wetfeet.com; and "WorkExchange Global Network Expansion Continues," *Business Wire* (May 30, 2000).

[2]Nancy J. Perry, "The Workers of the Future," *Fortune*, "The New American Century" (spring–summer 1991), pp. 68–72.

[3]Robert Reich, *The Future of Success* (New York: Knopf, 2000), p. 15.

[4]Quote from John A. Byrne, "Visionary vs. Visionary," *Business Week* (August 28, 2000), pp. 210–14.

[5]See, for example, Charles Handy, *The Age of Unreason* (Cambridge, MA: Harvard Business School Press, 1990); and Tom Peters, "The Brand Called *You*," *Fast Company* (August 1997), pp. 83ff.

[6]A good overview is provided by Robert B. Reich, "The Company of the Future," *Fast Company* (November 1998), pp. 124ff.

[7]See, for example, "Rethinking Work," *Business Week*, special report (October 17, 1994), pp. 74–87.

[8]Jeffrey Pfeffer and John F. Veiga, "Putting People First for Organizational Success," *Academy of Management Executive*, vol. 13 (May 1999), pp. 37–48.

[9]Jeffrey Pfeffer, *The Human Equation: Building Profits by Putting People First* (Boston: Harvard University Press, 1998).

[10]James N. Baron and David M. Kreps, *Strategic Human Resources: Frameworks for General Managers* (New York: Wiley, 1999), pp. 4–6.

[11]Reported in Ibid., pp. 471–502.

[12]Jeffrey Pfeffer, *The Human Equation: Building Profits by Putting People First*, op cit., 1998), p. 292.

[13]R. Roosevelt Thomas, Jr., *Beyond Race and Gender* (New York: AMACOM, 1992), p. 4.

[14]Ibid.

[15]Lawrence Otis Graham, *Proversity: Getting Past Face Value and Finding the Soul of People* (New York: Wiley, 1997).

[16]See also R. Roosevelt Thomas, Jr.'s books, *Beyond Race and Gender* (New York: AMACOM, 1992) and (with Marjorie I. Woodruff) *Building a House for Diversity* (New York: AMACOM, 1999); and Richard D. Bucher, *Diversity Consciousness* (Englewood Cliffs, NJ: Prentice-Hall, 2000).

[17]Information from *Working Mother* web site: www.workingmother.com.

[18]Quote from William Bridges, "The End of the Job," *Fortune* (September 19, 1994), p. 68.

[19]For a discussion of affirmative action see R. Roosevelt Thomas, Jr. "From 'Affirmative Action' to 'Affirming Diversity,'" *Harvard Business Review* (November–December 1990), pp. 107–17; and Thomas, *Beyond Race and Gender*, op. cit., 1998).

[20]See the discussion by David A. DeCenzo and Stephen P. Robbins, *Human Resource Management*, 6th ed. (New York: Wiley, 1999), pp. 66–68 and 81–83.

[21]See the example and discussion of BFOQs in David A. DeCenzo and Stephen P. Robbins, *Human Resource Management*, 6th ed. (New York: Wiley, 1999), pp. 77–79.

[22]Information from "There Are Questions You Shouldn't Answer," *New York Times* (January 30, 2001), p. 2.

[23]See discussion by DeCenzo and Robbins, op cit., pp. 79–90.

[24]See James N. Baron and David M. Kreps, *Strategic Human Resources: Frameworks for General Managers* (New York: Wiley, 1999).

[25]See Boris Yavitz, "Human Resources in Strategic Planning," in Eli Ginzberg (ed.) *Executive Talent: Developing and Keeping the Best People* (New York: Wiley, 1988), p. 34.

[26]Information from Thomas A. Stewart, "In Search of Elusive Tech Workers," *Fortune* (February 16, 1998), pp. 171–72.

[27]See Ernest McCormick, "Job and Task Analysis," in Marvin Dunnette (ed.), *Handbook of Industrial and Organizational Psychology* (Chicago: Rand McNally, 1976), pp. 651–96.

[28]Information from Gautam Naik, "India's Technology Whizzes find Passage to Nokia," *Wall Street Journal* (August 1, 2000), p. B1.

[29]See David Greising, *I'd Like to Buy the World a Coke: The Life and Leadership of Roberto Goizueta* (New York: Wiley, 1998).

[30]See John P. Wanous, *Organizational Entry: Recruitment, Selection, and Socialization of Newcomers* (Reading, MA: Addison-Wesley, 1980), pp. 34–44.

[31]"Key to Success: People, People, People," *Fortune* (October 27, 1997), p. 232.

[32]See Dale Yoder and Herbert G. Heneman (eds.), *ASPA Handbook of Personnel and Industrial Relations*, vol. 1 (Washington: Bureau of National Affairs, 1974), pp. 152–54; Walter Kiechel III, "How to Pick Talent," *Fortune* (December 8, 1986), pp. 201–3; *HRM Magazine* (April 1991), pp. 42–43.

[33]Information from Justin Martin, "Mercedes: Made in Alabama," *Fortune* (July 7, 1997), pp. 150–58.

[34]Reported in "Would You Hire This Person Again?" *Business Week*, Enterprise issue (June 9, 1997), pp. ENT32.

[35]Information from William M. Bulkeley, "Replaced by Technology: Job Interviews," *Wall Street Journal* (August 22, 1994), pp. B1, B4.

[36]For a scholarly review, see John Van Maanen and Edgar H. Schein, "Toward a Theory of Socialization," in Barry M. Staw (ed.), *Research in Organizational Behavior*, vol. 1 (Greenwich, CT: JAI Press, 1979), pp. 209–64; for a practitioner's view, see Richard Pascale, "Fitting New Employees into the Company Culture," *Fortune* (May 28, 1984), pp. 28–42.

[37]This involves the social information processing concept as discussed in Gerald R. Salancik and Jeffrey Pfeffer, "A Social Information Processing Approach to Job Attitudes and Task Design," *Administrative Science Quarterly*, vol. 23 (June 1978): pp. 224–53.

[38]Quote from Ronald Henkoff, "Finding, Training, and Keeping the Best Service Workers," *Fortune* (October 3, 1994), pp. 110–22.

[39]*Fortune*, "Key to Success," op cit.

[40]Quote from Peter Petre, "Games That Teach You to Manage," *Fortune* (October 29, 1984), pp. 65–72; see also, the "Looking Glass" description on the Center for Creative Leadership web site: http://www.ccl.org/products/lgi/index.html.

[41]See Larry L. Cummings and Donald P. Schwab, *Performance in Organizations: Determinants and Appraisal* (Glenview, IL: Scott, Foresman, 1973).

[42]Information from Dick Grote, "Performance Appraisal Reappraised," *Harvard Business Review Best Practice* (1999), Reprint F00105.

[43]See Mark R. Edwards and Ann J. Ewen, *360-Degree Feedback: The Powerful New Tool for Employee Feedback and Performance Improvement* (New York: AMACOM, 1996).

[44]Information from "What Are the Most Effective Retention Tools?" *Fortune* (October 9, 2000), p. S7.

[45]Information from "BET's Johnson Looks to Soar Higher," *Investor's Business Daily* (May 25, 2000); "BET.com Ranked #1 in Unique Visitors Among African American Sites," *PR Newswire* (June 6, 2000); quote from Associated Press wire reports (May 25, 2000).

[46]Charles Handy, *The Age of Unreason* (Cambridge, MA: Harvard Business School Press, 1990), p. 55.

[47]See Thomas P. Ference, James A. F. Stoner, and E. Kirby Warren, "Managing the Career Plateau," *Academy of Management Review*, vol. 2 (October 1977), pp. 602–12.

[48]Timothy Butler and James Waldroop, "Job Sculpting: The Art of Retaining Your Best People," *Harvard Business Review* (September–October 1999), pp. 144–52.

[49]Information from David Coburn, "Balancing Home, Work Still Big Concern," *Columbus Dispatch* (February 16, 1998), pp. 8, 9.

[50]See Betty Friedan, *Beyond Gender: The New Politics of Work and the Family* (Washington, DC: Woodrow Wilson Center Press, 1997) and James A. Levine, *Working Fathers: New Strategies for Balancing Work and Family* (Reading, MA: Addison-Wesley, 1997).

[51]For reviews see Richard B. Freeman and James L. Medoff, *What Do Unions Do?* (New York: Basic Books, 1984); Charles C. Heckscher, *The New Unionism* (New York: Basic Books, 1988); and, Barry T. Hirsch, *Labor Unions and the Economic Performance of Firms* (Kalamazoo, Mich.: W.E. Upjohn Institute for Employment Research, 1991).

[52]"Trade Union Membership," *Economist* (December 6, 1997), p. 114; Yochi J. Dreazen, "Percentage of U.S. Workers in a Union Sank to Record Low of 13.5% Last Year," *Wall Street Journal* (January 19, 2001), p. A2.

Example from Dennis Berman, "What's a Worker Worth?" *Business Week Frontier* (October 11, 1999), p. F4; additional information from corporate web site: http://www.saratoga-institute.com.

Chapter 13 Notes

[1]Information and quotes from Julie Flaherty, "A Parting Gift from the Boss Who Cared," *New York Times* (September 28, 2000), pp. C1, C25; Business Wire Press Release, "Employees of the Butcher Company Share Over $18 Million as Owner Shares Benefits of Success" (September 21, 2000).

[2]Max DePree, "An Old Pro's Wisdom: It Begins with a Belief in People," *New York Times* (September 10, 1989), p. F2; Max DePree, *Leadership Is an Art* (New York: Doubleday, 1989); David Woodruff, "Herman Miller: How Green Is My Factory," *Business Week* (September 16, 1991), pp. 54–56; Max DePree, *Leadership Jazz* (New York: Doubleday, 1992).

[3]Tom Peters, "Rule #3: Leadership Is Confusing as Hell," *Fast Company* (March 2001), pp. 124–140.

[4]Abraham Zaleznick, "Leaders and Managers: Are They Different?" *Harvard Business Review*, (May–June 1977), pp. 67–78.

[5]For additional thoughts, see Warren Bennis, *Why Leaders Can't Lead* (San Francisco: Jossey-Bass, 1996).

[6]Quotations from Marshall Loeb, "Where Leaders Come From," *Fortune* (September 19, 1994), pp. 241–42; Genevieve Capowski, "Anatomy of a Leader: Where Are the Leaders of Tomorrow?" *Management Review* (March 1994), pp. 10–17.

[7]See Jean Lipman-Blumen, *Connective Leadership: Managing in a Changing World* (New York: Oxford University Press, 1996), pp. 3–11.

[8]Two periodicals that follow current leadership topics in a variety of organizational settings are *Non-Profit Management and Leadership* and *Leader to Leader*, both published by Jossey-Bass.

[9]James M. Kouzes and Barry Z. Posner, "The Leadership Challenge," *Success* (April 1988), p. 68. See also their books *The Leadership Challenge: How to Get Extraordinary Things Done in Organizations* (San Francisco: Jossey-Bass, 1987), and *Credibility: How Leaders Gain and Lose It; Why People Demand It* (San Francisco: Jossey-Bass, 1996); *Encouraging the Heart: A Leader's Guide to Rewarding and Recognizing Others* (San Francisco: Jossey-Bass, 1999).

[10]Burt Nanus, *Visionary Leadership: Creating a Compelling Sense of Vision for Your Organization* (San Francisco: Jossey-Bass, 1992).

[11]Quotation from General Electric Company Annual Report 1997; p. 5. For more on Jack Welch's leadership approach at GE see *Jack Welch & the GE Way* (New York: McGraw-Hill, 1998).

[12]See Kouzes and Posner, op cit. (1988);

and James C. Collins and Jerry I. Porras, "Building Your Company's Vision," *Harvard Business Review*, (September–October 1996), pp. 65–77.

[13]Rosabeth Moss Kanter, "Power Failure in Management Circuits," *Harvard Business Review*, (July–August 1979), pp. 65–75.

[14]For a good managerial discussion of power, see David C. McClelland and David H. Burnham, "Power Is the Great Motivator," *Harvard Business Review*, (March–April 1976), pp. 100–10.

[15]The classic treatment of these power bases is John R. P. French Jr. and Bertram Raven, "The Bases of Social Power," in Darwin Cartwright (ed.), *Group Dynamics: Research and Theory* (Evanston, IL: Row, Peterson, 1962), pp. 607–13. For managerial applications of this basic framework, see Gary Yukl and Tom Taber, "The Effective Use of Managerial Power, *Personnel*, vol. 60 (1983), pp. 37–49; Robert C. Benfari, Harry E. Wilkinson, and Charles D. Orth, "The Effective Use of Power," *Business Horizons*, vol. 29 (1986), pp. 12–16. Gary A. Yukl, *Leadership in Organizations*, 4th ed. (Englewood Cliffs, NJ: Prentice-Hall, 1998), includes "information" as a separate, but related, power source.

[16]Lorraine Monroe, "Leadership Is About Making Vision Happen—What I Call 'Vision Acts,'" *Fast Company* (March 2001), p. 98; School Leadership Academy web site, http://www.lorrainemonroe.com/.

[17]Based on David A. Whetten and Kim S. Cameron, *Developing Management Skills*, 2d ed. (New York: HarperCollins, 1991), pp. 281–97.

[18]Ibid., p. 282.

[19]Chester A. Barnard, *Functions of the Executive* (Cambridge, MA: Harvard University Press, 1938).

[20]DePree, "An Old Pro's Wisdom," op cit.

[21]Monroe, op cit.

[22]Jay A. Conger, "Leadership: The Art of Empowering Others," *Academy of Management Executive*, vol. 3 (1989), pp. 17–24.

[23]For example, see Esther Wachs Book, "Leadership for the Millennium," *Working Woman* (March 1998), pp. 29–34; Charles Garfield, "Innovation Imperative," *Executive Excellence* (11/21/2000) from http://www.pcconnection.com/scripts/about/story03.asp.

[24]The early work on leader traits is well represented in Ralph M. Stogdill, "Personal Factors Associated with Leadership: A Survey of the Literature," *Journal of Psychology*, vol. 25 (1948), pp. 35–71. See also Edwin E. Ghiselli, *Ex-*

plorations in Management Talent (Santa Monica, CA: Goodyear, 1071), and Shirley A. Kirkpatrick and Edwin A. Locke, "Leadership: Do Traits Really Matter?" Academy of Management Executive (1991), pp. 48–60.

[25]See also John W. Gardner's article, "The Context and Attributes of Leadership," New Management, vol. 5 (1988), pp. 18–22; John P. Kotter, The Leadership Factor (New York: Free Press, 1988); and Bernard M. Bass, Stogdill's Handbook of Leadership (New York: Free Press, 1990).

[26]Kirkpatrick and Locke, op cit. (1991).

[27]See, for example, Jan P. Muczyk and Bernie C. Reimann, "The Case for Directive Leadership," Academy of Management Review, vol. 12 (1987), pp. 637–47.

[28]See Bass, Stogdill's Handbook of Leadership, op cit.

[29]Robert R. Blake and Jane Srygley Mouton, The New Managerial Grid III (Houston: Gulf Publishing, 1985).

[30]For a good discussion of this theory, see Fred E. Fiedler, Martin M. Chemers, and Linda Mahar, The Leadership Match Concept (New York: Wiley, 1978); Fiedler's current contingency research with the cognitive resource theory is summarized in Fred E. Fiedler and Joseph E. Garcia, New Approaches to Effective Leadership (New York: Wiley, 1987).

[31]Paul Hersey and Kenneth H. Blanchard, Management and Organizational Behavior (Englewood Cliffs, NJ: Prentice-Hall, 1988). For an interview with Paul Hersey on the origins of the model, see John R. Schermerhorn Jr., "Situational Leadership: Conversations with Paul Heresy," Mid-American Journal of Business (fall 1997), pp. 5–12.

[32]See Claude L. Graeff, "The Situational Leadership Theory: A Critical View," Academy of Management Review, vol. 8 (1983), pp. 285–91.

[33]See, for example, Robert J. House, "A Path-Goal Theory of Leader Effectiveness," Administrative Sciences Quarterly, vol. 16 (1971), pp. 321–38; Robert J. House and Terrence R. Mitchell, "Path-Goal Theory of Leadership," Journal of Contemporary Business (Autumn 1974), pp. 81–97; the path-goal theory is reviewed by Bernard M. Bass in Stogdill's Handbook of Leadership, op cit., and Yukl in Leadership in Organizations, op cit. A supportive review of research is offered in Julie Indvik, "Path-Goal Theory of Leadership; A Meta-Analysis," in John A. Pearce II and Richard B. Robinson Jr. (eds.), Academy of Management Best Paper Proceedings (1986), pp. 189–92.

[34]See the discussions of path-goal theory in Yukl, Leadership in Organizations, op cit.; and Bernard M. Bass, "Leadership: Good, Better, Best," Organizational Dynamics (winter 1985), pp. 26–40.

[35]See Steven Kerr and John Jermier, "Substitutes for Leadership: Their Meaning and Measurement, Organizational Behavior and Human Performance, vol. 22 (1978), pp. 375–403; Jon P. Howell and Peter W. Dorfman, "Leadership and Substitutes for Leadership among Professional and Nonprofessional Workers," Journal of Applied Behavioral Science," vol. 22 (1986), pp. 29–46.

[36]Victor H. Vroom and Arthur G. Jago, The New Leadership: Managing Participation in Organizations (Englewood Cliffs, NJ: Prentice-Hall, 1988). This is based on earlier work by Victor H. Vroom, "A New Look in Managerial Decision-Making," Organizational Dynamics (spring 1973), pp. 66–80; and Victor H. Vroom and Phillip Yetton, Leadership and Decision-Making (Pittsburgh: University of Pittsburgh Press, 1973).

[37]For a good discussion see Edgar H. Schein, Process Consultation Revisited: Building the Helping Relationship (Reading, MA: Addison-Wesley, 1999).

[38]See the discussion by Victor II. Vroom, "Leadership and the Decision Making Process," Organizational Dynamics, vol. 28 (2000), pp. 82–94.

[39]For a review see Yukl, Leadership in Organizations, op cit.

[40]Among the popular books addressing this point of view are Warren Bennis and Burt Nanus, Leaders: The Strategies for Taking Charge (New York: Harper Business 1997); Max DePree, Leadership Is an Art, op cit.; Kotter, The Leadership Factor, op cit.; Kouzes and Posner, The Leadership Challenge, op cit.

[41]See, for example, Jay A. Conger, "Inspiring Others: The Language of Leadership," Academy of Management Executive, vol. 5 (1991), pp. 31–45.

[42]Information from "We Weren't Just Airborne Yesterday," http://www.ifly swa.com/about_swa/airborne.html; quote from http://www.tamcoinc.com/kelleher.html (11/24/2000).

[43]The distinction was originally made by James McGregor Burns, Leadership (New York: Harper & Row, 1978) and was further developed by Bernard Bass, Leadership and Performance Beyond Expectations (New York: Free Press, 1985) and Bernard M. Bass, "Leadership: Good, Better, Best," Orga-nizationational Dynamics (winter 1985), pp. 26–40.

[44]This list is based on Kouzes and Posner, op cit.; Gardner, op cit.

[45]Daniel Goleman, "Leadership that Gets Results," Harvard Business Review (March–April 2000), pp. 78–90. See also his books Emotional Intelligence (New York: Bantam Books, 1995); Working with Emotional Intelligence (New York: Bantam Books, 1998).

[46]Daniel Goleman, "What Makes a Leader?" Harvard Business Review, (November–December 1998), pp. 93–102.

[47]Goleman, op cit., 1998.

[48]Information from "Women and Men, Work and Power," Fast Company, Issue 13 (1998), p. 71.

[49]A. H. Eagley, S. J. Daran and M. G. Makhijani, "Gender and the Effectiveness of Leaders: A Meta-Analysis," Psychological Bulletin, vol. 117 (1995), pp. 125–45.

[50]Research on gender issues in leadership is reported in Sally Helgesen, The Female Advantage: Women's Ways of Leadership (New York: Doubleday, 1990); Judith B. Rosener, "Ways Women Lead," Harvard Business Review, (November–December 1990), pp. 119–25; and Alice H. Eagly, Steven J. Karau, and Blair T. Johnson, "Gender and Leadership Style among School Principals: A Meta Analysis," Administrative Science Quarterly, vol. 27 (1992), pp. 76–102. See also the discussion of women leaders in Chapter 11, Jean Lipman-Blumen, Connective Leadership: Managing in a Changing World (New York: Oxford University Press, 1996).

[51]Vroom, op cit. (2000).

[52]Rosener, op cit. (1990).

[53]For debate on whether some transformational leadership qualities tend to be associated more with female than male leaders, see "Debate: Ways Women and Men Lead," Harvard Business Review, (January–February 1991), pp. 150–60.

[54]Quote from "As Leaders, Women Rule," Business Week (November 20, 2000), pp. 75–84. Rosabeth Moss Kanter is the author of Men and Women of the Corporation, 2nd ed. (New York: Basic Books, 1993).

[55]Peter F. Drucker, "Leadership: More Doing than Dash," Wall Street Journal, (January 6, 1988), p. 16. For a compendium of writings on leadership sponsored by the Drucker Foundation, see Frances Hesselbein, Marshall Goldsmith, and Richard Beckhard, Leader of the Future (San Francisco: Jossey-Bass, 1997).

[56]General Electric Company Annual Report 1997, p. 5.

[57]Gradner, op cit.

[58]See Steven R. Covey, *Principle-Centered Leadership* (New York: Free Press, 1992); and, Lee G. Bolman and Terrence E. Deal, *Leading With Soul* (San Francisco: Jossey-Bass, 1995).

[59]De Pree, op cit. (1989), School Leadership Academy web site, http://www.lorrainemonroe.com/.

Quote from John Huey, "The New Post-Heroic Leaders," *Fortune* (February 21, 1994), pp. 42–50. Information from corporate web site: http://www.gore.com/corp/about/profile.html.

Chapter 14 Notes

[1]Information from Eleena De Lisser, "Start-Up Attracts Staff with a Ban on Midnight Oil," *Wall Street Journal* (August 23, 2000), pp. B1, B6; and corporate web site: http://www.ipswitch.com.

[2]Quotes from Charles O'Reilly III and Jeffrey Pfeffer, *Hidden Value: How Great Companies Achieve Extraordinary Results Through Ordinary People* (Boston, MA: Harvard Business School Press, 2000), pp. 5–6.

[3]Example taken from Kevin Kelley, "I'm the Boss, That's Why," *Business Week*, Enterprise issue (June 9, 1997), p. ENT 32.

[4]For a comprehensive treatment of extrinsic rewards, see Bob Nelson, *1001 Ways to Reward Employees* (New York: Workman Publishing, 1994).

[5]For a research perspective, see Edward Deci, *Intrinsic Motivation* (New York: Plenum, 1975); Edward E. Lawler III, "The Design of Effective Reward Systems," in Jay W. Lorsch (ed.), *Handbook of Organizational Behavior* (Englewood Cliffs, NJ: Prentice-Hall, 1987), pp. 255–71.

[6]Michael Maccoby's book, *Why Work: Leading the New Generation* (New York: Simon & Schuster, 1988), deals extensively with this point of view.

[7]Example from Frank Hinchey, "Tops in Copper," *Columbus Dispatch* (August 27, 2000), pp. G1, G2.

[8]Information from Ellen Graham, "Work May Be a Rat Race, But It's Not a Daily Grind," *Wall Street Journal*, (September 19, 1997), pp. R1, R4. The story of Starbucks is told in Howard Schulz and Dori Jones Yang, *Pour Your Heart Into It: How Starbucks Built a Company One Cup at a Time* (New York: Hyperion, 1999).

[9]Information from Sue Shellenbarger, "Companies are Finding Real Payoff in Aiding Employee Satisfaction," *Wall Street Journal* (October 11, 2000), p. B1.

[10]See Abraham H. Maslow, *Eupsychian Management* (Homewood, IL: Richard D. Irwin, 1965); Abraham H. Maslow, *Motivation and Personality*, 2d ed. (New York: Harper & Row, 1970). For a research perspective, see Mahmoud A. Wahba and Lawrence G. Bridwell, "Maslow Reconsidered: A Review of Research on the Need Hierarchy," *Organizational Behavior and Human Performance*, vol. 16 (1976), pp. 212–40.

[11]See Clayton P. Alderfer, *Existence, Relatedness, and Growth* (New York: Free Press, 1972).

[12]The complete two-factor theory is in Frederick Herzberg, Bernard Mausner, and Barbara Block Synderman, *The Motivation to Work*, 2d ed. (New York: Wiley, 1967); Frederick Herzberg, "One More Time: How Do You Motivate Employees?" *Harvard Business Review* (January–February 1968), pp. 53–62, and reprinted as an *HBR classic* (September–October 1987), pp. 109–20.

[13]Critical reviews are provided by Robert J. House and Lawrence A. Wigdor, "Herzberg's Dual-Factor Theory of Job Satisfaction and Motivation: A Review of the Evidence and a Criticism," *Personnel Psychology*, vol. 20 (winter 1967), pp. 369–89; Steven Kerr, Anne Harlan, and Ralph Stogdill, "Preference for Motivator and Hygiene Factors in a Hypothetical Interview Situation," *Personnel Psychology*, vol. 27 (winter 1974), pp. 109–24.

[14]Frederick Herzberg, "Workers' Needs: The Same around the World," *Industry Week* (September 21, 1987), pp. 29–32.

[15]For a collection of McClelland's work, see David C. McClelland, *The Achieving Society* (New York: Van Nostrand, 1961); "Business Drive and National Achievement," *Harvard Business Review*, vol. 40 (July–August 1962), pp. 99–112; David C. McClelland and David H. Burnham, "Power Is the Great Motivator," *Harvard Business Review* (March–April 1976), pp. 100–10; David C. McClelland, *Human Motivation* (Glenview, IL: Scott, Foresman, 1985); David C. McClelland and Richard E. Boyatsis, "The Leadership Motive Pattern and Long-Term Success in Management," *Journal of Applied Psychology*, vol. 67 (1982), pp. 737–43.

[16]Developed originally from a discussion in Edward E. Lawler III, *Motivation in Work Organizations* (Monterey, CA: Brooks/Cole Publishing, 1973), pp. 30–36.

[17]See, for example, J. Stacy Adams, "Toward an Understanding of Inequity," *Journal of Abnormal and Social Psychology*, vol. 67 (1963), pp. 422–36; J. Stacy Adams, "Inequity in Social Exchange," in vol. 2, L. Berkowitz, (ed.), *Advances in Experimental Social Psychology*, (New York: Academic Press, 1965), pp. 267–300.

[18]See, for example, J. W. Harder, "Play for Pay: Effects of Inequity in a Pay-for-Performance Context," *Administrative Science Quarterly*, vol. 37 (1992), pp. 321–35.

[19]U.S. Department of Labor, Bureau of Labor Statistics, *Highlights of Women's Earnings in 1998*.

[20]Victor H. Vroom, "Work and Motivation (New York: Wiley, 1964; republished by Jossey-Bass, 1994).

[21]The work on goal-setting theory is well summarized in Edwin A. Locke and Gary P. Latham, *Goal Setting: A Motivational Technique That Works!* (Englewood Cliffs, NJ: Prentice Hall, 1984). See also Edwin A. Locke, Kenneth N. Shaw, Lisa A. Saari, and Gary P. Latham, "Goal Setting and Task Performance 1969–1980," *Psychological Bulletin*, vol. 90 (1981), pp. 125–52; Mark E. Tubbs, "Goal Setting: A Meta-Analytic Examination of the Empirical Evidence," *Journal of Applied Psychology*, vol. 71 (1986), pp. 474–83; and Terence R. Mitchell, Kenneth R. Thompson, and Jane George-Falvy, "Goal Setting: Theory and Practice," Chapter 9 in Cary L. Cooper and Edwin A. Locke (eds.), *Industrial and Organizational Psychology: Linking Theory with Practice* (Malden, MA: Blackwell Business, 2000), pp. 211–249.

[22]Gary P. Latham and Edwin A. Locke, "Self-Regulation Through Goal Setting," *Organizational Behavior and Human Decision Processes*, vol. 50 (1991), pp. 212–47.

[23]E. L. Thorndike, *Animal Intelligence* (New York: Macmillan, 1911), p. 244.

[24]See B. F. Skinner, *Walden Two* (New York: Macmillan, 1948); *Science and Human Behavior* (New York: Macmillan, 1953); *Contingencies of Reinforcement* (New York: Appleton-Century-Crofts, 1969).

[25]OB mod is clearly explained in Fred Luthans and Robert Kreitner, *Organizational Behavior Modification* (Glenview, IL: Scott, Foresman, 1975) and Fred Luthans and Robert Kreitner, *Organizational Behavior Modification and Beyond* (Glenview, IL: Scott, Foresman, 1985); see also Fred Luthans and Alexander D. Stajkovic, "Reinforce for Performance: The Need to Go Beyond Pay and Even Rewards," *Academy of Management Executive*, vol. 13 (1999), pp. 49–57.

[26]For the Mary Kay story and philosophy see Mary Kay Ash, *Mary Kay on People Management* (New York: Warner Books, 1985); see also information at the corporate web site: http://www.marykay.com.

[27]For a good review, see Lee W. Frederickson (ed.), *Handbook of Organizational Behavior Management* (New York: Wiley-Inerscience, 1982); Luthans and Kreitner, op cit. (1985); and Andrew D. Stajkovic and Fred Luthans, "A Meta-Analysis of the Effects of Organizational Behavior Modification on Task Performance 1975–95," *Academy of Management Journal*, vol. 40 (1997), pp. 1122–49.

[28]Edwin A. Locke, "The Myths of Behavior Mod in Organizations," *Academy of Management Review*, vol. 2 (October 1977), pp. 543–53.

[29]For a discussion of compensation and performance, see Rosabeth Moss Kanter, "The Attack on Pay," *Harvard Business Review*, vol. 65 (March–April 1987), pp. 60–67; Edward E. Lawler III, *Strategic Pay* (San Francisco: Jossey-Bass, 1990).

[30]See "Experts from Saturn Corporation and Transamercia Life to Discuss Alternative Compensation Systems, *Business Wire, Inc.* (November 8, 1999).

[31]Karthryn M. Bartol and Cathy C. Durham, "Incentives: Theory and Practice," Chapter 1 in Cooper and Locke, op cit. (2000).

[32]"As CEO Pay Rockets Higher, Shareholders Urge Companies to Share the Rewards More Widely," report by *Responsible Wealth* (April 5, 2000): http://www.responsiblewealth.org/press/CEO_shareholder.html.

[33]Information from Jaclyn Fierman, "The Perilous New World of Fair Pay," *Fortune* (June 13, 1994), pp. 57–61.

[34]Tove Helland Hammer, "New Developments in Profit Sharing, Gain Sharing, and Employee Ownership," chapter 12 in John P. Campbell and Richard J. Campbell (eds.), *Productivity in Organizations: New Perspective form Industrial and Organizational Psychology* (San Francisco: Jossey-Bass, 1988).

[35]Edward E. Lawler III, *From the Ground Up: Six Principles for Building the New Logic Corporation* (San Francisco: Jossey-Bass, 1996), pp. 217–18. See also Lawler's *Rewarding Excellence* (San Francisco: Jossey-Bass, 2000).

[36]Jaclyn Fierman, "The Perilous New World of Fair Pay," *Fortune* (June 13, 1994), pp. 57–61.

[37]Amanda Bennett, "Paying Workers to Meet Goals Spreads, but Gauging Performance Proves Tough," *Wall Street Journal* (September 10, 1991), p. B1; "Pay to Live On, Stock to Grow On," *Fortune* (January 8, 2001), p. 151.

[38]See Carl F. Frost, John H. Wakeley, and Robert A. Ruh, *The Scanlon Plan for Organizational Development* (Lansing, MI: Michigan State University Press, 1996).

[39]Information from www.intel.com and "Stock Ownership for Everyone," Hewitt Associates November 27, 2000): was .hewitt.com/hewitt/business/talent/subtalent/con_bckg_global.htm.

[40]Information from Susan Pulliam, "New Dot-Com Mantra: 'Just Pay Me in Cash, Please,'" *Wall Street Journal* (November 28, 2000), p. C1.

See *Restoring Competitive Luster to American Industry: An Agenda for Success* (Cleveland, OH: Lincoln Electric Company), Barnaby J. Feder, "Carrots, Sticks, and Growing Pains," *International Herald Tribune* (September 8, 1994), pp. 9, 10; corporate web site: http://www.lincolnelectric.com.

Chapter 15 Notes

[1]Information from Neil Gross, "Mining a Company's Mother Lode of Talent," *Business Week* (August 8, 2000), pp. 135–37; corporate web site: www.monitor.com/cgi-bin/templates/about.

[2]Jeffrey Pfeffer and John F. Veiga, "Putting People First for Organizational Success," *Academy of Management Executive*, vol. 13 (1999), pp. 37–48; see also Jeffrey Pfeffer, *The Human Equation: Building Profits by Putting People First* (Boston: Harvard University Press, 1998).

[3]See Mary Williams Walsh, "Luring the Best in an Unsettled Time," *New York Times* (January 30, 2001).

[4]Charles O'Reilly III and Jeffrey Pfeffer, *Hidden Value: How Great Companies Achieve Extraordinary Results Through Ordinary People* (Boston: MA: Harvard Business School Publishing, 2000), quotes from p. 2.

[5]Lyrics from "9 to 5" by Dollly Parton. Published by Velvet Apple/Fox Fanfare Music, Inc. © 1980 Velvet Apple Music & Warner-Tamerlane Publishing Corp. All rights reserved. Used by permission.

[6]This example is reported in *Esquire* (December 1986), p. 243. Emphasis is added to the quotation. *Note:* Nussbaum became director of the Labor Department's Women's Bureau during the Clinton administration and subsequently moved to the AFL-CIO as head of the Women's Bureau.

[7]Information from "old 1" and corporate web site: www.ey.com/global/gcr.nsf/US/Life_Balance_-_Careers_-_Ernst_&_Young_LLP.

[8]John P. Kotter, "The Psychological Contract: Managing the Joining Up Process," *California Management Review*, vol. 15 (spring 1973), 91–99; Denise Rousseau (ed.), *Psychological Contracts in Organizations* (San Francisco: Jossey-Bass, 1995); Denise Rousseau, "Changing the Deal While Keeping the People," *Academy of Management Executive*, vol. 10 (1996), pp. 50–59; and Denise Rousseau and Rene Schalk (eds.), *Psychological Contracts in Employment: Cross-Cultural Perspectives* (San Francisco: Jossey-Bass, 2000).

[9]Linda Grant, "Unhappy in Japan," *Fortune* (January 13, 1997), p. 142.

[10]For a thought provoking discussion of this issue, see Ben Hamper, *Rivethead: Tales from the Assembly Line* (New York: Warner, 1991).

[11]Studs Terkel, *Working* (New York: Avon Books, 1975).

[12]Sue Shellenbarger, "In Real Life, Hard Choices Upset Any Balancing Act," *Wall Street Journal* (April 19, 1995), p. B1.

[13]For an overview, see Paul E. Spector, *Job Satisfaction* (Thousand Oaks, CA: Sage, 1997); and Timothy A. Judge and Allan H. Church, "Job Satisfaction: Research and Practice," Chapter 7 in Cary L. Cooper and Edwin A. Locke (eds.), *Industrial and Organizational Psychology: Linking Theory with Practice* (Malden, MA: Blackwell Business, 2000).

[14]Information from Sue Shellenbarger, "Employers Are Finding It Doesn't Cost Much to Make a Staff Happy," *Wall Street Journal* (November 19, 1997), p. B1.

[15]Linda Grant, "Happy Workers, High Returns," *Fortune* (January 12, 1998), p. 81.

[16]Ibid.

[17]See Melvin Blumberg and Charles D. Pringle, "The Missing Opportunity in Organizational Research: Some Implications for a Theory of Work Motivation," *Academy of Management Review*, vol. 7 (1982), pp. 560–69.

[18]Based on an example in Edward E. Lawler III, *Motivation in Work Organizations* (Monterey, CA: Brooks-Cole, 1973), pp. 154–55.

[19]Information from David Whitford, "A Human Place to Work," *Fortune* (January 8, 2001), pp. 108–20.

[20]See Frederick Herzberg, Bernard Mausner, and Barbara Block Synderman, *The Motivation to Work*, 2d ed. (New York: Wiley, 1967). The quotation is from Frederick Herzberg, "One More Time:

How Do You Motivate Employees?" *Harvard Business Review* (January–February 1968), pp. 53–62, and reprinted as an HBR Classic in (September–October 1987), pp. 109–20.

[21]Herzberg, op cit. (1987).

[22]For a complete description of the core characteristics model, see J. Richard Hackman and Greg R. Oldham, *Work Redesign* (Reading, MA: Addison-Wesley, 1980).

[23]See Richard E. Walton, *Up and Running: Integrating Information Technology and the Organization* (Boston, MA: Harvard Business School Press, 1989).

[24]Richard Walton, "From Control to Commitment in the Workplace," *Harvard Business Review* (March–April 1985), pp. 77–94; and William A. Pasmore, *Designing Effective Organizations: A Sociotechnical Systems Perspective* (New York: Wiley, 1988).

[25]Quote from William W. Winipsigner, "Job Enrichment: A Union View," in Karl O. Magnusen (ed.), *Organizational Design, Development, and Behavior: A Situational View*, (Glenview, IL: Scott, Foresman, 1977), p. 22.

[26]See Karl Sabbagh, *21st Century Jet: The Making and Marketing of the Boeing 777* (New York: Scribner, 1996).

[27]Paul J. Champagne and Curt Tausky, "When Job Enrichment Doesn't Pay," *Personnel*, vol. 3 (January–February 1978), pp. 30–40.

[28]Barney Olmsted and Suzanne Smith, *Creating a Flexible Workplace: How to Select and Manage Alternative Work Options* (New York: American Management Association, 1989).

[29]See Allen R. Cohen and Herman Gadon, *Alternative Work Schedules: Integrating Individual and Organizational Needs* (Reading, MA: Addison-Wesley, 1978), p. 125; Simcha Ronen and Sophia B. Primps, "The Compressed Work Week as Organizational Change: Behavioral and Attitudinal Outcomes," *Academy of Management Review*, vol. 6 (1981), pp. 61–74.

[30]Information from Lesli Hicks, "Workers, Employers Praise Their Four-Day Workweek," *Columbus Dispatch* (August 22, 1994), p. 6; and Walsh, op cit. (2001).

[31]Example from the Business for Social Responsibility Resource Center: www.bsr.org/resourcecenter (January 24, 2001).

[32]"Networked Workers," *Business Week* (October 6, 1997), p. 8; and Diane E. Lewis, "Flexible Work Arrangements as Important as Salary to Some," *Columbus Dispatch* (May 25, 1998), p. 8.

[33]See Kemba J. Dunham, "Telecommuter's Lament," *Wall Street Journal* (October 31, 2000), pp. B1, B18.

[34]For a review see Wayne F. Cascio, "Managing a Virtual Workplace," *Academy of Management Executive*, vol. 14 (2000), pp. 81–90.

[35]Ibid.

[36]See Sue Shellenbarger, "Overwork, Low Morale Vex the Mobile Office," *Wall Street Journal*, (August 17, 1994), pp. B1, B7.

[37]Quote from Phil Porter, "Telecommuting Mom Is Part of a National Trend," *Columbus Dispatch* (November 29, 2000), pp. H1, H2.

[38]These guidelines are collected from a variety of sources, including: The Southern California Telecommuting Partnership (http://www.socalcommute.org/telecom.htm); ISDN Group (http://www.isdnzone.com/telcom/tips.htm).

[39]Steven Greenhouse, "Equal Work, Less Equal Perks," *New York Times* (March 30, 1998), p. C1.

[40]Timothy Aeppel, "Full Time, Part Time, Temp—All See the Job in a Different Light," *Wall Street Journal*, (March 18, 1997), p. 1, 10.

[41]See "Report on the American Workforce 1999" (Washington: U.S. Bureau of Labor Statistics); "1999 AMA Survey of Contingent Workers" (New York: American Management Association, 1999).

[42]Data and example from Sue Shellenbarger, "Employees Are Seeking Fewer Hours; Maybe Bosses Should Listen," *Wall Street Journal*, (February 21, 2001), p. B1.

[43]See Arthur P. Brief, Randall S. Schuler, and Mary Van Sell, *Managing Job Stress* (Boston: Little, Brown, 1981), pp. 7, 8.

[44]Robert B. Reich, *The Future of Success* (New York: Knopf, 2000), p. 8.

[45]Michael Weldholz, "Stress Increasingly Seen as Problem with Executives More Vulnerable," *Wall Street Journal*, (September 28, 1982), p. 31.

[46]Sue Shellenbarger, "Do We Work More or Not? Either Way, We Feel Frazzled," *Wall Street Journal*, (July 30, 1997), p. B1.

[47]See, for example, "Desk Rage," *Business Week* (November 27, 2000), p. 12.

[48]Carol Hymowitz, "Impossible Expectations and Unfulfilling Work Stress Managers, Too," *Wall Street Journal*, (January 16, 2001), p. B1.

[49]The classic work is Meyer Friedman and Ray Roseman, *Type A Behavior and Your Heart* (New York: Knopf, 1974).

[50]See Hans Selye, *Stress in Health and Disease* (Boston: Butterworth, 1976).

[51]Carol Hymowitz, "Can Workplace Stress Get *Worse*?" *Wall Street Journal*, (January 16, 2001), pp. B1, B3.

[52]See Steve M. Jex, *Stress and Job Performance* (San Francisco: Jossey-Bass, 1998).

[53]Reported in Sue Shellenbarger, "Finding Ways to Keep a Partner's Job Stress from Hitting Home," *Wall Street Journal*, (November 29, 2000), p. B1; Daniel Costello, "Incidents of 'Desk Rage' Disrupt America's Offices," *Wall Street Journal*, (January 16, 2001), pp. B1, B3.

[54]See Daniel C. Ganster and Larry Murphy, "Workplace Interventions to Prevent Stress-Related Illness: Lessons from Research and Practice," Chapter 2 in Cooper and Locke (eds.), op cit. (2000).

[55]Quote from Ibid.

[56]The extreme case of "workplace violence" is discussed by Richard V. Denenberg and Mark Braverman, *The Violence-Prone Workplace* (Ithaca, NY: Cornell University Press, 1999).

[57]See John M. Ivancevich and Michael T. Matteson, "Optimizing Human Resources: A Case for Preventive Health and Stress Management," *Organizational Dynamics*, vol. 9 (Autumn 1980), pp. 6–8. See also John M. Ivancevich, Michael T. Matteson, and Edward P. Richards III, "Who's Liable for Stress on the Job?" *Harvard Business Review* (March–April 1985), pp. 60–71.

[58]Robert Kreitner, "Personal Wellness: It's Just Good Business," *Business Horizons*, (May–June 1982), pp. 28–35.

[59]Developed from Kreitner, "Personal Wellness," and "Plain Talk about Stress," National Institute of Mental Health Publication (Rockville, MD: U.S. Department of Health and Human Services).

Robin D. Schatz, "Women's Work," *Business Week Frontier* (December 4, 2000), p. F48; see also Paola Gianturco, Toby Tuttle, and Alice Walker, *In Her Hands: Craftswomen Changing the World* (New York: Monacellli Press, 2000).

Chapter 16 Notes

[1]Information from "Importing Enthusiasm," *Business Week* (November 7, 1994); and corporate web site: www.Motorola.com/General/inside.html.

[2]Grove quote from John A. Bryne, "Visionary vs. Visionary," *Business Week* (August 28, 2000), pp. 210–14; Chambers quote from Charles O'Reilly III and Jeffrey Pfeffer, *Hidden Value: How Great Companies Achieve Extraordinary*

Results Through Ordinary People (Boston, MA: Harvard Business School Publishing, 2000), p. 4.

[3]See Edward E. Lawler III, *From the Ground Up: Six Principles for Building the New Logic Corporation* (San Francisco: Jossey-Bass, 1996), pp. 131 l.

[4]Cited in Lynda C. McDermott, Nolan Brawley, and William A. Waite, *World-Class Teams: Working Across Borders* (New York: Wiley, 1998), p. 5.

[5]See, for example, Edward E. Lawler III, Susan Albers Mohrman, and Gerald E. Ledford Jr., *Employee Involvement and Total Quality Management: Practices and Results in Fortune 1000 Companies* (San Francisco: Jossey-Bass, 1992); Susan A. Mohrman, Susan A. Cohen, and Monty A. Mohrman, *Designing Team-based Organizations: New Forms for Knowledge Work* (San Francisco: Jossey-Bass, 1995).

[6]Jon R. Katzenbach and Douglas K. Smith, *The Wisdom of Teams: Creating the High Performance Organization* (Boston: Harvard Business School Press, 1993).

[7]For insights on how to conduct effective meetings see Mary A. De Vries, *How to Run a Meeting* (New York: Penguin, 1994).

[8]A classic work is Bib Latane, Kipling Williams, and Stephen Harkins, "Many Hands Make Light the Work: The Causes and Consequences of Social Loafing," *Journal of Personality and Social Psychology,* vol. 37 (1978), pp. 822–32.

[9]See Marvin E. Shaw, *Group Dynamics: The Psychology of Small Group Behavior,* 2d ed. (New York: McGraw-Hill, 1976); Harold J. Leavitt, "Suppose We Took Groups More Seriously," in Eugene L. Cass and Frederick G. Zimmer (eds.), *Man and Work in Society* (New York: Van Nostrand Reinhold, 1975), pp. 67–77.

[10]John M. George, "Extrinsic and Intrinsic Origins of Perceived Social Loafing in Organizations," *Academy of Management Journal* (March 1992), pp. 191–202; and W. Jack Duncan, "Why Some People Loaf in Groups While Others Loaf Alone," *Academy of Management Executive,* vol. 8 (1994), pp. 79–80.

[11]See Leavitt, op cit.

[12]The "linking pin" concept is introduced in Rensis Likert, *New Patterns of Management* (New York: McGraw-Hill, 1962).

[13]See discussion by Susan G. Cohen and Don Mankin, "The Changing Nature of Work," in Susan Albers Mohrman, Jay R. Galbraith, Edward E. Lawler, III, and Associates, *Tomorrow's Organization: Crafting, Winning Capabilities in a Dynamic World* (San Francisco: Jossey-Bass, 1998), pp. 154–78.

[14]Information from "Diversity: America's Strength," special advertising section, *Fortune* (June 23, 1997); American Express corporate communication (1998).

[15]Example in Sue Shellenbarger, "Companies are Finding Real Payoffs in Aiding Employee Satisfaction," *Wall Street Journal* (October 11, 2000), p. B1.

[16]See Susan D. Van Raalte, "Preparing the Task Force to Get Good Results," *S.A.M. Advanced Management Journal,* vol. 47 (winter 1982), pp. 11–16; Walter Kiechel III, "The Art of the Corporate Task Force," *Fortune* (January 28, 1991), pp. 104–6.

[17]Developed from Ibid.

[18]Mohrman, et al., op cit.

[19]Ron Carter, "Team Concept Puts Workers and Bosses in Same Boat," *Columbus Dispatch* (October 27, 1997), pp. 8, 9.

[20]For a good discussion of quality circles, see Edward E. Lawler III and Susan A. Mohrman, "Quality Circles After the Fad," *Harvard Business Review* vol. 63 (January–February 1985), pp. 65–71; Edward E. Lawler, III and Susan Albers Mohrman, "Employee Involvement, Reengineering, and TQM: Focusing on Capability Development," in Mohrman, et al. (1998), pp. 179–208.

[21]See Wayne F. Cascio, "Managing a Virtual Workplace," *Academy of Management Executive,* vol. 14 (2000), pp. 81–90.

[22]Information from "Ford Team Find Ways to Recycle Car Parts," *Columbus Dispatch* (December 20, 1997), p. G1; and corporate web site: www.ford.com /default.asp?pageid=103.

[23]Wanda J. Orlikowski and J. Debra Hofman, "An Improvisational Model for Change Management: The Case of Groupware Technologies," *Sloan Management Review* (fall 1993), pp. 27–36.

[24]R. Brent Gallupe and William H. Cooper, "Brainstorming Electronically," *Sloan Management Review* (winter 1997), pp. 11–21; Cascio, op cit.

[25]William M. Bulkeley, "Computerizing Dull Meetings Is Touted as an Antidote to the Mouth That Bored," *Wall Street Journal* (January 28, 1992), pp. B1, B2.

[26]Cascio, op cit.

[27]See, for example, Paul S. Goodman, Rukmini Devadas, and Terri L. Griffith Hughson, "Groups and Productivity: Analyzing the Effectiveness of Self-Managing Teams," chapter 11 in John R. Campbell and Richard J. Campbell, *Productivity in Organizations* (San Francisco: Jossey-Bass, 1988); Jack Orsbrun, Linda Moran, Ed Musslewhite, and John H. Zenger, with Craig Perrin, *Self-Directed Work Teams: The New American Challenge* (Homewood, IL: Business One Irwin, 1990); Dale E. Yeatts and Cloyd Hyten, *High Performing Self-Managed Work Teams* (Thousand Oaks, CA: Sage, 1997).

[28]Bradley L. Kirkman and Debra L. Shapiro, "The Impact of Cultural Values on Employee Resistance to Teams: Toward of Model of Globalized Self-Managing Work Team Effectiveness," *Academy of Management Review,* vol. 22 (1997), pp. 730–57.

[29]For a discussion of effectiveness in the context of top management teams, see Edward E. Lawler III, David Finegold and Jay A. Conger, "Corporate Boards: Developing Effectiveness at the Top," in Mohrman, op cit. (1998), pp. 23–50.

[30]For a review of research on group effectiveness, see J. Richard Hackman, "The Design of Work Teams," in Jay W. Lorsch (ed.), *Handbook of Organizational Behavior* (Englewood Cliffs, NJ: Prentice-Hall, 1987), pp. 315–42; and, J. Richard Hackman, Ruth Wageman, Thomas M. Ruddy, and Charles L. Ray, "Team Effectiveness in Theory and Practice," Chapter 5 in Cary L. Cooper and Edwin A. Locke, *Industrial and Organizational Psychology: Linking Theory with Practice* (Malden, MA: Blackwell, 2000).

[31]Ibid; Lawler, et al., op cit. 1998.

[32]Example from "Designed for Interaction," *Fortune* (January 8, 2001), p. 150.

[33]See Warren Watson, "Cultural Diversity's Impact on Interaction Process and Performance," *Academy of Management Journal,* vol. 16 (1993); and Christopher Earley and Elaine Mosakowski, "Creating Hybrid Team Structures: An Empirical Test of Transnational Team Functioning," *Academy of Management Journal,* vol. 5 (February 2000), pp. 26–49.

[34]J. Steven Heinen and Eugene Jacobson, "A Model of Task Group Development in Complex Organizations and a Strategy of Implementation," *Academy of Management Review,* vol. 1 (1976), pp. 98–111; Bruce W. Tuckman, "Developmental Sequence in Small Groups," Psychological Bulletin, vol. 63 (1965), pp. 384–99; Bruce W. Tuckman and Mary Ann C. Jensen, "Stages of Small-Group Development Revisited," *Group & Organization Studies,* vol. 2 (1977), pp. 419–27.

[35]See for example, Edgar Schein, *Process Consultation* (Reading, MA: Addison-Wesley, 1988); and Linda C.

McDermott, Nolan Brawley and William A. Waite, *World-Class Teams: Working Across Borders* (New York: Wiley, 1998).

36For a good discussion, see Robert F. Allen and Saul Pilnick, "Confronting the Shadow Organization: How to Detect and Defeat Negative Norms," *Organizational Dynamics* (Spring 1973), pp. 13–16.

37Information from corporate web site: www.steinway.com.

38See Schein, op cit., pp. 76–79.

39Marvin E. Shaw, *Group Dynamics: The Psychology of Small Group Behavior* (New York: McGraw-Hill, 1976).

40A classic work in this area is K. Benne and P. Sheets, *Journal of Social Issues,* vol. 2 (1948), pp. 42–47; see also, Likert, op cit., pp. 166–69; Schein, op cit. pp. 49–56.

41Based on John R. Schermerhorn Jr., James G. Hunt, and Richard N. Osborn, *Organizational Behavior,* 7th ed. (New York: Wiley, 2000), pp. 345–46.

42Research on communication networks is found in Alex Bavelas, "Communication Patterns in Task-Oriented Groups," *Journal of the Acoustical Society of America,* vol. 22 (1950), pp. 725–30; Shaw, op cit.

43Schein, op cit., pp. 69–75.

44See Kathleen M. Eisenhardt, Jean L. Kahwajy, and L. J. Bourgeois III, "How Management Teams Can Have a Good Fight," *Harvard Business Review* (July–August 1997), pp. 77–85.

45Victor H. Vroom and Arthur G. Jago, *The New Leadership: Managing Participation in Organizations* (Englewood Cliffs, NJ: Prentice Hall, 1988); Victor H. Vroom, "A New Look in Managerial Decision-Making," *Organizational Dynamics* (spring 1973), pp. 66–80; Victor H. Vroom and Phillip Yetton, *Leadership and Decision-Making* (Pittsburgh: University of Pittsburgh Press, 1973).

46Norman F. Maier, "Assets and Liabilities in Group Problem Solving," *Psychological Review,* vol. 74 (1967), pp. 239–49.

47Ibid.

48See Irving L. Janis, "Groupthink," *Psychology Today* (November 1971), pp. 43–46; *Victims of Groupthink,* 2d ed. (Boston: Houghton Mifflin, 1982).

49These techniques are well described in Andre L. Delbecq, Andrew H. Van de Ven, and David H. Gustafson, Group Techniques for Program Planning (Glenview, IL: Scott, Foresman, 1975).

50Gallupe and Cooper, op cit.

51A very good overview is provided by William D. Dyer, *Team-Building* (Reading, MA: Addison-Wesley, 1977).

52Dennis Berman, "Zap! Pow! Splat!" *Business Week,* Enterprise issue (February 9, 1998), p. ENT22.

53Information from Jennifer Scott, "Working Better Together Is the Challenge," *Columbus Dispatch* (November 3, 1997), pp. 10–11.

54Katzenbach and Smith, op cit.

55Carl E. Larson and Frank M. J. LaFasto, *Team Work: What Must Go Right/What Can Go Wrong* (Newbury Park, CA: Sage, 1990).

56Quote from "Teach Your Leaders that Their Main Priority Is to Energize and Grow Their Team Around Themselves," *Fast Company* (March, 2001), p. 95.

57See Jon R. Katzenbach, "The Myth of the Top Management Team," *Harvard Business Review,* vol. 75 (November–December 1997), pp. 83–91.

58Developed from David Sibbet, *Process Tools* (San Francisco, CA: The Grove Consultants International, 2000).

Information from James Hannah, "Exec Touts Rigorous Retreats," *Columbus Dispatch* (October 8, 2000), p. G2.

Chapter 17 Notes

1Quotes from *Business Week* (July 8, 1991), pp. 60–61; for additional information see center's web site: www.ccl.org.

2Henry Mintzberg, *The Nature of Managerial Work* (New York: Harper & Row, 1973).

3John P. Kotter, "What Effective General Managers Really Do," *Harvard Business Review,* vol. 60 (November–December 1982), pp. 156–57; and *The General Managers* (New York: Macmillan, 1986).

4"Relationships Are the Most Powerful Form of Media," *Fast Company* (March 2001), p. 100.

5Alison Overholt, "Intel's Got (Too Much) Mail," *Fast Company* (March 2001), pp. 56–58.

6See Mintzberg, op cit.; Kotter, op cit.

7*Business Week* (February 10, 1992), pp. 102–8.

8See Robert H. Lengel and Richard L. Daft, "The Selection of Communication Media as an Executive Skill," *Academy of Management Executive,* vol. 2 (August 1988), pp. 225–32.

9Quotations from John Huey, "America's Most Successful Merchant," *Fortune* (September 23, 1991), pp. 46–59; see also Sam Walton and John Huey, *Sam Walton: Made in America: My Story* (New York: Bantam Books, 1993).

10See also Eric Matson, "Now That We Have Your Complete Attention," *Fast Company* (February–March 1997), pp. 124–32.

11David McNeill, *Hand and Mind: What Gestures Reveal about Thought* (Chicago: University of Chicago Press, 1992).

12Adapted from Richard V. Farace, Peter R. Monge, and Hamish M. Russell, *Communicating and Organizing* (Reading, MA: Addison-Wesley, 1977), pp. 97–98.

13Tom Peters and Nancy Austin, *A Passion for Excellence* (New York: Random House, 1985).

14This discussion is based on Carl R. Rogers and Richard E. Farson, "Active Listening" (Chicago: Industrial Relations Center of the University of Chicago, n.d.).

15A useful source of guidelines is John J. Gabarro and Linda A. Hill, "Managing Performance," Note 9-96-022 (Boston, MA: Harvard Business School Publishing, n.d.).

16Information from Carol Hymowitz, "How to Tell Employees All the Things They Don't Want to Hear," *Wall Street Journal,* (August 22, 2000), p. B1.

17Developed from John Anderson, "Giving and Receiving Feedback," in Paul R. Lawrence, Louis B. Barnes, and Jay W. Lorsch (eds.), *Organizational Behavior and Administration,* 3d ed. (Homewood, IL: Richard D. Irwin, 1976), p. 109.

18See Lengel and Daft, op cit. (1988).

19Information from Esther Wachs Book, "Leadership for the Millennium," *Working Woman* (March 1998), pp. 29–34.

20Information from Hilary Stout, "Self-Evaluation Brings Change to a Family's Ad Agency," *Wall Street Journal,* (January 6, 1998), p. B2.

21See Richard Lepsinger and Anntoinette D. Lucia, *The Art and Science of 360° Feedback* (San Francisco: Jossey-Bass, 1997).

22Brian O'Reilly, "360° Feedback Can Change Your Life," *Fortune* (October 17, 1994), pp. 93–100.

23A classic work on proxemics is Edward T. Hall's book, *The Hidden Dimension* (Garden City, NY: Doubleday, 1986).

24Mirand Wewll, "Alternative Spaces Spawning Desk-Free Zones," *Columbus Dispatch* (May 18, 1998), pp. 10–11.

25Information from Susan Stellin, "Intranets Nurture Companies from the Inside," *New York Times* (January 21, 2001), p. C4.

[26]Example from Heidi A. Schuessler, "Social Studies Class finds How Far E-Mail Travels," *New York Times* (February 22, 2001), p. D8.

[27]See Edward T. Hall, *The Silent Language* (New York: Doubleday, 1973).

[28]See H. R. Schiffman, *Sensation and Perception: An Integrated Approach,* 3d ed. (New York: Wiley, 1990).

[29]A good review is E. L. Jones (ed.), *Attribution: Perceiving the Causes of Behavior* (Morristown, NJ: General Learning Press, 1972). See also John H. Harvey and Gifford Weary, "Current Issues in Attribution Theory and Research," *Annual Review of Psychology,* vol. 35 (1984), pp. 427–59.

[30]See, for example, Stephan Thernstrom and Abigail Thernstrom, *American in Black and White* (New York: Simon & Schuster, 1997); and David A. Thomas and Suzy Wetlaufer, "A Question of Color: A Debate on Race in the U.S. Workplace," *Harvard Business Review* (September–October 1997), pp. 118–32.

[31]Reported by Kembar J. Dunham, "On Board," *Wall Street Journal,* (November 28, 2000), p. B14.

[32]Information from "Misconceptions About Women in the Global Arena Keep Their Numbers Low," Catalyst study: www.catalystwomen.org/home.html.

[33]These examples are from Natasha Josefowitz, *Paths to Power* (Reading, MA: Addison-Wesley, 1980), p. 60. For more on gender issues see Gary N. Powell (ed.), *Handbook of Gender and Work* (Thousand Oaks, CA: Sage, 1999).

[34]Information from Clare Ansberry, "The Gray Team: Averaging Age 70, Staff in This Cosmetics Plant Retires Old Stereotypes" *Wall Street Journal* (February 5, 2001), pp. A1, A15.

[35]The classic work is Dewitt C. Dearborn and Herbert A. Simon, "Selective Perception: A Note on the Departmental Identification of Executives," *Sociometry,* vol. 21 (1958), pp. 140–44. See also, J. P. Walsh, "Selectivity and Selective Perception: Belief Structures and Information Processing, *Academy of Management Journal,* vol. 24 (1988), pp. 453–70.

[36]Quotations from Dana Milbank, "Managers Are Sent to 'Charm Schools' to Discover How to Polish Up Their Acts," *Wall Street Journal,* (December 14, 1990), pp. B1, B3.

[37]Richard E. Walton, *Interpersonal Peacemaking: Confrontations and Third-Party Consultation* (Reading, MA: Addison-Wesley, 1969), p. 2.

[38]See Kenneth W. Thomas, "Conflict and Conflict Management," in M. D. Dunnett (ed.), *Handbook of Industrial and Organizational Behavior* (Chicago: Rand McNally, 1976), pp. 889–935.

[39]See Robert R. Blake and Jane Strygley Mouton, "The Fifth Achievement," *Journal of Applied Behavioral Science,* vol. 6 (1970), pp. 413–27; Alan C. Filley, *Interpersonal Conflict Resolution* (Glenview, IL: Scott, Foresman, 1975).

[40]This discussion is based on Filley, op cit.

[41]Information from the United Nations web site: http://www.un.org/News /ossg/sg/pages/sg_biography.html (February 22, 2001).

[42]Portions of this treatment of negotiation originally adapted from John R. Schermerhorn Jr., James G. Hunt, and Richard N. Osborn, *Managing Organizational Behavior,* 4th ed. (New York: Wiley, 1991), pp. 382–87. Used by permission.

[43]See Roger Fisher and William Ury, *Getting to Yes: Negotiating Agreement Without Giving In* (New York: Penguin, 1983); James A. Wall, Jr., *Negotiation: Theory and Practice* (Glenview, IL: Scott, Foresman, 1985); and William L. Ury, Jeanne M. Brett, and Stephen B. Goldberg, *Getting Disputes Resolved* (San Francisco: Jossey-Bass, 1997).

[44]Fisher and Ury, op cit.

[45]Ibid.

[46]Developed from Max H. Bazerman, *Judgment in Managerial Decision Making,* 4th ed. (New York: Wiley, 1998), Chapter 7.

[47]Fisher and Ury, op cit.

[48]Roy J. Lewicki and Joseph A. Litterer, *Negotiation* (Homewood, IL: Irwin, 1985).

Chapter 18 Notes

[1]Information from "The Littlest PC," *Business Week Frontier* (December 4, 2000), p. F12; "LynuxWorks partners with ZF Linux Devices," corporate press release, San Diego (June 19, 2000): www.linuxdevices.com/news/NS61925 09012.html; and corporate web site: www.zflinux.com.

[2]Information from "On the Road to Innovation," in special advertising section, "Charting the Course: Global Business Sets Its Goals," *Fortune* (August 4, 1997).

[3]Michael Beer and Nitin Nohria, "Cracking the Code of Change," *Harvard Business Review* (May–June 2000), pp. 133–41.

[4]Quote from John A. Byrne, "Visionary vs. Visionary," *Business Week* (August 28, 2000), p. 210.

[5]Quotes from David Kirkpatrick, "From Davos, Talk of Death," *Fortune* (March 5, 2001), pp. 180–82.

[6]Ibid.

[7]See Peter F. Drucker, "The Discipline of Innovation," *Harvard Business Review* (November–December 1998), pp. 3–8.

[8]Tom Peters, *The Circle of Innovation* (New York: Knopf, 1997).

[9]Peter Senge, *The Fifth Discipline* (New York: Harper, 1990).

[10]Ibid.; see also Brian Dumaine, "Mr. Learning Organization," *Fortune* (October 17, 1994), pp. 147–57.

[11]Information from corporate web site: www.kinkos.com.

[12]R. Duane Ireland and Michael A. Hitt, "Achieving and Maintaining Strategic Competitiveness in the 21st Century: The Role of Strategic Leadership," *Academy of Management Executive* (February 1999), pp. 43–57.

[13]Ibid.

[14]See, for example, Roger von Oech, *A Whack on the Side of the Head* (New York: Warner Books, 1983) and *A Kick in the Seat of the Pants* (New York: Harper & Row, 1986).

[15]Cited in Peter F. Drucker, *Management: Tasks, Responsibilities, and Practices* (New York: Harper & Row, 1973), p. 797.

[16]Information from David Kirkpatrick, "Software's Humble Wizard Does It Again." *Fortune* (February 19, 2001), pp. 137–42.

[17]Information from "Providing Rural Phone Service Profitably in Poor Countries." *Business Week* (December 18, 2000), special advertising section.

[18]Based on Edward B. Roberts, "Managing Invention and Innovation," *Research Technology Management* (January–February 1988), pp. 1–19, and Hamel, op cit.

[19]Based on Gary Hamel, Leading the Revolution (Boston, MA: Harvard Business School Press, 2000), pp. 293–95

[20]This discussion is stimulated by James Brian Quinn, "Managing Innovation Controlled Chaos," *Harvard Business Review,* Vol. 63 (May–June 1985). Selected quotations and examples from Kenneth Labich, "The Innovators," *Fortune,* (June 6, 1988), pp. 49–64.

[21]Peter F. Drucker, "Best R&D Is Business Driven," *Wall Street Journal,* (February 10, 1988), p.11.

[22]Developed in part from Quinn, op cit.

[23]See Roberts, op cit.

[24]Drucker, op cit. (1998).

[25]Reported in Carol Hymowitz, "Task of Managing Changes in Workplace Takes

a Careful Hand," *Wall Street Journal* (July 1, 1997), p. B1.

[26]Reported in G. Christian Hill and Mike Tharp, "Stumbling Giant—Big Quarterly Deficit Stuns BankAmerica, Adds Pressure on Chief," *Wall Street Journal*, (July 18, 1985), pp. 1,16.

[27]Beer and Nohria, op cit.; and "Change Management, An Inside Job," *Economist* (July 15, 2000), p. 61.

[28]Based on John P. Kotter, "Leading Change: Why Transformation Efforts Fail," *Harvard Business Review* (March–April 1995), pp. 59–67.

[29]The model and example are described by Beer and Nohria, op cit.

[30]Reported in Robert Rose, "Kentucky Plant Workers Are Cranking Out Good Ideas," *Wall Street Journal* (August 13, 1996), p. B1.

[31]The model and example are described by Beer and Nohria, op cit.

[32]Beer and Nohria, op cit.

[33]See Edward E. Lawler III, "Strategic Choices for Changing Organizations," chapter 12 in Allan M. Mohrman Jr., Susan Albers Mohrman, Gerald E. Ledford Jr., Thomas G. Cummings, Edward E. Lawler III, and Associates, *Large Scale Organizational Change* (San Francisco: Jossey-Bass, 1989).

[34]Example from *Fortune* (December, 1991), pp. 56–62; additional information from corporate web site: www.toro.com.

[35]The classic description of organizations on these terms is by Harold J. Leavitt, "Applied Organizational Change in Industry: Structural, Technological and Humanistic Approaches," in James G. March (ed.), *Handbook of Organizations* (Chicago: Rand McNally, 1965), pp. 1144–70.

[36]Kurt Lewin, "Group Decision and Social Change," in G. E. Swanson, T. M. Newcomb and E. L. Hartley (eds.), *Readings in Social Psychology* (New York: Holt, Rinehart, 1952), pp. 459–73.

[37]This discussion is based on Robert Chin and Kenneth D. Benne, "General Strategies for Effecting Changes in Human Systems," in Warren G. Bennis, Kenneth D. Benne, Robert Chin, and Kenneth E. Corey (eds.), *The Planning of Change*, 3rd ed. (New York: Holt, Rinehart, 1969), pp. 22–45.

[38]The change agent description is developed from an exercise reported in J. William Pfeiffer and John E. Jones, *A Handbook of Structured Experiences for Human Relations Training*, vol. 2 (La Jolla, CA: University Associates, 1973).

[39]Ram N. Aditya, Robert J. House, and Steven Kerr, "Theory and Practice of Leadership: Into the New Millennium," Chapter 6 in Cary L. Cooper and Edwin A. Locke, *Industrial and Organizational Psychology: Linking Theory with Practice* (Malden, MA: Blackwell, 2000).

[40]Pfeiffer and Jones, op cit.

[41]Information from Mike Schneider, "Disney Teaching Exces Magic of Customer Service," *Columbus Dispatch* (December 17, 2000), p. G9.

[42]Pfeiffer and Jones, op cit.

[43]Teresa M. Amabile, "How to Kill Creativity, *Harvard Business Review*, (September–October, 1998), pp. 77–87.

[44]Sue Shellenbarger, "Some Employers Find Way to Ease Burden of Changing Shifts," *Wall Street Journal* (March 25, 1998), p. B1.

[45]Ibid.

[46]John P. Kotter and Leonard A. Schlesinger, "Choosing Strategies for Change," *Harvard Business Review*, vol. 57 (March–April 1979): 109–12.

[47]Wanda J. Orlikowski and J. Debra Hofman, "An Improvisational Model for Change Management: The Case of Groupware Technologies," *Sloan Management Review* (winter 1997), pp. 11–21.

[48]Ibid.

[49]Overviews of organization development are provided by W. Warner Burke, *Organization Development: A Normative View* (Reading, MA: Addison-Wesley, 1987); William Rothwell, Roland Sullivan, and Gary N. McLean, *Practicing Organization Development* (San Francisco: Jossey-Bass, 1995); and Wendell L. French and Cecil H. Bell Jr., *Organization Development*, 6th ed. (Englewood Cliffs, NJ: Prentice-Hall, 1998).

[50]See, for example, Edward E. Lawler III, Susan Albers Mohrman, and Gerald E. Ledford Jr., *Employee Involvement and Total Quality Management* (San Francisco: Jossey-Bass, 1992).

[51]See French and Bell, op cit.

[52]Stephen Covey, "How to Succeed in Today's Workplace," *USA Weekend* (August 29–31, 1997), pp. 4–5.

[53]Tom Peters, "The Brand Called 'You,'" *Fast Company* (August–September 1997).

[54]Information from corporate web site: www.disney.go.com.

Information from "Tea Leaves, Entrails, and Crystal Balls," *Business Week Frontier* (December 4, 2000), p. F26; and World Future Society web site: www.wfs.org.

Photo Credits

Chapter 1

Opener & **Page 5:** ©AP/Wide World Photos. **Page 6:** Courtesy Viatru. **Page 9:** Courtesy Hudson Institute. **Page 10:** Courtesy John Schermerhorn. **Pages 15, 21:** ©AP/Wide World Photos. **Page 23:** Jon Feingersh/Corbis Stock Market.

Chapter 2

Opener. Courtesy Herman Miller, Inc. **Pages 39, 43:** ©AP/Wide World Photos. **Page 48:** Joe McBride/Stone. **Page 54:** Kevin Fleming/CORBIS.

Chapter 3

Opener: COVISINT, L.L.C. **Page 65:** Courtesy Ernst & Young LLP. **Pages 67, 69, 82:** ©AP/Wide World Photos. **Page 75:** Courtesy D'Artagnan

Chapter 4

Opener: Ed Honowitz/Stone. **Page 94:** Jim Erickson/Corbis Stock Market. **Page 95:** Courtesy United Parcel Service. **Page 100:** Jon Riley/Stone. **Page 102:** SPSS 10.1 for Windows. Reproduced with permission of SPSS, Inc. **Page 106:** Courtesy Daimler Chrysler Corporation. **Page 107:** Tobia Everke/Liaison Agency, Inc.

Chapter 5

Opener: Courtesy NTT DoCoMo. **Page 120:** Mark Peters/Liaison Agency, Inc. **Pages 121,123:** ©AP/Wide World Photos. **Page 126:** T. Anderson/The Image Bank. **Page 133:** Bever Borne with Air-Tech, Inc. **Page 136:** Keren Su/CORBIS.

Chapter 6

Opener: Courtesy Goldman Environmental Foundation. **Page 146:** Courtesy Peter Finger, Manhattan College. **Page 147:** Courtesy Tom's of Maine, Inc. **Page 153 (top):** Courtesy Council on Economic Priorities. **Page 153 (bottom):** Photo courtesy Malden Mills Industry, Lawrence, MA. **Page 156:** Bruce Hands/Stone. **Page 158:** Denis Scott/FPG International.

Chapter 7

Opener: Courtesy Manheim Auctions. **Page 177:** Jess Stock/Stone. **Page 184:** David Gould/The Image Bank. **Page 186:** Courtesy United States Army. **Page 188:** AFP/CORBIS. **Page 194:** Cari Single/The Image Works.

Chapter 8

Opener: ©AP/Wide World Photos. **Page 213 (top):** Courtesy freemarkets.com. **Page 213 (bottom):** (bottom): Lois & Bob Schlowsky/Stone. **Page 215:** Etienne De Malglaive/Stone. **Page 217:** John Lamb/Stone. **Page 219:** Courtesy Worthington Industries.

Chapter 9

Opener & **Page 233 (top):** ©AP/Wide World Photos. **Page 233 (center):** Courtesy Virgin. **Page 233 (bottom):** Reprinted with permission Black Enterprise Magazine, New York. All rights reserved. **Page 234 (top):** Courtesy Huizenga Holdings, Inc. **Page 234 (bottom):** (bottom): Courtesy The Body Shop, Inc. **Page 237:** ©Stanley Newton, Photo courtesy Anita Santiago Advertising. **Page 240:** John Gilimoure/Corbis Stock Market. **Page 243:** ©AP/Wide World Photos. **Page 245:** Courtesy Domino's Pizza. **Page 246:** Contents ©2001 by NBIA. All rights reserved worldwide.

Chapter 10

Opener: SuperStock. **Page 258:** Courtesy Siemens Corporation. **Page 265:** Bruce Ayres/Stone. **Page 268:** ©AP/Wide World Photos. **Page 270:** Courtesy Nucor Corporation. **Page 271:** Courtesy Intel Corporation.

Chapter 11

Opener: ©Jay Blakesberg. **Page 283:** Kaluzny Thatcher/Stone. **Page 286:** Todd Davidson/The Image Bank. **Page 295:** Courtesy Patricia Seybold Group.

Chapter 12

Opener: Courtesy WetFeet.Com. **Page 306:** Mark Wilson/Liaison Agency, Inc. **Page 307:** Jon Bradley/Stone. **Page 313:** Courtesy Southwest Airlines. **Page 315:** Courtesy Johnson & Johnson. **Page 323:** ©AP/Wide World Photos.

Chapter 13

Opener: ©AP Wide World Photos. **Page 339:** Victoria Pearson/Stone. **Page 346:** Courtesy W. L. Gore & Associates, inc. **Page 350:** ©AP/Wide World Photos.

Chapter 14

Opener: Taylor/Fabricius/Liaison Agency, Inc. **Page 364:** SuperStock. **Page 368:** Courtesy Silicon Graphics. **Page 376:** Courtesy Rocky Shoes & Boots. Inc. **Page 377:** ©AP/Wide World Photos.

Chapter 15

Opener: Paul Barton/Corbis Stock Market. **Page 389:** P. Crowther/S. Carter/Stone. **Page 390:** Bruce Jaffe/Liaison Agency, Inc. **Page 400:** ©AP/Wide World Photos. **Page 407:** Chip Henderson/Stone.

Chapter 16

Opener: ©AP/Wlde World Photos. **Page 421:** Courtesy Ford Motor Company. **Page 429:** ©AP/Wide World Photos. **Page 432:** Courtesy Worthington Industries. **Page 438:** Jon Feingersh/Corbis Stock Market.

Chapter 17

Opener: Courtesy Center for Creative Leadersip. **Page 448:** Marc Franccoeur/Liaison Agency, Inc. **Page 450:** Courtesy The Scotts Company. **Page 455:** Toby Seger/Liaison Agency, Inc. **Page 460:** Walter Hodges/Stone. **Page 462:** Louise Gubb/The Image Works.

Chapter 18

Opener: Courtesy ZF Linux Devices, Inc. **Page 474:** Danny Lehman/CORBIS. **Page 475:** Courtesy Kinkos, Inc. **Page 482:** Courtesy Toro Company. **Page 489:** Jose Pelaez/Corbis Stock Market. **Page 495:** ©Stone.

Name Index

Subject Index

SELF-TEST ANSWERS

Chapter 1

1. d	11. F	5. d	13. F
2. c	12. T	6. c	14. F
3. a	13. T	7. c	15. T
4. b	14. T	8. a	16. F
5. a	15. T	9. b	17. F
6. a	16. T	10. a	18. T
7. c	17. F	11. T	19. F
8. a	18. T	12. T	20. F
9. b	19. F		
10. b	20. T		

21. Managers must respect subordinates as mature, responsible, adult human beings. This is part of their ethical and social responsibility as persons to whom others report at work. The work setting should be organized and managed to respect the rights of people and their human dignity. Included among the expectations for ethical behavior would be actions to protect individual privacy, provide freedom from sexual harassment, and offer safe and healthy job conditions. Failure to do so is socially irresponsible. It may also cause productivity losses due to dissatisfaction and poor work commitments.

22. The manager is held accountable by his boss for performance results of the manager's work unit. The manager must answer back to the boss for unit performance. By the same token, the manager's subordinates must answer back to her or him for their individual performance. They are accountable to the manager.

23. If the glass ceiling effect operates in a given situation, it would act as a hidden barrier to advancement beyond a certain level. Top managers controlling promotions would not give them to African-American candidates, regardless of their capabilities.

24. Ohmae's term "borderless world" refers to the fact that more businesses are operating on a global scale and the countries are becoming very interdependent economically. Products are sold and resources purchased around the world, and business strategies increasingly target markets in more than one country.

25. One approach to this question is through the framework of essential management skills offered by Katz. At the first level of management, technical skills are important and I would feel capable in this respect. However, I would expect to learn and refine these skills through my work experiences. Human skills, the ability to work well with other people, will also be very important. Given the diversity anticipated for this team, I will need good human skills. I will also have a leadership responsibility to help others on the team develop and utilize these skills so that the team itself can function effectively. Finally, I would expect opportunities to develop my conceptual or analytical skills in anticipation of higher level appointments. In terms of personal development I should recognize that the conceptual skills will increase in importance relative to the technical skills as I move upward in management responsibility.

Chapter 2

1. a		3. b	
2. d		4. b	

21. Possible operating objectives reflecting a commitment to competitive advantage through customer service include: (a) providing high-quality goods and services, (b) providing low-cost goods and services, (c) providing short waiting times for goods and services, and (d) providing goods and services meeting unique customer needs.

22. External customers are the consumers or clients who buy the organization's goods or use its services. Internal customers are the individuals or groups within the organization who utilize goods and services produced by others also inside the organization.

23. The core culture of the organization consists of the values that shape and direct the behavior of members. An example would be a "quality" value that encouraged everyone to always do the highest quality work. The observable culture is found in the everyday activities of the organization. It may exist in the form of stories, rituals, and heroes. For example, reward ceremonies to recognize high-performance accomplishments are a ritual; the repeated reminder at such ceremonies of a popular high performer of the past is an example of recognizing heroes.

24. Subcultures are important in organizations because of the diversity of the workforce. Although working in the same organization and sharing the same organizational culture, members may also differ in subculture affiliations based on such aspects as gender, age, and ethnic differences. It is important to understand how subculture differences may influence working relationships. For example, a 40-year-old supervisor of 20-year-old workers must understand that the values and behaviors of the younger workforce may not be totally consistent with what she or he believes in, and vice versa.

25. I disagree with this statement since a strong organizational or corporate culture can be a positive influence on any organization, large or small. Also issues of diversity, inclusiveness and multiculturalism apply as well. The woman working for the large company is mistaken in thinking that the concepts do not apply to her friend's small business. In fact, the friend as owner and perhaps founder of the business should be working hard to establish the values and other elements that will create a strong and continuing culture and respect for diversity. Employees of any organization should have core organizational values to serve as reference points for their attitudes and behavior. The rites and rituals of everyday organizational life are also important to recognize positive accomplishments and add meaning to the employment relationships. It may even be that the friend's roles as creator and sponsor of the corporate culture and diversity leader are more magnified in the small business setting. As the owner and manager, she is visible everyday

to all employees. How she acts will have a great impact on any "culture" that is established in her store.

Chapter 3

1. c	11. F
2. a	12. F
3. c	13. T
4. c	14. T
5. c	15. F
6. a	16. F
7. c	17. F
8. b	18. F
9. a	19. T
10. b	20. T

21. An information system is intended to serve an organization and its decision makers by providing a convenient and accurate means of collecting, organizing, and distributing data in ways that make it meaningful as information. Today, such systems are widely used to improve operations and relationship within organizations and between organizations and their external environments – including supplier and customer relationships.
22. The success of any information system depends on (1) the technical quality of the system, (2) management support for the system, and (3) the participation and involvement of users in the design and continuous improvement of the system. Managers should avoid the following common information system mistakes. (1) Assuming that more information is always better. (2) Assuming that new equipment and software is always better. (3) Assuming that once a computer system is in place nothing can go wrong with it. (4) Assuming that the computer can do everything. (5) Assuming that human judgment is no longer important.
23. Decision making is just one part of the broader problem-solving process. Problem solving involves: (1) finding and defining a problem, (2) generating alternative solutions, (3) evaluating alternatives and making a decision to pursue one of them, (4) implementing the chosen solution, and (5) evaluating results.
24. A systematic thinking manager is going to approach problem solving in a logical and rational fashion. The tendency will be to proceed in a linear step-by-step fashion, handling one issue at a time. A manager using intuitive thinking will be more spontaneous and open in problem solving. He or she may jump from one stage in the process to the other and deal with many different things at once.
25. This is what I would say: Continuing developments in information technology are changing the work setting for most employees. An important development for the traditional "white collar" worker falls in the area of office automation—the use of computers and related technologies to facilitate everyday office work. In the "electronic office" of today and tomorrow, you should be prepared to work with and take full advantage of the following: "Smart workstations" supported by desktop computers; "voice messaging" systems whereby computers take dictation, answer the telephone, and relay messages; "database" and "word-processing" software systems that allow storage, access, and manipulation of data as well as the preparation of reports; "electronic mail" systems that send mail and data computer to computer; "electronic bulletin boards" for posting messages; "computer conferencing" and "video conferencing" that allow people to work with one another every day over great distances. These are among the capabilities of the new workplace. To function effectively, you must be prepared not only to use these systems to full advantage but also to stay abreast of new developments as they become available.

Chapter 4

1. d	11. F
2. b	12. T
3. b	13. F
4. a	14. T
5. c	15. F
6. a	16. T
7. a	17. T
8. b	18. F
9. c	19. T
10. c	20. T

21. Theory Y assumes that people are capable of taking responsibility and exercising self-direction and control in their work. Under these assumptions they should positively respond to opportunities for greater participation and involvement.
22. According to the deficit principle, a satisfied need is not a motivator of behavior. The social need will only motivate if it is deprived or in deficit. According to the progression principle, people move step by step up Maslow's hierarchy as they strive to satisfy needs. For example, once the social need is satisfied the esteem need will be activated.
23. Contingency thinking takes an "if—then" approach to situations. It seeks to modify or adapt management approaches to fit the needs of each situation. An example would be to give more customer contact responsibility to workers who want to satisfy social needs at work, while giving more supervisory responsibilities to those who want to satisfy their esteem or ego needs.
24. The external environment is the source of the resources an organization needs to operate. In order to continue to obtain these resources the organization must be successful in selling its goods and services to customers. If customer feedback is negative, the organization must make adjustments or risk losing the support needed to obtain important resources.
25. A bureaucracy operates with a strict hierarchy of authority, promotion based on competency and performance, formal rules and procedures, and written documentation. Enrique can do all of these things in his store. However, he must be careful to meet the needs of the workers and not to make the mistake identified by Argyris of failing to treat them as mature adults. While remaining well organized, there is room for the store manager to help workers meet higher order esteem and self-fulfillment needs, as well as to exercise autonomy under Theory Y assumptions.

Chapter 5

1. c	8. c
2. b	9. a
3. b	10. d
4. c	11. F
5. b	12. T
6. a	13. F
7. a	14. F

15. T	18. F
16. F	19. T
17. F	20. T

21. The North American Free Trade Agreement, NAFTA, provides the framework for Mexico, the United States, and Canada, to free the flows of investments, products, and workers across their borders. This agreement creates a large consumer market and is an opportunity for businesses in all countries to take full advantage of all of North America as a resource and customer base.

22. MNC/host country relationships should be mutually beneficial. Sometimes host countries believe MNCs take unfair advantage of them. The complaints against MNCs include taking excessive profits, hiring the best local labor, not respecting local laws and customs, and dominating the local economy.

23. The power-distance dimension of national culture reflects the degree to which members of a society accept status and authority inequalities. Since management involves positions of superior and subordinate status, the nature of the relationship may vary from one culture to the next.

24. For each region of the world you should identify a major economic theme or issue or element. For example: Europe—the European Union should be discussed for its economic significance to member countries and to outsiders; Americas—NAFTA should be discussed for its current implications as well as potential significance once Chile and other nations join; Asia—the Asia-Pacific Economic Forum should be identified as a platform for growing regional economic cooperation among a very economically powerful group of countries, Africa—the new nonracial democracy in South Africa should be cited as a stimulus to broader outside investor interest in Africa.

25. Kim must recognize that the cultural differences between the United States and Japan may affect the success of quality circles and work teams. The United States was the most individualistic culture in Hofstede's study of national cultures; Japan is much more collectivist. Group practices such as the quality circle and teams are more consistent with the Japanese culture. When introduced into a more individualistic culture, these same practices may encounter difficulties. At the very least, Kim should proceed with caution, discuss the ideas with the workers before making any changes, and then monitor the changes closely so that adjustments can be made as the workers gain familiarity with them. The goal should be to improve operations with practices appropriate to the workers and culture.

Chapter 6

1. a	11. F
2. a	12. T
3. d	13. T
4. d	14. F
5. a	15. T
6. d	16. T
7. a	17. F
8. d	18. T
9. c	19. F
10. c	20. T

21. The individualism view is that ethical behavior is that which best serves long-term interests. The justice view is that ethical behavior is fair and equitable in its treatment of people.

22. The rationalizations are believing that the behavior is not really illegal, the behavior is really in everyone's best interests, no one will find out, and the organization will protect you.

23. The socioeconomic view of corporate social responsibility argues that socially responsible behavior is in a firm's long-run best interests. It should be good for profits, it creates a positive public image, it helps avoid government regulation, it meets public expectations, and it is an ethical obligation.

24. Government agencies implement and enforce laws that are passed to regulate business activities. They act in the public's behalf to ensure compliance with laws on such matters as occupational safety and health, consumer protection, and environmental protection.

25. The manager could make a decision based on any one of the strategies. As an obstructionist, she may assume that Bangladesh needs the business and it is a local matter as to who will be employed to make the gloves. As a defensive strategy, the manager may decide to require the supplier to meet the minimum employment requirements under Bangladesh law. As an accommodation strategy, the manager may require that the supplier go beyond local laws and meet standards set by equivalent laws in the United States. A proaction strategy would involve the manager in trying to set an example by operating in Bangladesh only with suppliers who not only meet local standards, but who actively support the education of children in the communities in which they operate.

Chapter 7

1. d	11. T
2. a	12. T
3. d	13. T
4. d	14. T
5. d	15. F
6. b	16. F
7. d	17. T
8. a	18. F
9. c	19. T
10. a	20. F

21. The five steps in the formal planning process are: (1) Define your objectives, (2) determine where you stand relative to objectives, (3) develop premises about future conditions, (4) identify and choose among action alternatives to accomplish objectives, (5) implement action plans and evaluate results.

22. A strategic plan sets long-term enterprise direction. For example, a strategic plan for a local bank might be to expand regionally to become the dominant bank in rural communities of fewer than 5000 population. An operational plan helps to implement a strategic plans. An operational plan for the bank may be to acquire three banks per year that serve communities of the target size and location.

23. Benchmarking is the use of external standards to help evaluate one's own situation and develop ideas and directions for improvement. The bookstore owner/manager might visit other bookstores in other towns which are known for their success. By observing and studying the operations of those stores and then comparing her store to them, the owner/manager can develop plans for future action.

24. Zero-based budgeting begins each new budget cycle from a "zero" base. This means the budget must be totally justified based on future needs. For example, a 6-month advertising budget for the sports department in a discount retailer would be negotiated based on projected campaigns and sales. It would not be done as a percentage increase or decrease to the budget that had been given in the prior 6 months.

25. I would begin the speech by describing MBO as an integrated planning and control approach. I would also clarify that the key elements in MBO are objectives and participation. Any objectives should be clear, measurable, and time defined. In addition, these objectives should be set with the full involvement and participation of the employees; they should not be set by the manager and then told to the employees. Given this, I would describe how each business manager should jointly set objectives with each of his or her employees and jointly review progress toward their accomplishment. I would suggest that the employees should work on the required activities while staying in communication with their managers. The managers, in turn, should provide any needed support or assistance to their employees. This whole process could be formally recycled at least twice per year.

Chapter 8

1. a	11. T
2. b	12. F
3. c	13. T
4. c	14. F
5. d	15. F
6. b	16. T
7. c	17. F
8. a	18. F
9. b	19. T
10. c	20. T

21. A corporate strategy sets long-term direction for an enterprise as a whole. Functional strategies set directions so that business functions such as marketing and manufacturing support the overall corporate strategy.

22. A SWOT analysis is useful during strategic planning. It involves the analysis of organizational strengths and weaknesses, and of environmental opportunities and threats.

23. The BCG matrix analyzes business performance in terms of market share and market growth rates. This results in classification of business performance into dogs, cash cows, question marks, and stars. In the GE Business Screen, the two dimensions for analysis are more sophisticated. Market size and growth are one part of industry attractiveness, which also includes such factors as capital requirements and competitive intensity. Market share is only one of the factors analyzed for business strength, with others including technological advantage, operating costs, and more. The GE Business Screen results in classifying business performance as winners, question marks, average businesses, profit producers and losers.

24. Strategic leadership is the ability to enthuse people to participate in continuous change, performance enhancement and the implementation of organizational strategies. The special qualities of the successful strategic leader include the ability to make trade-offs, create a sense of urgency, communicate the strategy and engage others in continuous learning about the strategy and its performance responsibilities.

25. Porter's competitive strategy model involves the possible use of three alternative strategies: differentiation, cost leadership, and focus. In this situation, the larger department store seems better positioned to follow the cost leadership strategy. This means that Kim may want to consider the other two alternatives. A differentiation strategy would involve trying to distinguish Kim's products from those of the larger store. This might involve a "made in America" theme or an emphasis on leather or canvas or some other type of clothing material. A focus strategy might specifically target college students and try to respond to their tastes and needs rather than the larger community population. This might involve special orders and other types of individualized service for the college student market.

Chapter 9

1. d	11. T
2. a	12. F
3. b	13. T
4. b	14. T
5. b	15. T
6. a	16. F
7. d	17. F
8. a	18. F
9. b	19. T
10. a	20. F

21. Entrepreneurship is rich with diversity. It is an avenue for business entry and career success that is pursued by many women and members of minority groups. Data show almost 40% of U.S. businesses are owned by women. Many report leaving other employment because they had limited opportunities. For them, entrepreneurship made available the opportunities for career success that they lacked. Minority-owned businesses are one of the fastest growing sectors, with the growth rates highest for Hispanic-owned, Asian-owned and African-American owned, in that order.

22. The Internet is host to the "dot.com" entrepreneurial firms that are so characteristic of the new economy. There are many opportunities to create businesses that operate through the Internet, or to create new opportunities for an existing business by adding an Internet-driven component. Some firms are direct sellers, engaging in "e-tailing" ventures; others may provide auction locations are linkages that allow other businesses to find and work with one another. For someone with creativity and informed about technology, the Internet offers low barriers to entry for many entrepreneurial new ventures.

23. The limited partnership form of small business ownership consists of a general partner and one or more "limited partners." The general partner(s) play an active role in managing and operating the business. The limited partners do not. All contribute resources of some value to the partnership for the conduct of the business. The advantage of any partnership form is that the partners may share in profits, but their potential for losses is limited by the size of their original investments.

24. This is the realm of "intrapreneurship," or entrepreneurship that takes place within the context of a large organization. One of the ways to stimulate entrepeneurship in such settings is to make it a valued part of the culture.

In other words, to reward entrepreneurial behavior and not discourage it. Another way is to set up entrepreneurial units, sometimes called "skunkworks," that are allowed to operate free from any constraints of the larger organization. The creative teamwork in these units can be a major force for entrepreneurship.

25. My friend is right, it takes a lot of forethought and planning to prepare the launch of a new business venture. In response to the question of how to insure that I am really being customer-focused, I would ask and answer for myself the following questions. In all cases I would try to frame my business model so that the answers are realistic but very position in driving my business by a customer orientation. The "customer" questions might include: "Who are my potential customers? What market niche am I shooting for? What do the customers in this market really want? How do these customers make purchase decisions? How much will it cost to produce and distribute my product/service to these customers? How much will it cost to attract and retain customers? Following an overall executive summary, that includes a commitment to this customer-orientation, I would address the following areas in writing up my initial business plan. The plan would address such areas as company description–mission, owners and legal form, as well as anindustry analysis, product and services description, marketing description and strategy, staffing model, financial projections with cash flows, and capital needs.

Chapter 10

1. a		11. T
2. c		12. F
3. d		13. T
4. a		14. F
5. b		15. T
6. c		16. F
7. b		17. F
8. b		18. F
9. b		19. T
10. a		20. T

21. The product structure organizes work around a product, and the division or unit would be headed by a product manager or executive. The geographical structure organizes work by area or location. Different geographical regions would be headed by regional managers or executives.

22. The functional structure is prone to problems of internal coordination. One symptom may be that the different functional areas, such as marketing and manufacturing, are not working well together. This structure is also slow in responding to changing environmental trends and challenges. If the firm finds that its competitors are getting to market faster with new and better products, this is another potential indicator that the functional structure is not supporting operations properly.

23. A network structure often involves one organization "contracting out" aspects of its operations to other organizations who specialize in them. The example used in the text was of a company that contracted out its mailroom services. Through the formation of networks of contracts, the organization is reduced to a core of essential employees whose expertise is concentrated in the primary business areas. The contracts are monitored and maintained in the network to allow the overall operations of the organization to continue even though they are not directly accomplished by full-time employees.

24. By reducing levels of management, the organization may benefit from lower overhead costs. It can also benefit as lower levels find they are in closer and more frequent contact with higher levels, and vice versa. Communication should flow more readily and quickly up and down the chain of command, as there are fewer levels to pass through. This should also mean that decisions are made more quickly.

25. Faisal must first have confidence in the two engineers—he must trust them and respect their capabilities. Second, he must have confidence in himself—trusting his own judgement to give up some work and allow these others to do it. Third, he should follow the rules of effective delegation. These include being very clear on what must be accomplished by each engineer. Their responsibilities should be clearly understood. He must also give them the authority to act in order to fulfill their responsibility, especially in relationship to the other engineers. And, he must not forget his own final accountability for the results. He should remain in control and, through communication, make sure that work proceeds as planned.

Chapter 11

1. b		11. T
2. d		12. F
3. b		13. T
4. a		14. F
5. c		15. T
6. b		16. F
7. d		17. F
8. b		18. T
9. b		19. T
10. c		20. F

21. The term contingency is used in management to indicate that management strategies and practices should be tailored to fit the unique needs of individual situations. There is no universal solution that fits all problems and circumstances. Thus, in organizational design, contingency thinking must be used to identify and implement organizational particular points in time. What works well at one point in time may not work well in another as the environment and other conditions change.

22. The environment is an important influence on organizational design. The more complex, variable, and uncertain are the elements in the general and specific environments, the more difficult it is for the organization to operate. In general, stable and more certain environments allow for mechanistic designs since operations can be more routine and predictable. This calls for more organic designs.

23. Differentiation and integration are somewhat conflicting in organizational design. As differentiation increases, that is as more differences are present in the complexity of the organization, the more integration is needed to ensure that everything functions together to the betterment of the whole organization. However, the greater the differentiation the harder it is to achieve integration. Thus, when differentiation is high organization design tends to shift toward the use of more complex horizontal approaches to integration and away from the

vertical ones such as formal authority and rules or policies. In horizontal integration the focus is on such things cross functional teams and matrix structures.

24. The focus of process reengineering is on reducing costs and streamlining operations efficiency while improving customer service. This is accomplished by closely examining core business processes through the following sequence of activities: (1) identify the core processes, (2) map them in a workflows diagram, (3) evaluate all tasks involved, (4) seek ways to eliminate unnecessary tasks, (5) seek ways to eliminate delays, errors, and misunderstandings in the workflows, and (6) seek efficiencies in how work is shared and transferred among people and departments.

25. This situation involves the basic contingency notion of organizational design. There is no one best way to design an organization and different designs serve organizations well under different circumstances. The first person is most likely working for an organization facing rather routine and known environmental demands. This allows for the organizational design to become more vertical and mechanistic, focusing as it does on predictable problems and outcomes. The individuals who remain in such a design are probably compatible with the internal climate of such an organization and thus find it a good "fit" resulting in reasonable levels of job satisfaction. By contrast the second person probably works for an organization facing uncertain challenges in a dynamic environment, with the result that it is by design a more adaptive or flexible structure emphasizing horizontal rather than vertical operations. In this case the design fits the demands of the environment and it is also most likely to satisfy those individuals who remain with it over time. Thus we have a good demonstration of two aspects of contingency factors in organizational design: the environment-structure-performance fit and the structure-individual fit.

Chapter 12

1. a		11. F
2. b		12. T
3. c		13. T
4. d		14. F
5. b		15. T
6. c		16. T
7. d		17. F
8. b		18. F
9. b		19. F
10. c		20. T

21. Internal recruitment deals with job candidates who already know the organization well. It is also a strong motivator because it communicates to everyone the opportunity to advance in the organization through hard work. External recruitment may allow the organization to obtain expertise not otherwise available internally. It also brings in employees with new and fresh viewpoints who are not biased by previous experience in the organization.

22. Orientation activities introduce a new employee to the organization and her or his work environment. This is a time when key attitudes may be set for the individual and during which performance expectations will also be established. Good orientation communicates positive attitudes and expectations and reinforces the desired organizational culture. It formally introduces the individual to important policies and procedures that everyone is expected to follow.

23. The graphic rating scale simply asks a supervisor to rate an employee on an established set of criteria, such as quantity of work or attitude toward work. This leaves a lot of room for subjectivity and debate. The behaviorally anchored rating scale asks the supervisor to rate the employee on specific job behaviors that have been identified as positively or negatively affecting performance in a given job. This is a more specific appraisal approach and leaves less room for debate and disagreement.

24. Mentoring is when a senior and experienced individual adopts a newcomer or more junior person with the goal of helping them develop into a successful worker. The mentor may or may not be the individual's immediate supervisor. The mentor meets with the individual and discusses problems, shares advice, and generally supports their attempts to grow and perform. Mentors are considered very useful for persons newly appointed to management positions.

25. As Sy's supervisor, you face a difficult but perhaps expected human resource management problem. Not only is Sy influential as an informal leader, he also has considerable experience on the job and in the company. Even though he is experiencing performance problems using the new computer system, there is no indication that he doesn't want to work hard and continue to perform for the company. Although retirement is an option, Sy may also be transferred, promoted, or simply terminated. The latter response seems unjustified and may cause legal problems. Transferring Sy, with his agreement, to another position could be a positive move: promoting Sy to a supervisory position where his experience and networks would be useful is another possibility. The keys in this situation seem to be moving Sy out so that a computer-literate person can take over the job, while continuing to utilize Sy in a job that better fits his talents. Transfer and/or promotion should be actively considered both in his interests and in the company's.

Chapter 13

1. d		11. F
2. d		12. F
3. b		13. T
4. a		14. T
5. c		15. F
6. a		16. T
7. b		17. F
8. c		18. F
9. b		19. F
10. a		20. F

21. Position power is based on reward, coercion or punishment, and legitimacy or formal authority. Managers, however, need to have more power than that made available to them by the position alone. Thus, they have to develop personal power through expertise and reference. This personal power is essential in helping managers to get things done beyond the scope of their position power alone.

22. Leader-participation theory suggests that leadership effectiveness is determined in part by how well managers or leaders handle the many different problem or decision situations that they face every day. Decisions can be

made through individual or authority, consultative, or group-consensus approaches. No one of these decision methods is always the best; each is a good fit for certain types of situations. A good manager or leader is able to use each of these approaches and knows when each is the best approach to use in various situations.

23. Position power—how much power the leader has in terms of rewards, punishments, and legitimacy. Leader-member relations—the quality of relationships between the leader and followers. Task structure—the degree to which the task is clear and well defined, or open ended and more ambiguous.

24. Drucker says that good leaders have more than the "charisma" or "personality" being popularized in the concept of transformational leadership. He reminds us that good leaders work hard to accomplish some basic things in their everyday activities. These include: (1) establishing a clear sense of mission, (2) accepting leadership as a responsibility and not a rank, and (3) earning and keeping the respect of others.

25. In his new position, Marcel must understand that the transactional aspects of leadership are not sufficient to guarantee him long-term leadership effectiveness. He must move beyond the effective use of task-oriented and people-oriented behaviors and demonstrate through his personal qualities the capacity to inspire others. A charismatic leader develops a unique relationship with followers in which they become enthusiastic, highly loyal, and high achievers. Marcel needs to work very hard to develop positive relationships with the team members and to emphasize in those relationships high aspirations for performance accomplishments, enthusiasm for the work and for one another, integrity and honesty in all dealings, and a clear vision of the future. By working hard with this agenda and by allowing his personality to positively express itself in the team setting, Marcel should make continuous progress as an effective leader.

Chapter 14

1. c	11. F
2. d	12. F
3. d	13. T
4. b	14. F
5. b	15. F
6. d	16. F
7. c	17. T
8. b	18. F
9. d	19. F
10. a	20. F

21. People high in need for achievement will prefer work settings and jobs in which they have (1) challenging but achievable goals, (2) individual responsibility, and (3) performance feedback.

22. Participation is important to goal-setting theory because, in general, people tend to be more committed to the accomplishment of goals they have helped to set. When people participate in the setting of goals, they also understand them better. Participation in goal-setting improves goal acceptance and understanding.

23. Motivation is formally defined as the forces within an individual that account for the level, direction, and persistence of effort expended at work.

24. Herzberg suggests that job content factors are the satisfiers or motivators. Based in the job itself, they rep-

resent such things as responsibility, sense of achievement, and feelings of growth. Job context factors are considered sources of dissatisfaction. They are found in the job environment and include such things as base pay, technical quality of supervision, and working conditions. Whereas improvements in job context make people less dissatisfied, improvements in job content are considered necessary to motivate them to high performance levels.

25. In answering question 21, it has already been pointed out that a high need achiever likes moderately challenging goals and performance feedback. Goal-setting with the participation of both manager and subordinate offers an opportunity to choose goals to which the need achievers will individually respond and which also serve the organization. Through goal-setting, furthermore, the manager and individual subordinates can identify performance standards or targets. Progress toward these targets can be positively reinforced by the manager. Such reinforcements can serve as indicators of progress to the high need achievers, thus responding to their desires for performance feedback. All in all, the existence of good goals gives the need achiever something to work toward; it gives the manager something against which to offer reinforcements in a positive manner.

Chapter 15

1. d	11. F
2. c	12. T
3. c	13. F
4. c	14. F
5. a	15. F
6. b	16. F
7. b	17. T
8. a	18. T
9. b	19. T
10. b	20. T

21. A psychological contract is the individual's view of the inducements he or she expects to receive from the organization in return for his or her work contributions. The contract is healthy when the individual perceives that the inducements and contributions are fair and in a state of balance.

22. Growth-need strength helps determine which individuals are good candidates for job enrichment. A person high in growth-need strength seeks higher order satisfaction of ego and self-fulfillment needs at work. These are needs to which job enrichment can positively respond. A person low in growth-need strength may not respond well to the demands and responsibilities of an enriched job.

23. The type A personality is characteristic of people who bring stress on themselves by virtue of personal characteristics. These tend to be compulsive individuals who are uncomfortable waiting for things to happen, who try to do many things at once, and who generally move fast and have difficulty slowing down. Type A personalities can be stressful for both the individuals and the people around them. Managers must be aware of type A personality tendencies in their own behavior and among others with whom they work. Ideally, this awareness will help the manager take precautionary steps to best manage the stress caused by this personality type.

24. The compressed workweek, or 4–40 schedule, offers employees the advantage of a 3-day weekend. However, it can cause problems for the employer in terms of ensur-

ing that operations are covered adequately during the normal 5 work days of the week. Labor unions may resist, and the compressed workweek will entail more complicated work scheduling. In addition, some employees find that the schedule is tiring and can cause family adjustment problems.

25. The high performance equation states that: Performance = Ability × Support × Effort. The multiplication signs are important. They indicate that each of the performance factors must be high and positive in order for high performance to occur. That is, neither ability nor support nor effort can be neglected by Kurt or any of the managers/team leaders in his plant. Furthermore, the factors are straightforward in their managerial implications. Ability is an issue of proper selection, training and development of all employees. Support involves providing capable employees with such things as clear goals, appropriate technology, helpful structures, and an absence of performance obstacles such as poor rules and procedures. Effort involves making sure that the environment is motivation and offers varied intrinsic as well as extrinsic rewards. Only by giving direct and serious attention to each of these factors can Kurt and his management team take full advantage of the insights of the high performance equation.

Chapter 16

1. d	11. F
2. b	12. T
3. b	13. T
4. d	14. F
5. b	15. F
6. d	16. T
7. b	17. F
8. c	18. T
9. a	19. T
10. b	20. T

21. Input factors can have a major impact on group effectiveness. In order to best prepare a group to perform effectively a manager should make sure that the right people are put on the group (maximize available talents and abilities), that these people are capable of working well together (membership characteristics should promote good relationships), that the tasks are clear, and that the group has the resources and environment needed to perform up to expectations.

22. A group's performance can be analyzed according to the interaction between cohesiveness and performance norms. In a highly cohesive group members tend to conform to group norms. Thus, when the performance norm is positive and cohesion is high, we can expect everyone to work hard to support the norm—high performance is likely. By the same token, high cohesion and a low performance norm will act the same—low performance is likely. With other combinations of norms and cohesion the performance results will be more mixed.

23. The textbook lists several symptoms of groupthink along with various strategies for avoiding groupthink (see notepad 16.3). For example, a group whose members censure themselves from contributing "contrary" or "different" opinions and/or whose members keep talking about outsiders as "weak" or the "enemy" may be suffering groupthink. This may be avoided or corrected, for example, by asking someone to be the "devil's advocate" for

a meeting and by inviting in an outside observer to help gather different viewpoints.

24. In a traditional work group, the manager or supervisor directs the group. In a self-managing team, the members of the team provide for self-direction. They plan, organize, and evaluate their work, share tasks, and help one another develop skills; they may even make hiring decisions. A true self-managing team does not need the traditional "boss" or supervisor since the team as a whole takes on the supervisory responsibilities.

25. Marcos is faced with a highly cohesive group whose members conform to a negative or low-performance norm. This is a difficult situation that is ideally resolved by changing the performance norm. In order to gain the group's commitment to a high-performance norm, Marcos should act as a positive role model for the norm. He must communicate the norm clearly and positively to the group. He should not assume that everyone knows what he expects of them. He may also talk to the informal leader and gain her or his commitment to the norm. He might carefully reward high performance behaviors within the group. He may introduce new members with high-performance records and commitments. And, he might hold group meetings in which performance standards and expectations were discussed with an emphasis on committing to new high-performance directions. If his attempts to introduce a high-performance norm fail, Marcos may have to take steps to reduce group cohesiveness so that individual members can pursue higher performance results without feeling bound by group pressures to restrict their performance.

Chapter 17

1. b	11. F
2. a	12. T
3. c	13. T
4. b	14. F
5. c	15. T
6. b	16. T
7. b	17. F
8. d	18. F
9. c	19. T
10. a	20. T

21. The manager's goal in active listening is to help the subordinate say what she or he really means. To do this, the manager should carefully listen for the content of what someone is saying, paraphrase or reflect back what she or he appears to be saying, remain sensitive to nonverbal cues and feelings, and not be evaluative.

22. The halo effect occurs when a single attribute of a person, such as the way she or he dresses, is used to evaluate or form an overall impression of the person. Selective perception occurs when someone focuses in a situation on those aspects that reinforce or are most consistent with his or her existing values, beliefs, or experiences.

23. Win-lose outcomes are likely when conflict is managed through high assertiveness and low cooperativeness styles. In this situation of competition, the conflict is resolved by one person or group dominating another. Lose-lose outcomes occur when conflict is managed through avoidance, where nothing is resolved, and possibly when it is managed through compromise, where each party gives up something to the other. Win-win outcomes are

associated mainly with problem-solving and collaboration in conflict management, which is a result of high assertiveness and high cooperativeness.

24. In a negotiation, both substance and relationship goals are important. Substance goals relate to the content of the negotiation. A substance goal for example may relate to the final salary agreement between a job candidate and a prospective employer. Relationship goals relate to the quality of the interpersonal relationships among the negotiating parties. Relationship goals are important because the negotiating parties most likely have to work together in the future. For example, if relationships are poor after a labor—management negotiation, the likelihood is that future problems will occur.

25. Harold can do a number of things to establish and maintain a system of upward communication for his department store branch. To begin, he might set the tone for the department managers by using MBWA—"managing by wandering around." Once this pattern is established, trust will build between him and other store employees, and he should find that he learns a lot from interacting directly with them. Harold should also set up a formal communication structure, such as bimonthly store meetings, where he communicates store goals, results, and other issues to the staff, and in which he listens to them in return. An E-mail system whereby Harold and his staff could send messages to one another from their workstation computers would also be beneficial.

Chapter 18

1. b	11. T
2. a	12. T
3. d	13. F
4. c	14. F
5. c	15. T
6. b	16. T
7. c	17. F
8. a	18. F
9. d	19. T
10. a	20. F

21. The possible internal targets for change include the following. The tasks being worked on including organizational mission, objectives, and strategy. The people doing the work, including their attitudes and skills. The culture or predominant value system of the organization. The technology being used and the integration of technology and people. The structure of the organization.

22. Lewin's three phases of planned change are: Unfreezing—preparing a system for change; changing—moving or creating change in a system; and refreezing—stabilizing and reinforcing change once it has occurred.

23. In general managers can expect that others will be more committed and loyal to changes that are brought about through shared power strategies. Rational persuasion strategies can also create enduring effects if they are accepted. Force-coercion strategies tend to have temporary effects only.

24. The statement that "OD equals planned change plus" basically refers to the fact that OD tries both to create change in an organization and to make the organization members capable of creating such change for themselves in the future.

25. In any change situation, it is important to remember that success-ful planned change only occurs when all three phases of change—unfreezing, changing, and re-freezing—have been taken care of. Thus, I would not rush into the changing phase. Rather, I would work with the people involved to develop a felt need for change based on their ideas and inputs as well as mine. Then I would proceed by supporting the changes and helping to stabilize them into everyday routines. I would also be sensitive to any resistance and respect that resistance as a signal that something important is being threatened. By listening to resistance I would be in a position to better modify the change to achieve a better fit with the people and the situation. Finally, I would want to take maximum advantage of the shared power strategy, supported by rational persuasion, and with limited use of force-coercion (if it is used at all). By doing all of this, I would like my staff to feel empowered and committed to constructive improvement through planned change.